# PAGANS AND CHRISTIANS

ROBIN LANE FOX

# Pagans
# and Christians

Alfred A. Knopf, Inc.  New York  1989

THIS IS A BORZOI BOOK
PUBLISHED BY ALFRED A. KNOPF, INC.

Copyright © 1986 by Robin Lane Fox

All rights reserved under International and Pan-American Copyright
Conventions. Published in the United States by Alfred A. Knopf, Inc.,
New York. Distributed by Random House, Inc., New York.
Originally published in Great Britain
by Viking, Penguin Books Ltd, Harmondsworth

*Library of Congress Cataloging-in-Publication Data*

Lane Fox, Robin.
  Pagans and Christians.

  Bibliography: p.
  Includes index.
    1. Christianity and other religions—Roman.
  2. Rome—Religion.   3. Church history—Primitive and
  early church, ca. 30–600. I. Title.
  BR128.R7L36   1986        270.1       86–2752
  ISBN 0-394-55495-7

Manufactured in the United States of America
Published January 12, 1987

# Contents

List of Maps — 6

Preface — 7
1. Pagans and Christians — 11

## PART ONE
2. Pagans and Their Cities — 27
3. Pagan Cults — 64
4. Seeing the Gods — 102
5. Language of the Gods — 168

## PART TWO
6. The Spread of Christianity — 265
7. Living Like Angels — 336
8. Visions and Prophecy — 375
9. Persecution and Martyrdom — 419
10. Bishops and Authority — 493

## PART THREE
11. Sinners and Saints — 549
12. Constantine and the Church — 609
13. From Pagan to Christian — 663

Notes — 683
Index — 787

## MAPS

Major pagan cities of Asia Minor and Syria, 100–250 A.D.    *pages* 28–9

Client cities of the oracle at Claros, attested in the Greek
East during the Imperial period    *page* 174

Christian Churches in the Mediterranean known to have
been founded before the persecution by Diocletian, 304 A.D.    *pages* 274–5

Gregory's travels, 235–260 A.D.    *page* 529

The western centres of Mani's mission, 240–300 A.D.    *page* 548

# PREFACE

The subjects of this book need no apology for their importance. There have been many books on paganism and many more on early Christianity, but although there have been fine comparisons of their beliefs and philosophies and their views of each other, I know of no book which puts their practice side by side in a context of civic life. Eventually, books set their own pace, and although mine is long, I sympathize with the reader who felt that it should have been longer in order to do justice to its subjects. Those who try to cover two different areas of scholarship tend to satisfy experts in neither, while every general view of ancient society invites exceptions and provokes dissent. While writing about pagans, I have kept in mind the many Christians to whom they are not now familiar. While writing about early Christians, I have considered the many readers and connoisseurs of classical antiquity to whom Christian texts are unknown or a distant memory. I hope that each will gain from finding their areas of knowledge set beside others. Modern Christians tend to regard many of the early Christians with distaste. I have, however, been made aware that early Christianity is often best understood by those who would never wish to write about it.

Historians of the ancient world face two constant problems, a scarcity of evidence and the relation of its particular pieces to wider generalizations. At times, I have tried to establish the value of one piece of evidence against another or to prove the particular authority of a written text. This method is common to much legal investigation, but it is not legalistic. At others, I have tried to generalize, while citing particular statements and evidence which seem to me to have wider significance. About many people in antiquity we know only what others of a different sex or class wrote and sometimes not even that. Generalizations are therefore precarious, easier to refute than confirm. I have cited particular evidence both to give constant warning of the type of support on which I have relied and to convey its vivid style and expression, distinctive qualities about the ancient world and reasons why it continues to fascinate me.

It has been an exciting time to be writing this book because significant evidence has continued to be found on the subjects of each chapter, especially in newly published inscriptions and papyri, ever-growing sources with which I have struggled to keep in touch. Ancient history is not a static or finite subject: a lifetime ago, much that I discuss was not even available for study. Nor is this branch of it "ancient" to us or somehow dead and buried. While I have been writing, the Virgin Mary has been reported to be "appearing as never before"; a statue which seems to move is drawing a crowd as large as any in my field of study; born-again Christians, liberation theology, martyrdoms and the "moral majority" are but a few of the contemporary features which have caused me to reflect more deeply on the subjects which I have discussed. No generation can afford to ignore whether Christianity is true and, if it is not, why it has spread and persisted and what is the proper response to it. Historians have a particular contribution to make to these inquiries.

The origins of this book go back to my upbringing and to Eton school days when we were expected to teach ourselves the history of the Church before Constantine, to study a Gospel and the Acts in Greek and then to alarm visiting examiners with the results of our efforts. At Oxford, I coincided with a golden age of the subject, when it was possible to be taught by G. E. M. de Sainte Croix, to attend the lectures of Peter Brown and Henry Chadwick and to meet and talk with E. R. Dodds and Gervase Mathew. To them and their writings I owe much that I now seem to know. I have retained a constant awareness that they have expressed so much more in their own books and that they could have improved mine throughout. I was also fortunate to coincide with a new generation who approached these topics from other angles: I have gained much from the help of Stephen Mitchell, S. R. F. Price, S. N. C. Lieu, Garth Fowden, R. C. T. Parker, David Potter and C. J. Howgego, and from T. D. Barnes, whose important book on Constantine overtook my final chapters. In 1983, H. W. Parke kindly lent me chapters of his forthcoming book on the oracles of Asia Minor, and N. J. Richardson lent me the text of his lecture on religious experience in Homer's poems. Both saved me from errors and omissions, but I have let our differences stand. More specifically, Ian Tompkins checked the text and notes of Chapter 10 and removed several mistakes; Susannah Elm did the same for Chapter 7 and taught me much from her studies of its topics. I owe a particular debt to the vigilance and insight of Mark Edwards, who helped me with the notes to Chapters 8, 11, and 13. S. J. B. Barnish was my most perceptive critic: he caused me to rethink my general picture and exposed various faults in Chapters 5 and 9. Throughout, Patricia Morison made me aware of ideas I would otherwise have missed and encouraged me by commenting acutely on what I was writing. I would also like to acknowledge all I have learned from the writings of A. D. Nock and A. J. Festugière, J. Geffcken and A. Harnack, and my old and admired companions, Joseph Bingham's unsurpassed work on Christian antiquities (published in 1708) and, of course, Gibbon on the entire subject.

Books differ by their differing emphases, but I hope to have established something new on the topic of pagan oracles, the story of an early martyrdom and a text ascribed to Constantine himself. The chapters on visionary experience bring together evidence from Homer to Constantine which is otherwise kept in separate, specialized studies: they also add a few details which are not even kept there. In other chapters, I have tried to present a considered point of view without being uncritically up-to-date or, I trust, too unaware of previous studies. A difference of emphasis can be as telling as a new discovery, but here, too, I have tried to establish many particular points in passing. My use of works published since 1982 has necessarily been selective. I have been writing since 1977 and books have kept appearing on topics with which I thought I had finished. I have pressed on, not regardless, but omitting only those ideas which the latest books refuted. Where we overlap, I have been reassured by our agreement.

I would not have written this book if Worcester College, Oxford, had not given me a special research fellowship which I held in 1976–77: without their remarkable generosity, I would have become another lawyer. New College then kindly gave me an early term of sabbatical leave in 1983 which enabled me to complete the second half of the book. It has made its own martyrs, and without the exceptional skill of Anne Robinson, who suffered and typed my awful manuscripts over several years with impeccable speed and accuracy, it would never have been laid to rest. My deepest debt will, I hope, be obvious from the notes. Fifteen years ago, in bed, I found myself reading a French book on the indigenous names of Asia Minor. It began as an extended review of the errors of a recent German predecessor, but it seized my imagination late at night and made me aware of a standard and a range of evidence which were quite beyond my reach. Since then, I have been one of those classicists for whom research on antiquity is also research on the voluminous writings of Professor Louis Robert, its greatest scholar. Many of my moments of discovery have been made in his work: it is my particular regret that as I write this conclusion to so many years of learning from him at one remove, I have just heard of his death. It deprives this book of the chance of the review which would have done most to correct it and instruct me.

New College, Oxford
1985

# 1. Pagans and Christians

The transition from pagan to Christian is the point at which the ancient world still touches ours directly. We are heirs to its conclusion: on either side, participants shared an education which, until recently, we widely maintained. Like most transitions, it was a slow process, marked by unforeseen moments of sudden significance. While Christianity spread, many of the pagan gods were already a thousand years old. The contrast between the old gods and the new can be sensed in accounts of six individuals, two pagans, two Christians, two Emperors, in the years when the transition gathered speed.

In the mid-third century, to honour the pagan gods was still to expect their protection, in cities or in battles, at home or on travels abroad. They were old and proven companions whose very antiquity earned them respect, among young and old, Emperors and subjects, in the city of Rome or the provinces. In the year 242, this respect was still evident as the young Roman Emperor Gordian III prepared to march east for the safety of the Empire's frontier; Persian armies were on the move, sacking cities as they approached Syria. Gordian was untried, a boy of some sixteen years, and before he left Rome, he paid a distinctive respect to the gods. He opened the gates of the temple of Janus and ordered a new athletic festival in honour of the goddess Athena. His ancient choice was well advised. His enemy, the Persian monarchy, was also proclaiming remote descent from the classical past, from King Darius and the princes who had once invaded the Greek world. In preparation, Gordian honoured the warrior goddess Athena, who had defended her city of Athens against those same Persian princes 720 years before.[1]

This type of ancient display was not new on such an occasion: in 2 B.C., while his grandson prepared for an eastern campaign, the Emperor Augustus had opened the gates of Janus, flooded the Circus in Rome and staged a massive naval battle between teams called

Persians and Athenians, a show whose relics survived in Gordian's own day.[2] Honours for the old Athena sat well with the regional and literary connections of Gordian's family. Their undistinguished name is traceable to Greek-speaking Asia Minor, perhaps to Cappadocia, now inland in southern Turkey. Gordian's father had had contact with Greek high culture. He had conversed with the masters of Greek oratory and claimed a kinship with the grandest of them all, the rich and pre-eminent Herodes of Athens: it was probably a kinship of student to literary master, not a true kinship by marriage.[3] In extravagant language, the young Gordian had already been welcomed in the Greek world. The people of Ephesus had honoured him as the "new Sun," the ruler who "had restored and increased for his universe the ancient peace of life."[4] While he marched east, cities on or near his route asked for the right to attach his name to their athletic festivals. Others issued coins whose types alluded to hopes of victory, while Roman Imperial coins proclaimed the "felicity of the age," the "loyalty of the soldiers" and the protection of Jupiter himself. After some early victories, Gordian was killed on the eastern frontier, a death which came to be blamed on treachery in the high command.[5]

In the cities through which Gordian passed, the careers of pagan notables were still honoured by durable public inscriptions. His piety was theirs, and one recent discovery can speak for most of them, a text whose finder confessed that its "circumstances, perhaps, are somewhat commonplace."[6] Near little Cibyra Minor, an ancient site in southern Turkey, the wife of Aurelius Longinus set up statues in honour of her husband and daughter. The family owned land in this small town's territory, but Longinus's career had been drawn elsewhere, to the "most brilliant and glorious" city of Side, some thirty miles to the southwest, on Turkey's southern coast. On the base of his statue, a long inscription described his achievements as Side's people had honoured them. Aurelius Longinus had been a high priest in the cult of the Emperor "with piety and honourable generosity" and during office he had won favour by making gifts to the councillors and citizens. He had paid for civic shows "with great munificence" during his priesthood. He had served "with dignity" as an official of the "festival known as the Apolline," and then, too, he had given generously to the council and citizenry. He had held a magistracy of the agora, or marketplace, "with integrity." He had served as a guardian of the peace "with courage and care," words which suggest that he had led men in the field, perhaps against the area's many bandits. He had taken his turn in charge of the corn supply and had collected local debts. He had sacrificed on behalf of the "most dignified Council." He had "escorted the sacred grain supply three times to the people of Syria," an intriguing task which turns up on the inscriptions of other third-century notables in the area.[7] It is best related to the provisioning of Imperial armies on their marches east through Asia: Longinus had left with the grain ships from Side's fine harbour and sailed to Syria to deliver the cargo which Emperors demanded from the city's neighbourhood. This dutiful citizen had served with his wife as a priest of Side's protecting goddess Athena, whose temple and portrait loom large on the city's coinage. He had presided over the animal hunts and the gladiatorial combats which had been bequeathed to the city by a Roman dignitary, the governor of Galatia, in the year 177. This task, too, he had carried out "gloriously and with great munificence." He had also been an overseer of the "water store," perhaps one of the city's several cisterns which connected to its vast aqueduct, perhaps the baroque Nymphaeum which stands by its main gate. He had "been useful to the city in many other services and positions of responsibility and had proved himself always one of the best."

This inscription belongs in the earlier third century, although its exact date is not certain. The games called Apolline are probably the "Pythian Gordianic games" which Gordian approved for the city, and if so, they place Longinus's career in the years from c. 230 to 250, where his three "escorts of the sacred grain" belong neatly with the Roman campaigns which end in 244.[8] Longinus becomes an exact contemporary of Gordian's march, a man to whom Rome's new games for the old Athena seemed entirely apposite.

Like hundreds of other city notables, Longinus lived out a measured career of high office and expensive public service. At a similar date, the matching life of a man of letters can be caught from inscriptions in Athens.[9] There, one T. Flavius Glaucus commemorated a member of his family with a fine statue and described himself in its inscription as "poet, rhetorician and philosopher." He numbered sophists and philosophers on both sides of his family. His father's line ran to "key-bearers" in the cult of the healing god Asclepius and to high officials in the mystery cult at Eleusis. His grandmother, niece and uncle were the subjects of neat verse epitaphs which were presumably composed by their family poet, T. Flavius Glaucus himself. He belonged in the tentacular family circles of old-world Athenian piety, among Platonist philosophers whose ancestry traced back across a century and a half to intellectual friends of the pious Plutarch. He knew his Homer and could turn neat epigrams on masterpieces of classic Greek painting. His career had included a spell in the Imperial service as "advocate of the Treasury" and ranks as one more example of that cheering link between literary interests and the duties of administration which turns up so often in this age of education in the arts. His grandmother had crowned the Roman Emperors when they celebrated the mysteries at Eleusis in the year 176. She and he belonged to a family which called itself the "first in spacious Hellas and the East." She met painlessly with death, "death sweeter than sleep and mightier than Argive young men," an allusion perhaps to the two young men of Argos who had died so fortunately in the first book of Herodotus's histories.

T. Flavius Glaucus lived and wrote in the mid-third century, a man of traditional piety and letters who had been born and educated among the highest provincial society. His literary talent is the pair to Longinus's sonorous career. Its measured classicism belonged with an age of civic life when local power and economic patronage rested largely in the hands of a few notables. During the third century, their class had not been static.[10] The gap had continued to widen between its richest and most powerful families and the lesser members who also served their cities. Civic office entailed growing burdens of time and expense, while the scope for careers at Rome diverted some of the most eligible bearers. Longinus and Glaucus's family were willing benefactors, but even so, their careers intertwined with the avenues of Roman Imperial service, "escorting sacred grain" or serving the Imperial treasury and alluding to their links with senatorial families in the verses on their tombstones. As local civic life still gave them a valued esteem, their careers and qualities were still honoured by prominent local inscriptions, carved and displayed on stone. However, this "epigraphic habit" was already dwindling: significantly, it would not be maintained in this style by their sons and grandsons.

While these traditional benefactors still led their cities, another man, of similar culture and property, had abandoned the natural ambitions of his class and was rising to fame in a different community. Thascius Cyprianus, Cyprian in Christian tradition, had practised in Carthage as a public speaker, teaching Latin rhetoric and pleading as an advocate in the courts of law. In the mid-240s, he gave up his profession, sold the greater part of his property and gave the proceeds and most of his remaining income to help the Christian poor. Some years later, he

looked back on his progress in an elegant letter which he addressed to a
fellow Christian, formerly a pupil of his pagan teacher of oratory.[11] In
it, Cyprian connected the change in his convictions with his distaste
for displays of rank and riches, the mainsprings of Longinus and his
class. He endorsed the moralists' attacks on corruption, the insecurity
of riches, the indecency of the theatres and gladiatorial shows. His
self-portrait may have been stylized with hindsight, but it is telling
that he could represent his faith to others in this way: he had chosen a
style, a setting and a stock of themes which were common to educated
pagans. He makes no specific connection with a particular time of
political strife which had affected Carthage and its province a few
years earlier. Rather, he stresses his discovery of something personal
which he had previously doubted: that a man could be "born again."
In a corrupt and violent world, Cyprian called himself a "born-again
Christian." "Let fear be the guardian of your innocence," he wrote: he
had found a new hope and a new explanation of misfortune. He had
been unmarried at the time of his conversion, and as a Christian, he
remained celibate for the rest of his life. "Patience," meanwhile,
became a key word in his writings, the patience which made Job a
model for Christian life. "He who endures to the end is saved":
Cyprian responded to these powerful words in Scripture.

After renouncing his property, Cyprian found himself propelled
rapidly to the bishopric of Carthage by the support of a Christian
"people," which included the favour of slaves and women. As a
bishop, he became engaged in fierce arguments over the very nature of
his community. While pagan members of his class professed a staunch
civic patriotism, Cyprian was obliged to write letters and attempt to
influence fellow Christians in Spain and southern Gaul, Rome and the
East, as far as Cappadocia. At home, his ecclesiastical "province"
extended over three separate provinces under Roman rule,[12] and in
each, his advice was required on practical matters, the dress and
conduct of virgins, the commemoration of martyrs, the diluting of
wine at Holy Communion. He debated matters of great moment with
fellow bishops in Church councils whose deliberations were believed
to be guided by a "holy Spirit"; as bishop, Cyprian remained conscious of God's continuing guidance in dreams and revelations. The
style and allusions of his former, pagan rhetoric passed almost completely from his writings.[13] Instead, he found a new voice through the
Latin Scriptures, whether he was praising the merits of almsgiving or
compiling quotations against the Jews. Longinus and his class

professed a "love of honour" in the many gifts which they made to their cities; Cyprian, by contrast, praised giving because it could buy forgiveness of sins.

No pagan civic notable attracted a biography, but soon after Cyprian's death, his fame was enlarged and defended by a remarkable "life," composed by a companion of his final months. Like Cyprian, its author was a man of sound literary education: the "life" stressed Cyprian's exceptional faith, his rapid promotion and the charity which had touched Christians and pagans alike. It ignored the fierce arguments of Cyprian's career and focussed on a period to which Christian ideals gave special prominence: death and its approach.[14] Cyprian's career as a bishop had been dogged by the challenge of martyrdom and persecution. In a first crisis, he had withdrawn into hiding and tried to sustain his leadership by letter. In a second crisis, seven years later, he had been tried and banished; twelve months later, in summer 258, he was arrested again and put on trial for his life. He contrived to die in his own city, Carthage, and as he prepared for his execution, he was watched by crowds, some of whom had climbed the trees for an unimpeded view. Before kneeling, Cyprian asked that his executioner be given twenty-five pieces of gold. The deacons helped him to remove his outer tunic, and "almost the last thing Cyprian saw was a little pile of cloths," thrown by the crowd "to catch the martyr's blood and become relics for the faithful." No pagan notable had ever looked down on such a sight. His body was left lying until nightfall, "because of the pagans' curiosity," before it was escorted to a prominent cemetery, a magnet for future Christian burials.[15]

In the age of Gordian and Cyprian, Christianity was the persecuted faith of a minority. Nobody who marched with the old Athena or watched the public executions at Carthage expected to live to see it promoted and patronized throughout the Mediterranean. Yet only one lifetime later, in the mid-330s, such a change had become evident. When another Emperor, Constantine, prepared to campaign against the Persians, he put no trust in the old Athena.[16] An emblem of the cross preceded his march and its sign stood on his soldiers' shields. On Sundays, the troops had to meet, whatever their persuasion, and "at a given signal, offer to God with one accord a prayer which they had learnt." They addressed it to the one God, and after thanking him for past victories, they prayed for future benefits, among which was a long life for the Emperor and his sons. Christian priests are said to have been assigned to the army units, the first mention of military chaplains in history: before going east, Constantine asked bishops at his court to accompany him, and when they agreed, is said to have revealed to them the plan of his march. Then he ordered a huge tent to be stitched in the shape of a church for their use on the campaign. In it, he intended to join them in prayers to God, the giver of victory. He had always taken with him a "tent of the cross" in which he worshipped before joining battle. "After he had prayed earnestly to God," claimed Eusebius, writing a laudatory work, *On the Life of Constantine*, "he always received some revelation of God's presence and then, as if divinely inspired, he would leap up from his tent. At once he would set his troops in motion and exhort them not to delay but at that very hour to take up their swords. In a pack, they would fall on the foe and hack them down, beginning with their young men . . ."

Not only had the god of battles changed: Eusebius's own account was something new, a Christian's work of praise "on the life" of a deceased Emperor, which quoted the Emperor's own documents.[17] Its purpose and emphasis could not conceal the continuing ambiguities. Although the Emperor was a Christian, most of his troops were not, and their prayer was directed to "god, the giver of victory and all good things," without explicit Christian colour. The conversion of the Emperor could not change the beliefs and practices of most of his subjects. He could, however, grant favours and privileges to the "moral minority" whose faith he had accepted.[18] He built them magnificent churches; he exempted their clergy from civic duties; he gave their bishops power over judicial affairs, making them judges from whom there was no appeal. He also acknowledged the new ideal of charity. Previous Emperors had encouraged schemes to support small numbers of children in less favoured families, the future recruits for their armies. Constantine gave funds to the churches to support the poor, the widows and orphans.

Laws in his name touched on central areas of Christian concern, but it is still disputed how far each law reflected the Emperor's own Christianity; other laws in his reign showed no Christian influence and professed no Christian motive. There was no direct reference to Christian charity in his legal rulings, not even in a law which offered funds to parents who were too poor to bring their children up. Christian though this law might seem, it only expressed a fear that the parents might otherwise sell their offspring or turn to crime. At the same time, the penalties of laws against slaves or moral offenders showed a most un-Christian harshness, greater than any known previously.[19] Laws alone could not compel pagan practice to cease: most of the governors who were supposed to enforce them were themselves still pagans. However, in Constantine's reign, the transition from pagan to Christian did gain a new pace and prominence. We can see it most vividly in stories of an exceptional Christian.

Some twenty years before Constantine patronized Christianity, a boy, Hilarion, was born to pagan parents in a Syrian village just south of Gaza, a conspicuous centre of pagan cult. He was sent at their expense to a secondary teacher in Alexandria, proof that they were people of property and that Hilarion would normally have grown up to serve, like Longinus or Glaucus, as a city councillor. His life took a different turn, as we know through a text which St. Jerome composed c. 380, about ten years after its hero's death. Other accounts of Hilarion already existed and Christians who had known him were still alive in and near Palestine, where Jerome wrote. His work was not a historical life, but belonged to another type which Christianity popularized: hagiography, or the story of a saint. Jerome's "life" was a great success. It was translated "most elegantly" from Latin into Greek by one of his friends, whose version we probably possess. Already, the translation improved the tale, as did other imitators whose embellishments can still be followed in our various manuscripts.[20]

The value of this "life" does not depend on its degree of historical fact: it bears witness to the transition in another way. It shows the type of story which Christians liked to credit in an exceptional person whose long life had spanned the years before and after Constantine's reign. With them, we can look back on Christianity in action, as a time of quickening transition gave it greater scope.

In Alexandria, Hilarion's schoolmasters are said to have admired his gift for rhetoric, but before he could follow the usual career as a pagan speaker and public figure, he abandoned his school. Aged fifteen, he is said to have struck into Egypt's desert to find Antony, the Coptic-speaking Christian hermit. After two months in Antony's company, he is said to have returned to his home village and promptly given away his property. Behind the coast stretched the desert, and there Hilarion "fixed his dreary abode on a sandy beach between the sea and a morass, about seven miles from Gaza." At first he slept in a hut of reeds, then in the cell scarcely five feet high which was still on view when Jerome wrote the hermit's life. His diet remained a topic of interest. In his twenties, said Jerome, he had eaten bread and salt and lentils soaked in cold water. In his thirties, he changed to dry vegetables and when at the age of thirty-six his skin began to peel and his eyesight deteriorated, he dressed his vegetables with oil. Aged sixty-four, he gave up the bread and ate nothing but crushed vegetables for the next sixteen years. Holy men made achievements of diet interesting, and Jerome purported to give the exact details.

In the desert, Hilarion's fame soon spread. It does not depend on Jerome's testimony. We know from Sozomen, another Christian, writing *c.* 420, that Hilarion had exorcized a friend of his grandfather and turned the man's family to Christianity, succeeding where Jewish and pagan exorcists had previously failed: Sozomen's grandfather became a Christian too. Sozomen's siting of the event conforms to Jerome's topography and is a useful check on Hilarion's place and fame.[21] It is through Jerome, however, that the tales of Hilarion took their liveliest shape, naming known individuals and addressing Christians who had sometimes known Hilarion personally.

In his desert cell, Hilarion was thought to have coped with almost everything. He helped flustered women who wished to have babies. He cured family illnesses for an anxious mother on a long journey south with the children. Once, he straightened a charioteer whose neck had stiffened from driving, and calmed a lunatic member of the upper classes who had been carted in chains all the way to Syria from a city on the Red Sea. Animals were well within his competence. He tamed a Bactrian camel which suffered so badly from the hump that it needed ropes and thirty attendants to control it. He also upset the odds on the racecourse. A prominent Christian in Gaza was said to have asked Hilarion to bless his horses, as his archrival in the city, a pagan magistrate, was using a sorcerer to help his own team, which was winning continuously in the city's games. Hilarion gave a blessing to the horses, their stables and the racecourse, and next time out they romped home to resounding Christian cheers. Of the betting, unfortunately, we know nothing, but "the decisive victory in those games and many others later," Jerome commented, "caused very many people to turn to the faith." His comment throws an unusual, Irish light on the reasons why people were thought to have become Christians.

This story reminds us how life went on in the cities after Constantine's conversion, but its setting was not one of relaxed compromise

between pagans and Christians. When the pagan Emperor Julian came
to power, people in Gaza are said to have petitioned for the hermit's
prompt arrest: there was no love lost between a Christian holy man
and pagans who still sat on the town council. However, Hilarion was
away visiting Antony in Egypt. From there, he went by camel to
Libya and by boat to Sicily, where he prophesied and caused great
trouble to the local demons. Then he sailed slowly eastwards round
Greece to Cyprus, where he died, aged eighty, to the usual Christian
wrangle over his relics and the pieces of his body. From the first
demon to this final contest, the stories of his career had broken utterly
with the pattern of propertied families a lifetime earlier. "Nothing so
astonishes me," wrote Jerome, "as his power to tread honour and
glory under foot." Hilarion had moved freely in a world which spoke
Syriac as well as Greek. His business was not only with the lower
classes. His most ardent clients included visiting Roman officials, city
notables and the wife of a future praetorian prefect of the East. He had
done much good and no obvious harm, healing by faith and using his
notable powers of insight to give clients of all ranks his spiritual
advice.

Hilarion, it was believed, had become a Christian before Constantine, at a time when Christians still risked persecution and their future
was insecure. When he was born, there was no holy man of Antony's
talent in the desert and no widespread interest in a life of solitary
retreat. The first impulse to this life of perfection preceded Constantine's conversion, but then the social climate changed: Hilarion's own
retreat coincided with a time of rapid transition, when townsfolk and
people of high position would venture out to the Christian perfectionists, newly residing in the desert. Jerome's stories show what Christians liked to remember of their holy men: their poverty and charity,
their awesome abstinence, their insight, their blessings and their way
with demons and miracles. They also show the continuing ambiguities in civic life: the transition from pagan to Christian was still in
progress and Hilarion was at risk from pagans in his neighbourhood.

In this book, I wish to explore themes which the piety of these six
individuals suggests. I will begin with the traditional cults of Gordian
and Longinus and many others like them, a piety which stretched
back, I wish to argue, to themes which are familiar to fellow lovers of
Homer and Herodotus. Among Christians, I wish to explore the
themes which ran meanwhile through Cyprian's life: conversion
and the social distribution of the churches, visionary guidance and

celibacy, martyrdom, persecution and the role and choosing of the
Christians' lifelong leaders, their bishops. In each case, these themes
lead outwards to other, less prominent people whom no biography
honoured and whom inscriptions concerned less directly, if at all.

After setting these two types of religion in a social context, I wish to
pursue them through the obscure and difficult years between the
reigns of Gordian and Constantine. This age was one of quickened
transition on many fronts, but it is very poorly documented. I hope to
add to the evidence which historians can trust for the years between
250 and 325. Where possible, I have begun from texts which recent
discoveries have recovered or freed from persistent suspicions of
fiction: the pagan oracles which are preserved in late Christian handbooks, the diary of a martyr awaiting death in prison, the letters
ascribed to a future Christian bishop. I have tried to explain how the
life of a Hilarion could become so admired and attractive, and how a
primary cause of change, in the balance of the two religions, was the
conversion of Constantine himself. Here, I wish to vindicate a text
which is longer than any other to be ascribed to a previous Emperor; I
wish to establish it as the speech of Constantine himself at a demonstrable day and place. If rightly placed, it settles disputes about his faith
in Christianity. It also bears on the religious differences which I have
tried to bring out across the previous two hundred years.

To what, finally, did Constantine's conversion lead? It was only a
landmark in the history of Christianization, that state which is always
receding, like full employment or a life without weeds. The degree to
which people were ever Christianized is a problem which still runs
through medieval history, the "age of faith." It recurs awkwardly in
eighteenth-century studies before foundering, as always, on the
observable experience of our own lives. Christianity had never
preached an outright social revolution. There was no "liberation
theology," no sanction for a direct assault on the forms of social
dependence and slavery. In the Christian empire, the army still
fought, and the soldiery did not intervene for one religion against the
other. Distinctions of rank and degree multiplied and the inequalities
of property widened.

Was Christianity, perhaps, not so very novel in the pagan world?
Even before Constantine, Christians and pagans have been seen as
members of a "common Mediterranean religious culture," in whose
changes the role of foreign ideas was minimal, nothing more than
"alien thistle-seeds, drifting into the tidy garden of classical Greco-

Roman culture."[22] I wish to establish the opposite view. Early Christianity arrived with very distinctive roots. Grafted onto the Old Testament, it was not easily smothered, not even by the established ground cover of the pagan towns. The Christian groups retained and passed on ideals which have continued to recur in their history, giving it familiar patterns.

These roots did not die away, although proofs of "pagan continuity" have been sought in the developing types of Christian worship. The cult of saints and worship at the graves of the dead have been seen as a pagan legacy, as have the Christian shrines of healing and smaller details of Christian practice, dancing, feasting and the use of spells and divination.[23] Emphasis on these "pagan survivals" has opened long perspectives. In the West, it has led to the study of popular religion and medieval folklore as if they were living alternatives to Christian culture. In the East, it has encouraged the myth that Hellenism endured from pagan antiquity to Byzantium and far beyond, to become the national heritage of modern Greeks.[24] However, almost all of this continuity is spurious. Many of its details were set in Christian contexts which changed their meaning entirely. Other details merely belonged in contexts which nobody wished to make Christian. They were part of a "neutral technology of life" and it would be as unreal to expect them to change "as to expect modern man to Christianize the design of an automobile or to produce a Marxist wrist-watch."[25]

Christianity's impact cannot simply be judged by the failures of its ideals in the practice of the later Roman Empire. It brought other fundamental changes, in people's self-awareness, and in their opportunities and social organization. The Church and its careers and ever-growing possessions became major new forces in economic and social history. Its forms of worship distorted the town plans of established cities and created new centres which showed a new type of hospitality to a broad clientele.[26] Christianity taught the ideal of charity and the spiritual worth of the poor, teachings which did lead to new practice, though never to so much as idealists hoped.

Through Christianity, the concept of sin was also spread widely in the pagan world. The subsequent history of sin is largely the history of its triumph, but awareness of its nature did lead to the growth of new agencies to cope with its effects. In turn, they, too, became new centres of power and economic consequence.[27] Christians often neglected Christian virtues, but Christian attitudes and rewards were publicized to the point where Christians could not simply forget them. They changed the ways in which people regarded life's great encounters, between man and woman and also between people and their gods, encounters which are a central theme of this book. They changed attitudes to life's one certainty: death. They also changed the degree of freedom with which people could acceptably choose what to think and believe. Pagans had been intolerant of the Jews and Christians whose religions tolerated no gods except their own. Yet the rise of Christianity induced a much sharper rise in religious intolerance and the open coercion of religious belief. Christians were quick to mobilize force against the pagan cults and against their own unorthodox Christian brethren, a reaction which was not the late creation of Constantine and his reign. The change from pagan to Christian brought a lasting change in people's view of themselves and others: to study it is to realize how we, still, live with its effects.

# Part One

///////////////////////////////////////////////////////////////////////////////////////////////////////////////

*"I wish there was one person in my life I could show. One instinctive, absolutely unbrisk person I could take to Greece and stand in front of certain shrines and sacred streams and say 'Look! Life is only comprehensible through a thousand local Gods. And not just the old dead ones with names like Zeus —no, but living Geniuses of Place and Person. And not just Greece, but modern England! Spirits of certain trees, certain curves of brick wall, certain chip shops, if you like, and slate roofs—just as of certain frowns in people, and slouches. . . I'd say to them, 'Worship as many as you can see—and more will appear!' "* . . .

Martin Dysart, in *Equus* by Peter Shaffer

# 2. Pagans
## and Their Cities

///////////////////////////////////////////////////////////////////////////////////////////////////////////////////

I

By the reign of Gordian, the pagan gods could look back across centuries of uninterrupted worship. In the cities, their cults were supported by their claims to tradition and antiquity, supports which recur as commonplaces in pagan literature, from the orators of classical Athens to Libanius's speech "On Behalf of the Temples," composed in 386 A.D.[1] The cults of the gods had helped men and their cities to come so far for so long. Life, maybe, was bleak, but who was to say that it would not have been very much bleaker if these cults had not been maintained? These arguments did not exclude change: new gods were accepted; old gods were welcomed in new manifestations; details of worship and ritual were added or forgotten. Although the last new pagan god, Mithras, was introduced to the Latin West by the late first century A.D., the pagan cults did not become static: even the old state priesthoods at Rome, the Arval Brothers and the Vestal Virgins, show lively changes of detail during the first half of the third century.[2] However, the old argument from tradition survived continuing changes in matters of practice. It survived because it was essential to the way in which people wished to understand pagan cult.

The argument from tradition continued to outweigh the scepticism which was sometimes expressed by members of the educated class. Past thinkers had written very penetratingly on the nature of the gods and religious practice and had aired much which modern theorists of religion have had to rediscover. Cults and images, some had said, were valid only because they existed already and encouraged civic cohesion; the nature of god was unknowable, and negative theology was the sole way of discussing it; as for men's ideas of the gods, they were modelled on the social relationships which men experienced among themselves on earth.[3] Subtle though many of these arguments were, they attracted next to no interest and had no practical consequences in the Imperial period. They slumbered, until Christian

*Major pagan cities of Asia Minor and Syria, 100–250* A.D.

teichus
Sinope

**BLACK SEA**

NTUS

mpeiopolis

Amisus
(Samsun)

Themiscyra

Side

Cerasus

Trapezus

Phazemon

Eupatoria
(Magnopolis)

a
anicopolis)

Amasea

Cabeira
(Neocaesarea)

Comana Pontica
(Hierocaesarea)

Nicopolis

Satala

Megalopolis
(Sebastea)

Tavium

Eriza

**ARMENIA**

**CAPPADOCIA**

Halys

yssa

Mazaca
(Caesarea)

Melitene

Ingila

Comana

Tigranocerta

Nazianzus

Arabissus

Tigris

arsaura

Amida

Cucusus

Tyana

Nemrud Dagh

ustinopolis
Podandus

Samosata

Flaviopolis

Edessa (Urfa)

Nisibis

Anazarbus

Hieropolis
(Castabala)

Doliche

Apamea

Carrhae (Harran)

Cilician
Gates

Tarsus

Adana

Mopsuestia

Issus

**MESOPOTAMIA**

peiopolis)

ba

Elaeusa (Sebaste)

Hierapolis

Corycus

icia

Antioch

amis

Beroea
(Aleppo)

**SYRIA**

Euphrates

—— Boundary of the Empire
- - - Provincial boundaries

0        100        200 *miles*
0    100    200    300 *km*

authors revived them and used them against pagan opponents.[4] Meanwhile, the major philosophies in the Imperial age did more to supplement religious cult than to undermine it. Arguments against contemporary practice were sporadic and not concerted; their main result was to commend a philosophic type of piety which could usually coexist with established worship.[5] Critiques of myth were hardly more radical: they were not so much concerned to reject the entire tradition as to prune it of its absurdities, as a modern historian might prune it too, and to read the awkward parts as allegories of a deeper truth.[6]

Philosophers were few, even among the educated, and despite their writings "superstition" was not confined to the lower classes. In practice, religious overinsurance spanned the social boundaries and was evident, perhaps as it always had been, in members of the upper class too.[7] Its other, more sceptical members tended to follow the majority and pay the civic worship which their fathers had paid before them.[8] A degree of agnosticism did not lead to outright atheism, except, perhaps, among a few of the most dogmatic astrologers: we hear of one, but only in a fine Christian fiction, the "Recognitions," whose core probably goes back to the early third century.[9] Perhaps this Christian text exaggerated, for the astrologers whose books survive were not so extreme: astrology and cult were not mutually exclusive.[10] In the early Christian period, atheism, in our sense, was not an option. "Atheists" were either Epicureans who denied the gods' providence, but not their existence, or Jews and Christians who worshipped their own God, while denying everyone else's.

Nowadays, "pagan" is a term sometimes used by people who may accept that a god exists but who cannot believe the stories and preferences which the "revealed" religions have ascribed to theirs. It is also used by the worldly majority, those who have been exposed to Christianity, and dislike it, or who have not taken the doctrine seriously but have gone along with it because it offers something to their own wish to mark life's progressions, from the cradle to the grave. In antiquity, pagans already owed a debt to Christians. Christians first gave them their name, *pagani*. The word first appears in Christian inscriptions of the early fourth century and remained colloquial, never entering the Latin translations of the Bible. In everyday use, it meant either a civilian or a rustic. Since the sixteenth century, the origin of the early Christians' usage has been disputed, but of the two meanings, the former is the likelier. *Pagani* were civilians who had not enlisted through baptism as soldiers of Christ against the powers of Satan. By its word for non-believers, Christian slang bore witness to the heavenly battle which coloured Christians' view of life.[11]

"Paganism," too, is a Christian coinage, a word, like "Judaism," which suggests a system of doctrine and an orthodoxy, as Christian religion knows one. By modern historians, pagan religion has been defined as essentially a matter of cult acts.[12] The definition has an obvious aptness. Pagans performed rites but professed no creed or doctrine. They did pay detailed acts of cult, especially by offering animal victims to their gods, but they were not committed to revealed beliefs in the strong Christian sense of the term. They were not exhorted to faith: "to anyone brought up on classical Greek philosophy, faith was the lowest grade of cognition . . . the state of mind of the uneducated."[13] Although followers of Plato's philosophy began to give the term more value in the later third century A.D., no group of pagans ever called themselves "the faithful": the term remains one of the few ways of distinguishing Jewish and Christian epitaphs from those which are pagan.[14] There was also no pagan concept of heresy. To pagans, the Greek word *hairesis* meant a school of thought, not a false and pernicious doctrine. It applied to the teachings of different philosophical schools and sometimes to the medical schools too. Significantly, some pagans denied it to the Sceptics because they doubted everything and held no positive doctrine themselves: Sceptics, in turn, opposed them, wanting to be a *hairesis*, like other schools. Among pagans, the opposite of "heterodoxy" was not "orthodoxy," but "homodoxy," meaning agreement.[15]

The modern emphasis on paganism's cult acts was also acknowledged by pagans themselves. It shaped the way in which they tried and tested Christians: Christians were required by their judges to pay a gesture of worship to the pagan gods, an "act" which did not concern itself with their accompanying beliefs. To ensure the "peace of the gods," it was thought, this act sufficed. In 257, the two reigning Emperors stated this point in a letter to one of their provincial governors: they required the Christians, "those who do not follow Roman 'religion' (*religio*)," to "observe Roman religious ceremonies."[16] The Emperors, however, did not use the distinction so simply as do our modern summaries of paganism. The paying of ceremonies was sufficient to please the gods, but cult acts alone, they implied, did not amount to "following the Roman *religio*." What, then, did? The meaning and derivations of the Latin word *religio* had

long interested the ancients themselves.[17] It could mean the awe from
which any religious cult begins. It had a force as the opposite to
*superstitio*, the excessive fear of the gods. In the Christian period, it
gained a meaning as one or other religion: "our *religio*," Christian
authors wrote, as opposed to "yours." It is in this wider sense that I
assume the Emperors' letter used it, and so I will begin by surveying
the ceremonies and their civic context; then I wish to explore other
aspects of "following a *religio*," in the wider sense. I will concentrate
on the Greek cultural area, and admittedly, there is no term comparable to *religio* in Greek. However, there is a comparable area of
concepts, at least when the word is used in its wider sense. They do not
rest on dogma or orthodoxy or revealed texts, and thus I will describe
them not as religion but as religiousness. In its most extreme sense, the
practice of nothing but cult acts would be impossible. The very idea of
action involves intention or motive or purpose and some relation to
belief, if not in a strong Christian form. It may also evoke unconscious
associations in the performers and observers, which we must respect,
though as historians we cannot catch them in our network of surviving articulate evidence.

For this purpose, my broad limits of time are the early second to
mid-third centuries A.D., from the reign of the Emperor Hadrian
(117–138) to the end of the Severan dynasty (in 235). Much more is
known about pagan cult in this period than in the years which follow:
my primary aim is to evoke the range of pagan cults and accompanying religiousness while the Christian churches were putting down
their roots. I also wish to imply how much would have had to be
abandoned if the bleaker, modern histories of the sequel, from c. 235
to 300, were to prove correct.

To write about pagan cult is, inevitably, to select, and I have
selected my area with the contemporary Christian evidence in mind.
At this period, the two great languages of culture were Greek and
Latin, both of which extended beyond their original area. Greek was
current in most of the areas which had a Christian bishop before c. 250:
it was part of the high culture of a great city like Carthage in North
Africa, or in Lyons, to which, as to Rome, it had been brought by
immigrants from the East. It was the most international language in
the Empire. Latin had been spread through the West by particular
foundations or reorganizations of towns and by the presence and
recruitment of the Roman army.[18] In the Greek East, neither of these
influences was strong. Its new towns were organized as centres of

Greek, not Latin, culture, and in some important Eastern provinces the military influence was largely irrelevant. The most vital seat of Greek culture was the western coast of Asia (now Turkey), and here there was almost no recruitment into the Roman army and no contact with resident legions: Roman citizenship, therefore, was most common among prominent individuals in the province before its general extension in 212. In both the East and the West, Greek and Latin were surrounded by local languages whose importance we will confront when we turn to the Christians' missionary aims. These local cultures had their own religious traditions, of which those in Egypt and the Syrian area were especially prominent.

So many overlapping and coexisting cultures make general descriptions of "paganism" extremely difficult. Indeed, there is a merit in studying pagan cults only on a small, regional scale, not least to bring out their variety and, by implication, their contrast with the more uniform religion of Jewish and Christian contemporaries. Local variations were as abundant as local language and culture, and they often proved more tenacious, even when Greek or Latin became dominant. In Egypt, animal worship persisted beside the cults which Greeks and Romans introduced and continued to arouse strong passions: in the late first century, two neighbouring towns in Egypt declared open war after attacks on each other's sacred animals. This fervour struck outsiders as very bizarre: animal worship, Greeks remarked, must have been introduced by an early Pharaoh on the principle "divide and rule."[19] It coexisted with an elaborate daily "divine service" of the gods' images, much of which was comparable with practices which were known two thousand years earlier, in the Pharaohs' Old Kingdom. In Egypt, the duties of the hereditary priesthoods were very detailed and the number of festivals was very high: the village of Soknopaiou Nesos centred on a cult of a crocodile god, and in the Imperial period festivals in the god's honour took up more than 150 days a year. Only the priests had the time to attend to all of them, and full-time priests created full-time work for themselves; in this matter, religious bureaucracies are like any other.[20]

Although Egypt's priesthoods were exceptional, their cults were not the only curiosities in the Empire. In Anatolia, people honoured a Holy and Just divinity, complete with attendant angels; in Syria, temples had characteristic staircases; processions gave a prominent place to the image of the god, carried in a litter; fish were sacred and protected in everyday diet; the worshippers of certain Syrian gods would tattoo their wrists and hands with a vow to a particular divinity. They dedicated durable model hands in this style, which still survive and illustrate the patterns for us; sometimes, their men pierced their ears and wore earrings. Christian authors later ascribed these "punk" habits to hated fellow Christians, heretics from the same Syrian areas.[21]

Was this multiplicity and local variety a source of weakness? People held the priesthoods of several different gods at once; temples housed several cult images: altars proliferated. By the late second century, Apollo's great precinct at Didyma was so crowded that a visitor referred to its "encirclement with altars of every god."[22] Did people begin to lose their way? Pagans, it has been argued, "lived with a bewildering mass of alternatives. There were too many cults, too many mysteries, too many philosophies of life to choose from: you could pile one religious insurance on another and not feel safe."[23] People might adhere to one god as their particular protector, but they did not convert to one god only. Pagans had never had a wider choice of god than during this period, and yet these various cults show no sign of competing for people's sole adherences. Competition for converts was the business of philosophies only. Is not bewilderment at the range of choice a judgement coloured by Christianity? No pagan complained of it, and multiplicity had its strengths. As we shall see, it helped people to explain their misfortune in external terms, by error, not by sin. Pagans might be neglecting one angry divinity among many, whose mood accounted for their hardships.

By the Imperial period, however, were pagans beginning to merge these multiple gods into a single whole, a pagan "drift into mono-theism" on which Christian teaching could capitalize? Pagan hymns, dedications, engraved gems and amulets do honour a pagan god as "one" or combine its name with several others.[24] This style of address is frequent from the first century A.D. onwards and is particularly evident in the cult of Serapis. We can contrast this developed theology with Serapis's simpler forms in the Hellenistic period: not until the first century do we meet "one Serapis," "Helioserapis," "Zeus Helios Serapis" and so forth.[25] Perhaps this grander style of address increased the attraction of Serapis's cult for yet more worshippers. By honour-ing the god, they were conscious of honouring a very high divinity to which the lesser divine powers were subordinate. A similar inflation affected other divinities, Artemis at Ephesus, Asclepius at Pergamum or Isis "the one who is All."[26] However, it did not amount to monotheism, because it did not exclude worship for lesser gods too. "One Zeus" or "one Serapis" was "the great Zeus" or "the one" for a worshipper at a particular moment. So, too, there might be a Supreme god, but he did not exclude worship for his many subordinates. "Most High" gods or an abstract divinity enjoyed many local cults, in Asia Minor, Syria and other cities. Occasionally, but by no means always, they owed a debt to the religious language of a local Jewish community, but they did not adopt Jewish monotheism.[27] They were not the only god in heaven and their priests might be priests of other gods too. Coexistence remained the hallmark of pagan divinities, from the age of Homer to Constantine. The philosophers respected it too, for all their emphasis on a supreme god.

To what, then, did this merging and agglomeration of titles amount? It has been understood as a definite syncretism, or merging of cults, which gained momentum in a "vast religious landslide" and eventually dragged pagan cults downhill in the course of the third century.[28] This syncretism tends to receive most weight from those who see the history of paganism as a gradual corruption by Oriental influences: syncretism merged the gods of the East with the traditional cults and thus undermined their stability. Such clear oppositions between "Eastern" and "traditional" cult are no longer convincing, and the very category of Oriental religion has been severely reduced in significance.[29] Often, this syncretism did more to enlarge a god's appeal than to undermine it. As the higher Greek and Roman cultures spread, they met local divinities whom they interpreted as forms of the gods whom they already knew. Characteristic threesomes of gods had long been worshipped in Syria, and in due course they received the names of well-known Greek gods too: so far from losing identity, they became intelligible to more visitors. Syncretism took various forms, but usually it was a harmless consequence of this Greek or Latin acculturation. At other times it was a mode of address, which had no clear consequence for practice. Syncretism was no new development, least of all in Egypt, and under the Empire it coexisted with copious evidence for exactly the opposite, seen in the detailed portraits of gods on coins, in precise details of cult statues, in worshippers' concern to bring exact copies of the image of their local divinity when they travelled and above all in their acceptance that gods could be seen and heard and identified. Of this precision, I shall have more to say.

In general, studies of pagan cult in the Imperial period have tended to emphasize the foreign and the exotic gods. By implication, these gods are seen as a significant bridge to the Christian sequel, or as symptoms that all was not well in the pagans' heaven. By contrast, I will say most about the pagan cults of Greek tradition; then I will explore the presence and oracles of the gods, using evidence which is almost entirely Greek. The so-called Oriental gods, Mithras, Serapis, Isis and others, were themselves Greek creations. Their appeal cannot be reduced to one common thread of novelty, to a concern for the afterlife, perhaps, or to a myth in which the god shared humans' sufferings, or to a greater emphasis on the emotional and the ecstatic in their rites.[30] Their cults were too varied to be compressed in one way, and their new importance should not be exaggerated. Some of them remained gods with strong local constituencies, although travellers took them far and wide: none had a strong missionary drive or an aim of excluding other cults. Those "Orientals" which were most widespread did not differ in kind from the traditional civic gods. Certain aspects were perhaps more prominent: their presence in dreams, their healing and saving powers, their exotic ceremonies. These differences were only differences of degree. "Oriental" gods sometimes laid claims to a great antiquity and to a universal power throughout the world and the business of life. This breadth was central to their appeal, attracting people whose idea of the gods had enlarged with their idea of the universe. To a keener devotee, they could offer the idea of predestination, whereby he or she had always been marked out for a particular cult.[31] This style, however, did not amount to an alternative paganism. Priests and worshippers of these gods held priesthoods of the traditional gods at the same time.[32]

Nor will a province of "magic" be my primary source of examples. In antiquity, magic was itself a religious ritual which worked on pagan divinities.[33] It was not a separate technology, opposed to religious practice. To the ancients, magic was distinguished from respectable rites and prayers by the malevolence of its intentions and the murkiness of the materials which it used. It was not a new force, different in kind from conventional cult: cults, too, compelled their gods with symbols and aimed to work on them for beneficial ends. We know much more about magical technique in the Imperial period, as more evidence survives on the papyrus of practitioners' working books. Was it, therefore, a new and ascendant force? The art had gained much from the Greeks' contact with the Near East, especially Egypt; under the Empire, we find amulets and magical gems of an expensive style;

their users were not humble people, no more than the courtiers and senators in Imperial Rome, on whom the charge of magic could be plausibly fixed. In the mid-first century, we have the vivid letter of one young user of the art, Thessalus the student-doctor, who prefaced it to a work on medical "astro-botany" and addressed it, as so many authors did, to the Roman Emperor. In it, he tells how he found that the bolder magical rites were no longer being practised by the native priesthood in Egypt's ancient temples. He had not, however, turned to magic because traditional religion was dying away.[34] His aim was itself religious, to meet a traditional god, Asclepius, face to face and learn from him the secrets of the herbal doctors' art. Finally, Thessalus claimed, he had found one elderly priest who obliged him: in this light, the growth of subsequent Greek texts on magic helped to enlarge and organize an art which was dying in its former Egyptian sphere.

The art of magic was varied, but it divided, broadly, into two.[35] Most of its spells can be defined as a type of sorcery which was used for competitive ends. They enlisted a personal spirit and deployed the power of words and symbols in order to advance a suit in love or in the law courts, to win at the games, to prosper in business or to silence envious rivals. Significantly, this sorcery was a learned art, preserved in texts and usually worked by experts for their clients. It had always been practised in ancient societies, but it had become more organized through Greek contact with Eastern techniques. Its types of spell did not undermine the place of the gods. They supported the gods, if anything, by helping to explain failures: people could blame adversity on the "evil eye" or the malevolence of a rival, rather than on heedless, ungrateful divinities.

In the Imperial period, Greek magical texts also catered to clients who had more spiritual aspirations. They served their wish to win immortality for their soul, to escape the confines of fate and necessity and to confront a Supreme god alone, in a personal "introduction."[36] This more spiritual type of magic reflected issues which the growth of philosophic piety had helped to spread: it did not itself create them. Honours for the gods were like dealings on an ever more complex heavenly exchange. Everybody invested, hoping to profit and some- times to enjoy the gods' close protection. Spells were the illegal insider dealing of people who were overambitious to achieve a personal end or to attain to the higher source of power behind the baffling macro- economy of the heavens. Magic was not the "real" religion of most people: it flourished, not by opposing the surrounding religiousness, but by trading on it.

In this pagan religiousness, there is, I believe, a common core despite the many variations in local practice. It is not lost by drawing largely on evidence in Greek and Latin. From Britain to Syria, pagan cults aimed to honour the gods and avert the misfortunes which might result from the gods' own anger at their neglect. Like an electric current, the power of the gods had great potential for helping and harming; unlike electricity, it was unpredictable and mortals could do no more than attempt to channel its force in advance. Any account of pagan worship which minimizes the gods' uncertain anger and mortals' fear of it is an empty account. This fear did not preclude thanksgiving, but thanks, in Greek prayer, were interwoven with ideas of propitiation. These ideas centred on the offering of gifts. In prayers and offerings, there was an explicit concern to "give to the givers," the gods, in the hope of future favours.[37] Some people stressed that these offerings were best made voluntarily, but there was generally a strong hope of a return: this same precept, "give to the giver, not to the person who does not give," was rooted in traditional Greek advice on the business of living. So, too, was a lively concern for personal honour. It is not, then, so surprising that the gods were concerned with honour and the due offering of gifts. They shared the attitudes which guided their worshippers' relations with one another. They were not just superior patrons, but powers of immense superiority: they were particularly touchy, then, about honour and were not committed to giving regular gifts in return.

I intend to concentrate on Greek and (less so) Roman worship of angry divinities because this worship was the dominant piety in the towns, and it is in the towns that the Christians were concentrated. This type of paganism is the one which they knew and at times distorted to suit their own arguments. Such, however, was the range of the towns and provinces that here, too, the gods varied. Christian authors tended to attack the old and traditional Greek and Roman divinities, but throughout the Empire the gods of these high cultures had absorbed other local gods. This absorption took many different forms. In the towns of North Africa, the Latin names tended to dominate and it becomes hard to disentangle a local prehistory for most of the gods whom they describe. In Gaul or Asia Minor, local epithets became attached to the gods of the Greek or Roman pantheon: they made an "Apollo Lairbenos" or "Apollo Anexiomarus," in whom, again, a distinct "native" identity is hard to separate. In the more rural areas, Greek gods were honoured with epithets which often reflected their power over crops or forces of the weather: a Greek name had also been given to the older gods of "Justice" and their attendants. To find cults with the most evident native constituents, we have to look to the more remote areas. In mountainous Pisidia or inner Anatolia, an inscription to a god might be expressed in Greek, but the native name was still recognizable. The form of the inscription was distinct, not the shaped and personalized stone of Greek tradition, but a relief cut into a rock face, praising the god without recording the worshipper's own name.[38]

Meanwhile, there was a further complexity: the influence of Greek and Roman cults on one another. The influence of Greek gods, art and myth on Roman religion was old and pervasive: we began with one of its latest instances, Gordian's games for the Greek Athena. The impact of Roman cults in the Greek East is more elusive. The Roman army, certainly, observed a calendar of official cults which was a continuing agent of Romanity.[39] Soldiers, however, continued to honour their local divinities beside it, without any hindrance or objection: for centuries, the army remained an "oasis of religious freedom." In the Greek East, Romans were resident in several cities and owned land as a major benefit of Empire, and perhaps it is through their presence that Roman cults and their influence show up in Greek cultural settings. Occasionally, we find the Roman festival of roses, or Rosalia, in honour of a dead man; perhaps the festival of the new consular year, the Kalends of January, had already spread: perhaps, too, Roman influence explains the growing tendency to honour the dead not as heroes but as "divinities," which is evident by c. 220 in certain areas of the Greek world.[40] In one area, however, the ruling power of Rome did leave a dominant mark on its subject cities' religion: the cults of the Emperors and select members of their family, alive and dead.

Like magic, worship of the Emperor, a living man, has sometimes been seen as a significant sign of religious decadence. We have one explicit discussion of the motives of an Imperial priest, and it considers the matter entirely in terms of social prestige and the honour of an inscription. Certainly, the social aspects were prized. In North Africa, a priesthood of the Imperial cult stood at the summit of the positions which religion could offer to eminent citizens. In the first two centuries, these cults led to some flamboyant architecture and became a new arena for competition by the provincial upper classes: in Britain, the competitors were said to have "poured out whole fortunes under the pretext of religion."[41] It is not, however, because of this social element that I have nothing specific to say of the cult and its ceremonies: it was not alone among cults in offering scope for social display and competition. I will say less about it directly because it, too, was connected in so many of its forms with the existing cults of traditional gods and drew vigour from their association.[42] The gods were honoured for their power and their capacity for benefaction: the concept of "divine power" is very prominent in dedications to pagan gods in the Imperial period. Like gods, the Roman Emperors were agents of unpredictable power and benefaction: in the Greek world, cult had been freely paid to living rulers since the age of Alexander the Great. It was not, then, surprising that Emperors, too, received divine honours from their subject communities, a worship which was not always imposed from above: in Ephesus, during the reign of Claudius, the Roman governor had to intervene and stop misplaced celebrations by his subjects. People were attempting to sell priesthoods to any bidders, whatever their birth and family, in order to celebrate cults of the Imperial family on the slightest pretence of good news from Rome.[43] Worship of the Emperor was a cue for profit and yet more holidays: in the Latin West, the calendar of the Romanized towns contains a conspicuous number of festivals which are attached to events and members of the Imperial family.[44] Provincials themselves exploited the cults, but their opportunism does not reduce the whole business to flattery. The cult, it has been emphasized, took varying forms, associating the Emperor in varying ways with the gods and their ceremonies. On one strict modern view, it did not involve piety at all, because rulers, dead or alive, were never honoured with piety's touchstone, the votive offering which was made in recognition of a god's recent help.[45] That definition is too strict, while the other extreme view, that the cult was simply a cult of loyalty, is ambiguous. Perhaps for some people it was, but why, then, was it a cult, taking religious forms? What did these forms mean to many others? Generally, the cult attached itself to the lively, traditional religiousness, and this religiousness is my subject. The cult, therefore, increased the pagan ceremonies among which Christians lived, and although it was not the prime motive for their persecution, it was present, at times explicitly, in the accompanying circumstances.[46]

Cults of the Emperor flourished in the cities and were capped by provincial cults which were hosted by one or other major city in a province's self-styled league. They did not extend to local cultures or to the smaller townships and villages. By concentrating on the towns, I, too, have passed over many of the rural cults which extended beyond them. Yet the ultimate rise of Christianity has been connected with a crossing of this barrier, in a significant "winning of the countryside": is my omission, then, a serious restriction? In fact, the line between town and country is one which we can easily define too clearly. The gods themselves helped to bridge it: a focus on urban cult does not exclude the "country" entirely, a point, lastly, which is worth exploring.

Long before Christian pilgrimages, pagan townsmen walked or rode a fair distance to rural festivals on their country properties or further still, to recognized shrines in holy places.[47] These sites lay beside caves and chasms, high up on hilltops, in groves or out by the haphazard seats of the Nymphs and gods of healing, the springs and hot pools. The country landscape had made its own, notable contribution to the myths and presence of the pagan gods.[48] At Dokimeion in Phrygia, the very drops of blood from the dying god Attis could be seen in the red streaks which ran on the white marble quarries of the city's holy mountain. On Samos, people explained the redness of the local stone as due to the blood of Amazons who had been killed there by Dionysus: the very bones of his elephants survived in the island's remarkable fossils. Near Seleuceia, the monster Typhon rumbled in the torrent of an underground river and had to be neutralized by a Byzantine church at the entrance to his mythical resting place. It is only accessible after a steep descent and would not stand there without this pagan presence. Cave after cave claimed to have sheltered the infant Zeus, from Cretan Ida to the handsome cave near the great temple to Zeus at Phrygian Aizani, while a multitude of other caves were connected with the underground worship of Dionysus. At Thibilis, in North Africa, the magistrates processed and climbed yearly to a cave of the god Bacax which lies more than ten miles outside their town: their inscriptions on the site continue into the 280s. These tours from cities were made not only to natural oddities.[49] Some of antiquity's finest temples lay outside a city at several hours' distance, the shrine of Hera on Samos, of Asclepius on Cos or the famous Plutonium by the natural caves outside Nysa. There was a sacred feeling about the rural settings in which so many temples stood. A vivid series of second- and third-century inscriptions were found in the Phrygian shrine of a local "Apollo Lairbenos," whose visitors could hardly miss the divinity of its site. The temple stood on a hill of coloured rocks high above the Maeander River valley, where "curtains of red, brown and yellow seem to be draped along the face of either bluff . . . this desolate canyon might still be the haunt of gods." Here Apollo guarded his precinct watchfully. The Olympians and their myths were at home in Mediterranean settings, not in the broad deserts and river plains and regular monsoon winds of the further East. Landscapes receive the pagan gods they deserve, and the gods were not so urban that they ever lived only in towns.[50]

Urban artists and authors did not belittle the connection of their gods with rural nature. On the whole, they idealized it. It was the setting for their novels, for Horace's least ironic odes, for a charming poem by Martial, for Apuleius's plea to his judge that his opponent was the sort of scoundrel who would not bother to honour country shrines.[51] To Aelian, an urban man of letters, we owe a brilliant word picture of the relation between the gods and the landscape in the divine vale of Tempe during the second century.[52] The trees, he wrote, arch thickly over the banks of the famous river Peneus, which "glides gently like olive oil." Among them, the nearby peoples came together to offer sacrifices, hold parties and drink. "So many people offer sacrifices so continuously that those who walk or sail nearby are accompanied by the sweetest smell . . ." Well-born boys were sent from Delphi to sacrifice "conspicuously" every ninth year at the altar where Apollo was believed to have purified himself. They wove themselves crowns from the very laurel with which Apollo had encircled his brow. Their type of lively worship was one which we would never guess from the jibes of contemporary Christian texts.

Perhaps a similar image of a "divine landscape" encouraged painters in the big villas and town houses to show the countryside schematically as a landscape marked out by small shrines. The country was not remote from the richer townsman's life. The smartest town houses in Sicily or Africa, Pontus or northern Greece might belong to estate owners who returned to their properties for that pearl of all sports, their hunting. As we can see in their villas' mosaics, they prefaced the chase with offerings on small, private altars to the appropriate gods.[53] The hunters' gods were country gods, Pan and the deities who assisted their sport and were thanked for its catch. On the farms, too, the rustic divinities were honoured, and as the mosaics remind us, urban landlords might visit the fields at harvesttime:[54] they did not look down on these gods as a type of superstition. Pliny took pride in repairing and adorning a shrine of Ceres on his estates to which crowds flocked for a yearly festival: the soothsayers approved his action. He wrote with love of the Clitumnus springs, their setting, their temple and their oracular practice. Some of the inscriptions on the site seemed absurd to him, the sort of thing we still find, but others, he felt, were admirable.[55] When Christian monks began to destroy pagans' rural shrines, Libanius told the Emperor that "shrines are the very soul of the countryside."[56] They gave the farm labourer hope and increased his keenness by allowing him to pray for the health of the crops. So the land produced more, he said, the peasant was not poor and the landlord's yield was greater. Both classes, he alleged, gained from these temples' presence, and although we might be more cynical, it is revealing that he, a townsman, could argue this.

Did the townsman, however, travel with an idealized image of the country and its gods when he went out for a festival or a tour of his estates? In many provinces, the citizen's Greek and Latin were not the languages of many of the peasants and dependent workers. These people paid simple honours to their own gods and powers of country life, the type of worship which we can glimpse in Virgil's *Georgics* behind its prologue of glossy Greek divinities: in the Italian country-side, farmers offered daisy chains on plain turf altars to gods of the fields. These gods were not dignified by the traditions of classical art or a place in Greek mythology. They were the forces with which country people lived: these rural gods were "simpletons," said urban authors, when compared with the gods of the towns.[57]

Even so, there was not a total barrier between the two. Country gods also turn up among a city's cults, because the townsmen, too, depended on them for food and for the health of their market gardens and suburban plots. There was nothing specifically rustic about the association of pagan cults with trees and springs. Shrines in towns and country alike were surrounded by fine canopies of trunks and branches, their sacred groves. The gods were extremely jealous of their safety, the oaks of northern Lydia, the fine cypresses of Cos or the pines in the special groves of the cults of Attis. Guarded by the gods, these woods attained a great age and maturity. They offered refuge to suppliants and escaped prisoners; they also housed deer and dogs, cattle, snakes and unusual birds. So ubiquitous were snakes that at Claros their absence in the sacred grove was a miracle, due to Apollo himself; elsewhere, there were places where dogs would not hunt animals into the dark coverts of a divinity. In Sicily, on the slopes of

Etna, a local temple was said to house over a thousand sacred dogs who would fawn on the visitors. At night, they earned their keep: they escorted peaceful drunkards back to their houses and were said to bite those who tried to misbehave. It was the very essence of a sacred grove to encourage myths and good stories.[58]

These groves were carefully tended, a feature of pagan towns and their territories anywhere from Britain to Syria. Here and there, the cults themselves did devour mature trees.[59] There was a "Hera of the tree cutting" on Cos, a Dionysus in Asia Minor whose priests carried uprooted trees and in the great shrine at Syrian Hierapolis a yearly festival when big trees were brought into the goddess's precinct. Live goats, sheep and birds were hung on the branches among fine robes, gold and silver. Then the entire tree and its decorations were burnt to the ground. These ceremonies were exceptional, and they did not diminish a general care and admiration for the well-tended grove. Since the classical period, civic decrees had warned against illicit "wooding" and gathering in the gods' plantations; local magistrates were to exact fines from freeborn offenders and whip the slaves, one or two strokes being equivalent to each drachma of a free man's fine. The persistent rules remind us that the offence was very tempting in a harsh Mediterranean winter.[60] Round Hecate's great shrine at Lagina, in southwestern Asia, eunuchs and public slaves tended the noble trees of the goddess and worked under the strict orders of the priests to replant any specimens which died. Decrees were concerned with replanting as well as preservation, for almost every cult aspired to rural sanctity, and nowhere was gardening more devoted.[61] Well into the Christian era, in the third or early fourth century, some effusive epigrams were cut into the rock of the acropolis at Lindos, on Rhodes; they honoured a priest of Athena, Aglochartos, for feats of silviculture which rivalled, they said, the gods of myth. To that bare, dry site, he had transplanted the goddess's grey-green olives, "decorating it with the scented branch" at his own expense. Christians, by contrast, were soon to practise some determined felling at either end of the Mediterranean. St. Martin was remembered for killing some great old trees in Gaul, and in the east, in the sixth century, John of Ephesus made several assaults on Asia's sacred timber. The triumph of Christianity was accompanied by the sound of the axe on age-old arboreta.

Just as the countryside ran into the town, so an ebb and flow of people joined the two landscapes in honour of the gods. Out from the town went the citizen, wanting quiet, a particular cult or natural holy place: quiet brings understanding, said the philosophers in this period, and that is why people build shrines in lonely places, to Pan, the Muses and Apollo.[62] Our modern lines between town and country become blurred by the enduring willingness of Mediterranean people to walk and commute. A walk of three hours or more is not considered excessive by modern Greek islanders commuting to distant plots of ground: perhaps in antiquity, too, the farmer would travel from the town where he resided to temporary shacks, like the modern *spitakia*, on his outlying fields.[63] At holidays, there was scope for still longer journeys, from town to country and also from country village to town. By a reverse traffic, countrymen walked into the cities' major festivals. The habit has been adduced to explain the timing of the sacred calendars in classical Attica: the festivals in the outlying demes tend not to overlap with the big festivals in the city, presumably so as to allow the countrymen time to attend the major celebrations. With them, the surrounding country sent the necessities of every cult, the animals for sacrifice, whose stabling and maintenance required the cooperation of townsman and country dweller: in 215, when the Emperor Caracalla tried to ban the flight of country dwellers into Alexandria, he exempted those who were bringing necessities for sacrifice.[64]

At the festivals, townsmen and country visitors heard the same hymns and praises of the gods. They saw the same statues and pictures and heard the stories which filtered downwards from the only culture, the shared assumptions of educated men. It is hard to draw firm boundaries when country dwellers, too, came to consult a great oracular shrine or when a society of gardeners and another of shell-fishermen can be found in a great city, worshipping a Most High god. Their worship, in third-century Miletus, was shared by a notable city councillor who was also a prophet of the god: he was honoured by the gardeners, fellow worshippers of the Most High. "Higher" theology and rural piety were not totally opposed. Views on the gods could circulate by word of mouth, like so much in the cities' culture: countrymen did not read as a habit, but neither did most townsmen. In a charming dialogue (c. 100 A.D.), the orator Dio told how wise Charidemus had learned about the world from a peasant who had spoken "with a decidedly rustic lilt." He had told him that men were the gods' guests at a banquet, that the world was built like a rich man's mansion, that its dinner tables were the meadows and shores, that the

Seasons waited on their hosts in heaven, but that the human guests behaved with different manners and were rewarded accordingly by the watching gods. Was Dio, for once, not distorting reality entirely? Countrymen, too, had their periods of leisure, their opportunities to visit temples and hear visitors' tales.[65]

It was, as always, the variety of language which imposed the real barriers, but here written evidence fails us almost entirely, and we cannot pursue ideas of the gods into the remoter rural hinterlands or dialects. This failing, however, is not too serious for the scope of this book, because the early Christians were bound by it too. The Christian churches kept no animals for their rites. They were marked, as we shall find, by an urban centre of gravity and their priests served townspeople in urban places of worship. In their first centuries, the pagan gods still brought the towns and countryside into persistent contact. Not until the mid-fourth century, after Constantine, and the rise of the holy men and rural martyr shrines, were the Christian communities turned likewise to the countryside beyond.[66]

# II

Gods, like men, live in a social context, and as pagans and Christians met almost entirely in towns and cities, we need some idea of their social order in this period. No sketch can account for all the exceptions, while generalizations can only convey what was more or less the case, more often than not. This sketch aims to give the right emphasis, even where details remain uncertain: into it, we can fit the pagan cults and eventually the Christians and their social distribution.

The Greek-speaking areas of the Empire abounded in towns, not to mention the larger "villages" which often aspired keenly to "city" status. By "city," historians mean a "city-state," which controlled a hinterland: they do not generally mean a large city in our sense. The size of the hinterland varied greatly: a valley, perhaps, for a hill town in Anatolia, or a huge territory, including over fifty dependent villages, for Carthage, a prominent seat of Christians. Their populations fluctuated and are largely a matter of guesswork, informed in varying degrees by evidence. Most cities probably ranged from five to fifteen thousand people, but a select minority were vastly larger. Their size has also been deduced from varying evidence. Surveys of the city territory and guesses as to its population's density credit Ephesus with c. 150,000 residents, Palmyra with c. 200,000; by analogy, the great city of Antioch cannot have been smaller. For Rome, c. 200 A.D., a total of at least a million, including visitors, is at the lower end of the estimates.[1]

Ancient sources suggest the figures for Rome and give others of varying authority: an inscription gives an official figure for the "free" population of Apamea in Syria at the turn of the era and suggests c. 200,000 people in all; another official estimate is transmitted at one remove for Alexandria in Egypt and suggests well over half a million; from tax records, Josephus believed, another seven and a half million tax payers were recorded in the rest of Egypt (c. 70 A.D.). Galen, a contemporary resident, implies that Pergamum, c. 160, held 120,000 people, including slaves. Other figures are harder to control. On the eastern frontier, Seleuceia-on-the-Tigris was known to be enormous, although neither of the texts which credit it with 400,000 to 500,000 people is reliable. In central Anatolia, a better source gives 400,000 people to Caesarea, the main city of Cappadocia. The figure has been emended to 40,000, but Caesarea was one of the only cities in this large and very fertile area and perhaps we should conclude that people knew it to be enormous too.[2]

None of these calculations can claim accuracy, nor did the cities' populations remain constant. Earthquakes and epidemics were a constant hazard; by c. 200, separate figures suggest only c. 300,000 people for Alexandria, falling further by the mid-third century; Roman troops sacked Seleuceia in the 160s and Persians sacked Caesarea in the 260s. Nonetheless, these figures point to an order of magnitude which is very significant. Their size vastly exceeds the size of cities in Europe c. 1600, a date when London is credited with c. 200,000 residents, Rome with c. 150,000; not until the mid–nineteenth century did Egypt's population approach 8 million again.[3]

If the size of the biggest ancient cities was distinctive, their age patterns surely were not. Visitors and immigrants distorted the distribution of ages in a city at any one time, but life expectancy for individuals was not enhanced by medicines or diets superior, say, to those of French towns in the *ancien régime*. Like France of the eighteenth century, the ancient world was prone to crises of famine or epidemic: "one third of the human race," opined Buffon, "perishes before reaching the age of 28 months; half, before the age of 8 years." Modern studies do not greatly disagree, using his contemporaries' records.[4] In antiquity, the prospects cannot have been better. Infant mortality was almost inconceivably high, a "constant slaughter of the innocents"; one counterbalance, however, was the lower age of marriage for girls.[5] It is easy to be parochial on this topic, when early marriage is still typical of societies outside Western culture, but there is clear evidence in the Latin inscriptions of the Western Empire and the Greek papyri in Egypt that girls could be married at the age of fourteen or earlier. In eighteenth-century France, marriage was postponed, especially in poorer households, in order to limit families: in antiquity, this pattern is not so evident, because of the widespread habit of exposing female babies at birth. Adult girls were in shorter supply and thus their age at marriage tended to be low. In Egypt, early marriage, though attested, is not universal in our evidence: in Egypt, however, it was recognized that the exposure of children was less common, a discrepancy which may bear on these examples of later marriage, traceable in the papyri.

Habitual exposure of babies was a further brake on the size of a family and the balance of the sexes. As in early modern Europe, child-birth was also a constant killer of mothers. By being married young, girls did have a greater chance of producing heirs, but the risks of death in labour probably cancelled the possible gains to the family. For men, too, we can appeal to early modern analogies and assume that the likelihood of death was higher at certain phases of life. Once a male had reached adolescence, he had a better chance of surviving to his late forties, war and plague permitting. Some people lived much longer, but in antiquity, too, "big family groups were assorted survivors. Few children knew both grandparents, and to live long meant, most often, loneliness among a generation of strangers."[6]

During these patterns of life, the towns of each province (with very few exceptions) were subject to governors whom the Roman Emperor instructed, guided and answered when they faced difficulties. The Emperor was petitioned very freely by subjects of varying status, hoping for a response to their benefit from the highest power in their lives. Knowledge, however, of the Emperor and his activities remained very patchy, as we can see from one of the best of all texts on the "Emperor in the Roman world":[7] "people have definite knowledge that there is always a living Emperor," wrote the aristocratic Synesius of his countrymen around Cyrene in the year 408, "because we are reminded of this yearly by the Imperial agents who collect taxes, but it is not clear exactly who he is." Some people, Synesius claimed, still thought that Homer's King Agamemnon was in power, while the honest herdsmen believed that he had a friend and minister called Odysseus, a "bold man, but clever at finding ways out of difficulties." "Indeed, they laugh when they speak of him, believing that he blinded the Cyclops only last year." The touches of Homeric myth are probably Synesius's own, but his picture of the local ignorance of names and history is entirely credible.

Some provinces contained Roman legions, but there were culturally important areas, including Greece and Asia Minor, which did not. Here, as elsewhere, governors and Imperial officials exerted considerable control over cities' finances and dispensation of justice, but there was also an interest in keeping cities sound: they were responsible for amassing the taxes which were paid yearly to the Emperor.[8] In a striking image, Plutarch had reminded a young notable from Asia (c. 100) that Roman senatorial shoes, worn by the province's governor, loomed ever above his contemporaries' heads. Political freedom was indeed curtailed, to the point where politics, on a strict modern definition, have been declared defunct. Plutarch, however, was exaggerating. Governors toured their provinces yearly, visiting only a few centres, and then usually once. In the absence of Roman troops, local policing in the towns was rudimentary. There were civic "night captains," with small detachments of helpers, but, naturally, no local standing armies. When Rome's armies passed nearby, burdens of billeting, supplies and transport were indeed parcelled out in a harsh, arbitrary fashion. But in Asia and other ungarrisoned regions, neither senators nor the military were a constant presence.[9]

Freedom, however, is a relative concept, which an age may lack consciously because it is aware of a time when it had enjoyed more of it. The curbs on local finance and justice were, historically, very severe, although there was scope, of course, for evasion. Citizens of any property and fitness were also liable for inescapable duties, required by the Empire: the provision of transport and lodging and, in this period, the collection of the prescribed amounts of taxes. In a striking scene, the Jew Philo (c. 40 A.D.) tells how a theatre audience, probably in Roman Alexandria, had cheered boisterously at a line in a Greek play referring to "freedom."[10] Alexandrians were perhaps exceptionally conscious of their loss of it, but the scene can be generalized. Greek cities were aware of a great, free past, and in relative terms, we must allow for their sense of a loss of civil and political liberty. It underlay the culture of this period, and we can justly diagnose it, even when contemporaries do not emphasize it. On a broader view, it was itself an ally of the Christians' alternative freedom, stored up in a "city of heaven."

The limits of freedom were evident in the cities' own types of constitution. Any sketch must reckon with Rome, which had no self-government, Alexandria, which had no city council, and the townships of Egypt, which began by having no councils but received them shortly after 200. The Christians were a prominent presence in these exceptional cities, as also in the largest centres of population. My sketch, however, is fitted to a more typical pattern, essentially the Greek-speaking cities of all but the largest size. We do not as yet have a clear idea how the largest cities were run and how far they cohered: perhaps only in Rome, where we have inscriptions, can these questions be studied in any detail. My suspicion is that the big cities, too, fell into quarters and districts, making them an aggregate of the smaller "typical" cities to which my sketch applies. There are exceptions to almost every generalization about civic life, as the cities of the Empire varied widely in size and siting and natural assets. Despite the exceptions, my sketch is intended to cover many more places than it fits only in part.

In the Greek-speaking cities, "democracies" were generally professed, but in practice, affairs were managed locally by the magistrates and councils. The art of civic influence lay, if not exactly in "politics," in skilled manoeuvring and man management: the orator Dio emphasized the value for a civic career of studying Xenophon's *Anabasis*, that story of the manoeuvring of a group of Ten Thousand with no formal constitution.[11] In each city, the number of councillors varied. There might be as few as 30 in the West, though nearer 100 was a more conventional number; in the East, councils ranged from 50 up to 600 in cities as large as Ephesus. Members were elected, and had to be at least twenty years old. There was an entry fee on election, but the degree of competition varied locally. Councillors had their responsibilities, and throughout the period it was a bigger problem to find willing councillors than to select them. Effectively, the core of the councils had turned into hereditary elites, thinned largely by the vagaries of death, infertility and accidents or overspending. Then, less distinguished people might have to be promoted: Roman laws and governors discouraged this social mobility, unless absolutely necessary. It was out of the question for a poor man to serve. For a start, he could not have afforded the entry fee. It was also forbidden for a former slave (freedman) to serve, but office was open to his children, and it is evident, in the Western towns, that those who could afford it took the opportunity. In the Greek East, sons and grandsons of freedmen were present in the council at Athens by the 170s. Presumably, they could be found elsewhere, but we cannot detect them in Greek inscriptions.[12] In the early third century, the Emperor Severus also allowed council service to Jews who were resident in the Diaspora outside Palestine. The ruling has been considered a mark of great honour, but most Jews, like Gentiles, will have been wary of the burdens which it brought. During the difficult years of the mid- to late third century, the famous rabbi Yohanan was said to have given some curt advice to Jews in Palestine: "If you are mentioned for the city council, head for the neighbourhood of the river Jordan."[13]

In many towns and in the villages which were just below civic status, the (all-male) citizenry still met in assemblies. However, their main function was to acclaim the candidates for office and approve the proposals of the council or the presiding magistrates. By the third century, genuine elections were rare, outside the cities of Africa. Throughout the period, governors had been ready to intervene if the city assemblies in their province proved too turbulent: we also find them sending proposals by letter for a city's approval. Assemblies were themselves restricted groups which excluded women everywhere and sometimes dependent villagers or people whose trades were lowly. Not every resident in a city was a citizen of it. Some were visitors, including migrants of sufficient standing to undertake expensive civic duties, if pressed. Conversely, prominent citizens might belong to two or more cities at once in the Greek East or Latin West. The practice survived Roman discouragement, and if the cities quarrelled, these "double citizens" did have scope to mediate.[14]

The primary social division was still the division between slave and free, except, however, in Egypt, where slavery (on the Greek model) was never widespread. The evidence is not so full as to end dispute, but it is still convincing to describe the cities as "slave societies."[15] The issue is not the number of slaves and the precise fraction at which a society then becomes a slave society: it is, more simply, that the upper, propertied class derived its main income, on the likelier view, from slave labour, through their direct use of it and through its use by the tenants to whom they let farms.[16] There were no slave revolts in this period: the problem, rather, was to maintain an economic supply of persons. Within the free population, divisions into rich and poor, "better" and "humbler," were frankly expressed. The "people" (*demos*) of a Greek city become the "poor," quite simply, in the language of their rich benefactors' inscriptions. Meanwhile, in Roman

law, different penalties were being defined for people of different
status: essentially, "one law for the propertied, one for the poor"
established itself in the Antonine age. Before these new categories,
Roman citizenship lost its former legal value. In 212, when it had been
emptied of this privilege, it was extended throughout the Empire,
exposing its holders to further taxes.[17]

Had the rule of the "more honourable" ever been in danger, the
Imperial power would have supported it openly. We do hear of civil
strife in cities, between council and assembly, town and harbour,
excluded residents, even, and the citizen body.[18] In other cases, we
must allow for strife within the ruling order, where feuds and quarrels
were notorious. The city's order of councillors was not the peer group
which their praise of "concord" aspired to make of it. A few families
everywhere were vastly richer and more powerful than the others. By
the 170s, the divisions between these top councillors and other
members of their order are very apparent in Roman legal texts. The
very rich could set a standard of display which was hard to equal and at
the same time use their power to pass unwanted burdens to their
inferiors. From the 170s onwards, unwillingness to serve as a councillor also becomes more marked in our evidence.[19] A serious plague in
Asia was perhaps partly to blame, but so were the growing burdens of
time and expense.

A similar thinning of candidates affected the cities' various magistracies. Prominent citizens were elected to these jobs, or simply
appointed, in order to run the civic amenities and hold office, usually
for a year. These jobs were the positions which men like Longinus of
Side listed proudly on their inscriptions: the provision of games and
grain, oil for the gymnasium or that crippling necessity, fuel for the
heated baths. "Voluntary services," or liturgies, had become attached
to magistracies, joining two spheres of civic activity which classical
democratic Athens had formerly kept separate.[20] While the distinction
between an office and a liturgy was still observed in inscriptions, in
practice magistrates were expected to give and show voluntary
munificence. Donors and benefactors had thus emerged as the major
public "type" in the cities' upper class of notables. The obverse was
the dodgers in their midst, people who claimed one of the various
exemptions from voluntary service which Roman law respected, or
who tried to pass the most expensive types of magistracy to somebody
better placed to take them. There was a continuing tension between
service, exemptions and offers which could not be refused, and this

tension adds force to the professions of willing generosity which appear for us in donors' public inscriptions. The motives and achievements of these donors were central to the civic culture within which Christians lived. It was they who financed the amenities of life and from them civic culture was delicately suspended. To their ideals, as we shall see, the Church opposed a contrary image of community and good conduct: it is important, then, to explore their ideals further. They propelled the religious cults, too, in many of their forms.

Donors were quite open in public about their motives. Their inscriptions made them a cliché, from North Africa to the Greek-speaking East. Sometimes, they cited a "love of their home town": in the Greek East, magistrates donated statues of Eros, or Love, to their cities. Very often, they referred to their "love of honour," or *philotimia*, a word which had grown to cover their gifts themselves, especially if they were gifts of games or gladiatorial combats. The word which they vaunted, *philotimia*, had a murky past in one branch of Greek literature and philosophy. It was a word fit for tyrants or Alexander the Great. Herodotus had mistrusted it, and it had roused the moralists' disapproval, from Euripides to Plutarch.[21] Benefactors cared little for moralists. Instead, they revelled in the acclamations of the crowds and in the number of applauding voices, listed exactly at the end of their honorary decrees. They were "nurturers" of their city, "fathers" or "mothers," "founders" who adorned it with buildings, "adorners," givers like the Ocean or the river Nile. If a rich man dreamed of a river, said dream interpreters, he could anticipate a career as a benefactor. People who "loved honour" flooded their "sweetest homeland" with a tidal wave of gifts. In some cities, they included women of great property, to whom direct political office was denied. Their prominence, naturally, is no ground for generalization about the status or freedom of lesser members of their sex.[22]

Cities only profited from a limited range of rents, dues and taxes and thus they depended on their notables for the financing of their services and public life. There was no direct taxation of the rich, and these gifts were not exactly a "tax on status." Unlike surtax, they enhanced the givers' prestige and gave a useful insurance against envy. There was even a scope for "honour" in the rich man's obligation to provide grain below the market price in times of shortage. This duty could be very heavy, but some people turned it to further advantage by "overachieving" and making exceptional gifts from their estates.

These gifts were hardly innocent. They expressed and confirmed the power of the generous few before the rest of their city, the poor. By an advantageous bargain, the few donated while the many applauded and, continuing to be dependent, acquiesced peacefully. The arrangement was not a democratic device, transposing the older political power of the many into a new material pressure.[23] Informally, the poor could threaten a riot, but they had no formal power to extort. Rather, a primary impulse for giving lay in the givers' own class, among their fellow donors and notables, past and present. How could a Damas in Miletus give less than his father or grandfather had given? How could one great family in the city be seen to give less than another?

Rivalry within the class of givers was matched by keen rivalries between neighbouring cities: it was shameful if a theatre or temple was left in a state much worse than the adjacent city's. Intercity friction was not empty, even when it did not concern the use of assets like ports or territory. Better civic amenities supported claims to higher status and brought greater profits from more visitors and users. Inevitably, a few cities were very much smarter and more distinguished than others. To literary men in this period we owe a sharp perception of the barbarous dullness of small provincial towns:[24] the richer local families sent their children abroad for a proper schooling; people of exceptional talent were grateful to be made citizens of greater cities elsewhere; gradually, the most eminent local families entered the ranks of the Roman Senate, six hundred men who could consider themselves the "better part of the human race." It was miserable for a man of talent to live in some backwater, unvisited by good theatrical companies and graced only with third-rate games. However, awareness of the dullness of minor towns did not stop people from vying to improve them, least of all in the Greek-speaking East.[25]

The lives of these public benefactors were complicated by the accidents of birth and death. Inheritances were shared among sons and, sometimes, daughters: too many children could ruin an estate, and exposure of babies was therefore practised by rich families as well as by the poor.[26] Alternatively, a rich man, like Pliny, might die childless and set a new scale of generosity to his peers by bequeathing some very large legacies to his town in the absence of heirs. The costs of giving tended to spiral, helped upwards by two expensive crazes: heated baths and the shows of wild beasts and gladiators in the arenas. It was a singular mark of glory in public inscriptions if a notable had hired enough pairs of gladiators to sustain a programme of fighting for several days. If they fought to "cutoff point," the sporting slang for death, so much the better: inscriptions noted this fact, too, with pride. Shows of gladiators were still deplored by a few moralists, but they flourished in the major Greek cities, seats of the cults of the Emperor to which the fights were attached. Donors also paid for wild beasts to be "hunted" in the arena, not only bears and wild boars from forests in their province's hinterland, but panthers sometimes and even a few unhappy seals. Expert fighters sometimes fought with these beasts, but so, too, did groups of condemned criminals: the crowds watched while the criminals stood unarmed, ropes round their necks and bonds, too, on their arms. Rich donors paid for these victims, just as they also paid for the beasts and professional fighters. In 177, a decree of the Senate obliged the donors by limiting the price which cities could legally charge for the criminals. Christian martyrs were unlucky to coincide with this particular compound of benefactions, Imperial cult and shows which distinguished the high-ranking cities.[27]

In most cities the number of capable givers was very small indeed, perhaps three or four main families. To see them from the outside, we can look to two lively contemporary sources, the great Greek collection of dreams and their meanings by Artemidorus, whom we will consult later in more detail, and the famous Latin romance *The Golden Ass* by Apuleius. Composed in the late Antonine age (c. 160–170), this work of fiction depicts a province of Greece in which the noble families expect to know each other from one town to the next, while the rest of their townsmen engage in "intense observer participation." As one such observer, the contemporary Artemidorus assumes a similarity between the power of the rich and noble and the power of the gods: dreams of statues, he remarks, signify the doings and prospects of the cities' notables, the class whom these monuments honoured. To Apuleius, we owe a brilliant portrait of the officious severity and contempt for inferiors which a magistrate "of the market" might exhibit in a Greek city, even before a former school friend. To Artemidorus, too, it was not untoward that a magistrate would dream he was showing contempt for those whom he governed.[28]

A class which could exert such economic and political dominance is not prone to receive tributes from modern social historians. However, we must not be miserable philistines. "Love of the home town" meant something distinctive to a class who had a clear idea of the beautiful and attempted to realize it. A firm idea of taste was an attribute which they shared with their admirers, the age of Gibbon. In their literary works and their sculpture, they aspired to a demanding classicism, modelled on distant masters of the fourth century B.C.[29] Like all classicism, theirs has the charm of slipping somewhat, but it also gave its artists a style. There was no division between the upper class, the men of taste, and the people who studied and wrote, practised philosophy and indulged in public speaking: the one group comprised almost all of the other. Style was the man, a mirror of his moral worth, and top people cultivated it keenly. Books were reviewed fiercely for their errors of vocabulary; displays of oratory were a valued public entertainment: masters of the art assumed that their hearers had come equipped to note down their finer turns of phrase. The age's most spectacular feud between two great public figures was thought to have started from a dispute about taste in music.[30] Above all, taste was expressed in architecture, where designs broke with pure classicism and indulged in a splendid baroque vitality. As a result, the upper classes of the second and third centuries are the modern sightseer's best friends. They liked to hear their city's buildings praised in speeches, and the Emperor and his governors shared the same concern: governors were encouraged to see to the restoration of collapsing buildings. They were also to prevent the demolition of old architecture: "planning permission" was among the Empire's instruments of civic control.[31] It did not deter benefactors from a confidence that they, too, could build and improve. Their motives were not only honour and self-esteem. The fashion was for fountains, ornate nymphaeums, "odeons" for music and speeches and long colonnades. Donors wished to improve the "capabilities" of the cities which they loved. One very aristocratic donor in Ephesus, the orator and sophistic speaker Damianus, built a mile-long colonnade of marble from the city to the temple of "Diana of the Ephesians" so that visitors could attend in rainy weather: he gave the temple a banqueting hall of rare Phrygian marble; he also showed concern for the landscape. He planted his estates with fruit trees for their crop and their shade; he designed his houses in the city's suburbs "sometimes in the town style, sometimes in the manner of grottoes," like rich contemporaries in Italy who also played on the conceits of a "townscape" or "country in the city" when designing their grand villa gardens.[32]

Taste and learning are no longer automatic allies: the buildings and literary expression of the Antonines' modern critics would themselves be a butt for the Antonines' sense of malice. It has not been so unusual for a small landowning class to dominate the towns of history, but the Antonines did combine taste with rarer capacities. The ideal of their texts on ethics was a dignified self-control, in which reason governed the emotions and intelligence guided a man through adversity. Their men of letters idealized youth and beauty and admired elegance and education. Their gifts of memory and apt quotation were formidable. At their best, they could exploit the gap between their own self-awareness and the inherited themes of art and literature, enhancing life and easing its painful transitions. They had a keen sense of the *faux pas* and an equal awareness of what was expected. They were too subtle for "brotherhood," with all it evades: friendship was an art to them, with recognized limits.

They also had a rich capacity for enjoyment, in music and the spoken word, theatres, buildings and athletics. Their enjoyment could also involve great violence, in the gladiatorial shows and the pitting of wild beasts against the cities' convicted criminals. Although war was far removed from most civic notables' experience, outside the city many of them enjoyed their hunting: here, the sport had been transformed by the import of better hounds, the last great advance in the art until the improvements in hound breeding during the eighteenth century.[33] It is necessary to emphasize this scope for enjoyment. Anxiety, as we shall see, has been detected in the religious and intellectual life of the period, but culturally, we must remember, it was not in evidence, and indeed, cities were better equipped than ever to cope with it. The fashion for heated bathhouses was increasing and competing with the older civic gymnasia. The baths were a splendid counter to anxiety, among Christians and pagans alike: when Augustine first learned of his mother's death, he thought at once of bathing, "for I had heard that the bath owes its Greek name to the fact that it drives anxieties from the mind."[34]

In a Greek city, however, even the baths might be built for the use of the upper class only: beneath this small minority, how did the city spread itself? The order of city councillors would cover 5 percent, at most, of a city's adult male population, and by the third century the gaps between the upper and lower layers of this order were conspicuous. Beyond them, the absentees, to our eyes, are a separate, identifiable middle or merchant class. The upper landowning clique did not own all of their cities' land. There were small farmers, who owned some land and probably rented other plots, too: they might live in a city and commute, as we have seen, to their properties. At the same time, there is evidence for a multiplicity of petty trades and crafts, attested among the cities' minor artisans.[35]

Economic relations in the cities remain obscure, and therefore disputed, but the most plausible model is to accept the absence of the middle or merchant class as significant and develop a scheme round the rich minority and the groups who are well attested. The notables derived a yearly income from the rents and surplus crops off their farms and then spent their proceeds in the towns. By the "multiplier effect," their spending spread from person to person and filtered downwards: in the towns, evidence supports a widespread use of money for transactions, even for those of a small, everyday size. Spending from above encouraged the conspicuous specialization of trades: there was demand, too, from the small farmers and cultivators. They were not self-sufficient or engaged in minimal subsistence farming. They, too, could specialize on parts of their land, sell a crop in the towns for cash and return, in Virgil's charming picture, with some tool or goods for their own use.[36] In times of shortage, towns-people might remove the best of the harvest for their own use, leaving little for the producers to eat. Those times, however, were exceptional.[37] Although towns were not essentially centres of production, neither were they idle centres of consumption and nothing else. They were also centres of exchange and servicing and the temporary hiring of labour. There was no class of wage-earning employees, but there was scope for casual hired work, in porterage, harvesting and seasonal tasks. Here it was uneconomic to maintain slaves for work which fell only in a few months. A petty craftsman could supplement his earnings by taking such work and also by cultivating any small plots of ground which he might own in or beside the city. There was not an absolute division between the crafts and the land.[38]

Does the absence of a trading or middle class imply a detachment of "land" from "business" and a low level of economic activity? In practice, land and business were not exclusive alternatives; land-owners sold their surplus crops; the local assets of the cities' terri-tories also varied widely, encouraging trade between cities in their particular specialities. The absence of a trading class is a fact about the social order, not about the volume of the towns' economy.[39] Trade could be handled elsewhere in the pyramid, by the slaves or former slaves and dependents of the landowning rich. The upper class were not "in" business, but they certainly profited from it, by owning the ships and crops, the natural assets and funds which dependents could hire or dispose of on their behalf. This pattern was modified by the siting of the town, whether it lay on or off the sea or the navigable rivers, or whether it stood on a caravan route in Syria and the Near East: a more direct patronage of trade characterized the upper class of these "caravan cities," while access to the sea offered scope for the small man, too, to own modest boats. If a freed slave, or a rich man's dependent, contrived to amass funds for himself in the process of his master's business, he might buy his own independence, continue to trade and aspire, in turn, to become a landowner: such mobility was rare, too rare to constitute a merchant class.[40] In short, like the city's culture, the economic life of the towns was propelled from the top. This model, though without the supporting base of agricultural slavery, is not unfamiliar if we look just beyond the classical world and our industrialized Western city. Until recently, the combination of trade through social dependents and a specialized, self-employed range of artisans, selling their own goods and not working in factories, characterized the bazaar economy of modest country towns in the Islamic world.

Socially, such a model is bleak, with little to span the gap between the rich few and the dependent, or servicing, many: lower still lay the base of slave labour, in the household, the farms (here and there) and the humble trades. This bleakness, I believe, is true to life.[41] The social pyramid tapered much more steeply than we might now imagine when first surveying the monuments and extent of the major surviving cities. By itself, a specialized ability in a craft was not a source of upward mobility. Its adepts were often slaves themselves, and even if they were not, they were competing with slave labour, which kept the price of their own labour low. The most upwardly-mobile figures were the veteran soldier, the athlete, the retired gladiator and perhaps (if we knew more) the traders in slaves themselves.

The very bleakness of the social pyramid may help us, paradoxically, to see how the upper families maintained order. The ultimate sanction of Roman troops was very important, but locally the social order also worked to the notables' advantage. Their households were staffed by slaves who would pay with their lives whenever theft or crime was detected against the master's property. They were a vital, unpaid police force who were bound, in the last resort, by their lack of legal status and their sheer disposability. We meet criminals in the literature of the period, but they are not a distinctive urban underworld: they are bandits, essentially, who menace travellers and exploit the wild countryside. Bandits, more than burglars, are an explicit concern of Roman governors and lawyers: in cities, the houses of the rich, guarded by slaves, were not an easy target for theft. So, too, the very dependence of the free artisan on the upper orders assisted those orders' continuing rule. The ties of dependent status were compounded by those of custom, loans and financial support. It did not seem in the interests of such people to rise against the notables who sustained them.

From their vantage point on the pyramid, were the rich ultimately indifferent and without much sense of social responsibility? To slaves, they were often callous, to judge from some shocking anecdotes of violence and heartless comment. Christian authors were quick to enlarge the picture: in famines, they hoarded grain; they gave nothing to the destitute; they saw no merit in the poor.[42] Taken to extremes, these views would require a degree of heartlessness among freeborn pagans which cannot quite convince an eye trained on their literature and philosophy. Indeed, there were the shows in which criminals were thrown to the beasts, shows, however, which were enjoyed by all social classes and only opposed by a very few moralists. Criminals were criminals, no longer fellow citizens. But there were also gifts and distributions from the pagan rich to their lesser contemporaries: certain cities came to have definite groups of "grain receivers"; there were also social benefactions. We know most about these gifts from the inscriptions of one hugely rich donor, Opramoas, in Lycia (now southwestern Turkey):[43] apart from his gifts of games and a mass of civic buildings, we have recently found him offering to pay for the primary schooling of all the citizen-children at Xanthus, boys and girls alike, and to contribute to their upkeep; he gave funds for burial to people in need and paid the dowries of poor families' daughters; he made donations to two thousand people at once, besides giving the more usual "distributions" to local councillors in the cities. Newly found inscriptions allow us to trace a progression in his giving and see how it enlarged with time: in the year 140, the region of Lycia suffered a great earthquake, which, it has been suggested, marked a turning point for Opramoas and raised the scale of his gifts. Pagans were not expected to stand idly by at these times of recurrent disaster. We now have a letter of Gordian, in the 240s, coaxing the "free" city of Aphrodisias to act on a decree of the provincial League of Asia and offer help and shelter to victims of a nearby city's earthquake.[44] The province's council had decreed aid and cooperation, and the Emperor was concerned to nudge a free city to support the effort. Pagan heartlessness can be overestimated.

The paternal language for benefactors, the "fathers," "mothers" and "nurturers" of their citizens, was not entirely empty. Yet there were limits, too. Even Opramoas worked firmly within a framework of civic values, benefitting those who were already members of civic communities. "Philanthropy" remained firmly intertwined with "love of the home town." So, too, the corn doles of certain cities were benefits for citizens only, as many as 1,100 people in one Lycian town but, on the whole, people who were not destitute. In other distributions, women received the least, if anything: non-citizens generally received nothing. Above all, inscriptions of this type tend to record the exceptional: Opramoas has no known equals, and few donors were even comparable. It is significant that, like a fellow donor, Pliny, he had no children. To give publicly on this scale was exceptionally honourable, but there were other types of gift which also won honour, without showing "charity." Opramoas's giving was not a religious good work, concerned to lay up treasure in heaven.

How, finally, did people mix and circulate in this stratified urban setting? The notables' position was clearly marked. We meet in literature, though not yet in Greek archaeology, their splendid houses just on the edge of the town. They had privileged seats of honour in the theatres, whose seating and design were altered to conform to rank and degree.[45] These changes were accepted by the rest of the audience, whose compliance was relied upon. Among their beneficiaries, accessibility was still a recognized virtue, but somewhat *de haut en bas*: the ideal of philanthropy presupposes a superior type of philanthropist, above his fellow men. Pre-eminent in life, the rich were also marked off by their way of death. Their funerals were public occasions which still needed laws to control their extravagance in several Greek towns. Their tombs and funerary precincts dominated the civic burial grounds on the outskirts of the city, while the ideals of the benefactor were carried over beyond the grave.[46] The "very special dead" aspired to be honoured by rites of commemoration, which were financed for the future by their own donations. The poor, by contrast, could expect no private grave at all, except as a rich man's dependent. They would receive no proper funeral, unless they belonged to an association which saw to its members' last rites. Even so, these associations often depended on a rich patron's support.

At the level of most people's lives, we must reckon with both a severe lack of privacy and a constant circulation. In the East and West alike, humble people in the cities grouped themselves in small associations, dependent, too, on obliging patrons. These little groups were a counter to our modern ailment of urban loneliness, groups like the "friendly society of the purple dyers on the Eighteenth Avenue" in the town of Thessalonica, where the streets had impersonal numbers in a formal rectangular plan.[47] Among people of minor property, privacy was further undercut by universal customs of inheritance: everywhere, properties were split among male and (sometimes) female children, resulting in an extreme fragmentation of goods. We see the results in our only relevant source, the papyri in Egypt. Here, people own inconceivable fractions of almost anything, one-twelfth of a house or a field, a tiny piece of a garden, a donkey or a camel. Such fragmentation has obvious consequences. Even when it becomes more theoretical than real, it restricts privacy, requiring cooperation and preventing concealment of private business and, probably, private religion. It also entails movement, between one plot of ground and the fraction of another, between a twentieth of one house and a quarter of another: in Egypt, daughters, too, received fractional inheritances, which they brought with them at marriage, compounding their family's scatter of holdings. Like peasants in pre-revolutionary China, sons and daughters in Egypt coped with twentieths and thirtieths of a field in plots which were spread around their local township. Their scattered holdings probably differed only in degree, not kind, from those which families divided elsewhere.[48]

These distributions of people can be demonstrated from other evidence. The leases in Roman legal texts envisage the leasing of tiny fractions of an apartment to tenants: living space was the rare privilege of the rich.[49] There is also, simply, the abundant evidence for people travelling from place to place, a mobility to which the first Christian missionaries could attach without attracting comment. "Love of the home town" and intercity rivalry must not obscure the connections between one place and another. Between cities, people intermarried and did business and also lent and borrowed money: the problems of mutual debt and credit had loomed large in earlier attempts to merge Greek cities into one. The upper class included people who were citizens of other cities, too: how, then, are we to interpret the feverish civic patriotism which their culture expressed in cities outside Rome? It can, of course, flourish, even if the realities are more complex: it was not only the interest of a small ruling elite. Civic rivalries could animate "the people," too, if their city's titles and status were under threat: they were supported by the lively circuit of athletic games and the cities' pride and honour in their own athletic victors.[50] Yet the dominant note is not the only note, perhaps least of all when sounded so stridently. Like the Jews' synagogues, the Christian communities were proving able, meanwhile, to draw converts to an alternative "third race," whose only city lay in heaven. Politically, local citizenship meant less and less and was frequently a restricted privilege: why should many residents remain content with observer participation in a place where they happened to have been born or set free? Not everybody was rooted to one home town, not even those at the top of it. If the realities were more fluid, we can see one way in which the early Christians could establish themselves in the midst of such strident evidence for civic life. We can also see why, as their numbers and status rose, they then adopted the old civic ranking of cities as the natural type of their churches' organization. Like the dead, buried on its edges, the home town was a point of focus which still mattered to more people than not. The Christians began by transposing the idea of the dead and the city to heaven; then they fitted them into their hierarchy and thus, inevitably, into their rivalries too.

# 3. Pagan Cults

## I

So much for the civic setting and the religiousness which is our subject; how can we best connect the two? In the Christian period, paganism has been given a history by studies which look for contemporaries' written statements of scepticism or credulous acceptance of "superstition." From the Antonine age onwards, paganism has been attached to a general rise of irrationality. From the third century A.D. onwards, it has been claimed, "oracular sayings circulated more widely, prophets spoke more often in the marketplace, magical feats were more credulously studied and imitated and the restraints of common reason became a little less common, decade by decade, even among the highly educated."[1] It was Christianity's good fortune, on this view, that it coincided with a time in which people would believe anything. By a different route, the outlook of the educated class in the Antonine age has been characterized as an "age of anxiety." Materially, this age occurred at the height of Roman peace and prosperity, yet, it has been suggested, this same age saw an inner failure of nerve, a preliminary to the mid-third century's years of hardship and disorder.

There are objections to both these approaches. To measure paganism by expressions of educated scepticism is to concentrate on a very small fraction of the cities' upper classes. Such expressions are at risk to the chance survivals of our written evidence: the second century has itself been characterized as an "age of faith," yet it is evident from scenes in its copious remains that Cynics, Sceptics and true Epicureans still flourished, writing little that survives among the widespread publicity for the "providence" of the gods. Did these doubters really vanish in the third century, or do we only happen to hear less about them? How new, indeed, was the contrary current? The most evident rise in a literature of the "irrational" belongs much earlier, c. 200–150 B.C., where it coincided, significantly, with a demonstrable loss of civic freedom. By the Imperial period, people were sorting and

organizing texts and practices which had begun far earlier: suggestively, their interest has been seen as a rationalization of the irrational,
rather than a new surrender to it.[2] Arguments about the relative scale
of scepticism also assume that authors, our evidence for it, continued
to practise what they wrote. In the late first century A.D., Plutarch
repeated the old arguments against "superstition" in a youthful work.
He has been counted as evidence for a surviving, and significant,
opposition to "credulity,"[3] but we must remember that he spent his
later life as a pious priest at Delphi, writing essays on divine punishment and the evident terrors of the next world. Readers of the Acts of
the Apostles can only wonder how the second or third century could
possibly be more "credulous" than the first, even among the highly
educated. It is not, then, very helpful to divide the Imperial period into
ages of relative irrationality.

The idea of anxiety is no easier to pin down. Anxious individuals
can be found in any age with a personal literature: they are not the
aptest characterization of the slaves and dependent workers on whom
the burdens of Antonine civilization lay. In human relationships,
indeed, we hear more about anger than anxiety.[4] Philosophers in the
second century showed a continuing interest in anger and its problems: the Emperor Marcus's personal *Meditations* frequently mention
his struggle with them; anger takes on a new dimension to attentive
readers of Galen's treatises. Galen had seen his mother fly into a rage
and bite the servants. He describes his journey with an irascible friend
who split the heads of two slaves when they muddled the luggage;
anger was the man's besetting passion, as it clearly was for others in
their dealings with the servile classes. "Many friends" were reproved
by Galen's father when they had bruised themselves by striking slaves
in the teeth: "They could have waited a while, he used to say, and used
a rod or a whip to inflict as many blows as they wished, acting with
calm reflection . . ." Should the Antonine "age of anxiety" be
rephrased as an "age of anger," rooted in the social order and its
division between master and slave?

To sum up an age by a single emotion is to focus on a few
individuals and to simplify even those few. However, the idea of an
"anxious age" took this objection into account. It aimed only to
characterize a minority in the educated class, and within their number,
the Platonist philosophers in particular. If this minority had led their
cities' culture, this location might be significant. However, these
philosophers were only a fraction of a wider, more disparate class of

notables, and their written theories on the age-old problems of evil and its origins were neither distinctively "anxious" nor new to the Antonine age. Written opinions tell us nothing about philosophers' own practice in life, let alone the practice of their social equals who made excellent fun of the eternal gap between philosophers' writings and conduct.[5] Anxiety itself is too vague a diagnosis, neither apt nor new. The major anxieties of this age were not spiritual, but physical and geological, the plagues and earthquakes which beset whole cities, not a few individuals in their inner life. We do hear of medical anxieties among some of the educated class, but it is not clear that these were signs of a new "hypochondria": physical weakness and a concern for health had long been thought typical of men of letters, the main source, inevitably, of our evidence.[6] If the idea of anxiety is to have any significant force, it must be narrowed to something more precise, the particular detachment of people's inner life from an outer life of expected ceremonial and tradition. This type of detachment might indeed be a prelude to a greater age of change, just as a detachment from the "stage play" round of the external world among cultured Elizabethans and their authors can usefully be seen as a prelude to the great cultural changes of seventeenth-century England.[7]

To explore this idea of anxiety, we can best begin, not with "individuals' thoughts in their loneliness," but with cults as practised in their cities. The gods were known through their images, many of which resided in temples: in Egypt, the priests' daily liturgy was to open the shrine, offer food to the god's statue and attend to its cleanliness. In the Greek world, some, but not all, of the temples of civic gods were kept shut for the greater part of the year.[8] There were notable exceptions, however, and some cities prescribed daily hymns to be sung by choirs at the morning opening of a shrine; otherwise, by finding the shrine's keeper, a visitor could usually enter and pray before the god's image. The central "cult acts" for the civic gods occurred on the days of their festivals. Then, people processed, sang hymns and sacrificed in the gods' honour. Sometimes they processed from a fixed point in the city to a particular shrine or altar: cities and temples had their "sacred ways" and particular monuments along the route. By tradition, envoys would go out to summon other cities to attend certain festivals, a not inexpensive task whose cost, like the cost of secular embassies, was often borne by the envoys themselves.

Inside the city, participants in festivals generally wore clean white robes and accompanied their own chosen animals for sacrifice. The temples were hung with garlands and so, sometimes, were the private houses. Ritual worship was not confined to those who processed: people might pay libations or offer sacrifices on small altars beside their own residence.[9] In a world without weekends, these festivals were the only "holidays." Quite often, the statue of the god joined the tour, sometimes parading in its new robes, sometimes being escorted for a yearly washing.[10] These occasions were familiar to Christian observers, who later used them as a setting for legends of their martyrs. In southwestern Asia, at Panamara, a statue of Zeus was taken from his celebrated shrine and brought on horseback for his "visit" (*epidemia*) to nearby Stratonicea. These occasions were matters of civic self-respect and supported a city's identity. The tour of Zeus was shown on Stratonicea's local coinage: in Gordian's reign, the coins of Magnesia-on-the-Maeander show the city's statue of Hephaestus, processing on its stretcher, with four bearers. It was a great honour to carry sacred objects in a civic procession, and, like other great honours, it fell to the most distinguished families. To live in a city was to be accustomed to these interruptions of normal life, which broke up the calendar and honoured the gods. We know something of the calendar for the shrine of Capitoline Jupiter in Egypt's Arsinoë in the year 215. Only parts of it survive, but even in these fragments, we find that the statue of one or other god was anointed three times, crowned twenty times and taken on at least three processions between the end of December and the end of April in the year 215. Pagan cults created the divisions of civic time.[11]

These processions and festivals were merry occasions and were alive with all sorts of music.[12] Bands played various wind instruments and every sort of drum, while even the smaller villages tried to hire themselves a "symphony" by binding travelling performers to a contract. Their music was often the cue for dancers, whose art is one of our saddest losses from the ancient world. Processions also meant hymns, old hymns recopied in the Imperial age, newer hymns and prose panegyrics whose authors were sometimes commemorated: at Thespiai, in Boeotia, we learn of a competition for the best marching hymns, to be sung in processions. As the poets never tired of celebrating, a festival was also the *paseo*, or promenade, of an ancient city. It brought well-bred girls briefly into the open, ripe for a well-aimed romance. It also brought on the whores, not just the sacred prostitutes of a few remaining cults but girls like those whose masters Dio cited, trailing them round Greece from one festival to the next. At the level of the procession, the impact of a pagan cult can still be sensed in the journeys of the Christian images through the cities of southern Spain during Holy Week. Their content and context are Christian, not "pagan" survivals, but they are similar expressions of religious honour, based on the quarters of the city. The elements are familiar to anyone who has tried to picture an Antonine festival, the art and antique sculpture, the flowers, embroidery and candles, the marching ranks of well-dressed children, the spontaneous singing, the acclamations of the crowd before the seats of the city notables, and once again, the prostitutes, those necessary supports for fidelity and virginity in a Catholic country.

As civic life spread with the growth of new cities and as the resources of Greek culture expanded, processions became attached over time to ever longer festivals. For days on end, even weeks in the agricultural off-season, people in a city could enjoy a programme of music and oratory, drama, all manner of athletic contests and that unstoppable inanity, the pantomime. Cities held their own competitions, which, in turn, competed for talent with the cities nearby. There were prizes for every kind of virtuosity, for acrobatics, conjuring, spoken panegyrics, announcing, blowing the trumpet, and "Homerism," the valiant miming of scenes from Homeric epic. Already, in their Greek homelands, theatres endured all manner of non-theatrical uses, culminating in the vile contests of gladiators and the wild-beast "hunts."[13]

At one level, then, the public cults merge into a study of the life which attached itself to religious occasions. Their festivals drew crowds, and the crowds, naturally, were good business. It made sense to combine festivals with local fairs and with the Roman governors' assizes, involving the gods in two constant human activities: shopping and litigation. Cities, understandably, pressed hard for permission to raise the status of their festivals or somehow to join the circuit of the governors' tours. Elevation was not only a matter of civic pride. It had great economic benefits. Touring governors and better festivals brought more visitors, needing services, food and lodging. In turn, the visitors increased the gods' audience.

In this setting, the antiquarian culture of the cities' men of letters was not "irrelevant." A new civic pedigree could make the reputation of the least-known city, and no pedigree was more respected than a link with the gods and founding heroes of Greek myth. Ancient tradition was the touchstone of civic life, and where it did not exist, there was scope for inventing it. At Aizani, in Phrygia, we can still admire the results.[14] This outlandish site claimed descent from the Arcadians of ancient Greece, along with several other cities whom the continuing process of Hellenization had offered a place in the geography of Greek myth. It was probably in the late first century A.D. that the people of Aizani began to build a splendid temple of Zeus; their envoys then persuaded other cities to take their city's origin seriously, and Aizani entered the select company of the Panhellenic League, whose delegates met at Athens. Already, its antiquarians had done well by it, but their myth was backed by religion: just outside the city, they claimed, was the very cave in which the infant Zeus had been nursed. Claiming the infant Zeus, the city gained honour, visitors and a temple of particular design. The claim, naturally, was contested by other cities that had caves: Zeus's birthplace, like his tomb, became a topic of keen intercity rivalry, giving scope to public speakers and, again, to antiquarians, who could oppose traditions as well as invent them.

At Aizani, a temple and its festivals made the city's fame and fortune: did life in such a city become guided strongly by respect for the gods? Any activity, social, legal or political, could be preceded by prayers to the gods, but simply by association with a festival, these accompanying activities did not become "sacred." Rather, the religious core of a festival were the offerings which were made to the gods: incense, libations of wine, cakes and animals for slaughter. Considerable care could go into the choice of the proper ceremonial beast: priests and city notables of all periods needed a practised eye for an animal.[15] On Cos, admittedly in the late fourth century B.C., we learn how the divisions of the town's citizen body each presented a well-groomed ox on parade in the marketplace while the magistrates sat and picked the prize animal for their gods. When they had chosen from nine or more candidates, they prayed and made a proclamation. Then all the oxen were driven back onto the agora, and if their chosen ox "bows his head, let him be sacrificed to the goddess." In antiquity's cattle shows, the same animal never survived to win for the second year running. Perhaps the parade continued on Cos as a "tradition" in the second century A.D. It is then that we still meet a rite called "the driving of the oxen" in the city of Miletus, whose purpose, presumably, was to pick the best victims for sacrifice. The animals' horns were gilded; at Astypalaea, we know that the chosen animals were stamped, in case their owners tried to win the honour of processing with them while dodging the sacrifice at the end: such offenders were formally cursed. In Egypt, the "sealing" of suitable beasts was a constant task for the priesthood, which they rendered in return for a fee.

In the Greek world, the chosen animals were killed to the piercing cry of female spectators, "the customary sacrificial shout of the Greeks." The animal was sprinkled with water, which caused it to shiver and thus signify its assent to the act. A hefty blow of the knife or axe then felled it, either "pre-stunning" or killing it. In practice, the ligaments of the legs might be cut, to stop it bolting, but there was no question of bleeding an animal to death while conscious. The meat was then roasted and distributed among priests and participants: a sacrifice was the one recognized occasion for consuming meat in the diet of the Greek (but not Roman) cultural area. Some people took the context very seriously. In the Imperial period, we have recently learned, the servants of Meidon ate "unsacrificed meat" and poor Meidon was struck dumb by the local god, Zeus Trosos.[16] He only recovered his voice three months later after a dream had told him to put up a monument to the incident. It turned up recently in Pisidia. While Paul's Gentile Christians were being told to avoid meat offered to idols, Meidon and his pagan servants were learning from hard experience to eat nothing else.

At this basic level, pagan cults did indeed satisfy the emotions; they allayed hunger. Sacrifices were one more festive element in occasions which were not in the least anxious: on every count, festivals were enormous fun, and their ordered piety was the recognized opposite to excessive fear of the gods. In their books, moralists did insist that gods were not swayed by lavish offerings: Pythagoreans and reforming groups did stand aloof from the cults of cooked meat which the cities patronized; emphasis was also laid on worship "with a pure heart," a maxim which did extend to certain cults and shrines.[17] In the cities, however, blood sacrifice was not passing out of fashion as a result.[18] In the year 250, a pagan Emperor demanded it throughout the Empire and thus caused the Christians to be persecuted; in the fourth century, subsequent Christian Emperors deliberately tried to ban it. Its supposed "decline" is worth refuting. In texts and inscriptions, there is indeed plenty of evidence for pagans' use of incense and candles, lamps and hymns in a constant "service" of bloodless piety. We can see this worship in the old daily liturgy of the Egyptian temples and we can document it thickly in the cults of Asclepius or in pagan cults of an abstract divinity or Most High god. From time to time, as we shall see, Apollo himself approved this bloodless worship in oracles which he delivered under the Empire. Christians, eventually, repeated much of it, but it was not a new or distinctive fashion. The burning of incense was as old as historical cult in Greek temples and its use in honour of Asclepius was quite conventional. The two types of pagan service did not exclude one another. In other oracles, Apollo listed detailed blood sacrifices which his client cities were to offer. The Egyptian gods also received their bulls and cows in due season and we now know that Asclepius's major shrine at Pergamum required the offering of a piglet before entry into its Greater Incubation Chamber.

Was bloodless cult simply cheaper and quicker than the offering of an animal? If we think of cattle, sacrificed on civic occasions, the answer seems clear enough. Variations in time and place prevent certainty, but inscriptional evidence for their cost puts them in a price range which was only conceivable for people of a certain substance. In northeastern Lydia, we have the inscription of a worshipper who apologizes to his god for his stone monument, but asks him to accept it, as he is unable to pay the sacrifice which he had vowed previously.[19] We might think that inscribed stones were much more expensive and troublesome than animals, yet how many other votive reliefs were put up as substitutes for bulls and cows? Pigs, however, were vastly cheaper, as were sheep, especially ewes: a pinch of good incense was no doubt cheaper than either, but it was not an everyday commodity. The bloodless alternative to sacrifice owed something to ease and economy, but nothing to growing scruples about shedding animals' blood. When pagans could pay for it, they did, and the scruples of a few philosophers made no impact. Several temples preserved the skulls of exceptional carcasses, and rich people continued to offer them, not only Emperors like Julian and Heliogabalus but lesser persons of extravagance, like the aristocratic lady Polleinos, who sacrificed a hecatomb in Miletus in the early third century "in accordance with the divine oracles" of Apollo, or like the dutiful son near Leptis who sacrificed fifty-one bulls and thirty-eight goats, a true Iarbas, at his father's tomb in the fourth century A.D.[20]

The second and third centuries also saw a widespread interest in bulls' testicles.[21] Men and women alike offered these choice parts in private and public ceremonies, which are known from their Latin inscriptions. From 160 A.D. onwards, they are known to have been connected with the cult of Cybele, the Great Mother, and also with offerings "on behalf of the safety of the Emperor": once, the Emperor Pius granted an exemption from legal duties to an individual who offered them in this way and no doubt local bulls greatly regretted the offer. Worshippers went to great lengths: in 160, one Carpus transported a pair of bull's balls the whole way from Rome's Vatican Hill to Cybele's shrine at Lyons. We know that eventually, by the late fourth century, worshippers would sit in a trench and be spattered with the blood of a bull which was sacrificed above their heads. The date at which this highly prized "blooding" began is disputed, but it was not the rite of a culture which had started to soften on the topic of sacrifices. Animal bloodshed remained central to pagan cult, and when Christian Emperors banned sacrifice, they were aiming at the living heart of pagans' cult acts.

Animals continued to be offered to the gods; the circuit of festivals continued to grow, increasing up to and beyond the age of Gordian. Processions were reorganized with ever greater detail and munificence, old processions like those from Miletus to Apollo's great shrine at Didyma or from the city of Athens to Eleusis, new processions like the Komyria at Zeus's great shrine of Panamara.[22] In the early Christian periods pagan cults did not only shape civic time: they also shaped that well-worked category, "civic space." On site after site in the Antonine age, we can watch shrines and altars absorbing yet more space and money. "Planning permission" did not prevent the gods from receiving some new and spectacular housing. This extravagance is the background to the philosophers' writings on cult and religion, a background we would never guess from contemporary Christian attacks on "dying" pagan rites and mythology. New temple building is particularly well known in the civic and provincial cults of the Emperors. As this cult was prestigious and relatively new, the spate of new temples was not so surprising. Yet it was accompanied by new shrines for many of the old gods, too. From Asia through Syria to North Africa, the example of three cities may help to convey the scale of it.

At Gerasa (Jerash), in modern Jordan, we can only gaze and wonder at the scale of the second century's religious architecture.[23] Off the centre of their colonnaded street, the Gerasenes found the money for a massive temple of Artemis whose precinct excelled anything in Baalbek or the Near East. So, no doubt, they had intended. Its outer portico was flanked by shops, "a true Burlington Arcade," in an archaeologist's opinion, and fronted the steps and open space of a temple precinct which was over two thousand yards square. The temple and its surrounds marked the peak of Antonine civic ambition in the 130s A.D. Artemis's shrine was matched by a remodelled temple of Zeus at the far end of the main street, off the city's famous oval piazza. It was a near-rival in the number of its steps and pillars, though not in area. At the focal points of the city's plan, the gods changed the face of Jerash between the 130s and the 180s.

At Side, Longinus's home town, the area of the second- and third-century city has only been excavated in part, but a strong religious presence is also obvious.[24] In the region of the agora stood an elegant rounded temple, surrounded by twelve engaged Corinthian columns. Dated to the middle or later second century, it was probably a temple of Fortune. At the southern end of the main street stood another, older temple, entered from the east: it was probably a shrine for an Eastern divinity, perhaps Men. From a handsome inscription, we learn of a cult of "Zeus Helios Serapis," as at Jerash; another temple, outside the main city plan, contained a statue of Dionysus, and may have honoured this god. This shrine, too, has been dated around the mid-second century A.D. Near the "temple of Men," at the end of the main street, stood two large temples, also of late second-century date. They overlook the sea by Side's famous harbour and have been explained as the temples of Athena and Apollo, the divinities whom we know as Side's protectors on her coins and inscriptions. A recently found inscription has revealed a "festival of disembarkation" for the goddess Athena, which was donated by one Audius Maximus to the "citizens of Side." In another inscription, we find a "festival of disembarkation" for Apollo and "all the people of Pamphylia," which was given by a man whose name points to a later date, after 212 A.D. These festivals have been well understood as festivals for the disembarkation of the statues of Athena and Apollo from the nearby shore. The first festival was restricted to Side's citizens: the second went a step further, no doubt on purpose, and extended the occasion to all Pamphyliots. In the later second century A.D., we should picture the arrival of two great statues for the city's large new temples. Shortly afterwards, a festival honoured Athena's arrival, and then, a generation later, another festival commemorated Apollo's. Both were the gifts of very rich men.

Further west, in North Africa, the city sites of this period are so large that archaeologists have not yet revealed any one in full. Surprises are in store, but at Sabratha, in Tripoli, we can appreciate the centre of a city which was not in the first rank but which relates very neatly to a literary text.[25] It was at Sabratha, in the year 157, that Apuleius, author of *The Golden Ass*, pleaded in self-defence against a charge of sorcery. His speech, as published, is a remarkable *tour de force*, and is well worthy of a great performing sophist. Here and there, it alludes to cults which we can see in Sabratha's town plan. In the first century A.D., to the northwest of its Forum, Sabratha had had a modest temple of Serapis which was built of sandstone. A rather larger temple to Liber Pater (Dionysus) stood at the Forum's west end. The customary temple of Jupiter overlooked the Forum off its platform and was probably dedicated to Jupiter, Juno and Minerva. The glory of the site was an enlarged temple of Isis, set some way to the east of the city centre. It rose on the very edge of the shore, where its portico of Corinthian columns still stands just above the beach. The site was particularly favoured for this goddess of the sea and her festivals which prayed for calm sailing. From inscriptions, we know this temple to have been rebuilt and dignified with the name of a governor of the province in the 70s A.D.

A century or so later, Sabratha's temples had been greatly enlarged and improved. The citizens had imported marbles and remote Egyptian granite in honour of the gods. In court, Apuleius appealed to his audience's initiations into the mysteries of Liber Pater. These rites were celebrated in Liber Pater's enlarged shrine, which had recently been adorned with new stones and a smart new portico. Three grand new temples had entered the second-century city: a large shrine of unknown dedication to the south of the Forum, a lavish temple which was dedicated to the Emperors Marcus and Verus and an ornate temple of Hercules which had been dedicated in the year 186. In the second century, Sabrathan notables had suffered from acute lithomania, and their shrines were huge buildings for the gods. A Christian bishop is known in Sabratha by the 250s, but his converts lived in the shadow of this pagan magnificence.

This public flourish of the pagan cults is all the more interesting because at many sites it is a change from the preceding period. The cults and shrines of many Greek-speaking cities show signs of considerable disorder by the last decades of the first century B.C. Among several examples, none is clearer than a debate in Athens, perhaps to be dated to the Augustan era rather than the 60s B.C.[26] Not only had Athenians encroached on their gods' precincts and taken over the temple land as if it was their own. Many shrines, it was feared, had been defiled by childbirths and other impurities during years of neglect. In their assembly, the Athenians voted on a proposal to restore and safeguard these shrines, and for once, we know the voting on a matter of religion: 3,461 voted in favour, while 181 voted against. The meeting had been large by the standards of this period: the consequent "revival" was not artificial.

This picture of disorder could be extended. By a neat irony, the lifetime of Jesus appears to have coincided with a temporary low point in the shrines and externals of much pagan worship. No sooner was he dead than they began to spring back to life in a resurrection which nobody could deny. In the second century, new buildings improved or created many of Christianity's greatest enemies, not just the cult of Emperors, which was prominent, but not primary, in the known episodes of persecution, but other lasting seats of pagan cult, the huge temples of Baalbek in Syria, the revived shrine of Serapis in Alexandria, Pergamum's precinct in honour of the healing god Asclepius, the great oracles of Greece and Asia. There were always some local exceptions, as Pausanias remarked on his travels in Greece. On major sites, however, the town plans are clear enough. In the second century flamboyant building for the gods succeeded an age of relative quiescence; it then slowed to a virtual halt in the mid-third century.

At a general level, reasons for this new flamboyance are not hard to find. It belongs with the "love of honour" and the "love of the home town" which we traced among the cities' benefactors. Buildings like those at Jerash and Sabratha are a lasting witness to the peace of the Antonine age and the prosperity which it had brought to its leading citizens. In the pre-Christian era, their peace had been intermittent and insecure: by the mid-third century, it was once more in doubt. Between lay an age of surplus in which display and competition still flourished in the cities' upper class. The home town was still a greater focus for these notables' "love of honour" than a career in Roman service. Although the upper class of the bigger cities was itself dividing into an upper and lower layer, the numbers of potential competitors were not so few that display had lost its point. Their revenues arrived yearly from rents and sales of surplus crops, and there was little scope, or concern, for further investments seeking yet larger returns. The continuing cash surplus was better spent on public display. Buildings and decoration multiplied in the cities' squares; the gods were beneficiaries from an age of peaceful agriculture, whose ownership was concentrated in a few hands. They also benefited from the Emperors, especially (in Asia) from the favours of Hadrian.

In two particular forms, we can connect this honour for the gods with mortals' own "love of honour" among themselves: the forms involve "promising" and the sale of priesthoods. A recognized art of promising linked competition for civic office with material gifts to the town.[27] Some donors simply promised a gift to their cities on their own initiative, but most promises were not so spontaneous. They prefaced the promiser's candidacy for a magistracy or a priesthood or his attempt to exchange an onerous magistracy for a lighter one. Competition with peers and predecessors kept up the momentum. We know most about these promises in Latin inscriptions from North Africa, where civic elections continued to be contested in the early third century, but we also find them in the Greek East, where we can glimpse the elaborate bargaining which lay behind them. As promises tended not to be fulfilled, city councils tried to force their donors to put them into writing. They were also aware that promises were exploited to escape still heavier burdens of service. Inevitably, these problems found their way to the Emperors' notice, presumably by petition: they ruled that all promises which had been made to acquire, or avoid, office must be met by the promiser or, if necessary, by his heirs.

Like other interests in the city, the gods gained fine shows of stonework from the promises of notables who were seeking office. They also received promises which took far too long to complete. In the North African cities, promises of statues became a near-mania and temples were also very popular.[28] We can watch their fate over time, growing with a family's happy events, expanding with personal rivalry or lingering on from father to son and finally passing to a poor granddaughter who added yet more funds and at last raised the promised temple to Apollo off the ground. The gods, one feels, took a back seat in these donors' aims. Dedication day saw yet another round of presents, gifts for the city council, games and a feast for the citizens.

The cults of these temples created new priesthoods, and there, too, there were undercurrents which we can discern but not trace exactly. The burdens of a priesthood have not impressed historians of the Greek city: "the duties of priests were purely mechanical, their qualifications formal, and their posts were, as a rule, lucrative."[29] Perhaps no position is ever quite so easy, and there were priests, as we shall see, who brought rather more to their job. The gains of others were tempered by the need to give and even, at times, to buy.

Unlike a magistracy, a cult often had funds of its own: gods received rents from land, offerings to their collection box, taxes on sacrifices and, sometimes, the right to legacies. With considerable skill, Greek cities then multiplied their priesthoods and put them up for sale. The practice is best attested in inscriptions of the third century B.C. from cities in southwestern Asia, but it is evident, from the governor's ruling at Ephesus, that the practice had continued freely in the early Imperial period.[30] At Ephesus, complained the governor, priesthoods of the Imperial cult were being sold "as if in a public auction." In the Egyptian temples, vacancies in the hereditary priesthoods were also sold, again to the distaste of the Roman administration. The practice was a neat evasion of a profound pagan scruple: the appropriation of sacred funds. By selling priesthoods, cities profited indirectly from their gods' own riches. The priest paid the city: the gods repaid the priest by ceding him part of their income. To support these "offers for sale," cities resorted to the arts of a well-judged flotation. In the first century A.D., a decree in Miletus put the priesthood of Asclepius up for sale and then prescribed the sacrifices which other magistrates were to offer to the god throughout the year. The priests received parts of these offerings: the hides, entrails and prime cuts of meat. By defining the calendar of offerings, the city ensured a good price for its sale of office: the practice scandalized the Roman governor at Ephesus. In some cases, priests are known to have been granted exemptions from civic service or the promise of free meals at the city's expense. Evidence for these exemptions is pre-Roman, and they may have been curbed in the Imperial period, but they, too, were excellent reasons for bidding for a priesthood or regarding one as the summit of a civic career.

Simple in outline, the sale of office raises many more questions than we can begin to answer. The evidence for it is scattered from the third century B.C. to the second century A.D., but it is surely only the tip of an enduring iceberg. Bidders sometimes bought a hereditary right to the job; sometimes they bought it for only a few generations; at other times they sublet their purchase and turned it into a partnership. In some cases we find the god himself appointed to the high annual office at his shrine. The best-attested instance is Apollo at his oracle of Claros in the Antonine age: the god held office thirty-eight times in fifty-four years.[31] The oracle was then at its peak, and it was presumably not because of financial hardship or indifference among mortal givers that Apollo took the honour so often. Rather, the temple had such exceptional funds that it could finance itself and keep up its own momentum. Elsewhere sales of office would promote ostentatious piety. Having paid for the job, a priest would wish to make the most of his cult and encourage others to make offerings. Equally, some priests had paid nothing for their title, and by the Antonine age, some priests must have been holding offices which an ancestor had artfully bought in the past. Their continuing gains from a cult's income would help to support the "voluntary generosity" which their inscriptions then recorded proudly.

By no means every priesthood was sold, but there were pressures, nonetheless, to make a cult conspicuous. Priesthoods were a source of honour, and like its other sources, the magistracies, they could attract promises from willing candidates. Indeed, they were a much better bargain. Magistracies needed time and expense, but the gods' own income contributed to the costs of their festivals. Priests did not have to pay for every animal which was offered to the gods, but they did receive parts from every beast which others presented. At the end of the ceremony, priests took the "table offerings" or those "placed at the knees or lap" of the cult image, cuts which were set aside for the god but which the god, very tactfully, never ate. In return, there was a social pressure and advantage in putting on a fine show. Like magistrates and benefactors, priests were impelled to make gifts and "distributions" to groups in their city. A favourite occasion for these festival gifts was the assumption of office by new incumbents.[32] Generosity made them known to the city as a whole and gave their tenure a good start. They gave money, food and wine; they gave vintage wines, sometimes, and even "unmixed wine," a gift for which a Greek word had to be specially coined. Roman governors were alert to the dangers of troublesome generosity by which civic notables could bid for favour and risk starting faction.[33] Priesthoods, however, remained an unregulated chance to give and win favour from fellow-members of a town. They alone brought an income back to the givers, in return for their display.

These undercurrents are not inconsistent with an enduring pious concern to honour the gods. That concern was more or less constant among the cities' prominent citizens in this period, as the writings of philosophers did nothing seriously to dent it. But its visible extravagance varied from one period to another: these undercurrents help us to see why, and also to attach its rises and falls to the style of the cities' social order. How, then, did generosity to the gods relate to donors' other public gifts and how did it relate to their cities' cohesion?

Interestingly, expenditure on pagan cults and temples is not prominent among the gifts of the two second-century benefactors whom we know best: Opramoas in Lycia or the great Herodes in Greece, of whom his biographer has concluded, "it is men, much more than gods, whom he strives to please."[34] In his text of advice for a young notable (c. 100 A.D.), Plutarch repeated the conventional advice of the moralists and urged him to spend his money on the gods, the temples and their ceremonies. He was not, however, speaking for the habits which his class practised. He was complaining against contemporaries who were doing the opposite and wasting bigger fortunes on shows and gladiatorial games. In Ephesus (in 145) we see the problem: one Vedius had donated an impressive monument, but was then assailed for not having given games instead, and his munificence had to be commended by the Emperor. The stadium and the theatre were the major sources of instant popular honour.[35]

However, their honours were impermanent. So, often, were foundations which were endowed with capital assets: public property, as Pliny observed, was neglected, as if it were nobody's property. Educated donors might prefer to give a monument for cultural purposes: an odeon or a library publicized their own texts and attached their gift to the wider international world of culture. It is clear, however, from an artful letter in which Pliny introduced his gift of a library to Comum that the wider public did not necessarily welcome this type of gift. Why should they house a costly monument to one man's literary taste or a small odeon in which a few hundred people could listen to highbrow music and oratory? Of the more practical gifts, harbours, aqueducts and new agoras were enormous projects, requiring space and joint subscriptions. For all but the very richest giver, the gods were an easier alternative. Temples could be large or small, and there were never too many for another to be unwelcome. They also allowed self-advertisement. "Who builds a Church to God, and not to Fame, Will never mark the marble with his name . . ." Not so the builders of pagan civic temples. In the classical democratic city, there had been firm restraints on inscribed dedications in the donor's own name. In the Imperial period, by contrast, Emperors were required to rule that only the donors' names, and no others, should stand on temples and civic buildings. Those who paid, therefore, were assured of an advertisement.[36]

At the same time, temples had incontestable links with the well-being of the community, because the gods showed providence for the city as a whole. At a simpler level, the gift of a temple could be remarkably cheap. The best evidence for gifts and their prices derives from North Africa: there, games for a few days could cost up to 100,000 sestertii, though at that price, they included gladiators and the added excitement of panthers. In the little town of Muzuc, a temple of Apollo cost only 12,000: was this sum really the total cost, or did the donor give only part of a much larger whole? If it was the full sum, a little temple could be a very canny promise indeed.[37]

Standing further back, we can also see how a city's processions and festivals confirmed the social order. In a famous text, Aristotle had once advised oligarchies to urge the holders of civic office to meet expensive undertakings as part and parcel of their job.[38] They should offer splendid sacrifices, he suggested, and prepare public monuments so that the people should enjoy the feasting and admire their city's adornment. Then they would gladly "see the constitution persist." In Aristotle's own day, few cities, he complained, observed this advice: the notables of the Antonine age were wiser. Ultimately, their dominance could rely on the support of Roman power, but they had to maintain good order, meanwhile, in populations which greatly outnumbered them. Festivals showed off the city in its social hierarchy: people processed in a specified order of social rank, the magistrates, priests and councillors and even the city's athletic victors, if any. This ordered procession was seen as a continuing tradition, whereby the city had always honoured its gods and thus survived in their care for so long. The revivals, or inventions, of tradition were not "artificial": they reinforced the image of an enduring city, true to the forbears who had helped to make it great. The bigger the city and the more fluid the audience, the more urgent was this image. The image of tradition also conformed neatly to the exercise of power. The notables ran in a very few families, so long as the accidents of birth and death permitted. "New men" could never be excluded entirely, as families did die out, but the style of the ruling order was emphatically one of traditional continuity. Civic cults mirrored their style. At festivals, the prominent families honoured the gods, evoking the sense that they and their ancestors had always done so on "their" city's behalf. Their womenfolk, too, found a role, as priestesses in the public cults which required them: through religious cult, above all, the "silent women" of antiquity enjoyed a public place.[39] For the sake of the community's well-being, the prominent families processed, old and young, male and female, showing those indefinable qualities of deportment and good looks which they combined with their honorary wreaths and robes. This type of display conforms closely to the "consensual pageantry" which historians have begun to discern in the festivals of other urban societies.[40] It also showed "love of the gods," a quality which public speakers praised before their city audiences and urged as a reason for concord at times of civic tension. The role of the cults in displaying and supporting such "concord" was not necessarily explicit in the participants' minds. However, the effects of an action are not confined to its intentions. Processions and festivals did not "legitimate" or "justify" the pre-eminence of the leading notables: there was no longer a real alternative. Implicitly, however, they reinforced it: we should remember how even the bigger cities were remarkably underpoliced. It is in this light that we can appreciate the social role of public cult. It evoked "strong collective images of concord" in the life of the town and its territory, implicitly supporting the social order and distinguishing the town among its competing neighbours.[41] While evoking an image of the community enduring through time, cults and their honours also fed accompanying intercity rivalries. As these cults' public face began to be dimmed in the later third century, we will expect to see changes in the cities' social order and prosperity, rather than a growing indifference or detachment of men from the outer round of ceremonial: evidence for such detachment exists much earlier and there is no sign that it was rising or seriously impinging on most of the notables' lives. Their building and "promising," "bidding" and giving suggest the opposite. Seen solely as a social performance, the cults' "consensual pageantry" could span the line between towns and their countryside. As a civic tradition, it helped, too, to pass the ideal of the good citizen from one generation to the next. In a fine decree, datable c. 220, the people of Athens resolved that in future the escort of the sacred objects from Eleusis to Athens and back again should be accompanied by the city's youth, the ephebes, "crowned, walking in order" and carrying full weaponry.[42] They were to join in the sacrifices, libations and paeans along the way so that "the sacred objects should be safer" (probably), "the procession longer and the ephebes should grow to be more pious citizens by following the city's honours for the divine." Characteristically, this decree was presented as a return to ancient practice. These same ephebes became the adults of the dark years after Gordian: it is not plausible that their former duties simply counted for nothing when their city and its gods came under stress.

# II

Before we turn to these cults' religious purpose, we must face a prior question. The notables, we have seen, were a small fraction of a city's population: were the cults of the gods essentially their preserve on defined public occasions? If so, we could imagine very easily a growing detachment elsewhere, in the majority of a city's residents, spectators at occasions in which they were not central participants. Civic cults, however, were only some of the many times for regulated worship in a pagan city. If we look beyond them, we can appreciate the gods' role on every level of social life and their pervasive presence, the "infernal snares," as Gibbon described them, in early Christians' existence.

Beside the gods of the civic festival calendar, there were also the temples of cults which had migrated into a city with this or that group or individual. If an individual bought a suitable site in a town, he could establish a cult of a god and lay down rules for its continuance. In the Imperial period, civic permission is not known to have been an issue on religious grounds, but there might have been local objections, based on personalities and factions.[1] In Lepcis Magna, in the early third century, the temple of Serapis must have begun in this way, perhaps as the cult of Greek immigrants from Cyrene or its neighbourhood: in second-century Attica, at Sounion, we have the rules which another migrant, "Xanthos the Lycian," inscribed for a shrine of the god Men. Like Xanthos, the god was originally at home in Asia Minor, and Xanthos himself was a slave who was starting a cult for fellow slaves.[2] Here we find the level at which "outsiders" on public occasions could express their own honours for the gods: we cannot assume that outsiders were specially prone to Christian conversion because they did not have a personal role or reward from their city's pagan calendar. They could reproduce cults for their own benefit.

Some of the great healing and "Eastern" gods had first spread and established themselves through these individual foundations.[3] In turn, they came to earn public cults of their own, which were financed by the city and its priests. Of these "Oriental" gods, only Mithras remained a "private" god, worshipped by small groups who met in his subterranean shrines. His cult was the privately funded worship of a few males: "there was, if anything, less chance of the Roman Empire turning Mithraic than of seventeenth-century England turning Quaker. To say this is not to under-estimate Mithraism or Quakerism."[4]

Less visible in the town plans is the worship which was paid by individuals in their homes or private properties. We meet the individual not just in his votive dedications, the model limbs, locks of hair, model feet, ears and footprints (usually signifying, "I stood and worshipped here") which turned many ancient temples into lumber rooms as curious as shrines of the miraculous Virgin.[5] The householders of Alexandria had their cult of the "Good Daimon": houses and gardens had private altars; Greek households had their cults of the hearth, or of Zeus, "Zeus Ktesios" (Zeus of possessions). Family cults helped to define the circle of family membership: wives were expected to follow their husband's family cults, and adopted heirs were to honour their adopted family's cults and ancestors. In Roman religion, the cults of family and household were especially prominent: we find signs, too, of their export to the towns of the Latin-speaking West.[6] The gods were also a persistent presence in schools. Their festivals were school holidays and their cults a companion to the rhythms of the school year. Around the year 200, the Christian Tertullian draws a vivid picture of a schoolmaster's life in a North African town, the offerings to Minerva from the fees of the new pupils, the sacrifices at every turn and the days of prize-giving when civic dignitaries would come and join in paying conspicuous cult to the gods.[7] In these schools, Christians, too, were taught their lessons.

Everywhere, the gods were involved in life's basic patterns, in birth, copulation and death. The gods marked the various stages in human life, being honoured with "rites of passage" at moments of significant change: adolescence, marriage and childbirth. These mortal changes marked men off from their gods, and were marked, in turn, by the various pollutions which specific rites could dispel.[8] Ritual observance restored mortals to a fit state for keeping company with the divine, and so these rites of purification continued, wherever people were born, had sexual relations and died. Ritual honours did not cease with a person's death. Those who had property aspired to be honoured and remembered by ceremonies which were often

performed at their tomb or grave and for which they left funds and
properties. In the Imperial period, these duties were often bequeathed
to the freedmen of the family or to an association which the donor had
joined, or created for this purpose. Donors were acutely aware that
their own families were likely to die out and thus, explicitly, they
looked to these more enduring units to keep up their honour. Within a
few decades, therefore, a dead man might expect to be honoured by
people whom he had never known, and naturally, there was a
tendency for these rites to lapse into neglect.[9] There was a further
motive, however, for endowing them generously. Properties which
were attached to that "religious place," the tomb, were argued to be
exempt from a dead man's creditors. The Emperor Trajan ruled that
they were not, but there is a lasting gap between rulings of Roman law
and continuing funerary practice. It is far from certain that Trajan's
ruling settled the dispute, and if it did not, cult after death remained a
man's best retort to the debts accrued in his lifetime.[10]

In the Imperial period, these funerary foundations were common
practice. Like living benefactors, their donors aspired to continuing
fame through their gifts, and to achieve it, they added to the groups, or
associations, who met freely in pagan cities in order to pay cult to the
gods.[11] These associations took various forms, varying between the
Greek and Latin cultural zones. In the Latin West, groups of "humbler
people" met specifically as "funeral societies," celebrating a patron's
memory and contributing funds to ensure themselves a decent funeral
when they also died. In the West, too, societies in honour of a
particular god, or gods, grew like extended families beneath the
presidency of the master or mistress of a household, like the four
hundred worshippers of Dionysus who had grouped themselves
beneath the patronage of one Agripponilla in second-century
Tuscany. In the Latin-speaking towns, there were also groups of
workers, associated by a common trade, who would meet and dine in
honour of a divinity. They, too, were grouped beneath a richer
patron's care.

In the West, religious associations tended to assume the character of
extended families and hence, like the Roman family, they sometimes
included slaves and freedmen among their membership. In the Greek
East, slaves were rarely members beside free men; the sexes, too, were
almost always segregated. Women are sometimes found in a male
club, but essentially as priestesses of a god who required female
servants. Sometimes, too, they were honoured as benefactresses, but

they were not therefore members of the club beside the men. Like men, they had religious clubs of their own.

In the Greek East, clubs for the sole purpose of burial were not traditional: funerary rites were only one purpose among many. On other points, however, there were similarities between the Greek and Latin areas. In the Greek East, too, groups would form round a common trade or round a donor who wished to be remembered posthumously. In both areas, the role of the rich donor was very important. Beneath him, members of a cult society held office, passed votes and decrees and honoured themselves with titles which were copied from civic life. The style of an association, both Greek and Roman, wore the clear stamp of the style of civic life: a benefactor stood at its head, followed by a range of "magistrates" and voting members, copying the civic hierarchy to which they were often too humble to aspire. In these clubs, the patron, like the civic benefactor, exerted influence and earned praise in return. Roman law, therefore, was concerned to control the clubs' orderliness, and in the Empire it attempted to rule that a person could not belong to more than one club at a time. Slaves were only to be admitted with their masters' permission and meetings were to be kept within reasonable limits. On the matter of multiple membership, the law, we can see, was freely ignored.

These associations did not influence the form of the Christian Church, but they are the obvious pagan model through which to bring out certain differences in the Christians' own organization. For the moment, it is enough to evoke one example. Of the Greek religious associations, none is fuller or better preserved than the revised rules of the Iobacchi in Athens.[12] They worshipped the god Dionysus and have left a vivid inscription of one of their meetings, in April 176 A.D. First, they received a new high priest, the rich Herodes Atticus himself. The former high priest became his deputy after more than forty years of service and then read out the statutes which two earlier priests had drawn up. Those at the meeting were overjoyed. "Hurrah for the priest," they shouted; "Revive the statutes: you really should," "Long life to the Bacchic society," "Engrave the statutes," "Put the question." The vote in favour of the statutes was unanimous.

Like a civic assembly in miniature, the Iobacchi voted and acclaimed their leaders. They had a hierarchy of officers, a president, a chief bacchus and a patron. The sexes were segregated: all Iobacchi were men. At this meeting they were reviving rules which had been drawn up by former priests but had then been allowed to lapse. Perhaps the election of the rich Herodes had given the society fresh heart. Like civic decrees, the rules were inscribed on a pillar: we begin to see the elements of a popular meeting and a "civic" organization which helped to make these societies a focus for people's interest and support. The particular rules which they inscribed are also revealing. They set out the terms and expenses of membership and the reduced fees of enrolment for an Iobacchus's son. New candidates had to be approved by a vote, not just the vote of some club committee, but a vote of all those members who attended. Members had to pay a "fixed monthly contribution" for the wine which was drunk at their monthly meet-ings, their society's anniversary and the particular festivals of their god. Rules of conduct were very precise. Singing, rioting and clap-ping at meetings were all strictly forbidden and members who failed to attend without good reason were fined. Heavy penalties attached to anyone who started a fight or insulted a fellow member. If anyone came to blows, his fate was to be decided by a meeting of all Iobacchic members and a public vote. "Orderly officers" were appointed by lot, and when anyone caused a nuisance, he would find such an officer at his side, bearing the wand, or thyrsus, of the god. When the wand was laid beside him, the offender had to leave the room at once. If he refused to go quietly, he was entrusted to the Iobacchic bouncers, men with the apt title of "horses," who shoved him out of the company. True, the Iobacchi were drinking wine, but these careful rules say much for the problems of insults and bad behaviour in a small society which restricted itself to men. All Iobacchi were meant to be friends, but their meetings were times of festivity and some of the members, plainly, found the effort too much for them.

At the meetings, the god received sacrifices and such offerings of drink as befitted the occasion. The priest had to offer a libation for the "return of Bacchus" and "pronounce the speech of theology" which the retiring president, during his forty years, had instituted "out of public spirit." The meat and drink were divided among the various officials, some of whom bore the names of gods, titles like "Dionysus" and "Aphrodite," which were distributed among the members by lot. These names have been explained as parts in a sacred drama which the members then acted, although this theory is not provable. During meetings, speeches were only to be made with the express permission of the priest or vice-priest.

We can sense very clearly what an Iobacchus found in these aspects of his club. Once, a month, he felt that he was paying particular honours to gods who were "his" at that moment. These honours were laid down by rules and were more personal than those of a civic sacrifice at which he was only one in a crowd. Socially, he met and dined with fellow members whose behaviour was carefully regulated. His vote was very important whenever new members were discussed or older members were disciplined. He shared in the fortunes of fellow members' lives, and if anything particular befell him, like marriage or fatherhood, selection for a civic office or the high honour of the Panhellenic Council, then he had to treat his fellow Iobacchi to drink offerings "worthy of his rank." The Iobacchic group was much more than a burial club, but it also handled members' deaths very neatly. When a member died, the society provided a cheap wreath in his honour "not exceeding five denarii in value" and one jar of wine for "all those who have attended the burial." Those who did not attend were not allowed the drink.

The rules of conduct say less about the religious aspects of a meeting, but they do not allow us to conclude that religion was largely absent. The god's "return" was a subject of special celebration honouring his "presence"; there was a speech on theology, and if there was a sacred drama, it may have concerned the worshippers' souls in the next world. We do not know the details, any more than we know what it meant to be chosen as "Dionysus" in the lottery. These cult societies were clearly much more than the ancient equivalents of a good London dining club. The Attic Iobacchi were only one group among many small Bacchic societies throughout the world. We meet others in inscriptions, surviving from Italy to Lydia, and their officials and titles tell us a little more about the religious mysteries and rather less of the social programme. As the Iobacchi listened to the high priest's speech of theology, they evidently felt they belonged to a worldwide company of worshippers. Their branch, they felt, was the best on earth. "Now you prosper," they shouted as they passed the rules, "now, of all Bacchic societies, you are the First": from place to place, the Bacchic cults' practice was similar, but it was not identical. At Athens, the Iobacchi included people of high status who might rise to important civic positions: they met, almost certainly, in the shrine whose prominent ground plan lies between the Areopagus and the Pnyx hill. Were they not a rather exclusive group, like most other cult societies once they had been formed? A membership of up to forty was a normal size for these Greek-speaking groups in honour of a god, and it was customary to offer easy terms of membership to sons and descendants. Here we can already see a contrary social appeal in the Christian community: it was a bigger society, open to all comers, with no distinctions of rank and degree. The minor Iobacchus, meanwhile, had his Iobacchic vote and once a month he could exclude the people he hated most from the company which he most enjoyed. "Correctors of Greece" might lay down the law for Athens's public courts; Herodes himself might struggle with his opponents in the Emperor's distant presence. If he won, there would be more and better wine for the society. If he lost, the Iobacchi would still meet to celebrate the successes in lesser members' lives. Boring speeches were banned, and all the while there were easy terms for members who put down their sons to be Iobacchi too.

In a passage of remarkable vehemence, the ageing Plato had denounced all private cults and proposed the death penalty for anyone in his ideal city who established a shrine on private ground or sacrificed to gods outside the city's list. Private cults, he believed, would weaken a city's cohesion and give individuals the means of pursuing success for their own selfish ends. The suggestion had a long literary life, from Cicero to Apuleius, who quoted it in his speech of defence in Sabratha.[13] Yet, as often, Plato was out of tune with practice. In the Hellenistic period, cult societies had proliferated in many cities, giving citizens and non-citizens a focus for their loyalties and a non-political sense of community. By the early Empire, the household cults in cities like Pompeii and Herculaneum had confirmed Plato's worst fears. Their private houses and gardens contained many small shrines which were dedicated not merely to the Roman forces of hearth and store but to the personal gods of the Greek East, Isis, Serapis and many others.[14] Plato's severity had found few supporters. Private associations flourished far and wide, from Gaul to Syria: in the Syrian cities, "companies" of worshippers were very prominent and at Palmyra, especially, they are attested by the copious "invitation tickets," which asked members to attend their banquets. People did not feel a conflict between these cults and their civic gods. Like a philosophy, an "association" did not weaken the civic cults: it supplemented them. Often, its members met in dining rooms which were attached to major civic temples. Yet, in another sense, Plato was right, for these cult societies did represent a separate area of religious activity to which people turned specifically for religious ends. Some continued to turn to the Jews' synagogues; rather more began to turn to the Christian community. It was through the household and the house church that Christianity and its otherworldly "assembly" first put down its roots, then grew to undermine the old civic values and the very shape of the pagan city.

# III

Such, then, were the main areas of the "ceremonies," or cult acts, which pagans paid to their gods. They were bound up with every aspect of the social order which we sketched for a "typical" city. The older, nineteenth-century view that the ceremonies themselves had created that order, defining the members of a family, the citizens of a city and the orders of its "guilds" and corporations, is no longer convincing: cults alone did not define these groups, although they did sustain and give them a public expression. They were a field for the notables' "love of honour," but they were not confined to the notables only. They were intertwined with every grouping, each level of a city's social existence.

Of the ceremonies themselves, we have also seen something in passing: the offerings of animals, the libations, or drink offerings, the speeches of the *theologoi* who praised the gods,[1] the processions, or "pomp of the Devil," as Christian Latin called it,[2] the vowing of inscribed and sculptured monuments or other tokens of respect, fulfilled in return for, or hope of, divine favour. Pagans had their fixed patterns of prayer and hymns and their gods, too, received incense. These types of honour belonged to a "neutral technology" of worship which the Christians appropriated and set in a new context. Here and there, even the blood sacrifice of an animal has been practised by Christian communities. In the early Church, however, the imagery and language of sacrifice was diverted from blood offerings for the demons to the Christians' own offerings of alms and first fruits to their bishop.[3]

What, however, was required beyond these ceremonies if a person was to "follow Greek (or Roman) religion"? So far, we have looked at the cults as detached observers, trying to catch their effect as social acts in a social order. Yet they were, of course, religious acts for their performers, consciously addressed to the gods. Naturally, a person had to believe that the gods existed; what else besides?

We can begin with the observable cult acts themselves: did the central ceremony, the offering of an animal, have further associations for a pagan, perhaps not an orthodoxy or even a single meaning, but a pattern of religiousness which it evoked? Generally, sacrifices followed rules and patterns. Different cults tended to receive different animals and the victims were generally divided into categories. Gods of the earth and underworld tended to receive dark animals which were offered by night and burnt in full, the origin of our word "holocaust." Other gods, but not heroes, tended to receive light animals, while the people of first-century Mytilene, it has been aptly noticed, wondered how to accommodate the cult of the living Emperor and ended by offering him spotted animals, neither black nor light, for a figure who was neither quite human nor divine.[4] There are exceptions to these categories, because no central priesthood enforced them, but in general, they persisted and remind us that the rites were not entirely haphazard and devoid of further associations. To "follow" pagan religiousness was, in part, to accept them, at civic sacrifices or at the offerings which individuals made in fulfilment of a vow to a god.

The difficulty, for historians, is to know how far to pursue such "meanings" and by what means. We can turn to the inscribed sacred laws and rules for the cults which cities or individuals organized. They specify certain types of dress and behaviour, as if the details were very significant: however, were they merely attempts to give a cult a recognizable form? Almost always they list prohibitions, not positive commands: worshippers must abstain briefly from drink or from sex and other temporary pollutions; sometimes they must avoid certain foods and exclude certain types of person. Obviously, the rules are concerned to observe the general limits of "impurity," which mark off the world of men from the world of the gods. Less obviously are they concerned to reinforce deeper meanings in the cult acts themselves.[5] How, from a record of these prohibited practices, can we deduce any more? The problems may become clearer if we look at one of the civic rites of the Antonine age. No source for their practice is clearer than Pausanias, who observed them personally while travelling in Greece, and of many examples, his account of a rite for Artemis, held at Patras in Achaea, is particularly vivid.[6] Patras's cult statue of Artemis the huntress had been a present from the Emperor Augustus. Every year, the people held a "festival of the Laphria" in the goddess's honour "which was peculiar to their place." They made a barrier of tall logs round the altar, "still green," so that the stockade would not burn.

They piled the driest wood on the altar, for kindling, and then smoothed the approaches to this pyre by laying earth on the altar steps. On the first day, the people walked in a procession of the "greatest grandeur" for the goddess. A virgin priestess brought up the rear, riding in a chariot which was drawn by tame, yoked deer. On the next day, the people made their offerings and threw living game birds onto the altar with wild boars and deer, gazelles, the occasional wolf and bear cub and other fully grown animals. The altar was stacked with fruit from their orchards and then they set fire to the logs. "Thereupon," wrote Pausanias, an eyewitness, "I saw a bear and other animals forced out by the first leap of the flames, or escaping at full tilt. Those who had thrown them in brought them straight back to the fire and their funeral. The people have no record of anyone being injured by the animals."

Perhaps we should not be too solemn about this festival's details. They had obviously gained their own momentum and the animals' antics were half the fun. Pausanias thought it a local peculiarity, and on that point, archaeology so far supports him. Every offering was burned up, so that nothing was saved for the participants, and perhaps we should look no further than the wish to pay Artemis especial honour by especially conspicuous consumption. The rite then acquired the impetus of a good day's blood sports. Nonetheless, the details were not all haphazard. Artemis the virgin huntress was honoured by a virgin priestess and, like the goddess, the priestess had tamed wild deer. The animals were appropriate to Artemis's natural interests and, to its participants, the details of this cult represented her appropriate honours. They were also a source of local pride which crossed all classes and all barriers of "superstition." "The whole city," wrote Pausanias, "prides itself over this festival and so, just as much, do the individuals."

Once again, we return to the connection between a festival and a city's sense of identity. It should not be minimized as a source of "meaning" in itself, but if we try to penetrate further, we come up against the absence of any accompanying myth. In their lack of one, the Laphria are not untypical. Sometimes antiquarians do try to explain by a myth why this or that city acted ceremonially in some particular way. Historians would seldom trust their opinion for anything else, and their explanations may well be their own speculation: did the Athenians really observe their festival of the Pitchers in silence because of an incident in the mythical past of Orestes? Without

such interpretations, we can only try to interpret the rite itself.[7] The
details may cohere: its type of priest or priestess, its type of sacrifice,
the accompanying conduct of the worshippers, which may be very
distinctive. The best-known calendar of festivals is the Athenians',
and it is clear that many of the ceremonies evoked the concerns and
relationships of citizens and families. Certain festivals were the business of women only, and it is evident that they concerned the due
relation of the sexes and took contrasting forms to that end.[8] Others
concerned the prosperity of fields and crops and honours for the dead.
These areas of reference were common to the civic calendars of other
cities. Children and marriages, the family past and present, the vintage
and the harvest: these "collective images" were evoked by cult acts, to
a degree which histories of their "emptiness" or "irrelevance" in the
Christian period have not fully taken into account. Just as a procession
showed off the city's social order in a "consensual pageant," so the
sequence of these rites in the calendar evoked an image of stable,
enduring order, realized across generations and seasons, within families and between men and women. For example, the Athenians
continued to celebrate their festival of the Anthesteria throughout the
Imperial period: it was an occasion for giving presents to three- or
four-year-old children; it marked a first stage in a citizen's progress
from birth to death; it celebrated the opening of the wine of a new
year's harvest; it allowed drinking, to be conducted, however, in
silence at separate tables; the rites evoked an atmosphere of ill omen
and then moved on to honour the family's dead (probably) and to
celebrate the fertility of the fields. These rites, and other, less obvious
ones, extended over several days and brought the people to jostle and
process through the city's streets. This much we can grasp with some
confidence, without exhausting the full range of the ceremonies.[9]
Different people responded at different levels to their sequence of
possible references, but the sequence was not entirely lost in all the
drinking and the fun. Unlike Imperial Rome, a city like Athens had
both a real and an "ideal" continuity of membership, enduring
through its history. Citizenship still defined a civic community to
which these interwoven references could attach. They persisted because they evoked a pattern of relationships which was still relevant to
the civic order.

Over time, practice in these civic cults could change or be reinter-
preted. It might even continue to seem rather old-fashioned: antique
ceremonies did persist, even when people recognized that they were

rather quaint. Over time, the Anthesteria itself took a further turn at Athens. By the third century A.D., people would masquerade as nymphs and bacchants and recite "Orphic theology" during the festival.[10] The rites had acquired more, not less, meaning with age, one further reason why they had continued to be practised.

This attachment of a myth to the ceremonies is very suggestive. Myth and ritual had generally developed separately in the Greek and Roman world: pagan critics and philosophers could thus belittle the gods of myth and poetry without upsetting the continuing practice of cult. When Christian authors borrowed their examples, their polemic was no more effective. Literal myth was irrelevant to practice and its credit was preserved by seeing it as an allegory, whose oddities concealed deeper truths. In the Imperial period, the Anthesteria was only one of the many cults to which a "theological myth" had been attached. The compound was also present in the widespread "Bacchic" cult societies, whose myth was expressed in an artistic imagery and was probably understood as a religious allegory.[11] In the cult of Mithras, the recurrent imagery of the shrines and monuments accompanied a suggestive set of titles for the cult's officiants.[12] Gods like Serapis and Osiris, Attis and Isis also had myths of their past activities, which some of their worshippers would know and recall. These cults joined a myth and a ceremony together: the compound was particularly strong in cults which kept their "myth" secret. In the Imperial period, these "mysteries" abounded in many types of cult. They were paid as a preliminary to consulting an oracle, as part of the cult of Attis or Dionysus, as an element, even, in the worship of the Emperors.[13] To Christian scholars, the mystery cults once seemed the "real" pagan religion, the most tenacious seat of opposition to Christianity. The perspective is itself a Christian one: mystery cults were no more tenacious than the gods of many civic shrines and festivals. In a mystery cult, however, the relation between a mythical "secret" and a cult act was very close. By definition, we do not know what the particular mystery was, but plainly, it varied from cult to cult, as people continued to be initiated into many mysteries, not into only one. Their myths did not necessarily concern the initiate's own future, or even the fate of his soul. There were various interpretations of what a myth actually meant: according to one "naturalizing" theory, the myth of Isis and Osiris which was told in connection with their mystery rites symbolized the growth of crops and the fertility of the fields.[14]

By the Imperial age, the multiplication of these mysteries and the evidence for cults with a closer connection to myth do bring paganism into areas where Jews and Christians could offer a firmer and clearer compound. Where the Bacchic societies offered a myth of their god,[15] Jews and Christians offered history; the pagan mysteries conveyed a secret experience, whereas the Jews and Christians offered a "revelation" based on texts. They also united cult and religious philosophy, and here, too, they could capitalize on common ground. Since the third century B.C., pagans had developed a type of religious philosophy by which they explained and directed man's personal sense of God. This individual piety required no formal cult, and we find it expressed freely in the texts of Platonist philosophy; in the early Imperial period, it had spread further, to the "hushed lecture-room atmosphere" of the pagan Hermetists. These people met and studied the texts of revelation, which their divine guide, the Thrice-great Hermes, was believed to have bequeathed to them. We cannot place these groups socially, but their ideas do connect to higher religious philosophy.[16] Their commonplaces dwelt on the various paths by which people could come to God. They could turn inwards and contemplate their soul, learning to approach God by the old Apolline principle of knowing themselves. Alternatively, they could turn outwards and marvel at the beauty of the world, its flowers and seasons, the order of its lands and seas and, above them all, the reasoned harmony of those divine watchers, the stars. Like the great hymn writers of the eighteenth century, authors in this branch of theology emphasized the proofs of God which were written large in the world's natural beauty, whereas the other branch looked inward, to the mystery of the soul. These two fine paths became the neutral property of educated men, shared by pagans, Jews and Christians, although Jews in Alexandria first altered the pagan arguments. A man, they said, could not "know himself" and thus "know God." First, he must "un-know," or despair of knowing himself, and then resign himself to the "grace" of God. The aim, however, was the same: the "likening of man to God," in a favourite Platonist phrase, and the consequent stability and calm which set a mortal beyond change and chance and above the rule of Fate.[17] This philosophic religiousness was not an obstacle to the Christians' theology. Gratefully, their authors borrowed it and fitted it to their new ideas of Christ and Redemption.

To be a "follower of pagan religion," however, a person did not have to accept this philosophic theology. Nor did he have to attend a

mystery cult, or a cult in which myth and ritual were closely compounded. They were options, no more, although their emergence
does point to an interest which Christians, too, could satisfy. Myth,
however, had a further and more widespread role: it confirmed men's
awareness of that constant presence, the anger of their gods.

To appreciate this role, we need only attend to Pausanias again on
his tour round the Greek cities. Pausanias did not accept the odder
stories of myth: he liked to rationalize their wilder details and retain
only a manageable core. However, one type of myth neither he nor his
informants doubted: the tales of the past anger of a god, which had
been shown in famines or earthquakes and averted by oracular inquiry
and an appropriate local rite or shrine.[18] He and his sources remind us
how fragile all civic life had remained, against the constant dangers of
geology and the weather. To "follow pagan religion" was generally to
accept this tradition of the gods' appeasable anger. A few philosophers
argued against it, but the vast majority ignored them, and it was
precisely this fear which impelled people to persecute Christian
"atheists," dangerous groups who refused to honour the gods.

To Roman theorists, one role of *religio* had been to counter unwar-
ranted fear of the gods, a fear which we know now in an individual
type, anxiety about life after death. On the topic of an afterlife,
however, "the sentiments of the ancients admitted of infinite
variation."[19] Many of those who have left any word on the topic
denied it altogether, in their epitaphs, their poems, their books: for all
his interest in rites and shrines, Pausanias thought the idea of an
underworld in which the gods kept men's souls was absurd. Bodily
resurrection was preposterous, as anyone knew who looked at the
bare bones in a tomb. Where would the flesh come from? If the flesh
did return, the problems, remarked that characteristic Antonine,
Artemidorus, were unimaginable: how could all those resurrected
people get their property back?

There were, however, less sceptical currents. If anything survived,
it must be the soul, and the soul could ascend or descend after death.
Public paintings showed the punishments of Hades and there were
those who knew unease because of their stories; Lucretius's great
attack on them (c. 60 B.C.) had not been a war against shadows.
Philosophy did not create these beliefs, but it helped to give them
clearer form. Plato and Pythagoras had bequeathed to their followers a
clear image of rewards and punishments in the next life. In Plato's
*Republic*, the elderly Cephalus admitted that since he had been growing old, he had been troubled by the fear that he might have to expiate

in Hades the faults which he had committed during his long life. A "true Greek,"[20] however, he also suggested that this fear might only be a pathological consequence of old age. The Platonists were less sceptical: as Plutarch aged, he grew into a detailed concern for divine punishments and the fate of the soul after death.[21] Other Platonists differed little, and their arguments concerned only details, whether the punishments in Hades were symbols for the pangs of an uneasy conscience, or whether people would be reborn as animals in their next life.

However, very few people were serious Platonists, and it is hard to judge how far these concerns extended to a wider public, Cephalus's heirs. Epitaphs do not refer to the reincarnations which Plato had credited, but perhaps this silence is only a fact about epitaphs and their conventions. Art and funerary reliefs on the subject are also notoriously hard to judge: they have suffered from overinterpretation, seeing meaning where there may have been little or none. Archaeology is hardly more helpful. In the Imperial period, there was a growing tendency to bury the dead, not to burn them, but the cause of this change is quite obscure, and we cannot assume that it had a connection with changing views about a future life.[22] Perhaps the best evidence for such a concern is the nature and spread of mystery cults themselves. Not every mystery cult related to the participants' future after death, but it is evident that some of them did. Attacking the Christians, Celsus the Platonist (c. 170 A.D.) remarked that the idea of "eternal punishments" was accepted by priests and initiators into the pagan mysteries; Christian teaching on the afterlife was on a par with the terrors of the "mysteries of Dionysus."[23] He implied that these mysteries, too, were concerned with a life after death, and here we can support him from a different angle. When Plutarch wished to console his wife in the face of death, it was to these Dionysiac mysteries that he referred her, as also to the "traditional account" of the Platonists: they would have taught her, he assumed, that death was not simply the end and a dissolution.[24] In the later second century, Celsus assumed that the rites of Mithras assisted the soul on its ascent through the heavenly spheres; at Eleusis, the rites do seem to have aimed at a happy disembodied future beyond the grave; at the end of *The Golden Ass*, the hero Lucius experienced a simulated journey above and below the earth in the mysteries of his goddess Isis.[25]

People could worship a god without being initiated into these mysteries; not everybody bothered; open scepticism was still expressed. However, we hear more of the small Bacchic groups of initiates in the Imperial period and some of the other mysteries are themselves creations of that date.[26] A concern for life beyond the grave was perhaps more evident among more people than previously; to some people, it could seem compelling, as we can see from the Emperor Marcus's own private *Meditations*, in which he positively struggles to maintain his Stoic philosophy and deny a personal afterlife against his strong urge, otherwise, to believe it.[27] In mystery cults, initiations offered reassurance, whatever the fate of the soul after death. If it ascended to the heavens, initiation helped to ensure its safe passage through the opposing powers: initiates sometimes learned a password. If it went down into a literal underworld, initiation spared the dead the chillier terrors and the gloomier halls of residence. Were initiates also commanded to continue to behave well, like confirmation candidates, in order to attain these blessings? Sometimes, perhaps, they were: the rites at Eleusis are twice connected with continuing "holiness and justice" on the initiate's part, although these virtues were probably conceived in general terms: not to break oaths, not to kill or steal.[28] Among pagans there was no question of punishment for a passing evil thought in everyday life.

These types of belief were neither universal nor clearly defined. Only some pagans credited this future existence, and none, certainly, imagined a second life, body and all. There was a vagueness about what exactly bodiless existence meant for the individual: Plutarch, at least, thought that souls after death would still recognize their friends.[29] There were also the stories of punishments in Hades. Some people, certainly, assumed they would be eternal, a belief which Christians did not create. There was more doubt about the literal torments of the myths. Certain authors, especially Platonists, could argue that these tales were worth preserving nonetheless, as instruments with which to terrorize the ignorant. Plutarch, however, does also hint that "few" people believed them literally.[30] Spiritualized torment and vague oblivion were probably more widely credited, though Plutarch's knowledge of public opinion is not likely to have been very broad.

On any view, this range of opinion had a lack of coherence and any orthodoxy which could begin to compare with Christian teaching. Nothing, therefore, in pagan culture ever corresponded to the death-bed scenes and prayers for the dead which surfaced so quickly in Christian company. Among pagans there was no concern to die with "sins" forgiven or to pray for the state of friends and family beyond the grave. Pagans met to honour the spirits of the dead, to commemorate a dead person or to appease and nourish his disembodied soul by offerings of drink and blood from a sacrificial animal. Pagans prayed to the dead, whereas Christians (like Jews) prayed for them. Fearing their own inevitable Judgement, Christians also asked the dead to intercede on their behalf. Among Christians, feasting and celebrating at the tombs of the dead persisted, but intercession joined the older commemoration and gave a new meaning to the occasion.[31]

In pagan religiousness and cult acts, we have returned repeatedly to the ideas of fear and constant insurance, responses which lent force to the argument from tradition. The gods had been honoured always, and who would say what would happen if they were not? Fear for an afterlife was certainly present, though not universally: the more general fear was the more immediate, one which polite religiousness in Europe has lost, the fear that the gods might intervene and be "manifest" in everyday life. This fear extended to the "divine" souls of the dead: for every person who feared his fate after death, there were more who feared the dead's own anger in this world against the living. Here, pagans did hold beliefs, beside their religion of cult acts. Here, too, their religion connected with morality. The gods were held to be present, ready to uphold oaths or punish "impious" acts, beliefs which were present in both the Greek and Latin world.

The gods' presence also raises the question of their identity. Under the Empire, it has been claimed, a generalized concept of "divine power" had begun to take precedence over discrete divinities.[32] Certainly, people wished and expected their gods to work for them, or against others, through their prayers and spells, vows and offerings. Power was the essence of divinity, the bridge by which kings and rulers, too, had been granted "godlike honours." Did this explicit concern with power efface a lively sense of the gods' separate natures, leaving the Christians' "divine power" to step into the gap? Did it undermine that central theme of religiousness, the presence of the gods and their forms of contact with men?

The nearness and distance of divinity are poles between which all religious experience wavers. We have seen the cult acts of the pagan cities and touched on their wider areas of reference, yet the picture of festivals, temples and votive monuments remains a picture of externals. It lacks a sense of where the gods were felt to be. The Christians were only too conscious of the gods' presence, and the theme is particularly well documented in the second and third centuries A.D. It is especially through the themes of the gods' presence that the idea of "anxiety" has been attached to the Empire's religious life. In their ceremonies and civic life, pagans have so far resisted such a diagnosis: was it, however, more evident in this basic type of religiousness? The presence of the gods came to each generation with a long and hallowed prehistory, and the path to it is a long one, from the Homeric world to the Platonist philosophers of the fifth century A.D.

One early Christian witness brings out the theme very clearly, as he looks out at pagan communities in the Apostolic age. The scene is famous, the visit of Paul and Barnabas to the Roman colony of Lystra, that "thriving, rather rustic market town" which had been founded some sixty years earlier in the Augustan age.[33] There, the Acts of the Apostles describes how Paul and Barnabas were believed to have healed a cripple "lame from his mother's womb." At once, the crowds acclaimed them in their native dialect, saying, "The gods have come down to earth in the likeness of men." Barnabas they called Zeus, and Paul, Hermes, because of his gifts as a speaker. The priest of "Zeus before the city" prepared to sacrifice a group of bulls at the god's shrine before the gates, until a speech from "Hermes" disillusioned him.

This scene, the delight of Raphael, has received rough justice from biblical critics. It can be argued convincingly that the author was not present himself on the Apostles' journeys, but it is a further step to claim that he invented the scene to suit his purpose. Critics have quickly stepped so far, until the scene has become lost as a literary fiction, part of the author's subtle aim in constructing a story which passed as history. "Is it really conceivable?" asked Acts' greatest modern commentator. "It is highly improbable that the priest of Zeus would immediately believe that the two wonder-workers were Zeus and Hermes, quite apart from the fact that the animals had first to be brought from the pasture, and the garlands woven . . . In applying to Luke the yardstick of the modern historian, we do him an injustice."[34] His fiction has been traced to the influence of a pagan myth and left to moulder there. In Ovid's *Metamorphoses*, the gods are said to have been entertained unawares in Phrygia by two elderly peasants at the time of the great Flood. On the thinnest evidence, this myth has been located by modern scholars near Lystra and accepted as the source of Acts' incident.[35] The author, it is said, cast this local legend in a new

Christian dress in order to fill out a journey of whose details he knew nothing.

This theory has enjoyed a long life, but it never had anything to recommend it. Its geography is wrong, and although Acts' author has been given some odd disguises, none is odder than that of a man who knew fragments of Ovid and their Greek sources and distorted them to suit his picture of St. Paul.[36] Although he himself was not present at Lystra, he can be shown to have known and accompanied the Apostles elsewhere. Was he merely padding out their earlier days in Lystra with a plausible incident, another in his artful series of the misunderstandings which people attached to the Christians and their teaching? Might he not, instead, have heard the story from Paul and Barnabas themselves? The men of Lystra were said to have spoken Lycaonian, a language which no Apostle understood. Yet they were also supposed to have acted visibly on their error, while most, perhaps all, of them could also understand Greek. Is, then, the story true or is it what Paul and Barnabas liked to say of pagans in a "rather rustic market town"? The story named appropriate gods.[37] A statuette of Hermes and an eagle, bird of Zeus, have been found near Lystra; the two gods are coupled in an inscription from this general region; on a sculptured relief, we can see how people locally pictured these divinities, round-faced and solemn, with long hair and flowing beards, a searching gaze and the right hand held prominently across the chest. Such a Zeus looks uncommonly like our image of a wandering Christian holy man: in these reliefs, we, too, can sense the elusive features of a Paul or Barnabas.

These local reliefs do something to make the Lystrans' error intelligible. They were not alone in their mistake. Later in Acts, the author was present in person on the island of Melite, where "barbarians" saw Paul shake a serpent off his hand into the campfire.[38] They waited, expecting him to fall sick; when he survived, they changed course and hailed him "as a god" for his miraculous power. Like others, not least the Lystrans, they had to be convinced before they jumped to the wrong conclusion: the "barbarians" were not deceived without reason. Nobody has yet found this incident in Roman poetry. Like his informants for the scene in Lystra, Acts' author believed this response was natural. Nor, indeed, were pagans alone in it. In Caesarea, said Acts, the "God-fearing" centurion, Cornelius, had been guided by a vision to Peter's presence: on seeing him, he bowed and made a gesture of worship. "Rise up," said Peter, "for I too am a man."[39] In

Acts' view, he had greeted Peter as if he was a visiting angel. Here, the author was not present himself and could only draw on hearsay. An earlier chapter in Acts tells the story of the serving girl Rhoda, who called on the disciples' rooms in Jerusalem to inform them that Peter had escaped from prison. Peter, she said, was on his way to them, but at first they disbelieved, "saying that it could only be his angel."[40] In Acts, the smallest details are often the most revealing: when John Chrysostom published his homilies on Acts in the later fourth century, how natural, he thought, had been the Apostles' error, for "every man, it is true, has an angel." How wise, too, had been their author: first the Apostles mistook Peter for a heavenly being; then they saw him in person and realized their mistake. If they had not begun by making this mistake, said John, they might have made it when Peter departed: then they might never have realized their error.[41] The comment was revealing: so close, for John Chrysostom, too, did the world of angels lie to the world of men.

In the view, then, of an early Christian, pagans might think at any moment that they were seeing and welcoming a god; the first Christians, meanwhile, thought that they might be entertaining angels, not always "unawares." If this view of pagans is accurate, it shows us beliefs which they held, quite apart from their evocative ceremonies and their widespread building of temples. When the ceremonies and buildings faltered, these beliefs would not necessarily weaken. Are these Christian episodes accurate, and if so, how and where was this presence of the pagan gods supported, if not by some general anxiety at the core of pagan religiousness?

# 4. Seeing the Gods

## I

By the early third century, the presence of the pagan gods was clearly attested in a question and answer, set up on stone on the edge of the city of Miletus. The question had been put to Apollo himself by Alexandra, priestess of Demeter, near whose shrine, then, the stone is likely to have been displayed before it was found on the hill outside the city. "Ever since she has taken on her priesthood," the stone said, "the gods have been appearing in visitations as never before, to the girls and women but also, too, to men and children. What does such a thing mean? Is it the sign of something good?"[1]

Like nothing else, Alexandra's question takes us into the world which the author of Acts assumed to surround his Apostles. Not only in Lystra, but in old civilized Miletus, the squares and colonnaded streets were stalked by the gods, bringing close encounters into the life of every man, woman and child. It also takes us into our world. Just as the visiting gods perplexed the Milesians, so the Virgin Mary, visiting often, is perplexing even now the village of Medjugorje in western Yugoslavia. In Medjugorje, only a very few privileged children see and talk with the Virgin herself. In Miletus, the gods did not discriminate: they appeared freely to young and old, man and woman.

We are not told why this rash of divine appearances had broken out. Alexandra connected them with the beginning of her priesthood and we know from inscriptions elsewhere how the virtues of priests could affect the moods of the gods. We hear of no rush to Miletus, none of the two million pilgrims who have travelled to Herzegovina in the past four years, hoping to sight the Madonna. In Miletus, the visits were slightly alarming, and they pose a problem of translation: were they appearances of "gods to the girls and women, children and men," appearances which might be seen in dreams, or were they daylight appearances of gods "in the form of" women, children and men, an exact parallel to the belief of the men of Lystra? Each translation has been suggested, and to decide between them, we need to look into the forms of contact which pagans still accepted between men and gods. Alexandra was the priestess of Demeter Thesmophoros, whose festival, the Thesmophoria, was traditionally celebrated by women only. That fact, too, may help us to understand her question. For all its interest, this inscription was not brought to bear on the case for an "age of anxiety," yet the discussion which first brought it to life stressed the apparent "religious crisis," the "breathtaking anxiety" of the question, the note of "anxiety and exaltation" which seemed to match other evidence in contemporary inscriptions from Greek Asia. Is it, then, the missing proof of deep unease, the mood of a pagan city while the Christians were putting down their roots?

Like her fellow residents in Miletus, Alexandra had turned to Apollo himself for an answer. Like other oracular questions and answers which have been found in Miletus and Apollo's nearby precinct, her answer was inscribed on the same stone as her question. We must allow for the expense and trouble of this display, but it did not stand alone: a second oracle was inscribed in an identical hand on the side of the same block, another reply from Apollo, which ran to some twenty lines, praising the goddess Demeter and her gifts of corn and other crops of the earth.[2] All men, it said, should honour the goddess who had saved mankind from a diet of nothing but meat, but the people of Miletus should honour her especially. They were noble and favoured by the gods and therefore performed their mysteries to Demeter. The surviving text breaks off with an address to a woman, "you, devoted to the secret honour and service [of the gods], who pursue the end of stability in life": were these words, perhaps, addressed to our same Alexandra, praising her devotion to Demeter's cult and mysteries?

If so, we can understand the inscriptions' origin. Just as cities inscribed judgements which were favourable to them, so Demeter's priestess inscribed two texts from Apollo which praised her goddess and herself. The god's reply to her first question is almost entirely illegible, but eight surviving words show that the text ran at length in hexameters, which spoke of the "coming and going of gods among mortal men" and their "watching," it seems, for their honours on earth. The explanation sounds familiar, an echo of the epic poems whose metre it copied. Apollo, it seems, allayed anxiety by a style and metre which looked back to Homer, and if Apollo's resort was to Homer, then it is from Homer, too, that we should still begin in order to pin down something in the religious sensitivities of a city a thousand years after his poems.

No one who knew his Homer could miss the easy company of gods with men. In the Greek epic, the gods were not merely a divine audience, who looked on like aristocrats from a distant grandstand. They visited their heroes, "standing beside" them as "evident helpers," exact phrases which continued to pin down their presence until the end of antiquity. Homer's picture helped to fix subsequent descriptions in literature and thus, too, men's expectations in life.[3] If they were already a pattern for Homer, they may look beyond his poems to a pattern already accepted in reality. To study them, then, is to look two ways, to beliefs which Greeks may already have accepted and to the imagery which helped to fix those beliefs clearly for posterity.

In the epic poems, the gods mixed with men by daylight, gods in disguise, like Paul and Barnabas, or gods made manifest by signs of their power. When Athena led Odysseus and Telemachus through the suitors' hall, the sudden light from her lamp glowed on the rafters, alerting Telemachus to the presence of a god: "Hush," said Odysseus, "for this is the way of gods who live on Olympus."[4] This "way" was not visible to all alike: Odysseus, but not Telemachus, could see his helper Athena, just as Achilles, but nobody else, could see his mother, Thetis, standing beside him. Once, in the *Iliad*, Ajax boasted that there was no difficulty in detecting the gods, for they were "easily recognizable." However, his boast was made at a moment of departure when the gods did not care if they gave themselves away.[5] When the gods were first encountered, they were much harder to unmask: it was one of Aeneas's little distinctions that he detected Apollo in the guise of a herald, simply by the sound of his voice. Otherwise, men had to guess. They might deduce from the sudden prowess of a hero that a god was standing beside him in battle; the whole army might realize that a god was approaching because of the sight of a dark cloud in the sky or the omen of a sound or light from heaven. Like the white light at Medjugorje, these general clues of a "presence" were seen by crowds. Like portents, they were different from the clues of a god's personal attendance in which he took on human disguise.

In either epic, this personal attendance was frequent, because the gods had favourites to whom they were helpful "protectors." There were a few exceptions: until Sophocles's play, no god is known to have "stood beside" the tenacious Ajax. At times, these helpers touched their friends physically: they pulled Achilles's hair or held his hand.[6] The heroes already had the "personal religion" for which historians have searched in later texts: the care of the gods for individuals was taken for granted. "Never have I seen gods so openly befriending anyone," said Nestor of his guest Telemachus, "as Pallas Athena stands beside this man . . ." Befriending, then, was not uncommon, and only the degree of it, in this instance, was unusual.[7] Old Nestor, so wise and pious, was the sort of man who could pick it up distinctly, whereas others were less favoured, even when the presence benefited them. The gods could also deceive their favourites, a habit which Homer exploited for irony.[8] When Odysseus reached Ithaca, he failed to recognize his helper, Athena, whom he claimed not to have seen in all the years since he left Troy: cautiously, he greeted her as a goddess, although he had not realized who she was. At the end of the *Iliad*, old Priam, afraid and defenceless, had set out on his mission to Achilles's camp, and on the way he met a handsome young man who turned out to be a friendly guide. "Some god," Priam told him, "has held his hand over me," in a phrase so favoured by posterity: he felt that he had been directed to such a happy meeting, for, to judge from the young man's looks, he "must have parents close to the gods." As yet, Priam had not realized he was talking to Hermes in person. Homeric irony is strongest in the dealings of gods and men, where it helps to confirm the picture of the gods' superior power.

Irony was readily contrived, because the gods almost never revealed themselves by name when they first met men: only at the end of their encounter did Hermes declare his identity, unasked, to Priam. Usually, the god himself had to give the first clue, and he conformed to a typical sequence of changes.[9] He would reveal his beauty and show that essential divine attribute, height. He would give off a sweet scent or a dazzling light and might speak in an awe-inspiring voice. His rapid enlargement was followed by departure in a sudden flash.

Without these voluntary self-revelations, gods could continue to escape human notice:[10] "Who would ever see a god," asked Circe, "going to and fro, unless he wished to be seen?" Just as gods could be missed, humans, like Paul and Barnabas, could be mistaken. When Athena cast a divine beauty over Odysseus, his son Telemachus jumped to the wrong conclusion and assumed the stranger to be a god: "Please be propitious," he begged, mistaking his own father, "and spare us . . ." Like the Lystrans, he had been misled by a sudden miracle. Odysseus, however, was more artful. When he was first surprised by the young Nausicaa, he addressed her "cunningly," using "gentle words." Not knowing her name, he alluded to the possibility that she might be a goddess, to judge from her form and beauty: Nausicaa did not trouble to correct this compliment in her reply. Through Homer, the mistaking of beautiful women for goddesses passed into Virgil and the ancient romances. From there, it was picked up by Chaucer, Spenser and each of the heroines of Shakespeare's romantic plays: "No wonder, sir," Miranda answers, "but certainly a maid."

These scenes are the work of a poet who is already a master of the convention that gods meet men. He can also, surely, assume his hearers' familiarity with the theme. To Homer, our first poet, we owe the first expression of the idea of "accommodation," whereby gods suit their presence to individuals' capacities. Not everyone could see a god or sense his presence, unless the god appeared in an unusual weather sign above a crowd or an expectant army. Like Peter Pan, the gods were best seen by the pious or their special protégés, a limit which put their presence beyond refutation; those who failed to see them had only themselves to blame. When the gods did appear, they showed themselves in a pattern of signs which was fixed already for Homer: among them was beauty, the one sign which a mortal, too, might give off inadvertently.[11] There was no end to the gods' human disguises, as old men and women, heralds and, frequently, young and beautiful people: in one of its two translations, Alexandra's question makes sound Homeric sense. Did the gods also appear as animals? Occasionally, Homer's gods appeared "like birds," but there is no certain episode when a god turns completely into a bird, although he may become "like a bird" in a few particulars.[12] Essentially anthropomorphic, the gods stalked the world as mortals, disguising themselves so well that people could never be totally sure that a stranger was all that he seemed. Two famous scenes enlarged on these hidden depths, and neither was lost on posterity.

In the heroes' world, we are only seeing the second phase of a very much older relationship, a subtlety which the poems maintain very cleverly.[13] In an ideal past, we are told, the gods had behaved differently, and this past lived in Homer's ideal community, Phaeacia, whose King Alcinous put the point very clearly. When Odysseus was guided suddenly into his palace as an unexpected guest, the King mistook him for a visiting god. "Always before," he told his courtiers, "the gods appear clearly to us when we offer glorious hecatombs. They dine beside us, sitting where we sit, and if anyone meets them, even while travelling alone, they do not hide anything. For we Phaeacians are close to them, like the Cyclops and the savage tribe of giants." Happy Phaeacia was a land of this ideal relationship, persisting between men and gods, but Odysseus's arrival, said Alcinous, seemed to herald a lesser phase of it. He seemed to be a god by the manner of his entry, and if he was, said Alcinous, he did not bode well. He had not come openly, but in disguise: "the gods," it seems, "are planning something new in the future," an end to their days of open coming and going.

Back on Ithaca, this change in the relationship was openly acknowledged. When the leader of the suitors was rough to the stranger Odysseus, the rest of the pack rebuked him: "All sorts of gods," they said, "in the likeness of foreign strangers range in their prime through men's cities, watching over their insolence and orderly behaviour."[14] The belief was not a poetic fancy. Like the chorus in a tragedy, the suitors were plain witnesses who set off the epic heroes, and their remark, we shall see, recurred like none other on this subject in the literature of the next thousand years. The gods were not only an audience of watchers, eternal, impassive, but moved now and then to care for a human's predicament. Their minions also spied and took notes, far into late antiquity.

These details are scattered through two long epics, but they cohere in a way which shows Homer to have had a subtle picture in mind. Was it only a poetic device? Alcinous was speaking in an epic poem where the gods met poetic heroes, wrapped them in clouds and granted them invisibility. This world of the heroes was not reality. Homer also used meetings with gods for irony and contrast, his own poetic effects. However, their details follow such a pattern and their phrases recur so precisely that it is hard to believe they are only his fiction. Can we confirm this impression? Scenes of a meeting between a god and groups of men or women are found on certain engraved rings of Minoan date (c. 1400 B.C.) and are among the earliest pictures of gods in the Aegean world.[15] However, Homer's debt to this remote Minoan religion is now highly questionable and we cannot be sure whether these scenes refer to a specific experience, let alone to one which survived some seven centuries into Homer's own age. On their own evidence, the epics' "close encounters" have also been upheld for their psychological coherence. They belong, it is said, with the poems' distinctive vocabulary for mental and physical states, which "lacked" a word for man's unified consciousness.[16] This gap is said to conform to contemporary life, because people in the eighth century B.C. (it is said) lived at a particular phase in mental history, before a single consciousness imposed itself. Their minds were divided and their frequent encounters with the gods were simply the visions and voices of their divided minds. The *Iliad*'s theology was thus lifelike, because it was consistent with its primitive mental vocabulary. As the idea of consciousness arose, the gods retreated before it, taking their last bow in the *Odyssey*, which was composed at the end of the age of the "bicameral" mind.

This theory is an ingenious fantasy, but it is philosophically unsound and quite false to Homeric psychology, which amounted to more than the words for its separate parts. The rest of this chapter is a rebuttal of its supposed historical sequel. The gods did not retreat before some newly unified sense of the mind. They continued to appear in a manner close to Homer's, long after human thought had explored its own subtleties.

Homer's visions are better defended by the contemporary poetry of Hesiod, which was set outside the heroic world. Like the ordinary suitors in the *Odyssey*, Hesiod had no doubts that the gods were invisible spies who ranged the world of men.[17] Like Homer, he (or an imitator, c. 550 B.C.) also knew of the ideal past when men and gods had dined and kept open company. The Homeric picture is also supported by its own remarkable consistency. Phaeacia enjoyed one type of contact, the heroes another, which was more oblique. We hear less of a more remote contact, meetings with gods in dreams. The gods do send dreams to the sleeping heroes, but they are never dreams of the god in his own person.[18] Either the god comes in human disguise to a sleeping mortal or he sends a dream in the shape of a familiar friend: in the *Odyssey*, Athena enters Nausicaa's bedroom "like a breath of air" and appears in her sleep disguised as one of her girlfriends. In a marvellous scene, she sends a dream to Penelope in the form of a sister who seldom visits her. Through a dialogue with her, the sleeping Penelope learns of Odysseus's "divine escort" and wakes in joy at the "clear and evident" dream which has sped to her. By night and by day, therefore, Homer's gods restrict themselves to the same type of contact. They do not appear openly, but they visit people in human disguises, whether they are awake or asleep. Surely Homer did not suddenly create this cautious and coherent picture, which, as we shall see, was distinct in certain particulars from later experience?

On one point, however, there is an obvious continuity: intimacy with a god was not easy. At Lystra, Acts said, the priest of Zeus had hastened to pay the new Zeus a sacrifice: "Be propitious," Telemachus had begged, "and spare us . . ." It is quite untrue that Homer's gods and men kept easy, fearless company: from the first awesome simile of the *Iliad*, when the Sun god came down "like the night," to the last intervention of Athena in the battles of the *Odyssey*'s suitors, men trembled in terror before the presence of their gods.[19] The gods themselves knew their power: "The gods are hard to cope with," remarked Hera, "when seen very clearly." This remark, too, was kept alive across the next thousand years. When a god unveiled himself, he could dazzle his favourites and show a most unpredictable power: Apollo struck poor Patroclus to death; Aphrodite took such a stand before reluctant Helen that she cowered and then "the divinity led the way." After those three Greek words, the later language of "master" and "servant" for god and man was not a conceptual innovation.[20] Even to their favourites, the gods might be present because they were angry and resentful. "Perhaps it is some god," remarked Aeneas at the prowess of an opposing hero, "who has conceived spite against the Trojans, angered because of the sacred offerings: hard, indeed, is the anger of a god." These lines from the *Iliad* were not one of posterity's favourite quotations, but they expressed ideas which continued to motivate people: they could stand as the epigraph to any study of pagans' persecutions of Christians.[21] When a god did reveal himself, we can understand why so often he began with the words "have no fear . . ." "I am Apollo," he usually explained, or Poseidon, or a helping dream, a god or his messenger. This language of fear and reassurance became a fixed expression for the experience: "Peace be unto you. Why are you troubled? . . . Behold, my hands and feet, it is I myself." In the third Gospel, written by a man of the Gentile world, the resurrected Jesus addressed a similar sequence of words to his Apostles in their upper room.

We should allow, then, for two sides to a hero's encounter with a god. Once, he believed, the gods had been mortals' companions with whom they had sported and joked, conversed and sometimes made love. Heroes had already lost the fullness of this intimacy, but it had survived in a lesser degree. It could lead to sudden chance meetings, but these close encounters were deceptive, and when revealed, they led to human awe. Awe does not exclude joy and exalted emotion, although in Homer's poems, no hero confessed to elation when a god revealed his presence. The hero did not court the gods or strive to meet them. He chanced upon them, and as the first terror left him, he might beg for practical, earthly favours. It took a very special hero, a child of one of the gods, to dare to protest to a god face to face. Other heroes were more restrained, and mere mortals, naturally, would observe the greatest restraint.

Once isolated, this mixture of awe and intimacy runs through so much Greek writing on the gods, from Homer to the Acts of the Apostles. Did it derive largely from Homer's poems? Looking for pagan "scripture," we fasten on Homer's epic as the "bible" of the Greeks. Every schoolchild in the Empire had encountered it, every educated person had had a chance to succumb to its picture. Even in wretched Olbia, on the Black Sea, the wandering orator Dio (c. 100 A.D.) flattered his audience on their passion for Homer and his poems.[22] The "presence" of gods, however, is described in contexts where Homer's influence is hardly plausible, and even among men of letters, his examples passed down in a few favourite lines, remembered and chosen out of many more. The language of later texts and inscriptions matches the language which is used in his epics, but their relationship may be subtler than a direct borrowing. The epics, perhaps, had themselves picked up everyday language and beliefs (we cannot ever prove this), enhanced them and passed them on more vividly to those who read or heard them. Others, meanwhile, kept the same unembellished beliefs, which surfaced independently in texts and monuments under the Empire.

They persisted, above all, in the many stories of myth. The absence of a connection with ritual allowed many stories to spread beyond one occasion or locality: both within and without ritual, many of them brought gods among men. As late as the mid-second century A.D., we can listen carefully to Pausanias's informants during his travels around Greece and realize how these stories were still alive.[23] Myths had lost their surface meaning for sophisticated minds and had become a source of rococo decoration for many artists and poets, but these minds were still a tiny minority. Frequently, myths of divine punishment and "presence" explained the origins of the cities, cults and statues which lay on Pausanias's route. They spanned the same two extremes, awe at the gods' jealous anger and an ideal intimacy, shown in the gods' special favours for heroes or pious mortals who had died or suffered nobly. In turn, these past mortals became heroes, themselves deserving cult and greatly multiplying the potential centres of godlike anger on earth. "Heroic temper" was central to their super-human presence: localized and carefully appeased, they might have "no other claim to worship than their unrelenting anger with the world . . ."

These local myths of punishment and anger implied the wisdom of self-restraint and vigilant worship by mortals. Communities were well advised to respect these morals in view of their own visible past: moments of divine anger and divine friendship had created much of their surrounding landscape and some of their oldest monuments. Pausanias himself rejected the wilder stories and rationalized the details in many others, but his instinct was to accept, if possible, a large, historical core, and his travels strengthened his ability to believe. To learn these stories, he did not have to read: he heard them from local informants, just as any visitor to a shrine or festival could hear them too. Myth was not the preserve of professors and anti-quarians, and since Homeric epic, it had enlarged the scope for divine encounters: it made them classless. The myths told how gods had visited the poor and the old folk as strangers in disguise, giving scope for yet another reversal and transformation by which gods showed their power: they helped the least likely people, who, we might nowadays add, were unlikely to be transformed, in the age of Homer or Pausanias, by any human agent. Myth also kept alive the idea of the "fall" from Phaeacia's past and its possible reversal. Through myth, people knew the idea of a Golden Age, when men had been so pious that the gods moved freely among them. Unlike Phaeacia, this state might yet return, and thus it was a theme which Emperors in the later third century A.D. could still exploit in their publicity.[24] The Golden Age was to be accompanied by no Last Judgement, no setting of history to rights. It was potentially ever-present, not fixed by the will of God, and in it, man and god would again keep open company amid a generous, burgeoning world of nature.

If myth kept alive these possibilities, poetry helped to remind men how to respond if ever they should occur. In the Homeric hymns, as in the *Odyssey*, we find a further parallel for the men of Lystra: when the god reveals himself to unsuspecting mortals, they respond at once by offering to set up a cult.[25] To the Greek mind, cults began naturally from a close encounter: in that way, many of the oldest cults explained their origin and many newer dedications and cults came to exist. On the Attic stage, we meet gods through another dimension, the voice of a god, not his visible person. This aspect, too, was present in Homer,[26] and no Attic theatregoer could have accepted a modern view that meetings with pagan gods were essentially visual, whereas God, in the Old Testament, being one and remote, was encountered by his voice. The Jews' God did indeed speak, not "appear": when a Jewish dramatist cast the story of Exodus as a Greek tragedy in the second century B.C., God was played by a voice, not an appearing figure in the Greek manner.[27] However, polytheism, too, could be heard as well as seen. Among the Greeks, too, the voice of a god was a theatrical convenience, never more brilliantly exploited than by Sophocles in his *Ajax*.[28] Sounds from the gods were varied and familiar, the sounds of Pan in nature, the noises which counted as omens from heaven, the inner voice, even, of Socrates's daemon. In the early fourth century A.D., Iamblichus still distinguished carefully the experience of hearing divine voices among the various types of epiphany.[29] As many pagans heard the gods as ever sighted them: perhaps, too, they smelt them, as awareness of a sudden beautiful scent was an accepted sign of a divinity's presence.

The poets of archaic Greece continued to show the two sides to a divine encounter, the awe and the intimacy, not only because they were enshrined in Homer but because they suited the poets' idea of the gods and allowed them to write the rarest of literature: great religious poetry which was not sanctimonious. These moods were beautifully expressed in Sappho's two addresses to Aphrodite, in one of which she is the first poet to imagine herself "overheard by God": Aphrodite comes to her with that exquisite feature of the Greeks' religious imagination, a divine omniscient smile. To Christian readers, this intimacy has often seemed playful and its poems a literary conceit, but Aphrodite was nearer than the remote Father and Son, and nearness did not diminish divinity.[30] Pindar encountered it too, meeting one of the heroes on his road to Delphi: later traditions credited him with several encounters with gods and their images from which he began cults in their honour, as any pagan would.[31]

There is a clear difference between these epiphanies and modern accounts of a presence or encounter in Western culture. Nowadays, the sense of presence is connected closely with an "affective state" altering the subject's emotional mood into joy or warm elation, fear, too, or inner contentment. The experience of "seeing" another connects, as Sartre argued, to the consciousness of "being seen": the presence seems to be watching or helping the person who senses it. In antiquity, some of the same sensations were reported: fear, scent, light and sometimes touch. But in pagan culture, these presences were agreed to have their own existence, "gods in disguise," independent of mortals who might intrude on them, to their cost. The experience of emotional warmth and reassurance and a sense of unity with surrounding nature were not the hallmarks of an encounter with a present divinity in early Greece.

In classical Athens of the late fifth century B.C., we might feel that the presence of the gods had become a convention to sophisticated minds. The experience had been exploited in the theatre, where actors appeared on an upper level of the scenery or flew onstage in theatrical machines. The force, however, of Greek tragedy was bound intimately with interventions of the gods, and they lie at the heart of Sophocles's tragic art, in Athena's visible presence to the deluded Ajax, Oedipus's farewell in the sacred grove at Colonus and above all in the *Antigone*, where the chorus summon the gods to Creon's city in a moment of distress, only to receive the "arrival" of a human messenger instead. The gods, as in Homer, are known more by their power than by their discrete personalities: "when gods appear at the end of a tragedy, their divinity is always recognized at once by the chorus, their identity never . . ."[32] The angry presence of heroes and "gods in a small way" is taken for granted by the entire plots of plays, ascribing to the dead the "heroic temper" which is so manifest in Sophocles's heroes.[33]

When these interventions became trite, tragedy tended to melodrama, an effect which has often been found in Euripides: "on the whole, I should say, Euripides was not much interested in epiphanies, regarding them as little more than a dramatic convenience. He was not much concerned to invest them with any excitement or sense of mystery . . ." Yet the tone of some of his plays suggests that this "belief" had not been entirely diminished. In the *Ion*, the hero still fears to look on a god at the wrong moment and strikes a chord of sympathy in the audience. In the *Bacchae*, we can catch something of the poet's own religious sensitivity in the hush which he casts on nature and the tremors he gives to the earth before the god Dionysus appears. The stage conventions of epiphany meant less to him, but not the underlying notion.[34]

Nonetheless, these encounters were staged in plays and only brought their gods before mythical heroes of the past. When Euripides began to treat them as a convention, had they lost all connection with life and its expectations? Here, hymns throw a bridge between literature and religious life, and the hymns which were composed by Callimachus between the 270s and late 240s B.C. raise the problems of tone and sincerity in an age of sophisticated minds. Three of his hymns, especially, are connected with civic festivals, although their manner makes it hard to credit that they were meant for recitation on the festival's day. Each, however, begins with a lively sense that the god or goddess is about to be present among the onlookers.

In the first of them, "sharp-eyed Athena's" statue, we deduce, is about to be escorted from the goddess's shrine in Argos for its yearly washing.[35] "Come out," call Callimachus's Argive women to the goddess who is lodged in her temple: her wooden image has been cleaned and polished and also, we must imagine, robed, for "whoever sees Pallas, keeper of cities, naked, shall look on Argos for the last time." This prologue leads into the myth of Teiresias and Pallas at her bath: "the laws of Kronos order this: whoever looks on one of the immortals when the god himself does not choose, the sight shall cost him a heavy price." The picture is brilliantly drawn in two contrasting tones. Although Athena pities Teiresias, she is obliged to blind him for his spying, as she must obey the divine law. Teiresias, therefore, is blinded, but he receives a special insight into the ways of the gods, and thus becomes a "seer." The hymn ends as the goddess is at last coming out among her female worshippers who wait to "receive" her: her statue, we assume, is supposed to be visible in all its finery. "Welcome, goddess, when you drive out your horses and drive them back again: keep safe all the heritage of the Danaans." Athena's statue is emerging in her chariot for her yearly journey, like a Spanish madonna from a church in Seville during Holy Week.

In the hymn to Apollo, by contrast, the god's statue never emerges. His presence is perceived through its effects on Cyrene's great shrine: its doors seem to tremble and its laurel to shake: "Look," sing the choir of young men, "Apollo is hammering at the door with his fair foot." He is "visiting" his shrine, but not everyone can see him, as insight depends on the beholders' own virtue and piety. As one person can see more than another in a child or a garden, a landscape or a painting, so the assessment of visiting strangers was an art for pious connoisseurs. As the god drew near to Callimachus's crowds the young men struck up the song and dance. "We shall see you, archer Apollo, we shall see you, and then we will no longer be mean and lowly." There is none of the awe, because the god is coming openly, to be seen of his own volition. There is intimacy and a note of exaltation, although the hymn ends before the god himself is seen.[36]

Both of these hymns convey a crowd's eager anticipation of the presence of their god: only at Argos does the song end with a sighting when "now, truly," after several false hopes, Athena is visible in her statue. Together, these hymns express very neatly two poles of an epiphany, the sighting of a god in the form of his image and the sensing of a presence which only the pious can perceive. These two poles will recur in much we will examine, but first there is a question about the evidence itself. Callimachus was a sophisticated man from a sophisticated court, where a "visit from a god" was a familiar metaphor:[37] should we really take his hymns seriously? Opinions have divided sharply, but perhaps we should separate Callimachus's own point of view from those of the spectators whom he wished to evoke. Personally, he might be detached from his poem, although he intended it to convey what these festivals meant to others.[38] His playful touches do not tell against this: once again, awe and intimacy stand side by side, but it is in the mythical sections, not the cults' settings, that the wit and lightness are most obvious. Myth could prompt one tone, action and cult another, for the piety evoked in the hymn to Apollo at Cyrene is unmistakable. Like two other hymns on the gods' presence, this poem was set in a Doric city where we might, on other evidence, expect the most traditional cults to flourish. We see them through the gods' particular choirs and welcomers: in Cyrene, the young; in Argos, the women. These poems help us to sense what a detached, but acute, observer could attribute to a post-classical city on a public religious occasion. Callimachus and his sophisticated readers could enjoy the scenes of simple piety which the poetry conveyed. These readers, however, were a small minority, whereas the simpler, pious majority were not detached from the myths and expectations which surrounded their gods.

Far into the second and third centuries A.D., this piety of the majority survived the wit of poets and philosophers. The old hymns continued to be copied and sung, while the newer ones said much the same, though with more extravagance.[39] At Elis, Pausanias was assured by the residents that Dionysus attended their festival personally. His "visit" induced a flow of miraculous wine and we happen to have the old, enigmatic hymn in which the Sixteen Maidens of Elis called on the god to "come, rushing with foot like a bull's." Perhaps they sang it while driving a bull in the god's honour.[40] At Argos, the site of Callimachus's hymn to Athena, Plutarch told how the inhabitants "threw a bull into the deep and summoned bull-born Dionysus from the waters with a trumpet," an instrument which had heralded many epiphanies of the god, not least in Callimachus's own Alexandria.[41] Homer had given no prominence to boisterous Dionysus, but his cult had added vigour to the patterns of Homeric belief. Appearances did not die away: they attached, as we shall see, to yet more gods in different periods, who were honoured freely as present and "manifest" divinities. It is not until the fourth century A.D. that we first hear of a great pagan festival of epiphany which had developed, on present evidence, in the Imperial period.[42] Held in Alexandria, it celebrated the birth of the abstract god Eternity (Aion) and the revelation of the maiden goddess Kore in the form of her statue. This innovation in the city's cults was celebrated on January 5–6 and was clearly a popular occasion. In the fourth century, the Christians spread their own festival of Epiphany, a very different rite. Its practice owed nothing to this pagan ceremony, but it is no coincidence that it was placed on the same date in the calendar.

Prayers and invocations match the language of hymns and they, too, throw an obvious bridge between literature and life.[43] We know them best from Greek lyric poetry, especially the lyrics of the great Attic dramatists, whose requests to a god to "appear" are modelled on the daily hymns and prayers of cult. The best, once again, survive in Sophocles: in the *Ajax* his chorus prays for Apollo to come "with kindly mind and in easily recognizable form." The song was sung in a false dawn of joy and relief which was soon to be betrayed by the plot, and this context may explain its bold request. On the stage, as in cult, these songs were set off by the rhythms of dancing. "Pan, Pan . . . ," calls Sophocles's excited chorus and we must imagine the call against that beat of the foot which Horace ascribed to his rural ditch digger, "beating the hated ground" thrice over in a welcome for Italy's equivalent of Pan. These prayers remind us how the gods shared man's elation and happier moments as well as his anxieties: in Aristophanes, as in Sappho, gods are invited to drink with the celebrants of peaceful rustic festivals, and in short songs of balance and grace, the choruses call on the gods to "appear" and "stand beside" the actors' predicaments. These prayers have two particular features. They call on the gods by names which relate to their forms in their man-made statues; sometimes, too, they request in advance the manner or mood in which the gods should appear. Both these features had a long and influential life. "Advance requests" for a god to come in a particular mood were exploited by later poets, never better than in Milton's *L'Allegro*. In antiquity, they did not become mere decoration: prayers of invocation continued to inaugurate a god's new cult or temple or statue. The god was thought to respond to them literally, as we continue to find in cults of Asclepius, founded during the Imperial period.[44] As we shall see, the assimilation of a god to his cult statue also remained very close at all levels of society and experience. Gods were thought to attend individuals' prayers, too, and we will find scrupulous individuals asking the gods' own oracles how best to address a divinity in prayers. These scruples were still lively in the third century A.D. and are reflected in a series of hymns to the gods, composed in the Imperial period and ascribed to the mythical Orpheus.[45] People also wore carefully made amulets, engraved with scenes and legends which ensured that a particular god would come in the mood for a "good encounter."[46] This euphemism was applied to the more awesome divinities, especially to goddesses, and above all to Hecate and other fierce female visitors by night. By invoking a goddess in a particular mood, mortals could limit the dangers of her presence. These features of prayer led naturally into the arts of the sorcerer and the spiritual "magicians" whom we know from texts of the first Christian centuries. They show how hard it is to draw a line between "magic" and "religion" in terms of magic's techniques of compulsion. Religion used them openly too, a point which weakens the study of magic as a new type of irrationality.

When people prayed, they expected their gods to come, from the age of Homer to the last Platonists in the fifth century A.D. They did not expect to see them so much as to sense their "manifest" presence. Like a child to its parents, they tried to prescribe in advance the mood of their visiting superiors, for in gods and demigods, "irreconcilable temper" was anticipated and widely feared.

Were the gods also seen openly without a formal invocation? Here, too, we touch on patterns of psychology which our own modern case histories may not do much to illuminate: in antiquity, unlike our own age, "appearances" were part of an accepted culture pattern which was passed down in myth and the experiences of the past, in art, ritual and the bewitching poetry of Homer.[47] The ancients, however, did not see their gods without cause, and here the idea of "anxiety" does carry weight. In the ancient world, as in our own, the evidence suggests that people were most likely to see something when under pressure or at risk, though there is also a visionary current in their moments of peace with the natural world. Nothing was more hazardous or anxious than a journey, especially a journey by sea, and on this topic, life and literature met.[48] When the poets prayed to divine "escorts" for their friends at sea, they were not merely playing with a literary genre. Their poems attached to a continuing pattern of religious beliefs and acts which were as old, once again, as Homer, where so many of them can be detected in Athena's guidance of Telemachus on his first sea voyage. There were fixed prayers for a fair voyage and fixed honours for gods at embarkation and disembarkation. Travellers honoured the gods of temples which were passed at sea and continued to believe that a god's presence could attend the ship, guide it in a crisis or be seen, when the weather was rough, in the fire and clatter of a sea storm. Art and literature coincided in the monuments which sailors dedicated after a safe return. At sea, the gods were always near, and in the fire of a storm, Castor and Pollux were unmistakable, "flaming amazement" like Ariel on the prow.

As at sea, so in the crisis of sickness, the gods were agreed to come close to worshippers. Mostly, they were seen in dreams, as we can still discover from the double scenes on several votive reliefs which were put up in Attica during the fourth century B.C.[49] On one side, they show the sleeping mortal attended by a god, on the other the god and mortal in close contact. These reliefs have been well explained as a scene of the patient asleep and a scene of the patient and god as experienced in his simultaneous dream. The records of "miracles" at Asclepius's shrines do include cases where a patient is said to have met the god or his agent in mortal disguise outside the temple.[50] Perhaps, in these emergencies, people did allege such encounters, and if so, the stories are not the elaboration of temple priests: the "road to Emmaus" had been preceded by the "road to Epidaurus."

Divine sightings also throw light on those "touchstones of ancient piety," the votive reliefs which were put up by individuals to a particular god. In Attica, the earliest-known examples centre on minor divinities, Pan, the nymphs and the river god Acheloös. Precisely these gods were later singled out as among the "visible" gods whom people were particularly prone to perceive with their own senses. Several of the reliefs show the mortal in divine company: "it is the rule in these dedicated reliefs for the mortals to be about two-thirds the height of the gods: the goblin, goat-god Pan is generally smaller than his fellow-immortals."[51] The neatest origin for these pieces is a vision or a meeting, although the presence of Acheloös raises fascinating problems. Half man, half bull, he shared with the Greeks' other gods of water the ability to turn himself into terrifying animal shapes, and if he was seen, it can only have been in a dream. Pan and the nymphs were more accessible, not least in their natural haunts, where, perhaps on a warm or peaceful day, they spoke or seemed to appear. They also attracted particular devotees, or "servants," who might live in their company in a rural retreat or pay regular honour at their shrine.[52] These works of Greek art give meticulous, rational shape to events which, to us, are rooted in the irrational: they are utterly lost in our museums, those "aquariums of conditioned air." Greek votive reliefs of all periods owe a large debt to sightings of their gods. They confess it in inscriptions which refer to their dedication "according to a dream" or "at the god's command" and in reliefs which sometimes give us a snapshot in stone of the sighting which their patron had enjoyed. They have been found in all regions of the Greek-speaking world and although they have never been collected and fully described, a sample allows certain negative points.[53] Votive monuments were not restricted to freeborn donors: we have one from a slave who had seen the "mother of the gods." Priests were sometimes the donors, but by no means always: there was no control over the inscription and dedication of these monuments and they multiplied the proofs of religiousness beyond any official priestly class. Women dedicated them too, though they did not give the majority, accounting for no more than a sixth of the fullest recent list. There is, of course, no correlation between the number of votive monuments and the number of dreams of gods which one class or sex enjoyed. We can, however, say that these dedications in stone were not the preserve of women and priesthoods, or the business of men only. Like Miletus's visions, they span the sexes and the social classes, high and low.

As always, the "appearances" of gods did come under attack: Plato complained of Homer's support for such absurdities and was inclined to see them as a particular delusion of women. Although we know of one Spartan woman who had tall stories to tell about her visits from divinities and although we can believe anything of Alexander the Great's mother, here, too, other evidence does not suggest a female majority. At the healing shrines of Asclepius, stories of miraculous cures were posted up to impress the visitors, but women occur in only a third of the surviving texts and the priests who finally wrote them up were all men.[54] Convinced disbelievers were very few, and it is worth comparing the belief in fairies which flourished in Northern Europe until only recently. Here, too, we might feel that a presence which had seemed genuine to men of the sixteenth century faded away and died before the advance of reason. However, while Marx and Darwin wrote, the fairies lived for many more who never read such books. Unlike the Olympians, fairies lived in very close dependence on the human race.[55] In antiquity, the nymphs were said to whisk away small children from their parents' homes, but unlike nymphs, the fairies depended on men for food and tools and for their special recruits, the babies which they stole and swapped for changelings. Fairies were nearby authors of human misfortunes and thus they were easily encountered. Like the gods, they haunted the wilder landscapes, but they favoured the forests and wooded roads which were such particular European hazards. Although Pan was revered as the "good guide" through rough country, in ancient literature there is a striking absence of Europe's "pixie-leading," the guiding of travellers through thick woods by supernatural guides. The ranks of the fairies were more clearly distinguished in order of merit: pixies were not mere brownies and those who saw them knew the difference. Around 1900, there were two classes of Manx fairy and there was no mistaking the lower order, who were smaller and more vindictive. They dwelt apart from other breeds and from men, "in clouds, on mountains, in fogs, on the hideous precipices or in caverns on the seashore where they were frequently heard to yell." Like Homer's gods, the fairies were prone to be partisan: "The little gentry take a great interest in the affairs of men," remarked an Irishman in Sligo in 1908, "and they always stand for justice and right. Any side they favour in our wars, that side wins. They favoured the Boers, and the Boers did get their rights. They told me they favoured the Japs and not the Russians, because the Russians were tyrants. Sometimes, though, they fight among themselves. One of them once said, 'I'd fight for a friend, or I'd fight for Ireland.'"

On this point, above all, the gods and the fairies agreed. Homer's armies had sensed the presence of gods in the weather signs and clamour which surrounded battles, and they also believed that the gods stood by, assisting a warrior's prowess. Throughout antiquity there was continuity on this topic, between life and literature, one age and the next. In the sixth century B.C., the Spartans took the "bones of Orestes" into battle as their military ally and accompanied the army with their images of Castor and Pollux. When only one of the kings went to war, they took either Castor or Pollux, but not both. The Spartans were more precise, but only slightly more "superstitious" than subsequent armies.[56] This presence is not a matter on which the opinions of the educated and the rank and file divide. In the First World War, troops and clergy alike believed in the "angel of Mons" who haunted no-man's-land, attended their attacks and cared for abandoned bodies. Throughout antiquity, attempts to limit the presence of gods to the mystic belief of a minority or the delusions of women and the lower classes founder on the facts of war. In the 230s, the historian Herodian dwelt on this point while describing Maximinus's recent siege of Aquileia. During operations, the soldiers saw the god Apollo appearing in the style of his image "frequently" above the city and fighting for it. It is not certain, said Herodian, whether they really saw it or whether they invented it to exculpate their defeat: "appearances" were sometimes alleged by generals in order to encourage their men. Significantly, Herodian did not reject the troops' word, because the circumstances, he said, were so singular that anything was credible.[57] These old habits died hard. In 394, Rome's pagans made a last stand by the river Frigidus in northern Italy and placed images of the god Zeus with golden thunderbolts as their visible allies on the surrounding hills. They lost the battle, and the Christian victors, said Augustine, parcelled out the thunderbolts and made a joke of them.[58] In the fifth century A.D., therefore, Zosimus's pagan history was heir to a long tradition when he told his readers how Alaric had been astonished by the sight of Athena Promachos bestriding the walls while he started his siege of Athens. How Gordian would have applauded! She strode on the walls in her armour "exactly as she had been portrayed by Pheidias" and looked as threatening as Homer's Achilles. The city survived, and Zosimus accepted the story, one of the last and best examples of the influence of art on pagans' ideas of their gods.[59]

In Homer, the gods had favourite places, just as they had favourite individuals, and it was believed that they would not see them go to ruin. To the end of pagan antiquity, this belief persisted. Gods "held their hand" over cities, as Solon had charmingly reminded the Athenians: they did not forget him, as we can see from the brilliant wordplay which the comedies of Aristophanes spun round the idea and its language. His jokes presupposed that the audience knew Solon's words by heart.[60] Sieges brought these protectors into focus, just as sickness conjured up an individual's god. They were "present" to the

besieged and the besiegers alike, and it was because of this presence
that Roman generals formally "summoned out" the gods when they
began to besiege a city.[61] Cities had their "presiding" divinities, and
cities which had famous shrines continued to describe themselves as
"dear to the gods." The occasions of the gods' appearances were listed
in local histories and temple chronicles, where they had coincided, on
the Homeric pattern, with dedications to the god: these books could
be items of public concern, approved by the city assembly and based
on patient research in older records and evidence. "Appearances" gave
shrines prestige and antiquarians a job: meanwhile, they continued to
feature in crowded civic life.[62] At Magnesia on the Maeander, the local
Artemis was said to have "stood beside" the entire people during the
construction of a temple. Just as the prayers of the Athenians invited
the gods to "stand beside" the mass meetings of their classical
democracy, so Dio of Prusa, on his travels through the first-century
Empire, told the men of St. Paul's own Tarsus that their founding
heroes, Perseus and Heracles, attended and watched over their public
assemblies.[63]

Through myth and Homeric poetry, the visits of the gods continued to draw on a deep reserve of potential experience, which poets
and artists could exploit but which most people did not exclude from
life's possibilities. They were supported by actual sightings, which
were not imagined from nothing, because they occurred at times of
strain or anxiety when a "presence" was most readily set before the
mind's eye. These beliefs were not the strange fancies of a small
minority. They were sensitive to the entire social and political climate
and could lead to solid, persistent practice. We see this connection
most clearly in the later third century B.C., when cities were beset by
the warring Greek kings. In these times of collective tension, whole
cities claimed sightings of their god, and once they had seen him, they
would try to capitalize on the event. They sent their envoys on a
tireless round of the neighbouring cities and kings, pleading for their
town to be acknowledged as "inviolable" in the wake of this divine
presence. If the envoys failed, the gods might appear a second time,
encouraging a second diplomatic circuit to see if the great powers
would grant "inviolability" to the gods' favoured homes.[64] This age
of persistent war had been good for visibility. Sightings of gods were
indeed intertwined with anxiety, but the concept now loses its force as
the characterization of any one age in antiquity. Like the gods and their
anger, anxiety was ever-present. It was not the distinctive tone of

the Antonine age: it was a constant strand in experience, bringing the gods into mortal view. The strand was a part of "following pagan religion," apart from the ceremonies which had to be paid to the gods.

# II

Close encounters, therefore, had always exerted an influence on Greek poetry and art, religious cult and military and diplomatic practice. Throughout antiquity, a culture pattern linked them to the framework of the mind, in which they surfaced with a baggage of associations as old as Homer and the stories of myth. As religious culture changed and social relationships altered, we might think that more people, like Callimachus, would become detached from this inherited pattern and thus look on these experiences with irony or nostalgia. By the early Christian period, the forms of religious life had grown, but the idea of divine encounters had not faded: it had grown with them.

Close encounters had affected the various philosophies, not least because their masters were concerned to argue against them.[1] Plato's concern with the vision of God, Aristotle's account of the "friend of the gods," the Stoics' transposition of "visible" gods to the stars in heaven: in their different ways, these concerns owed something to popular ideas of the gods' "presence" which they wished to refine or oppose. Their influence was particularly clear in the teachings of Epicurus, who offered his own account of why gods were "evident" and tried to explain their appearances by night: from these, he accepted, man had derived his entire, mistaken idea of divinity. In the Christian era, Platonists used analogies from Homer to explain their master Socrates's guidance from an inner god: they ended by defending the Homeric "spies in disguise" whom Plato himself had ridiculed. Stoicism, meanwhile, allowed the Emperor Marcus Aurelius to continue to write of the gods as "helpers" and "assistants," "visible" as stars in the sky but also present as friends and instructors in his dreams. Authors tended not to be sceptical about these assistants: Dio the orator and Dio the historian, Galen the doctor, Plutarch, who was never so sceptical as to withhold a story of the gods' past appearances, and once again, Pausanias on his travels in Greece and the East. Though he tended to explain away the grosser features of certain cults, he respected the old tradition of the days when men and gods had dined together.[2] When he saw vapours rising from a hero's tomb in Asia, he accepted them as a proof of the dead man's presence. He knew his Homer and could quote with approval Hera's words on the danger of seeing gods "manifestly." They had been confirmed, he remarked, very recently, when a governor of Egypt had bribed a man to enter a temple of Isis without the goddess's invitation, and she had punished him severely.

By the Christian era, "paganism" tends to be studied through its Oriental cults and mystery religions, its magical texts and the wisdom of "Thrice-great Hermes" and the art of "theurgy," by which philosophers and educated men tried to work on their gods and compel their attendance. This emphasis is too restricted. Each of these aspects attached to the gods' older "presence," enlarging it, rather than limiting it. Since the Hellenistic age, the newer gods from the Greek-speaking East had helped to extend the old, familiar patterns of "encounter," and in turn these patterns had helped their cults to spread. The "presence" of Isis was invoked to help mortals in lawsuits and on journeys,[3] and was experienced by adherents who gazed fondly on her statue. Very soon after his creation, the god Serapis had spread widely because he was accessible in dreams and appeared and gave commands to people of all classes. Evidence for gods being thought to attend their own banquets and sacrifices is known from the sixth to fourth centuries B.C., yet it surfaces again for us in the small invitation tickets to the "couch" of Serapis, known to us from the second century B.C. onwards.[4] Attempts to minimize these objects as cards for social dining clubs have foundered, finally, on the discovery of a ticket in which the god himself invites the guest. These feasts were held in temples or private houses and brought men to a worthwhile party under the patronage of their god. Serapis, said an elegant hymn, was both "host and guest" of his worshippers. His role as host has been verified, and his presence as guest deserves to be credited. From Palmyra, we have quantities of similar tickets, inviting visitors to dine with this or that god.[5] They are not some Syrian curiosity. Unusually well preserved, these heavenly meal tickets are the pair to the parties which Serapis held throughout the Mediterranean. Entertainment of the gods was a familiar practice: in *The Golden Ass*, Apuleius describes how a baker's wife set the dinner table lavishly in her husband's absence and "waited for the advent of her young adulterer, like the advent of a god."[6]

In the mystery religions, too, the old patterns of a god's appearance were not displaced. There was an idea that gods might appear especially to people who had been initiated and would help them in their subsequent crises. This idea may not have been widespread, but the connection went deeper: so far as the texts tells us, the idea of an encounter was central to the entire mystery rite.[7] Descriptions of an initiation suggest that it induced the compound of fear, revelation and reassurance which was already detectable in Homeric poetry: the initiate was "the one who has seen," after "laborious circuits and journeyings through the dark, terrors of every kind . . . amazement . . . a wonderful light . . . songs and dances and holy appearances." "I came into the presence of the gods below and the gods above," says our one personal account of an initiation, "and I adored them from the closest proximity." In this old area of vision, the mystery experience seems to have been concentrated. When we find spells and magical texts promising to summon and reveal the gods, they attach, once again, to an existing strand in conventional religiousness. Magic offered a technique for bringing close encounters to pass: it was a systematization of an older hope, not a strange innovation.

Evidence for these magical practices has been connected with a change of mood in the Imperial period, giving a new twist to possible visions of a god: "In an age of bureaucracy and of the pressures of material civilization like ours and material needs less tempered by charity, such religious individualism let men somehow think they saw the things above the iron heaven which shut them in."[8] However, the visionaries of the Antonine age were not oppressed, humble men and their "religious individualism" grew from less immediate roots. It extended right back to Homer and his epics' awareness that "not to everyone do the gods appear": it also shared common ground with the old forms of prayer. These visions were not a response to social claustrophobia. In no religious culture has there been a necessary link between "misery and mysticism," least of all in the Antonine and Severan age. Pagans who strove to see the gods were often comfortable people, educated, ambitious and not unduly ground down by "bureaucracy." Their visions were not a passive escape but a positive search for knowledge. People wanted to know the secrets of higher theology, not because they were oppressed, but because the schools and philosophers had raised so many more questions than they had been able to answer.

Homer had not explicitly linked visions of the gods with moral and spiritual excellence: the gods tended to be seen by friends or favourites to whom they wished to appear. Here, as elsewhere, philosophy added moral depth to an old Homeric form, and by the Christian era, the "vision" of a god was attached explicitly to pious spiritual effort. By the mid-second century, the new art of theurgy aimed to "summon" the gods by symbols which they themselves had revealed. Its masters distinguished it sharply from magic, because it required a spiritual and moral excellence in its practitioners.[9] It appealed, then, to philosophic minds, especially to Platonists from the later third century A.D. onwards. In some remarkable chapters, the Neoplatonist master Iamblichus (c. 300) lists the exact distinctions between the appearances of gods, angels and demons. He and his select readership clearly knew the experiences of sound and light on which these chapters rested, although the sighting of a fully fledged god seems quite exceptional, on Iamblichus's account of it. No mortal eye or mind, he says, could ever contain the size or beauty of a pure divinity's arrival.

Shortly before the birth of theurgy, pupils of the wise pagan god, the Thrice-great Hermes, were already aspiring to a spiritual experience of God.[10] Their texts vary in level and quality, but again, these aspirants were not only poor or lower-class devotees: they included people of education who could write good Greek and develop themes from Platonist philosophy. In their more spiritual texts, we meet a new note of mystical union with God, the god of the philosophers, not the "helpers" of Homeric epic. Here, the relation between a sense of presence and the "affective state" of the subject becomes more explicit: emotion is a criterion of an encounter with God. The subject's identity becomes joined or merged with the Other he seems to encounter. The sight of Him, the texts taught, shuts out sound and brings stillness and immobility: it comes and goes, varying with the beholder's capacity. It is an apprehension of God through the "eye of the soul," not the eye of the body, and in this new sense, it develops the older types of encounter. "Everywhere, God will appear to you, at times and places where you do not look for Him, in your waking hours and your sleep, when you travel by sea and by land, when you are speaking and when you are silent . . . And do you still say, God is invisible? Say not so." The Hermetists' texts vary in their scope and advice, but "if I were to try to sum up their teaching in one sentence, none would serve the purpose better than, Blessed are the pure in heart, for they shall see God."

Each of these options enlarged the range of divine appearances. Neither excluded the other or blocked out the traditional encounters of myth and Homeric poetry. In this proliferation, we can distinguish various levels of presence: an unseen presence, by night and day; an encounter, face to face, between god and man; visits of gods in unperceived disguises; the nightly "company" of god and man enjoyed in dreams. If we explore them in turn, we can place the predicament of the people of Lystra and Miletus.

Since Homer, all these hints of a divine presence had come under a single Greek word, *epiphaneia*. It raises a further development since Homer: the cult paid to living men and rulers, "gods" whom anyone might encounter without disguise. In 196 B.C., the title *epiphanes* had first been taken by a king, Ptolemy V, to mark the sudden show of godlike power which he had displayed in a particular crisis for his kingdom.[11] Neighbouring kings copied this honour and by the second and third centuries A.D. it was a conventional Greek title for a divine ruler. This level must be added to our picture, though more as a consequence than its cause.

The unseen presence of the gods is the most obvious and the easiest to document. Because the gods were an unseen presence, men had always questioned them in oracles and invoked them in prayers, oaths and curses. These practices flourished in the early Christian centuries and were most vividly expressed in the models of large ears which worshippers dedicated in many temples, especially those of Isis and Serapis, and to which they directed, or whispered, their requests. The gods were thought to hear silent prayers, and by the high Empire that frequent epithet "listening" was added to their names in hymns and vows.[12]

The unseen power of a god could be highly localized and concentrated, for instance in the area of "asylum" which was defined round shrines and temples. Within this limited area, the god was thought to protect suppliants, and those who moved inside it were often conscious of a nearer divine presence. In these precincts, gods kept a sharp eye on their own assets and treasures and exerted a local vigilance which was invoked or described in many inscriptions. The most vivid are found in the villages of northeastern Lydia, where violators of the god's property, cutters of his trees, attackers of his birds or inadvertent thieves of his belongings proclaim their punishments and make amends by a declaration of their crime in public inscriptions. In the year 194/5, "Stratonicos, son of Euangelos, in ignorance cut down an oak of Zeus of the Twin Oak Trees and because of Stratonicos's lack of faith, Zeus summoned up his own power." He almost killed the offender, who "recovered from great danger and made this dedication by way of thanks"; "and I proclaim, let nobody ever belittle Zeus's powers nor cut down an oak again."[13] Inscriptions from the same area refer to a process called "setting up the sceptre," by which the villagers invoked the justice of their local god or goddess. The cases give us some of our liveliest glimpses of village life from the first to the mid-third century A.D.[14] When an orphan was suspected of maltreatment or when clothes were stolen in a bathhouse, the villagers held a "trial by sceptre" and summoned an all-seeing god. When three pigs went missing from a herd, the suspects "did not agree" to this appeal to the sceptre, but the appeal occurred nonetheless, and before long the gods had killed every one of them. When a stepmother was accused of poisoning her stepson, up went the sceptre, and before long she and her own son died. We know of these cases because surviving kinsmen inscribed them on stone and put up their record in order to appease the gods. The "twelve sceptres" were invoked to protect tombs from violation, "implacable sceptres" which would punish an offender's family forever. Here, the rods themselves had become agents, but behind them lay a divine presence, hunting down offenders by symbols which were modelled on the staffs which the priests of the gods carried. In the Roman governor's absence, the gods had their own tribunal to settle villagers' rumours and wrongdoings.

These texts of "confession" are vivid witnesses to a divine presence: are they, however, a local peculiarity in concept as well as form? We must not misread them as proof that a divine presence hung heavily over every life at every moment: they are only set up in the wake of an act which ignored the gods altogether. In these Anatolian villages, men were as willing as any Republican Roman to act first and risk payment later. They merely paid distinctively. They were not humble men either: the inscriptions were cut by specialists, and the stone and its carving were expensive. Their belief in the gods' anger was no local peculiarity. Any city blamed it for famines and earthquakes, and as these misfortunes were ever-present, so were the gods.

In easier times, were the gods sensed as constant, invisible protectors, not only of cities but of men in their daily lives? It depended somewhat on the rank of god. Olympians belonged with Homeric heroes, and Zeus was too lofty for all but a king.[15] However, Hermes and Heracles were less remote; Homer had already described Hermes as the most companionable god. They attended men on their travels and were thanked for their guidance in inscriptions after the event:

"May you be kindly, Heracles," as a traveller asked in his inscription, found in Rome, "since you are always present to me, as I pray to you, and always hold your hand above me." The word "always" was not idle.[16] In the Greek world we meet nothing quite like the possessive language of certain Latin inscriptions whose families refer to "my Minerva" or "our Hermes." Instead, the gods were praised as "assistants" and "helpers," recurrent words in the religious writings of the Emperors Marcus and Julian.[17]

By the Christian era, this invisible company had become connected explicitly with moral worth, a theme which was neatly developed by the orator Maximus of Tyre in one of the lively speeches which he published in the late second century A.D. and which are readily imagined in the setting of a public lecture to a city's educated men.[18] What, he asked, was the truth of that old mystery, Socrates's divine guidance? Surely Homer had explained it best when he wrote how the gods appeared to his heroes? Just as Athena guided Odysseus, so a divine sign directed Socrates and other virtuous men. Of course, he went on, you are not so vulgar as to think that Homer meant these "gods" in a literal, physical sense: Maximus had a gift for discounting his audience's commonsense views without argument. By gods, he said, Homer had meant divine powers, the *daimones* which accompany virtuous people, which "share their life" and, in that same charming image, "hold their hand" above them. Although Maximus allegorized one aspect of Homer's epiphanies, he took the other at face value. He rounded off his speech with the Homeric suitors' lines on the gods as "spies in disguise."

This bright little sketch presupposes an audience who liked to reflect on man's daemonic guidance. Written, surely, for performance, it was not divorced altogether from life, and its theme certainly was not new. It even attached to people's birthdays.[19] The Greeks ascribed certain days to particular gods and tended to honour them as the days came round in each month: they had an idea, too, of a man's attendant daimon and also the idea of these general "patrons" of the days of their birth. The Romans had an old and lively belief in each man's attendant "genius," which was born with him and was honoured, therefore, by each individual on his birthday.

This sense of divine, invisible guidance can be followed in individuals' writings, never more so than in those of the orator Aelius Aristeides, who lived with a heightened sense of the gods' company. In his writings Aelius touches on so many forms of divine contact that his comments are better reserved for the moment, as an invisible presence is only one aspect of their whole. Instead, it can be followed through a lesser divinity, who warns us, once again, not to think that this "presence" died away with time.

No presence has been more haunting than Pan's, and in the Roman world it was never better expressed than by Horace, who wrote so warmly of his protection by the gods and the attendance of Pan on the health of his country farm. Pan had visited Horace "often," though he had never met him face to face. The hills echoed with his divine music: "the poet acknowledges the origin of his prosperity in a spirit kindred to that in which an Italian calls the bread *'la grazia di Dio.'*"[20] On one view, Horace had been hearing the god's final cadence: Pan, a traveller told Plutarch's friends, had died in the age of Tiberius.[21] Christians later made much of this report. By a favourite pun, "Pan" was also the Greek "all," so his death stood for the death of all demons. Their Pan pun was premature, for his was the one reported death of Tiberius's reign which nobody believed. Cults of Pan continued in the very heart and identity of cities,[22] the "Pan hill" in the middle of Alexandria or the grottoes and springs of Caesarea Panias, where the god's person persisted on the city's third-century coinage. Pictures of Pan abound on the coins of second-century Asian cities, too, although they do not entail a local cult, and in Gordian's reign, Pan appears conventionally on the sudden burst of local coinage from little Arneae in Lycia, Pan with horns and a hand on a naked nymph.[23] Pan, meanwhile, had been discovered in new places, deep in the Egyptian desert, where pilgrims and travellers honoured his cave, Pan *"qui affectionne les hémi-spéos."* He could guide travellers, "Pan of the good journey," or rescue sailors on a becalmed ship. His presence had not faded, and in the mid-second century, Artemidorus's great collection of dreams assumes that Pan was frequently seen by night. One of Artemidorus's friends had been warned by Pan in a dream that his wife was trying to poison him through one of his best friends. The friend, it turned out, was having an affair with her.

At large in the landscape, Pan was still the god whose range of interests was to intrigue the Edwardian novelists. He was Pan the unhappy lover, Pan the mischief-maker, Pan the author of sudden sexual forays against girls and boys alike.[24] Proverbially, women who were said to have been pleasured by several men in sequence were still known as "Pan girls." Sexually voracious, Pan was also the disappointed suitor. Up in the woods and hills, men still heard Pan's bewitching music, a lasting intimation of his presence. *"Pan était là, bien présent, proche mais invisible, une voix sans corps."* In a song of exquisite sadness, he lamented to the mountains his loss of the nymph Echo.

Pan did not only surface in sounds and dreams. At midday, he was supposed to sleep on the hills, and it was then, at the hour of his keenest temper, that Hyginus saw him and was cured by his help, as his inscription of second- or early-third-century date expressed it when found in Rome, "not in a dream, but around the middle course of the day." Pan, it seems, had appeared openly to Hyginus and (perhaps) "all his sons."[25] In the early fourth century, Iamblichus still referred to "those seized by Pan" as a distinguishable class among people who had made contact with gods.[26] Pan's caves in Attica continued to draw pilgrims long after Constantine's conversion.[27]

Nowhere is his invisible presence more evident than in the novels of the Imperial period.[28] In Longus's *Daphnis and Chloe*, Pan's presence was felt and heard more often than seen: he arrived in Longus's plot to rescue his friends by an awesome power and music, clamouring all night and piping till the gates of dawn. In the adventures of Leucippe and Cleitophon, his presence took a local turn. This romance has retreated in date to the first century B.C. and perhaps further, but its final books contain Pan in an intriguing context. In a cave just outside Ephesus, the heroine was put through an ordeal which was reserved for servants of the goddess Artemis. Shut in the cave, the girls were tested by Pan for the presence or absence of their virginity. If the pipes of Pan were heard by those outside, the girls were adjudged intact; if a low moan was heard, their honour was impugned. The music, of course, sounded strictly in the minds of the onlookers: who was to say what a wind in the nearby pine trees signified? This ordeal reads true to life and is recoverable from an epigram which refers to the practice. When most dramatic, the novel may be most exact, and we do not know when, if ever, before Constantine, this practice ceased.

Like Callimachus's hymns, these novels made use of a pastoral art, involving their worldly readers in the pleasure of simple rural happenings. However, their pastoral tales were not purely wishful thinking, like the tales of Pan which appealed to that childlike streak in Forster and Saki, James Stephens and Kenneth Grahame. In the second and third centuries, Pan was indeed both Friend and Helper, and for a living sense of his presence, we have only to ask the gods themselves. When a group of rural visitors asked Apollo's great shrine near Miletus to explain a calamity, the god told them the cause in a splendid hexameter oracle.[29] Nine woodcutters had been found dead in the country, and in answer, Apollo explained that there had nearly been many more. "Golden-horned Pan," the servant of Dionysus, had been charming the nymphs with his song. His staff, said Apollo, had been held in one hand, his pipes in the other, and as he passed by, the shrillness of his song had stunned all the woodcutters within range. The sight of the god had overawed them, and every single one would have died had Artemis not intervened. She was angry with Pan, so she checked him. "Pray to Artemis," said the oracle, "if you want her as a protector." The date of this superb oracle is unknown, but a second- or third-century date is attractive, as it stood in the collection of oracles which Porphyry compiled, c. 260–290 A.D. It brings together so many threads. Country dwellers had come to consult Miletus's oracle, seeing no opposition between urban and rural piety; the god blamed the woodcutters' deaths on a culprit who could not be pursued. Had there not been Artemis and a truly Homeric division in heaven, the disaster would have been much worse. The morals were piety and prayer and thanks to Artemis, which neatly avoided the hunt for a human scapegoat. Above all, Pan and his presence were pictured as artists typically showed them. Pan's fellow gods had no doubt that he was still a living presence.

Up in the caves and hills, Pan still piped and was moved to anger, while around him, the gods kept watch on their property and spied invisibly on human wrongs. There were also the local heroes and "gods in a small way," localized agents of spite and random temper, as well as of friendship and neighbourly help. Among them, in the Imperial period, were some of a community's "very special dead." Individuals honoured dead members of their families as "manifest heroes" or "manifest gods," and in some cases, the epithet meant more than "distinguished" or "conspicuous": it meant that these people had appeared in dreams and visions and, in one or two cases, worked wonders to help the living.[30] This "demonic" presence of special dead people was yet another Satanic snare among which early Christians lived: most of our evidence for it is evidence from the early Christian era. These beliefs traded on the general acceptance of potential "epiphany" and were a further complicating part of pagan religiousness; they were beliefs, not emotions, and were not evoked solely by rites or acts of cult. Acceptance of the gods' invisible protection, "holding their hand" above men,[31] was still a part of what it meant to be a pagan, and in towns, especially, their presence drew near through those lasting objects, the statues.

In classical Athens, the statues' presence had impressed itself firmly on men's image of their gods. The effects were already latent in the *Iliad* and evident in Aristophanes's comedies, where men greet a god's statue as their "neighbour" and speak freely of a statue's hand as the hand of a god.[32] By the Antonine age, we hear more of these responses, but they are not the proof of a new irrationality. Rather, we are seeing the same beliefs from a closer angle, and we will have to return to them to understand the gods' visitations by night. The simple rustic was not the only person who identified a god with his image: Augustus, no less, showed his annoyance with Poseidon for a spell of bad weather by banishing his statue from a procession.[33] Because the gods were present through their images, petitions were pinned to their thighs and legs. In his speech of self-defence, Apuleius listed everyday acts of piety which would incur no suspicions of magic: would you think I was a sorcerer, he asked his judges, if I wrote petitions on the statues of the gods? His audience, clearly, thought it standard practice.[34]

Two cities in Asia have left a less expected testimony, coastal Syedra and the Roman colony of Iconium, where St. Paul enraged the Jews by his preaching. In each city, fragmentary inscriptions have revealed the same detailed orders for a trio of statues in which the god Ares was to occupy the central place. He was to be bound by the chains of Hermes, who stood on one side, while Justice "passed judgement" on him, standing on the other. This remarkable group was not a decorative work of art. It was intended to keep Ares in check by showing him as a bound suppliant. These cities were afraid of attacks from the bandits in the nearby hills, people whom Ares was thought to assist as their local war god. This remedy might have passed as a local aberration, had the orders not been shown to derive from the high authority of Apollo at his oracle of Claros. Symbolically, the statues were thought to work on the god's mood, and the remedy was not a vulgar superstition: Claros spoke the accepted theology of the age. Once, according to Homer, the gods had bound Ares in a jar; in Sophocles's *Oedipus*, the people of Thebes had prayed for Ares, the deadly war god, to be sped away to the north and slaughtered by Zeus's thunderbolt.[35] Perhaps he actually went there, for a Byzantine epigram refers to a statue of Ares which was believed to keep the barbarian Goths out of Thrace so long as it remained resting on the ground: Thrace, said the ancients, was also called "Ares's Land," after its prominent god.[36]

Ares, however, was not the only god on whom the province's safety depended. In 421, the governor of Thrace heard reports of a buried treasure in his province and learned from the inhabitants that its site was holy ground. It turned out to contain three silver statues which had been consecrated in the old pagan fashion in order to fend off northern barbarians. He wrote to ask the advice of the Christian Emperor, Theodosius II, who was probably his father-in-law: the Emperor told him to dig them up, three solid-silver statues with long hair and ornate robes and their hands bound symbolically behind their backs. They had been buried facing north, towards the barbarians, perhaps in the strategic Succi pass. No sooner had they been removed than the barbarians invaded, three different tribes, one for each statue.[37] Might these images have been ordered initially by Apollo at Claros, whose clients included cities in Thrace? When the Empire became Christian, were they buried, facing north, by inhabitants who wished to save them? In Thrace, the "decline and fall" of the Empire is directly linked with the symbolic presence of its gods.

If a statue of a god could keep off barbarians, it could also ward off plague and famine. Apollo at Claros prescribed his own statues and images as a defence against epidemics, while other oracles, too, prescribed statues against drought. The identification of god and image was very strong at all levels of society, and on some of their statue bases, the gods are made to answer the old forms of prayer which had "summoned" them. "I am come," they say, "standing always beside" the citizens, the Emperor or the men in the city's gymnasium.[38] We can understand why ambassadors, when they left their cities, took images of their gods to assist them, shipping them from Alexandria to Rome, or from Miletus to Syria. Statues accompanied litigants to court, or to the Emperor's presence: in 217/8, we can read from the Emperor himself how he had venerated the image of Apollo which the city's ambassadors had brought from Miletus to his audience.[39] At Side, "festivals of the disembarkation" of Athena and Apollo commemorated the "arrival" of the gods by sea, in the persons, evidently, of their cult statues. It was not, then, quite so peculiar when the Emperor Heliogabalus dragged the statues of various goddesses to Rome in order to be vetted for a marriage with the image of his favoured Sun god: the historian Herodian remarks that the marriage of his Sun god with a Moon goddess was privately celebrated throughout all Italy, presumably with the appropriate images.[40] If gods could come and marry in the person of their statues, there were fears, too, that they might depart without warning. It is to these fears, surely, that we can best refer the chains with which certain statues were held to their positions.

Statues were not only the symbols of a god's presence. From the first century A.D. onwards, we know of secret rites which were thought to "animate" them and draw a divine "presence" into their material.[41] Egyptian practice lay at the origin of this, and far into the Christian Empire, papyri still prescribed the spells which could be written on a slip and posted into a statue in order to "inspire" it. Yet this practice, too, was not "vulgar": the philosophic arts of theurgy exploited it, while suspicions of it had attached to men of letters and figures in high society far earlier. It connected with the common assumption that a god could work "good deeds of power" through his graven image, a belief which is best brought out for us in a famous decree datable to the third century A.D., when it stood in the council chamber of the city of Stratonicea.[42] The statues of Zeus and Hecate, in this same council chamber, are said to "perform good deeds of divine power," for which all the people sacrifice and burn incense and pray and give thanks. Since that is so, these gods who are "so extremely manifest" deserve still greater honours in future: choirs of neatly dressed children are to sing daily hymns in Stratonicea's council chamber and at the nearby shrine of Lagina. The miracles worked by these statues were celebrated daily by choirs in honour of the gods.

Stratonicea's honours were not an "Oriental" oddity, but a particularly vivid instance of a general belief, which happens here to survive for us.[43] This belief had such vigour that it also encouraged fraud, a neat example of which was detected during a patient modern restoration.[44] A pleasant marble head of a Greek philosopher was found to have been remodelled so that a circular hole opened in the centre of its mouth. Puzzled by this reshaping, its Danish students tried "connecting this funnel-shaped hole with a twelve-metre bronze tube which was led through an almost closed door . . . [When they spoke down the tube] the effect was powerful and strange . . . the head acted as a verse-oracle, with a voice which would sound to an emotional mind both weird and mysterious." Originally, the head had been a portrait of Epicurus, the philosopher who would have ridiculed this superstition, and perhaps the remodelling was mischievous. If so, it is not the only example of pagans' revenge on the "godless" doctrines of Epicurus, but it is the most arresting.

Through such artifices, the gods were made especially "manifest" to those who looked on their images. Some of the best stories of pagan artifice were taken up by Christian authors who tell of temples with sky-blue ceilings, lights reflected in water and fireworks which suggested the fiery departure of a god.[45] These "special effects" were particularly vivid in the worship of Mithras, conducted in the chambers of his small, dark, subterranean shrines. Because men expected their gods to be "present and manifest," who could blame the priests if they helped the gods to live up to expectations? Again, the line between religion and magic vanishes. A practical textbook by Hero of Alexandria included advice on making statues of the gods which moved automatically, doors of temples which opened by unseen mechanisms and optical devices which suggested the approach of a god. These devices traded on general assumptions. In pagan mysteries, frescoes at Pompeii imply a role for mirrors in the rite of initiation: the converts first saw the god "through a glass darkly," then turned to his mask "face to face." When Callimachus hymned Apollo's arrival, he stressed the god's impact on trembling doorways and opening gates. At Teos, a choir was appointed to sing a hymn each morning at just this occasion, the opening of Dionysus's temple doors. It is a neat conjecture that the doors in the gables of certain Greek temples were made to fly open at festivals in order to reveal the god's "presence."[46] At Corinth, the excavators of the temple of Dionysus found a pattern of underground channels and piping which they considered to be the priests' device for turning a stream of water into an apparent flow of wine. At Jerash and elsewhere, there were temples with similar "miracles."[47]

These devices relied on the acceptance of a god's presence in or near the place of his image. The most articulate sources for this presence are Christians of the second and third centuries: "If you believe in your gods' miracles through man-made statues," asked Theophilus, "why do you not believe in God's resurrection of the body?" Christians knew their way round these local miracles remarkably well: when Athenagoras remarked on the statues of Neryllinus, it was only one particular statue, he specified, out of many which had powers of prophecy and healing. Through these precise allusions, Christians show us what their pagan neighbours accepted. Through their statues, the gods did not undertake to punish the wicked systematically, a task which would have rapidly worn them out. Instead, they used some of their images for occasional "good deeds" whose very irregularity proved them to be divine.[48] So convincing were the deeds that Christians did not reject them. They merely referred them to another source.

This referral is very significant. Pan still piped, the gods still showed their anger and stood invisibly beside favoured men: to contemporaries, the evidence of the statues seemed indisputable. To account for it, the Christians cited the demons.[49] To their heirs, early Christians have at times seemed obsessed with these figures, who have earned them a black mark as "claustrophobic" or "guilt-ridden" individuals. There are many explanations, but part of the demons' prominence derived from this simpler cause. Like pagans, Christians still sensed and saw the gods and their power, and as something, they had to assume, lay behind it, by an easy, traditional shift of opinion, they turned these pagan *daimones* into malevolent "demons," the troupe of Satan. They were most demonic when they were most plausible, lurking under the statues and working wonders and visions as if from the gods who were represented. It was irrelevant that nobody ever saw them. Their power was manifest, but among Christians, too, only the pure and the virtuous could see their physical bodies. Far into the Byzantine period, Christians eyed their cities' old pagan statuary as a seat of the demons' presence. It was no longer beautiful: it was infested.[50]

Now that the gods watched and worked through their statues, did they still need to prowl among mortals in disguise? The Homeric suitors' words on "spies in disguise" did enjoy a long literary life, in Maximus's speeches and Julian's writings, biographies by Eunapius and the late Platonism of Proclus.[51] The "spies" were "like strangers," yet did people really believe what these men of letters continued to quote? There is no straightforward inscription or dedication to support them, and for evidence, we have to look to a difficult area, the romances of ancient fiction, and then assess their tone.

We can begin with a third-century theory which claimed to detect the gods in disguise among men. It stands in the fictional *Ethiopic Tales* of Heliodorus, a work for which two dates have been proposed, one around the 220s, the other in the aftermath of Julian's reign, around the 370s. The case is far from settled, but of the two, the earlier is preferable, suggesting that the book may be connected with the literary sophist Heliodorus the "Arab," who pleaded in the presence of the Emperor Caracalla and lived to an old age in Rome.[52] His novel was artful and cannot be taken as a direct statement, but its many dreams and visions are of unusual interest. At Delphi, an Egyptian sage called Calasiris saw the gods Apollo and Artemis by night, "not in a dream but in waking reality." Later, he explained to his questioners how he had recognized the gods so clearly and why these divine appearances were not unusual. The gods and the lesser divinities, he explained, often appeared in mortal form, though less often in the disguise of animals. Once again, Homer was proof of this. In the *Iliad*, one Ajax had told the other how the "shins" and paces of the gods left "traces" and how the gods were "readily recognized" by men. Calasiris expounded the meaning of this famous text. Men, he said, must be wise to perceive a god, for the gods remain hidden from those who are not "in the know." To the expert, the eyes betray a divine intruder, because they stay open and never blink. When a god moves, his feet glide forwards side by side, just as they appear in the upright stance of his statue. Calasiris confirmed this opinion by revealing a double meaning in Homer's words, which was only visible to the eyes of a wise reader.

Heliodorus gave these views to an Egyptian in a novel and did not endorse what he presented so obliquely. But it brings together themes of unusual interest. Once again, the gods are only to be seen by the wise or the virtuous, and again, Homer and Egypt combine with the types of statues and the hidden senses of poetry to produce a theory on the gods' "traces." These are revealed not only in dreams but in "waking reality." Before long, the philosopher Iamblichus also ascribed his views on the presence of the gods to the wisdom of an Egyptian priest: by their dress and way of life, the priests of Egypt were believed to be especially favoured with visions of their gods. In this novel, these later discussions are anticipated, and although the speaker is artfully characterized, his view does not read altogether like a joke.

In our other ancient novels, the gods' disguises serve a different, Callimachean purpose. They emphasize the charming, naive world which we, the readers, are lulled into sharing, while seeing through its fiction. So marvellous are the novels' young heroes and so simple their spectators that cases of mistaken divinities abound.[53] Of the gods' qualities, beauty is the most human, and the beauty of the novels' heroines led to all sorts of wrong identifications and Homeric errors. In *The Golden Ass* (c. 170 A.D.), Psyche is widely honoured as a "new Aphrodite," to the detriment of the cults of the old one. In the *Ephesian Tales*, the young Anthea is mistaken for Artemis or her creature, and when she and her lover reach Rhodes, their beauty persuades the Rhodians to pray to them and offer public sacrifice: they hoped, like Telemachus, to placate the visitors as "kindly" gods. The theme, naturally, dogged the fictional progress of the pagan wise man, Apollonius. Nowhere, however, is it better described than in a romance by Chariton, which was probably written in the middle to late first century A.D.[54]

Chariton's home was Aphrodisias, a particular seat of the goddess Aphrodite. In his novel, the fair Callirhoë was sold into slavery and transported to Miletus, where the onlookers are said to have mistaken her for Aphrodite herself. The goddess, wrote Chariton, was particularly "manifest" to the neighbours around her country shrine and also to visitors who came out from the city. Once again, these excursions to country gods linked pagan towns and their hinterland. Callirhoë looked like Aphrodite "made manifest," and when a rich prospective buyer came out to see her, he at once called her a goddess and quoted lines from Homer to express his faith. After this welcome, all the people of Miletus are said to have rushed out and adored her as Aphrodite. When she entered the city for her wedding, rumour had raced through the city. "Aphrodite is marrying," they all called out. The sailors bowed before her in terror, and the city had been garlanded since dawn. Everyone prepared to sacrifice before his own house while stories circulated about the bride's identity. The "commoner sorts of people," wrote Chariton, "were convinced by her beauty and her unknown origin and believed that she was a Nereid come from the sea, while the sailors spread the story that the goddess herself was present, come from the estates of Callirhoë's husband-to-be." When Callirhoë had finished making herself up, their last doubts vanished. "Aphrodite is marrying," they all shouted at the first sight of her, and scattered their purple robes and garments, their roses and violets before her path. The city was emptied, even of its children. "The crowd was packed tight, as high as the roof tiles . . ." The story then took a sinister turn: "On that day, jealous divinity was once more moved to anger."

Some of the details in this memorable scene can be matched with the real world. We have seen how the honouring of a fair or favourite woman as a goddess was a politeness which goes back to the *Odyssey*. From the cult of living rulers, we can match the crowd's acclamations and the private altars which were prepared outside the houses along Callirhoë's path. Above all, the girl's appearance was greeted with fitting words from Homer. When her buyer first saw her, he repeated the words of Penelope's suitors on the gods in disguise as "invisible spies."

This scene in a pagan romance is the perfect match for the conduct of Acts' men of Lystra and was narrated, most probably, at a similar date. The sailors and "more vulgar types," wrote Chariton, were especially prone to mistake a human for a nymph or a goddess. Acts, too, ascribed this response to men who spoke Lycaonian or mumbled like "barbarians" on Melite. Just as Callirhoë's rich buyer bowed down and hailed her as a goddess, so the well-meaning centurion, Cornelius, greeted Peter by bowing as if to a divinity. In the novel, this mistake stressed Callirhoë's beauty; in Acts, it brought out Peter's modesty and tact. Like Callimachus, these two authors were distanced from the simple mistakes which they chose to describe: were they themselves mistaken, repeating a stereotype of the simple peasant whom they did not understand? It seems unlikely. Acts' author was present himself on Melite and knew Paul and Barnabas, the victims of the Lystrans' mistake. Both stories may derive from Christian witnesses who were embellishing a central truth. Chariton does not seem to think that a god could never keep company with men: he merely wants us to smile at the Homeric error of his crowd in this one particular case. In Acts, the men of Lystra were misled by a miracle, performed in their presence. Their reaction, surely, is not untrue to life, no more than the reaction of the men on Melite. The dubious point in the story is not the crowd's reaction, but Paul's miracle of healing, a doubt which historians have not been able to settle.

With the help of Homer and the pagan novels, we have vindicated Acts' illuminating scene. To all but a few of the highly educated, the gods were indeed a potential presence whom a miracle might reveal.[55] They might leave their traces or they might be those handsome strangers who had appeared at noon on the hillside. They were present, watching and visiting, and if few of Homer's heroes had seen them without a revelation, who were second-century mortals to expect a clearer sign? They could only guess, but it was in the nature of these "gods" that the guesses, when exposed to proof, were invariably wrong. The postscript to Acts and to Chariton's pastoral novel has now been found on stone. From northeastern Lydia, we have the votive monument and text of a man who made his dedication "on behalf of the traces of the gods" in the year 184/5.[56] The brothers Ajax had once discussed these "traces" in Homer's *Iliad*: they are honoured in a few, but only a few, of the model stone footprints which worshippers left in shrines of the gods. This latest honour came from a person, Artemon, whose profession can only be restored as *topiarios*, or landscape gardener. Artemon had not quite seen the gods, but he had seen something almost as wonderful, their trail of footprints, traced into the very landscape which he loved and served. The novels and the men of Lystra were not so far removed from contemporary country life.

This level of epiphany added something, finally, to the cults of living men. By an inherited "culture pattern," people looked for beauty and power, the sudden flash, the transformation in circumstance which hinted that a god was present. Consequently, flatterers and beneficiaries detected these qualities in the gifts and the "arrivals" of "divine" Emperors. When Diocletian and his fellow Emperor crossed the Alps in 291 A.D., a court orator played on the old potential themes. "For the first time, your holiness radiated from the eastern and western peaks of the Alps . . . all Italy was bathed in a glowing light . . . Watchers were moved with wonder and also with doubt, asking themselves what gods were rising on their peaks or descending by such steps from heaven . . . When you were seen more closely . . . altars were lit, incense was burned. People did not invoke gods whom they knew from hearsay, but Jupiter close at hand, visible and present: they adored Hercules, not a stranger, but the Emperor himself."[57] It was glorious rhetoric, but it also attached the Emperors to the living belief that gods, in a show of power, might visit men. Its orator did not believe a word of it, but can we be so sure that all the spectators had been equally down-to-earth? That God could visit man was the least novel feature of Christian teaching in a pagan's eyes.

## III

What, then, had happened in Alexandra's Miletus? Here, there had been no mistaken identities, no single "divine" stranger, no sudden miracle. Gods in quantity had been "manifest" as never before, "standing beside" people of every age and either sex. In fiction, again, we can find a match for the perplexity of the city's priestess. In Petronius's *Satyricon* (c. 60 A.D.), another priestess, Quartilla, comes to threaten the main characters because they have been spying on her secret religious rites.[1] These ceremonies were confined, like

Alexandra's, to women only: I pity you, she tells them, because the gods are watching us all: "our region is so full of ever-present divinities that it is easier to find a god than a man." The scene, it seems, was set near Ostia in Italy, in a Campanian coastal town, but Quartilla was not a straightforward character. First she wished to scare the male intruders; then she intended to seduce them. Once again, the author was detached from the simple words which he gave to a fictional character: were there, however, people who thought in this way, not only in Italy but Miletus, too?

For the purpose of Alexandra's question, the idea of gods "in disguise" was surely not relevant. How could Alexandra and her sources be so sure that these strangers were really gods? Even in Homer, the heroes had needed signs and miracles before they could see through the gods' concealments. Gods "in the form of young children" would be most peculiar: the other translation is surely right, gods "appearing not only to the girls and women but to the men and boys, too." The emphasis in these words was very relevant. Like Quartilla, Alexandra was a priestess of rites which were for women only, yet here were the gods appearing to the opposite sex, men who did not take part in her particular cult. No wonder it seemed an omen, as if women had taken to sitting in the men's gymnasiums.

How, though, had the gods appeared? Were they seen directly, as in happy Phaeacia, or were they seen at one remove, through the contact of dreams? This choice leads us to the two other levels of epiphany, open face-to-face meetings and visions by day and night. Then we can choose between them for Miletus's precise experience.

We have seen the traditional settings for an open encounter: a crisis or a time of strain. In the Antonine and Severan age, battles and sieges were remote from most cities' experience, but personal crises were more constant, the strains of sickness or bereavement. We have a fine account on papyrus, c. 100 A.D., of a vision seen by a sick young author, "not in a dream, or in sleep, of a very large figure with a book in his left hand, dressed in white": he was a god, and he reproached the beholder for his long delay in publishing a promised account of his great deeds.[2] Near Nakrason, in northeastern Lydia, one Epicrates (c. 100 A.D.) recorded on two impressive stones his bequests and their financing of an elaborate funerary cult. They honoured Epicrates's son, "not just at the wish of an affectionate father, but because the hero visits me very vividly in dreams, signs and other appearances."[3] In his bereavement, Epicrates did not only dream at night of the son he had lost. He believed that he still saw him "clearly," and so far from being reticent about this, he inscribed it publicly "in seemly lettering," believing that his readers would not consider it odd. Throughout antiquity, pagans believed that the spirit of a dead man might be visible beyond the grave: posthumous "appearances" were no novelty.

However, stresses and strains of this type cannot explain the events in Miletus. These stresses affected individuals, whereas Miletus was alive with glimpses of the gods, granted to all sorts of people "as never before." Had magic and spells come into this collective process? In the Imperial period, magical texts did aim to "introduce" their followers to a divinity or to the attendant spirits whom their spells alleged that they could conjure up. Their chants and recipes did claim to draw Apollo and the Sun god into a worshipper's presence: through piety and philosophy, the "eye of the soul" could eventually hope to contemplate a divine power.[4] In the papyri of the later magical texts, we find detailed instructions for "autopsy" and direct sightings of the gods, but the one literary account of such a personal vision insists that it was very exceptional, the medical student Thessalus's vision of Asclepius, which he obtained with the help of the elderly priest in Egypt.[5] Only Thessalus's tears and threats of suicide obliged the man to assist him by conjuring up Asclepius "alone in his sole presence," after Thessalus had remained pure for three days: the tone of his narrative proves that this escapade was not granted to lesser men. In later papyri, we can still see the drawings which were thought to summon a god, a small squat figure with a sword gripped in his hand.[6] The dark materials of these spells kept company with special effects, lights, flames and arts of autosuggestion: Thessalus seems to have gazed into the surface of a bowl of water.[7]

It is hard, however, to know how widely these arts and aspirations were practised. After an exorcism by Paul, said Acts, people in Ephesus burnt their magical books of spells on a bonfire, to the value of "50,000 pieces of silver."[8] Perhaps some of these spells did conjure up gods and make them visible in people's lives, like the djinns who still haunt urban life in Cairo, but it seems unlikely. To find such a spell, Thessalus had to seek the only able priest in Egypt, and it is from Egypt and the Near East that most of the later evidence derives. The tone of Alexandra's question implies that Miletus's "visits" were spontaneous and quite exceptional. There is no connection, surely, with the world of sorcery and spells, arts which remained erudite, preserved in texts and libraries.

Miletus's own situation may be relevant, as a city centre for travellers and visiting sailors who came in from the nearby coastline. In the Imperial period, sea journeys were still a spotter's delight.[9] In a final twist to one of his speeches, Maximus of Tyre told his audience how he, too, had witnessed Castor and Pollux and Heracles, "not in a dream, but in waking reality." The words were emphatically placed, to close his speech with vigour. Sailors had lost none of their piety, and in places, their expectations were high. Every visitor to the Black Sea knew the special island of Achilles, and in his report on the area, a visiting governor, Arrian, informed the Emperor Hadrian how "some said" Achilles appeared to them in broad daylight on the prow or mast of their ships, "as did Castor and Pollux." Maximus, indeed, knew a man after Homer's own heart. Near the same island, visitors had "often" seen a young, fair-haired hero dancing in armour and had heard him singing a paean. Recently, one sailor had dozed off on the island itself, and Achilles had led him to his tent. Patroclus was there, he reported, pouring out the wine, while Achilles played the lyre. "He said that Thetis was also present, as was a group of other, minor gods." Had this been the mood in Miletus, too, in the harbour, perhaps, or the turmoil of some equinoctial gale?

On these occasions, open encounters were not entirely dead, but they did tend to centre on certain sacrosanct places. After Homer, no place was more liable to them than Troy itself: Maximus also told his listeners that Hector was "especially manifest in the Trojan area." For a sense of what this meant, we can look to a more remarkable work, Philostratus's dialogue On Heroes. It is more often dismissed than discussed, but it suggests, like nothing else, what educated readers were prepared to enjoy without altogether disbelieving, while the Christian "contagion" was the faintest of stains in the pagan cities. Its author's identity has caused problems, but he fits admirably as the Philostratus who lived from the 160s to the mid-240s and belonged among the literary sophists of his age.[10] He enjoyed the company of the Emperor Caracalla's wife and probably attended the court on its journey east in Alexander's footsteps between the years 213 and 217. On Heroes drops one reference to an athletic victor, Helix (the "Creeper"), which dates it after 213 and almost certainly after 217, perhaps many years after. Philostratus knew the highest people in high society: once, he conversed with Gordian's father on the topic of the Greek sophists. His book is extremely valuable as an insight into educated tastes.

Philostratus, friend of the Gordians, applied a notable gift to the style and context of his fictional dialogue. One day, he wrote, a Phoenician sailor had come up to Troy because his ship was detained by adverse winds. There, he met a resident farmer who tended orchards and vineyards of exceptional beauty. As the autumn weather was fine and the day stretched far before them, they sat in the shade of the trees and discussed the ways of Homer's heroes and the personal details which their poet had omitted. The setting was imagined with singular art. The author knew literary men from the old Phoenician cities and stressed his Phoenician's Ionic Greek dress and manner, which were cultural fashions in his age. The Phoenician, he said, had come with that frequent problem of polite society in the second and third centuries, a dream whose meaning he could not understand. He had dreamed of some lines of Homer, a type of dream which was not uncommon among the literary sophists, who knew the poems by heart. With Homer on the brain, the Phoenician had gone up to Troy in search of a "sign or saying" to interpret a dream which bore, he believed, on the prospects for weather at sea. If the Phoenician was artfully typecast, the vinedresser, too, was no ordinary rustic. He had been born a man of property, but had lost much of his estates to his guardians after his parents' death. Just enough remained for him to live in the city and study with "teachers and philosophers," but the slaves who farmed the land for him were corrupt. He had received such a poor return that he had decided to go back to Troy and take the ground in hand himself. Like the Phoenician, the vinedresser appealed to the literary tastes of the age—a cultured student in the role of a simple peasant, a man who could use his Homer and Plato to bring out the beauty of his idyllic retreat while working peacefully in the fields.

The vinedresser had not been gardening alone. He was privileged, he said, to have the best advice, which was passed on by the hero Protesilaus, with whom, at Troy, he kept constant company. Homer's old landscape was not a quiet orchard, but a noisy haunt of the ancient heroes, "present visitors" who called and strode across the plains, "standing forward" as companions and counsellors for those who pleased them. None was more favoured than the vinedresser, who enjoyed a special relationship with the hero Protesilaus, although it was not always easy, as Protesilaus had his moods and could take offence at human misconduct. He had been cross when the vinedresser had first returned from the city to his fruit farm, but he had softened when his new pupil took his advice and adopted the proper rustic dress. Since then, they had hit it off very well. Protesilaus gave tips on growing fruit and explained the little bits of Homer which the vinedresser had misunderstood and wrongly applied to his art. The picture was irresistible: the vinedresser turned to Homer's poems for advice on growing vines, and when he mistook their meaning, the hero saved Homer's credit by explaining what they really said. It took a Homeric hero to teach a former man of letters the arts of better gardening.[11] Others were less fortunate. Protesilaus retained a strong moral sense and had once set the dog on a pair of scheming adulterers who had come to visit Troy under false pretences.[12] Straightforward young lovers, however, touched his heart, because in them he saw a mirror of his former life. Even so, he preferred the vinedresser's company and his garden of fruit. He "keeps me straight" with the farming, said the vinedresser, and whenever the animals fell sick, he acted as a wise vet. While the bunches of grapes hung as heavily as swarms of bees above them, the hero told his friend the Trojan stories which Homer had omitted or mistaken.

Philostratus had aimed his story at educated readers who loved their Homer and liked to entertain suspicions that there was more in nature and the universe than Aristotle had contrived to classify. He wrote with a style which showed the better side of his age's Greek prose, artful, but never diffuse in the manner of its set speeches. His inspirations were obvious to men of letters: Homer and perhaps the miracles which Protesilaus performed while the Persians retreated in Herodotus's last book. But it is particularly significant that he added his own local knowledge, stories which were told on his own Lemnos and traditions which were current in nearby Aegean islands.[13] He also gave space to visible proofs of the heroes, especially the giant skeletons which had recently come to light on nearby beaches and headlands. Many passersby had noticed them, bones fit for fifteen-foot heroes, as tall as Protesilaus himself. To prove it, Philostratus took his readers on a grand tour of the old bones of the third-century Empire.

This evidence was not his invention. Similar skeletons had raised problems which only the oracles could solve: at Claros, Apollo had had to tell puzzled questioners the nature of huge bones which they had found in a riverbed. The reasons lay in geological history. Relics from the age of the dinosaurs were still plentiful in the third century, and were exposed by the winds, the seas and the farmers. Even the Emperors collected them. Carcasses of long-dead monsters had been mistaken for the bones of heroes at least since the mid-sixth century

B.C.; Philostratus was heir to those Spartans who had first unearthed the Pleistocene bones of "Orestes." Protesilaus, he said, had been asked about an eighteen-foot skeleton, while another, thirty-five feet long, had lain on the headland at Sigeum and provoked passing sailors to tell many stories about its identity.

The Christians' Resurrection left no bones, no evidence, not even, at this date, a so-called shroud. Yet who could doubt the heroes' existence when these Pleistocene corpses proved their enormous physique? When the Phoenician asked if the heroes were really visible in the plain around Troy, the vinedresser had no doubts. "They are seen, indeed, they are seen even now, large and godlike, by the herdsmen and shepherds on the plain." They came striding and clattering over the fields, an omen for those in the neighbourhood. If they were dusty and worn, they foretold drought, and if blood was seen on their armour, it warned of sickness. Visitors had to tread warily and watch their tongues. Only recently a boy from the Near East had insulted Hector's actions in the *Iliad*, and had promptly been killed in the river, on Hector's instigation, as soon as he walked below Troy.

If they were seen at Troy, might they not have been stalking Miletus, too? However, the great German scholar Wilamowitz believed that Philostratus was merely sporting with his readers and agreeing with nothing that he wrote.[14] We have had to allow for authors' ironic detachment from the scenes they evoke, but although *On Heroes* has an obvious pastoral atmosphere, it does not read at all like a *jeu d'esprit*. It enchants its readers with a picture which they could still entertain, and from his other works, Philostratus is known to have excluded no plausible fancies; who was he to be sceptical when he had known a woman on Lemnos who insisted that she had slept with a satyr? Philostratus used a mass of local details and stories which bore on others' good faith, while the tone of his dialogue is not ironic. The Phoenician trader comes to Troy, doubting the heroes' existence, and he leaves with a new faith, converted by a living protégé of Protesilaus. He no longer scoffs; he learns one of life's lessons. Among his business and petty commerce, he is to trust what Homer tells him. He is still full of questions when evening descends on the dialogue, and such is the art which evokes the setting and engages our sympathy that we cannot be meant to laugh at him, as if he had been duped into faith by romance.

Reluctant to accept this implication, others have passed off *On*

*Heroes* as a book for a special occasion. It belonged, they have claimed, with the Emperor Caracalla's journey to Troy in 214, which retraced the tracks of Alexander the Great and his hero Achilles. Philostratus had indeed visited Troy,[15] but although he had excellent contacts at court and may have followed the Emperor eastwards, there is no force in this suggestion. *On Heroes* was written at a date which is almost certainly after 217, and it shows no interest in the Emperor or his journey, already at least three years in the past.[16] Later, Philostratus returned to these Trojan subjects in his "Life" of Apollonius, where the heroes also appeared. Surely, he wrote *On Heroes* because the idea appealed to him. The book was not a *roman à clef* alluding to contemporaries, or a text tinged with magic and mysticism. These theories mistake the cosy Homeric piety of a well-connected man of letters in the late Severan age. As night fell on the dialogue, the Phoenician was looking forward to a talk with Protesilaus on the topography and punishments of the old, classic underworld. His interests were quite straightforward, the problems of myth which Protesilaus, the reborn hero, could solve. There were no questions on mysteries, no interest in salvation. "Whoever does not think you, vinedresser, to be an exceptional friend of the gods, he himself is detested by them."[17] "Friendship" was still a "friendship" as Homer had understood it, no more, no less. We must allow for men who agreed with Philostratus at the head of the Greek cities, men who were keener to find their Homer proved true than to drift into monotheism or let a revealed religion invade their private lives. Philostratus's readers and friends included the family of the future Emperor Gordian. *On Heroes* belongs with his games for the old Athena, belief in the old traditions and no sympathy with Christian "atheism."

Was this Homeric potential realized in Miletus, not between one man and his hero but between people of all ages and the host of "visiting" gods? Indeed, this type of Homeric piety was not dead. It still had its literary uses, suggesting a charming picture which might be true: in the 380s, Eunapius gave a beguiling account of the two divine strangers who had visited the future philosopher Sosipatra and caused her father to quote the familiar lines of Homer on "spies."[18] More immediately, we meet this piety in writings of the Emperor Julian, for whom the gods were still manifest protectors, "standing beside" him to help him through life.[19] In a magnificent myth, Julian hinted at his youthful encounter with the gods and his personal "ascent" to heaven, where they had commissioned his task among men. Julian told this myth because it stood for a serious truth, his own sense of divine company and guidance, based on a personal Homeric encounter. It is this "company" which is stressed repeatedly in the speeches to or about him which were made by the orator Libanius.[20] The gods, he says, assisted Julian in his marches to war; Zeus was his protector, Athena his "fellow worker"; they were "spies" to such good effect that they forewarned him of plots and conspiracies against his life, a heavenly system of counterintelligence. Some of these themes might only be flattery, but Libanius insisted on a more personal note. "You alone have seen the shapes of the gods, a blessed observer of the blessed ones . . . you alone have heard the voice of the gods and addressed them in the words of Sophocles, 'O voice of Athena' or 'O voice of Zeus' . . ." On the heights of the great mountain behind Antioch, Julian had indeed seen Zeus himself, while sacrificing in his honour. The gods were his "friends and protectors," Libanius insisted, "just as" Athena had once stood by Homer's Achilles. Julian, the last pagan Emperor, has been studied for his interests in "Eastern" gods and magic, but these interests kept company with an older consciousness, the potentially visible presence of the traditional gods. To miss this presence is to diminish the man whom the Christians feared like no other for his resolute sense of mission.

Julian, however, was a king who offered frequent sacrifices and knew the Homeric poems in detail, a source of enhancement for his own life and writings. He, perhaps, might see the "forms of the gods," but he was exceptionally blessed, their "special friend," like the vinedresser at Troy. In Miletus, the old and the young were not so favoured or exalted: if the old potential had been realized and if the gods had been roaming in broad daylight, the Milesians would have had to be very brave or very pious to behold them so clearly. "Not to everyone do the gods appear . . ." "The gods are hard to cope with, when manifest . . ." It was one thing to read of the old Homeric intimacy, another to experience it "as never before." Contact with the gods was likelier at a distance, in the safe privacy of sleep. To find the "visitations" in which gods "stood beside" the Milesians, it is right, surely, to look here, to epiphany's most open level.

Its potential was never better expressed than by Synesius, while a philosopher. "None of the laws of Necessity stops me being more successful than Icarus while I am asleep, from passing from earth to soar higher than an eagle, to reach the highest spheres . . . and thence, from afar, to look down on the earth, to discourse with the stars, to keep company with gods, an impossibility in our world. For what is said to be 'hard' "—here, again, he alludes to the words of Hera in the *Iliad*—"is then easy. 'The gods appear clearly'" (the Homeric words of Hera again). "They are not in the least jealous. A dreamer does not return to earth; he is there already."[21]


# IV


In their dreams, pagans of all classes and backgrounds kept the closest company with gods.[1] From this type of experience, philosophers had derived man's entire conception of divinity: they had been led astray, said the Epicureans, by their dreams of exceptionally large and beautiful figures whom they mistook for the gods' images.[2] The ancients were not uncritical in their attitude to what they saw: no people ever has been. At many levels of subtlety, they distinguished dreams which arose from the worries of the previous day or from hunger or an unusually heavy meal.[3] These "visions," they knew, had no significance. The others intrigued them, to the point where their theorists multiplied schemes of the different types and frustrated our modern attempts to derive them all from a lost or half-known original.[4] The source of dream images and their methods of contact with the dreamer's soul aroused a lively debate: it is not quite true to claim that "antiquity was interested more in the outcome and less in the cause."[5] Dreams of the gods raised particular interest: were they sent by the gods themselves, or did the soul reach upwards while the senses were sleeping and somehow make contact with higher reality? Opinions divided, and only the Aristotelians wrote sceptically about the very existence of any "divine" dreams at all. Few paid any attention, and by the Imperial period, their views had been merged with the more positive statements of Stoics and Platonists. Plato had written some promising things on the contact of the soul and the lesser *daimones*, while the Stoics, more prosaically, sorted dreams into groups and left a special place for dreams of the gods. Many dreams, they accepted, were "heaven-sent," and in one class, the gods themselves spoke directly with the dreamer: it is this belief that we find so clearly in the *Meditations* of the Emperor Marcus. There were also visions seen "not in a dream but in waking reality," whose subjects might often be gods.

This Greek phrase was very old, and Homer had already known it, but it was not so simple as we might think. In the *Odyssey*, it occurs twice, but it does not contrast a dream with a vision which is experienced in waking hours.[6] It applies to features within a dream itself, features which are either so realistic that they seem to occur or else of significance, a "happy reality" which will come to pass. The novels, too, copy Homer's usage, although the phrase had a second meaning, as commentators pointed out in antiquity. It could also mean a "vision seen after daybreak," and Iamblichus was usefully precise about this meaning. As sleep left a man, he wrote, and his mind became alert, he was prone to a heaven-sent condition which was quite different from a muddled and deceptive dream. The eyes remained shut, but the mind was free from earthly encumbrance, and as wakefulness returned, "the voices," wrote Iamblichus, could speak directly to the soul. These "waking visions" were common in the last moments of sleep when the soul was not distracted by food or worry. Not everybody accepted their validity, not even in the fourth century A.D., but they persisted, visions which we would class as "hypnagogic fantasies" and which often brought gods or their voices to men:[7] in modern encounters, too, the edges of sleep are particularly favourable moments.

So firm was belief in this nighttime "company" that men did their best to encourage it.[8] Sorcerers offered spells for conjuring up prophetic dreams and considered the arts of "dream-seeking" and "dream-sending" to be a central part of their business. Men wore amulets of a god and travelled with them as if they were pocket divinities, fingering them or gazing on them before sleeping: Calasiris, in the *Ethiopic Tales*, poured libations and prayed at evening for propitious dreams. Fasting was a helpful preliminary, as was avoidance of the heavier foods: the Greeks' diet, it was said, particularly favoured visions, because their food was light and dry. That view, admittedly, was expressed in the days before moussaka. Above all, dreams were courted deliberately in temples with special "incubatory" chambers, from the Britons' Lydney in Kent to the great centres at Pergamum and Aigai in Asia.[9] Serapis, Isis and Jupiter Dolichenus all encouraged dreams in their devotees, but no god was more prodigal than Asclepius, whose cult reached a new magnificence during the second century. Once again, this cult was not symptomatic of some new hypochondria or anxiety, let alone of the tensions of "colonialization," as Greek culture spread into yet more areas of the

East.[10] Polite society had long been intrigued by medicine and places
of healing and the Antonines' literary interest in both was not novel.
Rather, Asclepius flourished because, like Lourdes, the sites of his cult
were being given a new splendour by benefactions in the Roman age
of peace. The shrines improved and, in turn, they drew famous
clients. There was no opposition from doctors to the practices of
"incubating" and seeking cures in dreams from the god.[11] Since the
later first century B.C., the surviving records of dreams of Asclepius
say less about sudden miraculous cures and rather more about precise
medical practices which the god prescribed. Doctors talked to Asclepius's clients and visited his temples. They dedicated shrines to the god
or paid for improvements in his facilities, seeing no inevitable clash
between his "faith"-healing and their own. Asclepius, therefore,
picked up his visitors' science. In his temples, people shared surround-
ings which made dreams of the gods particularly frequent. Through
Plutarch, we know of the compound of sixteen spices which Egyptian
priests used to burn in the evening in order to encourage sweet dreams
in their visitors. Like the "incense of Epidaurus," this compound was
a scent, not a drug.[12] When the ancient recipes of the compound were
made up and tested, they had no effect, apart from giving wine the
sharp tang of retsina. Priests were alive to the distorting effects of
stimulants, a point which Philostratus brought out well, in the debate
which he gave to his fictional hero Apollonius at the court of an Indian
king. Wine, the sage explained, was avoided by those who wished to
have prophetic dreams, and this was why dreams in the early morning
were so much more revealing: by then, he said rather optimistically,
the influence of drink had worn off.[13] At Amphiaraus's charming
temple in Attica, the priests, he remarked, forbade the drinking of
wine for three whole days before the client slept in the shrine and
hoped for a dream of the god. The priests also forbade food for a day
beforehand and required the worshippers to sleep on the skins of a
sheep which had been sacrificed to the god.[14]

There is no undue mystery about the frequency of divine dreams in
such shrines. They attracted clients from all the free social classes,
many of whom had come from a distance to join a society of sleepers
who were all hoping and striving for as clear a dream as possible. For
several days, they had not eaten. They took no wine, and their
stimulants were what they heard and saw. Shrines like Pergamum
were frequented by priests and *theologoi*, men who wrote hymns to the
gods and talked piously to visitors among the short stories of miracle

cures which they displayed publicly. At Asclepius's shrine below Pergamum's hill, the temple had its own library and a small, elegant theatre for plays and recitations, staged, no doubt, on stories of the powers of the god.[15] Long underground tunnels joined the various shrines, sleeping chambers, perhaps, though their exact purpose is uncertain. Aristophanes was not being mischievous when he described how the long, tame snakes of Asclepius's shrines glided between the sleepers at night in their dark rooms: on Attic reliefs of the fourth century B.C. we see snakes licking the sleeping patient, and cures on display referred to this "licking" of the snakes. At Pergamum, as night fell, the worshippers had the choice of the Lesser incubation chamber or the Greater, for which the offering to the god was more expensive. Like certain nineteenth-century spas, some chambers, perhaps, were more polite than others. At Oropus, we know, the sexes were supposed to be segregated.[16]

In these chambers the entire company were urging each other to dream as divinely as possible. Even so, dreams came in fits and starts and missed some individuals altogether. These lean spells befell everybody, however responsive, and visitors who were becalmed in a bad patch had to ask a priest to dream on their behalf. Usually, however, the atmosphere was its own best narcotic. It was intoxicated, above all, by the presence of religious works of art.

Since the age of the epic heroes, statues and paintings had become a fundamental influence on the way the divine world was "envisioned." It is particularly significant that the dreams and visions in Homer show none of art's effects, for Homer had composed the epics before portrait statues had been widely available: we have seen how, by night and day, his gods appeared always in disguises, taking the form of other men and women. How else could they appear clearly, with separate identities? As Greek sculpture developed, it fixed mortals' ideas of their gods as individuals: the distinct "personality" of the Greek gods has been questioned, but art was an enduring mould which helped to form it.[17] By the Christian era, many of the gods' best-known statues were old and classic images cast like enormous Buddhas in bronze or gold, with ivory eyes and silvered teeth. At last we can appreciate their impact, as we are the first generation since antiquity to see masterly bronze statues of divine Greek heroes. In 1972, the Italian seabed, off Riace in Calabria, restored to us two bronze heroes, nearly two metres high and larger and stronger than life: to look on them is to give shape to the idea of superhuman power.[18] Both are the masterpieces of a classical Greek artist of the fifth century B.C., but the greater of the two has a gaze of confidence before eternity which distinguishes it from masterpieces of the Christian Renaissance. It survives with eyes and eyelashes, lips and teeth, and restores to us the facial expressions which so haunted the ancients' imagination. Is the statue's gaze welcoming or awesome in its boldness? The answer lies in the eye of each beholder.

In ancient temples and cities, statues of this type, if not quality, were abundant, even after the Romans had looted many of them, taking them, as Dio once told the Rhodians, to a "better" home where they would be seen and cared for in a capital city.[19] Statues of the gods would sometimes be much larger than our two bronze heroes, reaching fifteen feet or more in an effort to express the gods' super-human size. Perhaps only those who have felt the awe of the great gold Buddhas, recumbent like stranded whales in an Asian temple, can begin to grasp what this colossal statuary meant to the eye and emotions. As cult statues in temples, these works were decked with the gods' attributes and symbols, a further source of awe. Their authority provoked an interesting debate.[20] Were they products of the artist's own imagination or of his attempt to render the image of the gods which was already enshrined in poetry? Were they revealed to the artist first, by the god himself in a dream?

The "presence" of these statues varied from region to region. In the temples of Syria and the Near East, cult statues of the gods were enclosed or curtained from worshippers' eyes.[21] Only on particular days did they come out on procession, borne in a litter or wheeled in a chariot. The sight of these secluded figures induced particular emotion in worshippers who would not see them otherwise, without special leave from a priest. In the Greek world, too, cult statues were sometimes curtained off or kept in locked temples. In their mystery cults, too, the Greeks seem to have exploited the power of a hidden image that was rarely and briefly revealed: in the fourth century A.D., the orator Themistius hints that in some mystery rites, robed statues were stripped bare to the sight of initiates. In other shrines, however, they were accessible to any visitor, while outside the shrines, the images were familiar in public places, even in public baths. In each region, the image of a god left a powerful, potential imprint on the mind: in the Near East, they were a seldom-seen mystery; in parts of the Greek world, familiar, constant companions.

In this varying company of statues great and small, dreams of the gods begin to seem less surprising. Their frequency has been ascribed to men's vague ideas of what counted as a god's appearance: when every figure dressed in white was construed as a god, *"on comprend de cette façon que les épiphanies divines aient été nombreuses."*[22] This view does not give due emphasis to works of art.

Thanks to one author, we happen to know the dreams of the early Antonine age better than any before or after in antiquity. In five remarkable books, Artemidorus of Daldis explained his theory of dreams' significance, the meanings of their common types and how, in his experience, the accepted meanings had turned out to be true.[23] His interest was in dreams' predictive power, not in their "analytical" relevance to diagnoses of a person's past or present. He had spared no efforts to find out the truth. He had read his predecessors' books and developed theoretical distinctions of his own. He had associated with the despised "street diviners," with whom he had swapped experiences, and he had also visited the major games and festivals of "cities and islands" from Italy to the Greek East,[24] where he had questioned the spectators and competitors, the athletes, rhetors and sophists who attached such interest to dreams of their personal prospects.[25] He had travelled from Asia to Italy and Rome, where his conversation and notes embraced all classes, a well-to-do woman in Italy who dreamed she was riding an elephant, members of the upper classes in the Greek cities, orators, Roman knights, a tax collector, convicts and criminals, the poor, the sick and the slaves, among whom, said Artemidorus, he "knew a slave who dreamed that he had stroked his master's penis," and another who dreamed that the master stroked his. Like no ancient author since Aristotle, he had engaged in tireless empirical research. He had the stamina of a field worker with theories which badly needed proof: "for Artemidorus, experience was a kind of watchword."[26]

Research and observation, he insisted, were essential to the dream interpreter's art.[27] In each case, he had to consider local custom, the oppositions of custom and nature and the dreamer's previous thoughts and wishes. Many dreams were not predictive, because they merely duplicated thoughts and wishes in the dreamer's own mind: sometimes, Artemidorus had had to discover details of his clients' sex life in order to predict the meaning of their dreams correctly. The dreams of dream interpreters themselves were especially misleading, because they were people who thought constantly about the symbols which made others' dreams significant: in antiquity, too, "interpreters" found that the greatest difficulty was to interpret themselves. Above all, these interpreters had to consider who their client was: the meaning of a dream varied according to profession and social class, and Artemidorus's interpretations presuppose many of the social attitudes on which we have already touched in civic life. Older writers on dreams had stated that the poor were analogous to the places where men throw out dung. Artemidorus did not express disagreement, although a poor man could hope to profit from certain dreams, dreams of eating his own body or of growing extra feet, a type of dream which promised trouble for the rich, but for the poor, the acquisition of slaves. Woods, mountains and chasms signified fear and distress for everyone, but especially for the rich, "as in these places, something is always being cut up and thrown away." The meaning says something for the fears of richer travellers, moving between their beloved cities. Although a dream of marriage stood quite bluntly for death, there was no fear of a wider "class struggle" in the dream interpreters' art. The rich were at risk to fortune and hazard, not to their social inferiors. The symbols for their household slaves were cowering, timid mice: the more they saw, the merrier.

Experience, however, was not Artemidorus's only guide. His interpretations also proceeded by analogy and wordplay and by associations which were based in myth and literature.[28] Sometimes, they could be simple: if a woman dreamed of a garden, for instance, she would be slandered for promiscuity, as gardens were full of seeds. Others could be complex, and they tell against the prevailing view that Artemidorus was a humble man. His Greek is a treasure house of rare, precise terms, but it is not demonstrably "lower-class" and his contacts went far beyond the simple, loquacious man in the street.[29] He was a citizen of Ephesus, either through his father or through a special grant to himself as a cultured man of learning.[30] His mother came from the Lydian city of Daldis, an "insignificant little town," he said, which he thanked for "raising" him and to which he offered his first three books on dreams. Quite possibly, his parents belonged in their cities' upper ranks. Their son had been well educated, but he knew details which befitted a man with links at Daldis; he was familiar with aspects of the local Lydian cult societies and with his local "ancestral" Apollo, Apollo Mystes, who had appeared to him "often" in dreams and "pressed" him to write his book.[31] The god, however, had not resolved the tension between Artemidorus the dogmatist and the skilled researcher who had observed so much. The dreams of athletes and performers from his own Asia, the curious local cults of Dionysus, the various types of bullfighting and bull-leaping, the small cult associations, or *symbioseis*, which we find in his own Lydia—all this evidence he had to fit to his theories, and he shows the dogmatist's strong resentment of criticism and disbelievers' "envy" as he struggles to make his theory fit.

This range of research and inquiry has to be stressed, because it gives his books a unique value for the social history of his age. They also had a prolonged effect, being translated promptly into Arabic after the Muslim conquests and greatly widening the meaning which ninth-century Muslims found in their dreams. In England, by 1720, they had gone into twenty editions, and their influence was far greater than the use which historians now make of them. In all their interpretations, there are only two or three examples of the Emperor in a client's dream: one man dreamed that he had pulled teeth from "the king's" mouth, foretelling victory in a lawsuit in his presence; another dreamed of "King" Agamemnon, a Homeric image of the "Emperor" in Greek eyes.[32] As the Emperors' subjects petitioned them on such a huge range of topics, this relative silence in the evidence is unexpected. The energy which modern English people now divert into dreams of their royal family went in the Antonine era elsewhere, to dreams of extreme sexual detail and to dreams of the gods.[33] As we shall see, to read Artemidorus's collections of sexual dreams is to realize the scale of the challenge which faced Christian views on chastity and "pure thoughts." To read his dreams of the gods is to realize what their "company" and "presence" still meant. They are the clearest difference between ancient and modern patterns of night life.

Artemidorus grouped the visions of gods into types and classes, using a popular philosophic distinction, but he also repeated many of his own observations. They bear, therefore, on the wide public whom he had questioned.[34] "After long experience," he said, he had come to know that dreams of sharing Hercules's life, meals or clothing were very inauspicious. "Often" he had studied dreams of owning or wearing the clothing of a god. They signified a future appointment as a trustee, the appearance of riches, he explained, without the reality. This dream, we can see, was a dream for high society only, where Artemidorus must have studied it, questioning people's trustees and taking down their dreams and their sequels. At a similar social level, he met a man who had dreamed that he was the Sun god: before long, he became chief magistrate of his city. Offenders, too, attracted his interest: people who dreamed they were stealing the stars "generally" turned out to be temple robbers, while he knew a man who had insulted a god and then dreamed that he was working off his crime by cleaning the god's statue. Dreams of entertaining the gods were more ambiguous. To the rich, they signified misfortune, but to the poor, a sudden prosperity. Artemidorus gave no examples, and here his interpretation rested on the stories of myth in which the gods visited humble men. Artemidorus did not believe all myths indiscriminately; the battle of gods and giants and the story of Endymion and the moon struck him as absurd and out-of-date. However, he accepted the tales of the gods' presence in disguise, and his acceptance is a significant support for men's living belief in it.

How did the dreamers know that they were seeing a god, and if so, which god was visiting them? Large figures, dressed in white, were conventional types of divinity, but they bore no signs of personality, and unless they spoke, the question of identity was left open. Even when they did speak, they could not be expected to be direct, said Artemidorus: usually, they gave riddles and hints, which the interpreter had to explain.[35] The gods made excellent business for his profession. At times, the signs of a god do seem very slender: once, Artemidorus described how a dream of a boy would mean Hermes, two boys Castor and Pollux, three clothed women the Fates, three naked women the Hours. Yet the general drift of his theory is against these vague equations, because the gods are known by their attributes: if they appear without them, they signify trouble.[36] These attributes were known through art, and here Artemidorus assumes a direct influence of art on dreams.

Like the sleepers in Asclepius's temples, his clients imagined the gods in the forms which their statues had sanctioned.[37] To dream of a god's statue, said Artemidorus, was the same as dreaming of the god himself. The two looked the same, although a god was able to move, whereas an image could not: what mattered was not only the image but its exact material and attributes. Different meanings attached to the gods' local types, to the "severe" Artemis of Perge and Ephesus, whom we can still see standing stiffly on these cities' coins, or the more friendly Artemis who was known elsewhere. Artemidorus had observed the gods very carefully, because their manner and attributes were so essential to the meanings of what they said. "Whenever the gods are not wearing their customary dress or whenever they are not behaving as they ought, whatever they say is only a lie." Gods seen without their ornaments and weapons, like our two bronzes from Riace, were very inauspicious.

In antiquity, statues of the gods did not usually carry an inscription to identify them: instead, men knew them by their style and attributes. In the Imperial period, they had never been more certain what their gods looked like. Their images crowded the squares and temples of their cities and were cast in a form which was not disposable: they had dominated ideas of divinity across many generations. Like Artemidorus, Philostratus, too, pictured the gods and heroes with the eye of an artist, attaching particular weight to the mood and tone of their expressions.[38] This emphasis on the gods' expression was prominent in the orator Aelius's accounts of his many dreams.[39] Were the gods looking awesome or joyous, downcast or welcoming? Once again, we can appreciate this concern anew with the help of our Riace bronzes, where the survival of a hero's eyes and teeth has conveyed at last the full potential of a statue's gaze. Like modern beholders, the ancients, too, felt the awe in their gods' expressions: would they have seen only the confidence and optimism in our bronze's mouth and eyes? Perhaps there was no single response, as Yeats well realized: "Pheidias gave women dreams, and dreams their looking-glass . . ." Observer and statue reacted on one another. The recovery of the two bronze heroes has been followed by the recovery of an appropriate text.[40] In the Lycian city of Oenoanda, continuing finds of a huge stone inscription have restored to us an Epicurean's view of the gods and their images in the second century A.D. To contemporaries, Epicureans were "atheists," but this text is true to their founder, Epicurus, when it dwells on the power of images on mortals' ideas of their gods. "Some gods are angry with fortunate men, as the goddess Nemesis seems to be to most people. But the statues of gods should be made cheerful and smiling so that we may smile back at them rather than fear them." The sight of the two Riace bronzes and the awesome gaze of the greater of the pair help us to see what the Epicureans meant.

Other observers, too, were sensitive, Pausanias on his travels, many performing orators and the authors of literary word pictures, describing works of art. Of several examples, the best comes from Syrian Antioch, which housed a magnificent statue of Apollo by the master artist Bryaxis, a colossal image of gold with jewels for eyes. We can still appreciate the upright stance of its Apollo in his long, fluted robe, a bowl in his right hand, a lyre in his left, while the weight is slightly lifted from his right leg: the statue was copied on types of the city's coinage. In 362 A.D., this huge image was destroyed by a fire, and the pagan orator Libanius paid his respects in an emotional speech: "My mind sets its shape before my eyes, the gentleness of form, the tenderness of neck . . . the golden lyre: it seems to sing a song, as somebody once heard it, so they say, playing the lyre at midday . . . Ah, happy ear!"[41]

Colossal statues, too, combined awe with a friendly quality, never more than in the cults of Asclepius. His "far-famed" statue evoked profound emotions, an image into which "the god infused his own powers," wrote the third–century man of letters Callistratus, "and within which the power of the indwelling god is clearly manifest . . . in a marvellous way, it fathers proof that it has a soul. The face, as you look at it, entrances the senses . . ." Callistratus had put into words what thousands had already felt in the god's many shrines.[42] "Continual contemplation" of a divine statue is best detected in the last book of *The Golden Ass*, where the hero, Lucius, gazes daily on the image of his new protectress, the goddess Isis. The quality of this piety has been well emphasized, but it was not so different in kind from the hours of contemplation by many worshippers at the healing shrines or by those who gazed on amulets and carefully fashioned images in order to conjure up visions of a god. The gods came in pocket-sized models, so that anyone could travel with them and keep them handy.

No discussion of this level of "epiphany" can omit the experiences of the best-known client of Asclepius. From the 140s to the 170s, we have a sequence of the divine dreams which the orator Aelius Aristeides recorded in his *Sacred Tales*, and although only five books survive out of many more, they show us this same impact of religious art. Aelius's dreams and inner life have startled many of their readers.[43] They seem like a constant neurosis which is only typical of one verbose and unhappy individual, and indeed, they have a particularly monstrous conceit. They dwell freely on meetings with the Emperor, filling the gap which Artemidorus's sources have left.[44] As if one royal family was not enough, Aelius's dreams rose to dreams of two at once, the Emperor and the reigning king of Parthia, and with them, Aelius, making a speech by special invitation. Not even Alexander the Great was too eminent: "I dreamed that on the right of Pergamum's temple, there was a monument for me and Alexander, divided by a partition . . . he lay on one side, I would lie on the other . . . I rejoiced and reckoned that we both had reached the tops of our professions, he in military, I in rhetorical ability. It occurred to me too that he was very important in Pella and that those here in Pergamum were proud of me too."

Professional orators like Aelius spent their lives on a crippling course of memorizations, perfecting a style and vocabulary while learning the classics by heart. It is not, then, so surprising that Aelius dreamed freely of the classical authors and their presence with him: here, we can match his dreams to those of his literary contemporaries.[45] No more can his dreams of the gods be isolated and analysed as a personal complex. They were reinforced by a culture pattern, and differed in degree, but not kind, from those of the wider public whom Artemidorus had recently been questioning so tirelessly.

Like many literary men, Aelius was of sickly constitution, but his visits to Asclepius's shrine at Pergamum were particularly prolonged. His career as a speaker imposed its own nervous strains, which we should respect and not belittle, and in the *Sacred Tales* he relates his dream experiences of Asclepius and the other gods. The old patterns of language and response run through these tales, as the gods "stand beside" him, "manifest" and often almost tangible. Aelius even dreams that he is dreaming of the gods, in a particularly intense pattern of experience: he knows the intimacy and something, too, of the terror and awe. In a famous passage, we also meet the accompanying emotion of joy: in a good night's dreaming, Aelius noted, the gods would seem marvellously large and beautiful, bathed in the light which befitted them.[46]

Occasionally, the gods did appear in disguise, on the old Homeric model: Hermes once appeared as Plato, and Aelius was quick to detect a god in the form of a mortal acquaintance. On the whole, however, they conformed to their images in art: Asclepius and Serapis in Athens, Hermes and the god Apollo as honoured in Pergamum.[47] Once, dreamed Aelius, he seemed to hold the head of Asclepius in his hands and try to force it to give a nod of assent; the god, however, held his head steady, presumably as he did in his statue. Once, Aelius dreamed that this statue had changed to another type with a downcast expression.[48] Once again, when Aelius lay very near death, Athena herself appeared "as Pheidias had sculpted her," breathing a scent from her "aegis," which looked like wax. Appropriately, her large, beautiful form seemed to quote lines from Homer's *Odyssey* and tell her dying man of letters to "endure." Aelius seemed to feel his body slipping away and to be "conscious of himself as if he was another," yet even at this moment, others in his room, he said, could hear the words which Athena spoke. How Gordian, once again, would have applauded: as his life nearly ended, the orator Aelius dreamed first of the theatre, then of Homer's Athena, quoting the *Odyssey*'s words of encouragement.[49] At another point, he wrote, "I seemed, as it were, to touch Asclepius and to see that the god himself was come, and to be 'between sleeping and waking' and to long to look up and to be in anguish that he might depart too soon and to strain my ears to hear some things as in a dream, others 'in waking reality.' My hair stood straight; there seemed to be tears of joy, and the pride of my heart gave no offence. Who could describe these things in words . . . ?" When Aelius told one of the doctors, his favourite Theodotus, he "marvelled at how divine these dreams really were." He did not think that they needed curing.[50]

So close was the identity of god and statue and the relation of both to Aelius that once "I noticed in a dream a statue of me. At one moment, I saw it as if it were me, and then again it seemed to be a large and beautiful statue of Asclepius." Once, he dreamed that other worshippers were ushered away by Asclepius's statue, but that the god's hand told him to stay. "And I was delighted by the honour and the degree to which I was being preferred and I called out, 'The One and Only,' meaning Asclepius, but he said, 'It is you.'" Dreams reinforced his sense of a special relationship:[51] of all ancient authors, Aelius comes nearest to Sartre's observation that "being seen by another is the truth of seeing another," and to our psychological notion that the "other" may in fact be a projection of the feelings and emotions of the observer.

The proper context for this vivid night life is not our modern myth of "analysis," but the culture pattern which emerges from the solid evidence of votive sculptures and a brilliant series of chapters by Artemidorus. From Northumberland to Syria, Spain to the Black Sea, people continued to put up votive monuments and dedications in response to "warnings" or "visions" of their gods in dreams. A divine dream might motivate a city's "people and council" to a public act: it might encourage a civic dignitary and his wife to revive a divinity's civic cult.[52] Frauds were a recognized hazard, especially in so-called dreams of healing, and people could be quite wary. We have the inscription of a man in North Africa in 283/4 whom the god Saturn had seemed to be "warning" in a dream. Evidently, the man had had his doubts, for he waited till Saturn's "saving help" had proved itself and then he put up the monument which he had vowed, dedicating it "in return for having found faith."[53] The tradition of these dreams could survive a considerable degree of wariness and minor scepticism, not least because it was supported by cases of divine anger: people who neglected a dream might be chastened and then make due amends. The dreams could be as complex as anything in Aelius's tales. Like one devotee of Serapis (c. 50 A.D.), people might "receive" tokens from their gods, written letters, even, which they "found" next morning and read for advice on achieving their ends and excelling their rivals.[54] Not every sighting had a known origin in art: at Pergamum, a female hymn singer honoured Night, Initiation and Chance "in accordance with a dream"; other people in Pergamum honoured Virtue, Self-control, Faith and Concord, while one town council and citizenry in Thrace commemorated the pagan Most High god.[55] Had they seen these abstractions in person, and if so, had artistic traditions helped them to focus what they saw? We only have their monuments, hints at a lost experience.

We cannot "analyse" these dreams, not least because their cultural setting was so different from our own. Art and statuary, Homer, the poets and polytheism, ideas of the gods as "friends" and "helpers": these patterns made the gods a frequent company to people of all classes, of whom Aelius only happens to be the most articulate. In Artemidorus's terms, his dream of Athena would have been highly favourable.[56] It was seen by a man of high position, well educated and suited, therefore, for a dream of an Olympian god who was quoting poetry. Athena had come as a friend, with her proper attributes: her aegis looked "like wax," but it was not waxen, a bad omen, as it would have suggested magic. Meanwhile, other clients, known to Artemidorus, hint at a range of dreams of divinities, beside which Aelius's take a modest place.[57] To dream of Artemis, said Artemidorus, with no clothes on was most inauspicious: the myths supported that conclusion. Aphrodite was more ambiguous: if you saw her topless, said Artemidorus, that was a good omen, but a full frontal view was only auspicious for prostitutes. As for sex with the gods, that was a fine dream, so long as it was not sex with any of six goddesses from Artemis to Hecate. Sex with Aphrodite was pro-pitious, but the act alone was not enough: it also mattered whether or not the dreamer thought he had enjoyed it.

Behind the portrait busts of Antonine dignitaries and the family trees which wind through their cities' inscriptions lies this nighttime company, enjoyed with the gods. Men of all ranks saw them and heard them: the higher their class, the better their omen. They seemed to touch them and they even dared to go to bed with them. Historians have been slow to restore this night life to the men whom they study for administrative careers. As night fell, they recaptured the lost ideal of Phaeacia and the pre-Homeric past. If we miss this nightly screening of the gods, we reduce pagan religiousness to a "paganism" of cult acts, brightened only by personal cults which appealed to the emotions and made their worshippers "new." We also miss the level at which the people of Miletus had been startled by their gods.

If Chariton's romance matches the Lystrans, Artemidorus gives the context for Alexandra's question. The gods had been "standing beside" the Milesians "with great clarity": exactly these words were used by Artemidorus when he described how Apollo had inspired him to his great work. These "visitations" were not open encounters by daylight, but nightly visits in dreams. The gods had not retreated in the age of the unified mind: was this outbreak in Miletus really the sign of a new and anxious "exaltation"? Ultimately, perhaps, the city's statuary was to blame, and then the dreams spread, for dreams are as catching as measles. One mother dreamed, perhaps, of a god and told her children; they dreamed too, and so did her husband, the family next door and the boys and girls at school. What did it all mean? they wanted to know. Apollo related it to Homeric habits of the gods. In a dream, the sight of a god was not necessarily dangerous, because he came of his own choosing in a manageable, visual form. He was not surprised against his will or seen in disguise, spying on human wickedness, that idea of Homeric divinity which had persisted from Homer to the Emperor Julian.

This long tour of the various levels in pagan "epiphanies" has emphasized how much endured since Homer's age. Between life and literature, there was not a divide but a mutual relationship, in which the one, as so often, enhanced the other. One of the finest studies of later Greek piety has stressed Plato's role as the "father of Hellenistic religion."[58] This judgement considered religion to be a personal quest for God, a theme of which we do hear more in the works of Plato and which passed, under the Empire, into the devotional literature of the Thrice-great Hermes. Plato, in another sense, was not the most prolific parent. His Socrates had ridiculed the visits of gods in human form and dubbed them a mischievous notion of Homer, but Homer and the patterns which lay behind him survived such criticism. The revived Platonism of the second and third centuries accepted the visible appearances of gods as a fact to be courted and explained. Long after Constantine, a Platonist like Proclus was denying the opinions of Socrates and defending Homer's grasp of the varying levels of epiphanies in a brilliant combination of this chapter's themes. Reinforced by art, Homer and the Homeric "visitations" fathered many more children than Plato's contemplation of God.

To cover these examples in art and fiction, poetry and life, is also to restore a sense of what the early Christians faced. "What is clear," a fine theological study of visions concluded, "is that Christianity came into a world tantalized by a belief that some men at least had seen God and had found in the vision the sum of human happiness, a world aching with the hope that the same vision was attainable by all."[59] The opposite, in fact, was true. Pagans kept nightly company with their gods and those who sported in dreams with Aphrodite needed no new route to heaven. Among pagans, these "visits" were freely enjoyed, and there was no restraining orthodoxy, no priestly authority which restricted the plain man's access to a nightly contact with the gods. Art and the long centuries of literature had combined with myth and the general setting of its stories to contain these visions in harmless traditional forms. Their beneficiaries took no stand against authority and did not claim to know better than their civic leaders in the matter of pleasing the gods. The divine dreams of Artemidorus and his friends sounded no call for reform or orthodoxy and took no interest in history. In Artemidorus's sample, they were not concerned to take men on a tour of the next world or to menace them with fears of what might happen after death. Dreams did predict people's imminent end and its manner, but visions of the next world and its torments were most prominent in philosophic dialogues and perhaps in the theologies of small religious groups. Many people dismissed them, the absurd inventions of women and children.[60]

Among pagans, visions and dreams continued to spread new cults to new places, seldom with missionary fervour, but nonetheless without the intervention of priests or a religious hierarchy. The old Homeric ideal of the "close encounter" still haunted men as a possibility, while the myths and the living tradition of a Golden Age sustained the belief that the gods might one day return quite openly, if only men would lay aside their own injustice and wickedness. These beliefs had their own subtleties, without any scripture to enforce them. Among pagans, too, "blessed are the pure in heart," from Homer through Callimachus to the Hermetists and Iamblichus, "for they shall see God." "Your sons and your daughters shall prophesy," in Miletus as in Joel's Israel, "while your young men shall see visions and your old men shall dream dreams."

The Christians could not deny this. The "visits" were based on observable experience, not poetic convention, and if we had to choose one region in the second and third centuries where the evidence was most undeniable and the conventions reflected life, it would have to be Egypt, from Thebes to the Upper Cataract. There, stretched a land of immemorial antiquity whose temples and cults had the great prestige of history. In their temples, the priest still saw the gods: equipment for these sightings continued to be listed in their shrines' inventories.[61] Outside the temples, people turned to the experts for spells, but the epilogue to all epiphanies in this period is best found in a broken monument, the colossus which stood in the Valley of the Kings. An earthquake had unsettled this old, enormous statue in the first century A.D., and before long, its Greek visitors began to notice how the stonework gave off a sound.[62] The statue, they believed, was their own Memnon, with whom they had connected the Pharaohs' necropolis. By the later first century, visitors heard Memnon's voice in the statue's whisper. From far and wide they came to hear it, hard-bitten Roman soldiers, women, men of letters, the Emperor Hadrian and his entourage. There was no formal cult of Memnon and no oracles are known to have been sought from his voice. The Egyptians have left no evidence of any interest in the topic among all the material on the site. The statue was a wonder for Greeks and Romans only, a whispered intimation of their hero's presence. Sometimes he spoke and sometimes he was silent: Hadrian's followers had to visit twice before they heard him.

Those who heard carved their names and testimony on Memnon's vociferous remains. They went to infinite pains.[63] It was not enough to place an inscription on the statue's lower foot: we can see one such "first shot" recarved at a second attempt, higher up. For the visitors wished to carve their names on the side where they would bask forever in the rising sun, the hour at which Memnon spoke, while bathed in the light of dawn. In the year 122, one Charisius recorded his satisfaction and carved his memorial in east-facing sunlight: "I had heard as a child of the speaking ship Argo and of the whispering oak of Zeus. But only here have I seen and heard for myself." Further south, by the Nile Cataract, we can match these texts with inscriptions which run on a temple to the god Mandulis, set at the frontier post of Talmis. In this puzzling divinity, Greek visitors saw a form of their own Sun god. As in the Valley of the Kings, so here at distant Talmis they experienced his presence, seeing him in the sudden beams of early sun. Here, too, their inscriptions covered the temple's east-facing wall in order to catch the moment when the god revealed his power in the early morning light. Who were the Christians to deny these epiphanies? Memnon continued to speak throughout the Antonine and Severan period until his stones, we believe, slipped slightly and took away his voice. Mandulis drew pilgrims throughout the entire third century, people who recorded their particular moment, "today, I have seen," in a flash of personal joy.[64] The two experiences have been contrasted, as if Mandulis, seen in the sunlight, was the true piety, while Memnon, heard at dawn, was only a traveller's curiosity. Memnon was honoured in literary verses: "*Le vrai dieu du Colosse,*" concluded their editor, "*n'était pas Memnon, mais Homère.*" The distinction is rather too sharp. All we have seen, from Homer to Miletus, reminds us how literary language reflected and enhanced the experience of life. If men wrote like Homer on Memnon's upper body, they did so because the Homeric language best did justice to the "presence" which they wished to record. From the epics to Egypt's epiphanies, less had changed for most people's religious life than historians have tended to believe. At Mandulis's shrine, one Maximus inscribed a metrical *tour de force*, describing how he had dreamed that he was bathing in the Nile and hearing the song of the Muses: then the god Mandulis stood forward with Isis, and Maximus was inspired to write Greek without barbaric errors. After reading Artemidorus's researches, how can we be so sure that this "vision" is only a literary convention, unsupported by experience? Its metre was no more ambitious than many oracles which nobody would call a literary fiction. At Talmis, the gods were seen in the sunlight; in the Valley of the Kings, a hero could be heard at dawn; everywhere, by night, the gods crossed the open frontier with the world of men. We have restored to the Christians' contemporaries their visions and sightings, beliefs beside their ceremonies. It remains to tune our other senses and catch their gods as they spoke from their shrines.

# 5. Language
# of the Gods

An east-facing aspect, bathed in the dawn, was not peculiar to Egypt's piety. It made old Memnon speak; it revealed the sun god at Talmis. Throughout the ancient world, it was the holiest aspect for anyone's prayers. Pythagoras and Socrates were thought to have prayed to the east, as were the contemplative Jews whom Philo described in first-century Egypt. Wise men in India were said to favour prayers at dawn, a habit which was shared by the elephant. From India to Africa, elephants were believed to honour the rising sun: in sixth-century Byzantium, beasts which had been captured from Persia would bow to the east when they filed past a church. Then they made the sign of the Cross with their trunks, an amazing fact, which, said John of Ephesus, "we have often seen with our own eyes." From their Jewish origins, Christians inherited the gesture, and Tertullian complained that the Christians were misunderstood because they turned to the east and prayed at dawn. Pagans sometimes believed that they were worshipping the sun.[1]

In the late second or third century, prayer to the east found an unexpected home which leads us directly to the language of the gods. The small city of Oenoanda lies in the Lycian uplands of southwestern Asia Minor and remains one of the best-preserved witnesses to the spread of civic life in the Hellenistic age. By the year 200, the men of Oenoanda had their squares and colonnades, a well-cut theatre, an imposing set of baths and a shrine to Asclepius which a successful doctor had donated.[2] Through the city's centre ran a "vast wayside pulpit of stone" which was the gift of a certain Diogenes. Its blocks were faced with a textbook statement of the Epicurean philosophy which contemporaries often reviled for its atheist views.[3] In his old age, Diogenes bequeathed it, a hundred yards long, "for the salvation of men, present and future." "The philosopher," it told his fellow citizens, "does not want the power and authority of Alexander." Men must "realize what disasters have befallen others through the ambiguity and intricacy of oracles' replies." On a recent estimate, some twenty thousand words of text remain to be found, but the search for them has not been easy. By the 260s, Diogenes's heirs were pulling his sermon to pieces and using the stones for rebuilding their city's walls. Parts of it ended up in their west gate. Not everyone agreed with their donor's faith in Epicurus, and on the value of oracles, we have recently learnt, there were those in the city who disagreed.

At a steep point of approach to the outer circuit of their walls, men in Oenoanda chose a block of the Hellenistic masonry and shaped its central boss into the outline of an altar. They cut four lines of hexameter verse onto this altar's face and allowed two more to spread into the smoothed space below. The stone stood high to the right of a doorway which led back into one of their wall's defensive towers and looked out over a sharp drop below the wall. It was noticed, however, and copied by the early modern travellers in Lycia, but it was not understood until a second inspection was risked from the end of a rope in 1966.[4] Since then, study of the text has continued at the highest level.[5] In this primary home of Epicurean wisdom, we now have words from a god on the city wall, which run in hexameter verse as follows:

> Self-born, untaught, motherless, unshakeable,
> Giving place to no name, many-named, dwelling in fire,
> Such is God: we are a portion of God, his angels.
> This, then, to the questioners about God's nature
> The god replied, calling him all-seeing Ether: to him, then, look
> And pray at dawn, looking out to the east.

The text had been carefully sited. It was carved high on the wall's northeast aspect at a point which catches the first dawn sunlight along the rise and fall of the perimeter. The site was suited to the message of the god.

Two courses of stone below the text stood a second altar with a ledge for a lamp.[6] It was dedicated to the Most High god by Chromatis, a female name which tended to be borne by former slaves or their children. At Oenoanda, paganism takes a novel turn and it begins to seem as if all religions flow eventually to similar themes. Unshakeable, without one name, an all-seeing god was master of the angels, while beneath stood a lamp for the hours of darkness. Like Zoroastrian villagers in far-off Persia, people in Oenoanda rose early in the half–light to tend a flame and pray to the east, while the sunlight struck the text on their city wall. The text described God in a style which Jews and Christians could well understand. The inscription is not unduly handsome and it is only one among the many which survive elsewhere on matters of religion. However, it deserves its fame. Its implications have been brilliantly studied, but its origin and vocabulary can still be explored with profit. They are a thread to pagan oracles, in each of which we can hear the gods.

The language of Oenoanda's text has a precise and familiar origin. It begins with a burst of negative theology which defines God by what he is not. These definitions were a commonplace among Platonist philosophers in the early Imperial period. The vocabulary was characteristic of hymns and the higher theology and we can match most of its language. "Self–born," or "natural," had already been used of a god in classical Greek tragedy;[7] "motherless" is a less frequent epithet than "fatherless," but Galen used it for the First Principle and the Emperor Julian applied it to the mother of the gods. In the first century A.D., Philo was familiar with the word's philosophic use in these same contexts.[8] "Giving place to no name, many–named . . .": this type of paradox was as old as Heraclitus's philosophy (c. 500 B.C.) and is well attested in pagan hymns and theology by the first century A.D.[9] Among philosophers, we would expect these high epithets to apply to a Supreme god, placed beyond this world. The fifth line, however, called God "all–seeing Ether," while the second said that he dwelt in fire. This equation was not, in itself, unphilosophic, although we might have expected a higher name for God himself. Aristotle had added a fifth element, Ether, to Plato's fourth, Fire, and in the second century A.D., several Platonists reconciled the two views "by a certain sleight of hand." The Stoics had eased the merger, and the result was so familiar that Artemidorus listed "Ethereal Fire" among the major Olympian gods.[10] The mention of "angels" raises no problem in a pagan context. Angels occur freely in pagan cults of abstract divinities in Asia Minor;[11] however, the tone of this text suggests that it had derived the word from school theology. Platonists used it for the intermediaries between gods and men, while Aelius the orator told how Athena "sits by her father and gives orders to the *angeloi*," or lesser gods.

A Platonist of the second or third century might well have been speaking in the first three verses. In fact, says the text, they were the words of a god. In a brilliant study, they were promptly traced to a further context, the books of two Christian authors.[12] Shortly before the year 500, the unknown author of ten Christian books, *On True Belief*, quoted a pagan oracle which contained these lines at its further end. It had been given, he said, "to Theophilus" when he asked, "Who or what is God?" Earlier, the Christian author Lactantius had quoted the opening lines in the first book of his *Divine Institutes*, which he composed, c. 308, shortly before Constantine's conversion. He made one Christian alteration in the text's theology and claimed that these lines were the "beginning" of a twenty-one-line text in which a god was agreeing with the Christians. One of the lines earned a third Christian mention, in the work of John Malalas. In the sixth century, he quoted a text which was supposed to be the Delphic oracle's answer to the Pharaoh of Egypt when he asked, "Who is the first among the gods and the great God of Israel?" The text, alleged Malalas sportingly, "was inscribed on stone and still preserved in the temple at Memphis." He had no idea of its origin and his text was an obvious pastiche, but it contained the old phrase on the gods as "angels," a "part" of God.[13]

Lactantius had been more accurate. The text, he said, had been given by "Apollo at Colophon" when somebody asked him, "Who is God?" Here, Lactantius was probably following the pagan Porphyry, who had recently published a work called *Philosophy from Oracles*.[14] In its preface he had stressed the importance of citing the exact words of the gods, and if Lactantius borrowed them, his view of their origin deserves to be trusted.

Problems remain about the full nature of the response. Lactantius quoted these lines as the "beginning" of twenty-one lines of verse, but the author of *On True Belief* gave a text in which they stood at the end. His text should perhaps be divided into two: an answer to Theophilus and a separate answer which the Oenoandans received, other pieces of which can then be recovered from verses elsewhere in his book.[15] For our purposes, its origin is more relevant. "Apollo at Colophon" is the god of the great oracular shrine at Claros, a major seat of the gods' wisdom in the second and third centuries which we have come to know through excavation and finds of inscriptions. With their help, we can recapture the course of a consultation, for the ruins of the site support our best ancient description, a paragraph by Iamblichus, written in the early fourth century. He was not writing from personal experience, but he had found a good authority.[16]

Visitors to the temple at Claros entered the sacred valley and approached through the big triple gate which stood before the shrine. Beyond it stretched the sacred grove, where now there is only dust, and a hundred yards or so to the north stood the altar and Doric temple of Apollo. The approaches were lined with statues on stone bases, many of which were statues of Romans from the late Republican age. The altar was enormous, as were the colossal statues of Apollo, Artemis and Leto, up to twenty feet high, who made a family grouping in the shrine itself. On coins, we can see the particular type of Apollo, a huge half-naked divinity, seated at ease, whose right hand holds laurel and whose left rests on a lyre.

The god, we are told, was questioned by night, although not every night was fit for an inquiry. While visitors waited for a sacred night to fall, they were prepared for the process which lay ahead. At the beginning of the second century A.D., we know only of a "prophet" in the inscriptions which have so far been published. This single spokesman fits the picture of the oracle which was drawn by the historian Tacitus, himself a governor of Asia, and thus able, if he wished, to learn about the site.[17] A priest, he said, was chosen from a fixed number of families and "generally summoned from Miletus." This priest heard only the number and the names of the consultants; then he went down into a "cave" and drank the sacred water. Although he was "generally ignorant of letters and poetry," he gave responses in verse on the "topics which each questioner had in mind." We know nothing of the priest's despatch from Miletus to Claros in the inscriptions which survive: Miletus, however, had its own vast oracular shrine where citizens served as prophets and played an important role, as we shall see, as poets of the god's words. To date, the inscriptions confirm Tacitus's picture of a single male attendant at his time of writing. Tacitus implies that the man's method of answering was something of a miracle, and we must try to account for it. If the priest did not ask for his questioners' questions, his verse responses can only have been general and rather stereotyped. Perhaps the god kept to certain familiar verses and "inspired" his priest to utter one or other set. One hostile visitor, Oenomaus the Cynic, called at the site, perhaps c. 120 A.D., and alleged that the same obscure verses were given out to different questioners.[18] It may be wrong to trust him too closely, but his picture does fit neatly with the implication of Tacitus's words.

By the mid-130s, however, the inscriptions reveal a change. The prophet is joined by a "thespode," or "singer of oracles," and unlike the prophet, this thespode serves for life.[19] He brought a greater expertise, and by the time of the Oenoandans' visit, the giving of oracles was split between a prophet, a thespode and a secretary. There was also a priest: how, then, are they likely to have shared out the work?

Iamblichus tells us that "many religious rites" were performed before the god was consulted. A sacrifice on the great altar was surely one of them, and the natural official for this rite was the priest. We know, too, from inscriptions that some of the visitors were initiated into a mystery rite, apparently as a preliminary to the consultation. As elsewhere, these rites would involve expense: one leader of a city's delegation assisted the initiation of all the young choirboys whom he led, "out of love of honour and the god," and presumably he paid the bill himself. These secret rites greatly enhanced the occasion.[20] Meanwhile, the envoys were waiting for the appointed night, and while they waited, they talked. No doubt they talked to the priest and the secretary and probably to the thespode, too, telling them about their city and their problems, and starting the simple process by which a good counselling service works. They gave away enough to suggest an answer before they asked the question for which they had come. The temple staff listened innocently and so, therefore, did Apollo. There was no conscious fraud, no insincerity. Mortals could not bother gods without preparation, as a god would rebuke a questioner who asked too abruptly for too much. As the night approached, the prophet himself was absent. Iamblichus tells us that he fasted for a day and a night before the consultation began, and he also tells us of his withdrawal to "shrines untrodden by the crowds," where he abstained from human business and prepared himself to receive the god "untarnished."[21] He seems to refer to something more than the prophet's retirement at the moment of consultation. For twenty-four hours, then, the prophet had been out of sight, fasting, praying and freeing himself from the bother of the world. Iamblichus claims that he had already begun to be "enthused" by the god, but he may be elaborating the time of inspiration in order to suit his particular argument.

When the sacred night fell and the lamps had been lit in the sanctuary, the staff and the questioners met by torchlight before Apollo's Doric temple. Above them loomed the colossal statues of the gods. The prophet reappeared, and together they prepared for the journey to Apollo's inner shrine. Some of the visitors' inscriptions mention that they had "entered"; Tacitus and Iamblichus knew

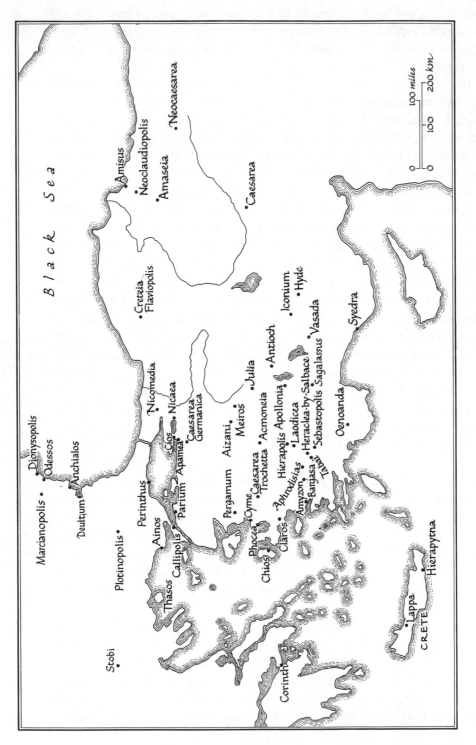

*Client cities of the oracle at Claros,*
*attested in the Greek East during the Imperial period*

nothing of this experience, but the "entering" or "crossing of the threshold" was evidently an extra ceremony which only a few of the clients chose.[22] On the evidence to date, those who "entered" were also among those who underwent mystery rites.

If others refused, they could be forgiven, for we have now learnt from the archaeologists what the word implied. By the light of torches, the prophet and thespode and perhaps the secretary stooped into one of the two low tunnels which ran underground to Apollo's sacred spring. They bent themselves for a journey through a low, narrow corridor which was roofed in marble of a deep shade of midnight blue. The corridor ran for some thirty yards and changed direction seven times before it stopped at the door of two underground chambers. Here was Tacitus's "cavern," vaulted suitably in stone. The sides of the first room were fitted with stone benches and housed an "omphalos," or navel stone, of deep blue marble, like the famous omphalos at Delphi. It signified to visitors that they had reached the oracular centre of the earth.

A narrow corridor led from the first chamber to the second room, where the god kept his sacred spring. The spring survived to reward its French excavators only thirty years ago, for the water table is high at Claros, and its rise now hampers access to the tunnels. The prophet, we must assume, passed into this inner chamber. Iamblichus states clearly that the prophet, not the thespode, drank the water, and on this point, too, we must follow him.[23] He helps us to make sense of their relationship. The prophet had not eaten for a whole day, and was primed by his rites and his hours of isolation. Whenever he drinks the god's water, says Iamblichus, he "is not in control of himself and does not follow what he is saying or where he is, so that he finds it hard to recover himself even after uttering his oracle." Was this inspired utterance really cast immediately in neat iambic verse? Some of the surviving oracles are metrical tours de force and they make this notion impossible. There was, after all, a thespode. First came the incoherent sounds of inspiration, induced by the solemn occasion and the expectations which surrounded the sip of Apollo's water. Then came a second, ordered voice, the voice of the thespode, or "singer of oracles," who put into intricate verses the basic message which Apollo had inspired. The thespode had had a day or more in which to reflect and to listen to his questioners' news. By divine insight, Apollo's verses neatly matched the problem in hand.

Questioners who had stayed above ground heard these sounds at a distance as they echoed through the underground corridors of stone. If they were sitting in the antechamber, they had the thrill of a closer proximity. Perhaps the secretary sat with them on the benches, taking down the thespode's version in the recently developed skill of shorthand before the words had slipped from human memory. Together again, the temple staff and their clients branched off down a second tunnel and turned seven times through a similar maze of midnight blue. Then they emerged into the sacred night, the blaze of torches and the lingering smoke of incense.

Such was the consultation which lay behind the words on Oenoanda's wall. The "questioners," surely, were people from Oenoanda, not distant questioners whose answer happened to be known to people inside the city. They had gone to Claros armed with an intriguing question: "What is the nature of God?" The prophet muttered, the thespode took up the challenge in verses of the best oracular theology which was known to his age. It is in oracles, too, that we can match it: "unshakeable" is a word known in another oracle's text, while the nearest parallel to the first two lines are verses in a "Sibylline" oracle, which a Jewish author had composed in Greek, probably around the turn of our era.[24] The questioners returned with twenty-one lines of oracular wisdom, which they shortened into a manageable text. They then inscribed six lines where an arched doorway led back to a tower in their outer wall. It was not the neatest of inscriptions and its site was sheer and inaccessible. But it basked on its altar in the morning sun.

Did the city approve their despatch, and if so, when did it send them? The answers remain uncertain. The city's wall was abandoned in favour of a smaller inner circuit and the date of this change is probably the 260s A.D. Did a private group of questioners inscribe the oracle in the 270s when the outer wall had gone out of public use?[25] It is notable, however, that no other text was cut into this wall's facing and that the oracle was rather special. It was placed carefully for its relation to the rising sun. The shape of the lettering does not establish a firm date, but the years around 200 have been proposed for their form: in the 270s, the text would be a great rarity, one of the only inscriptions to survive from any Greek city in Asia at this period. The text's language suits either date, but on balance, the earlier is preferable, when it fits with the well-known "epigraphic habit" of the age. Then, other cities displayed in public the results of their journeys to Claros. They put up Apollo's texts on their public squares and temples or obeyed his orders and put the image of "archer Apollo" above their gates, like a holy icon, to protect them in times of plague.[26] Diogenes had already given a huge text of philosophy to Oenoanda: visitors to Apollo then brought the gods' own view of the nature of God. An oracle raised the tone of the place, and although the inscription was quite modest, it is easier to suppose that the city's authorities had approved the reworking of a single block, so carefully sited in their city's outer wall. Later, Chromatis added her lamp below it and inscribed her small altar to the Most High god, in full awareness of the text above: perhaps she identified its "all-seeing god" with the Most High god whom she worshipped in a local pagan cult. By then, perhaps, the wall was no longer the city's public defence, and she walked to the old perimeter to tend her lamp beside a former tower.

As a text for one city, the inscription is of great interest. Once again, it takes us beyond a city's cults to beliefs which could animate pagans' actions. People dreamed of the gods and sensed their presence, but over and above their cult acts, they could ply them with theological questions. In answer, they could receive a text of divine wisdom, echoing the views which their philosophers liked to teach. They could discuss it or contest it, feel proud of it, inscribe it and obey its clear commands. How unusual, though, was this type of advice?

By a happy chance, we can trace Apollo's influence beyond the wall of this one remote city. In the second and the early third century, his shrine at Claros drew delegations from a far wider network who acquired a fortunate habit on arrival.[27] They arranged for their names to be inscribed and their visits dated wherever there was space on the shrine's blocks of marble. During the second century, the site turned into an archive for any researcher on civic and religious life, for inscriptions ran everywhere, on the statue bases, on four of the steps which led up to the temple, on the very columns of the temple and its Doric façade. Some three hundred texts have now been recovered, and although they are not yet published in full, enough has appeared during the past seventy years to make Claros the centre on which views of pagan worship in the Greek East during the Antonine and the early Severan period can be firmly based. The earliest civic inscription which has so far been reported is a record of envoys from Perinthus on the Sea of Marmara whose visit falls late in the reign of Trajan, perhaps around 110 A.D. The texts tend to date themselves by the years of the shrine's officers, but their system of dating has been unravelled and we now know that the surviving inscriptions extend to a date around 205 A.D.

The major cities of mainland Greece and old Ionia are almost entirely absent from the client cities who chose to inscribe their names.[28] These clients extended widely: west, in a year of crisis, to Stobi in Macedonia, south to certain cities inland in Caria, north to the northern coast of the Black Sea, quite often to Thrace, to the cities of Pontus and, here and there, to places in Phrygia and Cilicia. The delegations came mostly from the lesser or more recent centres of Greek city culture: Oenoanda was keeping appropriate company. Usually, they lacked an oracular cult of their own and any connection with Delphi or Miletus at the time of their foundation, and so they turned to Claros, rather than to these old, alternative shrines. In most years, cities sent envoys who inscribed their names and left us proof of their religious pilgrimage. The picture is even better than that.[29] The envoys often came with a choir from their city, a choir of boys or of boys and girls, so that we can watch the musical children of these cities coming again and again to hymn the god. A walk to Apollo's great temple was a high point in childhood for these groups of singers. Sometimes, they were a batch of seven singers, or nine, or twelve, numbers which were pleasing to the god. Off they set from their city with their distinguished "sacred envoys," their choirmasters or hymn teachers and their *paidonomos* (or "tutor"). Sometimes, too, they took their cities' local poets, minor names in the history of Greek literature who had nonetheless won fame and prizes at the many contests and recitations in the Antonine age, unsuspected talents like Permissos, son of Nothippos, prize-winning poet and teacher of hymns by appointment "for life," who visited Claros persistently in the mid-second century, a man with the name of a poetic river on the Muses' mountain. His job passed to his son, Permissos, who reached his city's council and in the 170s described himself as "poet extraordinary" from Laodicea on the Lycos.[30]

Within these small choirs for Apollo, we can watch the intricate family relationships, as brothers and sisters travelled together: several choirboys were sons of prominent fathers who travelled, too, as the hymnodes or city delegates. Choir service ran proudly in these families who passed it from father to son, and included men of great position in their home cities. Often, the trip to Claros was a long, lonely walk of many hours' duration through mountainous country. More distant clients sent envoys, but not a choir, and in the nearer delegations, the fathers were probably glad to be travelling, too, and seeing that their children came to no harm. The "tutors" and attendants would be men over forty years old, who were supposed to know how to control themselves on a lengthy walk with choirboys.

We can also watch the careers of the children who attended Claros's shrine, beginning as choirboys, then passing on with age and occasionally returning later as choir leaders and delegates. Some of them came again and again, fifteen, twenty-nine, even thirty-three times, according to the inscriptions of two modest Carian cities, from which two fathers came to Claros at least twenty-nine times, their sons at least fifteen times, making their families the best-attested pilgrims in the pagan world. Hymns and oracles were a way of life for these people, men who led their delegations on a long annual walk and needed no "higher" religion to satisfy their needs. Some cities chose a "priest of the children" from among their eligible youth, and the choirboys of our later inscriptions grew into the civic notables of the years of Gordian's reign: they would not readily desert a past in which they had walked to Apollo, shuffled, cleared their throats and sung him the hymns of their local poet.

Once, we can watch a former choirboy's progress from Claros to the very edges of the Empire. During the reign of Hadrian, T. Statilius Solon visited Apollo in the choir of his Carian city, Heraclea-by-Salbace, a place which was a keen, almost a yearly, client of Claros. Afterwards, T. Statilius Solon passed into the ranks of the Roman army, and almost certainly he is the same Statilius Solon whom we can detect as a centurion in an army inscription on Hadrian's Wall in Britain. He is obviously the Statilius Solon who honoured a dead friend in a Greek and Latin inscription from Brigetio on the Danube. He had carried his memories of Apollo from Claros to the borders of Scotland and the banks of the Danube River.[31] We must allow for the presence of these Clarian "old boys" when we find their Apollo being consulted by distant cities or by an army unit on Hadrian's Wall. At one stage in life, they had walked and sung: they knew the words of Apollo's hymns and grew up trusting the shrine where once they had honoured the god.

Apollo at Claros was consulted not only by civic delegations.[32] We meet individual questioners in our texts, a nephew of the Emperor, a Cynic philosopher, a merchant from Pontus, the orator Aelius's helper and, in fiction, the parents of two young lovers, puzzled by the causes of their apparent "sickness": the Clarian god's oracle is central to the plot of a novel by Xenophon, composed c. 150–250. A certain Symmachus and his sons consulted Apollo about the health of their crops and inscribed his answer at Yaliniz-Serai, in northeastern Phrygia.[33] Perhaps Claros's Apollo can now be detected farther south. Just to the west of the Euphrates, in the Kurdish mountains, his advice may have reached a valley of ancient royal monuments. A steep hill overlooks the shrines of the kings of Commagene and a fine Roman bridge: on its slope, one Candidus re-erected and inscribed an "age-old altar" on the advice of "Apollo's immortal prophecies" and set up a statue of Zeus the king.[34] Candidus was a victorious Roman general who served in the Eastern campaigns of 195 A.D., and Apollo, perhaps, was the Clarian, whose advice was so often sought on statues and restorations elsewhere. If so, the site is the wildest and most spectacular of any which has preserved his advice.

At Claros itself, no texts of Apollo's oracles have been found. We know, however, that there was a record office, and in the burial ground of nearby Notium, we have the epitaph of one Gorgos, honouring him as "elderly and very bookish" and referring to him "culling" the "page of the singers." The text, datable c. 150–110 B.C., has been well explained as a tribute to a prophet at Claros who had gathered up the "pages" of previous oracular poets at the shrine.[35] They were surely kept on the site in some perishable form: in the second or third century A.D., one Cornelius Labeo could quote an oracle's text in his book *On the Oracle of Clarian Apollo*.[36] He can hardly have toured the client cities in order to find his verses, although it is in the client cities that we still find them on stone, sometimes with their questioner's name before Apollo's verses. Durable inscribed texts from Claros derive from the client cities, not the shrine itself: the words on Oenoanda's wall are true to this epigraphic pattern.

While Christians travelled to the Holy Land and marvelled at God's wrath against the Jews,[37] pagan choirs were travelling yearly to Claros, to sing and to see their delegates "enter" the temple tunnels. However, the ceremonies at Claros were not unique. There were other famous oracles in Asia, but none larger or more famous than the temple of Didyma, which stood outside Miletus, city of the visiting gods. This gigantic shrine had recovered from the disorders of the late Republic and had promptly started a pattern of inscriptions which forms a pair with those at Claros. Not only did the god's questioners inscribe some of their questions and answers in the precinct and the adjacent territory of the city. Since the early 30s B.C., Apollo's prophets took to inscribing their names and careers on a newly constructed Doric building which stood in Didyma's sanctuary.[38] Like the visitors to Claros, they cut their names all over its surface, on the walls, the columns and its decorations. While Claros flourished, Didyma persisted, two seats of Apollo whose stones have left a sample of the language of the gods.

We know of no rivalry between the two shrines, but there were certain differences. At Claros, Apollo was made visible in a huge, half-naked statue of late Hellenistic style, urbane, relaxed and at ease with his lyre. At Didyma, he was represented in the most widely travelled holy image of Greek history.[39] Back in the archaic age, shortly before 500 B.C., the sculptor Kanachos had cast an Apollo in bronze for the shrine. Naked, the god held a bow in his left hand and a stag in his right, which could be moved by an artful mechanism. The god's hair and expression had the stiffness of the pre-classical age, and at Didyma, this image had a special veneer of history. In 494 B.C., the Persians had removed it to Susa after their sack of the city: in the wake of Alexander's conquests, it was kindly returned by King Seleucus, Apollo's protégé. Five centuries later, in the Imperial period, it still stood at Didyma's altar beside the temple, an archaic image which had the venerable awe of a travel to Persia and gave a curious, old-fashioned shape to Apollo's form.

At the two oracles, the patrons of the surviving inscribed texts also vary. At Claros, they are the delegations of cities. At Didyma, in the Imperial period, cities did continue to consult the god,[40] but all but one of the inscribed oracular texts are answers to individuals, most of whom are known as Milesian priests or members of the prophets' families. Not all were Milesians by origin. One of the prophets had come from Cyzicus, a city which had consulted the god, while a curious inscription refers to another prophet who was "summoned by the god" and promised and performed many generous duties for Miletus and its cults.[41] The man was a doctor, Pomponius Pollio, a Roman kinsman, evidently, of two namesakes who were governors of Asia in 151/2 and 167/8. How did the god's "summons" come about? The first move, presumably, was made by Pollio, one of several Roman senators at this period who were drawn to the oracles of Greek Asia. In return for his office, he "promised" valuable work on the site's buildings and Sacred Way: his offer, perhaps, was referred to Apollo for approval, and so the god "called" this stranger to his service. The duties were very expensive, and at Didyma, too, we find

the familiar compound of "volunteering" and a shortage of candidates, attested intermittently in the second and third centuries. Some
prophets, therefore, were particularly proud of their service and
generosity: their exceptional concern was sometimes approved by
Apollo himself, encouraging them all the more to inscribe their names
and honours on the site.

Apollo's language at Didyma did not differ noticeably from his
language at Claros. At Didyma, he gave a prominent benefactor of the
province of Asia some solemn phrases on holy Dawn and the Supreme
god, calling him "leader of Ethereal Fire."[42] The text belonged in or
before the 140s A.D., and a few decades later, Claros gave the
Oenoandans verses which touched on similar themes. The shrines'
agreement was not surprising. Although Miletus no longer staffed
Claros, the thespodes and prophets of the two shrines shared the same
education. They tended, however, to prefer different metres. At
Didyma, almost all Apollo's surviving answers are cast in hexameters.
At Claros, he also used hexameters, but sometimes he broke into
iambics or more complex metrical forms.[43]

The method of consultation also differed. At Didyma, the god
inspired a woman, his prophetess, but she was attended by a prophet,
whose career usually included civic service in Miletus. Once again, we
owe our best description of a consultation to Iamblichus, whose
words must be pictured against the ruined site. Questioners could not
intrude on Apollo whenever they wished. In the second century A.D.,
they travelled down the paved Sacred Way from nearby Miletus or
arrived on the nearby shore by boat. Before them stood the enormous
oracular temple of Didyma, whose thick columns and staircases still
amaze us and whose vast inner courtyard defied every plan for its
completion. While the questioners waited and sacrificed, they could
lodge in the housing which we know to have spread on the second-
century precinct, or *paradeisos*, as it was still touchingly described, in a
word of Greco-Persian origin.[44] The prophetess followed "a rule of
complete purity," presumably sexual purity. She bathed, and as at
Claros, so at Didyma she prepared for the god by eating nothing. She
fasted not for one day, but three, and "a multitude of sacrifices"
preceded her work: famished, she lived meanwhile in the inner shrine
and "was already possessed by the divine light, enjoying it for a long
while," at least in Iamblichus's view.

The method of consultation is uncertain, as the temple's ground
plan is ambiguous. Two staircases lead down into the huge inner court

and two staircases lead up onto the roof. A large opening, like a window, stands above ground level and gives onto the fore-temple: perhaps the questioners received their answers here. Apollo delighted in choirs and singing, and at Didyma, as we shall see, he approved them in an oracle of mid-third-century date: here, too, we must imagine choirboys accompanying his consultation.[45] Perhaps the questioners waited outside in the fore-temple while the prophet and other officials went down the vaulted inner staircases to meet the prophetess in the enormous area of the unroofed inner shrine.[46] Iamblichus lists various ways in which the prophetess might be inspired, and these ways are not alternatives, but differing aspects of a single ceremony. The priestess held a rod "handed down from the god," like the rod which Apollo was said to have cut from a bay tree and given to the legendary founder of Didyma's priesthood. She sat on an *axon*, a fascinating word which ought to mean a rotating, cylindrical block: in archaic Greek, an *axon* pointed upwards vertically, like a post, but the priestess must have benefited from a slight shift in its subsequent meaning. The *axon* was set beside the small sacred spring which welled up at the rear of the inner court. The water wetted her feet or the hem of her prophetic robe and gave off a vapour which she "breathed" when she received the god. Unlike the prophet at Claros, she is not said to have drunk it.

The prophetess made noises of inspiration, and the prophet stood by to turn them into verse. He changed yearly and was perhaps assisted in his poetry by one of the secretaries or temple staff: here, we can only guess. The prophetess needed time to recover after her long fast and her solemn contact with the god, and presumably she stayed in the inner shrine, lost in the anonymity which still surrounds her. Only once do we know a prophetess's name, and then, c. 200 A.D., she belongs to a very well-born family.[47] If she is a typical case, the job was not held by simple, unlettered persons: perhaps the prophetess added more to our surviving oracle texts than we imagine. The prophet's, however, is the name which we know most often. He returned with his companions up the vaulted passageway of stairs: did he then climb higher, ascending the upper staircases to the roof space above the forecourt? Alternatively, he appeared at the huge window which the doors had closed from the forecourt's view. The god's response was announced with due ceremonial at one or other site, and copies were made available for questioners at the nearby record house.

At Claros, the prophet tunnelled far below the ground, while at

Didyma, the prophetess sat on the *axon* and made contact with a surface spring.[48] Both shrines focussed on water in their differing ways, and both set a problem to Greek theorists who wished to explain why prophecy and inspiration were general forces but were connected with these particular local pools. How, from contact with Apollo's water, did texts of such lofty theology emerge? For an answer, we can look to a third site, Delphi, which is lit up for us by three dialogues by Plutarch, set at dates between the mid-60s and c. 120 A.D. They show us better than any other texts what company Apollo had begun to keep.[49] In the Imperial period, the site of Delphi was frequented by teachers and men of letters, travellers, philosophers and those eternal funds of vivid and useless information, the Greek guides. Through their persons, Plutarch's Delphic dialogues allowed a hearing to many philosophic views on the value and nature of oracles. He introduced a Cynic and an Epicurean who dismissed them as frauds,[50] a Stoic who defended them too uncritically and then, at the end, a speaker with Platonist sympathies who settled the topic in terms with which Plutarch would have sympathized. His characters were a wide-ranging company, from whom Delphi heard many cosmopolitan stories, the tales of people who had travelled in Egypt or visited the distant Siwah oasis, the views of an Alexandrian philosopher on a tour of Greece, the reports, even, of a tour in Britain and the Scottish islands round Mull. Delphi in the 80s had heard from Scribonius Demetrius, a schoolteacher who had travelled to these places, although his home lay in distant Tarsus. He told stories of the old god Cronos, who was said to be chained on a Scottish island: other islands, he said, were haunted by the spirits of great men whose deaths caused appalling storms at sea. We know Demetrius for his dedications to Ocean and a sea goddess which were found on two bronze tablets while the railway station was being built at York; Plutarch knew him for his learning and remote tales.[51] These visitors gave Apollo access to the latest modern geography, while others brought philosophy and speculative theology. Plutarch's Delphi gave scope to his friend Serapion, a man whom we know as a Stoic and a poet and as the author of advice on the proper ethics for doctors.[52] Plutarch dedicated a Delphic book to him, as he dedicated another on the gods Isis and Osiris to a Delphic priestess called Clea. They give us a priceless glimpse of the atmosphere which hung round Delphi and help us to understand the tone which Apollo assumed elsewhere.

Clea is a woman who stands for much we might otherwise miss in evidence based on the masculine world.[53] Her parents had been friendly with Plutarch and he greatly respected her learning and knowledge. She was an informed worshipper of Isis and a reader who could be interested in Pythagoras's doings in Egypt. Plutarch's book to her has been classed as one of the most difficult of surviving works in Greek, yet Clea was thought able to cope with it, a woman, said Plutarch, who must not take the stories of Egypt's gods too literally. A second work in her honour, *The Brave Deeds of Women*, was not so heavy. Plutarch and Clea had been lamenting a female friend's death, and Plutarch had started to tell how the virtues of men and women were identical. He finished off his pleasant conversation by sending her stories in which women showed men's courage. "Concerning the virtues of woman, Clea, I do not hold the opinions of Thucydides." He did not cite the usual examples of feminine courage; these, he said, were "well known to a woman who keeps company so solidly with books." Instead, he sent her some curiosities, as befitted a lady of letters who was familiar with Egyptian theology, books on the nature of the gods and the masculine virtues of Greek and Roman members of her sex.

Lesser versions of Clea, one feels, were among the society women to whom Christianity appealed. It, too, had a theology, tales of female heroism and scope for female endeavour, albeit of a sexless variety. Plutarch's other Delphic tract was addressed to Serapion, a Stoic, and discussed the difficult meaning of the letter "E" which was inscribed so prominently at Delphi. Plutarch cast the text as his memories of a discussion which had been held at the shrine in his youth, in the mid-60s A.D., when Nero was roaming in Greece. His text is a telling companion to the Apollo who spoke to Oenoanda, and Plutarch arranged his dialogue with skill.[54] He recorded wryly his own youthful views on the enigmatic "E," his passion for mathematics and number symbolism, and by contrast, the dry, logical explanations of his elder, the logician Theon. The climax was a speech by Plutarch's own teacher, Ammonius, who had travelled to Delphi from Athens and brought a higher philosophy to problems posed by Apollo.

This speech is preceded by some revealing details. We hear how residents of Delphi and a priest at the shrine attacked the more fanciful theories of the meaning of their puzzling "E." A "Chaldaean," Plutarch hinted, had recently explained it by a theory of the planets: when we find astrology and favourable words for "Chaldaean" wisdom in Apollo's answers, we must allow for the presence of like-minded visitors within earshot of the god.[55] Plutarch also alludes to tales of the *theologoi* which anticipate much in our subsequent oracles. These self-appointed spokesmen called Apollo "indestructible and eternal" and enlarged, too, on his transformations into a fiery substance and the form of the god Dionysus. When we find an Apollo describing his identity with the Sun, Dionysus and the Seasons, we must remember the loose theology of these speakers at his shrines.[56] They raised these questions for visitors but did not answer them exactly. Visitors then put the problems to the god.

When Ammonius ended the debate, his speech was already concerned with the central question which was to be put to so many later oracles: what is the relationship between the Supreme god Apollo and the others? His answer, perhaps, was individual, but already in the mid-60s, it touched on much which we later hear from the gods themselves.[57] The Supreme divinity, he said, is one, "eternal, uncreated, undying," "immovable, timeless, undeviating": Apollo, for Ammonius, is this Supreme god, higher even than the Sun, with which many confuse him. A lesser power oversees the world and the multiple forms of the gods, but we must praise Apollo the Supreme god with the words "thou art," while honouring his constant advice to "know ourselves," our mortal nature and frailties. This Platonist philosopher was a younger contemporary of the Alexandrian Jew Philo, in whose works we find a fascinating match for this elevated way of thought. It had been current among teachers in Philo's Alexandria: in one late text, Ammonius is said to have come "from Egypt" to Athens, where he taught and held high office. Perhaps he, too, had studied in Alexandria and learned these views there.

The argument is less important than its tone. Here at Delphi were clever men disputing on the "meaning" of an old, meaningless symbol. It was a totally misguided effort, but they revelled in it, airing every option, astrology and number symbolism, logic and a lofty Platonism on the relation of God to Apollo and his fellow divinities. Their belief in the significance of puns and wordplay was applied to the names of the gods, and Plutarch wrote up their discussion in his later years, claiming to have remembered it precisely: Apollo, as we shall see, was equally retentive. In the 60s, said Plutarch, Ammonius seemed to us all to have "proved correctly that the god Apollo is no less a philosopher than a prophet."[58] Subsequent oracles all over the Greek-speaking world are a gloss on Ammonius's proof.

When we next meet the Delphic oracle in literature, the atmosphere around it is hardly less elevated. It was probably in the early third century that Heliodorus gave a brilliant picture of Delphi in his fictional *Ethiopic Tales*, an aspect of his novel which has been misread as "Delphic propaganda."[59] When the Egyptian priest Calasiris arrived at Delphi, he was said to have been hailed spontaneously by the god as his "friend," an honour which had attached to legendary visitors in the archaic Greek past. When news of its repetition spread, Calasiris was plied with honours and stayed at Delphi to examine life at Apollo's shrine. Sometimes he busied himself with the "many varied sacrifices which were offered to Apollo by visitors and locals alike," and sometimes, like Plutarch, he conversed with the philosophers "who flocked to the temple as if to a true temple of the Muses." Their conversation had not changed, although a century or so had passed since Plutarch's books. "They began by asking me questions on the gods and Egyptian cults . . . they wanted explanations of the Pyramids and the Labyrinth. They did not forget any one of the oddities of Egypt; discussing and listening to Egyptian matters is what attracts Greeks most." Clea would have been in her element.

This impression of Delphi is not pure fiction: we know of one man from Delphi, in the Imperial age, who did visit Egypt's Valley of the Kings and inscribed his name on the site.[60] Back home, no doubt, his stories interested Apollo's shrine. An elevated philosophy also distinguishes the most famous Delphic oracle to have survived from the later third century, a poem which caught the imagination of W. B. Yeats. When the Platonist philosopher Plotinus died in the year 270, the most pious and diligent of his pupils sent to Delphi to ask about the destination of his soul. Apollo excelled himself.[61] Long ago he was believed to have hailed Socrates as the "wisest of men" and his favour for Platonism had not been lost on its exponents. In the mid-second century, we find the head of the Platonic school attending the games at Delphi, and an inscription on stone lists the Delphians' honours for a cluster of Platonist philosophers who extend across the generations in the second-century schools. With time, names were added to this list, and they suffice to prove that Platonist philosophy was still drawn closely to the shrine.[62] Did these Platonists serve in some capacity the god who was thought to have praised their master? A eulogy of Plotinus was a natural sequel to this prolonged relationship, and so eloquent is Apollo's long text that we can only regret the loss of most of his Delphic answers in the previous century and a half. Subtle echoes of Homer kept company with a learned allegory of the soul, based on a scene in the *Odyssey*: Plotinus himself had used an allegory from the *Odyssey* in a similar context, and imagery from the *Odyssey* found a home in the books and funerary art of subsequent pagans and Christians.[63] Plotinus, said the god, had enjoyed the gift of divine light. He had aspired beyond this "blood-devouring life" to the "blessed sights" which his soul enjoyed. Buffeted by the seas of life, it had returned to the heaven of Plato and Minos "and all the choir of Love." This remarkable oracular poem was not a fake, as the scholarly Porphyry cited it with great respect. Had one of Apollo's prophets attended Plotinus's classes? The god approved the philosopher whose metaphors he duly borrowed.

At Claros and Didyma, the tone was not different. People travelled no less far to consult Claros, and although we know nothing of the thespodes' education, some earlier priests and personnel are suggestive.[64] In the Hellenistic age, Claros was the home of the poet Nicander, who had probably served Apollo's shrine and was credited with books on "all oracles." His surviving poems are among the most contorted in Greek literature, but oracles would welcome his "combination of a repulsive style with considerable metrical accomplishment." The "very bookish" Gorgo was a match for him, a "painstaking" researcher into old oracular poems and a "lover of wisdom." At Didyma, in the 60s A.D., the prophet Damas had shown great zeal in restoring the old traditional rites in his city; in the mid-third century, another prophet, Ulpianos, was praised by Apollo for attending to the "old sayings," presumably the texts of an earlier age. In the second century, another Milesian prophet styled himself "successor of Plato": he would have revelled in Plotinus's Delphic obituary. Men of such education ensured that Apollo kept abreast of the schools: we will have to ponder and place a remarkable text from Didyma in the third century in which Apollo decried colossal statues and lavish sacrifices because the "gods are not in need of possessions."[65] Ultimately, this statement owes a debt to the philosophers' theology, as do texts in which Apollo used puns and clever wordplay on the "meanings" of the gods' own names.

Like many shrines, oracles had libraries and archives, while attracting talk of local history and natural wonders from their many clients and travelling visitors. They gave scope to one of the most persistent and distinctive types in Mediterranean civic life: the antiquarian. Apollo, as we shall see, could speak with rare learning, and we can detect a pleasant, close relation between the minor names of learning and the gods. They were the poets who wrote the hymns for Claros: at Ostia, near Rome, inscriptions show us the demigods Castor and Pollux answering three questions about one Septimius Nestor in elegant verse.[66] "How well has Nestor sung the story of your birth?" "How long will his literary fame endure?" "To which god should his statue be dedicated?" Nestor, from Greek Asia Minor, was a man of letters who enjoyed a wide following in the early third century A.D. He wrote erudite poems on curious stories, odd facts about farming and the habits of hyenas. He rewrote the entire *Iliad*, avoiding in each "book" the particular letter by which it was numbered. The statue of Nestor has been found, but unfortunately it lacks its head.

The clients of oracles were people who wished to know and argue, to be reassured or guided through their many choices of thought and action. Such a public ought to have interested Artemidorus while he compiled his book on dreams. Apollo, he wrote, had "stood beside" him "very clearly" and had inspired his work. Artemidorus had toured the games and festivals of Mediterranean cities: surely he stopped at Claros, so close to his "second city," Ephesus? He had personal contacts among the choirs of at least one client city: at Claros, he could revel in "*ce public d'informateurs de choix . . . cette affluence de dévots inquiets et confiants . . . Quel milieu idéal au point de vue psychologique.*"[67] The gods' horizons had grown with their prophets' education, as Philostratus, too, had recognized: he shows the point clearly when he imagines how the pagan wise man Apollonius once forced his way into the oracular shrine of Trophonius in central Greece.[68] "I wish to descend," Apollonius said, "on behalf of philosophy." Dressed in his philosopher's cloak, he descended into the oracular cave and reappeared "seven days later" at Aulis with a complete book, filled with the questions which he had asked. They concerned one issue: "What, O Trophonius, do you consider to be the most complete and pure philosophy?" Trophonius was said to be delighted with the style of this consultation, and Apollonius came up from the cave with a volume which was "still preserved" at Antium on the coast of Italy. Philostratus said that the people who lived around the oracle had told him the details of this episode, and the book, he believed, had been sent to the Emperor Hadrian, that connoisseur and patron of oracles and oddities. It had been shelved in his palace, he said, and still drew many tourists in the early third century. It befitted the tone of contemporary Didyma and Claros, for "it contained the views of Pythagoras," wrote Philostratus, "since the oracle was in agreement with this type of wisdom." This fascinating relic has not had the attention it deserves, although it summed up one aspect of oracular culture and thus attracted visitors for so long.

"What is God?" asked visitors to Claros from Oenoanda: their question was not so unusual for an Apollo who consorted with philosophy, and we can match it to texts which survive from the shrine. At Claros, Apollo once spoke on the nature of the Supreme god Iao: "in winter," said Apollo, "he is Hades; Zeus, when spring begins; the Sun, in summer; in autumn, delicate Iacchus." At Didyma, Apollo called the highest god Aion, or Eternity, a versatile concept which was also connected with Ethereal Fire and this same idea of a cycle of the Seasons: again, Apollo was reflecting a theological fashion, for the concept Aion enjoyed a greater prominence in the art and theology of the Imperial period.[69] Dawn and an east-facing aspect were also proven tastes of the god: Apollo at Claros told Symmachus and his sons to set up his altar, facing east to the sun. It is probably to Didyma that we should trace a fragmentary request and oracular answer which were discovered at Ephesus.[70] They concerned the siting of a statue of Eros and an altar to the great gods and they also spoke of "life-enhancing Dawn." The altar on Oenoanda's wall was true to this wider pattern of advice.

For further questions of this type, we have only to turn to Christians who seized on these oracles of higher theology and claimed that they proved the truth of their own. If they needed a little improvement, Christians were well able to give it. Christian authors gutted the pagan oracular books and saved the better pieces as Christian proof texts which improved, like wine, with the keeping. Yet, as they were verse texts, their metre set limits to their rewriting, and on the whole, their fragments have survived without too much alteration. Some of the fifth century's most turgid Christian sermons come to life when they cite an oracular gem which plainly goes back to a pagan Apollo. The richest Apolline collection survives in our shortened version of the work *On True Belief*. Shortly before 500 A.D., its unknown Christian author added four books of pagan oracles and prophecies to the previous seven in which he had set out Christian doctrine. They were only a pendant to his exposition of the truth, but this lowly role allowed some intriguing Apollos to have their say.[71] Old Apollos and pagan divinities are still trying to speak to us in many of the extracts.

The questioners from Oenoanda find their closest company in the pagan questions and answers which our epitome of this Christian book has preserved.[72] "When somebody asked Apollo if only the Most High is without beginning or end, he replied as follows . . ." "When somebody asked when he should worship the Ineffable god, Apollo showed that every place is in his power and that he receives worshippers everywhere. His reply was . . ." "When somebody asked if he could come near to God by careful attention to his life, Apollo answered . . ." In this oracle, Apollo denied that his questioner could attain "such a godlike privilege," as it was reserved for the Egyptian Hermes, "Moses of the Hebrews" and the "wise man of the Mazacenes," none other than Apollonius the pagan philosopher. This reply is not a Christian forgery, as it omits Jesus from its list. Like his prophets, Apollo respected the mirage of Eastern wisdom, the godlike figures of the past and the legendary Apollonius, a pleasant insight into the range of a third-century prophet's reading.

These oracular answers have a language and balanced phrasing which we can match with other pagan oracles and hymns. Although they are preserved in Christian handbooks, the majority are obviously genuine. *On True Belief* quoted a splendid text which had stood in the second book of Porphyry's *Philosophy from Oracles* and existed, then, by c. 290 A.D.[73] Its wording makes Oenoanda's answer seem rather prosaic, as it distinguished three grades of pagan "angels" at different removes from the pagan Highest god, "the all-powerful, most Kingly and sole Father of mortals and blessed Immortals." After a while, the theology of higher divinities tends to repeat itself, whatever the religion. Apollo's words could almost have served as Christian hymns.

The point was not lost on Christian preachers. There has been little interest in a mid-fifth-century sermon "On the Trinity," wrongly ascribed to Didymus the Blind, but like Books 9 and 10 of *On True Belief*, it quotes in profusion the words of pagan gods, many of which are impeccable in metre and vocabulary.[74] "Immortal God, supreme, dwelling in Ether, Imperishable, Unshakeable, Eternal, always the same": these quotations and several others make Oenoanda's answer seem really quite conventional.[75] It is clear that questions on God were not the curiosity of one small Lycian city and that Oenoanda was one among several inquirers.

Can we pin any of the texts in Christian sources to an original date and place? A brilliant series of conjectures has shown how excellent were the questions and answers which the author of *On True Belief* preserved. We only have a brief epitome of his book, but three of its quotations preserve the questioner's name, and in one case, we can add another from a separate Christian source. "A certain Poplas asked if it was proper to send to the Emperor about monies for a public show . . ."[76] The unusual name Poplas has been traced to Aelianus Poplas, prophet of Apollo at Didyma around the year 220. He had served as a priest of the Imperial cult and had asked his god whether he should go on an embassy to request the Emperor's financial support. He had held every sort of civic magistracy in Miletus and had volunteered for the job of archiprytanis, but nonetheless, he turned to Apollo to guide his ambition. A second oracle shows him at a lower ebb. His property had begun to diminish and his health was failing, so he asked Apollo who could help him. Poplas's two questions remind us of the costs of civic munificence, the ups and downs of the highest careers, the role of the Emperor and the problems of paying the expenses of shows in the Imperial cult. His family intertwined with Miletus's great prophetic dynasties, and Poplas's nephew survived to serve the god. Poplas the prophet suspected no fraud and practised no deception, but when life was hard, he turned to Apollo for advice and ensured that the answers survived for posterity.

"A certain Stratonicus saw a dream and asked Apollo if he should believe it." The dream concerned Stratonicus's length of life, a type of dream which Apollo once sent to the orator Aelius. The name Stratonicus is very much more common, but a Stratonicus is known as a prophet at Didyma in the 30s B.C., while another turns up there c. 180 A.D., although he is not known to have been a prophet.[77] "When somebody asked Apollo about the fate of the soul after death . . .": the same oracle was quoted by Lactantius the Christian, who traced the question to "Polites the Milesian." We know just enough about the top men in Miletus to prove him right.[78] A Polites had dined there with Mark Antony in the 30s B.C., but our man is surely the later Polites whom we know to have visited Rome in the year 177 A.D. Like Poplas, he was well aware of the hazards of an embassy to the Emperor. He, too, was a man of *philotimia* who went to plead on his city's behalf, "asking" permission for their new festival, the "Didymeia Commodeia," whose games honoured the Emperor Commodus. We also find this Polites's name on his issues of Miletus's coins, among whose types stands the image of Apollo Delphinios, implying that Polites had served as his "crown-bearer." Polites, then, had been honoured on Apollo's behalf, and when he wanted to know about life after death, he turned to the god in his shrine at Didyma. The prophet that year had a philosophic schooling, and so, therefore, did the god's answer. "While the soul is still in the body," said Apollo, "it tolerates the pains which cannot hurt it. When the body fades and dies, the soul ranges free through the air, ageless, forever unwearied."

This late Christian handbook has preserved four oracles whose questioners can be connected with prominent Milesians and prophets of Apollo at Didyma. When it names a fifth, the chances are high that he should be found at Didyma too: questioners at Didyma inscribed their names and questions on the site or in nearby Miletus, and thence, they could pass easily into the books of Porphyry and others. "Theophilus," says our Christian epitome, "asked Apollo, 'Are you God, or is somebody else?'" There is no shortage of men called Theophilus in the inscriptions of Greek cities, but the named questioners in this collection have been men from Didyma, and there, sure enough, we find Julius Theophilus, son of a prophet of Apollo and himself a priest of the Emperors.[79] His career extended after 215, to judge from his service in the city's festivals. He was the contemporary of Poplas and the near-contemporary of Polites, and belonged with other third-century Milesians who referred points of religion to their god.[80]

Not only were Oenoanda's question and answer not untypical: the questioners now turn out to have moved in impeccable company. In the years between c. 170 and 230 A.D., prophets and civic notables at Didyma were asking similar questions. The tone of these higher questions must not be misjudged, for they were not necessarily "anxious," like the "troubled" practical questions of Poplas. They could also arise from curiosity and a continuing interest in theology among people who had studied philosophy and knew that the philosophers had raised more questions than they could ever hope to answer.[81] The natural counterpart to their inquiries is the young Galen, whose father had sent him round each of the philosophic schools in the mid-second century, but had asked him not to commit himself too hastily to any one view. Oracles could settle these doubts and contradictions.[82] The opening scenes of that fascinating Christian fiction, *The Recognitions*, show how the young pagan Clement had been worried by the problem of the fate of the soul after death. After a vain search for the truth, he was said to have met St. Peter and come to rest as a Christian. The main core of *The Recognitions* was probably written c. 200 A.D.; a few years earlier, Polites had asked his Apollo the same question and found the answer directly from a god. Apollo, however, could not be pressed too hard. We should possibly attach to Theophilus's answer several lines in which the god admitted that he knew only some of the truths about the highest heaven.[83] The Supreme god, he said, lived in isolation, and Apollo could only rely on hearsay about his nature. Although he knew more than he was willing to reveal, he told his questioner to stop bothering him, "asking what is not right and meddling in higher things for the sake of your own wisdom." When Apollo was at a loss for an answer, he could still put his clients in their place. At Claros, too, his tone was similar, and the style was copied cleverly by a novelist.[84]

How many people, however, does this evidence concern? Priests and prophets are the very people whom we would expect to hold fast to oracles and honour their god by inscribing his texts. Are we only studying a few untypical enthusiasts? It seems not, for Apollo spoke to a much wider audience, as we continue to learn from the Oenoandan text and another type of inscription in his clients' home cities.[85] We have a widespread group of inscribed Latin dedications which follow a similar formula, though some of them misspell it: "to the gods and goddesses," they say, "according to the 'interpretation' of Apollo at Claros." Their spread is remarkable. They have turned up near Nora in Sardinia, where the text is now kept in a small village church, in cities in North Africa, re-used in the wall of a church in Dalmatia and far away on the Empire's extremities, in Housesteads' fort on Hadrian's Wall, where the text was put up by a Tungrian cohort. This British text, at least, must be dated after 140 A.D., because of the cohort's movements. The others are likely to belong in the second to mid-third century A.D., befitting the pattern of civic life and the history of visits to Claros. Were they all the result of an Emperor's central initiative? The suggestion has been made and accepted, but it has nothing in its favour.[86] There is no evidence of such a central edict, nor is it easy to imagine an Emperor with a "religious policy" which required them, or an Empire so willing, in its remote corners, to obey such a curious command. None of the texts mentions the Emperor or his well-being, and it is far from clear that they are all of a similar date. They are better understood as dedications which grew up naturally during the mid-second to the mid-third century A.D., sometimes in answer to a consultation by the place concerned, sometimes, perhaps, on reports of others' consultations. If the texts had a common motive, it may have been fear of the great epidemics of plague which threatened civic life in this period. The formula, however, is tantalizing: how far did Claros's "interpretation" go? Presumably, it amounted to a list of the proper honours to divinities who would keep a fort or city safe and healthy. Did Apollo also soar higher and send a touch of his "negative theology" to groups who asked for his "interpretation" of the gods? After Oenoanda's text, we cannot exclude the possibility. When people feared misfortune or wished to know the truth, they asked Apollo himself, from the borders of Scotland to the highlands of Lycia, from Sardinia to Banasa and Cuicul in Africa. Here, indeed, was a demon whom the Christians rightly feared. Apollo at Claros spoke to the Greek and Latin world alike, and the similarity of these brief texts suggests a certain standardization in the directions which he gave.

In one case, we can pursue such questions on gods beyond Claros and Didyma, and trace them far up the course of the Nile.[87] It was probably in the early third century that an unknown traveller journeyed to Talmis on the Nile's Upper Cataract and recorded his moment of divine revelation. He had seen signs of the power of the god who was honoured in the large temple and he had "pondered and busied himself very much with them." At Talmis, there was no prophet and no sacred spring, but the traveller prepared personally for the god's revelation and "made himself a stranger to all vice." He prayed and offered incense, and he watched as the sun rose. At the hour when Oenoanda's altar was warmed by the dawn, the god Mandulis gave power and breath to his image and his shrine. Even here, the statues of the gods seemed to whisper philosophy, far up the course of the Nile. What he had wanted to know was this: "Are you the Sun god, or not?" Here, the question was born of travel and personal experience, not the indecisions of the philosophical schools. At dawn, in Talmis, the god revealed the truth: "I knew you then, Mandulis, to be the Sun, the all-seeing Master, king of all-powerful Eternity." Once again, the idea of Eternity featured in an individual's theological text.

From Egypt to Ionia, we can enjoy a rare opportunity, oracles on matters of philosophy and texts in which gods discuss themselves. When had these theological oracles begun?[88] Only a tiny, random sample survives, but it belongs exclusively in the Imperial period: already in the first century A.D., Plutarch's speakers at Delphi had considered asking Apollo about his relation to the other gods. They would not, however, have received an answer in philosophic verse, because that verse style belonged with a clear oracular "revival," which dates from the reigns of Trajan and Hadrian (98–138 A.D.). Soon afterwards, questions to gods on philosophy were presupposed by the story of Apollonius and the "book" which he composed in Trophonius's cave: this story was abroad by c. 160, at the latest. At a similar date, jokes about gods and philosophic questions appealed to Lucian's sense of satire: clearly, then, they had become a contemporary fact of life.[89]

By the 170s, Polites the "crown-bearer" was asking Apollo about the soul. From these philosophical topics, it was a small step to the higher theological questions. They grew naturally out of a simple problem: the title or form of address which a particular god preferred. As gods began to multiply their names and attributes, questions of their identity gained in urgency: we find one such question imagined in *The Golden Ass*, composed c. 170. In the first and the early second century A.D., we have already remarked a greater tendency to merge gods' names and relate them to a Supreme god: this idea was not new, but its language does loom larger in our texts. As a consequence, we then find signs of the theological oracles. Theophilus may well belong in the early third century, as may the Oenoandans and their "inquiry." Other such texts owe their survival to two collections, Porphyry's, compiled c. 270–300, and Cornelius Labeo's, of less certain date but perhaps a mid- to late-third-century work. The texts which these authors preserved had existed earlier, but perhaps not very much earlier. It may well be through Porphyry that Eusebius the Christian knew a text in which Apollo discussed himself: "Helius, Horus, Osiris, king, son of Zeus, Apollo . . ." Like his prophet, inevitably, Apollo combined the names of the gods: he "controlled the reins of the dawn," he said, "and the starry night," and he was "king" and "immortal Fire."

Awareness of these texts can help us to understand several currents in later pagan piety, which have seemed much odder when isolated from the language of conventional gods. Intellectually, the second and third centuries A.D. have been judged to have preferred revelation to reason. This priority was not new, but Porphyry, a thinker, it has been said, "with an incurable weakness for oracles," has seemed to sum up the decline.[90] By c. 300 A.D., at the latest, he had gathered a collection of texts from the gods into three or more books, entitled *Philosophy from Oracles*. They have been dismissed as a youthful excess: "*les superstitions qu'il voudrait ennoblir sont par nature trop grossières . . .*" and his contact with the "rationalism" of his great teacher, Plotinus, has been thought to have won him away from this false turning. This dating rests only on guesswork. Philosophy, we now see, was evident in the words of the gods whose texts were inscribed at Didyma and nearby Miletus: perhaps Porphyry engaged in some shrewd epigraphy to collect the Didyma texts for his book. It may well have been a work of his maturity, for he had no doubts about its importance. He thought that the collection gave a means of salvation to its more perceptive readers. Can we justly criticize him? Like their own prophets and thespodes, the "gods" knew the school texts of Plato. If Apollo at Delphi had spoken like a Platonist during Plato's lifetime, the master would have welcomed his support. In the oracular revival of the second and the early third century, there were philosophers serving as prophets: Platonists and Stoics, perhaps a Pythagorean, even an Epicurean.[91] The Platonist names inscribed at Delphi are evidence of their philosophy's continuing links with Apollo: we can suspect a similar relationship at Apamea in Syria, where an oracular shrine of Zeus kept company with a circle of Platonists in the third and fourth centuries A.D.[92] It is not too surprising that people accepted the gods' own evidence when it seemed to agree with their own.

This rising current of "philosophy in oracles" also helps us to understand an influential fraud. In the second century, a collection of "Chaldaean Oracles" began to circulate and was later to surface noticeably in intellectual life from the later third century onwards. Porphyry wrote a commentary on them and their devotees beguiled the Emperor Julian. The neatest way to account for their origin is to assume that the Oracles first appeared anonymously in the earlier second century. They were supposed to be the Chaldaeans' Eastern wisdom on the rites and nature of the gods, and as time passed, these obscure, high-flown texts gained a growing authority.[93] Nobody knew their precise origin; nobody could fully understand them, and Platonist philosophers struggled to write an explanatory commentary. Their reputation was made. They were a jousting ground for the hyperintelligent, and they purported to describe the arts by which a pure and spiritual man could compel the gods. Now we can add another ingredient. Like the best type of fake, they closely resembled their genuine relations, for high-flown philosophy was also spoken by the established second-century gods. One of the Chaldaean Oracles' keenest modern students fell into their trap. He credited them with Apollo's answers to Theophilus and the Oenoandans, before the latter's text refuted him by turning up on the city wall as words from Apollo himself.

Like Apollo, these "Chaldaean" verses expressed much which was being argued by the philosophers. Part of their theology is close to views which we can find in our few fragments of the Platonist philosopher Numenius, who wrote in the earlier second century and took an interest in Eastern wisdom, including the views of "Moses," and the means by which gods could be attracted by their own symbols and images. "Some sort of bridge," concluded a great connoisseur of later Platonism, "must have linked the two systems, but I find it hard to be quite sure which way the traffic ran."[94] Perhaps Numenius or a close associate composed the Oracles and published them anonymously. The point of their subsequent success is that we, too, cannot be sure where the fiction begins and its sources end. Nor, perhaps, could Apollo. One Apollo, known to Eusebius and subsequent Christians, ascribed "wisdom" to the "Chaldaeans alone"; another said that only those who had a "sacred token of the gods" could see the gods themselves.[95] Are these texts so obviously fakes? If Apollo's prophets read and accepted the Chaldaean Oracles, the god, too, would pick up these views, both of which match the Chaldaean Oracles' teaching.

The continuing sensitivity of the gods to contemporary teaching helps us to appreciate other aspects of Porphyry's book. He is not known to have cited "Chaldaean" texts in it, but he did know texts in which Apollo approved Eastern wisdom. He also knew texts in which the gods discussed their relation to astrology and the power of the stars: like their prophets, the oracles had absorbed this system of thought.[96] The second book of Porphyry's *Philosophy* gave space to this topic, and also to the "compelling" of gods to attend a "recipient": priests and philosophers believed in these arts and so, therefore, did their gods. They also revealed their favourite names and the very words of their hymns:[97] we can well understand how similar hymns and oracles continued to be composed and passed off as the verses of prophetic "Orpheus," and why the invocations and higher theology of learned magic were sometimes recorded as "oracles" from a god. The style was easily copied, and the Orphic hymns and the magical papyri drew on widespread expectations. In the early Christian era, "paganism" had thus become more than the sum of the acts performed in its cults: it had acquired its own body of divine wisdom. When Christian Emperors banned cult acts, this doctrine was still able to survive and re-emerge. It is central, once again, to an understanding of the Emperor Julian, a man to whom the gods' own oracles were as evident as their "manifest" presence.

Julian was aware that the Chaldaean Oracles deserved respect, although his understanding of their meaning is unlikely to have gone very deep. He, too, had experienced the gods' sudden "presence" in their statues and greatly respected the theurgists among his contemporaries.[98] His conversion away from Christianity owed much to the sense of immediacy which these pagan philosophers could still elicit from their gods. In Christianity, he had found nothing like it. As Emperor, Julian took up the office of prophet at Didyma, and also stepped into its intellectual legacy. Like Theophilus, he believed that Apollo was the "master-founder of philosophy," and like other local questioners at Miletus, he accepted that the gods revealed their own hymns and titles. He knew as well as any third-century prophet at Didyma how the god "bore witness" to his pious servants. "Many of the gods' utterances," said Julian, confirmed the respect which was owed to their priests, and he quoted a splendid text from Apollo which stated the favour of gods for pious men. They kept their "swift eye" on human conduct, and confirmed their constant, Homeric presence. Like the text for the Oenoandans, these lines combined high-flown adjectives with concepts of Platonist and Pythagorean style. Julian did not only live by the words of the pagan gods: he died to the sound of them.[99] In his last hours, he was consoled by a charming oracle from the Sun god, or Apollo, on the fate of his soul: it promised him deliverance from the sufferings of his mortal limbs and a place in the "Ethereal Light" of his father's heavenly court, the place from which his soul had descended to human form. How Polites the "crown-bearer" would have sympathized with this response. If we miss the importance of these oracles for Julian, we mistake his piety for an esoteric intellectual reaction which none of his cities could have been expected to share. Rather, he was the great heir of the third century, when the gods had spoken philosophy to their clients.

Such, then, is one side to the language of the pagans' "rootless and compromise gods." In pagan company, it finds its last honours in the writings of Proclus the Platonist, c. 470–480 A.D.[100] When he cites an "oracle" on the soul's aspirations to return to heaven, he does not identify it as one of the various Chaldaean Oracles cited in his text. The verses belong to another source, perhaps to Apollo at one of his two great shrines. Not every soul, the god says, will realize its wish, nor will a life spent in "sacrificing" assist it: somebody, it seems, had asked if constant offerings to the gods could bring a person's soul to the heavens. Apollo denied that it could, opposing "wisdom" to external piety, and once again spoke philosophy to a questioner. Philosophy, however, was not the only side to Apollo's business. It was combined with advice on specific practical problems, the oracles' staple diet. What, then, was the scope and manner of this standard advice and in what sense, exactly, had oracles "revived" in the early Christian era? There were other puzzles in contemporary theology, not only the nature of divinity but the identity of a new God, Christ. At Claros, people were told to pray to a Most High god, facing east at dawn. In some texts, Apollo uttered no favourable words for blood sacrifice or cult in a temple; elsewhere, his clients were wanting to know how the Supreme god related to other divinities. Had the Christians sharpened these questions' relevance, and by the third century was Apollo trying to map out common ground between the two sides?

# II

To attempt an answer, we must come down from the heights for a while and look at the wider oracular landscape in the second and third centuries. At one end, it is clearly focussed. In the early 80s, Plutarch set a dialogue at Delphi whose speakers assumed that the oracles were in decline.[1] They wondered if the prophetic current at each site was fading or if the shrines had died away because the local populations had dwindled. The sceptics in their company were more forthright, suggesting that oracles were simply a hoax. Perhaps we can connect these discussions with a text from Apollo himself. Porphyry's book quoted an oracle in which the god had been asked about the status of Claros and Delphi. Other sites, Apollo said, had come and gone, having "gushed out on the back of the earth as springs or swirling breaths of vapour." Some of them "had been taken by Earth below the bosom of the ground," while others had expired with the passage of time. Only three major sites survived, he said: Claros and Delphi and also the "inspired water of Didyma." The remark allows us to place the text: Apollo at Didyma had been asked about his sister shrines at Claros and Delphi, and in reply, he had praised them as the sole survivors beside his own.[2]

In the early second century, this "decline" of the oracles began to be reversed. By c. 200, Christians still wrote polemically as if the gods had fallen silent, but they were ignoring the contrary facts at the sites to which they referred.[3] Even so, the change is still discounted: "What," we have recently been asked, "can one make of the assertion that oracles, 'it is true, enjoyed a recovery in popularity in the second century'—for which a single inscription is cited, recording help sought by a city in Sardinia from Apollo in Claros? Such characterizing of the feelings and thoughts of fifty million people on any day out of thirty-six thousand has something ludicrous about it.'"[4] Perhaps the full range of evidence can remove some of the absurdity, not one inscription but more than three hundred civic dedications at Claros alone, beginning c. 110 and witnessing, in the 130s, the rise of the thespode and a change in the way the site worked. At Delphi, Plutarch lived to see his earlier dialogue on "decline" be put out of date. He ends a second dialogue, c. 120 A.D., with words of delight on a recent transformation of the shrine's amenities, a benefaction which we can connect with the Emperor Hadrian.[5] His generosity had brought new life to the site, although Plutarch's text ascribes the revival to Apollo himself.

Delphi was not alone in receiving material favours at this date.[6] At Didyma, we know of benefactions to the shrine by the Emperors Trajan and Hadrian, and again, they helped the oracle's prestige. In Alexandria, by c. 130, the great temple of Serapis had recently been rebuilt and its "manifest" god was better placed than ever to impress his worshippers in oracular dreams. In Syrian Apamea, the oracular temple of Bel was constructed during Hadrian's reign. In Pergamum, benefactors in the Hadrianic age changed the face of the great precinct of Asclepius, a god who also gave oracles to questioners. Around 140, the "old and never-dying" Apollo at Patara began to speak again, and at Claros, the dedication of the great Doric temple bears the name of Hadrian. The oracle's flowering even induced a rival in the neighbouring city of Ephesus. Between 105 and 120, an enthusiastic Ephesian magistrate, Dionysodorus, spent large sums of his own money on repairing altars throughout the city and honouring the cults of all the gods. In the city's *prytaneium*, a central civic building, he installed an oracle, "making a chamber fit for the gods." In a decree, the people and council of Ephesus then stated that this oracle should remain "in perpetuity" where Dionysodorus had placed it. Its god was Apollo of Ephesus, not Apollo of Claros: the shrine was Ephesus's retort to nearby Claros's prowess and it stood in the heart of their great city's ground plan. Once again, cults flourished on the intercity rivalry of the age.

These texts have been joined by another, a very pleasant surprise.[7] From Cyzicus, on the Sea of Marmara, we now have an inscribed oracle from Ammon's shrine in distant Libya, given to the city's "worshippers of Ammon," whose names follow its text. The oracle had been brought all the way from the god's oasis at Siwah, once favoured by Alexander the Great: it was inscribed between 123 and 132 A.D. Some fifty years earlier, one of Plutarch's speakers had been lamenting the oracle's sad decline and reporting his journey to its site of former glory. Now, we find it reassuring worshippers as far afield as Cyzicus and sending them skilful hexameter verses. They were told, in turn, to go with offerings to Apollo at Claros, evidence of one shrine's support for another. We glimpse a whole pattern of oracular interrelationships which Plutarch's essay on "decline" had never countenanced.

As these oracular sites enjoyed a new life, they were joined by their obverse: forgery. The Chaldaean Oracles were faked in the years of oracular revival; in remote Paphlagonia, as we shall see, a prophet of Asclepius was accused of fraud when his oracle began to draw clients from far and wide during the 160s. The possibilities were summed up in the person of the Sibyl. If Sibyls wished to die, nobody in the Roman period respected their wishes. Sibylline oracles proliferated, extending far beyond the verse collections which still survive. Prophetic Sibyls spoke up for pagans, then Jews, and eventually they would speak for Christians, too.[8] Literary men with a gift for hexameters composed prophecies which they ascribed to the Sibyl and cast in obscure, allegorical language, drawing on a pool of Sibylline prophecy which focussed on political and collective disasters. There was no knowing where a new Sibyl might suddenly surface. From Perinthus, on the Sea of Marmara, we have iambic verses which members of a Bacchic cult society chose to inscribe in the second century A.D. "Good luck to you. An oracle of the Sibyl: When Bacchus shall be sated, then blood and fire and dust will be mixed together." We know nothing of the cult officers who put their names to this brusque text, men with names like Spellius Euethes.[9] Their text is a reminder how Sibylline verses had spread and multiplied: did authors sometimes believe that an ancient Sibyl appeared to them and inspired the texts herself? We will meet this question again in early Christian company.

By the second century, the Sibyls' ancestry had become a civic and cross-cultural battleground. Nobody had established who was the first Sibylline woman, or when she had lived. Indeed, how many Sibyls were there: ten or more? Which was the oldest: the Cumaean, the Erythraean, the Jewish, or the Babylonian who claimed to have spoken before the Flood? Cities competed for the Sibyl's birthplace and waged a minor version of their wars for the birthplace of Zeus or Homer. Was the true Sibyl a woman from Marpessus or, more plausibly, from Erythrae? In the year 162, Erythrae staked a definitive claim.[10] Her local "cave of the Sibyl" was visited by the Emperor Verus and was then adorned with statues of the Sibyl and the Sibyl's mother and equipped with a channel for her spring. "No other is my country," said the accompanying verses, polemically, "only Erythrae . . ." Here in Erythrae, the Sibyl was emphatically at home. She had lived for 900 years, said the texts, and her prediction that "Erythrae will blossom again" had at last been proved true. The city had just welcomed a "new Erythros," a second founder, the Emperor Verus himself. A Sibylline prophecy flattered the city and the Emperor, and very soon the Sibyl's image appeared firmly on Erythrae's coins.

Her new monument united much in the oracular culture of the Antonine age. A passing Emperor had taken an interest in yet another ancient centre of prophecy; its site had been embellished, and its new form then distinguished its city above all competing rivals. It had also benefitted from a fraud, a "Sibylline" prophecy which had been composed to predict this "second flowering" of Erythrae. We do not know this prophecy's date, but the events of 162 were held to have proved its truth. Age and uncertain origins lent respect to all manner of predictions. We have a Sibylline poem which "foretold" the eruption of Vesuvius and God's vengeance on the Romans: in fact, it was written shortly after the event of 79 A.D., but when Plutarch met its verses out of context only twenty years or so later, he thought they were an old, genuine prophecy in which the ancient Sibyl had proved her foresight.[11] If Sibyls could hide their origins, so could anonymous "Chaldaean" oracles or "ancient" oracles like the prophecy of "Hystaspes" which predicted a fiery end to the world. The older the prophecy, the more impressive it seemed to some of its readers in the antiquarian culture of the time. People were aware of a great length of time between themselves and these prophets' lives, but their words were still relevant: no great technological change had divided their era from much of life in the Roman Empire. Past seers had special credentials: they were children and brides of the gods or pious prophets of the ancient East. Almost nobody had a convincing test to distinguish an old text from a fake. The point was not lost on contemporary Christian authors.

In the second century A.D., the second flowering of oracles was true enough, affecting Apollos, Sibyls and competitive forgeries. Was it, though, a "recovery of popularity"? Once again, the greater prominence of a religious feature has been explained psychologically, in terms of rising credulity or the growing "anxiety" which gnawed at the heart of the cities' age of peace. From this view, it is a simpler step to explain the rise of Christianity, a faith which cut through pagan doubts and fears. Before, however, we accept this perspective, we should be clear what an oracle was and how, like the Sibyl, it related to competitors.

In the Greek world, observed Sir J. L. Myres, an oracle "has been defined as the conjunction of an uncanny place and a canny person."[12] The canniness of men like Poplas and Polites should not be set too highly, for they went sincerely and innocently about their business. The uncanniness of place was more relevant, a crowning example of the connection between cults and the landscape. Not for nothing are many of the old Greek oracles the most bewitching sites to survive from antiquity, not only Delphi and the sacred valley of Claros but lesser sites, too: the cavernous passage at Lebadeia or the oracular site of Ephyra, which was recently rediscovered in northwestern Greece beside two rivers, on a hill and inside a maze of passages.[13] The Greeks themselves had connected inspiration with peculiar places. Participants in Plutarch's dialogues wondered seriously about the quality of Delphi's air and its alleged vapours: was there a local "current" of prophecy which came and went at the different sites at different times? What, indeed, was so special about Claros's spring or Didyma's pool? Iamblichus, in the early fourth century, was still asserting the importance of place against Porphyry's doubts.[14]

The role of the person also aroused a lively interest among intellectuals. Sceptics took one view, but others were divided: did the god enhance a prophet's mind, casting a spark, perhaps, or playing on it as an instrument, or did he suspend reason altogether? The views were not mutually exclusive, but enhancement made more sense if you looked at the verse oracles: the style and metre were too feeble to be the god's own. Suspension made more sense if you considered the prophet or prophetess. At Delphi, Plutarch saw a prophetess go raving mad when consulted at an inauspicious moment, and at Claros and Didyma, said Iamblichus, the prophet (or prophetess) was "enthused" and "inspired."[15] Oracular inspiration continued to derive from a hungry trance, and debates on its nature were to have a long history. They were picked up by Christian leaders in the 160s and 170s who used them against their own "false" prophets. Later, they were translated into Arabic and interested some of the Muslim philosophers who wished to explain their own Prophet's gifts.

Major oracles, therefore, were a recognized combination of man, god and place. This combination was elaborate, and there was also scope for one or other part of it: a place without a person or a person in no one place. There were also techniques which relied on neither element. In the second and third centuries the pagan cities enjoyed all the forms of supernatural advice which historians of early modern Europe collect and analyse in later Christian contexts. There was only one exception: witchcraft. Pagan society knew no "Devil" with whom individuals could make a pact, and thus no torture and persecutions of "false" prophets and prophetesses. These features were a consequence of Christianity.

To see the oracular revival in focus, we must do justice to its full range of options. Prophetic places were as abundant as ever in the Imperial period, and many of the most famous were connected with the presence of a deity in dreams. A nest of dream oracles still flourished in southwestern Asia where the old heroes spoke, Sarpedon, Mopsus and Amphilochus: in the 80s, Plutarch's speakers savoured a story of Mopsus's dealing with a sceptical Roman governor of Cilicia. When some Epicureans urged the governor to test the shrine, the hero guessed his agent's question and confounded him.[16] From Gaul to Palmyra, gods and heroes also gave guidance by signs and omens at their shrines and sacred springs. At Memphis, a divine meaning was found in the words of children who played in the court of the temple of Apis.[17] Serapis gave oracles in Alexandria and also appeared in dreams, while the ugly curious god Bes had sprung into fashion in the Imperial period to serve Greek and Roman visitors to the Valley of the Kings in Egypt. He received their written petitions and gave answers, Bes the "entirely true, the giver of dreams and oracles, never-lying, acknowledged throughout the world, heavenly . . ." On the walls of his temple, visiting athletes inscribed prayers for themselves and their families: shown in their sports costumes, they match the athletes whose questions were known to Philostratus and whose dreams were so keenly researched by Artemidorus. The future mattered to these sportsmen, as it also mattered to the sick, for whom there were also the widespread cults of Asclepius. Almost everywhere, the god Asclepius gave advice to clients in dreams, but sometimes he uttered oracles too, which were distinguished from the guidance of his nightly presence. In a classicizing age, almost any past hero could surface and give advice: at Athens in the Imperial age, we even have a text from Harmodius and Aristogeiton, the heroes of the city's "liberation" in the late sixth century B.C. They were the proper people to speak in an antiquarian's dreams.[18]

We have only to follow Pausanias again in mid-second-century Greece to appreciate the range of available prophecy. Once a year, in Argos, a bull was sacrificed and the priestesses were made to prophesy by drinking its blood. At the charming shrine near Oropus, clients still wrapped themselves in sheepskins and dreamed of the healing hero Amphiaraus.[19] The most awesome consultation was reserved for the hero Trophonius at Lebadeia in nearby Boeotia, whose terrors far exceeded Claros's.[20] A client lived for several days in a shrine of the Good Daimon and Good Fortune, sacrificing freely, abstaining from hot baths and waiting till the diviners proclaimed a favourable night from their study of the entrails of a ram. Then he was led to be washed and anointed by two young boys. The priests took him to drink of the two springs, Memory and Forgetfulness. He gazed on a secret image, prayed, worshipped, dressed in a linen tunic with ribbons, and put on a pair of local boots. He was taken to the oracle's entrance, a chasm into the ground, down which he climbed on a thin ladder and then passed, feet first, into the lower darkness, holding cakes of honey. Underground, he was taught about the future, "not always in the same way, for one person sees, another hears." He returned feet first through the same narrow hole and was revived by the attendant priests, who set him on the Chair of Memory and asked him all he had seen and heard. He had to dedicate his findings on a tablet at the shrine, none of which, unfortunately, has been found. He emerged "gripped with terror and quite unaware of himself or those around him," but later, his wits returned to him and also, added Pausanias, "the power to laugh." We know of this remarkable ritual because Pausanias himself had endured it. The shrine was not moribund. By the mid-fifth century Christians had placed a martyr shrine near the cavern's entrance: if the oracle had not been active at a late date, they would not have troubled to neutralize it with a shrine of their own.

Wherever there was water, indeed, there was a possible source of prophecy.[21] The major oracular shrines used its powers: Claros and Didyma had their springs, while Delphi's Cassotis was piped down to the oracular temple, appearing to enter it, although it cannot be linked exactly with the rites of inspiration. At a simpler level, people threw offerings into water to see if they swam or sank, while holy springs everywhere upheld the sanctity of oaths. From Gaul to Sicily, suspects were subjected to hot geysers which scalded perjurers, and in Cilicia, there was a special spring which made them choke. Everywhere, springs were able to heal and cure, helping men and also the animals on whom human life depended. In Thrace, however, certain streams were thought to make horses more than usually uncontrollable.[22] The shrine of Demeter at Patrai had a spring into which visitors dipped a mirror on thin cords: then they prayed, burned incense and gazed into the glass, "which showed them a sick person either living or dead." The oracle answered questions of health and sickness only. There had once been a similar spring at Cape Taenarum "which showed ships and harbours," but by the time of Pausanias, it was said to have been spoiled for ever by a woman who had washed her dirty clothes in it.[23]

The specialization of these oracles is a further sign of their abundance. Uncanny places were everywhere, and without any expensive ceremonies, people turned to them for knowledge of the future. In the early third century, the historian Dio was as intrigued as Pausanias, fifty years earlier, by the properties of these places and went out of his way to investigate them.[24] At Apollonia, he described the two jets of flame which were still active above ground and onto which clients threw incense, having made their prayers. If the flame shot up, the prayer was to be granted, but if it died away, the answer was unfavourable. Here, the oracle refused questions on the awkward topics of death and marriage.

Meanwhile, prophetic persons were to be found everywhere, in the cities, the countryside, in every cultural zone of the Empire. If we are right to date the "Chaldaean Oracles" to the Hadrianic age, it was then that a new art, theurgy, had begun to take shape among certain intellectuals. Educated theurgists then combined these rites with an emphasis on pure living which any prophet at Didyma or Claros would have understood. Following up "traces" left by the gods, they insisted that their art was distinct from malevolent magic. Its masters are not to be confused with the lunatic fringe of modern parapsychology or mediums at a séance. They were developing the ideas of prayer and oracular wisdom which were shared by most of their educated contemporaries and the great contemporary shrines.[25]

At a less esoteric level, street prophets were strongly in evidence. We hear much about prophetic women,[26] "pythonesses," as they were popularly known, but it is not true that oracular "possession" was a distinctively female gift or essentially imagined in the metaphors of man's "possession" of women.[27] There were male "pythons" too, and at shrines like Claros and Patara, women played no part. More generally, possession was believed to attend the "young and the somewhat simple" of either sex: in Plutarch's day, the Delphic prophetess was still a simple country girl. When the city of Laodicea-by-the-Lycos sent its delegations to Claros, it sent its own local "prophet of Apollo" and "priest of the children," both of whom were young boys, like the city's choral singers.[28] Childhood and prophecy, these people assumed, were natural allies. The boys looked so innocent and so unspoilt. No barrier of worldly experience blocked them from divinity; no cares and distractions marred their godlike beauty. They were expected to speak, so their tongues ran away with them and their fantasy took wings. Private practitioners were quick to exploit the possibilities, and spells for obtaining a prophecy made ample use of a child's transparency to God.[29]

Cynically, we might feel that children were most open to trickery and autosuggestion. The ancients, however, were more trusting. In court, Apuleius reminded his audience how the vulgar and learned agreed on this point, that the powers of divination and prophecy resided especially in small boys.[30] Their explanations varied, but personally, Apuleius believed in the young soul's innate power of divination, which could be lured by music and sweet scents to revert to its primal nature, half-mortal, half-immortal, so that it foretold events to come. Others disagreed. Prophecy, they said, was the gift of the divine intermediaries, or *daemones*, who moved between gods and men and could enter into a child who was handsome and quick-witted, and then "he would give prophecies when touched on the head and clothed in a fair, white cloak." Earlier in this century, children, dressed in white, were still being given a prominent role in the drawing of the winners in Italian state lotteries.

These prophetic techniques were matched by others, in which no woman or child was required as an intermediary, because they turned on significant chance and a relevant use of the lot. This service had become freely available in cities during the Antonine age. At Pharai in

Achaea, said Pausanias, the image of Hermes was set behind a stone hearth onto which were clamped lamps of bronze.[31] "Inquirers of the god come to it at evening and burn incense on the hearth. They fill the lamps with oil and light them and lay a local coin called a 'copper' on the altar to the right of Hermes. They whisper their question into the god's ear. Then they stop their own ears, leave the marketplace and, just outside it, unblock their hearing: whatever words they then hear they consider to be an oracle. The Egyptians have a similar custom at the temple of Apis." The busy client could also consult the gods by throwing dice or knucklebones. Pausanias remarked how sets of dice were left lying on small ledges below statues of Hermes or Heracles, and one of the continuing gains from archaeology is the discovery of ever more stone fragments of these dice oracles and their inscribed lists of answers.[32] Examples have been found in Phrygia, in a differing form in Cilicia and also in Pisidia, and there are other examples from Thrace. Their forms varied and two main types are now evident, although the procedure was always similar. The questioner approached, threw the set of five or seven dice and looked up their combination of numbers on the inscribed list of answers. "Five threes: Zeus and Athena. Now is the time for you to attempt what you have come to ask about. The gods will fulfil everything according to your intention. Zeus and Pallas Athena are sending you victory . . ." Again, these answers were not the result of pure chance. They were attached to particular gods and abstract powers, while the method itself was said to have been conceded by Apollo to the care of the god Hermes.

These oracles were not the hidden interest of a lower-class minority. The better-preserved examples seem to have stood on rectangular monuments in cities and were surmounted by a statue, presumably the statue of a god. The majority were found on stones which belonged closely to a public temple or to a section of their city's gateways. Several of the answers address visitors or passersby and are well suited to their placing in crowded public thoroughfares. One set, from the Pisidian city of Anabura, stood above a public vote of thanks to its donor, Attalos, a man who "loved his country, and was a Founder and Benefactor."[33] These titles belong with an immensely grand civic figure. This type of consultation had a near-relation in alphabetic oracles, texts which required a questioner to pick model letters of the alphabet and read off the appropriate answer beside each letter on a list. This type, too, was widespread, and we have one good example from

Oenoanda itself.[34] Like the dice oracle, it gave answers in verse and favoured a riddling, enigmatic style: "You are kicking against the pricks: you are struggling against contrary waves: you are searching for a fish in the sea." Answers could only be very general when the questions were so vague and impersonal. Like the dice, these oracular "alpha-to-omegas" were under the care of the gods Apollo and Hermes. Most of the local variants draw on a similar core of answers and suggest that these oracles had had a common origin. Had they spread from a major oracle centre of Apollo, perhaps Delphi itself, which may have imposed the basic core and style and left others to elaborate it?

The texts of these oracles are datable to the second and third centuries by the style of their inscription and make an interesting parallel to the revival of the major inspired shrines. Like cash cards, they made the gods' resources swiftly available without priests or complex offerings. Although the patterns of answer vary locally and the answers are usually banal, most of the sets share a common concern with men's prospects for travel and trade.[35] They are concerned to predict the shape of the future, not to analyse problems in the past. Each answer in a dice oracle came under the care of a particular divinity, distinct gods who had extended their service as one more "infernal snare" in the cities in which the early Christians were putting down roots.

"Prophets," too, were alert to the scope for ready-made, practical questions and answers. If there was no dice oracle to hand, a client could turn to an "expert" and his impressive oracular books. We happen to know one example from a sequence of finds on papyrus.[36] It first came to light when a papyrus of the later third century revealed parts of a long list of Greek questions. At first, they seemed to be destined for a traditional oracle and their bleaker examples were misread as a proof of the "mood" of their age. Soon afterwards, they were related to a longer and older collection, the so-called Fates of a legendary sage, Astrampsychus. These Fates had only been known in Christian manuscripts of a later date, but the papyri have proved that they already existed among pagans by the later third century A.D., and probably earlier. They have sufficed for a brilliant decoding of the system by which they worked. The questioner chose an appropriate numbered question from an "expert's" book, whereupon the expert matched the question with a numbered answer and gave his client a response which seemed to be chosen by an act of Providence. We do not know when Astrampsychus's Greek almanac originated, but its surviving range of questions contains inquiries which only suit a date after the mid-first century A.D. Significantly, its questions suit the various social classes, high and low alike. While matters of marriage and health, love and inheritance interested everyone, others varied with the client's rank. "Shall I become a councillor?" "Shall I go on an embassy?" "Will I be sold into slavery?" Astrampsychus catered for more than a hundred eventualities and helped expert owners of his almanac to earn a living by following the simple rules. His clients were not only humble and uneducated people, nor was his book short-lived. It passed, with similar Fates, into the Middle Ages, when it was still used.

Astrampsychus's text is only one symptom of a wider pattern of practice. Throughout the ancient world, it was normal to prefer divination to indecision. Intellectuals did not argue the interesting problem of whether or not the preference was rational. Although a few remained sceptical, most of the others merely argued about the forms which divination took.[37] Here, there was a rough distinction between the value of oracles which a god inspired and these lesser techniques which relied on human materials. A few writers denied that the lesser techniques had any merit, but their complaints did not stop men from practising them, any more than attacks on macro-economics have stopped administrators from trusting its theories. The prizes were too tempting. It was left to Iamblichus to include both types in his Platonist philosophy and abolish the old distinction between inspired prophecy and minor divination.

Techniques of this type offered help where help was always welcome: they also attached to a congenial intellectual climate. Like us, the ancients were deceived: just as macro-economics has traded on mathematics, or sociology on science, in antiquity, too, dubious attendants found a home in the company of rational astronomy, mathematics and medicine. In its simplest forms, divination rested on an argument from analogy and the interpretation of "signs." More generally, this type of thinking was rooted in other arts which flourished in second-century culture, the study of dreams and the stars, the flimsier sorts of medical prognosis and even the study of people's eyes and faces. Artemidorus's interest in predictive dreams and their "allegory" is akin to oracular divination and its art of conjecture by signs and analogies. The astrologers, too, claimed divine inspiration for their art, although the better theorists claimed

only to study "signs" and tendencies, not determinant causes.[38] Like
dreams, the stars were grounds for a speculative prediction, although
the macro-economy of the heavens was too complex to be caught in
any one causal theory. A few thinkers denied there was anything in the
theory at all,[39] but it took more than a good argument to kill an art
which promised so much. Perhaps the summit of divinatory skill was
the art of telling people's nature and prospects from their faces. In the
Antonine age, the great sophist Polemo drew together all previous
learning on this riveting topic and added examples from his own
experience.[40] By studying people's faces, he had foreseen all sorts of
trouble, problems for Hadrian while hunting, for a bride on her
wedding day in Samos, for a woman in Perge who was walking,
wearing her veil, to the temple of Artemis. Naturally, also, Polemo
could see through his rival sophists by assessing the shape of their
hideous faces, a fact which he reported in a torrent of extreme abuse.
While the tireless Artemidorus was collecting and analysing dreams,
Polemo, the prince of sophists, was judging his fellow men from the
style of their walk or the thickness of their hair. Like Artemidorus's,
the art required a use of analogy and wordplay, combined with a
strong sense of social categories and "types" of character. Of course,
other intellectuals would have mocked it, but the future lay with these
types of study. In the Antonine age, Ptolemy compiled his great guide
to astrology; Artemidorus amassed books on the art of dreams;
Polemo described the predictive power of physiognomy. Their books
passed through Syriac into Arabic and fascinated the court societies of
Muslim rulers. With the help of Polemo, people could pick a decent
slave, long after his book's composition: slaves, like horses, were
judged by their eye, that unerring "mirror of the soul."

     These arts were not new, but their great literary authorities were
writing at the height of the oracles' revival, in the second century A.D.,
a time when the gods' "providence" was freely acknowledged. In the
past, each of these arts had owed something to Greek culture's contact
with the older civilizations of the Near East. Like a younger, freer
economy, the Greek world had pillaged its neighbours' techniques,
refined them into general theories and made prophecy, divination and
oracles a major Greek industry. In the early Christian era, "information technology" was blossoming under the care of the pagan
gods: was it, however, an entirely free enterprise? In an Imperial
age, divination was strictly banned if it concerned the prospects of
Emperors: what might not follow from the horoscopes of the

Emperor and his rivals? Control, however, could go beyond these awkward subjects, as we have learned from a recently published papyrus which well sums up the continuing range of the technology and the varying views of its worth.[41]

In the year 198/9, it shows a prefect of Egypt ordering his district governors in very strong language to ban the "chicanery" of oracles and divination. "Encountering many who believed themselves to be deceived by the practices of divination, I swiftly judged it necessary, in order that no danger should ensue upon their foolishness, herein to enjoin clearly that all people must abstain from this hazardous inquisitiveness." Officials who failed to carry out the order were themselves made liable for its penalty. "Hazardous inquisitiveness" amounted to "oracles or written scripts given as if from a divinity or the procession of divine statues." This rite with statues was an old Egyptian practice, but the "written scripts" are more tantalizing. Probably they are the pairs of questions which we find on papyrus and to which a god seemed to "give" an answer.

Why had the prefect been so bothered? His edict cannot be dated exactly, but it falls within the months in 198/9 when the Emperor Severus is known to have visited Egypt. On this visit, Severus is said to have investigated the country's secret texts and made many of them inaccessible: did the prefect issue his order after he had seen Severus's interest? However, no word in the text requires this connection and its ban goes wider than divination concerning the Emperor. The prefect, it seems, had been shocked by the swindles of prophets and diviners, and so he struck at their entire undergrowth. He failed, but his edict is excellent proof of their vigour and their continuing capacity for dividing opinions about their merits.

It is necessary to bring the range of these techniques together, not just for their antiquarian interest but also for the wider question of mood. If we set the "decline" and "rise" of the inspired oracles against this mass of evidence, their explanation has to be sought in a different direction. Theories of a psychological change, or a "new mood," are no longer helpful. There had been no sharp rise in credulity, no pressure from new, unsatisfied anxieties. Almost all of this range of persons, places and techniques had been credited for centuries, flourishing because they met enduring needs. In the second century, inspired oracular shrines were merely establishing themselves once more in the market: the market itself was not new.[42] The questions, then, are how and why the oracles re-established themselves. What did they offer which other services did not and what was needed for them to be able to offer it impressively?

Oracles were not concerned to defeat the rival services: at one level, they joined them. The temples, too, used techniques of drawing lots and gave simple answers to written petitions: at Claros, there is evidence of an oracular use of dice, and at Didyma, of an early use of knucklebones. No doubt, the clients took their questions to several authorities and sampled a range of advice, but perhaps they felt that the answers from a temple had more authority. Perhaps, too, they were glad of the privacy, a rule which private diviners could not be trusted to observe. In Egypt, during the second and third centuries, we can sample the questions which were put to various gods and temples by a technique which did not involve inspired speech: they were written on papyrus, and in Upper Egypt, papyrus survives.[43] The bulk of the surviving questions follow more or less the same form. They address their god, pose their question in a conditional "if" and then add "give me this" or "bring out this" as their final sentence. Some neat papyrology has helped us to understand their phrasing. The questions were often written on one and the same papyrus and then detached into halves. One half phrased the question negatively, "if I should not go," the other, positively, "if I *should* go." The two slips were then sealed and submitted to the god for his choice, and the client phrased his request as "give me" or "give me back" this piece of papyrus. We do not know how the god chose the answer, but perhaps his priest simply drew it from a jar: possibly, the god pointed to it by means of his statue, the old Egyptian rite whereby the god's statue was borne on his priest's shoulders and tossed or turned to direct him to one of two alternative answers which lay on the ground before him. Whatever the method of answer, we do have a precious range of questions which extend from the Hellenistic period into the Christian empire. They are very homely:[44] "Isis: are you the origin of my trouble and will you give me help?" "Am I to stay in the job of tax collector?" and that question of agonizing luxury: "Which of two women shall I marry?" These questions are personal versions of those which we also find in Astrampsychus's book of Fates. At this level, the gods came naturally, because they had such obvious uses to the anxious and the ambitious alike. They were a marriage bureau and a career service, a medical surgery and a farmers' bulletin.[45]

Their service could only survive and retain credit at this practical level by setting limits to the suitable forms of a question and answer.

The gods were prepared to consider a choice between alternatives, but if mortals asked for too much, they risked provoking a god's displeasure. If mortals did not pose alternatives, they ought to cast their questions as requests, "whether it was preferable and better" to do this or that.[46] The god, then, could not be refuted. If he advised action and the result was disastrous, questioners were left to reflect that the alternative would have been even worse. Many of the questions concerned clients' prospects in love and business, travel and public service, and distinguish their clients from contemporary tribal societies whose diviners are more concerned to analyse the past than to choose between options for the future. Life in antiquity was less uniform, even in small Egyptian townships, where there was a strong emphasis on prospects and choices between possible futures. Among the surviving questions, there is less of the obsessive concern with adultery which has characterized the tribal oracles, fondly described in the modern Sudan. Occasionally, questioners did ask the god specifically about a culprit, and here, perhaps, there were risks. Did the priests of an oracular crocodile god indulge in careful preliminary questioning before they put such questions to their god? Observers of modern oracles have commented on these preliminary discussions and on the gods' convenient gift for rude, dismissive replies. So, too, in the Greek-speaking world, we have seen how gods could rebuke their questioners' "insolence" if their questions went too far. Respect for the gods' anger and temper was a good insurance for the system, and faults, meanwhile, could always be blamed elsewhere. By Porphyry's time of writing, there were several alternatives. An oracle might have been given by a lesser daemon, who did not know the truth: mundane questions, Porphyry warned very tellingly, were particularly liable to attract an untruthful spirit. Otherwise, the gods' natural truthfulness might be interrupted while they came down from heaven. The lower, earthly regions fell under the powers of fate and the stars, forces which interfered with the gods' normal service and distorted clear transmission.[47] In these and other ways, one false science supported another, preventing users from seeing the culprits: themselves.

# III

In this maze of techniques and oracular practice, where did the consultation of great shrines and inspired prophets belong? Were most of their questions significantly different, questions which concerned the world of the gods, perhaps, whereas divination and the other oracular arts concerned the world of men? To test this distinction, we can look at the intriguing sample of oracular consultations which clients inscribed on durable materials in the Imperial age. The surviving texts are a random sample, and insofar as they were inscribed for posterity, they may be one-sided: the more impressive and solemn answers were perhaps more likely to be displayed and preserved. They also raise difficult problems of dating. Sometimes we can find a clue which fixes them more closely, but often we have only the style of their lettering by which to judge, and on this alone it is very difficult to place an inscription within the second or third century. Nonetheless, the texts do illustrate a major side of life at classic oracular shrines. First we can set their concerns beside the questions of God and the soul with which we began. Then we can use them to put a newcomer in perspective.

For a start, the oracles which survive in inscriptions at or around Didyma show the problems which could arise over details of cult. At Didyma, the treasurer, Hermias, noticed that the altar of Fortune had been crowded by newer buildings in Apollo's *paradeisos*, and thus was no longer visible: could he please move it to join the other gods' altars in the circle around Apollo's own main altar? Apollo agreed, in a single vague hexameter: "It is right to honour all the immortals and worship them all." This same Hermias recorded another question asking the god what was "dear" to him, and again Apollo answered in a single line. "It is better and finer to act with traditional purpose." When were these questions posed?[1] Their lettering has been placed both early and late in the third century A.D., but the earlier date now prevails, after the recent discovery of Hermias's longer text. He was deeply concerned for the details of cult and the wishes of the god whom he served.

A similar problem troubled Damianos the prophet, a man who had come from Cyzicus to serve Miletus's shrine. He had noticed there was no altar to Kore the Saviour goddess from his native city among the "encircling altars of many gods": could he, then, put one by the altar of her mother, Demeter? Kore, he claimed, was Apollo's "most holy sister," a curious genealogy for the goddess, our Proserpine, but one which Apollo did not rebut: "Perform the honour of joining the encirclement," the god replied. Damianos described himself as a "lover of the gods" and returned, keenly, with a second question:

would Apollo also be "legislator" of the "pious form of address in hymns" for Kore, whose altar was being honoured? Apollo replied, "Let us invoke her as Saviour with fair cries at times of sacrifice, gentle to encounter with her mother Demeter."[2]

This question and answer are full of religious interest. Damianos, too, referred the placing of an altar to Apollo himself: this "lover of the gods" had been "troubled," he said; he besought "master Apollo Helios of Didyma," an equation of Apollo and the Sun which the god himself had probably approved at the shrine in an oracle and which was in evidence by 200 A.D., at the latest. In reply, Apollo assumed the age-old patterns and fears of a divine epiphany. While offerings were made to Kore, she must be "called" with propitious cries of invocation. She must be hailed as Saviour, her native title in Cyzicus, and be greeted as "gentle to encounter," a phrase which carefully prescribed her mood in advance of attendance. These old patterns of prayer and divine presence still mattered to the god and his prophet: as in Homer, "the gods are hard to encounter openly." Damianos's question has been ascribed to the later third century A.D. on very tenuous grounds, but "master Apollo Helios" is a title known earlier and a date in the first half of the century is now much more likely for his text.

The dating of these two questions is important, because their rites and language have been taken as proofs of Didyma's declining years. In fact, they belong in the age of Poplas and his associates, when a general loss of vigour was not in evidence. The crowded "encircling" altars, the equation of Didyma's Apollo and the Sun, the encroachment onto the shrine's "precinct": none of these changes was a consequence of the mid-third century and its hardships, let alone of a growing apathy as Christianity then spread. With the passing of time, Didyma had become packed with ever more pagan gods and altars, and like his prophets, Apollo retained a lively sense of the awe and presence of gods when "called." These oracles were not the products of a growing religious indifference: they belong with Alexandra's question on the gods' "visitations" and the praises of Demeter, inscribed on her same stone. Their concern for the gods' mood and identity recurs in a further text, which was found some distance from Didyma, but had almost certainly been transported from an original home at the shrine. Its upper part is missing, but the rest of it introduces us to a female questioner, who was returning, like Damianos, to put a second question.[3] "You told her to propitiate

Hera, but where should she do so?" Evidently, there were several
shrines of the goddess Hera, presumably in Miletus itself, and Apollo
replied in some lofty and puzzling verses: she should worship Hera at
the "halls of an effeminate man" near baths for tired, elderly limbs and
the dances of virgins to the flute. Perhaps a particular shrine of Hera
stood near a set of baths and the shrine of a god which was served by a
eunuch priest. Whatever the reference, the question and answer turned
on a familiar concern: how exactly to "propitiate" a god, a word
which oracles at Didyma favoured, and which temple would have the
best effect? Again, the moods of the gods were not to be risked
without due care. It is to Didyma that we can trace another text,
known to Christian authors, in which Apollo told the people of
Rhodes to "propitiate" Attis, Adonis, Dionysus, apparently running
the gods' names into one.[4]

Prayers and sacrifices were not the only activities which continued
to involve gods in mortal life. Their presence was also freely invoked
in oaths: Tertullian, c. 200, complained of the problems for fellow
Christians who wished to borrow money but had to swear oaths by
the pagan gods to their creditors.[5] What was the proper form of an
oath? If Apollo could "legislate" on prayers to Kore, he could also
define the terms of an oath by the gods. In his book on oracles,
Porphyry quoted an elegant text in which Apollo at Didyma listed the
various gods and their functions, and showed a precise grasp of their
separate identities without any trace of "monotheism." A second text
survives as his answer to one Rufinus, who wished to know how his
sea captain should swear an oath. The text is an inflated statement in
hexameters, requiring the poor man to stand with one foot in the sea,
the other on dry land, and to hold sea and shore in either hand. He
must invoke the heaven, the earth and "the life-giving leader of
Ethereal Fire": "this is an oath which the exalted dwellers in heaven do
not themselves ever dare to dishonour." This text is particularly
important, because we know this Rufinus as a Roman consul and an
immensely rich benefactor of Pergamum, where he built the circular
Pantheon. After his death, Apollo answered another problem of cult:
he told the men of Pergamum where to bury this magnificent hero
"because of the past excellence of his life." This millionaire and great
public figure had the particular obsession of his type. He was anxious
that his ship captain should not dare to cheat him, and so he consulted
the god on his enterprise. To distinguished men like Rufinus, there
was no rigid line between the details of trading and their own social

respectability. There was also no doubt about the value and presence of the gods in both.

Vows, too, involved gods in mortals' willingness to stand by an obligation. We have seen the quantity of stone reliefs and dedications "vowed" in the hope of favour or in obedience to a dream, but did the gods themselves always want such a vow to be fulfilled? In the marketplace at Miletus, one Ulpius Karpas inscribed his question to Apollo: "whether it is 'dear' to Serapis for him to perform his vow."[6] We know this Karpas as a member of Miletus's council and a prophet, in his own right, of a Most High god in the city in the early third century. He turned to Apollo, not to the god whom he served, when he wished to know another god's preference. Then he inscribed the consultation proudly in public.

If Apollo could define the preferences of other gods, he could also speak on his own. It is in this light that we can best make sense of Didyma's fragmentary text on songs and sacrifice which was inscribed on the reverse of a marble block in the wall of the Prophet's House. Just enough survives for the drift of the oracle to be clear.[7] Apollo emphasized that the immortal gods did not need "possessions," or gifts of hecatombs and offerings of gold and silver colossal statues. What Apollo preferred was song, especially if it was sung just before his oracles were delivered. "I enjoy all singing, but particularly songs which are old." In the past, he concluded, he "drove away plagues, putting to shame the grievous threads of the Fates." In the 270s, Apollo at Delphi did refer rather coldly to mortal life as "blood-devouring," and in texts like the Oenoandans', blood sacrifice is not an evident "command."[8] In the Didyma text, Apollo was protesting more generally at excessive gifts, whether animal victims or works of art. He ended by referring to the very origins of his cult, a time when he was believed to have rid Miletus of plague with the help of a mysterious alphabetic hymn. Its symbols were remembered and still known to Clement, a learned Christian author, at the turn of the second century.[9] His musical defeat of the plague was relevant to a text on the value of song.

What is the origin of this remarkable text, which shows a true "philosophy in oracles" and survives without its question? The inscriptions of a great family at Didyma may allow us, at last, to place it.[10] From the family of Poplas the prophet, we have a text in honour of a lady who offered a due "hecatomb" and poured libations at the oracular shrine, all "in accordance with the oracles of the god." The precise degree of her "kinship" with Poplas is not known, but this pious lady is a younger member of his line, active, then, c. 230–250 A.D. It is particularly interesting that the back of this same stone was cut with a long, proud text which gives us our fullest family tree of Poplas and his prophetic relations. It then quotes Apollo's oracular praises for Flavius Ulpianus, a prophet who was commended for his respect for ancient oracles and his care of "sacrificial business." This prophet is one of the latest whom we know in Didyma's inscriptions and probably held office in the 250s.

At this date Apollo's own words were still praising a prophet who sacrificed keenly, and due hecatombs "in accordance with the oracles" were being paid at the shrine. The oracle text on song cannot already have existed at Didyma on a block of the Prophet's House; otherwise, these pious servants would have been flouting the explicit words of the god. On other grounds, the text has been dated late, to the end of the third century, where it has been seen as Apollo's "swan song": the choirs in his cult, on this view, had been forgotten, and as soon as the god tried to revive them in this text of spiritual piety, the Christians silenced his shrine altogether.[11] It may, however, be the opposite, not a swan song but an accompaniment to an oracular restoration.

The pious sacrificing prophet, Flavius Ulpianus, had a prophetic cousin, Aelius Granianus Ambeibios Macer, no less, whose statue was dedicated elsewhere in Miletus by his wife, Agatho. Her inscriptions called him "dear to Phoebus." His statue also stood near the temple, where its inscribed base was rediscovered, showing Macer to have been a man of notable talent. This member of a great Milesian dynasty was also a victor in one of the city's great third-century festivals: he won the contest for the best "encomium," or speech of praise. He had also been lyre player in Miletus's cult of Apollo Delphinios, "advance lyre player," on the likeliest translation, who played before the central moment of cult: he seems to have held this honour while a boy, when he had also been a "choir leader," presumably in Apollo's cult. As the years passed, Macer married well and, like his father, became prophet of Didyma's Apollo. In his year of office, we know, his wife donated a roof and stucco to the colonnade round the Prophet's House. Macer, we have also learned, "restored ancestral practices" in the cults: a notable scatter of inscriptions still honours him and his great forbears at the shrine.[12]

Is not Ambeibios Macer the missing clue to Apollo's "swan song"? Other members of his dynasty had recently been slaughtering hecatombs and showing expensive care for sacrifice "in accordance with Apollo's oracles": they are known, too, for their patronage of large monuments and statues elsewhere at Didyma. Around 200, we know of the lavish work of a daughter of another great Milesian family: she dedicated a statue and a silver relief of the gods, which may have been a scene of the birth of Apollo and Artemis.[13] This type of costly display was not true piety to Macer's mind. When he volunteered for the job of prophet "at his own promise," he undertook a different gift, a part of his "restoration of old customs." He revived the prominence of choir song, an art which he had practised personally in his youth. Through his musical prophet, Apollo spoke in support and added a mild reproach: the gods did not want statues and hecatombs, the piety of Macer's rich cousins, but they rejoiced in choirs and enchanting song. Songs, said the god, were to be sung "before" the oracular words were delivered. In his youth, Macer had served Miletus's other great cult of Apollo as the official lyre player at this very moment, playing for the god "before" the rites began. There may, indeed, be more. Macer's own father was also a prophet, Granianus Diodorus Phanias, and he, too, had shown an exceptional talent: he had been a victor in one of the grand "circuit" games in the Mediterranean. Competitive sport was not alien to great upper-class families: in Miletus, Poplas's family included a boxing victor, while other prophets had winning athletes in their line.[14] However, the elder Granianus may have been a literary victor, a public speaker, perhaps, at the great festivals. If so, the performing arts ran in his son's blood, and so, very possibly, did philosophy: at Didyma, one "Phanias" described himself as "successor of Plato" and also served as Apollo's prophet. It is quite possible that he belonged earlier in Macer's family, where the name Phanias recurs.[15] Once again, Apollo proved only as wise as his prophet. Ambeibios Macer was a lifelong musician and a prize-winning man of letters, well able to write hexameter verse: philosophy ran, perhaps, in his family's past. In his year of office, Apollo spoke to him in favour of song; his words were well chosen and the text wore the stamp of philosophic piety.

This text, we now see, was not a swan song:[16] it pointed to lively concern and rivalry between two branches of a rich prophetic dynasty. One year, the god had received hecatombs "in accordance with his oracles"; in another, he disclaimed hecatombs and praised ancient music instead. Inevitably, Apollo agreed with his yearly prophets, and when Macer "restored" ancient customs, the god endorsed the change. How great, indeed, had this change been? Had the choirs really ceased altogether in the years of Poplas and his fellow enthusiasts? In Miletus's other great cult of Apollo they had not,[17] for Macer was still leading choirs as a boy and playing a prelude on his lyre. Perhaps Macer merely revived an old, neglected hymn and set it at a new moment, just before the prophetess spoke from her seat. These very points were singled out for approval in Apollo's oracular text: at the same time, the god belittled cruder piety, the hallmark of Macer's cousin and kin.

These texts on cult were wholeheartedly conservative; they praised the "old" music and "old ancestral customs"; they endorsed attention to the old oracles and ordinances and to "ancestral purpose" in worship of the gods. They take us through the early third century A.D. into the 240s and 250s, the age of the Emperor Gordian and the first edicts which required sacrifice to the pagan gods. These Milesians needed no religious "revival" from above: Apollo and the details of his honours had not lost their interest for people who led his cult. They questioned their god for oracles of the type which we suspected: answers to details of change and practice in matters concerning the gods. Divination and dice oracles could not handle this business with authority. Nor could they sort out a running problem which even gods could not escape: troubles with the staff.

If Apollo could define cult practice, he could also give the final authority on priesthoods. From Claros, he sent a "testimony" to the purity of Prisca, a priestess of Artemis who had served the goddess for sixty years in her Macedonian city of Stobi.[18] The city consulted him with a small delegation in the mid-160s, the years of plague. Maybe the envoys also drew his attention to their chaste, long-serving priestess whose family was so prominent in the city's upper class. Then, or separately, Apollo applauded her virtue, perhaps confirming the continuing wisdom of her life appointment. Questions of tenure certainly concerned him. From Claros, he sent a most obscure answer to the people of Aizani which seems to bear little resemblance to their question.[19] They had asked if a particular priest should remain the priest of the Founder, evidently beyond his usual term of office. Perhaps there had been a dispute, but Apollo's answer sufficed to settle it and was inscribed on a building, perhaps the Founder's shrine. The text seems to allude to an oracular riddle from Herodotus's first book and may have been an answer from Claros in the years before the lifelong thespode improved the quality of the oracles.

These questions, once again, concerned affairs of the gods, not the political affairs of men. If tenure is one staff problem, correct selection is always another. At Didyma, in the late second to the early third century, we find Apollo easing the process, again in the highest social circles.[20] Saturnilla was a very well-born lady who had been married and borne children, but then, perhaps as a widow, she was appointed to a priesthood of the virgin Athena. Thereupon, some questioners asked Apollo for his opinion of her suitability. The god noted their delay in raising the matter and commented, it seems, on the contrast of Aphrodite, goddess of sexual love, and the virgin Athena. Nonetheless, Athena, it seems, had accepted their choice, and even though Saturnilla was not a virgin, her appointment, said Apollo, could stand. It seems that willing and eligible virgins were in short supply during these years, but Saturnilla's exceptionally good birth reconciled Apollo to her choice. She was connected with Roman senators and athletic victors, and her sons were so pleased with these sub-Homeric verses and their theological wordplay that they inscribed them as a memorial to their mother's honour.

If Apollo could approve the servants of other gods, it is not, then, so surprising that he also spoke about his own. Recently, we have learned that he "appointed" a prophetess at Didyma whose name, Tryphosa, is the only one we know in all the years of the office.[21] In the Imperial period, again, Apollo intervened to endorse a woman's appointment: the honour was specially recorded in a family inscription, suggesting that it was not the god's usual practice. What, then, of his male prophets? Here, they could hope for a separate honour: a divine "testimonial." Cities passed honorary decrees "testifying" to the virtues of their magistrates: the gods caught the habit and "testified" to their servants.[22] The habit was probably more frequent than we realize: we find the god of a prophetic spring at Palmyra "testifying" to civic dignitaries, while artistic reliefs in the city show gods making dedications to human benefactors. At Didyma, the prophets' inscriptions show something similar, Apollo's good references for his yearly prophets.[23] In the 60s A.D., he bore "witness to the holy soul" of Philodemus, who was the only man to have held the job of prophet and crown-bearer in one and the same year: Philodemus inscribed this honour above carvings of his four crowns of office. In the Imperial period, he "greeted" his prophet Posidonius, who had been chosen by lot "three times over," perhaps for three different jobs in one year. "Eternity will not forget his glory . . ." said the accompanying verses, perhaps words of Apollo himself. To the glory of another prophet, said his verse inscription, the "witness" was not a man, but a god: he was "cared for by divine Apollo." In the mid-third century, Apollo "testified" to the noble forbears of Macer the musician, perhaps in a "testimonial" to his mother, herself a priestess and a cult official: we can follow this "nobility" across four generations from prophet to prophet. His cousin, the prophet Flavius Ulpianus, went one better: the god, said his inscription, bore witness to him "often." Beneath, a verse text praised Ulpianus's care for "fleecy sheep" and remarked that Apollo would therefore reply "in turn" to his questions. The answer went on to commend Ulpianus's sacrificial activity. This "testimonial" was a unity, but it has not been rightly understood. Apollo was not complimenting this great prophetic family, the dynasty of Poplas and others, on its sheep farming and share in the trade of Miletus's wool. The "fleecy sheep" belonged with Ulpianus's sacrifices, the very "hecatombs," we have suspected, which Macer's Apollo then decried.

Like the oracles on tenure and selection, these testimonials have taken us into the highest social circles at the shrine. And yet, there was no Apollo: in all sincerity, the prophets were congratulating themselves. A public memorial was part of a prophet's reward: from the walls of the Prophet's House, we have a long range of inscriptions which commemorate the "pious" prophet of each year. Sometimes, they go further: around 200 A.D., Andreas, son of a famous prophet and civic figure, recorded his ancestry and previous offices and his "doing all else that I could with moderation."[24] Beneath, a set of verses asked Apollo the king to "look on him with gentle eyes." Did Apollo "testify" to Andreas, too, although his inscription did not say so explicitly? We cannot be sure, but we can say something about the manner and occasion of one type of "testimonial" for those who received it.

In the early to mid-third century, the god gave a very special honour to Ulpius Athenagoras, a prophet and civic magistrate.[25] He gave him an oracle "automatically," in the Greek word *automatizein*, which meant to "act or speak without prompting." Spontaneous oracles of this type had not surfaced in our inscriptional evidence since the Delphic legends of the seventh century B.C. One day, off his own bat, Apollo applauded this prophet who had also volunteered for a high civic office in the same year. The event, then, was exceptional, suggesting that Apollo's "witness" was not usually spontaneous but that it resulted from a specific question. The wording of Posidonius's testimonial implies that it was given at the prophet's inauguration. The prophet, it seems, put on his robes and his simple crown and prepared for the heavy expense of office, standing before his contemporaries. If they put a question to the god – "are you pleased," perhaps, "with our chosen prophet?" – he would then bear "witness" to his merits. These occasions were not the only time for "testimonials": Flavius Ulpianus had received them "often." But they are the ones we know best.

Like Apollo's advice on tenure, these "testimonies" helped traditional pagan religion to run smoothly. They confirmed the choice of a prophet and also gave an honorary return to the very people who were spending great fortunes on the burdens of office. Apollo's words could also be conciliatory in a wider sense. At Didyma, we have seen him steering a rivalry between sacrifices and ancient songs, conducted, most probably, by cousins within one dynasty. From Delphi, at an identical date, we have recently been made aware of a text for a similar occasion.[26] In the mid-third century, the city of Side, in southwestern Asia, received a smart new podium of stone, the site, most probably, of musical contests in the city's "Pythian" games. In addition to some artistic reliefs, it bore two sets of four hexameter verses which were each addressed to an individual. They gave moral advice on the practice of modesty and approved their addressee's "moderate thoughts." The podium was dedicated by two city councillors, father and son, and the evidence of the "Pythian" festival, of Side's cults and her civic coinage has allowed the referral of these poems to Delphic Apollo himself. Not only are they remarkable evidence for Delphi's clientele and poetic abilities as late as the 250s, when the shrine has often been thought to have fallen silent. The verses also praise the Apolline virtue of "moderation" in two city councillors, contrasting it with the "glittering robes" which were the dress of a high official, probably the agonothete, who took care of athletic festivals. It is perhaps too adventurous to see an outright quarrel behind these verses, as if the two city councillors had donated a fine monument for the festival, thereby annoying the senior official who would otherwise run the show. Like Didyma's text on music, the lines do endorse one party's innovation, but they combine this favour with generalized words of approval, reminding benefactors that they please the gods by their hearts, not the trappings of their office.

It is a small step from these questions on cults and their staff to questions on possible human trespass into objects and areas which concerned the gods. For a start, oracles could identify unnatural oddities, the sort of discoveries which Romans discussed and some-times agreed to declare a "portent."[27] Between c. 110 and 115 A.D., the people of Perinthus visited Claros because they had found something odd in their territory. Their inscription is not specific, but it may have been an image of a god lost long ago in some distant spot: they "set it up" after their discovery. Like the miraculous icons which are "found" in the country districts of Catholic Europe, these lost statues of gods roused religious concern. To solve the problem, the people of Perinthus sent some very high-ranking citizens to Claros, leading nine little choirboys, six of whom were their own sons. At Didyma, c. 200, a very fragmentary text tells of problems caused by another such "image" and mentions the role of a dream and the need to "propitiate" the result. One of the most famous instances enjoyed a new public life in the second century A.D. Back in the Hellenistic age, the people of Magnesia, near Miletus, had sent to Apollo at Delphi for advice on an image of Dionysus which they had found one day in a thicket. Apollo told them to send for some Maenads and start a cult of the god in their city, among its "great and mighty people." Good oracles never died, least of all when they honoured a cult and flattered a city's virtues. In the second century A.D., some four centuries after this text's delivery, a keen worshipper of Dionysus inscribed it again and displayed it on a pillar in Magnesia.

Lost images were only one of many such problems.[28] When an unnamed Roman Emperor ordered the widening of the Syrian river Orontes on its course to Antioch, the workers unearthed the bones of a giant skeleton. Off went envoys to Claros, whose Apollo pronounced the body to be the hero Orontes "of Indian descent." Philostratus later relished this story: it took a god to make sense of a dinosaur's bones. Apollo also coped with oddities from the sea: at Didyma, he upheld the existence of Tritons, "creatures of Poseidon, a watery portent," and his text was cited with respect by a pious man of letters in the later second century A.D. We can see, once again, how Alexandra the priestess had turned naturally to Apollo when beset by that supreme curiosity, the visits of the gods in dreams.

These problems arose from the trespass of men into the sphere of the gods. It is in this light that we can understand another type of trespass, feared by building contractors in Miletus, as we learn from their publicly inscribed oracle, which they set beside an upper flight of steps on the back wall of Miletus's theatre.[29] The building contractors for a part of the building had asked the god "whether they should carry out the vaults and arches" and "whether they should consider work given by their native city or work of some other kind." The question has been read as an episode in a building strike: could Apollo ever have been more useful than when letting two sides agree without losing face? His involvement, however, had another cause. The work had been under the supervision of one of his prophets, but the man had recently died. Not unnaturally, the workers turned to Apollo to discover whether to go ahead with his prophet's plans. Apollo answered in the style of an "expert" in arbitration and conciliation. He contented himself with verbose generalities on the value of brains and brawn, the need for a good architect and sacrifices to Athena and muscular Hercules. The inquiry probably belongs in the reign of Hadrian when major work on Miletus's theatre was taking place.

As this answer shows, there was scope for advice from the god in almost any personal enterprise: clients might wish to be told which god they should honour in order to have the best hope of success. Divination would not tell them, whereas an inspired oracle would, and it is in this light that we can appreciate a marvellous question and answer, given c. 150–200 A.D., which stood on the walls of Miletus's temple of Serapis.[30] "Apphion, also known as Heronas, from Alexandria" asked Apollo about his prospects in the arena. He was beautifully aware of the gods' constant assistance in his life: he was a theatrical "star" and his ancestral gods, he said, "stood by" him, "as you do too, master, in whatever business he undertakes." His question was this: would he "acquit himself gloriously at all times in his act of dancing on tiptoe and training bulls and will he be serving [Apollo?] with a fair name?" Apollo told him to pray to various gods and enjoy them as his "protectors": Apphion, it seems, was a bull tamer who danced on the bulls' bare backs. He needed the gods' reassurance on the "glory" of his act, and when he received it, he was so proud that he inscribed it prominently on the shrine of Serapis, the god whose "swift eye" Apollo told him, once again, to "propitiate." The text has the clumsy style and construction which we would expect from a bull tamer using his own words. Once again, it was not enough to receive an oracle which praised a questioner, a place or a cult. It was as well to inscribe it for others to read and admire for ever: did the priests, perhaps, of Serapis encourage the carving of this pleasant text? Oracles profited from that general connection in antiquity whereby the texts which were inscribed tended to be texts which reflected well on one party, or very badly on another.

These and other questions are very lively, but they are a far cry from the free Greek past, when Delphi's Cretan priests had helped Sparta with her constitution and were said to have encouraged the first Greek tyrants. At Delphi, Plutarch's debaters looked wistfully back to the old days when oracles had settled foreign policy and advised their clients on wars. Yet there was still scope for important business, and Plutarch was being too negative. At Didyma, Poplas the prophet asked how best to approach the Emperor for financial aid: in Athens, we have an oracle from Asclepius which was inscribed on a small cult table and told one of his worshippers how best to approach the governor of Achaea and to intercede with him for favours.[31] We can identify the man as the governor in 209/10 A.D. and see how the gods' horizons had moved with the times. No longer the crisis of war, but the problem of access to Roman officials, prompted Greek questions to the gods. What, though, of questions from and about the Emperors themselves?

Here, we enter a dangerous, but tantalizing, field. The establishment of the Emperor's rule at Rome had given a new focus for divination and "information technology": power now centred on an individual, and there was special profit, therefore, in knowing the course of an individual's career. At Rome, the older style of state divination had declined with the new requirements of a monarchy:[32] in the Greek world, kingship was no novelty, but we hear rather more of oracles for present and future rulers, not least because Roman Emperors ran in less stable dynasties and there was greater scope for an outsider, or a sudden change. At Didyma, Apollo was believed to have given a favourable response to the young Trajan; certainly, Trajan favoured the shrine conspicuously when he became Emperor. According to Dio, the temple of Zeus Belus at Apamea was believed to have uttered some robust Homeric lines to the young Severus when he consulted him while a private citizen. Perhaps Trajan heard something similar at Didyma. Out of context, a set of Homeric verses could be very ambiguous.[33]

Publicly, the establishment of new dynasties was indeed linked with signs and reports of approval from the gods, a pattern which runs from Vespasian to the fourth century A.D.: in this light, Constantine's favour for Christ was only one episode in the long history of usurpers' religious publicity. However, neither we nor contemporaries could distinguish clearly between real consultations made before the event and stories which an Emperor or his supporters liked to circulate afterwards. Inquiry about an Emperor's future remained a treasonable offence, punished by severe penalties. The repeated history of laws against the practice suggests that it retained its attractions, but the inquiries, surely, were best conducted in private, not at a shrine with thespodes, prophets and secretaries.[34] According to Dio, the shrine of Zeus Belus at Apamea gave an elderly pretender in the Severan period some different Homeric lines, contrasting an old and weary ruler with a victorious new warrior. Zeus Belus was not such a fund of Homeric jokes, especially as the same three lines are later said to have been given to an unfortunate rival of Constantine. They were obviously a witty invention, an art from which Severus later suffered. After his accession, he was said to have consulted Zeus Belus again, only to be answered with a line from Euripides: "Your entire household shall pass away in blood." Had this line ever been uttered, it was a shrewd bet on any Imperial dynasty, but the story, surely, was a fiction, answering the claim that Zeus Belus had favoured Severus's appointment.

However, the succession and prospects for it were not the only ambiguous matters of state: what of existing Emperors and their prospects in war? Here, despite Plutarch, there was an old and continuing field for prophecy.[35] In the Imperial period, warring rulers asked the shrines for advice; in the Christian Empire, they would ask Christian "holy men." Trajan is said to have consulted Zeus at Baalbek about his prospects in war in the East and to have mistaken a hint of his death in the answer. The consultation, at least, was plausible: throughout antiquity, generals needed to know which gods to honour in order to fare "as well as possible." There may also be truth in a story that the Emperor Carus, in the 280s, marched East against Persia with an oracle's support. Once again, Julian was heir to a long tradition when his Eastern campaign in the 360s was encouraged by words from the gods.

Was there scope, perhaps, for those who feared an Emperor, as well as for those who wished to be Emperor themselves? Here, questions were particularly dangerous, but not every oracular shrine was public, and once, at a private temple, we need have no doubt about this type of consultation.[36] We know it from Dio's own researches into the history of Condianus, a senator who had suffered the worst excesses of Imperial tyranny. During the 180s, the Emperor Commodus arranged the murders of Condianus's elderly, distinguished uncle and father and the death, too, of his brother. Condianus escaped by a trick and wandered as a marked man through the Empire. On his way, he consulted the hero Amphilochus's dream-oracle at Mallos and left a drawing of his dream on a tablet at the shrine, which showed a child strangling two serpents and a lion pursuing a fawn. We know about this tablet because Dio himself saw it as a young man when his father was governing Cilicia in the 180s. Condianus, it seems, had enjoyed an apt, if ambiguous, dream, which, as Dio discovered, could be referred to Hercules, a god whom Commodus especially honoured. Just as Hercules had strangled two serpents, so Commodus had already strangled Condianus's father and uncle and was hounding Condianus, the innocent "fawn." In a dream-oracle, the initiative lay not with a prophet but with the client's own imagination. The "meaning," therefore, could be relevant and more explicit: the tablet is an excellent insight into the terrors of Imperial rule and their impact on an individual's mind.

It was not, then, entirely just of Plutarch to imply that oracles' scope had shrunk with the passing of free political life. Monarchy created its own, momentous demands. In general, its questions are not likely to have differed from the type which we find inscribed by other individuals: which gods should be honoured and how best should the honours be paid for matters to go as well as possible? These questions did not only attach to new ventures, a war or the gift of a podium, a bareback dance on a bull or the building of a theatre. They attached to existing doubts and problems, tenure for life, the finding of statues and heroes' bones, a sudden deluge of dreams of the gods. These questions were unified by one constant presence: awareness of the gods' potential anger, fear of it and a wish to "placate" it and avert it by correct performance. The newly found oracle from Ammon in Libya begins with a significant reassurance: "do not be afraid, Cyzicus," if your citizens honour the god in this particular way.[37] Ultimately, therefore, epiphany and oracles meet on this shared ground. It helps us to appreciate the oracles' best-attested role: they performed a service which some have used as a key to religion's entire function, the "explanation of misfortune."

When two Asian cities feared raiding barbarians, we have seen how Apollo at Claros equated their troubles with the god Ares and advised them to bind his statue in order to ward them off. This belief in the power of statues has a fascinating counterpart in the higher theology which Claros preached. We have seen, too, how Apollo at Didyma explained the supreme misfortune of the group of woodcutters found dead in a field: Pan, he said, had been responsible for this "chain-saw massacre," and but for his enemy, Artemis, it would have been very much worse. It is not, then, surprising that less visible enemies were also within the oracles' competence.[38] On the very Acropolis of Athens, beside the Parthenon, stood an image of mother Earth emerging from her block of stone and raising her hands in prayer: Pausanias, who saw it, explained that she was praying to Zeus to rain on her in a time of drought. The inscription on the rock has been dated to the Hadrianic age, c. 120 A.D., and it ascribes the image to an oracle's command. At a similar date, or perhaps slightly earlier, we have an inscribed question to the oracle of Apollo at Gryneum in Asia Minor, asking about the proper honours to assist the crops. At Nicomedia, in Bithynia (northwestern Turkey), it is evidently to Claros that we should trace a verse text which advises honours to the Moon and the Winds in a time of drought. Here, the god addressed a "ruler of the city": as we shall see, the great crises of the age caused cities to send very prominent citizens as envoys to Apollo's shrines. These envoys belonged to families whom we know in happier times for their buildings and speeches and gifts of theatrical shows. In hard times, they feared the gods' evident anger: they were also people who presided over the persecutions of Christians.

Terrors had always made excellent business for Apollo, and there were never worse terrors than the plagues and earthquakes in the Antonine and Severan age. At Didyma, Apollo's cult was connected by its very origins to the banishment of plague: in the 250s, Apollo still recalled how he had "shamed" the threads of the Fates and kept off the epidemic. The shrine must have been consulted in these later crises, but the visitors happen not to have recorded the results on stone. Instead, we know about Apollo's remedies in a fascinating selection of oracles, most of which derive from Claros's client cities. They carry no date, but the main four probably belong in the great epidemic of the 160s when Roman troops were returning from the East and brought home a disease whose effects read horribly like smallpox.[39] The oracles, said observers, were packed with frightened clients, especially Claros, and in these years, our inscriptions by visiting cities include several distant cities who never inscribe their names at Claros again. At Odessos in Thrace, we find a man who had been on an embassy to Apollo and had "driven away disease" from his fellow citizens. Here, it seems, the oracular remedy worked. In Thrace, near modern Edirne, we learn of a group of statues which four women presented "in accordance with the oracles of Clarian Apollo" and which may have stood on a civic fountain to watch over the purity of the water. The most thorough instructions, however, survive elsewhere.

Three cities have left us pieces of Clarian Apollo's oracles on plague: Pergamum, Callipolis (near modern Gallipoli) and humble little Caesarea Trochetta, a small town in Lydia. The latter two were treated to a metrical and linguistic *tour de force*.[40] The god pitched his style very high and lamented the disaster (crying "Woe! Woe!" to each city) while changing from hexameters to three different types of metre in his long, emotional answers. None of these texts explained the plague; they only prescribed remedies. The Caesareans received a vivid verse picture of the plague "brandishing in one hand a sword of vengeance and in the other raising the deeply mournful ghosts" (probably) "of newly stricken mortals." Only part of the god's remedy survives, but it runs true to his old-fashioned manner. The "divine law," he said, required his clients to draw pure water from seven fountains, which they had fumigated carefully. They must then sprinkle their houses with these "nymphs who have become kindly" and must set up an image of Apollo the archer, bow in hand, in the middle of their plain. There, presumably, he would "shoot away" the invading enemy, the plague itself.

Callipolis was ordered to set up a similar statue, "the warder-off of plague," and was also told to offer blood from sacrificial animals to the "gods below the earth" and to burn all the animals' meat with spices.[41] The pyre of this holocaust was to be sprinkled with "shining wine and grey sea water": the victims, a goat and a sheep, must be black. No doubt Caesarea had had similar orders for a sacrifice, but they are missing from the surviving verses.

Of the three texts, the finest is Pergamum's, which moves in stately hexameters and spends the first nine lines on flattery of the citizens' ancestry, their closeness to the gods and their especial honour from Zeus himself.[42] On Pergamum's steep hill, said Apollo, the infant Zeus had been placed just after childbirth: his statement refuted a host of competing cities which claimed that they, not Pergamum, had received the newly born god. It was no wonder that the people and council of Pergamum decreed that the reply should be inscribed on pillars and displayed "on the agora and the temples." It also offered advice. Apollo wished to please his son, Asclepius, who resided so conspicuously in the city, and so he told the leader of Pergamum's delegation to return and divide the city's youth, or ephebes, into four separate groups. He called them "wearers of the chlamys," or the military cloak which alluded to their honourable Macedonian origin, and he told each of their groups to sing a hymn to a particular god while their fellow citizens feasted and sacrificed in support. This festivity was to last for seven days, a point which makes Pergamum the most favoured of Claros's three known consultants. Each libation was to be joined by prayers that the plague might depart "to the distant land of far-off enemies," perhaps to Parthia, whence it came. The young men's hymn to Zeus happens to survive in Pergamum, a splendid composition which calls on Zeus to "come propitiously" and honour the city with his presence. His companions were to be gods of civic and social concord, while he himself was hailed with high honours. He was the "dweller on the heights of the Titans," the realm of the Sun, and was the ultimate master of the crops and seasons. Claros had probably prescribed the exact words of this solemn, archaic hymn in hexameters, a classic text of belief in the gods' epiphanies.

These remedies were quite useless. They were bad news for their animal victims, better news for sculptors of Apolline statues. They did not, however, impair trust in the god. Like a shrewd prophet, Apollo predicted no easy result: if there was a second outbreak, he told Callipolis, he would promptly send another remedy. The course of divine anger was not predictable, yet in the end, Apollo would be proved right. Eventually, the plague would stop, and if it stopped slowly, the anger of the gods was to blame, not the quality of Apollo's advice. The survivors, finally, would give him credit, while the dead could express no dissenting opinion.

Although none of these texts gives an explanation of the plague's arrival, they each remind us how polytheism could account for any outcome: disasters could be blamed on the anger of one of its many gods. For a clear statement of this point, we can look, lastly, to oracles recently found at Hierapolis, in southwestern Turkey. A leading citizen brought them back from Apollo and inscribed them on blocks of stone in his city (the modern Pamukkale). The plague, they explain, was due to the anger of mother Earth at the slaying of her child, Python.[43] This explanation is of great interest. It referred the present calamity to a distant episode of myth, a thousand years and more in the Greeks' prehistory. The "angry displeasure of the gods," said the text, was paining "many cities and peoples," and the remedy was to offer "libations and perfect hecatombs" to escape their "generous anger." The people must kill appropriate victims for Earth, Ether and the gods of the underworld, and around all the city gates, they must set images of Clarian Apollo, "shooting from afar with his holy arrows." When the "evil powers have been appeased," the god commanded, "boys and girl musicians [should] go together to Claros, with hecatombs and glad libations." "Often," he complained, he had saved the city, but he had not received his share of a meat sacrifice. If the citizens did what he said, in future they would be richer and safer, because they were descended from the god, "through the hero Mopsus and Apollo Kareios."

This text is very illuminating. Once again, said the god, the plague was best defeated by images of archer Apollo and by sacrifices to the elements, of which Earth's huge holocaust is described in puzzling, archaic language. Once again, there was a touch of civic flattery: Hierapolis, said Apollo, was descended from a local Apollo and the hero Mopsus, a legend which we can trace on the types of the city's coinage in the second century A.D.[44] The text goes on to show us how a delegation to Claros could come about. The god himself had prescribed it, in exactly the form which the temple inscriptions at Claros then show us: similar instructions, we now know, were given by Ammon of Libya to his worshippers in Cyzicus, a city which we would otherwise connect with Delphi and, in one case, Didyma. Claros benefited from the advice of other gods, and at Hierapolis, we may note, Apollo only ordered attendance when the plague had passed. Did he, perhaps, fear infection himself? Not speaking, as yet, for Macer, he insisted that his clients offer him meat: hymns and prayers were not his exclusive taste, and the gods were also to have their hecatombs.

The origin of this oracle is not made plain to us, but it is not the advice of the local Apollo Kareios. On one view, it could be ascribed to the Clarian god, but it plainly distinguishes the Apollo who is speaking from the Clarian Apollo whose images are mentioned in the third person.[45] Hierapolis is not present among the consultants at Claros whose lists have so far been published, and the city looked elsewhere for its presiding Apollo. It was an early colony of the Seleucid kings, and like other such colonies, it was connected with Pythian Apollo at Delphi. Cults and games of Pythian Apollo were very prominent in the city, while a recently found relief in the city's theatre shows the town of Hierapolis holding Pythian Apollo himself.

The oracle was inscribed by an individual "at the command of Apollo Archagetes," or "founder and leader."[46] At Hierapolis, this title was particularly prominent for Apollo on coins and in civic inscriptions: as elsewhere, it points ultimately to Apollo at Delphi, the great colonizing god. There are two alternatives: either the oracle was given at a local shrine of Apollo the Founder or else it was sought from Delphi herself.

The local alternative has met with general support: the city did have a local oracular temple whose verses were said by Livy (c. 10 B.C.) to be "not unpolished," and like its fellow colony Laodicea, Hierapolis would have had local prophets in its citizenry.[47] The existence of a local oracle of Apollo did not stop Laodicea from sending choirs constantly to Claros: perhaps the local god, as in our text, commanded them to go. The god does say, "Attend to Apollo Kareios always: for you are my descendants." However, we might have expected him to say, "Attend to me," if Kareios was speaking: the text was from "Apollo the Founder," not Kareios, according to its preface; there is scope, still, for looking to Delphi instead. We know that another Delphic oracle was sought by the nearby city of Tralles in the Imperial period. It was "given" to a "priest," a member, once again, of a very grand family in the city.[48] As it is a verse text, it must belong after Plutarch, and its recipient's name fits the second century A.D. It ascribed an earthquake to the "thousand-year wrath" of the gods and advised a cult and honours for Poseidon, the god of tremors. Once again, it prescribed the exact adjectives by which a god should be invoked.

At Hierapolis, too, the god spoke of "grievous anger" and "wrath" in heaven. The explanation was similar to Delphi's, and so, above all, was the accompanying myth.[49] It was at Delphi that Apollo's arrows had slain the serpent Python, the event which Earth was "resenting." Exactly this scene appears on two splendid coin types from Hierapolis, showing Apollo shooting the serpent Python with his bow. They are unique types in all Asia, and the earlier of the two belongs in the co-reign of Marcus and Verus, precisely the time of the great Asian plague. Hierapolis survived and proudly showed the god's words on her coinage. The scene is Delphic through and through: it has no connection with Kareios's myth and attributes. At Delphi, Apollo was "founder and leader" of the city, her general "ancestor," as the god said. It is quite likely that the oracle, with its Delphic explanation, derived from Delphic Apollo in person.

If so, we have found a great rarity, one of the only verse texts from

Delphi in the Imperial age. It ought to belong before the earlier third century, because of the coin types and the treatment of the text's stones: when another shrine of Apollo was rebuilt in the city, they were taken and recut for use in it.[50] This rebuilding can hardly be later than c. 230, suiting a date for the text in the 160s: builders in Hierapolis were less respectful of their old oracle texts than those in cities elsewhere. To Christians, Hierapolis was the city of St. Philip and his seven prophetic daughters: the recent finds show how rich it also was in inscribed pagan oracles. It had an alphabet oracle, we also know, which gave neat proverbial answers by the usual method; it had these fine Delphic texts and several others known as yet in fragments only, which had been sought and inscribed from the gods. They conform to the pattern we have come to expect.[51] In one, a god laid down the rights of his spokesmen to receive parts of sacrificial meat, and in another, a god approved the wisdom of "nobly born" people, perhaps "kings," and commented on their benefits from wise second thoughts and a sensible way of government. A fourth response addressed the city as a whole and referred to its "questioning" about "the waters." The god rebuked any person, on the likeliest rendering, who "seems to themselves to be wiser than the immortals," and then went on to give advice about the "waters" and the land. Perhaps the city had consulted him in a time of drought.

These recent additions to oracular wisdom in the Imperial age are not unrepresentative. They praised the governors of a city with moral generalities which kept them up to the mark; they advised on details of cult which could cause dispute; they explained and gave cures for drought and plague; meanwhile, the alphabet text offered quick responses to those who wanted instant proverbial wisdom. These further texts' full wording and origins are not certain, nor do we yet know exactly where and when they were first displayed in the city, but their general tone conforms to other oracular business in the second and early third centuries, adding a fine poetic flourish from Delphi. Oracles told men which gods to honour in order to prosper and which to placate in order to avert misfortune. They did not blame misfortune on mortals' sins. They named supernatural culprits, and traced their actions to enmities in heaven. Artemis was hostile to Pan, Earth to Apollo, virgin Athena to loving Aphrodite: disruptive barbarians were allotted to the god Ares, plague to the "threads" of the Fates.[52] In a splendid verse text, recorded as given from Baalbek, Zeus is said to have blamed Poseidon for smashing his temple's columns. He told a third party, probably the Sun god at the shrine, to threaten Poseidon's rule over the sea and remind him: "It is wise, Poseidon, to listen to elder brothers . . ." Poseidon, it seems, had shattered the pillars in an earthquake.[53] Even if the text was a fake, it seemed plausible because it made one god pin blame on another, like oracle texts elsewhere.

We can see, then, how inspired oracles had continued to find a market. They belonged with the themes we have studied in the previous two chapters: cults of continuing vitality and the continuing belief in the anger and presence of the gods. Everybody could use them, benefactors, country people or ambitious stars of the arena. They had survived because they were useful, protecting their cities ("often," as Apollo told Hierapolis),[54] "propitiating" the gods constantly and helping their cults to move correctly with the changing times. To us, many of these questions can seem overscrupulous, but they show how the small details of practice still mattered to men in the cities' upper classes, men like the enthusiast Damianos, who called himself "lover of the gods." Because the gods were "present" and manifest, it was necessary to ask them about changes in cults and about discoveries which might concern them. Otherwise, they might be "unpropitious" and "stand by" men in an angry mood. The old compound of awe and intimacy was still alive.

These questions were not born in a static, indifferent age. Mostly, they arose from the central problem of religious innovation, on which there is a clear division between the Greek and the Roman world. At Rome, innovations were generally supervised by the board of "fifteen men" who had access to the collections of Sibylline books.[55] These old oracular sayings were consulted for advice on new cults or changes in existing worship, and often their meaning relied on their human consultants' judgement: in principle, they were a closed "canon" of divine wisdom. In the Greek world, however, these questions were put directly to the gods.

What style, exactly, was thought to befit the gods' replies? Around the year 120, Plutarch's debaters at Delphi had lamented the disappearance of oracle texts in verse.[56] Their absence, they said, had particularly undermined faith in oracular sites. Plutarch also admitted that people objected to the current texts' "extreme simplicity," which undermined belief in inspiration. "People," said his final speaker, "yearn for riddles and allegories and metaphors in prophecy, much as children prefer rainbows and comets to an honest glimpse of the sun and moon." The age of poetry, he felt, was over and the routine questions of his age no longer invited ambiguity.

Plutarch's general view was shortsighted. At Didyma, verse oracles seem to have been given in the first century A.D.; at Claros, before the 130s, the "prophet" did give verse answers, although they were probably standardized. After Plutarch's death, long and elaborate verses sprang back into prominence at the great shrines, at Ammon's oasis in Siwah (as we have just discovered) and even at Delphi, as we see in her texts for Tralles and Hierapolis, Side and the dead Plotinus. In Plutarch's day, the Delphic prophetess was a simple country girl, yet by *c.* 200 A.D., she is known to have been a very well-born lady.[57] Had this change helped the quality of the oracles? At Claros, the lifelong thespodes clearly made an improvement: perhaps Delphi's return to verse owes more than we know to the rise of this better class of prophetess.

While Plutarch wrote, the dice and alphabet oracles were already giving puzzling answers, again in smooth hexameter verse. Although they were not quite a rainbow, they were decidedly more complex than a plain, clear sky. "From dusky night there once appeared a ray bringing light . . ." "Realize the coming purging of body and soul . . ." When an oracle had to answer general questions in pre-arranged answers, we can well understand why it used this enigmatic style. To judge from Plutarch, the style would not affect many clients' belief in the system.

At the shrines, however, Plutarch was correct on one cardinal point: at this date, the inscribed oracular texts do not use ambiguity. In Plutarch's view, the reason for its decline was, ultimately, political. People no longer asked great questions of state, and on topics like plagues and harvests it was enough for a god to give simple, general replies. The stories of questions by future Emperors took a different line, but perhaps, as we concluded, they were apocryphal. Was Plutarch's reason really the sole one?

Ambiguity fitted neatly with an age of deep respect for the gods and the limits of their gifts. The gods revealed only so much, and no more: their text then threw the final responsibility back onto man's intelligence, giving him signs with which he could later share the blame, while essentially blaming himself. In the Imperial period, this respect for the gods was still deep and intact: why, then, was ambiguity rare in its surviving oracles? It was not easily contrived, and even in the age of Herodotus, we can overestimate its use. We have not seen questions which asked inspired oracles to predict the future in any detail: to our eye, the gods were asked questions in forms or on topics in which they could not be proved wrong by events. Even in the classical period, the majority of "ambiguous" oracles may have been fictions, invented or elaborated after the event. Then, too, oracles were not generally a source of detailed prediction, open to disproof. Plutarch, perhaps, was misled by these past fictions and gave a narrow political reason for a feature which had always lain in oracles' very nature. It helps us to see why other types of prophecy flourished. For a true "prediction," people would look to one of the so-called Sibylline texts, where warnings of ruin and disaster sheltered under the pretensions of age and fictitious authority. Inspired oracles gave advice on "appeasing" gods, a slow, uncertain business: to use the gods and to profit more immediately from their attendance, people turned to sorcery and spells. Some of the oracles' business did overlap with the diviners' and astrologers' questions: problems of marriage, theft and business were also submitted at their sites, though probably only for answer by drawing lots. The claims of "all-knowing" street prophets and sorcerers were much more extreme than the distinctive core of oracular business, the guarded wisdom which the gods inspired people to speak or dream. Only the oracles had the prestige of official consultation by cities, a point which continued to mark them off from rivals, but their inspired answers were usually quite general.

Archaism and obscurity, not ambiguity, typified the shrines' oracular verse. They always had typified it, as we can see from Aristophanes's brilliant parodies performed in the late fifth century B.C.[58] By the Imperial period, however, these qualities were a pronounced fashion in mortals' learning and literary style: the language of the gods now magnified a fashion among mortal contemporaries. The gods spoke in archaic phrases, straining for rare words and coining plausible Homeric forms.[59] Like philosophers, they found meaning in wordplay on the gods' names and qualities: in the second and third centuries, puns were an art of gods as well as men. To their clients, poetry seemed most inspired when it was most lofty and verbose, a cloud, if not exactly a rainbow. Underneath, however, the message was straightforward: "I bid" you to choose or honour this priestess or that god. In their directness, oracles thus differed from their obvious near neighbours, the messages of gods in dreams. At night, it was only to be expected, said Artemidorus, that the gods should speak indirectly to man and that their veiled meanings should need interpretation.[60] At Didyma, Stratonicus actually asked Apollo what a dream meant.

Ultimately, Apollo could not help reflecting the prevailing atmosphere. As Yeats came to realize from Mrs. Yeats's automatic writing, there is a necessary connection between human input and divine output. Apollo knew his Homer and his school philosophy; in an age of keen civic rivalry, he knew his local history and gave clients the compliments which their cities liked to hear. In this taste, too, Apollo was the mirror of his times. He respected cities' ancestry and pre-history in myth, and sometimes he warmed to these themes with a keenness which exceeded his orders: the men of Pergamum received nine lines of antiquarian allusions to their favour from Zeus and their city's noble pedigree, "the Telephids." Hierapolis was reminded of its ancestors Mopsus and the nearby Apollo Kareios, and the oracle inspired the city's subsequent choice of coin types. At Didyma, Apollo honoured the people of Miletus as the "sons of Neleus who fell prey to an arrow." These allusions were wonderfully rare and delighted their clients in an age which valued these ancient myths of origins and honorific tales of city foundations. Apollo could take his place beside the most ingenious of the orators who toured and flattered the cities: his diction and wordplay on place names were shared, too, by Sibylline prophecies, composed in the same period. These long verse fictions would have pleased any Clarian thespode, and their compo-sitions remind us how widely these talents were practised among minor men of letters.[61] At Claros, meanwhile, those cities that lacked a cultural history were less fortunate. Caesarea Trochetta could just pass as "Ionian," but Syedra in Cilicia was more problematic and Apollo escaped by resorting to puns. The people, he said, were Pam-phylians (of all tribes) and therefore *pam-migeis* (all of a mixture).[62] Their many component peoples lacked an obvious con-nection with Greek myth, and Apollo honoured them with a play on words. What, one wonders, had he made of the Oenoandans, whose people combined Lycians, Greeks and Pisidians in a single city?

Who, then, was this Apollo, master of so many complex puns and metres, and gifted with such antiquarian facts about the cities which gratefully inscribed his words? Deep below Claros's Doric temple sat a thespode who listened to the prophet's cry. Throughout the second century, he put its meaning into verses and helped the god to express his view. We know the thespodes from inscriptions, where we can follow their infrequent changes after many years in office.[63] In the years from the late 130s to the 140s, Apollo was explained by a very solemn figure, Claudius Asclepides, who called himself a Heraclid, no less, "descended from Ardys" through his father's family. His name looked back to the old Lydian kings, some nine centuries earlier, the predecessor of Croesus, whom Apollo had vainly tried to save. From the 150s to the mid-160s, Regginus Alexander; from 177/8 to 185/6, the job passed back to a Heraclid, Tiberius Claudius Ardys. Did these Heraclids first come from Lydia to Claros in the 130s as the new thespodes and had prophecy always run in their family? It is a fine picture, a thespode who traced his family back to the Lydian kings, advising cities on plagues and drought, sending "interpretations" to Hadrian's Wall, paying fulsome compliments to "noble Pergamum" and telling the men of Syedra they were "all mixed up." Who better to know these antiquarian details than poets who believed they were in the Heraclid line? Just as Homer's gods were still "standing beside" men as "evident helpers," so the gods were still speaking on the topics of religious practice, correct "propitiation" and the right course to follow in moments of anger of the gods. The age of Herodotus was not yet dead.

# IV

The language and business of these oracles allow us, finally, to appreciate the most notorious cult of their age. While Claros and Didyma flourished and the gods still spoke at lesser shrines, they were joined by a prophet whose shrine has seemed wholly preposterous. Emerging in the 150s, it forms a serpentine tailpiece to the age's oracular culture and says something, too, about the nature of contemporary pagan cult. It arose in Paphlagonia, a place which was way beneath a Heraclid's dignity. It centred on a man and his model snake.

On the southern coast of the Black Sea, the Paphlagonian town of Abonouteichos had sat obscurely beside its poor, unwelcoming harbour. It had attracted no comment in guidebooks to the coast, except that its anchorage was unpredictable. Visitors relied on the prevailing west wind to take them safely round the capes and small seaside settlements which marked the adjoining stretch of coast: not for nothing did the West Wind continue to appear on Abonouteichos's coins. Access by road was no easier. A Roman road had begun to be built along the seacoast, but the stretch which connects to Abonouteichos is missing from the road tables and had probably never been built. The town's hinterland was not easily negotiated. It soon ran out into ravines and the steep forests of the mountain range behind. A Roman road did run inland through the centre of the province, but it was cut off from Abonouteichos by the intervening forest and chains of mountains. The approach route was a local track through rough country.[1]

This Paphlagonian township is a resounding proof that it took more than geography to keep a good shrine down. From around 150 to the mid-170s, people flocked to this distant point where Providence seemed to have broken afresh into the world.[2] Its god gave personal advice to Romans of the highest rank and sent an oracle to the Emperor himself. The cult concerned two figures, a prophet Alexander and a long, coiled snake called Glycon. Together, they rivalled Claros in their power to draw clients from far and wide. The snake Glycon was honoured in two inscriptions from Dacia, a Danubian province, while cities in Galatia and Bithynia showed his portrait on their civic coinage long after the prophet's death.[3] How could "paganism" have come to such a pass, a snake with shaggy hair and two human ears on its head? Recently, he has turned up in two new aspects. He promoted statuary and fathered children.

The north and south shores of the Black Sea were linked to each other by networks of trade and exchange and also, we now know, by religious pilgrimage. On the north shore, several cities sent delegates to Claros, and before long, their citizens also called at Abonouteichos.[4] At Tomi, a carefully buried cache of statues was recently unearthed, containing images of sixteen pagan gods. Among them was a large model of Glycon whose coils would have unravelled to a length of some fourteen feet: Glycon, as a hostile witness told us, was indeed "very bulky." His cult, we were told, sprouted "paintings, images and carvings, some of bronze, others of silver" and others, we now know, of stone. Another model of Glycon has been reported at Dorylaeum, in Phrygia.[5] The snake, however, did not stop at self-portraits. When Caesarea Trochetta received its oracle on plague from Claros, it inscribed it on a statue base, presumably a statue of the Apollo whom the god had told it to set up.[6] The cost was met by the city's priest of Apollo the Saviour, "Miletus son of Glycon, the Paphlagonian." Glycon was a common name, but this combination is suggestive. "Miletus" was an excellent name for a man from the coast of Paphlagonia, where claims to a Milesian origin were popular in the cities. A "son of Glycon" is very tantalizing. At the new shrine in Abonouteichos, women are said to have consulted the god Glycon in the hope of conceiving children. The question, we know from

Dodona, was quite frequent at oracles, but Lucian, who knew the place, alleged that the new prophet fathered children himself. Might Miletus's mother have looked to Glycon and told the world that she had borne a child by the shrine's oracular snake? If so, people in Caesarea believed her and made her son from Paphlagonia their local priest of Apollo. Divinity ran in his veins.

The shrine's stamina and popularity are no longer in doubt. Not only was it a new growth which coincided with the flowering of Claros: it was a shrine on whose workings we have a sharp eyewitness account.[7] During the 160s, probably in 165, a literary man, Lucian, travelled north from Cappadocia with his father and family, and while his family forked west, paid a visit to Abonouteichos in the sole company of his manservant. He wrote up the event some fifteen years later and hardly disguised his disgust. The prophet, he claimed, had tried to murder him. He was a dangerous fraud who conned the local "fat and uneducated," people who had thick accents and were only good for chewing garlic. When the prophet held out his hand for Lucian to kiss it, he claimed to have seized the opportunity. To the fury of the spectators, he bit it instead.

Lucian's sketch is a reminder that oracles still found their critics and that scepticism was still alive: as he chose to present it, the antagonism between the prophet and his disbelievers amounted almost to war. He sent his story to his friend Celsus as a warning against the tyranny of hope and fear and made such fun of the Paphlagonians and two elderly, credulous Roman governors that it is easy to share his viewpoint and write off the shrine as pure folly. Yet its clients stretched widely and its snake persisted for more than a century in other cities. How can we recover history from a satire of such venom?

Even now, his sketch is read too literally as history without due allowance for his gifts of parody and satire. We should be wary of abuse which reappears in Lucian's other satirical pamphlets and is plainly his own invention: it tells us more about Lucian and his audience than the nature of the oracle. However, Lucian did observe details at the shrine, although he distorted them by alleging fraudulent motives. If we ignore these motives and the patchwork of his literary jokes, we are left with a hard core of behaviour which was not so very peculiar. Lucian also cited questions and answers from the oracle, and although he had an Aristophanic gift for writing hexameter parodies, his mischief is generally evident. It did not extend to every example: on one occasion, we can check him, and prove that his quotation was honest. He claimed that he had seen some of the god's answers which a keen devotee had inscribed in gold: if he had wanted, he could have consulted such clients' copies and noted them precisely. The line is hard to draw exactly: are we merely showing that Lucian's parody conformed to oracular language and practice elsewhere, or can we also show that the prophet and his shrine were not uncharacteristic? It is certainly not enough to accept the idea that Alexander was a "fraud" or a hoax. He served for some thirty years, long after a hoax would have worn thin. Where we have any control, Lucian is not inventing the entire picture. Here, we can set the actions which he distorts beside their proper contemporaries, not magic or mysticism, but second-century oracles and the cults of Asclepius. If there is a key to the prophet's success, it lies with what we have just seen.

Lucian tells a brilliant story of the beginnings of the prophet's fraud. Alexander "the false prophet," he said, had left home as a young man and drifted through a dubious study of medicine and sham philosophy. When his good looks faded, he fetched up with Cocconas, a wretched songwriter from Byzantium, the first known melodist, then, in that city's musical history. Together, they tricked a rich Macedonian woman, bought a huge, tame snake at Pella and decided, after a quarrel, that Abonouteichos was the best place for a fraud. They faked oracles at Apollo's old temple in Chalcedon and sent them to the Paphlagonians, predicting the god's arrival. They invented prophecies to the same effect from that irrefutable fake, the Sibyl, and left them to spread among Paphlagonian high society. When the crowds in Abonouteichos heard that Asclepius was coming with his father, at once they began to build him a temple.

The earlier scenes in this story are probably pure satire: the Macedonian episode was devised to ridicule the prophet Alexander, namesake of Alexander the Great. The later details are more tantalizing. Other local cities, we know, consulted Apollo's oracle at Chalcedon about changes in their cults, and there is a hint on Abonouteichos's coins that her people were not totally deceived.[8] In the reign of Antoninus, the city of Abonouteichos issued coins which showed Asclepius meeting the goddess Health. Each of the divinities carried a snake, but only later do the coins allude to the prophet's particular snake, Glycon. In Lucian's story, Glycon and Alexander were present from the start and the temple was hurriedly built to receive them. But the coins suggest that the city's concern for

Asclepius may have preceded the prophet's intervention. There were springs and holy places of Asclepius in their surrounding territory and the god was already popular in many Black Sea cities. The temple, it seems, was independent of Alexander's "fraud."

Lucian has a fine time with the scenes of Asclepius's arrival. The Paphlagonians gaped and their thickset jaws dropped ever further as their prophet streaked through the city and claimed that Asclepius was hatching that very moment from a well-placed egg in their temple's foundations. The god emerged as a snake and "grew" rapidly into Glycon, the pet whom the prophet had concealed. All we can say about this lively satire is that its elements were familiar in other sites' cults of Asclepius.[9] The god's "arrival" to a temple was a highly pitched affair, and several cults were said to have begun with his physical transfer to a new shrine in the form of a travelling snake. These stories were current from Mytilene to Rome's temple of Asclepius on the Tiber: eggs, too, were honoured in his cult, and marble and granite eggs survive from his shrines in nearby Thrace. The epiphany of any new god lent itself to satire. At Abonouteichos, snakes, eggs and the prophet played a part, but Lucian no longer allows us to see the details straight.

Why, then, was Alexander given charge of the city's shrine? Lucian claims that the idea was his confidence trick from the start. He also describes him as the pupil of a doctor who had learnt his art from Apollonius of Tyana: "you see, dear Celsus, from what sort of school the fellow came." Is this only his malicious invention? It is a surprisingly precise claim. Among the many legends about Apollonius the wise man, it seems safe to agree that he had been a follower of Pythagoras and that many of his pupils had gathered in the Cilician temple of Asclepius at Aigai.[10] There, said Philostratus, Apollonius turned the shrine into a "holy Lyceum and Academy, until every type of philosophy echoed in it." Had Aigai been the seat of Alexander's teacher and perhaps of Alexander's studies, too? Lucian goes on to remark that the prophet's picture appeared in his city's coins with the attributes of Asclepius and the hero Perseus.[11] Here, he is probably accurate, as the coins could otherwise refute him. Alexander, he said, had returned home and amazed the citizens by his dress, his long hair and his claim to be Perseus's descendant. Why did the prophet bother to stress this ancestry?

Perseus had local connections in Paphlagonia, where his picture stood on the coins of nearby Amisus and Amastris and pointed to the meeting of Greek and Persian culture in the region's past. Was Alexander claiming a local nobility? Perhaps, but he may also have been alluding to his own training.[12] Perseus was the founding hero of "god-favoured" Aigai, where Apollonius had once taught: respect for this ancestry was still lively in the mid-second century. It could explain the prophet's double descent, from Perseus the founder of Aigai and Asclepius the god of its temple. It also fits Lucian's home for his teacher, and if the guess is correct, it puts the prophet's appointment in a less suspicious light. He had returned to Paphlagonia after several years' study at one of Asclepius's major shrines, and when his city was building the god a new temple, who better to run it than the young man who knew Asclepius's ways? He was a man of culture and Pythagorean philosophy. At Delphi, Apollo kept company with Platonists, and at Claros and Didyma, his prophets and thespodes wrote verses on God and the fate of the soul. Asclepius was no less urbane. At Pergamum, his great temple was thick with sophists and orators, doctors and men of philosophy. How could poor Abonouteichos hope to compete? At Gangra, a major city centre in the south of the province, we find that an order of "ephebes," for education of the young, was only being established as late as the 180s A.D.[13] Civic education, it seems, was still rudimentary in Paphlagonia, where parents sent their children abroad for study, yet here was a Pythagorean who knew the proper ways of the god. So far from being a hoax, Alexander was one more contemporary prophet, capable of bringing philosophy to bear on oracles.

At Pergamum, Asclepius sometimes gave his clients oracles, and at Claros, Apollo was sometimes consulted by individuals on their health. At Abonouteichos, the prophet combined the services of Claros and Pergamum, the two most flourishing and cultured shrines of the Aegean seaboard. We must not deny his shrine all novelty. People could distinguish a god with a new genealogy and then worship him as a "new Dionysus" or "new Isis":[14] Alexander introduced a "new Asclepius" who was manifest in the form of Glycon, the snake. The image was not so peculiar. Snakes had often uncoiled themselves in cults of Asclepius, and if Glycon had human ears, these were no odder than the ears of gods like Isis or Serapis which expressed their role as "listeners," the standard epithet for so many gods in the Imperial age.

The shrine's business, too, becomes less peculiar when set against oracles elsewhere. Lucian complained how the god "bore witness" to his prophet through the snake Glycon, yet at Aigai, Philostratus happily recorded how Asclepius had "borne witness" to his hero Apollonius.[15] We have seen how the Apollos at Claros and Didyma were free with these testimonials. At Claros, consultants of Apollo were initiated into the mysteries, and likewise, Abonouteichos installed a longer cycle of mystery rites; Lucian claimed that they honoured the prophet's divine birth and led up to sex with a well-born priestess, the wife of a Roman official. At Claros and Didyma, the highest class of people asked Apollo who was God: at Abonouteichos, they asked about Glycon's identity: "I am Glycon," said the god, "I am come to bring light to mortal men."[16] Apollo at Claros told client cities to display his portrait and allow it to "shoot away" the plague, yet when Asclepius and Glycon gave the same order, Lucian ridiculed it.

At Hierapolis, one Apollo had spoken well of another and fostered Claros's cult: in Libya, Ammon at Siwah also referred clients to Claros, home of Apollo the Sun god.[17] In Paphlagonia, it was not so unusual when the new prophet referred clients to the old Aegean shrines, Didyma, Claros and the rest, advice which did not befit an obvious hoax. As his own clients spread, they knew very well what a major oracle offered.[18] Their cities in Thrace and on the Black Sea already sent delegations to Claros, while cults and dedications for Apollo can be traced in other nearby Greek colonies: those founded from Megara honoured Delphic Apollo, while a dedication to "Apollo at Didyma" survives from a Milesian settlement. Asclepius had already spread widely in these prospering centres of Hellenism, so that visitors were not such innocents, ripe for a fraud. At Pergamum and Aigai, Asclepius prescribed the rarest remedies to patients who saw him in dreams. At Abonouteichos, Alexander often dreamed on his clients' behalf, although his alleged recipes for bear's grease allowed Lucian much mirth.

Much of the shrine's daily business was the familiar diet of a local oracle, the sort of requests which were being handled in Egypt by any competent crocodile god. There were questions on marriage and runaway slaves, burglary and bother with the neighbours, although Lucian tells us more about questions on adultery than our other sources for oracles reveal: he alleged indignantly that the god sometimes cited correspondents who did not even exist. At Hierapolis, Apollo approved the wisdom of city magistrates; at Abonouteichos, the Roman governor of Asia was told how best to educate his son. At Didyma, Poplas would ask his god about an embassy to

Rome; in Paphlagonia, clients asked whether it was better to go to Italy by land or sea.[19] Polites the crown-bearer at Didyma asked Apollo about the soul; at Abonouteichos, an elderly Roman governor was said to have asked about his past and future lives. It was probably Lucian's fiction that he was told that he had first been Pelops, then Menander, and would end up as a sunbeam: Rutilianus, said Lucian, "began to imagine he had become one of the heavenly bodies."

Details of procedure were not too unusual. The prophet charged a fee, like all other shrines, although Lucian alleges that he also paid agents to fan out and increase his business in the cities. He kept *theologoi*, like Delphi, and sacred exegetes, and like other shrines of Apollo, his shrine used choirboys, allowing Lucian to claim that the prophet corrupted them whenever he fancied. He received many of his clients' questions as sealed inquiries, like shrines elsewhere. He also charged more for special "self-spoken" oracles in which the god himself replied through Glycon's person. There was nothing odd about this division of business: it can be found at classical Delphi. If Glycon seemed to speak, that was a clever trick, but other shrines were clever too.[20] Eager clients pressed the prophet to pray on their behalf and intercede, like a friend, with his god. This personal role was not so novel. At Pergamum, clients asked a priest to dream on their behalf when they were having a lean time at night. At Aigai, said Philostratus, a person approached Apollonius and asked him to "introduce" him to Asclepius, with whom he stood in such esteem.[21] Philostratus knew this habit, although he made his hero reject this particular instance. "What need has a man of introductions," said his Apollonius, "if he be morally good?" At Abonouteichos, as elsewhere, people were not so high-minded.

At Didyma and Claros, the gods spoke the Platonist theology of their prophets. At Abonouteichos, Lucian insists, the prophet was a follower of Pythagoras and was therefore a monstrous fraud. Alexander's philosophy does seem to be more than Lucian's invention, and if he had trained at Aigai, its style befitted him. At Delphi, Apollo mixed with the top Platonists, and at Didyma, his prophet might be a "successor" of Plato. At Claros, a thespode like Ardys knew all about middle Platonism. Some of these shrines' oracles had Pythagorean touches of language, as did the statements of priests and "theophants," inscribed elsewhere.[22] We need only recall Apollonius's "book," on show at Antium, in which an oracle had dictated Pythagoras's views on philosophy. As at Claros, so in

Paphlagonia: the god's oracles were most peculiar when most true to their prophet's education.

Why, then, did Lucian hate him? The cult was new, whereas Didyma and Pergamum were old and traditional, and it also aspired to an old Ionian pedigree. Lucian had tried to bestow this aura on a temple cult in his own Syria which he described in the ancient style of Herodotus.[23] Alexander the prophet went one better: he petitioned the Emperor and obtained permission for his town to change its awful name. Abonouteichos became "Ionopolis," a pure Ionian city in an area where many cities aspired to descent from Miletus and where the image of Ionian Homer stood on the coins of nearby Amastris, while a neighbouring town was "Doros," or Dorian.[24] The name survives in the modern Inebolu, for it was through its prophet that this Paphlagonian port became respectable. Lucian had been brought up on Rome's eastern frontier, where Syriac was spoken in the streets: his satire was the work of one *arriviste* deeply despising another.

He also hated the prophet personally, and when he tells how Alexander tried to marry the daughter of his grandest Roman client, we do begin to suspect his ambition. He was "prophet for life" and hierophant of the Mysteries at one and the same time, yet the honours were paid to Glycon and his god, not to the prophet's own person. It was not such a dangerous ambition, to wish one's city to be given an old Ionian name.

When the prophet died, no successor was adopted. Perhaps he had left funds to pay for his duties in perpetuity, but instead, the shrine was entrusted to a doctor.[25] This choice is revealing, a reminder that the shrine's business was medical, the typical field of Asclepius and the Pythagoreans.[26] It combined this art with the giving of oracles in a well-chosen area. The mid-second century saw growing prosperity in many of the Black Sea cities, a region whose rise has often been overlooked. Lucian's satire on the local "fat and uneducated" disguises people who were rich and willing to send their sons abroad for studies in Alexandria. Did Ionopolis seem a less daunting shrine than Claros for these cities which were not even reddish-brick? At Claros, Apollo told Syedra that her citizens were "all mixed up": Paphlagonians would have been utterly beyond the pale. But at Ionopolis, the prophet is said to have taken questions in Celtic and Syriac as well as Greek: Celtic for people from nearby Galatia, Syriac for visitors from cities down the roads of the eastern frontier.[27]

The oracle, in short, succeeded because it flowered in an undersupplied area and combined the features we have followed at such length. Glycon appealed to men's willing sense of the "presence" of a god. He was a "new" form of an old god in an age which did not unduly respect originality. He spoke philosophy; he answered questions on future prospects; he prescribed cures. He met lasting needs in a style which was slightly livelier than the accepted style of the old Aegean shrines.

If Alexander had been a fraud, he was exactly the fraud which his contemporaries deserved: much of his practice conformed to the general practice of great oracles elsewhere, at a time when those oracles were enjoying a renewed prominence. It is, then, to this prominence that we must return in conclusion. A simple "rise in credulity" is not its explanation. Before the oracles began to revive, many forms of "credulous" divination were already flourishing; when they did revive, educated scepticism was not dead, as Lucian and others demonstrate. It is better to begin an explanation from the business which the inspired prophets handled. They concentrated on questions concerning the gods' own preferences, and it is from the lasting belief in these gods' presence that this service could re-emerge. As a constant presence, the gods could both help and hinder, "standing beside" people and their cities or showing a very lively anger. As civic notables revived the gods' "ceremonies," oracular shrines revived too. They could guide small details of practice and help to assure the gods' own favour: the new text from Ammon to Cyzicus is connected with the ceremony of "displaying the crown of Ammon" in the city and evidently assures its clients that they will be safer if they honour the god in this way and send appropriate sacrifices to Apollo, a Sun god too, at Claros. There was a necessary mutual exchange between flourishing cults, flourishing oracles and honours for the gods.

It is clear from Plutarch that this abiding thread in pagan "religiousness" also needed material support. The smarter the shrine, the greater its clientele. At Didyma, in the 60s A.D., we can see a preliminary local revival: Claudius Damas revived "traditional" choirs and ceremonies in the cults of Apollo after a prominent career as a great civil magistrate.[28] At Claros, the temple had begun to be rebuilt before Hadrian's final benefaction. When the Emperors did assist the shrines' rebuilding, they were not giving funds to a vacuum: before Hadrian, Plutarch and some of his friends had been only too keen to see the oracles revive. Benefactions did not create belief, but they did allow it to spread and flourish. At Miletus, Trajan paid for the cutting and paving of a sacred way to the shrine at Didyma. Early in his reign, he held the office of prophet and "crown-bearer," the major honours at the site. The festivals to celebrate his office brought visitors from far and wide, and perhaps it is through them that we find the city of Tyre choosing to put up a fine honorary dedication at Didyma.[29] Word spread from these occasions that Apollo was back into his stride: at Didyma, Apollo was at one point granted the right by the Romans to receive mortals' bequests. Roman lawyers cite him as a prime example of a god who enjoyed this privilege, and evidently, the grant was an official ruling, probably from an Emperor.[30] Did Trajan or perhaps Hadrian, another benefactor, confirm it at the shrine? Inspired verse oracles needed financing to maintain their staff, and these rights were very valuable. Better buildings and festivals brought more visitors, paying more fees and making more offerings: Lucian considered twelve to fifteen talents a sufficiently monstrous sum for him to attribute it to Alexander's shrine as its yearly income from fees alone. More visitors and bigger incomes also helped the oracles to improve their style: the "Heraclids" became lifelong thespodes at Claros and verse returned to Delphi. It is evident from Plutarch that this change in oracles' quality would also increase the clientele.

Why, though, did so many cities process so dutifully to Claros and inscribe their names between c. 110 and 205 A.D.? The earliest of these inscriptions precedes the final dedication of the Clarian temple and the changes in its staff: does it mark the beginning of the cities' attendance or only the beginning of a new "epigraphic habit"? Even that new "habit" is significant; at the very least, we can conclude that second-century cities chose to publicize their delegations as never before. Within their numbers, we can also see new cities joining the circuit and inscribing, in years when epigraphy was the recognized practice. How can we explain these changes?

At the simplest level, again, attendance on Claros owed an obvious debt to the Roman peace and an age of more settled prosperity for the civic notables. They felt safer in travelling far and had the funds to pay for the choirs and trainers: in Paphlagonia, too, the oracle had flourished on peace and prosperity in its inaccessible site. As the cities' "ceremonies" and buildings received more funds from local donors, there was a greater need for an outside spokesman on the gods' own wishes: oracles could solve problems of tenure and appointment and prescribe cult titles, hymns and appeasement of the gods. Once visitors had begun to visit the newer, smarter Claros, the practice would multiply because of the intense intercity rivalry of the age. Hierapolis had an Apollo of its own and felt no need to send a choir to Claros, until Apollo ordered one. But what of a town like Tabai, when nearby Heraclea was known to have gone to the god? Should she not go too, and if Tabai then went, should not Heraclea go more often, thirty, thirty-five, forty times over the period?[31] Perhaps a particular priest at the shrine first suggested that a civic delegation should inscribe and date its visit on the stones of the site while the temple was beginning to be improved. Civic journeys to oracles were an old and familiar feature of Greek life, but in the second century, there was a particular reason why an "epigraphic habit," once started, should blossom. Whatever the particular cost or encouragement at Claros itself, one city's visitors would not wish to lag behind another's delegation. In turn, the cost of inscriptions increased the shrine's funds.

Intercity rivalry was joined, most opportunely, by a more basic motive: fear. The improvement of the shrines happened to precede an intense sequence of plagues and earthquakes, perhaps more intense than any in the previous century. We can see this pattern in the texts at Hierapolis: the city consulted Apollo's oracle in a time of plague and was then ordered to send a mission to Claros. In Paphlagonia, Alexander, too, referred business to the major shrines. The pattern is beautifully clear, now, at Cyzicus, where Ammon from distant Siwah told the city "not to be afraid" but to go with sacrifices to Claros and honour Apollo, "making mention of me, too."[32]

As a result, a city would go obediently and add its name to our Clarian inscriptions, and then, for the sake of its safety, it might come again and again. At Claros, we can see the end product: some cities' texts say that their choirs had come "in accordance with an oracle." One good reason, then, for the shrine's greater host of delegations lies in its own self-advancement: like Alexander the prophet, it commanded people to come. The improvement of the shrines was accompanied by these oracles of "bidding" and perhaps, too, by envoys, encouraging old clients to resume attendance. The great calamities then lent weight to this movement. At Claros, some cities came once only, sending delegates (but no choirs) from further afield. A crisis brought them to the god, and in turn, the shrine's fame spread ever further, to Sardinia, Africa and Hadrian's Wall. Meanwhile, former clients and choirboys helped to spread its repute.

We have seen how processions and "traditional" ceremonies did reinforce an image of the cities' social order, enduring through time. How did this oracular revival relate to this order, at the shrines and in the client cities? "In the Antonine age," it has recently been suggested, "the oracles had maintained their strong, collective associations. They were valued because they could speak for the city as a whole on questions that affected the city as a whole . . . they did so largely because they had been studiously maintained for that purpose by local benefactors . . . By such means, the ruling groups in the city were able to exercise a control of its religious life that went far deeper than mere display. It was they who interpreted the oracles."[33] Are these ideas of "control" and its setting true to what we have seen?

The range of the evidence does not entirely support them. Didyma flourished, although all but one of the inscribed texts spoke to individuals,[34] not to "a city as a whole," nor, so far as we know, did oracles from sites like Mallos or Patara. At Claros, it was not the upper class of the client cities who interpreted the god's oracles: the job was done by the thespode, who was appointed for life. His texts were verbose, but they were wholly free of ambiguity and needed no further interpretation, beyond a sense of Homeric Greek and rare compound words. Were clients like the Oenoandans really concerned with "control" and against what, indeed, was "control" needed? Not, indeed, against religious upstarts or individual "holy men": on a strict definition, there were no pagan "holy men," for in pagan Greek the word "holy" applied to places, but not to people.[35] There were stories of "godlike" seers who could indicate the will of the gods, like travelling oracular prophets. The best known is Apollonius, the legendary wise man who was believed to have advised cities on their cults and ceremonies in the mid-first century A.D. He was not believed to have faced opposition from traditional oracles. He taught at Aigai and his "biographer," Philostratus, remarked how the shrines of Claros and Didyma honoured him warmly. The Christian book *On True Belief* has preserved a third-century text in which an oracle praised Apollonius's wisdom.[36] In pagan "religiousness" there was no fear of heresy, no urge to orthodoxy and clerical "control." The real Apollonius cannot be untangled from the admiring legends, but pagans' religious fear was a fear of the random anger of gods, not the ambitions of upstart men. It is to this enduring thread that oracular questions and answers attached.

What, too, of the idea of a "studious maintenance" of oracular shrines by benefactors to suit a "purpose," related to their own power? Like all other culture in this period, an oracle was suspended from the time and money of the upper class. At Didyma, the prophets of Apollo were drawn from a narrow range of interconnected noble families. At Claros, the prophets were no humbler, while two of the thespodes claimed to be blue-blooded Lydians. The choirs and civic envoys to Claros were drawn from their cities' educated families: they included civic priests and people like Cornelius (Mu)ndicianus Crocus "of the Philopappidai," who evidently belonged in the highest society of Stobi before he travelled to Claros as the city's envoy.[37] The newly found text of Ammon to Cyzicus was connected with some important figures in the city, a "displayer of the crown of Ammon," a rich donor of the inscription and "pious" worshippers of Ammon who were people of rank, active in the cult of the Emperors. These persons of quality did not entirely lack a return. They advertised their attendance, at Claros and sometimes, too, at home. At Didyma, as elsewhere, the god did also "testify" to the virtues and family trees of willing prophets. However, we know of no person who used these words as grounds for civic, secular advancement: they were the copingstones on careers which had already been mapped out. In Miletus, Damas, the benefactor and restorer, issued coins in his year of civic office with the types of the Apollo whom he had served.[38] Others did likewise, but the god, not the donor, took most of the honour. When Damas was prophet for a second time, he was aged over eighty, acting not for his future career but for motives of correct piety. The "testimonials" at Didyma went to the few great prophetic families who had already held major civic offices or were combining them with "voluntary" service at the shrine. Perhaps the recipients prized them in their rivalry with each other: they did not prize them as a means of "control" of people outside their own small class. Oracular service was not consciously pursued as a device for power. It was one more reinforcement of an order which was not being challenged. The notables went to Claros for their city's safety and prestige: because they went, they could be felt to be doing their best by the gods. They met the great expense of the priesthoods, and in return, to coax them to give freely, the gods "witnessed" publicly to their merits. The consequent support for their position was incidental: it was not the reason why they undertook these tasks in the first place.

Like "control," "studious maintenance" is too external a view of oracular activity. The lists of Apollo's prophets had their interruptions, when nobody "volunteered" for the job: at Didyma, the methods of selection are implied by the prophet's inscriptions.[39] If several candidates stood forward, a choice was made between them by that time-honoured arbiter, the lot. In some years, only one candidate's name went forward: he was then chosen "without the lot" and sometimes in response to his own preliminary "promise." Such offers were not always forthcoming. Once, c. 120, the job is known to have passed directly from a distinguished father to a twenty-one-year-old son; once, in the mid-first century, there was no prophet at all. "Studious maintenance" is not quite the term for this delicate balance of "volunteering" and uncontested office: prophets, it seems, were not always easily found. At Claros, the pattern is clearer because the dated records are better: in thirty-eight years out of fifty-four, the god himself held high office at the shrine.[40] His funds, not the donors', financed it in the years of its great attendance. At Patara, in Lycia, we can watch the revival of an old, respected oracle and see the relation of benefactor and shrine from the beginning.[41] "After a long time of silence," the local Apollo began to give oracles once again, yet the primary impulse was an earthquake which had troubled southwestern Asia in or around the year 140. Only when Apollo had already begun to speak did he attract a modest benefaction from the prince of all Lycian donors, Opramoas. This great giver did not "coax the shrine back into life" or try to dominate it. He adorned it, one among his many other buildings, and never held office at the site. The inscriptions in his honour received the gift politely, but discreetly: "*perhaps,*" said the text warily, "Apollo also took pleasure in this moment because of Opramoas's piety . . ."

Oracles, then, were not an explicit source of control or power for individuals: rather, Apollo coaxed benefactors who might otherwise be reluctant, and also helped to contain the mutual rivalries within their class. These tensions were common to all offices which relied on holders' "love of honour," and Apollo, here too, reflected the atmosphere in which he lived. At Side, his verses praised moderation and a good disposition in benefactors whose gifts were open to dispute. At Didyma, he confirmed the musical piety of one prophet against his cousin's extravagance. At Hierapolis, he praised the government of well-disposed leaders. Oracles were not so much a source of civic power as arbiters, so that religious life ran smoothly.

At Claros, the latest-known civic inscription belongs c. 205 A.D., but the shrine did not then cease to draw clients. On a coin of the late 250s, we see the figures of thirteen city envoys standing round a bull as it is sacrificed before Apollo's temple: the cities are probably the members of Greek Asia's distinguished Ionian League. At Didyma, the sacrifices of Ulpianus and the musical piety of Macer, his cousin, belong in the same period; in the third century, we have our one Imperial inscription from a civic delegation, reminding us how much we have lost from Didyma's own client cities and "colonies."[42] In the 250s, Delphi still spoke for Side; in the 240s, the image of the local oracular Apollo still featured on Patara's coins. The shrines and their client cities were not immune from the great disorders of the 260s and 270s, but even then, as we shall see, those calamities did not undermine the continuing role of their gods.

What, though, of the theological oracles with which we began? The first datable text is the answer to Polites at Didyma given c. 170–180. Those which survive in later Christian books are most likely to derive from Porphyry's collection: if so, they must have existed by c. 260–270. They show very well how philosophy supplemented cults and conventional piety, adding "beliefs" to ceremonies to make a *religio*, as the Emperors then described it. They show a lofty, abstract theology in which the Supreme god was defined by negative attributes. Sometimes, they place him beyond the Elements or equate him with Eternity, "which was and is and ever shall be."[43] They also equate Apollo and the Sun god.

These tendencies and modes of thought had already been evident in Plutarch's dialogues, which were set at Delphi c. 66–85 A.D.: they were not a new development of the third century. As for the equation of Apollo and the Sun,[44] it was already made by "many people," as Plutarch's speakers accepted. The relations of Apollo to Dionysus and to Fire were topics which even the guides and local *theologoi* at Delphi discussed quite freely. So was the idea of a Supreme god, whose names and forms might vary with the yearly cycle of the seasons. When these questions were put to the gods themselves and inscribed or preserved for collectors, they were not a sign of a new, growing pagan doubt. There were sound, healthy reasons why such questions should occur within paganism itself: Miletus had priests and cults of a Most High god; curiosity is a sign of liveliness; the relation of the Supreme god to other gods was a genuinely interesting question; in reply, Apollo's answers were not monotheist, recognizing only one God. It has, however, been the essence of this chapter that Apollo was sensitive to atmosphere. These texts, then, cannot be considered without regard to the true monotheists in the pagan cities, the Jews and the Christians who were winning converts meanwhile.

In Miletus, we have a famous third-century inscription from "Jews who are also devout worshippers," carved on seating in the city theatre. Whether these Jews are Jews by birth or Gentile converts, they are clearly a group of some prominence, willing to share in their city's culture.[45] We have another intriguing text, also from the theatre, in which each of the seven archangels is invoked in a separate panel: "archangel, protect the city of the Milesians and those who live in it."[46] Its date is uncertain, but not earlier than the third century A.D., and Jewish ideas are surely present, although the text may not originate from a practising Jew. It is, then, very apt that Didyma spoke on the Jewish religion which was evident in the city's public places.[47] Lactantius quotes a text in which Didyma's Apollo praised the Jews' respect for law and their worship of the "Creator of all." According to Augustine, Apollo had been asked on this occasion whether "reason" or "law" was preferable; in Greek, perhaps, *logos* or *nomos*. In reply, he adduced the Jews to support his argument for "law," or *nomos*. This text had probably been found in Porphyry's collection and existed, therefore, at Didyma by c. 260: the first of Porphyry's books also quoted an Apollo who approved the wisdom of Eastern peoples, especially the Chaldaeans and the "enviable" Hebrews, who worshipped "in a pure manner" a single God and believed in the seven zones in heaven.

At Didyma, Apollo spoke on God and the Most High; at Claros, on the nature of "Iao," a Greek version of the Jews' Yahweh, who was known in popular spells and sorcery. People did ask explicitly about the Jews, and it is hard to believe that none of the theological questions on "God" owed any impulse to the presence of prominent Jewish groups in the second- and third-century cities.[48] If Greek-speaking Jews attended Miletus's theatre, they could also discuss and dispute with the pagan citizenry. Apollo's texts are firmly pagan, but they do discuss God in a language which Jews could endorse. It is quite credible that, at times, the questions arose from the presence of Jewish groups and sympathizers, a presence which is emerging into clearer prominence from the growing evidence of the second- and third-century cities in Greek Asia.

The Jews were not the only alternative presence in these years, for the Christians, too, were winning converts. Here, the oracle for

Oenoanda has been seen as Apollo's attempt at a compromise, answering a question which began from pagans' disputes with Christian atheists.[49] Its text, indeed, used language which Christians later applauded; it needed only a small Christian revision: it called the gods "angels" and ordered no sacrifices in their honour. However, the words of oracles elsewhere suggest that any resulting compromise was not deliberate. The Christian author of *On True Belief* cites a text in which Apollo foretold disaster for "those who have forsaken the ways of their ancestors." He quotes it as the god's rebuke to Jewish questioners, but may it not have begun as a rebuke to Christian converts?[50] Apollo certainly spoke on the subject, and we owe to Porphyry's book a plausible text in which Apollo gave a degree of praise to Christ. He was a wise man who worked miracles and died a "bitter" death: the miscreants were the Christians, who insisted on worshipping his mortal body when it had been torn and disfigured by nails. Their cult was absurd: God Incarnate, said Apollo, was a myth.[51] Porphyry also knew that a distressed husband had asked an oracle how best to dissuade his wife from Christianity. Apollo held out little hope: it was easier, he said, to write on water or fly like a bird than to shift a woman from such impiety, the worship of a man who had been put to death in irons. Christ's soul was immortal, but not his body, and the cult was thoroughly misguided.

Nowadays, these views might find sympathy from the Churches' very bishops, but at the time, they were not grounds for a compromise. Apollo found the Jews' religion easier company than the Christians'. In their language and remedies, explanations and praises, oracles were thoroughly traditional, and were valued for being so. In Plutarch's dialogues, it was his friend Serapion, the Stoic and poet, who defended a divine origin for every single word in oracles' texts.[52] "We must not fight against the god," said this literalist, "nor abolish providence and divinity along with prophecy. We must try to find solutions to apparent obstacles and not betray our fathers' pious belief." Greeks and Romans agreed alike on this great conservative case for their cults. At Didyma, c. 200, Apollo repeated it as a matter of course to the inquiring treasurer Hermias. In the 250s, he praised prophets like Macer and Ulpianus, people "to whom it was axiomatic that nothing could be both new and true."[53] Oracles united respect for "ancestral practice" with a strong awareness of the awe and potential anger of the gods. These attitudes, as we shall see, underlay the cities' persecutions of Christian "atheists." When the oracles diagnosed divine anger, they prescribed archaic rites of sacrifice and hymns for an appeasement by their clients, but Christians, in these same cities, could not participate in these divine "commands." The origin of cities' local outbursts against their Christians is usually concealed from us, but it may owe something to the prior advice of an oracle on rites and honours. At Abonouteichos, it seemed plausible to Lucian to allege that the "false" prophet told his crowds to throw stones at "atheist" Christians and Epicureans. By 250, the connection between oracles and persecution is clearly attested.

This oracular activity, as we shall see, extends beyond the mid-third century, and with its help, we can correct one perspective in Gibbon's unsurpassed account of the rise of Christianity within the Empire. By the third century, "human reason," he believed, "had already obtained an easy triumph over the folly of Paganism. . . . Yet the decline of ancient prejudice exposed a very numerous portion of human kind to the danger of a painful and comfortless situation." They could not bear the fruits of reason's triumph: rid of their superstition, they were all too ready to find it elsewhere. They were "almost disengaged from their artificial prejudice, but equally susceptible and desirous of a devout attachment . . ." Christianity met their need: "Those who are inclined to pursue this reflection, instead of viewing with astonishment the rapid progress of Christianity, will perhaps be surprised that its success was not still more rapid and still more universal."[54]

Gibbon mistook the views of a few unrepresentative thinkers for a "vacuum" which he ascribed to the majority. From the men of Lystra to the people of Oenoanda, we have seen a different world, one where the gods were still "evident," standing beside their clients in dreams and guiding them with words or signs of their will. There was no "disengaged" majority: there were those to whom pagan worship came naturally and those who expressed a stronger articulate piety. Pagans, too, had their gods as "helpers" and "fellow workers," an evident company who might accompany a man "always." Potentially helpful, they had not lost their old Homeric capacity for sudden awe and anger. Their company might reassure a city or an individual, but their continuing "mildness" and "ease of encounter" could not be taken for granted. In their cults and honours, the "traditional purpose" still mattered, as the language of gods themselves proclaimed. Wherever the cities' benefactors financed it, it helped to reinforce the image of an enduring community, true to its past. It also linked town and country in a mutual exchange of visitors.

Respect for the ideal of "tradition" did not exclude changes in reality, and by the second century A.D., certain currents in pagan cult are prominent in our evidence. More techniques aimed to secure and tame the "presence" of the gods; more techniques tried to elicit the future and ensure the best course through it. The cults of the household and city had been joined by the cults of small societies, a pattern which had a long history of development but which shows a particular intensity in the evidence of the Imperial age. People could now turn to groups for particular religious worship as a specialized activity within their cities' life. The evidence for religious mysteries in these groups, especially mysteries in the cult societies of Dionysus, is overwhelmingly evidence of the Imperial period. At that time, mystery rites begin to be attested for other cults, for Isis or Serapis, the oracle at Claros, even the worship of Emperors. Some, though not all of them, promised greater ease for the soul after death, reassuring pagans of an anxiety which was widespread, though not universal. There were worshippers, too, who felt protected by a god against the arbitrariness of fortune, the malice of sorcery and envy or the limiting constraints of the power of the stars: newer techniques exploited or charted these forces but did not necessarily weaken the appeal of "protecting" divinities, who were present in dreams and images. While art and the ancient cult statues continued to define people's sense of the gods, philosophy continued to discuss the concept of a Supreme god, his qualities and relation to the other divinities. Oracles then made this language the language of gods themselves: were they really only the interest of a few enthusiasts and a very small literate elite? Perhaps this position can never be entirely refuted, not even by the public inscriptions of theology, which many people might not read, or consider. It calls, in the end, for an intuition about the concerns and discussions of people in large and small Mediterranean towns where work is not constant, all day, every day, and the spoken word is vastly more influential than the written. Grand epithets for God are not hard to assimilate, wherever people meet and know Greek: providence and a Supreme power, the nature of the heavens and the various types of worship are not questions which only interest professors, and they are not unsuited to a long afternoon between harvests or a wet winter's day. At the very least, these debates on the higher theology bear witness to a continuing uncertainty: who was to say who the highest God might be? If the Supreme god was unknowable, who was to say which one of the many cults of different peoples was right or wrong? At its heart, therefore, pagan theology could extend a peaceful coexistence to any worship which, in turn, was willing to coexist in peace.[55]

We have dwelt on the lasting traditional "religiousness" and its continuing vigour, at least to the mid-third century. Yet we should not mistake it for "religion" in the strong Christian sense. In the Imperial period, some people in the cities were turning to find this different alternative, in the Jews' synagogues and the Christian churches. Both these religions continued to attract outsiders, especially the Christians' faith. Their converts, we have seen, were not abandoning a static or dying religious culture. Rather, they were joining the most extreme option in a period when religious issues were very lively; their chosen option joined cult and philosophy; it gave a clear code of conduct; it promised hope and an absolute triumph over death and Fate. The Supreme god of the Platonists and the oracles is, ultimately, a remote figure, more negative than positive; it has that distance and chilliness which is best sensed, still, in the very style of the Pantheon in Paris, a building put up by its deliberate heirs. The Christians, too, could cite prophecies in a world where past oracles were widely respected; they knew exactly who God was, in an age of discreet uncertainty: their God was a God of history, proven in events; above all, he had sent a Son, to redeem men by actions of total selflessness. It is time, then, to turn to the Christian option, in the years until 250; then we can set it beside the pagan cults and oracles and follow them both through the difficult years to Constantine himself.

# Part Two

///////////////////////////////////////////////////////////////////////////////////////////////

"*The Christians, O king, have found the truth by going and seeking for it. . . . They do not do to others what they would not wish to be done to themselves. They comfort those who wrong them and make friends of them: they labour to do good to their enemies. . . . He that has gives freely to him who has not. If they see a stranger, they bring him under their roof and rejoice over him as if over their own brother: they call themselves brethren, not after the flesh but after the Spirit and in God. . . .*"

Aristides, *Apology*, 15 (to the Emperor Hadrian, c. 130 A.D.)

"*Very rarely, no never, does it happen that someone comes to us with the wish to become a Christian who has not been struck by some fear of God.*"

Augustine, *On Catechizing the Uninstructed*, 5.9 (400 A.D.).

"*I do not care whether you expect some well-turned phrases today. It is my duty to give you due warning by citing the Scriptures. 'Do not be slow to turn to the Lord, nor delay from one day to the next, for His anger shall come when you know not' . . . I cannot be silent: I am forced to preach on it. Filled with fear myself, I fill you with fear.*"

Augustine, Sermon, in *Miscellanea Agostiniana*, i (1930) 199.

# 6. The Spread of Christianity

///////////////////////////////////////////////////////////////////////////////////////////////////

I

In the mid-third century, while the oracles still spoke and Apollo answered his clients, villagers in the Arsinoite nome of Egypt were troubled by questions of a different nature. When God brought the world to an end after six thousand years, would they enjoy a thousand years of fleshly pleasure in their own bodies, or was the reign of the saints to be disembodied and less robust? The question had divided and split their communities. A local bishop had argued the case for a fleshly resurrection and based it fairly on the Book of Revelation. He had published his argument as a challenge to those teachers who turned the text into allegory, and after his death, his argument had lived on, winning credit among the teachers of the local Christians. Perhaps it would have survived indefinitely, had it not encountered a tireless visitor. When Dionysius, bishop of Alexandria, came down to the district on other business, he heard the argument, disliked it and summoned the "elders and teachers" in the presence of Christian "volunteers." They brought him their bishop's book "like some weapon or unassailable wall," Dionysius recalled, and for three whole days, from morning to night, he took its statements one by one and proved that they were unfounded. Finally, the leader of their doctrine stood forward and declared himself convinced. The contrary view was routed; the hearers relaxed in agreement: there could never, they all accepted, be scope for sex after death.[1]

This incident takes us far from the pagan cults and beliefs which we have confronted. Thinking pagans had worried more about the beginning of the world than about its possible end. There was no question of the body being "resurrected": the facts were obvious to anyone who opened a grave and saw bare bones. There had been no three-day debates, no refutations of views which were "heretical." No pagan philosopher had travelled from his city to small townships in order to establish the meaning of Greek texts for the local residents.

These villages, wrote Dionysius, had been torn "for a long while by schisms and apostasies of entire churches": schism, like heresy, was entirely alien to the pagan religiousness which we have examined. The visiting bishop, Dionysius, was a highly educated teacher who knew school philosophy and the art of rhetoric. Yet he responded to the villagers' interest. He commented graciously on their "love of truth," their "sensible stand," their "following of an argument," qualities, he said, at which he had "marvelled enormously" in such people. In these communities, Christian doctrine had touched and divided simple men and women whom higher education never reached. To learn philosophy, these people would have needed money and the time to migrate to Alexandria. To learn the Christian faith, they had only to attend to their local elders and teachers, who preached for no fee in their village. If they went astray, a great Alexandrian bishop, visiting from the city, might spend three days correcting their errors.

On this occasion, they were talked out of a belief which had a long and respectable history.[2] Initially, it had been a Jewish belief, part of the various chronologies for the world's ending. On early authority, an elaborate "saying" of Jesus had been quoted in support of a fleshly millennium, although the Gospels never preserved its words. In the 130s, the philosophically minded Christian Justin defended the notion vigorously, as did Irenaeus a generation later. Yet the belief still troubled fellow Christians. Dionysius explained away the plain words of Revelation as an allegory, and when Irenaeus's tract against heresy was translated into Latin in the early fifth century, the translator omitted the millennium from its text. To many thinking Christians it had become an embarrassment.

Those who direct attention to the end of the world invite dispute over its nature and disappointment over its timing. In a brilliant image, Paul had compared the End with a mother's birth pang. The End, his image implied, was inevitable in a world already pregnant with its own destruction, but nobody could know exactly when it would strike. When his converts in Thessalonica began to be persecuted, they mistook their suffering for the first tribulations of which Paul had spoken. Forged letters, as if from the Apostle, encouraged their mistake. There were other false alarms in the following centuries, and a constant spate of Christian forgeries, but none was so tragic as these, the first on record. The End, meanwhile, was elusive. "We have heard these things even in the days of our fathers," Christians were already saying in the 90s, "and look, we have grown old and none of them has happened to us." In the 130s, Justin addressed a book to the "most cultured and philosophic" Emperor, Pius, in which he greatly enlarged the world's time span: God, he explained, was delaying the End because he wished to see the Christians spread throughout the world. By 200, Tertullian admitted that fellow Christians were praying that the End would not occur in their lifetime. By the 250s, the birth pang took a novel turn. Cyprian, bishop of Carthage, explained to fellow bishops in North Africa that they should not be too depressed by the evidence of Christian misbehaviour. It was itself the harsh prelude and a proof that the End was about to break.[3]

Persecutions still revived an immediate hope or fear, but by the mid-third century most people considered the End to be beyond their own horizon. Jesus had denounced all attempts to know the "times and seasons," and Christian leaders had rejected the various arts of futurology. Yet the End was soon given a date with the help, once again, of contemporary Jewish traditions.[4]

One day, the Psalms had said, was "like a thousand" and the Creation had lasted for six days. The world, then, would persist for six thousand years, to be graced by the seventh day of rest, the thousand years' reign of the Saints on earth. When, though, would the six thousand years end? Had they finished already, or was there still time to run? There was no limit to the evidence, if people looked carefully at Scripture.[5] Hippolytus, bishop of Rome, greeted the third century with an array of ingenious arguments. When carefully studied, the measurements of the Jews' Ark of the Covenant amounted to five and a half cubits, the symbol of five and a half thousand years. Had not John also written that the birth of Christ occurred "about the sixth hour," halfway through a day? Five kingdoms had already fallen, according to Revelation, and amounted to five thousand years: "half a day," to the Lord, was a further five hundred. When the "incorruptible ark" of Jesus's body replaced the old ark of the Jews, five and a half thousand years had therefore passed and a further five hundred remained before the End in 500 A.D. This chronology was not without a purpose. An alternative dating had fixed the six thousandth year in 202, the occasion of Hippolytus's calculations. The year caused some false starts, but when it passed without further event, hopes were deferred to the alternative, 500. To Christians of the mid-third century the End had receded over the horizon.

While the End refused to begin, where were Christians to be found?

The scenes in the Arsinoite nome raise basic questions of their class and language, geography and distribution. Bishop Dionysius preached in Greek, yet many of the villagers knew Coptic: he referred to elders and teachers in the "villages," yet he himself came from a great city. Was his audience the more prosperous Greek population from the nome's bigger townships, mere "villages" to an Alexandrian's eye, or did they also derive from the humbler, more uniform "villages" which we know from excavations and which were to contain Christian churches by the age of Constantine, fifty years later? The area was not isolated. In the 260s, shortly after Dionysius's bishopric, we have papyrus fragments of a letter which a well-placed Christian had written from the city of Rome to "brethren" in the Arsinoite nome.[6] It approves their purchase of linen cloths, befitting the linen workshops which we know in the town of Arsinoë. It refers to a "father" and a man in Alexandria who was to hold the brethren's proceeds from sales of the linen. Another man would hold money in Alexandria to refund the author's expenses. This three-cornered business links a Christian visitor in Rome with Christians in the Arsinoite nome: the two men in Alexandria bear the same names as a mid-third-century bishop and his successor and are probably none other than these famous Church leaders. The text reminds us what wide contacts Christians from the area enjoyed soon after Dionysius's visit. It is characteristic of our evidence for the presence of Christianity: mysterious, oblique, yet attached to the endless travel of people, goods and ideas in the Roman Empire and its areas of contact.

The number and identity of Christians before Constantine are disputed subjects because most of the relevant evidence is of this type. We have scraps of information which remind us of the possibilities, and in this chapter, I will pick and choose among them, citing the scraps which seem to be most significant. The broad question of scale is the most difficult to decide, because we have only one statistic.[7] A staff of 154 ministers of varying rank (including fifty-two exorcists) and "more than fifteen hundred widows and poor people" were said by the bishop of Rome to be supported by Rome's Christians in the year 251. The statistic does at least derive from a letter which the bishop wrote himself. From these figures, Gibbon guessed that the Christians in Rome numbered 50,000 in a city of a million inhabitants and suggested a general ratio of one Christian to every twenty pagans. The guess was too high, not least because widows and the poor were strongly represented in the Church's membership. Even if the figure is more or less right, we cannot project a total for Rome, the capital, onto other populations in the Empire. Rome was an exceptional city, a magnet for immigrants and visitors, where Christians had rapidly put down roots. Elsewhere, Christians were distributed patchily, if at all: in the mid-third century, there was still no bishop and no church in Salona (Split) and before the 250s, no Christians in Libya or in certain villages in the Mareotic district, connected by a road to Alexandria, which they almost adjoined.[8]

When describing their religion's success, Christian authors, from Acts onwards, were quite uncritical in their use of words like "all" and "everywhere." This habit lends particular weight to the one contrary assertion: in the 240s, Origen, the Christian intellectual, did admit that Christians were only a tiny fraction of the world's inhabitants. We can support his remark with two general arguments, one from silence, one from archaeology.

Although we have so much incidental material for life in the Empire, the inscriptions, pagan histories, texts and papyri make next to no reference to Christians before 250: the two fullest histories, written in the early third century, do not even mention them.[9] If Christians were really so numerous, we could also expect some evidence of meeting places which could hold so many worshippers. At this date, there were no church buildings on public ground, yet the tradition of regular attendance at services was very strong. Christians met in enlarged private houses or rooms.[10] There might be several meeting places in a city, but the space for each congregation cannot have been large. Around 200, a fine Christian novel imagined how one Theophilus, a rich patron in Antioch, had to send for the builders and enlarge his reception rooms as soon as Christians entered his house and started to multiply. The scene was plausibly imagined, but how large was the increase? At Dura-Europos,[11] out east on the Euphrates, this expansion can be followed on site. The Christians began to use a decent private house which had recently been built round a courtyard with rooms of fashionable pagan decoration, including a frieze of the god Dionysus's exploits. It may be right, then, to place their earliest meeting place elsewhere in the building, in a small room off the courtyard which was able to hold some thirty people. During the 240s, a bigger hall for sixty people or so was being made down the courtyard's west side by knocking two rooms into one, just as the Christian novel remarks. Perhaps the earlier room was now reserved for teaching while a small baptistery was equipped next door and decorated with symbolic paintings. The street door was marked with a red cross to signify a Christian "church house," private, but with community uses.

At Dura, during the 240s, the space for a Christian meeting increased from a capacity of thirty persons to one of sixty. Members, no doubt, were impressed by their "great" advance. Statements by Christians about their "growth" should be read with a very critical eye for the figures from which they begin. The point is well made in a "biography" whose accuracy is beset with difficulties but whose taste for the miraculous is not in doubt. In the Christian Empire of the fifth century, we have various versions of a "life" of Porphyry, bishop of Gaza, which purports to be written by Mark, the deacon. Perhaps it was, in its original Syriac form, though the question is still open.[12] On any view of its origins, the text was concerned to emphasize the wonders which amazed pagan Gaza between 392 and 420, eighty to a hundred years after Constantine's conversion. A first miracle is said to have won 127 converts in the city, a second, 64; the Greek version of the text goes on to tell how later wonders brought another two hundred people to God. It is not too important for our purpose whether this text is historical: what matters is that its author thought this scale of conversion was suitably remarkable. Gaza was a staunch pagan city, but other places were not graced with stories of evident "signs and wonders." If one or two hundred converts were an amazing harvest from a miracle, we can only wonder how many were won where miracles were less obliging.

Although Christians' numbers are elusive, the volume of their writings is conspicuous. In the later second and third centuries, most of the best Greek and Latin literature which survives is Christian and much more has been lost. Its authors wrote largely for Christian readers, but we must not mistake eloquence for numerical strength. The general arguments still point in the other direction. To read these books is to attend to a small, but extremely articulate, minority.

It is one of this minority's achievements that there are still so many histories of the Christians' expansion and mission, but hardly a note of the people who tried being Christians, could not bear it and gave it up. Christians have made their history into a one-way avenue, with the further implication that "paganism" and Judaism were so gross that nobody would have wished to return to them. Yet c. 110, Pliny was greatly exercised by former Christians in his province of Bithynia and Pontus who had lapsed up to twenty years earlier. It was because of them that he wrote to Trajan and acquired the famous rescript which governed the Christians' standing before the law. He does not tell us what modern historians assume, that these Christians had only lapsed for fear of persecution. We know of individuals who lapsed for other reasons: the well-born Peregrinus, who became a Cynic philosopher; Ammonius, who taught Origen his philosophy; perhaps Aquila, who is said to have been baptized but returned to the Jewish faith and retranslated the Greek Scriptures, excluding Christian misinterpretations; and the young Emperor Julian, who left Christianity for Platonist philosophy and cult.[13] We do not hear of anyone who left Christianity for simple paganism without any accompanying philosophy: perhaps this silence is significant and a lapse from Christianity did always lead to a favour for some systematic belief. Much the most attractive belief was full-fledged Judaism. We hear very little of Jews who became Christians after the Apostolic age, but much more of Christians who flirted with Jewish teaching: the shift was especially easy for women, who could convert without the pain of being circumcised. The acts of Church councils in the Christian Empire bring the continuing problem of these Christians back into view, long after Christianity had ceased to be persecuted. Histories of Christianity still tell a story of unimpeded growth, but the picture was always more complex at its edges. There were losses as well as gains, although Christianity, like all growing "movements," had more to say about the gains. By no means everybody who started to take an interest in Christianity "became" a Christian or died as one. The long process of "becoming" and the continuing losses at the margin are further arguments for keeping the Christians' numbers in perspective.

Nonetheless, Christians spread and increased: no other cult in the Empire grew at anything like the same speed, and even as a minority, the Christians' success raises serious questions about the blind spots in pagan cult and society. The clearest impressions of their growth derive from the Church historian Eusebius, who was writing after Constantine's conversion, and from the maps which can be drawn of Christian churches in North Africa: these maps are based on the list of bishops who attended an important Church council in the year 256.[14] The council's acts survive, although they do not give a complete list of the North African churches, as the bishops from certain areas did not attend the meeting.[15]

Eusebius has been most influential because he divided the Christians' expansion into phases. The first surge, he believed, occurred

with the Apostles' mission, the second in the 180s, the third shortly
before Constantine's conversion. In this chapter, the second of these
phases concerns us most. In the 180s, we do happen to know of
Christians in more prominent places and there does seem to be a rise in
the number of such people in Rome, Carthage and Alexandria.[16]
Perhaps Eusebius was overimpressed by mention of their names and
assumed that numbers as a whole were growing: like us, he had no
records or statistics on which to base his ideas of a widespread growth.
However, an increase in prominent Christians is itself an interesting
change and will need to be set in a broader context.

The idea of these phases of growth obscures a simpler question: was
Christianity growing apace in the towns which it had reached in the
age of St. Paul, not only growing among a few prominent people but
advancing like an ever-rolling snowball among the anonymous
majority, people who persevered and in due course were baptized? Or
was it entering more towns, where it simply won some two hundred
souls in the first ten years who intermarried, attended one or two little
house-churches, chose a bishop and added another static Christian dot
to the map? It is clear that numbers grew in Rome between Paul's
death and the long list of bishops and minor clerics in 251. In other
large cities, Carthage or Alexandria, we should allow for a similar
growth, although its rate and scale are elusive. Elsewhere, Christians
scattered widely, and by itself, their diffusion would account for a
general impression of their increase. In 256, two of the three secular
provinces of North Africa had at least 130 bishops: when plotted on a
map, they cover most of the known townships and often inhabit
towns less than ten miles apart.[17] This dense pattern of bishoprics is
most remarkable, but it does not make the Christians into a local
majority. Although it shows how widely their presence was scattered,
this particular pattern may have arisen from aspects of their local
history and organization. This fact, too, needs a context, but it need
not be one of dramatic, continuing growth.

It is in terms of its scatter, rather than its density, that early
Christianity can best be studied. Although there are many obscurities,
there is just enough evidence to refine explanations, refute older
theories and narrow the possible answers. There is a notable uneven-
ness between the East, where we know a little, and the Latin West,
where we know almost nothing. It has been suggested that in the West
Christianity spread especially with traders from the Greek East, and
that in North Africa it developed closely from the existing Jewish

communities and then prospered through this strong Semitic heritage which was shared by the Punic-speaking population in the Roman province.[18] Neither theory seems so convincing nowadays, although it is not clear how they should be replaced. We know next to nothing about the earliest Christians in Spain, Germany and Britain: in the 180s, Irenaeus of Lyons did refer to "settled" churches in Spain, Gaul and Germany as if they had been formally founded. Tertullian can hardly be trusted when he stated c. 200 that Christians were to be found among "all" German and northern tribes and that they existed in northern Britain beyond the reach of Roman rule. We can suspect, instead, that they were at least known in southern Britain, though the date and historicity of the first British "martyr," St. Alban, are highly disputable.[19]

The theory of traders and Eastern migrants to the West encounters similar problems. It is in Rome and Lyons that we have evidence for Greek-speaking Christians with Greek names, and in Rome, certainly, the faith had arrived from the East before St. Paul. However, we do not know if these Greek Christians had already been converted before they came West or whether they were only converted after settling: the "traders" are not distinguishable. It has recently been argued that in Lyons, Christianity in fact arrived from Rome, not the Greek East, weakening the argument still further.[20]

In North Africa, the likeliest guess is that Christianity did reach the main city of Carthage with Greek-speaking migrants: later details of the Church's liturgy support this Greek origin and do not conform to Roman practice.[21] In the more western region of Mauretania, the Christians' origins are much more obscure, and it has recently been suggested that here the churches looked to Rome, not Carthage or the East.[22] Throughout the African region, the theory of a strong Jewish contact and legacy is still unproven. It touches on a great uncertainty. West of Rome, in North Africa, Gaul and Spain, there is no sound evidence that there were any settled communities of Jews at all in the Apostolic age. There are a few incidental hints that this silence is significant.[23] It may well be that the Jews had in fact spread into the West before the wars with Rome wrecked their homeland in 70 and 135, but as yet, we cannot exclude the alternative, that Christians and Jews arrived in the West together, competing, if not for converts, at least for patrons and places of settlement. The idea of a strong Jewish legacy in African Christianity, appealing to Punic-speaking Semites,

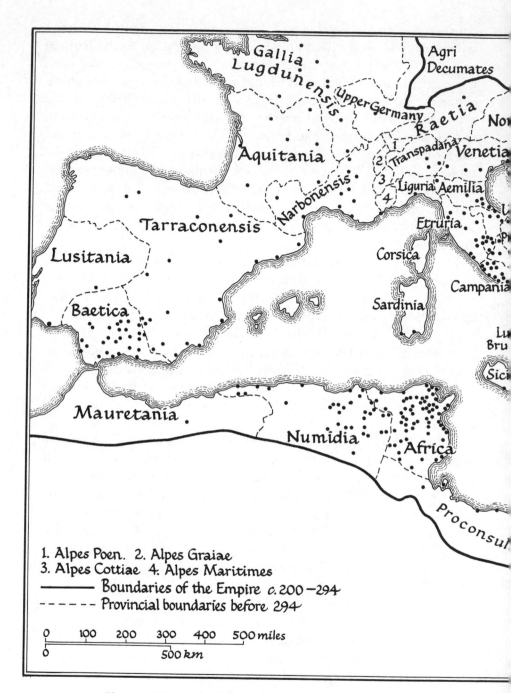

Christian Churches in the Mediterranean known to have been founded
before the persecution by Diocletian, 304 A.D.

Dacia

Chersonesus
Taurica

...nia

...natia

Moesia

Thrace

Macedonia

Bithynia and Pontus

Galatia

Cappadocia

Armenia

Epirus

...ulia et
...alabria

Asia

Mesopotamia

Cilicia

Syria

Achaea

Rhodes

Lycia and
Pamphylia

Cyprus

Phoenicia

Crete

Judaea

Cyrene

Arabia

Egypt

is quite unproven, and on linguistic grounds, as we shall see, it is not convincing.

In the West, in short, early Christianity has lost its history, but there is one general point on which we can be more confident. An older view that heretical types of Christianity arrived in many places before the orthodox faith has nothing in its favour, except perhaps in the one Syrian city of Edessa.[24] In Lyons and North Africa, there is no evidence of this first heretical phase and the likelier origins are all against it. In Egypt, the argument has been decisively refuted from the evidence of the papyri. Details of practice and leadership did differ widely, but the later existence of so many heresies must not obscure the common core of history and basic teaching throughout the Christian world.

In the Eastern Empire, the spread of the Christians is marginally clearer, though the origins of the local churches are most obscure. They confronted a lively variety of sites and languages, the great Greek city of Ephesus, the incestuous families of Egypt's townships, the royal valley of Petra, the tribal camps in the adjoining desert, the huge conglomeration of people and houses across the border in Parthian Ctesiphon, and always beckoning beyond, the roads to Iran and the East and the sea route of the Persian Gulf, where a whole day's journey can be seen in a single glance to the horizon. To know these sites is to wonder how Christians wormed their way into them, the developing temples of pagan Pergamum, the hotter and less predictable society of Edessa in Syria with its Macedonian name and the Arabic spoken in its streets, the smaller townships of inland Phrygia, where the gods were invoked by sceptres and the people were known for their sober ethic and their aversion, even, to swearing oaths.

The best early evidence for the eastward diffusion of Christianity lies in the allusive verse epitaph of a Phrygian bishop, Abercius, and its hints of his journeys: "to Rome he sent me to behold a kingdom and to see a queen in golden sandals and robes: a people I saw there who have a fine seal: I also saw the plain of Syria and the cities and Nisibis, crossing east over the Euphrates. Everywhere I had fellow [kinsmen] having Paul as my [guardian] . . ." Abercius's journey belongs well into the second half of the second century and he implies that he met Christians "everywhere" he went. Nisibis lay far beyond the river Euphrates in the region of Adiabene, whose queen mother and heir had become Jewish converts in the 30s A.D.[25] Did this Jewish presence help Christianity to gain its foothold? Certainly, we must allow for this type of contact in the general area of Syriac-speaking culture which stretched from Antioch to Adiabene, but a Jewish contact was not Christianity's only point of entry.

In 165, Nisibis was recaptured by Rome and brought under her control: in 196, it received the honorary title of "colony." When Abercius visited, it was within the Empire's boundaries. We can compare the military post at Dura, to the west on the Euphrates. Its Christian community in the 220s and 230s has been connected with the presence of Greek-speaking troops in the Romans' service, not with natives or local Jews: a few names were found in inscriptions from the Christian house-church, and almost all of them were connected with Greek or Latin names, not native names in Dura.[26] Fragments of an early version of Scripture were found in Greek, not Syriac: the church's wall paintings were not very similar to those in the Jewish synagogue. These hints are reminders of the possibilities, nothing more, but they warn against tracing the core of every community to converts from Jews and local families. At Nisibis, too, the Christian presence may owe as much to the presence of Roman troops as to any Jewish or native element. At Dura, the Jews' synagogue continued to grow, looking much more impressive than the Christians' little house-church.[27]

One of the most striking features of Rome's eastern frontier is the movement of people and ideas across it: Christianity was no exception, and no single pattern of transit will explain it in regions which saw so many travellers, traders and movements of men with their gods. The Christians in Dura with Greek names were only one of many possible types. Further south, we can already find Christians with a strong Jewish heritage who lived beyond the reach of Rome. During the second and third centuries, groups of Baptists could be found in the district between the mouths of the Euphrates and Tigris rivers, where they lived under the nominal control of the Parthians. They acknowledged Christian teachings among severe beliefs which had the stamp of Jewish influence. Here, they had presumably begun as a splinter group from Jewish settlers and we have come to know only recently how they combined a respect for Jesus with a strong stamp of Jewish practice and an honour for their original leader, the prophet Elchesai, who had taught in Mesopotamia c. 100–110 A.D.[28] Their sect, then, was quite old and traced back to a heretical Christian teacher, busy in this area at an early date. It is a reminder that very varied sects and small groups could multiply in the Mesopotamian area, just out of the range of Greek and Roman historians: Christian groups, already, were not limited to the area of Roman rule.

These Baptists' district was frequented by traders and travellers who moved freely between the cities of Roman Syria, the Persian Gulf and India. The new religion could travel yet further eastwards and in Christian tradition there are two distinct stories that it did. The area was the setting for scenes in the fictitious "acts" of the Apostle Thomas, which were compiled in Syriac, probably at Edessa, before c. 250. They told how Thomas, a carpenter, had seen Christ in a vision and had been sold into the service of King Gundophar, the Parthian ruler whom we know to have ruled at Taxila in the Punjab during the mid-first century. The story was well imagined.[29] Like Thomas, goods and art objects from Roman Alexandria and Syria were reaching the Indus River and its upper reaches in the period of Gundophar's reign. However, we do not know if there is any truth in the legend of Thomas's mission. Possibly some settled groups of Christians did exist in the Punjab and encouraged this story of an Apostle's visit to explain their origin. If so, they are a sad loss to history. In Taxila, during the first and second centuries, they would have lived in a society of rich household patrons, some of whose houses adjoined a large Buddhist shrine. Here, we would have to imagine the two religions' meeting, made without the intervening barrier of pagan gods.

The second story of an Indian mission is largely true. Eusebius reports that an educated Christian, Pantaenus, left Alexandria, evidently c. 180, and went as a missionary to India, where he found Christians who already claimed to trace back to St. Bartholomew.[30] They owned a copy of Matthew's Gospel in "the Hebrew script" which the Apostle was supposed to have left with them. Contacts between Alexandria and the southwestern coast of India make it easy to credit this visit. Eusebius reports it as a "story," but he seems to be expressing his own surprise at the adventure, not his doubt at its source. The Gospel "in Hebrew letters" need not disprove it: "Hebrew letters" may refer to Syriac script, and we cannot rule out an early Syriac translation of the Gospels for use in the East.

If Christians availed themselves of these wide horizons, they were not alone among the travellers on Rome's eastern frontier: soon afterwards, the Christian teacher Bardaisan was able to give us the best ancient description of India's Brahmins from his vantage point at Edessa, in Syria. In a pupil's memoir of his teaching, he also alluded to

Christians in "Bactria," beyond the Hindu Kush Mountains, though not specifically in southern India.[31] His silence does not refute the stories of Christians in that region: he was not giving a complete list of churches. He does, however, cast light on Christianity in his own Edessa, where it attracted something more remarkable: the patronage of a king.

The old city of Edessa lay beyond the Euphrates, to the west of Nisibis, and its fictions have left an enduring mark on Christian history. Its king, Abgar V, was believed to have exchanged letters with Jesus, "copies" of which were on show in Syriac in the city's archives by the late third century: the disciple "Judas Thomas" was believed to have visited this Abgar, to have cured him and many others at the court and then converted him. Copies of the "letter" to Abgar were later inscribed and distributed across the Empire as far as Spain. They became objects of pilgrimage and special power for their city, and at Edessa, they were eventually joined by a "miraculous" image of Jesus's face, a fake "portrait" which originated in the mid-sixth century.[32] The origin of this legend is tantalizing and open to historical dissection. A later King Abgar, Abgar VIII, was described by Africanus, a Christian scholar who visited his court, as "a holy man": another acquaintance, Bardaisan, refers to an Abgar who "believed" and "decreed that anyone who castrated himself should have his hand cut off." Probably, this Abgar is also Abgar VIII. His decree had a specific aim, as it struck at a local pagan practice, but it is very hard to accept that two local Christians would describe a king whom they knew personally as "believing," let alone as "holy," unless he was a Christian sympathizer.[33]

King Abgar VIII's sympathies are all the more tantalizing because his career brought him into conflict, then close contact with Rome. Reinstated as a king, he eventually journeyed to Rome, where he enjoyed a magnificent reception late in his life.[34] We do not know if he was already, or still, a Christian supporter at the time of his visit. However, his sympathies may well have encouraged the legend of the earlier Abgar's letters from Jesus. A king's Christianity deserved a noble ancestry, so the Edessans invented one. Perhaps we can also pin down their emphasis on "Judas Thomas," the city's supposed evangelist. We have learned recently that the heretical prophet Mani corresponded with the people of Edessa in the mid-third century and sent them his "apostle" Addai, also called "Thomas," as the preacher of his new missionary gospel. Perhaps this heretical Thomas was exploiting an existing Edessan interest in "Judas Thomas," the supposed "apostle" of Christ. More probably, the Edessan Christians replied to his heretical presence by stressing their own connection with the "true" Judas Thomas, the Christian evangelist.[35]

We do not know the degree or effects of King Abgar VIII's Christian sympathies: they have left no mark on his coins or his city's monuments. Nonetheless, they are the first pointer to Christianity's appeal to a ruler. Locally, they served Edessa very well. Whereas Nisibis had no royal connection with Jesus, Edessa could now boast letters and an apostolic visit. Thirty miles away, her old rival, Harran (or Carrhae), remained famously pagan, perhaps partly in response to Edessa's new identity. While Edessa's fictions drew pilgrims and tourists from all over the Christian world, Harran was to remain a pagan stronghold, obscured by its neighbour until it profited ingeniously from the Muslim conquests. Then, its pagans claimed a new identity as the lost "Sabian" worshippers whom the Arabs' Koran had mentioned. Edessa's rise is one more chapter in the lively history of the rivalries of local cities.[36] As with the new Ionopolis, religion gave her a fresh claim to fame. Her neighbours' contrary response is another proof of the patchiness of early Christian conversions: one town's faith could be its neighbour's poison.

In the East, however obscurely, we have seen some of Christianity's ways of spreading, with travellers and perhaps with traders, through the presence of troops from the Roman East and among groups who had followed Jewish practice. By 210 it already extended from humble Baptists to the court of a local king. These means of entry were joined by two others: war and persecution. Persecution always scattered Christians, and in the 250s, we know of many who withdrew to the countryside in order to escape it.[37] At the same date, schisms began among Christians themselves, and again, the "true" Christian minorities tended to withdraw from their fellow Christians in order to keep their sect alive. Pagan and Christian intolerance were constant agents of diffusion, and it is to them, therefore, that we can best trace the thick scatter of bishops in North Africa's towns. Sometimes, perhaps, a community asked for its own bishop in order to keep up with its neighbour, but such a quantity of bishops was especially advisable in a province where heresy and schism led an early, flourishing life.

If persecution could push Christians into remote townships, it could also push them across the Roman frontier. In the late fourth century, some of the towns in Mesopotamia claimed that their churches had attracted Christian exiles from the Roman Empire who had fled persecution during the reign of Hadrian. The claim is unverifiable, but similar pressures may have brought Christians soon afterwards into another eastern kingdom: the wilds of Armenia. Again, we have learned recently that Christians were thought to be prominent in the company of its king in the mid-third century. The source for this point is a later story by followers of the heretic Mani which depicted their own mission in the area.[38] It may well be correct on this detail, an anticipation of the kingdom's conversion in the age of Constantine: perhaps here, too, the first Christians were seeking a safe retreat.

Wars, we also know, were effective spreaders of the faith elsewhere between Rome and her eastern neighbours. In the Near East, the 240s and 250s saw resounding victories by the Persian monarchs and the consequent return of prisoners across their borders among the spoils. Their captives included Christians, inadvertent imports from the West. In a famous inscription, the chief Magus at the Persian court later told how "demonic" teachings had been destroyed in the Persian Empire (c. 280–293), including those of the "Nazareans and Christians," terms which seem to refer to two different types of Christian. The neatest explanation is that the "Nazareans" were native Aramaic-speaking Christians converted inside the Persians' Empire by some unknown type of contact, whereas the "Christians" were royal imports, originally prisoners from Greek-speaking towns. Their Greek language isolated them from wider contact with Iranian society, yet even here there were some odd opportunities.[39] In the 270s, one prisoner, the charming Candida, is said to have risen high by her personal talents. She was taken prisoner and brought to the Shah's harem, and if we can trust a detailed Syriac version of her martyrdom, her "astonishing beauty" earned her the greatest favour with King Vahram. She ushered in a sequence of Christian sympathizers among the many grades of queen and concubine at the Persian court. Her progress was not without precedent. At Rome, in the 180s, the Emperor Commodus had already favoured a concubine, Marcia, who used her backstairs influence to intercede for Christians who had been sentenced to hard labour in the mines. The men were more obdurate: when the powers at court altered, Candida was put to death by the Shah's new advisers.

These various avenues of Christianity's spread are all informal, but they recur in later Christian history, repeating themselves from the fourth to the ninth century. What we lack is anything more formal, any sign of a mission directed by the Church leaders. Except for Pantaenus in India and one other whom we will examine in a later chapter, we cannot name a single active Christian missionary between St. Paul and the age of Constantine.[40] Should we look for other obstacles besides the attitude of Christians themselves? In the Near East and the areas beyond the Euphrates, missionary religions were exposed to obvious barriers of language. By the 250s, we can see the consequences in the preaching of a new and determined heresy, the "Gospel of Light," which was spread by the young missionary Mani. Unlike Jesus, Mani had conceived his religion to be a universal faith within the immediate duration of this world. Before long, he and his fellow apostles were using Greek and Syriac, Coptic and Persian to teach it in the Near East. Some Christians, by contrast, give the strong impression of identifying their faith with the Greek language only. In the later fourth century, a strong body of Christian opinion held that at Pentecost the miracle of the tongues had affected the crowd, not the Apostles. So far from giving the Christians the gift of languages, it had enabled all their audience to understand Greek.[41]

In antiquity, a refusal to translate a creed or culture was the privilege of a ruling power: Alexander and his successors used Greek, which they imposed on their supporters and even on their Macedonians; the Romans kept their laws and legal teaching in Latin; the Arabs kept their laws and religion in Arabic. Language proved itself the "perfect instrument of Empire," as Christian conquerors of the New World later described it. The Christians did not emerge with the backing of superior force or a history of conquest behind them: to have confined their teaching to the Greek of their Gospels would have been untrue to this pattern of language and culture. It is not, then, so surprising that Christians soon came to have translations of their texts.[42] Books of Latin Scripture are attested in 180 and were probably much older in their parts or entirety. By c. 180, Gospels are attested in Syriac, the language which served as a common medium from the coast of Syria to western Iran. In Egypt, by the 270s, the Gospels are known to have been heard in Coptic: in 303, the "reader" in a small Egyptian church was "illiterate," presumably in Greek, and therefore read the Bible from a Coptic text: his father's name, Copreus, meant "off the dung heap," a man, then, of humble status who had been exposed at birth but rescued by others from death. Teaching in these versatile languages was older than our first attestations, as we can deduce from

Origen's underexploited contrast between Plato and the Christians. Writing in the late 240s, he remarked that if Plato had wished to spread his truths to barbarians, he would have preached them in Syrian or Egyptian languages. He implied, then, that Christians were already using both.

Were there other languages in the Empire which had a living literary tradition?[43] Hebrew was one, more vigorous than was once believed, but elsewhere the picture is more dubious. Inland in Asia Minor, we continue to find inscriptions in which Phrygians invoke their gods in native Phrygian curses, but these fixed formulae do not make Phrygian a literary language which could cope with a written translation of Scripture. In the early third century, the lawyer Ulpian did remark that a type of trust would be acceptable under Roman law whether it was composed in "Greek or Latin, Punic or Celtic or some other language." His words have been pressed to show that people of property were writing documents in Punic and Celtic, but in context, they are hypothetical: his essential point is to contrast a trust with a will, which had to be written in Latin only. We need better evidence that any of these dialects had a literary use.

In Punic, however, we can find hints of it.[44] The Phoenicians had first exported this Semitic language to North Africa, southern Spain and Sardinia c. 800 B.C. Its areas became Roman provinces, and although simple stylized inscriptions in Punic did persist in North Africa, at least until c. 200, they are known only in contexts which used or presupposed Latin too. The main exception exists outside Africa, in a text from Sardinia which records public dedications by the "people of Bitia," an Emperor's name (Marcus Aurelius) and the titles of local magistrates. The text was cut in an archaic style of lettering, harking back to the eighth century B.C., when Sardinia had had other such inscriptions, not far from Bitia. Nonetheless, this hint that civic notables could still read and write Punic does find support from St. Augustine, c. 400 A.D. He tells how Christians in North Africa could compose psalms in Punic, arranging them in the form of an acrostic. People who were capable of such artistry could certainly have written translations of the Gospels. Yet no Christian is known to have exploited Punic's forgotten potential.

The omission may not be too significant. The heretical followers of Mani had no hesitation about using non-classical languages, but they, too, are not known to have used Punic for their texts. Like the Christians', their mission concentrated on townspeople, among whom we should allow for widespread bilingualism, in Latin or Greek as well as Punic. Anyone who was skilled enough to read or write was likely to know Greek or Latin anyway. The neglect of written Punic is less telling than the more general lack of official encouragement. None of the other translations of the Bible is known to have been promoted by Church leaders or officials: when Tatian produced his "Gospel harmony" in Syriac as well as Greek, it was a personal work, undertaken to serve his own heretical interests. Yet even this apathy should not be pressed too far. We think naturally of a written canon of texts and Scriptures, but the acceptance of a basic body of written books was a slow development in the early churches. Above all, a lack of official interest in written translations need not entail a lack of missionary interest. In eighteenth-century Europe, many keen Christians argued that the Bible should not be translated from Latin for fear that vulgar Christians would then read it for themselves and find the wrong things in it. Preaching, meanwhile, continued in vernacular languages, while "experts" monopolized Scripture in a learned tongue. "In 1713, the Papal bull *Unigenitus* condemned the proposition. 'The reading of the Bible is for everyone.'"[45]

In Christianity's spread, the relevant question, therefore, is not whether Christians exploited all possible literary languages for their Scripture, but whether they were hampered by ignorance of spoken dialects in their missionary work. Here we enter very difficult ground, not least because the very nature or occasion of any "preaching" is itself obscure. Church services were held in one of the major written languages of culture: even in the fifth century, we find interpreters rendering what was being read and spoken in Greek or Latin into a second, vernacular language for the congregation's benefit.[46] During a service, we are not even sure when "preaching" was usual or who undertook it. We have no historical text which refers to formal, open-air sermons outside a church after the Apostolic age. For "preaching," then, we should think essentially of teaching to individuals and small groups whom Christians encountered on their travels. Even so, a traveller did not have to go far in the Roman Empire before he confronted the effects of Babel.[47] Celtic was spoken in the West, Iberian in Spain, Punic and a Libyan dialect in Africa, Coptic dialects in Egypt and "Arab speech" in parts of the Near East. At Edessa, pagans and Christians alike wrote in Syriac, but the names of the city's families suggest people who spoke a form of Arabic. In the hinterland of Pontus, so many languages were recognized that Rome's great enemy of the 80s B.C., King Mithridates, had been credited with fluency in twenty-two: some, but by no means all, died out in the Imperial period. Educated townsmen did not hesitate to project a picture of rural dialect onto the countryside beyond them. Around the mid-third century, a pagan novel assumes that on entering Cappadocia its hero had needed a native-speaking guide. He was embarking on lands which St. Paul had never touched. Lucian, we have seen, complained how the "false prophet" and his snake had given replies to questions in Syriac and in Celtic, presumably for the benefit of nearby Galatians, whose names and inscriptions show a Celtic tenacity. The complaint had to seem plausible.

Did Christians preach in these spoken dialects? The absence of written Christian translations in these languages proves nothing, as they lacked any literary history and often any alphabet, let alone a literate public. Unfortunately, our written evidence throws very little light on the question of Christians' speech. There is only one reference to "barbarian dialect," and it occurs in the preface to the books on heresy which were composed in Greek by Irenaeus of Lyons, c. 180. Apologizing for his Greek prose style, he referred to his "exertions" in barbarian dialect, a remark which has long been upheld as a proof of his preaching in Celtic.[48] The deduction is not justified. Even if Celtic was needed in the modest hinterland of Lyons, a Roman colony, Irenaeus was only making a lettered man's excuse for his literary style. His remark has even been referred to his use of "barbarian" Latin, current in the Latin-speaking colony. That extreme view is also unconvincing: no Greek of the period called Latin a "barbarian dialect." Instead, we should remember the witty apologies of Ovid, another man of letters who wrote on the edge of the classical world. In exile at Tomi, Ovid referred playfully to "speaking Getic and Sarmatian." The remarks were only the amused comments of a literary man lost in a sea of barbarity which he wished to emphasize: Ovid never bothered with dialect. Irenaeus's comment was set in the preface of his long work, where an apology for style was quite conventional. It was a literary disclaimer, not a genuine excuse.

This allusion has to be treated carefully because it is the only one to survive in all the evidence for the churches before Constantine. However, our written evidence derives from Christians who wrote in the bigger cities, and we cannot be entirely sure what a minor preacher in a small African or Pontic township may have tried for his missionary ends. We cannot rule out exceptional individuals, Christians like

Ulfilas, whose parents had been taken captive by the Goths on a raid in
Cappadocia, c. 260. Ulfilas then invented a Gothic alphabet in the 350s
and taught the people the Scriptures in his own translation, "omitting
only the books of Kings because the Goths were already too fond of
fighting."[49] When we have wider evidence in the fourth century and
later, we find monks who did allow for a wide linguistic diversity in
their monasteries. Of many examples, the best is Father Theodosius,
near Antioch, in the early fifth century. He used to herd four groups
together to sing bits of the mass in their own tongues and in their own
churches: Greek, Armenian, "Bessian" and that uncharted dialect, the
speech of lunatics who were possessed by demons. This chorus of the
cuckoo's nest ascended, men said, in perfect harmony. The sequel was
less informal. The three sane choruses processed into one inner hall
while the lunatics kept silence outside. Within, however, the final
liturgy was read in Greek.

By the period of these monasteries, the countryside was being
Christianized more widely and the problems of dialect had become
inescapable. Even so, a strong note of snobbishness and contempt for
barbarous speech remained in the sermons of urban bishops. We can
even find it in the preaching of John Chrysostom (c. 390). At Antioch
and Constantinople, he paid scant respect to the Gothic- and Aramaic-
speakers in his audiences while haranguing them in Greek.[50] No doubt
the same attitudes had coloured many lesser men, leaders of urban
churches in the years before Constantine.

Did these attitudes cut the Church off from many accessible converts? Here, we must be more careful, for the evidence of barbarian
dialect is often accompanied by evidence of an easy bilingualism. At
Lystra, the people were believed to have hailed Paul and Barnabas in
Lycaonian and promptly to have understood a sermon in Greek. As a
bishop, Augustine was aware of the value of Punic-speaking clergy
and took pains to promote a young priest because of his linguistic
gifts. Yet he also tells how farmers in the countryside round Hippo
would translate a conversation to and fro between Latin and Punic. We
should not pin a knowledge of dialect too closely to one social class:
there must have been a degree of "shame-faced bilingualism" even
among educated Greek-speakers, not least among bailiffs and tenants
who had to deal with their local work force. The Christians' use of
Coptic and Syriac made Egypt and a great wedge of the Near East
accessible to their teaching if they chose to follow up the opening. The
likelihood of a bilingual audience was high in and around the towns,

and much lower, naturally, in the remoter villages and further countryside.[51] The linguistic barrier thus merges into a wider one, the line between town and country.

Christianity's impact on the towns and countryside has been variously assessed. Before Constantine Christianity has been confined to the towns: it has been characterized as a "cockney" religion, which clung essentially to the humbler members of big cities; between c. 250 and 310, by contrast, it has been held to have "won the countryside" and made its promotion under Constantine more or less inevitable.[52] The variety of views reflects the extreme scarcity of evidence, but also a varying conception of where a line between town and country can be drawn significantly. Like early Islam, Christianity was a faith which presupposed convenient places of meeting. Its congregations had to finance the continuing costs of a bishop and his staff. It is not, then, surprising that bishoprics were distributed by cities or that early Christianity, like early Islam, is essentially known in an urban setting. Throughout antiquity, the towns were the seats and agents of religious change.

There are, however, some hints of a wider presence. In c. 110, Pliny wrote as a provincial governor to his Emperor, Trajan, and told him that the Christian "superstition" pervaded the local "villages and fields" as well as the towns. He had encountered it on an assize tour, perhaps as far afield as Amastris in Pontus on the southern shore of the Black Sea (northern Turkey).[53] Was he, perhaps, exaggerating? Recent persecutions, including his own, may have scattered Christians into the countryside, but the picture is not one of a narrow, urban faith. We do not know if the Christians concerned spoke anything other than Greek: further west, in Pliny's Bithynian district, the villages round Nicomedia are known as seats of the Greek language from their local inscriptions. His remark is of uncertain scope, but it does warn us that the line between town and village was not everywhere a strict one and that Christians, like others, could cross it, perhaps especially in times of persecution.

The evidence does not end abruptly with Pliny.[54] In 257/8, Eusebius refers to three Christian martyrs who, "they say," were living in the countryside before going up to be tried in the nearby city of Caesarea; between c. 245 and 270, we have the legends and oral traditions of a widespread conversion of "villages" in "inland Pontus," worked by one exceptional missionary; in 248, Origen does rebuke Celsus's sneer at Christian exclusiveness by referring to Christians who "have undertaken to go round not only cities but villages and farmsteads too, in order to win more believers in God"; in the first councils after Constantine, rules are laid down in the East for the duties and role of "country bishops," who must, it seems, have existed previously in Anatolia and Palestine; earlier, in North Africa, the acts of the council in 256 reveal four bishops out of more than eighty whose sees may have lain in village communities, not recognized towns or their constituent parts.[55]

There is a difference, however, between a rural mission and a rural presence, and throughout the years before Constantine, Christians had a special reason for retreating to the countryside: they were liable to persecution in the towns. In 250, we already hear of Christians in Egypt retreating into the mountains and desert: Eusebius's three martyrs may only have taken refuge outside Caesarea, until their consciences pricked them and they returned and "volunteered" to die. While in retreat, this type of Christian may sometimes have persuaded other country people to become Christians too, but the results owed nothing to a deliberate "mission." The episodes in "inland Pontus" raise problems of historicity which we will have to examine later: their framework, however, is essentially the group of Greek-speaking cities which made up Pontus's provincial "league." The story is exceptional, and we will see how it grew with the telling. The "country bishops" are more tantalizing.[56] They are not securely attested until the years after Constantine's conversion, when Church councils in the East tried to regulate their duties. By 325, they existed in Palestine as well as in inland Anatolia and Pontus, and we also hear of local "country elders." In the underurbanized regions of Anatolia, there were few recognized cities for Christians to serve, and yet a strong Christian presence is obvious in the area by the mid-fourth century. Significantly, the "country bishops" are compared by one council with Jesus's seventy Apostles "because they serve the very poor." They did not operate entirely away from recognized towns, but they do seem to have been active in humble circles, presumably in villages, to account for their name: their same concern for the poor emerges from Bishop Basil's letters, written in the 380s to country bishops in central Anatolia.[57]

When, though, did such "country bishops" begin? Here, Origen's remark is suggestive. He does not limit the activities of his rural missionaries to the past. He stresses their poverty and their willingness to travel with few goods; was he, perhaps, thinking of country bishops already serving the poor in Cappadocia and Anatolia, regions which he had visited? Perhaps he was also thinking of Christians in the Syriac-speaking Near East, around and just beyond other places which he knew. Here, as in Palestine, barriers of language did not divide so many townships from their territories. From other evidence, we can glean a picture of Christian "sons of the Covenant" in this area, wandering as "strangers" through the country and its roads, heirs to the Syriac tradition of holiness and a life apart.[58]

Like the Christian presence in Anatolia, this evidence blurs the suggestion that Christianity was a religion solely of the bigger towns. How far, though, does it point towards a true rural mission? Once again, it is hard to draw a firm line between town and "country," when so many "villages" were themselves seats of a culture which reflected urban forms. At its most extreme, the worlds of peasant village and town were indeed separate worlds, as we can see especially in the Syriac evidence. Whether early Christianity went across this extreme dividing line remains highly doubtful: there was no missionary "winning" of the countryside around cities like Antioch and Apamea until a generation or more after Constantine's conversion.[59] There was no specific appeal to the rural peasantry in anything which is known from the earliest Syriac sources. The four "rural" bishops known in Africa in 256 are not necessarily bishops outside a community which focussed on a village; only in the fifth century does a similar list reveal bishops of particular estates or country regions.[60] When we do find evidence of a rural mission, its bias is still significant. In the later Christian Empire, the conversion of country people was often the work of monks or holy men. Here, there is none so telling as the little-known exploits of one Symeon, nicknamed the Mountaineer, whose life at the start of the sixth century was later written up in Syriac by John, his friend and, eventually, the bishop of Ephesus. John himself was remembered as a great converter of the countryside, so his comments on Symeon's mission are doubly revealing.[61]

Around 510, Symeon had found himself beyond the territory of Claudias, in mountains on the very edge of the Euphrates's west bank. He was intrigued by a large sprawling village, visible in the hills, and on asking some visiting shepherds, he was appalled to find that they had little or no idea of Scripture. They had heard a few things from their fathers, but they had never seen a copy of a book. They never went near a church except to baptize some of their children: indeed, they confessed that as herdsmen "we live on these mountains like

animals." "Well said, 'like animals,' my sons," Symeon was believed
to have answered, "yet animals are much better than you . . ."

Symeon kept on pondering this meeting: "How is it that these men
are like animals on these mountains?" A sense of divine mission
entered him and he ascended to one of their places, "a sort of village."
He saw a small church, shaded by a vine, but found it filled with
wood, stones and dust. The older men approached him for a blessing
and revealed that they had no priest: "it is not our custom." Symeon
took up residence in the church and, after inquiry, invited all the
families to hear him. As he preached, they stared in amazement, "like
some idiotic animal," John commented, "which only gapes and stares
when a man tries to teach it." The older men, again, knew a little of the
Scriptures by hearsay: the others had no idea. First Symeon scared
them with tales of hell and then he told them to go away and fast.
When he asked them why their children had not been made "sons of
the covenant" and been taught in church, they told him, "Sir, they
have no time to leave the goats and learn."

Touched by this admission, Symeon announced a great family
service for the following Sunday. At the end, he told the parents to
leave the church while he gave their children a special present. Ninety
girls and boys stayed behind; Symeon and a friend forcibly segregated
thirty of them, locked them into the church and cut off all their hair
with a razor. When he let out these shaven children of God, their
mothers were appalled. Symeon merely laughed and then warned
them not to provoke his curses: rudely, they told him to "try cursing
the Huns, who are said to be coming and wrecking Creation."
However, two of his opponents died soon after Symeon's execrations,
whereupon the others submitted and gave him their children. Symeon
provided writing tablets and the Scriptures and taught the girls and
boys to read and write, schooling them until adolescence. The hills
echoed with their newly learned hymns, and for twenty-six years
Symeon wielded authority in the mountain villages. The story is not
only an excellent example of a holy man who forced himself on
villagers against their will. It is told in a way which puts its hero's and
narrator's views of rustics beyond doubt. They were brute "animals."
John talked often to Symeon and heard him tell of the "savagery of
that people, their subjugation and all the torments they had inflicted
on him." We begin to see why totally rural missions were slow to
start.

These attitudes do not belong with ideas of the Church's early "winning of the countryside." Even the "country bishops" faced formidable difficulties. Although countrymen might sometimes pick up the new faith while visiting a nearby urban centre, there were difficulties in taking the faith out to them. Access to dependent workers on the bigger country estates relied on the connivance of the upper classes or their agents, people who had to be exhorted to build private estate churches and convert their farm workers far into the Christian Empire.[62] Before Constantine, such access and support were rarely, if ever, available. Within the towns, meanwhile, bishops were hard pressed to maintain the Christian unity and discipline for which God held them personally to account. Their duties were thought to involve arbitration, not missionary conversion: in a pagan Empire, it is not surprising if they shrank from further expansion and attended to this responsibility. It is hard, too, to exclude altogether the priorities of Church finance. "Mass preaching" was most likely to attract poorer converts and increase the burdens on the Church's charity. The clergy, meanwhile, were paid from dividends off their congregation's offerings. Like it or not, there would come a point at which too many rustics and slaves would strain the Church's resources. It was more useful, though not more pious, to win three or four richer converts and thread them through the obliging "eye of the needle."

Essentially, the evidence for an early "winning of the countryside" in the third century lies elsewhere on the scale between town and country. It does not concern the rustic peasantry, but many persons in small townships, people who had some contact with the forms of a higher culture. Here, Christianity is especially evident to us in the provinces of Egypt, Phrygia and North Africa. In 180, a group of martyrs in North Africa came from towns with outlandish titles, but even though some of them had Punic names, they all spoke Latin and read a Latin Bible. They were condemned to death by the penalty of beheading, which was becoming a privilege of the "more respectable classes," and if the governor was being precise, they must have been men of a recognized social status in their home towns.[63] In 256, the bishops at North Africa's council are very frequently bishops from bizarre townships, strung out along the main roads, not always towns of recognized status but almost always identifiable from other evidence on the African provinces' map.[64]

Inland in Asia, we have the direct evidence of inscribed funerary monuments at a similar date. In the small towns of mountainous

Phrygia, their texts identify their patrons as "Christians for Christians." This openness was not a proof of militancy or heretical belief.[65] The patrons of these monuments were using the same materials, even the same workshops, as their pagan contemporaries. The earliest dated text belongs in 248/9, and the series of these Greek epitaphs record their Christians among scenes of ploughs and oxen, vines, horses and shepherd's crooks. The women, both pagan and Christian, were shown with their spindles and their wool: some patrons also put up pictures of their pens and writing tablets, proof that they knew how to write.[66] This significant constituency was neither rustic nor lower-class, but it can be aptly compared with the evidence of Christian papyri of the later third century in Egypt. These texts derive from lesser townships as well as from the more prestigious metropoleis: their Greek form and style have been classed with the "tradesmen and farmers and minor government officials, men to whom knowledge of, and writing in, Greek was an essential skill but who also had few or no literary interests."[67]

In these smaller townships, Christianity was not giving direction to a new "rejection of classicism and a renewal of native, pre-Roman ways of life." There was no such "renewal" and no concern to preach in Phrygian or write Scripture in Punic. The art of these smaller townships has been best understood as the rise of a "sub-antique" style which grew from the debris of high classical forms.[68] It sought to participate in a wider culture, not to reject it. As the faith of a "universal Church," Christianity sat well with this type of self-expression. Its widespread presence in these smaller townships makes it something more than a "cockney" religion based essentially in the bigger cities. The significant point is not that it prospered in these larger, untypical city centres but that it was in them that it found its literary expression. Of the major Christian authors between 100 and 250, all except Irenaeus wrote in one of the Empire's few great cities of culture, Rome and Carthage, Alexandria, Ephesus and Antioch. However, these well-educated authors are not necessarily the best evidence for early Christian life as a whole, especially if we only attend to the views which they express in their own persons. It is often more useful that they criticize explicitly the simpler views of the Christian majority, people who thought that Christ would literally return on a cloud, who believed that Peter had confounded Simon Magus's attempts to fly,[69] who did everything to avoid martyrdom and who knew better than to heed moralists' complaints about smart clothing and the pagan games, athletics, hairstyles and the irresistible ways of women. In the smaller townships, higher education was not locally available, and in the larger cities, very few Christians could afford it.

Christianity, then, was present in towns and cities of all ranks and degrees; its Gospels, by the mid-third century, were preached in the major literary languages, but not (so far as we know) in minor dialects; Christians were not totally unknown in the surrounding countryside, but they were very much the exception. There was certainly no "winning of the peasantry" in the Greco-Roman world of the third century. How, then, were Christians distributed round the other great barriers of the age: sex and class?

# II

Paul had admitted to being "all things to all men," and our best account of a Christian mission, the Acts of the Apostles, bears him out. Paul's churches included slaves and people who needed to be told "not to steal": Paul himself referred to the "deep, abysmal poverty" of his Christians in Macedonia. Yet his converts also included people "in Caesar's household," slaves, presumably, in the service of the Emperor. At Corinth, he converted Erastus, the "steward of the city," another eminent post which was often held by a public slave: it is quite uncertain whether this man could be the Erastus whom a recent inscription in Corinth's theatre revealed as a freeborn magistrate, the aedile of the colony. He attracted women of independent status and a certain property, people like Phoebe, the "patroness" of many of the Christians at Corinth, and Lydia, the "trader in purple," a luxury commodity. These women ranked far below the civic, let alone the Imperial, aristocracies.[1] But Acts adds a higher dimension which we might not otherwise have guessed: Paul was heard with respect by one member of Athens's exclusive Areopagus and by the "first man of Malta." He received friendly advice from "Asiarchs" in Ephesus, men at the summit of provincial society, where they served at vast expense as priests in the Imperial cult. On Cyprus, he impressed the Roman governor, Sergius Paulus, by a miracle which he worked in his presence. This connection with the highest society was not Acts' invention. The contact with Sergius Paulus is the key to the subsequent itinerary of the first missionary journey. From Cyprus, Paul and Barnabas struck east to the newly founded colony of Pisidian Antioch, miles away from any Cypriot's normal route. Modern scholars have invoked Paul's wish to reach the uplands of Asia and recover from a passing sickness; Acts ascribed this curious journey to the direction of the Holy Spirit. We know, however, that the family of the Sergii Pauli had a prominent connection with Pisidian Antioch: an important public inscription in the city honoured a Sergius Paulus who is probably the governor of Cyprus's son. One of his female descendants, probably his granddaughter, married a very powerful man of the city, and it was perhaps through her family's support that he attained the great height of the Roman Senate in the early 70s. The Sergii Pauli's local influence was linked with their ownership of a great estate nearby in central Anatolia: it is an old and apt guess that these connections go back to the time of Paul's governor.[2] They explain very neatly why Paul and Barnabas left the governor's presence and headed straight for distant Pisidian Antioch. He directed them to the area where his family had land, power and influence. The author of Acts saw only the impulse of the Holy Spirit, but Christianity entered Roman Asia on advice from the highest society.

In c. 110, Pliny wrote to Trajan that Christians were to be found in Pontus among people of "every rank, age and sex." Around 200, Tertullian repeated the same phrase in an essay addressed to the provincial governor of Africa.[3] Since the great studies of the 1890s, evidence for the social composition of the early Church has not increased significantly, but the topic has attracted an abundant literature. On a broader view, rather more has been added by continuing study of the first Christian inscriptions, known from c. 200 onwards.[4] In Phrygia, we have the epitaphs of "Christians for Christians," one of which is datable to the mid-third century. We know of Christians who served on the city council of a Phrygian town and of a Christian who paid for the expense of civic games as the official "agonothete" and also served as the "first magistrate" of a Bithynian city. These unexpected figures all belong in the third century. So, too, does a cultured Christian lawyer, Gaius, whose elegant verse epitaph, around 250, stressed his contentment with relative poverty, his devotion to the Muses, his conventional views on death and pleasure and his ingenious concern for number symbolism. His tomb lay in Phrygian Eumeneia, the city where we know of Christians on the town council, and it also contained "Rouben," a Christian with a Jewish name whom Gaius evidently revered. "Rouben" remained a powerful figure, even after death. The epitaph of a neighbouring Christian's tomb invoked "God and the angel of Rouben" against anyone who disturbed it. These texts take us into the less familiar sides of Christian views on death: burial with or beside a respected Christian figure and faith in a dead man's angel as a continuing protector in daily life. If Rouben had once been a Jew, the picture is even more intriguing.

Also in Eumeneia, we find the unexpected figure of a Christian athlete, nicknamed Helix (again: "the Creeper"), who had won prizes in a whole range of pagan games from Asia to Brindisi. Like many athletes, he enjoyed citizenship in several cities, and in Eumeneia, he was a councillor and member of the body of elders (*gerousia*). If Christians in other cities had only put up as many inscriptions as these confident figures in Eumeneia, what curious diversity might we not discover? From an epitaph at Nicomedia, again in Bithynia, we know of a third-century Christian who was a wood-carver, originally from Phoenicia; in Phrygia, we find a Christian butcher; in Ostia, the Italian port, we know of a Christian whose names correspond suggestively with those of a member of the boat owners' guild in the year 192. This evidence is particularly valuable because it widens the range of Christians' activities beyond the constricting horizons of so many Christian tracts.[5] It reminds us that their authors' ideals were not necessarily typical. It does not, however, show us the humblest Christians, people who did not pay for the expense of inscriptions. This type of evidence only concerns the better-off, but at least we are continuing to find a few Christians in their varying social contexts.[6]

It is as well to begin a broader survey at the very bottom. The bottom, throughout antiquity, meant slaves, and in slavery, the Church met a social barrier which the Jesus of the Gospels had nowhere discussed. Paul's short letter to Philemon nowhere suggested that there was a Christian duty to free a slave, even a Christian slave: Christian commentators on the letter took his silence for granted.[7] His other letters confirmed the view that social status was not relevant to spiritual worth and that believers should remain in the status in which they were called. Slaves should "serve the more," honouring their higher master, or *kyrios*, Christ. However, it is worth dwelling on Christian views of slavery, less, perhaps, for the appeal of their faith among slaves than for its appeal among those classes who still relied on them. Slaves were essential to the households of the rich, the mines, the agriculture of both tenanted and directly farmed estates in many provinces of the Empire. It is in this sense that we can still describe it as a slave society: slavery was entrenched in the social order of most regions in the second and third centuries.

Christian leaders did nothing to disturb it. When Christian slaves in an Asian church community began to propose that their freedom should be bought from community funds, Ignatius of Antioch advised firmly against the suggestion. He feared, he wrote, that they would become "slaves to lust." Like the Stoics, these Christian leaders began from a principle of the equality of man, yet argued that worldly differences of status should continue undisturbed.[8] The greater slavery was man's slavery to his passions. As if to prove it, pagan slaves continue to show up in the ownership of Christians, even of bishops. In Africa, Tertullian discusses the interesting case of a Christian whose pagan slaves had adorned his house with the trappings of pagan worship for a celebration of the Emperor's successes. Though innocent himself, the Christian was "chastised" in a vision. However, the right type of religion could not always be enforced. In Spain, c. 320, acts of the province's first known Church council advised Christians to "forbid, so far as they could, that idols be kept in their homes. But if they fear violence from their slaves, they must at least stay pure themselves." This fascinating glimpse of tenacious paganism in the household is matched by an absence of advice that Christians should convert their slaves as a matter of course.[9] Paul's letters already showed the varying practice: there were some "households" of Christians, but others where Christians lived in a non-Christian establishment. Paul had not left any encouragement for mass baptism in Christian masters' "families."

This silence is all the more telling because it contrasts with much Jewish opinion and a certain amount of practice.[10] Jewish teachers cited biblical texts to support the view that a Jewish master should circumcise his Gentile slaves. If the slaves disagreed, it was a common opinion that they should be given a year to think the matter over. If they still refused, they should be sold to a pagan master. These opinions were not altogether ignored. After the Jewish revolt of 132–135, the Emperor Hadrian restricted the circumcision of Gentiles, a practice whose prime victims, presumably, had been the pagan slaves of Jewish owners. The circumcision of slaves had played an important part in the spread of the Jewish faith and the conspicuous numbers of Jewish freedmen. By circumcision, slaves were "brought under the wings of the Shekinah." The medical handbooks of pagan doctors are a reminder that the operation was extremely painful.

A Church order of discipline, deriving from the early third century, proposed that all potential Christians must bring references with them when applying for teaching and that the slave of a Christian master must be denied baptism unless his owner had given him a good testimonial. The slave, then, was not alone in needing a reference, but the burden lay on his master's good faith: only if his master permitted was he allowed to hear the faith. The advice resembles the rules of many pagan religious societies where slaves were only to be admitted with a master's prior approval. Christians, however, faced a further category of applicants: slaves of pagan masters who came, nonetheless, to be taught. Here, there could be no question of asking for permission, and instead, the slave was told to "please" his master in order to avoid the risk of "blasphemy" and trouble. Whenever we cite this order, the so-called Apostolic tradition of Bishop Hippolytus, we face the same set of problems: is it evidence for practice, and did anyone observe it? Even if they did not, its value for the accepted attitudes of some Christian leaders is not in doubt. Its priorities are not those of a faith concerned to free slaves from their masters, or to urge masters to let them be released.[11]

On the conduct of slaves, Christian texts were unanimous. The Pauline epistles stated very clearly that slaves must submit, and for most Christian authors their words sufficed. If they were expanded, they were emphasized: slaves must obey masters as the "image of God." The grammar of Paul's commands has been traced to Semitic influence, but it is quite unclear if orders of this type were already current among Jews in their synagogues.[12] It is also unclear whether simpler Christians were naturally inclined to obey the advice. The repeated address to slaves perhaps suggests that some of them were minded to act differently. In a mixed household, disobedience could bring Christians into further disrepute: the orders to slaves in 1 Timothy address Christian slaves in pagan service and tell them to submit "the more" in order to avoid blasphemy.[13] At most, Christian slaves were consoled and comforted. One hint of this attitude occurs in the apocryphal Acts of Thomas, the text we have explored in connection with Edessa. When Thomas saw slaves carrying the litter of a noble lady, he reminded them that Jesus's words of comfort for the "heavy laden" referred to them. "Although you are men," he said, "they lay burdens on you like animals without the power of reason;

those with power over you suppose that you are not human beings, as they are." But he did not preach open disobedience.[14]

Once again, we might isolate this Syriac evidence as untypical of the Greek world, but it does find a direct parallel in the writings of Clement, the educated Alexandrian (c. 200). When Clement attacked the idleness and lack of exercise of ill-behaved contemporaries, he ended by urging them "not to use slaves like beasts of burden." He was not only thinking of the unhealthiness of being carried in a litter. He went on to exhort Christian masters to show "patience, equity and philanthropy" when dealing with slaves. Moral advice to the master was not unknown in pagan philosophy, especially Stoicism, but Christians, this text reminds us, could add it to their spiritual ideals.[15] Did the advice somehow humanize the relationship, as if a truly Christian master was no longer a slave owner, but a fellow man? Such a view puts too heavy a weight on ideals in the face of a debasing relationship. Christian masters were not specially encouraged to set a slave free, although Christians were most numerous in the setting of urban households where freeing was most frequent: our pagan evidence for the practice is overwhelmingly evidence for the freeing of slaves in urban and domestic service: the pagan authors on agriculture never discussed freedom for rural slaves, not even for slave bailiffs. Among Christians, we know that the freeing of slaves was performed in church in the presence of the bishop: early laws from Constantine, after his conversion, permit this as an existing practice.[16] This public act does not entail an accompanying encouragement to perform it. We do not hear of any, and indeed freeing did not presuppose an opposition to slavery. Many masters required slaves to buy their freedom or to leave a child in their place, so that a younger slave could be bought or acquired on release of an older, wasting asset. To free slaves for nothing was much rarer, and only once, in a work of advice to Christians in third-century Syria, do we find Christians being exhorted to spend money on freeing slaves. It took more than a random word of advice to stop Christians from using whatever slaves they could: pagan slaves were better value, economically, as they would not have to stop work on a weekly day of rest. In Sardinia, a collection of slave collars has recently been studied and dated to c. 400 A.D. Some of them were stamped with the sign of the cross and a telling name: "Felix, the archdeacon."[17]

In one particular, indeed, Christians narrowed antiquity's most travelled route to freedom. Before baptism, Christian men were required to marry or give up their concubines.[18] If, as often, the woman was a slave, she would presumably be freed first. After baptism, sex with a slave was a promiscuous sin and strictly forbidden to Christians. Yet pagan masters' sexual interest in their male and female domestic slaves frequently led to their eventual freeing. To well-behaved Christians, this route was closed.

To the churches, we can only conclude, these niceties were irrelevant. Christian teaching was not concerned with worldly status, because it was inessential to spiritual worth. So far from freeing others as a spiritual duty, some Christians were prepared to enslave themselves voluntarily. In Rome in the 90s, one group of Christians sold themselves into slavery in order to ransom fellow Christians from prison with the proceeds. Not until the fourth century and the rise of monastic communities do we find clear hints of Christian attempts to better the slave's position. In the 340s, the Council of Gangra threatened excommunication and the dire "anathema" against anyone who provoked slaves into disobedience "under pretext of piety": we would much like to know whom the council had in mind. Monks, certainly, were cautioned against receiving fugitive slaves into their company, as many Christian leaders took a wary view of runaways.[19] In the pagan Empire, slaves who had a grievance against their masters could seek asylum at any statue of the Emperor or within the precincts of certain specified temples. Their case was investigated and if justified, they were sold to another master or made into temple slaves of the god. In the Christian Empire, slaves could take refuge in church, but they were returned after inquiry to the same master. The only remedy was a rebuke to whichever party deserved it; Christians aimed to reform the heart, not the social order.[20] The appeal of their faith did not lie in a reversal of the barriers which disfigured pagan society. When we find Christianity among the higher classes, we should allow for the effects of this welcome reticence.

Where, then, did its centre of gravity lie? Not, surely, among slaves, when such care was advised before accepting them into the Church and when no orders were given for teaching a Christian's slaves the Gospel as a matter of course. We should recall the social order which we sketched for all but the largest cities: the absence of clearly defined middle or "merchant" classes and the sharply tapering pyramid, in which a narrow group of benefactors and notables paid for the amenities of civic life for the "people," the "poor." In such a social order, a Christian community of any size cannot be equated with a broad "middle class" or only with its known converts of higher position. Two or three inscriptions which mention Christian town councillors do not make the Church into a faith predominantly for the higher classes. "Not many wise men after the flesh, not many mighty, not many noble are called, but God chose the foolish things of the world." So Paul told the Corinthians; we must do justice to the exceptions, while looking for a guide to the "foolish" majority. Outsiders had no doubt.[21] "In private houses nowadays," claimed the pagan Celsus, c. 170, "we see wool workers, cobblers, laundry workers and the most illiterate rustics who get hold of children and silly women in private and give out some astonishing statements, saying that they must not listen to their father or schoolteachers, but must obey them. They alone know the right way to live, and if the children believe them, they will be happy. They whisper that they should leave their teachers and go down to the shops with their playmates in order to learn to be perfect . . ." The Christian Origen did protest at this allegation, but his book answering Celsus assumed the existence of Christians superior to the simple majority in the Church. Other Alexandrians wrote in the same manner, and it was left to Tertullian to accept the low status of many Christians and argue from their crude faith to the "natural" Christian instincts of the human soul. Significant evidence lies in the gem of early Latin Christian literature, the *Octavius* by Minucius, a work whose date is best placed between Tertullian and Cyprian in the early third century, perhaps c. 230.

This charming dialogue reports the conversion of a prominent pagan, Caecilius, by the Christian Octavius. Set at Ostia by the seaside, it is imagined in the "summer recess," while the law courts were shut at Rome. Three eminent advocates meet and discuss their beliefs, agreeing finally on the Christian faith. The Ciceronian style and colour of the dialogue were themselves a demonstration that Christianity could appeal to a man of high culture. So, too, was the dialogue's conclusion: it is highly likely that Caecilius was a local dignitary from North Africa, known in inscriptions at Cirta. Yet when he begins by complaining that Christians assemble the "lowest dregs of society" and "credulous women, an easy prey because of the instability of their sex," the Christian Octavius cannot entirely refute him.[22] He merely answers that everybody is capable of thinking and arguing, that the ordinary man can discuss theology too, that a rough literary style does not obscure clear thought and that "poor people of our rank have discovered the true wisdom." The assumptions in his answer are very revealing. In the writings of Clement, c. 200, we find a sharp awareness that Christians in Alexandria were divided between the simple, believing masses and those few who wanted a more intellectual faith without lapsing into heresy. This division, too, suggests a Church of many humbler Christians with a few educated and broader minds in their midst. In the *Octavius*, the impression is confirmed by a Christian author who attaches it to a social context: "most of us," Octavius admits, "are considered to be poor."

The hard core of these churches' membership lay in the humbler free classes, people who were far removed from higher education and at most controlled a very modest property of their own. It is against this silent majority that the exceptions should be seen, although the exceptions generally wrote the surviving texts and addressed exceptional Christians. To find a text which emphasized the mission to the poor, but not the rich, after the earliest period, we have to look to the fictitious "Acts of Peter and the Twelve Apostles."[23] It is thought to have begun as a text of the mid- to late second century. While other apocryphal acts in Greek tended to place the Apostles in the highest provincial society and sometimes dropped very well-chosen names, this fiction told how Jesus dressed as a poor seller of pearls and went out into the cities. The rich heard his sales talk, looked down from their balconies and sneered at his pretensions. The poor and the destitute pressed round him, asking at least for a glimpse of so precious an object as a pearl: "We will say to our friends proudly that we saw a pearl with our own eyes, because it is not found among the poor." Jesus promised not merely to show one but to give it to whoever followed his route in poverty and came to the holy city. The seller of pearls then appeared as Christ, who sent the Apostles on their mission, ordering them to show no favour to the scornful rich. The story is best set in Christian Syria, where the values of poverty and dependence on God lived among the wandering "sons of the covenant." In Alexandria, by contrast, the intellectual Origen could write frankly that "not even a stupid man would praise the poor indiscriminately: most of them have very bad characters."[24]

The bias of most of our early Christian texts inclined in his direction. A scarlet tradition of woes against the rich had lain to hand in the Jews' apocalyptic literature.[25] However, the proper use of riches was a topic which no surviving letter by Paul had discussed. Educated Christians in Alexandria were heirs to the old allegorical skills of Philo and his Jewish contemporaries, and it was their achievement to deny the tradition's plain meaning by widening the eye of the needle and shrinking the camel to a pinhead. Clement's pamphlet "Whether the Rich Man Can Be Saved" presupposed some very rich Christian converts who wished for advice on their predicament. He was aware of a certain paradox, as he pleaded for the rich man's salvation and advised him not to give everything away; he told him to take on a chaplain in his personal household to teach him ethics privately and intercede for the good of his soul.[26] Riches were in themselves "morally indifferent," as the Stoic philosophers taught: what mattered was their use. For a Christian, their best use was almsgiving to the exceptionally pious, the poor. Almsgiving would assist the rich man's salvation, while the poor, in return, would pray hard for his soul. The Sermon on the Mount seems a distant antecedent.

Around 200, a similar audience lies behind several of Tertullian's writings in Carthage.[27] Like Clement, Tertullian has a connoisseur's eye for fashionable females' makeup and hairstyles, and he also discusses the difficulties of Christians who have to hold civic office. Citing the precedent of Joseph, he enlarges on their proper attitude, while revealing that these questions had only been raised recently in the churches: Tertullian gives the impression of a community for which the problems of high society were being felt and experienced more widely for the first time.

In the 170s, Celsus had criticized Christians who refused to "hold office in their fatherland." He must have been referring to local civic magistracies, and among his protests at the Christians' low status, his comment is unexpected.[28] By the mid-third century, however, inscriptions from the Phrygian town of Eumeneia show us Christians of this rank. They were serving the city as councillors, a presence which literary texts had not led us to anticipate. The class of city councillors was socially rather varied, and by 250, quite humble men of modest fortunes might find themselves compelled into its duties. The duties involved pagan worship, but somehow these Christians compromised and avoided giving offence.

The best evidence for prominent Christians lies in the letter of an Emperor. In 258, Valerian prescribed penalties for Christian senators, men of "egregious" position, Roman knights, respectable women (*matronae*) and Imperial slaves. Their properties were to be confiscated if they persisted in their faith. Perhaps some of these categories were more imaginary than real, for by the 260s, Eusebius could name only one senator who was a Christian, a man who had been particularly prominent near Eusebius's own Caesarea. But modern studies of the senatorial order are unable to pin down any other.[29] Were all Valerian's Christian suspects somewhat hypothetical?

There is no doubt about the faith of certain Imperial slaves. In Paul's first churches, "those in Caesar's household" had sent their greetings to the Christians of Philippi. In the 90s, the bearers of the "epistle of Clement" to Corinth bore names which suggest that they had been slaves in the Imperial *familia*.[30] Irenaeus and Tertullian both used Christian "slaves in the royal household" as an accepted example in their writings. We can support them from three excellent types of evidence: a letter, a graffito and a group of inscriptions.[31]

In the Severan period, a funerary inscription at Rome reveals a Christian, Prosenes, as a servant "of the bedchamber," who stood very high in the Emperor's household; another puts a young Christian in the training school for the elite of Imperial officials. Both types of Christian are supported by literary evidence. To these inscriptions, we can add the famous graffito at Rome, found in 1856, which sketched a man with a donkey's head hanging on a cross. It was captioned "Alexmenos worships his God," and from Tertullian we learn that a similar "blasphemy" had been paraded in the arena at Carthage. The Roman graffito is unusually interesting because of its place of discovery: it was scratched in the *scola Palatina* at Rome, on the wall of the training ground for many of the Emperor's most capable servants. A parody of Christianity was thought especially apt there, and if we look closely at one of the letters of Cyprian, bishop of Carthage, we can support the impression. In 258, Cyprian had a foreknowledge of the Emperor's legal rescript, which is only intelligible if he knew highly placed Christians in the Emperor's entourage: Dionysius, bishop of Alexandria, remarks how Valerian's household was "full of the faithful," and this type of evidence helps us to locate them without undue surprise.

Imperial slaves spanned a wide social range, and these hints of Christians in their midst at Rome do not exhaust the possibility of Christians in the order as a whole: others may have existed on the Emperor's many properties throughout the Empire, although their identification has often been hypothetical.[32] "Egregious" Christians of equestrian or higher status are more elusive in our evidence: we must remember, however, "most excellent" Theophilus, to whom the third Gospel and Acts were dedicated. As we shall see, this "most excellent" sympathizer was a figure of very high standing.

In a different group of servants, the free soldiery, we find clear evidence for Christians by the later second century. Their presence raises many more difficulties than we can solve, whether they were converted while serving or whether, less probably, they were Christians when they were first recruited; how, indeed, they coped with the long calendar of pagan sacrifices which coloured army life.[33] The army's lack of religious commitment in the later conflicts of the fourth century is a fact of the first importance. We should allow, once again, for Christians who were ready to compromise to a degree which their leaders' moral sermons would not contemplate. The few military martyrdoms which are known to us before 300 arise from the victim's own unusual intransigence. Tertullian (c. 200) tells of a Christian who refused to wear his wreath on a pagan occasion, and we can best understand the story by connecting this refusal with an exemption which was enjoyed by the pagan worshippers of Mithras. Only when fellow Christians mocked the man for masquerading as a Mithraist was he interrogated. He was not put to death until he had refused to compromise after two separate interviews. It is quite clear that other Christians in his unit had had no such scruples and had been allowed to survive without bother.

We know much more, inevitably, about Christians who were prominent for their education, especially in the Greek-speaking world. Like the Christian magistrates and councillors whom we meet in inscriptions, they had the leisure and fortune to acquire a higher education, and from an early date there were Christians able to communicate with the literary culture of their age. As a "religion of the book," Christianity had a particular relationship with texts.[34] In Rome, several paintings in the burial chambers of the catacombs show Christians arriving at the Last Judgement clutching their books. When the governor of Africa asked a group of Christian prisoners what they had brought with them to court, they replied, "Texts of Paul, a just man." One of the fundamental contrasts between pagan cult and Christianity was this passage from an oral culture of myth and conjecture to one based firmly on written texts. In the first communities, there had already been a significant break with contemporary habits of reading: Christians used the codex, or book, for their biblical texts, whereas pagans still vastly preferred the roll. The Christian codex was made of papyrus, not parchment. It was more compact and better suited to people on the move, and it was an easier form in which to refer to and fro between texts. This Christian revolution lies at the beginnings of the history of the modern book; for scriptural texts, on present evidence, it seems to have been universal.

Gradually, this concern for the book extended to pagan culture too. In Paul's letters, we are reading an author who is capable of alluding at second hand to themes of the pagan schools but who remains essentially an outsider with no grasp of their literary style or content: Paul's echoes of pagan philosophy derive at best from the culture of other Greek-speaking Jews, but not from a pagan or philosophic education. His companion, the author of Acts, has also been mistaken for a Hellenistic historian and a man of considerable literary culture; in fact, he has no great acquaintance with literary style, and when he tries to give a speech to a trained pagan orator, he falls away into clumsiness after a few good phrases.[35] His literary gifts lay, rather, with the Greek translation of Scripture, the Septuagint, which he knew in depth and exploited freely: to pagans, its style was impossibly barbarous. In the 90s, the author of the "epistle of Clement" showed a more elegant manner, but his allusions to pagan culture, though more unusual, were still secondhand.[36]

In the early second century, the picture changes importantly.[37] A Christian, Aristeides, addressed an "Apology" to the Emperor Hadrian and described himself specifically as "the philosopher from Athens." The contents say little for his philosophy, but the claim and the form of this piece are most revealing. Aristeides was followed by at least six other apologists in the Antonine age who compared and defended their faith beside pagan myths and philosophies. In the Antonine age, a shared literary and philosophical education united senatorial Romans and prominent figures in the Greek-speaking cities. It helped the wide and disparate upper class to communicate on common ground and to maintain a sense of personal contact. Respect for this common culture was shared by Emperors and their households: by presenting Christianity in similar terms, Christians of varying education attempted to join the high culture which distinguished the period and gave cohesion to its governing classes. The claim to be a philosopher from Athens was beautifully suited to the Emperor Hadrian's cultural interests. We can be fairly certain that no second-century Emperor bothered to read these long apologies. One of them, Athenagoras's Embassy, was cast in the form of a speech, but it is not credible that a Christian was allowed to weary the Emperor's patience by delivering it in his presence while his faith was a criminal

offence. The setting is a literary fiction.[38] However, it is quite credible
that some or all of these apologies were despatched or delivered to the
Emperor's officials. They are no odder than several other petitions
which reached him, and in one case, it does seem that a pagan critic
was aware of their contents. In the 170s, the pagan Celsus's book is
best understood as rebutting the impudent link between Platonism
and Christianity which apologists like Justin had proposed in petitions
to the Emperor.

   In the Severan age of the early third century, the known addressees
of Christian books are rather different. They are no longer the
Emperors but their womenfolk. We know of letters which Origen
addressed to women in the Imperial family, while Hippolytus's book
*On the Resurrection* is dedicated to an unnamed "queen." The apologies
disappear, along with that particular surge of cultural exchange
between prominent citizens, senators and Emperors whose exceptional degree had characterized the Antonine period. In the early third
century, we find Christians among people of a wide and varied
culture, wider, even, than the first apologists'. Naturally, they are
most evident in the books which were written in the big cities, and
they are nowhere more evident than in the guide to Christian conduct
which Clement composed in Alexandria c. 200. This remarkable
work, the *Paedagogus*, urged an ethic of simplicity on Christian readers
in language which was the very denial of its ideal.[39] Readers were
expected to savour a *tour de force* of literary erudition which paraded its
pure Attic style and its knowledge of Homer and the old comic poets.
Like his teacher, Pantaenus, Clement was steeped in the ethic of Stoic
philosophy. To its moderate precepts, he added the comfort of God's
attendant Word, present and willing to assist each Christian in his
progress. Yet he also respected the later Stoa's accommodations to
rank and degree, its disdain for vulgar and ignoble actions and its sense
that the wise man was set far above the common herd. Clement's
passionate attachment to culture was evident in every section of his
book: his educated ear even led him to misunderstand Scripture,
mistaking a lowly use of Greek in the Gospel of Luke. Some of his
examples of worldly extravagance were more bookish than real, but
they are proofs, nonetheless, of the range and stamina of a cultured
Christian author and his audience. The pagan schools had produced
nothing more dazzling. Clement wrote for the smart minority in the
Church of his home city, whom he impressed by alluding to anything
under the sun, to the marvels and wonders in nature, strange facts

about pregnancy, the use of the mastic tree as a source of chewing gum and the deplorable sex habits of the female hyena. In Carthage, Tertullian had sounded a similar note, combining philosophy, rhetoric and the massive erudition of the higher schools. Culture, in these great cities, was finding fluent expression in Christian books.

By the 230s, we can watch this combination in a Christian, Julius Africanus, whose work and life spanned most of the interests of educated society. This fascinating figure implies in his writings that his "ancient fatherland" was the pagan colony Aelia Capitolina, which stood on the site of Jerusalem.[40] Early in the third century, he visited the court of Abgar VIII at Edessa and was sufficiently intimate with the courtiers to ride with them out hunting. His picture of their skills is very lively. He admired the extraordinary marksmanship of Abgar's young son and remarked how he once shot a bear in both eyes, using two consecutive arrows. He witnessed an even better display of archery by Bardaisan, whom we would otherwise mistake for a sedentary Christian and an armchair intellectual. Eusebius then implies that in 222 Africanus went on an embassy to the Emperor Severus to win support for the rebuilding of the local site of Emmaus: if so, we would much like to have his speech, as the Christian associations of Emmaus must have been in his mind. There is no reliable evidence that Africanus had ever been a Jew, but his culture is unmistakable. He tells us himself that he was appointed architect for the "handsome library" which Alexander Severus built "in the Pantheon" at Rome and completed c. 227. He was also a traveller, a critic and man of letters. He visited the supposed site of Noah's Ark; he toured the Holy Land; he knew various manuscripts of Homer which lay in civic libraries from the old site of Jerusalem to that fine city Nysa in Caria. He had travelled to Alexandria to hear a Christian philosopher and he conducted a famous correspondence with Origen: when Origen cited the episode of Susannah in the Book of Daniel as if it was history, Africanus showed crisply and decisively that the story was fiction. His *Chronography* set the comparative dating of Jewish, Christian and pagan history on a sound and influential footing. His literary *Miscellany*, or *Kestoi*, had the range of a polished man of letters, discussing anything from magical spells to battles with elephants, weaponry and a host of little-known facts about horses and how to keep them sound.

By the end of Africanus's life, men of good education were emerging as bishops in the bigger cities of the Empire. We can match them

with Christians of similar tastes whom we can detect in the contemporary papyri.[41] We began with the intriguing papyrus letter which a
Christian in Rome sent to brethren in Arsinoë c. 265. It is no less
intriguing that a subsequent Christian jotted the opening of the Epistle
to the Hebrews in one of its margins and added verses from Genesis in
another, using not one, but two Greek translations of the Bible.
Clearly, he was a person with a particular interest in texts. Perhaps
another was Hermogenes, magistrate and councillor in Egypt's Oxyrhynchus, who used the back of a page from a copy of Africanus's
*Miscellany* to write his will, adding a special compliment to his wife's
fitting conduct during their married life. The page came from a
Christian's text, and the compliment has been seen as a Christian's
touch of courtesy. This interest in culture and philosophy was not
confined to the grandest Christians. In Rome of the late 180s, we
know of Greek-speaking Christians from Asia Minor who were led by
one Theodotus, a "leather worker by trade, but very learned
nonetheless."[42] They studied Euclid's geometry, Aristotle's philosophy, and "almost worshipped Galen," an author who had once
remarked on the Christians' reluctance to argue their first principles
instead of relying on blind faith. These Christians were a living reply
to his criticisms, but in due course they were excommunicated by the
bishop of Rome. A strong opinion held that heresies originated in the
various Greek philosophies from which they descended like
"schools."

What, finally, of Valerian's other category, the "matrons," or
women of respectable birth? Here we can be more positive. Not only
were Christian women prominent in the churches' membership and
recognized to be so by Christians and pagans: in Rome, c. 200, we
have a precious insight into their social status and balance in the
community.[43] Bishop Callistus, himself a former slave, was reviled
for a ruling which permitted Christian women to live in "just concubinage" with Christian men whom they had not formally married.
Although his rule was mocked as a licence to adultery, it must be
understood through the marriage laws of the Roman state. If a
highborn lady married far beneath her rank, she was deprived of her
former status and legal privileges: Callistus's ruling belongs in a community whose well-born women outnumbered its well-born men.
This impression meets us in other Christian evidence,[44] in Tertullian's
remarks on women who preferred to marry "slaves of the Devil"
rather than humble Christian men, Valerian's rescript on Christian

"matrons" and the concerns of the first Church council in Spain to match an excess of Christian women to a deficiency of Christian men. Well-born Christian women were sufficiently familiar to attract a sharp comment on the Christians' "female Senate" from the pagan Porphyry c. 300; we know of governors whose wives were Christian sympathizers, as were female members of the Severan Imperial house; high-ranking women took good care of Origen in Alexandria; when Apollo spoke on the problem of Christian obduracy, he was answering a pagan husband's question about his Christian wife. In Rome, Bishop Callistus was trying to allow prominent women to take Christian partners without suffering a legal penalty. The problem was not unknown elsewhere in society. Marriages between women of high status and prominent slaves in the Imperial service were already familiar and had caused problems of legal disability: in a Christian community, men of high, free birth were rarer and Callistus allowed women their social *mésalliances* in order to evade the secular laws.

This conspicuous female presence in the churches can be taken further. Like the Jewish communities, the churches offered charity to widows. Unlike the Jews, many Christian teachers followed Paul in regarding remarriage as a poor second best, while a minority declared it entirely sinful. One of the major demographic contrasts between an ancient and a modern population lies in the ancients' higher proportion of young widows. Because the age of girls at marriage was frequently very low, as low as thirteen, older husbands were likely to die first, leaving their wives to the second marriages which secular laws encouraged: under Augustus's rules, widows were penalized if they did not remarry within two years. In the churches, however, widowhood was an honoured status and remarriage was often seen as a concession to the weak: an early council legislates strongly against women who marry two brothers, presumably in sequence, the natural course for a widow in many pagan families after one brother's early death.[45] Christian teaching thus tended to keep widows as unattached women, and their presence became significant. Only a minority of the "fifteen hundred widows and poor people" whom the Roman church tended in 251 would have been widows of any property, yet this minority was not without effect. The rules of female inheritance in most of these women's home cities would allow them to control or inherit a proportion of their husband's property. The Church, in turn, was a natural candidate for their bequests. Before Constantine, we do not know under what legal title these bequests were made, but it is not long before we have vivid evidence of their importance. In July 370, the Emperor Valentinian addressed a ruling to the Pope of Rome that male clerics and unmarried ascetics must not hang around the houses of women and widows and try to worm themselves or their churches into their bequests, to the detriment, even, of the women's families and blood relations. It is even more revealing that, twenty years later, in August 390, his successor deplored these "despoilers of the weaker sex," yet admitted reluctantly that the law was unworkable and would have to be abolished. Ingratiating monks and clergymen had proved too strong for secular justice.[46]

Nor did the churches profit only from widows. They exalted virginity, and their young female membership actually practised it, a point which greatly struck Galen in Rome. Again, these women grew up without any family, yet they were heiresses to parts of their fathers' and mothers' property.[47] Bequests were antiquity's swiftest route to social advancement and the increase of personal capital. By idealizing virginity and frowning on second marriage, the Church was to become a force without equal in the race for inheritance.

It is highly likely that women were a clear majority in the churches of the third century. We hear something of the mixed marriages of pagan husbands to Christian wives: on this general topic, Paul's moderate advice prevailed, that the Christian partner should not simply divorce his pagan equivalent. Yet we never hear of a Christian husband with a pagan wife. In a powerful comment, Tertullian remarks on the ease with which Christian wives found willing pagan husbands: the husbands were keen to seize and abuse their wives' dowries, treating them as their "wages of silence" about the women's beliefs. Perhaps we should only note the continuing evidence of Christian women and leave the proportions to guesswork:[48] in 303, however, when the church in the North African town of Cirta was seized during a persecution, it is suggestive that only sixteen men's tunics were found, whereas there were thirty-eight veils, eighty-two ladies' tunics and forty-seven pairs of female slippers.

Pagans would not have been surprised by such an imbalance: the wife, said their moralists, should strictly adopt her husband's gods and "bolt the door to excessive rituals and foreign superstition." It was a well-established theme in their literature that strange teachings appealed to leisured women who had just enough culture to admire it and not enough education to exclude it: few women were as well equipped as Plutarch's admired friend Clea. "It is not possible," Strabo had remarked around the years of Jesus's birth, "for a philosopher to influence a group of women by using reason, nor to exhort them to piety and faith: for this, he needs to use superstition too." Christians, on one view, had merely proved him right: the Resurrection, complained Celsus, rested on nothing better than the tales of hysterical females.[49] The male leaders of the Church shared the stereotype. The "letter of Timothy" accepted a general view of woman as the prey to emotion and irrationality, whose nature made her a natural culprit for the spread of heresy. Tales of the promiscuity of heretical teachers enjoyed a wide currency and the theme became a standard accusation.[50] They were a distinctive Christian slander, as women were particularly prominent in Church life, but perhaps we should not always dismiss them. The afternoons were long in a Gnostic's company; myths of the Aeons and Abysses were complex and impenetrable: the case histories of Montaillou remind us that there were many ways of pledging support for a man with a rare and special doctrine.

By the mid-third century, this feminine presence showed in the Christians' ideas of their founders. Just as Jesus was shown in art as a philosopher and teacher, so his mother, Mary, had been upgraded socially, to rival the smarter women in the Church. She had already been given rich and well-born parents in an influential fiction of her life: by the 240s, Origen was praising her deep reading of the Bible, and in subsequent art, she was raised to the status of a bluestocking.[51]

The next four chapters concentrate on aspects of the Church in or around the mid-250s: we can summarize its general composition with some confidence. The Christians were a small minority, hardly known in the Latin West or the underbelly of Northern Europe, on which so much of the military effort of third-century Emperors was to be expended. They were not only concentrated in the bigger cities, but they were prominent in towns of varying rank and degree; they used the living literary languages, but not, so far as we know, the many local dialects. Their centre of gravity lay with the humbler free classes, not with the slaves, whom they did little to evangelize. There were Christians in the army and in the Imperial household, though, so far as we know, no more than one, perhaps two, Christian senators. Women of all ranks were conspicuous and there was a notable presence in some churches of women of high status. This profile has had to be deduced indirectly, but it matches, most gratifyingly, the one sample of a church's membership which we can appreciate in any detail between the Apostolic age and the conversion of Constantine. In the early fourth century, we have the records of an interrogation of church officers in the North African city of Cirta.[52] Apart from its high proportion of female clothing, this church included a teacher of Latin literature, who was also a town councillor, albeit only in the second generation of his family; a fuller, who could nonetheless be alleged to have distributed a huge bribe; a woman of the highest status, a *clarissima*, whose bribes were twenty times bigger and had disrupted, people said, an entire election in her own Carthage; a *sarsor*, or worker of coloured stones for decoration; an undifferentiated body of simple laymen, harassed by a crowd of "rustics" who were not Christians themselves but were alleged to include prostitutes and quarry workers, people who could be bribed and incited: there were also the loyal Christian gravediggers, underground heroes of the Christian cemeteries and catacomb tunnels, the diggers whom we can still see with their picks and lamps in wall paintings of the catacombs in Rome.

On one final point, we can be more confident. In pagan cities, young men were frequently organized in groups and societies of self-styled "youths," yet we never hear of Christianity spreading horizontally between people of the same age. In 203, the Carthaginian martyr Perpetua tells a graphic story of her own resistance to her pagan father's pleas. "He fell before me weeping," she recorded, "and I pitied him as he called me no longer his daughter, but mistress and lady." Yet Perpetua and her companions owed their faith to an older Christian, Saturus, just as Cyprian owed his to the older Caecilius, and Justin remarked on the decisive advice of an elderly Christian whom he had met by the seashore. In Edessa, a pupil recalled how the great Bardaisan had rebuked a fellow pupil, Awida, who had started to put theological questions to his own "age-mates." "You should learn from somebody older than them," Bardaisan told him: Christianity did not open a generation gap in families.[53] It tended to spread vertically, not horizontally, from older teachers, from a Christian parent or a Christian head of a household.

# III

In the first Christian churches, amid all this social diversity, an ancient hope had been realized.[1] During Creation, said the Book of Genesis,

God had taken clay and fashioned man: then he "breathed into his face the breath of life and man became a living soul . . ." By his very nature, each man possessed this personal puff of divinity. It resided in him and linked him potentially to God. This element had not been forgotten by its Jewish heirs. St. Paul's contemporary the Alexandrian Philo still maintained a lively sense of it in his many books on Scripture.[2] A breath of divine Spirit, he believed, lived in all men from birth as their higher reason. It was allied to their inner conscience, the presence which "accused" and "tested" them and made them aware of their own misdeeds.

Would God ever send a second instalment, a further gift? Once, he had given it to individual prophets, but by the first century B.C., surviving Jewish literature had little to say on the possibility.[3] Philo did believe such a gift was available, but only to exceptional individuals who had engaged in a long and arduous progress through faith to self-knowledge. At last, through God's grace, they would receive a fresh gift of his Spirit which would "drive out" reason and possess them with divine ecstasy. Philo himself had known a faint approximation to this state. He had felt it, he wrote, in the course of his studies on Scripture, when sometimes he was granted a slight inspiration, in a sudden "flash," we would say, the "bright idea" of a scholar. Careful study of Philo's writings shows how rare and faint these scholarly "flashes" were.

Only in one place do we find a strong sense of the Spirit's guidance and its imminent coming to a Jewish community at the Last Day: in the scrolls of the Dead Sea sect, awaiting the end of the world. In the first Christian churches, both Jewish and Gentile, this presence suddenly came true. While Philo hoped for a gift of the Spirit to the minds of exceptional men, humble Christians across the Aegean were experiencing this very contact in their hearts, a presence which made them cry out, "Abba, Father," in a sudden burst of immediacy. The Spirit, said Paul, was bestowed on their communities as a "deposit" or "advance payment" against the greater gift of the Last Day. It amounted to more than an empty "speaking with tongues," that recurrent experience in Pentecostal history: this "speech" is no sudden gift of linguistic skill, but a random jumble, as neutral observers have often demonstrated.[4]

Among the first Christians, the Spirit belonged with a continuing change in personality and in people's understanding of themselves. It was attached, nonetheless, to the old Scriptural tradition. Though "alive" in the power of the new Spirit, Paul retained the fine and ancient imagery of Genesis. He, too, stressed the Spirit as a continuing link between God and man, like the first puff of divinity given by God at Creation. To Paul, as to Philo, the Spirit was the source of man's knowledge of himself, a power of conscience which pagan teaching had not recognized. The Spirit was divine, distinct from the "spirit" which pagan philosophy made an immanent power in the world. It distinguished the higher man from the lower, and in Paul's Christian churches, it was now present in a sudden new outpouring, the source of love and joy, peace and kindness, the reward of faith, the mark of the new "sons of God." To become a Christian was to learn of this new and immediate miracle: a potential change in human nature itself.

In Acts' opinion, the Spirit was the primary force in the mission's early direction. It "seized" and guided its Christian beneficiaries and helped them to preach and prophesy.[5] Paul's epistles differed only in their emphasis: in Paul's opinion, its effects in his first communities would have amazed any pagan who saw them: and if properly used, would begin to convert him. Such overt enthusiasm could not last. As the End receded and a Church hierarchy developed, the Spirit became dimmed, though not removed, from early Christian life. The force which had accompanied the first missions no longer impelled preachers to new places. There was less of its direct action to astound outsiders. Conversion had always depended on other presences too, and as time passed, it was through them that Christian numbers rose.

Gibbon identified five causes of the Christians' continuing missionary success: an "intolerant zeal," derived from the Jews but purged of their "narrow and unsocial spirit"; the "menace of eternal tortures"; the miracles and "awful ceremony" of exorcism; the "serious and sequestered life," whose "faults, or rather errors, were derived from an excess of virtue"; the government of the Church, with its scope for ambition and authority. Modern accounts tend to stress one or other aspect and lose Gibbon's delicacy of phrasing. They also relate conversion to the social order and particular groups within it. There is more to be said about the Jews and their "narrowness"; our previous study of pagan worship tells against the idea that people were generally "sceptical" before Christianity brought a new faith. How, then, can Gibbon's views be enlarged and adjusted?

It is as well to begin with the scope of conversion and the means by which outsiders could become aware of the new religion. Those means were not greatly advertised and promoted by the Church's own leaders after the Apostolic age. There were no public harangues, no mass meetings to evangelize pagan crowds. Compared with the preachers of popular philosophy, Christians kept a low profile. The leaders of a modest third-century church were advised to post a lookout on the door to check visiting strangers, while a Church order of conduct, as we saw, advised that potential converts should bring a good reference with them and be introduced by a fellow Christian. It remained a firmly held view of the Church leadership that unmarried Christians should marry Christians only: Paul had advised the same to Christian widows. These restrictions were not idle advice.[6] They tell very strongly against extravagant views of the churches' growth, once a core of believers had been won in a new town.

In these towns, Christianity's most public advertisement was martyrdom. Although most people in the crowds of spectators would simply have thought that these criminals were stubborn and totally misguided, a few might have second thoughts, wondering what exactly was this "atheism" for which such old and harmless people faced death, girls and women among them. Only Christian authors claim that these second thoughts sometimes led to conversion, but they are readily believed.[7] Martyrs were also capable of impassioned speeches whose warnings and threats of hell were not lost on their hearers.

However, martyrdoms were rare occasions, and for most of the time, Christianity spread informally between individuals. Here, the lack of privacy in most people's lives was very relevant. The fraction of a rented apartment or the bazaar economy of petty artisans left ample scope for inquiry, a little private encouragement and the circulation of news. For all Celsus's contempt, it was at work or in private houses that he located the Christians' approaches to "women and children." If we look beyond their moralists' texts, we can see that Christians' lives were not so "sequestered" as Gibbon implied. They continued to serve in the army, attend pagan weddings and parties and enjoy the games and shows in the circus. The history of the persecutions reveals pagan communities who could easily identify their suspects, although they found it harder to catch them before they hid or ran away. By the mid-third century, the public epitaphs of "Christians for Christians" in a few Phrygian towns were quite open about their families' faith to anyone who bothered to stop and read them: the older view, that they commemorated heretics, was partly based on the false belief that orthodox Christians were always secretive.[8] Of course, Christians knew how to hold their tongue and lie low when necessary, but at other times, they could try a little exhortation on a suitable friend. In an eighth of a rented room or a twentieth of a house in an Egyptian township, it was simply not possible or necessary to conceal one's prayers or worship of God from everyone's eyes.

Within the family, there was obvious scope for exhortation and dispute. Mixed marriages were not commended, but wives in an existing marriage might be converted and then an avenue opened for further conversions. In Christian opinion, backed by St. Paul, the wife should not leave her pagan husband but should try to win him over too. In higher society, she seldom succeeded, but there was hope for her subsequent children: fathers might object less to the mother's instruction of the girls or to her prudent baptism of infants at a time of sickness in order to stave off the stories of hell.[9] Some, a very few, of these infants might survive, perhaps impressing the father with the power of his wife's new God. It is in this domestic context that many of the Christian exorcisms of non-Christians were probably worked. We should not be misled by the apocryphal legends of public "contest" or the later crowd scenes which gathered round Christian saints, blessing and cursing in the different setting of the later Christian Empire.[10]

Above all, we should give weight to the presence and influence of friends. It is a force which so often escapes the record, but it gives shape to everyone's personal life. One friend might bring another to the faith; a group of friends might exclude others and cause them to look elsewhere for esteem. When a person turned to God, he found others, new "brethren," who were sharing the same path. Here, the earliest Church orders of discipline conform to a description by Origen and the precepts of the first councils.[11] Interested parties would rank nominally as "Christians" from their first reception, but two or three years had to pass before an interested party could progress to baptism, advice which remained constant across the third century. No doubt there were shortcuts, and thus the advice had to be given, but Origen's words are proof that it was not a vain counsel. Christians were not made in a hurry, unless they happened to have been baptized as an insurance by one or other Christian parent. The Christian apprentice, or catechumen, was watched for signs of misconduct. He was taught the details of the faith by fellow Christians and allowed to attend the church services in a special group, with his fellow apprentices. At the community's meal, he was supposed to receive "bread of exorcism," which was distinct from the baptized Christian's bread. He had no place at the Lord's table when the baptized Christians met and dined and prayed mindfully for their host. During the years of instruction, he was not supposed to sin, and if he did, he would be demoted for a while to the status of a "hearer" who was not receiving instruction. When his preparation was complete, he was brought forward for the final weeks of teaching, accompanied by fasting, frequent exorcisms and confession of sins. Only then was he fit to be baptized.

Perhaps this pattern was shortened sometimes but it does not conform to some modern historical views of the Church. The understanding of conversion is not the understanding of an unrecoverable first moment when a person decided to go along to church and give the sect a try. It is certainly not a process dominated, or largely explained, by sudden miracles. Historically, it is less significant that Christianity could bring in a diversity of persons for a diversity of initial reasons than that it could retain them while imposing these long apprenticeships. The years of instruction and preparation became, in their turn, one of the faith's particular appeals. People felt that they were exploring a deep mystery, step by step. They were advancing with a group of fellow explorers along a route which required a high moral effort.

The length of this journey is one further reason for keeping the total number of Christians in perspective: their faith was much the most rapidly growing religion in the Mediterranean, but its total membership was still small in absolute terms, perhaps (at a guess) only 2 percent of the Empire's total population by 250. Within this small sample, was it especially likely to appeal to particular social groups? This dimension is one which we would now stress more explicitly than Gibbon.[12] The social context and position of Christian converts does not allow us to lay down "laws" or to predict Christianity in this or that group, but it does suggest tendencies, especially negative tendencies, and it bears on the faith's more general appeal.

A simple theory of "social compensation" will not stand up to the evidence. The link between Christianity and victims of worldly oppression was neither simple nor obvious. The Church was not primarily a haven for slaves and least of all for slaves in the mines or dependent workers on the land, yet on these groups the burdens of the towns and the Empire lay most heavily. In contrast, recent social

theories of the Church have tended to emphasize the more prominent
named Christians and to relate them to notions of status and social
mobility. These attempts tend to overlook the churches' hard core
among the humbler free residents in a town.

They have been applied most freely to the age of the Apostles,
where Acts and Paul's epistles do allow us a glimpse of specific
converts. Here, however, we are often witnessing secondary conversions. It is quite clear that Christian preaching began by attracting
sympathizers from the Jews' own synagogues, sometimes full converts, but also, notoriously, the "God-fearers," who were probably
Gentile hearers, not full members of the Jewish community.[13] Here,
Christianity was not drawing people primarily because of their particular social class or status, but because of their prior attraction to
Judaism. The more we know from the cities of Greek Asia, the less it is
possible to reduce the Jewish presence to a "narrow and unsocial"
minority. In the Diaspora, the evidence for prominent local synagogues is greater after the final war in Judaea (135 A.D.): the communities continued to win supporters and converts and attract interest from
Christians themselves. Inscriptions in Miletus, Smyrna, Aphrodisias
and several Phrygian cities put the social respectability of the Jewish
communities beyond doubt. Above all, we have to adjust to the
discovery that a central building in the main area of civic life in Sardis
was taken over by the Jews as a synagogue and enlarged for their use,
perhaps in the late second century and certainly by the mid-third.[14] In
Caesarea and Antioch and Carthage, Jews were a powerful and
continuing presence, although Christian authors are varyingly informed about their life.[15] In the early third century, the Emperor made
Jews eligible for service on the cities' councils, a testimony to their
property and education. Even by 250, it is not clear that the Christian
community would have been the most conspicuous in many famous
cities. Until recently, the best-known testing ground was Dura-
Europos, out east on the Euphrates, where the Jewish synagogue was
bigger and much better-decorated than the little house-church and
was continuing to be enlarged after the mid-240s. However, Dura was
a distant town and even the Jewish paintings in the synagogue have
been related to special concerns of Jewish teachers in the East.[16] It did
not seem a typical site to compare with religions further west, but the
recent discoveries in Greek Asia have made it easier to see the
continuing strength of its Judaism as a wider pattern elsewhere. It
would be fascinating to have the history of a Jewish Eusebius,

describing the Jews' continuing prominence and growth in the Diaspora until 300 A.D.

Between the two communities, however, the traffic seems to have gone essentially in one direction. After the Apostolic age, we do not hear of Christians preaching as missionaries in synagogues. The Jews were alert to the danger; the Roman authorities had distinguished the Christians and allowed them to be persecuted; the failure of the Jewish wars further divided the Church from its Jewish ancestry. As an old and unpersecuted religion, Judaism did continue to attract Christian sympathizers, whereas Christians did not attract more than the odd Jewish renegade. In the Antonine and Severan age, therefore, Christian conversions were no longer secondary conversions and social theories might apply more directly to the process.

In the Apostolic age, Christianity has been connected with two particular social theories: "social mobility" and "status inconsistency."[17] Do they help us to place the subsequent converts more clearly, after the break with a ready-made Jewish clientele? We must be wary of claiming that the faith appealed "primarily" to such groups "because" of these social features. Much depended on how, if at all, the various groups encountered Christian preaching. If the first converts tended to be people of modest property, living in towns, the reason may lie, not in their particular view of their "status," but in the fact that they happened to hear most about the faith from people to whom they could relate. The scarcity of converts in the highest or lowest classes may reflect on their lack of occasion to learn about Christianity from a teacher whom they could take seriously. The class and ability of the teacher are as relevant as any inconsistency in the social position of the hearer.

In the years after Constantine's conversion, there is indeed some force in a connection between social mobility and Christianity: the faith seems particularly prominent among the new governing class who were promoted to the Emperor's Christian court and the new city of Constantinople.[18] However, this connection cannot be carried back with confidence into the previous centuries. Then, Christianity was a persecuted atheism which sat very badly with the aims of men "on the make." It was very sparsely represented in the army, the Empire's greatest centre of social mobility, and its roots lay in the Greek-speaking towns where social mobility was limited. The Emperor's promotion and patronage were the main agents of social advancement, yet Christianity was not particularly prominent in the two orders which were most open to it, the Senate and the Imperial "household." Although we know of Christians among the Emperor's slaves, we lack their biographies and we cannot distinguish those who converted after a sudden advancement from those who had already brought their faith from their family backgrounds. We cannot, then, argue that social promotion encouraged these Christians' conversions in the first place. When Justin was brought to trial in the 160s, he was accompanied by Euelpistus, "a slave in Caesar's household," who had had Christian parents in Cappadocia, probably before he passed into the Emperor's service.[19] His promotion did not influence or coincide with his faith: it merely brought him to our notice. Social mobility did not necessarily turn a person against prevailing traditions. If it distanced him from his humbler origins, it also made him embarrassingly keen, as always, to be accepted in the social circles to which he had aspired. The literature, the poetry and the inscriptions of the Imperial period are eloquent witnesses to the efforts of the parvenu to copy traditions and be thought respectable. The Christianity of the new men at Constantinople should be seen in this light: by then, the court looked up to a Christian Emperor.

What, then, of the notion of "status inconsistency," the condition of people whose view of their status does not altogether agree with the status which others ascribe to them? The concept has been applied to Paul's first communities, to the "independent women with moderate wealth, Jews with wealth in a pagan society, freedmen with skill and money, but stigmatized by origin, and so on."[20] People's views of their own status are enchantingly complex and unexpected, and perhaps "consistency" is a rarer condition than its theorists imply. Yet even in these particular groups, "status" may not have been the inconsistent element. The "Jews with wealth" could find an ample role in their own synagogues; known Christian "freedmen with skill and money" are not easily found and their sense of "social stigma" can be exaggerated if we look only at the judgements of Rome's ruling class: here, any "status inconsistency" was short-lived. The children of freedmen are well attested in our Latin evidence for that socially accepted class: the councillors and magistrates of the towns. Their families' ambitions often lay in this conventional direction: freedmen are a primary source of public inscriptions in Latin, an accepted claim to honour by which they, too, could bid for public esteem. It was not, then, for lack of prospects that they adopted a persecuted faith. The "independent women" are better attested, but "status inconsistency" may not be the aptest term for their condition. Their sex universally denied them the social role which their economic position gave to its other possessors. Their status meanwhile, was only too clear, and we have no evidence that women did other than accept it. It is quite untrue that Paul and the teaching of his epistles coincided with an existing movement for "liberation" among women, which they curbed.

A person cannot be the victim of "status inconsistency" without some conscious awareness on his own part; for the condition to apply, he himself must hold a conscious variant view of his own social position. We do not know that any type of Christian convert held such views. Even if they did, we still have to fathom why they resolved the inconsistency by taking to Christianity rather than to any other cult. The Jew had his synagogue; the prosperous freedman, the cult of the Emperors; the woman, the priesthoods of other divinities, through which, already, she could enjoy a public role. Why, then, become a Christian? The view that such converts wished to dominate a new cult and earn "clients" is also implausible. The concern for "clientship" belonged in social orders higher than those of almost any known Christian convert. Nor was the Christian community designed for easy "dominance." The first churches had no fixed leaders, and when they did develop them, they adopted a system of leadership by life appointment. Unlike the pagan cult society, the Church thus kept apart the roles of benefactor and leader: dominance was not easily assured.[21]

It is this aspect, rather, that we can usefully explore. By its own image and moral stance, the Christian community stood opposed to the open pursuit of power. It did not resolve "inconsistency" by offering a new outlet: rather, it claimed to sidestep status and power altogether. We would do better to view its appeal not against inconsistency but against a growing social exclusivity. Christianity was least likely to attract the people who were most embedded in social tradition, the great families of Rome, the upper families who filled the civic priesthoods and competed in public generosity for the gods. There were exceptions, but it was also least likely to attract the teacher and antiquarian who were steeped in pagan learning. It could, however, offer an alternative community and range of values to those who were disenchanted by the display of riches, by the harshness of the exercise of power and the progressive hardening of the gradations of rank and degree.[22] Only a simple view of human nature will expect such people to be none but the poor and the oppressed themselves.

There were people, too, who turned away from the power and property which others of their rank admired or exercised. It will cause no surprise if some of those who were most disenchanted contrived, nonetheless, to attain power and rank in their new community, or if others believed in charity, provided that charity did not have to begin at home.

On a longer view, the rise of Christianity owed much to a broader initial change, a loosening of the civic cohesion of the Greek city-state. Even in the classical city, the citizen had not been limited to his city's public cults, but as groups of non-citizens multiplied through migration from place to place and as tighter restrictions were placed on the holding of local citizenship, the general connection between a city's cults and its citizens had been greatly weakened. In the Roman period, the gap between citizenship and residence in or near a city was compounded by the growing gap between citizenship and the exercise of political power. As civic life depended ever more on a city's notables, the home town meant most to the sum total of its residents when contrasted with the honours of another town or when busy with its own shows and athletic games. It was one thing to exhibit a keen "observer participation" in the doings of a town's great families, but it was not the same as belonging to a community and feeling that one's presence mattered.

As the political value of citizenship declined, the older type of community and equality had receded in civic life. During the second century, the frank expression by Roman judges of "one law for the more honourable, another for the more humble" compounded the explicit division of cities into a few rich notables and the people, now openly called the "poor." Differing penalties for these differing classes did not supplant a system of legal equality: previously, Roman citizenship had brought legal privilege and there were gainers, as well as losers, from the change. Although the distinction only applied in criminal cases, its bluntness speaks for a wider attitude which is very significant. Officially, the "more humble" were now declared particularly vile and servile, and nothing prevented governors from treating them like slaves. Respectable contempt is quick to filter downwards. Governors could be quite blunt about their priorities: "If you were one of the rustics," the governor of Egypt was alleged to have told Phileas, the Christian bishop, in the year 303, "who have given themselves up out of need, I would not spare you. But since you have acquired such a surplus of property [the very word: *periousia*] that you can nourish and care not only for yourself, but the city too, please spare yourself for this reason and pay a sacrifice to the gods."[23]

Christianity had begun to spread before these legal categories had been openly stated and accepted. They were, however, already implicit in superiors' dealings with their inferiors, so much so that the Christians' contrary image of community had immediate point. As the first Messianic hope receded and the end of the world became less of an issue, these social divisions had continued to harden throughout the second century. Christianity's contrary values thus gained in relevance, although the two primary points of its doctrine lost their immediacy.[24] While pagan priests and magistrates competed in their "love of honour," Christians termed it "vainglory." While civic cults paid honour to the presiding "manifest" divinities of the town, the Christians' "city" lay in heaven and their "assembly" was the assembly of the people of God "throughout the world." The cults and myths gave pagans a focus for their "feverish civic patriotism," yet Christians obeyed one law, the same from city to city. Those whose loyalties were less engaged by the home town, or enlarged by travel beyond it, could respond to this image of a universal "assembly" and ethic. They saw it put firmly into practice. At their festivals, the great pagan families made distributions to the small class of councillors, to the male citizens and lastly, if at all, to their women. Christians brought their funds to those in need, men and women, citizen and non-citizen: Christian "charity" differed in range and motive from pagan "philanthropy": it earned merit in heaven and sustained those dear to God, the poor. The idea of "doing unto others as you would wish them to do unto you" was not foreign to pagan ethics, but there was no precedent for the further Christian advice to "love one's enemies."[25] At its best, such selflessness has always been its own best argument, but never more so than in the civic life of this period. Admittedly, Christians did not always live up to it, least of all in their attitude to the slaves whom they continued to own: if Christian women beat their maidservants to death, so an early council in Spain decided, they were to be punished with several years' denial of communion.[26] The mild scale of punishment was hardly less revealing than the existence of such sinners. We should remember, however, the words of Plutarch and Galen's friends, that it was worse to batter a door than a slave and that a lashing was appropriate, so long as it was not administered in anger. Rational pagan philosophy was capable of even greater heartlessness.

To the poor, the widows and orphans, Christians gave alms and support, like the synagogue communities, their forerunners. This "brotherly love" has been minimized as a reason for turning to the Church, as if only those who were members could know of it.[27] In fact, it was widely recognized. When Christians were in prison, fellow Christians gathered to bring them food and comforts: Lucian, the pagan satirist, was well aware of this practice. When Christians were brought to die in the arena, the crowds, said Tertullian, would shout, "Look how these Christians love one another." Christian "love" was public knowledge and must have played its part in drawing outsiders to the faith.

On taking an interest, they found other values exalted which pagan society did not assert. Among pagan authors, "humility" had almost never been a term of commendation. It belonged with ignoble and abject characters. Men were born "sons of God," said the Stoics, and thus they should cherish no "humble or ignoble" thoughts about their nature. The humble belonged with the abject, the mean, the unworthy. Christianity, however, ascribed humility to God's own Son and exalted it as a virtue of man, his creature whom he had redeemed.[28] Through its Jewish heritage, Christianity idealized "abject poverty," *ptocheia*. It was not specifically material poverty, but poverty in the broader sense of an utter dependence on God. Pagans had never seen any spiritual merit in the status of the poor. *Ptochoi*, they thought, were down-and-outs, worse than poor men of a certain independence.

These alternative values belonged with a powerful ideal of community. From the start, Paul's letters had abounded in the language of a "family" and a brotherhood, supported by his luxuriant use of compound verbs, formed with the prefix "together." This language was not entirely novel. In the papyri, pagans, too, address each other as "brother":[29] Christians, however, combined this language with a tighter control on their group. The cohesion of brotherly "equals" required the rigorous exclusion of anyone who threatened to confuse it: Paul was already reminding his Corinthians of a man whom he had excommunicated and handed over to Satan. Among pagans, "anathema" had begun as the word for a "dedication" to the gods, but had then been extended to cover the "dedication" of a person to the powers who were invoked in a curse. Christians were heirs to its extension. As in the Jewish sect of the Dead Sea scrolls, so in the first Christian communities, an "anathema" dedicated victims to Satan and thus to eternal hell.[30] At the Council of Gangra, we may recall, the "anathema" was the bishops' punishment for Christians who encouraged slaves to disobey their masters.

This tightly guarded "brotherhood" can be contrasted with the cult societies which we encountered in the example of the Iobacchic group at Athens. Whereas pagan trade societies and most of their religious groups segregated the sexes among their membership, Christians included men and women alike. In the Greek world, slaves were generally excluded from these pagan groups: Christians even admitted slaves of pagan masters.[31] The Iobacchi's awareness of a worldwide group of Bacchic worshippers was exceptional: among Christians, however, the universal (or "catholic") Church was a constant presence.[32] In any one town, their membership was several times greater than the largest known cult society's. Unlike any such society, they were reviled by crowds in the stadiums as a "third race," distinct from pagans and Jews: the classical city had had no room for this "state within a state."[33] Its organization differed from any known in pagan or Jewish cult. The powers and elections of its bishops were distinctive, as were its roles for giver and leader.[34] In a pagan cult, the patrons and givers were also the leaders: their ranks and titles offered the members "pale and vulgar reproductions of the hierarchy of a real aristocracy." In the churches, a bishop might happen to be rich, and electors soon saw the advantage if he was, but officially, the richer Christians gave alms, while a separate hierarchy administered their use. This hierarchy was chosen to serve for life. In a growing Church, therefore, the number of richer Christians would far exceed the number of vacant posts in the hierarchy of power. Divorced from office, "benefaction" was seen as almsgiving, a charity for all alike.

By its form and ideals, therefore, the Christian "brotherhood" offered very different scope to the potential benefactor. At the same time, it did not have the blunt, unsettling appeal of a faith which directly assaulted social barriers. It sidestepped them in the name of spiritual equality, while leaving them in place. This pattern had already been traced by Stoicism, which had remained the dominant ethic among the philosophies. It allowed Christianity to appeal to many more people of higher rank and property than if it had attacked their riches and status in plain material terms.

Although the growing exclusivity of civic life gave force to the Christians' alternative image, it did not, by itself, produce converts. They had to be held by Christian teaching and the Church's type of community during the long years of apprenticeship. For a start, this teaching introduced them to Satan, a novel "explanation of misfortune."[35] Through his demons, it explained what we have identified as the living heart of pagan religiousness: the oracles and epiphanies and accompanying anger of the gods. Paganism was reclassified as a demonic system: it was most misleading when it seemed to be most effective. To deceive people, these demons worked mischief by curing and occasionally predicting the future, yet, finally, they would go bankrupt, however impressive their interim results. Satan, their manager, had entered the last stage of a long "rake's progress." Since Jesus's mission, God's old accusing agent had been cast out of heaven and left to wander as his adversary on earth.[36] While Jewish teachers feared Satan's continuing access as an accuser before God, Christians knew that he had fallen for ever and that his rival kingdom had only a brief while left.

With this new and powerful myth of evil went an altered perception of the supreme misfortune, death. Unlike the pagans, Christians did not die or fade into the disembodied life of the soul. Their remains were contained in "cemeteries," or sleeping places, while their souls were stored in the capacious bosom of Abraham. At the Last Day, the dead would awake and return to bodies of varying degrees of glory. Pagans had not been clear or unanimous in their belief in an afterlife, but those who credited it could look to mystery cults for insurance in their future. Christians were much more positive. Since Jesus's death, they had not only won immortality: they had triumphed over death itself. They would rise, body and all, and like the pagan burial clubs, their Church offered every adherent a proper place of rest. Unlike the burial clubs the Church offered it whether or not a person had paid contributions for the purpose.[37]

Both these "explanations of misfortune" had their darker side. If Satan was the source of error and evil, false teaching and wrongdoing were not merely mistaken: they were diabolic. The division between a Christian community of goodness and an outer world of evil could easily become too pronounced. The idea of Satan magnified the difference between "true" and "false" Christians and between Christian sinners and saints. So, too, the triumph over death was a triumph for believers only, and even they had to pass a searching Last Judgement. There was an ample place, therefore, for plain fear in Christian conversions, and Christian authors did not neglect it: their martyrs' words on hell and the coming Judgement were believed to be an advertisement every bit as effective as their example at the stake. Terrors in the next world were not unfamiliar to pagans, but Christians insisted on their certainty and imminent realization. Clever Christians were well aware of their power: just as a Platonist like Plutarch could write freely on the terrors of the underworld as an "improving myth," so Origen argued that the literal terrors of hell were false but they ought to be publicized in order to scare the simpler believers. In Acts, it was when Paul talked of "justice, self-control and the judgement to come" that Felix, the corrupt governor, "begged him to stop."[38] This teaching was reinforced by an equally powerful ally, the Christian idea of sin. Sin was not just the sin of an action, or even an intention, but also the sin of a thought, even a passing interest in an appealing man or woman. This combination of rarefied sin and eternal punishment was supported, as we shall see, by books of vision and revelation which were probably more widely read than modern contempt for "pseudepigraphic" forgeries allows: acquaintance with the Apocalypse of "Peter" would make anyone think twice before leaving the Church. If fears for Eternity brought converts to the faith, one suspects that they did even more to keep existing converts in it.

Like Satan, therefore, the Last Judgement was a force which Christians exaggerated and then claimed to be able to defeat. The teaching impressed people who already knew the sting of death and misfortune, the gap between good actions and good intentions and the continuing core of a paganism which could be seen as well as heard. These forces, the Christians said, were defeated by their miracles of bodily resurrection and exorcism, Gibbon's "awful ceremony." Did these signs and wonders, perhaps, account for many conversions to the Church?

There is no doubt that wonders were felt to occur. Pagans had had no organized order of exorcists, because they accepted no organized "kingdom of Satan": invasive *daimones* of ambiguous status were sometimes cast out by spells or particular lines of Homer, but the experts in this field were the Jews. Their Most High god had no name and was felt to be particularly powerful against lesser spirits who could be identified, named and expelled: to name a force, then too, was to tame it and bring it nearer control. To the Jews, demons were not the ambiguous intermediaries whom pagans placed between gods and men: they were outright agents of evil, the troupe of Satan himself. The Christians' view was similar, yet they insisted that their own exorcists succeeded where Jewish exorcists failed.[39]

We know too little about the process and its case histories to test the truth of this claim. Both Jews and Christians aimed to make the "demon" name himself and confess his own divine master: we have one early polemic against verbose formulae uttered by Christians in order to seem impressive; Cyprian pictures the action of the Spirit on a man's inner demon in terms which are a compound of torture, burning and beating. Ejection, it seems, involved a rough combat of powers, with few holds barred. Unlike the Jews, Christians did also assert that Satan was doomed by Christ's kingdom and perhaps they did lay a greater emphasis on faith. In a tantalizing scene in their Gospels, Jesus is said to have remarked that he could not work wonders among an unbelieving people.[40] Once, he was believed to have healed a child who had not seen him, but in this case the exceptional faith of its father sufficed. His followers, one suspects, never worked miracles at long range. Faith and a willingness to accept the exorcist's grim and awful explanation were probably central to these cures by sudden release. Perhaps Jewish exorcists required some such faith, but they were not heirs to stories of such a master and founder of the art as Jesus in the Gospels. Pagans, certainly, never worked in such a tradition or demanded faith as a precondition.

To educated pagans, exorcism was tommy-rot. The Emperor Marcus classed it with idiocies like cockfighting, and the philosopher Plotinus reacted with real horror to the notion that an imbalance of nature could be corrected by a supposed expulsion of intruders.[41] Yet these intruders were exactly what Christians detected and tried to remedy. They extended their myth into new areas. In the past, the misfortune of epilepsy had been understood as the effect of the heavenly bodies: it was caused by the sympathy of the universe working on an excess of one "humour" in a patient's constitution. To Origen, despite his knowledge of philosophy, epilepsy was the work of an intruding demon and therefore curable by Christian exorcism.[42] Pagan thinkers had seen health as a "concord" or "blend" of opposing qualities, terms which interrelate with their language for the body politic. Christians connected health with faith and an absence of sin, a state which had to be maintained against outside invaders and tempters. Their image of the human body conformed to their image of the Church as a sinless Body, set apart from a demonic world.

The fame of the Christian exorcists was widely known. Their apologists appealed repeatedly to their achievements, and according to Tertullian, they had even been summoned to practise in the household of the Emperor Severus: in this case, historians may wonder if they succeeded. Exorcisms were not the "short, sharp shock" we might imagine: they worked "sometimes," remarked Theophilus, a Christian author in the 180s. Candidates for Christian baptism underwent several, and while they waited between treatments, we can understand how they might grow to a faith in the accompanying "myth" and help the process, finally, to seem successful.[43]

Did these exorcisms win many new converts in the first place? The orders of Christian exorcists were always busy with fellow Christians who needed the "awful ceremony" repeatedly before baptism. However, their fame did influence others.[44] In Acts, the author tells how a misuse of Jesus's name by Jewish exorcists at Ephesus led to a sensational mishap which terrified "all the Jews and Greeks" and brought added honour to the faith. Miracles certainly continued to be credited; in c. 177, at Lyons, the doctor Alexander was martyred, a man who was by birth a Phrygian but who had spent many years in Gaul and was "known by everyone for God's love of him: he was not without a share of the charisma of the Apostles." Presumably, he worked miracles of healing. His contemporary Irenaeus wrote that miracles were still frequent, but when he adds that "very often indeed" the "spirit of a dead man has returned at the prayers of the brethren" after a period of intent fasting, the claim slightly weakens his point. In the 240s, Origen was more restrained: "traces" of miraculous power, he said, still persisted "in some measure" among the Christians. Between the Apostolic age and the fourth century A.D., we know of no historical case when a miracle or an exorcism turned an individual, let alone a crowd, to the Christian faith. The silence may reflect on our ignorance, but as Justin observed in the 130s, miracles only impressed their eyewitnesses. Although the legendary "acts" of Apostles laid great weight on the signs and wonders which their heroes worked, they were not historical texts, nor were they written to win pagan converts: they aimed to impress Christian readers and spread the views of a minority of fellow Christians through vivid fiction.

A successful exorcism would certainly win credit, and if it was worked on a pagan, it would probably make him a believer. No doubt cases occurred, but it is also significant that this type of conversion was alleged of a Christian heretic in order to discredit him: evidently, it was not felt to be a very honourable motive for entering the Church.[45] In view of the long apprenticeships which followed, it was not a sufficient motive. Even in Acts, Paul does not only heal and cast out demons: he preaches and instructs, persuades and discusses for days and nights on end.[46] It is this tireless work which he recalls persistently in his letters to his churches. To believe that Christians were fully won by the sight of a wonder or an exorcism is to shorten a long process and ultimately to misjudge the extreme canniness of Mediterranean men. These events might awaken their interest, but why should they accept that the God behind them was the only god and that all their previous gods were false? Whereas pagan cults won adherents, Christianity aimed, and contrived, to win converts. It won them by conviction and persuasion, long and detailed sequels to the initial proof that faith could work.

It is not, then, surprising that Christianity made the least-expected social groups articulate. The "free speech" of unlettered Galileans had already alarmed the authorities in Acts. It continued to characterize their followers.[47] Cyprian was troubled by a turbulent female, a seamstress by trade; Dionysius marvelled at humble villagers' debates and arguments in Egypt; in the 170s, the group of Christians who studied Aristotle and Scripture in Rome were led by a leather worker. It was an old slander that a particular doctrine was fit only for women and the lower classes, but when pagan critics repeated it against Christian teaching, they were not false to the facts. These people also formed schisms and supported heresies, adhering to particular principles and points of doctrine not because of miracles but because the ideas appealed to them. Christianity's theology combined simple ideas which all could grasp but which were also capable of infinite refinement and complexity. They made converts because they won faith: it was not just because of some past miracle that simple Christians were prepared to die agonizingly for their religion.

This conviction extended to thinking people, too, both the early Christian authors and their audiences. In the pagan cities, popular philosophy had begun to claim the authority of the gods. We have heard how their gods spoke the higher wisdom of Plato, and we have seen that their worshippers were sometimes exhorted to worship "with a pure heart." The Christians, meanwhile, united ritual and philosophy and brought the certainty of God and history to questions whose answers eluded the pagan schools. While men like Lucian and Galen surveyed the philosophers' disagreements with a certain detachment, Christianity captured their near-equals, Justin and Tatian, by giving them a firm dogma. They idealized faith and gave a powerful counter to anxiety.[48] Among second-century authors, it is the Christians who are the most confident and assured. There is a magnificent optimism in the theology of Irenaeus and its faith that by redemption man could rank higher than an angel; confidence is never far from the writings of Justin and his "sunny open-heartedness and innocent optimism . . . even when it leads him into naivety. Nothing could be less haunted than Justin's mind and conscience."[49] Expectation of the End did not lead most Christians into pessimism about the world or the flesh. Their authors wrote as warmly as any Stoic about the "providence" of God's Creation. They looked to the future reign of themselves, as saints, and the resurrection of their bodies, improved and enhanced. Their asceticism, as we shall see, was grounded in positive, conscious aspirations, not in an alienation from the material world.

This confident tone cut through the doubts of the pagan schools and the note of anxiety which we have sometimes caught in questions to the pagan gods. It also went with a sense of Christianity's newness. So much of Christians' writing in the second and third centuries can be related to the need for a balance between the newness and the tradition of their faith. Here, too, we must allow for the setting of contemporary pagan culture. In the Antonine age, to be old and traditional was to be respectable, for a city or a philosophy, a cult or an individual: respect for antiquity extended to the very ways in which men of culture spoke and wrote. In many of their books, Christians excelled this intellectual fashion. Through their Jewish heritage, they could claim to be heirs to the ancient "wisdom of Moses," which Greek philosophers had borrowed without acknowledgement. They could go back further to the "practice of Abraham" and even to the "philosophy" which God had laid on man at his Creation and which Jews and other peoples of the East had subsequently corrupted.[50] Of the world's major religions, only Buddhism made a complete break with tradition at its birth: Christianity made no such claim. It could meet the traditionalist culture of pagan contemporaries on equal terms.

However, there was a tension in stressing Christianity's "antiquity" too strongly, and some fellow Christians felt it. Many of them were new converts, made, not born, to their faith. Some of them were content to relate the change in their beliefs to existing philosophies: all the literary Christian "apologists" were such people, converts from paganism who were concerned to make sense of their new faith by stressing its continuity with older wisdom. Others did not wish to lose the sense of a deliberate break with the past, and this wish lay at the root of the great Christian heresies of the second century. Already, before Christianity, pagan writings had begun to emphasize revelation and personal "awareness" as the sources of a new religious knowledge which gave truths about the gods and the world, the fate of the soul, the exercise of reason.[51] To this existing pagan literature of knowledge and revelation, Christians brought the wholly new idea of man's Redemption. The more extreme "newborn" Christians developed these ideas into a separation of their new "knowledge" from God's previous Creation and the dark and ignorant past. This tendency was exemplified in the writings of "knowing" Christian Gnostics, who dissolved history and the Gospels into a complex myth of Creation and the human predicament.[52] Even so, these "knowing" Christians were not pessimists reacting against an anxious age. Like Buddhist mystics, they knew their souls were eternal, waiting to return to their heavenly home. Unlike existentialist philosophers, they combined their talk of "alienation" from the material world with a faith in salvation and spiritual renewal.[53] Other Christians were more specific. At Rome in the 140s, the recent convert Marcion shocked the Church by denying any connection between the Gods of the Old and New Testament. By rewriting Scripture, he presented a powerful case. The Creator, he argued, was an incompetent being: why else had he afflicted women with the agonies of childbirth? "God" in the Old Testament was a "committed barbarian" who favoured bandits and such terrorists as Israel's King David. Christ, by contrast, was the new and separate revelation of an altogether higher God. Marcion's teaching was the most extreme statement of the newness of the Christian faith. Combined with virginity and a rejection of marriage, it became "Marcionism" and continued to attract followers, especially in the Syriac-speaking East, far into the fourth century.[54]

This pursuit of newness through heresy did not weaken the strength of the Church. Like "structuralism" in literary studies, pretentious heretical teachings provoked sensible Christians to state their own faith in history and tradition and to set out the texts of their Gospels more firmly and explicitly. Heretical ideas and groups survived, catering for those who wished to be perverse, but by c. 180 Christianity had been strengthened by great conservative statements, none finer than Irenaeus's "Overthrow of the So-Called Knowledge" and

"Demonstration of the Apostolic Teaching": it is particularly apt that papyrus fragments of a handsome early copy of the "Overthrow" have been found in Egypt's Oxyrhynchus. It had been written very soon after the work's appearance in Lyons, from where it had hastily travelled east as a weapon in the battle against heretical folly.[55]

Unlike any pagan cult or heretical system, the main stream of Christianity took its stand on history. It also cited its antiquity and its Jewish prophecies, some of which, in Greek mistranslations, appeared to have been fulfilled.[56] Both were powerful weapons in a culture which respected tradition and oracular prediction. Surviving texts say less about Jesus's own personal qualities, but perhaps we should be wary of minimizing this aspect just because our few discussions of conversion ignore it.[57] The example of the Lord was urged on martyrs in prison and later was imitated by Christian holy men: did the model of his life really fail to impress the other Christians who do not happen to have written books? It is, however, true that articulate, thinking Christians tended, rather, to emphasize the general certainty which they found in their new faith.[58] Justin told of his tour of the philosophers in search of a satisfying doctrine, and Tatian wrote of his own independent disgust with the grossness of polytheism. Fictions repeated this theme: in the *Octavius*, a discussion of the role of Providence led to an intellectual conversion without any concern for Scripture. The long and ingenious Christian novel *The Recognitions* begins with the young Clement's anxiety about the immortality of the soul, a worry which left him only when he met St. Peter. Our study of questions to Apollo has shown how these topics could indeed turn people to their gods. We might think that no Christian encountered the Scriptures until after his conversion, as their Greek was too repellent to outsiders' taste. Yet Tatian cites his meeting with biblical writings as a decisive turn when doubts had begun to trouble him: he found "doctrines other than those of the Greeks, and more divine," in books whose speakers lacked "arrogance and excessive art." He admired the "easy account of Creation," the "foreknowledge of the future," the "extraordinary" precepts, the idea of One God. He was persuaded, then, by the Old Testament as well as the New. To his admiration of biblical Greek, it may be relevant that his own first language had been Syriac.

To Greek-speaking converts, the "Messiah" had lost all its meaning: many of them did not even understand the idea of "anointing" contained in the Greek word "Christ." By the mid-second century, the end of the world was also receding in many Christians' expectations. Yet the faith whose texts had emphasized these two ideas was still spreading and growing and by the later second century was making the progress among more prominent people which Eusebius rightly noted. Perhaps we can now see why. Since the 160s, there is clear evidence in legal texts of the division between the rich minority and a humbler majority in the ranks of the cities' councils. Exemptions and migration had thinned the ranks of potential benefactors, and service in these bodies was quite often unwilling. These tendencies were not new, but they had attained a new prominence. They brought lesser people into the councils' recruitment. They widened the gap between existing members, leaving a few powerful and very rich benefactors among many who found office more burdensome. At the same time, the division of legal penalties into "one law for the rich, another for the poor" had become explicit. The older restraints of "modesty" (*aidos*) and "insolence" (*hybris*) in Greek city life were losing their force.

Both these tendencies worked to Christianity's advantage. The recruitment of lesser families into civic service might bring existing Christians or their friends into the upper orders of a town. The social divisions within the upper order and between that order and the rest gave particular force to Christianity's contrary image. It could appeal to people with a conscience, without unsettling the material distinctions of their rank and riches. Above all, Christianity had come to be presented as a teaching to which people of rank could respond. The general social changes of the later second century coincided with a crucial inner change in the faith's public image. It is no accident that the progress Eusebius noted followed and overlapped with the efforts of thinking Christians to relate their faith to existing philosophies and ethics. Even if the Christian apologists' books were not widely read, their existence was a proof that Christianity was now respectable. It offered the certainty which eluded the philosophical schools and an ethic which was not entirely dissimilar. The teaching could now be heard from educated people, not stray Galilean missionaries, and as converts began to be won in higher places, more people could hear of the faith from people to whom they could relate. In turn, they attracted more texts on points of particular interest to them, from Clement or Hippolytus or even, in some moods, Tertullian. The dimming of the End and the fading of the Messianic hope were not obstacles to this progress. If anything, they helped it.

The continuing spread of Christianity, therefore, was not only due to its offer of goods which pagan "religiousness" had never centrally comprised. It was also due to faults in pagan society. In cities of growing social divisions, Christianity offered unworldly equality. It preached, and at its best it practised, love in a world of widespread brutality. It offered certainty and won conviction where the great venture of Greek philosophy was widely perceived to have argued itself into the ground. By 250, it was still the persecuted faith of a small minority, but its progress was sufficient to reflect on a growing failure of the pagan towns.

# 7. *Living Like Angels*

## I

The lasting impression left by the early church membership is one of social diversity. Yet it went with an ideal of human equality: in Christ, taught the Christians, all were equal and the distinctions of rank and degree were irrelevant. In church meetings, educated people had to sit as equals among other men's slaves and petty artisans. On both sides, the tensions were already evident in the churches of the Apostolic age.[1]

While belittling rank, Christians also taught the vanity of worldly competition: the "love of honour" which propelled pagan cult and civic life became "vainglory." These contrary values had their appeal, but they were not without consequence. It is the fate of groups who claim to abolish competition that they invert it and cause it to emerge elsewhere. In early Christianity, there was an obvious field to which competition could be transferred. If Christians were socially equal, spiritually they were acknowledged to be more diverse. The sayings of their Gospels already implied a double standard of achievement and understanding. "If you would be perfect, even as your father in heaven is perfect . . ."; in matters of conduct, the sky, it seemed, was the limit. Paul's letters had already recognized a distinction between a first- and a second-class Christian achievement, and as time passed, the gap increased. All Christians faced the same final test, but while the majority hoped only for a modest pass, a few aspired to congratulated honours. Christianity gave scope for this boundless perfectionism, while keeping in touch with those who aspired to much less. In pagan philosophy, there had been one ideal for the supremely wise and virtuous, another for persons of lower capacity, but philosophers were rare and the supremely wise were rarer still. Among pagans, no supernatural rewards and punishments attached to the ethic of perfection, and nothing in their religiousness required it as a lifelong ideal. We have seen how Christianity extended Scripture and theology to a very wide range of persons. There was a further innovation. It brought the tensions and evasions of a double standard into the experience of every Christian man and woman.

The effects were visible in the very structure of each church community. If the years of preparation were one part of the faith's appeal, they also promoted divisions of merit and progress. By c. 300, there were novice "hearers" as well as the "catechumens," who were receiving instruction before baptism.[2] There were also good and bad catechumens: Tertullian complains of Christians who used the interval before baptism as an excuse for concerted sinning, their final fling; the acts of the first councils after Constantine consider the same problem, and the further problem of catechumens who do not attend church for a long while and suddenly turn up, demanding baptism.[3] The catechumen's official period of two to three years' preparation was variously spent, it seems. The baptismal rite was preceded by repentance of sins and frequent exorcism, giving an important role to the churches' retained exorcists. After baptism, Christians had only one last chance of forgiveness. Even so, the history of forgiveness had been a history of falling barriers whose every collapse was resisted but never regretted subsequently.[4] First, all Christians were granted the second chance; then the second chance was extended to deadly sins, to adultery and to lapsing or pagan observance during persecution. Practice varied locally, but the second chance became attached to a ritual of fasting, weeping and humiliation.

Around 200, we see it in North Africa, where the idea of a pure Christian Church was strong: Tertullian describes how "Christian sinners spend the day sorrowing, and the night in vigils and tears, lying on the ground among clinging ashes, tossing in rough sackcloth and dirt, fasting and praying."[5] Sometimes a penitent adulterer found himself "led into the midst of the brethren and prostrated, all in sackcloth and ashes . . . a compound of disgrace and horror, before the widows, the elders, suing for everyone's tears, licking their footprints, clasping their very knees . . ." By the mid-third century, grades of sin and penance had begun to be defined, varying from a few weeks' correction to a lifetime of entreaty. In a church of the 250s, several classes of Christian were to be found: inside were gathered the virtuous and the minor sinners who were banned only from communion; outside waited the "standing" sinners in the porch and the serious cases who were required to grovel and ask for their brothers' prayers as they went in and out of the building.[6] If we miss this weekly evidence of the group's inner divisions, we miss the flavour of early Christian life. Whose turn would it be next? God alone could forgive, the Christians believed, and he could forgive anything in his mercy; meanwhile, prayer by the assembled Christians and restoration to his Church were near-guarantees of his pardon. The process gave ordinary Christians a role and importance beside their priests: they, too, could intercede with God, causing the sinners to beg abjectly for their assistance.[7] It is disputed whether sinners were obliged to make a public confession, but one passage in Origen implies that they were, and two of Bishop Cyprian's letters assume such statements, once from Christians who had lapsed during persecution, once from Christian "virgins" who had lapsed in the bedroom. Personal sins became fascinating public knowledge. In the 450s, Pope Leo I considered public confession an "intolerable habit," evident among Italian bishops. In many churches, it seems, it had long been recognized, linking shame and group solidarity to healing through humiliation.[8]

These procedures were grim, and Christians could make use of them only once. It is clear from Tertullian that many Christians disregarded them altogether and preferred to keep their sins to themselves and God.[9] Others took them discreetly elsewhere. Martyrs, as we shall see, had the spiritual power to give a swift remission: around 200, while writing for rich Christians, Clement recommended that they should adopt holy individuals from among the poorer "brethren" who could pray and advise them as "friends of God." How could a civic notable be seen grovelling on a church path? The richer Christians could keep their own adviser in their household, and in Clement's view, the adviser need not even be a priest. Nonetheless, the idea of one, and only one, repentance was still generally accepted.

These gradations helped to compound the quality of a Christian church. If there was only one chance after baptism, was it not wiser to put off baptism and continue sinning meanwhile?[10] In the fourth century, the problem explicitly worried Church leaders, as Christians delayed full commitment until their deathbed. Delay was all the easier because of the humane Christian view that a novice or apprentice should not be denied early baptism if he seemed about to die. In the third century, the full scope of this manoeuvre does not seem to have been appreciated. Tertullian still saw the problem to lie in the opposite direction, in the habit of baptizing infants. "Why," he complained, "should the age of innocence hasten to the forgiveness of sins? If the burden of baptism is understood, its reception will be feared more than its delay." He could not have written in this manner if the cunning postponement of baptism were widespread in Christian life. The practice of infant baptism was not without critics, but many churches accepted it and the hard facts of life encouraged them. As infant mortality was so miserably high, parents had a good claim that a baby should be baptized before its probable death: the point is made clearly in Latin inscriptions in the later Christian Empire.[11]

Time, and this practice, added to the divisions between Christian believers. In the third century, Origen had some hard words for the snobbishness of Christians who had a long family history of the faith: they were worse if they could point to a bishop or dignitary in their ancestry.[12] They felt superior to newly made converts, yet these people had renounced much and endured two or three years' teaching before baptism. Their religion was very much alive and perhaps, in their turn, they would look down on Christians who had merely been baptized as infants. Infants had made no choice, and perhaps the faith did matter less to many of them later.

These divisions in the churches' membership are the setting within which the overachievers belonged. There is always a place for aims and ideals which are difficult, and Christianity was particularly able to satisfy those who respond to a life of difficult struggle. In this chapter and the next two, they will loom large. Are they really Christians, we may wonder nowadays, recoiling from their self-mortification, their visionary tours of heaven and hell, their eager anticipation of martyrdom? Yet they could cite texts in the Gospels to support their ideals. The extreme forms of overachievement were not approved by many of their contemporaries, but the values which underlay them were Christian, nonetheless. At first sight, they may seem to resemble ideals in pagan ethics: are they, then, proofs of a continuity between pagan and Christian ways of life?

These questions are easier to study because they lie on the surface of so much early Christian literature. Not only did the overachievers attract polemic and approval from fellow Christians: they helped to multiply the texts which supported their own practice. Their methods were very simple: where no authority existed, they invented texts and ascribed them to authors who never wrote them.

It is possible to put this practice in context and draw distinctions between its types.[13] In the Hellenistic age, Jewish authors had already availed themselves of this literary form: the Christians were merely one more group in the field. Like their Jewish contemporaries, they lacked the critical concern for history and its sources which would have excluded these fabrications. There were a few doubters, but some very notable believers: despite its critics, wrote Tertullian, the Book of Enoch (composed c. 150 B.C.) must be genuine, as Enoch had lived in the days before the Flood.[14]

Narrative fictions tended to name no author, the "Acts of Peter" or the "Acts of Thomas," whereas bogus letters of discipline and "re-velation" tended to claim a false authorship, the "Apocalypse of Peter" or the "Teaching of the Apostles." In either case, the deceit had one primary aim: success. By withholding his name, the writer lent authority to texts which had none. The practice was not insignificant when the texts discussed points of religious conduct. It had begun promptly, characterizing several of the New Testament's epistles and, on one view, some or all of the Gospels themselves. However we try to justify the authors' practice, at bottom they used the same device: falsehood.

In the churches, the strict regard for authority and the growing respect for "orthodoxy" gave added point to this type of invention. It was also propelled by the interests of overachievers. These authors wished to support their behaviour by texts of a spurious authority, and if we look at the contents, we can see the conduct which they specially commended. Nobody wrote in this style on the surrender of riches or on support for the poor. Perfectionist texts described other qualities: virginity, visions and martyrdom. Despite initial appearances, each brings Christian practice into a contrast with pagan society. Each has remained central to Christian piety ever since: we can explore them one by one, beginning with Christian teaching on sex and its suppression.

# II

Christian teachings on sex and remarriage were part of a wider ethic, concerned with desire and human sin: explicit words on the subject were not many, though the Gospels omitted some supposed sayings of Jesus. No area of Christian teaching has had more effect in subsequent Christian lives: it extended widely, to divorce and second marriage, abortion and contraception, homosexuality, the degrees of "kindred and affinity," the status of women and the merits of never indulging in sex at all. Christians are still its troubled heirs, but was its original motivation one which is still alive and pertinent? In its early historical context, was this teaching new or did it, perhaps, coincide with similar changes in pagan sexual practice which influenced it in their turn?[1] Is much of the teaching, as we tend to believe, obsolete because it was tempered to the times in which it was given?

In their sexual code, Christians were conscious of standing apart from the pagan world. To find a virtuous people on earth, they remarked, a man had to look far away to the Seres, the people of China, who lived justly and in sexual modesty and were therefore not afflicted with famine and disease.[2] In the second and third centuries, accepted sexual practice in the Roman Empire had a range and variety which it has never attained since. It varied somewhat between cultural regions and perhaps between social classes: we cannot, however, identify a "bourgeois" code of morality, or even be sure that divorce and adultery were more frequent and more tolerated in upper-class society.[3] Here, these variations are not at issue, for we need only sketch the range of accepted pagan practice which Christians could confront. As always, we should be wary of isolating one "Greek" and one "Roman" attitude: different Greek-speakers and Romans regarded practices differently. Yet even this diversity points to a change. Among Christians, more conduct was regarded with one, and only one, attitude.

In Egypt and much of the Near East, brothers married their sisters. Whatever its origin, this custom helped family property to cohere under a system of inheritance which recognized both male and female shares. These marriages led to children, expressions of mutual affection and sometimes to dowries from the couples' families. They were not tolerated by Roman law and the highest city culture, but they were not merely lower-class or reserved for couples who did not know Greek. In the Imperial age, they were still evident in the Greek-speaking population of the Egyptian townships, a setting in which Christians soon made a mark. They were also widespread in Mesopotamia.[4]

In many cultural regions, "bisexuality" was also taken for granted, for "Greek vice" had not faded with the classical age. In civic life, homosexuality between young men, or an older and younger partner, was socially acceptable.[5] Among many examples, the most telling is Apuleius's speech of self-defence, written in the Greek- and Latin-speaking milieu of high civic culture in Roman Africa. Like an orator in classical Athens, he cited his youthful poems to boy-lovers as a point in his favour. His speech was set before an educated Roman governor, in answer to a capital charge.[6] In his work on dreams, Artemidorus distinguished "natural" and "unnatural" sex, and although he classed lesbianism as unnatural, male homosexuality, he assumed, was not. In his personal diaries, the Emperor Marcus thanked the gods that he had not "touched Benedicta or Theodotus," girl or boy, in his youth. He did not regard the one as more of a potential lapse than the other. Pagans' sanctions against homosexuality concerned male prostitution and political ideas of the good citizen.[7] In classical Athens, laws had punished the male citizen who hired his body and then dared to stand for office or address the assembly: the penalty was death, as also for pimping and procuring, though other Greek cities may have been more lenient. Among Romans, the most acceptable homosexuality was an act conducted by citizens on slaves or foreigners. In early Rome, an obscurely attested law does seem to have punished all homosexual activity between citizens themselves. Christian authors still alluded to it, but it is clear that the law had long been defunct in normal political life. In Rome, as in Athens, there was special objection to those who were passive partners in a homosexual act. In classical Athens, full physical submission caused a person to be derided. By the mid-third century A.D., Roman laws asserted strong penalties against male prostitutes but also proposed the confiscation of half the goods of a citizen who willingly submitted to another man. No cases are known to have been brought under it.

By historical contact, and perhaps, too, by a polite evasion, Romans had long regarded their homosexuality as "Greek love." In the second century A.D., Greek culture was at the height of its esteem, and wherever we have literary evidence for continuing "pseudo-homosexuality," we find it being praised or taken for granted, in Artemidorus's tireless researches on dreams, in literary dialogues on the relative merits of sex with a man or a woman and, as late as the 380s, as a thriving light industry in the schools, banquets and social life of Antioch.[8] Nor was it confined to Greeks. Other peoples indulged in it in their differing cultures. The Romans, wrote Tatian, a Christian who knew their city, "consider pederasty to be particularly privileged and try to round up herds of boys like herds of grazing mares." In lists of national characteristics, pederasty was considered the particular distinction of Gauls.[9]

Before marriage, a young man could also turn to slaves or prostitutes. Although overindulgence was frowned on, it was not defined. It worried parents, not as a practice, because married men shared it too, but because it was expensive: "the proper analogy today [1939] would be drawn from betting."[10] As for the girls, the legal sanctions against seduction confirm that they were expected to remain virgins for their first partners. However, they were often married very young, easing the problem of premarital chastity. Their early marriage has been justly connected with their relative scarcity, caused by the exposure of more female babies than males: in Egypt, the exposure of children was thought to be less prevalent, and it is in Egypt that we find evidence of a lower proportion of early marriages. Some of the victims of exposure were brought up by others to meet the demand for slaves, and in the Greek world, there was a continuing argument about the financial rights of people who brought up these exposed "foundlings" and then had them reclaimed: Roman law took a kinder view of their recompense.[11] Exposure is reflected in some, but not all, of the uses of the Greek proper name Kopreus: "off the dung heap."

Exposure was only one of several checks on reproduction. Abortion was freely practised, and the medical sources distinguish precoital attempts at "contraception."[12] The line, however, between the two practices was often obscure, not least in the case of drugs which were taken to "stop" unwanted children. Limitation of births was not confined to the poorer classes. Partible inheritance was universal, and as the raising of several children fragmented a rich man's assets, the number of his heirs was often curbed deliberately. As men of all ages slept with their slaves, natural children were a widespread fact of life.[13] However, they followed the servile status of their mother, while laws of inheritance and social status did discriminate against any who were born from free parents. Between rich married couples, we hear remarkably little about the problems of disputed paternity, even in cases of inheritance. The higher aristocracy, it seems, had an Edwardian gift for containing the sexual adventures whose results are anyway so hard to detect.

Few women, if any, expected to remain spinsters. Marriage was generally a matter of agreement between partners, validated before suitable witnesses. Within it, adultery was essentially a female crime, and married women were generally victims of a double standard of morality.[13A] They were not, however, denied pleasure: sex with women, observed its defender in one of the literary "dialogues" on love, gives equal exchange of enjoyment. The couples part happily when they have affected each other equally, "unless, that is, we believe the seer Teiresias and accept that a woman's pleasure is double a man's share."[14] Doctors were well aware of females' enjoyment of sex and even sought to connect conception with moments of simultaneous orgasm. Galen shared the prevailing view that women, too, produced sperm, that its presence increased a woman's sexual pleasure and that it delighted men, too. It even gave pleasure to eunuchs, remarked Galen, knowledgeably: "and you could not look for a clearer proof than that."[15]

In marriage, the primary imbalance was age. The man was very often the older partner, and so most women who survived childbirth could anticipate an early widowhood.[16] Remarriage was a matter which aroused various conflicting responses.[17] They show occasionally on Latin epitaphs, sources which would tend to mention a point of special significance or obscure an unfavourable quality. In a large sample, twenty-eight epitaphs were found to record that a woman had stayed a widow, sometimes stating explicitly that she stayed true to her love for her first husband: Virgil played on these feelings in his portrait of the widowed Dido's dilemma. However, thirty-one epitaphs record a woman's remarriage quite openly, while some belong on tombs which they publicize as the tomb of a husband and his successive wives. Epitaphs do use the term of praise "a one-man woman" (*univira*), but the word does not usually mean a lifelong widow. It refers to fidelity within a marriage, not lifelong fidelity to one husband: it praises a faithful wife on the occasion of her own, or her partner's, death. In the Imperial period, indeed, the Roman marriage laws urged the widows of citizen husbands to remarry within two years. There was evidently some interest in whether a man would marry a virgin, a widow or a girl whom somebody else had seduced: in the 330s, a handbook on astrology alludes repeatedly to this point as a matter of interest in people's horoscopes. The allusions suggest that the first marriage to a virgin was thought more favoured, but the authors were also aware that such marriages did not necessarily last as well as others.

Marriage, finally, was only one social form of cohabitation and it was valued because it legitimized children and eased the transmission of property. Many men lived with a partner as "concubine", especially if she came from a different social class: the practice of "living together" had been greatly extended by aspects of Roman law.[18] Until the end of the second century, soldiers in the Roman army were not allowed to marry while in service; in Egypt, marriages between Romans, Greeks and Egyptians were prohibited by legalized "apartheid," an attitude of Roman Imperial rule; since Augustus, severe penalties attached to marriages between Roman citizens who were members of different social classes. There is an easy, age-old answer to a barrage of socially prejudiced law: give up marriage and cohabit instead. No social stigma, therefore, attached to such unions or even to children born under them: a primary consequence of Roman law among provincials was an increase in "illegitimate" children. Of course, there were also men who lived with a wife and a concubine at the same time.[19] Though the details varied in local laws, divorce between married partners was essentially a matter of consent.

For a more private insight, we have only to look to Artemidorus and his invaluable fieldwork.[20] Sexual dreams among his clients and informers had a range which would stretch most modern analysts' experience in a lifetime. They dreamed of everything imaginable, sex with their children, their animals, their parents, fur on their penis, teeth and mouths in their backsides. To Artemidorus, these dreams were interesting because of their predictive power, not their diagnostic relevance. He knew people who dreamed of sex with a child under five or as passive partners with animals; mothers were envisaged in every sort of position; an important landlord, known to Artemidorus, ran into debt and killed himself some months after dreaming he had had sex with himself. Poor men who dreamed they had sex with their sons could anticipate a big bill: they would end by sending them to fee-paying schools. Fathers dreamed freely that they had sex with their married daughters: "often," Artemidorus knew, rich fathers made bequests to their daughters after these dreams, "against their initial resolution." Historians of property and inheritance have not allowed for this impact of night life on daylight patterns of reality.

In waking life, this sexual variety did not amount to shamelessness or lack of restraint. Shortly after Paul's lifetime, we catch a glimpse of pagan practice in his home city of Tarsus, through a civic speech by the visiting Dio.[21] He reproached Paul's fellow citizens for their shameful habit of "snorting." Their city echoed with it, he protested, like a brothel, and the sound, we know, was connected with sexual activity. Yet Dio could both make fun of it and expect sympathy, and in a familiar Mediterranean mixture, this city in which men "had a snort" in the brothels was also a place where the women went veiled from view through the streets. It is quite untrue that pagans lived in unfettered sexuality before Christianity came.[22] In a telling aside,

Artemidorus remarks that men who resorted to city prostitutes experienced "shame" and financial expense. Adultery was a crime, and if there had been no scruples, the point of some raffish literature would have been lost. In the second century A.D., Rufinus wrote neat Greek epigrams on erotic adventures and encounters: "Does anyone throw his woman out naked when he happens to find a lover with her, as if he has not enjoyed adultery himself, as if he is one of Pythagoras's followers?" The whole point of the poem was to be audacious, though not entirely untrue to life.[23] Sexuality, in the pagan Greek world, was governed by the profound restraints of honour and shame. It could be infringed by "insolence" (*hybris*) and was upheld by "modesty" (*aidos*), essential but untranslatable terms.

Homosexuality was also to be kept within limits. Although it was idealized, it was considered largely from the person of the active partner. Doctors considered active homosexuality to be natural, though in Rufus's view (c. 100 A.D.) it was more exhausting than heterosexuality because it was more violent.[24] Passive homosexuality was another matter.[25] There had been a familiar medical debate on the causes of this perverse preference, which was compared with the tastes of women "who pursue other women with an almost masculine jealousy." Some said that it was a disease of the mind, others an inherited defect at birth which had become ineradicable ever since it had entered the human race. It was generally agreed that there was no queer like an old queer: unable to perform, he was obliged to endure, although his appetite became more intense with age. The active partner "takes an exquisite pleasure," says a belittler of the practice in a literary dialogue on love (c. 150 A.D.), whereas his victim "initially suffers pain and tears, though the pain does wear off a little with time . . ." Pestering old men and overindulgers were equal objects of abuse. Although the civic gymnasiums were recognized breeding grounds for homosexual romance, the rules of membership in one known example (admittedly c. 150 B.C.) had excluded "pederasts," among others. Here, love affairs had been for respectable amateurs only.[26]

These social conventions were supported by law, religion and philosophy. Legally, they were complicated by the Roman marriage laws which the Emperor Augustus had introduced and which persisted, with frequent refinements, throughout the period. While encouraging children and discouraging marriage between certain social classes, they also laid down penalties for extramarital affairs and adultery: their elaboration by third-century Emperors used phrases like "the chastity of our times."[27] A married man was liable for criminal punishment if he made love with another freeborn woman of high status (committing *stuprum*): he was also punished if he was proved to have condoned his wife's adultery.[28] These severe laws applied to Roman citizens and were not popular. By the Severan period, abortion was also a crime, but only if practised to the detriment of a husband's interests. It was not a crime by its very nature.[29]

The sanctions of religion were milder and more varied. In many pagan cults, rules of sexual purity governed entry into a temple and sometimes participation in worship.[30] Generally, they excluded people who had recently had sex or specifically committed adultery, but the exclusion was usually brief. Before sleeping in Pergamum's great shrine of Asclepius, clients were expected to have abstained from sex for two days: elsewhere, one day, or a quick wash, sufficed. Different cults viewed the matter differently, and we cannot generalize about long-term changes. In the late second century B.C., the rules for a public cult in Pergamum demanded a day's interval after sex with one's wife, but two days' interval after sex with somebody else's, yet in the same period, a privately founded cult in Lydia required members to swear only to have sex with their wives, or if they were bachelors, with unmarried women who were no longer virgins. Here, the rules were turning into a code of conduct, although this cult is exceptional in our evidence. As time passed, the gods did not expect ever more from their worshippers.

These prohibitions defined the state in which pagans could best approach their gods. They were phrased negatively and applied for a fixed period of time: without their inscription and display, people might simply have overlooked them. They never enjoined continuous abstinence on their participants. Priesthoods, however, did sometimes require rather more. Some cults were only served by virgin priests or by women who were not sexually active.[31] It was hard to be sure of their conduct, and we have already seen how the oracles were asked to resolve problems. Prolonged virginity was a rare requirement, and hence, in part, we find it recorded honourably in inscriptions throughout the Empire's various zones. In Rome the Vestal Virgins persisted through pagan antiquity, if anything with a stronger sense of their "divine" choosing. In the Lebanon, two inscriptions of second-century style refer to a virgin who became the prophetess of the Syrian goddess and also served the god of a local shrine.[32] In the first inscription, she records her abstention from bread for twenty years "at the order of the god"; in the second, she is honoured for her career and is said to have lived for "a hundred years." As prolonged virginity was exceptional, we can see why people in Stobi asked Clarian Apollo to applaud their long-serving "chaste" priestess, Prisca. Elsewhere in Macedonia, a contemporary, Alexandra, lived at Pella as a virgin for twenty-seven years before marrying, a condition which she only survived for a further eight and a half months.[33] She had undertaken her vow "at the command of Ephesian Artemis," the great goddess whose cult had spread into Macedonia and other provinces. This command implies that Alexandra had been dedicated to the goddess as a young woman: we know of such virgin attendants in the cult, not least through the vivid novel *Leucippe and Cleitophon*.

Alexandra, however, graduated to a married life, as all virgin priestesses could. At Rome, the Vestal Virgins served for a minimum thirty-year term, after which they could take a husband. Not many did, because they were first taken into "captivity" in the years before they were ten and were only set free when the best of their childbearing years were past. If they did marry, the result was sometimes felt to be ill-fated, like Alexandra's own brief marriage.[34] Only a few exotic "Oriental" cults went further and required priests who were physically eunuchs. Whereas virginity in a priestess was universally respected, self-castration found many critics in the Greco-Roman world. It continued nonetheless, among people, even, who were brought up to the higher languages and culture. An altar inscription of March 24, 239, at Lectoure, recalls how a lady "received the potency" (*vires*) of one Eutyches. The words described emasculation, and as the day was the "Day of Blood" in the cult of Attis, the occasion was presumably the castration of Eutyches, a priest in the service of the god. The woman received the pieces.[35]

Outside these few, controversial priesthoods, abstinence and asceticism were urged as lifelong ideals of behaviour only by some of the schools of philosophy. Their primary impulse was the concept of "life according to nature" and the mastery, or destruction, of desire by reason. Some authors attacked abortion and "unnatural" homosexuality, while urging that sex should be confined to its natural occasion, the deliberate production of children. The ideal life, some said, was free of all desire, and the ethic of abstinence applied to everyone, even to married couples.[36] There was, however, a wide variety, even within a single school:[37] some Stoics could urge the extreme limitation of sex, while another, Epictetus, proposed a milder ethic for his followers: "Stay pure, if possible, before marriage; confine yourself to what is lawful; don't be a nuisance, or start reproaching those who do indulge; don't keep on drawing attention to the fact that you do not." A usual setting for discourses on love and marriage was the charmed circle of a philosopher's pupils and friends or close kin. Plutarch sent proverbial sayings on good matrimonial conduct to a young newly wed couple, while Porphyry included advice on suppression of sexual desire in his letter to the elderly wife whom he had married, late in life. Did this type of literature do anything more than charm and amuse its coterie of readers? When Plutarch commended sex for reproduction only, one wonders if his young couple paid the slightest attention.[38] "Cats, it is said, are driven mad by the smell of sweet oils . . . as women are affected likewise, not by scents but by their husbands' sexual affairs with others, it is wrong to upset them so much for such a tiny pleasure." It was charming prose, like its French translations which appealed to the libraries of eighteenth-century seducers but did not interrupt their lives of *liaisons dangereuses*.

Philosophers were also heirs to an idealized respect for homosexual love. The great Neoplatonist Plotinus was not best pleased when a rhetorician delivered a speech to his study group on the theme that a pupil should obey his teacher, if necessary to the point of agreeing to sodomy. The theme, however, was developed from Plato's own *Symposium*.[39] Much fun was made of the eternal gap between philosophers' ideals and practice. The fun extended to household objects of art: there are several examples, of which the best is a second-century vase showing philosophers haring avidly after a handsome boy.[40] The ethic of continence and self-control was for a very few, and then it tended to elude them. Lapses, however, were of no consequence for their fate after death. Perhaps the most regular "abstainers" were athletes, who believed that the avoidance of sex improved their results. Artemidorus ended his dream book with the example of an athlete who had dreamed that he cut off his private parts and was crowned afterwards. He took it as a sign to stay "uncorrupted," without sex. He won several great prizes, Artemidorus knew, until he broke his rule, and promptly "retired ingloriously."[41]

As we know slightly more of the philosophers' writings in the Imperial period, the literature on abstinence seems to grow with time.

In the Greek novels of the period, we can gain a similar impression: the stress on the heroine's virginity becomes most emphatic in the plots of the two fictions which are probably the latest, neither being written before c. 200.[42] Yet these impressions are not grounds for social generalizations. Apart from the chances of survival, the philosophers were writing for a tiny minority whose ethical ideal was not their contemporaries': the novelists were no more representative. What we know through laws, histories and inscriptions refutes the idea that a widespread change in pagan sexual practice or attitudes was gathering its own momentum. Most of the Greek medical writers continued to recognize that an active sex life was good for a person's health. Even in females, the advantages of virginity were disputed, as we shall see. Among men, there was no argument. Galen attacked the old theory of Epicurus that sex was always hostile to good health. In his working life, he had seen so many counter-examples.[43]

There were some people, he said, who needed sex regularly, as otherwise they felt heavy in their heads and lost their appetites: "I have known people of this type give up sex out of modesty," a fascinating insight, "but then become slothful and listless . . ." He had even known a man who gave up sex because of grief at his wife's death, though he had enjoyed it "constantly" in the past: the poor man's appetite had gone to pieces. Reflecting on these cases, Galen realized that they all derived from a clear complaint, "retention of excess sperm." Resumed sexual activity soon put them to rights, and as women produced sperm too, the same remedy would work for them. He had seen a most unhealthy widow who was suffering all sorts of nervous pain, but the midwife had started to massage her private parts, whereupon she released a "thick sperm" and had a physical pleasure "as if from sex." Plainly, she, too, had been suffering from "retention." It seemed quite clear to Galen that this "retention of sperm" was more painful and serious than menstrual tension.

If Galen had met a Christian monk or nun, he would have known exactly what to prescribe for them. He was not alone in his view: a fellow doctor, Rufus, agreed that sex was a good cure for melancholia and for epilepsy and headaches in adolescents. It should not be overdone, but it did prove easier for those who were in the habit of it. They should keep fit by a moderate diet and exercise, nothing so strenuous as wrestling or throwing javelins. Sex was tiring, in Galen's view, because the sperm was composed of vital spirit and orgasms were related to a heating of the blood in the male and female. It was best, Rufus thought, to make love after a light meal, and activity should be followed by a rest or sleep. A little gentle horse-riding was an excellent preparation.

To turn to these authors' Christian contemporaries is to enter a different world. Nobody was concerned with the balance of the body's humours or the good effects of sex on health and pent-up sperm, male and female alike. Christianity aimed to effect changes in this field: it did not coincide with them. Once, and once only, had a pagan thinker anticipated Christianity's effect. In his old age, Plato had considered how best to limit sex and abolish homosexuality in his ideal state. There was little hope, his speakers agreed, without an extreme sanction, the fear of God.[44] Once again, a late view of Plato was to find its realization in Christianity.

# III

A central part of Christian teaching on sexual conduct derived directly from the Jews.[1] Like the Jews, Christians opposed much in the accepted practice of the pagan world. They vigorously attacked infanticide and the exposure of children. Both continued in "Christian" Europe for centuries, but the teaching had effects on patterns of inheritance wherever it was taken to heart: it caused more heirs to survive and property, therefore, to be fragmented into smaller pieces. Christians also followed the assumptions of the Old Testament and identified adultery with murder and fornication with apostasy from God. Abortion was a more complex matter.[2] The Mosaic law had punished it, if it harmed the mother: when Exodus was translated into Greek, the translators introduced a concern for the child, varying with its status as a formed or unformed embryo. Most of the early Christian texts attack abortion simply as "murder of the creation of God," but some do stop to wonder when exactly the embryo is a living thing. In essence, they then follow this Greek distinction of two stages in its existence. On incestuous marriages, early Christian texts said less, although the faith had spread rapidly in areas in which brothers married sisters. The matter, however, was considered by a council in Antioch in 325: the marriage of brothers to sisters was equated with murder, while marriage to a niece was equivalent to adultery and required the same expiation by grovelling and begging forgiveness. This type of ruling was very pertinent to many Christians' family life, especially in the Greek world, Egypt and the Near East: here, too, there were consequences for inheritance, although they were not singled out as motives by Christians themselves. Marriage to a close kinsman was particularly likely for a widow or a young heiress: by condemning these marriages, Christian councils may have encouraged rather more widows to remain unmarried and more heiresses to adopt virginity. The marriage of a woman to two brothers, surely in succession, was judged by an early council (c. 320) to deserve excommunication for life. We do not know how early these teachings developed in the churches, but it is suggestive that the fictitious Acts of Andrew (probably before 300) attacked the intermarriage of close relations in the propertied upper classes.[3] As for homosexuality, Paul and the early epistles agreed with the accepted Jewish view that it was a deadly sin which provoked God's wrath. It led to earthquakes and natural disasters, which were evident in the fate of Sodom. The absence of Gospel teaching on the topic did not amount to tacit approval. All orthodox Christians knew that homosexuals went to hell, until a modern minority tried to make them forget it.[4]

Nonetheless, there were topics on which Christians did go beyond mainstream Jewish opinion. One was an ingenious allegory which seems to have begun with the Christian author of the "Epistle of Barnabas" (c. 100): why, he asked, did the Mosaic law declare hares, hyenas and weasels to be unclean? They were types of sexual vice, he explained, as their odd habits and the details of their rear anatomy proved. These animal facts had been noticed by pagan observers, and when this Christian author applied them to the Mosaic law, he produced a new group of names to be used in sexual polemic. Hares, he explained, stood for homosexuals and hyenas for oversexed seducers, while weasels were people who indulged in oral sex. Moses had banned them for these reasons, and the unholy trinity then passed through Christian literature into the learning of medieval authors.[5]

This language of abuse was trivial beside the real innovations in Christians' teaching: their views on remarriage and divorce.[6] Here, Christianity was not suiting its ethic to the prevailing morality or tempering it to the mood of the times. It went beyond anything practised by Jews or pagans and its teaching has troubled consciences ever since.

In Mark's Gospel, Jesus was said to have forbidden divorce in a saying which made no exceptions and greatly alarmed the disciples.[7]

Nothing in Jewish life can have prepared them for this extreme attitude: not even the sect whom we know in the Dead Sea scrolls took any such stand against the practice. Although the woman could not legally initiate the change, divorce in Jewish marriages was not a matter of religious scruple: the Hellenized Jew Josephus (c. 80 A.D.) remarks that it could occur for "many sorts of reason" and he seems to have divorced his own wife when he became bored with her. Jesus's age, like our own, was very free with its divorces: his teaching went flatly against its practice, as against ours, and although priority is still disputed, it is likelier that the "permitted exceptions" in Matthew's Gospel were an addition to the simpler original text. Among Jews and Gentiles, this prohibition was novel and a lasting source of complication. When Christian Emperors eventually tried to limit divorce by law, they were foiled by their subjects' prompt evasions. It was among those Christians who had stayed closest to their Jewish roots that Bishop Epiphanius, in the late fourth century, discovered to his horror a willingness to tolerate up to seven consecutive marriages.[8]

On the matter of a second marriage after either partner's death, Jesus was not remembered for any explicit advice. There were, however, a few Jewish widows who had already set the example which Christians idealized: the story of the heroic widow, Judith, was already current as an inspiring tale in Greek; in Luke's Gospel, we meet "Anna the prophetess" in the temple precinct, a Jewess who had had a husband "for seven years from her virginity" and after his death had lived in widowhood to the age of eighty-four. She was thought to be especially close to God, and in her style of life, she was indeed a prophet of the future.[9] It was St. Paul who expressed the subsequent Christian ideal on the topic, implying that his view was endorsed by the Holy Spirit: he was probably not at odds on the matter with his Apostolic contemporaries. He stated that a woman's remarriage after her partner's death was a poor but excusable second best and that it ought to be to a Christian partner.[10] On the whole, subsequent Christian writers, even Tertullian, remained true to his priorities, although perfectionists did continue to argue that remarriage was never permissible in any circumstances.[11] The Pastoral epistles proposed that Christian bishops should only marry once, setting a good standard. By the earliest Church councils, "twice-married Christians" were excluded from Church offices.[12]

The topic, however, was too complex for any one sentence of advice. If an innocent partner divorced an adulterous one, could he or she remarry? The bulk of the early Fathers accepted that the husband of an adulterous wife could indeed remarry (citing Matthew 5.32) but that the wife of an adulterous husband could not (citing 1 Cor. 7.39). Contradictory though the texts could seem, there was no doubt that Paul had advised the very best Christians against remarriage. This teaching was extremely pertinent in a society in which many girls were married so young and widowhood was so likely. In the Christian Empire, the new emphasis shows up in Christian epitaphs.[13] The old Latin praises of the "one-man woman" vanished almost entirely: fidelity, without divorce, was expected of every Christian. Instead, praises of chaste widowhood become more frequent, and a state to be endured for thirty, even sixty, long years. As we have seen, pagans could admire this rare devotion, although nothing in their society required it: it testified to lasting affection and avoided a stepparent for any surviving children. Christian apologists could thus cite their teaching on second marriage as grounds for respect before a pagan audience. Widowhood, however, was admired for a very different reason: not the love of a former husband, but dependence on God.

Together, the teachings on divorce and the priorities in remarriage impinged on much which pagan practice and subsequent domestic life would otherwise have taken as it came. Their impact was felt everywhere, in dreams and visions, in Church appointments and even as the core of the best of the fictions which early Christians wrote, in awareness of the pagans' own romances. Whereas pagan novels explored the trials of young lovers and their lapses from their high ideals, the neglected *Recognitions*, ascribed to Clement, turned on a distinctively Christian plot. Probably composed c. 200, it developed round an old man's fears that his long-lost wife must have sunk into adultery because her horoscope had predicted it. As he then discovered from St. Peter, astrology was vain, adultery a matter of free will and his wife, when restored to him, entirely free from the lapse which was "worse than many murders."[14]

Those who demand a strict sexual ethic tend also to police it. Husbands who tolerated their wives' adulteries were to be punished quite severely, according to the bishops at an early Council in Spain (c. 320): it made no difference if these long-sufferers were being generous or showing Christian forgiveness. For a widow to succumb to a man whom she then went on to marry was an offence which required penance. Men were not exempted: in Christian Latin epitaphs, there are praises for the *virginius*, the virgin man at marriage, though the word's relative scarcity perhaps suggests that the virtue was not particularly common.[15]

What, meanwhile, of the proper occasions for sex, for those Christians who still had to resort to it? Here, the Alexandrian authors, especially, took over the philosophers' convention, that sex "according to nature" was sex for the purpose of children only.[16] Obviously, the principle excluded sex during pregnancy, a habit, as Stoics had also urged, which placed man even lower than the animals: only Lactantius let it pass with a frown, as a necessity, not a lapse. On deliberate contraception, the texts before Constantine said next to nothing, and, presumably, those who favoured "natural" sex regarded it as excluded without further comment. General polemics against abortion probably subsumed it, and it is enough that the one explicit mention of interrupted intercourse presents it as the beastly habit of Gnostics. Older techniques found a new meaning.[17] In pagan texts, the leaves of a willow tree, soaked in water, were a recognized contraceptive potion, the "destroyer of fruits," as Homer called it. In Christianity, they became more drastic. "As for our harps," said the Psalmist, "we hanged them on willows . . .": the harps, explained a Christian author, were bodies, the willow "chastity," because "a potion of willow flowers in water extinguishes sexual desire." An old pagan precaution was now seen as a means of suppressing sexual activity altogether. The change was indicative of something much wider. From its very beginnings, Christianity has considered an orderly sex life to be a clear second best to no sex life at all. It has been the protector of an endangered Western species: people who remain virgins from birth to death.

In modern Christianity, there are more than 1,600,000 adults vowed to virginity. In his Revelation, John had already seen a heaven positively teeming with virgins, 144,000 of them, he said, men who were singing to their harps and had never defiled themselves with a woman: they were one group whom John understood as soon as he saw them, without verbal explanation of their condition.[18] Among Christians, as Jesus had stated, there was to be "neither marrying nor giving in marriage" in the time of the Resurrection. Some Christians claimed that that time had already dawned, and others thought it good to anticipate it. As a result, the ideal of virginity was widely preached to Christians in this life. To attain it, there were even some extremists who disarmed temptation: at the Council of Nicaea, Christians who castrated themselves had to be excluded from the priesthood; in the

130s, Justin told of a young Christian who had asked a doctor in Alexandria to castrate him, but as castration had been banned by recent Roman laws, the doctor had to apply first to the provincial governor, who refused permission. This intriguing episode is not only an insight into the limitless "in" tray of a Roman governor. It is particularly telling, because Justin relates the young man's aim as something admirable.[19]

"Concerning virgins," Paul had told the Corinthians, "I have no commandment from the Lord": he and his readers were quick to fill the gap. Female Christians claimed to live as sisters among themselves, while the ideal of sexless cohabitation was urged, and practised, by married Christian couples. In the Syriac-speaking churches, it seems likely that only male Christians who had vowed celibacy were allowed to be baptized.[20] In c. 172, Tatian, pupil of Justin, returned from Rome to the Near East with teachings which denounced marriage and enjoined chastity on all Christians, yet he was not so far removed from several Church leaders. In the mid-second century, we know from Eusebius how the bishop of Corinth corresponded with the bishop of Cnossos in Crete, encouraging him to consider the weaker Christians and not to lay the burden of chastity on everyone. The bishop of Cnossos replied that next time he should send nourishment for adults, as his flock could not continue to live on such slops until the end of the world.[21]

When the churches included such perfectionists, we cannot ignore the "apocryphal" texts and fictions which urged an extreme opposition to sex. They were not to everyone's taste, but in one case, the "Acts" of Paul and Thecla, they were invented by an Elder in the orthodox Church. They told how Thecla, a noble virgin in Iconium, had sat "entranced like a spider" at her window, listening to Paul's message that men and women must utterly renounce sex and marriage. Like Jewish novels in Greek, these stories did owe an ultimate debt to the literary form of pagan fiction. In pagan novels, however, the plots have been summed up as not a "Whodunnit?" but a "When will they do it?" In Christian fiction, couples of good family learned never to do it at all.[22]

The techniques of persuasion took various forms. Like Paul, the Apostles might be shown preaching lifelong virginity to young people, even to fiancées: in itself, this picture was not heretical, but three of the "Acts" went further. They told how an Apostle had broken up marriages in very high society by dissuading the wife from sex: in the "Acts" of Andrew, the Apostle told one such society woman that marriage was "foul and polluted" and that her renunciation of sex would restore the Fall of Adam through Eve. In each case, this disruption was followed by the Apostle's martyrdom in an angry pagan society.[23] Probably, the same pattern occurred in the incomplete "Acts" of John, in which John was dissuaded three times from marriage by visions of Christ. By the mid-third century, "Acts" of Thomas were available, composed by an author, probably a Syrian, who did show signs of an extreme enthusiasm for sexless living.[24] He invented some startling stories of the Apostle's impact on the nobility of western India, how one wife had run out of her husband's bedroom, wrapped in the bed curtain, and slept the night with her nurse, and how another couple saw Jesus in their bedroom on their wedding night, explaining that sex was foul and that marriage should never be consummated. Of all possible guests at a society wedding, an apocryphal Apostle was the worst.

People read these stories, and as time passed, their dubious origins were too easily forgotten. In the mid-third century, as we shall see, they were developed by Manichaean heretics who used them, in turn, to support their own ascetic ideal.[25] Perhaps of all "non-Acts," the most chilling is a Christian "Act" of Peter, which was cited by Augustine against the Manichaeans, who accepted it. A gardener, it was said, had one virgin daughter and had begged Peter to pray for her. He asked the Lord to give her what was "useful for her soul," whereupon she died. When the gardener begged for her to be brought back, she was resurrected, but was raped soon afterwards by the slave of a Christian lodger. In fact, she had been fortunate. Peter also had a good-looking daughter of his own, to whom a rich pagan had taken a fancy while she was bathing with her mother. At the time, interestingly, she was aged only ten. Before he could rape her, she was struck down with the palsy and crippled on one side of her body: "as the Lord liveth," Peter used to say, "this is expedient for her and me."[26]

These apocryphal texts were not necessarily less read and known than many orthodox ones: how exactly should we place them? Typically, they show the Apostles preaching chastity to the wives of pagan governors and notables, and when they succeed, they are martyred by the angry husbands. In the churches, we do know of high-ranking female converts, even governors' wives; chastity was admired by everyone, and here at least these fictions dramatized a pattern which was not incredible. We do not know if women read them or, on one view, wrote several of them, but among their more extreme miracles and scenes of overachievement there is a note of explicit preaching and moral example which is distinct from anything in the genuine Acts of the Apostles. These fictions' savage attacks on sexuality had no good words for married believers unless they gave up the whole nasty business.[27]

The arguments of these fictions correspond to several notorious heresies, though they fit no single type. During the second and third centuries, many heretical groups taught that marriage was Satanic and akin to fornication; some connected it with the work of an inferior Creator.[28] Followers of Marcion spoke of the body as a "nest of guilt"; secret sayings were ascribed to Jesus in which he reviled childbirth and praised the androgynous state of man at Creation. In the "Gospel of the Egyptians," Christ was said to tell Salome that all would be known when "you have trampled on the garment of shame; when the two become one and the male with the female is neither male nor female." In the first Paradise, it seemed, the sexes had not been differentiated: little-known words of Jesus spoke of the time when the "inner" and the "outer" would be exchanged, the sexual organs combined and the old perfection restored.

Within and without the Church, these views met well-merited opposition. A few heretics preached sexual indulgence, especially the exotic Carpocrates, whose seventeen-year-old son wrote a book advising sexual and material communism; it has continued to receive a bad Christian press: "the scribblings of an intelligent, but nasty-minded, adolescent of somewhat pornographic tendencies."[29] By the orthodox, Tatian's extremism was opposed; the author of the "Acts" of Paul and Thecla was deposed and most Christian authors did remember that the highest ideals did not apply to everyone, but to each according to his capacity. We must do justice to this range of opinion which was headed by Paul himself. It would have had no patience with the wilder views of apocryphal Apostles.

Nonetheless, in their milder moments these "Apostles" did pose a dilemma, as did the heretics themselves. Their arguments were infuriating, but their ideals came near to accepted Christian perfectionism. We can see the difficulty from the reply which Clement made to heretical teachings while writing in Alexandria.[30] On the one hand, he insisted that marriage was preferable to not marrying, because it gave less scope for selfishness and more for self-denial. However, he also believed that it called for a sterner resistance to temptations, because a wife, children and belongings multiplied such snares. When he set out his own matrimonial ideal, it amounted to sexless marriage, lived as if between a brother and sister. His aim was to define a way for the thinking, committed Christian who aspired beyond the simple believer, and while attacking sexual heresy, he ended, significantly, by repeating much of its content.

Like poets, therefore, early Christians had very little to say in praise of marriage. "Let marriage be honoured in all circumstances," stated the author of the Epistle to the Hebrews, exhorting his readers not to sin against it, perhaps by rejecting it altogether.[31] Those authors who were most directly influenced by a Jewish context were at first most favourable to marriage's cause. After Clement, no Christian author wrote anything so positive about the married state, and even Clement's views had hardly been straightforward praise.

In Carthage, Tertullian's various treatises against remarriage are conspicuous for the arguments which they muster against any form of marriage at all.[32] Their purpose was not to revile marriage altogether, but their arguments do tend repeatedly in that direction. Virginity was simply better, and married couples should give up sex and return to it. In 251, Cyprian, bishop of Carthage, was telling his Christians that plague in the city had its advantages: it allowed the Christian virgins to die intact. Once again, the Christian fiction *The Recognitions* bears witness to the arguments which could be used in public discussions. In a bold speech against astrologers, "Peter" reminds the "huge crowds" which have gathered to hear the debate that they "are smeared with sins, as if with pitch. . . . Perhaps you say, 'If someone falls in love, how can he contain himself even if he sees before his eyes the river of fire?'" Peter replies that true believers know the full power of fear: "Imagine human punishments, and see what force fear has. . . ."[33]

In the orthodox churches, meanwhile, virgins were admired bearers of the Christian standard. Tertullian implies that in North Africa they were sometimes maintained by their fellow Christians and honoured with gifts for their fine aspiration.[34] In the Eastern churches, we are lucky to have the Syriac text of two early letters, "On Virginity," which were certainly composed before Constantine and seem, from their biblical quotations, to belong in the third century.[35] Falsely, but typically, they are ascribed to Bishop Clement of Rome. Their author was particularly concerned with the perils and abuses which beset the life of the celibate male "virgin" as he travelled from one community to the next. Writing to male and female virgins, the author is best imagined as a celibate Christian in the Syriac-speaking Church who was concerned for the conduct of fellow "sons of the covenant."

Virginity, he warns, is no excuse for boasting and conceit, advice which reminds us how it is nothing but the most selfish of human ideals.[36] Nor, he cautions, is it an excuse for reckless licence. In fascinating detail, he protests at male virgins who cohabit with female virgins, travel with them in solitary country, feast and drink freely at parties in their company and drop into their houses "on the pretence of visiting them, reading them the Scriptures or exorcising them." In the pagan world, no virgin girl could have wandered at will on a distant road with a visiting unmarried man; no male could simply intrude as he pleased into other houses' female quarters. The warnings are their own best comment on reality, a world of small Christian groups in which virgins bickered and spread gossip, alleged an urgent "exorcism" in order to call on a female and teach her the strangest heresies. As these visiting virgins were usually supported from a community's hospitality, they had time in plenty on their hands. Our author protests against their "idleness" and adds that an exorcism must not be performed with a long, eloquent preamble, as if to parade the performer's learning. He goes on, in the second text, to describe his own habits. Whenever he finds himself short of a bed in a village or small group of houses, he looks for a fellow celibate or, with due caution, for married Christians. He avoids female company, and if he gives a blessing, he ensures that the female recipients' right hands are hidden in their robes, like his own, which they can touch only through a garment. What, he then asks, airing a rare peril, if he finds himself far from his own church in a place where the only Christians are females? He looks for the oldest of the Christian old crones and asks her quietly for a room apart. She carries the lamp and brings him whatever he needs; serving girls, of course, are quite untrustworthy. And what, finally, if he happens to find himself in a place with only one Christian, a female at that? "We do not stop, nor pray . . . we run from it as before the face of a serpent." An extreme Jewish-Christian sect, followers of the prophet Elchesai, seem to have equated sexual desire with the bite of a poisonous snake or rabid dog. Their seat, too, was in the Near East, especially in southern Mesopotamia.[37]

"Where," it has been asked, "did all this madness come from?"[38] To many spectators, the ideal did not seem mad at all. In one of his best asides, the author of "On Virginity" reproaches celibate Christians who attend pagan parties and sing in choirs for their supper, "singing the Lord's song in a strange land."[39] Pagans, it seems, liked the rhythms and new vigour of the early Syrian hymn chants and found their virgin performers a fine after-dinner turn. In the 170s, Athenagoras the Christian composed an "Embassy" speech, addressed as if to the Emperors: "of course," he stated, "virginity brings a man near God." The remark was thought to be self-evident to educated pagan readers. One of the Emperors, we may reflect, was Marcus Aurelius, a man who had given thanks in his private diaries for his sexual restraint as a young man and who, in a world-weary moment, described sex as "internal attrition and an expulsion of mucus with a sort of spasm." When Galen encountered Christians in Rome at the same period, he was impressed by their willingness to abstain from sex, men and women alike.[40]

The topic had provoked continuing discussion among fellow doctors in the Greek world, and echoes of a debate on virginity in females still reach us in the writings of Soranus at Ephesus, earlier in the second century.[41] "Continuous virginity" struck the pagan doctor Soranus as an excellent way of life. Admittedly, some doctors argued the opposite, and cited the case histories of widows who remarried and found that they enjoyed easier periods. Soranus drew analogies from the animal kingdom and was especially impressed by virgins' observed resistance to diseases. It was evident, he said, in virgin priestesses of the gods, and for this reason, he endorsed it. We need only recall the hundred-year-old virgin priestess who was honoured by inscriptions in the Lebanon.

This discussion, however, is not evidence for a growing favour for the virginal life among pagan contemporaries. In the Hellenistic age, philosophers had already expressed views on the merits of chastity, even within marriage, and as a result, they had made the matter interesting. Soranus was responding to them, not to the demands of particular clients; few people could afford to consult him anyway, and the views of doctors were not widely known. Nor were they unanimous. Others argued against virginity, while we only have to remember Galen's diagnosis for that most distressing complaint, "retention of excess sperm" in males and females.

Christians did not invoke the medical arguments for virginity, but they could assume a degree of pagan sympathy for their apparent "madness." If pagans could appreciate the Christians' ideal, did it perhaps owe a general debt to the pagans' example and teaching, absorbed when the Gospel began to be preached in the Gentile world?

This theory would see a wider drift into the chastity to which Christianity attached itself, emphasizing a current which was only latent in its Gospel teachings. Certainly, the pagans' arguments were very useful. To support the case for virginity, authors like Jerome did draw on unacknowledged pagan philosophers, not least on Porphyry, whose work *Against the Christians* was anathema to the Christian Empire but whose work *On Abstinence* remained a secret gold mine for Christian essayists.[42] Like pagans, Christians urged that a period of abstinence befitted those who approached God. Paul was only the first to advise that it should precede intense times of prayer: Origen even stated that people should not pray in bed, as it was the scene of their lovemaking. These scruples are widespread in human societies, and among Christians we need only look to the legacy of Jewish Scripture for their inspiration.[43]

Did virgin priesthoods, perhaps, set the Church an example, encouraging Christians to excel the practice of rival pagan cults?[44] In the churches, virginity occupied a different place. Celibacy was not required of priests in the Church, though the demand for it grew in the fourth century. As for eunuch priests, self-castration did not equip Christians for the priesthood: it disqualified them, according to the Council of Nicaea. Whereas the Vestal Virgins were an order, defined by symbolic dress and legal rights and duties, Christian virgins were individual volunteers. Their status was their own choice, not an allotment in childhood. Virgins who were "commanded" by "Diana of the Ephesians" might seem a closer parallel to Christian practice, but they were not virgins for life and it is quite implausible that Christians deliberately copied the practice of pagan cults which themselves they considered demonic. Pagan philosophy was no more of an "origin": the first teachings on virginity emerged from Christians who had had no close contact with its schools. Although an author like Tertullian could cite pagan analogies, they embellished a case and conviction which rested on other supports.[45] Perhaps at an unreflecting level, the first Gentile Christians may have accepted that virginity belonged with the holiest life because they knew the connection already. However, their explicit arguments and their conscious motivation were based on other grounds.

A primary source of this "madness" was Jesus himself in the Gospels. He was remembered for commending "eunuchs for the sake of the kingdom of heaven" (Matthew 19.12), and in Luke's Greek, he seemed to state that followers must "hate" their own wives and children. In the single most influential text (Luke 20.35–36), he stated that Christians who are worthy of the next life "neither marry nor give in marriage: neither can they die any longer . . . they are equal to the angels and are children of God, being children of the Resurrection." It needed only a slight shift of emphasis to refer the absence of marriage to this world, not the next. The texts were supported by Jesus's own example and the singular condition of his mother. Jesus had never married, and although our evidence is far from decisive, it seems at present that Jewish bachelors in their thirties were a rarity in Palestine, except for a minority who were influenced by the sect whom we know in the Dead Sea scrolls: to find other examples, we have to look to the scriptural interpretations of the deeply Hellenized Jew Philo.[46] As for Mary, her virginity was firmly stated in the "Gospel of James," which already existed in the early second century. Childbirth had done nothing to impair it: the doubting Salome had been encouraged by the midwife to insert her hand to test its presence, and had burned her fingers very badly as a result. "Christ and Mary," Jerome later argued, "were both virgins, and thus consecrated the pattern of virginity for both sexes." Indeed, they did: in Rome, between the 360s and 380s, there were stately houses whose female residents, and a few men, lived "in prolonged and rigorous fasting, the wearing of coarse, even squalid clothing, the neglect of personal appearance, the avoidance of personal comforts like baths and, above all, in chastity . . . Their devotion was profoundly Jesus-centred."[47]

As they stood, these Gospel texts gave clear encouragement. Usually, the "eunuchs for the sake of the kingdom" were understood in a broader sense, as referring to those Christians who adopted virginity or practised abstinence during marriage: the "equals of the angels," however, were taken more strictly, meaning Christians in this life, not the next.[48] There was also the famous chapter of St. Paul to the Corinthians (1 Cor. 7). In it, Paul does seem to be answering the questions of Christians in Corinth who were themselves preaching abstinence, even between married couples. While approving their fine ideal, Paul answered more gently that it must be accommodated to each man's capacity, and if people could not observe it, they should marry and not risk extramarital sin. One partner must not deny sex to another who wanted it, but ideally, it was best to be unattached, because "the time is short" and the "End nigh." Paul made it clear that the unmarried state left Christians without cares, and helped them to think of God alone. Marriage, he insisted, was not wrong, but it emerged from his text as an evident second best: Peter, meanwhile, was keeping a wife.[49]

Almost every subsequent author took Paul's remarks out of context and made a strong passage even stronger.[50] "It is good for a man not to touch a woman," he had begun, in answer: the words became his own final view on the subject. These scriptural texts carried great weight. Some Christians, Origen remarked, "practise total chastity, others marry only once because they think that the person who marries, or marries a second time, is damned." If we turn to the Syriac and heretical texts of the Scriptures, we can well understand their error.[51] Tatian's Gospel text was widely used in the Syriac-speaking Church, but it deliberately changed the meaning and order of several Gospel sayings in order to give them an ascetic message. After Jesus's conditional "if thou would be perfect," Tatian added: "take up your Cross and follow me." Similar changes in the text and its order were made by Marcion's followers, whose ethics strongly opposed marriage and remained influential for centuries among Eastern Christians. These dishonesties were clever and of great moment: "we are often surprised," concluded their modern scholar, "in finding how the simplest means were employed to the greatest effect." In Greek, Clement knew heretics who cited Luke 14.20: "I have married a wife and cannot come," in order to show that marriage excluded Christians from the Last Supper. Tertullian's four tracts against remarriage rested heavily on these same deceits: tendentious translation of the Greek New Testament into Latin, distortions of proof texts in St. Paul and mistaken references to a non-existent passage in the Old Testament.[52] As Paul had insisted that remarriage was not wholly wrong, Tertullian had to argue his case against the plain meaning of the texts. His wish proved too strong for the natural sense of Scripture: were his errors unintended, or were they a conscious means to an end? The question is still debated, but surely, most of the "errors" were deliberate, to suit his general case. Meanwhile, the cluster of fictions, pseudo-acts, "revelations," secret "Gospels" and "sayings" of Christ kept up the pressure.

The influence of these texts and their misunderstandings were extremely important for first-class Christians, but it is not a sufficient explanation of their practice. Why did their authors and forgers advance them in the first place? Why did they attract such interest, whereas texts on poverty and the use of riches tended to be weakened and played down?

The question of origins has become more answerable in recent years, though we cannot claim a direct derivation or transfer of ideals. Jesus had connected celibacy with the angelic state, which was attainable after the Resurrection, and had hinted that the End would be easier for those who were unencumbered; Paul, too, linked virginity with the imminent end of the world. In Jesus's lifetime, one sect among the Jews is now known to have taken a strict stance against prevailing sexual ethics.[53] Among the "Covenanters" of the Dead Sea sect, there was opposition to polygamy and to marriage between nieces and uncles, as practised by other Jews. There was also, it seems, an inner core of the sect who practised celibacy, though they were males only. Philo knew of a related community of contemplative Jews outside Alexandria, and from his own experience, he stated that not only men but women among them lived as celibates in a life of prayer and spiritual effort: the women were mostly quite old and lived in segregated quarters. It is plausible to see this group as an offshoot of the Qumran sect whom we know in the Dead Sea scrolls. There may have been other such groups, but already, the imagery which we find in their texts shows a considerable similarity to the imagery of the celibate life in Syriac-speaking Christianity. We cannot know how conscious or direct the connection was, but in these Jewish groups, celibacy was already a model of excellence, among people who stood apart from the Temple's cult. The example had already been set, before Jesus's lifetime.

"Virginity," remarked the Christian Methodius, c. 300, "was a late plant from heaven,"[54] yet before Christians faced Gentile philosophy or the chastity of pagan priesthoods, they were aware of the plant in their own home soil. Their founder's ideals were not those of the Dead Sea sect, but this general model of holiness cannot have been lost on him: the plant's subsequent flowering owed much to his explicit words of support. Did it then coincide with deeper motives? Psychologically, it has been claimed, early Christians set a low value on the material world and thus turned their guilt and frustration inwards against their own bodily desires.[55] Among orthodox Christians, such a total "devaluation of the material universe" is hard to identify, even among the monastic Fathers. Rather, we should begin from the conscious motivation which Christians themselves cited; then we can consider the supporting practicalities and lastly return with caution to a possible unconscious drive.

The esteem for virginity was connected with an optimistic theology which invites us to see the ideal positively.[56] By virginity or chastity Christians aspired to the state of the angels. They reversed the Fall which had occurred through the "error" of Adam and Eve and thus they returned to the sexless state of humanity in the wake of Creation. It made no difference which of the two versions of Creation the authors chose for their purpose. "Male and female created he them," in the first version: clearly, mortals had once united both sexes in one person. Before Eve's creation, in the second version, Adam knew neither sex nor marriage, and the arrival of both events could be blamed on subordinate woman. With sex and marriage, death had entered the world, and when death had again been overcome by the Resurrection, sex and marriage would pass away.

By practising virginity, Christians aspired to reach back before the Fall, to profit from their Redemption and to recover a childlike "simplicity" of heart.[57] Virginity encouraged single-mindedness and dependence on God alone. Whereas sex took a person's mind from God, abstinence, as Cyprian put it, allowed people to "hold themselves free for God and Christ." This praise of simplicity and single-mindedness exalted human achievement by greatly limiting its scope. It denied man's capacity for living in complexity, for pursuing desirable ends which might not be mutually consistent, for enlarging his sympathies and own understanding by engaging in several pursuits at once. To return to a childlike Paradise was to exclude almost everything and understand next to nothing: "single-mindedness" is a dangerous, enfeebling myth. By Christian authors, these human complexities were left out of account. "Virginity," wrote a Latin author, probably Novatian, a Roman Elder, in the early 250s, "makes itself equal to the angels: it excels the angels, because it must struggle against the flesh to master a nature which the angels do not possess. What is virginity, if not a magnificent contemplation of the life to come? Virginity is not the exclusive possession of either sex."[58] Through virginity, a Christian equalled the angels, those rivals whose exact status was still being debated so keenly by the rabbis but whose ultimate judgement by Christians had been assured by words of St. Paul.[59]

It is one thing to deck an ideal with high-flown imagery, another for the pursuers themselves to believe it. Did virgins themselves really strive to rival the angels, as these texts said? The pursuers of virginity did also enjoy an attractive practical freedom.[60] Women escaped the high risk of death in childbirth and avoided the unwanted child whom good Christians could no longer expose or abort. It is very relevant that Christian girls, to judge from a sample of 180 Latin inscriptions, continued to be married at very early ages: a fifth married before the recorded age of fifteen. There were sound reasons for this continuity. As Christian texts taught, early marriage was the antidote to youthful spirits and the hideous sin of premarital sex. We can see, however, from the ancients' medical books what physical problems the marriages of prepubescent girls were capable of causing.

For a Christian girl, therefore, "marriage to Christ" was not such a daunting prospect, compared with a marriage, at the age of fifteen or less, to an older Christian husband: if she happened to be an heiress, her likeliest marriage partner in the Greek world and the East was a close kinsman, a union which Christian rulings judged to be as sinful as murder. Not that every virgin had been able to choose her fate: if parents could select husbands, they could also vow their girls to future virginity in the hope of divine favour. A newly found letter by Augustine addresses the problem of a widowed mother who had made such a vow in a crisis and then found that her daughter grew up to object to it. In return, the mother offered to remain celibate herself: already there had been virgin "mothers, sisters and daughters," in Tertullian's experience.[61] The "virgin mother" was a widow who vowed sexual abstinence after her first marriage. In the churches of North Africa, widows and virgins were seated separately, although the same Greek word could apply to them both. Third-century authors allude to their "promise," made personally to God. The first councils speak of a "pact," perhaps a formal declaration before the Church, but they also show that virgins lapsed, marrying or falling for a man. In Cyprian's view, it was better for these fallen virgins to marry and save themselves from hell. The early councils agreed, punishing virgins' marriages and casual affairs, a sign that a virgin was not expected to set aside her vow as soon as a suitable man appeared.[62]

Unlike pagans, therefore, Christians did aspire to virginity for life. They might, however, time their decision to suit their family's future. In the Syriac-speaking churches, two separate words applied to the abstainer, and the easiest explanation is that one referred to lifelong celibates, the other to married couples who had agreed on abstinence for the rest of their shared lives.[63] Such couples did exist as a central group of "virgins" in each zone of the early Church: Tertullian argued that they deserved greater admiration, on the principle that it was harder to give up a pleasure which you had once known than one which you had never had. Sexless couples were "virgins by virtue," not "virgins by innocence, or happy bliss."[64] Yet they might also be couples who had already had a child and whose interest in sex was declining with age.

These practicalities do not diminish the appeal, to some people, of perfection for perfection's sake. Christians had been freed from the details of the Jewish law and its daily observance, but those who wished for an obvious contest, where merit and failure were clearly marked, could now find it in a battle against their own instincts. The ideal had the simple merit of being difficult, but self-centred. Its practice distinguished Christians from their nearest, thriving relations: the Jews in the synagogues of their cities. In the Syriac-speaking churches, celibacy was a precondition of baptism, and as Christians moved between the two cultural zones the extreme Eastern example may not have been lost on Western perfectionists.

Perfectionism was helped, once again, by aspects of Church life. Widows were frequently encouraged not to remarry, but without a husband, what was to become of them? Tertullian commended the taking of a widow into a man's household in a "spiritual marriage": she would be useful with the housework, he added frankly, and there was no reason why a Christian bachelor should not take several widows at one time. Economically, the Church did aim to support its widows, like the Jewish communities from which this charity was copied: what, though, of the true virgins, girls who never married at all? Unless they came from a Christian family, they faced particular problems. They could not work on their own account in pagan society, because pagans did not reckon with spinsters, except as priestesses, or with women who travelled or worked without any family connections. Virgins did not feature in the list of people whom the Church in Rome was supporting in 251, although Tertullian does hint that virgins were sometimes maintained by fellow Christians and honoured with gifts: in the fourth century, there was a minority view that the tithes of the faithful should go to virgins, among others.[65] These supports were not enough to keep a girl in assured comfort, and virgins could not count on them. Their ideal was easier if they were rich themselves or could look to richer fellow virgins for support. The restrictions on their economic life do help to explain why it is among women that we find the first hints of a celibate household community, c. 300: men could cope more easily on their own. From the texts of

Tertullian and Cyprian, meanwhile, there is no mistaking the riches of many of the virgins in Carthage, girls who could afford their high ideal.[66] Perhaps it often relied on the support of a few richer girls for themselves and their fellow competitors.

In their absence, a virgin would turn to the household of the bishop or one of the clergy: the bishop dispensed the charity of the Church and his duties included hospitality to visitors and those in need. We know that by the 260s the residence of virgins with bishops or priests was familiar, and it was probably much older, as it had acquired a special Greek name.[67] Once again, perfectionism kept uneasy company with the practicalities of life, and in several senses, the relationship went too far. The early councils roundly condemned the random support of virgins in a clerical household and limited the practice to close kin. If we look at Cyprian's letters, we can see why.[68]

In bishoprics near Carthage, young virgins were cohabiting with Christian men, with clerics, even, and deacons, with whom they were said to be sleeping chastely in the same bed. The risks were obvious, and Cyprian was quick to deplore them. When reports of scandals reached him, he ordered that the suspect virgins should be examined internally by midwives to see if they had lived up to their vows. Not that this examination sufficed: they "may have sinned," he recognized, "in parts of the body which can be corrupted, yet cannot be examined," and thus the entire practice of "cohabitation" must cease at once. How old and widespread was it? An answer turns on the difficult words of Paul to the Corinthians, which advised a man to marry (or marry off) "his virgin" if he began to desire her: if he could live with her without desire, thought Paul, well and good.[69] Who were these virgins "of" the earliest Christian men? Daughters and fiancées have been advanced as an answer, yet neither quite fits the advice: Paul cannot have advised fathers to marry their own daughters, nor is he obviously proposing a prolonged sexless "betrothal" between a good Christian and "his" virgin fiancée which was to last for life: "his virgin" is an odd phrase for a fiancée, and there was no reason why such a couple could not have declared a spiritual marriage, formed by their mutual consent. The older view is more likely, that the "virgins" are Christian girls whom Christian men had taken into their households. Perhaps, like Ignatius, Paul was alluding to "virgin widows," cohabitants for the mutual care which Tertullian commended. Widows needed this care, if they were aiming to be good widows and not remarry. It is, however, possible that virgin girls were also included in his category and that Paul, looking to the end of the world, approved a relationship which subsequent councils condemned.

We have no idea of the numbers of these overachievers, but we must allow for these types of refined torture while picturing the personal lives of the early Church membership. From these household companies, one strand in monasticism developed naturally, though the ideal was steeped from the very beginning in the dangers of lapsing, deceit and boasting: Ignatius already warned explicitly against virgins who were too pleased with their achievement, while Tertullian drew attention to the continuing risks of the pagans' "evil eye" as a counter to the virgins' self-congratulation.[70] Was the ideal not inevitably too individual, encouraging this type of personal conceit?

Among pagans, the chastity of the Vestal Virgins was associated with the well-being of the Roman community: if they lapsed, they might provoke the anger of the gods. Among Christians, God's anger was no less lively: did virgins carry the same burden on behalf of their Church as a whole? Before Constantine, at least, it seems that they did not. Virgins were not ranked into a specific order, and their recruitment was voluntary, a matter for "copycat" emulation: young contemporaries, said Tertullian and Cyprian, should urge each other on and compete in its attainment.[71] Neither Cyprian nor Tertullian alludes to fears that lapses by a virgin would pollute the pure Church, and as both had occasion to use this type of argument, we can conclude that, as yet, it was not current. Instead, they advised that sinful virgins should be checked and segregated, "like infected sheep and diseased cattle," but only because they might otherwise corrupt their companions.[72] Before the age of Constantine, we do not meet the idea that virgins were working for the purity and favour of the Church before God. Rather, the relation was reversed: the accepted image of the Christian community tended to support the virgin's own personal ideal.

Christians, Paul taught, were members of the Body of Christ: the image was most unusual and perhaps it had first dawned on him on the road to Damascus, when Christ's words connected persecution of the Christians with persecution of his own person. This Body was deathless and therefore "incorruptible," but also, by the same Greek word, "uncorrupted."[73] The language of uncorrupted holiness was supported by a very rich use of the imagery of marriage. Cold though Christians were in their estimation of earthly marriage, they applied its language keenly to their ideal relationship with God.[74] At baptism, we first learn from Tertullian, the Christian's soul became betrothed to the Holy Spirit. The Church herself had been married off much earlier. Paul had already told the Corinthians that he had "espoused them to one husband that I may present you as a chaste virgin to Christ." The Church was then visualized as a Virgin, the bride of Christ himself, pure, unblemished and "uncorrupted"; her person was visible to the eye of faith in the least likely book of Scripture, the erotic chapters of the Song of Songs. At the same time, this virgin was a Mother, mother of the Christians whom she brought to God.

This imagery grew from Jewish texts, their stress on Israel as God's chosen bride and their equation of idolatry with fornication; by Christians it was applied to individual virgins, to whom it has clung ever since.[75] They were virgin Brides of Christ, their heavenly Bridegroom: "you married Christ," Tertullian reminded them, "to him you gave over your flesh, to him you betrothed your maturity." To lapse, Cyprian taught, was to commit "adultery to Christ." Christ, Jerome explained to a girl, was the supreme "opener" of virgins: "when sleep overtakes you," he wrote to the young Eustochium, "your Lover will come behind the wall, thrust his hand through the opening and caress your belly . . . you will start up, trembling all over, and you will cry, 'I am wounded with love.'"

In pagan Rome, details of dress and legal privilege had implicitly matched the Vestal Virgins with married women; in the Christian churches, the imagery was made explicit in hymns, texts and sermons. Like the Virgin Mary, the Christian virgin was both bride and mother; by the mid-fourth century, this enduring theme of Christian virginity had taken shape.[76] It was tied to a maze of images and associations which had never been asserted in pagan religiousness. Pagan philosophers had never exploited Jerome's imagery of sublimated sexual desire when praising the virginal life. Their praises had never been unanimous, and they were part of a wider discussion of the "natural" and the unnatural, of self-control and the passions, and the ideal of a perfect mastery of soul over body. Christian authors adorned their ideal with quite different colours, with the reversal of the Fall and the attainment of angelic status, with "betrothal to Christ" and multiple rewards in the life to come. Whereas pagan philosophers wrote for their own limited circle and dedicated their essays on marriage and sexual conduct to friends or marital partners, Christian tracts and fictions addressed Christians as a group; Tertullian and Cyprian addressed their texts specifically to female virgins. In the legendary "Acts," too, it was the well-born woman who set the example of Christian chastity to her male partner.

This ideal of virginity cannot be related to an internalization of guilt and frustration: the women who took it up are not known for their "devaluation of the material universe." Rather, we might wonder about the unconscious motives of those who wrote texts and encouraged them: were Christian tracts on virginity expressions of a deep anti-feminism by which the male Church leadership desexed the women whom they did not understand, and perhaps even feared? Women, indeed, were barred from the Church's leadership, and although they could serve as deaconesses, they could not teach.[77] Women had so much to overcome. By Mary, said the second-century theologians, the Fall of Eve had at last been reversed: formerly, woman had been the "gateway of the Devil," though now she could be closed and restored, by maintaining her virginity. It was in those sects which esteemed virginity or single marriage most highly, the Marcionites and the Montanists, that women were allowed to baptize and exorcize, teach and hold office.[78] As virgins, they had reversed the Fall and were freed from the encumbrances of children and marriage: in Tertullian's plan for them, they were left only with life's inescapable burden, the housework. The good Christian woman was told to renounce makeup and jewellery, fine hairstyles and elegant shoes. We can well understand why outsiders were known to complain at the dowdiness of women who became Christians. In the "Acts" of Paul, Thecla offers to cut her hair in a male crop so that she can accompany the Apostle. The scene did conform to reality. The Council of Gangra (340) banned the wearing of male clothing among female ascetics.[79]

Nobody, however, was forcing these women to pass as men. The male bishops at the council tried to stop them, and the simple truth was that women could not wander at large in a male pagan world unless they disguised their sex. By virginity, Christian women did obtain an inverted type of freedom, and it would be wrong to assume that the books of their male authors were meekly obeyed. Some of the livelier virgins wore fine jewellery, smart hairstyles and little or no covering for their heads in church. Behind Tertullian's and Cyprian's essays stand virgins who knew their own minds and were not so readily coaxed into the ideals of a minor female college. They had their own subtle arguments from Scripture, and in Cyprian's Carthage, they had enough property to make rich virgins a recognized problem.

The well-born women who were imagined in the legendary "Acts" found their match, c. 250, in Cyprian's congregations, where virgins wore gold and necklaces, plaited their hair and sported smart earrings.[80] Above all, virginity was urged on men as well as women, on married couples and individuals alike: it did not originate as a means of suppressing "disruptive" women.[81] It was, however, pregnant with its own failure and it is here that the unconscious impinges most obviously on the ideal.

Both men and women, it was widely believed by the doctors, produced seed as a fact of nature. Not only men, but women, too, were thought to be prey to erotic dreams, "fantasies" which caused them to discharge their "seed" while asleep. Try though Christians might, the pursuit of virginity increased these emissions.[82] Virginity frustrated total chastity and a detailed literature then grew round the complications, involving the arts of fasting and dieting in the lives of Christian perfectionists. The less a man ate, the more infrequent his wet dreams were found to be. By extreme fasting, too, a woman could interrupt her menstrual cycle and seem to reverse the "curse of Eve." It was to such an end that this perfectionism gradually drove itself: deliberate fasting and careful control of all thoughts before sleeping, in order to outwit the very nature which the ideal itself was stimulating.

In its origin, motivation and practice, this esteem for virginity was something entirely new. It owed nothing to pagan example or the "mood of the times." It became a distinguishing feature of Christian life, where it created its own forms of organization, and has survived ever since wherever the faith takes root. It inspired its own poetic imagery, using the symbols of whiteness and transposed erotic desire: in a church of the age of Augustine, we would have found the virgins seated apart, screened behind a balustrade of chill white marble.[83] To become a Christian was to live with this constant evidence of the striving for perfection. Nothing in pagan religiousness compared with it.

Striving, however, was not attainment, and the majority did not strive at all. Behind the marble barrier, virgins continued to lapse and misbehave, and beyond it, the sexual revolution remained strictly an ideal. How could a woman remain virtuous when the whole organization of her social existence conspired against her? She had only to go to the public baths, where men and women bathed naked together. "Frequently," Cyprian admitted, "the Church mourns over her virgins as a result; she groans at their scandalous and hateful stories."[84]

If we had to choose one "hateful story" for its splendid impudence, it would have to be the conduct of a Christian priest in Cappadocia displayed during the 370s. So far from secluding his church's virgins, he ran away with them and was later reported at a festival, a pagan one, it seems, at which he showed them off as chorus girls. The spectators admired their routine, and when their parents asked for the girls back again, the priest refused, insulting them.[85]

On a wider front, immediately after Constantine's conversion, the acts of the early councils remind us of real life. By their concerns, they refute the notion that Christian preaching had coincided with some wider retreat in sexual conduct, to which the teachings of pagan philosophers had also attached. They warn, too, against minimizing the importance of sexuality for contemporaries, because we, in our turn, have lived through such a sudden emphasis on it. The early councils are concerned with its endless complications.[86] They presuppose Christians who still turned to slaves and prostitutes, boys and other men's wives, who had sex with animals and even (on one interpretation) encouraged fellow Christians to do the same. Virginity, maybe, gave Christians the status of angels, but others put their own construction on man's lordship over the beasts. Perhaps the best comment on Christian practice was dropped by John Chrysostom, addressing the church in Antioch, c. 390.[87] "There ought to be a wall inside this church," he said, "to keep you apart from the women, but because you refused to have one, our fathers thought it necessary to barricade you off in these wooden partitions . . . I hear from other people that in the past, there was no need even for partitions. In Christ, there was 'neither male nor female . . .' But now it is quite the opposite. The women have learned the manners of the brothel, and the men are no better than maddened stallions."

# 8. Visions and Prophecy

///////////////////////////////////////////////////////////////////////////////////////////

## I

The best Christians did not only aspire to the condition of the angels: they kept company with them. They could expect to see them; they might even hear them. "The angels will come among you," said Jesus in the "Gospel" of Thomas, "like the prophets," the seers who lived in the Christian communities. In the earliest Church, no cleric was proposed for such honours as a visiting prophet. "Whenever you open a jar of wine or oil," advised the early "Teaching" of the Apostles, "take the first fruits and give them to the prophets." There were true and false prophets, but if a true prophet chose to settle in a community, this early text proposed that he should be kept at its expense.[1]

To us, "epiphany" and visionary experience seem a constant part of Christian life, from the first vision of angels at the Tomb to the continuing appearances of the Virgin Mary in the modern Catholic world. Great religious art has sanctioned and ennobled the connection; we can still share contemporaries' shock over Caravaggio when he broke with the tradition and chose a rougher idiom for the contact of angels with men. We are heirs, above all, to the Counter-Reformation, when visions were exploited in high art and literature as an advertisement for faith. The experience is still lively.[2] In the past thirty-five years, the Virgin has made 352 "appearances" which the Catholic Church has accepted as genuine, quite apart from her continuing attendance on non-Catholic Christians in Syria and Egypt. The period since 1900 ranks as a golden age of visions in Spain, for whose equal historians must go back as far as the years from c. 1400 to the 1520s. In 1947, the Virgin appeared, crowned with roses, in Stockport, in the north of England. Since 1981, she is claimed to have appeared more than two thousand times to a small group of adolescent visionaries in the village of Medjugorje in western Yugoslavia. Her most recent site for a visit was a gardener's potting shed in Poland.

Perhaps it is proof of her good taste that she has not been sighted in St. Tropez since October 1954.

Historians of the early Church have tended to overlook that they, too, are living in this golden age of visions: encounters and sightings have not yet occurred in scholarly libraries. Whereas the beneficiaries may take Christian visionary experience for granted, historians can still ask questions of its forms, occurrence and literary expression. Among contemporary pagans, we have studied the enduring sense of the gods' presence: how, if at all, did the Christians' sense differ and did the pagan pattern influence its newer companion in the Gentile world? Visions differ according to the piety of differing groups and periods, for they lie in the beholder's eye: does the emphasis in known early Christian visions differ in kind or degree from pagans'? There is, indeed, one new dimension, affecting all we will study. While pagans could reflect on Homer and the myths, enhancing what they saw in life, Christians looked to past appearances which were recorded in their Scriptures. They were not myth, but "revelation." Among Christians, "epiphanies" thus related to distinctive ideas of authority and heresy: in Spain, "it is apparently because of the activities of the Inquisition that only a handful of visions occurred between 1525 and 1900."[3] Reports of modern "epiphanies" tend to claim that they are something special, even unique. Is there, nonetheless, a continuity of imagery and response, running from Homer, or at least the Gospels, to the current sightings of the Virgin in Herzegovina, pointing to something basic in religious experience which existed before any revealed religion and which Christian stories thinly clothed?

Already in Jesus's own lifetime, epiphany and visionary experience accompanied his baptism and commission and recurred in the Transfiguration. No pagan had been granted such an experience, seeing a change from the human to the supernatural and back to the human. However, the response to it conformed to the familiar pattern. Knowing the awe in such intimacy, the chosen Apostles were scared at what they saw; the mark of transfigured divinity was a radiant white-robed presence, as so often in previous encounters; by an age-old reaction, Peter wanted to build some little monuments to mark the spot. Once again, "not to everyone do the gods appear . . ." As Origen remarked, the degree of the vision depended on the piety of those who saw it. Only three disciples were picked by Jesus for the experience.[4]

It is tempting for a classical historian to turn from the Greek world to the Gospels in Greek and match these continuing patterns directly with pagan antiquity. Homer, however, was unknown territory to the first Christians, and behind their stories lay a third tradition, enhancing their experience and perhaps even influencing their Lord's decisions. The Transfiguration was understood in terms of the epiphanies of Jewish Scripture and apocalyptic texts. In the Old Testament, God was not seen personally. He was manifest in darkness and clouds, voices, thunder and the tremors of nature: these beliefs surface in the scene in John's Gospel when "there came a voice from heaven" to Jesus on Palm Sunday and some of the bystanders "said that it thundered, while others said an angel spake to him."[5] The Jewish prophets' and seers' books of revelation hint at their authors' physical visionary experience: the supernatural was met through sounds and heavenly voices, brilliant light and angelic helpers on earth. These descriptions do resemble the Greeks': the Greek translators of the Old Testament sometimes used language and details which went beyond the Hebrew and increased the similarity.[6] However, Jewish visions were closely attached to history, unlike the pagans' "encounters." The two traditions' similar details do not blur this essential difference of form. It is to the Jewish tradition and its historical depth that the Gospels' "epiphanies" looked.

This tradition helped to express, but itself it did not create, the central Christian experience, an encounter with the risen Lord. In the pagan world, visions of a person soon after death were not uncommon. Epicrates's inscription recorded publicly how his son was still appearing to him in "visitations and visions"; the ancients had their ghost stories, the Roman love poets their reproachful mistresses who appeared from beyond the grave.[7] Christians, however, advanced the extreme claim that the object of their visions had risen physically from the dead. Visions of him abounded. Some ten years later, Paul was taught in Jerusalem that Christ had been "seen" by Peter, then by the Twelve, then by more than five hundred brethren at one time, then by James, then by all the Apostles.[8] Of these copious appearances, only those to Peter and the Twelve can be closely identified with any in the Gospel tradition. Although much has been lost from the visionary record, and what survives is often at variance in its details, the gaps and inconsistencies do not undermine Paul's tradition. To critics, however, some of the stories of visions do seem to have developed as defensive legends, taking forms which countered obvious objections. When the women returned from the Tomb, said Matthew, they saw

Jesus and "came up and took hold of his feet." At other times, he asked them to feel him or to poke fingers into his wounds. They "ate salt with him" and watched while he ate or cooked their breakfast over a campfire. These stories were very explicit and had no pagan counterpart.[9] They countered the criticism that, like so many others, the disciples had merely seen a vision of their dead, beloved companion. The seers were not simply recorded as believers. The events at the Tomb had already occurred, but in Matthew's Gospel, some of the Apostles still doubted, even when Jesus "appeared" and was worshipped: is this unexpected note of doubt historical, or was it contrived to answer the charge that the beholders had been convinced too easily?[10]

Among pagans, no god had been concerned to prove his bodily reality; in Jewish texts, God never appeared in person on earth. In both traditions, divine beings appeared more discreetly, in dreams or in disguises, ways sanctioned by the angels of the Old Testament or the exquisite range of Homeric imagery. It is particularly interesting that some Christian "appearances" did take this form, despite their interest in asserting a bodily Resurrection: they remain, as a result, the most beguiling.[11] In the Garden, Mary Magdalene mistook the Lord for the gardener, until he merely spoke her name: unlike the gods of pagan myths, he revealed himself by no greater power. By the Sea of Tiberias, he conformed to the older pattern: he was only recognized by his disciples when he helped them with their fishing. On the road to the "village called Emmaus" two of the disciples met Jesus, but were denied recognition of him. As he walked beside them, the "stranger in Jerusalem" heard their disappointed hopes, their tale of the empty tomb, the women's vision of the angels. He expounded the Scriptures "concerning himself," until his companions' "hearts burned within them." Entering with them, he shared their room, and when he blessed their bread, their "eyes were opened." They knew him by a characteristic action, whereupon, like a god in Homer, he prepared to depart. The story obeyed old patterns of epiphany, and although there is great art in its invention and telling, there is no mistaking the feeling behind the form.

Nonetheless, like all the "appearances," these stories raise famous problems. Only in Luke are the Apostles told to stay in or near Jerusalem: in the other texts, Jesus orders them to go ahead into Galilee, where the "appearances" occur.[12] How, if at all, can the road to Emmaus fit this discrepancy? The appearance by the sea has been suspected as an addition to John's Gospel: were these stories legends, shaped, perhaps, by Greek traditions of the "gods in disguise" which might have been known to their two Evangelists, the most open to Greek ideas? However, the first Christians had an ample tradition of epiphanies in their own Jewish Scriptures, whose angels had visited mortals "unawares": it was on this angelic pattern that the Gospel authors drew to express their stories of Jesus in disguise. These stories, it so happened, were those which a pagan could best accommodate.

There is an interesting range, too, in the reactions of the beholders. In John's Gospel, those who see are not afraid, not even at first, when beholders traditionally had to be reassured. They know the intimacy, not the awe, in a "Christ epiphany" on earth: they are greeted with their name or the familiar word of peace. In the Jewish Scriptures, however, beholders were as aware as any pagan of the fear and terror when first they saw an angel or a heavenly light, and in the other Gospels, the witnesses conform to this pattern of description. The text of Mark ends abruptly with word of the visitors' fear at the Tomb, a point which has been thought to lay deliberate emphasis on "human inadequacy, lack of understanding and weakness in the presence of supreme divine action."[13]

In many pagan cults, "epiphany" had led to a wish to publicize the event and set up a permanent shrine or priesthood. Stones were vowed in Lydian villages to record the gods' manifest power and appease it by open advertisement; cults of Isis or Serapis led to the publication of the gods' "good deeds" in inscriptions, with rules for worship or texts on the divinity's power. Early Christianity was also born from visionary experience, but it responded to it with special vigour. The experience caused conversion, a faith in only one God, not a favour for one among many. It also fired a sense of mission with which no pagan cult could compete: Christians' visions impressed their seers with the added force of history and fulfilled prophecy. All the while, they seemed to say, this was what had been meant. At Jesus's baptism or Paul's blinding moment of vision, a heavenly voice and an appearance marked the start of a new career. The Apostles' own missionary impulse derived from their visions of the Lord after his death. Although Luke's Gospel implies that he specifically commanded the mission to the Gentiles, Acts' history of the hesitations and subsequent uncertainties makes such a specific vision unlikely.[14] At each turn in the subsequent journeys, however, further words of the Lord, dreams or actions of the Spirit encouraged the major changes of direction. The author, Paul's companion, knew some of them on good authority. In language which was common to pagans and Greek scriptures, angels "stood beside" Christians by night and day. Like gods to pagans, they appeared at moments of tension, in the dark anxieties of prison or on ships during storms at sea.[15] During the first crisis of martyrdom, God and Christ were seen by Stephen, about to die. As among pagans, so among Christians: moments of extreme anxiety brought divinities into view.

Like the gift of the Spirit or the ideal of virginity, this angelic presence was not unknown to some of the Christians' Jewish contemporaries. In the sect whom we know in the Dead Sea scrolls, the presence of angels had already become a lively feature of community life.[16] Also expecting the end of the world, the first Christians had a strong sense of angelic companionship.[17] Here, their belief in "epiphany" differed scarcely from the simple Lystrans'. When Peter escaped from prison and was reported to be at the door in Jerusalem, the Apostles could not believe it: they thought that it must be his angel. In the Epistle to the Hebrews, Christians could be told "to show love unto strangers: for thereby, some have entertained angels unawares." As in Homer or in the Old Testament, so in Christian company there was no knowing who an uninvited guest might be. In the epistles, the Christians' type of experience begins already to be defended and defined against false imitations. The author of "Peter's" second letter assures his readers that he himself witnessed the "glorious appearance in power of Jesus," heard the heavenly voice and was present at the Transfiguration: he was not relying on mere fables. Among the Colossians, by contrast, there were people who trusted other visions, worshipping angels and "vaunting the things which they have crossed the threshold and seen . . ."[18] Whatever their identity, these people were reproached in language which echoed contemporary pagan cult. Paul's word for "crossing the threshold" is the word for visitors who "entered" a temple like Claros's and penetrated its tunnels. The "angels" are perhaps the pagan "angels" who had long been worshipped near Colossae inhabiting its local springs and waterfalls, seats, eventually, of the Christian angel Michael.

Meanwhile, there was much more to the rise of Christianity than met the eye. In Paul's opinion, the birth of Christianity accompanied a huge, invisible upheaval among the powers in heaven.[19] This great supernatural revolution was mirrored in an inner change in every believer, an "illumination of the knowledge of the glory of God in the face of Jesus Christ." Unfamiliar ideas of God's "glory" and a constant inner change in each believer entered the older Greek tradition of a spiritual vision of God.[20] In Paul himself, this spiritual change led to heavenly revelations and a personal tour of the upper heavens.

What, meanwhile, did visionaries see and describe to win such esteem in the early Church? Paul himself nowhere described what he witnessed in heaven, and instead we look nowadays to the trumpeting and thunder of the Book of Revelation and its debt to Jewish apocalyptic texts. Like the Jewish seers, the author left hints of his own experience: he was "in the Spirit"; he saw and he heard; once, he wept, for fear that no one would read out the scroll which he had seen in heaven.[21] There is, however, another text, which stops short of this open door into Paradise. Known as the "Shepherd" of the visionary Hermas, it was set near Cumae in Italy at a date which probably falls in the 90s: it names Clement as a leader of the Church, most probably the church in Rome.[22] This jewel of the non-canonical writings nearly earned a home in the canon of Scripture, and the early papyri continue to show how it found a Christian readership.[23] It has not been so honoured since, as no full Greek text of it survived from antiquity: modern study and scholarship have touched it lightly. Yet its author is the early Christian whom we know best after St. Paul. His use of language conforms to the very gift of simplicity which the angels praised in his person. He combined the symbolic power of a visionary with the self-awareness of a sinner who had learned the errors of his past.

Appreciation of Hermas and his book has not progressed beyond two blind alleys. Like Revelation, his writing has been studied for literary precedents, as if traditional details in small parts of his visions disprove the authenticity of the entire work.[24] Visions, however, are not "fictitious" because they draw on their seer's own learning: like any Apollo, Hermas was only as wise as his personal culture. The contrast between traditional imagery and "original" truth is misplaced. Nor is his book an "artificial allegory."[25] Symbolic allegory was part of the Jewish prophetic tradition and, in turn, it influenced what prophets saw. Hermas combined it with a personal history which ought to be taken at face value.[26] He began his book with a personal statement, like the "confessions" of a witness in a modern Church of the Spirit. He tells us who he was, a slave who had been sold by "the man who brought me up" to one Rhoda, in Rome. He does not tell us what modern scholars have conjectured, that he was a slave from Judaea, a captive, perhaps, in the Jewish revolt. Nor does he mean that he was brought up by God. His wording suggests a foundling who had been brought up, like so many in antiquity, for subsequent sale. In Origen's view (c. 240), he was the Hermas greeted by Paul at the end of his letter to the Romans. Probably, this idea was only a guess, but we cannot altogether exclude it.

"After many years, I recognized Rhoda," he continues, "and I began to love her as a sister." These words are more cryptic, but it emerges that Rhoda had become a Christian, hence the "recognition," and therefore that Hermas "loved her as a sister," the Christian mistress of his household in which he was a Christian slave. Revelations have sometimes been seen as characteristic of the socially distressed and excluded. As a slave, Hermas might seem to qualify, but his visions did not derive from social protest or the notion that the world would be set to rights for those who joined his group. They began from a personal awareness. One day, he had seen Rhoda, his mistress, bathing in the Tiber. As he helped her from the water, he thought how fortunate he would be if only he had such a wife. "I only thought of this, nothing else . . ." His scene must be read as it stands, the contact of a slave with his mistress while she bathed in the Tiber, like many before and since.[27] It might not have been so bad, but Hermas was already a married man.

After a while, he was walking towards Cumae, "praising God's creations, how great and powerful they are." While he walked, he "went into a slumber," or trance, and seemed to be seized by the Spirit, which lifted him beyond rough country to a level plain.[28] There, as he prayed, he seemed to see Rhoda, his owner, who told him "she had been taken up," presumably by death, "to denounce his sins against her." Hermas wondered what these sins could possibly be, until she reminded him of the "wicked desire in his heart." The heavens shut, and Rhoda disappeared: Hermas, not unnaturally, was thrown into alarm. How could he ever propitiate God for his sin? Jesus's words on "adultery of the eye and heart" lie behind this fear, the cause, we might feel, of the entire vision in a "subconscious mind" which was beset by the Christians' new ethic of perfection.[29] He had not seen a dream; he had gone into a trance, imagining a landscape with no exact reference.

While Hermas pondered, he saw a second vision, a white chair, covered with fleeces of white wool, on which sat an elderly lady in white reading a book. "Why so downcast?" she asked. "Hermas the long-suffering, the never-angry, Hermas who is always laughing?" Hermas's sin had been bad, especially from the "master of self-control," but it was not on that account that God was so angry with him. Hermas's household, she explained, lay at the root of the trouble: he should consider his unbelieving children and even the behaviour of his wife. The woman began to speak, saying things which so scared Hermas that, unlike the author of Revelation, he could not bear to listen to them. But she ended on a brighter note, promising the imminent rule of God. While she was speaking, four young men appeared and lifted her by the elbows, whisking her away to "her seat, the East." "She left, looking glad, and on parting, said to me, 'Courage, Hermas . . .'" The men, we may conclude, were the four angels of the inner host of heaven, while the East was the seat of Paradise. If a god departs to the East in a dream, said Artemidorus, it is a propitious sign.[30]

For a year, Hermas published nothing; then, while walking to Cumae at the same season, he was reflecting on his vision and felt himself transported in the Spirit to its former place.[31] On waking, he seemed to pray and see the same woman. When she asked if he could still preach her message, he told her that he could not remember it, but must be given the book to copy it out. The idea of a written copy is conventional in visions, whether pagan, Jewish or Christian: the "book from heaven" guaranteed the message, not least in the seer's own mind.[32] In this case, however, Hermas could not understand the message. Only when he had fasted and prayed for fifteen days was its meaning revealed. As he read it, it told him to reprove his family and to discipline his wife and her lying tongue: "in future, you are to live with her as with a sister." On a matter of more general interest, it promised Christians one last chance. Every Christian who repented wholeheartedly would be forgiven his sins up to the day on which Hermas made known his book, but afterwards, they would have no further opening.[33] As for Hermas himself, his ascetic self-control and simplicity of heart had saved him, despite his "bad dealings and neglect of his family." Somewhere, too, there lurk local problems which we hardly see: "Tell Maximus," said the book, "affliction is coming on you, if you deny a second time . . ." Hermas was ordered to quote to him the words of "Eldad and Modat," a lost prophetic book which reminds us of his wide knowledge of Jewish aprocryphal texts.[34] The "denial," perhaps, was denial during persecution, possibly the persecution in Rome in the early 90s.

Until now, Hermas had been victim of a fascinating error. He believed that he had been seeing the Sibyl, the deathless prophet of pagan and Jewish tradition, one of whose pagan seats, after all, was at nearby Cumae. This mistake was corrected that same night. A "beautiful young man" explained in a dream that the woman was the Church and that she looked so old because she had existed since Creation. Thereupon, she appeared again, and told Hermas to send two copies of his writing, one to Clement, presumably the bishop of Rome, the other to Grapte, who could teach it to the widows and orphans. He must also read it out "to this city" in the presence of the presiding Elders. We do not know where this city was, but it is proof of Hermas's early date that as yet it did not have a single recognized bishop.

No Christian visionary was ever more loyal to the Church than Hermas.[35] He thought that he met its figure; he learned that the Church had existed since Creation; he revealed his visions to its proper authorities. Hermas saw and heard revelations for the sake of the community through which he had his visionary gifts: no pagan prophet or dreamer had ever worked in such a context. The elderly Church promised him a further vision, and after constant fasting, Hermas prayed to the Lord for its fulfilment. That night, the woman "was seen" again, and after rebuking his importunity, she agreed to meet him at his chosen place, "a remote and beautiful field." When Hermas arrived, he first saw an ivory bench, clothed with linen rugs and cushions. Like so many subjects of a divine "epiphany," Hermas began to take fright. Being Christian, he confessed his sins repeatedly to God.

Soon the Church's figure appeared, touched him and dismissed her six angelic companions. She asked Hermas to sit on the bench beside her, and when he replied that only Elders should sit there, she corrected him and seated him on her left hand: the right hand, she said, was reserved for Christian martyrs. What does this vision say for Hermas's own status? He was not himself an Elder, yet the Elders, not the bishops, were the group to whom he deferred. As a virtuous Christian perfectionist, he ranked next after the martyrs, but his rank was not based on any title or office: any penitent Christian, it seems, could aspire to the same honour. The woman raised her shining staff and showed him the vision she had promised. On a surface of water, it seemed, a Tower was being constructed from stones of varying quality. The Tower, she explained, was the Church, whose building was nearing completion, and the stones were the varying classes of Christian sinners and penitents.[36] Some of them were unusable in the Tower's masonry, and soon the building would cease. Meanwhile, Hermas had good news: he need not ask for forgiveness, but for righteousness, in which his family could share.

Hermas, the Church remarked, was not especially worthy of these visions, for there were others who were more deserving. He could, however, publish them to help the wavering Christians, those "in two minds."[37] His superiors, evidently, were the martyrs whose visions, as we shall see, were a recognized gift: the Church's remark is one of their earliest witnesses. As she left, she told Hermas to publish his vision when three days had passed. She then warned Christians against "eating" excessively while others went hungry: the reference, surely, was to spiritual food. As a parting shot, she denounced the leaders of the churches and those who took the most honoured seats; they were like sorcerers, she said, with poison in their hearts. Then she disappeared, only to return by night and tell Hermas to fast rigorously in order to find answers to his further questions.

That night, a young man appeared and explained the continuing changes in the Church's person. Each time Hermas had seen her, she seemed to be younger and fairer: the reason, the angel stated, was that Hermas himself had improved and progressed. Once again, we meet the theory that visions vary with their seer's capacity. As if to prove it, a final vision followed, in which Hermas escaped from a fearsome monster and the Church appeared as a fair virgin. The monster was a symbol of future "affliction," the torment, it seems, which awaited all Christian sinners at the imminent end of the world.[38] Saved by his faith, Hermas then returned home. There was, however, to be no respite. After praying and taking his seat on a couch, he saw a figure, "glorious to behold," who was dressed in the garb of a shepherd. The figure explained that he was the angel of repentance, who had been sent to dwell with Hermas for the rest of his days.

Can we really believe the sequence of these visions, the chair and the angels, the rendezvous in the country, the Church and these visiting strangers? Hermas was not raised up to heaven: he sought most of his visions by prayer and fasting and understood them by long and careful dialogues. Each of his visions arose out of the one which he had seen before, but their connection is no argument against their reality: Jewish prophets sometimes began their visions by pondering a book, and Hermas began his by pondering the visions which he had had previously. His fasting is particularly noticeable.[39] In pagan cult, fasting had been a preliminary to dreams of the god, prayers, spells and oracular statements at Didyma or Claros; in the Old Testament, the example of Daniel was often cited. Modern studies of prolonged fasting stress their subjects' apathy and irritability, introversion, emotional instability and marked lowering of sexual interest: if Hermas continued to take very little food, he would, on the Christians' own reckoning, find life with his wife "as a sister" more easily attainable. In Hermas's own view, fasting was an ally for prayer and prompted God to attend to its requests: we will have to explore this conscious motive, but it does not exclude the unconscious psychological effects which we, too, recognize. Here, Hermas's pattern of vision also owes an obvious debt to Jewish apocalyptic texts. Jewish seers, too, were enjoined by God to fast: in the "apocalypse of Esdras" the seer is told to go to a meadow and eat nothing but the flowers of the field. The book, the angels, the sensations of fear and trance are all traceable to apocalyptic texts, but as we shall see, they do not explain the particular, personal quality of Hermas's visionary odyssey.

The arrival of the angel of repentance marked a new phase in Hermas's revelations. It is a commonplace in early Christian history to distinguish spiritual experience from moral obedience. Hermas, however, united both. The angel began by instructing him in twelve new commandments. The commandments were not rules of thumb, and it is a travesty to call Hermas a "formalist, to the backbone."[40] The new commandments urged virtues, not mere obedience. They enjoined simplicity and a pure heart, faith and self-control: they were discussed between the two of them in terms which bring Christians' peculiar problems to the fore. "Sir," begged Hermas, "allow me to ask you a few more questions . . . If a man has a Christian wife who commits adultery, does he sin if he continues to live with her?"[41] He must divorce her, said the angel, at once: angels agreed with a hated law of the Emperor Augustus. What if he then remarried, or if a widowed Christian married a second time? It took an angel to define the priorities in an ethic whose complexities were already bothering the Church.

One by one, the commandments took shape. They repeated the teaching on the last repentance; they described the continuing presence of two conflicting angels in Christians' lives; when Hermas became aware of the lies in his sinful past, he wept bitterly, like that other seer, the author of Revelation. The idea of these "commandments" owes an obvious debt to contemporary Jewish teaching: in this form, they helped Christians who wished to live by clearer rules. When their sequence finished, Hermas was granted a series of symbolic visions in each of which the angel explained problems. Once, the angel found Hermas fasting, but belittled this routine practice: abstinence must be joined, he said, with fasting from evil desires and with the gift to the poor of the goods which would otherwise have been consumed.[42] The advice is frequent in later Christian texts, giving a new context for the fasting which assisted "visions."

In one such vision Hermas seemed to be travelling on a plain where angelic shepherds were guarding sheep. One angel stood forward with a knotted staff and a huge whip, and whenever a sheep was frisking and well fed, he would take it and put it down a sheer ravine, thick with thorns and briars. "And his look was very sour, and I was afraid of him because of it." This angel, the angel of punishment, was promptly commissioned to dwell with Hermas and chasten him for his household's sins. "Sir," he asked, "the glorious angel is embittered with my household, but what have I myself done wrong?" "They cannot be afflicted," said the shepherd, "unless you, the head of the house, are afflicted too." This hideous note of collective punishment was alien to the company which pagans recorded with their gods in dreams.[43]

Other parables taught Hermas other lessons, how the rich should support the poor in a Church and how the poor should intercede for the rich man's soul, a balance between social classes which was to persist for centuries in Christian teaching.[44] Finally, the angel explained that Hermas had progressed so very far in virtue that he could now see his visions directly: their source throughout had been the Holy Spirit. To complete his earlier revelation, he was whisked in the Spirit to Arcadia, a fascinating choice of location for revelations in a shepherd's company.[45] Arcadia was the landscape for Virgil's pastoral poetry: had Hermas known of it, or perhaps its long-lost source? Amid twelve mountains, he saw a huge white rock on which six men were handing stones to an attendant troupe of virgins. They, in turn, were building the Tower. While Hermas watched, he learned the fate of the stones, until a huge inspector came to examine the progress. The inspector ordered the shepherd to sort the Tower's materials: Hermas was left to spend the night in the company of the virgins, the holy powers and virtues of God. He spent it, he wrote, as "their brother, not their husband . . . and they began to kiss me and embrace me, to lead me round the Tower and to sport with me. And I seemed to become a younger man . . ."

As for a virgin, so for a visionary: Christian images of discipline and correction had this powerful obverse, a stress on simplicity and a return to childlike innocence, man's state in Paradise before the Fall. Among pagans, said Artemidorus, it was auspicious for an old man to dream of becoming slightly younger, but to dream of becoming a child meant death.[46] In Christian company, it signified something else, a return to a childlike state of "single-mindedness." After a night of prayer in the virgins' company, Hermas discovered more details of the building and returned home. The Church, he had seen, was almost finished, but completion was being delayed to give Christians a final chance to repent. Then his angel bade the shepherd and the virgins leave him, having promised that he would prosper if he continued blamelessly in their company. Hermas's book was written and the angel rose from the couch. "He told me, however, he would send the shepherd and the virgins back once again to my house . . ."[47]

Perhaps this text is its own best commentary, an insight like none other into the mind of a visionary in the earliest Church. How, though, should Hermas be placed? His personal history cannot be turned into allegory, as if his "household" was really a Church which he led.[48] He makes it plain that he himself was not a dignitary, an Elder or a bishop. Though married, he practised "self-control" and was known for his exertions. He prayed and fasted, enlisting two potent allies of visionary gifts. Although he nowhere calls himself a prophet and refers throughout to his simple frailty, his visionary odyssey is surely the work of a "prophet" as the early Church orders knew one: a Christian, gifted with the Spirit, who deserved the community's highest respect. New teaching on Christian repentance could only be given through the Spirit's authority: nothing less had the power to "bind or loose." While Hermas was sending his book to the churches, it is apt that a fellow Christian visionary, Elchesai, was publishing a similar message of one last repentance to Christians in the East. The angels whom he saw in Mesopotamia were larger and more awesome, but in East and West, the setting was the same.[49] By c. 112, a lifetime after Jesus's death, the churches were so beset with sin that they needed a chance to wipe the slate clean and begin all over again.

Hermas's visions did not only draw on the tradition of Jewish angels and prophetic imagery. They were distinctive because they owed something, too, to the imagery of divination and pagan inquiry, in which a man, whether Jew or pagan, could ask the gods and angels for advice.[50] It is this tradition which explains details of his visions of the Church. The chair and the ivory bench, their coverlets, the sitting position, the use of a staff, the words of greeting and inquiry: these features can all be matched with the patterns of inquiry which we find in pagan texts of oracular spells and in questions to an attendant divinity. In one of his visions, Hermas was shown a false, proud diviner, seated on a bench and misleading his Christian clients. Plainly, these consultations were known to him, as to Jews and perhaps also to fellow Christians versed in the "neutral technology" of prophecy. This pattern of inquiry gives Hermas's visions their particular quality and tone. They are not awesome glimpses of lightning and destruction, falling demons and punishments in hell. They pose personal questions and receive answers suited to their questioner's spiritual merit.

Like the clients at ancient oracles, Hermas does not only know the terror of a divine encounter: he is also rebuked by the Church and his angel for cheekily trying to know too much. He could only know what was good for him and he could only see what he was good enough to behold. His visions were so clear because they rested on near-perfect piety, on fasting and exceptional virtue, prayer and a marriage which was to continue without sex. Only then could the Spirit reveal answers to a Christian's questions and cross the wide abyss between God and sinful man. Hermas's visions were beset with Christian hopes and fears, sin and "double-mindedness,"[51] punishment and forgiveness, childlike virginity and adultery, social distinctions and the imminent end of the world. They are a printout of Christianity's impact on a sensitive Christian soul. If they share some of their origins with pagans' dreams and Jewish visions, it is because the sources of these experiences are constant in human nature: Hermas prayed and fasted intently. He then saw the Sibyl, the Church and the angels whom his own culture and training disposed him to see in a trance.

The teaching on one further chance of repentance was enough to ensure Hermas a lasting readership in the Church. After him, we continue to hear of prophets and prophetesses in the Christian churches: in the 170s, pagan critics knew of their high esteem.[52] None, however, has left such a text, perhaps because none spoke with authority on a point of such general importance. Perhaps, too, none had Hermas's particular genius or winning way with words. The idea of questioning God and the angels gives way in our evidence to texts of pure revelation. Only Hermas drew on the ancient imagery of divination and met his heavenly companions with more curiosity than fear; the imagery occurs in no other text, except for a curious passage in the legendary "Acts" of Thomas. Already, Hermas knew there were "true" and false prophets: by c. 200, the "true" prophet had been more closely defined and there was less scope for Hermas's type of writing.

What, then, was the sequel to this exceptional intimacy with the divine? We can approach it through the same categories which we used for pagans and which are as old as the history of epiphany: the encounter with a stranger in disguise; the unseen presence; the dream; the waking vision. Then we can consider how Christians responded to the idea of oracular questions and inspired answers, the classic conjunction of "canny persons with uncanny places."

After Hermas, the "close encounter" with a heavenly stranger fades from the literary record. Through Scripture, Christians lived with memories of angels on earth in the past, like the divine "spies" who stalked the myths and poems of their pagan neighbours. Yet nobody encountered Christ in disguise, after the scenes at Emmaus: nobody recorded their own "entertainment of angels, unawares." There were sound theological reasons. Among Christian authors, the very word "epiphany" was referred to a future event, Christ's promised Second Coming. What need did he have to appear meanwhile? God's Son, said Athanasius, had taken a human form as part of God's plan for Redemption: if God wished "only" to appear, he could have revealed himself in other ways.[53]

While Christians awaited the last act of history, they could not expect to see the principal actor in the intervening scenes. As the drama was fixed, there was no cause to send warners and watchers to study and alter its direction. Since the Ascension, Paul and Stephen had seen Christ in heaven, a "Christophany," as modern theology calls it, not a "Christ epiphany" on earth. For the time being, Christ's own person had withdrawn. Meanwhile, Christian authors turned back to the past epiphanies and angelic visitations in the Jews' Old Testament. By the oak tree at Mambre or the Burning Bush, Christ was detected in the episodes of ancient Scripture.[54] Epiphany gained a longer Christian prehistory, while believers waited in an interlude before its final episode.

Among pagans, the gods still "stood beside" mortals and "held their hand" over individuals and their cities; among Christians, meanwhile, an unseen presence was a guide and guardian.[55] Each church had its angelic protector, while Matthew's Gospel had sanctioned the idea of a guardian angel, watching over every child: on the small Aegean island of Thera (Santorini), inscribed epitaphs honour the "angel" of this or that person and are best understood as Christian texts, dating from the third century onwards. An "angel of baptism" attended each Christian's immersion, although it is too simple to claim that afterwards each baptized person was freed from the conflicts between heavenly powers.[56] Hermas learned otherwise, and his angels of punishment and repentance are a reminder that Christian angels, too, had harsher, opposing aspects; the richest exponent of guardian angels, Origen, makes it clear that a conflict between good and bad angels continued during every Christian's life. Meanwhile, for every angel, there was the potential presence of a demon, equally impenetrable to mortal eyes.

"You stand before the heavenly Jerusalem and its mighty host of angels; you are in the presence of the joyous assembly," the author of the Epistle to the Hebrews had written. From the start, Christian worship on earth matched angelic worship in heaven, and the one, thought Origen, attended the other.[57] Just as gods "stood by" the meetings of a city, so angels, thought Origen, attended church with each of the Christians whom they guarded. They took pleasure in the reading of Scripture, although Christians were too sinful to see them with their own eyes. Before Constantine, therefore, the idea of a double Church, human and angelic, was known, although it was not emphasized in Christian ritual. As yet, there was no large Christian architecture, no art to enhance this idea of "presence" at a service. Rather, Christians looked forward to the final "epiphany" of Christ; as yet, there was no January festival of Epiphany in the Church's year.[58]

At night, as Artemidorus recorded, the pagan gods used to cross the open frontier between their world and the world of men. Did Christians also dream freely of their God and his angels as the nightly companions in their sleep? Without a Christian Artemidorus, the question is hardly answerable, but enough survives in written literature to suggest a certain difference. Christians were especially wary of the validity of dreaming.[59] Not only did they share pagans' awareness that daytime anxieties and physical discomforts could cause dreams of no significance. To it, they added a keen sense of the demonic.[60] How could pagans be seeing true dreams, or dreams of their "gods" and statues, unless the demons were deceiving them at night? Sexual dreams were unavoidable facts of life, but Christians ascribed them, too, to demonic intervention: if demons inspired these two frequent types of dream, might they not cause every other type of appealing vision? Inconsequential dreaming had made good business for Artemidorus and his art. Among Christians, it was classed as demonic, not significant, and its unformed and unconnected images were dismissed as rubbish. They were printouts from the demons' system, that pathetic "information bank" which could confuse or rearrange, but not create.[61] To search for meaning in these incoherent fragments was to turn away from Jesus's words against attempts to "know the times and seasons." Dream interpreters, therefore, were banned from Christian baptism.[62] For Christians, the only true dream became the clear dream whose symbolism was thinly grounded in Scripture. In these significant dreams, the characters spoke a direct message, warning, correcting and disciplining.[63] The dreamers themselves shared in the action, obeying a heavenly command, to "come" or "follow me."[64] No interpretation was needed. Following their Latin translations of Scripture, Christians in North Africa described significant dreams and visions as a "showing" (ostensio). Unlike pagans, they worked with an ideal of "revelation," whose characteristic, said Augustine, was its clarity, appealing to the mind as well as the eye.[65]

This difference of emphasis had consequences for Christians' inner psychology. By several pagan philosophies, the soul had been credited with a natural power of divination. As man's reason and body were at rest, the soul retired into itself and apprehended truths of the higher realm, the "home" from which its immortal nature had descended.[66] Christians reduced this natural power to a vague and imitative striving; in it, Tertullian said, the soul acted out a mime, like a driver or gladiator gesticulating without his equipment. In most Christians' view, the soul retained no pre-existent knowledge.[67] The only significant dreams were those which God sent through angels, yet here, too, Christian dreaming had a quality of its own. Unlike a pagan's, it lacked the ubiquitous aid of art.

Nobody remembered what Jesus had looked like.[68] Citing Isaiah, one wing of Christian opinion argued that he had chosen a mean and ugly human form. By c. 200, he was being shown on early Christian sarcophagi in a stereotyped pagan image, as a philosopher teaching among his pupils or as a shepherd bearing sheep from his flock. To

Christians, the pupils were "disciples," and the flock, the Good Shepherd's. These conventional images had little of the impact of a great pagan cult statue or portrait. The question of early Christian sculpture has been reopened by a group of small figures, presently ascribed to an eastern Greek workshop of the mid- to late third century A.D.: in them, scenes from the story of Jonah keep company with a group of elegant portrait busts and suggest that a cultured Christian had owned the series.[69] Jonah's life was a favourite subject for early Christian wall paintings in the underground catacombs in Rome; it symbolized God's power to save and grant repose. These small sculptures are not portraits or icons. Like the type of the Good Shepherd or the scenes in the tomb paintings, they are symbolic scriptural works, expressing more than they show.

As these statuettes remind us, Christian bishops and authors did not speak for everyone when they opposed all representational art.[70] The wording of their views suggests that other Christians thought differently, putting paintings on their church walls and unsuitable scenes on their signet rings. But, however much we search for this "early Christian art" and ponder the meanings of the crude paintings in the Roman catacombs, we cannot bridge the gap between its schematized, symbolic style and the artistic patronage of the upper classes in the pagan cities, which multiplied the store of fine pagan statuary and figure portraits of the gods. Only one group of early Christians, the heretical Carpocratians, are known to have owned portraits of Christ: significantly, they and similar sects were accused of courting spurious dreams. In a famous scene, the "Acts of John" (c. 300) told how a pagan convert had attempted to paint John's portrait in Ephesus, but the Apostle had denounced him for daring to perpetuate his form in the material world. To paint an Apostle was as offensive as to photograph an early American Indian chief. The exceptions are very modest. By the mid-third century, variable figures of Christ, with and without a beard, could be seen in wall paintings of the house-church in Dura; in Rome, the souvenir trade had started promptly: small pottery objects were available, c. 250, stamped with portraits of Peter and Paul.[71] By contrast, the pagan cities were crammed with forests of statuary whose powers and imaginative impact were undeniable. Christians accepted their supernatural effects, but referred them to the demons. These creatures lurked beneath the pedestals in forms which only a pious eye could see.

Early Christian art was based firmly on Scripture and used a densely compressed symbolism which expressed much more than it represented. It has been described as "signitive" art and to see its works or dream of them was not to exhaust their essential message.[72] This "signitive" style meets us elsewhere in early Christian life, in epitaphs, prayers and especially in the early hymns.[73] Christians sang and listened to texts: they did not gaze on idealized forms of their God. Just as Jewish visionaries had started their visions while pondering and reading texts of Scripture, so Augustine was finally converted by reading a biblical text: the father of Gregory of Nazianzus was won by dreaming that he was singing a sentence from the Psalms.[74] The effects show in the very style of Christian visionary literature. The absence of religious sculpture was supported by the Jews' acceptance that God could never be comprehended by mortal eyes: the result, said the Book of Exodus, would be death. Not until Origen did Christian theology begin to dwell on a possible mystical union between Christians and their God. Even then, the achievement was exceptional, requiring a long training of soul and body, and it lacked a sharp visual outline. It depended on that lasting faculty, diffused through Platonist philosophy, not the physical eye but the "eye of the soul."[75]

In the Book of Revelation we can see the consequences for a Christian's imagination.[76] Like Hermas, the author does not see God as a person. God appears in the abstract, like a precious stone, blazing in brilliant red and white. Only in the "new heaven and new earth" is he visible directly: we may aspire, Irenaeus believed, to the vision of God, but only at the end of this world. As for Christ, he is revealed symbolically, as "one like a son of man." He is imagined through his supernatural attributes, not through features fixed in art. The visions draw heavily on impressions which are "not visual so much as auditory and dynamic." The seer understands what he sees through the messages which he hears: it is the "new song" of the host in heaven which enables him to understand the puzzling Lamb whom he has seen; a voice has to identify the multitudes who are dressed in white and explain the avenging angels on horseback who are to butcher a third of the human race. These figures are presented through similes and symbols, not through the clear definition of art. Christ, the Lamb, appears with seven horns, while his seven eyes shine like fire and his feet like burnished bronze: "altogether," as Jung concluded, "it must have looked pretty awful."

This imagery of the supernatural has prompted a powerful contrast between the minds of Jews and of Greeks.[77] To the Greeks, it is said, divine beauty was visual and harmonious, whereas Jews conceived it through sound and voice and the dynamic effects of light and colour. On one side, we have seen, the contrast is posed too sharply. In Greece, too, the gods were heard as well as seen, on the stage, in oracles, in statues. Greeks, too, could picture a present divinity in terms of the play of light. On the other side, however, the contrast is just, a fact not so much about Semitic language and its structure, for language can bend if it must, as about the absence of anything remotely comparable to the Greeks' fine art of their gods.

Behind Revelation, as behind Hermas, stretched a different source, the conventions of late Jewish visionary literature from Daniel and Enoch to the apocalypses and heavenly tours which we meet in the books of Baruch and Ezra.[78] In Revelation, the author's vision is strongly conditioned by what he has heard and read: what, though, of known Christian dreams which were not so dependent? In the absence of art, they tend to vaguer contours, to God as an elderly "Father" or Christ as a radiant young man.[79] The figure of Christ was capable of immense height and brightness, wearing a youthful smile and robes of intense light. These contours were shared by pagan dreams of divinity: are they, therefore, a lasting core of experience, "archetypes," in Jung's view, embedded in the human mind? There is no need to believe this fancy. If a person began to picture God, immense size and radiance and beauty were obvious "superhuman" features by which to imagine his presence. As these visions were written down, the tradition strengthened the pattern, influencing the dreams which others then saw.

Although Christian dreams lacked the stimulus of art, they did enlist a powerful ally: hunger.[80] We have seen how Hermas began by fasting and praying for days, even a whole fortnight. Here, there was ample scope for the overachiever. Early Christians fasted weekly on Wednesdays and Fridays, although the Western Church then added a Saturday fast, to the East's eventual disgust. The length of a day's fast varied, allowing overachievers to "superimpose," as the practice was known, and continue without food until cockcrow. Fasting preceded baptism and accompanied all prolonged penance: until c. 250, and perhaps later, Christians' one total fast ran from Good Friday to Easter morning. Yet the history of Christian fasting was a history of gradual extension. Very soon, there were overachievers who fasted throughout Holy Week: a forty-day fast during Lent was not the early Apostolic practice which later churchmen suggested.[81]

In the pagan world, fasting was deliberately practised at cults and oracles to elicit significant dreams and "receive" the gods' inspiration. Even if people did not fast, what they ate was known to matter: pagan doctors were well aware that a man's dreams and psychic experience were livelier if his diet was drier. Prolonged "dry fasts" were also observed by Christian groups who placed particular trust in continuing visions and prophecies: as for total fasting, Christians' practice was grounded in other motives.[82] They did not wish it to be confused with the positive aims of pagans, as if God was to be "seen" by deliberate acts of physical denial. Instead, they claimed that fasting was an act of humiliation which abased a believer and assisted his prayers before God. This motive encouraged prolonged observance: the more a Christian fasted, the more he humbled himself before his Lord. Some authors also insisted that a true fast should be accompanied by abstention from every wicked thought or deed: long fasting became a spiritual exercise whose visionary sequel might be a gift of God's grace. Believing in man's sinful nature and "humility," Christian perfectionists starved their bodies and directly provoked their powers of vision. To the same end, chastity was a magnet. As at the pagan shrines, God was particularly drawn to virgins and to celibates like Hermas. Among older women, he favoured dependent widows.

As fasting and celibacy assisted visions, it is not surprising that we read most about "epiphanies" in the apocryphal texts of over-achievers, especially the "Acts" of Apostles which preach the value of sexless living.[83] In these texts, they fall into two broad groups. Some of the visions motivate turns in the story, and perhaps they are merely based on the genuine Acts, their model. There are others, however, which occur at particular moments, after prayer or fasting or at baptism. Here, their descriptions seem more personal. An angelic presence did attend baptism, an event which also took place after long fasting and confessions. In the Eastern churches, it occurred at night by torchlight, for candidates who were celibate. In the "Acts," baptisms are said to be accompanied by heavenly voices and by visions of light or of Christ himself. In the "Acts" of Peter, one such baptismal vision suggests the author's own experience. If, like his characters, he had fasted systematically, he was probably familiar with what he described.

Two related themes do suggest a degree of personal awareness in their authors. When Christ is seen by characters in these stories, his appearance varies according to the nature of his beholders. From

Homer to Hermas, the theme, by now, is familiar. If nobody knew what Christ looked like, some such variation was anyway a fact of Christian experience. At other times, Christ's figure varies in itself, being seen in opposing shapes and stages, now great, now small, now an old man, a youth or a child. In modern visions, the small size of a saint or the Virgin Mary has been related to the smallness of the particular icon or image which influenced the seer's eye.[84] In an age of few, or no, images, this variability had a different sense. In the "Acts" of John, the Apostle explains how Jesus had appeared to James as a child, then as a youth, but to himself, as a handsome, balding figure with a thick beard. "Never at any time did I see his eyes closed, but always open . . .": we may recall the Egyptian, in Heliodorus's novel, and his views on the "unblinking" eyes of gods. Sometimes, Jesus's body had felt hard, sometimes soft: John could not always feel it, or see its footprints.

This changeable type of vision was connected to John's knowledge of the Transfiguration, an event which seems to have attracted visionary Christians' particular interest. It is exactly this episode which introduces a notable scene in the "Acts" of Peter.[85] In Rome, an audience of "women and widows" are listening to this very text, when Peter stands forward and begins to expound it. He describes how, at the time, "each saw, as he was able" and how God, meanwhile, is a union of opposites, "now great, now small, now young, now old . . ." "At the ninth hour," the blind widows in his audience ask him to heal them, and after his prayers, are rewarded with an indescribable light. They regain their sight, and each describes what she has seen: some saw a handsome old man; others, a young one; others, a small child. Peter then praised God, "who is constant and greater than our thoughts . . ."

This variability occurs in other religious traditions and has been connected with the problem of God's relationship to time and change: like eternity, he unites all contradictory times and ages in one and the same person, whereas "many-shaped Satan" changes merely from one beast to another.[86] Here, the point may only be that God's power transcends opposing qualities: the perception may be grounded in the experience of select Christian readers.[87] The "Gospel of Philip," a third-century work, also describes how Jesus varied in size, according to the varying eye of those who beheld him.[88] It then reminds its readers: "You saw the Spirit, you became Spirit; you saw Christ, you became Christ . . ." Perhaps they enjoyed this varied experience at baptism: the "secret teaching" of John, a second-century work, also agreed that Christ's experience was multiform. Although Christian authors agreed that the nature of a vision varied with the moral capacity of the beholder, unorthodox sects, it seems, did experience rather more, in contrast to the churches' low view of their moral worth.

Their texts, however, observed careful limits. They did not write up their visions in their own person or cast them as dialogues between themselves and a prophetic "other half." They ascribed them to figures whom the Gospels had sanctioned: Peter and Paul, James and John, prophetic Philip and Mary Magdalene, who had sighted Christ in the Garden. It is wrong, then, to claim that the early Gospel tradition had deliberately narrowed the number and type of Christ's "appearances" in order to exclude this type of heresy.[89] No such exclusion was possible: heretics attached their texts to the few visionary figures whom the Gospels had to include. Heretics, too, accepted that "revelation" needed a higher authority than personal experience. If their own visionary life showed through the text, essentially it was passed off as what the Apostles had seen but the Gospels never revealed.

In the orthodox Church, there was no concern, initially, to put up personal monuments to dreams or visions. There was also no continuing connection between dreams and new missionary ventures. It was not that dreams were no longer an impulse to conversion: Origen claimed to know many people like Paul, whom a vision had turned from hatred of the Gospel to a willingness to die for it.[90] Inside the Church, however, continuing dreams were not worthy of special credence or commemoration. By c. 400, Christians in North Africa were indeed putting up altars and memorials to martyrs as seen in a dream or vision: their bishops then ordered that these monuments should be overthrown, unless people resisted their demolition, and that altars should not be spread about on the authority of dreams or "empty revelations."[91] In the earlier Church, the cult of the martyrs had been essentially a matter for the community as a whole. Visionaries belonged to a wider group which awaited God's return. They spoke on its behalf, and in this expectant company there was no strong reason to put up a monument to an individual's personal experience. The reticence extended to dreams of innovation or missionary significance. In early modern Europe, a familiar type of dream revealed "miraculous statues" in a remote place and encouraged Christian missions and piety in distant rural areas. In the early Church, no dreams encouraged the founding of new house-churches or missions into the countryside. There are no known missionary visions in the orthodox Church between the age of the Apostles and Constantine. This silence in our evidence connects with the churches' relative lack of missionary endeavour. It gains significance against what we know of the heretics: visions and dreams marked a turning point for them, the persistent founders of "new" groups. The greatest heretical missionary, Mani, was propelled by dreams and visions, as we shall see, and by his sense of a constant angelic presence.

The apocryphal visionary texts and this connection between visions and heretical missions can only have encouraged the churches' opposition to casual visionary claims. We can follow their concern from debates, once again, in the long Christian novel *The Recognitions*, and the accompanying homilies, ascribed to "Clement." At length in these fictions, St. Peter inveighs against "mendacious" dreaming, refuting the heretic Simon Magus, who set visions above mere reality.[92] In a dream, Peter argues, we cannot use reason or ask a question aptly. How, then, are we ever to know if a dream is from God or a demon? As unrighteous men see "true" dreams too, we cannot simply judge by the moral nature of the dreamer.

These texts derive from Jewish-Christian circles and were written, most probably, c. 200. Their emphasis falls on two aspects of wider significance, which many Christians accepted. The vision of God was the gift of the "pure in heart," yet who could be so pure as to attain it since the Apostolic age? Pagans, too, had connected visions with a virtuous nature, from Homer to the Neoplatonist texts: Christians had greatly raised the threshold for human virtue by their views on sin and perfection. Faith in "appearances," meanwhile, was the faith of Simon Magus, the father of Christian heretics. Here, Peter's sermon corresponded with the view of the orthodox Church: visions might convert Christians, but they continued to impel and "instruct" heretics only.

The distancing of orthodox Christians from dreams and visions was helped by the Christians' view of their community and by their hopes for its history; nonetheless, it could not bring down an iron curtain on patterns of the unified mind. As among pagans, so among Christian contemporaries, visions still occurred, not least because the same anxieties and tensions beset minds in a similar culture pattern. Among pagans, the gods were never more manifest than in times of storms and sickness, battles and collective fear. Where pagans saw gods at sea, Christians saw angels, "standing beside" them already in Acts, the book of Paul's companion on his tempestuous voyage to Rome.[93] Although Christians waged no battles, instead they feared persecution, an anxiety which was more personal and hardly less acute.

In pagan Miletus, the gods had stood beside man and woman, young and old, in dreams whose root cause escapes us; in Carthage, c. 250, the young and old were equally affected in the Christian Church. Uneasy dreams abounded, seen by Cyprian the bishop and by the "innocent boys" in his company, Christian children who received revelations in an hour of need.[94] As in Miletus, so in Carthage: God "stood by" the young as well as the old. He spoke clearly to the simple, childlike mind, just as the Virgin has "spoken" recently in Portugal and Yugoslavia. Unlike a pagan priestess, a bishop needed no oracle to explain these visits' meaning. In Miletus, we do not know the dreams' purpose; in Carthage, their cause is only too plain, a fear that persecution was about to beset the Church.

Among pagans, too, the onset of death had induced moments of visionary insight and visits by warning dreams. In Plutarch's lives of great men, warning dreams frequently foretell to the hero the manner or approach of his end; they have even been emphasized as one of Plutarch's primary interests in choosing particular biographies. Among Christians, by a different route, these patterns of anxiety gained a new urgency.[95] Jewish traditions of martyrdom had already forged a connection between martyrs' deaths and visions of heaven, and in Christian company, they were reinforced by promises in the Gospels. Jesus had foretold that the Spirit would attend those people who confessed his name. Persecution then took the form of a trial and public execution and provided martyrs with a long and intense anxiety. Prisons, meanwhile, added yet more visionary assistance. They crowded their prisoners and denied them regular food: the prison staff used to burgle much of the charity which Christians brought to the cells. Hunger and fear were joined by sleeplessness and a general mood of expectation, because a long imprisonment for its own sake was a rare and expensive punishment in an ancient town. Every inmate was awaiting trial and sentence in a setting which was hot, cramped and dark. These "sensory deprivations" are fast breeders of visions, seen with remarkable rapidity by subjects placed "in a dark room." It is not, then, so surprising that the promises in the Gospels were freely realized. Visions abounded, and like the prisoners in

Solzhenitsyn's First Circle, the waiting Christians kept up morale by telling each other their dreams.

While unorthodox Christians pondered the Transfiguration and wrote safely of visionary experience, humble fellow Christians were experiencing visions directly in the interlude before their deaths. Martyrdom was an ideal which visionary "knowing" heretics tended to belittle, yet as the Church had hinted to Hermas, the martyr was the worthiest receiver of visions from the Lord.[96] Our knowledge of visions after Hermas is largely knowledge of those which martyrs and their friends preserved.

In Carthage's prison, in March 203, the conditions were acutely unpleasant, and felt to be so by a young well-born Christian, Perpetua. Aged twenty-two, she had been baptized in prison, where she had also given birth. She was keeping a prison diary in Greek, one of the most intimate of all early Christian texts.[97] "I was absolutely terrified," she wrote, "because I had never experienced such darkness." Her brother encouraged her by reminding her of the rewards: "Respected sister, you are now in great esteem, such esteem that you may ask for a vision and it may be shown to you whether it is to be martyrdom or release . . ." Perpetua "knew she was talking with the Lord": the gift was the consequence of her recent arrest and baptism, not of a long-lasting strand in her nature. Awaiting death, she wrote down her famous visions, how she ascended into Paradise, where an elderly shepherd received her; how she saw her young brother who had died with a badly disfigured face; he seemed to be trying vainly to drink at an otherworldly fountain until his sister prayed and later saw that his fate had been eased. On the night before Perpetua died in the arena, she dreamed that she fought with a large diabolic Egyptian and overcame him before Christ, the heavenly umpire. When she and her companions went out on the morrow, they knew, through her visual preview, that their crowns in heaven were assured.

Is this visionary power in prison the key to Paul's own heavenly tour of Paradise, taken perhaps during one of his many arrests? The gift was neither heretical nor denied by orthodox Christians, and the visions in Perpetua's diary were excellent proof that a seer is only as productive as his or her previous experience. Her own visions had the simple imagery of a serpent and a ladder to heaven, an elderly shepherd and her suffering brother, pure fountains and an athletic battle with a large wrestler. Her most Christian touches of colour derive from the imagery of the baptism which she had just experienced. They were followed, however, by the visions of one Saturus, an older Christian who was more mature. He described how he and Perpetua had ascended to heaven, "floating face upwards, though lying on our backs." His vision of Paradise owed more to the imagery of other texts of Revelation: he saw walls of light, ranks of angels, roses, even, and cypress trees inside the heavenly garden. He also heard a rebuke for the local church which the angels administered to two clerics, seen grieving outside the gate. The visions of these two martyrs are extreme examples of the Christians' own theory, that visions varied in depth according to their beholder's nature.[98]

The visions in Perpetua's diary were published and studied and their Latin translation influenced other martyrs in Africa.[99] The best evidence for such visions is almost all North African, preserved in Latin, but we should probably not invoke some local "visionary" temperament to explain it. The style may be distinctive, but African texts are perhaps only those which happen to survive. In 259, the African martyrs Marian and James kept company in prison with one Aemilianus, a respectable man of high equestrian rank.[100] He "had reached his fiftieth year, but he was still a chaste virgin" (*puer*): in prison, he prayed continuously and fasted by a double "superimposition," taking no food at all for two days at a time. It was not, then, so surprising that, while dozing at midday, he saw his pagan brother in a dream. His brother seemed to taunt him about his life in the "darkness and hunger of our prison," but "I replied that even in a prison the soldiers of Christ enjoy a brilliant light and in their fasting have the food of God's own word." In his dream, his brother seemed to press him about his fellow Christians' fate: were not some of them more special than others, and could he not say who would enjoy the greatest rewards? Aemilianus hinted that two of the company would be most honoured, though they had had to wait for the longest time: this questioning is its own best comment on the suppressed concerns of the dreamer, a high-ranking man who had abandoned his pagan family and was living as an equal among inferior fellow Christians.

The two Christians to whom he referred were James and Marian, partners in the gift of visions. While they had been travelling by a rough road to prison, their companion on the coach ride remembered how James had fallen into a slumber and seen the figure of Christ, promising the martyr's crown. He remembered the scene with particular relish: "O sleep more intense than all our waking hours," he wrote, "in which they were allowed to hear and see Christ, offering himself for his own at every place and every time . . . The restless jolting of the carriage was no obstacle, nor midday, which was blazing, then, beneath an unclouded sun. There was no waiting for the secrets of the night . . . by a new kind of grace, the Lord has chosen a new time for revelation to his martyrs."

The old pagan notion, "not in a dream but a waking vision," thus found a novel variation in the experience of Christians under arrest. Little did their captors know what was being screened before them, in the private world of their prisoners' dreams. Yet, as we would expect, the approach of death induced a certain narrowing of subject matter. With the sole exception of Saturus, none of the visionaries addressed themselves to problems and persons in their church. Saturus was a mature Christian who had already won several converts, but generally, martyrs foresaw their own fate and the manner of their death. Being Christians, they also dreamed of their brethren and their rewards beyond the grave; they saw fellow martyrs who had been killed a short while before; they had visions of Paradise and heavenly banquets and prizes won in combats with Satan.[101] Often, these visionary prisoners were the simpler Christians, less able to give bribes and evade arrest. There was less likelihood of bold doctrinal visions emerging from their company: unlike the heretics' visions, their dreams were only significant for a short while before they were silenced. As their end approached, these people were less concerned with points of authority and doctrine than with their own consciences. While Aemilianus dreamed of his pagan brother and a slight social anxiety, Montanus dreamed, like Hermas, of uneasy moments in his past: "and our flesh became so bright," he reported, "that our eyes could see into the intimate secrets of the heart. And on looking into mine, I saw some stains . . . And I said to Lucian, my fellow martyr, 'You know, those stains are there because I did not immediately make up my quarrel with Julian . . .'" In the next life, the martyr expected to return to a childlike peace and a harmless simplicity of heart. "Go," said the angels to Saturus and Perpetua, "go away, and play . . ."[102]

These detailed visions were constructed from brief moments in their subjects' rapidly moving thoughts. Once again, in the fragments they preserved and elaborated, we catch the impact of Christianity on individuals' attitudes and ideals. Pagans, too, had dreams of warning and imminent death, but nothing in Artemidorus's great collection corresponds to this compound of correction and prize combat, simplicity, triumph and consciousness of sinful thoughts.

## II

The Church authorities could respect the Spirit as these martyrs experienced it: what, though, of its availability to other Christians at other times? In the pagan world, oracles and oracular techniques answered questions on cult and personal prospects for a wide and unrestricted range of customers: could not the Christian Spirit answer questions from its believers, just as dice oracles, caverns, streams and street diviners answered problems for a pagan clientele? Could not the Church, too, give an oracular service, helping Christians with their continuing doubts and problems? In one of his visions, Hermas had been shown some faithful Christians, seated on a bench, while a "prophet" was seated on a chair. The "wavering" Christians were approaching this diviner and asking him a question we can well understand: "What, please, will happen to us?" The "prophet," Hermas learned, was a false prophet, betrayed by his boasting, his way of life and his habit of taking money. It even seems that he was a pagan diviner, answering Christian problems.[1] Denied their own arts of futurology, Christians, it seems, were already turning for oracles to any service which would give them.

In this area of "neutral technology" there was scope for more experiment than the orthodox texts reveal. Divination remained a sin among practising Christians, but we now have a startling reminder of the overlap between pagan and biblical ways of using it. In the highlands of Phrygia (central Turkey) we have the epitaph of one Zosimus, a man of good birth and the "Most High people," who was praised for "writing on a tablet whatever men request and desire and telling the future on a folded tablet to wise questioners." To this end, Zosimus used "inspired Scriptures and Homeric verses."[2] In these remote villages, prophecy took various forms: the reference to the "Most High people" and "inspired Scriptures" shows that Zosimus was not a pagan. Perhaps he belonged to the sect of the Most High god, which is known inland in Asia, but more probably he was a Christian, using Homer and the Bible to answer questions by random selection or lot.

Like the old pagan almanacs, Zosimus was using written Scriptures: might not the Spirit, too, give prophetic advice? It was an option which would not, perhaps, leave Christian life until it had been fully tested. While pilgrimage to Claros had been at its height and Abonouteichos was drawing the crowds, Christians in Asia were made aware of an oracular voice which addressed their own particular problems. In the wilds of Phrygia, a Christian, Montanus, with several male helpers and two prophetesses, began to speak the words of the Holy Spirit. We cannot place the only sound evidence for the date when his prophecies began: the mid-150s or later 160s are both possibilities.[3] By 177, the Spirit was very widely known. "Lo!" it said, through Montanus, "man is like a lyre, and I strike him like a plectrum. Man is asleep, and I am awake . . ."[4] It posed in the sharpest terms the question of the Spirit's access to whomever it chose to dignify.

As critics agreed, Montanus's followers were not intellectual heretics. They parted from fellow Christians only in their acceptance of the Spirit's new words, and they persisted far into the sixth century, suffering legalized persecution from their "brethren." Modern study of their sect has tended to follow the orthodox Church's perspective.[5] Montanus has been classed as a "millennial" prophet who was merely roused by the famines and earthquakes of the 170s, and his millennial teaching has been seen as a Phrygian oddity. In one of the Spirit's "oracles," a Montanist prophetess was said to have seen Christ, dressed as a woman, and heard that "here" (or "thus") the "new Jerusalem will descend." She believed, said the critics, that the reign of the Saints would begin at Pepuza in Phrygia, a site as bizarre as little Abonouteichos before it changed its name. Unlike the new "Ionopolis," it remained Pepuza, a site so obscure that it has eluded all attempts to find it on the map.[6]

This approach reduces Montanus to one more oddity of "Phrygian" cult whose local hopes were misplaced: he joins those worshippers of pagan angels, prophets, prophetesses and cults of an abstract divinity which we know in Phrygia through pagan inscriptions. Did not one of his critics allege that he had once been a pagan eunuch priest in an ecstatic Phrygian cult? To see him in those terms is to surrender to his critics and their wish to belittle his appeal: the strict and sober Phrygian character was regularly belittled by scornful critics who lived in the older Greek cities. Nobody remembered who exactly had seen the vision of the new Jerusalem, nor is it clear that they translated it correctly: it was good male fun to allege that Christ had appeared to the women as a female. In the 160s, it was not so very special to believe in an imminent millennium.[7] According to one chronology, it was scarcely forty years away. We hear of no great rush to Pepuza, while earthquakes and famines were nothing new in the history of Asia.

Perhaps the Spirit's origin owed something to the surrounding prophetic culture in Phrygia, to which other Christian prophets were attached: its grave, puritanical ethic well suited the mood of the Phrygian villages. Yet the appeal of the sect exceeded and outlived its supposed local venue for a Second Coming and any local temper in its birth. Puritans were not confined to Phrygia, and by c. 200, the "new prophecy" had spread through Antioch as far as Carthage. Christians found more in it than a misplaced millennial hope.

Rather than emphasize the sect's view of the millennium, we should turn to its view of the Spirit. This view was less conventional. While playing on a passive lyre, the Spirit spoke in the first person: "I am come, neither angel nor envoy, but God the Father." Its words were collected carefully from the male and female mouthpieces and were published, it seems, on their hearers' testimony. Their critics and one of their supporters, Tertullian, cite fragments of the words of the Spirit which give us a feel for its interests.[8] The Spirit, we find, spoke on vexed points of early Christian conduct which were largely familiar from the worries of Paul and his churches. Should Christians remarry? How long should they fast, and in what way? Would the Resurrection be fleshly, or in a spiritual body? Should the Church forgive sins? These questions were perennials in Church life, as old as the timing of the end of the world. Montanus was not concerned to be heretical, or to vaunt his superior knowledge. Tertullian, who accepted his words, makes this quite plain. The words of the "Paraclete" were a new and "richer" discipline, or way of conduct.[9] They attached to Jesus's promise in John's Gospel that further truths would be revealed by the Spirit, as a future gift. Through Montanus and his females, the Spirit was bringing Christian "discipline" up to date. It defined a way for the higher-class Christian: no remarriage, no forgiveness of sins in church and a "dry" fast during a fortnight, five days a week.

While pagan questioners in Paphlagonia asked the prophet Alexander about their children and their prospects, Christians were turning to their Spirit in Phrygia for an ethic which defined their higher achievement. Both prophets aroused critical allegations that they were paying their staff to spread their fame.[10] By very different routes, both brought notoriety to their obscure home towns. Whereas Alexander's cult attached to the oracular culture of his age, Montanus, on one point, was less conventional. He and his Spirit gave a prominent role to those "gateways of the Devil," women.

In Montanist groups, women were honoured as "prophets" and

"participants," as we also know from their inscriptions.[11] Montanists admired Eve, the source of knowledge, and praised Moses's prophetic sister. At their meetings, seven virgins would enter, carrying torches and wearing white robes, like the Wise Virgins of Scripture, whereupon they would weep and urge repentance on their hearers. In a famous oracle, the Spirit urged Christians not to be ashamed by people's opinions: better to die "not in soft fevers, beds and abortions, but in martyrdoms . . ." The text was not an encouragement to "voluntary" martyrdom: it was once argued that such provocation was an essential part of Montanus's message, but the argument was not soundly based. Rather, by this text's choice of examples, did not the Spirit have female martyrs in mind?[12]

To Origen, in the 240s, true prophets were male, not female, and were proven by their moral conduct, not their "possession." In his views, we see the assumptions which Montanus had failed to overthrow.[13] His Spirit was equated with a type of "ecstasy" which orthodox Christian opinion promptly defined out of court. Montanus claimed that in himself and his followers, the Spirit was speaking in its own person. It was this direct quality which made his "new discipline" so attractive and so dangerous.[14] In reply, a cluster of pamphlets from leading Asian Christians asserted that "true" prophecy did not suspend its prophet's faculties. It enhanced them while the speaker was still conscious, a person of proven experience and worth. "True" prophets spoke in humility, in their own person. They were people like Paul and Ezekiel, or even St. John, whose Revelation reported what "in the Spirit" he had seen.

Against these views, the Montanists asserted their novelty, and their argument, it seems, affected their use of Scripture. John's Gospel had promised a further Spirit which would aid men's understanding: this "Paraclete," the Montanists said, had descended on their "new age."[15] This view had difficulties, not least with Pentecost and the Book of Revelation. From one of Montanus's critics, we can perhaps deduce his original argument.[16] To refute the "new prophecy," critics had to insist that the Apostles had waited in Jerusalem for twelve whole years after Jesus's death and that St. John had indeed worked wonders in the Spirit in Ephesus. What were they refuting? Perhaps the Montanists argued against former "gifts" of the Spirit and thus denied the story of Pentecost and the "ecstasy" of the Book of Revelation. Like modern Christian scholars, they may have pointed to Mark's Gospel, in which Jesus told the disciples to go to Galilee and stay there: how, then, could they have received the gift of tongues, as they were not even in Jerusalem? Montanus is usually assumed to have accepted John's Revelation "in the Spirit," but critics soon pointed out that it contained some awkward remarks: it attacked "Jezebel," a false prophetess, in one of the cities where Montanists became strong. Montanus, perhaps, implied that John had not really had the true Spirit, whereas he and his followers were the first to receive it.

The arguments rolled on for forty years and eventually came to rest on the definition of "ecstasy."[17] In the Greek Bible, said the critics, the word had never applied to true inspiration. When God created Eve, he cast on Adam an "ecstasy" which was only a deep sleep; in Acts, Peter seemed to deny that "ecstasy" was relevant to prophecy. The argument was an old one, already aired by Philo and other Jews in Alexandria; orthodox Christians added arguments from the contemporary Platonist debates on the nature of the contact between pagan gods and oracular priests. While the Platonists left the possibilities open, Christians borrowed their case for a gentle enhancement. They ranked Montanus's "suspension" as demonic.

The result was all too predictable. Montanus became a "false" prophet, an ecstatic who was possessed by Satan. His teachings were damned by Asian bishops, and in the 170s, he was excommunicated. He did not, it seems, accept his fate. The course of the dispute runs neatly if we assume that he promptly appealed for support to the bishop of Rome.[18] If so, the first invocation of Rome was by a prophet suspected of Satan: Rome, it seems, was sympathetic to his case. If we allow for this preliminary, we can then understand the sequel. Christians in Asia went higher still, to a group of Christian martyrs who were awaiting death in the prisons in Lyons. Who better to test the new words of the Spirit than these acknowledged bearers of the Spirit's gifts? Some of the Christians in Lyons had links with Asia, the province from which the words had originated. Not for the last time, Christians in prison sided with sober orthodoxy. They wrote a sheaf of letters to Rome's bishop and despatched a delegation with Irenaeus himself, a man whose works combined deep respect for the Spirit with an equal concern for orthodoxy. The Montanists were thus declared frauds by the Church's highest authority. Delegations of bishops set out for Pepuza, and we have the sworn testimony of one of them that a fellow bishop tried to seize a prophetess and exorcise her.[19]

Five generations, at most, after "Pentecost," Christian leaders were exorcising fellow Christians, mouthpieces of the Holy Spirit. The heart of Montanism had not lain in heresy or millennial teaching, let alone in militant apocalyptic. It lay in a faith that the Spirit could speak personally, bringing Christian "discipline" up to the mark. Thus the sect could survive the deaths of its first prophet and his prophetesses and spread back to the West with new envoys.[20] It returned to Rome in the bishopric of Zephyrinus (c. 198–217), when the older views had nearly been forgotten. It troubled Antioch and by this time reached Carthage, where it attracted the widower Tertullian. At first, sparks from the Asian crisis had flown from Phrygia to Rome and west as far as Lyons: the fire was then dowsed, but its embers continued to glow for several generations. The new "discipline" appealed to over-achievers, to "Elect" minorities who wished to find an authority for their sterner effort. Its rebuff closed one option in the Spirit's future and, in its wake, the third person of the Trinity went further into retreat. Random ecstasy was no longer a possible source of authority in the Church. The Spirit became a silent guiding presence, granted at baptism to each Christian and present, but not so vociferous, in Christian life.

One result of the crisis was to link the Holy Spirit very closely with the personal qualities of its bearer. The advantages are still keenly felt: "if Montanus had triumphed, Christian doctrine would have been developed not under the superintendence of the Christian teachers most esteemed for wisdom, but of wild and excitable women."[21] Agreed sayings from the Spirit would also have entailed an even greater orthodoxy. However, the victory by Church leaders did have consequences for their own position. The visions of Hermas and Saturus had rebuked the Christian leadership, but now it was ever more plausible to deny that such visions were genuine. In the modern Catholic Church, the problem of true or false visions and "ecstasy" has not gone away: since 1981, have three girls and a boy in Medjugorje, in Yugoslavia, really seen and heard the Virgin two thousand times? The question is still being discussed in terms of partial or total ecstasy, with credit going to the latter, "suspension," not enhancement. The argument, eventually, has gone Montanus's way. It has, however, been joined by other requirements; one test for a "true" trance is now to stick long pins into the young participants and watch for any awareness. Another is to weed out all references to the Church's hierarchy. In 1965, a female visionary in Lourdes was judged not to have seen the Virgin because her vision criticized the Pope and the Second Vatican Council. A primary obstacle to acceptance of the children at Medjugorje has been their message from the Virgin, criticizing the local bishop's treatment of the Franciscans. As Paul had warned, Satan might masquerade as an "angel of Light":[22] what Christian, except a martyr, was so pious that he could be sure of seeing Christ? If the Spirit enhanced its speakers' minds, it was most likely to result in a true utterance if these minds were already of proven worth. From the start, Church councils were said to be guided by the Holy Spirit. "It seemed good to the Holy Spirit," wrote Acts' author, reporting the decisions of the first council at Jerusalem: the Spirit was most evidently true when it "enhanced" Church leaders.[23]

In glimpses of the third-century Church, we can watch the consequences.[24] Even after Montanus true visions were not confined to bishops. Part of an early "Apostolic" order proposed that in each church a widow should be given the role of "seeking revelations whenever necessary"; in Cyprian's letters, visions on Church conduct are still received by Christians other than the bishop, even by "young and innocent boys"; by third-century authors, the idea of direct, ecstatic inspiration could still be entertained. The concept of inspiration had not passed a watershed in Christian company, from random "ecstasy" to a constant angelic guidance and advice in dreams.[25] However, approved dreams now had an obedient tone which was unlike anything in Artemidorus's pagan book: they told a congregation when to pray and whom to choose as a bishop. Cyprian describes how a brave confessor, Celerinus, had hesitated to accept the duties of a clergyman until the Church herself appeared to him in a vision and urged him to accept. Plainly, this particular vision was not demonic.[26]

We can see the restraints in a valuable story, told by Tertullian in his treatise *On the Soul*. At the time of writing, his views on "ecstasy" and fasting reveal that he was not yet a committed Montanist, and although the point has been disputed, he seems to be describing a scene in the orthodox Church.[27] "Among us," he wrote in Carthage, "there is a 'sister,' gifted with revelations. She talks with angels, sometimes even with the Lord . . . She sees and hears mysteries." She was also gifted with a particular Christian insight: "she sees into the hearts of some." Her gifts extended to healing, "giving medicines to those who ask."

We would dearly like the memoirs of this gifted female, but her context is illuminating. Like the young visionaries at Medjugorje, since their first sightings, she enjoyed her ecstasy in church during a service. The readings of Scripture, the Psalms, the sermons and the prayers "supply materials for her visions." After the service, the laity (*plebs*) were sent away, and the "sister" would tell what she had seen. Her visions were "most carefully collected so that they might also be tested." On the occasion in question, she had seen a vision which supported Tertullian's views on the soul.

This type of experience was far from a free play of the Spirit, to be accepted at face value, whatever its topic. It was tested and reserved; it was stimulated, even, by the services in church: a "sister," entranced during Sunday service, was not likely to upset a bishop's teaching. If she did, her vision could be rejected as false or demonic. When, though, were such visions known to be true? In Cyprian's letters, it is noticeable that the acceptable visions tend to be visions of testing and correction, visions which reproach the Christian community's lapses and predict the onset of persecution. In Cyprian's own visions God also "castigates" and "warns" insistently, though the warnings had useful implications. Cyprian's letters allude to his own "revelations" and visions from God as a source of guidance in his role as bishop.[28] His critics attacked him, the "dreamer, Joseph," but we should not see this emphasis on visionary power solely as his response to his own difficult position. Prophetic gifts had been ascribed to bishops before him and were claimed by other bishops in his province. "Among other things which God deigned to show and answer," wrote Cyprian to an enemy, "he added this: 'So, then, he who does not believe in Christ making a priest will believe very soon in Christ avenging a priest.'"

At the pagan oracles, the gods "testified" to the virtues of their servants; in Cyprian's Church, God warned of the consequences of opposing his chosen bishop. At Didyma or Claros, Apollo discussed the gods' identities and the fate of the soul after death; among Christians, God explained problems of doctrine and met a constant concern over details of the next world. Each of these types of dream took distinctive forms in Christian company.[29] It was perhaps excessive when one bishop, Dionysius, alleged that he had only inspected a heretical text when an angel appeared to him and advised him to take the risk; the allegation, however, would never have been made by a pagan. In the pagan world there was no forbidden theological literature. It was perhaps less novel that respected Christians were said to have been told their particular creeds by visions of angels or even by a dialogue between an Apostle and the Virgin Mary. Among pagans, the rules for a cult were sometimes revealed in a dream, but there was no similar concern for literal wording and orthodoxy.

On the matter of the next world, Christians sharpened a widespread pagan uncertainty and, inevitably, there were consequences for their visions here, too. Death, perhaps, is feared in any culture, but we can sympathize with a bishop, known to Cyprian, who was terrified as his own end approached.[30] In this case, a young, radiant figure did appear in a vision to console him: "What," he asked in rebuke, "do you dare to be afraid to leave this life?" It was a fear which other visions did more to magnify than reassure. Here, too, Christians were heirs to Jewish apocalyptic texts, to which they soon added others, reinforcing points in their own ethic.[31] So-called "Apocalypses" of Peter and Paul purported to give guided tours to hell and its punishments: distinctively, these Christians singled out sexual sinners, the parents of exposed and aborted children and girls who had been promiscuous before marriage. In the Christians' afterlife, these texts revealed, homosexuals and lesbians were being pushed repeatedly over the precipices onto rocks below. Acquaintance with Peter's "Apocalypse" was enough to scare any Christian's conscience: we happen to know that this "vision" was still read as a holy text in the churches in Palestine on Good Friday during the fifth century.

At this date, there was still no concept of purgatory, "correcting" all but the very few between their death and Resurrection. The idea of remedial punishment was reserved for the aftermath of the Last Judgement, before Christians passed into the company of Christ and the angels.[32] The options, then, between death and this judgement were relatively clear: either an immediate torture, like Dives, or "interim refreshment," like Lazarus, in the bosom of Abraham. Tours of the next world, therefore, were not yet concerned with the theological problems which purgatory would later raise. Their bulletins concerned one of only two locations: Paradise, for martyrs only, or hell's torments, for the worst sinners. As a result, most of these early "tours" had a dark and alarming quality. They were instruments of discipline whose range and precision exceeded any pagan visions of the underworld.

"With the path of dreams blocked," it has been suggested, "the way was open for nightmares . . . medieval man would not reconquer the dream-world for a long time to come."[33] There is no denying the authority which was given to these particular nightmares, but the connection between the two experiences was not one of cause and effect. The early Christians did not "block" dreams: they merely argued that many of the most frequent types were demonic or without significance. As for the "nightmares," the most famous were literary works which may not derive from a genuine vision. The prominence of dreams of the next life was not caused by a "block" on other subjects. It derived, simply, from the extreme weight which attached to the afterlife in Christian circles and the ways in which it laid such a high requirement on human nature.

Like Hermas's dreams or the dreams of martyrs, these underworld visions wore a characteristic stamp. They concerned the concept of sin which Christians emphasized and the duality of fierce correction and childlike innocence and rest. These shades of meaning had not coloured pagan "epiphanies," and again, they bring out a constant area of impact of Christianity on Christians' minds. Among Christians, indeed, the place and scope of an "epiphany" were significantly different. Before Constantine, the central hope of "epiphany" was focussed on future history. As yet, neither the liturgy nor any widespread sacred art enhanced the sense of a visible presence, potentially "evident" and "manifest" at any moment. Between the age of the Apostles and the Christian Empire, there was ample reason why "epiphanies" in Christian company should have been more restricted than in most other periods of Christian history.

In Christian company, the old idea of "epiphany" did indeed take on different contours. It has not lost them since: tours of purgatory, advice on twice-weekly fasting, the criteria of "true" trance and ecstasy, the relation between visions and the growing capacity of visionaries, the status of visions which criticize the official Church, all these elements are still present and keenly disputed in the Virgin's evening "visits" to the children of Medjugorje, the new Pepuza. The Virgin appears in the form, essentially, of her statue in church: she was first seen by children among whom were those who had known a recent bereavement and acute illness. Her latest "sightings" are not "unique." They conform to a pattern as old as Christian experience and in details draw content from it. There is one exception: in the early Church, no angel or vision revealed "secrets" which the seer should keep quiet and never agree to reveal.

"Not to everyone do the gods appear . . ."; the old Homeric view had acquired new depth in early Christian experience. The company of angels was reserved for the most virtuous natures, as Hermas had already exemplified. Perfectionism did not cease with Hermas, and it is in its light, finally, that we can best understand the most celebrated recent find of early Christian documents. In Upper Egypt, across the Nile from Diospolis Parva, twelve "books," or codices, with leaves from a thirteenth, were unearthed in a jar in 1945, the famous "Nag Hammadi Library" of fifty-seven Coptic tracts. Much has already been written on their contents, their spurious Gospels, their connections with known "Gnostic" heresies of the second century, their imagery of Creation and their mysteries of higher theology. Historically, however, particular interest lies in their origin. They are not an "early Gnostic Christian's" library: none of the "Gnostic" Christians bothered to read or write Coptic.[34] The collection is not a single library, nor is it uniformly heretical, nor even entirely Christian. It includes a poor translation of a section of Plato's *Republic* and a pagan letter of "Eugnostos the Blessed": the letter was then given a Christian preface and conclusion and presented in another copy as the "wisdom" which Jesus revealed to his Apostles after his death. The "Library" also includes three texts which are known in a pagan setting: a prayer and two discourses of Thrice-great Hermes, the pagan god.

Of these three pagan texts, the prayer has a fascinating postscript which is carefully inscribed in a decorated rectangle.[35] "I have copied this one discourse of his [Hermes]. Indeed, very many have come to me. I have not copied these too, because I thought that they had come to you. I hesitate to copy these for you, because perhaps they have come to you already, and the business may burden you . . ." Other texts have other postscripts, which refer to "the father" and "the brethren." What, then, was this community which was so well supplied with pagan Hermetic literature?

When the bindings of the codices were first opened and their padding examined, the materials in one of them proved that it dated after the year 348. Another referred to a Christian monk, and first thoughts were that much of the padding derived from a nearby Christian monastery whose members had owned the books.[36] Further study has shown that other suggested references to the monks and their community are only one possibility among several, and sometimes not even that, but the general theory has not been refuted: it still explains the evidence more tidily than any other.[37] Barely five and a half miles from the discovery of these books lay a major monastic community, founded by the great Pachomius, father of this type of monasticism in Egypt: his own first monastery was only three miles distant. In theory, the filling of the bindings could have derived from any rubbish heap elsewhere, but the brilliant conjecture that the books, too, belonged to monks is still the most economical.[38] There were no "Gnostics" at Nag Hammadi in the mid-fourth century and certainly no study group of Coptic-speaking "Hermetists," pagans who wished to own so many Christian books beside their own. Coptic, however, was the language of the majority in the early Pachomian monasteries: after c. 350, we know that rumours of rampant unorthodoxy caused their members' opinions to be checked. Our texts seem to fall into three separate collections, which were gathered, perhaps, by their owners and then hidden near a deserted pagan temple when the books in their monasteries began to be questioned and sought out.

The picture is intriguing. By c. 350, we have a group of Christian monks who owned such a quantity of texts from the pagans' spiritual master, "Thrice-great Hermes," that a scribe had hesitated before sending them any more. By c. 300, we know, Christian authors already welcomed "Thrice-great Hermes" as a pre-Christian witness to their Christian theology.[39] The Library's extract from Plato's *Republic* also gains a new relevance.[40] As mistranslated in Coptic, it refers to the virtue of "casting down every image of the evil Beast and trampling on them, together with the image of the Lion." Monks were the supreme destroyers of pagans' religious art, the "image of Beast and Lion." For monastic readers, the passage was only too aptly chosen.

In these books, texts of revelation and "tours of heaven" are abundant. Some were originally Jewish while others are Christian, but seriously heretical; others are pagan: three extracts from Hermes and a longer text called "Zostrianos."[41] To the first monks, it seems, any guide to heaven and the vision of God was as good as another. It did not matter if the text was pagan, Christian or heretical, so long as it suited their piety and its aims.

The founder of the monasteries, Pachomius, is said in his Greek biography to have "seen the Invisible God in purity of heart, as in a mirror."[42] Certainly, he enjoyed one type of vision, the power of seeing deeply into the hearts of the Christians whom he controlled. It was Pachomius's gift to know his fellow Christians better than they knew themselves; beholders were aware of his intense, searching gaze, that self-revealing quality which they ascribed to the neutral surface of Father Pachomius's eye. Did Pachomius also see upwards as well as inwards? He was questioned on reports of his mystic visions, but the case was never established against him. He did, however, use a cryptic alphabet with a mystical significance which has still to be deciphered. His aim, it seems, was to keep company with the angels, whatever the results. It is not, then, surprising that lesser monks in his community were studying with interest the texts of previous heavenly visions.

By subsequent monks, we know, the gift of sleep was despised and rejected.[43] They prayed and fasted intently, and by breaking the night with their vigils, they aspired to "sleeplessness." Consequently, they set little store by dreams, preferring the waking vision, a goal which some of the texts in the "Library" had attained. While striving for their high ideal, they could read how others had achieved it: "I have found the beginning of the power that is above all powers," one of their "Library's" texts proclaimed, "the power without beginning. I see a fountain bubbling with life. I have said, 'O my son, I am Mind. I have seen . . . no words can reveal it . . .'" The speaker was a pagan disciple of Hermes whose author, plainly, had known the vision of God.[44]

However, between the monks and attainment of this vision lay barriers which differed in degree from those which pagans had acknowledged. How could Christians be sure that their visions were of God, not a demon? When man was so profoundly sinful, how could he ever be so pious as to see God? From these distinctive Christian questions, two scenes in our texts gain a new relevance.

In the mid-fourth century, the life of Antony, the first Christian hermit, was publicized in Greek by Athanasius, bishop of Alexandria. It is easy to doubt the work's purpose and credentials: a bishop of such a high Greek education was an unlikely biographer for a simple Coptic-speaking holy man who had lived most of his life in isolation. Much has been conjectured of the work's intention, its interest in claiming the new Christian perfectionists for the orthodox Church, its concern, perhaps, to combat contemporary heresy.[45] However, it gives its hero a very long speech to his Egyptian brethren which has a more immediate aim. In it, Antony is made to distinguish a vision which is sent by God from a vision which is sent by demons. His criterion is one of emotional effect, whether the vision brings only fear or fear followed by joy: the criterion has recurred frequently in Catholic theology, perhaps most famously in the trials of Joan of Arc. "When they come to you by night," said Antony, "and wish to foretell the future, or say to you 'we are angels,' pay no heed, for they are lying. In a true vision God and his angels take away fear . . . It comes quietly and gently, and at once, joy and gladness and courage rise in the soul . . . whereas demons bring fear and hatred of others, fear of death and remembrance of kin and family." The monk should ask his divine visitor a question as old as Homer, to whose heroes this sequence of fear, then "courage" had also marked an epiphany of the gods. "Ask them, 'Who are you?' and 'From whence are you come?'" "The holy ones will change your fear into joy," as Christ, indeed, had changed it for the Apostles after the Resurrection.

The author of this speech was plainly aware of the aims and pitfalls of contemporary monastic life. The speech sits very neatly with the contents of the Nag Hammadi texts. Monks did aspire to angelic contact, to a state in which their protectors would "stand beside" man, as of old, "face to face," in a "waking vision, not a dream." This company of the angels was most evident to the overachiever, as Hermas had already testified: from Hermas's book, this sense of angelic company had greatly struck Origen and his perfectionist view of human nature. Monks, the new perfectionists, were heirs to this theme in Hermas and Origen, so much so that lesser Christians addressed them as "your angel" and believed that they lived "in the state of angels":[46] once, it was believed, when Antony had been suffering from slothfulness, he had seen a man in his own likeness, busy at his work. Like Hermas, Antony had been graced with an angelic corrector: his angel appeared disguised as himself, further emphasizing the perfect Christian's upward potential, aspiring to the angelic state.[47]

Perfection, however, is a receding ideal and Antony was exceptional. Like a book or a garden, a painting or a musical performance, human nature is a thing never perfect to those who feel responsible for it. Monks were deeply aware of the gap between their imperfect selves and the vision of God. Here, the contrast with pagan religiousness is beautifully caught in one of their stories: one day, a pagan visitor arrived at the Christian monastery in Scetis and lodged in Abba Olympius's cell.[48] After a while, he asked his host a natural pagan question: "Leading this way of life, do you really have no visions of your God?" "No," Abba Olympius answered, "we do not." "When we perform rites to our God," said the pagan, "he hides nothing, but he reveals his mysteries to us all. With all these toils and vigils and silences and acts of asceticism, do you really mean to say you have no visions at all? You must, indeed, have wicked thoughts in your hearts which separate you from God: that is why he will not reveal his mysteries." Abba Olympius left his visitor and reported these words to his fellow monks. They did not reject them as unworthy: there had been no retreat from the ideal of "company with God," no ending of a long debate in religious history. Indeed, there had not, for as we now suspect, these very monks read texts of the pagans' experience, striving to share it themselves. "Indeed," the monks replied, "it is so. Unclean thoughts do keep God away from man." The higher a man set the ideal of virtue, the further the vision of God withdrew. "Always before," King Alcinous had warned in the *Odyssey*, "the gods have appeared to us clearly when we offer glorious hecatombs . . ." Ever more elusive, the encounter was now placed in the life to come. "The gods are hard to cope with," Hera had warned in the *Iliad*, "when seen very clearly . . ." In Christian company, God would be greeted with weeping, by Christian holy men who shed tears in his presence for their own and their fellow Christians' sins. To prepare for their last meeting, God, too, made new arrangements. If only the pure in heart could see God, then Christian viewers needed correction after their death and before this last encounter: "epiphany" became a seed from which that ultimate fiction, purgatory, grew in Christian thought.

# 9. Persecution and Martyrdom

The most excellent Christians in the early Church were neither the virgins nor the visionaries. They were the Christians whom pagans put to death. The spread of Christianity, the conversions, the over-achievement took place in an era of persecution. In heaven, said the authorities, the rewards of a virgin were sixty times greater than an ordinary Christian's, but a martyr's were a hundred times greater, the highest of all. Christians' deaths were idealized as martyrdoms, "second baptisms" which effaced all previous sins and ensured an immediate crown in Paradise.

Persecution has been an enduring fact of Christian history: "it is by no means impossible that in the thirty years between 1918 and 1948 more Christians died for their faith than in the first 300 years after the Crucifixion."[1] In early Christianity, it did not cease in the age of Constantine: Christians promptly began to persecute their fellow Christians. Beyond the Roman Empire, others fell victim to intermittent purges by the kings of Persia: elaborate stories of their martyrdoms continued to spread in the fifth century. The old patterns died hard. During the 850s, fifty Christians were martyred at Cordova in Spain in a long sequence of arrests and hearings which were forced to the attention of the Muslim cadi.[2] The detailed Latin narratives of their martyrdoms described their trials as if they still took place before a "consul" armed with the fasces, or rods of authority. Their pattern reminds us how much endured in these occasions across the centuries: the concern of the judge to find a compromise; the effect of one martyrdom on other "volunteers"; the careful recording of events by men in prison; the enthusiasts' "rash itch for destruction"; the idea of martyrdom as a prizefight by "warriors"; the moderate views and evasions of the Christian majority; the prominence in martyrdom of well-born girls. There was also the publicity for violent suffering: when Flora, a Christian virgin, was released after torture, "I gazed upon the skin of your holy neck," wrote the future archbishop of Toledo, "torn by the blows of the whip and the wound which had bared your lovely hair and which you deigned to show me personally."

As a result, the ideal of martyrdom has remained alive in world history, since its first formulation by Jews in the mid-second century B.C. Christianity has never lost it, and it was probably through contact with Christians, not Jews, that early Islam picked up its analogous language and theology for those who die for the faith. The legacy is still tragically fresh. In the war against Iraq, the Iranian dead are publicized as martyrs whose instant reward has been granted in Paradise. Dreams of a martyr's glory impel boys to volunteer, as Christians once volunteered for trial. They risk gassing and chemical burns, the modern heirs of the fires and wild beasts.

In the early Church, martyrdoms were exceptionally public events, because Christians coincided with a particular phase in the history of public entertainment: they were pitched into the cities' arenas for unarmed combat with gladiators or bulls, leopards and the dreaded bears. As we have seen, these displays were financed and chosen by the great men of the cities "out of love for their home town": by the second century B.C., the phrase "love of honour" could refer directly to a show of lurid violence. People liked it, and donors courted popularity through this potent psychological form. Violence made excellent viewing, and the crowds could be utterly callous. "Well washed, well washed," called the crowd in Carthage when martyrs in their arena spattered themselves in blood. Their shout was a hideous misuse of a popular salutation which was uttered in the public baths.[3] Christian victims were particularly appealing: they included a good proportion of women, not merely slave girls but well-born women and virgins, as Origen remarked. Trained female gladiators were known in both halves of the Empire, but among Christian "criminals," women were as prominent as men. When the well-born Perpetua and her slave girl Felicitas entered Carthage's arena, "the crowd were horrified when they saw how one was a delicate girl, the other fresh from childbirth with her breasts still dripping milk." First they called for them to be clothed more modestly. Then, like a crowd at a bullfight, they roared their applause while the girls were brought back to die before the wild beasts.[4] This same high-pitched mixture of torture and female martyrdom was later to inspire the baroque dramas of Corneille and Dryden and the works of art which Christians patronized in their own counter-Reformation.

The intransigence of the braver Christians made a great impression on their brethren and also impressed itself on pagans. When the Emperor Marcus wrote his thoughts on suicide in his private *Meditations*, he contrasted an orderly, reasoned choice of death with the Christians' "sheer opposition" to the rational order. The comparison was not entirely logical, but there is no good reason for deleting illogicality from the Emperor's private thoughts.[5] It is a striking example of the martyrs' public reputation.

In their own limited terms, the Roman governors often strove for a compromise with the Christians before them. If a Christian refused to eat sacrificial meat, might he not offer a simple pinch of incense? Could he not sacrifice "at least" to the Emperor, as if the Emperor was not such an intractable divinity? Perhaps he could "swear by the fortune of the Emperor," just a simple little oath.[6] The governors knew a little about their opponents, but not very much. Our stories of their interrogations are all Christian stories, the soundest of which were slimmed down to a dialogue in a "protocol" style. Even if they were shaped for a Christian audience, they had to seem plausible. It all sounded so odd, this doctrine of Resurrection, body and all, and this trust in books by St. Paul. "Was he not a common sort of chap who spoke Aramaic?" a governor of Egypt was said to have asked Bishop Phileas in c. 305, after centuries of persecution. "Surely he was not in the same class as Plato?" "Well, then," another despairing governor had asked in Smyrna, in March 250, "do you pay attention to the air? If so, sacrifice to the air instead." "I do not pay attention to the air," replied his prisoner, "but to him who made the air, the heaven and everything in it." "Tell me, then, who did make it?" "It is not right for me to tell."[7] This childlike obstinacy was very irritating. "Do you want to wait a few days to think it over?" asked the governor who tried Colluthus, also in Egypt in the early fourth century.[8] The Christian story of his trial has been recovered recently in a Coptic version which bears the stamp of other early Christian versions of their martyrs' hearings. "I can see it in your face; it tells me that you want to be saved." How could Colluthus want to be killed? "Don't you see the beauty of this pleasant weather?" asked his hopeful judge. "No pleasure will come your way if you kill yourself. But listen to me and you will be saved." "The death which is coming to me," Colluthus was said to have answered, "is more pleasant than the life which you would give . . ."

Christians on trial were maddeningly unwilling to betray themselves. According to Acts, the first martyrs had "gazed steadfastly" to heaven, wearing that well-known look of intent, Christian assurance. Pagans who knew how to tell a man by his face had no time for "steadfast gazing": according to Aristotle and the books on physiognomy, it revealed a man who was impudent. The Christians' view was very different: the martyr was a living "mirror of God" who stood a greater trial than any governor knew. As the Jesus of the Gospels had so bleakly asserted, anyone who dared to denounce him before men would be denounced in turn by his word before God. Without this dimension, we cannot fully appreciate the martyrs' motivation.[9]

To pagan eyes, Christians compounded their impudence by being evasive. Even under torture, there were Christians who refused to reveal their name or social class, home and place of origin. They simply said they were Christians who belonged to a "universal Church." In February 310, a governor in Caesarea faced five Egyptians who had betrayed themselves as Christians but, when questioned, hid their former names and said they were called Elijah, Daniel and so forth. When they told the judge that their city was Jerusalem, he refused to take them literally, and began to torture their leader. "Ours," he said, "is the country of the pious only, and they alone have a share in it. It lies towards the East, towards light itself, towards the sun . . ." The judge had no time for this talk of a never-never land. He "shook with impatience, thinking that Christians had perhaps established a city for themselves somewhere at enmity and odds with the Romans." When scourging and further torture revealed nothing, he ordered immediate death by decapitation.[10]

During their years of persecution, Christians are not known to have attacked their pagan enemies: they shed no innocent blood, except their own. In his letter to the Romans, Paul had described the pagan governors as necessary ministers of God's wrath and had urged the Christians to submit to authority. They remained true to his advice, never rebelling against the Emperor's temporal rule. Why, then, were they ever persecuted and how had persecution come about?[11]

Not until the year 257 were Christian services and places of meeting attacked. Before this date, action was taken only against Christian individuals, but its legal grounds and the degree, if any, of official encouragement have been much discussed. Before 250, there are only three references to concerted action against Christians which deserve any consideration from historians:[12] there is word of "new edicts" in

Asia in the 170s, a "decree of the Senate" in the 180s and an alleged order against Church leaders from the Emperor Maximin in the mid-230s. The first is known from the "book" which Melito the Christian addressed to the Emperor Marcus: he refers to it in terms which make it plain that the "edict" was not the Emperor's own. Probably, the "edict" was due to the enthusiasm of a new provincial governor who had announced a special readiness to hear Christian trials. The "decree of the Senate" occurs in a florid Greek version of a martyrdom whose other details are inexact. As it stands, it cannot be trusted. As for Maximin's "order," it is Eusebius's false deduction from general remarks by Origen. An Imperial edict against the Christians has thus been removed from the early history of the subject. Between the reign of Trajan and the year 250, persecution is better understood as a response to pressure from the Emperor's subjects than as his own initiative, enforced from above.

Indeed, the Emperor did more to protect the Christians than to stamp them out. When the Emperor Trajan replied to inquiries from his governor Pliny, he ruled that Christians must be given a proper trial before their own accusers and that judges must not give weight to anonymous attacks. This reply, issued c. 110, was essentially confirmed by the Emperor Hadrian in 122/3 when "the provincials," perhaps the provincial council of Asia, petitioned his governor for greater licence.[13] The ruling set the legal framework for the Christians' trials and gave them no mean protection. Legally, Christians were "not to be hunted out." Accusers had to endure the delay and expense of prosecution before a governor who visited their nearest assize city perhaps once in a year. We now know rather more about the volume of other business awaiting him, from a series of numbered petitions, surviving on papyrus. It has been estimated that over 1,804 petitions were presented at the assizes at Arsinoë in just over two days in March 209: "if we calculate that the prefect's office remained open ten hours a day—the maximum allowable length—then the petitions were handed in at a rate of better than one a minute."[14]

Historians have tended to leave persecution to its legal framework, but if we remember how overburdened this framework became, we must allow for other types of conflict and their private resolution. Christians might be married to pagans or surrounded by pagan families and parents. In one instance, we know of a matrimonial wrangle between a Christian wife and a pagan husband which reached a court of law. It was an unusual case, and more often, one presumes, these disputes were settled unofficially behind closed doors. An early-third-century Church order refers to such "domestic chastening": we know of pagan slave owners who abused their Christian slaves; in 303, seven girls from Thessalonica admitted to studying their Scriptures in secrecy, "considering their own family worse than enemies." When a persecution broke out, they fled to the hills. In 203, the well-born Christian Perpetua recorded in her prison diary how her loving father had visited her in the cells and had been so enraged when she called herself a Christian that he "threw himself at me to tear my eyes out." By reducing the history of Christian persecution to a history of its legal hearings, we miss a large part of the victimization.[15]

Even the majority of martyrs' trials, as described by Christian contemporaries, do not conform to the spirit of Trajan's ruling. Only twice do they show accusers as well as Christians before a governor's tribunal. Their stories may omit the prosecutors and focus deliberately on the martyrs, but there are clear cases, too, of Christians who were being illicitly "hunted down." We do not know what caused the hunt for Polycarp in Smyrna, probably in 155/6, or the hunt for Christians in Lyons c. 177. There is a tension here between the Emperors' rescripts and the practice of governors who had the general duty of seeing to their provinces' peace and quiet. The governors' procedure and sentences are sometimes "irregular," and as their overriding concern was order, the discrepancy need not surprise us. The ban on "hunting" could never be absolute. When persecution threatened, Christians tended to withdraw or hide, and without some informed pursuit their leaders would never have been found at all. The stories of their arrests, therefore, are our best sources for governors' police troops in action.[16] Initially, the troops worked with the local "peacekeeping" forces of a city, but when the Emperors' edicts ordered persecution in the mid-third century, they had an important role as "flying squads," seizing Christians from retreat. The authors of our martyrdoms have an exact grasp of these troopers' titles, even when writing in Greek: they remind us that these local detachments, at major "stations" in a province, were known in detail to the inhabitants, much as we might identify the various types of military aircraft, brought in to keep our peace.

There is a gap, however, in the Christians' own narratives: no early story of martyrdom explains the origin of a city's persecuting fervour. From other evidence, we can imagine good reasons, while always remembering that different people may have hated or feared the

Christians for differing reasons. Now that persecution has been freed from an explicit Imperial order, its motives have been well studied at different social levels, among provincials and their city leaders, governors of provinces and, however negatively, the Emperors themselves.

At a popular level, Christians attracted blackmail and slander: in Rome, as early as 64, it was plausible to accuse them of morally outrageous conduct. Who knows how many heirs and neighbours wanted a condemned Christian's goods? Melito wrote to Marcus that the persecutors were "covetous of Christians' property": one Christian story tells of accusations against the Christian soldier Marinus by people who wanted his job.[17]

Secondary motives are present in any persecution, but they do not account for the continuing outbursts in the cities or the particular form of the governors' trials. Here, the Christians' "atheism" was the basic cause of their maltreatment. Some intellectual pagans decried the forms of contemporary cult, but almost all concurred with them when necessary; the Christians refused to concur, and their lack of respect was intolerable. It was also dangerous. "Perhaps some god has conceived spite against us, angry because of the sacrifices: hard, indeed, is the anger of a god . . ." These Homeric verses still spoke for a widespread fear and attitude. If a god was dishonoured, he might send his anger against the community, in the form of famine, plague or drought. "No rain, because of the Christians," had become proverbial by the mid-fourth century.

The persecutions, therefore, connect neatly with the features which we identified as the living heart of pagan religiousness: honour and anger, and the appeasing advice of oracles. Persecution would have occurred at any period, because it attached to the bedrock of this religiousness, as old as the age of Homer, in which it was first expressed for us. The persecutions are good evidence that the essential continuity of pagan religiousness was still significant. It was not the preserve of a few antiquarians: it still animated whole cities.

The primary role of "atheism" helps to explain the course of the governors' trials. Nobody minded too much what Christians did or did not believe. A gesture of honour to the gods and conformity to tradition was all that was required of them.[18] As a governor told Bishop Dionysius, there would be no objection if the bishop would only worship the pagan gods as well as his own. In Africa, Tertullian knew of a governor who had tried to help Christians acquit themselves. Some allowed them to offer a pinch of incense instead of meat and strove to find a "convenient" form of words. They wanted worshippers of their own gods, not martyrs for a faith. The whole procedure was lacking in religious zeal. The fear of "atheism" in the abstract was not so strong that governors or Emperors before the mid-third century ever tried to stamp the Christians out.[19] Some of the philosophers dismissed belief in the "anger" of the gods as mere superstition, an attitude which one Emperor, Marcus, certainly professed to share. Persecution occurred nonetheless in his reign, at a local level where the fear of "atheism" had been brought to life by particular events. Particular ignitions were necessary if a city or a crowd were to call for Christians to be arrested. We seldom know their exact nature, though droughts, plague and famines were the most frequent causes. In turn, they caused cities to consult oracles and receive the gods' advice on the rites with which to appease sudden anger in heaven. These rites involved sacrifices, acts which the Christians could not join. There may often have been an indirect link between oracles and local bursts of persecution.

In a crisis, fear of the gods' anger came to life, supported by oracles, epiphanies and the traditional culture of the cities: even the most philosophic governor or city magistrate would think twice if faced with a possible riot. Governors, meanwhile, had their own interests to consider. As members of the senatorial order, they shared its respect for Roman morals and tradition. Governors were sensitive to charges of treason or disloyalty, not least because they could be prosecuted in Rome for failing to take them seriously. Most of the governors were heavily indebted to the reigning Emperor for their position, and it is no surprise that they refer Christian suspects to the Emperor's cult.[20] Several times, we find governors offering the challenge of an "oath by the Emperor's genius," or in Greek, his "fortune." As Christians themselves said that they could pray for the Emperor's *salus*, in the sense of his "salvation," but not his "safety," could they not compromise and swear the oath too?[21] These requirements are never cited as the cause of the Christians' arrest in the first place: provincials did not denounce them because of their refusal to pay cult to the Emperors. The issue is only aired in the courtroom by governors themselves, and at times they air it as an easier way out for the people on trial. That, perhaps, made it doubly diabolic in Christian literature.

In 180, a governor in Carthage remarked before passing sentence that the Christians had been given a chance to return "to the Romans' custom," or *mores*. This note of frustrated Romanity recurs elsewhere, as does the stress on morals. In the second century, especially, extreme gossip accused Christians of a lurid range of immorality. Their Eucharist was insulted as cannibalism; their secret meetings were said to practise incest and child murder and to resort to group sex when the lights were turned down in church. The better-informed Greek pagan authors do not mention these slanders, not even Celsus in his fierce attack on the faith. However, Christian authors rebut them as if they were common currency in both the West and the East before c. 230: they also apply them to fellow Christians whom they deemed heretical. It is not, then, surprising that they had continued to circulate in high society: in the 160s, Fronto, the literary tutor of the Emperor Marcus, referred to Christian immorality in a speech where it served, most probably, as a passing example in an invective against a pagan.[22] In Lyons, c. 177, wild charges of immorality inflamed a persecution which had already broken out. They were not, however, its origin. After Pliny's letter, written c. 110, it was generally known in the ruling classes that the extreme allegations of Christian vice were false. Coercion to "Roman *mores*" was something more general, a wish to oblige a return to Roman "discipline," the inherited way of behaviour. The form of the governors' trials puts the moral slanders in perspective. If a Christian suspect honoured the gods, he went free. No suspicion of past immorality was held against him, because immorality was irrelevant to the essential grounds of the trial. Bygones, therefore, were allowed to be bygones.

As a result, lapsed Christians were also tolerated, a principle which was first set out in Trajan's answer to Pliny. Pliny had been faced with people who had once been Christians but had given up the religion: he investigated the rumours of immorality and found them completely unfounded. Should past belief be held against a man who had done nothing else wrong? He thought it should not and wrote to Trajan for confirmation. Trajan agreed with him.

If there had been no lapsed Christians, Pliny would probably not have troubled Trajan with his procedure: he had already beheaded those Christians who were not Roman citizens. Formally, the nature of their crime was by now their "name" as Christians, and there, on the whole, the matter has been left. In any given case, governors may have felt personal outrage at other aspects: the apparent treason and disloyalty, the success in influencing other converts, the obstinacy, the "steadfast face," the un-Roman behaviour with the rumours of immorality in the background. Christians disturbed the peace of a province, and detracted from the gods' honours and most governors would agree that "atheists" might provoke anger in heaven. If many governors in the second century had been asked to be more precise, one suspects they would simply have said that Christians were Christians; they had been persecuted elsewhere, and precedent required governors to take up accusations and persecute them again, without too much thought for the niceties.

These conclusions risk becoming circular, as if Christians were persecuted because they were Christians. They raise a more difficult problem: why were Christians persecuted, whereas Jews, meanwhile, were not? The Jews, too, were exclusive "atheists." Many provincial cities detested them, and many Romans enjoyed anti-Semitic slanders. Since the years of friction in Hellenistic Alexandria, malicious Greek authors had vilified the Jews' early history and had accused them of a past in which they had sacrificed foreigners. Their rites were insulted, mere "pig worship," and their circumcision was thought ridiculous. They diverted income from the pagan temples, and initially, they did not put their property at a city's service. Like Christians, first-century Jews were keen pursuers of converts. Unlike Christians, they involved the Romans in three major wars between 70 and 132.[23]

Jews, however, could not be brought to trial for their atheism, or their "name," a fact whose explanation begins where Gibbon sought it, in the antiquity of the Jews' worship. Romans respected the old and venerable in religion, and nothing was older or more venerable than Jewish cult: "the Jews were a people which followed, the Christians a sect which deserted, the religion of their fathers."[24] Unlike the Christians, they had a Law whose wisdom, as we have seen, impressed Apollo at Didyma. There were other points in their favour. The stories of Jewish crimes and immorality were focussed on the Jews' remote past and were less vivid than the stories of contemporary Christian "cannibalism." Jews did not idealize virginity and caused less bother to their converts' mixed marriages. Synagogues were well-known buildings, some of which stood in prominent civic sites, whereas the Christian meetings in house-churches were new and secret and more mysterious. Publicly, the Jewish cult was more familiar. Until the destruction of the Temple, it had involved the sacrifice of animals, and it had not been visibly disloyal: Augustus is said to have paid for victims to be offered "on his behalf," and the upper-class Jewish priesthood had had a strong history of support for Rome.

After the final war in Judaea and the destruction of Jerusalem in 135, Jews' attitudes to the Roman Empire continued to vary.[25] Generally, Roman rule was regarded with little enthusiasm, the "reign of Esau" or Daniel's Fourth Beast, and prayers for its ending were offered in the synagogues. However, Jewish writings on the subject, in the second and third centuries, showed a certain caution. Like the Christians', they varied between covert hostility and a worldly submission: "better the Devil you know" until God brought the Messianic age. Roman rule was God's punishment for Israel's sins. Unlike the Christians, some Jews also had a long history of public support for pagan rulers. Synagogues in Hellenistic Egypt had been dedicated "on behalf of" the ruling Ptolemy, a practice which was still alive in the reign of the Emperor Caligula. Among certain Jews, this loyalism did not die, not even after the 130s. When the Emperor Verus visited Sardis in 166, the city's prosperous Jewish community is now thought to have commemorated the occasion in a Hebrew inscription, set in their synagogue. In Ostia's synagogue, c. 200, a Greek inscription recorded the gift of an ark for the Scriptures and was headed by a Latin invocation for the "safety," or *salus*, of the Emperor. Christians, too, said they could pray for the Emperor's *salus* (safety, but also salvation): it is doubtful, however, whether any such inscription for a Roman Emperor would ever have been found in a house-church.

These differences of emphasis were all significant, but the basic difference lay in the history of patronage. In the Hellenistic age, Jews had been settled as useful soldiers in several regions by the ruling Hellenistic kings. Some of their most prominent seats in the later Diaspora, in Cyrene, Phrygia and Sardis, had developed from this royal service. The Jews had also been prompt allies of the Roman advance in the Near East: in the late Republic, they had found a great patron and champion in Julius Caesar. His privileges for the Jews in Rome set a framework for relations which Augustus and his first heirs respected. In the early Empire, Jews, the former soldiers, were exempted from military service in the Roman legions.[26] Nonetheless, individual Imperial responses continued to protect them from attack by their neighbours in pagan cities, and their privileges were not totally revoked after any of their great revolts. While Christians were persecuted, Jews were officially tolerated. In the later second and the third century, we have the growing evidence of a prominent

Jewish presence in the civic life of great cities in the Greek East.

At first, Christians had enjoyed the same toleration from Roman governors, who regarded them as a sect within the Jews. In 51/2, Gallio, the governor of Achaea, dismissed Jewish complaints against the Christians as an internal religious dispute: he "cared for none of these things."[27] Yet by 110, Pliny was writing as if he could have expected to attend Christian trials in his earlier career as a senator: what, since Gallio, had gone wrong?

The outlines of an answer are latent in the Acts of the Apostles and its story of the trials of St. Paul. Eventually, Paul was shipped from Caesarea for trial in Rome, and as he travelled, an angel is said to have promised him that "he must stand before the Emperor." In Acts, angels' predictions were not mistaken, although this particular prediction was not pursued in the book.[28] Its story ends abruptly with Paul's open arrest in Rome for two years, and afterwards, Paul must have "stood before the Emperor," on a trial by Nero or one of his senior officials, perhaps the prefect of the city with powers to inflict death. Many theories have been given of Acts' "purpose," its concern to spread orthodoxy, to portray an idealized Paul, to write some supposed "salvation history" or to justify the Gentile mission in its scheme for the end of the world and its reiterated "plan of God." Answers would do better to begin from the work's preface and its abrupt conclusion.

Acts and its companion volume, the third Gospel, were dedicated to "most excellent" Theophilus, who wished to "know more exactly" about the faith "of which he had heard." Only one other type of person is called "most excellent" in the two books: a Roman provincial governor. The usage of contemporary Emperors and the incidence of the title in inscriptions and the papyri confirm that "most excellent" people were people of very considerable rank and position:[29] Theophilus, then, is the cover name for a highly placed figure in Roman circles. Acts' abrupt ending is explained if "Theophilus" knew the sequel to Paul's years of arrest. "Theophilus" had heard of Paul's trial and execution: perhaps he had attended both. He wished to know the truth of a faith which had interested him but now lay under this recent cloud. Acts and the third Gospel are the first, and greatest, of Christian apologies to be addressed to highly placed pagans.

Why, then, was Paul tried and condemned? The course of his

imprisonment has been discussed repeatedly in terms of Roman law and obscure allusions in the texts of later Roman jurists. A neglected approach lies through Acts' companion volume, the third Gospel, where Paul's trial is matched by the narration of the trial of Jesus. Of all four Gospels the third is the most insistent that Jesus was innocent, and was freely pronounced to be so by all who heard him. To emphasize this truth, the author included fictitious hearings of Jesus while under arrest and gave bystanders' fictitious remarks at the time of the Crucifixion.[30] He exaggerated, but he was serving a basic truth: Jesus was totally innocent. In Acts, the tone is similar. Throughout the missionary journeys, the Christian faith is emphasized by the many scenes in which pagans misunderstand it. When Paul is arrested, he, too, is shown to be innocent. Only when the Jews were about to lynch him for a crime in the Temple which he had not committed did the Roman troops intervene and rescue him.

The sequel is more intricate. As a Roman citizen, Paul was entitled to a privileged respect for his person. He could also "appeal" from a Roman's trial: the right had once obtained in the city of Rome, but had extended and then become attached to the person of the Emperor.[31] However, there was only point in "appealing" if a citizen felt that he had a better chance at a privileged hearing by a second authority. For two years, Paul did not claim this privilege but stayed quietly in the Roman governor's prison in Caesarea, out of reach of his Jewish pursuers. We do not know why he had not "appealed" earlier, but perhaps he felt safer where he was and did not wish to risk this second hearing. By itself, his long delay does not disprove the existence of this citizen right.

After two years, however, Festus, a new governor, arrived, where-upon the Jews hired a professional orator and set out to mislead him. They expanded their initial charge that Paul had introduced Gentiles into the Temple, and two years after the event, began to allege that Paul preached "contrary to Caesar" and "contrary to the teachings of the Jews." The mention of "Caesar" was a new departure, and before the governor could respond, Paul took advantage of it. He "called on" Caesar, as Acts describes, using the Greek term for the Romans' right of "appeal." Perhaps Paul feared the consequences if he said nothing: he now risked condemnation on this new charge by a governor who did not know the facts. Equally, the governor was glad of the opening. He dared not ignore this serious allegation of action "against Caesar," for fear of his own subsequent prosecution. After conferring with his advisers, he decided to inquire no further. He agreed to rid himself of the problem and despatch Paul to Rome.

Perhaps he would have despatched him even if Paul had not appealed: actions "against Caesar" were best heard by Caesar himself. However, said Acts, before the governor despatched him, he introduced him to high-ranking Jewish visitors, Agrippa and Queen Berenice. In Acts' version, these Jews declared him entirely innocent: "If he had not appealed to Caesar," the governor was said to have remarked, he could have gone free. Acts' narrative conforms here to its author's account of Jesus's trial:[32] Christians, he showed, were agreed to be innocent and Paul was only tried in Rome because he had stood by rights of his citizenship. We may doubt that the governor would really have let the Jews' allegation pass. When Paul left for Rome, probably in 59, he joined a boatload of other prisoners (who were not citizens "on appeal"), and with him went a letter from Festus, the governor, which presumably mentioned the Jews' latest charge of "acting contrary to Caesar."

In Rome many cases were awaiting trial through Nero's indifference, and two years passed before Paul appeared before a court.[33] Acts does not pursue the story, because "Theophilus" already knew it, but eventually Paul "stood before Caesar." When first arrested, Paul was supposed to have taught the wicked Felix about "justice, continence and the world to come." "Felix," said Acts, "then begged him to stop." Perhaps Paul talked of the heavenly king; perhaps he refused to swear by the Emperor in answer to the governor's accompanying letter. Whatever happened, he was sentenced to death, and the precedent was set. The Emperor's justice had distinguished Christians from Jews, a point which was not lost on senators, the provincial governors of the future.

In 64, the city of Rome was burned in the Great Fire, and Nero and his advisers knew only too well where to find their scapegoats. They burned the Christians, a persecution with which his brutish praetorian prefect, Tigellinus, was associated by posterity.[34] After Paul's trial, the Christians were the obvious group for Nero to blame. The precedent was ever more firmly established, and persecution began to extend to the provinces, too, as their governors were willing to accept charges of the new crime. "I have not been present," wrote Pliny to Trajan, "at the trials of Christians": by implication, other men of his rank already had been. By the mid-90s, we can trace a persecution to Rome and give force to Pliny's remark.

The "persecution of Domitian" has been rejected by recent historians, but phrases in the "First Epistle of Clement," a Christian letter from Rome, prove that persecution indeed occurred in the capital during Domitian's reign.[35] There were good reasons why Christians had come to the officials' notice. Domitian had ordered a tax on Jews to be exacted with particular care, and the hunt for Jews in Rome was taken to unusual lengths: Suetonius recorded his presence in a "very crowded council" when a very elderly suspect was formally debagged to see if he was circumcised.[36] Christians were at risk to this inquisition, because many were former Jews or Jewish suspects. If they denied their Jewish liabilities in order to escape the tax, they asserted their Christianity, an offence which was even worse.

The effects went down in history. "Many Christians were martyred under Domitian," we are told, an event which was connected with the year 94. We know this from a remarkably good source whom Eusebius and later Christian chronographers preserved for us. It was not Christian, but pagan, the "history of Bruttius," perhaps the contemporary Bruttius Praesens, whom we know as a friend of Pliny and an intrepid commander on the eastern frontier.[37] After this quotation from his history, Christian sources went on to list Flavia Domitilla, a lady of senatorial connections, among the victims. Unfortunately, we cannot be quite sure that her name was given by Bruttius, too, but there is a strong possibility that it was. Nor is the persecution connected directly with Domitian himself, although Eusebius also quotes the early authority of Hegesippus the Christian for a story which involved the Emperor personally.[38] He is said to have sent for surviving members of Jesus's family and brought them from Judaea to Rome to inquire about the new Messianic king. From an early date, Christians were capable of all manner of fictions to prove their own innocence, but we cannot entirely rule out this strange report. After questioning them, Domitian is said to have found them harmless and set them free. Certainly, there had been a persecution at Rome, and probably it involved a high-ranking lady and therefore came to the Emperor's notice. Being Domitian, he might, then, have pursued the rumours of their source: the question stays open.

We have seen, then, how the Romans came to distinguish Christians from Jews. Riots and disturbances in the Jewish communities did not suffice to alert them. To draw the distinction, the Emperor or his judges in Rome had to hear a Christian who was accused of conduct "contrary to Caesar." By a chapter of accidents, the first Christian in this position was Paul: his defence and sentence brought about the new age of persecution. By the second century, the precedent was well established and Christians were being accused for the "name" of Christianity. However, the history of this charge is unintelligible if it is written without its missing first chapter. It is one of the unrecognized effects of Paul's later career that it caused Christians to be persecuted by Romans.

# II

"The Christians are not to be hunted down . . .": Trajan's famous answer to Pliny was reasserted by his successors even when cities petitioned them for something more urgent, and continued to govern the legal fate of the Christians until the mid-third century. In these relatively favoured circumstances, it takes two to make a martyr, and many people agreed to a bargain instead: the richer the Christian, the more he had to lose and also the more to offer. Bribery, therefore, became a recognized art of Christians who stood in fear of their lives: around 200, Tertullian alluded to whole churches which had bought their way out of danger and to one particular martyr, Rutilius, who had fled "frequently" from persecution and bribed his potential informers until he was suddenly arrested, tortured and martyred, much to Tertullian's relish.[1]

There was also the reluctance of Roman governors. Sometimes they banished Christians instead of killing them; sometimes they sentenced them to work in mines and quarries, where they served, their heads half shaven, under constant threat of the lash.[2] These punishments lacked the public finality of the death sentence: until 180, no governor in Africa was known to have put a Christian to death. In the late 240s, Origen insisted with rare candour that "few" Christians had died for the faith, and then only when God thought the moment ripe. They were "easily numbered," he said.[3]

However, the history of the persecutions is not only a history of the gaps in Roman provincial government. It is also the history of Christian ideals, expressed in texts of martyrdom which have been suspected of forgery, mistrusted as "unreal" or passed over with repugnance. Their provenance is varied, but undoubtedly there are contemporary stories among their number, the best of which are priceless evidence. Yet even the contemporary stories are now known to have been capable of variation. In c. 305, the bishop Phileas was tried by the governor of Egypt: a Latin version of his hearing was the first to be found and was then checked against a second find, a manuscript of tenth-century date. Then a Greek version appeared in a papyrus text copied c. 320–350, where it probably belonged in a collection of other martyrs' stories.[4] This text was similar to the Latin, but not identical, and of far greater value, as it belonged so close to the event. But then a second papyrus, of similar date, was discovered, also containing parts of a Greek version. It is reported to be similar to the other Greek papyrus's text, but not identical, and to be very close to the Latin.[5] Phileas's trial seems to have circulated in different forms from a very early date: one, perhaps, was a fuller "apology" for Christianity; the other was for use in Christian meetings. These remarkable recent discoveries add to the problems in trusting even an early martyr text as "the" version of what happened.

One of the versions of Phileas's trial may have been read at Christian meetings to commemorate the martyr. Christians did keep these anniversaries with public readings, "both as a memorial for those who have already competed," proposed the earliest-known example, the martyrdom of Polycarp (c. 155–165), "and as a training and preparation for those who will follow suit."[6] In this case, the purpose was not necessarily maintained: the text had to be revived and re-edited some eighty years later. However, it was perhaps the text, not the ceremony, which had become worn with age, for these "anniversaries" continued to be noted elsewhere, as we can see from Cyprian's letters in third-century Africa.[7]

These stories helped to reinforce the image of the martyr: our text of Polycarp's death states explicitly that it was a "training" for future martyrdoms. The martyr's rewards were believed to exceed those of any other Christian overachiever. His death effaced all sin after baptism; pure and spotless, he went straight to heaven. "There are two things," wrote Melito, bishop of Sardis, in the 170s, "which give remission of sins: baptism and suffering for the sake of Christ." "Your blood," wrote Tertullian, "is the key to Paradise."[8] Martyrs bypassed the long delays, the intervals of cooling and refreshment, the minor corrections and discipline, the years of waiting in Abraham's bosom. They sped straight to Christ and his Father, "friends of the Lord," said Cyprian, "who are hereafter to judge in his company." In the calendars of martyrs' festivals, death marked their "birthdays" into eternity.

In Christian texts, martyrs were idealized as athletes and prize-fighters in a supernatural combat. Their struggle was less with worldly officials than with the Devil, who stood behind them. Justin had already written to tell the Emperor Pius that persecution was not the work of Emperors, but of wicked demons: historians of administration have been slower to take his point.[9] Christians transposed the imagery of the earthly arena and its pagan games to their own martyrs' combats with Satan. Their martyrs were believed to enter the arena with some very powerful allies. As Jesus of the Gospels promised, the Spirit answered for the martyr when on trial for his faith. This text in Matthew's Gospel was a favourite quotation of Bishop Cyprian in the 250s, who had no doubts about its continuing truth: in 250, he believed, one particular martyr's voice had been "full of the Holy Spirit" when he cried out to the Roman governor during tortures, "You will see the contest tomorrow."[10] To us, perhaps, the prophecy seems rather obvious, but on the morrow the martyr did indeed win his "crown," perhaps in Carthage's festival games. Jesus did not only stand by his Gospel promise: to the eye of faith, he was sometimes present by association. In c. 177, at Lyons, the slave girl Blandina was suspended upside down on a post in the arena, and Christian spectators described their perception in a letter: "She seemed to hang there," they wrote, "in the form of a cross and by her concerted prayer she aroused great eagerness in those who were struggling too, for they saw, in their struggle and with their physical sight, him who was crucified on their behalf in the person of their sister Blandina . . ."[11]

How had this powerful ideal of the martyr been constructed? In its essentials, it was not new. Its origins lay firmly in Jewish piety and literature which had been inspired, once again, by the critical years of the Maccabean revolt against the Hellenistic king Antiochus IV (173–164 B.C.). At that period, immortality, let alone a resurrected afterlife, had not been the hope of the vast majority of practising Jews. After the revolt, the heroes were idealized as martyrs, present in heaven before the throne of God.[12] Of the surviving literature, two books hint particularly at this belief: the second book of Maccabees (probably composed c. 120–100 B.C.) and the fourth (composed by c. 60 A.D.). "Those who die for God," the latter book assumes, "live unto God."[13] The promise of eternal life had also been used to encourage opponents of Roman misrule. Then, the Jewish war of 70 A.D. bequeathed the memory of thousands more Jews who had preferred to die rather than betray their Jewish faith and the details of its practice. The great revolt in Judaea of the 130s added further martyrs to Jewish history, of whom the later traditions of the rabbis particularly remembered heroic scholars and teachers. In due course, the deaths of the early Jewish prophets became adorned with stories of painful martyrdom, a process which had already begun by the Christian era.[14]

Numerically, Christian martyrs are a poor second to their Jewish forerunners, and inevitably, this Jewish legacy shaped the way in which the Gospels and the Christians described their heroes' deaths. In Acts' narrative, Stephen, the first Christian martyr, enjoyed the characteristic vision of God; in Revelation, the martyrs, like the Maccabees, are pictured in heaven before God's throne.[15] The letters of Ignatius (c. 110) have been studied for parallels with the Jewish Maccabean books, especially with the fourth, which may well have been composed in his own Antioch, a city where the martyrs' memories were fresh. Exact parallels, however, have been overstated and the debt is more general, suggesting, too, certain differences.[16]

To Ignatius, the prison bonds were "spiritual pearls," an emphasis on the martyr's gift of the Spirit which was bolder than any known in previous Jewish texts.[17] In another forceful metaphor, he describes his "lust" for death and his hopes of being ground by the teeth of wild beasts into the "pure bread" of Christ. Again, this imagery is essentially Christian. In Jewish texts, the death of a martyr could be stressed as a ransom and atonement for the sins of the entire nation, like a grand atoning sacrifice in the Temple cult. The imagery did not totally escape Christian authors, least of all Ignatius, but there was less scope for it, as Jesus's death was considered to have atoned already for humans' sin. The idea of personal oblation was more apt, and it seems that Ignatius was exploiting the idea of his death as a Eucharistic offering in which his blood was to be the wine and his body, crunched by beasts, the bread of God.[18]

Above all, Christians could be referred to the model of Christ's own sacrifice. The contemporary authors of Polycarp's martyrdom understood the event in these colours, and in the 250s, Cyprian's letters continued to set the ideal before Christians in prison. Imitation of Christ was a counter to excess ambition and suicidal display.[19] In Jewish history, martyrs had died for the Law and its observance. Among Christians, martyrs died because they refused to honour the pagan gods. Before them lay the example and promises of Jesus, who had gone passively to his death, refusing to explain to his judges the truth, in his view, of his mission. The element of personal surrender was not lost on some of his heirs.

There is also a difference of literary effect. The surviving Jewish texts which hint at the martyrs' rewards are texts on martyrdoms in the distant past, the deaths of the patriarchs or prophets or the Maccabean heroes. They dwell on tortures and say little, if anything, of the martyrs' own response and personal experience. Their style is verbose and they lack the detail and courtroom protocol which the best Christian narratives deploy. A select few of the Christian texts were the work of eyewitnesses and even, as we shall see, of martyrs themselves. They have a range of detail and frank expression which makes them priceless evidence for perceptions of the trials and prisons of their time. Some of them, too, were the work of literary Christians, friends of the poor sufferers whom they wished to honour. The most effective of their texts unite literary opposites, the unbearably violent with the serene and the incorruptible. Perhaps Jewish texts, if we knew more of them, had used the same colours, but in their Christian form, they give their narratives a lasting power.

Martyrs endured appalling tortures and succumbed to the beasts in the arena, horrors which Christian narrators did not evade. But they did not suffer, enjoying "anaesthesia" and an "analgesic state."[20] They were "not harmed" by the flames at the stake: their faces "glowed," their bodies "regained" the bloom of youth. Their visions of Paradise and their scenes of death evoked a contrasting joy and tranquillity. They pictured that green peace which meets us later as the background to so many subsequent Christian mosaics. Among the best of these contrasts are the memoirs of the African martyr Marian.[21] "Our road," he told of his vision before death, "lay through a country of lovely meadows, clothed with the lush foliage of green woods, shaded by tall cypresses and pine trees which beat on the very heavens, so that you would think that the place was crowned, amid all its winding perimeter, with green groves. In the middle was a hollow abounding in the teeming veins of a crystal-clear fountain . . ." There is no better literary evocation of the traditional "pleasant spot" in all third-century Latin. When the martyrs reached their place of death, their friend and narrator could not resist a last pen picture to point the contrast. The place itself, he wrote, was like Paradise, in contrast to its scene of physical violence. A river ran in a valley between high hills on either side "like a theatre," so that the "stream in its hollow drank the martyrs' blessed blood." Pagan scenes of divine encounters had joined intimacy and terror; Christian stories of martyrdom linked obscene violence with natural serenity.

By a similar pairing of opposites, their texts turned suffering into triumph. Martyrs, wrote Cyprian, "were only breathing, heavenly things." They delighted the Lord with the "sublime, the great, the acceptable spectacle," the "flow of blood which quenches the flames and the fires of hell by its glorious gore."[22] This type of "theology" repels most modern readers, and even at the time, superior "Gnostic" Christians did not fail to challenge it. Awareness of the Truth, they said, assured a man's salvation, whereas death for the Name was a hideous waste. Like Muslims in hostile countries, these heretical Christians exalted the wise virtue of dissimulation, saying one thing while meaning another in their hearts. At best, they believed, a martyrdom might help to purify the sinful, but it was quite irrelevant to Christians who had true "knowledge."[23]

It is easy to sympathize with these critics and suspect that authors' theology of martyrdom varied in direct proportion to their own chances of suffering the pain themselves: Cyprian, after all, wrote as a man who had hidden himself prudently in a year of major persecution. However, the ideals extend across too wide a range of evidence for the suspicion to stand. "Today, we are in heaven," exclaimed the Scillitan martyrs in Africa, when sentenced by a puzzled judge.[24] The same visions of tranquillity and "company with the Spirit" are known from the evidence of martyrs themselves. Here, the richest source once again is the Greek diary which Perpetua kept in her prison at Carthage. In her own words she recorded the grand vision which she had experienced on the night before she was thrown to the beasts. Before Christ, the heavenly umpire, she seemed to be defeating a loutish Egyptian wrestler, one of the heavy sweating Egyptians who competed in the cities' games. Having thrown this symbol of the Devil, she received apples, the prize in Apollo's games at Carthage, the occasion of her imminent death.[25] To the last, Perpetua's dreams saw her trial as a triumph over Satan, in which Christ was to be a constant presence, accompanying her as closely as possible. When I have to face the wild beasts, she told her jailor, "another will be within me who will suffer for me, and I shall be suffering for him." On the next day, wrote a Christian spectator, Perpetua advanced calmly into the arena and assisted a young gladiator to kill her, "having guided his wavering hand to her throat." Readers of her diary can easily credit the bravado which impressed the audience.

In turn, her diary influenced other narratives: we can also compare it with a precious group of Latin letters which have survived among Cyprian's correspondence.[26] They derived from simple Christians in prison while they awaited their deaths. Like Perpetua, they fully accepted the ideals of triumph. They were eager, they wrote, to "quit men in order to stand among angels," to "become the colleague of Christ in suffering." "When torn by all instruments of cruelty," they wrote to Cyprian, we "aspire to overcome torture by the tortures themselves" and "not to shudder at our own blood, streaming forth." Simple men, they quoted text upon text from the Gospel's promises: "When we read and compare these things and the like in the Gospels, we feel, in our Lord's words, 'torches' put under us to kindle our faith; not only do we no longer dread the enemies of the truth, we even challenge them . . ."[27]

Beside these assurances, we can set a more personal exchange of letters, made between the young Celerinus in Rome and the confessor Lucian, who lay in Carthage's prison.[28] "I know," wrote Celerinus, "that each one in your position no longer regards the world, but hopes for a heavenly crown . . ." He went on to beg Lucian to absolve two of his female friends who had lapsed very slightly, and in return, he received a remarkable note. The confessors in Carthage, it said, had been crammed into two inner dungeons and left to die from thirst and hunger and overcrowding. For nearly two weeks, Lucian had been suffering. For five days before writing his letter, he had only had scraps of bread and water. For a further eight days, he had endured total starvation in close confinement. Yet he still wrote and upheld the common ideals: "now," he said, "we have attained to very brightness itself." Starving slowly to death, Lucian was "fulfilling those wishes" he had "always dreamed of." The ideals helped this simple confessor to attain his end, the hungriest author of any text to survive from antiquity.

Like the hope of future brightness, the gift of the Spirit was not the invention of authors who were looking safely on. As we have seen, it was a true visionary power, reported by its recipients, supported by expectations and enhanced by the enforced fasting and "sensory deprivation" in the fearful heat and darkness of the city prisons. It was no respecter of persons: like several other beneficiaries, Perpetua had not even been baptized. Its gift, however, made condemned prisoners into the highest authorities in the Church. The Spirit enabled them to "bind and loose," forgiving fellow Christians' sins, and to pronounce on heresy and orthodoxy. Just as the words of Montanus and his "Spirit" were taken all the way to Lyons for an opinion from Christians in prison, so it was a serious matter when condemned Christian "confessors" later spoke out against Origen and his doctrine from a mine in Egypt.[29]

There is no doubt, then, that the entire theology of martyrdom sustained and animated many Christians when under arrest. They believed their Gospel's promises and warnings, and to those who believe, martyrdom needs no justification. To those who do not, it must seem questionable; can a belief only survive if its holders die for it? Christians, certainly, were quick to exploit their martyrs' legacy, their deeds, their anniversaries, the little pieces of their bodies. Martyrs became such a part of the Church's identity that their effect transcended the moments between their sentence and consequent oblivion beyond the grave. The survivors, in short, gave martyrdom its most solid consequences. Despite the rhetoric, martyrs were not a very prolific "seed of the Church." Some of their observers are said to have converted to Christianity, but not many;[30] their public endurance perhaps did more to convey their faith's intensity than to propagate it. Had Christians compromised, as Gnostic Christians thought they should, it is far from obvious that Christianity would not have spread as it did. Its greatest expansion followed the Emperor Constantine's conversion, which owed nothing to martyrs' examples. In its greatest age of growth, martyrdom was no longer an option, as Christians were a favoured and protected group.

A religion of compromise would not, however, have been a Christian religion. Behind every martyrdom, whether or not the texts chose to dwell on it, lay the self-sacrifice of Jesus himself.[31] To be a Christian, baptized or not, was to recognize the supreme value of this selfless death at the hands of misguided authorities. At its heart, Christianity glorified suffering and passive endurance; did this ideal and its rewards perhaps encourage Christians to seek arrest in the first place?

Martyrdom brought great publicity and near-universal admiration. It had no use for sophistication or for a complex awareness of the complexities in human choices. It required a simple, persistent response, which was admirable even if it irritated others and had only to be repeated to attain its end. This compound of qualities has an appeal for various sorts of person, but it appeals especially to the young or the inexperienced and to those who do not reflect habitually that all may not be quite as it seems. Such a habit of reflection does not come easily, and among the early Christians there were particular forces working against it, the certainty of faith, the misguided ideals of single-mindedness and simplicity of heart. To the overachiever, the rewards and esteem of martyrdom had a clear and final attraction. Why live, if death brought a martyr to Christ? In a vivid anecdote, Tertullian described how a group of Christians had approached the governor of Asia on his assize tour in 185 and begged him to put them to death. He refused to oblige most of them, remarking that they were free to use cliffs and ropes if they wished. Although the story may not be true, it purported to give the governor's answer in Greek and was meant to seem plausible.[32] "Volunteering" did indeed occur: in 258, according to Eusebius, three men in the countryside outside Caesarea heard that fellow Christians were winning "crowns" in the city and began to reproach themselves for holding back. "With this in mind, they went together to the governor and attained their end . . ."

Simple "volunteering," however, was not to most Christians' taste. Several authors, including Origen and Clement, warned against it, and Cyprian told his Roman governor that the discipline of the Church did not permit his Elders to give themselves up of their own accord. Ignatius wrote extravagantly of his "passion for death" as he travelled in bonds to Rome, but he was also anxious that fellow Christians might try to frustrate his urge.[33] On closer inspection, the majority of known "voluntary martyrdoms" turn out to be more understandable.[34] Almost all of them were secondary martyrdoms, sparked off by the sight or news of fellow Christians who were being tried, abused or sentenced: even Eusebius's three heroes were thought to have been prompted in this way. Elsewhere, the urge was more immediate. In the heat of the moment friends and spectators declared their common loyalty with the poor victims of injustice. When the governor of Egypt, in the last "great" persecution, sentenced some Christian virgins to a fate worse than death, Hierocles the Christian leapt at him, according to Eusebius, knocked him over and hit him as he lay on the ground. Such passion ran in the family: Hierocles's brother had earlier shown hardly less audacity against a governor in Caesarea. The courtroom was a great breeding ground of spontaneous Christian protest. Whole groups gave themselves away, in surges of indignation at unjust decisions, and there were some touching scenes of loyalty: in 310, when the noble and highly educated Pamphilus was sentenced to death in Caesarea, his eighteen-year-old slave demanded permission from the back of the courtroom to receive the body for burial. The demand betrayed him and he too went heroically to his death. In the heat of the moment, martyrdom proved infectious, for reasons of indignation and group loyalty which we can well understand.

We must allow, too, for the impact of the persecutions which the authorities initiated from the year 250 onwards. Once the order to persecute had been given, Christians might indeed make a public protest and thus draw attention to their faith. In the year 305, Eusebius describes how a rumour had spread at Caesarea that Christians would be thrown to the beasts during a great festival. As the governor approached the amphitheatre, he was astonished to meet six Christians with their hands bound, demanding to be killed in the arena. He imprisoned them and ordered them to be beheaded instead; significantly, they were all young men. A year earlier, on April 29, 304, "a man named Euplus shouted outside the veil which curtained off the prefect's chamber in the most illustrious city of Catania, in Sicily. He said, 'I want to die; I am a Christian.' And the illustrious governor said, 'Come in, whoever it was who shouted out.' " Thereupon, Euplus is said to have entered, carrying his copies of the forbidden Gospels. The story is not demonstrably historical, but again, it was meant to be plausible.[35]

The sight of condemned Christians provoked some volunteers, and an existing persecution provoked others. Others were provoked by their awareness of a former lapse or the fear that people around them were about to lapse too. We know most about these motives from the disciplinary canons issued by Peter, bishop of Alexandria, in the last years of persecution, and we can judge their power from several earlier texts, especially Cyprian's letters.[36] Lapsed Christians, we know, might provoke a second arrest in order to court death and clear their deadly sin, and we can appreciate the fears if we attend to Cyprian's vivid sermon, "On the Lapsed." Cyprian composed it in Carthage in mid-251, after a year of concerted persecution, and although he may have been fulminating on purpose, his case histories had to seem plausible to his audience. The "lapse" of offering a pagan sacrifice involved more than the roasting of meat on a bonfire while mumbling a prayer to some ill-defined divinity. Sacrificers also had to eat what they offered, and Cyprian chilled his audience with tales of Christians who had not survived the effects.[37] One woman who had lapsed and eaten pagan meat had dared to go down to the public baths as if nothing had happened. On entering, she had thrown a fit. Another lapser had come to Holy Communion, only to find that the Eucharist turned to ashes in his hands. "How many are daily possessed by unclean spirits?" asked Cyprian. "How many are driven out of their minds and racked by a frenzy of fury and madness?" Sermons of this type kept up the pressure: if we look at modern case histories of shock after breaches of religious conduct, we may be more confident that Cyprian was not inventing the argument. According to Christians, demons sat on the very pieces of meat which were offered in their name and swarmed in the accompanying smoke and incense. By their demonic imagery, Christians took the "presence" of the gods at a sacrifice as literally as any Homeric hero, more literally, perhaps, than many pagan contemporaries. Christians, therefore, who had eaten a sacrifice had eaten demons with it. There were many proofs of their indigestion.

Only the other day, said Cyprian, a baby had howled in church during Communion and had refused to touch a drop of the wine from the chalice. The congregation ought to have guessed: the child's nanny, said Cyprian, had taken it down to pay sacrifice in its mother's absence and the officials had fed it on bread which was soaked in wine from a pagan libation. Babies' screams during "family service" were a vivid proof of the effects of a meal of demons.

It is important to give due weight to these threatening stories because they may help to explain why some lapsed Christians could not live with their sin and returned to efface it by provoking their own arrest. "Volunteering" is not quite the word for such conduct. Outside an existing bout of persecution, genuine cases of the "rash destructive itch" are hard to document. It is not true in any strong sense that Christians were only persecuted because they "asked for it." Too much advice and practice went the other way. In Matthew's Gospel, Jesus counselled flight during persecution, a text of which many bishops must have been glad; perhaps their predecessors invented it. As Ignatius knew, Christians tried to ransom prisoners by any available means and save them from death: himself, he had to beg the brethren not to interfere with his fate.[38] Most Christians needed no traditions to encourage them. To the historian, the minority who died or volunteered in a year of "great" persecution are far less significant than the vast majority who lapsed and survived. We must not be misled. Like tales of escape from a prison camp, martyrdoms were compulsive listening because so many in their audience had evaded their fate and artfully stayed put. Tales of voluntary martyrdom thus belonged in the early literature of overachievement. They were ascribed to heroes and heroines in the fictitious "Acts" of Apostles: like their teaching on sex and marriage, they were the ideals of extremists, exceeding sensible leaders' opinion. In the Christian Empire, when persecution had ended, they were then taken up by many of the legends of martyrdom, written by orthodox Christians too.

If we respect the worldly majority, we can appreciate a central role of the martyrs themselves. As immediate travellers to Paradise, martyrs were a unique point of contact between heaven and earth. They joined the great pyramid of heavenly intercessors who supported God and were so richly evoked by Origen: the angels, the Apostles, the patriarchs and, among them, too, the martyrs.[39] Intense prayer was bound closely to the martyrs' ideal and there were several stories of its proper use.[40] When the soldiers found Polycarp outside Smyrna, he had been praying continuously, day and night, "for everyone and all the churches throughout the world, as was his custom." Asking leave to pray for a further hour, he amazed them, old as he was, by praying for two, facing to the east. This use of prayer on earth was readily carried over into the image of martyrs praying and petitioning Christ in heaven. Prayer, their letters and stories hinted, was best when it was prayer for the peace and unity of whole churches. In Spain, in January 259, Felix the soldier begged Bishop Fructuosus to remember him personally as he prepared to enter the amphitheatre. Fructuosus answered in the hearing of all, "No, I must bear in mind the entire Church, stretching from East to West." In Palestine, in 309, the confessor Paul made prolonged use of his "sweet and resonant voice," beseeching God "for the reconciliation of his own people." Then he prayed for the conversion of the Jews, then for the Samaritans and other ignorant nations, including his own persecutors around him.

Prayer, at its best, could also help to heal the divisions which opened after a martyr's death. In the year 258, a close friend praised the restraint of one Lucius as he went out to die in North Africa. "Lucius was by nature mild-tempered with a pleasant disposition and a modest shyness. He had been weakened by a serious illness and the deprivations of prison, but he pushed ahead with only a few companions, for fear that an excessive crowd would begrudge him the shedding of his blood. He instructed his companions as best he could, and when the brethren said to him, 'Remember us,' 'No,' he answered, 'you must remember me.'" Prayers and memorials for martyrs could help to stiffen and unite a Church which was divided by lapsing and quarrels during persecution. It was to this unified prayer that Ignatius aspired, "that I may be found in the company of you, the Christians of Ephesus," adding a timely reminder: "you, who agreed with the Apostles at all times."

These communal scenes were particularly moving, but there was scope for more personal favours. At the moment of death, a martyr became precious property; in Carthage, the mature Saturus, a Christian, took a finger ring from his accompanying guard, dipped it in his own blood and returned it as a "pledge," telling the guard to remember "the faith and me." Among pagans, the blood of executed criminals was credited with special potency, especially in spells to cure epilepsy: had Saturus had these powers in mind?[41] If martyrs passed directly to the court of heaven, particular value attached to the parts of their earthly body. "May none of my body be left," prayed Ignatius in another context, "that I may not be a bother." His prayer was one of the least popular in the early Church.[42]

The race for bones and skin began early, as we can see from hints in the earlier martyrdoms. In the 150s, the Jews of Smyrna were said to have retained Polycarp's corpse for fear that Christians would start a cult of it. In 259, Spanish Christians hurried to gather the ashes of Fructuosus and his fellow martyrs, until "Fructuosus appeared to them in a vision and ordered that whatever each had taken of his ashes out of love for him should be returned without delay." Martyrs did not enjoy these indiscriminate dispersions; the vision glossed over an ugly competition. In the third century, the fictitious "Acts" of Thomas told how the Apostle had been killed by Misdaeus, an Indian king, how Misdaeus's son had fallen sick and Misdaeus had planned to heal him by taking a bone from Thomas's corpse and setting it on his child. The body, however, had gone, and Misdaeus had to take dust from its tomb instead, hanging it on his son's neck and healing him, the first beneficiary of a relic in any Christian text. If the idea was included in a fiction, masquerading as history, it was presumably familiar in people's lives.

These beliefs were not without foundation, and like so many religious innovations, they could point to "evidence": they received the support of dreams.[43] In prison, Perpetua's diary describes how she prayed for the fate of her young, dead brother and then saw in a subsequent vision how her intercession had been granted. Who would dispute such powers when their own dreams seemed to prove them right? There were also the dreams of survivors, seeing their recent blood-spattered victims. In 202/3, in Alexandria, the martyred Potamiaena appeared after her death to the soldier Basileides, a "disciple" of Origen who had escorted her to the stake; she told him that she had "interceded" with Christ for a favour and had gained her prayer that he should be martyred too. On the very next day, Basileides was beheaded: who could deny that martyrs were as good as their word? On earth, they could be alarmingly assertive. When Saturus and Perpetua celebrated their last day in prison, they mocked the "curiosity" of those pagans who gathered to watch. Grimly, they threatened them with the judgement of God. "Why do you look freely at what you hate?" Saturus asked. "Friends today, enemies tomorrow. . . . However, take careful note of our faces, so that you may recognize us on that Day of Judgement . . ." The crowd departed in astonishment, and "many believed" after this stern and confident threat.

How new were these beliefs in the power of martyrs' remains? There was nothing comparable in pagan cult: had Jews already retained relics and fragments of past martyrs for their faith? The rabbis and their texts do not discuss the matter, and although it might have flourished despite them, we would then expect some contrary comments on the subject. Martyrs, patriarchs, pious teachers and heroes certainly had their memorials, familiar to Jesus, who cited them in a Gospel saying. Significantly, they honoured past heroes, whose bodies lay elsewhere and did not themselves contain bones and corpses, so far as we know. These memorials were private foundations and were not a recognized part of public Jewish worship in the synagogues.[44] Among Christians, private patrons did honour the martyrs too, but from an early date their commemoration became part of official Christian worship. In due course, the cult attracted copious funds from Christian churches.

It is possible to trace this difference to a fundamental difference of ideas. Among the Jews, the idea of the immortal martyr had developed late in a religion whose Mosaic law had declared a grave to be unclean for the living. In Christianity, however, the dead were a primary focus of hope and interest from the beginning, "sleeping," merely, until the restitution or transformation of their former bodies.

There was no uncleanness about tombs and corpses, and there was good reason to treasure the bones or dust of a martyr already in heaven. In a telling piece of advice, a third-century Christian in Syria advised his fellow Christians to meet in their cemeteries, in contrast to the Jews, in order to read Scripture, pray and celebrate the Eucharist. They should pray for those who had "fallen asleep" and need have no fear of impurity.[45] Throughout his advice, this author was concerned to refute the teachings of others who insisted on a more literal observance of the old Jewish law. His advice points neatly to the difference between Christian and Jewish sensibilities. The new Christian attitude to the dead and their relics marked a break in previous religious life. Before long, church leaders were digging up corpses and breaking them into fragments, a type of grave robbery which pagans had never countenanced. The Christians' concern for bits of the dead continued to disgust non-Christian cultures: in 1601, when the first Jesuit missionary tried to make contact with the Emperor of China, the Emperor's minister of ceremonies warned against the bones that would be brought into the palace, "inauspicious pieces of refuse."[46]

Why, though, should the powers and favours of the martyrs be delayed until their death? At their trials, martyrs had passed their oral examination: then they waited in prison, assured by their sentence of first-class honours in Paradise. They had the gift of the Spirit: could they not use it meanwhile to help the mass of lesser Christians who feared a final judgement they were sure to fail? Through the Spirit, a Christian could "bind and loose," and as a martyr in heaven, he could use his prayers before God for others' sins.[47] These gifts were immensely popular. In a vivid comment on fellow Christians' worldliness, queues soon formed around the martyrs' cells. We have no idea when this practice began and we have no grounds for confining it to any particular region. We first see it clearly in the scorn which Tertullian poured on "the well-known darkness of prison" to which sinners and adulterers resorted in order to clear their lapses.[48] "No sooner has anyone put on bonds than adulterers beset him, fornicators gain access, prayers echo round him, pools of tears from polluted sinners soak him . . ." As a matter of course, a Christian woman might go to kiss a martyr's chains. In turn, Tertullian hinted, others took advantage of her. One good favour deserved another, and power had its temptations: "men and women are violated in the very darkness with which they are so familiar . . ."

Wherever there were martyrs, Christians were accustomed to put these beliefs to use. They were very distinctive, and they arose from the Christians' unique combination of martyrdom with formal trials and sentencing. As Jesus had promised in the Gospels, the Spirit accompanied the martyr from the very moment of his trial. The delays between sentencing and execution and the judges' habit of trying martyrs a second or third time prolonged its company among the prisoners. As a result, Christian "confessors" had opportunities which the martyrs of other world religions have lacked. The martyr heroes of the Jews died immediately in war and rebellion. In traditional Islam, the martyr was at first the warrior who died for the faith; then the name was applied to any Muslim who suffered instant accidental death.[49] For such people, there was no interval between sentencing and execution. In Christianity, it was not so much death as a confession while on trial which brought martyrs their power: not every confessor went on to die, and although there was a view that only those who did could give effective absolution, other confessors continued to exploit their "spiritual" gift.[50]

These differing patterns of martyrdom were matched by differing attitudes to intercession. In Islam, the Koran explicitly rejected the possibility of intercession by any intermediary before God. In Christianity, however, intercession emerged rapidly: in the first letter (falsely) ascribed to John, Christians were advised, "If any one sees his brother committing what is not a mortal sin, he must ask, and God will give him life for those whose sin is not mortal."[51] Before long, mortal sins, too, found a second home, with "bearers of Christ" in prison whose gift of the Spirit could "bind and loose." To understand the appeal of this escape route, we have only to recall the humiliating rite of penance: who would prefer to fast and grovel when a blessing from a Christian in the cells could efface a sin? Ideally, the martyrs' remissions were required to be followed by slow reconciliation in church, but it is clear that this ideal was not always upheld. Instead, veneration of the confessor became a widespread habit entrenched in many Christians' lives: it leads directly into the Christian veneration of living "holy men" which took over when persecution finally ceased.[52] By their self-mortification and "overachievement" these new perfectionists lived out the former ideals of humiliation, down to the very detail of the prison confessor's chains. In the Christian Empire, these "saints" became the new "athletes," raised to angelic status while alive. Like the cult of relics, they remained a distinctive part of Christian piety, from the age of Constantine to Tsarist Russia on the eve of the Revolution. Yet they had grown from a pattern which took root in the early years of persecution. It was through persecution that first-class Christians became marked off for use by the rest: the Christian view of the dead and the cumbrous pattern of Roman persecution gave those uses their particular forms, bequeathing a constant legacy to later Christian life.

# III

In the mid-third century, the initiative in persecution swung from the subjects and their cities to the Emperor himself. Persecution began to be ordered by Emperors' edicts, a change which brought the dangers and evasions into many more Christians' lives. The change is a turning point in Church history: what an Emperor could order, he could also suspend. It is in this light that the years from Gordian to Constantine are differently coloured in Christian history, an age when persecution came and went.

According to Eusebius, the change occurred rather earlier. The Emperor Maximin (235–238) so hated his predecessors' household, "which was composed for the most part of Christians," that he ordered a persecution of the leaders of the churches. Eusebius, it seems, was guessing.[1] We know of a local bout of persecution in Asia during Maximin's reign, but we also know of a severe earthquake in 235/6 which suffices to explain it. The bishop of Rome was also martyred, and at most Maximin or his officials may have heard the case, perhaps after local trouble in the capital. To support the idea of a general persecution, Eusebius only cited letters and works by Origen. One of them survives, and it exhorts two leading churchmen to stand firm "during the present crisis": from these remarks, Eusebius probably deduced a general order against the leaders of the Church.

A general edict departed from Trajan's ruling, and is best delayed fifteen years, for an Emperor who added Trajan's name to his own. In autumn 249, a coup brought Decius to power, a man some sixty years old and "to be compared," wrote Gibbon, "with the brightest examples of ancient virtue." By mid-December, this senator of mature ability had issued an edict which ordered sacrifice to the gods throughout the Empire. He prescribed its enforcement by commissioners who were to be chosen from local city councils. No such orders for local enforcement are known in previous surviving edicts, while there is not even a clear precedent for a universal edict which compelled all men to a course of action and did not merely regulate the rights of this or that group. When we know most of the Emperors at work, in the "eloquent provinces" of the Eastern Empire, we find them responding to requests which derive from their subjects, rather than from their own initiatives or an interest in change for change's sake. But Decius's edict stands at the head of a cluster of others whose "rising note of moral didacticism" breaks up this pattern over the next sixty years. The edict was a spontaneous, but futile, effort to make life better. If it was bad news for Christians, it was worse for the Empire's animals. They were killed in quantity for gods who did not exist.

The edict had not been entirely unexpected. Like swallows gathering by instinct for their autumn journey, Church leaders had already begun to feel that a sifting of their ranks was imminent. In its Indian summer, the Church, said Cyprian, had grown soft and lax. It had begun to cause uneasy dreams.[2] "It was revealed," said Cyprian, that an old father figure was sitting, with a young man beside him, "anxious, slightly indignant, holding his chin, with a sad expression on his face": this pose derived ultimately from the figures of mourners in pagan funerary art. Beside them, a tempter was netting the flock's weaker members and abusing them with peculiar cruelty. The dreamer, perhaps Cyprian himself, then asked what the vision meant: the divine figures lacked clear attributes, and once again a Christian asked in his vision for an explanation. The dream had been heavy with the images of testing and Christian laxity: soon afterwards, Decius cast his net. While Cyprian kept this dream to himself, Origen had already put a prediction in writing. In the late 240s, he was composing his refutation of the pagan Celsus's old and perceptive book against Christian belief, and already felt that clouds had gathered over the peace of the Church: when Christians, he said, are held responsible "for the strife which has now reached such a pitch," they will no longer be safe from persecution.[3] The words sit very well in early summer 248, when pretenders had emerged on the Danube and in the Near East against the Emperor Philip, Decius's predecessor.

Origen's fears were confirmed by their immediate sequel, a series of riots in Alexandria. We do not know exactly when these riots began, but in late 248 or early 249, without any Imperial prompting, pagans began to persecute the city's Christians. Dionysius, bishop of Alexandria, refers in the surviving parts of a letter to "a prophet of troubles for the city," a "poet" on the likeliest translation, "whoever

he was, who excited and roused the crowds against us."[4] We know
nothing more of this tantalizing figure who appears to be a pagan
exponent of oracles: was he the prophet of Serapis in the city, or did he
compose his own verses, like so many "Sibyls," and ascribe them
anonymously to the gods? He is the first known example of the link
between oracles and persecution which looms so large later: here,
quite plainly, the oracles were not seeking common ground between
Christians and pagans. This prophet caught the general mood and
heightened it, and for once, we may see reasons for the discontent.
Egypt's papyri suggest that a pattern of tax reform in the province can
be pinned to the Emperor Philip's reign. In the 290s, it has recently
become clear, the announcement of similar reforms touched off a
serious revolt in Alexandria: in 248/9, the Christians may have
suffered in similar riots as scapegoats for Philip's innovation.[5]

To take this further, we must fix the timing of Decius's edict. In
249, Decius killed the Emperor Philip in battle and emerged to power,
"a palmary specimen of the reluctant usurper." He needed legitimacy,
and his other actions show his efforts to achieve it. One local ruler in
Syria was already harking back to the Antonine dynasty and calling
himself "Antoninus." Decius looked further back and called himself
"Trajan," as befitted a military conqueror on the Danube. Like those
earlier usurpers, Hadrian and Severus, he was quick to issue coins with
fine portraits of dead and deified Emperors, his so-called ancestors.
His edict is likely to belong with this deliberate public image.[6]

As only one phrase is known from its text, its purpose and nature
remain matters of dispute, deducible only from evidence of their
impact. It appears to have demanded more than the usual sacrifice
which was made on the Emperor's behalf by his provincial governors at the start of each new year. The edict had already been issued by
mid-December and continued to be enforced long after the season for
these yearly vows had passed. In a general way, it conformed to the
motive of piety which other Emperors' edicts professed.[7] Decius
ordered a "sacrifice to the gods," not a sacrifice to or for the Emperor,
and left each town to honour its local divinities.

In 248, the Emperor Philip had celebrated a spectacular "millennium" of Rome with lavish pagan honours. Since then, parts of the
Empire had been through a difficult time. In 248, Goths and pretenders had troubled the Empire's northern sector, while famine
and sickness beset several cities in Asia.[8] Decius was an elderly
senator who would wish to foster the "peace of the gods" in a time of

crisis. Yet his edict had no precedent, and perhaps there was more to it.

With hindsight, fourth-century Christian authors explained the edict as Decius's response to the growth in Christian numbers.[9] They are most unlikely to be right. There is no good evidence for such an alarming growth in Christianity before 250; the core of the edict ordered a "sacrifice to the gods" without naming Christians explicitly; had Decius feared the Church's increase, he would have acted directly against its meeting places, rites and leaders. However, the edict does seem to have anticipated opposition, and hence it prescribed the local "special commissioners." The Jews were exempted, and the only opponents, therefore, would be Christians. Though not a cause, they do seem to have been recognized as a problem from the start.

Did their "atheism" weigh directly in Decius's motives, not, perhaps, as a growing force but nonetheless as a presence? There is no certainty, only deductions, but a recently found inscription has reopened the possibility. In the Tuscan city of Cosa, it honoured Decius as the *restitutor sacrorum*, "restorer of the sacred things," presumably the sacred rites.[10] It used the language of a pagan revival which was later to be applied to the pagan Emperor Julian, but in context, its meaning may be more limited. It was found in a small temple whose rebuilding has been dated to the mid-third century, a period in which Cosa was enjoying a recent urban revival, the "restoration" of its "republic," which is mentioned in other inscriptions. Decius's wife came from a good Tuscan family and his son had a Tuscan name. His "restoration of the sacred rites" may be his local favour to Cosa's temples, and on a minimalist view, it would tell us nothing about wider perceptions of his edict. There may, however, be more.

For a hint of it, we can only look to Christians, the edict's eventual victims. Once again, Eusebius claims that the Emperor acted "out of hatred" for his predecessor.[11] He was probably guessing on this occasion too, but he goes on to report a "story" about Decius's predecessor. Once, the Emperor Philip had tried to join the Christians' prayers at Easter, but the bishop had put him in his place. He told him to stand in the ranks of the penitent, and Philip had obeyed: according to John Chrysostom, a century and a half later, the episode took place in Antioch and the bishop was Babylas. Eusebius separated this "story" from the historical fact that Origen had addressed Christian letters to Philip and his wife.[12] Again, these letters may have been "open letters," proving nothing about the Emperor's own beliefs, but we happen to have the remarks of Bishop Dionysius to back them up. He described Philip's reign as "more kindly to us Christians," and he also referred to "those Emperors who are said to have been Christians quite openly" in a letter written in 262.[13] He must be alluding to Philip, whether or not he believed the story. If so, we can perhaps understand better why the Christians, Philip's friends, were persecuted in Alexandria after news of Philip's reforms and also why Decius, Philip's murderer, was so unusually eager to honour, perhaps to "restore," the older cults. His edict distanced him from rumours of Philip's religion and reinforced his own legitimacy.

Such an interpretation does justice to the rumours but remains, inevitably, uncertain. However, these rumours do mark a turning point in the style of Imperial government. Some sixty years before Constantine, an Emperor's edict was ushering in a persecution of the Christians; there had been stirrings of tax reform, a hint of Christianity in the Imperial family and an uneasy struggle between rival usurpers. Without the full text, we can only guess at Decius's motives, but we know much more about the progress of his edict, which brought together these themes of a "late antique" age. The edict was posted up in Rome in mid-December 249 and its effects were soon evident. In a letter from prison, a Christian in Carthage wrote to congratulate a young Christian in Rome for "driving back the great serpent, the champion of Antichrist." He seems to refer to a human judge, not to the Devil, and if so, the "great serpent" is probably Decius himself.[14] When Decius encountered the first Christian opposition, he may have wished to test the case for himself. He told this young Christian, Celerinus, to go away and think his atheism over. He wanted worshippers for the old gods, but he had not reckoned with the tradition of martyrs in Celerinus's ancestry and with his frequent dreams of a martyr's crown. At the second attempt, Celerinus contrived to be put to death.

Emperors' communications were always at risk to the winter, but Decius's edict passed swiftly to the provinces. "And then the edict came," recalled Bishop Dionysius in Egypt, "almost exactly like the one which our Lord had predicted. Everyone cowered in terror. At once, many of the more conspicuous Christians were affected: some stood forward in fear; others were brought along by their public business; others were dragged on by people around them. They were called by name and approached the unholy sacrifices, many of them pale with terror."[15] The edict reached Alexandria in January 250, and within four days, a soldier had been sent to hunt down Dionysius. Similar orders were being carried out in Asia by mid-February, and by mid-March they were well underway at Carthage. The text had not singled out Christians or their leaders for special attention, but the commissioners knew where to look.[16] Many of the bishops went promptly into hiding, leaving their flocks to cope for themselves. On a kinder view, they may have thought that their deaths would weaken their churches' resistance and cripple their recovery. Pagan Emperors were not accustomed to cults with clearly defined leaders who wielded such authority, and in 250, the lesson was well learned. Seven years later, the next persecuting edict singled out the churches' leaders for arrest.

Until mid-April 250, the surviving letters of Cyprian, bishop of Carthage, are more concerned with the lives of the Christians in prison than with the divisions which were opening in the churches. After mid-April, the problems of lapsing loom larger in his correspondence, and between April and midsummer 250, we first hear of an option from the edict's administrators, the notorious "certificates," which were signed by the pagan authorities.[17] These documents attested the bearer's lifelong pagan observance and his act of sacrifice in the presence of a local commissioner. From Egypt, forty-four written certificates have now been discovered on papyrus, each of which is signed and dated to the weeks between mid-June and mid-July 250.[18] They arise from the pressures of Decius's order and follow a set pattern: "to those appointed to see to the sacrifices: from Aurelia Charis of the Egyptian village of Theadelphia. I have always continued to sacrifice and show piety to the gods and now, in your presence, I have poured a libation and sacrificed and eaten some of the sacrificial meat. I request you to certify this for me below." Official signatures follow her petition. One of many, Charis's certificate survived in two copies, one for herself, one with a number for the official files.[19] Such duplication is a rare event in the remains of Roman administration: the purpose of these notes is more debatable.

The certificates have usually been read as statements by pagans, as if every inhabitant of the Empire had to sacrifice and obtain a certificate which was signed by a local commissioner and could later be shown on demand. If so, Decius's edict became a bureaucratic nightmare, extending, on this view, to every single person and imposing a massive burden on the commissions of four or five men who were attached to each city's magistrates. At Theadelphia, the same commissioner signed every one of our surviving certificates. Could five or fewer officials have coped with certificates for every single person or household in their care? We know of no such enforcement in the various edicts of the fourth century's "great" persecutions. In 250, the certificates are perhaps better understood as a second stage, aimed only at suspect Christians.[20] No surviving example is dated before mid-June, not necessarily because the edict was slow to travel to Upper Egypt, but because they were introduced as a further measure. Suspects who could produce a certificate were to be safe from further harassment. Again, the officials wanted lapsing, not martyrdoms.

If this view is right, one surviving certificate has obscured the documents' purpose. Its owner described herself as the priestess of a pagan crocodile god, but even if this claim was true, she may have had Christians in her family or a Christian phase in her earlier life.[21] Her pagan duties do not prove that every other pagan had to obtain a certificate. If the papers were only acquired by suspects, the batch from Egypt adds some forty possible Christians to the likely social background of the third-century Church. Revealingly, one group of the certificates derives from a ready-made batch which was written in the same scribe's hand on papyrus of the same shape and quality. Shrewd householders, it seems, had put their literate slaves to work in this sudden market for written texts. It was good business, as many of the Christian suspects were unable to write for themselves.

Among the surviving copies, the social pattern is suggestive. Nineteen derive from a find near Theadelphia in Egypt, and interestingly, at least thirteen are certificates for women: one is for a seventy-two-year-old man; another for a thirty-two-year-old who describes himself as disabled.[22] Women, of course, were a likely target as supporters of Christian "atheism." The old, the women and children: these are the victims who stand out in Cyprian's contemporary letters from Carthage. Enforcement, this sample suggests, ran as few risks as possible.

This role for the certificates is not proven, but it allows a reconstruction of the edict's course. At first, a "sacrifice to the gods" was demanded from the inhabitants of the Empire, excepting only Jews and probably, in their own capacity, the slaves. Local commissioners were appointed and duly announced the days for sacrificing. The crowds filed up to pay honours to the gods, and so far, local envy and gossip sufficed to bring "atheists" to the authorities' notice. Some of them promptly lapsed; others were imprisoned and tested repeatedly. The local officials wanted conformists, not martyrs, and would tend not to bring their stubborn Christians before a visiting governor until they had tried frequent pressure and inducements. Only the governors could impose a sentence, and they were not always keen to order death. After a trial, some Christians were banished and others returned to prison for a second attempt. When the mass of inhabitants had honoured the gods, the officials were only left with the problem of suspects and alleged Christians. At this point, they brought matters to a head by introducing certificates. Possession of these notes spared suspects from further harassment, and as a brisk trade developed, few Christians were left who were known to be standing firm. Throughout, enforcement had been haphazard. "Appointed days" of sacrifice had left Christians with the chance of going into hiding. People were not forced to return and register in their home cities. There were no scenes like those in the "great" persecution of the early fourth century, when soldiers read out newly compiled registers and called on residents to stand forward and sacrifice street by street. There is even a hint that a certificate for one member of a household sufficed to clear all others in its care.[23]

By March 251, persecution seems to have dwindled away, and soon afterwards, Decius met his death on the northern frontier. His edict has usually been judged a failure which was abandoned, but Decius had wanted worshippers, not martyrs, and in pursuit of a certificate, Christians granted his wish. Thousands of Christians lapsed and offered sacrifice, and many others bribed the commissioners, an act which added greatly to the edict's popularity among the class who had to enforce it: "there is nothing to be feared in the laws," Cyprian wrote, "because what is for sale is not feared."[24] In 250, Christians and pagans were quick to agree upon a price. On his return to Carthage, Cyprian drew a careful distinction between actual lapsing and ownership of a certificate: the distinction says much for the scope of the Christians' bribery. People of rank and property had been the most likely to be detected as Christians in the course of their daily lives. Not every rich Christian lapsed, and initially, some of the most prominent had been brought promptly to the test. However, Cyprian did recognize that the "chains of property" restrained heroism and did make bribery much easier.[25] There may have been a further loophole when the certificates were on offer. We find slaves among the sacrificers and even among the owners of surviving certificates. It is just possible that slaves, too, were expected to honour the gods, but it is much easier to interpret them as specific Christian suspects and as forerunners of a practice attested in the subsequent "great" persecution. Then, Christians did send slaves to sacrifice on their behalf and clear the household's name. Sometimes their slaves would be pagans, but not always: if anyone risked going to hell, it might as well be one of the servants.[26]

Why should those Christians who found themselves in prison show any greater restraint? Death, they believed, would make them perfect, assuring their instant arrival in Paradise: what, meanwhile, did it matter if they sinned? Cyprian knew the consequences in his own Carthage.[27] After their confessions, Christians were found to be boasting and drinking heavily. Christian women came down to the cells with their food and comforts and were unable to resist the appeal of these "friends of God." Promiscuity was said to be rampant: "eat, drink and make love, for tomorrow we die." The wages of sin were death, but a martyr's death effaced his sins for ever. His approval, meanwhile, effaced other people's. Cyprian could not deny the power of the confessors' dispensations, but in the year 250 they exceeded all reasonable bounds.[28] One confessor began to issue notes of remission in another confessor's name and continued, pleading his colleague's orders, long after the man had been martyred. Good confessors, said Cyprian, should issue a note or two at most: one for their mothers, he suggested, or perhaps their close relations. Bad confessors were prolific and bypassed the clergy entirely, while Cyprian, in hiding, could only watch with horror: "I hear that to some, letters like these are given. 'Let this person, with all his friends, be admitted back into Communion.' This was never done by those Christians who are already martyrs . . ." The torrent reached full spate in summer 250. "Without any discrimination or inquiry into individual cases," complained Cyprian, "thousands of letters were daily given against the rules of the Gospel." They were dangerous, these open visas to escape from hell. "Their uncertain and vague petition," said Cyprian, "leaves a wide opening when it says, 'This person, with his friends.' Twenty or thirty or more may then be brought to us, allegedly the families and kin, the freedmen and slaves of the person who received the letter."

The year of the edict, then, presented special tests to the bishops' and clergy's authority. While confessors kept company with Christ, a bishop like Cyprian was absent in hiding. The ironies are obvious. To well-behaved prisoners, Cyprian deferred magnificently: "What could be more sweet and sublime than now to be kissing your very lips which confessed the Lord with a glorious voice? But since I am not permitted to partake of this joy, I send this letter instead." "O blessed prison, on which your presence sheds light! O blessed prison, which sends the men of God to heaven!"[29] Cyprian's problems did not end when persecution ceased. After locking so many Christians into prison, the authorities let the survivors out. Some "confessors" had confessed more boldly than others: some were frauds. Many judges had given suspects a second chance and astute "confessors" had used the interval to run away. How did an overworked bishop know if so-called confessors deserved their name? They were only too alert to the benefits of travel. On a single boat from Carthage, we know of sixty-five "certified" confessors who arrived in Rome. Were all their claims genuine? Was, indeed, a "letter" from a bishop written by the bishop himself? While Cyprian encouraged the martyrs and attempted to sustain his own authority, his enemies tried to under- mine him by forging letters in his name. A new tone entered into humans' correspondence: "you have my epistle," wrote Cyprian, "I have yours. In the Day of Judgement, both will be recited before the tribunal of Christ."[30]

By the standards of an ancient edict, Decius's has left ample trace of itself, although its details are still not certain. The confessors dispensed certificates, the authorities dispensed certificates. Prudent Christians needed both: one from the authorities to avoid death, one from the prisoners to avoid hell. The confessors wrote to each other, the bishops wrote to the confessors and plied other confessors with copies. Christians, meanwhile, forged every one of these papers with the utmost abandon. They bought certificates; they coaxed and seduced confessors; they wrote letters as if from their bishop and gave pardons in other confessors' names.

As time passed, they also invented long legends of martyrdom and adorned the year 250 with a further host of martyrs.[31] One Maximus, they said, was stoned and cudgelled for his obstinacy. His fellow Ephesians, the Seven Sleepers, were said to have retired to their den. "You should love the Emperors," a governor was said to have told Acacius, "because you live by Roman laws." His answer was so wry that it was said to have been sent to Decius, who read it with a smile. St. Trypho was invented, the patron saint of gardeners, while east on the Euphrates, a Christian friend in the ranks was said to have urged Polyeuctus to "tear down the edict" and embark on the drama which later appealed to Corneille's sense of theatre. St. Mercurius emerged from nowhere and after his "death" was finally credited with murdering the Emperor Julian. St. Cassian excelled them all with a legend which earned him two churches, one at Imola, the other at Chaddesley Corbett in Worcestershire. His martyrdom points a moral for all Christian teachers. Cassian was a stern schoolmaster, and in 250, he was stabbed to death by the pens of pupils who could bear his austerity no longer.

The further the Decian persecution receded, the more its tales of heroism multiplied. However, among the legends and the mass of contemporary paperwork, we still lack one vital piece of evidence: an account of a martyrdom which can stand up to the doubts of scholars and historians. From the year 250, we have long known one such text, but doubts have continued to form around it. The last days of Pionius, a Christian Elder, purport to be set in the cultured city of Smyrna during the first February of Decius's edict. Its most recent editor was not impressed. In his *History*, Eusebius connected this martyrdom with the earlier reign of Marcus Aurelius: "given the vagueness of the legal background, it seems impossible to determine when Pionius and his companions were taken." "Our pious author," writing shortly before or after 300, may have "confused details from various periods." The "document seems reminiscent of the baroque rhetoric of the late Cynic diatribe." It has that damning weakness, "a certain atmosphere of the Hellenistic novel." Regrettably, it is a "pretence."[32]

It is, however, nothing of the sort. The story of Pionius is a brilliant sketch in miniature of all that we have surveyed. If carefully analysed, it shows us a martyr in the making, his ideals, his views of pagan culture, the great city of Smyrna, its sophists and its Jews. The story is also a rare textual challenge. Our Greek text survives in a manuscript dating from no earlier than the twelfth century A.D. Its colour and detail are confirmed by earlier versions: an Armenian translation which was made in the 430s, a Latin one which is known in fragments dating from the eighth century and a Slavonic translation which we know in a late-eleventh-century copy. In these languages, vernacular Christians were doing their best with a Greek original which was far earlier than our surviving copy. The versions match each other for the most part, although the Slavonic text omits the more difficult sections. The Armenian version attempted to be literal, and here and there it brought out the meaning of our Greek more clearly than editors since. No translation, however, was able to catch the culture of a Greek city. The details of Pionius's trial light up the place of Christians and martyrs in a great third-century city. They create the particular picture which brings the generalities to life.

The story begins in February, a month when the weather can still be cold to the point of snow in coastal Smyrna, the modern Izmir. When Pionius and his friends walked onto the city square through its double gate, the colonnades, we are told, were packed with a holiday crowd: "Greeks, Jews and women," in their Christian author's view of them. For a fortnight or so, a long drama was played before them in the wake of Decius's edict. The text has often been doubted, but even in this opening scene, the details can be brought to life by the site, its remains and the Armenian translation.

In the 250s, Smyrna's agora had been rebuilt after a recent earth-quake and is known in part from its archaeology.[33] Down the east and west sides of the square ran the colonnades which are mentioned in the Christian text. Two stories high, their pillared facades extended for more than 130 yards, the status symbols of a late Hellenistic city. In the northwest corner stood the double arch of an entry gate which is now known to have been dedicated in the reign of Gordian. Through the opposite gate, Pionius entered and walked northwards past the packed colonnades, leaving behind him a heavy pillared basilica. On an arch in the west colonnade stood busts of the Emperor Marcus and his wife, the patrons of rebuilt Smyrna; the building was dedicated to the "two goddesses Nemesis, all the gods and goddesses and the Emperors." It did not bode well for the Christians. They were being taken to the temple of these Nemeseis to pay sacrifice and eat the pagan meats. The temple has yet to be found, but the text shows that it stands on the square's unexplored south side. The Christians were determined not to enter it. Before their arrest, Pionius had put chains on his com-panions, "woven chains" in Greek and Slavonic, "iron chains" to a puzzled Armenian. The chains were a symbol. When the soldiers had found Pionius, he and his friends were already bound and waiting. In a gesture of Christian passivity, they had given themselves up in bonds of their own making. Here, indeed, was a rare haul, a group of Christians who were not exactly volunteers but were at last prepared to be stubborn and take themselves off to prison.

Word of the drama had spread like wildfire through the holiday crowds. They had come running to see this curiosity, "Greeks, Jews and women." They pushed and shoved, the "huge audience," the *immensus populus*, whom the Christian Perpetua had once noted in her diary in similar circumstances. "They climbed up onto the *bathra* and even onto the *kibotia*, trying to watch." The sentence has caused the oddest mistranslations, but their first perch is matched by inscriptions, while the Armenian translator made sense of the other.[34] The *bathra* are steps or pedestals or benches, including the seats which were built round a statue's base. When a Phrygian city wished Constantine to take it seriously, it reminded him of its forum and its "statues of past Emperors" and its seats, or *bathra*, which were "always crowded." In Smyrna, we know of these "seats" from inscriptions, in which one group of seats was reserved for the city's porters: they valued the honour so much that, cheekily, the Roman governor was asked to approve it. The *kibotia* should be "boxes," not "ballot boxes," as they were once translated, but "booths" or "sheds" in the view of their Armenian translator, paraphernalia left by stallkeepers, or by builders on Smyrna's market square. Scrambling for a perch on booths and benches, the holiday crowd peer in at the drama's first act. As they look on, the problems begin: whether this remarkable story, spun out across more than a fortnight, has any claims to be well perceived and whether it bears on the year of Decius's edict.

# IV

Nobody reveals where Pionius, the Christian Elder, passed his earlier years. He springs into history near Smyrna when he fasts and prays and foresees his own arrest, presumably in a vision. Christians later credited him with a prayer and a biography, but neither is genuine.[1] For Pionius, arrest and death are everything.

Eusebius knew a long text of his martyrdom, full of the sermons and trials and harangues of lapsed brethren which still distinguish our version. He connects it with the reign of Marcus Aurelius, whereas our text states that Decius was the Emperor, the year 250 and the months February and March. It gives this date at the start and finish of the story, and in one place, it lists the precise titles of the Emperor, adding Trajan, correctly, to his name. Other martyrdoms date themselves falsely by an Emperor's reign, but none descends to such details of name and title. The dating is kept up consistently, even in passing allusions to time. Without Eusebius, there would be no problem, but he was near to the event and knew a text of the same form as ours. Sometimes, his early dating has found favour; more often, it has weakened faith in the alternative. The problem can now be settled, by personalities who are named in the text.

Pionius and his fellow prisoners were arrested by a group of pagans who were led by Polemon, a temple official in Smyrna. "You know, of course, about the Emperor's edict," said Polemon, "and how it bids you sacrifice to the gods." "We know the edicts of God," replied Pionius, "in which he bids us worship him alone." In the reign of Marcus, only one late, fictional source refers to an edict of persecution which the Emperor issued himself. It is not to be trusted, whereas Decius's edict is only too familiar. Polemon was a famous name in Imperial Smyrna, and this Polemon fits very well as one of the edict's local commissioners, a member of those groups of "four or five men" whom Cyprian's letters remarked in Carthage at this period. Coins of Smyrna in the second and third century honour the city and her temples as "three times neocorate," and of the three temples so honoured, Polemon's was the temple of the two goddesses Nemeseis, an ancient cult in Smyrna.[2] Sensibly, the city had chosen a senior "temple warden," or *neokoros*, as one of the commissioners to enforce a sacrifice for its local gods.

When Pionius was arrested, he was keeping female company. For some while, he had been attended by a homeless Christian slave girl, and although the early Armenian translator omitted almost every scene which mentioned her, Sabina the Christian was one more excitement for Smyrna's holiday crowds. Like Pionius and his friends, she had decked herself in chains and followed her captors onto Smyrna's main square. These self-imposed bonds were a symbol of passive Christian surrender. "Look how she clings to him," the crowd shouted, "as if she has not yet been weaned." When she stood firm, the magistrates harassed her with that frequent threat to Christian heroines, a compulsory spell in the city brothel.[3]

When Sabina first joined Pionius, she said that she was on the run. She had been a slave girl, she claimed, but she had been bound and cast out into the hills by her mistress, the "lawless" Politta, who had wished to shake her out of her faith. The Christians had picked her up: "A great effort had been made," they said, "to free her from Politta and her bonds."

Politta is a name with a new and intriguing history. Up in the valleys northeast of Smyrna lies the lesser village of Apollonis, a former colony of Macedonian soldiers who had been settled near modern Palamut. Recently, it threw up the inscription of a certain

Eutychianus, business agent of a Flavia Politta. As the wife of a Roman citizen, she had come by an estate near Apollonis. This Flavia Politta, a Roman matron, is not unknown. She married Manilius Fuscus, a future governor of Asia, who may well have bought this estate while serving in the province, probably around the year 210. His origins have been traced tentatively to Spain, and he is known as a senator with strong views.[4]

Back in Rome, Manilius had already served as one of Rome's board of "fifteen men" who had authority over new foreign cults and controlled the use of the Sibylline Books. In 203/4, Manilius is known as their Master. The year had not been idle. Yet another round of "secular games," Rome's seventh, had been announced amid the usual rhetoric of a new age. The "fifteen men" were at the heart of it, if only as consultants of their Books. From inscriptions, this husband of "lawless Politta" can still be followed as he made his speech to the Senate. He warmed to the usual themes, the pagan Sibyl, the passage of the years and the dating of the games: "For the security and eternity of the Empire," he told the Senate, "you should frequent, with all due worship and veneration of the immortal gods, the most sacred shrines for the rendering and giving of thanks, so that the immortal gods may pass on to future generations what our ancestors have built up and all which they have granted to our ancestors and to our own times too."[5] This classic argument for pagan worship left no room for the new Christian faith.

Manilius could rely on the support of his wife. At the secular games, it was the custom for 110 Roman matrons, one for each year in the passing age, to go up to the Capitol and pray to Juno, goddess of marriage. Well to the fore went Flavia Politta, at one with the traditions into which she had married. She had gone down on her knees to plead with Juno, imploring her to favour the Senate and people, send health and safety to the state and look after the Roman legions.[6] Politta was no "lawless" mistress of a household. She had processed in the grandest festival of Roman cult at the start of the third century, her husband's golden moment.

In Asia, Flavia Politta did not only come by an estate. Her name has recently been discovered on the inscriptions of the Marble Court at Sardis, one of the most daring baroque buildings in the province. Dedicated in 211/12, this extravagant forecourt led into a gymnasium and a side room for rubbing down, whose surface had been gilded by the city with the help of funds from Flavia Politta and the fellow wife of a Roman consul. Her fellow benefactress was a lady of the highest Roman rank, whose mausoleum and sarcophagus later towered over a central place of honour at Sardis, the scene of her benefaction.[7] Pionius's girl must have been a slave in this family's household, perhaps of Flavia Politta herself, or if not, of her daughter. It only took a hint of Christianity belowstairs for a slave girl, around the 240s, to be out of a Politta's house for good. No wonder the Christians had told the girl to conceal her identity and call herself "Theodote," "gift of God." Behind a family like Politta's ran networks of high Roman friends who could divert the course of justice, intercede and help each other in cases of mutual interest before the governor of the province. Runaway slaves like Sabina could never feel safe from their influence.

"Frequent the most sacred shrines so that the immortal gods may pass on to future generations what our ancestors have built up . . .": with this powerful vignette, the date of Pionius's death is removed forever from Marcus Aurelius's reign. Politta and her Asian household are facts of the third century, fitting only with the date under Decius. There are other consequences. The girl Sabina adds to the list of Christian slaves who served in pagan households. Like some of her Christian contemporaries in Phrygia's Tembris Valley, she served on an estate in Roman ownership before exchanging her service for a new identity with Pionius, the Christian Elder.[8]

When Pionius was escorted onto the square, the officials tried to make him pay sacrifice, but failed and sent him to prison instead. A few days later, they succeeded in forcing his bishop to lapse. Whereupon they returned and dragged Pionius back to the altar of the two Nemeseis: "six soldiers had to carry him head first, since they could not stop him from kicking them in the ribs with his knees and interfering with their hands and feet." Before the altar, he found his bishop, bowed disgracefully in worship of the gods. He also found "one Rufinus standing by, one of those who were thought to excel at rhetoric." Stop it, Pionius, he said: do not strive for vainglory. "Is this your rhetorical skill?" "Are these your books?" Pionius replied. He quoted back at Rufinus the heroes of his pagan learning, martyrs like Socrates and men as upright, he thought, as old Aristeides who "practised philosophy, justice and perseverance."[9] So much for Rufinus's bookish studies. His texts should have taught him that a martyr's intransigence was not vain show.

Who, then, was Rufinus? Smyrna's coins are inscribed with the names of the year's civic magistrate, or "general," and on them the name Rufinus shows up intermittently from the reign of Pius (138–161) until Gordian III (238–244).[10] At first, he is plain Rufinus: then, from around 200, Claudius Rufinus; then, by 208, "Claudius Rufinus the sophist"; from the 220s, there is a gap, then finally "Rufinus the sophist," ten years, at most, before Pionius's arrest. The alternatives are several and obvious, but the best is to divide these men into two, perhaps as father and son. First came the plain Rufinus, then "Claudius Rufinus the sophist," who may have been born around 180 and survived until 250 to meet Pionius at the altar.

Their exchange takes on a new interest, central to the city culture of the high Empire. Rufinus, the former city general, was also a sophist, a master of public speaking and erudite oratory in an age which still set a high value on both. On their local coins, the Greek cities frequently name their yearly magistrates, and among them, we find the names of many sophists, showing that they put their riches to work for their fellow citizens' benefit. Only in one city, Smyrna, do these literary men of office announce they are "sophists" on the legends of their coins.[11] Smyrna was the city which "sacrificed more than any other to the sophists' Muses." It was a nest of sophists, lined with books and libraries, where men of culture discussed mathematics and Platonic philosophy and exchanged their classical proof texts round the city's own Museum.[12] A string of famous names on the coinage links Rufinus with the speakers and lecturers who had served Smyrna as city magistrates in the past. Even in the mid-second century, a repeated holding of civic office by one man had not been uncommon. Serving the city during fifty years, Claudius Rufinus measured up to the great public figures of his city's history.[13]

A Rufinus of Smyrna is known to have taught the rising star among young Greek sophists in the late 190s, but he is said to have been "more audacious than successful."[14] The story may be malicious, but it would best refer to the first Rufinus, a sophist of lesser note. In the younger Claudius Rufinus, the art bore richer fruit. On one of this man's coins, struck between 198 and 211, the Emperor and his heirs are shown seated, holding a scroll in their outstretched hands. An inscription adds force to the scene.[15] At some point after 198, and before or near to 211, the men of Smyrna sent an embassy all the way to Rome and the Emperors about Rufinus. As a recognized sophist, he enjoyed an exemption from all local duties and taxes. Perhaps, then, he was a sophist of "exceptional learning," one of the small inner circle of erudite teachers who enjoyed this exemption as a personal favour from the Emperors. If not, he had been chosen by Smyrna's council as one of the few exempt sophists whom the Emperors permitted to each city. Whatever his privilege, Rufinus had not been allowed to stand idly by it. The men of Smyrna had applied "voluntary compulsion" and involved their sophist in an offer which he could not refuse. He had served as the city's general, and the men of Smyrna went all the way to Rome to ask a favour on his behalf, that this "voluntary" office should not affect his general exemptions from local taxes and service. The Emperors agreed. Rufinus, they said, was distinguished for his *paideia*, or culture, and had obliged his citizens "out of love for his home town." His exemption was unaffected.

The scene on Rufinus's coin belongs in this context, although the motives of the city's embassy may not have been entirely innocent: afterwards, we find Rufinus as the "city general" yet again. The details add point to the scenes in Smyrna's marketplace. "Do not strive for vainglory," said Rufinus the sophist, by now, on the likelier view, a man of some seventy years. His learning and sense of honour had been commended by Caesars. His ideal of true value lay in public service, acclamations in the theatre and wild-beast shows, magistracies beyond the call of duty and civic buildings at personal expense. To die out of obstinacy, denying the gods in public, was a negation of such values, a theatrical self-indulgence. Yet Pionius was also an Elder, hardly less impressive in his mastery of learned allusions, albeit from the barbarous Greek of Isaiah, Baruch and Matthew. He, too, spoke forcefully in public, stringing quotations like beads among homely examples and moral denunciation. Rufinus had served Smyrna with a "love of honour" and a "love for his home city," yet these typical motives were "vainglory" in a Christian Elder's opinion.[16]

"Lawless" Politta and Rufinus the sophist were not people of the age of Marcus Aurelius. Nor was the governor who finally sentenced Pionius. He is known in an inscription from Eleusis whose exact date is uncertain but whose lettering is judged to be of third-century style.[17] Another city notable is more tantalizing. While Pionius refused to compromise, he was menaced, say all three versions, by one "Terentius," the official in charge of the wild-beast shows. On past form he ought to hold the rank of Asiarch, and on Smyrna's coins of the 240s, we know of just such a figure, "Marcus Tertius the Asiarch," who also held office as Smyrna's general.[18] Tertius, not Terentius: the names could easily be confused, especially as a Terentius had just been mentioned separately in the story. But the translations of the Greek text all name "Terentius," and if there was an error, it was made early.

One last individual can be fixed more exactly. In prison, says the Greek text, Pionius found "a certain Macedonia, a woman from Karine." If fictions, like forged paintings, betray themselves by their smaller details, this Macedonia proves that Pionius's story is not "late and obviously embroidered." Macedonia and Karine are names which tell a long tale, some of it new, but none of it accessible to "vagueness" or pretence.[19] Inland, up the Hermus Valley, recent inscriptions help to place the home of the Karenites in one of the villages which straddled the line between Smyrna and Sardis's assize districts. Macedonia was aptly named for such a home. These villages were peopled with settlers of Macedonian stock, first planted by Alexander the Great and his successors near the military colonies with which previous empires had garrisoned Lydia. These Macedonians by origin kept up their past in their names, their dress and the emblems on their coins. The lady Macedonia is named correctly for her obscure home and she also confirms that Christians were not sent back to sacrifice in their home towns. Karine, we now know, lay in Sardis's assize district, whereas Macedonia was imprisoned and tried in Smyrna. In 250, Christians were judged wherever they were caught.

These individuals vindicate the martyrdom's details, date it to 250 and refute Eusebius's view. Pionius can take his place with other martyrs, Mappalicus of Carthage and the Egyptian Christians, whom the letters of Cyprian and Dionysius place in late winter and spring of this year.[20] His martyrdom fills the gap in the year of the Decian edict and rivals Cyprian's letters as a source of events. Such is its exact detail that its origin raises a tantalizing question. All our texts, Armenian, Slavonic, Latin and Greek, begin by alluding to the "composition" which Pionius himself left behind him. This "composition" is said to be the story itself, written for the "advice" of fellow Christians, whom it reminded of Pionius's teaching.

Fictitious prologues and chains of authority have hampered other stories of martyrdom to the point where none can be taken on trust. The legend of Polyeuctus, set in the year 250, is an apt warning. The text claims to be based on the copy of a close Christian friend in Polyeuctus's regiment, but the story is a fiction from start to finish.[21] Christians' abundant gifts for forgery soon met the demand for stories of their martyrs' "last days." The martyrs, however, had not been reticent, for the filth and darkness of prison did not deter Christians from writing to their friends and brothers. The prison letters of Paul and Ignatius are only the best-known compositions by Christians under arrest. Lesser gems belong beside them, preserved among Cyprian's letters and sent to and fro by confessors in Rome or Carthage's cells. While Perpetua awaited martyrdom in Carthage, she had kept a prison diary in Greek.[22] So did her fellow prisoner Saturus, who wrote down his visions for posterity. Their editor did not blur the personal style and the exact details which suited their varying capabilities. Naturally, these diaries could only survive with the help of good friends. A third party put the various sources together and added the scenes of death itself, something which no martyr could record.

A few years after Pionius, in the persecution of 258/9, two vivid texts of martyrdom show the ways in which friends and martyrs combined their efforts.[23] Set in North Africa, they are extraordinary documents, and of the two, the story of Montanus, Lucius and Flavian is the more varied. It begins by describing itself as the martyrs' own letter, written while they awaited death in prison. The stories are circumstantial and the visions detailed and local. If Paul or Perpetua could write in prison, so, too, could these three Africans. They wrote for a martyr's proper ideal: peace among their fellow Christians and a life without recriminations "in the bonds of love." If anything, their narrative and their visions show how elusive these ideals had been, even between the martyrs themselves.

After a while, two of these prisoners were killed and only Flavian survived. The text then takes a new and appropriate turn. It claims, from then on, to be the work of a friend of Flavian who conformed strictly to his orders. He recorded the visions and events which Flavian chose to impart in the two days between his companions' martyrdom and his own death. At the moment of execution, "we were standing there at his side," wrote the friend, insisting on his own credentials, "we were joined closely to him, clinging to him so as to clasp our hands with his, showing honour for the martyr and affection for such a close friend." No other text divides its martyrdoms so carefully between two sources and explains their separate origins. To support them, the Latin style of the two sections differs detectably. The martyrs' prison letter has the weaker command of syntax and the lesser art with participle clauses. Flavian's "close friend" also piled up his clauses rather clumsily, but he risked some bolder touches of rhetoric and was obviously a man of some education. He is an interesting addition to Christians of rank and talent in the 250s. In their later life, martyrs, like master painters, discovered some very insistent friends: Flavian's copywriter was one of the keenest in Church history.

In the same year, he was rivalled by another "best friend," also writing in Roman Africa with as brave a story to tell. "As always before," he claimed a special intimacy with two martyrs, Marian and James. He had dogged them on their triumphant path to death. He had shared in their arrest by the soldiery; he had followed their journeys from prison to prison, as the magistrates passed them to the prefect and the prefect heard them repeatedly, hoping they would weaken. Like Flavian's "very best friend," he claimed an unimpeachable closeness to his subject. They "had clung to me," he insisted, "quite apart from their shared religion and sacrament, by the closeness of our life together and our domestic attachment." When fictions were so prolific, an author had to protest his authority. He was not just an intimate, but he was the sort of friend who never quarrelled: "Who could doubt how common a life we lived in times of peace, when one period of persecution found us living in undivided love?" It is revealing that such a statement had to be made: though arrested, the author was not martyred himself, perhaps because he was not a cleric, perhaps because he was of a status which earned him a lesser penalty.

Like Flavian's friend, but more so, this "inside source" was a man of considerable literary culture. Like Cyprian's own literary biographer, Pontius, these authors tell us much about the social standing which Christians in third-century Africa could command. When their friends faced death, they used their literary gifts to honour them. In prison, Christians wrote freely for fellow Christians; outside prison, friends worked their diaries into a coherent story. In the year 250, could not Pionius's martyrdom derive, as it says, from a similar combination?

The main text divides into several types of material. The connecting narrative is broken up by two powerful speeches from Pionius, two dialogues between Christians and pagan officials, some comments from the watching crowd and an idealized scene of Pionius's last words and death. The narrative's exact details have proved it to be a contemporary's work, and twice it breaks into the first person plural, as if the martyrs are describing events themselves.[24] When a spectator jeered at "the little fellow" who seemed ready to sacrifice, "he was referring to Asclepiades," says the text, "who was with us." "Us," here, is not the editor's general term for "us Christians." It refers to the martyrs, and at this point in the story, we can deduce that it refers to Sabina and Pionius only. Did Sabina, another "best friend," perhaps preserve our text for posterity? It claims to be Pionius's composition, and here, now, we can well believe it.

What, then, is the source of Pionius's speeches? The first does not survive in full: "Pionius said this and much else," says the text. The second, delivered in prison, is a passionate sermon, but both these speeches, as we shall see, are so full of exact detail that they cannot be the late fiction which has so often been alleged. Again, they need only derive from Pionius himself and his "composition." It gives us a clear hint of its origin. In Smyrna, Pionius and his friends welcomed their imprisonment as a chance to "discourse and pray by day and night." Their word for discourse was *philologein*, a word which was worthy of a literary sophist and appears nowhere else in early Christian literature. It was the word for scholarship and literary discussion and is well known in Smyrna's many inscriptions: Pionius made his prison a rival to the city's literary Museum.[25] Christians did not sit idly in the prisons' darkness. Confessors in Rome told Cyprian how they were studying their Bible, and then proved the point by citing proof texts on martyrdom. The evidence of prison scholarship is still written clearly on one surviving biblical manuscript.[26] A text of the Book of Esther cites its remarkable origin: "Copied and corrected against the Hexapla of Origen," runs its subscription, "as corrected by Origen himself. The confessor Antoninus collated. I, Pamphilus, corrected the roll in prison." Pamphilus was a devoted pupil of Origen, and while he waited in Caesarea's prison, he had practised his master's art of biblical scholarship. Pamphilus worked on Scripture, whereas martyrs like Perpetua kept diaries. Pionius practised prison "philology," and among it, he recorded his speeches and the story of his own captivity.

How, though, do we know about his trial and death? Pionius was interrogated twice, and his first trial is told in the style of a brief dialogue: "a notary," it remarks, "took everything down." If Pionius or his editor had wanted a record, one existed—this report, in pagan hands. However, other Christians cited their trials from memory and imitated this curt official form; Bishop Dionysius quotes details of his interrogation in a letter which depended on no written records.[27] This first trial, then, need only be based on Pionius's own "composition." At the second trial, "appointed officials" are again remarked to have taken the details down in writing, the first explicit allusion to the use of

shorthand by secretaries in a Greek city.[28] We know that the archives
and legal records of Smyrna were kept in the city's famous Museum.
In one fictitious martyrdom, Christians are said to have bribed the
keeper of a city's archives in order to acquire the pagans' version of a
trial. The claim had to be plausible in order to deceive its readers. Did a
Christian read the file on Pionius after the event? If not, Pionius could
perhaps have recorded his final interrogation or, more plausibly, a
spectator could have filled in the details and then added the scene of
Pionius's death. The martyr was given some brave last words while
the nails were hammered into his body: then, "after the fire had been
extinguished, those of us who were present saw Pionius's body like an
athlete's in his prime. His ears were not distorted; his hair lay
smoothly on his scalp . . ." These illusions could be a spectator's, just
as the author alleges. When Marian and James died, Christians in the
audience agreed that white horses snorted and galloped across the sky.

The story of Pionius the martyr, then, is far removed from "pretence." The bulk of it was so exact because Pionius had written it
himself in prison. A spectator idealized the death scenes and perhaps
added the final hearing, which he had witnessed or researched from
official sources. There is a distinction between texts like the trial of
Bishop Phileas, which do not go back to his own account, and texts
like Perpetua's and Pionius's, which are based on the martyr's diary.
The former could rapidly circulate in several versions, each with a
different emphasis, according to its use and editor. The latter remained
more stable, because the martyr's own version had authority: later
versions might make small errors and misunderstandings, but they are
variants of a different type. The core of Pionius's story is a text of rare
authority, true to its first contemporary form. It is our single narrative
of life in a great Ionian city in the mid-third century. It has much to tell
us about Pionius himself and the "Greeks, Jews and women" whom
he addressed.

On the same day, some ninety-five years earlier, old Bishop
Polycarp, friend of the Apostles, had gone to his death on a bonfire in
Smyrna. Pionius had been too young to see the event, but Polycarp
had since been a part of his life. The Greek texts of Polycarp's
martyrdom agree in a final note of its successive copyists. Pionius
rounds off the list: "I, Pionius, copied this from the former copy
which I tracked down. The blessed Polycarp revealed it to me in a
vision, as I will later show, and I collected the text, now almost worn
out with the passage of time." This search and copy were undertaken

in the "hope of joining the saints in the kingdom of heaven."[29]

The chain of copyists makes sound historical sense across nearly a century, and there is no good reason to reject it or to ascribe this allusion to Pionius to a later fake. Dreams and literary inspiration are a common pair in the ancient world, a convention which would affect, in turn, the dreams which men then had.[30] Just as the older Pliny began his book on the German wars because he dreamed that a great Roman general was standing beside him and urging him to rescue his triumphs from oblivion, so Pionius saw old Polycarp and heard him make a similar request. He had never seen Polycarp, and we know of no icons which could help him to focus the martyr's image. Instead, one suspects, he conjured up a picture of Smyrna's great martyr because martyrdom was already much in his thoughts. He copied Polycarp's story "in the hope that the Lord Jesus may gather me too into the company of his elect in the kingdom of heaven." Pionius, as we shall see, was helped by his city's calendar to follow his hero's path. His dreams compare with the dreams of his contemporary Lucian, who was imprisoned in Carthage at the same time and who had been dreaming for many years of the glory of imprisonment for Christ.[31]

A pattern of reading and writing reinforced these martyrs' resolution and confirmed their lifelong desire for their ideal. Like martyrs in so many subsequent prisons, it gave them a routine, while their imitation of the Gospel set them a selfless example which marked off their "martyrdom" from suicide or theatricality.[32] As Pionius copied his hero's text, he had also learned how death did not hurt: when Polycarp died, "it was not as if flesh was burning, but as if bread was being baked . . ." Pionius did not volunteer, or provoke his own arrest, but his reading and previous dreaming can only have stiffened his resolve to die. The self-imposed "chains" were part of a wider pattern of ambition and long-held ideals.

This student of previous martyrs was also a capable orator. Other martyrs recorded their dreams for posterity and set great store by visions which they saw while "in the Spirit." Not so Pionius, a man of literary culture. Uniquely, his diary preserved his speeches, not his dreams: one, a reply to the crowds, the other, a comfort to Christians in prison. When we read Pionius's sermons, we can well imagine their impact: like other Christian prisoners, the Elder used his martyrdom to make an alarming case for his faith.

When he first entered Smyrna's agora, he halted in his chains and addressed the crowd. "You men who boast of the beauty of Smyrna,"

our version runs, "and take pride in Homer, the son, as you say, of
Meles . . ." The address was worthy of any visiting orator's customary flattery.[33] Pride in the city's buildings ran high among its occu-
pants: in the late 250s or 260s, while honouring an athlete, Smyrna
called herself "first city in Asia for beauty and size, most glorious,
mother city of Asia, adornment of Ionia."[34] Pionius's taunt at her
vanity was well aimed, and so, too, was his sceptical reference to
Homer's origins. In Smyrna, Homer had his own shrine, a
Homereion. Smyrniotes had written books on his birthplace, claiming him as a son of Meles, their fellow Smyrniote. Naturally, a host of
cities pressed rival claims, and like them, Smyrna showed Homer's
image on her coins, the local "Homers." To Homer's alleged "com-
patriots," Pionius went on to quote the *Odyssey*. He had not only
studied the martyrs. He knew the outlines of pagan culture too:
Homer, Socrates and those who had died for philosophy.

Next, Pionius turned his oratory against the Jews who were massed
round the agora. He warned them not to gloat if Christians lost their
nerve, because Christians, he said, were only mortals like themselves,
people who were being treated unjustly. The Scriptures showed that
many Jews had sinned of their own free will. The Book of Judges was
packed with examples, not to mention the sexual and criminal sins
which ran through Exodus. Other Christians were standing firm, and
it was by them that the Church should be judged. The Jews, however,
had killed their prophets. They had also murdered Christ.

Eight years later, when Marian the martyr stood forward for
execution, he was filled, said his best friend, with the spirit of
prophecy. "Boldly and bravely," his friend and reporter remembered,
"he had repeated predictions that vengeance was imminent for the
blood of the just; plagues and captivities, he said, hunger and the
poisoned torment of every sort of insect."[35] Pionius, too, struck a note
which was worthy of an apocalypse. Like Marian, he was convinced
of the imminent end of the world. His own researches proved it, and
he told the holiday crowds how he had seen the coming wrath with his
own eyes.

Earlier in his life, Pionius had travelled to visit the Dead Sea. The
countryside, he had noticed, was burnt to a cinder, a fact which he
ascribed to its villagers' past misconduct. God's wrath, it seemed, was
seared into the landscape as a punishment and warning to sinful men.
Once scorched, twice shy: the Dead Sea, said Pionius, had withdrawn
its waters in fright, and after the sins of Sodom, it refused to receive

any human bodies. Bodies floated, Pionius correctly saw, but never sank beneath its surface, while the landscape gave off a cloud of smoke which was no stray fact of geology. It was a trace of the subterranean heating which awaited sinners at the Last Day. That day, Pionius told the crowds, was now imminent.

In Pionius's diary, the officials' response was neatly caught. "I wish I could persuade you to be Christians," he later told them as they tried to coax him away. "You can't make us willing to burn alive," they answered, roaring with laughter. "It is far worse," replied Pionius, "to be burned when you are dead": hell returned once again to the surface of a Christian's argument. Perhaps the Dead Sea seemed a little remote from Smyrna's audience, but if so, Pionius went on, they should consider the black cones of ash in their own Burnt Lydia, which stretched away on the borders of Smyrna's assize district. Charred and grotesque, it "stands for us down here," he said, "as evidence of men's impiety." For over a thousand years, pagans had happily thought otherwise. The volcanic landscape of Burnt Lydia was an old and awesome curiosity which they explained by one of Anatolia's longest-lived myths.[36] The land, they said, had been scorched by a dragon whom the god of the heavens had beaten in battle. The story was known to the old Hittite kings (c. 1200–1000 B.C.) and had passed to Greek travellers in the archaic age (c. 750). They equated the dragon with their monster Typhon, whom Zeus had slain, and located his presence in this scorched region, inland from their Aegean cities. Among pagans, a fault in nature was explained by an old and impersonal myth. Among Christians, it was traced to the faults of men themselves. The contrast goes far in the change from a pagan to a Christian way of life.

If Burnt Lydia was too far to seek, Pionius could strike nearer home. The text has been expanded, but his next allusion fell just outside Smyrna, on a range of hot springs and the famous Baths of Agamemnon.[37] To Christians who knew God's geology, these were no stray genii of the place. Smyrna's hot springs, said Pionius, were a hint of God's fires to come. They were ready and waiting under the world, and when men sinned badly, they already spouted up through its crust. As a man might point to the steam clouds from New York's manholes and argue to the fate which awaits that great city of sinners, so Pionius looked at the steam in Smyrna's landscape with an eye for the Christians' End. His speech had a further point. The pagans, he knew, blamed their earthquakes and natural hardships on the impiety of the Christians and the anger of their gods. Not at all, said Pionius. These hardships were a foretaste of God's coming punishment, provoked by pagan sin.

The 230s and 240s, the years of Pionius's training, were still a time of open horizons, when men of culture could travel for curiosity's sake. Just as a pagan might travel to Persia for Persian wisdom, to India or into Egypt, a Christian Elder had toured Judaea, noting proofs of the wrath of God. Christians had taken to pilgrimage very early in their history.[38] By the early second century, we know, a "cave of the Nativity" was being shown in the Holy Land, and by the 170s, Melito, bishop of Sardis, had visited Judaea "for the sake of his inquiries" into Scripture: Alexander, the bishop from Cappadocia, was also present on a pilgrimage in the early third century. In Pionius's lifetime, Origen's commentaries reveal a detailed interest in the Holy Land's geography, whose facts survive his gift for allegory. He had travelled to check the village where John baptized Jesus. He had seen the "extraordinary" wells which Abraham was said to have dug at Ascalon. He relocated the Gadarene swine in Gergesa, where the cliff over which they had charged was already being shown to visitors. Pionius's journey was in good company. On a pilgrimage, Christians could pinpoint their Gospels, for they were as interested in holy places as in any "holy men." They could see, too, how Jesus had been proved right: Jerusalem was indeed a ruined city, before their very eyes.

On the theme of God's punishments, Pionius next reminded the pagans of their hero Deucalion and the Jews of their Noah. Apologists had often compared these two traditions of a flood, and Pionius now argued they were "partial proofs," a foretaste of a greater whole. In a resounding sentence, he stated his own position. He "refused to worship the so-called gods and bow down to the golden idol." An impressive silence greeted his words. So he repeated them for good effect.

When Origen wrote his *Exhortation to Martyrs* in the mid-230s, he remarked how "everywhere, the golden image is set up against us." The Christians' art and literature compared their martyrs' struggles with the three young heroes who had refused to bow to Nebuchadnezzar's image in the Book of Daniel.[39] Although Decius had asked for a "sacrifice to the gods," not to himself, the cult of the Emperor stood prominently in the background to his edict's enforcement. In Smyrna's city calendar, the month from late February to March was named Philosebastos, "friendly to the Emperor." Portraits of the divine Emperor Marcus and his wife looked down from the agora's west colonnade. The cult of "the golden image" was not the cause of persecution, but it was a frequent accompaniment: Pionius's closing words were not an empty defiance. More than any other source, his diary lights up a provincial leader's view of this worship. First, Pionius was asked to sacrifice to the gods, and when he refused, Polemon, the temple warden, asked him "at least to sacrifice to the Emperor."[40] "At least . . .": the Emperor, then, was not such a full-blooded god in the eyes of a leading pagan in Smyrna. His cult might be present, but not even the persecutors saw it as the most divisive issue. It was a cult, they felt, which allowed a compromise. Unlike the other pagan gods, a living Emperor had no divine anger, no power to cause droughts or tremors. To Christians, however, his worship was quite unthinkable. Strictly, they would not even swear by the Emperor's fortune.

When Pionius stopped speaking, the crowd recovered from a brief hush and then began to clamour. They "demanded an assembly in the theatre," and Pionius, in his diary, gave the reason: "they wanted to hear more." Were they alarmed for their souls or merely enjoying a great performance? They wanted a popular gathering in Smyrna's theatre, but "friends of the city general," men like the sophist Rufinus, began to take fright. Their theatre can still be seen, a vast row of seats for some 16,000 spectators which look north, across the stage, to Smyrna's gulf and the sea. In such a place the officials feared a riot and a general inquiry, runs the Greek text, "about the bread."[41]

The text has often been altered, even by the Slavonic translator, who preferred to write "man" for "bread." However, there is no good reason for the change. Any city magistrate in the Greek East knew the dangers of a theatre meeting in which, during famine, he might be mobbed and pelted by crowds accusing him of hoarding grain. Early spring was a difficult time for food, a season when the cities had eaten the previous year's harvest and could not yet gather the next. In February 250, Smyrna was looking back on a recent rough patch which fills out the background to the persecution. When Pionius was bustled to the city prison, it emerges from the crowd's comments which he recorded in his diary.

"Ah, what education," some said as Pionius passed. "Indeed, it is so," added others. In Smyrna, culture was admirable in anyone, even a Christian. Pionius turned these regrets against his spectators. "Ah, such education," the crowd in Smyrna uttered, remarking in Pionius that same *paideia* which Emperors had praised in their Rufinus, the "so-called expert in rhetoric." "Not that sort of education," Pionius claimed to have answered, not the proof texts from Homer and the Panhellenic rhetoric. "Recognize, rather, the education of those famines, deaths and other blows by which you have been tried," the *paideia*, rather, of God in the Greek Old Testament, no tutor in polite letters, but the Father who reached for his switch in nature and chastized his children for their sins. Correction, not culture: the Greek Bible's rough notion of *paideia* had long proved embarrassing to Christians with a serious grounding in classical letters.[42] "And someone said to Pionius, 'But you too went hungry with us.'" How, then, could a famine be a "correction" if the virtuous had suffered with the others? "But I," said Pionius, "had hope in God."

The fears for the bread, then, were real enough. Pionius's last days were set against a background of recent famine, a proof of the gods' "anger" which Decius's edict was hoping to avert. Yet there is a significant note to the scene. In the 160s, the people of Smyrna had shouted for Polycarp's arrest without any Imperial prompting. In 250, Smyrna had been through a famine, and yet, so far as we can see, no persecution had resulted until Decius's edict ordered it. Faced with Polycarp's heir, the crowd listened in alarm and wonder and then regretted his evident culture. It had been very different a century before. The grosser stories of Christian crime, people now realized, were simply not true, and Christianity had become a fact of civic life. We will have to pursue this hint of a change elsewhere. Meanwhile, the city officials had far more to fear from their hungry fellow citizens than from one chained Christian Elder. They begged him to be sensible, and even came down to the prison to implore him to give in. It was all most revealing. When Pionius finished his speech, pagans stood forward and begged him to yield "because we love you and your life is so valuable for its character and virtue."

"Ah, such education": yet Pionius's attitudes were far removed from the pagans' own. Pagans visited the Dead Sea, but they only thought it a natural oddity: Galen knew people in Italy who sent for samples of its buoyant water and kept them as toys in their houses.[43] To pagans, the myth of Typhon and Zeus explained the volcanic landscape of Burnt Lydia, and famine was due to the random anger of "manifest" gods. But Christians connected these facts with human sin. Pionius's "education" was Cyprian's *paideia* too: "we are being whipped," he told his African churches, during persecution, "as we deserve. . . ." "It pleased the Lord to prove his family," wrote Cyprian of the year 250, "and we deserved yet more for our sins. But the Lord in his great mercy has moderated his anger . . ."[44]

After his first speech in the agora, Pionius was dragged to prison, only to find that Christians were lapsing on all sides: before long, the bishop of Smyrna succumbed too. We know from Cyprian's letters how one man's firm example could strengthen a host of lesser men. In Smyrna, Pionius was resolved to stand firm, and to help posterity, he put his next speech, on lapsing and the Church's predicament, into his prison diary.

In a lyrical sequence of scriptural metaphors, he lamented in prison the disarray of the Church. Like Esther and Susannah, she was being menaced by conspirators. Satan was winnowing the chaff, but "let no man imagine the Lord has failed, but only ourselves." The Christians in Smyrna had accused each other and had torn the Church apart with quarrels. As in Pontus or Africa, so, too, in Smyrna, the year 250 gave Christian worldliness free rein. But Pionius centred his speech elsewhere. He turned his oratory against the Jews.

In the main square, Pionius had already attacked the Jews for gloating over Christians who lapsed. Now he attacked them again because he heard that they were inviting "some of the Christians" into their synagogues. What lay behind this invitation? It has been seen as a friendly offer of protection, but the truth was not so innocent.[45] We would have to believe that Pionius's speeches were largely beside the point, attacking Jews who were really his Christians' best friends. His tone suggests a different pattern. Some Christians were scared of being tested and then lapsing, and "in despair," Pionius hinted, they were amenable to the Jews' overtures. The Jews' aim was to win converts in the crisis, among Christians who would prefer to join a synagogue rather than eat "demonic" pagan meat: such a secession was less fraught and less public. Once they came into Jewish company, Pionius believed, they would hear slanders about Jesus and the Resurrection. Rather, they must remember the Jews' own history, how they had killed Christ and the prophets. Reversing their own titles, Pionius reviled them as "rulers of Sodom and the host of Gomorrah." He was also convinced that they would spread a familiar slander: Christ, said the Jews, had died a criminal's violent death, and like other executed criminals, his spirit still roamed without rest. Christians, therefore, could conjure it up and had already brought it back to earth by their magical sign of the cross. The "Resurrection" appearances were caused by sorcery, said the Jews, practised on a criminal's restless soul.[46]

Pionius insisted that this story was spread by Jews and that Christians in Smyrna heard it from them. It would be too sceptical to ascribe it all to his own imagination and to doubt if in this crisis the Jews were concerned to undermine their Christian hearers' faith. Rather, we are being treated to one of our rare glimpses of Jews' continuing missionary interest, an interest, indeed, which Christians no longer extended so openly to them. Pionius thought the slander so urgent that he preserved a long refutation for his diary. In Smyrna, Jews accepted the prevailing pagan view of the souls of the "violently dead." They used it to accuse Christians of sorcery, and as the charge was dangerous, Pionius rose to the occasion. What restless criminal, he asked, had filled the world with disciples and with the miracles which still occurred in his Church? This faith in continuing miracles is revealing. Christ had not killed himself and was not, then, one of the "violently dead" who found no rest. Pionius shared the Church's execration of suicide, a death, naturally, which was quite distinct from martyrdom.[47] Jesus had been killed through no choice of his own, and as for the charge of sorcery, it was a skeleton in the Jews' own cupboard. Pionius had heard of this crime "since childhood": this Christian who visited Judaea and dreamed of earlier martyrs had known the Jewish Scriptures in his early years.

He explained his point by the Jews' own story of the witch of Endor. The witch, he argued, had not conjured up the dead Samuel, but had produced a demon who wore Samuel's likeness. If sorcery had failed to bring back the prophet Samuel, how could it possibly bring back Christ? Had not the disciples witnessed Christ's direct ascent to heaven? If the Jews denied the logic of this argument, Christians, he said, must simply state their own superiority. Christians lapsed under duress, whereas the sexual and religious sins of the Jews had all been voluntary.

The argument was unconvincing and unoriginal.[48] Tertullian had already discussed the same problem, using most of Pionius's proof texts and some of his phrases, as had Hippolytus, recently teaching in Rome. "Samuel in Hades?": Origen, too, had discussed Endor's witch in an essay in which he kept close for once to Scripture's exact wording. It was a story, he said, which "touches everyone," because it sets out the facts of life after death. The text, he claimed, could only be read as a proof that Samuel had indeed appeared in person: Pionius's contrary views had Christian opponents too. In Jewish sources, we can still catch echoes of the Jews' own doubts about the story's meaning. Their Rabbi Abbahu taught in Caesarea during the later third century and is said to have answered a "Sadducee" or "heretic" who asked him how Samuel could have appeared in person if the "souls of the just" resided beneath the throne of God. In Caesarea, exchanges between Jews and Christians were frequent: perhaps the "heretic" was a Christian, teasing the rabbi with the type of argument which Pionius proposed.

Why was Pionius's prison speech more concerned to attack the Jews than his pagan captors? His harsh words have been ascribed to a fourth-century editor, as if they did not befit a Christian in Smyrna in the year 250. Evidence in Smyrna suggests that they belong there only too well. No synagogue has yet been found in Smyrna, but a few precious inscriptions suggest a Jewish community of some size and rank. There were Elders and "rulers," Pionius's "rulers of Sodom." There was a "secretary of the host," his "host of Gomorrah," and in one case, we know this secretary to have been a Roman citizen.[49] The Jews and pagans of Smyrna had lived in close contact. In Hadrian's reign, an inscription lists "the former Judaeans" as a group among donors to the city's amenities. They were not, surely, Jews who had lapsed: they were Jews who had come to Smyrna "formerly" from Judaea and settled into its civic life.[50] In the early to mid-third century, a similarly relaxed relationship showed in the inscription which guarded the family tomb of one Rufina, "head of the synagogue."[51] It prescribed the fines which transgressors should pay to "the most sacred Treasury" or Imperial fiscus. Elsewhere, more cautious Jews tended to avoid this casual use of the pagan word "sacred." A copy of Rufina's inscription was to be deposited in the pagans' Museum, among the city archives, where it could settle future disputes. This prominent Jewish family was able and willing to use the pagans' civic facilities, while pagans were prepared to help them guard their tombs against infringement.

Behind these inscriptions lay a strong and powerful Jewish presence. Anticipating Pionius, the Book of Revelation had already damned the Jews in Smyrna as a "synagogue of Satan." In the 150s, Christians believed that the city's Jews had persuaded the pagan notables to petition the Roman governor and deter him from releasing Polycarp's corpse.[52] Whatever their truth, these beliefs are evidence for the Jews' high contacts in the city's life. They join the growing evidence for a prominent Jewish presence in the lives of eastern Greek cities in the second and third centuries:[53] we can compare Pionius's tone with a fellow pilgrim to the Holy Land, Melito, bishop of Sardis, the city whose synagogue has been one of the great discoveries of recent archaeology. In Sardis of the 170s, the Christian church was a poor relation to the strong Jewish community: preaching in a style like Pionius's own, this "eunuch bishop of Sardis" denounced the Jews as "Messiah-killers," criminals who had invented an "entirely new sort of crime."[54]

It was not only during persecution that the lure of Judaism continued to influence Christian practice. In other thriving cities, it also left its mark.[55] In Antioch, it was still being strongly attacked in Christian sermons of the 390s: "the synagogue on Saturday, the church on Sunday" was a familiar summary of practice. In the 430s, the Christian Council of Laodicea ruled in detail against Christian observance of the Jewish Sabbath, their acceptance of unleavened bread from Jews and their keeping of Jewish festivals. In Antioch, especially, there is a long chain of evidence for women who converted to the Jewish faith: women found conversion easy and painless, as they did not have to be circumcised. In Smyrna, surely, the Jews were not merely offering shelter: they were angling for apostasy.

We do not have enough evidence to plot variations in the Jews' reactions to the Christians in their midst. Some, clearly, continued to hope to convert them; others refuted their bogus use of biblical proof texts which meant something different in Hebrew from their free translation in the Christians' Greek. In the first century, we know, Jews did persecute and abuse Christian converts in pagan cities. Afterwards, we happen to hear less about this casual violence, and perhaps Trajan's ruling on Christianity reduced these attacks, after the first shock of Christian novelty: Jews and Christians were now legally distinct. We do hear, however, of a continuing war of words.[56] It lies behind Pionius's sermon and behind Origen's disputations with leading Jewish teachers in Caesarea.[57] The fear of Jewish slander was not a Christian invention, and we can see its effects in the form of Celsus the pagan's attack on Christianity. In the 170s, he set a Jew at the forefront of his work and gave him views on Christianity which are very close to later attacks by Jews on the new "Messiah." Jesus, he said, was only the son of a soldier named Panthera with whom Mary had committed adultery. He had learnt magic and practised sorcery among the worthless disciples with whom he begged for a living. The Jews had condemned him wisely, as the Resurrection was merely the tale of some bewitched fellow beggars and one "hysterical female." Much of this abuse matches the allusions to Jesus which occur in later, written versions of Jews' "anti-Gospels."[58] In the 170s Celsus the Platonist had clearly picked up the Jews' own slanders.

The war of words was not idle. It influenced Celsus and it is prominent in a second story of martyrdom which is also set in the year 250. It is not clear when the story originated or if it is based on a historical core: it was set in Pamphylia, on the southern coast of Asia Minor, where it joined several others, fictions, perhaps, from a local Christian.[59] It told of the capture and death of Conon, gardener on an Imperial property near Magydos, whose citizens had almost all fled when the governor approached. The governor, it is said, knew about Jesus's history because the local Jews had brought "records" to him and he had learned "precisely" that the Christians' God was only a man. They had explained Jesus's family, his works before the Jewish nation and here, too, his "violent death" as a criminal. There is no evidence that the author had copied this from Pionius's story: his point is simpler and quite different. Even if his text is essentially a fiction, it had to seem plausible, and this Jewish dismissal of Jesus was evidently current. In Pamphylia, too, there is nothing incredible in the story of the Jews' initiative before a Roman governor. Inscriptions from nearby Side in the third and fourth centuries reveal a prominent Jewish community and at least two synagogues.[60] We can see how the story of their "instruction" of the governor could arise, whether or not it was factual.

From Homer to the Dead Sea, Susannah to the witch of Endor, Pionius's speeches have taken us on a tour of the culture of a mid-third-century Christian. They are not the invention of a later editor: they survived in his own prison diary, sermons, not visionary dreams. Their themes belong in the city in 250: perhaps the diary can solve one final problem, the timing of Pionius's arrest and trial.

Like Antigone, Pionius had known that he was going to die. On the day before his arrest, he had woven his sets of symbolic chains and draped them round his companions' necks. Why had he been so sure of his arrest? The day, he knew, would fall on the anniversary of Polycarp's own death. Pionius had studied Polycarp's story and knew how his hero was said to have foreseen the time and manner of his arrest: "every word," said the text, "which he let fall from his mouth has been, and will be, fulfilled." The gifts of prophecy and foresight were linked explicitly with a bishop: Polycarp was said to have dreamed all the details, down to a vision that his pillow was burning, a proof that he would die at the stake.[61] Twice, for Smyrna's Christians, February was the cruellest month: across nearly a century, can we explain the martyrs' power of prophecy?

It owed much to Trajan's reply to Pliny. A Christian prisoner could only be put to death by a Roman governor, and recent studies have set his powers more clearly against their two basic limits, time and distance.[62] Capital justice was confined to the bigger cities of a province and only reached them when the Roman governor arrived as a circuit judge on tour: "delegation" of these capital powers to his under-legates is not established, despite some difficult texts in the Roman law books.[63] These assize tours are best understood as an annual event. They were well known in parts of Egypt, where their details had long been deduced with considerable subtlety from the papyri. The sequence of assize districts was then discovered for the province of Asia from an obscure text and confirmed by a recently found inscription.

The assize system now shows up as an old and constant fact of a governor's life in Asia too. New cities pressed to join the circuit, for an assize centre enjoyed easy access to justice, a claim to the governor's favour and a host of useful traders. Smyrna, naturally, was such a centre, lying on the governor's way north from his provincial seat at Ephesus. It is highly likely, then, that Smyrna is the scene of an apt, if partly preserved, piece of rhetoric on the subject by Plutarch.[64] Around 100 A.D. he was contrasting the passions of soul and body and appealed for an example to his audience's mood: "you see this large and motley crowd," he wrote, "which jostles here and surges in confusion round the governor's seat and the marketplace." Pionius had seen them well enough, surging and jostling in the same place. They had not come, said Plutarch, for religious worship, but "a critical fever drives Asia to lawsuits and contests of fixed date in this city, attacking it in yearly visitations. A crowd has burst into this single marketplace, like a flood of humours coursing through the body. It boils and 'dashes together the destroyers and destroyed,' as Homer put it. What fevers are the cause of this, what delirious attacks? If you examine each lawsuit like a patient, looking for its origin and nature, you will find that one is the child of a stubborn temper, another of a mad sense of competition, another of wicked desire . . ." These words might almost be a speech of Pionius the Christian, haranguing the sickened assize crowd in the same city of Smyrna while awaiting trial.

The Smyrna assizes recur in the career of Aelius Aristeides, two of whose speeches address Roman governors in the city.[65] Across an interval of several years, the governors were present at the same season and had come to attend to local matters of justice. This regularity begins to explain the martyrs' foresight. They were seized in the same month after an interval of nearly a hundred years because the Smyrna assizes recurred at the same date. Their prophecies can be narrowed further. Both Pionius and Polycarp were dragged into Smyrna "on a great Sabbath." This "great Sabbath" is a famous and unresolved problem. It was not a Christian festival: it was being observed by the crowd of "Greeks, Jews and women." It must be a Jewish or pagan occasion, seen through a Christian's eyes. There are firm grounds, not least the assizes, for believing it to have been both.

There is no doubt that Polycarp and Pionius were arrested in the last stages of a major pagan festival which had already extended over several days. When Polycarp was hauled into the stadium, the crowd "shouted at Philip the Asiarch to let loose a lion on him. But he replied that he could not lawfully do this as he had now completed the staging of the wild-beast shows." So, too, in the weeks of Pionius's arrest, the "certain Terentius" or Tertius was "putting on the animal hunts at that time." He told one of the Christians how he "would request him for the single-combat shows of his son." Here, too, the picture may be similar. "Terentius" did not want to use the Christian prisoners in his own animal hunts, as these hunts were already over. He would save them, then, for something separate, the gladiatorial shows to be put on later by his son. No doubt the boy hired the usual troupes of combatants, and a few condemned Christians would liven things up. First the days of the wild-beast hunts, then the separate event of the gladiators who fought each other, but never battled with animals: the division is borne out by monuments of gladiators in Asia, not least in Smyrna, a thriving centre of the sport.[66]

In late February, this long pagan festival can only be the city's ancient Dionysia. The date adds force to the other glimpses of Smyrna's assizes. Plutarch had accused the assize crowds of assembling from a feverish passion, not from a "wish to offer first fruits from Lydia's harvest to Akraian Zeus or to hold night rituals for Dionysus." The "Lydian harvest" suits the rural Lydian districts which are now known to have fallen in Smyrna's assize district. As for the cult of this Zeus, it stands prominently on Smyrna's city coins. The "rites of Dionysus" belong with the city's Dionysia, the occasion when Smyrna's assizes were held. The crowd, so Plutarch hinted, were ignoring their proper business of honouring Smyrna's gods and were clamouring for selfish justice instead.[67]

When Aelius addressed his governor, he, too, referred him to a sight of the moment. A sacred trireme, he said, was being escorted through Smyrna in honour of Dionysus. Here, the assizes and the Dionysia coincided in a pattern which made obvious sense.[68] The ancient world's only holidays were its religious festivals, days when crowds could pack a colonnade and litigants could best press a case. Business reached a peak, while the festival's games made up for any annoyance provoked by the long delays in hearing so many cases. At Smyrna, the coincidence brings the martyrdoms' context into sharper focus. Everything lay to hand: a crowd and a governor, assize trials and a programme of bloodshed in the stadium. Death in late February begins to seem a simple forecast for a man on the spot.

The "great Sabbath," however, remains to be explained.[69] Clearly, it was a single day in the longer course of pagan festival. The easy answer is that it was a Jewish holiday which overlapped with a day of Smyrna's Dionysia. When the Jews joined the "Greeks and women" as spectators in the colonnade, they, too, were on holiday. A day called "the Great Sabbath" is well known from John's Gospel and Jewish sources, but it falls at Passover and cannot be dragged back into late February 250.[70] There must, then, be other "great Sabbaths" besides this one, the "Great Sabbath" *par excellence*. Later Jewish sources refer to four, which were finally grouped in their calendar from mid-February through to Passover, but it is unlikely that they existed as early as the third century A.D.[71] Instead, we should look to the great Jewish festival of Purim, the setting for the Bible's tale of Esther and the Jews' deliverance from the Great King's persecution.[72] There are too many uncertainties in equations between ancient and modern calendar dates for the timing of Purim to be fixed exactly in the year 250. However, the approximate dating fits, and to support it we can look forwards to a law from the Emperor in May 408: it forbade the Jews to insult the Christians and burn a model of the cross at their festival of Purim, "commemorating Haman." This fascinating glimpse of the mood between Jews and Christians at Purim fits neatly with the tone of Smyrna's "great Sabbath." The pagans were enjoying their Dionysia, the Jews their Purim, and both were gloating at the Christians from their city's colonnades.

Such an easy relationship between a Jewish and a Gentile festival is one more warning against inventing a so-called Judaism from the texts of Jewish rabbis.[73] In Smyrna, nobody was any the less a Jew for ignoring the advice of one rabbinic author, that a Jew should do no business with a Gentile for three days before a festival. Jew and Gentile enjoyed the Christian spectacle, side by side round the city's agora. The scene fits well with other hints of the strong Jewish presence in Smyrna and its attitude to surrounding pagan culture. It may also throw light on a common pagan opinion that the Jews were worshippers of Dionysus under another name. If a city like Smyrna saw Jews relaxing at Dionysus's festival, the confusion lay particularly near to hand.

For the Christians, the assize circuit was an important pattern, as we can see from Cyprian's experience in Africa during the 250s. Although new cities pressed to join the assize list, Africa is a province where the timing of one section of the circuit stayed constant, to judge from our second- and third-century evidence.[74] In April, the new governor normally reached the province and took up his seat at Carthage. Carthage's "Apolline games" soon followed in the calendar, the occasion which made a martyr of Perpetua. In the year 250, we can perhaps see the result: Cyprian's letters suggest that from mid-April onwards, persecution in Carthage had worsened for imprisoned Christians. From Carthage, the governor then progressed on his summer tour, returning to Carthage in the autumn. This pattern was exploited by Cyprian, that master of visionary foresight.

In late summer 258, Cyprian did not wish to die in one of Africa's minor assize cities, the insignificant centre of Utica. Across half a century, August shows up as the season for Utica's assizes, while Carthage followed as the governor's next stop, his return to base after the summer's work. Cyprian wanted to die before his own church in a great city: "whatever a confessor bishop says at the very moment of his confession," he had written, "he says it in the name of all, inspired by God."[75] Thanks to the assizes, Cyprian said his last words before as large a crowd as possible, by being tried in his home town. While the governor visited Utica, Cyprian went into hiding and only came out when the assizes moved to Carthage.

Like Polycarp and Pionius, Bishop Cyprian was said by contemporaries to have foreseen the exact date of his death. In September 257, they said, he had already seen a dumb show in one of his dreams, in which a governor was sitting on his tribunal and writing out his sentence, while a young man stood behind his shoulder and explained by mime that the verdict was death.[76] Death, however, was only to occur on Cyprian's request, and so the dream allowed him time to put his Christian house in order. Cyprian was killed, said his friend and biographer Pontius, in September 258, exactly a year to the very day after this curious vision. This coincidence is quite credible. The dream had fallen in the usual season for Carthage's assizes, and if Cyprian wished to die in Carthage, the date, next year, would be repeated. The bishop claimed the Holy Spirit, but the Holy Spirit worked better when aware of the facts of Roman government.

In Smyrna, the martyrs' arrests coincided across nearly a century and the assizes explained their prophetic power. Pionius was beset by their presence. When he entered the city, the *agoraioi* of Smyrna implored him to compromise "because they were so fond of him." These admirers are more than everyday lawyers.[77] At the assizes, or *agorai*, a group of local advisers, the *agoraioi*, sat with the governor to help him reach his decisions. The governor was also helped by picked provincials, men who travelled the province in his retinue. In Smyrna, an earlier inscription reveals one of them, a man who had united his expertise in law with the headship of the city's Museum, the artistic centre and seat, too, of Smyrna's legal records:[78] literary culture and legal skill were not always separate arts in a third-century city. In 250, lesser fry, of a similar background, walked round Smyrna's seat of judgement and tried to divert Pionius from his death. "Listen to us, Pionius," they said, "because we love you, and you are eminently worthy of staying alive . . ." Like the crowd who heard his speeches, they hated to see a good man die. Could he not sacrifice, they said, and clear himself? The scene was very revealing. In Spain, in the year 259, Bishop Fructuosus was also besought by pagans who "loved him." Pagan friends continue to appear in Cyprian's biography, while Cyprian languished in prison.[79]

Among Christians, the pattern of the assizes was so familiar that it influenced their very dreams. In 258, the martyr Marian was gifted with the Spirit, as his insistent "best friend" recorded: "My brothers, I was shown a seat of judgement, high and white, standing far above the ground, in which, instead of a governor, a judge was sitting, a man of very pleasing countenance. And I heard a voice loud and clear saying, 'Bring up Marian!' So I began to climb up to the platform when

Bishop Cyprian appeared at the judge's right hand. He raised me up to a higher point on the platform and smiled and said, 'Come, sit beside me.' And it came to pass that all the other groups were heard in trial, while I, too, sat as assessor beside them.'"[80] In 258, the martyr Marian climbed the governor's tribunal in his dreams and sat with Cyprian and the assistant *agoraioi*, advisers of the sort who had pleaded with Pionius before a similar seat. A few days later, Marian was dead.

In Smyrna, the assize scene was set as usual, but the sequel was most unexpected. At a former assizes, Polycarp had been dragged straight before a governor to a stadium where the crowd was baying for his blood. He was promptly burned at the stake. In February 250, Pionius was brought before the local commission who were enforcing Decius's edict. They threatened and cajoled him persistently, but Pionius was kept in chains for more than a fortnight until the governor finally arrived. At first, he was interrogated, then hustled through the crowd to prison: people in the crowd called for his immediate punishment, but Polemon replied that "the fasces," the symbols of Roman authority, "do not go before us, so that we have authority," the Roman *imperium*.[81] In prison, Pionius described how he and his friends refused all their visitors' charity, whereupon the warders threw them into an inner dungeon and denied them any sustenance whatsoever. When Pionius and his friends then agreed to accept the "usual tips," the prison authorities ordered them to be brought back to the outer cells.

"While they were in prison, many pagans came down, wanting to persuade them, and when they heard their answers they were amazed." Soon, the bishop of Smyrna was obliged to lapse and Pionius was tested again. He refused, however, to appear without a governor, and so his interrogators used one of the governor's military officers to set a trap.[82] The governor, they said, had asked for Pionius to be transferred to his seat at Ephesus, and they and his officer were hoping to make him come quietly. Pionius saw through their deceit. The officer threatened him with his rank, a characteristic attempt of a soldier to browbeat a civilian, but they had to drag him, kicking and butting, to the altar. When he refused, in full view of the bishop, "the public official stood there, holding the sacrificial meat; however, he did not dare to go near anyone, but he ate it, the public official, just like that, in front of everyone . . ."

Throughout this long drama, the governor's seat had been ready and waiting, but business must have detained him at an earlier stop on his tour. Pionius's diary is only a fragment of a wider drama whose missing pieces lie elsewhere on the governor's circuit. Although they escaped Pionius and his crowds in Smyrna, they may not be entirely lost to us. There is a chance that the assize tour of early 250 may be the best known in the history of the Asian circuit.

When Smyrna's officials tried to deceive Pionius into "going with them to the governor," they told him that their master had asked for his despatch to Ephesus. Ephesus was the seat from which the governor usually began his tour, and it so happens that stories of trouble in Ephesus are prolific in the year 250. The city is the scene of the most famous of all legends of Christian persecution, the Seven Sleepers, seven Christian boys and their dog who were said to have taken to a cave to escape from Decius's edict. In 250, their legend is joined at Ephesus by the fiction of Maximus's martyrdom, which is dated impossibly to May 250. These martyrdoms are only legends, yet perhaps they reflect the prolonged Christian trials in Ephesus which had delayed Pionius's governor. The "edict of 250" fathered many fictions, but a certain truth lies behind these legends' setting in the city.

While the Seven Sleepers were driven to their den, Pionius sat in prison, preaching and writing his diary. From Aelius's earlier writings, we can reconstruct the usual stops on the Asian assize tour: Ephesus to Smyrna, then Smyrna north to Pergamum, where the governor ought to arrive in late March or April. In April 250, another martyrdom can be attached to his progress.

Eusebius refers to the "records" and "conspicuous confessions" of three martyrs at Pergamum and implies that they were martyred at the same time as Pionius. Two versions of their martyrdom survive and carry particular weight: one, an expanded Greek version, the other, a Latin translation which is nearer to the Greek original from which this expanded text developed.[83] The Latin text's preface and prescript date the martyrs to Decius's reign and refer correctly to the Emperor's edict which ordered "sacrifice to the gods." The governor is called "Optimus," but no "Optimus" is known, and there is force in the old guess that the name is the Latin translation of his title in the Greek original: "Most excellent governor," like "most excellent Theophilus." His name, then, is recoverable. The earliest calendars of Christian martyrs place these Christians' deaths at Pergamum on April 13. The year was 250, and if so, the "most excellent governor" was Quintilianus, processing north from Smyrna, having sentenced Pionius to death. In April, Pergamum was the assize tour's next stop.

In early March, Quintilianus heard from Pionius that Christians worshipped the Maker of the heavens. In mid-April, he was harangued by Christians in Pergamum's amphitheatre, that huge arena which spreads across the natural backdrop to the upper city's theatre, the steepest stage in the ancient world. The Latin version remarks that the crowds in Pergamum had been in a hurry. They had wished to light the Christians' bonfire before it started to rain. Perhaps this detail is true to life, and so, perhaps, is the speech which the Latin gave to the martyr Papylus as they hurried to bring the fire: "Here the fire burns briefly, but there it burns for ever, and by it, God will judge the world. It will drown the sea, the mountains and the woods. By it, God will judge each human soul."[84]

Just enough is known of the "most excellent governor" to sharpen the irony. It was no use telling Quintilianus a truth about the world to come. Inscriptions at Eleusis reveal that Quintilianus had followed high Roman fashion and been initiated into its pagan mysteries. The next world held no terrors for an Eleusinian initiate who held the rank of an honoured Eumolpid. Christians, he thought, were worshippers of the air: could they not, please, sacrifice to that? When Pionius refused to admit who made the air, Quintilianus had to tell him. It was "God," of course, "that is, Zeus, Zeus who is in heaven as king of the gods."

Earlier in Carthage, Perpetua had met with a deputy governor, a man who had built an altar in northwestern Spain "to the gods and goddesses to whom it is meet and right to pray in the pantheon": he had built it "for the safety of the Emperor."[85] In the 240s, Sabina the slave girl had been thrown out of a household whose pagan loyalties had been warmly expressed at Rome's last secular games: "for the security and eternity of the Empire you should frequent the most sacred shrines for the rendering and giving of thanks." Pionius and the martyrs of Pergamum had run into a staunch Eumolpid. Such men in Roman service still held to its traditions and fostered the pagan cults which had kept life going for so long. When times were hard, disaster reinforced the faith which they took for granted. The gods, they thought, needed to be honoured more vigorously until their anger passed away. For them, there was nothing which Decius had to revive. On circuit, the "most excellent Eumolpid" had made a brisk start: the Seven Sleepers were in their den; Pionius was on his cross; the local bishop of Smyrna had compromised and eaten meat for the gods; a bishop, a deacon and a Christian lady had been burnt in Pergamum before the April showers. Last year, the harvest for these cities had been very poor, but this year, the gods might be kinder. By early May, the crops would be ripening. On tour, the Eumolpid had already done his best.

In Smyrna, we have seen his actions through a victim's diary, but there was one last twist to his sentence and its execution. When the pagans fixed Pionius onto his cross, facing east, they fixed beside him "one from the *hairesis* of the followers of Marcion." To any Church leader, Marcion's heresy was the most shocking deviation from Apostolic truth. He had denied the Old Testament's inspiration and the continuity of its God and Creator with Christ. Bishop Polycarp had known how to deal with him. When Polycarp met Marcion, said Polycarp's pupil Irenaeus, he had greeted him as "the firstborn child of Satan." Pionius, we happen to know, was well aware of the saying. Our longer version of his postscript to Polycarp's martyrdom shows that he had quoted it for his readers' benefit.[86] Shortly before 250, Asia's Church leaders had met in Smyrna and agreed that heretics who wished to enter the true Church had first to be rebaptized. Bishops in Africa would soon be explicit: better a pagan, they asserted, than a heretic. While Pionius burned on his cross, his Christian observers were taught to see only "an athlete in his prime . . . his face, too, shone again . . ." If Pionius had thought anything, he could have turned to a sadder theme. Persecution had split a Church which was already divided by heresy: Smyrna's pagan crowds and their open respect for culture were better than bishops who lapsed and the "son of Satan" who was burning by his side.

# 10. Bishops and Authority

## I

We have seen the social diversity of the churches' membership, their varying standards of achievement, their scope for perfectionism, their virgins, their visionaries, their reactions to persecution. Like Pionius and his prison lament, we can only wonder how such communities could ever cohere. Within their diversity, enough people, ultimately, accepted and desired similar ends and were prepared to recognize authority for their sake. Cohesion was achieved through a distinctive style of leadership: to appreciate it, we must explore the ideals and position of Christian bishops.

Bishops viewed superior Christians with a mixture of respect, wariness and outright hostility. They respected the sexual perfectionists, but were wary of their conceit and capacity for forcing their ideals on others: such people were also a source of scandal, even in the households of bishops or clerics where the females tended to be brought up. Superior "knowing" Christians were more of a menace and sometimes lost any claims to be Christians at all. Many of them rejected bishops as part of an inferior Creation beyond which their own awakened insight had led them. Bishops' authority, some of them said, was a sterile creation for ignorant believers.[1] Their claim to uncontrolled, personal "knowledge" soon provoked the reward of pseudo-intellectual systems which defy the content of historical texts: they moved others to refute them, and state their conservative case very forcefully. By the third century, "Gnostic" views were the curious beliefs of minorities who had become rather passé: better books had been written for those who wished to be enlightened, knowledgeable Christians while remaining within the Church.

Superior "knowing" Christians also laid emphasis on their visions. The respect for the prophet and the visionary was an obvious danger to the rule of leaders appointed for life. In Hermas's third vision, the Church herself had told him to publish harsh words for the "leaders of the churches and those who occupy the foremost seats." They were like sorcerers, she said, and nursed poison in their hearts: "how can you hope to educate the Lord's elect when you have no education of your own?"[2] This type of heavenly pamphlet was not the most welcome reading for its senior recipients.

By the third century, however, visionary experience was the acknowledged gift of bishops, while rival claims to the Spirit were subject to careful testing. The most admired revelations were the dreams of martyrs, but on the whole they were most concerned with the martyrs' personal fate. The one surviving exception is the vision of the elderly Saturus, companion of Perpetua in Carthage in spring 203. "We went out from Paradise," he wrote, "and before the gates we saw Bishop Optatus on the right and Aspasius the Elder and teacher on our left, separated from each other, and looking sad. They threw themselves at our feet and said, 'Make peace between us . . .' And we said, 'Are you not our bishop and our presbyter, yet you throw yourselves at our feet?' Perpetua began to embrace them and talk to them in Greek beneath an arbour of roses. But the angels rebuked their interruption and told off Bishop Optatus: 'Correct your crowd [plebs],' they said, 'because they come to you like people returning from the circus and quarrelling about the teams.'"[3]

This vision was not an attack on an accepted principle of leadership: it was a call for proper leadership from those appointed to power. It was evidence of the bishops' predicament, not of their illegitimacy. In Carthage, the community was beset by factious rivalries which already resembled the hooliganism of a city's sports fans: discipline was the duty of a bishop with whom his own Elders might be at odds. It was left to two martyrs, one of whom was an unbaptized woman, to try to settle their differences. We can see from the letters of Bishop Cyprian, fifty years later, how the martyrs' behaviour to bishops varied: in one case, we find them deferring to his "glorious" authority, although he himself was in hiding; in another, they send him a letter whose superiority shows through almost every sentence.[4]

Martyrs, however, were short-lived, and the leaders of the churches were quick to record the dates of their deaths and honour them safely as community occasions. A greater problem were the "confessors," Christians who had been arrested and tried or sentenced to temporary punishments. When persecution ceased, they survived or were released. As agents of the Holy Spirit, they possessed a very great prestige. It was an official view, c. 200, that confessors could immediately be made priests and Elders, but not bishops: Cyprian's letters show how a Church leader had to defer to their authority, even if he also wished to chide and redirect it. Bishops themselves were not well placed to counter this type of prestige: when Cyprian greeted a Christian who had first been a confessor and was then made a bishop, he compared his arrival with the coming of Christ.[5] After the events of 250, we can well understand why. Like many other bishops, Cyprian had withdrawn into hiding. In Smyrna, the bishop had lapsed. Many in the Church were not slow to discover that age-old principle, that leaders are somehow too valuable to risk themselves in the front line.

As the persecutors themselves came to realize, the Christian leadership was a vital and distinctive part of their "state within a state": the next edict after Decius's singled out Church leaders as its particular target. Unlike any people whom we found in the pagan cults, Christian groups had accepted single leaders with wide powers, to be exercised for life. Was there any precedent for this type of authority, so essential to the degree of cohesion which Christian churches maintained?

Once again, the nearest parallel lies in the Jewish sect whom we know from the Dead Sea scrolls. The community's overseer had had to teach and arbitrate, grade the religious progress of his membership, supervise the sect's property and doctrine and act in all things as "father and shepherd." Like the early churches, the sect had acknowledged two types of banishment, one for a brief period, the other for life.[6] Our studies of the Holy Spirit, the close company of angels and the ideal of celibacy have led us repeatedly back to the Dead Sea sect: did Christians accept their bishops because this type of power was already familiar in Jewish sectarian practice? If a debt existed, it must have been indirect: the office of bishop did not emerge in the churches of the first Christian generation. Before bishops were sole accepted leaders, the Dead Sea sect had probably declined, taking its example with it.

In the Gentile world, lifelong rule by a single bishop was something quite new: it differed from any pattern of authority known in a pagan cult association. It was also a break with the practice of Jewish synagogues. Certainly, they had their leaders and dignitaries. In the first century the "chief of the synagogue" is known from Christian sources as the person who invited others to read the lesson from Scripture and expound it afterwards. He did not necessarily teach, and his general responsibility was for orderliness and the smooth conduct of the service. Presumably it was the "chief of the synagogue" who sat in the special "Chair of Moses": in the synagogue on Delos, one survives, a marble chair with a footstool. However, the chief's tenure and capacities were not necessarily the same in every community. In an inscription from Acmoneia in Phrygia, we find a "chief of the synagogue for life" with a mere "chief of the synagogue" mentioned next. When we later find a woman called the "chief" in Smyrna and children given the title elsewhere, we cannot assume the job was always a post of authority. "Chiefs of the synagogue" also record their personal spending on their synagogues' buildings: it was presumably because of their property that women and children were chosen for the job. The "chief of the synagogue" seems more like a benefactor and president than a bishop.[7]

What of the other titles that we meet in evidence from the Diaspora? They are mostly known from Greek and Latin inscriptions, c. 200 A.D. or later, and from the rulings of Constantine and subsequent Emperors which refer to the authorities among the Diaspora's Jews. We must be wary of reading these titles back into the synagogues of St. Paul's lifetime, two or three centuries earlier: we cannot even be sure of the nature, or formal definition, of an order of Jewish "Elders" when Christianity first emerged.[8] However, synagogues did need a firm authority: offensive members were banned; fines were imposed and floggings were ordered for religious offences. Beside the Elders, we hear of "rulers," and between them, the two must have governed the communities' affairs in Gentile cities. They will have heard cases between fellow Jews and seen to details of conduct which went beyond the regulation of worship: people record that they were both a "ruler" and a "chief of the synagogue," perhaps concurrently. The "rulers" are not known to have served for life; there were several, not one; we know of a ruler (c. 100 A.D.) who paid an entry fee for selection to his office, like a pagan magistrate. We also know of "fathers" and "mothers" of the community, who assisted it as donors and benefactors. If this was their only role, they were comparable to the big benefactors in second- and third-century cities who were honoured in the same family language. Like the "rulers," they were probably named on the model of contemporary civil practice.[9]

In Christian imagery, the bishop was heir to none of these titles. By the mid-third century, it could be assumed by Cyprian, bishop of Carthage, that bishops were successors to the priests of the Old

Testament.[10] Had Christians taken over the strand of priestly authority which Jews, meanwhile, had lost? The destruction of Jerusalem
and the Temple had ended the role of the Jews' own priesthood: to our
eye, the authorities in Jewish life of the second and third centuries were
the rabbis, or teachers, in the learned academies. Rabbis wrote and
expressed opinions, but did not direct a formal Judaism. During the
second and third centuries, however, tithes were still paid in Galilee to
priestly individuals, and we find self-styled "priests" in funerary
inscriptions from nearby Beth Shearim and in inscriptions in the
Diaspora: we even find a "priestess," buried in Rome. Not all of these
people were mere descendants of the old priestly families, without any
function, since we find Constantine giving immunities to "priests" of
the Jewish community. This favour equated them with the ministers
of a God and we cannot, then, entirely exclude some "priestly"
element in the third-century synagogues.[11] Its scope, however, is
uncertain.

Of one higher authority among the Jews, we are told much more,
but the reliability of Christians and rabbis on the subject may not be
very great.[12] In Palestine, from the second century onwards, Roman
rule recognized a single patriarch, and rabbinic sources preserve
several stories of the three successive Judahs who held this office from
c. 170 until the later third century. They claimed that the patriarch
regulated the calendar and declared fasts, imposed and received taxes,
banned unsuitable teachers and pupils and appointed judges. They
told of his contacts with Roman governors and the Emperors and
projected a picture of his high status. Christian sources enlarge on it.
Origen compared the patriarch to a king, when explaining the story of
Susannah, and referred to his own experiences in the land of the Jews:
people, he said, were still put to death "unofficially" by Jews with the
patriarch's connivance. However, his observation did not necessarily
apply outside Palestine: only the late Christian texts allege that the
patriarch sent "apostles" with encyclical letters round the Jewish
communities. In the Diaspora, recently, it seemed as if a newly found
inscription, datable c. 280, supported these notions.[13] At Stobi, in
Macedonia, its text laid down rules for the use of a synagogue building
and stated that the fines for any infringement should be paid to "the
patriarch." This rule has been seen as a sign of the Great Patriarch's
authority, extending to small, local details so far outside Palestine. In
the fourth century, however, the rulings of Christian Emperors
address Jewish "patriarchs" who are local figures: at Stobi, the

"patriarch" may only be a dignitary in the local community.

It is of great interest that the titles of rank in the Jewish synagogues were developing during the second and third centuries: we find "principals" and "fathers" as well as "priests" and "patriarchs." Once again, we can compare the multiplication of titles of rank in secular society and suspect that the pattern owed something to contemporary practice in the pagan world. While Christians spread, the Jewish communities in the same cities were not static: once again, we have lost a vital angle on the history of this period, because no books survive from Diaspora Jews in an age of change. However, even without them, we can see that these titles offer no parallel for the pattern of power in the Christian Church. There, by contrast, rule by a single leader emerged and spread as the dominant authority. Christians had taken up a type of leadership which was used by a small sect: they multiplied it in each of their communities. The church of each city looked up to its monarchical bishop, who was a leader appointed for life. "One God, one Christ, one Holy Spirit," the Christian laity called out in Rome after a dispute in the mid-third century, "and in a Catholic church there ought to be one bishop."[14] Their cry was all the more remarkable, as there had not been a hint of bishops in anything said by Jesus in the Gospels.

Other Christians had been quick to fill the gap.[15] In the 90s, a leading Christian at Rome wrote to the church in Corinth and explained how the Apostles had appointed "bishops" from their first converts. He quoted Isaiah to support the point: "I will appoint their bishops in righteousness." The text was a convenient misquotation. By the 170s, Irenaeus was confounding the heretics by citing a list of successive bishops of Rome, of which he himself, significantly, was the twelfth. The first, however, was his mistaken deduction from the epistles, where he had misconstrued an adjective as a bishop's proper name. By the early third century, Tertullian argued that the Apostles had appointed bishops in the major cities and that their churches had "records" which connected them to Apostolic appointments. This documentary evidence was probably his exaggeration, not their fiction. By 250, Cyprian was assuming that the Apostles had been bishops themselves.

The emergence of bishops in cities of the Greek East is visible in the letters which Ignatius sent to the major churches of Asia, c. 110.[16] His attempts to exalt the bishop's authority suggest the shock waves which the office had spread in certain quarters. We cannot be more precise about its origins and we must always allow for differing local circumstances.[17] In Alexandria, the Elders remained unusually important. Among the Syriac-speaking churches of eastern Syria and Mesopotamia, the sense of hierarchy and organization may have remained weaker. By the 170s, there is still no sign of bishops in the churches in southern Gaul.

From the third century, however, we are lucky to have a long description of the good bishop. It survives for us in a Syriac translation, whose original was composed in Greek.[18] It presented its contents as the teaching which the Twelve Apostles circulated after their council in Jerusalem. This fake authority is all too characteristic. We will return later to its excellent picture of life in a small church community, but here, we must pick out its ideals of good leadership. The bishop, it said, should be a blameless character, preferably aged over fifty and married to a Christian wife. He must not have remarried and his own children ought to be good Christians. He must be meek and chaste, merciful and adept at making peace. His own family should be examined as proof of his discipline and talents for sound upbringing. If possible, he should be learned and lettered. If not, he could be illiterate, so long as he knew the Scriptures. If the church was a small one and if all the members bore witness to him, the bishop could be a young man. Was not Josiah, after all, a good king of the Jews at the age of eight? Earlier, Ignatius had written in support of a young bishop whom some Christians were opposing in the Asian city of Magnesia. Young though they might be, bishops were able to serve for the rest of their lives.

Bishops needed one supreme gift in everything which these "Apostles" prescribed for them. They had to be men of keen discernment, a requirement which takes us to the heart of their difficulties. They had to distinguish the widow in genuine need from the widow who was not so badly off. They had to investigate the sources of Christian charity, and if the donors were heathens or sinners, drunk or lazy, they had to reject it. They were not to buy food with money of dubious origin and risk polluting the widows and orphans: if they had to accept such funds, they should spend them where they did least harm, on firewood. Dubious sources of finance included Roman officials who were stained with innocent blood, abusers of slaves, imprisoners of the poor and innkeepers of singular vice who diluted their wines with water. Bishops must also see to the education of orphans, especially when richer Christians were unwilling to adopt them as their heirs. They must discern false teachers and expel them from the church. Above all, they must investigate the truth of quarrels and slanders and reconcile the Christian participants.

It is here that the gift of discernment was most urgent. Paul had advised his Christians to take their disputes before fellow Christians, not before pagan courts of law: arbitration and conciliation became the formidable tasks of every bishop. Their art was to strive for reconciliation, not to dispense summary justice. The "Apostles" advise that the deacons should call out in church and ask if anyone present had anything against one of the brethren. If so, the bishop must reprove the bearer of the grudge and try to talk him out of it. He should call both parties and hear and reprove them on a Monday, giving the two parties a whole week until Sunday to make up their differences. The bishop should always hear the two sides together and conduct a careful examination of their character in order to decide which party must be telling the truth, a faith in character as evidence which was rather optimistic. Not every accusation was merited, and false complaints were a severe test of any bishop's insight. On no account, said the "Apostles," should he accept a heathen's testimony, but he should act slowly, imitating the slowness and diligence of a pagan court in a murder case, of whose workings the "Apostles" took an unusually favourable view. Like a "certified money changer," they said, the bishop must test his disputants. He must work to abolish lawsuits, not to pass judgement, and he must not hold back if the two parties resist him. Kings only reign over their subjects' bodies, said the "Apostles," but bishops reign over their bodies and also their souls. They can bind and loose on earth with their gift of heavenly power. If necessary, they can invoke the wrath to come and threaten the fires of hell.[19]

During the bishop's arbitration, the Elders could sit beside him, but throughout the process the greater assessor was Christ himself. Although the bishop was the mouthpiece of God, he was also under God's eye and was personally accountable for every false judgement. If he condemned an innocent man, he himself would be condemned at the Last Day.[20] He was also accountable for the conduct of his flock, a charge which obliged him to correct the local sinners. Deadly sins were thought to be beyond forgiveness, but progress could be made with lesser wrongdoing. The bishop should exclude sinners from church for two to seven weeks until they repented and were reconciled to Christian conduct. A bishop's reproofs were greatly helped by a unified, blameless community. If a sinner entered such a church, he would be "confounded and go out quietly, in great shame, weeping and feeling remorse in his heart. And when the whole flock sees the tears and weeping of that man, it too will fear, knowing that everyone who sins will perish."[21] The group, then, was chastened with fear, while the individual was humiliated in public.

These practices were not altogether an innovation. The Gospels and epistles had stressed the community's role in reproving a troublesome brother: Christians were advised to cut off contact with an offender after two warnings. Paul had already declared false teachers and "those who do not love Christ" to be "anathema"; they were given over to Satan, to whom the First Epistle to Timothy roundly consigned two "blasphemous" individuals. As the bishop became established, it was surely he who pronounced this sentence, just as we see bishops pronouncing it collectively in the acts of the earliest councils. Their penalties for sin range from a temporary denial of the Eucharist to excommunication, "ejection" and "anathematization," a solemn surrender to God's judgement.[22]

These sentences were extremely grave, and the bishop who controlled them was urged to be no respecter of persons. He must not fawn on the rich and famous or show hostility to the poor. He must strictly resist the bribes of sinners, as they would pollute the entire church. If a rich man entered church, he must ignore him and only make way for the poor man. The insistence on these values says something, it seems, about bishops in real life. The "Apostles'" advice finds a near-contemporary support in the vivid remarks which Origen passed while commenting on Matthew's Gospel in the 240s. "We terrify people," he wrote, "and make ourselves inaccessible, especially if they are poor. To people who come and ask us to do something for them, we behave as no tyrant, even, would: we are more savage to petitioners than any civil rulers are. You can see this happening in many recognized churches, especially in the bigger cities."[23]

We can well see how these tyrants had developed. More than any Emperor, bishops combined accessibility with the exercise of an awesome power. They "ruled in the place of God." They could suspend a cleric or an ordinary Christian, ban him from church and damn him to eternal punishment. It was hard for a man to be open and humble when any slander against his person was said to be a slander against God. "Love your bishop as a father: fear him as a king: honour him as God . . .": this ideal asked Christians to reconcile impossible opposites.[24] The bishop had to retain his own insight while attracting a difficult mixture of affection and reverential fear.

The outlines of this advice on bishops' conduct were much older than their clear statement by the "Apostles." They already existed in the epistles addressed to Timothy, where bishops were exhorted to teach and befriend strangers, to show sobriety and eschew quarrels and financial corruption. The theology echoed much which Ignatius's letters also expressed. The bishop, wrote Ignatius, was the "image of the Father." The man who disregards him "deceives not the bishop, who is seen, but deceives God, who is invisible." Whoever acts without the bishop is the "servant of the Devil."[25] Ignatius already had a strong sense of the potential awe of the Christians' leadership, and expressed it by emphasizing the power of a bishop's silence. "The more anyone sees a bishop to be silent, the more reverence should he feel towards him."[26] As silence was the quality of God himself, a silent bishop reflected God on earth: "He who possesses Jesus's word is truly able also to hear his silence, so that he may be perfect, so that he may act through his words and be known through his silences." Silent authority on earth reflected God's silent authority in heaven: the bishop was "the likeness of God," and the Elders "his council and the company of the Apostles."

The exaltation of the bishop as the "man of God," the high priest, the "bearer of the Spirit," was not, then, a new development in the churches of the third century. It owed nothing to new patterns of social relations developing in surrounding worldly society.[27] It was not the effect of any "common Mediterranean religious culture," supposedly shared by pagans, Jews and Christians. The language of the bishop's authority and inspiration went back to his very origin as a distinctive Christian minister: Ignatius had already praised him as the guardian of true doctrine who should pray for spiritual revelation of "things invisible." He should care especially for the widows, and before long, his household became a recognized haven for orphans and resolute virgins: we have a vivid record of such girls' turbulence in a papyrus record of the early fourth century.[28] Ignatius had already advised Christians to marry in the presence of their bishop, and although there was no formal ceremony of Christian marriage in the early Church, this proposal connected bishops promptly with the private lives of their membership. When Christians went on to commit adultery, the bishop was involved again. By the early third century, some of the leading bishops were prepared to absolve this deadly sin and their "power of the keys" was extended accordingly. The more the bishop could forgive in the Spirit, the wider his authority extended.[29]

Power brings its own temptations and suspicions, especially a power which requires such insight, persuasion and honesty. It is not, then, so surprising that we know most about early bishops when they fell short of these ideals. Their job involved the care of money and the instruction of widows and virgins, while the power to "bind and loose" carried its own temptations. We have only to read Cyprian's letters to discover bishops who were charged with succumbing to each of these specific sins: Cyprian knew how to suit his allegations to the particular temptations of the job. By Origen's standards, few bishops lived up to it.[30] "And the Lord said to Moses, Take all the chiefs of the people and expose them to the Lord over against the sun, and the anger of the Lord shall be turned from Israel . . ." "Perhaps," wrote Origen, when he reached this choice episode in Numbers, "I will give offence to certain people in discussing this text." The prospect did not deter him. Church leaders, he wrote, would not dare to compete for the rank and honour of their position if they remembered that they would be accountable for their own and their church's sins.

In the pagan world, oracles had applauded the piety of priests and warned against their violation in texts which were much to the taste of the Emperor Julian. The sanctions surrounding a bishop were of an altogether sterner order. The bishop was the successor to the royal and priestly leaders of God's chosen people and deserved a respect appropriate to his responsibilities. As Cyprian reminded one opponent, opposition to God's minister was opposition to God himself.[31] Scripture proved it, he wrote, from Deuteronomy to Acts: "the man who will not hearken unto the priest . . . shall die and all the people, when they hear, shall fear and act no more with presumption." The equation of dissent with the Devil and the threat of reprisals in hell for any opponent strike us as abominable innovations. These threats, however, were not the roots of a bishop's authority. They lay in the general manner of his job's origin and the particular form of his election.

Bishops had not been imposed on most Christians from outside or above. They had been selected with local approval, as the best means to cope with problems. In the absence of Apostolic precedent, their origins can only be guessed, but it is not unjust to suspect that bishops were born from conflict. At first the early churches had looked up to

"Elders," respected men who were of an age to remember the churches' founders. What, then, if the Elders disagreed? There was a need for a single "overseer" to settle disputes.[32] Like Ignatius's bishop in Magnesia, the chosen overseer might not be an "Elder" himself. Standing outside the group, this one individual could also take over the task of offering the Eucharist and administering the funds of a city's church. As Christians were supposed to be one Body, he could represent his local community in the affairs of the wider Church. As the membership grew, Christians in the bigger cities became divided among various places of worship. Services had to be held in houses or private properties which were put at the Christians' disposal. There was no single cathedral, or public "church." By giving authority to one leader, the churches were better placed to maintain uniformity and avoid disintegration. The bishop became a badly needed focus in a city when the menace of heresy required a concerted counterattack and when persecution threatened to tear the community apart. Above all, there was the overriding worry of the Last Judgement.[33] Here, the bishop was expected to answer for his flock's conduct before God and to work for the community's safety in the world to come. A good bishop was in everyone's interest, both in this life and in the next.

There were solid grounds, then, for the bishop's pre-eminence and we must not isolate him entirely from his fellow clergy. He sat on his own distinctive "chair," covered with linen in Cyprian's case: during a service, however, he was not raised above his congregation. High pulpits were thought an outrage: it has been calculated that Augustine, in his African church at Hippo, addressed his Sunday audience from a chair only five yards away from their front row.[34] Before the age of Constantine, the bishop wore no special dress and could always consult freely with his wider company of Elders. They might sit beside him while he gave judgement and around him while he taught in church. In practice, a bishop could expel an offending Christian without further consultation, but he would naturally consult his supporting clergy when appropriate.[35]

His pre-eminence was linked with two basic instruments: pay and appointments. In each case, the bishop was supreme, but his supremacy had to be exercised tactfully if it was to be accepted. It is quite clear from Cyprian's letters and other texts that a bishop could appoint his own choices to vacant jobs in the church; the "Apostles" compare his choosing of Elders and deacons with the wide powers enjoyed by

Samuel.[36] However, we can see from Cyprian's letters that a consultation with the clergy and "mass membership" was more usual in many churches. It is true that Cyprian appointed a reader, an Elder and several minor officials while hiding from persecution. Yet he wrote very carefully to his fellow churchmen, emphasizing the special circumstances which obliged him to choose personally. Some of his appointments, he pleaded, were already confessors, who had stood trial for their faith and whom God, he said, had already approved. The churches, therefore, would hardly wish to dispute them. It is evident from such a letter that consultation was the more normal practice whenever bishops wished a change of personnel.

It is also evident that they could not appoint an entire new clergy on the occasion of their own appointment. They had to live with existing Elders and clerics: we can detect a group of supporting priests who served Cyprian's daily business and ran his various errands for him, but they are essentially a power bloc whom he himself had attracted and built up.[37] A similar constraint attached to finance. The bishop, ultimately, dispensed the charity. He allotted funds to the widows, orphans and deserving poor. He also paid the clergy their shares.[38] This power allowed some skilful tactics: opponents, as Athanasius (c. 330) showed, could be struck off the list and paid nothing. However, both the bishop and the clergy depended on the good will of the laity for funds in the first place. At first, they were supported by a "dividend system," financed by the total of their Christians' offerings: the sum seems to have been paid monthly, and a bishop's share was probably twice as big as an Elder's.[39] The offerings included first fruits from crops and produce: Christian polemic against the letter of the Mosaic law did not extend to its rules on first fruits and tithes: tithes, on one view, were payable to the minor clerics, widows, paupers and virgins. The notion of fixed clerical salaries was considered an outrage as late as c. 200, in both Rome and Asia. It was the shocking practice of Christian sectarians and heretics. In the Christian Empire, however, it became the orthodox system in the East. Salaries are the heretics' one lasting legacy to Christian life.

The bishop who lost touch with his laity would find himself financially weakened and eventually with no funds for the task. Equally, if the laity failed to contribute, they robbed themselves of an ally in their search for salvation: the laity's offerings, said the "Apostles'" letter, pass through the bishop for the remission of their sins.[40] Above all, the bishop was their own man, however long he lived in office and however much they grumbled at him. "In almost all provinces," said Cyprian, the entire clergy and laity of the local church met to approve the bishop's election.[41]

However, his authority had a wider dimension: bishops were not merely local leaders whom the local Christian membership appointed. Their election and ordination required the participation of at least three neighbouring bishops: we know of elections by as many as seven or twelve or sixteen.[42] These visitors' role linked each bishop's authority to the universal Church in the community of God. This universality was an earlier support to the bishop's power than any supposed succession from the Twelve Apostles. The idea of a continuous chain of bishops, tracing back to the Apostles, is first apparent in texts of Hegesippus and Irenaeus in the mid- to later second century: they emphasize it to guarantee doctrine and orthodoxy, not to underpin the bishops' general authority. In the early third century, Hippolytus then emphasizes the transmission of the Spirit from Apostles to bishops, with the implication that the latter are special guardians of the truth. Finally, in the 250s, Cyprian's letters equate bishops and Apostles: the chain of succession has become an explicit argument for authority and obedience.[43]

Neither the laity nor the visitors exhausted the content of a bishop's election. A third dimension entered the process: the approval, or "judgement," of God. We hear most about this element from Cyprian, but it was not his invention, nor was it the response of Church leaders who found themselves under threat in the mid-third century.[44] It was grounded in the very prayer and ritual of a bishop's ordination. The texts of this procedure raise difficult problems of dating and elaboration, but the earliest material appears to have included a prayer to God for the gift of "the princely spirit to this, your servant whom you have chosen to the bishopric."[45] The prayer connected the bishop with God's choice and with the "princes" and "priests" of Jewish history: the Church, it said, was the heir of the "race of the righteous," descending from Abraham. The attending bishops prayed for the gift of the Holy Spirit to pass to their new candidate, while the entire assembly observed a silence to mark the occasion. Gifted with the Spirit, the bishop alone could impart the Spirit by laying hands on newly baptized Christians.

These beliefs were most unfamiliar to pagans. At their oracles, Apollo gave a divine word of reference to his ministers. At Didyma, he "bore witness" to his prophet's qualities, probably when the prophet was inaugurated. At the major shrines, the function of prophecy was divided between a thespode or "prophetess" and a prophet whom the god's words approved. Unlike a bishop, the prophet changed frequently, usually every year. His inspiration was tied to a place and a fixed ritual and was not transmitted from one prophet to others: it was not a continuous guidance at all times and places. Even when a god enhanced a prophet's faculties, the words were generally thought to be his own, not the speaker's.

The bishop, by contrast, was selected by the "judgement" of God; he was approved by the "suffrage" of the people and validated by the "agreement" of fellow bishops. He promised no donations; he assumed a "perpetual magistracy" for life without agreeing to any accompanying "liturgy" to be performed at his own financial expense.

However, when we pass beyond the ideal, the practical problems begin to multiply. Did the visiting bishops choose their candidate and submit him to the assembled people for approval or did the people nominate their own candidates? What happened if the people and the bishops disagreed, or if God was believed to favour somebody else? What exactly was this popular "suffrage"? If the judgement was God's, could people not argue that other methods might express it better? The questions do not end with the local churches, for the bishop was also the choice of the "Church universal": who, then, resolved disputes between bishops in different places? Details of the liturgy were a bishop's local responsibility, but questions of heresy and discipline raised theological issues about the very unity of the Church. Were all bishops autonomous, as Cyprian implied, while some were more equal than others, as his arguments presupposed? The ideal of unity could be employed, as always, to coerce dissidents, yet the very notion of a "bishop of the bishops" was still outrageous.[46] It was equated by Tertullian and Cyprian with tyranny and an unsupportable dictatorship, and was applied only to their opponents. This rhetoric was very stirring, but it set a heavy weight on "consensus." Could one church never interfere with another and fairly compel its leader? Only God, implied Cyprian, could judge a bishop's conduct, but did this view imply that no bishop could force another into line? What if a bishop misbehaved and his church wished to be rid of him? The problems arose very sharply after persecutions, and it took a firm series of scriptural texts from Cyprian's pen to reassure the laity that they were right in deposing lapsed bishops whom formerly they had elected.[47]

To answer these problems, we must examine the parts of the "electoral" process. The word "suffrage" had been imported into church elections from the language of secular elections and preferment: here, the churches in North Africa were no more immune than the synagogues in the Greek world to the language of surrounding society. In the third-century African cities, the elections of magistrates were still lively popular occasions: "popular clamour" could disrupt them, and as late as 325, in a very revealing law, we find Constantine acknowledging that the "suffrage of the people" played a part in the nomination of magistrates "by custom" in Africa, but insisting that only suitable candidates should be put forward.[48] This continuing secular "custom" is very relevant to the language and scandals of elections in the contemporary African churches. People were used to exerting suffrage, and the Church was not alone in giving a role to it: it differed, however, in including the suffrage of slaves and women. In pagan appointments, the word "suffrage" had declined from its older sense of free "voting" to a feebler "acclamation" at elections or a word of "support" in a letter of testimony for a job:[49] did the Church's usage, too, lie near the bottom of the slope?

Stories in Eusebius's histories and Cyprian's own life show that the people's suffrage could indeed be a force in its own right.[50] It is latent in Eusebius's simplest tales of election, tales like the appointment of Fabian to the bishopric of Rome. When a dove landed on the head of this obscure candidate, it signified his choice by the Holy Spirit and ensured his election by all the people and clergy. They had gathered, however, with other candidates in mind, suggesting that the people could have a general role as proposers. In the early third century, another story points in the same direction. When a faction arose in Jerusalem against the austere bishop Narcissus, he retired for peace to the Judaean desert, whereupon the neighbouring bishops presumed he had disappeared and appointed a successor. Narcissus then reappeared during his second successor's reign and "the brethren," said Eusebius, summoned him back to his old position. When Narcissus was too old to manage the job, God alerted the local Christians to an approved replacement. He sent them a vision by night in which he directed them to choose Alexander, a visitor from Cappadocia who happened to be touring the holy places as a pilgrim. The brethren waylaid him and the usual process was believed to have taken place. Neighbouring bishops became involved in the election and Alexander was approved as Narcissus's partner. By now, Narcissus was a very poor advertisement for life appointments. In a contemporary church letter, he was described as 116 years old.

The story was probably more legend than fact, but its elements did conform to the accepted ideas of a bishop's authority. Significantly, Narcissus's enemies were said to have been punished by God's vengeance, while he himself was remembered for his miracles, especially for the miraculous oil which he had produced one Easter and which survived in small quantities in Eusebius's own day. In the third century, a bishop could still be idealized as a "holy man." However, the legends of Narcissus's divine authority could not conceal that his austere manner split his church and obliged him to retreat in despair at the quarrelling. Above all, the election of his partner was remembered for the same three elements which Cyprian's letters stress: "divine judgement," the "agreement" of neighbouring bishops and the "approval" of the local membership.

The waylaying of a visiting Christian and his elevation to a bishopric were to have a long history: how active was the laity in the process? Eusebius's stories are told as if the "brethren" as a whole took the initiative: he knew two other examples in third-century Laodicea.[51] It is significant that the stories were presented in this way, although we may suspect the planned action of particular groups or individuals within the wider community. In Cyprian's own life, his admiring biographer found a further example. Cyprian himself was a recent convert, a man of considerable property and proven skill as a speaker and advocate in court. His rapid promotion to Carthage's great bishopric was brought about, said his fond biographer, by the laity's enthusiasm: "seething with ardour, the plebs swelled and the crowds besieged his doors . . ."[52] This popular backing overrode his very brief time as a Christian, though it helped to alienate the "gang of five," the five dissident Elders who then caused Cyprian such trouble in the conduct of his office. Perhaps the picture has been stylized to reflect credit on Cyprian, its hero, but again, it assumes that the people could bring decisive pressure to an election. No doubt, Cyprian's social position and property speeded his cause. In civic life, electors paid great attention to the candidates' willingness to promise gifts and perform civic services at their own expense. The laity could not be expected to abandon this familiar pattern whenever they met. The Church, too, needed money and service, and if Christians saw a rich candidate, they would anticipate charity for themselves and their community. By the later fourth century, the preferment of upper-class candidates was attracting widespread polemic.[53]

"Suffrage," it is clear from these examples, was not a fixed power of voting: Christians did nothing to reverse the word's decline "from vote to patronage." In contemporary pagan elections in Africa, "suffrage" could force an undesirable candidate forwards; it was also the acclamation which greeted a proposed name, and which was so hard for a candidate to refuse. A unanimous shout from a crowd or assembly was widely seen as an omen from the gods: there is an irony, here, for historians, as Greek theorists in the free, classical past had considered election by shouting to be "childish."[54] On both points, Christian suffrage overlapped, essentially, with its contemporary pagan counterpart, familiar from civic life. To Eusebius, a "unanimous shout" was a divine sign; Cyprian calls suffrage "divine" too, but suffrage did not exhaust the element of "divine judgement" which at other times he connects with the agreement and testimony of bishops and clergy only.[55] Suffrage was not a "right" of acclamation which alone could validate a candidate. The procedure was more fluid. It seems that visiting bishops and local clergy would put a suggested candidate before the people to see if they knew any "just cause or impediment." They might already have forced the clergy's hand, by waylaying a visitor or clamouring for someone like Cyprian, no doubt with the help of some skilful manipulation. If they disliked a candidate, they could withhold "suffrage" and stop his election. They might clamour for a rival, or they might rally unanimously and give the shout which seemed like a heaven-sent sign. Then the visiting bishops would "agree" and proceed to ordination while the people looked on. It is very doubtful if there was anything so formal as an election between two candidates, decided by the balance of popular noise. Nor was a unanimous acclamation a necessary part of the "judgement," let alone a popular right.

"Suffrage" remains imprecise, not only because our evidence is indirect, but because it was in essence informal: the people's dissent could stop an appointment or undermine one, and their assent could force one, if properly mobilized. However, only if "suffrage" was a real potential force can we understand the stories of bribes, faction and distortion at church elections.[56] In the mid-fourth century, Church councils ruled explicitly against claques who were placed in the crowd to distort its "suffrage" by their shouting. Among these watchers, the shouts of slaves and women were as good a suffrage as any. In the early fourth century, a rich woman was said to have used bribes to distort the course of an entire election in Africa. We know of no comparable actions by women in any pagan elections.

By this combination of the bishops' "judgement," the clerical "testimony" and the popular "suffrage," the new bishop was held to be "ordained by God." He was dignified by God and chosen by God: the threats of God's vengeance to anyone who opposed him rested firmly on the form of his public election.[57] If the people had approved him by "divine" suffrage, who were they to disobey his will? Not everyone, however, thought the electoral process was sensible.

In Origen, again, we have a contemporary in whom these uncertainties induced explicit distaste.[58] Churches, he remarked, received the leaders they deserved, and generally, they were more interested in rank and position than scholarship. People competed for the jobs, and most of them had more of an eye for the church's rich membership than for the Scriptures and their meaning. How wisely, by contrast, Moses had appointed Joshua. He had ignored his own sons and family. He had prayed for God's sign and had merely presented Joshua to the priests and people as a foregone conclusion. There had been no scope for the people's voice, which faction and bribery could corrupt, and no excuse for the intrigues of priests. These comments were not made at random.[59] In the mid-second century, we happen to know of a bishop who could already point to seven other bishops among his relations. Brothers and sons assumed office in subsequent centuries and there was always the chance that an ageing bishop would simply announce his successor: Augustine availed himself of old age's final tyranny by presenting "his" choice to his church before his death. In North Africa, in 259, the martyr Flavian gave a long "last testament" as he prepared to go to his execution: he "praised Lucian the Elder with a very fulsome eulogy and destined him, so far as he could, for a priesthood." "Not undeservedly," his "best friend" added in defence, "for it was not hard for him to have knowledge in the Spirit when Christ and heaven were so near . . ." We do not know what the other candidates thought of this long, unsolicited outburst.

The uncertainties and the skilled manoeuvres help us to see why so many appointments spilled out beyond the local church and became great Christian scandals of the third century. Any appointment involved the outside bishops, and if a choice was contested, there was as yet no order of primacy among the greater city sees. Rome had the most prestige, but had no agreed status as the senior power.[60] No hierarchy of metropolitan bishops stood above the local bishops in a province. In the absence of a firm hierarchy, local appointments risked becoming everyone's business. During the 90s, the deposition of clergymen in Corinth drew a warm letter from the church in Rome, pleading reconciliation and second thoughts.[61] In the 170s, the affair of Montanus passed from Phrygia to Rome and Lyons and back again: afterwards, Irenaeus is found writing from Lyons to the bishop of Rome to complain about the orthodoxy of one of his priests. In the 250s, Cyprian was writing from Africa to the bishop of Rome, urging action against a bishop of Arles. His synod intervened against bishops in Spain whose conduct encouraged the worst sort of rumour, and he devoted much energy to opposing a breakaway "bishop" in Rome who disagreed with his principles.[62]

It is a commonplace among historians that the cities, groups and individuals of the second- and third-century Empire pursued their interests by a flurry of letters, envoys and petitions to any higher authority which could possibly advance them. While pagans were travelling to Roman officials and the Emperor, Christians were engaged in an equally vigorous pattern of embassies, petitions and letters amongst themselves. They swelled the ranks of those endless travellers, speakers, letter-bearers and petitioners who crossed and recrossed the Mediterranean world: major bishops would use their own clerics to carry their letters, trusted postmen who would be less likely to forge them.[63] Their exchanges led to bishops' meetings in synods, events which are well attested in both West and East during the early third century. As a seat of the Apostles, the church in Rome had particular prestige when invoked in a dispute: Rome's primacy was to take shape from this early informality. What if the loser in a dispute refused to give up his position? If matters could not be resolved within the Church, might not one party follow the example of so many others throughout the Empire and appeal to the source with the most power to conclude it, the Emperor himself? Power, in the ancient world, had so often attracted the unresolved pleas and disputes of outsiders. Once established, it grew as much by unsolicited invitation as by imposition from above. It was only a matter of time, and desperation, before bishops somewhere invited an Emperor into their affairs.

By 272, we know of the first such appeal, and its reports sum up many of the ambiguities in the bishop's position.[64] At its centre stood one of the tragic figures of early Christian history, Paul, bishop of Antioch, who was finally excommunicated by a synod of bishops for reasonably holding that Christ was a man, not God. The dispute showed the relentless character of Christian authority. The visiting bishops interrogated Paul, while secretaries trained in shorthand took down the questions and answers. The bishops then addressed a circular letter on Paul's person and views to churches throughout the world and accused him of vices which sit very neatly with a bishop's exceptional responsibilities. Paul, they complained, had enriched himself by giving corrupt judgement, "though he was formerly poor and destitute": if this charge is true, Paul is a rare example of a bishop who had enjoyed a sudden social promotion through his election. His particular vices were the style in which he held court to settle disputes and his sinister power over women. These vices were easily credited in a bishop when arbitration was so important and female "suffrage" ranked equally with male. Paul was said to have offered help in lawsuits in return for money; he gave himself airs, strutted with attendants in public, exalted his bishop's throne in church and equipped himself with a secretariat, like a pagan magistrate. Women shouted applause in his presence, and their trained female choirs were alleged to sing psalms in his honour, even at Easter. Virgins were admitted to his household, but they succumbed to his advances and never dared to reveal their lapses. Paul, it was said, had already broken up with one woman and was now taking two "in the flower of youth and beauty" on his daily business, living in luxury wherever he could.

As Cyprian well knew, women, corrupt justice and financial embezzlement were easy charges to lay against a bishop. Paul was excommunicated, but he refused to surrender the church building. His enemies did not wait for God's vengeance. They invoked secular power by sending their dispute at once to the Emperor Aurelian. By invitation, an Emperor thus found himself requested to deal with Church affairs. The request, perhaps, was no odder than many which reached him, but his reply showed a grasp of Christian authority which can only have come from a sympathetic adviser in his service. He replied that the church building should be assigned to whomsoever the bishops of Italy and Rome approved. The answer respected Christian ideas of universality, and the decision duly went against Paul.

The affair had not only invited the Emperor into the business of the

Church. It illustrated the power of bishops to commune and excommunicate, and the tensions which could easily surround its use. This power had always found Christians who would criticize it, especially those Christians of superior knowledge and insight who claimed that the bishops' authority was imposed by an inferior Creator. Their views attracted a strong polemic, but their own practice was more interesting. Some of them avoided the contradictions of a church "election" by returning to that great device of earlier Greek society, selection by lot. Use of the lot still apportioned the equal shares in many families' inheritances, but politically, it was dead. In the second century, it was revived by Christian minorities who valued it, as Homer's heroes had once valued it too, as the expression of the will of God.[65]

"Nowhere," complained Tertullian, "is promotion easier than in the camp of the rebels where the mere fact of being present is a prominent service. So, today one man is bishop, tomorrow another . . ." The lot appointed the leader for the day, as Irenaeus described in meetings of Marcus, a pupil of the heretic Valentinus. As each member was equally inspired with the Holy Spirit, nobody officiated by a permanent right. Instead, they cast lots to find God's choice for the occasion. The practice contrasted sharply with "orthodox" elections and had a certain logic: if Christians were equals in Christ, why should one rule over another? The lot, as Greek theorists knew, restrained faction and discontent in the selection of officers from a company of equals. It was not nearly so childish as a choice by acclamation, or so arguable as preselection by an inner ring of clergy. When complaining of these practices, Origen himself entertained its use with a certain enthusiasm.[66] It was also much cheaper for the candidates, as it excluded bribery.

Selection by lot had a good scriptural precedent in the Apostles' replacement of the traitor Judas. The precedent was variously discussed and dismissed, but it did lead, finally, to one of the best reflections on a bishop's predicament. In the later fourth century, John Chrysostom took the text as his cue for a lament on the problems which beset the bishops of his age.[67] They were compounded, he said, by the bishops' great prestige, which no governor and no other visitor to "great houses of rich ladies" could possibly equal. Nonetheless, their problems still followed the patterns which we have sketched. Bishops, he complained, sought prestige, while treating their responsibilities too lightly. They forgot that they bore the burden of all their flock and that one single soul lost to God would count against them at the Last Judgement. Their freedom, however, was limited. In an acute comment, John raised the problem which besets authority in any company appointed for life: what should a new bishop do to the mediocrities whom he inherits from his predecessor as Elders and clergy? Should he risk sacking them all? If he did not, he was still responsible for their acts before God. In John's perfectionist approach, we catch clear echoes of Origen's complaints. We find other suggestive perceptions: the losers in an election, John remarked, should follow the Apostles' example and "believe that the choice is with God." Their talents might be great, but ill suited to a church's particular needs: God's disposition was for the best. Like every other appointment, a bishopric, it seems, roused strong feeling in failed candidates, that potent source of stasis, or faction, in so much of the theory and practice of ancient government. Properly construed, said John, the job was not one which the winner could treat idly: "the soul of the bishop is like a vessel in a storm, lashed from every side, by friends and foes, by his own people, by strangers." His authority had to combine the opposites of harshness and equity. We return to the ideals with which we began and to which John adds a telling postscript. People bothered the bishop day and night: they expected favours and resented discipline, but it was no use threatening them. "As for the fear of God, it does not influence people about their bishop in the slightest degree." If we trace a bishop's authority to threats, we miss the limits and the ambiguities of his position.

These ideals of a bishop and his authority were the practical setting in which Christian thought and teaching impinged on most early Christian lives. It is particularly important to do them justice, because so much of our early Christian literature happens to survive from a different angle. Relatively little of it is written by bishops and almost all of it derives from authors in the big cities of the Empire, Alexandria, Carthage, Rome and Ephesus. These Christian authors adapt pagan wisdom to a Christian framework and lead naturally to studies of early Christianity and the "classical tradition" or "classical culture." However, many of the texts in this vein discuss questions which only bothered those few Christians who had a degree of higher education. The most explicit may be the most misleading, the books written in answer or "apology" to pagan critics or addressed to the Emperor himself. As with the "apologies" which Greek-speaking Jews had addressed to the Hellenistic world, the main audience for these books was probably people of the apologist's own persuasion, Christians, not pagans.[68] In them, Christians tried to be as accommodating as possible to pagan culture and philosophy. They wished to show their faith to be reasonable and universal, the near-relation of Plato and the old philosophic wisdom of the East. These demonstrations were good for their author's reputation and good for the morale of Christian pupils and contemporaries, who liked to know that their faith could stand up to the highest schooling of the age. However, few pagan men of culture would bother with books which quoted Scriptures of such repellently bad Greek: Celsus was exceptional in acquainting himself with the heresies of Marcion and using a Christian heretic's views against his Christian opponents.[69]

How deep, then, did the continuity go between "Athens and Jerusalem," between Christians' lives and a classical education? The humbler Christians were not literate by habit, in the sense that they would read freely in complicated books. Although they took a keen interest in theological questions, this interest was based on preaching and discussion. For them, the outlook of their priests and bishops was the main guide or stimulus to disagreement. The bishop's teaching and authority rested on profoundly unclassical sources, yet it was the bishop who set a pattern for most Christians' lives, not only in the big cities but in the multitude of lesser towns from which no early Christian texts on higher theology emerged.

By the mid-third century, we happen to know something of several bishops' outlook, after a century or more in which their writings are poorly represented. We can even begin to see how bishops could graduate from their classical schooling, how far, indeed, the study of "Athens" guided their future practice in "Jerusalem." Of one bishop's progress, we can form such a picture: just as Pionius's diary helped to bring out the nature and problems of martyrdom, so a bishop's letters may help to connect the ideals of the "apologists" to practical Christian life. Gregory, bishop of Pontus, lived from c. 220 to c. 272. His life is known from several angles, from a detailed panegyric of his life which was delivered in his home town during the 380s, from doctrinal works whose claims to authenticity vary, from references in Eusebius's history, from a flourishing legend of his miracles in Latin, Syriac and Armenian and, above all, from an autobiographical letter which he addressed to his teacher, Origen.[70] We have Origen's own letter back to him and, later, an abbreviated letter of discipline which Gregory issued during his episcopate. A recent challenge to the identity of the letters to and from Origen has only served to underline their attribution to Gregory himself. They were collected by Origen's pupil Pamphilus and published in his defence of Origen, where Eusebius also knew them. The panegyric and the legend raise more awkward questions, not least because attempts to prove their use of Gregory's own letters have met with no success.

These differing sources open different perspectives. Through the letters, we can follow a bishop through his years of schooling to his practical use of authority. In his panegyric, we face once again the question of the scale of Christian conversions in the mid-third century. The legend remains less penetrable. Gregory's example and sayings were revered for a century and more in the churches which he had founded, and he joins the very small company of bishops who ever attracted hagiography. It is hard to control it, but Eusebius's history may give us an opening.[71] He knew Gregory's early letters, and also knew of Gregory's service as a bishop, although he had not known him personally. By implication, he did not rate Gregory among the greatest bishops of his age. Instead, he was a notable figure, perhaps nothing more, whose legendary miracles were not known to Eusebius, or else not worth recording. Among the legends of Gregory, it is as well to allow for this moderate view: Gregory's progress may be less untypical than oral tradition later implied. If so, its interest for historians is all the greater.

# II

Gregory was born Theodore, the son of pagan parents in Pontus who could afford to send him for a good education. At the age of fourteen, as he recalled in his letter to Origen, he lost his father and first made contact with Christian teaching.[1] The time was ripe for this encounter: fourteen, said the ancients, was the traditional year at which a boy began to use his reason. We do not know what part, if any, his widowed mother played in his Christianity, but we do know that she considered his worldly career. She sent him to a teacher of rhetoric in her city of Neocaesarea, choosing an art which was already well based there. Only a few years earlier, an author of a Roman law book had illustrated a vexed point by citing the case of "sophists, doctors and teachers" who migrated from a nearby city in order to teach in Neocaesarea. The place was not a cultural desert.[2]

The city itself housed an imposing monument to this type of study.[3] In the 170s, an unknown man of letters had built himself a large family memorial and arranged for statues to crown its facade. He guarded its future in an elegant Greek inscription which threatened vandals with a long list of divinities, the "all-seeing Sun," the most "ancient goddess" Curse and a minor divinity whose roots lie only in Attic Eleusis. The entire text matched a famous Attic model, the inscriptions on the family memorials which the great Herodes, "king of words," had scattered over Attica in memory of his kinsmen and friends. By the 170s, this unknown student from Neocaesarea had travelled west for a higher schooling at Athens and entered the circle of its grandest teacher, Herodes. Even there, there was no knowing what a student might bring home with him.[4] Another of Herodes's pupils, Amphicles, returned to Euboea and put up a text of similar shape for a memorial, it seems, to a son who had died young. Yet the curse which protected his monument had been lifted word for word from Deuteronomy and alluded only to a single God.

Schooling abroad was to transform Gregory, too, but the changes came about through a different career and contact: the law and Christianity.[5] Gregory's teacher in rhetoric proposed to teach him the elements of Roman law, a subject with which he was not unfamiliar. The study, he said with appealing modernity, would give the boy a "passport and qualification" from which he could always earn a living, whether he chose to plead as an orator in court or whether he "chose to be something else." In the culture of other second-century orators, we catch hints of a grounding in Roman legal texts; the "something else" is best seen in the developing careers of men whose legal skills brought them into the service of Emperors and governors. Under Marcus Aurelius, we find the first attested legal expert of provincial origin on the Emperor's advisory council, a man who bore a Greek name. Others followed, while similar openings drew legally competent provincials to the staffs of provincial governors. Second- and third-century inscriptions show two men of this type from Amaseia, a neighbouring city to Gregory's own: both served outside the province, as was obligatory.

The market for Roman law was growing. Already, in the mid-second century, several of Gaius's law books addressed subjects of interest to provincial readers. By Gregory's own lifetime, recent works by Modestinus and others met a similar need.[6] Since the edict of 212, Roman citizenship was widespread in the provinces, bringing

Roman law into yet more provincial lives, if they chose to use it. A bright young man from Pontus would no longer look naturally to Herodes's literary heirs in Athens. Law, moreover, was already present in Gregory's family. His brother-in-law was a talented legal man who had been summoned to "something else," a job as adviser to the governor of Syria. Although Gregory's own teacher was handling the law and Latin skilfully, the lessons were interrupted by a message from Syria which seemed to be heaven-sent. Gregory's brother-in-law sent a request for his wife to join him in Caesarea and despatched a soldier to escort her at public expense. Her two brothers were invited to keep the party company. As his next step, Gregory had already been considering a course in law at Rome, but he now realized that the prominent law school of Beirut lay near to his sister's destination. He and his brother accepted the offer and took up their free tickets for travel by the Imperial post, a privilege which he recalls with all the pride of a man sent first-class at official expense.

Departures of bright young men from provincial towns to more favoured cities were familiar occasions in third-century society, and Menander's handbook for orators told young students what to say when taking their leave.[7] They should praise the great city to which they were going, saying that it was a "workshop of the Muses," "a real Helicon." But they must praise their own city more strongly and promise to share with it their new fruits of learning. "You should go on to say: 'I shall draw my ration of literature and philosophy, I shall learn for your sakes and for our common country, and when I feel quite able to help the land that gave me birth, once again I shall long for this city and my family. For who, after meeting the Sirens or arriving in the land of the Lotus-eaters, would not prefer you here at home?'" Gregory's return, some eight years later, brought gifts of an unexpected nature.

While waiting with their brother-in-law in Caesarea, the two brothers were introduced to Origen, the great Christian teacher. The date of their meeting is uncertain, but it probably falls in the later 230s. Origen had several friends in Cappadocia, just to the south of Gregory's home city, with whom he had spent time during the persecutions of 235/6.[8] Perhaps these contacts guided Gregory to his presence in this cosmopolitan city of pagans, Christians and prominent Jewish communities. Gregory recalls how he was swept off his feet at his first meeting with a Christian teacher of genius.

In his letter of thanks and farewell, Gregory does not emphasize the aspects of Origen which overawe a modern reader, his astonishing memory, his extreme pursuit of chastity, and his capacity for work and writing, pressed to such extremes that even fellow Christians felt happier with epitomes and handbooks of his main commentaries and teachings. Gregory gives no hint of Origen's local debates with Jewish leaders or the ammunition which he derived from Jews who became Christians and brought him an inside knowledge of their explanations of Scripture.[9] He does not mention Origen's interest in Hebrew or his work on parallel texts of the Old Testament. For him, Origen was a teacher in Greek of Scripture, philosophy and ethics. When Origen first offered these subjects to Gregory and his brother, they hesitated for several days. Perfect piety, Origen told them, required a knowledge of philosophy; Gregory recalled how he presented the subject in the manner of the "protreptic" speeches with which pagan teachers tried to lure pupils into their branch of higher studies.[10] Gregory felt a familiar apprehension: philosophy was a subject on which he had hardly touched. After a few days' thought, the brothers succumbed to persuasion. Gregory's very soul was drawn to his new friend and master; he was like a second Jonathan, he later wrote, holding fast to his beloved David.

With hindsight, Gregory attributed his progress since youth to the approving care of his guardian angel.[11] In Origen's classes on Scripture, he would have heard much of these guardians, at Mambre's oak tree, by the threshing floor of Araunah the Jebusite or beside the young Tobias, urging him to endure. Origen emphasized them, fellow travellers through the labyrinth of Christian life. To our eye, however, Gregory's progress is not so unusual. It spanned a fashionable education, good family connections and a tutor who gave him direction when the world first opened before his path. The idea of a guardian angel helped a fortunate young man to break with his father's example, and to feel that his good fortune was guided by an approving power.

He was not alone in his idealization of a teacher of higher philosophy. Like the best pagan philosophers in the third century, Origen, too, was a teacher who worked outside the hierarchy of an old, established school. He attracted personal devotion, and bestrode a subject which had become ever more complex and remote from a plain man's schooling. He seemed a godlike master, an impression which other contemporaries shared. Like Gregory, Alexander of Cappadocia left his distant home and met Origen in Caesarea before ending his career unexpectedly as a bishop. Eusebius quoted a letter in which Alexander described the warmth of a meeting with Origen and traced it to the will of God.[12] Origen evoked a strong sense of guidance in visiting pupils.

In Origen's company, Gregory was tutored in a godlike mastery of soul over body and the age-old objective of "knowing himself."[13] His classes observed the natural progression of studies which Origen described in his own works. Classes in astronomy and geometry helped the young Gregory to refine his views on the beauty of God's Creation, while logic and readings in ethics replaced the study of rhetoric which had dominated his past. After this preparation, he passed to the study of Scriptures and the philosophers, "Greek and barbarian" alike: we know from criticisms by Porphyry that these "barbarian" philosophers were authors like Numenius of Syria, who wrote in Greek. Only Origen's better pupils were allowed to advance to a full philosophical course which used the Greek masters as the "handmaids of Scripture." The Bible dominated their training, not merely a book or two of the Scriptures but the entire Old Testament, as Origen recommended in his own biblical *Commentaries*. The philosophers supplemented this sweep of Scripture, except for the Epicureans, whose denials of Providence disqualified them from serious reading. To open their books, said Gregory, was to risk corruption.

Was there a distinctive "Origenism" which the master imparted to his pupils? Later quarrels over Origen's orthodoxy made Origenism a clearly defined doctrine, but Gregory and a fellow pupil, Dionysius of Alexandria, give us a chance to see its contemporary impact.[14] Gregory's church in Neocaesarea was later believed to have preserved the wording of his theological creed, "written in the saint's own hand." The wording survives, albeit with signs of its heirs' improvement, but the hard core is probably genuine and has justly been related to Origen's own views of the Father, the Word and the Spirit. The similarities are rather general, as are the traces of Origen's teaching which surface in the theology of Gregory's farewell letter. Neither divides the pupil from his master.

A second work, "To Theopompus," raises much more difficult problems.[15] It is ascribed to Gregory in a Syriac manuscript of the sixth century, in which it alone survives; it shows Gregory discussing theology among friends and then answering a pagan, Theopompus, who had protested at the doctrine that God could suffer. The theology of his answer is not true to Origen's own, a discrepancy which has been taken to prove that the work is not by Gregory, his pupil. Nobody else alludes to this work's existence and the case against his authorship is strong. It might belong to Gregory's years as a bishop when the atmosphere of discussion and philosophy would be particularly interesting. It can hardly belong to the years in Caesarea, where Origen's teaching would have suggested a very different argument.

Suspicion of this work is reinforced by a third, a "Paraphrase" of the Book of Ecclesiastes which was ascribed to Gregory by Jerome and subsequent Christians.[16] Seldom, if ever, studied, it is a fine example of a Christian's rewriting of an inconvenient text: "The wise benevolence of the author," concluded one of its few students, in the 1840s, "is more apparent than his critical skill. No book was more likely to puzzle a pagan inquirer than this, so the paraphrase gives it meaning and consistency, but over and over again, not Solomon's meaning, I am persuaded."

Gregory was not alone in his reaction to this puzzling text. We do not know who first wrote this world-weary classic of religious experience, presenting it as the wisdom of a preacher who had once been king of Israel. Its Jewish author probably lived in the later third century B.C. and was quite untouched by the Greek wisdom which historians have fondly ascribed to him. Very soon, his text was given an apologetic epilogue by a Jew who wished to defend it: early fragments have been found near the Dead Sea and show how Jews continued to rewrite its message to suit more conventional taste.[17] Christians worked with its translation into Greek and were more drastic with its contents. The preacher had questioned the meaning of life in the face of death with a sharpness unique in the Old Testament. On the way, he had expressed his changing views of the world and concluded that they, too, were vanity, no better than fleshly pleasures. Gregory and subsequent Christians accepted that the royal author was King Solomon himself and emphasized his weary view of pleasure: they rephrased his similar views on wisdom as the foolish views of his past. In their hands the text lost its subtlety and became a one-sided sermon on asceticism.[18] It contained so much which Christians could approve: words on the virtue of chastity and the vanity of idle laughter, the merit in obeying kings and the impossibility of finding even one chaste woman to every thousand chaste men on earth. A few of "Solomon's" lapses were simply omitted: "If two lie together," wrote the author, but not Gregory, "they are warm, but how can one be warm alone?" Other chapters were ruined. "Remember now thy

Creator in the days of thy youth": Gregory misread the "evil day which cometh" and saw it as the Christian Day of Judgement. The "grinders" were indeed brought low and the "daughters of music" were silenced. They were lascivious slave girls, thought Gregory, who were grinding in mills and piping at parties. No silver cord was loosed; no golden pitcher broken. Gregory wrecked the greatest scriptural dirge on ageing and death, and made Solomon warn promiscuous women about the imminent wrath of God.

Some books are too subtle for their contemporaries and heirs, and perhaps none has suffered more than Ecclesiastes. Ever since its composition, it has puzzled and eluded a host of lesser renderings, from its first Jewish paraphrase to its Greek translation and subsequent Christian misuse. Gregory's "Paraphrase" reflects very poorly on Origen's critical classes. It ignored the Hebrew version and falsified Solomon's authority in order to impose Gregory's own views. It stands at the head of the many similar Christian versions which extend from Gregory through Ambrose to Jerome and Gregory of Nyssa.[19] "Vanity of vanities, saith the Preacher": to Christians, the ascetic message seemed obvious. When Jerome wrote to Paula, a young Christian virgin, he urged her to study Ecclesiastes, as it would teach her to despise the things of the world.

Gregory's interest and the tone of his work are traceable to Origen himself.[20] At Caesarea, we know that Origen covered Ecclesiastes in his briefer expositions. He read it as part of a significant trilogy by King Solomon, in which it stood midway between Solomon's Proverbs and his mystical Song of Songs. Proverbs, he argued, taught morals; Ecclesiastes progressed to natural science, while the Song of Songs advanced to unseen eternal truths. Solomon's trilogy had linked the three subjects in ascending order, like the courses of instruction in the Greek schools of philosophy. Solomon, therefore, was a true philosopher whose very titles were full of meaning. Solomon, said Origen, was the type of Christ. His "words of Ecclesiastes" hinted at Christ's role as a preacher, gatherer of his own *Ecclesia*, the Church.

This trail of sensational misreading was not lost on his pupils. It excited Gregory; it also inspired a fellow pupil, Dionysius, the future bishop of Alexandria. Before the 230s, Ecclesiastes had aroused next to no interest in Christian literature, but then, quite suddenly, Origen's pupils produced two books on its text. Gregory paraphrased it freely; Dionysius seems to have commented at length on the opening chapters, and a newly found fragment, if genuine, implies that his commentary strayed further into "Solomon's" work.[21] His book has no known date, but its only modern editor had no doubts: "The general impression left on the reader will be that he is here in the presence of a mind which is either not yet matured or else altogether of a lower order . . ." Like Gregory's, his book seems to be an exercise which was inspired at school in Caesarea.

The pupils owed their subject to Origen's example: was "Origenism" the guide to their interpretation? Gregory composed a free, if dishonest, "Paraphrase," and only resorted to the mildest allegory; Dionysius keeps closer to the spirit of the original in our few fragments of his text. At most, he misunderstands it in a Christian sense. "There is nothing good for a man," said the Preacher, "but what he eats and drinks": the reference, said Dionysius, must be to mystical food. These explanations were a far cry from Origen's own search for hidden meanings.[22] We know one of his interpretations of a passage in Ecclesiastes, and as so often, it dug deeply for the words' allegorical secret. Does the pupils' neglect of allegory divide them from their master? Origen's use of it was strongly attacked by the pagan Porphyry and by fellow Christians, to whom he himself alludes in his biblical works. It was not, however, his particular invention. It had many precedents, pagan and Jewish, and in Caesarea, a former Jew had confirmed the approach's validity.[23] He had told Origen how Scripture was like a house full of locked rooms: God, he said, had confused the keys, and it was up to his heirs to fit the right key to each lock. Origen considered this view a "beautiful tradition" and showed himself an inventive opener of some very secret doors. His allegories were totally false to the plain meaning of Scripture. He believed, however, that they were given to him by God's inspiration and that they were the preserve of a few favoured Christians. "Only he who shuts can open": Gregory ascribed Origen's bold allegories to his personal gift of the Spirit and his help from God's word.[24] In his own commentaries, we find Origen taking a similar view. If, then, his pupils did not use allegory themselves, they were not implying that they disapproved of it. They thought that, as yet, they lacked the necessary gifts from God to practise it. Later, when Dionysius was a bishop, he did not shrink from the allegorical method when facing villagers in the Arsinoite nome. In Revelation, he explained, the text on the millennium was an allegory, not to be taken literally.

In Caesarea, then, works which are certainly by Gregory do not diverge from Origen's own principles: the point tells against the acceptance of "To Theopompus" as our Gregory's work. Contact with Origen broadened his theology and encouraged his sense of a guardian angel. It also inspired him to misread a neglected book of Scripture. We can set his own impressions and responses beside the letter which Origen later sent him and which is best placed as his answer to Gregory's "letter of thanks." In it, Origen warned his departing student not to let philosophy drag him down into heresy. He asked him to hold fast to his text of Scripture and remember that its meaning was God's gift in answer to prayer.[25] His pupils, it seems, obeyed him: Gregory's name was given to two works which answered pagan objectors. One was "To Theopompus," the other, the "Exposition of Faith," which answered a pagan, Aelian, and contained theological remarks about God and his Son: Basil later had to excuse them as Gregory's passing concessions to his opponent.[26] The text, he said, had suffered from subsequent miscopying, an excuse which reminds us how the theology of an innocent mid-third-century author could seem controversial to a later age with different interests. The work had tried to meet pagan critics on their own ground. Dionysius, too, left one book on philosophy. It is a routine attack on the Epicureans, the sect whose writings Origen had banned.[27] Neither pupil, it seems, put his philosophical studies to deeper, intelligent use. They played on the surface of classical thought, no more.

In his farewell letter, Gregory implied that his studies with Origen had extended over eight years. We know of other eternal students in antiquity, pupils who spent up to five years with the same sophist, but Gregory's words imply he had kept at other work besides. As he began his letter, he apologized to Origen for his Greek style: a different study, he said, was occupying his mind "strongly." Here, he referred to the study of Roman law in Latin.[28] After two of the clumsiest sentences in the history of Greek prose, he refuted his disclaimer by a fluent abundance which does not lack ingenuity.

Gregory, it seems, had not abandoned his legal studies as abruptly as he implied. The Roman laws, he said, were "our" laws, in an interesting and not untypical equation of Roman and provincial concerns.[29] They were "wise, precise and varied and marvellous and, in a word, most Greek." They were not an easy subject of study. These laws were not "reconciled," on the likelier of the translations, nor were they "learned by heart" without effort. To study Roman law was necessarily to learn Latin, a language which struck Gregory as "awesome, solemn and well suited to Imperial authority." His comment is one of our few appraisals of Latin's qualities by a Greek-speaker in an age when more Greeks than ever were learning it. His remarkable view of Roman law as "most Greek" may owe something to the textbooks in which he had met it.[30] Later in Beirut, students began their course with Gaius's *Institutes*, a work whose early use abroad is attested by a mid-third-century papyrus from Egypt. The *Institutes* cited differing views on a topic side by side and suggests how Gregory had found "variety and precision" in laws which were "so hard to reconcile." Like other third-century law books, Gaius's text reveals a distant debt to the concepts of Greek thinkers. By an unsuspected route, its laws did have a trace of the "Greekness" which Gregory idealized. Shortly before his lifetime, the renowned lawyer Ulpian, from Tyre, had praised Roman law as the "art of the good and fair," "whose priests, in a sense, all lawyers are." They encouraged virtue, he wrote in the preface of his textbook, and deterred vice while "aiming at true, not pretended, philosophy." The ideals of a legal teacher were not so remote from the ideals of Origen's classes in ethics.[31]

Gregory's judgements on law and Latin were those of a man who had not abandoned law school. Gregory's idealization of Origen was combined, it seems, with a continuing respect for his worldly career. Beirut, a Roman colony, was a living seat of the Latin in which Roman law was then taught.[32] We can see that by the 190s rulings from the Emperors were commonly posted there, and the convenience of these local documents may relate to the law school's contemporary rise. "Mother of the laws," Beirut was a city whose temptations and small rivalries stand out in the memoirs of her fourth- and fifth-century pupils. The pupils grouped themselves in "herds," or age groups, by their year of entry, with a "master" at their societies' heads. The years had their nicknames and extended the usual contempt to new arrivals. The new recruit found himself mocked and ragged as a test of his self-control. His fellow students were quick to master the pleasures of wine and the races, city women and a life with concubines, by whom some of them fathered children. Their four-year course competed with compelling ties of friendship and worldly experience, and like most of its kind, it lost the competition more often than it won it.

Conditions will have been little different in the 230s, and it is against them that we can picture Gregory's instruction, now in law, now in Christianity. Conversion is amply attested for other roving students:

as a lawyer and a Christian convert, Gregory also finds a contemporary match in the speakers in Minucius's charming dialogue or in men like Gaius, the Christian lawyer, who was buried in mid-third-century Eumeneia.[33] Like Gregory's own letter of thanks, these lawyers' literary portraits were not concerned to emphasize Christ or scriptural texts. The lack of these themes in Gregory's letters should cause us no surprise.

In his letter of reply to Gregory's farewell, Origen included a brilliant allegory, as befitted his spiritual gifts. He explained Exodus as a man's progress from Christian teachings to worldly studies. He then applauded Gregory's gifts as philosopher and lawyer in words which suit our picture of a student commuting between Caesarea and Beirut. He had "wished," he said, that Gregory would use his gifts to a Christian end.[34] Gregory himself had been more melancholy as his own letter to Origen drew to a close. He was falling, he wrote, from Paradise. He was a second Adam, banished into the world, a Prodigal Son setting out on his travels, an exile by the waters of Babylon, a returning Samaritan at risk to thieves on his way north from Caesarea.[35] Gregory the reluctant graduate was taking leave of his tutor with the proper extravagance. He was leaving Origen's "inspired presence" for "public places, lawsuits, crowds and pomp," the busy company of men, and "wicked men," at that. As Origen hinted, Gregory seemed to be expecting the life of a law-court orator and a public figure in Pontus.

"Pray for a good escort, a fellow traveller," he asked Origen, pleading for the despatch of a guardian angel to guide him along his route. He had studied philosophy and Scripture. He had kept up his law, and like his fellow pupil Dionysius, he had not lost his grasp of rhetoric. It is in their works that we first find themes and similes from Scripture applied ingeniously to the author's own predicament.[36] Together, they stand at the beginning of a new Greek manner in prose. Behind their fall from Paradise, however, there may have lain a more awkward reason.[37] By an Imperial ruling, students from propertied families were required to return for service to their home towns within ten years of study elsewhere. In the 280s, the Emperor Diocletian was asked to rule specifically on the problem of upper-class students who lingered at the Beirut law school until the age of twenty-five or more and thus avoided the claims on their time and money which were justly advanced by their home towns. By birth, Gregory belonged to the upper class of Neocaesarea. After eight years, the eternal student may have been obliged to return to his city in order to meet its demands.

A Beirut student could expect great things in the future if his city ever let him go.[38] An inscription from the mid- to later third century has shown us young Conon from Pamphylia, a Beirut law student, an assistant of Roman governors in Judaea and Antioch, Nicomedia and Egypt's Thebaid. He died prematurely in Egypt, where his father collected his body: the news of his death, said his epitaph, nearly killed his mother with grief. Neocaesarea's student returned with a different surprise. He had changed his name from Theodore to Gregory, the "awakened" or, equally, the "awakener." How, then, did his family and city respond to this Prodigal Son and his Christian call?

# III

If Gregory had disappeared from history on taking leave of his tutor, he would be classed among Christians who combined classical and biblical culture, who felt that Athens (and Beirut) had much to do with the new Jerusalem and who were not brought up to exercise worldly authority: Origen, his teacher, took a cold and critical view of the standard of Christian who led the churches. Gregory, however, does not disappear. His subsequent career raises questions of the scale and nature of the Christians' missionary successes. It also shows the relation between a Christian's writings and his resources as a bishop, when obliged to rule in the field.

A network of major Roman roads ran up the eastern frontier and linked Caesarea to Gregory's home; on his return, his career is mostly known through a difficult source, the panegyric which another Gregory, Gregory of Nyssa, delivered in his home town during November (probably) of the year 380.[1] Its stories were developed from the oral traditions of local Christians who were still very loyal to their image of Gregory, their churches' founder.[2] They held fast to his reported practices and believed that his creed was preserved in the church in Neocaesarea, "written in the saint's own hand." Families had passed down a living tradition of Gregory's words; we know how the grandmother of the panegyrist told her younger relations the sayings and stories of Gregory which she had heard, she said, from contemporaries. The panegyric's stories and emphasis were not their author's invention. A similar outline was already known to the

Gregory's travels, 235–260 A.D.

author's brother Basil, who cited it in a letter some years before the panegyric's delivery: he knew most of the stories of miracles and the legend of Gregory's feats as a "second Moses." The traditions of Gregory's doings continued to grow. In the fifth century, the stories were elaborated in Latin and added to the legend of a saint who was still a topic of "discussion," said their author, "in the north and east."[3] It is a separate question whether any of the stories had ever been true.

When Gregory arrived in Pontus, said the local tradition, he found only seventeen Christians. When he died, he left only seventeen pagans. These stories of mass conversion have often been used as history, the first clear hint, it is felt, of a rising tide of Christianity in the mid-third century which was to sweep Constantine with it, some sixty years later. To a great modern historian of Christianity's expansion, they have seemed an "extremely instructive sketch of the way in which the mission was carried out and how paganism was 'overcome,' or absorbed."[4] Yet wherever we can test the panegyric's stories, they are mistaken. They ignore Gregory's own description of his early years. They allege that both his parents died, that he became a Christian when he first saw how the philosophers disagreed to no purpose, that he studied in Alexandria, that he met Firmilian of Cappadocia, then Origen. The stories had outgrown Gregory's own letter, which the panegyric did not consult.[5]

When he returned home to Pontus with many offers of a job, he is said to have opted for a quiet spiritual retreat. However, the bishop of nearby Amaseia obliged him to become bishop of Neocaesarea and to embark on a career of miracles and mass conversion. Origen had written praises of a spiritual retreat, as opposed to holding clerical office, and his view would not, perhaps, have been lost on a pupil. However, Gregory's letter shows no such interest: the intervention from Amaseia does not conform to the usual pattern of a bishop's election; it is better to look to the panegyrist's own times. It is deeply misleading to use the panegyric as if it gives a correct historical image of Gregory's appeal in the 250s. The story was shaped to suit the tastes of an author and an audience in the 380s, and much of the shaping may be the author's own.[6] The relation between spiritual withdrawal and life as a bishop was an evident interest of the speaker himself; "compulsion" to clerical office was a particular feature of his age. When Gregory entered his home town, said the panegyric, neither his glance nor his expression strayed, to the amazement of his spectators. The scene recalls the entry of an Emperor or holy man into cities of the fourth century, where this "immobility" was widely noticed. Gregory, it was also said, had won repute by writing a note of banishment to a demon and driving it from a pagan oracle. Perhaps he did, but it was a nice touch of the panegyrist to make the keeper of the shrine appeal at once to the Emperor. In such details, we see something of the Emperor's continuing image in the mind of his subjects, the speaker and his audience. We do not see Gregory's own history.

Gregory's success, we are told, was assured by his protection of the Christians during a plague. Afterwards, the demons fled before a puff of his breath; Christians brought him their quarrels and disputes, which he settled as a good bishop should. While he practised his shrewd arbitration, flooding rivers returned to their beds and rough justice was done to the Jews. About Gregory's invitation by the nearby Christians of Comana to intervene in their election of a bishop, the panegyrist told a splendid story. Gregory rejected the local gentry's choice and gave his inspired preferment to a simple charcoal burner who turned out to be a philosopher in disguise, well able to speak educated Greek.[7] The gentry's dominance over clerical elections was a topic dear to the panegyrist's own heart, and here, too, we must allow for his shaping of the saint's legend.

As for the detailed stories of miracles, the chastening and conversion of the Jews are a commonplace,[8] and in two examples, we can see how stories had become attached to local landmarks. When the local river Lycus flooded, Gregory was said to have planted his stick as its marker and kept the water's course thereafter within bounds. Known locally as the "staff," Gregory's "original" willow tree was visible at the riverside and became the stock from which this story subsequently sprouted. Elsewhere, two brothers were said to have disputed the right to their father's lake, and they were preparing to arm their dependents and fight the matter out, an interesting hint of the scope for private armies among the large landowners of the area. Gregory put an end to their quarrel by twitching his cloak and drying up the property under discussion. The "vanishing lakes" and dried plains of inner Anatolia are common enough to explain how this local tale of a miracle began. Just outside Gregory's Neocaesarea they have an unrecognized relevance.[9] In the 1830s, William Hamilton travelled into Pontus and approached Gregory's home town with no idea of the legends of the saint. "It was impossible," he wrote, "to look on this rich and level plain without being convinced that it was the site of an ancient lake which had been drained by some convulsion . . . but I was surprised to find that the Turks themselves had a tradition that the plain was once a lake or sea, navigated by large ships. They pretended that formerly, a great chain was hung across the gorge below the bridge and our guides pointed out to what parts of the rock it had been attached. From this chain were suspended smaller ones, to which pieces of leather and skins were fastened by which the waters were kept in to form the lake. I could not learn at what period this event was supposed to have taken place, but . . . it is remarkable that a people so unimaginative as the Turks should have conceived such an idea." Before the Turks, Christians in Pontus had conceived another: they explained their curious landscape by a legend of Gregory, their saint.

These stories Christianized the local landscape, but they are not evidence for their hero's true career. Only twice does the panegyric allude to external events; Gregory was believed to have preached during a plague and went into retreat during the persecution of the year 250. Evidently, he was not martyred and his relics did not receive a cult, an omission which the panegyric neatly evaded. The stories also retained some plausible names of cities and local rivers and recorded the first man of property in Neocaesarea who gave Gregory the use of his house: in the panegyrist's own age, the local bishop bore the same name as this first patron and might have been his direct descendant in the city.[10] It is as well to remember that Pontus was a province of very large landowners and that Gregory enjoyed the birth and position to greet them on equal terms. They seem to have taken no exception to his activities, until Decius's edict required them to start a persecution. For the rest, there is only the mention of Gregory's church, "surviving" despite earthquakes and natural disasters in a "very conspicuous" place in the fourth-century city. It also contained the creed "written in the saint's own hand." Like the text, the building had probably enjoyed a few later embellishments.

Elsewhere, we can see from Eusebius how many concerns of Gregory's lifetime the speech has suppressed.[11] While Gregory preached, Pontus was vexed by the problems of rebaptizing heretics. During the 260s, the bishop of Rome sent aid to the nearby churches in a crisis. Then Gregory himself went south to Antioch to join in the hearing and assessment of the heretical bishop Paul. The panegyric omits every one of these episodes, just as it omits Gregory's partner, his brother Athenodorus, with whom he had attended Origen's classes. Like Gregory, Athenodorus was made a bishop in Pontus, a fact which we only know from Eusebius and which adds to our early examples of bishoprics which ran in families. Perhaps Gregory appointed his brother personally.

Can we, then, take the stories of mass conversion literally in a speech which builds on such a vague set of legends? They ignore practical problems. In other churches, candidates still had to be selected and prepared at length for baptism: did Gregory simply dispense with this pronounced feature of Church life?[12] Perhaps his social contacts gave him an unusual access to large local estates, but a mass conversion of the countryside raises the old problem of dialect.[13] In Pontus, people presumably spoke a dialect, like the adjoining Cappadocians. It was not entirely lost on educated local people: in the 370s, Basil, the Christian bishop, could cite the problems of the word "and" in "native Cappadocian" while arguing a complex point of theology in Greek. This piece of knowledge is not proof that he spoke the language freely himself. Perhaps many Pontic peasants were themselves bilingual, but it is hard to think that Gregory combined a mastery of "Pontic" with his Greek and Latin.

In the panegyric, the main episodes occur in the inland cities of the province, and here, we can give Gregory's legend a context. Most of the city sites have now been located, although none has been excavated. Study of Pontus is still in its infancy, but the surviving coins and inscriptions can be joined to a precious description by Strabo, the geographer, writing at the turn of the era. Together, they cast the scene of the Christians' triumph in an unexpected light.

Gregory's home and mission lay in the distinctive landscape of the old Pontic kingdom. By the late 230s, it had recently been detached and set beneath its own Roman governor for the first time: capital justice lay nearer than ever to the sites of Gregory's adventures.[14] Escape, however, was easy, away into the woods and hill forts which were later to house the Christian ascetics. The isolated clifftops bore ancient strongholds, framed against wooded mountains and river plains which teemed with vines, fruit and precious crops. Gregory's home town lay beside the steep river Lycus, which races between deep ravines and spreads here and there into pockets of exceptional fertility. In antiquity, the locals themselves felt the magic of this countryside.[15] The contrasts of sheer cliffs and deep valleys left a mark on the prose of Basil and his brother Gregory and moved them to a Homeric imagery of hanging forests and changing colours, until their pictures in words took on the tone of an Alpine sketch by Salvator Rosa. Through and beyond the river valleys branched the military roads which Roman governors had built and extended for their eastern campaigns since the Flavian era. "If a man asks you to go with him one mile, go with him twain . . .": Gregory's Christian preaching lay in regions where these exactions were frequent.

When Gregory arrived, said the panegyric, the Pontic countryside was totally under the sway of the demons. The remark gains point from the local antiquities.[16] Old sites of worship show up on the peaks of mountains outside the towns, while nymphs and local divinities watched moodily over their glades and springs. An hour or so's walk from several townships lay springs and pools of healing, holy places which were known by their latest identity as haunts of the god Asclepius. The countryside was the refuge of odd minorities, worshippers of fire in the manner of the Persian Magi, or devotees of the "Most High god."

The five cities of the area had formed into a local league of "inland Pontus" which organized a cult of the Emperors and held the accompanying shows and amenities.[17] However, their monuments were not confined to the usual equipment of cities with Greek pretensions. Before the Romans encouraged these city foundations, Pontus had enjoyed a royal history as the heartland of old Mithridates's kingdom. At Amaseia, images of the royal tombs were still shown prominently on the city's third-century coinage.[18] Cabeira, near Gregory's home, had housed the dynasty's palace and zoo, and the surrounding forests had been royal hunting grounds. They continued to be rich in game, as Christian ascetics later proved by hunting it and living off their catch. It was a rough country, through which the river Lycus hurtled with enough force to power the first recorded water mills in history: long after Strabo's mention, the nineteenth-century travellers remarked their frequency along the nearby river Iris.[19] This royal past had been combined with an older presence of gods and temples which its rulers respected, but did not create. We see it memorably in Strabo's descriptions, which were written from his own local knowledge around the turn of our era. The handsome coin types of the local cities bring his picture into the early third century and the years of Gregory's Pontic childhood: proudly, they reflect local cults and temples which were surely still in use.

At Amaseia, where Gregory found a bishop, people were still proud of the ancient cult which Greeks called Zeus Stratios, and which was practised on a hilltop at nearby Ebimi, an hour's climb from the city. Zeus Stratios was honoured with a fire altar whose picture stands on the city's coins with the types of a tree, sometimes a pine, an eagle astride a sacrificed bull and a four-horsed chariot in the sky above.[20] The city lay dramatically round two steep pinnacles of rock above the river Iris, a setting which is beautifully caught on the portraits of its early-third-century coinage. Matching Strabo's sketch, these coins show the city's two temples still thriving, one by the river, the other perched high up on the mountain peak. The first must be the city's temple of the goddess Ma, while the other ought to be Zeus Stratios's on his nearby hill, still honoured with the old local rites which had been quite unspoilt by the arrival of the city's first Christians.

At Zela, southwest of Gregory's home, a high mound housed an old temple of the Persians' goddess Anahita, whose priesthood had once dominated the life of the town.[21] The cult may have reached Zela through nearby Armenia in the Persian period, and in Strabo's day it was still flourishing. "All the local men of Pontus swear their oaths on matters of the greatest importance there," he wrote: the oaths perhaps included those inscribed vows and "confessions" to the goddess which are known from her cult sites in Lydia. The temple survived in the enlarged city of the Roman period and at least in the early first century, it continued to house sacred slaves. By then, its priests' powers had been reduced after abuses, but the rites had continued with great sanctity and the yearly festival of the Sacaea was still the occasion for men to dress in "Scythian" clothes, eat, drink and flirt with one another or with the women who came to drink in their company. As elsewhere, the women presumably included temple prostitutes.

We do not know if the slaves and women persisted during three centuries of Roman rule, but the local coins again bring pride in the old cult and temple into Gregory's youth, showing fire altars and the half-moon and other attributes of a Persian Artemis and her fellow Persian gods far into the third century. There may be a much later echo. In the early fifth century, the "girdle" of the Virgin Mary was deposed in a special church in Constantinople and various stories were told of its origin.[22] One story connected it with a relic which the Emperor Justinian had brought from Zela, the old temple city of Anahita-Artemis. As at Ephesus, so at Zela, the cult of two rival virgins coincided: perhaps this exact tradition refers to some relic of Artemis in Zela which Justinian had found and added to the new Virgin's shrine in his capital.

Outside Gregory's own city lay a shrine of the goddess Men, whom the province's rulers had invoked in their royal oaths.[23] The temple, in

Strabo's day, controlled a sacred village with "many temple serfs and sacred land which the priest alone can harvest." Its fate is complex, as the nearby town of Cabeira changed its name and ceased coining in the first century, while nearby Neocaesarea was founded in one or other early Caesar's reign. There, the third-century coins show a superb pillared temple from several angles, revealing that it housed the statues of two divinities. The neatest view is that these gods are the same two, Men and Selene, who had earlier been honoured jointly at Cabeira. If so, theirs was another cult which lived beyond Strabo's lifetime into Gregory's. Perhaps it kept up a system of sacred slaves and land, but they may not have survived the transfer of the cults to the new city.

At nearby Comana, beside the river Iris, cult and landscape drew neatly together.[24] Here, Strabo had described how the impressive shrine of the goddess Ma dominated the social and commercial life of the entire region. Vines covered the allotments in the temple estates and allowed the priests and temple devotees to live in enviable luxury. In the mid-first century B.C., the temple slaves had numbered six thousand, he said, and changes since then had merely enlarged the temple's lands. Again, we do not know their fate under later Roman rule, but the third-century coins still show Ma and her temple with its boldly broken pediment and pillared façade. Even if her slaves had died out, her seasonal festivals may have flourished as Strabo first described them. When the goddess had one of her "exoduses," visitors from as far as Armenia would swarm in for her religious fair. Comana, as Strabo knew it, housed temple prostitutes, and on the days of "exodus," the goddess expected them to serve the crowds. Few cities could offer such a mixture of trade and religious worship, processions, sex and a drinkable local wine. The drink was hardly less novel than the women: at nearby Sebaste, in the colder climate to the southeast, Gregory of Nyssa described the inhabitants as men who never saw vines at all unless they travelled. They listened to tales of wine, he said, as if it was the rarest luxury from India.

This long history of a pagan temple society is the unacknowledged background to Gregory's mission. Against it, he begins to seem like a hopeful nineteenth-century missionary let loose in heathen Tibet. The local coins were still portraying these temples and their images in his own lifetime, just as he left for Origen's classes: it is natural to take them as living, contemporary portraits, not as allusions to cults which had died away. The temples' estates and social dependents may perhaps have altered, but their gods, buildings and ceremonies were sufficiently vigorous for cities to display them as marks of their identity. Although we cannot be sure that every custom had continued since Strabo's day, there is a certain pleasure in imagining a pupil of Origen attempting to convert temple prostitutes and their clients in a city like Comana.

In 250, there were still sufficient pagans in Pontus to enforce a Christian persecution. We begin to see why, and we must add to these temples the usual patterns of civic life.[25] Coins show the Fortune of Neocaesarea, the "mother city," among five lesser cities of the league of inland Pontus, arranged beside the river Lycus. In the 130s Neocaesarea had sent a choir to Apollo at Claros. Third-century coins show her baroque buildings, her temples and her provincial cult of the Emperors. Whereas she claimed an Emperor as her founder, Amaseia claimed the god Hermes, the old royal tombs and the title of metropolis too. No doubt there was the usual civic rivalry between the two "mother cities."[26] Doctors and poets still speak from Amaseia's tombstones, while its arena echoed with a Christian's worst enemies, gladiatorial contests and shows of wild beasts. Their dreaded enemies, the bears, were hauled in for the occasion, being trapped in the surrounding forests. The cities of inland Pontus revelled in the usual games and festivals; from a Christian speech, around 400, we catch a lively glimpse of the festival of the Kalends of January, which had persisted in Christian Amaseia. It was a time of crowds and shows, pantomimes and the exchange of New Year presents among family members, patrons and social inferiors. In this speech, we are seeing an older occasion, familiar in civic life under the pagan Empire and one we should probably picture in Gregory's lifetime too. Most of these worldly audiences were not ripe for a missionary's preaching. "I have spoken in many theatres, I have travelled far and wide," said the tombstone of Gemellus the actor which was set up near the hill shrine of Zeus Stratios outside Imperial Amaseia, "and now I have paid my debt and gone my way. All this is simply dust." "I did not exist, I knew nothing," said Prinnas the gladiator's tombstones in a traditional farewell, "I was born, I exist no more, I know nothing: this does not bother me".

By a happy chance, we can relate this city culture to an episode in Gregory's panegyric.[27] "At the time of some traditional festival," said his panegyrist, a pagan crowd had packed their theatre for a civic show. Only Gregory stood outside, a lone Christian who muttered his disgust at the roars of the heathen audience. "Give us space," bellowed

the crowds to Zeus as they sat jammed elbow to elbow in their seats.
"Space, indeed, you shall have," replied Gregory's voice outside the
gangways, and space, indeed, they had, when a plague thinned their
numbers soon afterwards. Widespread plague beset Asia during the
250s: in the panegyric's view, this prophecy and Gregory's subsequent
role in the epidemic accounted for Christianity's great success.

Beginning in the reign of Gordian, the surviving coins of
Neocaesarea show the symbols and legend of a series of local Actian
games.[28] These new coin types ought to refer to a new set of games in
the city, and perhaps they took their cue from the Emperor's presence
in Asia, like the Actian games which a group of cities in southwestern
Asia began at the same date. If so, Gregory's return to his home town
coincided with a sumptuous new festival of pagan athletics. It was
hardly the likeliest setting for mass conversions to Christ. A coin type
of the 260s happens to survive, still showing the symbols of athletic
victory in these same Actian games. The festival, it seems, survived
Gregory's mission and fits neatly with the scene in the panegyric of his
life. The continuing imagery of pagan games on the city's coins
tempers the extreme stories of the Christian conversion of
Neocaesarea. Actian games honoured the local gods and continued to
draw pagan crowds in Gregory's home city long after the plague was
supposed to have won him his converts. These local games add weight
to a different episode: after the persecutions in 250, Gregory introduced festivals of Christian martyrs to the people of Pontus. He
planned them, said his panegyrist, as an alternative focus for converts
who were accustomed to the pleasures of heathen games. In the late
fourth century, this pragmatic motive was often ascribed by Christian
authors to their churches' cults of martyrs. Its relevance has been
questioned, but the continuing pagan games in Pontus during the 260s
give it a sharper edge. A city with such symbols on its coins was not
reduced to seventeen pagans by the time of Gregory's death.

In nearby Armenia, some sixty years later, the established shrines of
Anahita were only dislodged with the help of its king. He was
sympathetic to a subsequent Gregory, the kingdom's missionary,
who converted him at a date around the year 314.[29] In Pontus,
Gregory's impact is known from the continuing local respect for his
sayings and example. However, there was no king, and here a
Christian mass conversion is neither evident nor plausible. Over a
century later, the panegyric ignores the province's strong pagan
setting. It is not history, and its legends should not be used to

support the idea of a rapid growth in the mid-third-century Church.

Since leaving Caesarea, Gregory has wandered at the mercy of local legend and his panegyric's better stories. All we can do is point to their exaggerations and allow throughout for the tastes of its speaker and audience a hundred and twenty years later. If the work "To Theopompus" is really by our Gregory, it probably belonged in the years in Pontus and would cast yet more doubt on the panegyric's stories. It shows him discussing and philosophizing, like a Christian apologist, not a charismatic worker of miracles. Perhaps one man could be both at once, but the picture is not of Christians being gained in crowds and spared the usual teaching. Doubts, however, continue to form round this text's authenticity.

To return to history, we must turn elsewhere, to the so-called Canonical Letter, which survives from this period in Pontus and is unquestionably Gregory's own work. It has probably been shortened, but it passed safely into the main body of Church law and drew comments from late Byzantine editors.[30] Once again, it shows us Gregory through his own words, although, typically, the panegyric ignored it. The Letter belongs with a well-attested crisis, the raids on Pontus which brought Gothic tribesmen across the Bosphorus in the year 251/2.[31] These raiders had profited from deaths and faction in the Bosphoran dynasty which Rome had previously been subsidizing. On their first raid, these Goths, the Borani, took captives back with them to man their newly built fleet. On a second raid they used a calm summer to sail far and wide and sack the temples and city of Trapezus, seat of the Romans' Pontic fleet.

The Letter belongs in the aftermath of this second raid and addresses a nearby Christian "father," or *pappas*.[32] He had authority over a country district and was evidently a bishop, perhaps the bishop of Trapezus itself. Gregory had heard of some shocking misconduct: the Goths had stolen and scattered property; they had raped Christian women and obliged Christian captives to lead them to profitable targets. When necessary, Christians had strangled their fellow men, "Pontic people," said Gregory, with a touch of local indignation, marking off the members of this province as something special.[33] In the wake of the raids Christians had seized other people's lost property and were also detaining captives who had escaped the Goths' clutches. The raid had left Christians with awkward problems. Were the victims of Gothic rape innocent victims, the church leaders wondered, or had they encouraged the Goths to the act?

The barbarian raids of the mid-third century have been regarded by many historians as a prelude to economic ruin. There were Christians in Pontus who took a different view. They had seized windfalls and were asking high prices for escaped captives whom they had trapped. They had used the Goths to loot their neighbours' property. Throughout the episode, the poor had not risen against the rich.[34] Individual enemies, rather, had used the Goths to settle a varied range of old scores. In the aftermath, Gregory wrote a letter of authority and urged the "father" to adopt his own practices of discipline and authority. In his Letter, we see the church founder at work, the pupil of Origen and the Beirut school in a new, Christian role.

Gregory had inquired carefully about the Goths' habits. Before eating meat, he found, they did not offer it to their idols and did not pollute it with demons. Christian captives who had eaten Gothic food had no need to fear and make amends. Did not Scripture prove that man is defiled by "what goes out," not by "what goes in"? With embarrassing pedantry, Gregory applied this text to the Goths' female victims.[35] Rape, which "goes in," was not a defilement, a point which a humane text in Deuteronomy supported. What, though, of the looks and enticements which "went out" of the supposed victims? With the precision of a High Court judge, Gregory classed these victims as sinners, defiled by the looks which "went out" and urged the Goths to come "in." He ordered a search among the Christian communities for any women who were known, on past form, to be flirtatious. The result, no doubt, was a horrible witch-hunt.

Christians who had found windfalls were no more fortunate. It made no difference, wrote Gregory, if the Goths had dropped the spoils, for the principle "finders, keepers" amounted to theft. Black passages from Genesis and Deuteronomy were brought to bear on these Christians' misconduct.[36] Just as Achan in the Book of Joshua had sinned and stolen the spoils of God, so Christians in Pontus who retained this lost property were held to be provoking divine wrath. Like Achan's spoils, the Goths' lootings were "anathemata," goods dedicated to God, and if they belonged to anyone, they belonged to God's Church. For a similar theft, Achan, his sons, his daughters and all his animals had been stoned and burned. Just as all Israel had suffered for his greed, so these Christian profiteers were bringing down the wrath of God on every Christian's head. They must be "excommunicated," a threat of the bishop's strongest weapon. Fellow Christians who were retaining the Goths' former captives and hoping to sell them could expect no mercy. District "commissioners" must comb the countryside and catch them "so that the thunderbolts of God may not fall on those who practise such behaviour."[37] Otherwise, God's anger would fall on the entire community and "especially on those leaders who fail to hunt the sinners out." It would come, as it once came on Achan, a punishment of fire on sinners, their flocks and innocent relations. To avoid this fate, the accusations, wrote Gregory, must follow fixed rules.[38] Christian sinners must be urged to stand forwards and denounce themselves, whereupon they would find a place in their fellow brethren's prayers. The churches should not lose respect for the laity's judgement. General assemblies of all the faithful, wrote Gregory, must judge the gravest cases of Christian collaboration, while lesser offenders should be consigned to different remedies, guilt and public shame. They could hope for a gradual, public reconciliation, whose various grades Gregory defined with a fine precision. Extreme sinners must stand weeping outside the church door, while minor sinners could proceed by stages to a presence inside church for all but the sharing of the Eucharist. Although some have thought these stages a later addition to the Letter, they sit well at this date, when the churches were becoming patient schools for sinners. They are close to the advice to bishops which is given by Cyprian and by the third–century "Apostles'" letter on this topic.[39]

These Christians' misconduct throws a rare light on Christian charity in action. It has been excused as the result of a hasty mass conversion, but the mass conversion is uncertain and the conduct recurs in other churches where the legends of crowd conversion found no place. There is a further dimension to the Letter. Seventy years before Constantine entrenched bishops as civil judges, Gregory was ruling on crimes of property and violence as if only the Christians' justice was relevant. He says nothing about civil authority or the intervention of Roman governors. It is striking how soon, in the fourth century, civic life in Pontus and Cappadocia depends on the benefactions of the Christian patrons in its upper class: is Gregory's Letter already a sign that the Church had filled a very large gap in Pontic society and that it alone stood forward when Roman rule broke down? The conclusion is excessive. As a bishop, Gregory was only concerned with Christians and a Christian settlement of mutual disputes. His Letter says more about the lengths to which Christian investigators would go than about the "collapse" of a separate pagan framework of justice, which Gregory was not concerned to discuss.

On Gregory's own outlook, however, the Letter casts an invaluable light. In his youth he had learned public speaking and admired and studied Roman law. He had read the Stoics, Platonists and Peripatetics under Origen's open guidance. Yet none of his training survived his practical role as a bishop. Roman law had its own rules for theft or rape, and its own redress for the detection of lost property or the sale of escaped captives. They owed nothing to the separate and narrow province of sacred law. Roman justice held only the guilty liable for punishment and was praised for its express refusal to allow that the sins of one generation could ever be visited on another.[40] The concepts of intention and personal responsibility stood at the very centre of the pagan ethics which Origen expounded to his pupils. They were opposed by their entire origin and elaboration to the archaic doctrine of a collective liability for punishment. God's treatment of Achan, his sons, his daughters and his entire household was a shocking betrayal of the principles of classical law and ethics.

At Caesarea, Gregory had considered the laws of the Romans to be "most Greek." He had valued philosophy as a key to the meaning of Scripture. In Pontus, he turned to a different language and authority, the scriptural powers of a Christian bishop. Even if "To Theopompus" is his work, it does not remove the contrast: when writing and arguing, Gregory could still philosophize, though not exactly as Origen would have taught: when ruling as a bishop, classical culture fell away from his language and advice. As we have doubted "To Theopompus," the contrast is particularly strong. Gregory turned for authority to Scripture, not philosophy: "Jerusalem," not "Athens" was the setting in which his converts were taught to live. In the mid-third century, his progress is all the more telling because it does not stand alone.

As the age of the apologists ends, we begin to hear from other Christian leaders, from Cyprian and Dionysius, Novatian the Elder in Rome and the minor bishops of North Africa. Novatian was the most true to his philosophical schooling, an author whose theology drew on Platonism and whose writings did retain a clear stamp of his education.[41] The quality was not lost on Cyprian: Novatian, he said, was made harsh by "the mischief of worldly philosophy," not "mild" by the wisdom of the Lord. He was not entirely fair to him. In Novatian's Rome, there were Christians who marshalled the Old Testament to justify all manner of behaviour: why, they argued, could they not go to the games, if Elijah had driven a chariot and David had danced before the Ark? In the Scriptures, Novatian replied, lay the proper "spectacle" for Christians; they should contemplate the world and its sins, the rewards and punishments of God, the resurrection of the dead. The "mischief" of philosophy did not supplant Scripture in his priorities.

Like Gregory, Cyprian had also begun life as a pagan of rank and riches. He had had an oratorical training and could plead as an advocate: he carried his gifts for rhetoric into his Christian writings, which are steeped in the Latin Bible and the "scriptural orchestration" of his style.[42] Like Gregory and Dionysius, he was developing a new literary imagery from biblical sources, but the influence of rhetorical schooling and its forms did not affect his writings at the deeper level of content. As a bishop, he drew heavily on proof texts from the Old and New Testaments and from the books of scriptural "testimonies" to which he added his own volume. With their help, he defended the "priestly" status of the bishop.[43] He used text upon Jewish text to stress the purity of God's chosen ministers and the wickedness of those who defied their will. Like Gregory, he called down God's vengeance against Christians who disobeyed their leaders. The bishop, he wrote, was both priest and judge, hedged about by texts from Samuel and Deuteronomy which lent the Lord's support to his sanctity: "God commanded them to be slain who did not hearken unto his priests and obey the judges he appointed for the season . . . the proud and insolent are now killed by a spiritual sword, in that they are cast out of the Church. . ."

We know less of Dionysius's writings, but enough to compare his progress with his fellow pupil Gregory. Again, his rhetorical training did not affect the hard, scriptural core in his thought. As we shall see, he quoted dark texts from the Old Testament to explain political events: "I will visit the sins of fathers upon children unto the third and fourth generation of them that hate me . . ."[44] When asked by the bishop of Libya, he also gave his advice on a series of sexual topics. Men who had had wet dreams were referred by Dionysius to Paul's words on conscience, while menstruating women were to be banned from approaching the Eucharist, as they would defile the purity of the place of God. Not all Christians agreed, but Dionysius's ruling lies at the root of a lasting tradition in the Eastern Church.[45] Ideas of pollution and purity took precedence in his answers over the views of educated men.

By scriptural casuistry, these bishops applied their advice to questions which the Gospels had never discussed. They also explained and advanced their own authority in texts drawn freely from the Old

Testament. So, too, the "Apostles'" letter in Syria supported its ideal of the bishop by long quotations from Jewish Scripture, ranging from the careers of David and Samuel to books as arcane as the "prayer of Manasseh."[46] These sources reinforced a particular view of the Church itself. In September 256, a council of bishops met at Carthage to discuss the question of the rebaptism of heretics. The topic concerned the very nature and theology of the Church, and by a happy chance, the interventions of the lesser bishops have been preserved in the minutes of the council and transmitted with Cyprian's letters. Among their free extension of texts from the Gospels, notes of the Old Testament also sound clearly. "And Lucian of Rucuma said: It is written, 'God saw the light that it was good, and he divided the light from the darkness.' Only if light agrees with darkness, may we have anything in common with heretics . . ." "Pelagianus of Luperciana said: It is written, 'Either the Lord is thy God, or Baal is thy God.' So now, either the Church is the Church, or heresy is the Church . . ."[47]

It would be superficial to see these bishops' use of Old Testament texts as nothing but a cynical prop for their authority. God's words of anger and vengeance were useful allies, but the Scriptures also allowed bishops to give rulings and advice in a form which was not merely a personal opinion. In Scripture, a greater voice spoke, to which the bishop, too, was subordinate: this impersonality was never better remarked and commended than by Augustine: "If threats are made, let them be made from the Scriptures, threatening future retribution, that it should not be ourselves who are feared in our personal power, but God himself in our words."[48] Like Gregory, Augustine had left a distant province in search of a pagan education. Away from home, he, too, had coincided with a great Christian teacher: Ambrose was to be his Origen, Milan his Caesarea.[49] Augustine, too, returned home to rapid promotion as a bishop and a life of hard, practical rule over a flock who knew only too well how to sin. In this life, the contacts with Ambrose and his philosophic culture gave way to a bedrock of Scripture and the Old Testament. No Christian ever wrote more sensitively of the changes which this progression involved, but the progress itself was not untypical: Augustine speaks for a course which other Christian leaders travelled.

We have seen how the ideals of Christian perfectionists appeared to overlap with much which pagan philosophers could admire. Among pagans, too, virginity and chastity were fine ideals; pagans, too, sought the vision of God and respected prophecy; it was admirable to die for one's convictions, if those convictions were noble and worthy. Yet, in each case, the Christian ideals had a different motivation and a different core; the "life of angels" and the return to Paradise were quite irrelevant to pagan sexual ethics; Christian visions had their own obsessions and occasions; martyrdom was quite unlike a philosopher's noble suicide. We can now add the different type of authority which aimed to control and lead these ideals. Under its leadership, the rise of Christianity is distorted if it is merged into a common religious culture of "Mediterranean" proportions and a shared attachment to one education, common to Christians and pagans. Christian authors could indeed present their faith in philosophical terms and defend it before pagans, as if it was the heir to pagan wisdom. These books were significant, but ultimately they did not relate to the realities of Christian discipline. The election, powers and scriptural resources of the bishop were quite unlike anything in pagan experience. Beside good, critical philosophy, the bishop's resources can only seem archaic and alien. The living heart of a high culture cannot survive if it is transplanted into a different context of power and authority. The "continuity" of pagan and Christian culture founders on the powers of the bishop and that impersonal source of "threats," as Augustine saw it: the Scriptures.

Christianity could appeal to ideals which pagans could recognize: it gave scope for intellectual defence and the refinement of faith. Yet it was also grounded in this different type of authority, and it now remains to be seen how this authority fared in the years of transition from the age of Decius to Constantine himself. In the final years of persecution before Constantine, it has been said, "the pagan wing of the intelligentsia tried to outlaw their Christian rivals. They failed. What a Christian author like Lactantius or Eusebius could offer, by way of negotiation, was to shelter the elevating traditions of classical education under the umbrella of a revealed religion . . ."[50] Negotiations, we now see, were likely to be rather more awkward, for the umbrella itself had a tough and alien central support. More than the safety of an education was involved in the change from pagan to Christian, and persecution itself had strong unintellectual roots. It is in this light, rather, that we can ask how far Christianity had grown by the year 300, whether, without Constantine's support, it would have become the most prominent religion in the Mediterranean world, and how far, then, it made a difference to life.

# Part Three

///////////////////////////////////////////////////////////////////////////////////////

*"You must understand, sir, that a person is either with this court or against it: there be no road between. This is a sharp time, now, a precise time: we live no longer in the dusky afternoon when evil mixed itself with good and befuddled the world. Now, by God's grace, the shining sun is up, and they that fear not light will surely praise it."*

Danforth, in *The Crucible* by Arthur Miller

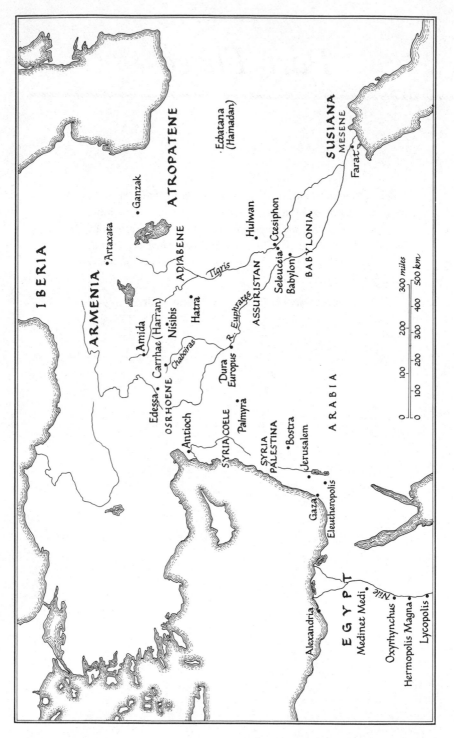

*The western centres of Mani's mission, 240–300 A.D.*

# 11. Sinners and Saints

/////////////////////////////////////////////////////////////////////////////////////////////////////////////////////////

I

The years between Gregory's mission and the conversion of Constantine have often been seen as the years of a Christian triumph. To bishops, they took on a different colour. In the year 250, Cyprian blamed Decius's persecution on the Christians' own sins: "We are being whipped," he wrote, "as we deserve." Fifty years later, the last great persecution was explained similarly, as God's punishment for Christian sin.[1] We have studied the Christian overachievers: in the age before Constantine, we must now do justice to the Christian majority, the sinners.

By obliging so many Christians to lapse, Decius's edict split the Church in an argument over its image of itself: was it a school for sinners or a narrower society of saints? The issue was debated keenly throughout the Christian world, engaging the full literary talents of Cyprian and Dionysius.[2] In North Africa, the treatment of the lapsed was joined by a further issue: if a Christian had been baptized by somebody outside the "true" Church, must he be baptized again before he could return to the fold? The two controversies were connected: a harsh decision on the lapsed put yet more Christians outside the Church, into schism and heresy. At first, Cyprian took a stern position on the readmission of those who had compromised: at Rome, he was supported by Novatian, then an Elder.[3] When persecution ceased, Cyprian's own position began to soften under pressure, while Novatian's remained firm. Rival bishops were elected in Rome and Carthage; strange alliances of opinion were forged by opposition; eventually, Novatian was forced into schism.[4] "Novatianists" held no heretical beliefs, but stood by the idea of a pure, uncompromised Church in which penance was long and offered to few. They troubled the Eastern and Western churches alike and persisted into the fourth century.

In the wake of Decius's edict, eligible recruits for Novatianism were none too plentiful.[5] At first, Decius's memory was damned by his successor, and in June 251, his edict was abandoned. The majority of Christians had lapsed in one way or another, but in late summer 251, Cyprian and his supporters could still persuade a council of African bishops to a cautious view on readmission. Each case of lapsing by acquiring a pagan certificate must be examined individually, with the implication that mild faults would not bar a Christian's prompt restoration. More serious cases needed penance of varying duration, while the lapse of offering a pagan sacrifice excluded a Christian until his deathbed. In all cases, God alone could grant forgiveness: repentance was essential and the Church's prayers and membership could help, but not assure, the outcome.

As in Pontus, so in Africa, this decision exposed Christian sinners to the threat of examination by their leaders. Events, however, overtook it. By spring 252, a widespread plague beset the African cities, and Christians were brought to their deathbeds sooner than their leaders had expected. There was also a fear that Decius's successor would respond to the "anger" of the gods by repeating the persecution. At a second council, in spring 252, the lapsed were granted peace, expressly in order to strengthen the Church for the coming assault. Some shrewd leadership had saved the African churches from a schism on issues which raised deep principles of theology. The Christian majority, who had bribed and sacrificed, were left in the knowledge that humanity and sense, despite some of their leaders, had won the day.

In the event, they had profited from a misplaced fear. Although a renewed persecution had been keenly awaited in Africa during 252, the only known victims were in Rome, where the bishop and several confessors were sent into exile. The Emperor had greater worries on his frontiers, and when he died in 253, the threat died with him.[6] For four more years, his successors took no notice. Then, in summer 257, they returned to the attack, choosing methods which suggest that they had learned from Decius's experience. In summer 257, the Emperors Valerian and Gallienus sent a rescript to their provincial governors and ordered that bishops and elders should be punished and that no Christians should hold a meeting or enter one of the "cemeteries." If they did, they should be put to death. In summer 258, a second Imperial letter was published; it enlarged on the matter and specified the penalties of death, exile and forced labour for Christians in various higher classes.[7] It was this letter which gave us an insight into the social composition of the Church.

We know nothing of the Emperors' immediate motives for their orders, beyond popular rumour, but we do catch an echo of their supporting way of thought in a reference to their letter of summer 257. It was then that they had distinguished the observance of "Roman ceremonies" from Roman *religio*, implying that the Christians were offensive because they refused to go through cult acts which honoured the gods and conformed to tradition, as Romans recognized it. It is suggestive that the second letter, in 258, was originally addressed to the Senate in Rome.[8] At the time, the Emperor Valerian was almost certainly in Syria, and the Senate may have prompted his letter by petitioning him to follow up the orders of the previous year. Persecution, it seems, was not unpopular in the highest circles of Roman society, and the emphasis on "Roman ceremonies" in the first letter fits well with this climate of opinion. The customs and religious traditions of the higher social orders had always been a profound concern of the Roman governing class. In 257/8, they were effectively upheld. Valerian and his partner struck directly at the Christians, whereas Decius had only disturbed them in a wider order intended to benefit the gods. None of the Emperors wanted martyrs, but since Decius, they had learned to aim at the Christians' weak points, their leadership, meetings and upper-class supporters. Their orders were much more aware of the enemy: the staff who drafted them knew the Christians' own word for the grave, the "cemetery," and used it in the first letter.[9] For the first time, Christians were not merely obliged to compromise. Their worship and common life were threatened with extinction.

In Christian history, this new approach had an unintended consequence. By focussing on bishops and elders, it closed the gap between two types of authority. It offered Church leaders the prestige of becoming confessors, while denying the honour to lesser men. Certain bishops were not slow to publicize the consequences.[10] Minutes of Cyprian's two hearings by the governor of Africa were composed and circulated for Christian readers. In Egypt, Bishop Dionysius could at last oppose a solid trial and confession to critics who complained that previously he had known neither. When the second Imperial letter was publicized, the penalties were made harsher: Church leaders were to be martyred, not exiled. However, the sequel suggests there was little popular support for the demand.

Before Decius's edict, the cities had initiated their own arrests and accusations of Christians: they feared, or were reminded to fear, these

"atheists" who would not participate in the cults which averted the
anger of the gods. This fear had not disappeared, nor had the proofs of
the gods' anger. In the 230s, earthquakes in inland Asia caused another
bout of persecution: in the 250s, Cyprian took care to refute an
intelligent pagan who argued that Christians provoked the gods'
anger and caused natural calamities, a contention which was still
worth answering at the end of the century.[11] However, the intervention of the Emperors and their edicts brought a new dimension. In the
250s, Imperial officials were directly involved in the arrests and
interrogations: in Smyrna, the cavalry commander warned Pionius
that he was a *princeps*, or officer of the governor, with a hint of
officious pride. In the persecutions of 257/8, Christian leaders were
rounded up by troops under the governors' authority, not by the local
cavalry and police of the cities themselves. Bishops Cyprian and
Fructuosus, Agapius and Secundinus were arrested by the governor's
troops without any local initiative: the "best friend" of Marian and
James recalled the arrival of an entire army unit at their country house
near little Muguae. "Nor was it, as in other places, one or two soldiers
from a local 'station' who did this, but a violent and wicked crowd of
centurions . . ."[12]

In the cities, the crowds still watched the hearings and executions,
but even the Christians' own narratives do justice to a change of
mood. In Smyrna, in the 150s, the crowds had bayed for the blood
of Polycarp; in Lyons, c. 177, they had encouraged the awful trials of
women and old men. In Alexandria, that great centre of crowd
violence, they were enthusiastic watchers of some great brutalities in
the local persecution which preceded Decius's order. However, we
then find another tone. In Smyrna, they regretted Pionius's death
through his own obstinacy; in Spain, they began to grieve for Bishop
Fructuosus because he was popular with pagans and Christians alike
and they thought it a shame that he was being led to the amphitheatre.
In Carthage, they were very curious to see Cyprian's last hours and the
fate of his body; at Cirta, we are told, the city was "seething" with
persecution in 259 because of the "blind fury of the heathen," but in
fact, the soldiers and the governor were the motive force in the stories
which followed. At Carthage, a "popular tumult" was admitted to
have been roused by the governor himself. In Egypt, Bishop Dionysius told how in 250 he had been rescued from his military captors by a
crowd of country people who had been preparing for a wedding feast,
but stopped to drag him away, dressed only in his shirt. They are not

said to have been Christians, but they put him on a donkey and sent him to safety. People did not like to see respectable elderly leaders being carted away by soldiers and officials. They had not started these persecutions, and although they watched them, they were not prepared to abet them. In 250, the martyrdom of Conon alleges that everyone except two city leaders had run away from a town on Asia's south coast as the governor approached, announcing that he was enforcing Decius's edict. The story may be embellished, but the fiction had to seem plausible to its Christian readers. At first, the Emperors and governors had done more to limit Christian persecution than to apply it thoroughly. In the 250s, they tried at last to enforce it, but like other legal rulings, their measures foundered on their own subjects' apathy. If asked to choose between Christians and visiting soldiers, most people would have preferred Christians.

If this distinction is right, we can better understand how events took another, unexpected turn for the Church. In 258, it must have seemed as if the faith was about to be driven out of any society which mattered. The process was overtaken by a further catastrophe: the Emperor Valerian was captured and killed by the king of Persia. In summer 260, his son and former partner, Gallienus, ordered the churches and cemeteries to be restored to the Christians. These edicts marked a turning point. We do not know if Gallienus had been a reluctant party to the previous events, as the Christians later claimed, or why he changed course: perhaps he feared the larger problems which were now before him in the East; perhaps he agreed that a total attack on the Church was excessive. To what, then, did his new edict amount?[13] We know of at least one martyrdom which followed its despatch, but it occurred in a province which was not at first under Gallienus's control: otherwise, we have no knowledge of martyrdoms, as opposed to Christian fictions of them, between 260 and the 290s. When we then find Christians being martyred, they are soldiers in the army. The charge against them is not their religion and their refusal to sacrifice, but their refusal to serve in the ranks, an offence which was punishable on other grounds. This charge is quite different from the older accusations of the "Christian name." The previous type of trial was no longer relevant, because Gallienus had ended it, restoring the Christian communities' property and leaving them free to enjoy it without the risk of accusations on the old Trajanic pattern.

The edicts of summer 260 thus granted the churches a degree of security for the first time in their history. We can watch their impact at two levels, in the general temper of Christian life and the particular efforts of Christians in the East to claim their legal protection. Like other edicts, Gallienus's were not always as good as their language. As often, it needed a further petition and response before several major groups of Christians were secure from others' attacks. Their reactions emerge from two telling letters by Bishop Dionysius, each of which sounds a note of particular interest.

The first is best dated between autumn 261 and early 262, shortly after a rival to Gallienus had been overcome in the Near East.[14] It was set at a time when events had been moving very fast around the Emperor, and in it Dionysius explained their course to a bishop in Egypt. The former persecutors, he remarked, and the recent pretenders had each been struck down by the vengeance of God. Now, quite suddenly, Gallienus had rejuvenated the Empire, dispelling darkness and restoring light in a manner which the bishop hailed in Messianic language from Isaiah. Although Dionysius was writing only to a Christian audience, he invited them to celebrate their festival day, "as the holier Emperor has already passed seven years of rule and is now completing his ninth."

This letter is extremely significant. Although it was written for Christians only, it expressed a very warm view of the new Emperor and encouraged the churches to a loyal celebration of his reign. Four years earlier, its author had assured his Roman judge that "we pray to our God unceasingly for the kingdom of the Emperors, that it may remain unshaken": loyalism, it seems, was a natural attitude for Dionysius. So, too, was faith in God's wrath. His letter explained the fate of the persecutors and pretenders as due to the anger of God. Like Gregory, his fellow pupil, he abandoned his Greek education and turned to the darker views of the Old Testament in order to interpret recent events: God, he quoted, had "visited the sins of the fathers upon their children, unto the third and fourth generation of them that hate me."[15] By his letter, Christians were enabled to grasp why history was happening, although the argument distorted events. In fact, Gallienus had shared power with his father during the recent persecutions, but the troubles, said Dionysius, were entirely due to the evil pretender who had emerged meanwhile. For the first time in Greek, we hear the combination of effusive support for an Emperor with the damning of his rivals, both of which were expressed in biblical terms. Fifty years later, the same themes surface in the writings of Christians who had to adjust to events round Constantine.

After this brief new dawn, a second revolt broke out in Egypt which is best placed shortly before Easter 262. It was on this Easter that Dionysius wrote a further letter to the brethren in Egypt, describing in a high biblical style how he and his fellow Christians found themselves besieged in a quarter of Alexandria by the attacking army of the Emperor.[16] To these events, we can attach an incident which the order of Eusebius's narrative has obscured.[17] The besieged Christians included the famous Anatolius, a Christian who was well educated in mathematics and rhetoric and was recognized as the city's leading teacher of Aristotelian philosophy. As a famine began, this Christian intellectual sent word to a fellow Christian, Eusebius the deacon, in the Roman camp: he, in turn, arranged with the commander that deserters to his side should be given a safe haven. Anatolius then persuaded the council of the besieged Alexandrians to allow the old, the women and the children to leave their company and burden the besiegers instead. Against some opposition, Anatolius carried this proposal before a public assembly. The order was interpreted broadly. Many were smuggled across to Eusebius, the Christians first, the rest later, and all were given a notable welcome by his Christian partner in the Roman camp. This episode is full of interest. It shows an intellectual, a known Christian, being able to initiate and convince a pagan public meeting in Alexandria, addressing a "council" and "assembly," in Eusebius's view, at which votes were still being cast. Meanwhile, a fellow Christian could approach and convince a Roman commander and work out a plan which reflects well on the clever agreement and humanity of two Church leaders whom the siege had caught in differing camps. Like Gregory in Pontus, these Alexandrian Christians had stepped naturally forward in a time of general crisis. When Gallienus's troops were victorious, this ruse gave the Christians an excellent claim to favour. Their leaders could tell the Emperor of their loyalty and recall their efforts at helping his besiegers' cause.

By autumn 262, this second revolt had ended, and we can well understand how Bishop Dionysius promptly petitioned the Emperor. Since 260, Gallienus's edict had not been applied by the various pretenders in the Near East, and the Christians needed a second statement if they were to benefit from it. We would dearly like to know how Dionysius's appeal reached Gallienus's court, which of his advisers acted as the Christians' contact and whether their plea was accompanied by proofs of their aid during the siege and even, perhaps, by extracts from Dionysius's letter in the previous autumn, which had expressed such unsolicited favour for Gallienus's victories. Whatever was said sufficed, for the Emperor granted the famous rescript which Eusebius knew and quoted. Its content is better known than its setting against the events in Alexandria.

Gallienus's original edict had granted peace and property to the Christian churches; the rescript reaffirmed the restoration of church property in Egypt and similar rescripts to other bishops confirmed the rights of churches elsewhere.[18] From 262 until 299, Christians were then left alone in a time of quiet which has often been seen as a time of expansion, the age of Christian "triumph" before Constantine.[19] These years are notoriously obscure and the evidence is unusually scattered and indirect. Before prejudging the sequel under Constantine, it is better to begin with a sense of the realities in a third-century Church. We can then wonder whether a "triumph" could develop from them without the active patronage of a Christian as Emperor. Persecution, Origen had observed, was not such a potent weapon of Satan as its absence: in the 230s and 240s, some of the most penetrating comments in his biblical works are those which look bleakly at fellow Christians' failings.[20] After 260, there were no persecutions to revive fears of an imminent End: Christians were more than ever at risk to boredom, that powerful enemy of religious commitment.

It is of a piece with this relaxation that during the third century rigorist views on sin were in retreat.[21] There were still many variations in the details of local practice, as we can see from the subsequent councils under Constantine, but we happen to know most about North Africa, through its Latin authors. Before the 230s, adultery had seemed unforgivable to many African bishops; to Cyprian, by 250 it was no longer an irreconcilable sin. In the year of Decius's edict, lapsing was still widely regarded by African bishops as a sin without remission; two years later, their views had had to soften, and in much of the Greek East this moderation had probably occurred rather earlier. Penance, meanwhile, was altering.[22] It had not lost its essential bleakness: in the 250s, Cyprian describes the same compound of mourning, fasting and public humiliation which Tertullian had so vividly depicted. It was defined, however, by categories of time and degree, a process which was evident in Gregory's letter of discipline. In Cyprian's writings, it becomes connected closely with something else: "the ugly theory of almsgiving as the stipulated price for forgiveness."

Cyprian's tract "On Works and the Giving of Alms" addresses a

Church into which the lapsers had only recently been readmitted. It stresses almsgiving as the route to a "white crown," a lesser precursor of the "purple crown" of martyrdom. Its publication should not be detached entirely from the recent persecution.[23] It is probably datable to the year 252, just after the discussions over the admission or exclusion of Christians who had lapsed in the Decian crisis. Many of these Christians were the richer members, who had more to lose and more to offer by way of bribes to their accusers. Had they been excluded, as Cyprian first suggested, their alms and contributions would have been lost to the Church, undermining the entire system of payments by dividend. This consequence must have been foreseen, though the surviving debates do not dwell on it. In 252, the lapsed were reinstated, and we then meet Cyprian's tract, urging people to give alms as a secondary route to a crown of honour.

On their reinstatement, there was still a contrast between the few perfectionists and the large, sinful majority: in Carthage, there were Christians who did penance simply because they had thought of lapsing, without actually doing anything wrong.[24] To broaden this picture, we can follow life in a modest church in Syria, where the tension is still evident between overachievement, a first-class performance and just enough of an effort to pass as a Christian. It is revealed by the precious text to which we turned for the duties and problems of the bishop. Preserved in Syriac, it was written originally in Greek and it is agreed that it derives from a third-century author: his learning and biblical quotations have been thought to exclude an earlier date.[25] He discusses martyrdom and conduct during persecution and urges charitable help for any Christians in prisons or the mines. These precepts might suggest a date before the edict of summer 260, but there is no certainty and the second half of the century is also possible. The dating is not too critical: the earlier its origin, the more deep-seated is its picture of Church life.

The text was written by a Christian in Syria, probably a Church official, who cast it as a long book of teaching and passed it off as a letter from the Apostles. They were writing, he pretended, after the first Council of Jerusalem, the scene of the debates on Paul's Gentile mission. This "letter" to all the churches filled one of the gaps which was left by Acts, Chapter 15. This forged "Apostolic" origin is another comment on contemporary Christians' ideas of authority and lack of historical sense. It was not, however, mischievous. Its author gave the text a false pedigree because he felt so strongly that his proposals were the right proposals for a Christian life. His text, then, is a doubly useful guide to the churches. It gives a strong view of Christian conduct, while pointing to alternatives which other Christians were advancing.

On their second appearance, the "Apostles" show a welcome measure of humanity. Parts of their letter make sense as an answer to perfectionists and Christian overachievers whose standards had been troubling plain believers' lives. One such group had been teaching the merits of sexual abstinence and extreme self-denial: in the Syrian churches, we have seen examples of such overachievers, the wandering ascetics and virginal "sons of the covenant." On these topics, the "Apostles" gave more flexible advice. Bishops, they ruled, did not have to be celibate. Sex was a fact of life and Christian parents should marry off their children as quickly as possible before they caught bad pagan habits and started to sleep around. If widows, especially young widows, found their status impossible, they could remarry as a "second best." Lapses were not wholly unforgivable: for the first time, the episode of Jesus and the woman taken in adultery was cited with approval in a Christian text. The "Apostles" approved penance and reconciliation for any sin, in terms which answered others who disagreed.

Another group was causing trouble by insisting that the precepts of the Jewish law must be observed in full. Again, these overachievers conform to our evidence for Christians elsewhere in Syria. In reply, the "Apostles" insisted on Christians' new freedom from the old covenant. The Ten Commandments, they said, applied to all men, but the detailed "second legislation" of Moses was death. Its laws of purity were a gratuitous burden. Christian women, said the "Apostles," should not even be ashamed of their monthly periods. They should not hide away or wash frequently. Their husbands were free to make love to them at any time of the month. This liberal view was not universal in the Church: we may recall Bishop Dionysius's contrary warnings to the churches in Libya, which still survive in the practice of the Eastern Church.

Although these differing calls for "overachievement" were addressing the simpler Christians, their lives seem becalmed on a millpond of worldly temptation and petty sin. The "Apostles" had the usual words of praise for martyrs, but they had much more to say on familiar difficulties: sex, charity and social class. We have already attended to their advice to bishops and their insistence that they should not show undue favour to the rich or well-born. The deserving poor should take precedence, just as the older Christians deserved respect from the young. In church, advised the "Apostles," younger people must give up their seats to the old. Children, Paul had written, must "submit" to their parents: the "Apostles" encouraged parents to stand up to their children and give them a good smack whenever necessary.

Women were more intractable. Before a service, the text said, one of the deacons must stand and watch at the door for strangers, taking special care to discover the marital status of visiting women. They must also be vetted for heresy, that besetting complaint of the female mind. Inside church, the company must be segregated "like the dumb animals": for the reality, we may recall John Chrysostom's words on the problems of church seating in Antioch. Women and widows must sit apart at the back of the meeting and never expound their faith to strangers: pagans would not take lessons seriously from a female. Instead, the women must state their creed and repeat it in answer to every question: we can see why educated pagans complained of Christians who asserted their views without argument. No Christian, male or female, should read any pagan books, the "Apostles" commanded: old and new Scripture sufficed, and anyone who wanted history could study the Book of Kings. Women, meanwhile, must not court adultery by using makeup or choosing smart clothes, and men should help them to remain chaste by refusing to grow their hair too long or to make clever use of the comb. These commands were not a rare, local oddity: an early synod of bishops in Spain denied communion to any women who had boyfriends with long or curly hairstyles.[26] The Christian ideal of equality entailed a persistent dullness in so many of its leaders' minds. It did, however, run into problems. In a fascinating chapter, the "Apostles" had to insist that Christian men and women must not bathe together in the same bathhouse. If there was only one mixed bathhouse in the town, they must use it at different hours. Rules to avoid mixed bathing were not unknown in pagan cities, but their observance was not universal. It was this type of problem which had first bothered Hermas the visionary; the "Apostles'" concern was shared by Clement in Alexandria and reminds us of the practical strains on observance of Jesus's teaching about "adultery of the eye and heart."[27]

While answering the overachievers, the "Apostles" themselves had not abandoned discipline: did their advice conform to the lives which fellow Christians lived? Here, they could not ignore the realities, which are best seen in their instructions to bishops and their long commands on the conduct of widows. In their churches, the status of "widowhood" belonged to all single women over the age of fifty, but younger widows, they said, should be supported too in order to dissuade them from a second marriage. We have noticed how in ancient society the relative ages of man and wife at marriage made widowhood especially frequent. No other text brings its Christian features so clearly before us.

The well-behaved widow, the "Apostles" advised, should pray wholeheartedly and join in no debates. She should sit at home and work wool. This advice conformed to a conventional pagan ideal of the good woman, but the reality was rather different. Widows, the "Apostles" went on, should not lend out money like usurers. Their remark suggests a Church in which women of property were familiar and financially active. They must not be jealous of each other's charitable gifts and must not compare the origins of every little handout. Although charity must be dispensed by bishops and deacons only, the "Apostles" did allow the names of almsgivers to be announced when gifts were bestowed. Widows, they said, must not compete or be smug about a gift which came from a particularly smart donor. They must remain quietly and gratefully in one house. They must not bicker against each other or flit from door to door with scraps of malicious gossip.

Life in a third-century church shows only too clearly through these long counsels. They do not suggest the birth pangs of a Church triumphant. They show a membership which had known better than to obey their authors' and leaders' counsels of dullness. Their life was a round of small temptations, furtive love, gossip among the widows, gambling and attempts to buy or influence the bishop's favour. A few extremists still worried those of their "brethren" who were susceptible, but conspicuous combats with Satan were rare and the majority were living to a different rhythm. The End had receded to the year 500 and persecution was no longer a preoccupation. In these churches, nothing much was happening, no missionary ventures, no concern to win new converts. It was hard enough to control the existing membership: inside the church, the "Apostles" ordered, a deacon must take good care to check the congregation and see that nobody was whispering or snoozing, laughing or making signs.[28]

# II

Sin and its perennial vigour were joined by a further problem: fellow Christians' deviant beliefs. Christianity had brought the notion of heresy to a pagan world which had never known it, and by c. 250, worthwhile battles had been won. The "bilingual ambiguities" of "Gnostic" Christians were no longer a major issue in Greek- and Latin-speaking communities. Better books had been written for Christians who wanted an intelligent faith and did not wish to disregard its historical foundation. Victory, however, caused the nature of the enemy to be further defined. In the 180s, Irenaeus had accepted that there were areas in which a range of theological views was still possible: this same sense of "legitimate disagreement" is still evident in Origen, an unusually philosophic Christian. The drift, however, was not in Origen's direction. In the Greek world, heresies began to be defined on questions which had previously been more fluid. None was more elusive than the relation of God the Father to his Son. In the 260s, Paul, bishop of Antioch, was interrogated for views which would probably have passed muster a century earlier.[1] By the fourth century, the views of some of his opponents themselves seemed embarrassingly unorthodox. If the history of forgiveness was one of falling barriers, the history of heresy was one of closing paths.

This drift did not go with a narrowing of intellectual interest and a general inability to cope with new arguments. If anything, it went with the opposite. These questions were very difficult and were only gradually narrowed down. It took several generations of argument for the next layer of subtlety to be seen: Paul of Antioch's examination raised questions which did not disappear with his excommunication. It was not, then, for lack of intellectual scope in the Church that Christians of education and intelligence began to be attracted to a new and unexpected heresy. Just when the major battles of belief might seem to have been won, a new system appeared, not a heretical interpretation but a new self-styled Gospel with its own apostle, deliberately modelled on St. Paul. Born in the early 240s, it rapidly drew converts in the cities of the Greek-speaking East, Iran and even India. Unlike the teaching of previous Gnostics and heretics, it was a missionary faith for all people, preached in "all languages" and quickly organized into a Church. Its success points a contrast with the contemporary orthodox communities. Its rise and appeal connect with our major themes of Christian perfectionism: visionary experience, sexual abstinence and, finally, martyrdom.

Its preacher, Mani, was a Syriac-speaking "apostle of Christ" whose horizons spanned the known world. Whereas other faiths had been parochial, Mani proclaimed his Church as the "Church of East and West alike." He spread it with the vigour of newly enlightened youth.[2] Aged twenty-four, he had experienced his own missionary calling and set off from his home in southern Mesopotamia to take his Gospel of Light through the kingdoms of northwestern Iran, where his father's family had local connections. He returned to Mesene in southern Babylonia, the "central market," as a Syriac hymn text called it, "for merchants from the East." Like St. Thomas in the Christians' legend, Mani then joined the company of traders and travelled east on a missionary visit to India. On his return, he headed north again through Iran, turning eastwards down the great road through Khurasan, the former route of Alexander the Great. In two years, from 240 to 242, he travelled through much of the reviving Persian Empire, entirely outside the provinces of Rome. Not yet twenty-six, he, and a few followers, had shown a missionary energy which matched any in the earliest Church. He had also sent missionaries across the Roman border, giving them instructions, his disciples said,[3] to "be wise and eloquent in every place" and to "be prepared to live in poverty . . ." He told them "how to keep company with women . . . he gave them the 'Treasure of Life' and his other books . . ." Various names were cited in Christian and later Manichaean sources as those of the first Western missionaries, and we cannot be sure exactly who crossed the Romans' frontier for the first time.[4] Before long, preachers had reached Palmyra, Edessa, Alexandria and Upper Egypt and were winning converts in places where they bothered the Christians' churches. By the 290s, they are evident to us in North Africa. Mani himself did not visit the West, so far as we know, but he gained some significant supporters in Iranian society before 276, the year of his interrogation and death at the order of Vahram, the new Persian king. His followers preserved a bold tradition of this "last journey," records of which, it seems, were taken down by one of his followers, like the records of Christian martyrs' trials which were kept by their "best friends."[5]

Mani's new Gospel and its missionary travels made a remarkable use of the freedom of movement across the Roman and Persian frontiers of the mid-third century. Mani's death gave his world religion the added appeal of a theology of martyrdom. It did not die with him: rather, his death helped it to grow. Unlike any of the great heretics of the second century, Mani founded a Church which was to survive as long as the Roman Empire and in the East would last for very much longer. It developed a "head," twelve deputies and an array of bishops and elders. Mani himself had conceived his new Gospel as a universal religion, explicitly contrasting it with the teachings of Buddha, Jesus and Zoroaster: this wide horizon could perhaps only have occurred so naturally to a man on the open frontier between the Roman and Persian empires.[6] While Christians were teaching in Syriac and Latin and beginning to use Coptic, Mani claimed to reveal a faith "for all languages." He himself wrote Syriac and cast one of his books in a rather heavy style of Middle Persian; he used Jewish texts in Aramaic, although at times he mistook their true meaning. His first missionaries in the West knew Greek, Syriac and Coptic, while in the East his trusted preacher, Mar Ammo, knew the Parthians' language and script: in eastern Iran, a wise man is said to have questioned Mani on the oldest script in the world, the "first of all," to which Mani replied, "Indian, 'Syrian' and Greek," apparently preferring his native "Syrian" Aramaic.[7] The Greek heresies of the previous century had never bothered with this range of languages, and it is Manichaeism which reminds us of the scope for multilingual preaching in the ancient Near East. Eventually, it was to spread into at least eleven languages and span the world from North Africa to China; there, it continued as a living faith from the T'ang dynasty to the 1930s. Of all the sub-Christian religious systems, "Manichaeism" has proved to be the most persistent and the most widely persecuted.[8] Like its founder, it suffered persecution in Iran and was then outlawed in the pagan Roman Empire. Christian Emperors maintained the death penalty for its leaders, and Chinese Emperors frequently proved intolerant. For nine years in his youth, St. Augustine was to be a "hearer" of the sect: when he first told his mother, she tried to shut him out of the house.

The impulse and nature of this extraordinary mission pose obvious questions to those who focus only on the orthodox Church. In the past fifteen years, we have come to know the early journeys of Mani in unimagined detail, through the discovery of a tiny papyrus codex of a Greek text, "On the Birth of His Body," and through brilliant reconstructions of parchments belonging to the sect in eastern Iran and Central Asia, where they had survived in fragments, torn up by Muslim conquerors. These texts have helped to make up for the

Coptic papyri whose contents had been surveyed but not published before their loss in Germany in 1945: it now seems that they matched the material which has recently been recovered in Greek.[9] As never before, we can watch this small band of missionaries on its travels throughout the Near East: like the first Muslims, the Manichees preserved "sayings" of their founder's early followers, extracts from which we now have in a miniature booklet, copied in Greek script c. 400 A.D. Some of the details may be embellished, but the framework of time and place is meticulous and the quotations from Mani's own books are invaluable. The narrative is not a fiction, not a work to be compared with the apocryphal "Acts" of Christian Apostles.

For our purposes, knowledge of this world religion has a special Christian relevance. We can now be certain that Mani grew up in a Jewish-Christian community of Baptists in Mesopotamia; his mission, we know, was earlier in reaching the West than many suspected; its successes make a powerful contrast to those which attended the Christians during his lifetime. The great missionary preachers of the years of the "peace of the Church" turn out to be Manichaeans, not Christians. They appealed to Christians, too, and earned sympathy in high society. We can develop these points from the new discoveries, while asking how such teaching would have struck Christians in the Church of this period.

Like Gentile Christianity, this new missionary Gospel was born from visionary experience and a reaction to religious tradition. Mani was the son of Iranian parents and was born in April 216 in southern Mesopotamia, a region which was then under Parthian rule. His mother was credited with royal Parthian descent and his father had moved south to Mesopotamia from his birthplace in Media. He brought up his son among a strict sect of Baptists whom he served as an honoured member. These Baptists observed austere rules of diet and washing and practised self-denial within a framework of Jewish-Christian beliefs. They honoured Christ and Elchesai, the "post-Christian" prophet, a counterpart to Hermas, whose books had appeared in Mesopotamia in the early second century.[10] As Mani grew up, he began to claim that Elchesai's teaching was being mistaken by his followers: this starting point is particularly interesting, as we know from Eusebius that Origen, in the mid-240s, wrote a vigorous polemic against Elchesai and his teachings. His attack was phrased against living "Elchesaites," proof that this sect still attracted interest outside its Mesopotamian homeland.

To progress beyond his father's Baptist group, Mani needed a particular source of authority. Like so many founders of cults and heresies, he discovered it where we have come to expect, in a classic series of visions.[11] He wrote of them himself, as we know from the Greek codex: from earliest childhood, he recalled, "I was protected through the might of angels" who "nurtured me with visions and signs, short and very brief ones, which they showed me so far as I could bear them": once again, angelic visions were related to the capacity of their beholder. Mani's began very early, making him the most favoured child in the rich history of antiquity's child visions. From his fourth year, he was conscious of angelic protection; aged twelve, he enjoyed a first revelation of his Heavenly Twin, the "most beautiful and largest mirror image of my own person," whom he eventually related closely to the Holy Spirit. The idea that each human being had a Twin, watching and guarding him as an angelic higher self, was already familiar in the heretical types of Christianity which were known to Mani in their Syriac form. These visions were sometimes awesome, coming "like lightning," but they also reassured him about the trials of the future. Mani continued to see visions and hear voices, although for the time being he said nothing. Then, when he was twenty-four, "the most blessed Lord" sent him his Twin in a second, most glorious appearance. He taught him "who I am and what my body is, and how my arrival into this world occurred . . . who is my Father on high and what order and commission he gave me before I put on this material form and before I was led astray in this abominable flesh . . . who is my inseparable Twin . . . he revealed to me, too, the boundless heights and unfathomable depths . . ."

This vision, Mani came to believe, was a "gift of God's grace"; "when he saw me," he later wrote of it, "he took pity on me and was moved with compassion . . ." Mani saw it as an act of redemption, while the secrets which he heard were his "treasure" and "riches" for all the world: he was to call one of his books "The Treasure of Life." Such knowledge could not be kept from his elders and betters in the Baptist sect. He began to argue with them and accuse them of mistaken practice. They appealed to his father and when he told them to test Mani themselves, they sent for him and gathered round him. "From boyhood, they said, you were doing well with us . . . You were like a composed young girl in the midst of us. But now, what has happened to you or what has been seen by you?" Epiphanies had made it impossible for Mani to go back to his old ways: after a dispute with one of the sect's leaders, he had seen the "whole world become like a sea, filled with the very blackest waters; I saw thousands and tens of thousands plunged into it . . ."[12] Mani seemed to be walking on a road laid above it, but his opponent, Sita, had fallen off under the water: "I could only see the slightest bit of his hair and I was greatly distressed. But the One who had cast him out said to me, 'Why are you worried about Sita? He is not one of your chosen Elect.'"

Mani's career, we now know, is the last great flourish in the history of heavenly epiphany before Constantine. His Twin promised to be his "Helper and Protector"; "if ever you are afflicted and call on me, I will be found standing near you." He knew the awe and terror, but also the intimacy: his followers supported his visions by comparing them with the apocalyptic visions ascribed to Jewish figures: Mani's own vision of a personal opponent, drowning and no longer one of his number, belonged in this beastly tradition.[13] Visionary experience accompanied Mani throughout his mission. Once, he saw one of his Iranian followers visible in glory beyond the grave: at another time, a vision of himself in his absence helped to heal and convert a prominent lady in Syria.[14] Throughout, the visions of his Heavenly Twin encouraged his travels and the despatch of his preachers. This core of experience became elaborated in his followers' oral tradition, and sometimes we can see it being used to reinforce points in their Gospel's teaching. Two particular fictions attached to pursuits they detested: hunting and gardening.

When Mani first returned to southern Mesopotamia, he was said to have converted the brother of King Shapur by a novel type of revelation. The prince was a proud garden owner who hated the new sect, surely because its teaching was opposed to working the soil and pruning plants and trees.[15] One day, Mani intruded into the prince's garden, whereupon the prince asked him aptly, "In this Paradise you preach, will there be a garden as good as mine?" He was then granted a heavenly tour of the gardens in Paradise and is said to have been converted by what he saw. This story was born, it seems, from the Manichaeans' known opposition to gardening: Mani is also said to have intruded on another prince and interrupted his hunting.[16] The sect detested this blood sport, too, and Mani's admonitions are said to have converted the prince while he was drawing a promising covert. In each case, the story has grown from the sect's own teaching. A knowledge of the mood on the hunting field or among owners of very good gardens is enough to refute these stories of conversion, worked by an uninvited spoilsport.

Critics later attacked the truth of Mani's personal visions, and in the newly found Greek codex, some of the stories are best understood as his pupils' defence of their master's visionary credentials. They attached Mani's visions to a long tradition, to the revelations of Adam and others, whose books had circulated spuriously beyond the time and place of their Jewish creators.[17] Mani himself attached his visions to the model of St. Paul. His Twin, he believed, had "redeemed" him from the sterile formalism of the Baptists. Although their final conflict occurred over rites of washing and the proper treatment of bread, it owed something, too, to Mani's readings of Paul, a man whom Baptists deplored as a troublesome Hellene. At first, Mani's visions perplexed them: was he a new prophet, like Elchesai? Then his rejection of their rites enraged them. Mani turned instead to the wider horizons of Parthian Mesopotamia. Through its traders and travellers, it offered a double prospect, west to Syria and Egypt and east as far as India. In its Syriac language, a young man could find texts of all manner of so-called Gospels, Jewish works, too, like the "Book of Giants," Christian speculations of Marcion and the cosmologies of Valentinus and Bardaisan.[18] Copying Paul's own wording, he called himself "Mani, apostle through the will of Jesus Christ," and set out on his long travels.

While the Spirit was muted in the contemporary churches, Mani's preachers arrived in their region, claiming access to a newly revealed truth. This is not the place to do justice to the power and range of their cosmology or their severe code of conduct: Manichaeans were taught to respect the particles of light and goodness, trapped in evil matter, the trees, the earth and all living creatures. Their aversion to hunting and gardening was part of a wider ban on eating meat and working the soil: good Manichaeans were antiquity's most scrupulous vegetarians. Stories told how vegetables had once wept to Mani when they were about to be cut, and palm trees had spoken when they were about to be pruned: centuries later, in the Central Asian deserts, Manichaeans would foster the culture of melons, fleshless vegetables of concentrated goodness and light.[19] Against the setting of the contemporary Christian churches, we need only stress two aspects: the Manichaeans' notorious dualism of good and evil and the structure of their community.[20] Mani described man and the universe as the scene of a constant struggle between an evil kingdom of darkness and the particles of light and goodness which it had ensnared. This struggle was a fact of the world's Creation and was played out daily in the hearts of every hearer. Once, God had sent his "call" through the heavens to his divine emissary, caught in the kingdom of evil and darkness: now, Mani brought a new "call" to his hearers in the earthly kingdom of evil and to it, too, they must awake. By recognizing the new "Gospel of Light," a hearer could assist the release of the particles of goodness which were trapped within himself. He could hope to progress to a higher existence in his next life; meanwhile, sin and wickedness were inevitable facts of his being which he could recognize but not correct. The Manichaean sects accepted a frank "double standard" of behaviour. Their few Elect members, male and female alike, lived a life of extreme asceticism and overachievement, sustained by the help and alms of their lesser hearers: food and alms could never be given to non-believers, as they would only imprison the particles of light and goodness in the matter they consumed. Even more than the early Christians', the Manichaeans' charity was thus turned in on their own group.[21] The hearers were "fellow travellers," not fully committed combatants. By merely assenting to the Gospel, they assured their own progress and eventual salvation while living with their sins, their concubines and moral failings and acknowledging a struggle which, as yet, they could not win. When they died the souls of the Elect went directly to the kingdom of light, those of the hearers into several reincarnations before following suit. Meanwhile, disbelievers, deaf to the new call, were destined for hell at the ending of the world; this Future Moment would follow Jesus's second coming and lead into the collapse of the entire world and a huge fire, burning for 1,468 years.

Like so many founding fathers in the history of thought, the young Mani had compounded ideas which, in isolation, were not new. Mostly, they derived from heretical Christian theorists, who had been well known in the Syriac-speaking East by the early third century: Mani was explicitly the "apostle of Christ," although he shared the heretical view that Jesus the Son of God could not have been the son of Mary or have suffered in his body on the cross.[22] In his hands, the ideas of his Christian predecessors became a powerful and coherent myth. They explained the confusion in their hearers' souls, their awareness of a strand of goodness, beset by sin and wickedness which they could recognize, but not control. They promised salvation, while trading on the great fear of punishment for all non-believers in a future existence.

They also made sense of the origins of the universe: the separation of good light from evil matter was central to their preaching and could be seen daily in the waxing and waning of the heavenly bodies, drawing and transmitting the particles of purified light from Earth.[23]

Their mission used impressive aids: books, pictures and a memorable imagery, sung in hymns and psalms. Manichaean hymn writers exploited sequences of metaphors whose imagery expressed much more than could be shown by a literal reading.[24] Their teachers could point to their own holy texts: Mani's letters, his own seven books, ranging from a "Living Gospel" to a version of the "Book of Giants," and their fictitious "Acts" of the Apostles which adapted the Christian versions and caused these fakes to rebound on the churches. Above all, their repetitive psalms and books had the power of works of art. While Christians still read their Scriptures in little books, or "codices," of no particular style or taste, the Manichaeans appealed to stately volumes whose appearance implied authority. In Central Asia, a desert oasis on the Silk Road to China has preserved for us fragments of a superb Manichaean codex of double folio size, made from thin white leather and beautifully adorned in artistic script. Such were Mani's "gorgeously bound volumes of parchment," as Augustine knew them. While orthodox Christians lacked icons and patronized mediocre objects of art, the Manichaean preachers could point to their own masterpieces. From the start, their great books were adorned by calligraphers and painters: Mani himself had an illustrated text of his complex teachings, and in the eleventh century, copies of Mani's "original" drawings were still to be seen in Ghazni, just south of the Hindu Kush Mountains. They included a diagram of the world and sketches of the Last Judgement.[25]

As a system of explanation, Mani's Gospel could appeal to intellectuals as well as to simpler men: by c. 300, in Upper Egypt, we already find a Platonist philosopher, Alexander, protesting in a book against the Manichees at the conversion of several "fellow philosophers" of his acquaintance. He knew Manichaean preachers who were "quite cultured" and "not unfamiliar with Greek myth and poetry": they compared the Greek tale of Giants with their own, and applied allegory to the Greek myths.[26] At the same time, the faith had attracted lesser people, the travellers and merchants to whom its ethics and origins were so well suited, petty artisans in the towns, the "speculators" whom Augustine later reviled: these urban people could live with religious restrictions on working the soil and culling animals and trees. The new Gospel even attracted a veteran soldier from the Roman army, who brought back to Palestine in the 270s a creed which he had acquired in the East.[27] In the later fourth century, we can see rather more of the range of Manichaean hearers from evidence in the Latin West. They included women, too, humbler urban sympathizers and also a scattering of young men and children. Sympathizers would sometimes give their children to the Elect for education: it was remembered that Mani himself had demanded and received the daughter of a noble family for whom he had worked a miraculous cure.[28]

We might wonder how this bizarre "myth" could ever appeal to people in very high society. We do not find Manichaeans among the male senatorial class in Rome, but their history is not one of "vulgar" superstition or lower-class credulity. The "Acts" of Christian Apostles were often set in a high society which was their authors' own fiction. The newly found stories of Mani and his mission are often similarly placed, but they do attach to known events in his life. In western Iran, Mani did indeed impress kings and princes. Like the Christian apologists, he wrote to his reigning monarch, the Persian King Shapur. Unlike them, he gained an audience, and royal favour as a result.[29] He was supported by noble families on the road east to the Oxus, and his great disciple, Mar Ammo, continued to foster these contacts.[30] Mani's final arrest was provoked by one such success. In the West, the scope of the Manichees' early mission has often been missed. When the Coptic papyri were first surveyed in the 1930s, they revealed the story that one of Mani's disciples had converted the "queen of Tadmor," or Palmyra, almost certainly the famous Zenobia, who ruled with such effect in the 260s. Puzzled outsiders claimed this woman variously as a Christian or Jewish sympathizer: was the Manichaeans' story correct? From the fragmentary Iranian texts, we have learned of the cure of a noble lady in Syria who saw Mani (probably) in a vision and dreamed that he had healed her by laying on his hands. In turn, this cure led to other conversions and the curing of her sister, a queen and a "wife of Caesar," perhaps Zenobia herself: it seems that the Iranian fragments agree on this point with the Coptic papyri which were lost before their full publication.[31] Mani did not only write and preach. Like a true Apostle, he healed and worked miracles. Shortly after his death, his preachers converted the powerful desert sheikh whose Arab kingdom was based at Hira. Cures and miracles retained importance in the sect's impact.[32] It was for his skills as a doctor and exorcist that Mani impressed members of the Persian court.

Like the Christians, then, the Manichees began by drawing converts from "every age, class and sex." They, too, worked wonders; they had Gospels, a Church imagery and an indomitable sense of mission. Inevitably, they trespassed on the Christians' ground, and in one sense, we can see that their arrival was opportune. They brought a revived sense of salvation and a new, updated revelation to a Church which risked going "soft." They explained the universe and human nature, the evil in Creation and the entire course of history. They were heirs to the ancient prophets and seers, from Adam to Elchesai, but they dismissed their grosser legacy. They rejected the curious doings of the Jewish patriarchs and the darker episodes in the Old Testament which Christians, too, had turned into allegories or found distasteful. Their Elect members set an extreme standard of perfectionism in their sexual habits and diet, the arena of Christian overachievement: the rest of their sect served only as "fellow travellers." While the churches came to terms with the world, there was no mean appeal in a sect with such a double standard. Those who wished to compete could do so, while the others could understand how and why they could not help sinning.

It is no surprise, then, that we find a vigorous retort to the Manichaean presence in a papyrus letter from a Christian in Egypt, writing in or before the 280s. The text is probably the work of a bishop, perhaps an "encyclical letter" on the subject composed by the bishop of Alexandria himself.[33] Its author knew his enemy, and how to abuse him. In our short surviving extract, he attacks the Manichees' denial of marriage, their supposed worship of the "sun and heavens," their "apology to bread" before eating it and their general "madness" (*mania*) which befitted followers of Mani, the "madman." He admits that a Manichaean text has come into his hands and repeats the dubious slander that the sect drank the menstrual blood of its female participants in order to maintain its immortality. No reader of this outburst can miss the threat which the Manichaeans were felt to be posing. A new Gospel, one feels, was worse than no Gospel at all: like the last pagan Emperors, Christians in the Christian Empire would insist that Manichaeans should be put to death for their beliefs.

# III

While the Manichees travelled and founded their Church, or "body," they left Christians between 250 and 300 with yet another problem to police and resist among themselves. Yet the arrival of new heretics and a new Gospel was a minor episode in the civic life of this period. Between the 250s and the early 270s, cities in the Empire were beset by barbarian raiders, plague and notorious inflation. The surviving historical evidence also undergoes a change.[1] From the 260s, the great Greek and Latin inscriptions shrink in numbers and say little, if anything, about their subjects' origins, families and local duties. No continuous literary history survives of the period, and in bulk and detail, the longest texts are written by Christians with a case to plead. After 268, almost every Greek city ceased to issue inscribed local coins. This break itself suggests a crisis: the leading citizens no longer wished to supervise new issues of their local coinage as one more civic duty. By its very sparseness, the evidence of archaeology confirms these signs of strain in the cities' upper class. In the 260s and 270s, new public building in the cities ceases to be identifiable by inscriptions and signs of new private building elude the archaeologist. Many town plans were divided by smaller, inner circuits of defensive walls, in Gaul or Lycia, and even in the centre of Athens. Elsewhere, civic amenities became part of the line of defence, the big amphitheatre in Tours or the "baths of Faustina" in Miletus.

During these dark and troubled years, "barbarian" invaders troubled many of the most famous places in the Empire: Antioch (c. 253), Ephesus (262/3), Miletus (c. 263), Caesarea in Cappadocia (260), Athens (267/8), Alexandria (270/1): in c. 272, a Roman army sacked Palmyra in Syria. Conspicuously, this list includes cities which are credited with the largest populations in the Empire, sites which had had 200,000 or more inhabitants during the mid-second century. "Diana of the Ephesians" was left with a shrine in ruins. The Heruls almost sacked Athens, and the Goths made a serious assault on Miletus. In the early 270s, a civil war which was fierce even by Alexandria's standards caused havoc in that fine city: it is probably to blame for the destruction of the tomb of Alexander the Great. What was the Eastern Empire without its Alexander? In his absence, the Persians' pressure on the cities of Syria and Mesopotamia led to a sequence of local kings and independent princedoms. Barbarian tribes in North Africa and hill bandits in Asia Minor added their usual flourish to the disorder. Cities emerged into the fourth century behind their distinctive late-antique emblems: solid, towered walls. In some places, the walls had had to be financed by funds which had once been given for games and entertainments.[2]

Of the bigger centres, only Rome and Carthage survived without attack. Even so, they were not safe. In the early 250s a plague touched them both, while infecting cities further east: in 262, plague broke out in Alexandria, too, while it was temporarily under siege. These upheavals in civic life were matched by problems in the Imperial household and the way in which the Empire ran. Between the 250s and the 280s, the Roman Imperial coinage was debased in a spectacular phase of inflation. The Emperors changed with bewildering speed, until Diocletian restored stable rule in 284 and shared it in 293, creating a college of four, the "Tetrarchy." The restoration of order brought its own burdens. The commands, recruitment and numbers of the Roman army were reorganized and a new system of taxation was adopted. By the sole reign of Constantine, in 325, people were paying more taxes to support more men in the Emperor's service, although the scale and dating of the increase are still uncertain.[3] The number of provinces and governors had also been multiplied: by Diocletian, governors were given deputies, their "vicars," and provinces were grouped into bigger regions or "dioceses." A generation later, the Christians' own organization followed this framework, giving these pagan words an unexpected history.

Art, finally, reinforces our sense of a new historical period.[4] Sculpture had always been a craft which passed from one master artist to his pupils: it was not enshrined in written texts. In the later third century, much statuary loses that old neoclassical elegance which would have charmed Canova. It becomes heavy and graceless, like the crowded lettering of contemporary inscriptions. Portrait busts take on strange proportions and sometimes show the eyes enlarged, staring outwards and upwards. These styles are not the only styles in art during the years from 240 to 300, and perhaps they seem more startling because earlier colossal statuary has not survived. Although they do not express some general "mood" of their times, they are related to their historical setting. The relation is still disputable: is their style the sign of a loss of competence, as the demanding art of classicism was no longer passed from one practitioner to the next in many settled schools? Or did it coincide with a change in taste among patrons, who chose, among other options, to be shown with this emphasis on inner tension, conveying the image of a greater resolve and a magnified spiritual life? On either view, these portraits are a reflection of contemporary historical change.

The great events of these years affected morale and, on one view, they altered men's loyalties to their gods in a single, traumatic generation. We may recall the explanation which Gregory's panegyrist gave for his hero's successes in "inland Pontus" at this period. Writing in the 380s, he cited a disastrous plague as the prime reason why so many pagans deserted their gods and became Christians. Readers of Cyprian's sermon "On Mortality," with its emphasis on God's blessing in granting an early death from sickness, may wonder if the option was always so appealing. However, modern historians have largely remained content with this type of explanation. Christians are believed to have met these disasters with the "essentials of social security" and to have offered a "community of human warmth." In the towns, Christians are said to have advanced among the "appalling economic and social conditions of the years from 250 to 284."[5] While some came to terms with worldly life, others are thought to have exported a new fervour into the countryside. Here, Christianity has been seen as profiting from social protest, which the Emperors' attempts to restore stability merely embittered by their expense. "Christianity began to give coherence and direction to those who saw in the reforms of the Tetrarchs nothing more than a system of unlimited extortion and oppression . . . to populations which were prosperous and articulate enough to feel a sense of grievance, and were prepared to break with their immediate past in order to express it . . ."

The widespread insecurity must also have left its mark on civic ceremonies for the pagan gods, but it is arguable how that mark impressed itself. Sixty years ago, the greatest scholar of late paganism had little doubt. He detected an abrupt break in dated inscriptions which honoured the pagan gods and saw it as occurring by the later 260s all over the Empire, from Rome to Egypt, Africa to Asia Minor. "This documentation must be regarded as conclusive. It is wrong to speak of gaps in the evidence. The state of the evidence demonstrates a historical fact." If not exactly dying, paganism was fading: "Even if it is improbable that the cults became entirely extinct, the absence of exactly dated inscriptions does demonstrate a decline of interest in rendering services to the gods."[6] After the 250s the living heart of paganism has been sought elsewhere, in the "Oriental cults," men's personal worship of Mithras, a stronger emphasis on the divinity of the Emperors and a growing "drift into monotheism" which flowed into the worship of the Sun god. From these points, it then seems an easier step from "late paganism" to faith in a single God. "The pagan state religion and Christianity were never closer in theology than at the time of the Great Persecution."[7]

However, we have seen the presence of an older religiousness, the beliefs beside pagan cult acts and the whole fabric of honour and appeasement. Only some twenty years before the years of crisis, Philostratus had been writing fondly of the Homeric presence of the heroes and their continuing miracles in the Greek world; the Emperor Gordian had marched East in the care of the old Athena; at Didyma, in the 250s, Macer, the musical prophet, had restored the old skills of choir song and excelled the lavish sacrifices of other members of his family. The sacred groves still stood, as did the temples and awesome statues; no curtain had fallen on the nightly screening of the gods in dreams. When inscriptions ceased at the shrines, every other type of durable inscription ceased too: their interruption is a fact about people's "epigraphic habits," but not necessarily about their religious commitment. We must ask, instead, whether years of danger and hardship would really have discredited the gods: did civic life suffer nothing but collapse? Will only a loss of belief explain the decline in the inscriptions of priests and benefactors?

A sequence of disasters would influence the pagans' most frequent argument, that the gods should be worshipped because they had always been worshipped before. It would not necessarily undermine it. If times were hard, pagans had their own explanation: the gods were showing their anger or quarrelling among themselves.[8] The remedy was not to abandon belief in them, but to try to identify and appease the aggrieved party. Apollo at Claros was no stranger to the problems of plague and barbarian invaders: he had already prescribed sacrifices to appease the angry elements and ordered statues to keep the war god, Ares, under control. In the 250s and 260s, the Goths and other invaders were blamed by contemporaries on Ares and his turbulence. Belief in this potential anger was still very lively and could explain and accommodate many years of misfortune. On this view, bad times were no argument against the old protectors in heaven: they were a proof that one or other had been neglected or honoured inadequately. Polytheism could account for all manner of calamities, citing gods who were the angry gods of myth.

Misfortunes had always been the business of oracles, and these dark years raise the question of the role of the old oracular shrines.[9] At Claros, a coin type shows the Ionian cities attending the temple for a sacrifice as late as the 250s. Inscriptions had already ceased on the site, but we cannot conclude that the oracle was silenced: its text to the Oenoandans has been dated, on one view, to the 270s, and the shrine was still considered active in the mid-fourth century. Delphi has been described as "shrouded in some obsolescent sanctity, aware only of some dream-like passing of the days," but Apollo, we now know, sent verse to Side in the 250s and gave the long verse obituary for Plotinus the philosopher in the 270s. The gap may lie in our information, not in the activities of Delphi's priesthood and prophetess.

At the great Asian temple of Didyma, we have superb evidence which combines Apollo's continuing presence with a barbarian invasion, and protection of pagans in the god's precinct.[10] In the 260s, probably in 263, a wave of Gothic tribesmen penetrated from the Black Sea as far south as Miletus. The huge temple of Didyma defied them, a potential fortress whose walls were over sixty feet high and whose entrance had been blocked by Milesian refugees. We know a little of these operations from a series of poems which were composed and inscribed c. 290 and were later transported on their stones to the subsequent Christian basilica. They have been linked to a less legible inscription which honours a certain Makarios for his part in (possibly) "repelling the strife of enemies."

The poems explain how barbarian raiders had been pressing hard, helped by the war god, Ares, but Apollo had looked after his own. When the Milesians were "worn out by pangs of thirst" and were penned into the temple by the "barbarian god of war," he commanded a spring to burst out, "bubbling with golden-flowing streams." This water was separate from the oracular spring and probably derived from a hidden vein in the temple's inner courtyard. The hero of the siege was Apollo himself, abetted by Makarios, a high-ranking pagan Asiarch who was a priest in the Imperial cult. Later, this miraculous spring was spoiled by "wicked men" and had to be protected by the governor of Asia, c. 290, to whose actions the poems were related. The spring had had healing powers, and its spoiling need only have been the work of a few vandals.

These poems have provoked some unsupportable theories: that Makarios was a Christian, that the oracular spring had dried up and ceased to function and that the events are proof of the oracle's decline.

The poems are not themselves oracular verses, but neither the spring nor Apollo had been abandoned. The god was the hero of the crisis. He had saved his suppliants by a miracle and repulsed the invaders, who were explained, within paganism, as the people of "barbarian Ares."

For centuries, hardships had brought the gods into view, in cities or at sea, on hillsides or in the bedrooms of the sick and dying. The mid-third century will have been no different. At Didyma, Apollo revealed a miracle; elsewhere, the gods must have returned in epiphanies to "stand by" the world of men; in one case, we can see how years of danger could confirm an oracle and heighten consequent piety. In the mid-third century, the city of Stratonicea in Caria sent a questioner to ask their nearby god Zeus at Panamara "whether the wicked barbarians will attack the city and its territory in the coming year." The god's answer was eminently worth preserving. "Seeing you fare so well, I cannot understand the cause of this question. For I was not sent to sack your city nor to make it a slave when it is free, nor to deprive it of any other good thing."[11] The questioners had been encouraged to put this question by their local god, Serapis. Zeus Panamara was confident in his predictions, and he was proved right. The barbarians came and went, Stratonicea survived into the fourth century only slightly the worse for wear and Zeus's fine words on his care and protection were carved on the walls of a building which has since been identified as the city's council chamber.

This enduring sense of the anger and presence of the gods was not to be refuted by events. Twenty years of hardship did not necessarily cause people to abandon their old gods; at times, dangers increased the evidence of the gods' protection. Nor could an age of disaster destroy the vigour of every city's life: the Empire was too varied and widespread and its communications were too poor. The eclipse of civic life tends to be extended over a long period, as if to include as many external disasters as possible, from the 240s to the 280s. The difficulties in so many of the biggest cities are significant, but not every region suffered equally; much of the map suffers more from obscurity than demonstrable gloom. Lesser towns in North Africa, hill settlements in the Apennines, the coastal society in Campania, the inner reaches of Pamphylia are but a few of the patches where we happen to have contrary evidence. The worst of the inflation charts a puzzling course, too: it seems to have affected North Africa later than other areas, for reasons which have not yet been explained. Its effects should not be overestimated. Barter and exchange were familiar options in Mediterranean life, most of whose centres of population supplied their basic foods from their own hinterland. The worst of the inflation's effects were probably felt in the time lag, while payments reverted to kind and people gave up the habit of everyday coinage. Differing groups suffered it differently, and not everyone will have lost on the way through. While the impact of the inflation is still unclear, a corrective to the darker theories now lies in the history of civic entertainment. In the years from 240 to 280, it is something we can know about, from coin types, papyri and inscriptions. As the evidence continues to grow, it is still open to interpretation.

We began this book in 242, with Gordian's new games in Rome for the goddess Athena and the games in the Greek cities to which he granted a new status. This pattern now extends into the early 270s, across a period when cities are supposed to have faced their darkest crisis.[12] The people of Gregory's Neocaesarea kept good company. In southwestern Asia, the cities of Caria and Pamphylia enjoyed festival games of a new status, which began in the late 250s. In Egypt, the Emperor Gallienus helped a revival of the Olympian games in Alexandria, just after one of the city's worst periods of troubles. The city of Panopolis began a new series of "Pythian" games with music and athletics in 264. Antinoöpolis started Capitoline games in 267/8. No doubt to keep up with them, Oxyrhynchus began its own Capitoline games with horse and chariot racing in 272.

This random evidence from Egypt is particularly significant, because it derives from the only province where we can look beyond the inscriptions. In Egypt, we have contemporary papyri, without which the state of the province would seem as bleak as many others'. Tribesmen raided the south; Alexandria was twice besieged; the great inflation was in evidence by the 270s. Yet these papyri have a double interest because they reflect twice over on organized civic life. During the 260s and 270s, they show the towns which were the hosts of new or improved games writing to other towns and confirming that, as victors, one or other of their citizens was automatically entitled to a pension from local funds. The awards to victors thus give a glimpse of wider civic life and of an athletic circuit which at times extends far beyond Egypt. The obligatory pensions for victors were no mean burden on a home town's funds: in the Egyptian town of Hermopolis, we have most evidence, and we happen to know of local athletes whose pensions were already costing seven and a half talents by

266/7.[13] This sum was not inconsiderable. Perhaps it was not so disastrous for the home towns when the great inflation effectively wiped out the costs of their former, ageing athletes.

These bigger and better games do not suggest an era of civic collapse or social disintegration. They drew crowds and they required advertisement and organization. In Egypt, however, there may have been special circumstances. Two of the new games were "sacred" games, a very high status which required the prior "grant" of the Emperor: their celebrations were obsequiously attached to Imperial victories and hopes for continuing rule. The nature of the "grant" is still uncertain.[14] Its frequent occurrence in the titles of such festivals suggests that it was no more than a "permission," allowing a change of status. However, certain towns in Egypt are also known to have enjoyed another "grant" in this period, a free distribution of corn to their citizens and perhaps these "grants" were material gifts. The Emperor Philip had reorganized taxes in the province by 248/9, and after some consequent troubles, "grants" from the proceeds may have been made to certain towns by way of conciliation.[15] If so, the surprising growth of new games may not have imposed such a financial burden on local donors in the hosting towns as it did on the home towns of victorious, pensionable athletes: essentially, the Emperor financed them.

Even if Imperial funds had been "granted" for part of the cost, these complex festivals reveal an underlying sense of community and a wish to show prominent vigour in pagan civic life. They simply do not fit the pictures of bleaker social historians. Perhaps we should allow for changes in the style of the games themselves, like the changes which occurred in English cricket between 1921 and 1936, from an age of "gusto and free, personal gesture" to one when "the catch-word 'safety first' became familiar, the nation's life contracted and care and want batted visibly at both ends of the wicket."[16] Here, however, we have no evidence to help us: we can only reflect that in the years in which Oxyrhynchus came to have two Christian churches and the Manichaeans began to annoy intellectuals in Upper Egypt, the same town had been enlivened with Capitoline games and all the dash and excitement of chariot racing. Even a city which had suffered barbarian attack could quickly recover and rejoin the circuit of major games and festivals. At Ancyra, invaders raided the city in c. 260, but we find no fewer than three major sets of civic games later in the decade, drawing performers back to this site astride the main roads of Asia.[17] A similar revival emerged in Syrian cities shortly after the Persians' invasions.

When this period is seen through its cities' games, the years from Gordian to the death of Gallienus do not seem typified by civic collapse: they have been seen, instead, as led by "a Delphic torch," applied to the "mobilization of Greek culture."[18] With the blessing of Apollo, cities from Asia to Egypt drew the crowds and touring star performers, bringing culture and entertainment into their lives. Actors and athletes alike had remained in high favour, and no more than a part of this revival can be attributed to finance from Emperors themselves. If a city could still organize a great athletic festival, it could also pay public honours to the gods. The games themselves were not secular occasions. They, too, honoured the gods, and we know that at Side a problem over a monument for the Pythian games inclined the parties, still, to appeal to Apollo at Delphi. Perhaps when other client cities of the oracle began Pythian games in this period, they, too, asked the god to approve the festival which was modelled so exactly on his own. Not until the Christian Empire did athletic games lose their pagan religious accompaniment.

In the papyri, again, we can see traces of continuing pagan festivals and cult, even in the most obscure and difficult decades.[19] In the late third century, we find the magistrates in Euergetis hiring actors and "Homerists," those bold performers who mimed the battle scenes from Homer; they were to "come as usual to share the holiday and festival of the birthday of Cronius, the greatest god." In 274, at Oxyrhynchus, we know of "image-bearers at the Theoreum of the Revealing gods": the images, it seems, still processed through the town with their bearers. In 282, the small village of Laura was still concerned to send a list of the children of its priests to the keepers of the district's public archives: their listing was the traditional concern of the authorities, and the children would become recruits for the priesthood in the next generation. When a local notable returned to Hermopolis from Gallienus's Rome in the 260s, the council honoured him with magnificent literary allusions and praises of "Thrice-great Hermes, our father's god, who always stands beside you."

In these public phrases and random hints of activity, the old gods were still being taken for granted. We can match them to several Latin inscriptions, preserved in the cities of North Africa. In Mauretania, just outside Setif, the worshippers of Cybele and Attis were actually spurred by a disaster to find better honours for their gods. After a fire, the ceremonial "tree-bearers" and the "faithful" (*religiosi*) restored the gods' temple in the year 288.[20] The "all-powerful holy gods" received new statues, of which Cybele's was made of silver. The shrine's colonnade was adorned with a painting which befitted the gods' dignity, while the chariot which bore Cybele's statue in her processions was given a new canopy, with woollen cords and tassels shaped like fir cones. These lavish expenses were met by a collection among the worshippers, paying as a private group.

Arguments from silence have become more questionable as more inscriptions continue to be found. No sooner had the great god Saturn been declared dead in Africa by a modern Christian scholar than a dated inscription turned up in his honour from the year 323; another then followed it, dated to 283/4, when it was put up "for the finding of faith" after a miracle had confirmed the god's warning in a dream.[21] Even when the fighting was worst and the confusion between rival Emperors most evident, there were always lulls and moments of optimism. In Syria, two fervent inscriptions praised Cronos for giving victory, perhaps in the very plain beneath their hill site, and exhorted readers to believe in the power of the god: they were cut in the year 252/3. At a hill shrine in the Lebanon, "Drusus the priest" honoured Nemesis and "Fair Occasion," "in the euphoria of the moment," it has been suggested, when the local fighting ceased.[22]

The continuing pagan ceremonies are best seen in Egypt's papyri, and they suggest that inflation did not destroy the traditional patterns of public cult in the towns. Private societies and burial foundations were more vulnerable if their endowments were fixed in money, but private societies had come and gone for many reasons throughout their history and their loss was not irreparable: some societies were endowed with land and enduring assets. Cults, meanwhile, were no more expensive than people chose to make them: the robes and temples, statues and altars existed already and only needed animals for sacrifice or wine and incense for offerings. The supply of cattle was not at risk to the inflation of the denarius: animals could be brought directly off the priests' and benefactors' farms. When we find a correspondent paying eight hundred drachmas for ten cakes of frankincense in a letter of "late third century" script, we are reminded that cult was not always a complex affair of processions, shows and blood sacrifices. Incense sufficed, and it was not expensive.[23]

When studying the new buildings, lavish festivals and oracular embassies of Antonine and Severan dignitaries, we kept returning to the role of competition between themselves and civic rivalry between their cities. The impulses of "promising" and "love of honour" and the bidding for priesthoods and office helped to explain the flowering of ceremonies and their inscribed records. In certain places, they did not cease, not even in the years of great hardship elsewhere. Latin inscriptions from cities in North Africa sometimes carry unexpected dates: at Dugga, that charming site, the reign of Gallienus in the 260s saw a robust civic renaissance. At Thala, a hill site in modern Tunisia, a leading citizen showed no foreboding in 265, when he inscribed the details of his spending in cash on a full restoration of an old, collapsed temple, his gift of victims for the gods, a banquet for the people (*populares*) and a fund for future priesthoods of the cult, which were to change annually.[24] Was this generosity a last flicker in a brief Gallienic time of peace? Even so, the response was still possible, despite the previous decades, and the sequel makes it hard to credit that such activity was only a modest postscript to a wider recession in which the majority began to desert their gods. In the eastern provinces of Africa, sixty-one inscriptions now survive, attesting new building works in cities during the 280s and 290s, much of which concerns the gods. Above all, scenes of civic life in the succeeding century show pagan processions, cults, festivals and dances persisting in many cities throughout the Empire in the mid- to late fourth century.[25] They were certainly not the result of an "artificial" pagan revival made by the local notables in the reigns of Christian Emperors. More persisted since the 250s than the gaps in our evidence once implied.

The decline in that evidence points to a broader change which was more social than religious. It is one which historians have well emphasized.[26] The durable public inscriptions of benefactors and priests had flourished in an age of competing families and civic pride. Public cults were occasions for winning esteem through generosity and, indirectly, for confirming the social order of a city through "consensual pageantry," largely financed by the notables themselves. During the third century, self-advertisement and rivalry with fellow townsmen lost some of its appeal. Some of the richer families in the cities looked to wider Roman careers instead: "love of the home town" did not die, but it lost some of its impulse, as the governors' controls on finance and social order became ever more detailed. The remaining local families in the ranks of potential councillors found themselves encumbered ever more with the duties and requirements of Imperial rule. The expense and bother of these tasks diminished the impulse to compete in "voluntary munificence" before fellow towns-men. No new "middle class" was emerging in the cities: rather, the pool of benefactors was narrowing while its obligations continued to increase. Where only one or two families found themselves left in social isolation as the richest notables in a town, there was less need for them to be seen to compete and to spend freely in asserting their own eminence. This impulse did not die out, least of all in the North African cities, but where such families were exempt, or absent in Roman service, a primary source of ceremonial was removed from civic life.

These changes were older and slower than any sudden barbarian raid or inflation. Combined with them, they are the nearest, at present, we can come to explaining the decline of the old "epigraphic habit" and the evident retrenchment in civic life. The times were not in favour of confident public gestures or permanent inscribed mem-orials, but beside their insecurity, there was this wider shift in the balance of benefaction. In the second and early third centuries, so much of the recorded giving is by local notables and holders of office. From the mid-third century on, the donors whom we find in inscrip-tions tend to be governors or Imperial officials or dignitaries who stand high in a career at Rome. Their gifts stretched back beyond the particular years of the third-century crisis, but that era marks a watershed in their importance.

At just this time, we can pick up some interesting evidence at Side, the city of Longinus in the 240s, with whose civic career this book began.[27] The city had enjoyed its lively civic festivals during the 250s, but a sudden barbarian raid had had to be repulsed in the 260s, and was followed by trouble from the nearby hill tribesmen. In the 270s, the city was still able to issue its own coins and engage in requests for honours to its civic temples. There are still signs of local munificence: after 276, a high priest and high priestess of the Imperial cult were honoured for their "love of honour," shown in their fine displays of wild beasts in the city's arena. However, the city's bigger benefactors lay elsewhere. In the 270s the "most glorious council," the "tranquil people" and the "most solemn, Emperor-loving, holy and great *gerousia*" of the city honoured the Roman Senate with a statue, perhaps for favours to their temples. When the city's harbour was dredged, c. 290, the thanks went to a Roman governor, the "founder of harbour and city." At a similar date, various quarters of the city honoured the gifts of one Bryonianus Lollianus and his wife. Bryonianus was praised as "founder and lover of his homeland," but although he claimed to be of senatorial family, this distinction may have been a recent honour: his main source of eminence was his career in Imperial service and his marriage to a very rich local bride. Bryonianus earned thanks at Side by paying for repairs to the city's great aqueduct, a gift worthy of a great millionaire in the heyday of the second century. The emphasis, however, was different. Lollianus had been exempt from civic obligations through his niche in Imperial service. His gift did not arise from the competitive pressures of a local peer group. It was of unprecedented scale, from a man whose service had otherwise been given outside his city.

At one great shrine in Asia, we do have evidence of continuing ceremonies and generosity, growing, even, in the mid-third century.[28] The prestigious cults of Zeus at Panamara and Hecate at Lagina, both in southwestern Asia Minor, had been perfect examples of the "love of honour" of the second and early third centuries. Their gods held banquets to which worshippers were invited from nearby cities: Zeus gave oracles, while "mysteries" and processions became attached to the two cults. Without inscriptions, we would think that both the cults died away in the years of crisis. At first sight, however, they grew: not until the mid-third century do we find the office of "mystagogue" at Panamara, and the peak of generosity was not reached until very much later.

In 311, the cult at Panamara blossomed through the willing munificence of a great priestly family. Sempronius Arruncius Theodotus was the son of three generations of priests at Panamara, and in 311, he joined forces with his sister to pay for thirty-four days of conspicuous extravagance. The festivals and processions at the shrines of Zeus and Hecate were celebrated with an exuberance which surpassed their previous style. During the processions, gifts were made to men and women of every age and rank in a rare show of generosity. The two donors assisted in the celebration of every "mystery" throughout the calendar year and then honoured their family's achievements in stone on the site.

These children of a great priestly family showed no disillusionment, no loss of heart in a time of hardship. A mystagogue assisted them, overseeing the pagan mysteries which were attached to the cult: he was a descendant of the other great priestly family of the place, one which had long attended to these mysteries' celebration. He was more than a local aristocrat: he was a philosopher "from the Museum," perhaps the great Museum of Alexandria in Egypt.

This combined munificence may seem to trace back to the Antonine age and its "love of honour," refuting ideas of a deep change of emphasis in spending on the gods. There was, however, another dimension. In 311, the armies of the Emperor Maximin were encamped nearby, engaged on a rout of bothersome "brigands." Maximin was promising favours to pagans who persecuted their Christians and mobilized honours for the old gods. Near Panamara, a bad harvest had caused the local olive crop to fail, but the soaring price of olive oil did not stop Theodotus and his sister from giving free oil to Maximin's entire army and from giving banquets to the councillors and citizens. There was a persecution of Christians in progress, supported by pagan philosophers, people like Panamara's mystagogue. In 311, the wish to impress the Emperor joined the intellectual mood of the times as particular motives for lavish display in honour of the gods. Only at Panamara has evidence as yet been found for munificence at such a date. Yet, beyond the pressure of the moment the same great families had persisted, unbothered by the previous years of crisis: even in a famine, they had enough stores of olives to supply an army. The underlying religiousness had not disappeared, no more than in the towns of North Africa or Egypt: it was this same shrine of Panamara which had reassured the nearby city of Stratonicea, some fifty years earlier, that its Zeus would not abandon them to the barbarians' raids. The text of the oracle still stood on the walls of the city's council chamber, proved right by subsequent events. The impulse, merely, was different, not the competitive generosity of local donors, lovingly inscribed, but a display provoked by the Emperor's proximity and the particular union of cult and philosophy at a particularly opportune time.

# IV

In the later third century, therefore, the ceremonies of the pagan gods were undergoing a relative lull. Belief, however, had not diminished with the retreat of ostentatious cult acts and the general decline in inscribed records: even later, there was to be no direct overlap between the cooling of pagan munificence and a willingness to spend and give to Christian churches instead. The gods still commanded a very large majority and the Christians had certainly not won the argument. On some points, the winners were pagans. In the early 270s the Platonist philosopher Porphyry had turned his talents to an *Against the Christians*, written in fifteen books.[1] He scored some acute points. He remarked from Paul's epistles how Peter and Paul had quarrelled: if so, he asked, how could the Apostles be infallible, as one group of their contemporaries had already thought them to be wrong? Some of the Christians' use of prophecy was bogus, and as for God's eternal punishment, the whole idea was illogical nonsense. Porphyry objected to the particularism of the Christian revelation: himself, he sought a more "universal way." His book was promptly banned when the Empire became Christian and was still being censored in the 440s.

Formerly, it seemed that Porphyry had had to admit, nonetheless, the worldwide growth of the contemporary Christian Church: it looked as if his attack was a response to the Christians' growing success.[2] Now, the quotations which seemed to support this view have been shown not to belong to the bulk of Porphyry's lost book. The question, then, of the Christians' achievement in these difficult years for pagan ceremony is more open than before.

To Eusebius, with hindsight, Christianity had enjoyed high favour in the years from 260 to 300. Connoisseurs of his history may note that he cites no details for a view which he presents as a rhetorical question. He names no Christian senators or governors and, as usual, gives no idea of the scale of increase which he assumes. The same reservations apply: the restraints on "mass conversion," the long history of Christians in high places, the familiar fact, by 300, of Christians who had had a good education. If we look ahead to the first Christian councils of Constantine's reign, we do not find Church leaders who are accustomed to a great rise in Christian numbers. They are concerned to restate the same cautious limits: there are to be no mixed marriages with pagans, if possible, and there must still be a long progress through two or three years of teaching for apprentice Christians. The need to reassert these principles may show that sometimes they were being disregarded. But it is extremely significant that the official view had not altered since c. 200. These rulings are those of a Church still caught unawares by its sudden promotion, not of one which had grown accustomed to a rising swell in the tide of conversion.

The case for Christianity's "triumph" has become confused with later evidence, with statements made after Constantine's conversion, with an untenable view of what counts as a "winning of the countryside" and with too generous a judgement of the significance of church buildings and bishoprics. In Nicomedia and Oxyrhynchus, we know that, by 300, Christians were meeting in churches which were no longer the inconspicuous house-churches of a patron's private rooms. At the start of the last persecution, in 303/4, a simple Christian in North Africa recalled witnessing the destruction of Christian "basilicas" in three modest towns. If his word was well chosen, these buildings were something more than mere house-churches, and if "basilicas" existed in these three African towns, they must have been widespread in the province: at Altava, almost certainly in 309, a newly found inscription reveals the building of a "basilica of the Lord" by a rich family of donors at the command of the bishop. It stood beside a memorial shrine to the donors' family and the local martyrs: even in the years of persecution, it seems, it was possible to construct these permanent buildings. Yet we also know that Christian buildings were easily stripped; at Nicomedia, in Asia, the church was swiftly razed to the ground. We should think in terms of modest halls, not the great Constantinian basilicas of the following decades.[3]

The burden of proof, meanwhile, lies with theories of a great Christian advance: if there was such a change in this period, where can we see it? Evidence of any sort is not abundant, but evidence for the Christians' growing presence is very tenuous indeed. In Phrygia, we hear of one town which had gone completely Christian before Constantine's reign, but it was probably exceptional.[4] In certain towns of Phrygia, we also know of Christians who had been holding office and serving on the councils in the mid-third century; in particular areas, Phrygia also gives us our greatest cluster of early Christian epitaphs. At least twenty were put up in the years between 240 and 300, on the latest collection of the evidence: no other province has left anything comparable and this scatter of Christian inscriptions is a further reason for thinking that the Christian presence in parts of Phrygia was unusually strong.[5] Even so, it did not extend to every Phrygian town or region. In 324/5, the little Phrygian settlement at Orcistus petitioned Constantine, referring to its totally Christian population and asking to be returned to its former status. It had lost its prominence, it said, because of the aggression of a neighbouring "city," presumably a pagan community. Religion could divide one town from another and fire an existing civic rivalry: as in Phrygia, so in Syria we find the Christian city of Edessa adjoining the stubbornly pagan Harran. Fully Christian communities were still very scarce: it is most revealing that Eusebius knew of only three little townships which were Christian in the entire Holy Land when compiling a book on its place names as late as 324/5.[6]

In North Africa, we can glimpse Christianity's public prominence from a different source, the evidence which rival Christians submitted to Roman officials and which stretched back fifteen years or more, to elections made in 303/4. At Cirta, they said, a "false" bishop had been elected by a crowd of "rustics" and "gladiators" (or quarry workers): "there were also prostitutes present . . ." Meanwhile, the "citizens," they said, had been locked into the martyrs' cemetery, while the "people of God" had been shut into a building called the "larger house." The truth of these stories is irrecoverable, but the implication is that an unsuitable bishop had been elected with the help of the riffraff of the town, people who were neither respectable "citizens" nor Christian members of the "people of God."[7] It is extremely interesting that a bishop's election could plausibly be presented as a major event in civic life; bribes, however, are said to have accompanied it, and money could create an interest in any section of the population. It is even more interesting that the "people of God," the laity, could be said to have been shut into one "larger house." False bishops in Cirta could rent a crowd, but it is quite clear that Christian believers were only a small minority in the place as a whole. At Carthage, the implications are similar: Christian elections could be turbulent, but believing Christians were not dominant.

In the Western Empire and the European provinces, evidence of all types is scarce, and perhaps we can only say that Christians have left no proof of a great and growing presence. It is significant that some important new beginnings are only attested later. In one case, we can see the beginnings of a new bishopric shortly before Constantine, and the town concerned is so prominent and accessible that it must make us wonder about the presence of Christians farther north. On the Dalmatian coast, the city of Salona (Split) had no bishop until c. 304/5, when a Christian from the Near East happened to migrate and set up a church there: with this Eastern migration, we soon find Manichees, dogging Christians who had come from their homeland.[8] Farther north and west, we can use a different argument. These areas were major seats of recruitment for the army, but it is relatively clear from Constantine's reign and its sequel that the random sample of the soldiery remained overwhelmingly pagan, although many Christians would have had no scruples about serving in their ranks.

What of the biggest cities, where life, one suspects, was most vulnerable to economic change and external forces? In one such city, Porphyry complained, it was no wonder that sickness had been so troublesome for so many years: the "presence" of the gods had been interrupted and Asclepius and the others had not been able to visit since Jesus was being honoured.[9] In Rome and Alexandria, we have hints of the Christians' various communities, although we do not know if either was in Porphyry's mind. In Rome, forty-six priests had been serving the city's Christians in 251: in Alexandria, the Christians are said to have been divided among at least ten separate churches by 310. Further arguments have been based on the names and placing of subsequent church properties in each city, but it is now clear that they cannot be pressed with confidence.[10] In Rome, the later third century does see an increase in the number of "catacombs," or burial chambers, which Christians began to use, often taking them over from former pagan users; in Alexandria, archaeology offers no support, and we do not even know if the local churches which commemorate third-century bishops' names were founded before 300. In both cities, it is plain that the upper class had remained firmly pagan: there was no question of a socially fashionable drift to Christianity which Constantine merely followed.[11]

These arguments from silence may seem fragile in a period when so little is known about anything. In one province, however, we can apply some control to it. In Egypt, again, we have the evidence of papyri, and if Christianity was a triumphing presence in the years between 260 and 300, we might expect to find it reflected in this small but random sample of evidence.[12] We continue to find copies of Christian texts and Gospels in this period, and there is support for the hints in other evidence that Christians were now preaching in Coptic. This habit did indeed enlarge their potential audience. We also have a modest number of letters, written between Christians themselves, of which the most revealing is a letter, dated c. 300, in which a Christian, probably a church official, encourages a "son" to donate land "to the place" "according to the ancient custom." The "place" is presumably a church and the "custom" points to an established pattern of gift or bequest by propertied Christians. Other texts and letters add to our evidence for Christians of a certain property and culture, but not on any unusual scale.

When we look for allusions to Christians in texts with a secular, non-Christian context, the harvest is very thin indeed.[13] By c. 300.

Oxyrhynchus had two churches whose presence served to identify their streets: it also had twelve pagan temples and a synagogue. It is hard to be sure what phrases establish a Christian author or a Christian presence in the papyri, but on a tight definition, there is next to nothing before 300 which is not related to problems of persecution. It is no great surprise to find two Christian families liable to serve on Oxyrhynchus's council. It is pleasant, but not too illuminating, to have two wills in which Christians (probably) pay a special tribute to the good nature of their wives. Perhaps new discoveries will broaden the picture, but the contrast with the pattern after Constantine's conversion will remain very marked. Then, Christians and their business intrude much more evidently into our evidence; between 260 and 310, many fewer papyri survive, but there is not a hint of any Christian "triumph" in what evidence we have.

This low profile is supported by the pattern of individuals' names. New discoveries and better collections of the evidence will enlarge our understanding, but at present, a negative point does emerge from the papyri.[14] As yet, we can trace very few examples before c. 300 of the personal names which Christians in Egypt later preferred to adopt or bestow on their children. These names are not unknown in our other Christian evidence before Constantine, and by the mid-fourth century the papyri suggest a very different pattern. From c. 340 onwards, references to Christians, churches and Christian authorities multiply, as do the numbers of favoured Christian names. On this evidence, the great expansion of Christianity belongs where we would expect it, after Constantine's victories, not before. Nor can we argue safely from the number of known Christian bishops. In 325, we know of fifty-one bishoprics in Egypt, but we do not know how many had existed there c. 300. Between these dates, the last, "great" persecution had intervened, a force which tended to spread Christian leaders into new hiding places. Rigorist Christians went into schism during this period and withdrew from their fellow Christians to form new Churches of their own. Of the fifty-one bishoprics in the year 325, it is suggestive that fifteen are only known otherwise as seats of the new, schismatic Church[15]: Christians split and scattered, but their total numbers did not therefore advance.

Some advance, no doubt, there was, perhaps especially in the bigger cities where the troubles had made most impact, but we should not exaggerate its scale. The social effects of the difficult years from c. 250 to c. 280 and the subsequent age of reform were generally to exacerbate the gap between the very rich and the men of modest property, the propertied classes and the rest. The religious appeal of Christianity was still intact, and this social climate favoured it more than ever. In public, some Christians did indeed practise charity and show a rare selflessness: in the 250s, it was the Christian Church, not the pagan cities, who made hasty collections to ransom their members from barbarian captors: in 262, during the plague in Alexandria, they tended their own sufferers, while the pagans were said to abandon their sick at the first sign of disease; during the siege of the same year, the two Christian leaders contrived to save many old and weak people, Christians first, then pagans, too, later. During the great famine of 311/2, the richer pagan donors were said to have given abundantly, but then hardened their hearts for fear that they would become beggars too. The Christians, however, would offer the last rites to the dying and bury them and distribute bread to all others who were suffering from hunger.[16] This good example cannot have been wasted, although the Christians in Gregory's territory remind us that Christian charity was not universal. Nor should we accept everything the Christians imply about the heartlessness of pagan men in the street. In the 260s, we have the sudden evidence of schemes to distribute free grain, working in certain towns in Egypt, a "grant" from the Emperor: it is, however, very telling that these distributions were for a fixed number of citizens only, evidently people of property and modest wealth.[17] The Christians, too, gave charity only to their own members, but they directed it first and foremost to the poor. There were limits, however, to this fine ideal. Like pagan foundations, Christian giving was also exposed to the problems of inflation as soon as it went beyond sympathy and burial. The churches in the bigger cities could not possibly cope with charity for the mass of unsupported residents. It took the enormous favours and endowments of Constantine to enable Christians to support the poor on a large scale; in Asia Minor, it also required the conversion of the large local landowners. Neither source of help was active before 312.

One final hint of a Christian "triumph" is less cogent than it appears. In winter 312, the pagan Maximin wrote a letter for his officials in which, under pressure, he revoked persecution of Christians in the East. In its Greek version, it told how his predecessors had had to act against the churches some ten years previously, seeing that "almost everyone" was deserting the worship of the gods.[18] This flourish of Imperial rhetoric is not evidence that Christianity had already won: "insincerity and plain mendacity shine through the resplendent phrases,"[19] and the Latin original of the text may have said "very many," not "almost everyone." By seeing events through Christian eyes, we risk overestimating the dominance of religious issues in this turbulent period. It may seem at times as if the starting or ending of persecution was a major instrument of political favour, but to many non-Christians these decisions may not have been so momentous: on the whole, they had left persecution recently to officials, without much enthusiasm. The Christians were not so numerous that their support had to be courted. In the total population of the Empire they were only a small minority, significant in some cities, most inconspicuous in others. Since 250, their numbers had probably advanced, helped somewhat by the general hardships of the age: the advance is significant against the rate of growth of any other cult, but it shows no sign of triumph or even predominance. We may be dealing with only 4 or 5 percent of the population. A cautious view of the balance between pagans and Christians helps to keep the course of the persecution in perspective. It also helps to explain why it started yet again.

In the origins of the last, "great" persecution, we can isolate three elements: the Emperors' recent military success; the moral and religious tone of their edicts and public piety; the support of Greek intellectuals, and thus of their echo, Apollo himself.[20] We cannot be sure of the balance among these elements, or of the relative roles of the two Emperors, Diocletian and Galerius. Our only evidence derives from Christian contemporaries or converts who wrote with hindsight. We cannot, then, know whether the views of the intellectuals followed, or helped to create, the Emperors' concern. But we can see similarities between this persecution and its predecessor, which had begun in 257.

During the intervening years, the Emperors' public piety had not altered. In the 260s, a new note had appeared on the coinage under Gallienus: its types showed the Emperor's investiture by a god.[21] This image presumably developed as a response to the many rivals and pretenders. However, it was not taken further by the Tetrarchy of four rulers when they gathered to restore the Empire in 293. The panegyrics which were spoken in their honour laid no special emphasis on the Emperors' own "divinity."[22] Like their poets and artists, they dwelt on their special protection by old Olympian gods, by Jupiter and Hercules, Mars and Apollo. This type of protection was

familiar to all Mediterranean men, who knew how the gods "held
their hand above" those whom they favoured: it was as old as the
Homeric world and the image of kingship in Greek thought. By their
governors and publicists, the Emperors were seen as restoring the
"golden times" of the long-lost "Golden Age": in Rome, a double
portrait bust shows Diocletian on one side, the figure (probably) of
Saturn on the other, god of that golden past.[23] These "restoring"
Emperors did not promote cult of themselves in any new form. Nor
did they favour the worship of Mithras unduly or the "Oriental" gods
before all others: the old belief that they did was derived from a single
Latin inscription of no general significance.[24]

In the 270s, the cult of a new Sun god had been promoted in Rome
by the Emperor Aurelian, but it did not exclude or undermine
worship of other gods too. In the Emperors' coin types and panegyrics, an imagery of the Sun is evident, but this "solar theology"
had no implications for their preferred type of worship: it expressed
the power of a supreme god or ruler and was not a new intellectual
creation of the period from 270 to 300.[25] Sanctioned by Plato, it had
older roots in art and philosophy, in the titles of Apollo and the
honours of earlier Emperors. The image of the Sun was only one
among the many other gods which appeared on these Emperors'
coins. When we do meet a ruler who favoured the Sun god, Constantine's father, Constantius, he did not impose his favour to the exclusion
of other gods. It is quite untrue that if his son had not turned to
Christianity, the Mediterranean world would have drifted into a
common "Sun worship." It is one measure of the difference between
the pagan Emperors and their Christian successors that the former
never had to devise and promote a deliberate religious policy for all
their subjects.

In the 280s, the Emperors were drawn yet again down the military
roads to the East, and as a convenience, they began to develop an
Eastern city as the seat of their moving court. They chose Nicomedia
in northwestern Asia Minor, a Bithynian city which praised Diocletian as its "second founder."[26] In this Greek-speaking milieu, they
were exposed to the writings, representations and dinner discussions
of Greek intellectuals. From Christian sources, we know especially of
three, who were reviled as the "authors" of persecution. Hierocles, an
important governor, was later to write a book exalting the pagans'
Apollonius as the superior of Christ; an unnamed philosopher used to
dine with the Emperors and ask them to persecute; the third was

Porphyry himself, who was known for his work *Against the Christians*.

In 260, persecution had ended after the Emperor Valerian's capture in Persia; forty years later, it restarted after a crushing victory over the Persian king. Should we see the Emperors as waiting until their credit stood high in the East before they risked another assault on the Church? Such a view overestimates the strength of the Christians and the unpopularity of the decision: Christians never fought back, and no pagans would go to war on their behalf. The writings and requests of the Greek intellectuals were not indications of a new fear: back in the 120s, provincial leaders in Asia had already petitioned Hadrian for sterner action against the Christians.[27] Rather, the persecution was born from success. Victory gave a new force to the ideals of Roman discipline and Roman god-given glory. At Damascus in May 295, Diocletian referred in an edict to the "discipline of our times," the past growth of Roman power "by the favour of the gods" and the union of law, morals and religion which was to be observed with "eternal respect." His edict concerned a social problem, the acceptable degrees of "kindred and affinity": his recent travels in the Near East had alerted him to a moral outrage, the incestuous marriages of some of his ordinary subjects.[28]

This language did not bode well for the Christians, and four years later, in 299, it was reflected in the omens, those mirrors of the mood of their observers. At a sacrifice, the diviners blamed the state of the sacrifices' entrails on people in the Emperor's company who had signed themselves with the cross. Christians were ordered to be purged from the army, although inscriptions continue to show us some much-travelled Christian officers in this period and one or two recent incidents had exposed other Christians' unwillingness to serve.

New datings from the papyri make it almost certain that this purge of the army was followed some three years later by an edict of ominous and significant tone.[29] It was probably in March 302 that the Emperor wrote from Alexandria of "the greatest crime," to abandon "what has been decided and fixed by the ancients." The edict was answering the inquiries of the governor of Africa, who had come into contact with a new problem, the Manichees: he had investigated the sect and knew of its books and double structure. Were they to be treated like Christians or not? The Emperor believed they were even worse: "the Manichees oppose what was once conceded to us by the gods" but they were also "poisonous" intruders from the enemy, Persia. They were to be punished by the death penalty. The Manichees, it has been suggested, may have provoked the Emperors to a general move against the Church. The sequence, now, looks different. The preliminary purge of Christians had been in progress since 299, and subsequently Manichees in Africa had been brought to the governor's attention: perhaps Christians had denounced them or perhaps they had been mistaken for orthodox Christians themselves. They did not bring persecution on the Christians: rather, the purge of the Christians brought the death penalty on them.

This rising note of moral and religious didacticism in the Emperors' edicts travelled north from Alexandria and in summer 302 came to rest at a site where it could only expect encouragement. It was then that the Emperors consulted Apollo at Didyma. We know the sequel only from a young officer in the ranks, the future Emperor Constantine, who recalled, some twenty-three years later, how the voice of the "god" had sounded from a "vast cavern" and complained that his ability to give oracles was hindered by the "just upon earth."[30] This ambiguous comment was understood as a reference to the Christians. We would dearly like to know more about this climax in oracular history, what question was submitted, how far the shrine had been revived for the purpose, whether its business had flourished recently and, above all, who was "Apollo" for this particular year. Philosophers were still serving as prophets of the god, and one of them was soon to suffer for his statements at Didyma: perhaps he was the very man who answered for the god to the Emperors. Among the clamour of the Greek intellectuals, there is no surprise that Apollo had picked up their vibrations. Perhaps his prophet had dined at Nicomedia; perhaps he had read Porphyry's book. In traditional style, his answer was inscribed on the site, though the surviving stone is too fragmentary for any certainty of interpretation. The gods agreed with the Emperors' growing inclination. On February 23, 303, the day of an antique Roman festival, the Emperors' first edict of persecution was posted at Nicomedia. The churches were to be destroyed, the Scriptures were to be burned and all services were banned. Christians lost their valuable privileges of rank and were excluded from all courts of law: in a matter of hours, the Christian building in Nicomedia was razed to the ground.

# V

The consequent "Great Persecution" became blurred, with hindsight, into a continuous process of martyrdom, ended only by the victories of Constantine and his colleague ten years later. This is not the place to follow its vicissitudes in any detail, or to relate them to the changes in the college of the four "co-Emperors" whose balance was upset between 306 and 312. Persecution came and went in varying bursts of ferocity. At the very start, a fire in the Imperial palace was unjustly blamed on the Christians in Nicomedia and led to a string of martyr-doms among Christians in the Imperial household. The first eight months were severe, leading up to an edict for the arrest of Church leaders. Then, in November, they were released: in spring 304, another edict commanded sacrifice to the gods by all the inhabitants of the East. Once again, its enforcement was haphazard in the absence of accurate registers. In the West, there is no solid evidence that this edict was ever applied outside Africa, except, perhaps, by a few governors at their own discretion. This silence greatly reduces the scope of persecution. Instead, Western Christians were asked to surrender their Scriptures and were deprived of their meeting places. Nowhere were they martyred systematically: "the so-called 'Great Persecution' has been exaggerated in Christian tradition to an extent which even Gibbon did not fully appreciate."[1]

In the East, we know much more about individual governors and martyrs because Eusebius wrote a pamphlet on them, especially on those whom he had known personally in Palestine. The East was also subjected to the Caesar Maximin, the ruler who did most to enforce persecution under his authority. From May 305 to summer 308, from autumn 308 to April 311, and finally from December 311 to winter 312, persecution was at its most severe in his provinces. Maximin was the one ruler who devised new and serious techniques against Christian suspects. In autumn 308, goods on sale in the markets were ordered to be sprinkled with libations or blood from pagan offerings. Checks on Christians were carried out at the city gate and even in the public baths. In the final phase, copies of scandalous "Acts of Pilate" were circulated to rouse hatred of Christ; prostitutes were tortured to confess to Christian debaucheries, while bishops were directed to a new, invigorating life as keepers of the Imperial camels or stable boys for the Imperial horses. Maximin also planned to organize pagan cult by appointing high priests in each province who were to wear white robes, the usual garb of holiness, and supervise daily worship of the gods.[2] He offered tax exemptions to cities which signified their willingness to persecute the Christians in their midst.

We cannot estimate the number of Christians who died in these proceedings, but the impact of a persecution was always greater than the numbers executed or sentenced to work in the mines. There were cases of conspicuous heroism, but we must also look to the vast majority, to the mood of the Emperors' pagan subjects, the devices of the Christian survivors and the reactions of two particular groups, Christian perfectionists and Christian authors, in the years while persecution was in force.

Like Valerian in 257/8, the Emperors were imposing persecution from above for reasons which originated within their own entourage. From our few authentic sources, we do not see their subject cities engaging on a prompt witch-hunt and hounding down their Christian neighbours. In one North African town, the magistrate was prepared to receive any old books from the bishop as if they were his Scriptures.[3] Elsewhere, we see civic leaders enforcing an order firmly, but with no particular fervour. As usual, all authorities were open to bribery, while some pagans were willing to sacrifice on a Christian's behalf. There was much connivance and profiteering, the primary effects of an Imperial edict. Although Eusebius exalted known cases of heroism in which several martyrs brought death on themselves by their own acts of provocation, most fellow Christians, as always, responded less dramatically. In the Great Persecution, the evidence for lapsing continues to increase, not least among clerics and bishops.[4] It is capped by the rules for penance and readmission of the lapsed which Peter, bishop of Alexandria, issued in 306.

His canonical letter makes Cyprian's early rigorist phase seem a distant eccentricity.[5] Three or four years' penance now sufficed to reconcile the grossest lapsers, if they had a conscience; reconciliation was no longer to be delayed till the moment of death. Provocative martyrs received a cool and guarded comment, whereas guile was respected: "against those who gave money that they might be undisturbed by trouble, no accusation can be brought." There can have been few more popular rulings in the history of the early Church. The bishop was aware that not all Christians were shameless: priests who had lapsed were not to be punished too severely for "fear that they may hasten their death by violence." Others had allowed their very hands to be burnt, rather than offer incense in the flames. But Peter was also a realist: Christians who had bought their safety had suffered a loss of property and were forgiven entirely, while those who had sent slaves or pagans to sacrifice on their behalf and written false documents, their particular art, were not too culpable. In a papyrus letter, we can see how one such Christian in Egypt had coped with the crisis by using his own family.[6] The first edict had obliged all litigants to sacrifice before pleading in court, but a Christian, Copres, writes to tell his sister how he had asked their brother, presumably a pagan, to go and sacrifice on his behalf before pursuing a lawsuit about their family property.

The pagans' response was also mixed. We have pagan petitions from the final phase, when Maximin was encouraging persecution in the East in 311/12. In a local copy, we can read the official complaint of the provincials of Lycia and Pamphylia, how they deplored the "detestable pursuits of the atheists" and stressed their "worship of the gods on behalf of your eternal majesty." In reply, Maximin promised to grant whatever the people asked for, perhaps, in this case, an exemption of the urban population from the poll tax. At Tyre, copies of his eloquent answer appealed to the natural order of the world, the gods' concern for the waving fields of corn and their pleasure at the punishment of wicked "atheist" error. These replies were locally engraved and distributed throughout the provinces which asked for them.[7]

Christians, however, alleged that these petitions had been solicited by Maximin himself. As his promise of favours became known, city leaders would indeed be quick to send letters: envoys from Nicomedia arrived in the time-honoured manner, with the "presence" of their gods' statues to assist their case.[8] These texts and embassies relied on the concern of a few educated pagans, zealots, perhaps, for the gods whom they honoured as priests and philosophers. In the cities as a whole, we should allow for a range of inconsistent attitudes: keenness among some members of the educated classes, apathy among others and uncertainty among most of the crowds. It was not that pagan cult was declining and that the persecution was a vain attempt at "revival." Pagan cults and gods were still widely taken for granted, but the change lay, rather, in their worshippers' attitudes to Christians. It was these attitudes the Emperors were trying to revive, not always successfully. By 300, Christians had been around for many years. The livelier stories of vice and crime were now known to be false, and in recent crises, some of their church memberships had really been most helpful and sympathetic. People did not have to be deserting their own gods, or converting to the Christians', to feel differently about yet another Christian inquisition. So far as they could see, the Christian leaders were harmless, educated people. Only if the gods showed anger in the form of a famine or earthquake might they begin to take sides against the "atheists" in their midst. In the final phase, feeling was indeed exacerbated by a severe famine in the East, yet Christians also made a good showing in some of the cities by their care for the victims, pagan and Christian alike.[9] It was harder, now, for a city to feel that every one of these people should be killed if they would not honour the gods.

The range of pagan responses is beautifully illustrated in three accounts of martyrdom, the postscripts to all we have seen in the narratives of the martyrs' followers and "best friends." At Ancyra, seven Christian virgins, probably Montanists, are said to have been stripped naked and conducted on a cart through the town on a day of festival: they were to be drowned in the nearby lake, scene of the ceremonial washing of a statue of a pagan goddess.[10] The brave Christian Theodotus, sheltering in the shop of a friend, is then said to have set out to recover their bodies, wishing to add their relics to those which he had previously rescued from a river and to house them safely in his chosen spot for a chapel. The effort caused Theodotus to give himself up of his own accord for trial and execution. His own body is then said to have escaped its pagan guards; they became drunk on wine from a passing wagon driven by the Christian priest of nearby Malos. While they snored, Theodotus's corpse travelled safely by this wine cart to his chapel's designated site; it lay in it thereafter, known to the story's narrator, Nilus, who claims to have been close to Theodotus, to have witnessed and researched the events and to have accompanied the martyr's last imprisonment.

This lively and detailed story is set in 311/12, the years of Maximin's last persecution, and its persons and local geography have recently been vindicated by finds of inscriptions. It is, however, more than doubtful whether Nilus was telling the truth, rather than a story which honoured Theodotus's martyr chapel. He was probably writing c. 360, perhaps in the reign of the pagan Emperor Julian, when Christians again feared persecution: the tale of the origin of Theodotus's relics is too neat to be easily credited. However, it is striking that the story still did justice to a range of pagan responses, the incompetence of the guards of Theodotus's body, the curiosity of a festival crowd, who saw seven naked virgins passing out of the city on a cart, and the indignation of Theodotus's governor, faced with a martyr who had brought about his death by giving himself up.

The two other stories are set at Edessa, that stronghold of good Christian fictions, but they deserve considerable respect.[11] They tell of the martyrdoms of two simple Christians and, somewhat later, a third, the deacon Habbib. The earlier of the two stories has the relative restraint, the legal accuracy and inner conviction of the best martyrs' memoirs: the dates with which it begins pose a problem, but they may have been added by a later hand. Shmona and Gurya, the story tells, were denounced to the governor for preaching Christianity in the villages outside Edessa. They resisted his every argument and threat and after several days' imprisonment in the "dark hole" were taken and tried by torchlight. They were duly sentenced to death. The problem was how and when to kill them: they, too, were despatched on a cart at cockcrow to be killed outside the town, for fear of the townsfolk who would protest and cause trouble. When the soldiers returned from a hill outside Edessa, crowds are said to have confronted them, asking, "Where have you carried off the confessors?" On discovering the truth, they poured out to find their bodies, "gathering the very dust on which their blood had been spattered."

Habbib's story is not dissimilar: when he goes voluntarily to offer himself up for death, the pagan soldier of the guard tells him to disappear and hide away at once in safety. When he does finally win the death sentence, "even some of the Jews and pagans took part in shrouding and burying his body with the Christian brethren."[12] Like the confessors, he had been active outside the city of Edessa: he was popular and he brought about his own death, not least because his family were being held hostage.

Both these stories purport to be told by a witness, Theophilus, who wrote the first only "five days" after the event and the second, too, from his own observation and researches. The example of the martyrs, he claimed, had made him become a Christian: "may the dust of the martyrs' feet, which I received as I ran after them as they went to be crowned, win me pardon for having denied Christ . . ."[13] Although Theophilus is at pains to stress the records of the martyrs' trials, which the notaries and officials had kept and published, his dialogues between the Christians and their captors are too florid to be entirely credible. Like Theodotus's, these three martyrs' relics were later revered at a shrine beside Edessa: the final version of their story may owe its publication to the existence of this memorial. Yet the setting of their story does carry conviction and, like Theodotus's, the narratives have accurate local colour.[14] Perhaps Theophilus did indeed witness the events which he later embellished with dialogues.[15] It is hard to be sure, but the same point emerges in both texts: even if the story is fiction, it no longer shows pagans baying for Christians' blood. Edessa's townsfolk were so sympathetic to the victims that they had to be killed in secret, and then their bodies became the concern of large crowds. The tone is very different from the days of the Lyons martyrs or Polycarp's death in Smyrna. The bulk of the townsfolk are more resentful of soldiers and officials than of Christians in their midst.

The history of persecution ends, in this light, as a history of failure:[16] its most positive consequence lies elsewhere, in the history of the Christian Church. Not only did it create the enduring cult of martyrs and intercessors: it split the churches into schisms, as "true" uncompromised brethren refused to serve leaders from the "false" compromised majority. It also scattered the believers more widely. Once again, the stories at Ancyra and Edessa show the effect of persecution in scattering Christians outside a town into the safer and easier settings of a rural village. It is against this background that we can best appreciate a novel companion of these persecuting years. While Christians in the East feared inquiry and trial in their cities, we learn in Egypt of the first Christian solitaries, withdrawing into the desert to live the perfect hermit's life. By 320, they began to be joined by the first monastic communities, places which grew rapidly to house several thousand souls behind their walls. The impulse began before the East was under Christian rule.[17]

In the view of subsequent historians and biographers, the decisive move to a solitary life was made by Antony, an illiterate Coptic Christian who decided in the year 305 to leave his retreat and go into the desert, encouraging others to follow suit. In 313, he retreated yet further: by 320, communities of monks were forming round Pachomius, a fellow Egyptian who had been press-ganged into the Roman army and had converted to Christianity when he saw the Christians' care and charity in times of adversity.[18] Before long, a new word, *monachos* (monk), occurs as a casual fact of life in a pagan papyrus. In June 324, a farmer, Isidore, writes to a government official and complains of an incident of assault, arising from a stray cow which had grazed his land.[19] Its owners, he said, would have killed him had he not been rescued by "Antoninus the deacon and Isaac the monk" on their way up to the village of Karanis. "Isaac the monk" is cited as a respectable figure who needs no further explanation to a pagan.

Antony's own first retreat lay near to the village where Isaac was sighted, and Antony himself was not isolated from other churchmen: Isaac was possibly one of his followers, coming up to the nearby community in the company of a "deacon," perhaps a deacon in a monastic group. By the 340s, other papyri do reveal more moderate Christian perfectionists, the *apotaktikoi*, people who had "signed off" but continued to live in villages and townships, controlling property and maintaining contact with Church officials. The urge to retreat soon took different forms, but the solitary style of Antony's life still lies at the head of their development.

These types of the celibate life were not entirely new: in the Syriac-speaking regions, Christians were already familiar as wandering "sons of the covenant," while we have seen how the ideal of a virginal life posed social and practical problems for its female devotees. It was best pursued in groups in a household, supported by the richer members: in the early fourth century, a fictional dialogue by Methodius, a bishop in Lycia, presupposes this very setting, a household company of virgins.[20] Perfectionism, we have also seen, was a constant theme in Christian experience, and in Egypt it had lost none of its urgency. The years of the Great Persecution also saw the first teachings of the heretical Arius, whose theology did not only extend to an abstract view of Christ's nature. It also reaffirmed man's capacity for salvation and perfectibility: "indeed we can become sons of God, like Christ," so Arius is said to have taught; "it is written, 'I fathered and raised up sons . . .'"[21]

This teaching reminded its hearers of their own potential, but it did not encourage them to realize it in an ethic of overachievement. Here, the example of the Manichees is more relevant.[22] Their Elect lived a life as austere and celibate as any Christian monk's and, by c. 300, they were a well-recognized presence in Egypt's Christian centres. Contacts between perfectionist *monachoi* and Manichees were known to be quite common in early-fourth-century Egypt; the fathers of the early monasteries imposed a food test to expel Manichaean sympathizers, knowing that they could not eat meat. In the newly found codex, Mani's father is said to have served the Jewish Christian Baptists' sect as a "house master," a title which was adopted by the Manichaeans too. Conspicuously, the same term, "house master," was to be used in the community life of the earliest Christian monastic groups. Direct derivation, however, of the monastic impulse from a hated rival heresy is quite implausible. At most, it was a goad, provoking yet more competitive effort.

A more immediate goad lay in the tensions of Christian life itself. The age of the first Christian solitaries was not an age of static social and economic life.[23] When Antony withdrew to the desert, the Egyptian villages were subject to two particular changes: they had been brought more directly under the authority of distant state officials and they were living through changes in their own pattern of landownership. In registers of local property, the absentee landlords and the state-owned land of an earlier age disappear in the early fourth century: more of the land seems to be passing to local proprietors. This increased "privatization" made the villages more self-contained, while giving scope to the ambitious and artful small landowner. The first monks of known social origin were not poor and destitute: rather, their withdrawal has been connected with the increased tensions of secular village life. In Christian eyes, however, the impulse was more immediate, not the tensions in worldly society, but the tensions among Christians themselves. The first Christian hermits retreated to the desert in order to escape from their fellow Christians.

Any reader of the Christian councils of the early fourth century can well understand this reaction; a life of overachievement could no longer be realized in the compromised company of an ordinary Christian church. In the later third century, the gap between the perfectionist few and the sinful majority had certainly not narrowed. Then, most brusquely, the Great Persecution exacerbated it. While Christians lapsed or gave bribes and told convenient lies, how could a perfectionist continue in their company? These disputes split the churches in schisms, a further distraction for those who sought the perfect life. Persecution multiplied the tensions among Christian "brothers": it also showed a way out of the dilemma.

In the year of Decius's edict, we first hear of Christians who had fled from the troubles and retired into the hills and deserts of Egypt and the Near East. Many were killed there by marauding Saracens, but Antony's first "master" is said to have been an elderly hermit surviving from that year. In the Great Persecution, the hills and countryside are attested as refuges all over the Mediterranean, in North Africa and Greece and in the stories set at Ancyra and Edessa.[24] In Egypt, the desert was a close and familiar retreat. By withdrawing into it, Christian perfectionists escaped the trials and compromises of the village: when Christian life was torn apart by recriminations in the aftermath, they could escape this bother too. As migrants, they joined the persistent circulation of people in Egyptian life: smallholders who were travelling between fractions of their families' inherited property, wanderers or vagrants evading tax. In this setting, Christians in flight were easily overlooked.

These developments were to mark all future Christian history, and in more than one way, persecution helped to bring them about. The first desert fathers cannot be identified with a type of follower whom they later attracted: the poor, the fugitives and the slaves whom they were accused of harbouring. The aim of the first "holy men" was to be perfect, to live a life in the "rank of angels," as the Gospels seemed to define it. Events conspired to support their aim: within a few years, the supreme achievement of martyrdom was to be withdrawn in the Christian Empire, while the life of a bishop was to become ever more of a tension between the chores of administration and accountability to God. The monastic life became the main avenue to perfection; at the same time, a far from perfect Christian majority had as great a need as ever for intercessors and agents of blessing and forgiveness.[25] The ending of persecution removed the confessor, the former bearer of the Spirit who could bless and forgive their sins. Instead, Christians looked to the new perfectionists, the heroes of the desert who could bless and curse and offer prayers in the continuing shadow of the Last Judgement. Not every holy man courted this function, nor did the function account for these people's rise. Yet as persecution ceased, the legacy of martyr and even confessor passed to these new perfectionists in the Christian world.

In an expressive Coptic legend, two Christians are said to have withdrawn from their village during the Great Persecution and found a hermit building a church in the desert.[26] After they had helped him finish, they decided to return and fetch their local bishop to dedicate the building. They were too late: on the road back to the village, they met their bishop on the run, retreating from the troubles. For those who gave bribes or prudently took flight, the Great Persecution begins to seem only as menacing as the nearest hillside or money box. This perspective may help us, finally, to appreciate two Christians who spent its years rather differently, the authors on whom our knowledge of this period rests.

Without Lactantius's Latin and Eusebius's Greek, we would have little idea of the events which come to a head with Constantine. There would be no means of writing the final chapters to this book. Their writings have earned them just accolades, as the Christian Cicero and as the father of Church history. To explore them more deeply is to appreciate their particular talents: in Lactantius, a sharp moral sense, and in Eusebius, a concern for precise, often accurate details and biblical exegesis. Both were authors with an above-average gift for rhetoric: both were prolific writers, capable of keen polemic. Philosophy was central to their ways of interpreting their faith, yet when the context required, they could distort the course of events to suit their argument. To live for a while in their company is to enter that tantalizing, literary world where not everything said is to be taken entirely at face value. Like their major works, which they had to revise, these authors proved able to move with the climate of the times.

The older of the two, Lactantius, had left his native North Africa to teach Latin rhetoric at Nicomedia, court of the pagan Diocletian. We do not know if he was born a Christian, or was a Christian convert when he moved, but by c. 302, his Christian sympathies were not in doubt. By then in his fifties, he withdrew from court when his fellow Christians began to be persecuted. Approving Christ's own "retreat" into the garden of Gethsemane, Lactantius avoided arrest and continued his literary works. He followed his pamphlets on the Creation with a more ambitious work, seven books of *Divine Institutes*, which aimed to explain Christianity's relation to the philosophical teaching of the schools. It set out Christian doctrine for the "general reader" of middling intelligence, just as Cicero had once set out the "offices," or "duties," of educated men.[27] While Lactantius wrote, persecution was still being enforced in the East; in the West, Christians had lost their places of meeting. To Lactantius, in late middle age, the time seemed ripe for the promised end of the world. He dwelt on the coming millennium, the rule of the Saints on earth and the hints of the end of the world which had been dropped by the prophetic Sibyl in her "ancient" verses. The proof, as we shall see, was to have an unimagined future. For Lactantius, history was moving to a well-prophesied pattern. Hideous though the prospect seemed, the End was inescapable: "it scares the mind, but I will say none the less, happen it will."[28]

While Lactantius worked on seven long books of Christian institutes, a second author, some fifteen years his junior, was proving more prolific in the Eastern Empire.[29] Eusebius, bishop of Caesarea, had been born in that city c. 260. As a young man, he had worked on Christian chronography and published a first edition of his *Chronicon* c. 303, if not earlier. In it, he drew freely on the published books of Christian predecessors and set out the relative datings of sacred and secular history, beginning with the birth of that pre-Christian father, Abraham.[30] The persecution found him in the company of his admired master, Pamphilus, a pupil of Origen, whose great library he had largely preserved in Caesarea. In Pamphilus's company, Eusebius became known as a fluent author. During the Great Persecution, he embarked on ten books of General Elementary Introductions to the Christian Faith, of which four concerned the scriptural prophecies of Christ's coming.[31] The work was intended to confound the Jews and heretics, and it reviewed text upon text in which God or his angels appeared or made contact with man in the Old Testament: God, Eusebius insisted, could not appear in person, so the references must be to his Word, as later revealed in Christ. The Introductions probably ended with texts from Christ's first coming to earth and looked to his future "epiphany" at the end of the world. On the matter of continuing "epiphany," it was resoundingly orthodox.

In this same period, Eusebius turned on that enraging critic Porphyry and his attack *Against the Christians*. Defence was also needed elsewhere. During the persecution, confessors in Egypt had begun to attack his admired Origen's teaching; so Eusebius and Pamphilus composed a *Defence of Origen* from the master's books and letters, which were preserved in their library. When the work was in its first form, Pamphilus himself was tried in Caesarea and martyred: Eusebius added a further book to their joint *Defence* and then composed a "Life" of Pamphilus as well. When persecution was briefly interrupted in 311, he turned to a further plan, a series on the deaths of the martyrs whom he knew personally in Palestine. The work survives for us in various revisions and editions which cannot be dated decisively, but it is a fair assumption that a first version was already composed, if not published, in late 311.[32] Like the "best friends" of earlier martyrs, Eusebius used his literary gifts to honour the Christians with whom he had been familiar before their deaths. In the later phase of persecution, the prominent pagan Hierocles issued a work praising the pagan Apollonius in contrast with Christ. Again, Eusebius sprang to the defence and promptly issued an *Against Hierocles*.

A natural question, which some Christians later prejudged, is what

Eusebius himself had been doing to avoid arrest in this period. Some thirty or more volumes had appeared in his name during the years of the persecution, an output which was assisted by his art of dictation to well-trained scribes. Like Lactantius, Eusebius had avoided excessive heroics: perhaps, like other Eastern bishops, he had lapsed. Yet, in him, too, the persecutions had kept alive the sense of an imminent end to the world. The General Elementary Introductions were adamant that the present persecutions were in accord with the ancient prophecies and that Christ would soon return to make his enemies his footstool. The final book, on one view, was strongly apocalyptic, looking forward to the imminent End and the one promised "theophany" since Christ had last visited men.

By a fine irony, both Eusebius and Lactantius, two ageing men of letters, were promptly overtaken by events. The world did not end: a new Christian future began instead. In autumn 312, the complex years of Imperial partnership ended with the victories of Constantine, a pretender who ascribed his success in the West to the Christian God. History had moved too fast for the works of its two Christian authors. To keep up with it, their books required revision, the *Chronicon*, the *Divine Institutes* and, in due course, the *Martyrs of Palestine*, in a sequence of "second editions" which still stretch the ingenuity of their critics.

It was in this unforeseen climate that Eusebius issued his *Church History*, the work on which all modern accounts of the early Church must rest. Large and justified claims have been made for the result, its careful citation of documents, its realization that "ecclesiastical history" was a separate branch of history. Yet such had been Eusebius's rate of writing in the previous decade that we should be wary of overestimating the scale of the undertaking. There is no good evidence that an edition of this work had existed in seven books as early as the 290s, while Eusebius was still young. There is no support in the manuscripts for such an edition, and there is decisive evidence in the shape and content of the sixth book that this central part of the *History* was only conceived and written after 309/10.[33] The work had had ready aids to hand. The *Chronicon*, as Eusebius admitted, was in existence to give the *History* its chronological frame and its sequence of Christian bishops. The *History*'s fourth book drew freely on published martyrdoms, misdating Pionius's, among several other slips. The sixth presupposed the existing *Defence of Origen*: like the seventh, it quoted freely from the writings of Bishop Dionysius. In its first form, the eighth book merely added a preface and conclusion to a version of the *Martyrs of Palestine* which Eusebius had already prepared, but perhaps not circulated. The ninth, too, relied heavily on documentary quotations. This type of history was not unduly taxing for a man who had already written basic handbooks, "outlines" and "selections" and fifteen books against Porphyry. He was an author, moreover, who dictated to practised scribes. Again, the exact scope of the *History*'s first edition will never be certain, but of the two serious possibilities, a first edition of nine books is the likelier, achieved in late 313. The detail, perhaps, is not too important. On either view, the *Church History* was born in the wake of Constantine's conversion, a fact which left Christian authors with so much so suddenly to understand. In his *History*, Eusebius told of many themes, of bishops and martyrs, of Christian relations with the Jews and the birth of heresies. But when he reached his own adult lifetime, he moved quickly over the churches' years of peace, from the mid-270s until the persecution, those years, said Gibbon, in which "prosperity relaxed the nerve of discipline." Of the last persecution, he remarked somewhat darkly how it had been sent by God to chastise Christian sins. He gave no details, and instead, exclaimed in general terms what favours and progress the faith had been making before the year 300: it was hard, we have suspected, for an author to be more exact.[34] Constantine's conversion had changed Eusebius's own perspective. He had moved from a vivid sense of the imminent End to a new sense that history was happening quickly and that a Christian needed to write and explain why his Church was now where it was. The "most audacious act of an autocrat" raised urgent questions about the Church's past and identity: in its wake, Eusebius turned to make a history from others' documents and his own existing works. We cannot know how long it took him, perhaps six months, perhaps much less, but we misjudge the work and its achievement if we detach it from its times.

# 12. Constantine
## and the Church

## I

To us, as to contemporaries, the conversion of Constantine remains an entirely unexpected event. Bishop Dionysius's letter in praise of Gallienus, the rumours of Christian sympathies in King Abgar of Edessa and in Philip the Emperor, the interest of an Empress mother in Origen's teaching: these events do something to prepare for the conversion of an Emperor himself. They do not, however, take us very far. At the start of the Great Persecution, Diocletian is said to have asked his wife and daughters to sacrifice to the gods: perhaps he wished them to set an example, not as Christian suspects but as the most prominent women in pagan society.[1] Although we can at times see Constantine as Diocletian's true heir in secular matters, his religious policy remains one of history's great surprises, "an erratic block which has diverted the stream of human history."[2] It was to be urged as an example on many Christian rulers in medieval Europe and it inspired its own memorials, from Piero's great cycle of frescoes in Arezzo's church of San Francesco to the spectacle which greeted the fiftieth Holy Roman Emperor in 1659: the Jesuit College in Vienna staged *Pietas Victrix*, a baroque opera which centred on Constantine's Christian vision and victories, before an audience of three thousand guests.

His conversion occurred at the least auspicious moment for Christian unity. In Rome itself, the Church had been without a bishop for several years in a series of disputes which turned on the right of Christians to lapse during persecution. In 303, their elected leader was said to have "handed over" the Scriptures to the authorities, and not until 311 was the issue settled. In Africa, a "true" Church of uncompromised "Donatist" Christians had broken away from their treacherous brethren. In Egypt, rigorist followers of Meletius had begun to organize a Church of their own. These divisions showed Christian intolerance at its worst: in prison, the bishop of Alexandria divided the cells with "a cloak, a blanket and a shirt" and announced through a deacon that Meletius's supporters were to stay on their own side of the curtain. In Carthage, one group was said to have posted armed pickets outside the prison in order to stop food and drink from reaching the other group inside.[3] Born during persecution, these great schisms were to plague Christian history in the next generation, and in the East they were soon joined by open heresy. It arose in Alexandria, where the priests of the city's many churches customarily read and expounded the Scriptures at twice-weekly meetings: one of them, Arius, began to pose the insoluble question of Christ's nature in terms which appeared to debase his relation to God. Constantine did not create these deep divisions: he inherited them. They stretched back to the 250s and 260s, when lapsing during persecution had first provoked schism and when the status of Christ had caused heresy in Syria and a theological rebuke to Dionysius, bishop of Alexandria.[4]

Never had the Church been so fatally divided: we can sympathize with those perfectionists in Egypt who had begun to withdraw from their fellow Christians in order to pursue their ideals in the desert. Yet by autumn 324, the Empire was to be united under one and the same Christian Emperor. A massive programme of building and benefactions was to mark the Church's new prominence in Rome and the provinces. It was a symbol of the change that Christians had to develop an architecture: in the East, they exercised it in a new Imperial capital, Constantine's own Constantinople. Previous Emperors, Domitian and Aurelian, had favoured a particular pagan god among many others and had honoured their choice with a cult at Rome or in his homeland. Constantine, too, promoted the Christians' cult as his personal religion, not as the official religion of the Roman state. He, too, built shrines for his god in Rome and at sites connected with its history. His patronage, however, amounted to a widespread policy which was publicized by laws, rescripts and letters throughout the provinces and which was encouraged by legal privileges, weapons which no other Emperor had used.

The religion of Constantine's own family is not entirely clear to us. His mother, Helena, is said by Eusebius to have become a Christian after her son's example: as Eusebius wished to praise Constantine, we do not know if this statement is correct or if it was made to give his hero as much independent credit as possible.[5] His father, Constantius, was said to have worshipped a Supreme god and certainly died a pagan, despite Constantine's later attempts to imply the opposite.

There is a hint, however, of something else. Constantius separated from Helena and married a second wife, Theodora, by whom he had six children, among them, one Anastasia. Her name had obvious Jewish or Christian associations, implying "resurrection." If she was given the name at birth, c. 300, we would much like to know whether her mother encouraged the choice. There is, however, another likelihood. She may have taken the name herself after 312 at baptism when other members of the family became Christians; if so, the name does not prove Constantine to have had a Christian stepsister before his conversion.[6]

In his youth, Constantine had known Christianity as a strong demonic force which the diviners and the priests of Apollo believed to upset their gods. He had been in camp during the incidents which led to the Great Persecution, and he had heard that Christianity was a detestable "atheism." Between c. 293 and 305, he had accompanied the court on its journeys and campaigns from Rome to the eastern frontier. He had lived at Nicomedia in the company of the intellectual enemies of Christianity, and when he left for Britain in summer 305, there is no evidence, and little likelihood, that he had been exposed to a detailed exposition of the Christian faith. He had gone west as a disappointed party in the dynastic rearrangements of the Emperors' co-rule, but in July 306, his father, Constantius, died at York and Constantine announced himself his successor. One of his first moves was the restoration to the Christians of the property which they had lost under the first edict of the persecution.[7] Lactantius's report of this move is probably reliable, but it implies nothing about Constantine's own Christian beliefs: the pagan Gallienus had done as much. Four years later, in 310, we know that Constantine was still pagan. In his presence, at Trier, a panegyrist reminded him in Latin of the cult which he had paid to a Gallic Apollo's temple in the previous year. He turned it into a complimentary "epiphany": "you saw, I believe, Apollo," holding crowns which symbolized an immense length of reign. In Apollo, he continued, the Emperor, "I believe," had seen features like his own, young and radiant, the features of the Child whose Golden Age the poet Virgil had predicted. The "epiphany" was the orator's extravagant invention, his "belief," as he neatly put it, but it was meant to please the Emperor, whose aid he then solicited for his local temple in the most material terms.[8] In 310, to equate the Emperor with Apollo was to flatter him.

In 311, another panegyric shows Constantine entering Autun in a fine scene of pagan greeting for the traditional arrival of an Emperor. "We brought out the images of all the gods," recalled the orator, and we welcomed you with "instruments of clear-pitched music."[9] During 312, however, the Emperor's outlook changed. The evidence for the change continues to be contested because of its very nature. It is not the direct evidence of eyewitnesses but the reports of subsequent beneficiaries of the Emperor's patronage, writing at varying distances in time and place from the event. Nonetheless, the outlines are not in dispute, though the personal details will never be certain. Perhaps the most vital link which we miss is the date of a particular connection at Constantine's court.[10] By early 313, we find the Emperor, now a Christian, sending monies to the bishop of Carthage and ordering him to bestow them on persons named by the list "which has been sent by Ossius." This Ossius was already established at the Emperor's side and may well have accompanied him into Italy. As he was the bishop of Cordova in southern Spain, we would dearly like to know how and when he had entered the Emperor's favour. Had he been drawn into his company, or perhaps into Helena's, in the wake of the offer to restore Christian property, made in 306? His influence on what follows may have been crucial.

On his father's death, in 306, Constantine had been recognized as a member of the Imperial college, the body of two senior and two junior "tetrarchs." His recognition had not been without embarrassment for his senior colleagues. From 306 to 311, the Emperors engaged in a complex series of attacks and counter-alliances, while Constantine bided his time in the West. By 310, he was publicizing his own "descent" from a previous Imperial house: in 311/12, he broke with the fragile consensus of co-rule and launched himself across the Alps into an invasion of Italy. By now in his fortieth year, he aimed his attack against Maxentius, whose rule was based in Rome.

His invasion was not a war of religion. Like himself, Maxentius was tolerating the Christians in his domains, and when war threatened, he increased his favours. Nonetheless, both contenders were pagans, and all over the Empire the pagan gods were much in evidence. The old "epiphanies" were far from dead. In the East, in 311, the Emperor Maximin wrote how the people of the cities had come to plead for a renewed persecution of the Christians, bringing the images of their gods with them. In the West, in 311, "all the images of the gods" had been brought out of Autun when the people came to welcome the pagan "arrival" of Constantine. As so often, a supernatural presence attended the embassies and diplomatic dealings of the pagan cities.[11] In Rome, the usurper Maxentius was said to be resorting to omens, Sibylline prophecies and a wide range of divination and pagan sacrifice.[12] The invader needed divine protection, a god to "hold his hand" above him, in the familiar pattern which we have seen so often at work.

The sequel has been endlessly discussed, but not without historical gain in the past fifty years. Our earliest hint is given by a panegyric which was performed in Constantine's presence at Trier in autumn 313. The speaker was himself a pagan and trod warily before a mixed audience. He praised Constantine's boldness in invading Italy "when almost all your companions and generals were not only muttering quietly but showing open fear . . . you felt the time had come against the advice of men, against the warnings of the soothsayers."[13] Had the pagan omens indeed been unfavourable on the march the year before? The speaker went on to develop the point. "To be sure, Constantine, you have some secret contact with that divine mind which entrusts care of us to the lesser gods and deigns to show itself to you alone . . ." While the omens were uncertain, Constantine, he said, was guided by a Supreme divinity. Perhaps there is more here than the pagan speaker's inventive oratory, phrased in a manner which the oracles had so often echoed: had the old gods really denied their aid to the usurper on his march?

Not every general who ignored omens was blamed for his neglect: the omens might have been misread and events might prove him right. But it required a man of the standing of Alexander the Great to carry off this boldness. If the omens had been doubtful in 312, we can well understand how Constantine was conscious of his lack of divine support. Before he engaged battle, he was said to have seen a vision, for which we have two Christian authorities, Lactantius and Eusebius. At first, in his *Church History*, Eusebius could not be precise about the form and origin of Constantine's divine aid.[14] He was writing in the East in or before 313 and as yet had enjoyed no contact with the court. Lactantius, the future tutor to Constantine's son, gave more detail. Within four years of the event, he wrote that Constantine had seen a dream "on the eve of battle," and that it ordered him to inscribe the "heavenly sign of God" on his soldiers' shields. His description of this sign has been emended and abandoned as "virtually incomprehensible,"[15] but we are able to confirm it through the evidence of Christian papyri. In copies of the Gospels, written c. 200, several papyri show the word "cross" (*stauros*) by a symbol which combines an upright cross, †, with a loop at its top, ⸶.[16] This sign makes sense of Lactantius's description, although in his view the sign stood for Christ. We cannot be sure where Lactantius was writing, or how he heard these details. But his account is the earliest which survives, and even if it was written in the East, a symbol as public as a shield inscription could have become common knowledge.

At least thirteen years after the event, the story had gained a clearer outline. The details were said to derive from Constantine himself, who had described them "on oath" in the hearing of Eusebius, the Christian bishop and, eventually, author of a work on the Emperor's life.[17] However much we might suspect his own fiction, this authority is too boldly emphasized to be the bishop's personal deceit. Constantine is generally supposed to have revealed the details to Eusebius in a private conversation, but it is perhaps easier to suppose that they formed part of a public speech in Eusebius's presence, perhaps a speech on the occasion of the great Council of Nicaea in 325. If so, other Christians heard them and the Emperor's oath seems more in place. Their outline, then, gives us the way in which Constantine himself had come to remember the event.

Eusebius was writing after Constantine's death, perhaps twelve years after this sworn testimony and at least twenty-five years after the vision. He may, then, have run some of the details together. Constantine, he stated frankly, had begun by feeling the need for powerful heavenly aid while his foe, Maxentius, was supposedly resorting to pagan spells and sacrifices in Rome. He reflected that all the followers of the old gods had come to a miserable end, whereas his own father, Constantius, had died a natural death. Constantius, he knew, had honoured the "one Supreme god," who had given him many "manifestations and signs" of his aid, but he did not know who this god had been. So he prayed to him to reveal himself and "stretch forth his hand."

These allusions to Constantius's piety were not Eusebius's invention. We know that Constantine himself liked to publicize them, for they stood in the open letter which he sent to the provincials in the East after his final victory in autumn 324. "My father," he stated, "was the only Emperor who uniformly practised the duties of humanity, and with admirable piety, called for the blessing of God the Father on all his actions . . ." So far as we know, this statement was a lie: Constantius was remembered and praised as a pagan and had allowed a persecution of the Christians in his territory. It may, however, be true that Constantius had acknowledged a Supreme god in the manner of the pagan oracles whom we have heard so frequently.[18] While remaining a pagan, he may have honoured a Supreme divinity, "self-born, untaught, motherless, unshaken," like the god whom the Oenoandans had inscribed on their walls. If so, our themes begin to come pleasingly together. In the later third century, we must allow for the effects of the "interpretation of the gods and goddesses" which the shrine at Claros sent throughout the Empire. For all we know, these theological oracles were still being sought freely: at Claros, the inscriptions cease, but not the shrine. Constantius's coins made a prominent use of the type of the Sun among other divinities, and Constantius left a proof of his piety in the army. Soon after his accession, a legion was named *solenses*, the "Sun's people," while another was entitled the "people of Mars." These titles can be referred to the Emperors' own initiatives, to the wish of Galerius, the self-styled favourite of Mars, and to Constantius, the special protégé of the Sun.[19] Where did this favour come from? Cults of the Sun god are attested in the general area of Constantius's home province, Dacia Ripensis, but we should also look more generally to Apollo, the great solar divinity. In 310, when the orator at Trier flattered Constantine's "vision" of "your" Apollo, he may have touched on ground very dear to the family's heart.

Like Theophilus or the Oenoandans, Constantine was said by Eusebius to have wondered, "What is God?" Eusebius does not make it clear that he heard this part from the Emperor on oath, and unfortunately, he may only have deduced it from Constantine's later publicity. By 324/5, Constantine liked to emphasize his father's piety; twelve years earlier, we cannot be so sure that this type of anxiety was in his mind.

On his march south, practical concern for the gods was surely more urgent. Like so many warriors, from Homer's poems onwards, the Emperor was diverted by a vision, and he swore in Eusebius's presence, thirteen or more years later, that he and "all the troops" had seen a "sign of the cross" in the noonday sky, inscribed with the words "By this, conquer." Constantine had gone to bed wondering what the sign in the sky had meant. That night, he was visited in his dreams by the figure of Christ, who was bearing the same symbol and commanding him, said Eusebius, to "use its likeness in his engagements with the enemy." Constantine awoke at dawn, told the miracle to his friends and began, said Eusebius, to fashion the famous standard which bore the letters "chi-rho" at the summit of a cross. Eusebius himself had seen this trophy, which was made of gold and jewels and bore a banner with pictures of Constantine and his children. His privileged viewing of the symbol occurred long after its construction: the children's portraits were a later addition.

In their different ways, the descriptions by Lactantius and Eusebius are referring to results of the same event. They should be combined, not contrasted, and their common core of truth can be detached in each case from error. Against the Emperor's own oath, Lactantius is wrong in placing the vision on the night before the battle, but his shield sign conforms to Eusebius's description of a "sign of the cross."[20] Eusebius, however, has slightly confused the details by connecting the vision with the Emperor's developed standard, the famous *labarum* with the sign of "chi-rho." He was particularly concerned with this standard because he wished to remark how he himself had seen it in the Emperor's private rooms. Was he, perhaps, running two memories into one? On oath, Constantine swore that he had seen a cross in the sky; then he gave Eusebius a "private view" of the standard, and the bishop connected this symbol with the vision. In autumn 312, Constantine was not exceptional in seeing the familiar sign of a cross against the sun: modern sun-watchers, too, have often reported the sighting of cross-shaped haloes.[21] The "chi-rho" sign, however, was much more complex, and at that date, it was not a familiar public symbol: despite much debate and searching, no "chi-rho" sign has been found in a Christian context which is datable with certainty to the years before Constantine's vision.[22] Instead, the sign had quite a different connotation, which also goes back to the papyri. In pagan papyri, scribes or readers used exactly this sign to mark a "good" or "useful" passage, "chi-rho" for the Greek *chreston*.[23] Did the Emperor's advisers suggest this clever abbreviation for "Christ" ("Chrestos")? Like other symbols in the years after the conversion, it had a double meaning, one for pagans, one for Christians. The "chi-rho" symbol is not attested until spring 315, when it is shown on a silver medallion as a badge on the Emperor's helmet.[24] Its name, *labarum*, continues to attract derivations from Celtic or European languages, but none of them makes sense of the object. As no explanation of the word's origin has yet been found, it cannot prove anything about the date or place of the symbol's origin.[25] After his victory, Constantine ordered a large statue of himself to be placed in the basilica which his opponent had been building in Rome. In his hand, Eusebius remarks, he held the "sign of salvation," plainly the cross.[26] At this date, he did not commemorate the "chi-rho" symbol, and Lactantius, it seems, was right about his early vision. The soldiers' shields were painted in 312 with the Christians' abbreviation of the word for cross, and the standard, most probably, was a simple cross, too, not so different from the "wooden crosses" which Christian authors described as the military emblems of the third-century pagan army.

None of this background detracts from the Emperor's own sworn evidence that a vision occurred. Plainly, Constantine referred his conversion to a type of epiphany whose broad outlines were familiar in contemporary religiousness. It is extremely interesting that he began by seeing a symbol where a pagan would surely have seen a divinity's person, focussed by its image in art. A man only sees in the sky what he is predisposed to notice or recall: evidently, Constantine was already guided by Christians in his interpretation. It is not surprising that we hear nothing about the vision until Eusebius wrote on his life, even though the event was supposed to have occurred in full view of the army.[27] The views of common soldiers escaped history at this period, and even if we had them, they lacked the Christian coaxing which disposed the Emperor to notice a deeper truth in what they saw. That night, the Emperor's dream was also shaped by Christian advice. Perhaps, like the pagans known to Artemidorus, he had dreamed of a conventional type of divinity, a young man of outstanding beauty, dressed in shining robes. He could hardly have been more specific, as no artistic image focussed his dream and nobody knew what Christ had looked like. He must have required a talk with Christians to confirm the stranger's identity. Like the "epiphany" in the sky, the dream is entirely credible against all that we have seen of this enduring religiousness, especially in battles and times of tension. The interest lies less in the vision's occurrence than in the way in which it was understood: the Christian interpretation was planted in the Emperor's mind, and if Ossius, the Spanish bishop, was already in his company, we must allow for the influence of the man who was to lead so many of the Emperor's subsequent dealings with the Church.

After the two visions, Constantine responded in a familiar manner to the interpretations which others had encouraged in his mind. He gave his symbol material form, like the altars, votive reliefs and temples which pagans constructed "in accordance with a dream." Perhaps he ordered a new standard to be built like a cross, reputedly on the model of his vision during sleep. He told the troops to paint their shields with the "symbol of the cross," seen, like so many visions before it, in a deceptively illumined sky. The choice of these objects was traditional. In pagan armies, the standards bore images of pagan gods; so, often, did the shields, as we can see from the shields of troops which are carved on Trajan's Column and are marked with a thunderbolt, the symbol of Zeus. What did Constantine himself make of it? Years before, in 302, he had been present at Didyma when Apollo complained that the Christians interfered with his "normal service." Of their god's strength, he had these personal memories. Perhaps he first understood it in the way in which his father had understood the Sun god, as a Supreme divinity of whom the others, as the oracles said, were "angels, a part." There were other, attractive aspects. His new Protector, Christ, appeared to be young and fair, as a panegyrist had recently described Constantine himself: on his arch of victory in Rome, Constantine's own portrait was to look strikingly youthful.[28] As Christians in camp could have told him, the protégé of Christ was raised above earthly fate, while his power was placed beyond the astrologers' art.[29] Nobody could argue that he was not fated to rule or that his rule was fixed in time: Christ had destroyed the very basis of "vain" astrology. If the pagan omens had indeed been pronounced unfavourable, what better to replace them than the new support of Christ? Civil wars and usurpations always increased contemporaries' interest in prophecies and horoscopes. In the year 69, when four Emperors had competed for power, their stars and omens were studied and remembered as a significant point in their biographies.

The proof of a god is best found in his protection, and before long, Constantine was amply rewarded. His campaign through Italy was extremely audacious. Only five years before, another army had attacked Maxentius in Rome, but had failed in the face of the city's massive walls.[30] In 312, against all expectations, Maxentius and his troops came out of the city to offer pitched battle. Perhaps there had been dissent in Rome, but Constantine, stationed outside, could see the hand of God in this unexpected chance. The battle was quickly decided in his favour. Nine years later, in autumn 321, another panegyrist, evidently a pagan, enlarged very cleverly on the accompanying host of heaven. "I believe," he said, in Constantine's presence, that "your father," Constantius, led an entire army of assistants "sent from heaven." This tactful "belief" in Constantius's presence was his way of pleasing the Emperor, and it shows that the connection between the father Constantius and the new God had already been made public knowledge. The heavenly army brought the best out of the speaker's rhetoric. "What appearance, what bodily vigour, what fullness of limb, what keenness of will is said to have been theirs?" Their shields blazed with heavenly light, enough to scare any opponent, but their presence was attached to the old tradition of pagan "epiphanies" in time of war. Once, said the speaker, Rome's army had been helped against the Latins by two figures, dressed in white, who had vanished after victory and proved that they were the demigods Castor and Pollux. This famous story of 338 B.C. was enshrined in Livy, an author, incidentally, who had already found Christian readers. The panegyrist used it artfully.[31] The greater scale of Constantine's support proved the truth of the old pagan story: if Constantine had been helped by an entire heavenly army, surely Rome had once been helped by a couple of mere demigods? The heavenly army also proved Constantine's own greatness and chaste self-control: once again, the degree of an "epiphany" depended on the moral virtue of the person who experienced it. In a single sweep, the orator respected pagan tradition and flattered the Emperor who excelled it. He hinted at his "higher" religion, without naming it openly.

Why should we believe the tradition of Constantine's vision, but reject the sightings of Apollo and this heavenly army which speakers mentioned in 310 and 321? There is a clear difference in the evidence. The speakers were public performers, pagans before a largely pagan audience. They paid traditional compliments, qualified by "I believe" or "it is said," and they claimed no knowledge of the Emperor's personal beliefs. Eusebius, too, praised the Emperor in his posthumous work *On the Life of Constantine*, but he cited the vision on the Emperor's own testimony, backed by an oath. No other event in the *Life* was presented on such authority, and although the work was highly favourable, it was not a speech or a flattery for an occasion.

Does the continuing combination of these pagan themes in praise of Constantine suggest that the Emperor had not really "converted" to a single Christian faith? Had he only adhered to Christ as one more god among many older divinities? We might well wonder where "conversion" came into the process. Constantine first saw a religious sign, and then saw a god who bore it: he responded as pagans so often had, and soon afterwards, he found that this god had a special power. Why should he exclude all other gods? Constantine, it has been well said, might have entered on Christianity as a man embarks on marriage, not realizing at first that it required him to give up his former, disreputable friends.[32]

These theories of a compromise or an undercommitted conversion have had a very long life. They emphasize one side of the court's publicity, the coinage and the panegyrics, and minimize the central evidence of Constantine's own letters, edicts and actions, which began in the very winter after his victory.[33] Naturally, there was scope for ambiguity and uncertainty in the eye of the beholder, and we can see them in several places: in the Roman Senate, in dealings with the East, in the earliest approach of Christians in Africa and, eight years later, among soldiers who were in Constantine's own presence. These groups were outsiders, looking on: they were not Constantine himself.

In Rome, after the victory, the pagan Senate had faced a difficult problem. They were expected to approve a commemoration of Constantine's successes, but their public statements could hardly accept his idiosyncratic faith. Like other victorious Emperors, Constantine was to be honoured with an arch, but its inscription and scenes in relief made a subtle statement of neutral theology. The inscription publicized Constantine's victory at the "instigation of divinity," without specifying which divinity had helped him to expel "the tyrant and his faction" and "rescue the Republic." When the arch was dedicated in 315/16, it showed soldiers of Constantine's inner bodyguard, but it made no reference to the new sign on their shields. It depicted them with the usual pagan helpers from heaven.[34]

This interesting silence does not undermine the Christian tradition. Lactantius was already writing of the "heavenly sign" while the arch was being prepared, and it is better to see its absence as a reflection on its pagan patrons and the pagan public in Rome. The accompanying scenes of Constantine's departure from Milan and his arrival in Rome were also studiously neutral.[35] The artists followed a recent tradition in the art of the pagan Tetrarchy. In the past, the heroes of a pagan triumph had been closely identified with the god Jupiter. On the arch, the artists now showed the Emperor sitting, not standing, in his chariot. Jupiter was no longer featured, and the departure and arrival of the Emperor were connected with the imagery of the heavenly bodies. The long scene of Constantine's departure stretched beneath a bold medallion of the descending chariot of the setting Moon, while the scene of his "advent" placed his person beneath a similar medallion of the rising Sun. After his victory, Constantine had not climbed the

Capitol in Rome to pay the usual offerings to Jupiter, but this "neutral" art need not be a tactful evasion of his new religion. The joint rule of the pagan Tetrarchy had already been related to these cosmic themes and the style was evidently in fashion. We find it amusingly expressed in a panegyric which was delivered in July 291 before a pagan Emperor.[36] When two pagan rulers had met in concord at Milan, said the speaker, "everybody except your closest companions *perhaps* believed what was worthy of your majesty, that the two lights of the Universe had lent you their chariots of Night and Day." The orator then disclaimed the notion: "Let us remove these foolish tales, let us speak the truth . . ." Artists were less realistic, and in 312, this style lay to hand as a way of expressing an Emperor's triumph.

Nothing, in short, suggested the Emperor's Christianity in the scenes on Rome's arch of victory: his guards were shown with pagan symbolism, not with their new Christian sign. In the East, there was a similar lack of public emphasis and a studious occupation of ambiguous, neutral ground. Constantine's senior partner in the Empire was now Licinius, whom he met at Milan in early 313. Licinius tolerated the Christians when necessary, but he was not a Christian sympathizer, nor was he seriously concerned with the fate of their property. On returning to the East, he had to fight his junior colleague, the keen pagan Maximin. Before he did battle, his troops were given a neutral prayer to recite to the Supreme god in words which avoided a direct reference to Christ or paganism. Lactantius claimed that this prayer had been dictated to Licinius by an angel in a dream, but it is a likelier guess that Constantine had agreed to it at this meeting as a suitable prayer with which to continue victories against non-Christian rulers.[37] It accommodated the wishes of both Emperors, the Christian Constantine and the pagan Licinius, and it duly worked. In June 313, after the victory, Licinius sent a famous letter to the governors in the East which was issued in his own name and Constantine's. We know it in Latin and a Greek translation, which refer to the Emperors' wish to appease "whatever divinity" or "active power" is in heaven. This text, however, was Licinius's version, based on a letter which had been sent to the East in the previous winter. It says nothing about Constantine's own choice of words.[38]

Nearer home, other groups were unaware how best to approach Constantine; others, too, continued to make of him what they wanted. When the Donatist Christians appealed to Constantine from North Africa, one of their earliest petitions, despatched almost certainly in April 313, alluded only to his father's "justice" and refusal to persecute the Church.[39] These Christians do not seem to have said anything about Constantine's own Christianity, perhaps because they were unsure of it, perhaps because he had already written to bestow favours on a "list" of their Catholic opponents and they feared his orthodoxy. Later, in Asia, the small town of Termessus was to adopt an openly pagan approach: it honoured Constantine in an inscription as "the (new) Sun," probably late in his reign.[40] Above all, we have the vivid dialogue of Constantine with a group of veteran soldiers which has survived in the law codes and is dated there to March 320.[41] On entering his military headquarters, Constantine was greeted by senior army leaders with a clearly pagan acclamation: "Constantine, may the immortal gods preserve you for us." There is no need to change the date or the placing of this incident, which was set in an unknown community near Serdica, in Thrace. The scene reminds us, more than any other, that the majority of Constantine's army and high command were still pagan in 320 and greeted him in their own pagan way.

Meanwhile, Constantine's own position is clear from his public letters and actions in the West. There, he had no need to compromise with Licinius. His honours for the Christians' God were profuse, and many of them grew out of the traditional patterns of Imperial favours for a cult or a privileged group. This continuity was only to be expected, and it does not imply that Constantine was still seeing Christ as one more god among many others: how better could he express his favour than by granting Christians and their cult the prizes which so many subjects had hoped to receive from Emperors before? Great generals of the past had honoured their gods of victory with cults and temples in Rome, and like them, Constantine soon gave the Christian God the splendid material setting which his cult had lacked. In Rome, God received endowments for two particularly fine shrines, St. John the Lateran, from Constantine himself, and a palace-church, the Sessorian basilica (subsequently S. Croce in Gierusalemme), from Helena, his mother, who was already, then, a Christian. We have a list of these churches' endowments, and it is suggestive that all their properties lie in areas which Constantine controlled by his victory in 312. Nothing acquired in the East in 324 attached to them, and it is highly likely that they were ordered before that date.[42] We cannot be more specific, but by 315 it was widely known that Constantine had already been honoured with an enormous statue, holding a "lofty spear in the shape of the cross." This huge monument, "ten times larger than life," stood prominently in the basilica which Maxentius had been building for secular use in Rome, but which was now dedicated to Constantine. In the twenty-five years between his victory and his death, Constantine ordered a sequence of huge church buildings, from Rome to the Holy Land. All were built largely at the Emperor's expense.[43] This deluge of Christian publicity exceeded any other programme in precious stone which was realized by a ruler in antiquity.

These enormous gifts were accompanied by language in his public letters which rapidly went beyond mere toleration. In the wake of victory, letters to Africa and the East proposed the restoration of Christian property. In spring 313, Constantine wrote again to the pagan governor of North Africa, exempting the clergy of the recognized Catholic Church from the burdens of civic office, what a pagan called "love of the home town."[44] This type of exemption had been courted and retained by several groups in pagan society: athletes, "exceptional sophists" and the rest, but this new grant was grounded in a distinct perception: the Christians' prayers, said Constantine, were intimately connected with the safety of the state.[45] It is very telling that he stressed this point in a letter to a pagan governor. The tendency of pagan legislation under the Empire had been to restrict this type of immunity to the one religious group, the priests of Egypt, who had enjoyed it in the Hellenistic age. Now an Emperor bestowed it on a far wider priesthood throughout his territory. Concern for the safety of the state befitted the thinking of a Roman Emperor, for whom religious rites traditionally maintained the "peace of heaven," but in this case, it realized an old Christian claim. As Origen had put it: "If Christians do avoid the responsibilities of civic office, it is not because they want to avoid public service. They keep themselves for a more divine and necessary service in the Church of God for the salvation of all."[46] It is in this Christian pressure, not in pagan "precedent," that Constantine's view had surely been formed.

This enormous favour was an open encouragement to false pretence: by 320, Constantine already had to legislate against rich pagans who were showing a fascinating ingenuity and were claiming exemption as alleged Christian priests.[47] This grant was accompanied by other, positive legislation whose full scope and dated origin largely elude us. In 321, we find Constantine ruling on the validity of bequests to the Church. Emperors had previously favoured their veteran soldiers' powers of bequest, but the law for the Church had a particular angle: it stressed the validity of a man's deathbed legacies to a church's funds, a topic which was particularly sensitive because of the clergy's special presence at the moment of death.[48] Again, "precedent" is not very helpful in this Christian context.

An accompanying mass of social and moral legislation raises questions of the degree of Christian motivation in each particular case.[49] Christian interests were obvious in the banning of crucifixion and gladiatorial shows, the making of Sunday into a holiday and the ending of the old marriage laws which had penalized celibates, childless couples and widows who did not remarry. When banning the branding of slaves on their faces, Constantine's law referred unmistakably to his particular God. Yet, other laws are less explicit, and their penalties are conspicuously savage. Argument over their origins persists, but it concerns the degree of particular Christian influence in each law, not the general Christian atmosphere. Several laws with secular concerns do not diminish the broader point, as they may have been drafted by a pagan on Constantine's staff. The problem, rather, is the definition of the point at which a Christian legislator is no longer a Christian, and those who recall the early Church councils will hesitate to pass judgement.

In return, Christians had been very quick to keep up a pressure of their own. In April 313, petitions besought the Emperor to intervene on one or other side of the dispute between Donatist Christians and Catholics in Africa. Constantine's advisers had been well aware of this division. In winter 312/3, his letters to Africa already specified that only the Catholic clergy were to be their beneficiaries and referred to the "list" of suitable clerics which lay in Ossius's keeping.[50] From Cyprian's correspondence, we have seen the close contacts between the churches of southern Spain and Carthage: Ossius, bishop of Spain's Cordova, was in touch with the various parties to the African dispute. Whereas some of the first Donatist petitioners seemed uncertain about Constantine's own faith, the Emperor's letters had been only too clear about them.

At first, Constantine tried by all possible means to assign this dispute to picked groups of bishops for settlement among themselves. He had been invited into a Church quarrel and he looked to Christians to get him out of it. In fact, they tried to drag him ever further in. From Rome to Trier to Milan, Donatist petitioners dogged him until, after two years, he investigated the case himself and declared the Catholic bishop innocent. However, his decision could not end the dispute inside Africa itself. He threatened to visit the province; his orders probably led to the riots in 317 in which Christians in the African cities killed one another. In 321, his letters changed course and again urged toleration and concord, proposing that the Catholics should leave their sufferings to the vengeance of God. The Donatists prospered on the kind invitation.[51]

In his public statements since 313, Constantine had stressed how he himself, the "servant of God," was answerable for the concord of his Christian subjects.[52] Pagan Emperors had been concerned tradition-ally with the "peace of the gods," but never with unity of belief among their pagan subjects. Constantine's language owed less to the tra-ditional role of an Emperor than to Christian views of the heads of their communities, the bishops whom God held accountable for their flock. The thunderbolts of God were poised at a new target, not the sinners, the thieves and the "discoverers" of lost property, but the Emperor himself, who wrote of his genuine fear of God's wrath against his person if he failed to preside over Christian concord in the Church.

These letters, edicts and statements have a consistently Christian note which far outweighs the careful neutrality in aspects of the Emperor's publicity or the continuing patronage of pagans in his service. Already in 314, he was writing about the "kindness" of "our" God to the bishops whom he had assembled for a council at Arles.[53] He illustrated the fact by his own history. At first, he said, there had been much in himself "which lacked justice," as he never believed that a god could see into the secrets of the heart: the very notion had posed problems to Latin translators of Scripture.[54] In God, Constantine was already implying, he had experienced this new moral scrutiny, and it had moved him profoundly. As a result, he had become God's "servant." "Service" brought obligations: as Emperor, he was deeply concerned for Christian harmony, fearing that discord might annoy God. It would also discredit the faith before pagans, for in time, he assumes, all men will see the folly of their ways. Meanwhile, his personal statements show no sign of undercommitment or of a misunderstanding which is any grosser than many other recognized Christians'. If the reports of his conversion gave no explicit place to Scripture, in that, we know, they were not alone.[55] In the earlier third century, we have only to look at the philosophic tone of Minucius's fictional dialogue and its assumption that arguments from Providence sufficed to convert an educated pagan gentleman without any biblical teaching. At the end of the century, the prolific Christian apologist Arnobius was said, like Constantine, to have been converted one night by a dream. After his first "conversion," Constantine then recognized the truth of his faith from the most powerful proof: his own success. During the march down Italy and its aftermath, we can imagine an old Christian argument finding a relevant use, the argument of an Origen or Dionysius, that Christians prayed for the furtherance and stability of the Roman Emperor.[56] As Origen asserted, "if the Romans ever pray with complete agreement, they will be able to subdue many more pursuing armies than were destroyed by the power of Moses."

After 312, Constantine still lived and ruled among an overwhelmingly pagan majority. His troops were almost all pagans, and so were his ruling class and the aides whom he inherited. They drafted his laws, they issued his publicity, they attended his panegyrics. Sometimes, but not always, Constantine insisted on his own preference;[57] sometimes, a Christian aide would insist on his behalf; but there was not time to control everything, and the mixed tone of the laws and the publicity surely does not say anything about Constantine's own commitment. Doubts about its depth derive either from a reluctance to welcome such an Emperor as a Christian or from a particular angle of vision among Greek-speaking pagans in the East. Since 311, we can see Constantine trying to legitimize his own Imperial ancestry: Christianity gave his family a shared religion which fitted well with his dynastic aims. It did not stop murders and scandals among his own immediate family, for the first Christian Emperor could not afford to indulge in Christian mildness. Yet his claim to Christians' respect can rest fairly on his huge donations, his express concern with unity, his hatred of schism and heresy and his refusal to coerce the pagan majority by the direct use of force. Beside these rare attributes, the tragic dramas of his own family were the inevitable lot of an Emperor, exposed to suspicion and false testimony in his own household.

The pagan Greek views are more readily ascribed to prejudice. Until 324, the East lived under the pagan rule of Licinius: at a distance, Greek-speaking pagans could easily have mistaken the strength of the Western Emperor's convictions. To belittle Constantine's Christianity, subsequent writers of pagan history postponed its date.[58] Some ascribed it to greed: to pay for Constantinople, Constantine, they said, became a Christian and plundered the pagan temples. Others ascribed it to guilt: Constantine, they said, converted to Christ after murders in his own family in 326. One stubborn group of pagans in the city of

Harran ascribed it to disease: Constantine, they said, had been a leper and had converted to Christianity when he learned that it did not exclude lepers from its company. To refute this Eastern point of view, we must end by looking elsewhere, to the single most tantalizing document which was ascribed to Constantine's person. It admits, at last, of a date and context: properly placed, it prevents us from explaining these pagan views as a venial misunderstanding. It settles for ever the question of the Emperor's commitment when he embarked on the rule of a unified Christian Empire in 324. While giving the flavour of his public statements, it unifies the themes of this book.

# II

Shortly after Constantine's death, Eusebius published his work *On the Life of Constantine*. It was not a biography or a straightforward work of history. It was a stylized work of praise and its general remarks about the Emperor and his habits have to be read with this purpose in mind. However, it also quoted documents, and ever since an extract from one of them was discovered on a contemporary papyrus, their credit has stood very high.[1] One document does not prove the truth of them all, but the probability is that Eusebius quoted his written evidence fairly. It shows us Constantine through his own public statements and has a surer value than the intervening chapters which express Eusebius's generalizations.

Near the end of the *Life*, Eusebius noted that the Emperor composed his orations in Latin, but that they were translated into Greek by special interpreters. This habit, he assumed, would earn high praise from his readers, and to prove it, he announced that he would add an example to the end of the *Life*, the speech which Constantine inscribed "To the Assembly of the Saints."[2] In our manuscripts of the *Life*, a long Oration to the Saints follows, exactly as promised. The best manuscripts describe it as the *Life*'s "fifth book," and if genuine, it is our longest surviving statement from an Emperor between Marcus's *Meditations* and Julian's letters.

When Constantine's great modern historian, N. H. Baynes, set the study of his Christianity on a sound and enduring course, he passed judgement, regretfully, on the Oration. It had been rewritten, he believed, by others' hands: "the student of Christian apologetic must give to the Oration prolonged consideration, but the student of Constantine's personal convictions must exercise self-denial."[3] The judgement, however, can be overturned.

Between Eusebius's date of writing and the date of our earliest manuscript, we have two lists of Eusebius's works, one by Socrates, in the 430s, the other by Photius, in the mid-ninth century.[4] Neither included the Oration in his list, and although their silence has aroused suspicion, it tells, if anything, in favour of the work's authenticity. They would not have listed it in Eusebius's writings if they thought that it was written by Constantine.

"Discourses" by Constantine survived until the mid-sixth century at the very latest, for John the Lydian referred to them then and knew their contents.[5] In a famous chapter of the *Life*, Eusebius sketches their characteristics.[6] The Emperor, in his view, was not the ill-educated man of action, the mere soldier of Danubian extraction on whom secular historians have tended to concentrate. He was also a tireless public speaker who passed sleepless nights in studying theology, who missed no chance to reason with his subjects and "secure a rational obedience to his authority." He would sometimes call an assembly, to which crowds flocked "hoping to hear the Emperor perform the part of a philosopher." His reign was an age of long Christian vigils and ever-longer speeches. Eusebius recalled how his own speech on the Holy Sepulchre had gone on and on in Constantine's presence, and "after some time had passed, the speech being of considerable length, I myself wished to finish, but this he would not allow . . ." Constantine stood up throughout, said Eusebius, and listened carefully to every point of theology. During his own speeches, the Emperor would stand up in reverence whenever he touched on a sacred topic. At a reasonable rate of delivery, the Oration to the Saints would have continued for about two hours, but its length does not prove that it was revised after the first performance. Eusebius's own speech on the thirtieth anniversary of Constantine's reign exceeds it by half as much again. The preaching and theology of Constantine's court did not observe the usual limits of time.

Whenever occasion offered, so Eusebius tells us, Constantine liked to develop his usual themes. First he would attack the folly of paganism, then assert the sole rule of God. He would move on to Providence, "general and particular," and he would explain the necessity of God's salvation. He would dwell on the divine judgement and prick his audience's conscience by reminding them of rapacity's rewards in the world to come. His hearers "received his words with loud applause, but their insatiable greed induced them, in practice, to ignore them."

These same themes are the backbone of the Oration to the Saints, but they are not discussed in exactly this order or manner, and the slight variations tell somewhat against the idea of a later forgery. If Eusebius or anyone after him had wished to forge or embellish a speech by "Constantine," they would perhaps have followed the pattern which was thought to be typical. Our Oration is sufficiently close to this pattern to be Constantinian, but not so close that it is pure imitation.

The ascription to Constantine is secure: Eusebius, the manuscripts and the contents, as we shall see, support it. However, has the Oration been revised and expanded by later hands, by the translators into Greek, by court officials before publication or by someone who used it as part of the "history of Christian apologetics"? The translators, in particular, have attracted the highest level of scholarly interest. Behind the Greek, the great German philologists of the late nineteenth century believed that they could still detect original Latin constructions poking through the prose.[7] The idea was developed and the Oration was translated patiently back into Latin, in a version, however, which failed to find a publisher or to survive the Second World War. Here, at least, we can be more positive. These great scholars had tended to minimize the changes in Greek oratorical prose between the age of classical Athens and the fourth century A.D. None of their Latinisms survives scrutiny, nor, indeed, should we expect such Latinism to be visible if we look more widely at other documents, quoted by Eusebius as "translations from Latin." They are not so literal as to preserve Latin syntax.[8]

Has our Oration, therefore, been greatly enlarged after delivery while passing into Greek? The Greek translation was already known to Eusebius, and it was not his own work. This difficult question is best postponed until we have fixed a place and time for the Oration's first performance. If, as we shall see, the Oration was delivered by the Emperor to a Greek audience, its first public hearing could already have included all the phrasing in our Greek text. Only if it was spoken to a Latin audience would the Greek version necessarily raise questions of alteration after delivery. Indeed, there is room for further doubt. Constantine, we know, addressed the Council of Nicaea in Latin, which interpreters turned into Greek. However, he knew Greek himself and one section of the Oration depends on this knowledge. It cites the poetry of Virgil in Greek and comments on phrases which could only occur in the preceding Greek translation.[9] Attempts to deny this point have failed: either, then, this entire section was inserted afterwards, or else the Emperor used the Greek text and its Greek interpretations during composition. The latter is surely the right answer, for the section on Virgil is tied closely to the Oration's argument. It is preceded by a long quotation of Greek verses from a Sibyl's prophecy which only made sense in Greek. Rather than reject these central sections, we should, perhaps, doubt Eusebius: if he only had a Greek copy of the Oration, how did he know there had once been a Latin original? In other documents, the fact of translation was expressed in the prefatory title, but our texts of the Oration carry no such clue.[10] Two of its long sections tell against an independent Latin original, expanded after delivery: was the speech a Greek creation from start to finish and did it prove rather more about the Emperor's language than Eusebius believed? At the very least, the Greek translators cooperated with the Emperor before the speech was made public.

These questions are a fascinating exercise in philology, but they cannot obscure a broader point. The Oration was not revised and clarified in any detail between delivery and publication. We can assert this because the speech contains some very oblique allusions to moments in the speaker's past, to its audience, its setting and timing. Together, these remarks allow us to fix the speech to a place and occasion, but they require a background whose pieces have only become clear to us again in the past eighty years. If the speech had been carefully revised before publication, these obscure allusions would have been explained more fully for their wider readership. They were left untouched and were surely beyond the range of a later forger.

While speaking on the vengeance of God, the author of the speech chose to support it by facts which he had seen on his travels: Memphis, he said, lay desolate and Babylon was now in ruins. How Pionius would have applauded these observations. They have now been placed decisively in Constantine's early career. As a young man, he had served as a tribune in the army, and in 297/8, he could have accompanied Galerius on his famous march to Ctesiphon.[11] If so, the ruins of Babylon lay conveniently beside his route. In spring 302, we now know that the Emperor Diocletian was in Egypt. Constantine was with him on his return journey, and it was probably then that

Eusebius saw him for the first time. Presumably, Constantine had been in Egypt too, and the fate of Memphis was evident to any traveller in the land.

These allusions, then, are Constantine's own, and no later author imagined them. What of the speech's setting? Its opening dates it plainly to a Good Friday. The "first pledge of Resurrection, the path which leads to everlasting life, in brief the day of the Passion has arrived." The audience includes Christian experts and laymen, "best-beloved leaders and you, my friends who are assembled, you blessed crowds who worship the Author of all worship." It addresses this audience in two separate phrases which perplexed most of the manuscripts and led to a confusion in the text.[12] The first addressed the "captain, endowed with holy virginity," the second the "nurse of tender and inexpert youth, whom truth concerns, whom kindliness concerns, from whose eternal spring flows the draught of salvation." The first phrase refers to an individual, a celibate Christian who led the Church; the second probably refers to the Church itself. Together, the opening addresses a Christian assembly which is presided over by a bishop and composed of laymen and experts. This setting suits its title: a speech to an "assembly of saints." The saints are Christians, "assembled" in a church service or perhaps in a synod, or meeting.[13]

If the opening gives us the setting, the end gives us a date and place. After a great survey of God's Providence and salvation and the copious proofs of both, Constantine turned to a personal topic: the favour of Providence for himself. Diocletian's army, he remarked, had passed to the "authority of a worthless person who seized the Empire of the Romans by force, but the entire army has been destroyed in many, various battles, while the Providence of God was freeing the great city."[14] There could be "no more evident proof of the judgement of God. The world itself applauds, the course of the stars shines more clearly and plainly, rejoicing, I think, at the punishment of the unjust." Three of the manuscripts found this flourish too much for them and left it out. But "what of the appeals to God from the oppressed," said Constantine, "and from those who were longing for their freedom? Are not these convincing proofs of God's Providence and his affectionate concern for mankind?" These "proofs" led once again to Constantine's view of himself. "When men praise my service, as one who holds the Empire by the inspiration of God, do they not, then, confirm that God is the cause of my prowess?"

He speaks as if these "convincing proofs" were very recent, a hint which is supported by the tenses of his verbs. Present participles refer to the "liberation" and the recent "cries of the oppressed," while the opposing army "has been destroyed," in a perfect tense which probably retains its force. In Greek, it suggests a sudden, recent triumph, although in other contexts the speaker, admittedly, has used it more loosely. Who, then, was the "worthless usurper" who had taken Diocletian's army? There are only two possibilities: Maxentius or Licinius. Maxentius, a frequent favourite, does not fit the reference. Before his defeat in 312, a few of Diocletian's former soldiers in the East may have deserted to his troops in Italy, but his army could not be described as Diocletian's, even by rhetorical licence. He was not "destroyed in many, various battles": his troops lost two sieges and a conventional land battle. Licinius, however, lost a huge sea battle and his troops were twice defeated on land. His army could be connected with Diocletian's without too great an exaggeration.[15] As we shall see, Licinius suits the allusion to "liberation" and the "great and dearest city." He also suits a silence in the speech. Constantine did not dwell on the fate of the "worthless usurper" himself, and if the man was Maxentius, the silence was very odd: after his defeat, Maxentius was said to have ridden in full armour into the Tiber and drowned himself. His death gave ample scope to Christian rhetoric, whereas Licinius's death was less appealing. After his defeat, he petitioned Constantine for mercy through his wife, Constantine's own sister. Publicly, Constantine announced a pledge that Licinius would be spared, but by mid-325, Licinius had been strangled.

The "usurper," then, was Licinius, and the speech insisted on his "destruction," not his temporary defeat. A sequence of "various battles" had brought about Licinius's downfall, an event which is fixed in autumn 324. The speech, then, was delivered on the next Good Friday, in the second week of April 325. Either Licinius was still alive or his recent death was too vexed a topic to be mentioned.

Where, lastly, was this Christian assembly held and where was the "great city" whose "liberation" had been so recent? Cities from far and wide have been canvassed as candidates, but the dating to 325 restricts the choice. The "city" is contrasted with Rome; in April 325, it can only have lain in the Eastern Empire, where Constantine resided in triumph.[16] Once again, we have just enough detail to find the answer.

To the kindness of God, said Constantine, he attributed his own good fortune and his many victories. The "great city," he continued, also acknowledges and approves this fact, as do its people, even if they had been briefly led astray and had chosen themselves an unworthy leader. Their choice was "immediately taken captive," and Constantine did not wish to discuss him further while making a pious speech in such sacred company. Instead, he went on, he must mention the Church's loyal piety during a persecution which the "tyrants" ordered against "all the communities." The Christian martyrs had not flinched and the tortures had persuaded nobody. How, then, said Constantine, addressing the author of all this wickedness, had you ever thought that persecution would do any good? The gods, perhaps, had seemed angry to you, or perhaps the ways of your ancestors required it. Perhaps you thought that some special power resided in images shaped like men and fashioned by artists and craftsmen?

Constantine, plainly, was speaking in the "great, dearest city." His allusions were never revised before the speech's general publication, but they were explained conveniently in a subsequent commentary. Manuscripts of the speech divide its length with short headings which help the reader to grasp the allusions in the text. These headings are not always very specific, but they surely go back to a hand which was contemporary with Eusebius's. To judge from similar headings in his other works, their author is almost certainly Eusebius himself.[17] They show us how a contemporary, probably Eusebius, understood the speech's reference. For the "dearest city" section, the heading explains that "the Emperor gratefully ascribes his victories and other good fortune to Christ and condemns the conduct of the tyrant Maximin, the violence of whose persecution enhanced the glory of the faith."

The heading has been ignored or emended, but instead, it ought to be tested as it stands. It makes excellent sense. As Caesar, then Augustus, Maximin had presided over repeated bouts of persecution in the cities under his authority and had allowed the violence to continue from 311 to 313. In summer 311, he seized the chance of Galerius's death and invaded Asia Minor, appealing to its subjects by offers of a change in tax. Moving up from his seat at Antioch, he fits very well as the "unworthy champion" of the "great and dearest city" whose citizens largely supported his advance. Maximin was "caught immediately" by two defeats in 313. His conqueror was Licinius in the wake of Constantine's own conversion.[18]

When Constantine turned to the Church's bravery during this final persecution, his language was less precise. "War," he said, had been declared by "the tyrants" against "all the most holy churches" and "there was not a lack of people in Rome who rejoiced" at this event. Perhaps he was alluding to the start of the Great Persecution in 303; perhaps he was thinking of Maximin's last persecution in the East and the rumour which he later exploited, that people in Rome had secretly connived with Maximin's conduct.[19] His words were too vague to be pressed, but when he turned to address the individual who had thought that persecution would succeed, his language was more suggestive. "Did you think that some special power resides in images . . . ?" The words suggest the famous action of Theotecnus, a pagan official in Maximin's domains who consecrated a statue to Zeus Philios in Antioch and received oracles against the Christians from its "special power."[20] Constantine, it seems, first touched on the "unworthy Maximin," whom the "people" of the "great city" had wrongly supported. Then he turned to a generalized picture of the persecutions before returning again to "most impious" Maximin and the particular folly of his ways.

If we follow the heading and apply these words to Maximin, the "dearest city" ought to be Antioch, Maximin's seat as ruler of the East. The case, as we shall see, is confirmed by Constantine's own movements, but already it suits some small details. Antioch was indeed a "great city," called by this very title in Libanius's speeches in the 380s and set beside Rome as one of the Empire's three or four great cities in artistic groups of the mid-fourth century.[21] In 311, its people were said by Maximin to have petitioned him to continue the persecutions: before a Christian audience in Antioch, Constantine's tactful allusions were well advised. At Antioch, too, we can explain a final detail which has troubled recent readers of the speech.

During his long address, Constantine spoke of the authority of the Sibyl and described her as a priestess of Apollo. Her parents had given her up to a "service which led to nothing fine or noble, but only to indecent fury, as in the case of Daphne." Apollo, the Emperor implied, had lusted after his priestesses and inspired them by sexual contact. This insult to pagan prophecy was popular among early Christian writers, but the comparison with Daphne was something new. It referred to Daphne the person, not Daphne the place: "Apollo hunted Daphne so only that she might laurel grow . . ." The allusion was apt anywhere, but nowhere more apt than before a Christian audience in Antioch. They knew the famous sanctuary in Antioch's suburb of Daphne, which was said to commemorate the Daphne of Apollo's attention. It even contained the very laurel tree into which Daphne had turned.[22] When denouncing Apollo's frenzy, the Emperor referred aptly to a local female victim.

The speech contains no other clues to its date, place and audience, but these few suffice. The day was Good Friday, the year 325 in the immediate wake of Licinius's defeat. The audience was an "assembly" of Christians, some of whom were experts in doctrine, all of whom were presided over by a bishop "endowed with holy virginity." The site lay in the Greek East, where Antioch emerges as the likeliest "great city." It remains to set these clues beside what we know of Constantine's movements in early 325. From some very varied sources, enough emerges to place the speech in an unexpected light.

# III

On September 18, 324, Constantine defeated Licinius for the last time, and on November 8, he marked out the boundaries of his new city, Constantinople. Between his victory and the following spring, he issued a flurry of public statements to enforce and explain his Christian purpose.[1] Eusebius alludes to six such documents in swift succession: a letter to the churches of God, which he does not quote; a letter to the heathen, which he translates from Latin into Greek and cites from a copy which was sent to the people of his own province, Palestine: it was ordered to be published like an edict throughout the East. Two laws, in Eusebius's view, banned pagan sacrifice and divination; each bishop also received a letter about the building and rebuilding of churches at the Emperor's expense: Eusebius quoted his own copy, the first letter, he said, which was addressed to him personally by Constantine. Lastly, he translated from Latin a long letter which was sent yet again to the East's heathen. Whereas the First Letter to the Heathen had said more about specific privileges for the Christians, this remarkable Second Letter sketched the Emperor's views of his faith. It explained recent history, Christian theology and the permissibility of paganism, mistaken though it was, for those who could not yet be convinced by the obvious Christian truth. Later than the others, it probably belongs in early 325.

This deliberate publicity by letter is very revealing. To the buildings, inscriptions and edicts of earlier Emperors, Constantine added a new medium: unsolicited letters for their own sake. We have evidence of others' publicity on Constantine's behalf in the Imperial coin types and panegyrics, but their relatively neutral allusions to religion are of small significance beside the explicit content of the Emperor's own "circulars" to his new subjects, pagans and Christians alike. It is at just this moment, in April 325, that we have placed the public, Christian statement of the Oration to the Saints. Intellectually, we now see, it belongs excellently with the Emperor's activities in the preceding months, and it also sits well with a type of document which Eusebius had acquired and used when writing his *Life*: public statements, sent through the East, in 324/5. Unlike the letters, the Oration was not translated from Latin by Eusebius or his aides: they knew a Greek version, perhaps because only a Greek text had ever existed.

Beside the three fully-quoted texts, we should probably set a fourth, which was addressed to a more distant audience. In winter 324/5, Constantine is said to have received an embassy from Persia.[2] In the *Life*, Eusebius states that "a personally written letter of the Emperor" was available to him in Latin and that he would cite it in a Greek translation so that it could be better known. It was addressed by Constantine to Shapur, the Persian king. We do not know how Eusebius came by his copy in Latin, which had apparently not been circulated widely, but its contents sit admirably with the Emperor's public statements in winter 324/5. The text, perhaps, was Constantine's answer to this Persian embassy.

The Persian and provincial letters bear a very strong resemblance to themes in the Oration to the Saints. They are grouped closely from autumn 324 to spring 325, and throw a powerful and consistent light on the Emperor's public views of his triumph. The First Letter to the provincials of the East emphasized how persecutors of the Church had all come to a horrible end, whereas observers of the divine law prospered and pleased God. Constantine himself was a proof of this truth. "Surely it cannot be thought arrogance for one who has been benefitted by God to acknowledge this in the loftiest terms . . . Beginning at the remote Ocean around Britain and those regions where, according to the law of nature, the sun sinks below the horizon, through the aid of the divine power I banished and utterly rooted out every form of prevailing wickedness . . . in the hope that the human race, enlightened by me, might be recalled to the fit observance of the holy laws of God . . ." The moral crusader from Britain claimed to have swept the world with the guidance of God.

The king of Persia received a similar statement.[3] "Beginning from the very borders of the Ocean," Constantine claimed to have freed and confirmed every people whom he met. He stressed his Christian faith: "this God I invoke with bended knees." He stressed his personal "horror at the blood of sacrifices" and the fire worship which was practised in Persia. His God brought justice and peace and confirmed the rule of kings, whereas pagan rulers came to a miserable end: Shapur was referred to the fate of the pagan Emperor Valerian, who had been "driven from hence by the thunderbolt of divine vengeance" and made a captive of the Persian king. Constantine expressed delight at the news of Christians "in the fairest districts of Persia" and commended them to Shapur's care, in the name of God. He also alluded to his own recent knowledge of God's wrath. He had seen the deaths of the persecuting rulers and the return of Christians to peace "through the Providence of God." "Those who had been 'groaning in servitude to the cruellest tyrants' have been restored through me to a happier state." The concluding language and tenses of the Oration bear a very close relation to these statements.

In early 325, the "Second Letter to the Eastern provinces" dwelt on philosophy and the Emperor's personal creed at greater length than did its predecessor.[4] Ever more strongly, it sounded notes which reach a climax in the Oration to the Saints. Divine forethought and intelligence, so Constantine began, are proved by the law and order of the universe. The authors of the Great Persecution have met a miserable end in hell: no reference, however, is made to the death of Licinius, that embarrassing event which perhaps still lay in the future. Constantine is God's "servant," as he describes himself in the Oration: "under God's guidance I have contrived and accomplished measures full of blessings." After the Fall, God's Son had brought light and salvation to sinful men, and the order of the world, wrote Constantine, now proves God's forethought. Without God's hand, the winds and the sea, the earth and the seasons would clash in fatal strife. In their harmony, God's power is self-evident, but although the remaining pagans are foolish and impious, Christians must live with them as their neighbours in peace. Paganism is gross and false, but "it is one thing to undertake the contest for immortality voluntarily, another to compel others to do likewise through fear of punishment." Though utterly contemptuous of the pagan cults, the first Christian Emperor was far more tolerant than the Christian bishops and holy men who surrounded and succeeded him.

In late 324 and early 325, themes, then, of the Oration were already sounding for the first time in Constantine's surviving letters to the

East. There was no mistaking his public image, and already in 324/5, the little town of Orcistus, in Phrygia, appealed to him for promotion; it cited its many civic amenities, its crowded forum, its Imperial statues, its water mills, but also the fact that it was a totally Christian community.[5] In spring 325, Constantine's plans and movements rest on more intricate evidence. On February 23, 325, Constantine was issuing laws entitled "At Nicomedia" and was probably still resident there. By June 1, 325, he was present at Nicaea for the great Christian council. Between February and June, his time was rather more active, a pattern which is confirmed by two fortunate papyri from Egypt, some local coins and another letter from his pen.[6]

On January 13, 325, a papyrus refers to the "coming visit" of the Emperor to Egypt, and on May 26, another refers to animals which "were despatched for the divine visit," again the visit of the Emperor. Constantine, clearly, had been expected to tour his new conquests and go as far south as the Nile. In a subsequent letter, he himself implies this very purpose.[7] By the hand of his trusted cleric, Ossius, he sent a letter to the heretic Arius and his opponent in Alexandria. In it, he revealed intentions which their quarrelling, he said, had frustrated. "When I stopped recently in Nicomedia, my plan was to press on to the East at once. But while I was hurrying towards you and was already past the greater part of the journey," on the likeliest translation of his words, "the news of this business reversed my plan, so that I might not be forced to see with my eyes what I did not think possible ever to reach my hearing." From Nicomedia, then, the Emperor had indeed turned south on a journey through the East to Alexandria and had nearly reached Egypt when reports of the Arian heresy obliged him to turn back. The local coinage along his route reveals how far he went.

At Antioch, a series of gold coins survives stamped with the legend "Adventus Augusti," or "arrival of the Emperor."[8] On technical grounds, they have been dated independently to spring 325, and although those grounds are not conclusive, their legend fits perfectly with the wording of Constantine's letter. The type and legend of this *adventus* issue were conventional, but at the very least they prove that the Emperor was expected to reach the city on his journey. Their "arrival" makes the necessary sense of Constantine's words on his "greater part of the journey" to Egypt. He reached Antioch in spring 325, heard the news of Arius and despatched Ossius with his letter to the heretic, while himself, he retraced his tracks.

This journey through the Eastern Empire ties up with two very different types of contemporary verse. One was the work of an exiled pagan senator, the Ovid of the Constantinian age. Publius Optatianus Porfyrius had held the governorship of Achaea but was exiled before the year 320, perhaps in a political scandal which involved his friends.[9] After his exile, he petitioned Constantine for leave to return and sent him a series of intricate poems which were "glittering in purple, silver and gold." As a poet, Porfyrius showed a brilliant art. He wove patterns and acrostics through his verses and spelt out allusions to their dates and patrons. The ancient commentators were hardly less adept at recognizing the hidden meanings than Porfyrius at constructing them. He was no Virgil, but in an age which is dominated, to our eye, by religious evidence, there is something to be said for a senator who could send a poem to a friend, concealing in its inner design the name of the man who was enjoying adultery with the recipient's wife.

Of his poems to Constantine, we have a group which belonged in the months between Licinius's defeat and Constantine's celebrations in July 325. Two of them sound an Eastern note in their flatteries.[10] One alleges that the "Medes and Parthians" now honour the new master of the East, the "lord of the Nile." The other pictures Constantine as passing through his Eastern conquests while "all Syene," in southern Egypt, begs him to give her his laws. Roman poets' allusions to Eastern places and peoples were usually more fulsome than factual. The details cannot be pressed, but the themes of Eastern travel and the mastery of Egypt sit very well with the hints of Constantine's plan.

The other poem is less direct. By 324, Lactantius had served as the Christian tutor to Constantine's son, and among his prose works, he is credited with a burst of Latin hexameters on that symbolic bird, the phoenix. The poem is plainly the work of a Christian, and the case for the Christian being Lactantius is sound, but not certain.[11] Among pagan men of letters, the phoenix had long exerted a particular spell. It created itself from its own ashes and united the mystery of a home in Egypt with the inauguration of a new age. Christians had been quick to use the bird as a type of their own Resurrection, a tradition which Lactantius followed. From its "happy home, far off in the most distant east," the young phoenix would rise anew from its ashes and fly to its "ancestral home" in the first flush of reborn perfection. Its colours evoked the best in Lactantius's imagination. Its feathers, he wrote, would shine with the bloom of poppies and pomegranates when it returned to Heliopolis, the city of the Sun. "Egypt comes hither to see the marvel of such a sight, and a jubilant crowd welcomes this rare bird . . ." There were two pagan traditions about the length of time between its appearances, either five hundred or a thousand years. Lactantius preferred the latter, perhaps because it suggested a new millennium.

As tutor to the Emperor's son, Lactantius could not have published such a poem without its subject reaching the notice of Imperial circles. Much in his prose works moves in harmony with the Emperor's own themes and theology: his poetry, too, would be known at court. The unfinished revisions of the prose works imply that Lactantius died in 325: if so, his poem on the phoenix existed before Constantine visited Egypt. Was there, perhaps, a closer connection? To support it, we have to look far ahead to John of Salisbury's *Policraticus*, a twelfth-century source of no independent value.[12] However, John's wide reading in classical authors shows through many of his anecdotes, and when at one point he lists examples of classical omens, most of them derive directly from Justin; then he remarks on the singular good fortune of a sighting of the phoenix. The point, he said, was proved by the foundation of Constantinople, the "new Rome" which was founded with good omen "after a sighting of the phoenix." His source for this statement is unknown, as is the exact date he had in mind: Constantine marked out the boundary of his new city in November 324, but it was not dedicated until May 330. The founding of Constantinople attracted tales of every sort of omen, and John may simply be wrong. But reports of the phoenix's reappearance may have been circulating in November 324, as his words imply, and if so, they give the planned Egyptian visit a special interest. Tales of a sighting of the phoenix had long agitated the learned men of Greece and senatorial Rome: did Constantine set out to tour his new conquests with high hopes for its ornithology, hopes which are reflected in Lactantius's poem?

In 325, his Christian visit to Egypt was not to go unwitnessed by the pagan world. A year later, in 326, we have the inscription of the noble Athenian Nicagoras, son of one of the city's most learned families and himself a Eumolpid, priest in the mysteries at Eleusis.[13] At the Syrinxes of Upper Egypt, by Memnon's talking statue, Nicagoras recorded his thanks to the Emperor: Constantine, he revealed, had paid for his journey to the land of the Nile. This conspicuous patronage of a pagan has long provoked comment on the first Christian Emperor. It was not, however, a proof of his lingering pagan sympathies and it may have had a particular motive. Nicagoras's family had had historical interests; he himself was a priest in the great pagan mysteries which concerned the afterlife. If Constantine had gone to Egypt with hopes of sighting the phoenix, who better to witness it than this leading pagan from Athens? The phoenix, Lactantius had written, was a bird "neither male nor female," reborn without sex from its ashes, "not the same, because she is, and is not, herself, yet acquiring eternal life by the blessings of death." It proved the idea of bodily resurrection and could teach the great pagans of Athens the truth about life after death.

With or without the phoenix, Constantine's tour of his Eastern conquests was sure to be a grand occasion. It would take him back to the scene of his travels some twenty-three years earlier, but now for the first time, the entire Empire was under the sway of one Christian ruler. Yet the visit to Egypt never took place. As the Emperor remarked in his letter, the Arian heresy turned him back. Between autumn 324 and the opening of Nicaea's council in early June 325, some of his concerns can still be reconstructed, and of the several reconstructions which the details allow, the following is the simplest. Its framework is certain and only the minor details are arguable at this critical point in Christian history, the prelude to the Council of Nicaea. Its events fix the occasion of the Good Friday speech.

When Constantine entered Asia, he was weary from his long and unfortunate tangle with the Donatists' schism in North Africa. By 324, a sequence of petitions and rescripts, councils and plain threats had already taught him that not even the fear of God's vengeance could force Christians to agree. His problems, however, were only beginning. Since c. 318, perhaps earlier, Arius's heresy on the nature and divinity of Christ had been a cause célèbre in the East. Under Licinius's rule, Christian synods had been banned, and when Constantine entered Asia, this violent dispute had probably not been aired very recently in public company.[14] Constantine probably knew of it, but not, perhaps, of its continuing vigour. By early 325, a "great and holy synod" of Christian leaders had been summoned to meet at Ancyra, and although this initiative is not traced directly to Constantine, its "great and holy" status implies his own involvement and encouragement. The site of Ancyra has been minimized as an inconvenient backwater, but we must remember that it stood on the main network of Asia's roads and on the main route to the West.[15] Bishops from each half of the Empire could have been summoned to meet at Ancyra in the first great synod since the Christian conquest of the Empire. Although we cannot date the first issuing of this summons exactly in the months from November 324 to April 325, the idea was a natural sequel to Constantine's final victory in the East, at a time when he need not have had the Arian dispute particularly in mind. It was only one good reason among others for a synod; the date of Easter needed discussion; the new peace of the unified Christian Empire ought to be celebrated; there were persistent problems of discipline and Christian sin. In the winter of 324/5, Constantine expected to travel south to Egypt: he could return to his Ancyra council after the visit.

To prepare his path in the East, we know that he sent Bishop Ossius, the Christian eminence of his court. We also know that trouble had arisen in Antioch.[16] The bishop of this major Eastern see had been a keen opponent of Arius, but on December 20, 324, he had died. Ossius's manoeuvres are not entirely clear to us, but we know that he intervened in both Antioch and Alexandria, and these interventions are best placed in early 325. To Antioch, we know, he summoned bishops from Palestine, Arabia and Cappadocia, who duly met there in April; by then, a new bishop had been appointed in the city. Probably, the appointment had been encouraged by Ossius when he first reached the vacant see. The contest taught him the extreme feelings which the Arian heresy still aroused, and hence, presumably, he summoned the Antioch synod at the same time in order to straighten matters out. If possible, he wished to avoid dispute before the Western visitors reached Ancyra in the coming summer. For the same purpose, he went on from Antioch to visit Alexandria, the root of the Arian heresy. There, too, he summoned a local synod, presumably of the bishops in Egypt; so far as we know, he was less concerned at this time with Arian problems than with the deposition of a schismatic bishop and his creations. These meetings and decisions took some time: by early April, he could return from Egypt to Antioch, where his synod was now meeting.

By a happy discovery, the Acts of this Council of Antioch were found in a Syriac version and published in 1905.[17] Their truth was vigorously contested, but the attack soon failed and Church historians have had to live with this unexpected prelude to the great Council of Nicaea. Before that synod, we now know, there was an attempt to "fix" Christian opinion in one of the bitterest regions of the Arian dispute. In 1958, a second discovery in a Syriac manuscript put the guidance of this council beyond doubt: Ossius's name emerged as its presiding bishop.[18] At Antioch, the Emperor Constantine's interests were advanced by his chief authority.

While the truth of these Syriac Acts was being debated, they were not brought to bear on an older problem, the date and nature of the Oration to the Saints. By the time their worth had been established, the Oration itself had been suspected as a later apologist's work or had been diverted to an untenably early date. While interest in its dating faded, the newly found Council of Antioch was overlooked as a possible venue. Yet "while I was hurrying towards you," Constantine wrote to Arius, "and was already past the greater part of the journey, the news of this business reversed my plan . . ." The gold coinage at Antioch attests the Emperor's expected arrival in the city; there, in spring 325, "news of this business" would have met him unmistakably at Ossius's council. The allusions in the Oration have already required a setting on Good Friday in April 325 before a Christian assembly which included doctrinal experts and looked up to a "virgin Christian" as its leader. The Council of Antioch brought such an assembly to the city: it was headed, we now know, by the celibate Ossius, the "captain" of "holy virginity." Antioch, as we have already suspected, is confirmed as the "great and dearest city." The Oration is not an apologist's fiction, nor is it the freely revised publicity of the Emperor's advisers. It is the Good Friday sermon of April 325, which was preached in Antioch to a church congregation, while the council, presumably, drew to its close before Easter. Nicaea, then, was not the first Church council to discuss the Arian problem in the presence of the Emperor's agent; it was not even the first council in the East which the Emperor attended and addressed. The Oration concluded Antioch's proceedings: we must follow carefully what the Emperor said.[19]

Constantine's speech has been criticized for incoherence and an inability to follow an argument through. These qualities have called its authorship in question, as if an Emperor could not ramble on the topic of God and the world. Its context at Antioch, on Good Friday 325, may help to excuse its digressions.

The "assembly of saints" was a church congregation of Christians, but it included the bishops and theologians who had gathered for the council. Such an audience was daunting. If Constantine was to hold their attention, he needed to combine the skills of a sermon and a scholarly communication. He could reassure the audience by repeating refutations of old and long-abandoned views: these conventional statements proved that he was one of their own Christian group and reinforced their sense that they were so much wiser than the world. He also needed some new evidence, things which he had seen or read and which his hearers, with their different background, would like to ponder and debate among themselves. Then he could end on the important note, the favour of God for his "servant" Constantine, as proved by history and the "liberation" of the previous autumn.

As a speech to a critical audience, the Oration has its merits. Its grasp of the Bible is not always firm and its allusions have a pleasant inaccuracy, but before its audience, these slips mattered less than the movement of the surrounding whole. Its style was no more verbose than other Christian sermons'. It would not have disgraced the young Gregory, straining to praise his Origen, but its shape and direction had rather more force.

Good Friday gave Constantine a powerful, if complex, opening. It was the day of promise and salvation, he began, and it proved that God's own Providence excelled the innate benefits of nature, which he himself created. The prophets had been inspired to preach this Providence, but men had ignored them and practised injustice until the coming of Christ. Christ had founded the eternal Church on earth, but the pagans had ignored him too. They had continued to fight among themselves and to lust for money, that particular vice.

After a brief address to Ossius and his audience, Constantine turned to refute pagan views about the world. A few passing comments on God and his Word came horribly close to heresy, but the general attack was more conventional. Idolatry was wrong and so was polytheism. There was only one God, and his Providence was proved by some hopeful theology: Adam and Eve, said Constantine, had been creatures endowed with reason and God had therefore revealed to them the difference between good and evil. The Emperor did not allude to the dark story of the Fall. Adam and Eve, he said, had merely grown into the gift of reason, just as God had bestowed on men the gifts of wild and tame animals and birds with the power of song. The order and beauty of this world were living proofs of Providence. Chance could never have created such flowers and seasons, mountains, rivers or seas. These examples were conventional and pagans had often used them: there is a particular irony in their use in this Christian context, as we happen to know that Maximin himself, the vilest of pagan "tyrants," had recently cited them in his rescripts to the Greek East, using them as proofs of the pagan gods.[20] Imperial rhetoric had a common store of themes, but it was important to reassert this commonplace in the Christian cause.

Constantine capped it with the first of his personal touches. After broaching these well-worn themes, he alerted the saints in Antioch by asking them to ponder the mysteries of natural hot springs. They were rare, he believed, but they were not random. In these hot springs, Providence combined the opposites of heat and cold and showed her infinite forethought in their natural clouds of steam. Seventy-five years earlier, the crowds in Smyrna had been told to see them differently, yet the Emperor's speech saw only the best in God's choice of possible worlds. By a fine irony, we may be able to trace this interest in hot water to its source.[21] In 310, the panegyrist at Trier had flattered Constantine with his "vision" of Apollo and then asked him to visit and favour his city. It was a noble place, he said, which possessed some unusual springs: "the spouting water, covered with steam, will seem, Constantine, to smile to your very eyes . . ." Constantine, it seems, took his panegyrist at his word: fifteen years later, far from Trier, hot springs surfaced in a kindly fashion in his speech to a Christian audience.

The evidence of hot springs was joined by the distribution of metals. The more precious the metal, the rarer were its seams, and if God, said Constantine, had made gold more common, nobody would have bothered to dig up the iron which daily life needed. The laws of supply and demand were suspended by the first Christian Emperor: "to trace the secret reasons for all these things is a task beyond human capacities."

His examples had caught his audience's interest, and carefully, he moved back to more usual ground. It was time to berate the philosophers. The mysteries of Providence proved the narrow limits of human reason. Socrates's critical questioning had merely enraged his fellow citizens and shown itself to be a menace to the state. Pythagoras had stolen his teaching from Egypt, and Plato had believed that there were many gods. Plato, however, had groped towards the truth in his *Timaeus* when he wrote about a first and second God. He had hinted that the soul was born from the breath of God, and he had written some excellent passages on future punishments in hell. Essentially, these pagan philosophers had strived to know the unknowable: Constantine's criticisms attached to a long tradition of pagan polemic against philosophy, some of which the Christians had already borrowed. Yet, though philosophers were bad, they were not so bad as poets. People said that poets were entitled to tell lies occasionally, but they joined their lies to impiety and wrote falsely about the gods.

In a few broad sweeps, Constantine had damned the free use of reason and had banished poetic imagination. It was time to be more positive. God, he said, had resolved to restore order and justice through the mission of his Son, a purpose which the prophets had foretold. There were two types of birth, said the Emperor, the eternal and the natural, and he described Christ's birth as the second, the natural birth of the pre-existent Word. His language here trod dangerously close to Arius's heresy, but a scriptural "type" helped to soften it. A dove, said Constantine, had alighted on the Virgin Mary, like the dove which had flown from Noah's ark. The comparison is found in no other surviving early Christian text. On earth, he continued, Christ had differed from the philosophers because he imparted true wisdom. His hearers had been wise and honourable men, not illiterate Galilean rustics, and they drew their lessons from Christ's miracles and from the portents which surrounded his death. After his Passion, God's grace had restored the face of the darkened world, by giving it its former beauty and studding it with heavenly stars. Lyrical for a moment, Constantine paused to refute two acute pagan objections: could not God have softened men's hearts to receive his Son, or could he not have given all men the same moral nature? The Emperor defended man's freedom to accept or refuse the gifts of Grace. He stressed the obvious virtues of Jesus's teaching, the predictions of the prophets and the knowledge of those whom God's prompting had saved from danger. They, above all, could recognize the power of faith. Here, Constantine seemed to hint at his own experience, a note which recurred in his following proof. While asserting the vanity of pagan sacrifice, animal and human alike, "I myself," he said, "was present and conducted researches and was an eyewitness of the pitiable fate of the cities Memphis and Babylon," old seats of pagan empires. The audience would welcome these reports from a man of so many travels who had seen so much more of the world.[22] God's wrath, once again, was at large in the landscape for anyone who cared to see it.

The destruction of Memphis had been worked in answer to Moses's prayers. As Constantine's speech gained strength, it enlarged on Moses's merits, on the wisdom which had been stolen by Greek philosophers and the cautious laws which had shaped the Hebrew people. One man's prayers suggested another's, the prayers of Daniel, who had once preached humility to "rapacious" Nebuchadnezzar:

Constantine, like Origen, had no doubt about these stories' truth. Like the three boys in the fiery furnace, Daniel had overcome a tyrant's persecution, and then, said Constantine, the "Assyrian kingdom was destroyed by the thunderbolts of God." The comment was peculiar to him, but it befitted the man who had seen the ruins of Babylon and explained them by the wrath of God. After Assyria's ruin, said the Emperor, Daniel had moved to the Persian court of Cambyses, where he worked his miracles and prayed intently three times a day. The Magi became jealous of this new superior, and so he was cast to the lions in the royal den. By faith and prayer, he triumphed yet again and caused Cambyses to throw the Magi to the lions in his place. "Formerly so gentle, the beasts rushed at once onto their victims and tore and destroyed them all with the full fierceness of their nature." Like Assyria's ruin by "thunderbolts," these events between Daniel and the Magi are known nowhere else. If the story was a free invention, it sits well with an Emperor whom contemporaries were urging to a Persian triumph and who had probably sent his Christian letter to the Persian king only a few months before. In Sassanid Persia at this time, the Magi were influential: Antioch, of all places, knew the horror of Persian invasions, and an audience in the city would be glad to hear of God's vengeance on Magi at the Persian court. As for Daniel, he remained a favourite in Imperial publicity: Eusebius tells how his image was set on public fountains in Constantinople, fashioned from bronze and gold.[23]

For Constantine's purpose, the heroes of Scripture were an insufficient proof of the powers of God. He wished to confound all pagan objectors by proving the truth from their own sources, and it was here that his speech moved from the commonplace to the less expected. He began by quoting the wisdom of that ancient pagan prophetess, the Sibyl, who had been a priestess, he said, from Erythrae and had served Apollo at the "serpent's Tripod" in Delphi. Her parents had devoted her to this service, but no good came of it, as she was troubled by the advances of the so-called god. The consequences were known to his audience through the fate of their own local Daphne. The Sibyl, however, had lived in the distant past, only "six generations" after the Flood. Although she was a frenzied old woman who usually spoke lies, on one occasion at Delphi she had spoken the inspired truth. To prove the point, Constantine quoted thirty-four Greek hexameters. Not only did they prophesy the Last Day when "all kings shall come to God's seat of Judgement and a stream of fire and sulphur shall flow from heaven . . ." but also the first Greek letter of each line spelt Jesus Christ, Son of God, Saviour, Cross, in a perfect Greek acrostic.

A Sibyl of Erythrae, who had served at Delphi, was very familiar to pagan tradition; so was her extreme antiquity, though Constantine's "six generations" were a particular precision which he perhaps derived from some Sibylline poem. A few of the verses which he quoted had already been quoted individually by earlier Christian authors, but none had showed any knowledge of this special acrostic which built up a longer text.[24] If they had known this astonishing proof, they would surely have quoted it. At Antioch, like the best type of speaker, Constantine was introducing new evidence into the debate. He had seen Memphis and Babylon; he had found a new meaning in Noah's dove; he had enlarged on Daniel's Persian career. Now he added a new prophetic text. He was alive, however, to the arguments of sceptics. "Most men disbelieve," he said, "even though they agree that the Sibyl was Erythraean . . ." They suspect that "someone of our religion, not without the gifts of the poetic Muse," had inserted false lines and forged the Sibyl's moral tone. These sceptics were already known to Origen, and give us one of our rare glimpses of pagans' responses to the Christians' spate of forgeries.[25] Yet Constantine thought he could disprove them. "Our people," he said, "have carefully compared the chronologies with greater accuracy," and the "age" of the Sibyl's verses excludes the view that they are a post-Christian fake. His proof of this comparison was unexpected: "It has been agreed," he wrote, that Cicero "chanced on this poem, translated it into the Romans' language and included it in his writings . . ." In fact, Cicero nowhere mentions such a set of verses. Once, in a sceptical passage, he noted that the prophecies in Rome's Sibylline books were composed as acrostics, but he did not cite examples.[26] To Cicero, the style of the acrostic was a proof of the exact opposite, that the verses were not divinely inspired. Acrostics, he said, required careful composition by an author who had firm control of his mind. Some Christian, known to Constantine and his advisers, had enlarged the Ciceronian argument. The Sibyl, he said, had prophesied Christ in an acrostic; as Sibylline acrostics were known to Cicero and recognized as genuine prophecies, Cicero had known the prophetic acrostic about Christ. "I cannot but think the Sibyl blessed," said Constantine, "whom the Saviour thus chose to unfold his gracious purposes for us." The proof was a fraud twice over.

Sibyls were familiar sources to Greek and Latin Christians, but

Constantine had a rarer proof. The advent of Christ, he said, had been predicted by Virgil in a Latin poem. No previous Christian text which is known to us alludes to this proof, and Constantine's Greek-speaking audience in Antioch were most unlikely to have met it in this or any other form. In or around the year 40 B.C., Virgil had honoured his patron Pollio with a poem which predicted the return of a new Golden Age. Its fullness would be brought on gradually and would grow with the birth and youth of an unnamed child. This great poem, our Messianic Eclogue, served Constantine's Christian purpose. He began with its seventh line, in a free Greek translation which changed its meaning: "thence, then, a new company of men has been revealed." In Latin, the line could have been given a clear Christian reference by its words of a new "child from heaven," but Constantine stood by the different version in Greek. This first quotation is a warning that the Emperor used a Greek translation of the Eclogue and not the Latin original which has been sought so often, but never established, beneath his detailed use of the poem. "In another place in his Eclogues," he continued, though quoting the first line of the same poem: it does not seem that the Emperor was quoting a body of verse which he knew very well himself.[27]

It was a remarkable moment in the history of public speaking, when an Emperor cited Latin's loveliest Eclogue to a Christian audience for a meaning which it never had.[28] Constantine stands at the head of a long and misguided tradition, the search for "typology" in Virgil's poetry. In the later nineteenth century, German scholarship was to study Virgil as if his work was biblical Scripture, predicting and alluding to themes beyond its immediate reference. This lasting tradition had an early ancestor: Constantine himself, whose detailed misreadings were most ingenious. "The last age of Cumaean Song has come," so Virgil had written. The Greek translation altered the sense, making a "saying of Cumaean prophecy" come "to fulfilment": Virgil, said Constantine, was hinting at the Sibyl of Cumae, whose prophecy he was quoting throughout. The Greek translation suppressed Virgil's pagan language, the "reign of Apollo," Apollo's love for "beautiful Linus," "Saturn's kingdom" and Pollio's "consulship": Pan was changed from a god into a mortal, Arcadia's natural son.[29] An echo of pagan cult survived in the advice that the Moon should "worship" the child, but Virgil, said Constantine, had hidden the Christian truth which he had already understood. He had been afraid of provoking the pagan rulers of Rome and so he had left these familiar landmarks of pagan worship. By stages, the Child would mature. His vision of "heroes mixed with the gods" became, in Greek, a vision of "the Just," the Christian souls with God. It was followed, in Greek, by the Child's future Coming, "guiding the reins of the world by the virtues his father gave him." "Nor is it right," in Greek, "for the flocks to fear raging lions . . .": how wisely, said Constantine, the poet had written, as "the faith of the kingly court will not fear savage dynasts." The allusion, he hinted, was to the "savagery" of persecutors of the Church: was there a hint, too, in the "faith of the kingly court," an allusion to Constantine's own Christian faith?

In a very free Greek translation, the robes of the young Child were said to breathe "fragrant flowers," or the Holy Ghost; gone was "the nature of the poisoned snake," the Serpent of the Fall. The text of the poem is then confused in our manuscripts, but Constantine's comments imply that his Greek had made a very strong reference to the death of "the destructive insults" of the Assyrians, the symbol, he said, of the disbelieving pagan.[30] Instead, he confirmed, "*amomum* is flourishing in every place"; in Greek, *amomum* was understood as the "blameless people," not as Virgil's Latin spice plant. The "blameless people" were the Church, and the "Assyrian" was the pagan whose ruined cities the Emperor had seen for himself.

As the Child matured, he would learn the "good deeds of the heroes," the just Christians, and see the "works of his mightiest father," in the nature of the created world. Meanwhile, human nature would advance to a gradual perfection. The fruits of God would be harvested from the brambles of men's past. "Honey," Virgil had said, "will flow from hard oaks," a reference, said Constantine, to the hardness of man's former nature and "perhaps" to virtue's sweet rewards after toil. Meanwhile, "a few traces of former deceit will survive . . .": "O wisest of poets," exclaimed Constantine, as he could hint at the truth but not pronounce it openly, "being no prophet himself." Virgil had feared "the danger which attached to those who refuted the ways of men's ancestors," but his words were a clever allusion to man's fallen nature. Men, said Virgil, would still sail and wage wars; recent history, said Constantine, had shown this clearly. Indeed it had, when Licinius's fleet had just been destroyed at sea. A "second Achilles will be sent to Troy"; the Saviour will wage a Christian Iliad, whose Troy is this world and whose Trojan enemies are the powers of evil. Mature at last, he will uproot the encumbrances of mortal life and rule the world in peace. The elements will applaud him and the arching vault of heaven will rejoice in sympathy while he takes his father's mighty sceptre. Well might Virgil pray for an added length of life in the hope of seeing and praising events of such tremendous moment.

This sequence, said Constantine, could never have been constructed for the birth and youth of a mortal baby, whatever the sceptics alleged. The Sibyl of Erythrae had once made a similar statement: had she not asked God why he obliged her to prophesy and did not keep her in the heavens until the blessed Second Coming? We do not know exactly which lines by a Sibyl Constantine was citing here, but he knew them in Greek, not Latin: they developed themes which finally found a home in the eighth of our collection of Sibylline texts. From the Sibyl, the Emperor returned to Virgil's last lines in a Greek translation which utterly proved his case. It removed the Latin's playful allusions and obscured its address to the newly born Child. Subject and object were reversed, while the famous textual puzzle of Virgil's final line was turned in a new direction.[31] No "parents," of course, had "smiled" on the Son of God, for he had never been created. "Nor have you touched the marriage bed, nor known a copious banquet." Virgil's reference was changed from future to past, to befit a virgin birth whose Holy Spirit knew nothing of feasting or the pleasures of sex with a goddess. This gross distortion of Virgil's lines seemed to rule out any child but Christ, and the Emperor's case was proven in the terms in which it had begun. "The Virgin is come, bringing a lovely king": the line was a godsend to its Christian reader, who took the Virgin to be Mary, not Virgil's goddess, Justice.

Has there ever been such a sequence of misplaced discoveries in a Christian sermon, let alone in a speech at the end of a Christian synod? The Christians of Antioch listened; the experts among them strained, no doubt, to remember Virgil's text. As a man might read *A Midsummer Night's Dream* in a Russian translation and cite it as proof of the class struggle, so Constantine found Christianity in Latin's loveliest Eclogue, when freely translated into Greek. The Greek version gave him the hints which the Latin had patently lacked. He quoted it in Greek, commented on it in Greek and assumed its Greek wording throughout. Even in antiquity, nobody had been sure whom Virgil had meant by the unnamed child. In Greek, these ambiguities seemed to have vanished. During composition, Virgil had had his own varied sources, poems, perhaps, on Hellenistic princelings, a hint or two from the lore of his ancestral Etruria, the great poem by Catullus on

the marriage of Peleus and Thetis, whose prophecies he subtly reversed. There may have been another source, more apt than Constantine knew. Twice, Virgil's poem evoked its Golden Age in terms
which resembled the hopes of the Jewish prophets, and once it
predicted the Child's career in a sequence which runs more smoothly if
it is read as the sign of eternal, Messianic rule. Behind this Jewish
colour, there may lie, after all, the person of the Sibyl. Its tone recalls
the poems which Jews had written in Greek hexameters and ascribed
to the Sibyl's impressive name. These surviving texts from the
Hellenistic period are the neatest match to Virgil's train of thought.[32]
In 40 B.C., Pollio, his poem's recipient, had entertained King Herod
and his Jewish friends in Rome. Was it through, or in honour of, these
contacts that Virgil gave his poem this touch of Jewish colour, as
found in a Jew's Sibylline verses—poems, however, which Constantine never knew?

To Constantine, the march of history was a more immediate
concern than this search for literary origins. The Sibyl had sensed its
march at Delphi; Virgil had buried it from hostile eyes in Rome; recent
history had proved it in obvious terms. The speech moved to its
climax, the power of prayer, the fates of the Christians' persecutors
and the rewards for service like Constantine's, rendered (he said) to
Christ and God alone. Delicately, Constantine moved from Virgil to
the "dearest city's" aberrations. He hinted at Antioch's ill-judged
support for the "tyrant" whom his hearers could recognize as
Maximin, ruler in the East. Addressing the deceased Maximin, he
moved to a broader contrast between pagan superstition and the
Christian faith. The rewards of imperial persecutors were visible in
their recent fates. Decius had died in the "Scythian plains," making
Roman arms the mockery of nomads. Valerian had been flayed by the
Persian king, who had dried his skin and kept it as an "eternal trophy"
at the Persian court. Courtiers had murdered Aurelian in Thrace, while
Diocletian had been driven mad by guilt for murdering so many
Christians. Nicomedia still told how a thunderbolt from God had
struck and burnt down Diocletian's palace. Once again, the Emperor
could add his own proof. He had seen this catastrophe as it happened, a
sign as vivid as the ruin of Babylon, which proved God's way with his
pagan enemies. As Christians had been blamed for the disaster, they
would be glad to hear the truth.[33]

Since the burning of the palace, there had only been Licinius, the last
"worthless usurper" who had just been "destroyed." Those who "had

been oppressed and had longed for their freedom, imploring the help of God," were free, now, in a just and fair society. "Does not this in every way prove the Providence of God and his loving care for the interests of men?"

The lesson followed from Constantine's own "service," which was grounded in the "inspiration of heaven." By praising this "service," he said, men praised the foresight of God. With supreme confidence, he linked his usurpation to the Christian movement which he had seen in human history. "Surely all men know that the holy service in which these hands have been busied has begun in pure and true faith towards God?" Prayer, said Constantine, preceded his every action for the common good, and prayer had been proved invincible. The lessons of Moses and Daniel reached their peak in Constantine's own prayer and triumph. "Men have witnessed battles and watched a war in which God's Providence granted victory to this host . . ." God, in short, had willed Constantine's victory in response to his piety and prayers, the themes which ran through history and his entire Oration.

When the Emperor at last sat down, he had treated the saints in Antioch to a remarkable tour of Christian thought. His speech was greater than the sum of its errors and false allusions. He had given them new evidence, Virgil and the Sibyl, Daniel in Persia, the oddities which he had seen in nature from Babylon to Gaul. He had also reassured them with familiar proofs. Much of his conclusion and its underlying theme had already been sent by letter to the Eastern provincials and to Shapur, the Persian king. In 324/5, much was being said on the deaths of the persecutors, Constantine's "service" and prayer to God, the ways of Providence, the proofs of history and the "liberation" of the oppressed. The Oration was exceptionally optimistic, and it helped its audience to understand why history was happening. There had been no irreversible Fall; there was no unmixed evil in God's Creation. Philosophy and paganism were as dead as the old Assyrian cities: Constantine had freed the East by his prayers and piety, and before them both lay the promised future of God.

The world being as it is, these hopes were not to be realized. At the Council of Antioch, three of the bishops who supported Arius refused to join the consensus. They were excommunicated, but they were allowed time for second thoughts before the imminent synod of Ancyra. One of the three was Eusebius himself. The Council of Antioch had presumably ended before the Good Friday on which the Emperor preached his sermon: by then, he can have had no illusions

about the power of Arius's doctrine. His own speech came dangerously close at one point to language which Arius would have permitted:
we can only relish the irony and reflect that these words are one more
proof that the speech was not thoroughly revised in later years.[34] The
extreme subtleties of the argument had escaped the Emperor's grasp of
Greek theology; he was aware, however, of its general significance.
We know that Constantine sent a letter by the hand of Ossius to Arius
and his opposing bishop in Alexandria, and we can best date its
despatch to the moment after the council had risen. In its appeal to
their good sense, the letter tried to play down the points at issue.[35]
Bishop Alexander, Constantine wrote, had been researching "un-
guardedly" into the meaning of an obscure text of Scripture while
Arius had answered him "inconsiderately." Arius's heresy, wrote
Constantine, was not "new," nor did it destroy their broad expanse of
common ground. It was best kept as a private speculation on a "tiny
and insignificant point," while the central Christian doctrines were
not in doubt. Within broad limits, Christians were not obliged to
agree: could not the two of them show charity and concord and reopen
their Emperor's road to Egypt?

The letter says much for the cunning of the man who drafted it. By
the last week in April, on the likeliest view, it had reached Egypt with
Ossius, but it made not the slightest difference. Ossius, one assumes,
sent immediate word of his failure to Constantine, who was by now
on his way north from the Antioch synod. By early May, the Emperor
made his famous decision. The imminent synod of Ancyra was to
become the "ecumenical synod" of Nicaea, a site which had many
advantages. It was nearer for the Western visitors and it lay well away
from the see of a determined opponent of Arius, Marcellus, the bishop
of Ancyra. In early May, therefore, Constantine could write the
celebrated letter which changed the council's site, and although we
only know its text in an Arabic and a Syriac translation, the emphasis,
we now see, was too apt to be anyone's but Constantine's own.[36] He
urged the visiting bishops to hurry: if the opening of the council was
hardly a month away, his pleas gain a special relevance. Again and
again, he asked for haste, repeating the plea four times in a single
sentence. After the failure of Antioch and Ossius's mission to Alexandria, time was running short: the recent synod had nearly been
unanimous and a rapid sequel might cut off the Arians from general
support. At the same time, Constantine remarked on the finer climate
of Nicaea, that charming lakeside city. The comment was apt, as

summer loomed in the landlocked city of Ancyra. He forbore to add that Nicaea was nearer to his own palace and that the new site allowed him to attend the council in person.

In the West, the Donatists had dragged Constantine into their dispute, much against his will: when he read one of their first petitions, in 313, he was said to have replied in anger, "You demand from me a court in this world, when I look forward to the court of Christ . . ."[37] Chastened by these experiences, the Emperor left less to chance in the East.[38] So far as we know, he first collided with Arius's heresy through the preparatory journey of Ossius, his own agent. Ossius then summoned the Antioch Council and presided over it: Ossius, we can deduce from the Acts, interrogated each one of its participants separately, and then, on the Good Friday, the Emperor's own Oration was preached to the congregation. At Nicaea, two months later, the pattern was similar. The Emperor chose the council's site and attended in person, while the attending bishops were allowed the privilege which had so impressed the young Gregory: free travel by the Imperial post. They stayed in Nicaea, all expenses paid, and when the council ended, they were invited to a great dinner to celebrate the Emperor's twentieth anniversary. Among his other innovations, it was Constantine who first mastered the art of holding, and corrupting, an international conference. On leaving his palace, each guest received a present, according to his rank. On entering, recalled Eusebius, "units of the bodyguard and other troops surrounded the palace with drawn swords, and through them the men of God proceeded without fear into the innermost rooms of the Emperor, in which some were his companions at table, while others reclined on couches at either side." It was "like a dream," he said, an anticipatory picture of the kingdom of Christ.[39]

The great council had opened on June 1 and met in the palace's inner hall of judgement. When Constantine entered in his robes and jewels, the Christian participants stood up. He asked their permission to sit and took up his position on a small stool adorned with gold. After a panegyric in his honour, he replied briefly, using the Latin which many Western bishops could follow, and under Ossius's presidency, he then sat in isolation, though he probably joined in the discussions.[40] No Acts of the council were preserved, perhaps because their contents were too controversial, but we do know the names of the signatories to the Creed which Constantine himself eventually approved and explained in a preliminary speech. Of the three Arians who had temporarily been suspended at Antioch, two, including Eusebius, came back into the fold. However, fellow Arians who had consented at Antioch now moved in the opposite direction, and ultimately, the signatures were not lasting. It was Ossius who first announced the Creed and signed it: from a precious fragment of the fifth-century Christian historian Philostorgius, we learn that the Creed was then taken round to each individual by Constantine's own notaries, led by Philumenus, the "master of the offices." This very high-ranking official controlled the palace secretaries and stood very close to the Emperor: once, we know, Philumenus had already shown considerable cunning when handling the Donatist leaders in the West. This secular official, a former Donatist "contact," brought the Emperor's authority directly into the climax of the council.[41] Although many Arians signed the Creed, their signatures, therefore, were given under pressure, and before long, they understood its wording in senses which suited their own case. At Nicaea, the Emperor himself imposed criminal sentences of exile on the bishops who refused to sign. He also investigated other reports of heresy.[42] In the 430s, the Christian historian Socrates knew from private sources the story that the Emperor himself had cross-questioned a Novatianist during the council, reportedly finding him unheretical. It was probably after the council, and certainly before 326, that Constantine issued a further letter: it was addressed to heretical sects and announced that their places of meeting would be confiscated. Throughout the proceedings, the Emperor's own interventions had been very forceful, and they ended on a clear note of intolerance. In the past, Christians had been persecuted for refusing to "go through the motions" and pay an external act of worship, "observing Roman ceremony," though they did not follow Roman religion. Now, by a Christian Emperor, fellow Christians were made liable to legal penalties because of their beliefs. Prayer had done much in history, but it was not so strong that it could bring Christians to agree. Others, perhaps, with the text of the Oration before them, may reflect that a mere two months before Nicaea, the Emperor himself had preached a sermon, one sentence of which trod unwarily on Arius's ground.

# IV

Constantine's Good Friday sermon shows the man's public image and style of argument at greater length than any other document. It was a public statement, and like other contemporary documents, it was circulated as Christian publicity. Its optimism and moral exhortation are not at odds with the tone of previous Emperors' public statements. Theirs was an age of effusive public language, and it is worth setting the speech beside the themes which handbooks commended to public orators. When an Emperor was crowned by a city, so Menander told his readers, they should begin the conventional speech by praising the Emperor for his distinguished family. If his family was undistinguished, they should try a different line: "Say, 'God from on high took pity on the human race, and wishing to comfort it with prosperity, contrived that you should be born, for the good destiny of the world. . .'"; Constantine's family was so undistinguished that he had to devise a new ancestry. Ambassadors should emphasize how "God sent the Emperor down to earth because he knew he was merciful and a benefactor . . .": they should add, "We plead with you and fall at your feet . . . the ambassador's voice is the voice of the whole city through which the women and children, the men and old men, pour forth their tears and plead with you to be compassionate . . ."[1] We catch an echo here of the Oration's sense of mission and "cries of the oppressed." The similarities are not surprising: Constantine had heard many panegyrics and his advisers knew how to write them. However, no handbook catered for the personal, Christian tone which ran through the Emperor's sermon. It was combined with philosophy, a view of history and his notes from personal experience. "We are struggling, to the best of our power, to fill the uninitiated with righteous hope, calling on God to assist our endeavour . . ." In his public letters, Constantine expressed pleasure at the spread of Christianity to new pagan converts: in the Oration, we hear the "first crowned Christian apologist."

At Antioch, in these very months, a fine gold coinage circulated, showing the Emperor receiving a figure of victory from the pagan Sun god. The legend declared, "To the Sun, Companion of Our Emperor."[2] The type had been struck in the city in the immediate aftermath of Licinius's defeat and had been borrowed from issues which were already current in the West. Nonetheless, small details in the design had been altered to suit the new military circumstances. The imagery was not a thoughtless transfer. Between the Emperor's own letters and sermon and this legend and image on his coinage, we have to make a choice: in the same city, at the same date, one is definitely Christian, the other explicitly pagan. The coinage has been emphasized as proof of Constantine's essential paganism, but the Oration and its setting refute this notion. We must prefer the Emperor's own elaborate oratory: if the coinage is out of step with it, the discrepancy reflects on the coinage's lesser historical value and the paganism of the majority of its users. It raises the same type of question as the arch in Rome, ten years previously, and in each case, for Constantine's own views, we should prefer his own words to the publicity which others issued on his behalf. The Oration's context finally destroys excessive conclusions from his coin slogans alone.

If Constantine trod warily, it was because he ruled a large pagan majority: he did not ban pagan cult, nor did he drop the Emperor's public role as *pontifex maximus*. In return, he can be allowed two particular forms of insurance, one for reasons of state, the other for the fate of his soul. In 320, the Colosseum was struck by lightning and the pagan officials in Rome went through the usual public rites of divination. They reported them to Constantine, who replied that these arts should be followed if a palace or public building was similarly struck. This public rite was necessary to calm public opinion: the results were to be sent to Constantine, who might, after all, have read them as a clue to the demons' purpose.[3] The other insurance was characteristically Christian: Constantine postponed baptism until his deathbed. The delay says more for his fears than his indifference. As Emperor, he was obliged to impose his rule by force, a necessity from which he did not shrink, and full Christian baptism was better reserved till this necessity was almost past. The Good Friday sermon was followed a year later by scandal in the Imperial household, the murder of his son, perhaps on false testimony, and the enforced suicide of his wife. Constantine's actions may still upset Christian consciences, but they have to be accepted as those of a sincere and convinced adherent of the faith, the man whose massive gifts and legislation first promoted it against all expectations, whose reluctance to coerce pagans was only too seldom shared and whose simple fears for God's anger at heresy made him the most tireless worker for Christian unity since St. Paul.[4]

Resolution of this old "Constantinian problem" leaves us free to turn to others. The Good Friday sermon has touched on many of the themes of this book, but the combination may strike us as strange: the Sibyl and the pagan oracles, the "presence" of God and the proofs of his anger, the place of philosophy, the hidden senses of poetry, the constancy of martyrs. How strange, though, was this combination in Constantine's own circle? How, indeed, was such a sermon composed and, on a longer view, in what sense does it mark a new age? The themes of his speech are all the more interesting because they do not stand alone. Not only do they relate very closely to his other letters and circulars which were composed in 324/5. On point after point, they make contact with intelligent discussion, or attempts at it, which are known to us in other authors of the years c. 300–330. It is notable that the details and the authorities of the Emperor's public statements are not, on the whole, those which Eusebius preferred in his own works. In 325, the Emperor's future biographer was a suspected Arian, far removed from the Emperor's inner circle of advisers. Instead, the Oration and the accompanying letters match many of the interests of Lactantius, the tutor to Constantine's son. The relationship of the family tutor to the Emperor's public statements is a spur to the imagination: which of them influenced the other?

By late 324, Lactantius was an old man, perhaps over eighty, and on a likely deduction from our texts of his major work, a man with little more than a year to live.[5] Nonetheless, he was still active. Two of our manuscripts of his long work, the *Divine Institutes*, preserve long, honorary dedications to Constantine, which he set before their first and seventh books. The tone of the latter, especially, suggests a date after September 324: it told how God was guiding Constantine to bring back justice, while the wicked "pay or have paid" the divine punishment for sins against the Church. The manuscripts support the case for this second edition, published in the wake of Constantine's victory in the East.

If so, Lactantius was adding these prefaces shortly before, or during, the composition of Constantine's speech. Perhaps at the same time he burst into verse on the phoenix: did he also influence the Oration to the Saints? The two authors shared notable ground, not all of which was conventional. Lactantius quoted freely from the Sibyls, fifty-seven times in his surviving works.[6] Lactantius, too, quoted Cicero in support of the Sibyl's wisdom. He accepted that Virgil and other poets had hidden their Christian intimations for fear of their fellow pagans. He quoted the same Messianic Eclogue, though much more briefly; he presented it as the Cumaean Sibyl's wisdom, which Virgil reported, and saw it as a prophecy of the coming millennium, although he rearranged its phrases to suit his case. In one fragment, we find him pairing the Sibyl with Virgil as a figure of exceptional authority.[7] Like Constantine, Lactantius stressed the virtue of justice, and in his revised preface, ascribed it to the Emperor himself.[8] On the topic of God's anger, Lactantius had devoted an entire pamphlet to the miserable deaths of the persecuting Emperors, a major Constantinian theme. When he first completed his *Divine Institutes*, probably by 311, he showed no direct knowledge of Plato's *Timaeus*. His Plato was still Cicero's, known in the Latin translation or its anthologies. Several years later, by 320, he wrote a shortened epitome of his longer work, and direct echoes of the *Timaeus* were then evident.[9] He had met it, presumably, in the intervening period: in 325, its echoes sounded at three points in the opening sections of Constantine's speech.

How, then, should we picture the two men's relationship? Did Lactantius give Constantine the substance of his speech, or did the Emperor show the family tutor a way of thought? The gainer, presumably, was Constantine, but even so, there were limits. Lactantius cited Sibyls, but never an acrostic on Christ; he used Virgil's poem, but never quoted it for the birth of Jesus. These differences may be more apparent than real: perhaps Lactantius had found new evidence in 324/5, after his main works had been written. In his pamphlet on the deaths of the persecutors, published between 313 and 316, Lactantius had blamed Galerius for the Great Persecution.[10] In the Oration, Constantine said nothing on Galerius's role and fate. Perhaps its Eastern context caused him to be silent, but his silence ignored Lactantius's former strong advocacy. It is revealing, too, that minor details in his views of the persecuting Emperors were subtly different from Lactantius's own. So, too, were his dismissals of Plato and Pythagoras. The Oration's theology omitted much which Lactantius had liked and could easily have asserted.[11] It said very little on his major theme of justice, on Jesus as a mediator, on the significance of man's upright stance or the metaphor of Christ as a stream from God's fountain. As a pagan witness, the "Thrice-great Hermes" was dear to Lactantius, yet absent from the Oration's proofs. Lactantius had stressed that the truth of miracles and the power of the cross had a symbolic and prophetic meaning. He said nothing about the wisdom of the Apostles, whom the Oration exalted.

Perhaps we should no longer look for a direct derivation, let alone for total composition by Lactantius himself. Instead, we should think of common discussions, shared by more participants and developing and growing as events unfolded: here, the Greek interpretation can find a place, encouraging the use of the Sibyl and Virgil in a Greek text. The Oration's use of Virgil is an interesting case in point.[12] In 310, the panegyrist in Gaul had flattered Constantine in language which connected him with Virgil's Messianic child. In 324/5, the exiled Porfyrius continued the conceit: "justice," he wrote in a poem for the Emperor, "will return, under your leadership," at the start of a new Golden Age. At the same date, however, Constantine was learning from some Greek-speaking Virgilian in his circle how the poem referred to Christ. Porfyrius's poem made a brilliant pattern which contained letters in an acrostic, shaped like the Emperor's famous "chi-rho." At the same date, Constantine was being shown an acrostic in the Sibyl's poems which spelt the name of Christ.

We would dearly like to know who first unveiled these "proofs" in court society. The Oration is a characteristic child of its time and it is not surprising that its philosophy, too, finds a near-contemporary parallel. Like Lactantius in his later years, Constantine touched on the themes of Plato's *Timaeus*.[13] His use of this difficult text was very limited, but it did not stand alone. At an unknown date, one Calcidius turned the *Timaeus* into a free Latin translation and commented on its views, dedicating his long book to one "Hosius," who, he said, had "enjoined" the task as one which he would otherwise have carried out himself. Despite recent doubt, it is still most likely that this Greek-speaking "Hosius" is Constantine's Ossius of Cordova, the man who stood at the centre of events in the months surrounding the Antioch Oration. One group of manuscripts asserts that Calcidius was Ossius's deacon, and it is plain from his wording that Ossius knew the great interest of Plato's text.[14] So, too, did Lactantius in his older age: did Ossius introduce it to him, too? Like the Oration, Calcidius understood the *Timaeus* through the eyes of subsequent "middle" Platonists. That, perhaps, was usual, and proves nothing.[15] The Emperor's allusions to Plato are too vague to be tied to anything specific in Calcidius's translation, nor, indeed, do we know if it existed in 325.[16]

We should think, then, of a growing body of evidence and theory at court, to which different individuals contributed differently in discussion. We can see only some of the pieces of this mosaic, but they suffice to suggest how the Emperor's speech attached to it. In Eusebius's *Life*, Constantine is praised as a natural thinker and theologian who was greatly engaged by questions of doctrine. In a limited sense, the Oration proves him right.[17] It includes touches which have to be the Emperor's own, the lessons of Memphis and Babylon, the proofs of God's anger, the favour of God for his new servant, Constantine himself. Whoever suggested the bulk of the speech, whether Ossius, Lactantius or unnamed interpreters in the weeks before April 325, they had had to take careful account of the views included by the Emperor himself.

At once personal, but typical, the Oration is thus our best public statement of the way in which the new Christian Emperor wished history to be seen. It makes a striking contrast with the views of the Emperor Marcus, at the end of the Antonine age, the period with whose pagan cults we began this book. The Oration was a public statement, whereas the *Meditations*, admittedly, were Marcus's private diaries. Nonetheless, they reveal two men with an entirely different image of themselves. Like Constantine, Marcus accepted the visible proofs of Providence in the design of the world. He, too, lived in a universe where all had been chosen for the best, yet he felt weary at the tension between the role which was given to him as Emperor and his own attempts to live up to Reason, while playing his allotted part. He was wearied by the struggle to conform to Providence, a struggle which revealed a man who had "faith and charity, but somehow lacked hope."[18] Hope was not Constantine's weak suit. He believed that God's personal Providence had guided history and was backing his own role as Emperor. God's Providence cared for Constantine, his servant, while God's anger beset the "worthless usurpers" who had perished during his rise.[19] To Marcus, it had seemed wholly mistaken to attribute anger to a god.

# 13. From Pagan to Christian

The public statements and circular letters of 324/5 mark the start of a new chapter in the life of the Greek-speaking city culture with which we began. To the ageing Lactantius, the Emperor's conversion had seemed to signify the dawn of the new millennium, a Virgilian Golden Age. Christian letters and speeches were distributed throughout the Empire, and Christian business became public business, visible in the great synods, buildings and privileges of the new era. To what, though, did it all lead? A sermon is only a sermon, and whatever Constantine might say at Antioch, people's lives were not so easily changed. In the 430s, the Christian writer Socrates began a *Church History* of his own, complaining of the exaggerations and omissions in Eusebius's *Life* of Constantine. Socrates was writing in the more fully Christianized society of the reign of Theodosius II, but when he looked back, he doubted the blessings of the Christian Emperor who had first become involved in affairs of the Church.[1]

This involvement was felt in two areas: the internal life of the Church and the relations between Christians and non-Christians. On the former, Socrates's doubts were misplaced. Constantine's generosity did not lead Christians off a former path of virtue: it intensified vices which already existed. Nor did his involvement split the Church for the first time: one Christian group appealed to him against another, just as in the 270s Christians in Antioch had already appealed to a pagan Emperor against their "heretic," Paul. Christian petitions began by being grounded in the control of property; they became disputes about claims to be the "true," then the "orthodox" Church. In the West, Constantine delegated the Donatist dispute to bishops' arbitration: he ended by involving himself and his agents. In the East, the role of the Emperor and his agents was more positive throughout. The Emperor's criminal sentences against Christians at Nicaea were followed by Church councils at which his own court advisers presided. As "servant of Christ," the Emperor wished only to bring about Christian unity. The Christians first involved, then frustrated his efforts to this end. At Nicaea, Christians were said to have begun the council by piling the Emperor's lap with petitions against fellow Christians: it was the Emperor himself who had the petitions burned.[2] After Nicaea, charges of criminal misconduct continued to be advanced by any one Christian party against the leaders of another. Constantine struggled with the results, and one of his greatest church buildings bore witness to his efforts. In 326, in Antioch, work began on the octagonal plan of the famous Golden Church. This huge building was known as the "Church of Concord," a title which has been traced to Constantine himself.[3] Concord was his aim at all times, but never more so than in Antioch, where the Emperor first collided with news of the Arian heresy and where, we now see, he had preached his Oration to a divided Church.

The style of Church life in the aftermath of his conversion emerges in vivid detail from the Acts of Christian councils summoned between 313 and 325. In the East we have the Acts of a council at Ancyra, held between 313 and 316, and another which followed it in Gregory's own Neocaesarea, probably before 325. In the West, we have Acts of the Council of Arles in 314 and the intriguing Acts of Elvira, a council whose date may have been misjudged. Such is its picture of Christian life that its relation to Constantine's own conversion is worth exploring more closely.

At Elvira, in southern Spain, Ossius was the presiding bishop, and his presence has generally been taken to date the council before his attendance on Constantine, in 312/3.[4] The case is not cogent: he could have returned temporarily to his home district at any time before 324. The Acts of Elvira take an interesting stance on matters of martyrdom. They are not concerned with Christians who might lapse while on trial, and they have nothing to say on persecution. This silence has generally suggested a date before 300, but the Acts also warn against Christians who falsely claim the status of "confessor" and win an unjustified respect. Between 260 and c. 295, no "confessors" had been created by the authorities. A date after 312 is preferable, when martyrdom was not an issue, but when "confessors" were still circulating in the wake of the Great Persecution. The Council did consider one particular type of "martyrdom": the death of Christians who tried to smash a pagan idol and were killed "on the spot." Before Constantine, we have next to no historical record of such zealots.

After Constantine, we can see at once how they could become a problem. Enthusiastic Christians, made safe in the new Empire, might start to demolish pagan idols of their own accord.

These two canons belong more readily after 312 than before. There is, however, a notable silence. The council has nothing to say on the familiar problems which followed the persecutions elsewhere: lapsing, betrayal and the "handing over" of Scriptures. The silence may be explicable. In southern Spain, the persecution may not have been so very harsh and the edict requiring sacrifice to the pagan gods was probably never enforced.[5] At Arles, a council had already discussed priests who were supposed to have "handed over" their Scriptures: accusations had to be backed by public documentary proof. Several bishops at Elvira had already attended Arles, and there would be no need to go over the matter again, after this moderate ruling had settled it. So, too, in the East, the council at Ancyra settled major problems of conduct during the persecution: a decade or so later, the local synod at Neocaesarea did not go over them again.

Elvira, then, can best join the other councils whose Acts throw a sharp light on Church life in Constantine's Christian era. It is all too plain that the Emperor had inherited many more problems than he created. These councils' common concerns are unmistakable:[6] interference by one priest or bishop in another's sphere of authority; moneylending by clerics; gross complexities in Christians' sex lives. There were penalties for husbands who connived at their wives' adulteries, very heavy penalties for women with lovers, minimal penalties for hardened male adulterers, who "must be approached on their deathbeds and asked if they promise to give up adultery: if they do, they may take communion; if they recover and then also commit adultery, they must not make a mockery of communion again." Bad though such sins were, they were seldom so bad that they should be left without forgiveness at the moment of death. At Neocaesarea, the bishops ruled that anyone who had avidly desired to sleep with a woman, but failed to realize his wish, had been saved by the grace of God. At Ancyra, the intriguing class of Christians who either had enjoyed or still enjoyed sex with animals was broken down by age groups and allotted long periods of penance. Married offenders, if aged over fifty, were to receive communion only at death. When the canon was translated into Latin, it was taken to be a ruling against homosexuals, and in the early medieval kingdoms, it was persistently cited as an authority against them.

We are still in a familiar world, where overachievers castrate themselves voluntarily, where pseudo-perfectionists claim to be living as "brothers and sisters" with the virgins in their house and where the majority gamble and go to the games, use sorcery and divination, pursue each other's wives or ask a Jew to bless the crops. Over them presided bishops who damned the theatre, the races and paintings inside church, who forbade women to write or receive letters in their own name and who were aware that Christian wives might be coaxed into lending their finest dresses for a procession of the pagan gods. Others simply joined the sinners, lending money, sleeping with the virgins and widows and laying slanderous documents against fellow members of the Church.[7] The prime obstacle to Christianization lay in the Christians themselves, their clergy as much as their ordinary followers. A double standard had always been present in Christian ethics: after Constantine, it became entrenched for the first time in civic life.

As Emperor, Constantine still fulfilled the public role of a pagan *pontifex maximus* and allowed the public cults to continue: he had begun as the patron of a small Christian minority, and he moved cautiously. In political affairs, he had to accept an army and a ruling class who were overwhelmingly pagan, and remained so throughout his reign. But his public language was unambiguous. Paganism was a false "error" and sacrifice a "foul pollution." Although both were probably allowed to continue for the poor souls who could not see the Christians' truth, the language which permitted them was not the language of a man tolerating equals. It was the language of a man suffering fools. The postscript to his Oration at Antioch was to be rather more robust: torture of pagans "in authority in the city" so that they admitted religious fraud. Constantine himself is not cited as responsible and here, perhaps, his Christian hearers outran his intention.

However, it took more than the Emperor's language to win a majority of pagans to the Church. We can see the Church leaders' initial hopes from the Acts of their first councils: at Arles, the bishops ruled that any Christian who held public office or who became a provincial governor should write and introduce himself to the local bishop. While he held power, he should then do whatever the bishop advised. This ruling did not show any grasp of the realities of power and it promptly needed revision at Elvira, a few years later.[8] At Elvira, the council was also noticeably milder to Christians who became one of the senior "two magistrates" of a Roman town: they must stay away from church during their year of office, which involved pagan cult and shows, but they could return as good Christians afterwards. If the bishops had been any harsher, they would have lost all contact with the high officials of their cities. Here, we see the predicament of a Christian leadership given sudden prominence in a predominantly pagan society.

Constantine could not oblige the Christian leaders by abolishing pagan cult: Eusebius alleges that he banned all sacrifices by a law, but this claim is highly contestable and was certainly not fulfilled:[9] most of the governors who would have had to enforce it were themselves still pagans. Nonetheless, Christianity did make notable progress in the Constantinian age, beginning a greater expansion outside the towns and attracting many more prominent converts.[10] Here, more than any ban on paganism, the ending of persecution had its effect. Christianity's subsequent progress owed less to legal prohibition than to a subtler compound, composed of legal privilege, the faith's intrinsic appeal and a continuing use of force.

By Constantine, the long tension between "love of honour" and immunity from civic burdens was given a new twist: the Christian clergy were exempted from civic duties. The arbitration and judgement of bishops was given a new legal backing: on the likeliest interpretation of a complex law, Constantine allowed the parties in a civil or criminal suit to appeal to a bishop's final "judgement" and "testimony." The bishop's decision was then binding on any other judge. Perhaps this law only covered disputes between Christians, but it was a remarkable recognition of the Christian "state within a state." So, too, was the recognition of the legality of bequests to the Church, even if they were made in a person's dying wishes. These privileges were a strong inducement to join the Church: in 320 and again in 326, Constantine already had to legislate against pagans who were claiming to be clerics in order to avoid their civic duties. This type of claim did not belong with a robust pagan "opposition."[11]

At the same time, the new faith became a great source of economic benefit. Not since the last year of Alexander the Great had a ruler spent so lavishly.[12] Constantine built and endowed a series of huge new churches, projects which were very dear to his own person: in a letter, we find him ordering the bishop of Jerusalem to build a new church on Golgotha at public expense, and twice asking him to report promptly to the Emperor in person. The many who benefited from the new circulation of funds will have found little to challenge in the prominence of the new religion. Pagan shrines, meanwhile, lost funds and treasures which were diverted or melted down to pay for the Christians' publicity.

As part of this new circulation, the Christians received and redistributed huge donations, some from Constantine himself.[13] Whereas the corn doles of pagan cities had been confined to citizens, usually to those who were quite well-off, the Christians' charity claimed to be for those who were most in need. Swollen by the Emperor's gifts, it helped the sick and the old, the infirm and the destitute. By the later fourth century, it had led to great hostels and charitable centres, most visible in the underurbanized province of Cappadocia, where the Christian fathers encouraged and practised its ideals. It is no coincidence that paganism ceased to trouble them in their letters, written in the 370s and 380s. In the East, a similar function was being met by the great monasteries which grew up near places of pilgrimage.

In this new climate of Christian favour and pilgrimage, Constantine was not alone in having decisive Christian dreams. In Cappadocia we learn from Gregory of Nazianzus how his father, a great landowner, was converted to Christianity by an opportune dream in the year 325: he had a Christian wife already and ended his days as the powerful bishop of the family's home town.[14] Others, too, were sensitive to the new opportunities: at Elvira, the bishops began with four strong rulings against Christians who entered temples and sacrificed to the gods after baptism or who served after baptism as pagan priests. It is easier to credit this double life if the council met after Constantine's conversion: prominent citizens were already willing to make a show of being Christians, while continuing to lead their home towns in pagan cults. Others were adept at playing the two loyalties against one another: they included the ingenious scoundrels who were pretending to be Christian clerics in order to claim exemptions from the expense of civic duties.

These judicious "conversions" did not make immediate Christians but they did bring the new faith into yet more households, where it could take root and become the natural loyalty of the next generation.[15] Christianity had not lost the appeal of a scriptural religion: it united cult and philosophy and still promised the various rewards and certainties which we have seen in it from the start. Conspicuously, it was able to hold many of the people whom it first attracted, and its bitter internal quarrels did not blind outsiders to its ideals. Here, we can share the views of Ammianus, a pagan from Antioch and the great historian of the fourth century. In his histories, he deplored the failings of many bishops and the savage hatred of Christians for each other, but he still saw Christianity as a "just and gentle" religion.[16]

As the new patronage made Christianity more confident, the "just and gentle religion" could turn round and answer pagan religiousness on its own terms. So far from keeping things going, the pagan gods had brought their "usurpers" to miserable ends. The Christian God now gave victory to the Emperor and helped him to bring an end to conflict: life did indeed go no worse with a Christian Emperor and no sudden calamity called in question his new faith. Christianity could thus destroy the strongest of all arguments for pagan worship, that it had always been practised and that its abandonment would be very foolhardy. The argument from success became joined to the growing impact of patronage for the Church in civic life. In 325, Constantine legislated against gladiatorial games and withdrew Imperial support: eventually, they died in every province of the Empire.[17] Public occasions became increasingly Christian occasions, as a new calendar of festivals and commemorations rivalled the old sequence of pagan games and festivals. Newly built churches became alternative centres of urban life, offering legal "asylum" to fugitives, becoming places where slaves, too, could be legally freed, where big crowds could meet inside buildings for worship and where people could even expect to find a suitable girlfriend.[18] The churches were not the only new centres. In a pagan city, the adult dead, traditionally, had been buried outside the city's walls. In the Christian Empire, the dead acquired a new importance, through the building of shrines on the bones of past martyrs. Constantine built a huge church to honour the martyrs of Nicomedia:[19] gradually his own capital, Constantinople, came to have martyrs' shrines within and without the walls. Like the churches, these new centres of power changed the focus of the cities and their social existence.

Even so, the pagan cults were not quick to die away: they had been the religion of the majority at the time of Constantine's conversion and not for another century did the balance tip decisively in the Christians' favour. They were, however, put under strain, quite apart from their loss of supporters to the Church. Lavish pagan cult had been intertwined with particular values and a particular social order in the cities' upper classes. During the fourth century, those classes narrowed further, while service to the home town lost almost every connection with the old "love of honour," spread widely within a competitive local elite. Pagan cults found their funds reduced and their ceremonies threatened, while the old forms of civic education no longer survived to support them.[20] After 325, we hear no more of the training of a city's youth as "ephebes" with the accompanying pagan ceremonial. By the 380s, nothing more is heard of the civic gymnasium and its officials. The reduction in the cities' incomes may have influenced their disappearance, but Christian attitudes may also have played a part. "The physical side of education languished in a Christian environment": in the cities, it had been linked with naked exercise, paganism and consenting homosexuality. The eventual "collapse of the gymnasia, the focal point of Hellenism, more than any other single event brought in the Middle Ages."

While "love of honour" and "love of the home town" no longer impelled the competitive buildings and "promises" of so many pagan benefactors, Christianity released the ostentatious patronage of its supporters. They gave not merely for worldly fame but to further their own eternal life, and in turn, these gifts helped to keep their religion at the centre of public life. It is more important that prominent support for the Christian religion can be traced to distinctive patrons at the Imperial court than that individual laws can be cited prohibiting pagan worship, yet needing always to be repeated. Between c. 380 and 450, this patronage was particularly influential.[21] In the 390s, Ossius of Cordova found his heirs in courtiers of Spanish origin who gathered round Theodosius I and showed a conspicuous Christian piety. From 423 to 451, the sister and the Empress mother of Theodosius II competed in an extravagant rivalry, citing Constantine's mother, Helena, as the model for their charity. They patronized relics and holy men; they favoured pilgrimages and monasteries; their rivalry even advanced the fateful creed at the Council of Chalcedon (451), which was to split the Church still further.

Pagan cult had benefited from the buildings and "love of honour" of its donors, but their gifts had been made from somewhat limited motives. By contrast, Christianity combined the exercise of patronage with a sense of spiritual progress, an ethic against sin and hopes of superior treatment in the world to come. It offered this combination to upper-class females as well as to men, and in Constantine's own lifetime both sexes were quick to take it up. In 326, the execution of Constantine's son and the "suicide" of his wife were immediately followed by the pilgrimage of his mother, Helena, to the Holy Land and her conspicuous spending on the holy sites of the Gospels. Between the 380s and the 450s, extravagant patronage by both men and women publicized the Christian faith and greatly extended its scope.

This ever-increasing prominence was backed by a distinctive rise in the use of force. Constantine's Christian successors tended to invert the thrust of his legislation. Their laws tended to curb the Christians' privileges, while acting more directly against pagan cult. Constantine's extreme favour for the bishops' "testimony" as a court of appeal had to be revised when they failed to live up to expectations. The laws on bequests were also reviewed. In 370, a strong law attacked Christian men, especially ascetics, who tried to win legacies for themselves or their churches from innocent women. In 390, it was abandoned as unworkable.[22]

Meanwhile, Christian intolerance of pagans had made gradual, but steady, progress. Against the Jews, intolerance could hardly have gone further than the attitudes Constantine inherited: they were a "deadly sect," said the laws in his reign, parricides, murderers of God's own Son. By his successors, it was made a crime for Christians to marry them.[23] Pagans, too, were not spared abuse in the Emperor's letters, but only six of their sites are known to have suffered in his reign. Perhaps the list was longer, but each of the known places was a special case.[24]

One, at Mambre, was a site of great holiness in the Old Testament; another, a shrine of Aphrodite, stood on the site of the Crucifixion and the Holy Sepulchre in Jerusalem. A third, at Aphaca, was an offensive Phoenician centre of sacred prostitution. The other three told a different story. At Didyma, Christians seized a prophet of Apollo and had him tortured, as also at Antioch. At Aigai, in Cilicia, they are said to have razed the shrine of Asclepius, a misfortune, however, from which it partially recovered.

Why were these latter shrines singled out so promptly? At Aigai, the pagan wise man Apollonius was believed to have "turned the temple into an Academy": this temple, or a nearby shrine, had been honoured with a fine pagan inscription in honour of "godlike" Apollonius, perhaps as recently as the reign of Diocletian. In the last phase of the Great Persecution, Hierocles, a prominent governor, wrote a book exalting Apollonius as the pagan superior to Christ. Not so long before him, Porphyry had compiled the books of *Philosophy from*

*Oracles*, which publicized texts from Didyma. At Didyma, the Emperors then underwent the encounter which set their Great Persecution on its course. When Constantine conquered the East, Christians therefore struck at Didyma and Aigai, the two shrines which were closely linked with the origins of their recent suffering: at Antioch, oracles from the local shrines had also embittered Maximin's persecutions and there, too, the prophets were duly tortured and obliged to confess "fraud." These reprisals are the counterpart to two written works by Eusebius, his polemic against the book on Apollonius and his "Demonstration of the Gospel," which disproved Apollo's oracles by quoting them against themselves.

In the early 340s, we find the first surviving Christian text which asks for something more, the total intolerance of pagan worship.[25] It was addressed by a recent convert, Firmicus, to Constantine's sons. In it, he pleaded for the persecution of pagans, but as a former pagan astrologer, Firmicus was perhaps protesting his Christianity with a special fervour. Nonetheless, contemporary bishops were already turning temples into churches, and by the 380s, we find them taking the initiative openly, abetted by monastic leaders and their followers.[26] From St. Martin in Gaul to the fearsome Shenoute in Egypt, there is a robust history of Christian temple- and statue-breakers. The laws could never move so fast: they relied for application on a class of governors who were often pagans themselves.

Force alone could not make converts, but it did weigh heavily with the undecided, and by the lack of divine reprisals it did show that the "anger" of the gods was no match for Christ. Importantly, the use of force was not usually mobilized by pagans in the first instance against Christians. There were some ugly incidents, essentially under Julian's pagan restoration, but pagans were capable of offering Christianity a mutual coexistence. As one pagan told Augustine, their gods were accustomed to "concordant discord."[27] While Christians worshipped their particular God, some pagans could simply see this worship as one more way among others. The old argument that Christian atheism caused divine "anger" had been refuted by events, while the pagan gods' own oracles had called their Supreme god "unknowable": who was to say if the Christians' way was not as acceptable to him as many others? Their piety, at first glance, was of the elevated, bloodless type which pagan philosophers commended: relics and martyr cult were perhaps aberrations. Intolerance had never been rooted in the long history of pagan philosophy and religious thought. After

Constantine, many pagans could still extend to the new worship a tolerance which its exclusivity refused to extend to them.

Pagan attacks on Christianity were attacks on its prominent "heroes": the virgins and holy men, monks and clergy. Such attacks made martyrs, and the victims were always replaceable. Christians, by contrast, did not attack individual pagans, after the torture of the oracular prophets at Didyma and Antioch. They attacked places to which the presence of the gods was attached. These attacks did more permanent damage, yet to ban sacrifices or close or demolish temples was only to limit cult acts. It was not to defeat the beliefs which we have studied beside pagans' religious practice. Nobody could dim the pagan stars, those visible reminders of the souls of the departed. Nobody could hope to control every nook and cranny in the Mediterranean landscape, although Constantine, said Eusebius, sent his emissaries into "every pagan temple's recess and every gloomy cave."[28] Their mission was apt, but impossible. Not even the entire army could have covered each cave of the Nymphs, the many caves which claimed Zeus's birthplace, the underground shrines of Mithras, the caves of Cybele and Attis or the many cavernous entries to Hades. Long after Constantine, the old Cretan caves still drew pagan visitors, couples like Salvius Menas and his wife, who climbed to the Tallaean cave every year: when his wife died, Menas came alone to make a double sacrifice on her behalf, "honouring the divine concerns of the gods."[29] The persistence of this subterranean pagan piety emerges clearly from two fourth-century inscriptions which were found in Attica's old cave of Pan at Phyle. One sophist recorded how he had climbed to Pan's cave "for the sixth time" to honour a pagan friend; another text marked the eleventh or twelfth visit of one Nicagoras, kinsman, perhaps, of the Nicagoras whom Constantine had sent to Egypt. These pagans were still pilgrims, as Claros had once known them. The fifth century saw persistent potholing by pagan men of letters and philosophy, in search of their old gods' "presence" below-ground.

Those other sources of "epiphany," the pagan statues, were also subjected to Constantine's demonstrations: Eusebius tells how his agents broke up divine statues and exhibited their stuffing as mere rubbish.[30] Yet there were far too many statues for such action to be more than demonstrative, and most of them survived, not least as decoration in Constantine's new capital. To neutralize them, Christianity had to divert attention elsewhere and to leave them as "demonic" survivals beside its own new centres of religion.

The age of Constantine has been aptly described as an "age of hiatus": we can carry this notion to our major theme, the "presence" of the gods.[31] This theme attracted heavy spending by the new Christian Emperor, under whom the sites of the gods' "presence" took a new, Christian turn. In 325, Constantine had been foiled of any hopes he may have had for the phoenix in Egypt; in the immediate aftermath of Nicaea, he amazed the Christian world by revealing something more spectacular. In response to local requests, he encouraged excavations to discover the site of Jesus's tomb. After finding a range of ancient burials, the workers were able, by some unknown criterion, to pick out one example as the "Holy Sepulchre." Plans for a vast new basilica were promptly announced and were joined by similar plans for shrines at Bethlehem and the Mount of Olives. There, caves "connected" with the Gospels' story had been seen by the Empress mother Helena, visiting the Holy Land as a pilgrim after the scandals in her family.

Shortly afterwards, Constantine's mother-in-law, Eutropia, reported yet another "presence." She had been visiting Mambre, one of the supreme sites in the Holy Land according to Jewish and Christian tradition.[32] It was at Mambre, in the Book of Genesis, that Abraham had met the three mysterious strangers, one of whom was the "third" whom nobody identified. Some of the Jews had already understood the scene as a meeting of their patriarch with God and his two powers; Christians understood it in terms of their own Trinity. At Mambre, Eutropia reported that the holy place of encounter was being defiled by pagan superstition: Jews and pagans were holding fairs and markets on the site. Constantine built a Christian shrine by the oak tree, scene of the biblical meeting, and adorned it with gold and precious stones. Characteristically, he did not suppress the Jews' and pagans' fair by legislation. It continued throughout the century, and the site's holy well continued to receive offerings, if anything in greater numbers.

This patronage of caves, sepulchres and holy oak trees had a focus which was altogether different from the easy world of pagan "epiphany." It owed much to the "discoveries" of Imperial females, touring hopefully on a pilgrimage: it honoured sites of a past "appearance," not the continuing presence of gods and angels. Its foundations lay in written Scripture, not in contemporary dreams and visions. The new sense of "epiphany" focussed on historical places, seen on pilgrimage, and "historical" fragments, the relics of the saints.[33] Perhaps we can go further.[34] Among pagans, portraits and sculptures had focussed the idea of divinity and helped their easy company with gods by night. In the Constantinian age, Christians were encouraged to see the pagans' statues as demonic, but they still lacked a figured art of comparable scale for themselves. At Elvira, the bishops ruled firmly that "there must not be pictures in a [or perhaps "the"] church, so that what is worshipped and adored may not be depicted on walls." Some Christians, perhaps, were already behaving otherwise, but the ban speaks for itself. The new Constantinople did contain statues of Daniel, of the Good Shepherd and other biblical figures, but the literary descriptions of Constantine's new churches are empty of references to figure paintings and representational sculpture. Instead, they mention abstract symbols, signs like the Christian cross. On the strength of this bias, Constantine has even been seen as a supporter of higher piety, offered without images.

The literary texts may not give a complete record, but they do suggest a marked contrast with pagan art and sculpture. This "hiatus" related to the contrast in religious experience which we met in our survey of Christian visions. In the Constantinian age, Christians still looked to one supreme epiphany, the Second Coming. They looked back, meanwhile, to the biblical epiphanies whose sites were being marked by fine new buildings. Their "oracles" were the old historical texts of Scripture; when Eusebius wrote five books called *Theophany*, he discussed the relation of the Creation to the Incarnation, not the continuing appearances of God to men. God did not "stand by" ordinary Christians as an "evident" helper: in Constantine's reign, there were no longer any martyrs for God's special company, except for the unhappy Christians whom "orthodox" Christians put to death. Instead, God's constant "companion" was said to be the Emperor himself. On Constantine's thirtieth anniversary, Eusebius aired the theme in his speech of honour, delivered in the Emperor's presence: "perhaps, Constantine," he inquired, "you will agree at your leisure to relate for us the abundant evidence of his presence which your Saviour has granted to you alone. Perhaps you will relate the repeated visions of himself which have addressed you during the hours of sleep . . ."[35] Eusebius hinted politely at his ruler's supreme guidance, but he was flattering him in a speech. Neither he nor Constantine was specific about any vision's content after the vision of the year 312.

Fellow Christians still acknowledged their unseen and impercep-
tible guides: the constant presence of their Holy Spirit and the
vigilance of their angels who came, as Origen had believed, to share
their meetings in church. In the new Christian Empire, however, this
"age of hiatus" was not to last for long.[36] By c. 330–340, a portrait of a
young beardless Christ had been set in a fine floor mosaic at Hinton St.
Mary in Dorset: probably, it derived from a church's decoration, a
portrait, perhaps, in its dome. As yet, it is the one mosaic portrait of
Christ which is known in a private house at this date, but if one existed
in distant Britain, there were probably others elsewhere. As the
century advanced, the Christian sense of "epiphany" was heightened
by further allies: the development of the liturgy and the rise of shrines
of the saints.

In the large, permanent interiors of the new churches, the Christian
liturgy could be held with a greater ceremony and visual impact. In the
Greek East, by c. 400, the idea of an "angelic presence" during Church
services was being emphasized by the siting and form of the Eucharist.
As Christians looked on at the ceremony beyond them, they sensed,
and even saw, angels who had come to attend the magnified rite. By c.
380–400, some of the greatest shrines of Christian saints were already
in existence, to be joined by many more in the course of the next
centuries. By the early fifth century, we know of the ownership of
private icons of saints;[37] by c. 480–500, we can be sure that the inside
of a saint's shrine would be adorned with images and votive portraits,
a practice which had probably begun earlier. By now, the image of
Christ and the saints had become fixed in a portrait art which was also
portable: as a result, the old relationship between art and dreams came
once more into play.

Like the old shrines of Asclepius, the saints' shrines were becoming
packed with works of art; like a pagan sacrifice, the Christian liturgy
was drawing a heavenly presence to its offerings. Some of the saints'
new shrines were placed deliberately as counters to old pagan temples
of epiphany: on the coast of Egypt, St. Cyrus and St. John "replaced"
a nearby shrine of Isis, just as St. "Therapon" replaced a famous
Asclepius on Mytilene. Once, pagan men of letters had "answered
back" to the Asclepius who appeared to them in his shrine at Aigai; by
the 380s, Christian men of letters were enjoying dreams and advice
from "scholarly" St. Thecla in her shrine on a nearby hillside.[38] Yet
these shrines were not merely "pagan" counterweights. They brought
their own Christian piety to a continuing culture pattern, the "epipha-

nies" which still occurred to the unified human mind. In sickness or in sea storms, in moments of stress or sadness, Christians continued to "see" their "helpers," as pagans had also seen theirs. While Christians accepted the pagans' experience and described it as demonic, they traced their own to God and his saints. In the past, Homer and religious art had enhanced what pagans saw; by the fifth century, the legends of the saints and an emergent portrait art were helping to focus the Christians' sense of a divine presence.

The age of Constantine has been seen as the final "ending of a debate" whereby Christians, especially the Christian monks, turned their backs on the pagans' easy access to the divine.[39] Yet the same needs and tensions endured, around which so many of the types of epiphany have always cohered. Finality was not so likely, and the history of oracles, visions and appearances does not have a tidy ending.

Like the "epiphanies" of the gods, the arts of pagan divination had also been grounded in human wants and experience. As Hermas had already been shown, these arts had their attractions for Christians, too.[40] The Christian Empire saw their absorption by Christians, not their rejection. Although the sites of inspired pagan oracles were classed as seats of the demons, the "neutral technology" of divination was promptly revised in Christian dress. The best evidence for its absorption lies in the continual attempts of fellow Christians to penalize its use. Business at the Council of Antioch had already included rules against Christians who practised divination. The rules continued to be affirmed, and if we look at our texts we can see why. In the third century, pagan clients had consulted the wisdom of "Astrampsachus's" book of oracular answers. They asked about their careers and marriages, their property and whether they were victims of a spell. By the fifth century, Christians were using the same book, although they had changed a few of the questions.[41] Whereas pagans asked, "Will my first wife stay with me?" Christians asked, "Will I remain a Presbyter?" Pagans had inquired if their running away would be detected; ambitious Christians now asked if they would become a bishop, to which the answer was "yes, but not quickly."

In Egypt, we can watch another old oracular technique being pressed into Christian service.[42] In Christian Egypt, God began to receive questions which were submitted on papyrus as alternatives for his choice: similar petitions had been offered to the pagan gods, requests whose grammatical form did not alter across seven centuries.

In Christian company, the social range of the surviving oracular questions is very revealing. They concern people who might become bishops, who feared the collectors of taxes and the burdens of civic office. They also include monks, for whom this old approach to a god was not improper. Here, no "debate on the holy" had ended: on this topic, there was no "debate" in the first place. Like epiphanies, futurology was grounded in human experience and its arts were much too precious to be rejected. By the sixth century, astrology, too, had established itself again with many Christians, despite the strong opposition of Christian teaching. Its art was the study of God's "signs," not his "causes," a view which pagan practitioners had also accepted. The arts of the horoscope and the old "books of fates" thus passed usefully into the Middle Ages.

The history of epiphany also wears a familiar face. A century after the "age of hiatus," Christian saints were appearing freely to Christians, "standing beside" them as "manifest protectors" in that exquisite Greek language which is as old as Homer. This continuity of language tempts us to see them as "pagan" intruders who kept alive a type of religious experience that was older than any revealed religion. The temptation should be resisted.[43] These "protectors" were no longer gods, but men with fictitious biographies, friendly "helpers" with well-known faces who had attained to the court of heaven. They were unpredictable and angry, like pagan gods and minor divinities, but they were also "patrons" before a Supreme God. They could intercede for their mortal clients, as a powerful noble might intercede for his dependents in earthly society.

These new "patrons" were not only present through their portraits: unlike any pagan god, they were "manifest" in their bones and relics. Christian beliefs about resurrection had first made these fragments into living, "manifest" tokens of power. Before them, visitors experienced a new "epiphany."[44] Visitors did not "see" their saint, as pagans had once seen Pan on the noonday hillside. Instead, they "saw" pieces of skin and bones, phials of blood and milk, which they greeted with the language of a revelation.

Above all, saints worked in a context of belief and explanation whose echoes had sounded so clearly in Pionius's prison diary. Like most pagans, Christians explained their misfortunes by God's anger, but this anger was aroused by the Christians' own sins. These beliefs, in turn, bred new public forms and practices. The saints in their healing shrines were not Asclepius in a thin Christian dress: they pinned sickness and failure on undisclosed sins and they prescribed cures which had a sacred and symbolic content. No client at pagan Pergamum could have been referred to anything so holy as the Christian "oil of the saints."[45] In their recorded miracles, the saints did not grant new and continuing revelations: whereas Apollo might speak like a Platonist, they quoted Scripture and the recorded words of Christ. The ceremonies and experiences at their shrines had a different intensity and psychological range. We can contrast the miracles of Cyrus and John with the cures enjoyed at Pergamum, the responses of pagan oracles with the answers which Christian solitaries gave to their clients, the scenes at processions of Christian relics with the urbane poems of Callimachus which had evoked the "arrival" of a god and the "exodus" of his statue through a city.

The new, Christian context showed clearly in men's response to misfortune. When God's anger seemed particularly evident, Christian cities and men of the world now turned to intercessors and begged them to plead for its relaxation. The justified wrath of God bred a new class of intermediaries, heirs to the Christian confessors in the old days of persecution.[46] In the Near East, people appealed to the prayers of the "holy men," solitary Christian overachievers; in fifth-century Byzantium, they turned to the Virgin herself, the advocate for the city in the awesome court of heaven. When natural calamities wracked the Mediterranean world in the mid-sixth century, they were met by the invention of Rogation Processions, beseeching God for human sins. The choirs for Apollo at Claros seem far away. Sin was a new explanation of universal scope and relevance: when the Arab armies finally swept across the Near East, Christians were encouraged to feel that they had only their own sins to blame for the catastrophe.

After the mid-fourth century and the pagan revival of Julian, the major pagan oracles disappear from our evidence.[47] The torturing of prophets in Constantine's reign must already have weakened Apollo's willingness to continue speaking: by the 360s, little shrines for the bones of Christian martyrs had impinged on Apollo's ancient precinct at Didyma and were interfering with reception on the old pagan frequency. The walls of the great pagan temple are scratched with Christian crosses, spidery signs which neutralized an older presence. By the late fourth century, it is doubtful if any maintained pagan prophet could be found at the major sites: subsequent references to pagan oracles as if they functioned are erudite and literary.

In the early fourth century, two ageing Christian authors had shown possible ways of "defusing" the words of the pagan gods. Eusebius had dismissed them as demonic and used them to refute their authors, whereas Lactantius had quoted them with Christian improvements and claimed them as proofs of the Christian faith. The future lay with Lactantius's method, as the Christians gained in confidence. In the first flush of the "new Empire," it must have been on the Christians' initiative that torture was applied to Apollo's prophet at Didyma and to others at Antioch, "people taken from the magistrates of the city." They were not humble, ignorant people, Eusebius asserted proudly: they were people of "wonderful and noble philosophy," at Antioch civic notables, at Didyma a "prophet and philosopher," last of the long line of cultured voices who had kept philosophy running in oracles, the voices of Polites, Theophilus, Macer and the rest.[48] Philosophic oracles had begun when Apollo's wisdom advanced with the culture of his prophets. They ended when Christians tortured the prophets who had recently helped to torture them too.

The Christians' reprisals silenced this type of continuing wisdom from the gods, and in due course, they could exploit its other aspects. Before long, their age of change was being eased, as so often, by being attached to an unrelated past. Anyone who wondered how so many great pagan thinkers had achieved so much without Christianity could now be reassured by a simple fiction: the pagans had been predicting it all the while.

Around the year 500, as the world was expected to end, the postscript to this type of history was written by the Christian author of the book *On True Belief*, to which our knowledge of late pagan oracles has owed so much. It only survives in an epitome, but even so, the preface to its books of oracles is very telling. "I have often noticed," it began, "the generous nature of theosophy," a word which was itself, it seems, a Christian coinage. It stood for the "wisdom of God" as opposed to the wisdom of mere philosophers. "The testimonies of pagan wise men must not be thrown away. It is not possible for God to appear and converse with men, but by inspiring the thoughts of good men, he gives them to the common crowd as teachers . . ."[49] As a pendant to seven books of Christian orthodoxy, the author added an eighth of texts from the pagan gods, among whom spoke the old Apollos of Didyma and Claros, answering Poplas and Polites, Theophilus and the long-lost Oenoandans.

By the sixth century, the balance had shifted decisively: the debris of pagan oracles and pagan *epiphaneia* was Christian property, maintained on sufferance in Christian books. In the 530s, just after the world had failed to end, we see the point made firmly in art.[50] When the Emperor Justinian founded a new city in Christian North Africa in honour of his wife, Theodora, a mosaic floor in his city showed the new priorities. Its design is all the more revealing because it was drawn, it seems, from a conventional pattern book. In the centre reclined the old Castalian spring of Delphi, dimmed and muted. In either corner flowed four livelier streams, the four Christian rivers of Paradise, new streams of the wisdom of God.

Henceforward, encounters with figures from the pagan past were encounters with the particular prophets whom Constantine had honoured in his Oration: Virgil and the Sibyl. They had first been publicized as Christian proofs by Lactantius, a man who had left North Africa to teach Latin rhetoric at a pagan court and had ended as the tutor to a Christian Emperor's family. Favoured by the Emperor, Virgil survived as a Christian guide, a "Christian before his time" who had sensed the Fall and the Christian remission of sins. If he had erred on the impregnability of Hell and the truth of the Incarnation, his grasp of the underworld did entitle him to lead the poet Dante on his travels through Purgatory.

Nothing, meanwhile, not even the fall of Rome, could cause the Sibyl to die. She had prophesied for Greeks and had spoken, too, for Jews; her books guided the Romans, and she survived as a witness to Christ. Among the pagan prophecies which Christians absorbed during the sixth century, there was already a story that the Sibyl had met Augustus on Rome's Capitoline hill and had prophesied the birth of Christ. Sibyls had always flourished on fiction, and centuries later the pattern was repeated; this literary fiction gave the Sibyl a lasting monument. On the site of her Christian prophecy, Christians built the Church of Maria in Ara Coeli, which was to loom above medieval Rome.[51] The Sibyl's future was assured, from the Capitol to the great floor scenes in Siena's cathedral and so to the frescoes of the Sistine Chapel. The centuries of pagan epiphany survived, but only through their legacy of prophecy, as a new phase had started in the history of "manifest presence." In the past, epiphany had multiplied the forms of pagan religiousness; from such a presence, the Christian religion itself had been born. When it ceases, religious experience will cease with it, yet "not to everyone do the gods appear . . ."

# NOTES

I have given notes to the pagan chapters and Chapter 12 by citing the author's name and the date of his book or article, giving a full reference to its title and whereabouts in my separate bibliographies, arranged alphabetically. Many of my references in those chapters were to collections of essays or conference papers and this system seemed preferable. In the Christian sections, Chapters 6 to 11, I have given the author, periodical or book title and date in the note itself. The titles in these sections are less cumbersome and the range of modern references deliberately more restricted. In each part I have amalgamated as many notes as possible under a single number in the text, so that they often refer to a sequence of statements just before or after the number itself.

## CHAPTER I

1. L. Robert, C.R.A.I. (1970) 11–17; on Janus, Eutrop. 9.2.2. and H. A. Gord. 26.3 with R. Syme, Historia Augusta Papers (1983) 132.
2. Dio 55.10.7 and Syme (1983) 131–2.
3. R. Syme, Emperors and Biography (1971) 167 on Gordianus in Asia Minor, esp. Cappadocia. On Philostratus, V.S. preface, I still side with V. Nutton, Latomus (1970) 719, esp. 725 on the meaning of the Greek: for another view, K. D. Grasby, C.Q. (1975) 127–9.
4. S.E.G. IV.523 with O. Benndorf, Ephesos I pp. 210 ff.; date, X. Loriot, A.N.R.W. II 2 (1975) p. 729 n. 554.
5. On G.'s route, most recently (but not finally), E. Kettenhofen, in S. Mitchell, ed., "Armies and Frontiers in Rmn. and Byz. Anatolia" (B.A.R. 156, 1983) p. 151, with bibliogr. on coinage. On games, Loriot p. 731.
6. G. E. Bean, T. B. Mitford, Denkschr. der Oesterr. Akad. der Wissensch. in Wien, Phil.-Hist. Klasse, 102 (1970) no. 19.
7. For evidence, S. Mitchell, in his ed. "Armies and Frontiers . . ." (1983) 131–50.
8. For problems, P. Weiss, Chiron (1981) 342–3 (the Nymphaeum); 331–41 (the games). Bean, op. cit. related the three "escorts" to Caracalla, Severus and Heliogab.; my dating is a possible alternative.
9. J. H. Oliver, Hesperia, Suppl. VIII (1949) 246–58, with the evidence; I G II² 3816 is not relevant, cf. J. Nollé, Z.P.E. 41 (1981) 197; I differ from Oliver p. 249, seeing a possible echo of Herodotus in I.G. II².3632 line 12.
10. A. H. M. Jones, Later Roman Empire (1964) 20; R. MacMullen, A.J.P. (1982) 233, the "habit."
11. G. W. Clarke, Latomus (1965) 633; Cypr., Ad Donat. 3.1 and 4 with (e.g.)

M. M. Sage, Cyprian (1975) 118–32: I would not call it "apologia," directed to C.'s pagan contemporaries. Herodian 7.9, for a background C. ignores. On patience, Cypr., De Bon Pat., esp. 13.

12. Cypr., Ep. 48.1–2.

13. A. Harnack, Z.N.W. (1902) 177; S. Deléani, Rev. Et. Aug. (1977) 221; J. Burnaby, Amor Dei (1938) p. 237, on alms giving.

14. On Pontius's Vita, most recently M. M. Sage (1975) 385–94.

15. Acta Cypriani 5.6 with P. B. Hinchcliffe, Cyprian of Carthage (1974) p. 130; Acta Maximiliani, 3.4.

16. Eus., V.C. 4.19–21 with 4.56 and 2.12 (cf. Sozom, 1.8): on "hēbēdon koptein," note Dionys. Hal. 2.16. "Chaplains" in Sozom. 1.8, doubted, however, by A. H. M. Jones, H.T.R. (1953) 239/40.

17. N. H. Baynes, Constantine the Great and the Christian Church (1972) p. 31 n. 5 on the correct (and often forgotten) title of E.'s *Life*.

18. R. Krautheimer, D.O.P. (1967) 115; C. Dupont, Rev. Hist. Eccles. (1967) 729; K. M. Girardet, Kaisergericht u. Bischofsgericht (1977); on family law, and the Augustan element, J. Gaudemet, L'Eglise dans l'Empire Romaine (1958) 514–61; on "charity," V.C. 4.28 with Cod. Theod. 11.27.1–2 and L. Robert, Rev. de Philol. (1967) 82–4 (important); here, too, P. Veyne, Le Pain et le Cirque (1976) 653 denies a "charitable" motive, citing the law's concern for public order and morals.

19. A. Watson, Phoenix (1983) 62–5; note esp. C. Theod. 9.12.1 and 9.24.1.

20. Text now in Vita di Martino, Vita di Ilarione . . . , introduz. di C. Mohrmann (Vita Dei Santi, IV, Fondaz. Lorenzo Valla, 1975) with C. Mohrmann's survey, pp. XL to LI. Gk. version, discussed by E. Fisher, Y.C.S. (1982) 193.

21. Sozom, H. E. 5.15, with interesting detail of the temples and name of the converts' village, "Bethelia."

22. P. R. L. Brown, Making of Late Antiquity (1978) 7; I question this "koine" from (say) 150–300 A.D., when I am more impressed by regional variations in pagan cult, the non-"Mediterranean" novelties in Christianity and such changes in Jewish piety as the acceptance of the rabbinic teachings on purity in (Mediterranean?) Galilee.

23. P. R. L. Brown, Cult of Saints (1981); P. A. Février, in 9 Congr. Internaz. di Arch. Crist. (Roma, 1975); E. Jastrzebowska, Untersuchungen zum Christlichen Totenmahl (1981); on dancing, J.-C. Schmitt, in La Religion Populaire en Languedoc, Cahiers de Fanjeaux 11 (1976) 127.

24. C. Mango, Byz. Literature in a Distorting Mirror (Oxford, 1975) and Jhrb. Oesterr. Byzantinistik 31, Akten 16 Internat. Byz.-Kongr. (1981) 337.

25. P. R. L. Brown, An Age of Spirituality: A Symposium (Princeton, 1980) 17–27.

26. A. H. M. Jones, L.R.E. II. 970–85; G. Dagron, D.O.P. (1977) 1.

27. P. R. L. Brown, Cult of Saints (1981) and E. D. Hunt, Holy Land Pilgrimage . . . (1982); on intolerance, G. E. M. de Sainte Croix, The Class Struggle . . . (1981) 451–2.

CHAPTER 2

I

1. Lys., 30.18; Lib., 30.31–6; S. Weinstock, J.R.S. (1961) 209–10.

2. J. A. North (1976), for Rome; L.R. (1980) 400 with Lucian, Alex. 14 and S.E.G.

XI.4; on Mithras, R. L. Gordon (1977), esp. 163–4; Arvals, A. Piganiol, C.R.A.I. (1946) 241; Vestals, Nock, Essays 1.252.

3. H. W. Attridge (1978); Varro, ap. Aug., C.D.4.21; 6.3–4 (Stoic: Aetius, S.V.F. II, p. 300, 8–10); J. C. McLelland (1976); on "gods" in man's image, theories rejected by Sext. Emp., Adv. Phys. 1.14–48; on "social relations," specifically, Aristot., Pol. 1252 B25.

4. G. Lieberg (1973) 63.

5. D. Babut (1974), for their roots.

6. See now P. Veyne (1983) 81–111.

7. E.g. Acts 13.6–12; Lucian, Alex. 30–33; R. Syme, Roman Papers II.762, a brilliant insight.

8. Note esp. Celsus, the Christians' critic, with M. Simon (1960) 309.

9. Ps. Clem., Recog. 8.2.2; cf. Suet., Tib. 69; Vett. Val. 5.9.

10. W. Gundel (1959) 55.

11. I still follow E. Löfstedt, Late Latin (1959) 75 ff.; Oros., Hist. 1.9 is surely a contrived derivation; cf. A. Harnack, Mission 1.430; C. Mohrmann, Vig. Chr. (1952) 109, for another view; E. Demougeot, Studi . . . Calderini . . . ed. Paribeni 1.337; H. Grégoire, Nouv. Clio (1952) 131. And so on. Cod. Theod. 16.2.18 (370) is the earliest use in the law codes.

12. A. D. Nock, C.A.H. 10.465: on Roman religion, admittedly, but I have generalized, I hope without inventing a view never held.

13. Dodds (1965) 120–1; R. Walzer (1949) 48; Lucian, Peregrin. 13, on Christians' lack of "akribes pistis."

14. Porphyr., Ad Marc. 24; L. R. Hell., 11–12 (1960) 424 n. 5.

15. Best is M. Simon (1979) 101, esp. 110–13 on Sceptics and on hetero/orthodoxy. More polemically, J. Glucker (1978) 166–92, for texts: p. 168 n. 18 denies any strong idea of "choice" in the word.

16. Acta Cypriani 1.1.

17. W. Warde Fowler, Religious Experience of Roman People (1911) 460–62.

18. P. A. Brunt (1976) 161, for general survey.

19. Plut., Mor. 380B: Juv. 15.33; Plut. Mor. 380A; D.S. 1.89.5.

20. J. A. S. Evans (1961); N. Lewis (1983) 91.

21. A. R. R. Sheppard (1980/1), with bibliography; S. Downey (1976); R. Amy (1950); S. P. Brock (1975) 106–8, on litters; Lucian, De Dea Syr. 45, with G. Goossens (1943); P. Perdrizet (1911), a brilliant study of tattooing; cf. Irenae., 1.20.4; Hippol., 7.32; Epiphan., Pan. 27; Clem. Alex., Ecl. Proph. 25.

22. W. Günther, Ist. Mitt. (1971) 97.

23. Dodds (1965) 133, citing Festugière; J. A. North, J.R.S. (1980) 191 wonders if cults did compete to monopolize devotion. The one text I know here is Eunapius, V. Philos. p. 436 (Loeb), referring, however, to a "pater" in the cult of Mithras, not (crucially) to other worshippers. A. D. Nock, Conversion (1933) is still definitive, on its own terms of reference (which I accept).

24. E. Peterson (1926), esp. 268–70; e.g., J. Keil, A. Premerstein, Denkschr. Akad. Wien 54 (1911) 109 n. 211: Men, at Saittai; J. Teixidor (1977) is conceptually misleading.

25. P. M. Fraser, Ptol. Alex. (1972) 1.192–3, 259; E. Peterson (1926) 227–40 and esp. O. Weinreich, Ausgewählt. Schrift. 1 (1969) 432; also, F. Cumont, C.R.A.I. (1919) 313.

26. M. Le Glay (1976) 366–8; A. Alföldi, Schweiz. Munzblätter 18 (1954) 25–31, on

Isis, "panthea"; M. Simon (1980) 517–8, excellent on Lucius's developing
awareness that his helping divinity is Isis, a fact revealed by her after several
stages in his addresses to her.

27. A. T. Kraabel (1969) 81, too firmly denying Jewish contacts; contrast, L.R., Op.
    Min. Sel. 1.411; B. Epig. 1961 no. 750; 1965 no. 412; S. Mitchell, Inscrip. of North
    Galatia (B.A.R. 35, 1982) no. 209, a Jewish one. Elsewhere, S. Sanie (1978)
    1092–1112, for non-Jewish uses. Each case must still be considered in its context.

28. J. Geffcken (1978) 14.

29. For summary, R. MacMullen (1981) 112–30.

30. M. Meslin (1974).

31. Apul., Met. 11.19, "iamdudum destinatum"; R. L. Gordon, Jo. of Mithraic
    Studies (1976) 119 and (1980) 19.

32. J. F. Matthews (1973).

33. J. H. W. Liebeschuetz (1979) 126–39, for recent discussion; Pliny, NH 28.10,
    but cf. 28.861; on "compulsion" and other definitions, H. Geertz, K. Thomas
    (1975); on amulets, esp. L. Robert, Jo. des Savants (1981), and Campbell
    Bonner (1946); generally, Nock, Essays I.176–95. Thessalus, ed. H.-V.
    Friedrich (1968), brilliantly studied by Festugière (1939), but I share the caution
    of Dodds (1973) 189 n. 2 about its ultimate authenticity. This, however, does
    not affect its value: it wished to seem convincing. For other works "to"
    Emperors (but not Thessalus's), F. Millar, Emperor in the Roman World (1977).

34. J. Z. Smith (1977) believes he had, unconvincingly: "rather than celebration,
    purification and pilgrimage, the new rituals will be those of conversion,
    initiation into the secret society and identification with the divine man"
    (p. 238). This is too sharp an opposition, and these "new rituals" need much
    clearer definition, as does the ubiquitous "divine man."

35. I have been best helped by A. F. Segal (1981); Brown (1972) 119 is the most
    stimulating study. A. Abt (1908), for techniques.

36. Nock, Essays I.176 ff.; also, the tour de force by E. Peterson (1948) on P.G.M.
    IV.1177.

37. H. S. Versnel (1981) 42, with J. W. Hewitt (1912); I am not thinking here of
    philosophers' theories of prayer. Hesiod, W. and D. 354/5; A. J. Festugière
    (1976).

38. H. Seyrig (1971) and (1973); P. A. Février (1976) 310, on Africa; J. J. Hatt
    (1965), on Gaul; in Asia Minor, L.R., B.C.H. (1982) 378; B.C.H. (1983) 541
    and esp. 553–80. In Spain, R. Etienne (1973) 153. In Britain, see now the
    excellent study by M. Henig, Religion in Roman Britain (1984).

39. W. F. Snyder (1940).

40. L.R., Jo. des Sav. (1975) 158–9: not always Roman, but P. Herrmann (1969) for
    an example; M. Meslin (1970), merely attested in 5th cent. but not, I suspect,
    originating then (contra, Brown 1978, 50); Schwarzlose (1913) on dead as
    deities. Note Février (1976) 317, on Capitolia in Africa in 2nd–3rd c.; for
    Roman domestic cults in the West, J. Alarcao (1969) and Février (1977), esp.
    522–3.

41. Epictet. 1.19.26–9; P. A. Février (1976) 314 n. 81; Tac., Anns. 14.31.

42. I anticipate S. R. F. Price (1984), a fundamental study: his emphasis on
    "representing power" is, to my mind, too conceptual, as if the rulers caused a
    real problem of categorization. Stories of the first decisive "divine honours," for
    Alexander, are stories of people who were exploiting the new possibilities, or

resenting others who did; they are not stories of people who were puzzled how to make sense of them. Balsdon (1950) and S. Weinstock (1972) 287 ff. for the setting; Nock, Essays I.34–45 for "power." L. Robert (1960) and (1966) for religiousness.

43. F. K. Dörner (1935) p. 15, line 11, with L.R., in Laodicée du Lycos: 1 (1969) 274.
44. Herz (1975): rather too adventurous in its reconstructions.
45. Nock, C.A.H. 10 (1934) 481, well handled by Price (1984): see now J.H.S. (1984) 91 n. 105–6.
46. Price (1984) on this. W. H. C. Frend (1965) 452, on Christianity, unconvincingly.
47. E.g. Theocr., Idyll 7; MacMullen (1981) 18, on "typically rural" cult theatres, in northwestern provinces.
48. Attis, L.R. (1980) 234–6; Samos, Q.G. 56 with Halliday's commentary and esp. R.E. 1A (Samos) 2168–71; Corycian Cave, J.H.S. (1891) 212; L.R., B.C.H. (1982) 355 ff., on Zeus; on Dionysus, e.g. D. M. Pippidi, B.C.H. (1964) 151, citing P. Boyancé et al.
49. J. and R. Alquier (1929) 129–168, on Bacax.
50. V. Scully (1962); M.A.M.A. IV p. 15.
51. Hor., Od. 3.18; Mart. 10.92, a lovely poem; Apul., Apol. 56.4.
52. Ael. V.H.3.1.
53. K. J. Dunbabin (1978) 47, 63–4; I. Lavin (1963) 181; Basil, Ep. 14.2; Greg. Nyss., Vita Macrinae (S. Chrét. ed.) p. 169; Apul., Met. 8.31; Arr., Kyneg., passim. Philokunegoi in Sheppard (1979) 180, with L.R. (1940) 323, for meanings; from Britain, R.I.B. 1041 is magnificent.
54. Dunbabin (1978) plates 95–6 (Zliten).
55. Pliny, Ep. 9.39; 8.8.
56. Liban., 30.9–10; 19.
57. Virg., Georg. 4.276; L.R., B.C.H. (1983) 526–42; de Sainte Croix (1981) 18, quoting Babrius, Fab. Aes. 2.6–8.
58. See now D. E. Birge (1982) and P. Debord (1982) 170 + n. 59, both since I wrote; T.A.M. V.1 (1981) 19 + B.C.H. (1983) 515, on Lydia; Val. Max. 1.1.19 and Dio 51.8.3, Cos with R. Herzog (1928) nos. 11 and 12; M. J. Vermaseren (1977) 115, Attis. Paus. 2.13.3–4; Philostr. V.A. 1.16. Ael. N.A. 11.7; Livy, 24.3.3; Ael. N.A. 11.2, and 7.9. On Claros, N.A. 10.49. Strabo, 5.1.9 + Ael. N.A. 11.20, dogs.
59. Dio 62.7.3; D.S. 3.42–3, 5.42–4; S.E.G. XIX.550; esp. L.R., B.C.H. (1977) 77–98 (was this why Gadatas penalized them? Meiggs-Lewis 12); Lucian, De Dea Syr. 49.
60. Lois Sacr. Cit. Grecques 37 or 84 line 85.
61. B.C.H. (1920) no. 78–80 + L.R., B.C.H. (1977) 85. Cf. G. E. Bean, J.H.S. (1954) 87 ff., no. 22. J. Bousquet (1976).
62. Plut., ap. Stob. 4.16 with F. Wilhelm, Rh. Mus. (1924) 466.
63. C. Renfrew, M. Wagstaff, ed. (1982) pp. 109–10.
64. J. D. Mikalson (1977) at p. 428; Grenfell-Hunt, Select Papyri, 215.
65. Eus., P.E. 5.190A; L.R. (1968) 595 + O.G.I. 755. Dio 30.25 ff., though I doubt the truth of 1.52–4. Following Aristotle, de Sainte Croix (1981) 116–7, 183–4 limits leisure unduly, I feel, in Mediterranean smallholdings where wives and families worked too.
66. P. R. L. Brown (1981) 42–3.

## II

1. Liebeschuetz, Antioch (1972) 92–8; D. Crouch, Mél. Univ. St. Jos. (1972) 241; P. M. Fraser, J.E.A. (1951) 103 and Diod. Sic. 17.52.6, Eus., H.E. 7.27 (250s); A. H. M. Jones, L.R.E. p. 698.
2. I.L.S. 2683 (Apamea); Jos., B.J.2.385 (Egypt); Galen V. (Kühn) 49; C. Hopkins (1972) 150–61 with Pliny N.H. 6.30; Zon. 12.23 with Amm. Marc. 20.9.1, doubted by Beloch, Bevölkerung . . . (1886) 240. In general, R. Duncan-Jones, Economy of the Roman Empire (1982) 259, with endnotes.
3. R. Mols, in C. M. Cipolla, ed. (1977) p. 42.
4. For France, the admirable book of J. McManners, Death and the Enlightenment (1981): p. 10 quotes Buffon; for antiquity, K. Hopkins (1966) cites U.N. model life tables and queries the evidence of epitaphs, as do A. E. Samuel et al., Death and Taxes (1971) 7 ff., with pp. 14–16 on the uses of Egyptian censuses instead; P. S. and E. Derow, Phoenix (1973) 80 ff., undermine the further argument from tax records.
5. On age at marriage, Hopkins (1965), citing the fundamental articles of M. Durry; for Egypt, M. Humbert, C. Préaux, Rech. sur le Recensement dans l'Egypte Romaine (P. Lugl. Bat. 5, 1952) 160–1 is fundamental, with M. K. Hopkins, Comp. Stud. Soc. and History 20 (1980) 333. For postponed marriage, McManners p. 69 (in France).
6. J. McManners, Death and the Enlightenment (1981) 73.
7. F. G. B. Millar (1977), with Synesius, Epistle 148.
8. A. H. M. Jones, Roman Economy (1974) chaps. 1, 2 and 5 are essential surveys.
9. Plut., Mor. 813E, with C. P. Jones, Plutarch and Rome (1971) 133, rightly; cf. Plut., Aemil. 5.2. Finley (1983), on politics; L. Robert, Laodicée I (1969) 261, on "generals"; cf. G. Lopuszanki (1951), on policing; O. Hirschfeld, Kleine Schriften (1913) 576–612, for the West; S. Mitchell, J.R.S. (1976) 106 on labour services.
10. L. Neesen (1981), on these munera patrimonalia, Philo, Quod Omnis Prob. Lib. 141, a very striking episode, set, I assume, in Alexandria.
11. Dio 18, 12–17, esp. 16, a fine passage.
12. P. Garnsey (1975); M. Gordon (1931).
13. Rabbi Yohanan, in M. Avi-Yonah (1976) 102.
14. Dig. 48.14, and Paul, Sent. 5.30, on elections; L.R., Rev. Philol. (1977) 8 n. 7, on letters; M. I. Rostovtzeff, S.E.H.R.E. (1957) 632 n. 33, misjudging the "incolae" in legal texts, as P. A. Brunt has pointed out to me; on double citizens, e.g. Dio, Or. 41 with C. P. Jones (1978) 92–4.
15. M. I. Finley, Ancient Economy (1973) 71 ff., stressing a "sufficient minimum" and also a significant "social location"; on the latter, I follow de Sainte Croix (1981) 52–3. Note that the so-called "slave hunt" by Veranius in Lycia (for doubts, de Sainte Croix p. 307–8 and 533) was a judicial process, not part of an insurrection: L. Robert, Et. Anat. (1937) 375–8 and B.C.H. (1978) 477 showed that V. sorted out slaves who were masquerading as free persons.
16. P. D. Garnsey (1975) p. 237/8 is less impressed by S. Gsell (1932) on slaves in North Africa than I am.
17. De Sainte Croix (1981) 303–26; 454–62; 518–37: with bibliogr.
18. C. P. Jones (1978) s.v. faction; Plut., Mor. 823F–825F; Broughton, in Economic Survey . . . 4.810–2 for examples.

19. P. D. Garnsey (1974), an excellent survey: what caused the three years of "anarchy" at Athens between 167/8 and 171/2: plague, or stasis? S. I. Rotroff, Hesperia (1975) 407–8.

20. L. Robert, Arch. Ephem. (1969) 27 n. 14 and H. W. Pleket, Talanta (1978/9) 78; for the realities, P. Veyne (1976) 274–5; L. Neesen (1981), on exemptions.

21. L.R., Laodicée I (1969) 259–60, on "love" of town; on philotimia in a bad sense, Hdts. 3.53.4; Thuc. 3.82; Pindar F210; Aristot., Ethics 1125B 22; Eur., Phoeniss. 532; A. Wardman, Plutarch's Lives (1974) 115–24; in a good, if competitive sense, already in Lysias 21.22 and 26.3 and 19.56 (on liturgies and expenditure); 33.2 (Olympics).

22. P. Veyne (1976) 341–67, with notes; L.R. Hellenica 11–12 (1960) 569–76; R. MacMullen (1980), on women; cf. C. Naour Z.P.E. 24 (1977) 265 line 16 for a "mother"; C. Roueché (1979), on "fathers"; on dreams, Artemid. 2.27; L.R., R.E.A. (1965) 304–5, on numbers of acclaiming voices. Lucian, Peregr. 15 is exact satire.

23. P. Veyne (1976) 326–7, for this view, alleging a tacit "pact."

24. P. D. Garnsey (1978) 227–8, with Fronto, Ad Marc. 1.10.5.

25. L. Robert, H.S.C.P. (1977), a classic account.

26. Musonius F 15B (Hense) is decisive evidence.

27. L. Robert (1940) 240–331 is classic: pp. 255–6 (on Polemo's attitude); p. 262 (fights to "death"); pp. 320–1 (in bonds). On I.L.S. 5613, I follow Millar (1977) 195.

28. Millar (1981) 69, though I also detect deliberate playfulness in the Ass's "world": e.g. Met. 2.20 ("Romana frequentia") at Hypata! Best of all is still E. Auerbach, Mimesis (1968) 60–63, a brilliant study of Met. 1.24–6. On dreams, Artemid. 3.63; 3.13 (gods); 4.44 (contempt): A. is also aware of the anxieties and hazards of high office.

29. E.g. C. Habicht, Altertüm. v. Pergamon, VIII.3 (1969) no. 33, p. 75; Isocrates, too, is a pervasive influence; on sculpture, J. Inan, E. Rosenbaum (1966) and (1980); philosophy, M. N. Tod (1957).

30. On book reviews, Galen 19.60–67; writing down speeches, Apul. Flor. 9.7 with 9.13–14; musical feud, Philostr. V. Soph. p. 166 (Wright), a nice use of "heterodoxos."

31. M. Lyttleton (1974); Men. Rhet. p. 382.10 and 386.23 (ed. Russell); Dig. 1.18.7; 50.10.7 (Pius), on restoring old buildings; P. Graindor (1930) 179 ff., on Herodes and pp. 223–4 (Odeons).

32. Philostr. V.S. p. 266 (Damianos), with G. Bowersock, Greek Sophists (1969) 27–8; also N. Purcell, C.R. (1982) 251.

33. Arr., Kyneg. esp. 2 with P. A. Stadter, Arrian (1980) 50–60.

34. Aug., Civ. Dei 9.12.32.

35. E. Patlagean (1977) 156–81, on the Corycos evidence.

36. Contra, K. Hopkins (1980) 104: e.g. F. Millar (1981) 72–3: for the papyri, E. Christiansen, Z.P.E. (1984) 271. Virg., Georg. 1.275. C. J. Howgego reminds me that it was the mark of a primitive (not typical) society to lack coinage in the Imperial age.

37. The much-quoted Galen VI (Kühn) 749–52 refers to an exceptional bout of famines.

38. On towns, K. Hopkins (1978) 35.

39. H. W. Pleket (1983), a very clear and important paper: note Damianos's private

"harbours" at Ephesus (Philostr., V.S. p. 266 f.). In general, P. Veyne (1979).
40. P. D. Garnsey (1981), for Italy.
41. R. MacMullen (1974), for emphatic statement of it.
42. E.g., Eus., H.E. 9.8.9.
43. A. Balland (1981), a superb study with full bibliography for the points I mention: "grain receivers," etc. Damianos also helped poor pupils and litigants: Philostr. V.S.266.
44. J. Reynolds, Aphrodisias and Rome (1982) 133 no. 21.
45. Apul., Met. 2.4 ff. and Damianos, Philostr. V.S. p. 266, for houses; on theatre seating, e.g. R. Heberdey, Forsch. in Ephesos II (1913) 127 ff.; L. Polacco (1981).
46. Plut., Solon 21.5–7; P. Schmitt-Pantel (1982), on benefactors.
47. R. MacMullen (1974) 62–87; L. Robert, Et. Anat. (1937) 535 n. 3.
48. R. Lane Fox (1985).
49. B. Woodward-Frier (1977), with Dig. 9.3.5.1–2.
50. L. Robert, H.S.C.P. (1977), with Dio Or. 38 and 41, spoken to the city assembly.

## BIBLIOGRAPHY: I

A. Abt, Die Apologie des Apuleius (1908).
J. Alarcao, Le Culte des Lares à Conimbriga (Portugal), C.R.A.I. (1969) 213.
J. and R. Alquier, Le Chattaba et les Grottes à Inscriptions Latines (1929).
R. Amy, Temples à Escaliers, Syria (1950) 82.
H. W. Attridge, The Philosophical Critique of Religion under the Early Empire, A.N.R.W. II, 16.1 (1978) 45.
D. Babut, La Religion des Philosophes Grecs (1974).
J. P. V. D. Balsdon, The Divinity of Alexander the Great, Historia (1950) 363.
D. E. Birge, Sacred Groves in the Ancient Greek World (Diss., Berkeley; 1982).
C. Bonner, Magical Amulets, H.T.R. (1946) 25.
J. Bousquet, Les Oliviers de Lindos, Recueil Plassart (1976) 9.
S. P. Brock, Some Aspects of Greek Words in Syriac, Abh. der Wiss. in Göttingen (Phil.-Hist., 1975), ed. A. Dieterich, 106–8.
P. R. L. Brown, Sorcery, Demons and the Rise of Christianity, in Religion and Society in the Age of St. Augustine (1972) 119.
P. R. L. Brown, The Making of Late Antiquity (1978).
P. R. L. Brown, The Cult of Saints (1981).
P. A. Brunt, The Romanization of the Local Ruling Classes, in Assimilation et Résistance, ed. D. M. Pippidi (1976) 161.
G. E. M. de Sainte Croix, The Class Struggle in the Ancient Greek World (1981).
P. Debord, Aspects Sociaux et Economiques de la Vie Religieuse dans l'Anatolie Gréco-Romaine (1982).
E. R. Dodds, Pagan and Christian in an Age of Anxiety (1965).
E. R. Dodds, The Ancient Concept of Progress (1973).
F. K. Dörner, Der Erlass des Statthalters von Asia Paullus Fabius Persicus (1935).
S. Downey, Temples à Escaliers: The Dura Evidence, C.S.C.A. 9 (1976) 21.
K. J. Dunbabin, The Mosaics of Roman North Africa (1978).
R. Etienne, Les Syncrétismes Religieux dans la Péninsule Ibérique, in Syncrétismes dans les Relig. Gréco-Rom., ed. F. Dunand (1973) 153.
J. A. S. Evans, A Social and Economic History of a Temple in the Greco-Roman Period, Y.C.S. (1962) 149.

A. J. Festugière, L'Expérience Religieuse du Médecin Thessalos, Rev. Bibl. (1939) 45.

A. J. Festugière, Anth'Hōn: La Formule en Echange de Quoi en Prière Grecque, Rev. Sci. Philos. Theol. (1976) 389.

P. A. Février, Religion et Domination dans l'Afrique Romaine, Dial. Hist. Anc. 2 (1976) 305.

P. A. Février, Natale Petri de Cathedra, C.R.A.I. (1977) 514.

W. H. C. Frend, Martyrdom and Persecution . . . (1965).

R. Garosi, Magia, ed. R. Xella (1976).

H. Geertz, K. Thomas, An Anthropology of Religion and Magic: Two Views, Jo. of Interdisc. History VI (1975) 71; 91.

J. Geffcken, The Last Days of Greco-Roman Paganism, trans. S. MacCormack (1978).

J. Glucker, Antiochus and the Late Academy (1978).

G. Goossens, Hiérapolis de Syria (1943).

R. L. Gordon, The Date and Significance of C.M.R.M. 593, J. Mithr. Studies II (1977) 148.

W. Gundel, Sternglaube, Sternreligion u. Sternorakel (1959).

J.-J. Hatt, Essai sur l'Evolution de la Religion Gauloise, R.E.A. (1965) 80.

P. Herrmann, K. Z. Polatkan, Das Testament des Epikrates . . . (1969).

P. Herz, Untersuchungen zum Festkalendar der Röm. Kaiserzeit (1975).

R. Herzog, Heilige Gesetze von Kos (1928).

J. W. Hewitt, On the Development of Thank-Offerings . . . , T.A.P.A. 43 (1912) 95.

A. T. Kraabel, Hypsistos and the Synagogue at Sardis, G.R.B.S. (1969) 81.

I. Lavin, The Hunting Mosaics of Antioch and Their Sources, D.O.P. (1963) 181.

M. Le Glay, Hadrien et l'Asklepeion de Pergame, B.C.H. (1976) 357.

N. Lewis, Life in Egypt under Roman Rule (1983).

G. Lieberg, Die Theologie Tripartita in Forschung u. Bezeugung, A.N.R.W. 1.4 (1973) 63.

J. H. W. G. Liebeschuetz, Continuity and Change in Roman Religion (1979).

J. C. McLelland, God the Anonymous (1976).

R. MacMullen, Roman Social Relations (1974).

R. MacMullen, Paganism in the Roman Empire (1981).

J. F. Matthews, Symmachus and the Oriental Cults, J.R.S. (1973) 175.

M. Meslin, La Fête des Kalendes de Janvier (1970).

M. Meslin, Réalités Psychiques et Valeurs Religieuses dans les Cultes Orientaux, Revue Historique (1974) 289.

J. D. Mikalson, Religion in the Attic Demes, A.J.P. (1977) 424.

A. D. Nock, Paul and the Magus, in Beginnings of Christianity, ed. F. J. Jackson and K. Lake, vol. 5 (1933) 171.

J. A. North, Conservatism and Change in Roman Religion, P.B.S.R. (1976) 1.

P. Perdrizet, La Miraculeuse Histoire de Pandare et d'Echedore . . . Arch. für Religionswiss. (1911) 54.

E. Peterson, Heis Theos (1926).

E. Peterson, La Libération d'Adam de l'Ananke, Rev. Bibl. (1948) 119.

S. R. F. Price, Rituals and Power: The Imperial Cult in Roman Asia Minor (1984).

C. Renfrew, M. Wagstaff, ed., An Island Polity (1982).

L. Robert, Les Gladiateurs dans l'Orient Grec (1940).

L. Robert, Recherches Epigraphiques, R.E.A. (1960) esp. 316 ff.

L. Robert, Sur un Décret d'Ilion . . . Essays . . . C. B. Welles, American Studies in Papyrology I (1966) 175.

L. Robert, A Travers l'Asie Mineure (1980).

L. Robert, Amulettes Grecques, Jo. des Savants (1981) 3.

S. Sanie, Deus Aeternus et Theos Hypsistos en Dacie Romaine, in Hommages à M. J. Vermaseren, III (1976) 1092.

W. G. Schwarzlose, De Titulis Sepulcralibus Latinis (1913).

V. Scully, The Earth, the Temple and the Gods (1962).

A. F. Segal, Hellenistic Magic, Studies in Gnosticism and Hellenistic Religions. For G. Quispel, ed. R. van den Broek, M. Vermaseren (1981).

H. Seyrig, Le Culte du Soleil en Syrie (1971) 337.

H. Seyrig, Le Prétendu Syncrétisme Solaire Syrien . . . , in Les Syncrétismes dans les Relig. Greco-Rom., Colloque de Strasbourg (1973) 147.

A. R. R. Sheppard, Jews, Christians and Heretics in Acmoneia and Eumeneia, Anatol. Stud. 29 (1979) 169.

A. R. R. Sheppard, Pagan Cults of Angels, Talanta, XI/XII (1980/1) 77.

M. Simon, Christianisme Antique et Pensée Paienne . . . , Bull. Fac. Lett. Strasb. (1960) 309.

M. Simon, From Greek Hairesis to Christian Heresy, in Early Christian Literature and the Classical Tradition . . . , ed. W. R. Schoedel, R. L. Wilken (1979) 101.

M. Simon, Anonymat et Polyonymie Divins dans l'Antiquité Tardive, Studi . . . A. Brelich (1980) 503.

J. Z. Smith, The Temple and the Magician, in God's Christ and His People . . . Studies . . . N. A. Dahl, ed. J. Jervell, W. A. Meeks (1977) 233.

W. F. Snyder, Public Anniversaries in the Roman Empire . . . , Y.C.S. (1940) 223.

J. Teixidor, The Pagan God (1977).

M. J. Vermaseren, Cybele and Attis (1977).

H. S. Versnel, Religious Mentality in Ancient Prayer, in Faith, Hope and Worship, ed. H. Versnel (1981).

P. Veyne, Les Grecs Ont-Ils Cru à Leurs Mythes? (1983).

R. Walzer, Galen on Jews and Christians (1949).

S. Weinstock, Divus Julius (1972).


BIBLIOGRAPHY: II

M. Avi-Yonah, The Jews of Palestine (1976).

A. Balland, Les Liberalités d'Opramoas, Fouilles de Xanthos, VII (1981) 173.

P. A. Brunt, The Romanization of the Local Ruling Class . . . , in Assimilation et Résistance, ed. D. M. Pippidi (1976) 161.

C. Cipolla, ed., Fontana Economic History of Europe, 16th and 17th Centuries (1977).

G. E. M. de Sainte Croix, The Class Struggle in the Ancient Greek World (1981).

M. I. Finley, The Ancient Economy (1973).

M. I. Finley, Politics in the Ancient World (1983).

P. D. Garnsey, Aspects of the Decline of the Urban Aristocracy . . . , A.N.R.W. II.1 (1974) 229.

P. D. Garnsey, Descendants of Freedmen in Local Politics: Some Criteria, in the Ancient Historian . . . , ed. B. M. Levick (1975) 187.

P. D. Garnsey, Rome's African Empire under the Principate, in Imperialism . . . , ed. P. D. Garnsey, C. R. Whittaker (1978) 223.

P. D. Garnsey, Independent Freedmen and the Economy of Roman Italy under the Principate, Klio (1981) 359.

M. L. Gordon, The Freedman's Son in Municipal Life, J.R.S. (1931) 65.

P. Graindor, Un Milliardaire Antique (1930, repr. 1979).

S. Gsell, Esclaves Ruraux en Afrique, Mélanges Glotz, 1 (1932) 315.

C. Hopkins, Topography and Architecture of Seleuceia on the Tigris (1972).

K. Hopkins, The Age of Roman Girls at Marriage, Population Studies (1965) 309.

K. Hopkins, The Probable Age-Structure of the Roman Population, Population Studies 20 (1966/7) 245.

K. Hopkins, Economic Growth and Towns in Classical Antiquity, in Towns and Societies, ed. P. Abrams, E. A. Wrigley (1978) 35.

K. Hopkins, Conquerors and Slaves (1978).

K. Hopkins, Taxes and Trade in the Roman Empire, J.R.S. (1980) 101.

J. Inan, K. Rosenbaum, Roman and Early Byzantine Portrait Sculpture in Asia Minor (1966).

J. Inan, K. Rosenbaum, Römische u. Frühbyzantinische Porträtplastik aus der Turkei: Neue Funde (1980).

A. H. M. Jones, The Roman Economy, ed. P. A. Brunt (1974).

C. P. Jones, The Roman World of Dio Chrysostom (1975).

R. J. Lane Fox, Aspects of Inheritance in the Greek World, in Crux, ed. P. A. Cartledge, F. D. Harvey (1985).

G. Lopuszanki, La Police Romaine et les Chrétiens, Antiqu. Class. (1951) 5.

M. Lyttleton, Baroque Architecture in Classical Antiquity (1974).

R. MacMullen, Roman Social Relations (1974).

R. MacMullen, Woman in Public in the Roman Empire, Historia (1980) 208.

F. G. B. Millar, The Emperor in the Roman World (1977).

F. G. B. Millar, The World of the Golden Ass, J.R.S. (1981) 63.

S. Mitchell, Requisitioned Transport in the Roman Empire, J.R.S. (1976) 106.

L. Neesen, Die Entwicklung der Leistungen u. Ämter, Historia (1981) 203.

E. Patlagean, Pauvreté Economique et Pauvreté Sociale à Byzance (1977).

H. W. Pleket, Urban Elites and Business, in Trade in the Ancient Economy, ed. P. D. Garnsey, K. Hopkins, C. R. Whittaker (1983) 131.

L. Polacco, Théâtre, Société, Organisation de l'Etat, in Théâtre et Spectacles . . . . Actes du Colloque de Strasbourg 7 (1981) 12.

L. Robert, Les Gladiateurs dans l'Orient Grec (1940).

L. Robert, La Gloire et la Haine . . . , H.S.C.P. (1977) 1.

C. Roueché, A New Inscription from Aphrodisias and the Title Pater Tes Poleos, G.R.B.S. (1979) 173.

P. Schmitt-Pantel, Evergetisme et Mémoire du Mort, in La Mort, Les Morts . . . , ed. G. Gnoli, J. P. Vernant (1982) 177.

M. N. Tod, Sidelights on Greek Philosophers, J.H.S. (1957) 132.

P. Veyne, Le Pain et le Cirque (1976).

P. Veyne, Mythe et Réalité de l'Autarcie á Rome, R.E.A. (1979) 261.

B. Woodward-Frier, The Rental Market in Early Imperial Rome, J.R.S. (1977) 27.

CHAPTER 3

The outstanding studies of paganism are the Essays of A. D. Nock (1972) and his brilliant study, Conversion (1933). J. Geffcken, The Last Days of Greco-Roman Paganism (1978, translation) has an unsurpassed range and momentum; Gaston Boissier, La Fin du Paganisme (1891) is still powerful and apt. J. H. W. G. Liebeschuetz, Continuity and Change in Roman Religion (1979) is an excellent study of the Latin literary evidence, Ramsay MacMullen, Paganism in the Roman Empire (1981) an excellent essay on the Greek evidence, though I would lay more emphasis on the gods' sense of honour and anger than on "the chief business of religion, to make the sick well" (p. 49). E. R. Dodds, Pagan and Christian in an Age of Anxiety (1965) is a brilliant study, despite my disagreement with one of its main themes. It prompted a fine review article by Peter Brown, reprinted in his Religion and Society in the Age of St. Augustine (1972) 74–93: his own chapters in The World of Late Antiquity (1971) are memorable.

I

1. R. MacMullen (1976) p. 37; E. R. Dodds (1965), for anxiety.
2. B. Reardon (1971) 237–8 on "rising credulity" in 2nd cent.; P. M. Fraser, Ptolemaic Alexandria I (1972) 434–44 on earlier pseudo-sciences; O. Murray, J.R.S. (1961) 263: "never was magic more rationally pursued than in the later Roman Empire."
3. By MacMullen (1981) 69–70.
4. Aul. Gell. 1.26; P. A. Brunt, J.R.S. (1974) 11, on Marcus; Galen, V. (Kühn) 1 ff., a fascinating text; I quote V.4 p. 17: note esp. pp. 21–2, on how best to whip slaves and why the beaters of slaves are less wicked than people who kick doors. Brown (1978) 40, on this "static electricity of violence."
5. J. F. Kindstrand (1980) 341 and now P. Oxy. 3659 with notes; in art, F. Cumont, Ann. Soc. Arch. Bruxell. 14 (1900) 401, the Herstal vase, c. 100 A.D.
6. Celsus, De Med. 1.2: "litterarum cupidi" are "imbecilles."
7. Brown (1971) 49–57, for a brilliant sketch; Julia Briggs, This Stage-Play World (1983) 197 ff.
8. A. M. Blackman (1918/9) 26; P. E. Corbett (1970).
9. On hymns, L.R., Et Anatol. (1937) 20; on processions, MacMullen (1981) p. 27 n. 41 and 45 and esp. F. Bömer's Pauly article, R.E. 21 (1952) 1878 ff.; Tertull., Apolog. 35 (197 A.D.); L.R. in Essays . . ., C. B. Welles (1966) 175.
10. S. Mitchell (1982); as for wooden xoana, P. Perdrizet (1906) 226–7 saw the truth.
11. A. Laumonier (1958) 298 and 305, for Panamara. U. Wilcken (1885) 430, on the calendar.
12. P. Collart (1944), a lovely study; J. Bremer (1981) on hymns, with now MacMullen (1981) 15–24 and I.G. 7.1773 (the competition). Dio, Or. 77.4, on the girls.
13. L.R. (1930), on pantomimes with Lucian, De Saltatione, passim; L.R. (1940), on gladiators; both are superb studies.
14. L.R., B.C.H. (1981) 330 and B. Epig. (1982) 399 on Aizani; IGR IV 573 and 576; on the temple, S. R. F. Price, J.R.S. (1982) 196; on Zeus, L.R., B.C.H. (1977) 121–32, a brilliant insight.
15. Syll.³ 1025; 1. Did. 199, with F. W. Schell, A.J.A. (1954) 25; L.R., Hellenica

11–12 (1960) 122–3; J. Evans (1961) 255–6; Aeschyl., Septem 269; Burkert (1983) 3–9, 68; details on butchery in P. Stengel (1910) 114 n. 2 and K. Jeppesen, The Maussoleion 1 (1981); L.R., Hellenica 10 (1955) 44–5, for ropes; E. Fraenkel, Elementi Plautini in Plauto (1960) 124 ff. and 409 ff. on contrast of Greek and Roman world over meat eating: in a drought or famine, of course, I assume Greeks ate dying livestock.

16. P. Herrmann, Das Testament des Epikrates (1969) 58 ff., on Meidon.

17. E.g. Philostr., V. Apol. 1.1.10; M. Detienne (1979), esp. 77 ff., for speculation; L.S.C.G. 139 (Lindos; 2nd cent. A.D.?).

18. Contra, M.P. Nilsson (1945); for the oracles, note I. Did. 217 and chap. 5 Pt. III and the Proclus text in Pt. I, end. C. Habicht, M. Wörrle, Inschriften . . . (1969) 167, on Asclepius.

19. E. Lane, Anat. Stud. (1970) 51; P. Debord (1982) 402–4, excellent on prices, and add A. Rehm, Inscr. Didyma (1958) p. 152.

20. I. Did. 375 and I owe to Joyce Reynolds the mid-4th cent. A.D. man at Ghirza, in P.B.S.R. (1955) 139.

21. Most recently, J. B. Rutter (1968) and R. Duthoy (1969); Frag. Vatic. 148 is local, in reference, and is not a ground for Empire-wide generalizations; Carpus, in C.I.L. 13.1751. K. and P. Lehmann, Samothrace Part 3: The Hieron (1969) pp. 42 ff. ascribe a remodelling of the interior, c. 200 A.D., to the taurobolium and "blooding," but their view is entirely speculative.

22. Milet. 1.3 (Delphinion) 134; Sokolowski, L.S.C.G. no. 8; Laumonier (1958), esp. 247 ff. (Ti. Claudius Lainas).

23. For summaries, I. Browning (1982).

24. G. E. Bean, Turkey's Southern Shore (1968) 71–2 and (1965) esp. 43–7.

25. P. Ward (1970) with bibliogr.

26. I.G. II$^2$.1035, where I still prefer the Augustan dating of G. R. Culley, Restoration of Sacred Monuments in Aug. Athens (Diss., 1973) to the post-Sullan dating of J. von Freeden, Oikia Kyrrestou (1983).

27. R. Villers (1939); P. D. A. Garnsey, J.R.S. (1971) 116; F. Jacques, Antiqu. Afric. 9 (1975) 159; P. Veyne, Le Pain et le Cirque (1976) p. 358 n. 270, citing L.R. and evidence in Gk. East. Digest 50.12.1–14, esp. 13–14; 50.4.16; Pliny 10.39.

28. R. Duncan-Jones (1982) pp. 63–88, for evidence; p. 88 on temple.

29. A. H. M. Jones, The Greek City (1940) 229.

30. On sales, see now P. Debord (1982) 63–8 and n. 110, with map; also pp. 101–16. S.E.G. IV.516.34 ff., for Ephesus; Evans, Y.C.S. (1961) 275, Egypt; Sokolowski, L.S. A.M. 52 (Miletus); D. Gill, H.T.R. (1974) 117, on "table offerings"; Debord p. 69 plus notes on exemptions, esp. n. 168 and n. 171.

31. F. Sokolowski, H.T.R. (1957) 133, on partners; J. and L. Robert, La Carie II (1954) p. 213, on Claros.

32. P. Schmitt-Pantel (1981) esp. 90 ff., on inaugural banquets.

33. E.g. Pliny 10.110–1; 116–7.

34. P. Graindor (1930) 229 and A. Balland (1981, under Ch. II.2) p. 174 ff.

35. Plut., Mor. 822 B–C with Stob. II.132 (Wachsmuth): Brown (1978) p. 36 n. 37 is slightly misleading if he implies this ideal was widely shared: see his pp. 35–8 for thoughts on a "model of parity." Vedius, in Syll.$^3$ 850.

36. Pliny, 7.18.2; 1.8.10–11 (Comum); Dig. 50.10.3.2 and 10.7.1 (on inscribing names).

37. Games: Duncan-Jones, p. 82; Muzuc, Duncan-Jones, p. 88 and no. 21.

38. Aristot. Pol. 1321A31, made famous by de Sainte Croix, Class Struggle . . .
(1981) 305–6; note, though, Ar.'s other thoughts on the matter, e.g. 1309A
15–25.
39. R. MacMullen (1980) 208 and M. I. Finley (1968) 129; Xen., Ephes. 1.2.7–8.
40. Most recently, e.g. D. Cannadine, Past and Present (1982) 107: his civic oyster
feast, of which we have heard much, and the "invention of tradition" are
themes very familiar to historians of Antonine civic life.
41. On cults and "images of concord," Brown (1978) 35 ff., a suggestive treatment.
42. L.S.C.G. no. 8.

## II

1. Most recently, R. Merkelbach, Z.P.E. 10 (1973) 49 ff.; Pliny 10.49–50, on
moving sites.
2. Sokolowski, L.S.C.G. 55: L.R. has promised a discussion (B. Epig. 1964.138).
Note the stress on Men's "appeasement," lines 11 and 16, and the worshipper's
"heart."
3. M. Malaise (1972) 71–110.
4. Nock, Essays I.458: still, to my mind, the best account. More speculatively,
R. L. Gordon (1976) and (1980).
5. F. T. van Straten (1981), for examples: M. Guarducci (1942/3), on footprints
and their various meanings.
6. Nilsson, Opusc. Sel. 1.25–34; on household cults: D. G. Orr (1978) and D. P.
Harmon (1978) with bibliographies for Rome; on wives, Plut., Moral, 140D; on
heirs (in classical Athens) M. Hardcastle, Prudentia (1980) 11, although I do not
believe that inheritance laws were "primarily" religious in aim. In West, see
chap. 2.1. n. 40.
7. Compare with Tert., De Idol. 10, H. Marrou, Hist. de l'Education (1965) 227:
eight days of religious festival in a school month on Cos c. 150 B.C.
8. R. Parker (1983) for a very important study of this.
9. F. de Coulanges, The Ancient City (E.T. 1980) 32 ff.; J. Crook (1967) 133–8,
for excellent summary; fear of the dying out of the family line is clearly the
motive for the developing practice, cited (but not fully stressed) by Hopkins
(1983) 247–54, who gives the bibliogr.
10. Gnomon Idios Logos (ed. Riccobono) 1, lines 8 ff.: T. concerned himself with
debtors to the fiscus, and we do not know if his law had any success.
11. S. Dill (1904) 251–86, accessible and good on Latin clubs: cf. F. M. de Robertis
(1971). On Greek ones, F. Poland (1909) is classic: pp. 289 ff., on sexes. M. N.
Tod (1932) 71 ff., an excellent essay, building on Poland; also P. M. Fraser
(1977) 58–70, with notes.
12. SIG³ 1109, translated by M. N. Tod (1932); datable, almost certainly, to 175/6;
cf Hesperia (1975) 406–7. Bibliogr. and notes, most recently, in F. W. Danker
(1982) 156–66, citing the rules for the Hellenic Society, in 1900, not an apt
parallel.
13. Plato Laws 909–10; Cic., De Leg. 2.25–6; Apul., Apol. 65.
14. D. G. Orr (1978) 1575.

## III

1. L.R., R.E.A. (1960) 316, on theologoi.
2. J. H. Waszink, Pompa Diaboli, V.C. (1947) 13.

3. L.R., Hellenica 10 (1955) 197–200, St. Nicolas and sacrifice; F. M. Young (1979), on imagery.
4. Nock, Essays II.582–93; Price, J.R.S. (1980) 35 and Hor., Odes 4.2, for Emperor.
5. Parker (1983) 352–6, on negative rules; M. Beard, J.R.S. (1980) 21 on "evocation" and its vast range, where "one imagines" a certain group being stressed.
6. Paus. 7.18.8, now with G. Piccolunga (1980), not, to my mind, successful in its search for a myth: pp. 282–3 repay thought.
7. W. Burkert (1983) 216–61, for survey.
8. R. C. T. Parker (1983) 81–3, for one interpretation, with bibliogr.; on women's rites, I. Chirassi Colombo (1979) and F. I. Zeitlin (1982), for recent types of study.
9. Burkert (1983) 226–47, preferring, however, "Carians" to "Keres," which I find hard to accept.
10. Philostr., V.A. 4.21.
11. R. Turcan (1966) and M. P. Nilsson (1957), with the important review by F. Matz, Gnomon (1960) 540; the subject is still open, and I tread warily.
12. On Mithras, R. L. Gordon (1976) and (1980) for one range of "evocation."
13. H. W. Pleket (1965), on Imperial cult, a very valuable study.
14. Firm. Matern, De Errore 2.6 and 3.2 on this "physica ratio": naturally, it was only one intellectual view, but he implicitly connects it with the mystery rite. For date, pp. 22–7 of the Budé ed.
15. Most recent "Bacchic" groups, one with a child mystes: L.R., B. Epig. 1982. 340 and B.C.H. 1983. 597–9, both in Asia Minor.
16. Here, Festugière, Révélation de l'Hermes Trismégiste (1944–54), esp. vols. II–IV; Nock, Essays I.30 ff.; II.647 ff. on the cultural level of the texts.
17. For a summary, M. Harl, Quis Rerum . . . (1966) 25 plus notes, on Philo; H.S Merki (1952).
18. A key word in Paus. is mēnima: e.g. 3.23.5, 4.24.6, 4.27.1, 5.1.7, 7.24.6, 8.7.6, 9.25.8–9. Cf. contemporary Delphi: Parke-Wormell, II. no. 471.
19. A. J. Festugière, Epicurus and His Gods (1969, E.T.) 56.
20. Plato, Rep. 330 D–E; K. J. Dover, Greek Popular Morality (1974) 261–8.
21. F. E. Brenk (1977), 23–7.
22. A. D. Nock, Essays II.606; 1.277.
23. Orig., C. Cels, 8.48; cf. 3.16; 4.10; F. Cumont, Lux Perpetua (1949) 219.
24. Plut., Mor. 611D, alluding (like Celsus, in C. Cels. 3.16) to Plato, Epist. 7.335R.
25. Celsus, ap. Orig. C. Cels. 6.22; Aristoph., Frogs 450 ff.; Apul., Met. 11.6, 11.23.
26. Recently, L.R., B. Epig. (1982) 340 and B.C.H. (1983) 597–9; Serapis's "mysteries" are not Hellenistic (P. M. Fraser, Ptolem. Alex. 1.265); cf. Nock, Essays II.798, for others, and, of course, Mithras and Isis (F. Dunand, Le Culte d'Isis . . . 1973, 3.244 ff.).
27. M. Aur., Med. 12.5.
28. In general, Nock, Essays, s.v. mysteries; esp. 2.792 ff.; ethical conduct, in Aristoph., Frogs 456 ff. and Epictet. 3.21.15 ("correction" of our lives).
29. Plut., Mor. 564B ff.
30. Plut., Mor. 1104A–1107C; few believers in 1105A–B and 450A.

31. V. Saxer, Morts, Martyrs, Reliques en Afrique Chrétienne (1980); P.R.L. Brown, Cult of Saints (1981); other refs in Chap. 1 n. 23.
32. Nock, Essays, I.34 ff.
33. Acts 14.8 ff., with B. M. Levick, Roman Colonies in S. Asia Minor (1967) 154.
34. E. Haenchen, Die Apostelgeschichte (1961) 374.
35. Most recently, A. S. Hollis, Ovid's Metamorphoses VIII (1970) 108–9, with refs to L. Malten and others since.
36. L.R., Jo. des Sav. (1961) 150 n. 53, detaching the Flood from Isauria's Lake Trogitis.
37. L. R., Hellen. 13 (1965) 29, statuette; W. R. Calder, C.R. (1910) 77–9, inscription; now, L.R., B.C.H. (1983) 539 and pl. 116, for reliefs which struck me, too, in 1976 on a visit there.
38. Acts 28.6.
39. Acts 10.26.
40. Acts 12.15.
41. Jo. Chrys., P.G. 60, 201–2.

## BIBLIOGRAPHY I

G. E. Bean, Side Kitabeleri (1965).
A. M. Blackman, The Sequence of Episodes in the Egyptian Daily Temple Liturgy, J. Manch. Eg. and Or. Soc. (1918/9) 26.
J. Bremer, Greek Hymns, Faith, Hope and Worship, ed. H. Versnel (1981) 193.
P. R. L. Brown, The World of Late Antiquity (1971).
P. R. L. Brown, The Making of Late Antiquity (1978).
I. Browning, Jerash and the Decapolis (1982).
W. Burkert, Homo Necans (1983).
P. Collart, Réjouissances, Divertissements et Artistes de Province dans l'Egypte Romaine, Rev. Phil. (1944) 134.
P. E. Corbett, Greek Temples and Greek Worshippers . . . B.I.S.C. (1970) 149.
P. Debord, Aspects Sociaux et Economiques de la Vie Religieuse dans l'Anatolie Gréco-Romaine (1982).
M. Detienne, Dionysus Slain (1979).
E. R. Dodds, Pagan and Christian in an Age of Anxiety (1965).
R. Duncan-Jones, The Economy of the Roman Empire, Quantitative Studies (1982).
R. Duthoy, The Taurobolium: Its Evolution and Terminology (1969).
J. A. C. Evans, A Social and Economic History of an Egyptian Temple . . . , Y.C.S. (1961) 147.
M. I. Finley, The Silent Women of Rome, in Aspects of Antiquity (1968) 129.
P. Graindor, Un Milliardaire Antique (1930).
J. F. Kindstrand, Date and Character of Hermias's Irrisio, Vig. Chr. (1980) 341.
A. Laumonier, Les Cultes Indigènes en Carie (1958).
R. MacMullen, Roman Government's Response to Crisis (1976).
R. MacMullen, Women in Public in the Roman Empire, Historia (1980) 208.
R. MacMullen, Paganism in the Roman Empire (1981).
S. Mitchell, The Life of St. Theodotus of Ancyra, Anatolian Studies (1982) 93.
M. P. Nilsson, Pagan Divine Service in Antiquity, H.T.R. (1945) 63.
P. Perdrizet, Ulp. Nikopolis Pros Mestoi, Corolla Numismatica . . . , B. V. Head (1906) 217.

B. P. Reardon, Courants Littéraires Grecs des II et III Siècles a.c. (1971).

L. Robert, Pantomimen im Griechischen Orient, Hermes (1930) 106.

L. Robert, Les Gladiateurs dans l'Orient Grecque (1940).

J. B. Rutter, Three Phases of the Taurobolium, Phoenix (1968) 226.

P. Schmitt-Pantel, Le Festin dans la Fête de la Cité Grecque Hellenistique, in La Fête:
Pratique et Discours (C. Rech. Hist. Anc. 42, Besançon 1981) 85.

P. Stengel, Opfergebräuche der Griechen (1910).

R. Villers, Essai sur la Pollicitatio à une Respublica, R.H.D.F.E. (1939) 1.

P. Ward, Sabratha: A Guide (1970).

U. Wilcken, Arsinoitische Tempelrechnungen aus dem Jhr. 215 n. Chr., Hermes
(1885) 430.

## BIBLIOGRAPHY: II–III

F. E. Brenk, In Mist Apparelled (1977)

W. Burkert, Homo Necans (1983).

I. Chirassi Colombo, Paides e Gynaikes . . . , Quad. U.U.C., n.s. 1 (1979) 25.

F. de Coulanges, The Ancient City (1864, E.T. 1980).

J. M. Crook, Law and Life of Rome (1967).

F. W. Danker, Benefactor (1982).

S. Dill, Roman Society from Nero to Marcus Aurelius (1904).

A. J. Festugière, La Révélation de l'Hermes Trismégiste (1944–54).

P. M. Fraser, Rhodian Funerary Monuments (1977).

R. L. Gordon, The Sacred Geography of a Mithraeum, J. Mithr. Stud. (1976) 119.

R. L. Gordon, Reality, Evocation and Boundary in the Mysteries of Mithras, J.M.S.
(1980) 19.

M. Guarducci, Le Impronte del Quo Vadis . . . , Rend. Pont. Accad. Romana di
Archaeol. 19 (1942–3) 305.

D. P. Harmon, The Family Festivals of Rome, A.N.R.W. 16.2 (1978) 1592.

K. Hopkins, Death and Renewal (1983).

M. Malaise, Les Conditions de Pénétration et de Diffusion des Cultes Egyptiens en
Italie (1972).

H. S. Merki, Homoiosis Theoi (1952).

M. P. Nilsson, The Dionysiac Mysteries of the Hellenistic and Roman Age (1957).

D. G. Orr, Roman Domestic Religion: The Evidence of Household Shrines,
A.N.R.W. 16.2 (1978) 1557.

R. C. T. Parker, Miasma (1983).

G. Piccolunga, L'Olocausto di Patrai, Entretiens Hardt 27 (1980) 243.

H. W. Pleket, An Aspect of the Emperor Cult: Imperial Mysteries, H.T.R. (1965)
331.

F. Poland, Geschichte des Griechischen Vereinswesens (1909).

F. M. de Robertis, Storia delle Corporazioni e del Regime Associativo nel Mondo
Romano (1971).

M. N. Tod, Sidelights on Greek History (1932).

R. Turcan, Les Sarcophages Romains à Représentations Dionysiaques (1966).

F. T. Van Straten, Gifts for the Gods, in Faith, Hope and Worship, ed. H. Versnel
(1981) 65.

F. M. Young, The Use of Sacrificial Ideas in Greek Christian Writers (1979).

F. I. Zeitlin, Cultic Models of the Female: Rites of Dionysus and Demeter, Arethusa
(1982) 129.

CHAPTER 4

The classic study of epiphany is F. Pfister's fine article in Pauly-Wissowa, R.E. Suppl. 4 (1924) s.v. Epiphanie, 277–323. I have returned to the subject because his dictionary article could not bring out the tone and context of the literary texts; the evidence has increased; Pfister had much to say on vocabulary, where historical change is not provable, and on titles in ruler cult; he gave less space to the evidence under the Empire. D. Wachsmuth, Kleine Pauly 5 (1975) 1598–1601 is brief, but gives a good bibliography; F. T. Van Straten's excellent study, Bull. Ant. Besch. (1976) overtook me and gives an excellent list of votive texts. N. J. Richardson generously lent me a text of his unpublished lecture on Homeric epiphany, after I read a version of this chapter at an Oxford seminar in 1983, whose members helped me then, and later. Collections of modern reports of this type of religious experience are being made in the Religious Experience Research Unit, Manchester College, Oxford: samples are published in A. Hardy, Spiritual Nature of Man (1979) and T. Beardsworth, A Sense of Presence (1977), whose stories I have used gratefully and compared repeatedly with their pagan predecessors.

I

1. Inscr. Did. (ed. Rehm) no. 496; L.R., Hellenica 10–11 (1960) 544, suggesting "in the form of" and emphasizing the note of crisis; F. T. Van Straten (1976) 17 n. 248, for the other view: I only encountered his note when this chapter was largely complete.
2. Most recently, with several conjectures, W. Peek, Z.P.E. 7 (1971) 207.
3. E.g. Il. 20.98; 20.121; Od. 3.221, 13.307 and 13.393; L. Robert, Hellenica VI. 109–10; Sylloge³ 814.36 ff. (Nero); O.G.I. 383.65 (Antiochus of Commagene); Epictet., 2.18.29; Marcus, Medit. 1.17.8 and 9.27 ("helpers"); 9.11 and 9.40 ("co-workers"). In the N.T., A. Wikenhauser (1939) 320; for Christian saints, e.g. Cyrus and John, P.G. 87.3443D and passim.
4. Od. 19.40–43.
5. Il. 13.72 (Ajax); 17.323–4 (Aeneas); Il. 5.174–91; 5.864 (cloud); 4.73 (star).
6. Il. 1.197; 21.286.
7. Od. 3.221 (Nestor).
8. Od. 13.312; Il. 24.361 ff.
9. N. J. Richardson (1979) 208 ff., 252 ff. is a definitive treatment.
10. Od. 10.573 (Circe); 16.178–9 (Telemachus), with E. Kearns (1982), though I doubt her general argument. Od. 6.149 and 160–1 (Nausicaa).
11. Od. 13.312; 16.161; beauty, in Il. 3.396, Od. 13.288.
12. F. Dirlmeier (1967): I owe knowledge of this to N. J. Richardson.
13. Od. 7.200 ff.; cf. 6.152 and 7.210.
14. Od. 17.485 with E. Fraenkel (1942); J. Griffin (1978).
15. F. Matz (1958), sometimes questionably; C. Sourvinou-Inwood, Kadmos (1971) 64.
16. Julian Jaynes, The Origin of Consciousness in the Breakdown of the Bicameral Mind (1976): I owe knowledge of this to M. C. Hart; cf. B. Snell (1953) 8.
17. Hesiod, W. and D. 122–3, 249 ff. and 259; F.1.6–7.
18. E. R. Dodds, Greeks and the Irrational (1951) 104–6, for the examples; Od. 6.20; Od. 4.795 ff.
19. Il. 1.47; cf. 24.170 (Iris); 24.533.

20. Il. 20.129–30; cf. Il. 3.420: the linguistic change, to "servant" of the gods, studied by H. W. Pleket (1981) 159 ff. strikes me as no real innovation.
21. Il. 5.177–8 (Aeneas); Il. 15.254–5; 24.171; Od. 4.825; cf. Luke 24.36.
22. Dio 36.9.
23. Paus. 5.5.4; 6.22.8; 7.24–5; 9.38.4; I quote the fine insight of B. M. W. Knox, The Heroic Temper (1964) 56.
24. H. Fuhrmann, Röm. Mitt. 53 (1938) 44: Diocletian and Saturn.
25. Hom. Hym. 2.270; 5.100; in 3.498–500 the god prescribes his cult; Plato, Laws 909E; Pfister R. E. Suppl. (1924) cols. 298–9.
26. Il. 2.155, 279; 5.439; 10.512; 18.203; 20.380.
27. On Ezekiel's drama, most recently H. Jacobson (1983).
28. Sophocl., Ajax 14–16 with Buxton (1980) 22 and Seale (1982) 144.
29. Iambl., De Myst. 3.2 (103.10).
30. Sappho F. 1–2, on which I concur with R. Jenkyns, Three Classical Poets (1982) 13–15; 28–30.
31. C. M. Bowra, Pindar (1964) 49–54, for the evidence of varying date; J. A. Haldane (1968); Pyth. 8.58–60 is a personal "encounter," despite recent denials of "autobiography" in the Odes.
32. J. D. Denniston, Euripides' Electra (1939), lines 1233–7, for both my quotations.
33. B. M. W. Knox, Heroic Temper (1964) 55–9 is admirable.
34. Eur., Ion 1551–2; Bacchae 1084–5, with E. R. Dodds's note and F. Williams's (1978) note to his line 18.
35. Callim., Hymn 5.33, 53, 100–1 and 136–41, with P. Perdrizet (1906) 226–7, on wooden statues.
36. 2.3–7 and 10–11 with F. Williams (1978), notes, and above all, O. Weinreich (1968) 67.
37. Herodas 1.9 with Headlam's excellent note (1922).
38. Fraser, Ptolemaic Alexandria (1972) 652–66 argues hard for "genuine religious feeling." This creates a problem over Anth. Pal. 6.147 (his p. 586); A. W. Bulloch (1977), for more sophisticated views.
39. J. M. Bremer (1981), esp. 203–15.
40. Paus. 6.26; Plut., G.Q. 36 with W. R. Halliday's compendious notes.
41. Plut., Mor. 364F and 671E (comparing the Jews' trumpets).
42. Nock, Essays I.388.94 for a magisterial discussion of the Aion festival, with p. 391 and n. 139 on the Christian sequel. Epiphanius, Panar. 51.22.10; E. Pax, R.A.C. s.v. Epiphanie cols. 903–4.
43. W. Kranz, Stasimon (1933) 185 ff.; Soph., Ajax 694; Hor., Od. 1.17 with E. Fraenkel, Horace (1957) 204 n. 4, a marvellous note. Aristoph., Thesmo. 312; Acharn. 263.
44. L. Robert, Et. Anatoliennes (1937) 162 n. 7.
45. O. Kern, Hermes (1917) 149, an excellent note; on the Orphic hymns, A. M. Athanassakis (1977), with translation; Kern placed them in the later 3rd cent. A.D., possibly at Pergamum.
46. On amulets, L. Robert (1981), esp. 20–25.
47. E. R. Dodds, Greeks and the Irrational (1951) chap. 4 is, of course, classic, here.
48. D. Wachsmuth (1967) is excellent, with full evidence; Hom., Od. 2.28, 420 ff. with W. pp. 72 ff.
49. F. T. Van Straten (1976) is excellent on this.

50. I.G. IV.952.28 ff. (Sostrata's cure).
51. M. Robertson, Hist. of Greek Art (1975) 375.
52. N. Himmelmann-Wildschütz (1957); T. B. Mitford (1980); L.R., B. Epig. 1981, no. 636, for more.
53. Van Straten (1976), p. 17; for the slave, J. B. S. Sterrett, Wolfe Expedit. to Asia Minor (1906) 226–7.
54. Plato, Rep. 381D–383; cf. Sophist 216 B–C; Laws 909E–910, on women; cf. Hdts. 6.69 and Plut., Alex. 3.1–2. Van Straten (1976) p. 17, for numbers, and discussion.
55. K. M. Briggs (1973); I quote W. W. Gill (1932) 106; Briggs (1978) chap. 10; on nymphs stealing babies, P. Borgeaud, Recherches sur le Dieu Pan (1979) 161 ff.
56. W. K. Pritchett (1979) is admirable, here; cf. W. Speyer (1980) 55, a very full study. Hdts. 1.68 and 5.75.
57. Herodian 8.3.9: for attitude, cf. Arr. Anab. 5.1.2.
58. Aug., Civ. Dei 5.26; Theod., H.E. 5.24.
59. Zosimus, 5.6.
60. Hom., Il. 4.40–55; U. Brackertz (1976); cf. F. G. Maier, Gr. Mauerbauinschr. I (1959) 69 line 12, on Colophon. Solon F4 (West); Aristoph., Knights 1173 f., a brilliant parody.
61. Most recently, J. Le Gall, Mélanges Heurgon (1976) 1.519; Macr., Sat. 3.9 does not state that this rite had been long dead.
62. E.g. Athena at Side; for "god-beloved" Aigai, L.R., Jo. des Savants (1973) 204, a unique case, he thinks; Et. Anatol. (1937) 24–6; Men. Rhetor p. 362.62 (ed. Russell, 1981). M. I. Rostovtzeff, Klio (1920) 203 and W. K. Pritchett (1979) 11–13, for records.
63. Sylloge³ 695.12 (Magnesia); Aristoph., Thesmo. 369–71; Dio 33.47; 34.38 with L.R., B.C.H. (1977) 96–108; Plut., Camill 6.1–2, a very telling comment.
64. W. K. Pritchett (1979) 30–41; K. J. Rigsby (1975), promising further lists; C. Picard, in Xenia (Athens, 1912) 67, where p. 78 n. 3 cited E. Hicks, Greek Inscr. in the British Museum, III (1886) no. 482 as proof that the dwindling cult of Ephesian Artemis was revived by fresh epiphanies in the 160s A.D. However, Hicks's reading was remarkably wrong: Artemis "is being honoured," not "dishonoured": H. Wankel, Inschr. v. Ephesos (1979) 1A no. 24, with p. 148, 9–10, for this. The epiphanies in line 14 are those in the past, not new ones in the Antonine age.

## II

1. Lucr. 4.722 ff.; Diogenes Oenoand. F 52 (Chilton); Marcus, Med. 1.17.5; 9.11; 9.27; 9.40; I take 12.28 to refer to the stars; Festugière (1955) p. 68 n. 39, on "enargēs."
2. Paus. 8.2.4; 9.18.4; 10.22.18, another good example of stories of Roman governors "testing" oddities and shrines in the provinces: there is quite a dossier of these stories in the 1st and 2nd cents.
3. Y. Grandjean (1975) line 10, for example.
4. F. Deneken (1881); L. Koenen, Z.P.E. (1967) with P. Oxy. 3693.
5. H. Ingholt, Recueil des Tessères de Palmyra (1955).
6. Apul., Met. 9.22.
7. D.S. 5.49.5; S. Eitrem (1926); Stob., Florileg. 120.28; Apul., Met. 11.23: "accessi coram."

8. Nock, Essays I.194; Dodds (1965) 100, for this idea: Muslim mystics (e.g. M. Molé, Les Mystiques Musulmans 1965) are one contrary example, among many.

9. Dodds (1951) 283–311, still best; Iambl., De Myst 2.3–9.

10. Festugière, R.H.T. I–IV (1944–54), one of the greatest works on antiquity; note esp. IV 152–62; 200–58; I.283 ff. (on magical parallels). Nock, Essays I.30–1, II.500–1 on the very varied range of cultural context in our "collection." I quote C.H. 11.20 ff.: also W. Scott, Hermetica (1924) 1.14.

11. Nock, Essays I.192–5.

12. R. MacMullen (1981) 34, with bibliogr.; O. Weinreich (1912) 41.

13. T.A.M. V. 179 B with F. Petzl (1978) 253.

14. Bibliogr. in T.A.M. V 159, 231; 317 (114/5, A.D.); 318 (156/7 A.D.); 172; 167 A (12 Sceptres: 98/9 A.D.); Z.P.E. (1982) 112–3 (26/7 A.D.). On this material, see now L.R., B.C.H. (1983) 518 ff.

15. Nock, Essays II.659–62.

16. Hom., Il. 24.336: Hermes the companion. I.G. XIV.1003 (Heracles) with L.R., Hellenica 13 (1965) 129–30. On hero shrines by houses, see now J. S. Rusten (1983).

17. Nock, Essays I.41 n. 61.

18. Max. Tyr., Orat. 8.5–7; Plut., Mor. 580C; Apul., De Deo Socr. 24; cf. Amm. Marc. 21.14.5; M. Riley (1977); Nock, Essays II.666–9.

19. W. Schmidt, R. E. 7.1140–3.

20. Hor., Od. 1.17 with E. Fraenkel, Horace (1957) pp. 206–7. P. Borgeaud (1979) is an excellent survey; W. Roscher, Lexikon (1897–1908) Bd. 3. s.v. Pan, is the classic study; cf. F. Brommer, R.E. Suppl. 8 (1950) 949, also a fine study.

21. Plut., Mor. 419B; "all" in Plato, Cratyl. 408B; then Stoics (Cornutus, 27) and Christians (Euseb., P.E. 124B).

22. P. M. Fraser, Ptol. Alex. (1972) 29 on the mysterious Paneion; Head H.N.[2] 786 and L. Robert, Hellenica IV p. 11, n. 1. Artemid. 4.72, however, thinks dreams of Pan in a city are inauspicious: perhaps only in the cities he knew.

23. K. Tuchelt (1969/70); L. Robert, Hellen. 10, 214–6. A. Bernand (1977) 269. Bernand (1972) nos. 27, 28. Artemid. 4.71–2.

24. Borgeaud 115 ff.; p. 117 n. 11 (Eratosth. 1.40, Pan-handling); Ps. Heracleit, Incredibilia 25 (Pan-bang). Borgeaud, 123–35 (music).

25. Theocr. 1.15; R. Callois (1937); Norman Douglas, Old Calabria, chap. 40; Kaibel, Epig. Graec 802 with J. Bousquet, Klio (1970) 37–9.

26. Borgeaud (1979) 162–71, with evidence; Iambl., De Myst. 3.10 (122).

27. A. Wilhelm (1929) 54; cf. J. Papadimitriou, B.C.H. (1958) 681. Also I.G. IV.53 with L. Robert, Hellenica IV (1948) 1.

28. Longus 2.25–9; C. Meillier (1975). Ach. Tat. 8.6 ff.: "aimables fantasies narratives," Picard, Ephèse et Claros (1922) 370 ff. But note the epigram cited by Borgeaud p. 126 n. 57.

29. Euseb., P.E. 5.190A.

30. P. Roussel, R. E. A. (1912) 277, an excellent study, with bibliogr.; L.R., Rev. de Philologie (1939) 200–1; H. W. Pleket, Gnomon (1975) 566 on a daimon, perhaps not a dead "hero." C.I.G. 3514 (Thyateira), for a grand family inscription.

31. D. M. Pippidi (1975) 135–6, with full bibliogr. on "hyperdexios"; L.R., Hellenica 10 (1959) 63–6.

32. Aristoph., Wasps 819; cf. Peace, 661 ff.; Knights 1169; Birds 518.
33. Suet., Aug. 16; H. S. Versnel (1981) 38–42, for more evidence.
34. Apul., Apol. 54; MacMullen (1981) p. 159 n. 78.
35. L. Robert (1966) 91–100; F. Sokolowski (1968) 519. Soph. O.T. 190, with Weinreich (1929) 182.
36. Anth. Pal. 9.805; Steph. Byz., s.v. Threikie.
37. Olympiodorus F27; K. Holum (1982) 118; B. Croke (1977); J. F. Matthews, J.R.S. (1970), esp. 95.
38. O. Weinreich, A.R.W. (1915) 38–45; M.A.M.A. VIII.446 with L.R., Hellenica 13 (1965) 129–131: are these types of inscription the source of the verses in Porphyry, ap. Euseb., P.E. 124A–B?
39. Acta Alex. 8.44–8 (Musurillo); L.R., C.R.A.I. (1981) 530 ff.; Milet. 1.7 (1924) no. 274; also Pan. Lat. 8.8.4.
40. Herodian, 5.6.3–5.
41. Corp. Herm. 17.10 and Budé notes; Corp. Herm., Asclepius, 23–4; 37; P.G.M. 5.370; G. Wolff (1856) 206–13, excellent.
42. A. Laumonier (1934) 85 with L.R., Et. Anat. (1937) 516.
43. F. E. Brenk (1977) 30; Plut., Camill. 6; Coriol. 38; Mor. 397C. Lucian, Philops. 18–20 is more sceptical!
44. F. Poulsen (1945) 182–3.
45. Hippol., Refut. IV.35–6.
46. MacMullen (1981) 125, with bibliogr.; Hero Alex. (Teubner Ed.) 1.175 ff. (doors); 1.405 ff. (statues); II.1.362–4 (mirrors); R. Seaford (1984); O. Weinreich (1929), a classic; P. Hommel, M.D.A.I. (1957) 30–2, on gables.
47. C. Bonner (1929); Paus. 6.26.
48. Theophil., Ad Autol. 1.18; cf. Lucian, Peregr. 27; C. Clerc (1915) 149 ff.
49. Clerc (1915) 44–5.
50. Tatian, Orat. 15; C. Mango, D.O.P. (1963) 59.
51. Maxim. 8.6; Eunap., V.S. (Wright) p. 407; Proclus, In Rep. 1.127 ff. (ed. and trans. Festugière, 1970).
52. Heliodor. III.12–13; J. J. Winckler, (1982); Philostrat. V.S. pp. 306 ff. (Loeb) for a possible author; I find the Julianic date c. 360–80 much harder to credit, and the arguments unconvincing.
53. R. Helm, Neue Jhrb. (1914) 191, in general. Cf. naturally, Philostr. V.Apoll. 4.31, etc.
54. Apul., Met. 4.28; Xen., Ephes. 1.2.7; 1.12; Chariton, Callirh. 3.2 ff., with K. Plepelits (1976) 4–9, summarizing theories of date; L.R. (1966, no. 2) 186–95.
55. For miracles, compare A. Henrichs's lengthy commentary on Vespasian in Alexandria: Z.P.E. 3 (1968).
56. P. Herrmann, K. Z. Polatkan (1969) 54–5 with emendation in B. Epig. 1970.522. M. Guarducci (1942/3) 322 on "traces" of various kinds.
57. Pan. Lat. 3.10.4–5.

III

1. Petronius, Satyr. 17.
2. P. Oxy. 1381.
3. P. Herrmann, K. Polatkan (1969) lines 32–6 with p. 28.
4. On magic, Nock, Essays I.176–94, esp. 180 is still the best historical discussion; T. Hopfner (1921), on techniques; Festugière (1932) 320 ff., on aims; P.G.M.

I. 104–10; 170 ff.; IV.930 (a "systasis"); "autopsy" in VII.727 ff. On "spontaneous auditory automatism," Dodds (1973) 191–2.

5. Thessalus (ed. Friedrich) chap. 18–22 with Dodds's important note (1973) p. 189 n. 2; even if it is not demonstrably historical it is valuable evidence of what was plausible.

6. P.G.M. VIII with Tafel 1. Abbild. 6.

7. Dodds (1973) 183–92.

8. Acts 19.19: Gentiles and Jews, together.

9. Maximus 9.7: cf. Arrian, Periplous 23 ("not incredible"); Max. 9.7, again; cf. I.G.X. 67, to the Most High god, after an "oracle" in a dream and a rescue at sea: 74/5 A.D.

10. Philostrat., ap. Suidas is a notorious battleground, but it does attribute the Heroicus to Philostratus II; the Troikos of Philostr. III is not the same work. On the date and identity, note esp. K. Münscher, Die Philostrate, Philolog. Supp. X (1907) 497 ff. esp. 517, 554; Dio 80. 10.2–3 and Philostr., Heroic. 147.8 and Gymnast. p. 174.5 on Helix, with J. Jüthner. Philostratos Über Gymnastik (1909) 87–8 and J. Jüthner, Festschr. T. Gomperz (1902) 205, for acute discussion. I forbear to give endless refs. to the Teubner, Heroicus, which can be read in full.

11. 11.4 (gardening).

12. 16 (adultery).

13. On the local stories, Münscher is correct; Hdts 9.120; G. L. Huxley, G.R.B.S. (1979) 145; Heroic. 8.3–13; 17.3 ff. (Rhesus); 18.6 (Hector). On size of heroes, T. Mantero (1966) 85 n. 15; Paus. 2.5; Philostr., Imag. 5.1.

14. U. von Wilamowitz, Glaube der Hellenen II (1932) 522.

15. Philostr, V.A. 6.27.

16. On dating, J. Jüthner, Philostratos Über Gymnastik (1909) 87–8, arguing for post-217. F. Solmsen, T.A.P.A. (1940) 556, at p. 559 on the "real reason," so often repeated, without any evidence. Philostr. had indeed visited Troy, Vita Ap. 4.13; Heroicus lacks any dedication, or any hint of an "Imperial" connection; Philostr. V.A. 4.16 ff. is similarly vague. E. Champlin, H.S.C.P. (1981) 210 is even less convincing: H. Grentrup (1914) 46 did not even establish Philostr.'s use of "Dictys." S. Eitrem, Symb. Oslo. 8 (1929) 1–56 wrongly looked for "magic" as a parallel: cf. T. Mantero (1966) who overinterprets, e.g. "synousia," at p. 64 ff.

17. Heroicus, 58.

18. Eunapius, Lives (ed. Wright, Loeb) p. 407.

19. Julian, 249 B–D; 233D; 250C; 275B; Or 7.227C–234C; cf. the idea that every site "links" man to the cosmos and the gods. Sallustius, ed. Nock p. 6.26 and 26.26 (the word "synapteia").

20. Lib. 12.89, 15.80–1, 18.167–8, in war; 13.27, "synergos" (cf. Marcus, Med. 9.11, 9.40); 12.86–8 and 18.162, 172 on spies. I quote 15.29–32; cf. Jul. 294D. None of the recent books on Julian discusses this.

21. Synesius, P.G. 66.1317.

# IV

1. E. R. Dodds, Greeks and the Irrational (1951) chap. 4 remains the classic account; here, I aim only to extend the study to examples in the Christian era

beyond his immediate scope. C. A. Behr, Aelius Aristides (1968) pp. 171–204 is essential to the task.

2. Lucr. 4.722 ff.; Diogenes Oenoandae, F 52 (Chilton).
3. Behr (1968) 176 n. 11e; Ps. Theocr. 21.40.
4. Behr (1968) 173–5, for an excellent survey.
5. Behr (1968) 171–2; Aristot., 462B20 and 464A22; Behr, p. 174 n. 11, importantly stressing Herophilus's theory, against Dodds; also note 11A, with Marcus, Med. 1.17.8. For Stoics, cf. Cic., De Div. 1.50 ff.; Philo, De Somn. 2.1 and F. H. Colson, Philo, Loeb V. 593 ff.
6. Homer, Od. 19.547; 20.90; Pindar, Olymp. 13.67; Aelius, Sacr. Tales 2.7, 2.18.
7. Iambl., De Myst. 3.2; Proclus, V. Marini 30; for a denial of their value, Macrob. Commen. In Somn. Scip. I.3.8.
8. E.g., P.G.M. VII. 664, 704, 740; or XII. 107; Synesius, De Insomniis 11, on diets; L. Robert, Jo. des Savants (1981), on amulets; R. Arbesmann (1949–51), on fasting.
9. E.g., C. Roebuck (1951); L. Robert (1973); M. Besnier (1902); on incubation, L. Deubner (1900); on miracles in Rome, P. Roesch (1982).
10. E. and L. Edelstein (1945); contra, I. Chirassi Colombo (1975) 96; for the growth of Pergamum, C. Habicht (1969) 8–16; for Cos, S. Sherwin-White (1978) 334–59, starting with a major, unified building plan of the mid-3rd cent. B.C.
11. On Galen, F. Kudlien (1981), with some caution; on doctors, S. Sherwin-White (1978) 276–9 with n. 108.
12. Plut., Mor. 383E with J. G. Griffiths, De Iside . . . (1970) and p. 571 on Parthey's experiment; Apul., Apol. 43 refers to scent, and so probably does Galen 19.462, though he does mention apparitions and loud noises as a consequence.
13. Philostr., V.A. 2.37.
14. Paus. 1.34.3.
15. C. Habicht (1969), passim, for clientele; cf. Behr (1968) 27–32, 41–51 for Aelius's Cathedra; A. Taffin (1960), on procedure; Habicht, pp. 161 ff., the lex sacra; pp. 180–1, on abstinence.
16. Dodds (1951) 114 (dogs and snakes); Lois Sacr. Cit. Grecques (Sokolowski) 69, 43–8, on Oropus.
17. J.-P. Vernant (1983) 323.
18. A. Busignani (1981) for photos only.
19. Dio Chrys. 31.151.
20. Dio 12.25; Plut., Aemil. Paull. 28.2, Strabo 8.354C, on Pheidias and Homer; cf. Dio 12.44–6.
21. H. Seyrig, Antiquités Syriennes II, pp. 111–2, with Lucian, De Dea Syria 31; L. Robert, Hellenica (1960) 470–1; P. E. Corbett (1970) esp. 151 n. 11; Themistius, Orat. 20.235.
22. A. Taffin (1960) 325.
23. On Artemidorus, esp. L.R., B.C.H. (1978) 538; Laodicée: 1 (1969) 309–12; also R. A. Pack (1955); Festugière edition (1975), for best trans. and notes.
24. Art., 5.1: note his access to other migrants, e.g. 4.1 and L.R., B.C.H. (1978) 539.
25. Athletes: e.g. 5.44, 48, 55, 75; 1.24; 1.57; 4.42. L.R., Fond. Hardt XIV (1967) 221: Art. and his athletic terms.
26. His travels: Pack (1955) 284 with 2.12 (Italian woman); 4.28 (the *eques*); 4.42 (tax

man); 1.49, 1.53 and 1.78 (slaves); I also quote C. Blum, Studies in the Dream Book of A. (1936). The key phrase is "hōs ego etērēsa": e.g. 2.18. At 4.24, A. refers to the Jewish revolt under Trajan. He adds "hōs eipomēn" (not in the best Ms., L), but he means, not "as I then predicted," but "as I have just said," i.e. in the previous sentence. A., then, was not active in Trajan's reign, a cardinal point in his dating.

27. Bk. 4, pref., on "enhypnia" (his own term); 4.4 (custom); 4.2 (nomos/physis); 4.59 (two clients' sex life); 4, pref. (p. 240, Pack), on interpreters; 2.9; 3.23 (cannibals); 1.48 (feet); 2.28 (woods); 2.65 (marriage); 3.28 (mice).

28. 4.11; e.g. isopsephism, in 3.34, 4.24; medical, 4.22; Theognis, 1.32, 1.66.

29. On his Greek, note general caveat by L.R., C.R.A.I. (1982) 62.

30. 3.66 (Daldis).

31. Apollo: 2.70, end; other local detail in L.R., B.C.H. (1978) 538 ff.

32. 4.31, with Pack, T.A.P.A. (1957) 192–3; 5.16 (Agamemnon); 4.84 is a general reference.

33. 2.34 with A. S. Pease, on Cicero, De N.D. 1.315.

34. 2.37 (Hercules); 3.14; 4.49; 2.36; 3.13 (but note 1.5, dining with Cronos); 4.63.

35. 4.71 (riddles).

36. 2.44 (Hermes and co.).

37. 2.35, esp. to 2.39; 4.72 (without attributes).

38. Philostr., V.A. 4.16, esp.; Heroicus 48–9.

39. Aelius, Sacr. Tal. 1.11; 1.17; 2.18; 2.41; 3.47; 4.40; 4.50.

40. M. F. Smith (1982).

41. L. Lacroix (1949) 320; Liban. 60.11 with Philostorg., H.E. 7.8.

42. Callistr., no. 10; Apul., Met. 11.19, and esp. 11.24 and 29: "clemens imago," with Festugière (1954) 80; F. J. Dölger (1934) 67; L.R., C.R.A.I. (1982) 517–35.

43. Most recently, G. Michenaud, J. Dierkens (1972).

44. Aelius, Sacr. Tal. 1.23, 1.33, 3.21 and esp. 5. 44–5; 1.46; 1.36; Alexander, 4.49.

45. Ael. 4.16; 4.19; 4.57; 4.60; C. Habicht (1969) no. 33, on Polemo; Philostr., V.S. pp. 109–112 K, on Hermocrates (cf. Habicht, no. 34). Ael. 4.25 is telling.

46. 2.32; cf. 3.46.

47. 4.57; on statues, 1.11; 2.18; 3.47; 4.40; 4.50.

48. 1.71; 1.11, changed statue.

49. 2.41, Athena. I presume "coram suo illo" in Apul., 11.30 means a statue dream.

50. 2.32–34; for Theodotus, 4.21. He was not opposed to divine cures: he was A.'s favourite doctor: F. Kudlien (1981) 117 ff. is mistaken here.

51. 1.17; 4.50; Brown (1978) 43–5 suggests a diagnosis in terms of "heat" and "dryness": this is not convincing. The cures and visions sometimes induce a warm glow (Behr, 164 n. 8 for texts), usually by bathing: I cannot see they "control" or "dissipate" a problematic, pre-existent heat. As for a prevalent "dry" image of the body in a Mediterranean "koine," I know of no evidence: Brown p. 44 n. 78 refers to a dry diet only.

52. The only catalogue is Van Straten (1976) 21–27, an excellent survey. I.G. Bulg. 680 (city); I.G. Bulg. 2338, for dignitaries of the mid-1st cent. A.D. reviving the cult of Artemis.

53. Artemid. 4.5 and Men. Rhet. 390 (Russell-Wilson, p.116), brilliantly spotted by MacMullen (1981) 17–18, both on frauds; A. Beschaouch (1975): "pro fide comperta."

54. R. Merkelbach (1973).

55. H. Hepding, Ath. Mitt. 35 (1910) 457–61; I.G. Bulg. 680.
56. Artemid. 2.35; 2.39 (wax).
57. 2.35 (Artemis); 2.37 (Aphrodite); 1.80 (sex).
58. Festugière, R.H.T., passim; Plato, Rep. 381D; Proclus, In Rempubl. 1. 109 ff. (ed. Festugière, 1970).
59. K. E. Kirk (1931) 54.
60. F. E. Brenk (1977) 16–21 and 214–35, a very interesting survey; note esp. Plut., Dion 2.
61. Festugière, R.H.T. I (1944) 45 ff. for a brilliant evocation.
62. A. Bataillé (1952), pp. 153–68.
63. A. Bernand (1960) no. 30 (Hadrian); pp. 10–13 and nos. 51–3 (placing); no. 19 (Charisius).
64. Nock, Essays I.357 is classic: pp. 368–9 (on "today"); pp. 361–3 (Maximus) and p. 363, dismissing them, however, as "conventional tours de force."

## BIBLIOGRAPHY: I

A. M. Athanassakis, The Orphic Hymns (1977).
U. Brackertz, Zum Problem der Schutzgottheiten der Gr. Stadt (Berlin, 1976).
J. M. Bremer, Greek Hymns, in Faith, Hope and Worship, ed. H. S. Versnel (1981) 193.
K. M. Briggs, Fairies in Tradition and Literature (1973).
K. M. Briggs, The Vanishing People (1978).
A. W. Bulloch, Callimachus's Erysichthon, Homer and Apollonius, A.J.P. (1977) 97.
R. G. A. Buxton, Blindness and Limits: Sophocles and the Logic of Myth, J.H.S. (1980) 22.
F. Dirlmeier, Die Vogelgestalt homerischer Götter, Sitzb. Heidelb. Akad. Phil.-Hist. (1967).
E. Fraenkel, The Stars in the Prologue of Rudens, C.Q. (1942)10.
W. W. Gill, A Second Manx Scrap-book (1932).
J. Griffin, The Divine Audience and the Religion of the Iliad, C.Q. (1978) 1.
J. A. Haldane, Pindar and Pan, Phoenix (1968) 18.
N. Himmelmann-Wildschütz, Theoleptos (1957).
H. Jacobson, The Exagoge of Ezekiel (1983).
E. Kearns, The Return of Odysseus, C.Q. (1982) 2.
F. Matz, Göttererscheinung u. Kultbild Im Minoischen Kreta (1958).
T. B. Mitford, The Nymphaeum of Kafizin: The Inscribed Pottery (1980).
P. Perdrizet, Nikopolis Pros Mesto, in Corolla Numismatica . . . B. V. Head (1906) 226.
H. W. Pleket, Religious History as History of Mentality, in Faith, Hope and Worship, ed. H. G. Versnel (1981) 152.
W. K. Pritchett, The Greek State At War, Part III (1979).
N. J. Richardson, Homeric Hymn To Demeter (1979).
K. J. Rigsby, A Hellenistic Inscription From Bargylia, G.R.B.S. (1975) 403.
L. Robert, Amulettes Grecques, Journal des Savants (1981) 3.
D. Seale, Vision and Stagecraft in Sophocles (1982).
B. Snell, The Discovery of the Mind (1953).
W. Speyer, Die Hilfe und Epiphanie einer Gottheit, eines Heros, eines Heiligen, Jhrb. für Ant. u. Christ., Erganzbd. 8 (1980) 55.

F. T. van Straten, Daikrates's Dream . . . B. Ant. Besch. (1976) 1.

D. Wachsmuth, Pompimos Ho Daimon (1967).

O. Weinreich, Religionsgeschichtliche Studien (1968).

A. Wikenhauser, Die Traumgesichte des N.T. in religionsgeschichtlicher Sicht, Pisciculi . . . F. J. Dölger (1939) 320.

F. Williams, Callimachus's Hymn To Apollo (1978).

BIBLIOGRAPHY: II

A. Bernand, Le Paneion d'El-Kanais (1972).

A. Bernand, Pan du Désert (1977).

C. Bonner, A Dionysiac Miracle at Corinth, A.J.A. (1929) 368.

P. Borgeaud, Recherches sur le Dieu Pan (1979).

F. E. Brenk, In Mist Apparelled (1977).

R. Callois, Les Démons de Midi, R.H.R. 116 (1937) 143.

Charly Clerc, Les Théories Relatives au Culte des Images chez les Auteurs Grecs du IIe siècle (1915).

B. Croke, Evidence for the Huns' Invasion of Thrace in 422, G.R.B.S. (1977) 358.

F. Deneken, De Theoxeniis (1881).

E. R. Dodds, Greeks and the Irrational (1951).

E. R. Dodds, Pagans and Christians in an Age of Anxiety (1965).

S. Eitrem, Die Vier Elemente in der Mysterienweihe, Symb. Osl. (1926) 39.

A. J. Festugière, La Révélation de l'Hermes Trismégiste, I–IV (1944–54).

A. J. Festugière, Epicurus and His Gods (1955).

Y. Grandjean, Une Nouvelle Arétalogie d'Isis à Maronée (1975).

M. Guarducci, Le Impronte del Quo Vadis, Rendic. Pont. Acc. di Arch. 19 (1942/3) 322.

P. Herrmann, K. Polatkan, Das Testament des Epikrates (1969).

K. Holum, Theodosian Empresses (1982).

L. Koenen, Eine Einladung zur Kline des Sarapis, Z.P.E. 1 (1967) 123.

A. Laumonier, Une Inscription de Stratonicée, R.E.A (1934) 85.

R. MacMullen, Paganism in the Roman Empire (1981).

C. Mango, Antique Statuary and the Byzantine Beholder, D.O.P. (1963) 59.

C. Meillier, L'Epiphanie de Dieu Pan, R.E.G. (1975) 121.

G. Petzl, Inschriften aus der Umgebung Saittai, Z.P.E. 30 (1978) 250.

D. M. Pippidi, Scythica Minora (1975).

F. Poulsen, Talking, Weeping, Bleeding Sculptures, Acta Archaelog. 16 (1945) 178.

M. Riley, The Purpose and Unity of Plutarch's De Genio Socratis, G.R.B.S. (1977) 257.

L. Robert, Documents de l'Asie Mineure Méridionale (1966).

L. Robert, Sur un Décret d'Ilion . . ., Essays In Honour of C. Bradford Welles (1966) 175.

J. S. Rusten, Geiton Heros . . ., H.S.C.P. (1983) 289.

R. Seaford, 1 Corinthians XIII. 12, J.T.S. (1984) 117.

F. Sokolowski, Sur l'Oracle de Claros Destiné à la Ville de Syedra, B.C.H. (1968) 519.

K. Tuchelt, Pan und Pan-kult in Kleinasien, Ist. Mitt. (1969/70) 223.

H. S. Versnel, Religious Mentality in Ancient Prayer, in Faith, Hope and Worship, ed. H. S. Versnel (1981) 1.

O. Weinreich, Theoi Epekooi, Ath. Mitt. (1912) 41.

O. Weinreich, Gebet und Wunder (1929).

O. Weinreich, Religionsgeschichtliche Studien (1968) 1–290.

A. Wilhelm, Inschriften von der Grotte des Pan u. der Nymphen bei Phyle, Jahreshefte Oest., Akad. 25 (1929) 54.

J. J. Winkler, The Mendacity of Kalasiris, Y.C.S. (1982) 93.

G. Wolff, Porphyrii Philosophia Ex Oraculis Haurienda (1856).


BIBLIOGRAPHY: III and IV

R. Arbesmann, Fasting and Prophecy in Pagan and Christian Antiquity, Traditio 7 (1949–51) 1.

A. Bataillé, Les Memnonia . . . (1952).

C. A. Behr, Aelius Aristeides (1968).

A. Bernand, Les Inscriptions Grecques et Latines du Colosse de Memnon (1960).

A. Beschaouch, A Propos des Récentes Découvertes Epigraphiques dans le Pays de Carthage, C.R.A.I. (1975) 101.

M. Besnier, L'Île Tiberine (1902).

F. E. Brenk, In Mist Apparelled (1977).

P. R. L. Brown, Making of Late Antiquity (1978).

A. Busignani, Gli Eroi di Riace (1981).

I. Chirassi Colombo, Acculturation et Cultes Thérapeutiques, in Les Syncrétismes dans les Religions de l'Antiquité, ed. F. Dunand, P. Levèque (1975) 96.

P. E. Corbett, Greek Temples and Greek Worshippers . . . B.I.C.S. (1970) 149.

L. Deubner, De Incubatione (1900).

E. R. Dodds, Greeks and the Irrational (1957).

E. R. Dodds, The Ancient Concept of Progress (1973).

F. J. Dölger, Das Apollo-bildchen des Kriegsamulette des Sylla . . . Jhrb. Ant. u. Christ. (1934) 67.

E. and L. Edelstein, Asclepius (1945).

A. J. Festugière, L'Idéal Religieux des Grecs et l'Evangile (1932).

A. J. Festugière, La Révélation de l'Hermes Trismégiste, I–IV (1944–54).

A. J. Festugière, Personal Religion among the Greeks (1954).

E. Grentrup, De Heroici Philostratei Fabularum Fontibus (Münster, 1914).

C. Habicht, Die Inschriften des Asklepeions (1969).

P. Herrmann, K. Polatkan, Das Testament des Epikrates (1969).

T. Hopfner, Griech.-ägyptischer Offenbarungszauber (1921).

K. E. Kirk, The Vision of God (1931).

F. Kudlien, Galen's Religious Belief, in Galen: Problems and Prospects, ed. V. Nutton (1981) 117.

L. Lacroix, Les Reproductions des Statues Sur Les Monnaies Grecques (1949).

T. Mantero, Ricerche Sull'Heroikos di Filostrato (1966).

R. Merkelbach, Zwei Texte aus dem Sarapeum zu Thessalonike, Z.P.E. 10 (1973) 43.

G. Michenaud, J. Dierkens, Les Rêves dans les Discours Sacrés d'Aelius Aristide (1972).

R. A. Pack, Artemidorus and His Waking World, T.A.P.A. (1955) 281.

L. Robert, De Cilicie à Messine et à Plymouth . . . Jour des Savants (1973) 161.

C. A. Roebuck, The Asklepieion and Lerne . . . (1951).

P. Roesch, Les Miracles d'Asclépius à l'Epoque Romaine . . . in Mémoires, III: Médecine et Médecins . . ., ed. G. Sabbah (1982) 171.

S. M. Sherwin-White, Ancient Cos (1978).

M. F. Smith, Diogenes of Oenoanda: New Fragments 115–121, Prometheus (1982) 193.

A. Taffin, Comment on Rêvait dans les Temples d'Esculape, Bull. Assoc. G. Budé 4 (1960) 325.

J.-P. Vernant, Some Aspects of Personal Identity in Greek Religion, in Myth and Thought among the Greeks (1983) 323.

CHAPTER 5

My debt to L. Robert will, I trust, be obvious, not only for his reports on his excavations at Claros but also for his brilliant studies of oracles and their texts, perhaps especially in the volume on Laodicée du Lycos (1969), in the remarkable study of the Theosophy (C.R.A.I. 1968), the prompt recognition of the Oenoanda text (C.R.A.I. 1971), the review of the Didyma inscriptions (Gnomon 1959 and Hellenica 1960) and the insights into Claros in La Carie II (1954). It is only through his studies that I have come to treat this subject at length. The best book on oracles in this period is G. Wolff's remarkable De Novissima Aetate Oraculorum, published at an early age in 1854. To his knowledge and his fine edition of Porphyry (1856), I owe much. A wide range of oracular verses was collected by E. Cougny in volume 3 of the Anthologia Palatina for the Bibliotheca Graecorum Scriptorum, 1890, as an appendix, pp. 464–561. The most recent sample is given by M. Guarducci, Epigrafia Greca, IV (1978) 74–122, necessarily brief, but including photographs of several texts. A summary of part of this chapter benefitted from comments at a London seminar in 1983 and especially from the advice of H. W. Parke, who then lent me his own chapters on this period, to be published in his book on the oracles of Asia Minor in 1985. Where we differ, I have been content to let my views stand, but I have gained greatly from the stimulus of his own acute study. I have also been saved from several confusions and errors by the vigilance of S. J. B. Barnish, who read the penultimate version and suggested many improvements. When L. Robert's publication of the Claros inscriptions is complete, yet more will be clear about the history of the site and its clients.

I

1. Festugière (1954) IV.245, n. 3; John of Ephesus, Eccles. Hist. 2.48 with F. J. Dölger (1920) 28; E. Peterson (1959) chap. 1; Tert., Apol. 16.9–11.

2. J. J. Coulton (1983) with M. Holleaux, P. Paris, B.C.H. (1886) 217; C. W. Chilton (1971) p. xxi. A. S. Hall (1979).

3. C. W. Chilton (1971) F2.5; cf. M. F. Smith, J.H.S. (1972) p. 154; M. F. Smith, Hermathena (1974) 120; M. F. Smith, Denkschr. Oesterr. Akad, der Wiss., Phil.-Hist. Kl., 117 (1974) p. 13; most recent finds, M. F. Smith with bibliogr., in Prometheus (1982) 193.

4. G. E. Bean, Denkschr. Oesterr. Akad. der Wiss., Phil.-Hist. Kl. (1971) pp. 20–2. A. S. Hall, Z.P.E. 32 (1978) 263.

5. Above all, by L. Robert, C.R.A.I. (1971) 597. Subsequent studies by M. Guarducci, Rendiconti dell'Accad. Naz. dei Lincei, 8.27 (1972) 335 and id., Epigrafia Greca IV (1978) 109–12 (with photo) and C. Gallavotti, Philologus (1977) 94 have not made their case.

6. Hall (1978) 263–9, with bibliogr.

7. Eurip. F593 Nauck; cf. Plotin. 6.5.1.; Clem., Strom 5.14.114, with J.

Whittaker (1969), (1975) and (1980) for further details. For Christian usage, cf. J. McLelland (1976); R. Braun, Deus Christianorum (1977) 47.

8. Galen IX (Kuhn) 934; Nonnos, Dionys. 41; 51 ff.; Corp. Herm. IV F4B; Philo, De Op. Mundi, 100: the 7 and "motherless" Athena; Julian, 166A–B; A. Cameron (1969) 240.

9. Heraclit., ap. Hippol. Ref. Haer. 9.9.

10. J. M. Dillon (1977) 170–1; Cic. De Nat. Deor. 1.39, with A. S. Pease; Artemid. 2.34.

11. L. Robert (1958) 103; A. R. Sheppard (1980/1) 77.

12. L. Robert, C.R.A.I. (1971) 597.

13. H. Erbse, Fragmente griechischer Theosophien (1941) 13.30; Lact., Div. Inst. 1.7; Jo. Malal., Chron. III 79E; S. P. Brock (1983).

14. R. M. Ogilvie (1978) 23 suggests a Christian source book between L. and Porphyry: I doubt if there was much time, and none is known.

15. I take "principium" literally, despite G. Wolff (1856) 229 ff. and many since: I will argue this elsewhere, tentatively suggesting Theos. Tubing. 34, 36 and perhaps 35 as the "disiecta membra" of the Oenoandans' original 21 lines.

16. The fundamental authority, again, is L. Robert, Les Fouilles de Claros (1954) and esp. in C. Delvoye, G. Roux, La Civilisation Grecque de l'Antiquité à nos Jours (1967) 302; Iamblich., De Myst. 3.11; on image, B.M.C. Ionia, pp. 42–3.

17. Tac., Ann. 2.54 with R. Syme, Tacitus (1959) II.469–70.

18. Oenomaus, ap. Eus. P.E. S.21–3, with P. Vallette (1908) 134–7.

19. L. Robert, La Carie II, p. 207 no. 139 and p. 211: a thespode in 136/7. In earlier inscriptions, so far published, he is lacking.

20. C. Picard (1922) 303–4: texts 3, 4, 5, 7 report "mysteries" only; 1, 2 and 6 mention "mysteries" before "entry." The latter, I believe, is thus distinct from the mystery rite: Paul, Coloss. 2.18 is not using "mystery" language, specifically. With text 7, M. L. West (1983) 169, on child initiates.

21. Iambl., De Myst. 3.11. 124.17, with 3.12.

22. Iambl. 3.11 (124.14) surely means "no longer visible to those envoys present above ground."

23. I differ from L. Robert (1967) 305, who takes Iamblichus's "prophet" to be the "thespode": if so, the prophet's role is very modest.

24. A. Cameron (1969) 240 and Orac. Sib. III.11–12 (Rzach), a very interesting parallel, making the Clarian text seem commonplace. The summary in the last two lines conforms to no other oracular inscription, and may be the questioners' own: it also runs off the central altar and fills the space below.

25. A. S. Hall (1978) 263–9 for this view; earlier date, L.R. (1971) 602, 610; from photographs, the letter forms look to my eye similar to blocks of Diogenes's text: M. F. Smith, Prometheus (1982) for these blocks.

26. M. L. West, Z.P.E. 1 (1967) 185, line 18; L.R., Documents de l'Asie Mineure (1966) 91–100.

27. L. and J. Robert, La Carie II (1954), index, s.v. Claros; earlier, T. Macridy, Jahresheft. Oesterr. Arch. Inst. 15 (1912) 45 ff.; with C. Picard (1922) 305 ff.; L. Robert, in Laodicée du Lycos (1969) 301 ff., 310; Studii Clasice 16 (1974) 74–80, esp. p. 77 on earliest attested delegation (n.b.: no thespode).

28. Map now in P. Debord (1982) 19 and 21, always with L. Robert (1954) and (1968) 591–2.

29. L.R., La Carie II p. 215; Laodicée (1969), pp. 301 ff. for what follows, too.
30. L.R. (1969) 304 n. 3.
31. L. Robert, La Carie 382 ff.; Rmn. Inscr. Brit. 1439; C.I.L. 3.11034.
32. Tac. Ann. 2.54; Euseb., P.E. 5.22; Ael. Ar., Sacr. Tal. 3.11–12; Xen., Ephes. 1.6; these cases blur the contrast with Didyma, sketched in L. Robert (1968) 592. For another oracle in fiction, Heliod., Aethiop. 10.41: oracles are more relevant to the plots than supposed "mystery religions."
33. A. Petrie (1906) p. 128.
34. T. B. Mitford, J.R.S. (1974) 173, for Candidus.
35. I. Cazzaniga (1974) 145 and 152.
36. Macrob., Saturnal. 1.18.19–21 with P. Mastandrea (1979).
37. Eus., Dem. Ev. 6.18.23.
38. Didyma, II (1958), ed. A. Rehm., pp. 155 ff., with bibliogr.
39. L. Lacroix (1949) 221–6, for an excellent discussion.
40. I. Did. 83 (3rd cent. A.D.): Rhodes had come "often," and here she sends a poet too, like Claros's clients.
41. Inschr. Did. 504 with L. Robert, B.C.H. (1978) 471–2; V. Nutton (1969) 37–48; R. Syme, Roman Papers III, p. 1323.
42. Anth. Pal. 14.72 with L. Robert (1968) 599.
43. K. Buresch (1889) 76–8 and G. Wolff (1856) 68–90, a fine study.
44. Iambl., De Myst. 3.11; W. W. Günther (1971) 97; Strabo 14.1.5, whose sacred grove is surely a paradeisos; I suspect Didyma was the "god" in Meiggs-Lewis 12, lines 27 ff.
45. Most recently, W. Peek, Z.P.E. 7 (1971) 186, with essential doxography.
46. B. Haussouillier, Rev. Phil. (1920) esp. 263 ff., for these ideas on the site.
47. Tryphosa, in W. Günther, Ist. Mitt. 30 (1980) 164, inscrip. no. 5.
48. J. C. Montagu, A.J.A. (1976) 304 for some stimulating ideas.
49. R. Flacelière (1971) 168 and his editions of the E (1941), Prophecies in Verse (1937) and Decline (1947) are all fundamental studies. I assume them for what follows: also, the recent papers by H. D. Betz and E. W. Smith, W. E. Rollins, and K. O'Brien Wicker, in H. D. Betz, ed. (1975) pp. 36–181.
50. Moral. 413A (Cynic); 396E (Epicurean).
51. Moral. 410A–B, with Ogilvie-Richmond, ed. Tac., Agricola (1967) 32–5: some have doubted this, e.g. Flacelière, Dialogues Pythiques (1974) 88.
52. J. H. Oliver, Hesperia, Supp. 8 (1949) 243; R. Flacelière (1951).
53. De Is. et Osir. 351E with J. Gwyn Griffith's notes (1970), p. 17, 95, 253 ff.; De Virt. Mul. 242E, 243D.
54. Moral. 384D–E; 387F (Plut. and numbers).
55. 386A–B (Chaldaean) with L.R. (1938) 15 n. 3; Roman astronomer of 1st cent. B.C. at Delphi.
56. Mor. 388F (theologoi).
57. 391 ff., Ammonius, with J. Whittaker (1969) 185; C. P. Jones (1966); only Eunap., V. Philos. p. 346 (Wright) links him to Egypt, perhaps by confusion with his namesake; Philo, e.g. Opif. 100; Somn. 1.60; 1.119.
58. Plut., Mor. 385B.
59. E. Feuillatre (1966) 45–67, 145 ff.; Heliod. 2.26.5 with Hdt. 1.65.2–3; Hel. 2.27.2–3. The "labyrinth" is the tombs near "Memnon": Str. 17.1.46.
60. M. J. Baillet (1926) no. 1427.
61. Porph., Vita Plot. 22; cf. 3.10 on Amelius, its pious authority.

62. A. Gell. 12.5.1; S.I.G.³ 868 with J. Dillon (1977) 233–8; M. Montuori (1982) argues that the Socrates oracle is Plato's forgery.

63. Vita Plot. 22 line 15 with Hom. Od. 5.399; another image in Plot. 1.6.8; cf. P. Courcelle (1944) 65.

64. A. S. F. Gow, A. F. Schofield, Nicander (1953) pp. 5–8; Alexiph. line 11; I. Cazzaniga (1974) 145; Damas, I. Did. 237 II and 268 with L. Robert (1967) 47–51; "old oracles," I. Did. 277. 18ff.; Phanias the Platonist, I. Did. 150; note the strongly pro-Platonist and anti-Epicurean epitaph for the son of "famous" Menander, discussed by L.R., Hellenica (1960) 484. Was this Menander the prophet praised in I. Did. 223A?

65. I. Did. 217, with R. Harder (1956): see Part III of this chapter.

66. M. Guarducci, Epigrafia Greca IV.113–7, with photos and bibliogr.: L.R., Bull. Epig. 1944 no. 205.

67. Artemid. 2.70, end, with L.R., Laodicée (1969) 312.

68. Philostr., V.A. 7.19–20 with E. L. Bowie, A.N.R.W. 162 (1978) 1672.

69. Macr. Sat. 1.18.19 (we must, with Jan, emend Iao to Iacchus): Theos. Tub. 13.1.15–28 (in my view, Didyma). Nock, Essays I.377–96, on Aion: the Maximus text and the dedication of Q. Pompeius and his brothers, S.I.G. 1125, show the idea's interest for individuals. The latter text, hinting at Eternal Rome, is variously dated, but must, on the Rome point, be Augustan, at the earliest: Virg., Aen. 8.37, for the idea. Nock, pp. 388–93 is surely right about the lateness of an Aion cult in Alexandria.

70. L.R., B. Epig 1946/7 182 and C.R.A.I. (1968) 591, relocating the text in J. Keil, Anz. Akad. Wien (1943) 7: it quotes its request, a Didyma characteristic.

71. Theos. Tub. (Erbse) p. 2 and paras. 42, 33, 44 with Nock, Essays I.164.

72. P. Battifol (1916) 177 and Nock, Essays I.160 are particularly valuable.

73. Wolff (1856) 144–5.

74. L. Doutreleau, Rech. Sci. Relig. (1957) 512, questioning the attribution; the text is in P.G. 39, and the oracles fall in Book 3; 758 A–C, 792A and esp. 888A resemble Oenoanda's text; 913B stands as Theos. Tub. 35 (via Porphyry?); 796C shares half a line with Theos. 43.17 and a Porphyry text. 965B has a rebuke to the mortal: cf. Theos. Tub. 21.15 (Erbse).

75. Eus., P.E. 3.15: not in Porphyry, Wolff (1856) 127–8; not obviously in Labeo, either, despite the claims of Mastandrea (1979) 168.

76. Theos. Tub. 22/3 with L. Robert (1968) 569–86; C. J. Howgego, Num. Chron. (1981) 147–8; for genealogy, and his philosophic cousin, A. Rehm, Inscr. Did. (1958) nos. 182, 277.

77. Theos. 24; L. Robert (1968) 586–9; Aelius Ar., Sacr. Tal. 2.18; a tantalizing Stratonicus in Artemid. 4.31, who "kicked the King" (Emperor?).

78. Theos. 37; Lact. De Ira 23.12; L. Robert (1968) 589–90; I differ, however, preferring Polites in P. Herrmann (1975) 154–5; for his coinage and connection with Keramos, L. R. (1967) 44; his coin type, Imhoof-Blumer, Gr. Munzen 648 no. 338.

79. As a delegate to Claros: Picard (1922) 303–4: from Amaseia; or Laodicea, with L. Robert, Laodicée (1969) 302 no. 21; as a second "divine" name, Ael. Ar. 4.16. But I still prefer I. Did. 372 with the tantalizing I. Did. 369, following Robert's own principle: C.R.A.I. (1968) 584, 598.

80. A. Rehm, Milet. 1.7 (1924) 205B with Robert (1968) 576, 594–8.

81. Plut. 381F; 386A; 393C; 400C–D; 435A for this problem.

82. Galen V. (Kuhn) 41–2; cf. Lucian, Hermotimus, passim; Justin, Dial. Tryph. 2.3 ff.; Ps.-Clem., Recogn. 1.1.
83. Theos. Tub. 21: I will argue elsewhere for this.
84. Macrob. Sat. 1.18.20; Xen., Ephes. 1.6.2: the parents decide to "paramuthēsasthai" the god's words (1.7.2), not "ignore," but "divert" and bring them true as best they can.
85. R. Thouvenot (1968–72) 221 gives the list, supplemented by unpublished material known to L.R. A. Taramelli, Notizie degli Scavi (1928) 254–5 judged the lettering of the Sardinia text to be 1st cent. A.D. G. Sotgiu, I.L. della Sard. 1.42 prefers the Birley thesis, and the 3rd cent. In view of Claros's own history, Taramelli's view is now unlikely: 2nd–3rd cent. seems better.
86. E. Birley (1974) 511, unconvincing: no such "inquiry" by Caracalla left any mark anywhere, even at Claros. On p. 512 he claims that "all" the Tungrians' texts at Housesteads are Severan: R.I.B. 1577 ff. show a wide diversity of lettering.
87. Nock, Essays I.357.
88. R. van den Broek (1978) claims that Nicocreon's oracle from Serapis is genuine, and thus pre-311 B.C.: Macrob., Sat. 1.20.7. This will not do. Its language conforms to Orphic hymns of late Hellenistic date (most recently, West, 1983, 240: this type of thought is not at issue earlier, certainly not in Aristoph., Eq. 74 ff., pace West n. 25). Serapis quite possibly did not have a cult in N.'s lifetime: Fraser, Opusc. Athen. (1960) 46 and (1967). In M., the answer is taken to equate Serapis and the Sun. This may be M.'s own idea, but if it is not, it is still a late equation, of the Roman period when, I assume, this "oracle" was forged. Nock, Essays I.167–8 used Max. Tyr. 11.6 to prove that Max. knew no theological oracles c. 180 A.D. The wording, in context, does not strike me in this way, and N.'s conclusion is forced.
89. Lucian, Zeus Elench. 3–6; Icaromenippus, passim.
90. Dodds, Greeks and the Irrational (1951) 287; J. Bidez, Vie de Porphyre (1913) 18–19; R. L. Wilken (1979) 130–1 unconvincingly suggests P. as the author of these books before the Great Persecution, connecting them to Div. Inst. 5.2: nothing supports this. H. Chadwick, Sentences of Sextus (1959) 66 links the "journey" in Porph., Ad Marc. 4, with an anti-Christian work: even so, not necess. our "Philosophy."
91. I. Did. 100 and 150; for Pythagoras and Alex. of Abonout., vid. infra; I. Did. 310, a Stoic; J.P. Rey-Coquais, Ann. Arch. Arab. Syr. (1973) 66–8; "Belios" Philippos, priest of Bel and successor of the Epicureans in Apamea. Cf. I. Did. 285, for another.
92. J. Balty (1981) 5.
93. Proclus (in Tim. 3.63) is the first author to connect the Or. Chald. to an author: surely (as Dodds saw) they began anonymously? By c. 400, pagans were linking the Rain Miracle with "Julian" too (Saffrey, 1981); the dates were difficult, so a second "Julian" was introduced, alive under Marcus. He then took credit for the Oracles, by the time of Suidas s.v. Joulianos.
94. E. R. Dodds (1961) 270–1; Numenius, ed. Des Places (1973) 18–19; F53 may connect N. with the belief in "animated statues." Note Saffrey (1981) 223–4 for a Syrian god and Syriac wording in a fragment of the Oracles.
95. Eus., P.E. 9.10 with G. Wolff (1856) 141–2; "autogenethlos" in Or. Chald. F39; Theos. Tub. 44.26, with F2 and F109.

96. Wolff (1856) 140–2; 143–74, with 166–70 on astrology.
97. I. Did. 504.25; M. L. West (1983); P.G. M. IV.165ff., for instance.
98. Eunap., V. Philos. p. 427–35 (Wright).
99. Julian 451B; 188A; 298A; 299C; 451B and 136A quote oracles; Eunap. F.26–7 (F. H. G. Müller IV) on his death; cf. Amm. Marc. 25.3.15.
100. Proclus, In Rempublicam III. 70 (Festugière ed. and trans.). I do not think the "sacrificing" refers specifically to a diviner, or augur: if it does, the text might belong in a theurgist's work, exalting his piety against theirs. Julian's court would appreciate it.

II

1. R. M. Ogilvie (1967) 108: date is shortly after 83.
2. Wolff (1856) 172, but p. 173 misses the likely origin.
3. Clem. Alex, Protrep. 2.11; Eus., P.E., pref. 5.
4. R. MacMullen (1981) 63.
5. Flacelière (1971) 168; Plut., Mor. 409C.
6. I. Did. 293; 318; 356; P. M. Fraser, Ptolemaic Alexandria (1972) 274–5, though the chronology is still unsure. J. Balty, A.N.R.W. (1977) II.8.126–9; M. Le Glay, B.C.H. (1976) 347; L. Robert (1954). D. Knibbe, Forsch. in Ephesos IX (1981) 27–8, with the brilliant study by Robert, B.Epig. (1982) 298.
7. R. Merkelbach, E. Schwertheim, Epigraphica Anatolica (1983) 147; I reject their suggested opposition between blood sacrifice and the offering of incense (not required by l. 10); l. 12 requires "sacrifices" at Claros. The key reference is surely the ritual of "displaying the crown" in l.4, to which the opening lines attach. I forbear, then, to cite the text (as yet, uncertainly read) for I.Did.217, below. On Siwah, Plut., Mor. 410A and H. W. Parke, Oracles of Zeus (1967) 230 ff.
8. Discussion in V. Nikiprowetsky (1970); D. S. Potter (1984, Oxford).
9. K. Buresch (1889) 78.
10. Paus. 10.12.4–8; H. Engelmann, Inscr. Eryth. v. Klaz (1973) 224.
11. Plut. 398E; 566E. Lact., Div. Inst. 1.6.13 on the problems; O. Windisch (1929) on Hystaspes.
12. J. L. Myres (1953) 15.
13. S. I. Dakaris (1963) 50, on Ephyra.
14. Plut., Mor. 437C–D; on Iamblichus, esp. J. Carlier (1974).
15. Plut., Mor. 437C–438D; 397C; Iambl., De Myst. 3.5 and 3.11.126 (cf. 127); cf. chap. 8, for Christians; R. Walzer (1957), on Muslims.
16. Wolff (1854) 21, with Zos. 1.57.2; Plut., Mor. 434D–F; Dio 73.7.1; Wolff, p. 30.
17. Wolff (1854) 37 with Dio Chrys. 32.13; Wolff, 13–16 and P. Perdrizet, G. Lefebvre (1919) XIX ff., with no. 492, and 481, 500, 526, 580; C. Habicht, Altertüm. v. Perg. VIII.3 (1969) 76.
18. I.G. II/III² 5007.
19. Paus. 1.34.1–4.
20. 9.39.4; Schol. on Lucian, Dial. Mort., ed. Jacobitz 4.66: I owe this to Garth Fowden.
21. W. R. Halliday (1913) 116–45, from which I draw most of the examples; H. W. Parke (1978) and his Greek Oracles (1967) 75, on Cassotis; Zos. 1.58 and Paus.

3.23.8, on offerings; Macrob., Sat. 5.18.21; Aristot., Mirab. 834B; Philostr., V. Ap. 1.6; Pan. Lat. 6. 21.7–22.2, on geysers.

22. Ael., N.A. 15.25.
23. Paus. 7.21.4–6; 3.25.5.
24. Dio 41.45.2 with F. Millar (1964) 14, 180 ff.
25. Most recently, M. Tardieu (1978); Des Places, Oracles Chaldaïques (1971) 20–24, with Aug., De Civ. Dei 10.9–29 and A. Smith (1974) 82, esp. 122 ff.
26. Dio Chrys. 1.52.6, with L. Robert, Et. Anat. (1937) 129 and R. Merkelbach, Z.P.E. 15 (1974) 208.
27. Acts 16.16; generally, Dodds (1951) 71 and n. 47; on females, R. Padel (1983) 12–14 (exaggerated).
28. Parke, Delphic Oracle I (1956) 35–9; L.R., Laodicée I (1969) 304 n. 3.
29. E. R. Dodds, Anc. Concept of Progress (1973) 190, 199 ff.; T. Hopfner (1926) 65.
30. Apul., Apol. 43.
31. Paus. 7.22.2–3.
32. C. Naour (1980) is the best study, with full doxography; E. N. Lane, C. Monum. Relig. Deae Menis. IV (1978) 53–5, for another fragment, copied in 1897; J. Nollé, Z.P.E. 48 (1982) 274, most recent; in the West, R. Meiggs, Roman Ostia (1973) 347 and pl. XXX.
33. R. Heberdey, Wiener Studien (1932) 94–5.
34. Naour (1980) 30; F. Heinevetter (1913), on alphabet texts, with F. Zevi (1982); R. Heberdey, E. Kalinka, Denkschr. Akad. Wien 45 (1897) 35, on Oenoanda.
35. Naour (1980) 34–6, on tone.
36. G. M. Browne (1970), (1976) and (1979) for fine scholarship on these texts, with full doxography. My examples, from P. Oxy. 1477.17, 16, 3; T. C. Skeat (1954), for afterlife.
37. J. S. Morrison (1981), for earlier arguments.
38. W. and H. Gundel (1966), for technique; Nock, Essays I.495–7, for inspiration, with Vettius Val. pref. 6; Ptolemy Tetrab. 1.2–3, for nuances, with L. Robert (1968) 215–6, on signs/causes.
39. Notably, Cic., De Div. 2.42–7; Liebeschuetz (1979) 119–26, for a good summary.
40. Polemo, ed. G. Hoffmann, in Script. Physiognom. Gr. et Lat. (ed. R. Foerster, 1893, Teubner) vol. I. I cite 138 ff.; 286 (cf. 288); 282; 160 ff. (on Favorinus). Users include G. Bowersock (1969) 120; L.R., Hellenica 5 (1948) 64; E. C. Evans (1941). In Arabic, note T. Fahd (1966) and Y. Murad (1939) 55; generally, B. P. Reardon (1971) 243–55.
41. G. M. Parassoglou (1976) and J. Rea (1977), with Liebeschuetz (1979) 7–29, on the impact of the change from Republic to Empire on divination.
42. Dodds (1965) 55–7, arguing, however, that the "conventional" oracles "never fully recovered their old popularity" in the face of greater competition. Epigraphy suggests otherwise.
43. W. Schubart (1931); H. C. Youtie, T.A.P.A. (1964) 325–7; A. Henrichs (1973) 115; M. Gronewald, D. Hagedorn (1981), with Coptic and demotic studies: also, A. Bülow-Jacobsen, Z.P.E. 57 (1984) 51.
44. I cite P. Mich. Inv. 1258, P. Wien Gr. 297 and K. T. Zauzich, vol. I (1978) 1–3, who suggests that the choice greatly agitated the author and affected his grammar.

45. E. G. Turner, Greek Papyri (1968) 149, on Sarapion, cf. P. Mert. 81, a mother and her son's travels.

46. W. G. Forrest, Camb. Anc. Hist. III. 3 (1982) 309; H. W. Parke, Oracles of Zeus (1967) p. 266 no. 11; Hdts 1.159, Macr. Sat. 1.18.20, for reproach. Cf. Lucian, Alex. 43.

47. Euseb., P.E. 5.10.11; cf. Orig., C. Cels. 7.3–6; Wolff (1856) 169–70.

### III

1. W. Günther (1971) 97; I. Did. 499; I. Did. 348. Note that Rehm suggested "2nd century A.D." for the latter and "late Imperial" for the former, though they refer to the same man. The new text is well before 250 A.D.; M. Guarducci, Epigrafia Greca IV (1978) 96, with photo; for residents at the shrine, an old feature, L.R., Gnomon (1959) 668.

2. I. Did. 504 with L.R., B.C.H. (1978) 471 and the important page, C.R.A.I. (1968) 583 and n. 5; also, O. Weinreich, D.L.Z. (1913) 2959 and A.R.W. (1914) 524–7; O. Kern, Hermes (1917) 149, all cited by L.R.; Rehm's "Diocletianic" date is undermined by L.R. (1968) 583 n. 5.

3. I. Did. 501 with L.R., C.R.A.I. (1968) 578 n. 1.

4. Socr., H.E. 3.23: I. Did. 83, for Rhodes's frequent consultations; "hilaskou" is a word used at Didyma, as elsewhere.

5. Tertull., De Idol. 23; Porph., ap. Eus. P.E. 5.7 with Wolff (1856) 123; A. Pal. 14.72; L.R., C.R.A.I. (1968) 599; C. Habicht (1969) no. 2, p. 23.

6. Milet. 1.7 (1924) 205B.

7. I. Did. 217; H. Hommel (1964) 140; W. Peek, Z.P.E. 7 (1971) 196, latest version and bibliogr.; I doubt his line 5.

8. Vita Plot. 22 line 32.

9. Clem. Alex., Strom. 5.8.47.4 with Callim. F.194.28 and 229 (Pfeiffer).

10. I. Did. 375 with 363 and L.R., Hellenica 11–12 (1960) 475 and esp. Gnomon (1959) 672–3, on reverse, I. Did. 277.

11. H. Hommel (1964) 140 n. 3, citing letter forms, but comparison of them (Rehm, p. 165) with a Diocletianic text (p. 116) shows clear differences, and I consider I. Did. 217, on style, to be earlier.

12. Delphinion no. 175; I. Did. 182, with L.R., Hellenica 11–12 (1960) 447–8; I. Did. 302–3 with the brilliant insight of L.R., Hellenica (1960) 460–3.

13. I. Did. 363, with prefatory note; I. Did. 370, 20 for silver relief, with L.R. (1960) 477 n. 2.

14. I. Did. 243–4; cf. I. Did. 179, L.R., Hellenica 11–12 (1960) 478–9; also I. Did. 261, with L.R. 454–5; P. Herrmann (1971) 297–8 and n. 20.

15. I. Did. 150, from the lettering a 2nd cent. text: note I. Did. 243.7 where Rehm suggests the word "autophanōn" is a Platonic pun, applied to Granianus Phanias's ancestors: very appropriate, if I. Did. 150 belonged to the family. The word, however, also occurs in the recent text for Saturnilla (G.R.B.S. [1973] 65), where its sense is not yet clear: it may refer to "noble ancestry" here too, or perhaps simply to Athena.

16. R. Harder (1956) 88–97.

17. I. Did. 182.17, for choirs for Apollo Delphinios in c. 220–30 A.D.

18. J. Wiseman (1973) 153; L.R., B. Epig. (1958) 266–8.

19. A. Körte, Ath. Mitt. (1900) 398; and L.R., Laodicée, I (1969) 337.

20. P. Herrmann (1971), with p. 296 on I. Did. 370; T. Drew Bear (1973).

21. W. Günther (1980) no. 5.
22. L.R., Hellenica 3 (1946) 21–3; H. Seyrig, Syria (1941) 245–8; J. T. Milik (1972); P. Veyne (1976) p. 351 n. 226.
23. I. Did. 229 with L.R., Hellenica 11–12 (1960) 449–53; I. Did. 282, with L.R., 456–9; I. Did. 223A; I. Did. 243 with P. Herrmann's ingenious suggestion (1971) 294 n. 10; I. Did. 277.
24. I. Did. 206–306; I. Did. 219, with L.R., Gnomon (1959) 673, for date.
25. I. Did. 279; H. W. Parke, J.H.S. (1962) 175; L.R., Hellenica 11–12 (1960) 458–9, for robes.
26. P. Weiss (1981) 317 with L.R., B. Epig. (1982) no. 450, a very important study.
27. L.R., Studii Clasice (1974) 75–7; I. Did. 500; Parker-Wormell, Delphic Oracle no. II. no. 338, suggesting a mid-1st cent. reinscription.
28. Paus. 8.29.3. and, differently, Philostr., Heroic. 8.5; Aelian, H.A. 13.21.
29. W. H. Buckler (1923) 34.
30. Milet. 1.7.205A with L.R., C.R.A.I. (1968) 578 and Et. Epigr. (1938) 106.
31. Theos. Tub. 22; I.G. $2^2$ 2963 with J. H. Oliver, G.R.B.S. (1973) 404, for dating.
32. Briefly, J.H.W.G. Liebeschuetz, Continuity and Change . . . (1979) 123–39.
33. C. P. Jones (1975); Dio, 79.8.6.
34. D. Grodzynski (1974); Dio 79.40.4; and Dio 79.8.6; for a self-confessed forger, Dio 78.16.8 is a fine example.
35. Aug., Civ. Dei. 5.26; Macrob., Saturn. 1.23.14 (an interesting story of "testing"); Aur. Vic., Caes. 38.4; Eunapius F26; also, Zosimus 1.57 with Sarpedon's "rebuke" to the Palmyrenes (surely a fake) and the advice to Aurelian, on which see G. Wolff (1854) 21.
36. Dio. 73.6.1–7.2.
37. R. Merkelbach, E. Schwertheim (1983) 147.
38. I.G. $2^2$ 4758 with G. P Stevens, Hesperia (1946) 4; cf. O. Kern, Ath. Mitt. (1893) 192, for something similar; G. E. Bean, J.H.S. (1954) 85 with C.I.G. 3769 and L.R., Laodicée (1969) 337; more speculatively, S. Stucchi, Divagazioni Archeologiche I (1981) 103, at Cyrene.
39. Queried by J. Gilliam (1961), ignoring the local coin types; Ael. Ar. 3.58; I.G. Bulg. 1.224 with L.R., Laodicée (1969) 305 n. 4; I.G. Bulg. 1.370; I.G. Bulg. III. 1475.8 is probably an oracle in iambics.
40. K. Buresch (1889) 101 ff.; I.G.R.R. 4.1498.
41. Kaibel, Epigr. Graec. 1034; C. Picard (1922) 389; O. Weinreich, A.M. (1913) 62 acutely cites the Apollo on the city's coinage, from Marcus's reign.
42. Buresch (1889) 70; I.G.R.R. 4.360 with C. Picard, B.C.H. (1922) 193–7 and perhaps Inscr. Perg. (ed. Fraenkel) no. 324.
43. The find: G. Pugliese Caratelli (1963–4). Text best in M. L. West, Z.P.E. (1967) 183; H. Lloyd-Jones, M. L. West, Maia (1966) 204.
44. L.R., B. Epig. (1967) 582 with L. Weber (1910) 195 n. 22: note that the coins could all be from the 170s, or later.
45. M. L. West, Z.P.E. (1967) lines 16 and 18 are decisive here; also the initial "Archagetes."
46. F. Kolb (1974), for Delphi; L. Weber (1910) 180, for evidence; also B. Epig. (1967) 580.
47. Livy 38.13.1; cf. L.R., Laodicée (1969) 304–5.
48. O. Kern (1910) with E. Groag (1907); the date cannot be fixed between c. 120 and 240.

49. West, lines 1–2, with L. Weber (1910) p. 178; Weber's own explanation concerns a myth I will discuss elsewhere.
50. G. Pugliese Caratelli (1963–4) for this point.
51. M. Guarducci, Epigrafia Greca IV.102–3 (with photo); West, Z.P.E. (1967) 3A and 3B; in 3B 10, I feel we must surely read "pinutoteros," to give "wiser than the immortals"; the text should be re-examined.
52. The Didyma text on music ends with a Herodotean flourish on Apollo warding off a plague, sent by the Moirai: I. Did. 217.
53. Anth. Pal. 14.75, with Wolff's brilliant explanation (1854) p. 23.
54. West, Z.P.E. (1967) 2B line 24, cf. G.R.B.S. (1973) line 6: Didyma, on Athena, the "cities' helper."
55. J. North (1976).
56. Plut., Mor. 396C; 402B; H. W. Parke (1981) esp. 109.
57. H. W. Parke, D. Wormell, Delphic Oracle I (1956) 36.
58. Aristophanes's forged oracles show bombast was typical, too, of the classical age: Peace 1063 ff.; Birds 967 ff.
59. T. Drew-Bear (1973) 65 ff. for examples; Theos. Tub. 38.5 (cf. Hesiod, W. and D.3); Wolff (1856) 124.44.
60. Artemid. 4.71.
61. I. Did. 496; Or. Sib. 13.130 ff., for example: the reworked text, published in Petermanns Mitteilungen 55.10 (1909) 268, from Caria with Hiller's comment.
62. L. Robert (1966) 91–100.
63. C. Picard (1922) 208–14; J. and L. Robert (1954) no. 139 p. 207 and p. 211; nos. 24, 26 with p. 116, and p. 381 with no. 144; nos. 28 and 196, pp. 117 and 382 and nos. 30 and 135 with pp. 117, 205 and 213. Ardys had already been prophet, before being thespode; no. 193, p. 381. Naturally, this note remains provisional until all the texts appear.

## IV

1. Arr., Peripl. 14; for West Wind, Waddington, Recueil, I (1912) 132, no. 19 (under Treb. Gallus); Tab. Peut. 9.2–10.1 omits road stages up to Abonout.: no milestones are known. G. Jacopi (1937) 8 for a visit, in rough weather, and for hinterland. R. Leonhard (1915) has good maps of Ineboli's immediate plain.
2. Lucian, Alexander, which I presuppose hereafter; R. Syme, Roman Papers 1.469 dates Rutilianus's governorship of Asia to 150/3, a linchpin in L.'s chronology.
3. C.I.L. III. 1021–2; P. Perdrizet, C.R.A.I. (1903) 62, for Antioch; it was still known to Mart. Cap., De Nupt. 1.18 in Africa: however, I wonder if the line was in fact Clarian, accompanying Apollo's images and statues against plague.
4. L.R., Et. Anat. (1937) 272–3, on Tieion. L. Robert, B.C.H. (1977) 60 n. 35. C.I.L. III.7532 for an Abonouteichite at Tomi (n.b.).
5. G. Bordenache (1965) with L. Robert (1980) 398; S. Mitchell informs me of the unpublished Phrygian one.
6. K. Buresch (1889) 10; Glycon is a common name in Asia Minor, admittedly. In 1977, I had suspected a link: L. Robert (1980) 407–8 has put it firmly on the map, but it rests on "the Paphlagonian" as much as the name "Glycon." S.E.G. 18.519 is worth pondering: "Nicetes son of Glycon," from Tieion, at Smyrna.
7. M. Caster (1938), on text. I.G.R. III.84 makes Avitus (Lucian, Alex. 57) govern in 165/6. A. Stein (1924) 257 on the other Romans. C. Robinson (1979) on L.'s

stock abuse: most studies of Alex. do not allow enough for L.'s own mendacity. Even L. Robert (1980) may have shown more about L.'s eye for local colour than about the truth of Alex. Lucian, Alex., 43 alleges gold texts. "Those within the kiss" in chaps. 41 and 55 are L.'s witty parody, using Alex. the Great: Arr. 4.10 ff.

8. D. M. Pippidi, Scythica Minora (1975) 101; Istros consults Chalcedon before introducing Serapis: N. Asgari, N. Firatli, Festschr. . . . F. K. Dörner (1978) 1–12, no. 10. E. Babelon (1900) p. 12 on coins, tentatively: Waddington, Recueil 1.130 no. 3 for the example, under "Hadrianos Antoninos," implying an early date in the reign. L. Robert, Et. Anatol. (1937) shows Asclepius cults at Chalcedon (Syll.[3] 1009); Tieion (p. 286). I. Chirassi Colombo (1975) 100–8, for evidence only.

9. A. J. Festugière, R.E.G. (1939) 231; L. Robert, Et. Anat. 162 n. 7; M. Besnier (1902); I have seen these stone "eggs" in several local museums in Thrace: cf. T. Gerasimov, B.I.A. Bulg. 29 (1966) 219.

10. Lucian, Alex. 5; Philostr., V.A. 1.7, with E. L. Bowie (1978) 1684–8.

11. Lucian, Alex. 11 and 58: Perseus.

12. Imhoof Blumer, Gr. Munzen, p. 38, pl. 3; L. Robert, Rev. Num. (1976) 36; at Aigai, L. Robert (1973) 184–200 and esp. B.C.H. (1977) 119–29.

13. G. Mendel, B.C.H. (1903) 326–30; in the 60s, Pompeiopolis was the metropolis (Gangra later disputes this in coin legends) and does have ephebes, I.G.R. III.1446. For Greek at Abonout., in 137/6 B.C.: T. Reinach, R.E.G. (1904) 252, a decree with a prominent role, still, for a temple priest.

14. L. Robert, A Travers . . . (1980) 400: Hadrian the "new Asclepius" at Pergamum was rather different: I.G.R. 4.341, I. von Perg. 365; on "listening," O. Weinreich, Ath. Mitt. (1912).

15. Lucian, Alex. 24 with Philostr., V.A. 1.8.

16. Alex. 43 (note "ou themis' . . .": typical?). Cp. Asclepius at Pergamum, on whether Hermocrates was immortal: Habicht, Inschriften des Asklep. (1969) no. 34.

17. R. Merkelbach, E. Schwertheim (1983) 147 line 12: Claros.

18. Alex. 29 with 43; L. Robert, B. Epig. (1958) 477 and Rev. Philol. (1959) 189; at Megarian cities, K. Hanell, Megarische Studien (1934) 164 ff. with I.G. Bulg. 315 line 10; on Milesians, F. Bilabel, Die Ionische Kolonization (1920) 106 ff. and Studia Pontica III p. 29 n. 18 and I.G.R. III.98.

19. Alex. 53 (journeys): 34 (transmigration) + 40 (A.'s soul). The oracular language has some very convincing touches: e.g. the vogue words "kelomai" (47–8) and "eparōgos" (28 and 40); the Homeric epithet, Il. 20.39, for Phoebus (36). The latter was genuine, but the rest may reflect on L.'s gift for parody, as does the long text for Marcus, Alex. 48.

20. Oenomaus had mocked "autophōnoi": Julian, 7.209B. Hippolytus, Ref. Haer. 4.34, for stock abuse. Macrob. Sat. 1.23.14–16: L. Robert, Et. Anat. p. 37 n. 2 for overnight consultations elsewhere.

21. Alex. 22, with A. D. Nock (1928); Philostr., V.A. 1.12, admittedly to a pestering visitor.

22. Note esp. Nock, Essays II.847: Pythagoreanism and cult at Smyrna, an important parallel.

23. Lucian, De Dea Syria: even if this is parody (I am not so sure it is), it is relevant to the other Ionopolis.

24. L. Robert, Et. Anat. 262–7 and A Travers . . . (1980) 408–19; the title may originate in 165/6, just after L.'s visit; Waddington, Recueil 1.131 no. 11, where Victory prob. connects with Marcus's title Parthicus. For Doros, L. Robert, Gnomon (1959) 20 n. 2.
25. Lucian, Alex. 60; cf. I. Did. 280, another doctor-prophet.
26. L. Robert (1980) 415 with Alex. 22; Iamblich., V. Pyth. 82 and esp. 29 (his favour for "kataplasmata," not drugs); Ael., V.H. 4.77.
27. Lucian, Alex. 51; Pontic coins were reaching Dura-Europos in the 3rd cent.
28. I. Did. 237; 268; 272; Delphinion 134; L.R., Monnaies Grecques (1967) 38 ff.
29. I. Did. 151.
30. Ulpian, Fragm. 22.6 (ed. Huschke, 1886).
31. J. and L. Robert, La Carie (1954) p. 115 and p. 216.
32. R. Merkelbach, E. Schwertheim (1983) 147–8, lines 5, 55–8.
33. P. R. L. Brown (1978) 36 ff.
34. The exception: I. Did. 83 (Rhodes), after M. Aurelius's reign and dated late by Rehm only on letter forms: note they "often" came, this time with a "poet" and "priest."
35. E. Williger (1922) 83: it was a very worn cliché to call a pagan man "theios": Plato, Sophist 216 B–D, for brilliant parody; Lucian, Alex. 61, Epicurus was "alethōs hieros": the adverb is significant. Cf. Julian on Iamblichus: Epist. 2, to Priscus, with Zeller, Philos. der Griech. 3.2, p. 738 n. 2.
36. Philostr., V. Ap. 4.1; Theos. Tub. 44.
37. Note the Odessa and Dionysopolis texts, cited at I.G. Bulg. 1.224; high-priestly delegates. J. Wiseman (1973), for Stobi; generally, J. and L. Robert (1954) 215 n. 1.
38. L.R., Monnaies Grecques (1967) 38 ff.
39. I. Did. 215A implies voting, by demes, for candidates for the lottery: perhaps 1st cent. A.D. Votes never occur in a text again: I. Did. 260, 282 and the difficult 214B, yet to be explained, all refer to the lot only. No lot needed for Fl. Andreas, c. 200, son of the great Andreas, I. Did. 286; was he unopposable? No prophet c. 60 A.D., before Damas: I. Did. 237 II. A 10.
40. J. and L. Robert (1954) 209–13.
41. A. Balland (1980) 89–93; T.A.M. II.3 no. 905, p. 341 (I assume "tacha" means "perhaps," not "soon") and p. 343. Contra, Brown (1978) 37.
42. B.M.C., Ionia p. 45; I. Did. 83. B.M.C., Lycia, p. 76–7.
43. Sex and Q. Pompeius's phrase in S.I.G.[3] 1125 (of uncertain, Imperial date); on Apollo and the Sun, cf. Heliod. Ethiopica 10.36 and I. Did. 501.
44. O.G.I. 755–6.
45. C.I.J. 748: most recently, M. Simon, R.A.C., Gottesfürchtiger, col. 1061.
46. C.I.G. 2895.
47. Lact, De Ira 23.12; Aug., Civ. Dei 19.23; Wolff (1856) p. 141.
48. M. Simon (1976), for sympathetic Jews and pagans.
49. L.R., C.R.A.I. (1971) 617–9.
50. Theos. Tub. 52.
51. Euseb., Dem. Ev. 3.7.1.; Wolff (1856) 181–2; Aug., C.D. 19.22.
52. Plut., Mor. 402E.
53. H. Chadwick (1966) 23, on Celsus.
54. E. Gibbon, Decline and Fall, vol. II, p. 59 (ed. Bury, 1909).
55. On this, see now A. Armstrong (1984) 1.

## BIBLIOGRAPHY: I

M. J. Baillet, Inscriptions Grecques et Latines des Tombeaux des Rois (1926).

J. Balty, L'Oracle d'Apamée, Antiquité Classique (1981) 5.

P. Battifol, Mélanges III: Oracula Hellenica, Rev. Bibl. (1916) 177.

H. D. Betz, ed. Plutarch's Theological Writings and Early Christian Literature (Leiden, 1975) 36–181.

E. Birley, Cohors I Tungrorum and the Oracle of the Clarian Apollo, Chiron (1974) 510.

S. P. Brock, A Syriac Collection of the Pagan Philosophers, Orient. Louv. Period (1983) 240.

K. Buresch, Klaros (1889).

A. Cameron, Gregory of Nazianzus and Apollo, J.T.S. (1969) 240.

I. Cazzaniga, Gorgos di Claros e la Sua Attivita Litteraria, Parola del Passato 29 (1974) 145.

C. W. Chilton, Diogenes of Oenoanda: The Fragments (1971).

J. J. Coulton, The Buildings of Oenoanda, P. C. Ph. Soc. (1983) 1.

P. Courcelle, Symboles Funéraires du Néoplatonisme Latin, R.E.A. (1944) 65.

P. Debord, Aspects Sociaux et Economiques de la Vie Religieuse dans l'Anatolie Gréco-Romaine (1982).

J. M. Dillon, The Middle Platonists (1977).

E. R. Dodds, New Light on the Chaldaean Oracles, H.T.R. (1961) 263.

F. J. Dölger, Sol Salutis (1920).

A. J. Festugière, La Révélation d'Hermes Trismégiste (1944–54).

E. Feuillatre, Etudes sur les Ethiopiques d'Héliodore (1966).

R. Flacelière, Le Poète Stoicien Sérapion d'Athènes, Ami de Plutarque, R.E.G. (1951) 325.

A. S. Hall, The Klarian Oracles at Oenoanda, Z.P.E. 32 (1978) 263.

A. S. Hall, Who Was Diogenes of Oenoanda?, J.H.S. (1979) 160.

P. Herrmann, Eine Kaiserurkunde aus der Zeit Marc Aurels aus Milet, 1st. Mitt. 25 (1975) 149.

C. P. Jones, The Teacher of Plutarch, H.S.C.P. (1966) 205.

L. Lacroix, Les Reproductions des Statues sur les Monnaies Grecques (1949).

P. Mastandrea, Un Neoplatonico Latino: Cornelio Labeone (1979).

J. C. McLelland, God the Anonymous (1976).

T. B. Mitford, Some Inscriptions from the Cappadocian Limes, J.R.S. (1974) 173.

M. Montuori, Note Sull'Oracolo a Cherefonte, Q.U.C.C. (1982) 113.

V. Nutton, The Doctor and the Oracle, Rev. Belge de Philol. et d'Hist. (1969) 37.

R. M. Ogilvie, The Library of Lactantius (1978).

E. Peterson, Frühkirche, Judentum und Gnosis (1959) 1.

A. Petrie, in Studies in the History and Art of the Eastern Roman Provinces, ed. W. M. Ramsay (1906) 128.

C. Picard, Ephèse et Claros (1922).

L. Robert, Etudes Epigraphiques et Philologiques (1938).

L. Robert, Les Fouilles de Claros (1954).

J. and L. Robert, La Carie II (1954).

L. Robert, Reliefs Votifs et Cultes d'Anatolie, Anatolia 3 (1958) 103.

L. Robert, Documents d'Asie Mineure Méridionale (1966).

L. Robert, L'Oracle de Claros, in La Civilisation Grecque . . ., ed. C. Delvoye, G. Roux (1967) 305.

L. Robert, Trois Oracles de la Théosophie, C.R.A.I. (1968) 568.

L. Robert, Les Inscriptions, in Laodicée du Lycos, I: Le Nymphée (1969).

L. Robert, Un Oracle Gravé à Oenoanda, C.R.A.I. (1971) 597.

L. Robert, Des Carpathes à la Propontide, Studii Clasice (1974) 74.

H.-D. Saffrey, Néoplatoniciens et Oracles Chaldaïques, Rev. Et. Aug. (1981) 209.

A. R. Sheppard, Pagan Cults of Angels in Roman Asia Minor, Talanta XII–XIII (1980/1) 77.

M. F. Smith, Diogenes of Oenoanda: New Fragments, 115–121, Prometheus VIII (1982) 193.

M. Tardieu, ed. Chaldaean Oracles and Theurgy, by H. Lewy (1978).

R. Thouvenot, Un Oracle d'Apollon de Claros à Volubilis, Bull. d'Archéolog. Marocaine 8 (1968–72) 221.

P. Vallette, De Oenomao Cynico (1908).

R. Van Den Broek, The Serapis Oracle in Macrobius, Hommages à M. J. Vermaseren I. (1978) 123.

M. L. West, The Orphic Poems (1983).

J. Whittaker, Ammonius on the Delphic E, C.Q. (1969) 185.

J. Whittaker, Neopythagoreanism and Negative Theology, Symb. Osl. (1969) 109.

J. Whittaker, The Historical Background of Proclus's Doctrine of the Authhypostata, Entretiens Fond. Hardt (1975) 193.

J. Whittaker, Self-generating Principles in Second Century Gnostic Systems, in The Rediscovery of Gnosticism, ed. B. Layton I (1980) 176.

R. L. Wilken, Pagan Criticism of Christianity, in Early Christian Lit. . . . , R. M. Grant, ed. W. Schoedel, R. Wilken (1979) 117.

G. Wolff, Porphyrii de Philosophia ex Oraculis Haurienda (1856).

BIBLIOGRAPHY: II

G. W. Bowersock, Greek Sophists in the Roman Empire (1969).

G. M. Browne, The Composition of the Sortes Astrampsychi, B.I.C.S. (1970) 95.

G. M. Browne, The Origin and Date of the Sortes Astrampsychi, Ill. Class. Stud. (1976) 52.

G. M. Browne, A New Papyrus Codex of the Sortes Astrampsychi, Arktouros . . . , B. M. W. Knox, ed. G. W. Bowersock (1979) 434.

A. Bülow-Jacobsen, P. Carlsberg 24: Question to an Oracle, Z.P.E. 57 (1984) 289.

K. Buresch, Klaros (1889).

J. Carlier, Science Divine et Raison Humaine, in Divination et Rationalité, ed. J. P. Vernant (1974) 249.

S. I. Dakaris, Neue Ausgrabungen in Griechenland, Antike Kunst, Beiheft 1 (1963) 50.

E. R. Dodds, Greeks and the Irrational (1951).

E. R. Dodds, Pagan and Christian in an Age of Anxiety (1965).

E. C. Evans, Physiognomy in the Second Century A.D., T.A.P.A. (1941) 96.

T. Fahd, La Divination Arabe (1966, Strasbourg).

R. Flacelière, Hadrien et Delphes, C.R.A.I. (1971) 168.

M. Gronewald, D. Hagedorn, Eine Orakelbitte aus Ptolemäischer Zeit, Z.P.E. 41 (1981) 289.

W. and H. Gundel, Astrologoumena (1966).

W. R. Halliday, Greek Divination (1913).

F. Heinevetter, Würfel- und Buchstabenorakel . . . (1913).

A. Henrichs, Zwei Orakelfragen, Z.P.E. 11 (1973) 115.

T. Hopfner, Die Kindermedien in den Gr.-ägptischen Zauberpapyri, Receuil d'Etudes . . . , N. P. Kondakov (1926) 65.

J. H. W. G. Liebeschuetz, Continuity and Change in Roman Religion (1979).

R. MacMullen, Paganism in the Roman Empire (1981).

F. G. B. Millar, A Study of Cassius Dio (1964).

J. S. Morrison, The Classical World, in Divination and Oracles, ed. M. Loewe, C. Blacker (1981).

Y. Murad, La Physiognomie Arabe et le Kitab al-Firasa Al-Razi (Paris, 1939).

J. L. Myres, Persia, Greece and Israel, Palestine Exploration Quarterly (1953) 8.

C. Naour, Tyriaion en Cabalide (1980) 22.

V. Nikiprowetzky, La Troisième Sibylle (1970).

R. M. Ogilvie, The Date of De Defectu Oraculorum, Phoenix (1967) 108.

R. Padel, Women: Model for Possession by Greek Daemons, in Images of Women, ed. A. Cameron and A. Kuhrt (1983) 3.

G. M. Parassoglou, Circular from a Prefect . . . , Collectanea Papyrologica, ed. A. E. Hanson I (1976) 261.

H. W. Parke, Castalia, B.C.H. (1978) 199.

P. Perdrizet, G. Lefebvre, Graffites Grecs du Memnonion d'Abydos (1919).

D. S. Potter, A Historical Commentary on the Thirteenth Sibylline Oracle (Oxford, D. Phil. 1984).

J. Rea, A New Version of P. Yale Inv. 299, Z.P.E. 27 (1977) 151.

B. P. Reardon, Courants Littéraires Grecques du II et III Siècle (1971).

L. Robert, Les Fouilles de Claros (1954).

L. Robert, Epigrammes Satiriques de Lucilius sur les Athlètes . . . , Entretiens Fond. Hardt 14 (1968) 179.

W. W. Schubart, Orakelfragen, Zts. Äg. Spr. u. Altertumskunde (1931) 110.

T. C. Skeat, An Early Medieval Book of Fate . . . , Medieval and Renaissance Studies 3 (1954) 41.

A. Smith, Porphyry's Place in the Neoplatonic Tradition (1974).

M. Tardieu, ed. Chaldaean Oracles and Theurgy, by H. Lewy (1978).

R. Walzer, Al-Farabi's Theory of Prophecy and Divination, J.H.S. (1957) 142.

H. Windisch, Das Orakel des Hystaspes, Verhondl. Akad. Wetensch. 28.3 (1929).

G. Wolff, De Novissima Oraculorum Aetate (1854).

G. Wolff, Porphyrii De Philosophia ex Oraculis Haurienda (1856).

K. T. Zauzich, Papyri von Elephantine, vol. I (Berlin, 1978).

F. Zevi, Oracoli Alfabetici: Praeneste e Cumai, in Aparchai, Nuove Ricerche . . . , P. E. Arias, ed. M. C. Gualandi (Pisa, 1982) II. 605.

## BIBLIOGRAPHY: III

W. H. Buckler, Labour Disputes in the Province of Asia, Anatolian Studies Pres. Wm. Ramsay (1923) 34.

K. Buresch, Klaros (1889).

T. Drew-Bear, W. D. Lebek, An Oracle of Apollo at Miletus, G.R.B.S. (1973) 65.

J. F. Gilliam, The Plague under Marcus Aurelius, A.J.P. (1961) 225.

E. Groag, Notizen zur Griechischen Kleinasiatischen Familien, Jahreshefte Öst. Akad. 10 (1907) 282.

D. Grodzynski, Par la Bouche de l'Empereur, in Divination et Rationalité ed. J. P. Vernant (1974) 267.

W. Günther, Inschriften in Didyma, Ist. Mitt. 21 (1971) 97.

W. Günther, Didyma, 1975–9, Inschriftenfunde . . . , Ist. Mitt. 30 (1980) 164.

C. Habicht, Die Inschriften des Asklepeions (1969).

R. Harder, Inschriften von Didyma Nr. 217, Navicula Chilonensis . . . , F. Jacoby (1956) 88.

P. Herrmann, Athena Polias in Milet, Chiron (1971) 291.

H. Hommel, Das Versorakel des Apollon von Didyma, Akten IV Internaz. Kongr. für Gr. u. Lat. Epigraph. (1964) 140.

C. P. Jones, An Oracle Given to Trajan, Chiron (1975) 403.

O. Kern, Die Herkunft des Orphischen Hymnenbuchs, Genethliakon C. Robert (1910) 99.

F. Kolb, Zur Geschichte der Stadt Hierapolis in Phrygien . . . , Z.P.E. 15 (1974) 255.

R. Merkelbach, E. Schwertheim, Sammlung Necmi Tolunay: Das Orakel des Ammon für Kyzikos, Epigraphica Anatolica 1 (1983) 147.

J. T. Milik, Dédicaces Faites par des Dieux . . . (1972).

J. North, Conservatism and Change in Roman Religion, P.B.S.R. (1976) 1.

H. W. Parke, Apollo and the Muses, or Prophecy in Greek Verse, Hermathena 131 (1981) 99.

C. Picard, Ephèse et Claros (1922).

G. Pugliese Caratelli, Chresmoi di Apollo Kareios e Apollo Klarios a Hierapolis in Frigia, Annuar. Sc. Arch. Ath. 41–2 (1963–4) 351.

J. and L. Robert, La Carie, II (1954).

L. Robert, Documents d'Asie Mineure Méridionale (1966).

P. Veyne, Le Pain et le Cirque (1976).

L. Weber, Apollon Pythoktonos im Phrygischen Hierapolis, Philologus, N.F. 23 (1910) 178.

P. Weiss, Ein Agonistisches Bema und die Isopythischen Spiele von Side, Chiron (1981) 317.

J. Wiseman, Gods, War and Plague in the Time of the Antonines, Studies in the Antiquities of Stobi, I (1973) 143.

G. Wolff, De Novissima Oraculorum Aetate (1854).

G. Wolff, Porphyrii De Philosophia ex Oraculis Haurienda (1856).

## BIBLIOGRAPHY: IV

A. Armstrong, The Way and the Ways: Religious Tolerance and Intolerance in the Fourth Century, V.C. (1984) 1.

E. Babelon, Le Faux Prophète d'Abonouteichos, Rev. Num. IV (1900) 1.

M. Besnier, L'Île Tiberine dans l'Antiquité (1902).

G. Bordenache, Il Deposito di Sculture Votive di Tomis, Eirene (1965) 67.

E. L. Bowie, Apollonius of Tyana: Tradition and Reality, A.N.R.W. 16.2 (1973) 1652.

P. R. L. Brown, The Making of Late Antiquity (1978).

K. Buresch, Klaros (1889).

M. Caster, Lucien et la Pensée Religieuse de Son Temps (1938).

H. Chadwick, Early Christian Thought and the Classical Tradition (1966).

I. Chirassi Colombo, Acculturation et Cultes Thérapeutiques, in Les Syncrétismes dans les Religions de l'Antiquité, ed. F. Dunand, P. Lévèque (1975) 100.

G. Jacopi, Dalla Paflagonia alla Commagene (1937).

R. Leonhard, Paphlagonia (1915).

R. Merkelbach, E. Schwertheim, Sammlung Necmi Tolunay: Das Orakel des Ammon für Kyzikos, Epigraphica Anatolica 1 (1983) 147.

A. D. Nock, Alexander of Abonouteichos, C.Q. (1928) 160.

J. and L. Robert, La Carie II (1954).

L. Robert, De Cilicie à Messines et à Plymouth, Jour. des Savants (1973) 161.

L. Robert, A Travers l'Asie Mineure (1980).

C. Robinson, Lucian and His Influence in Europe (1979).

M. Simon, Jupiter-Jahve, Numen (1976) 40.

A. Stein, Zu Lukians Alexandros, Strena Buliciana (1924) 257.

E. Williger, Hagios . . . (1922).

J. Wiseman, Gods, War and Plague . . ., Studies in the Antiquities of Stobi, I (1973) 143.

G. Wolff, Porphyrii De Philosophia ex Oraculis Haurienda (1856).

CHAPTER 6

The great work of A. Harnack, Mission and Expansion of Christianity (1908, E.T.) is an unsurpassed survey of the evidence; B. Grimm, Unters. zur Sozialen Stellung der Frühen Christen (1975) is a recent thesis, C. Andresen, Geschichte des Christentums (1975) a recent survey whose bibliographies I have covered. The best one-volume history is H. Chadwick's masterly The Early Church (1968). Ramsay MacMullen, Christianizing the Roman Empire (1984) was not available to me, but I prefer my view of conversion and had the benefit of his earlier article on miracles when taking the more cautious line in the text.

I

1. Dionys., ap. Eus., H.E. 7.24–5 with C. L. Feltoe, Letters . . . of Dionysius (1904) 106 ff. 1 Enoch 10.17, for sex after death; cf. still, Lact., Div. Inst. 7.24.

2. J. Daniélou, Hist. of Early Christian Doctrine I (1964) 377 ff., an excellent account of the various beliefs; Eus., H.E. 3.39.11–12 and Iren. 5.33.3–4, for the saying; Justin, Dial. 80, 118.2; Iren. 5.33–6 with H. Chadwick, Early Christian Thought . . . (1967) 130 n. 51.

3. 1 Thess. 5.3; 2 Thess. 2–3 and 1 Thess. 2.14–15; 1 Clem. 23.3; Just., Apol. 1.45; Tert., Apol. 39 with V. de Clercq, Studia Patristica (1967) 146; Cypr., De Unitate 16.1–2.

4. E. Schürer, Hist. of Jewish People (rev. ed. 1979) II.523–5 for Jewish views, matching the two main Christian ones.

5. Ep. Barn. 15; Iren., Adv. Haer. 5.28.3; Theoph., Ad Aut. 3.28 Hippol., In Dan. 4.23–4 with D. G. Dunbar, V.C. (1983) 313 ff. for the other texts.

6. P. Amh. 3A with H. Musurillo, Chron. d'Eg. (1956) 124: I accept that the names are not coincidental, but really do apply to Maximus and Theonas in Christian tradition.

7. Eus. 6.43.11.

8. J. J. Wilkes, Dalmatia (1969) 427–30, for summary; Dionys., ap. Eus., H.E. 7.11.13 and 16–17, with A. Martin, Rev. Et. Aug. (1979) 5–6.

9. Orig., C. Cels. 8.69.

10. F. Filson, J.B.L. (1939) 105; Ps. Clem., Recog. 10.71: the very important study by C. Pietri, Rev. Et. Aug. (1978) 3 devastates the earlier archaeological claims

that we can identify early "house-churches" in the lower levels of subsequent "tituli" in Rome. I entirely agree; J. M. Peterson, V.C. (1969) 264, for a different resort.

11. C. B. Welles, ed. The Excav. at Dura-Europos (1967) VIII.2, esp. 108–11.

12. R. M. Grant, Early Christianity and Society (1977) 9–11, using the text as history: I doubt its veracity, but the doubt does not affect my case.

13. Pliny, Ep. 10.96; Lucian, Peregr. 16; Porphyr., ap. Eus., H.E. 6.19.6, correct against E.'s own H.E. 6.19.10; on Aquila, see the intriguing Epiphan., De Pond. et Mens. 14–15 (blaming his continuing taste for astrology); not, however, mentioned in Iren., Adv. Haer. 3.24 and therefore suspect; Dict. Christ. Biogr. I (1877) s.v. Aquila, 150 ff., for texts. G. Bardy, La Conversion au Christianisme (1940) 294 ff., for discussion of the question: the councils, e.g. J. Parkes, Conflict of Church and Synagogue (1934) 174 ff.

14. F. van der Meer, C. Mohrmann, Atlas de l'Antiquité Chrétienne (1971) map 22.

15. M. M. Sage, Cyprian (1975) 2–6, esp. now Y. Duval, M.E.F.R.A. (1984) 493.

16. H. U. Instinsky, M. Aurelius Prosenes (1964); D. E. Groh, Studia Patristica 1971 (1976) part III, in Texte u. Unters. 117, p. 41, a very good study; Clement, Paedag. and Quis Dives?

17. Y. Duval, M.E.F.R.A. (1984) 511 is important.

18. W. H. C. Frend, Jhrb. Ant u. Christ., Ergzbd. 1 (1964) 124 ff. tentatively; on Punic, M. Simon, Recherches d'Histoire Judéo-Chrétienne (1962) 30–100, with Frend, J.T.S. (1961) 280.

19. Iren., Adv Haer. 1.10.2; Tertull. Adv. Jud. 7; on St. Alban, C. Thomas, Christianity in Roman Britain (1981) 48–50 doubts the date, but not the event.

20. For Gaul, F. D. Gilliard, H. T. R. (1975) 17 and alternatively, C. Pietri, Colloque sur les Martyres de Lyons (1978) 211.

21. T. D. Barnes, Tertullian (1971) 273–5.

22. Y. Duval, M.E.F.R.A. (1984) 519–20.

23. W. P. Bowers, J.T.S. (1975) 395; M. Monceaux, R.E.J. (1902) 1; T. D. Barnes, Tertullian (1971) 282–5.

24. F. W. Norris, V.C. (1976) 23, against W. Bauer; above all, C. H. Roberts, Manuscript, Society and Belief in Early Christian Egypt (1979) 49 ff.

25. M. Guarducci, Anc. Soc. (1971) 174; Jos., A.J. 20.17–48 and 54–91.

26. C. B. Welles et al., Excavations at Dura-Europos . . . VIII.2 (1967) 90; 108 ff., 114.

27. C. Kraeling, The Synagogue at D.E. (1979) 332–9: work began in 244/5; soon (p. 335), the seating is increased to c. 125 persons.

28. A. Henrichs, H.S.C.P. (1979) 357–67.

29. Act. Thom. 2; A. Dihle, Jhrb. A. und C. (1963) 54 and in Mullus, Festschr. . . . T. Klauser (1964) 60. J. Marshall, Taxila (1960) 27–8; 72–82.

30. Eus., H.E. 5.10 and Jer., De Vir. Illustr. 36.

31. Bardaisan, F.G.H. 719 F1–2, helped by conversing with an Indian embassy. Bardaisan, Book of Laws of Countries, ed. Drijvers (1965) pp. 60–61 (Kushan, not southern India).

32. J. B. Segal, Edessa (1970) 62–78, for survey; Averil Cameron, The Sceptic and the Shroud (London, Inaug. Lect. 1980) 7–14 is decisive, against any earlier date for the "image."

33. Jul. Afric., in Syncell. Chronogr. I (ed. Bonn) 676; Bar Daisan, Book of Laws,

ed. Drijvers (1965) p. 59. Rejected, without reasons, by Drijvers, in Cults and Beliefs at Edessa (1980) 14, surely wrongly.

34. Dio 79.16.2, correct in specifying Rome: against, Drijvers, A.N.R.W. 8 (1977). 895–6. For a new mosaic of Abgar VIII, Drijvers, Antike Welt (1981) 17: dated 277/8.

35. Mani's Letter, Z.P.E. (1970) 108 ff.; Cologne Codex 64.1 ff.; Drijvers has also stressed this connection, e.g. in Studies . . . G. Quispel (1981) 117; the earlier view, in J. B. Segal (1970) 67 ff., comparing the Jewish conversion story in Adiabene, is unconvincing.

36. J. B. Segal, Edessa and Harran (Inaug. Lecture, 1963).

37. Eus., H.E. 6.42.2–4; 7.11.23.

38. J. M. Fiey, Anal. Boll (1964) 189: on Armenia, W. Sundermann, Mitteliranische Manichäische Texte . . . (1981) pp. 45–9.

39. S. P. Brock, Abh. Akad. Wiss. Gött. 96 (1975) 91; Anal. Boll. (1978) 167, for Candida; Hippol., Ref. 9.7, a fascinating history: Eus., H.E. 6.3–4.

40. Eus. 5.10.7 is emphatically worded, as if continuing missionaries were a very remarkable fact: he can name only Pantaenus.

41. G. Dagron, Rev. Historique (1969), esp. 49–53, a fine study. In general, G. Bardy, La Question des Langues dans l'Eglise Ancienne (1948).

42. T. D. Barnes, Tertullian (1971) 276–8; B. M. Metzger, Early Versions of the N.T. (1977) 4 and 99 ff.; C. H. Roberts, Manuscript, Society . . . (1979) 65 ff., 73; P. Oxy. 2673. Orig., C. Cels. 7.60; on types of translation, and their problems, S. P. Brock, G.R.B.S. (1979) 69.

43. E. Schürer, History of the Jewish People . . . II (1979, rev.) 26–8; Dig. 32.11 pref., with R. MacMullen, A.J.P. (1966) 1.

44. F. G. B. Millar, J.R.S. (1968) 126; P. A. Février and S. Moscati, Riv. Stud. Or. (1968) 1 on Bitia; Aug., In Ps. 118.32.8 and P. Brown, J.R.S. (1968) 88 n. 23.

45. O. Chadwick, Popes and European Revolution (1981) 75 ff.

46. Itiner. Aetheriae 47 (in Palestine).

47. J. P. V. D. Balsdon, Romans and Aliens (1979) 137 for survey; Val. Max., 9.7.16, on Mithrid.; Xen., Eph. 3.1.2; Lucian, Alex. 51.

48. Iren., Adv. Haer., pref. 1.3; Latin, proposed by F. Millar, Colloque sur les Martyres de Lyons (1978) 187–93; on Ovid, R. Syme, History in Ovid (1978) 16–17; cf. Sen., Consol. ad Polyb. 18.9; Greg. Thaum., Letter to Origen, preface.

49. E. A. Thompson, in Conflict of Paganism and Christianity, ed. Momigliano (1963), on Ulfilas. For Theodosius, see P.G. 114, 505–8.

50. E.g. Jo. Chrys., P.G. 63.502 with the admirable study of E. Dekkers, in Ecclesia Orans (1979) 119.

51. Aug., Ep. 84.2; 209.3 and the fine study of P. Brown (1968) 85 with n. 23; J. H. W. G. Liebeschuetz, Antioch (1972) 62.

52. P. Brown, World of Late Antiquity (1971) 93, but cf. 62–5; W. H. C. Frend, J.E.H. (1956) 1.

53. Pliny, Ep. 10.96.9 with Sherwin-White's note, pp. 693–4, suggesting Amastris.

54. Eus., H.E. 7.12.1; Orig., C. Cels. 3.9; E. Kirsten, R.A.C. II.1105.

55. Y. Duval, M.E.F.R.A. (1984) 513–4.

56. E. Kirsten, in R.A.C. 2.1105, though the pre-Constantinian texts are all doubtful; Can. Ancyra 13., Neocaes. 13 and esp. 14 (the poor), Nicaea. 8. I have not pursued the problems of their exact status (see W. Bright, Canons of First

Four Councils, 1892, 34 ff. and the new Letter 20 of Augustine in the recently published collection, ed. J. Divjak, C.S.E.L., 1981).

57. Basil, Ep. 142.
58. R. Murray, Symbols of Church and State (1975) 28–9, with bibliogr.
59. J. H. W. G. Liebeschuetz, in Studies in Church History, ed. D. Baker (1979) 17.
60. S. Lancel, Actes de la Conférence de Carthage en 411 (So. Chrét. 194), 134–43.
61. E. W. Brooks, Patr. Or. 17 (1923) 229–47.
62. F. J. Dölger, Ant. u. Christ. 6 (1950) 297–320.
63. Act. Scill. (ed. H. Musurillo) 17: "decollati."
64. Y. Duval, M.E.F.R.A. (1984) 510–11.
65. E. Gibson, The Christians for Christians Inscriptions . . . (1978).
66. Provocative ideas here, in W. Ramsay, Expositor (1905) 209 and 294.
67. C. H. Roberts, Manuscript, Society . . . (1979) 21.
68. Contra, W. H. C. Frend, Martyrdom and Persecution (1965) 463; subtler view in E. Kitzinger, Early Medieval Art (1940). "Native" is a slippery term in art and archaeology.
69. Cf. C. Pascal's theory, in J.R.S. (1980) 169–70, with Suet., Nero 16.2; in general, G. af Hällström, Fides Simpliciorum, acc. to Origen (1984) 81 ff., though O.'s "simpletons" are not unsophisticated in all respects.

## II

1. Ephes. 4.28; 2 Cor. 8.2, in a rhetorical vein, perhaps; Phil. 4.22; on Erastus, Rmns. 16.23 with G. Theissen, Social Setting of Pauline Christianity (1982) 75 ff., though I do not accept his conclusion; Rmns. 16.2; Acts 16.4 with Averil Cameron, G. and R. (1980) 60.
2. Acts 17.34; 19.31; 13.8–12 with S. Mitchell, A.N.R.W. 7.2 (1980) 1073–4, summarizing the arguments of W. Ramsay: for the later marriage, B. M. Levick, Roman Colonies . . . (1967) 112.
3. Pliny, Ep. 10.96; Tertull., Ad. Scap. 5.2; shrewd warnings in E. A. Judge, J.R.H. (1980) 201.
4. E. Gibson, The Christians for Christians, Inscriptions . . . (1978) with no. 22; W. M. Calder, Anat. Stud. (1955) 38; A. R. Sheppard, Anat. Stud. (1979) 169: the Bithynian, after 212, F. K. Dörner, Reise in Bithyn. no. 159; L. Robert, B. Epig. 1953. 194; B.C.H. (1978) 414; on Gaius, L.R., Hellenica 11–12 (1960) 414 ff.
5. L.R., Hellenica (1960) 11–12, 414 ff.; B.C.H. (1978) 413 ff.; W. Ramsay, Cities and Bishoprics of Phrygia (1897) p. 534, no. 388; R. Meiggs, Roman Ostia (1973) 389.
6. F. Blanchetière, Le Christianisme Asiate (1981) pp. 458 ff., for fullest list of texts; p. 477, for other Christians on city councils.
7. G. B. Caird, Paul's Letters from Prison (1976) 215–7 did his best; Joh. Chrys., P.G. 62.704 has no such problems; 1 Cor. 7.21–4.
8. Ign., Polyc. 4.3; M. T. Griffin, Seneca (1975) 256 and 458.
9. E.g. M. Lyons (ed. Musurillo) 14; probably, M. Polyc. 6; Athenag., Leg. 35; Tert., Idol. 15; Canon. Elvira 41, with dating proposed in chap. 13.
10. E.g. Gen. 17.12; Ex. 12.44 and in general, J. Bamberger, Proselytism in the Talmudic Period (1939) 124–7, whom I have followed; on the circumcision ban, Schürer, Hist. of Jewish People 1 (1973) 538 ff.; Paul, Sentent. 5.22.4

specifically prohibits circumcision of Gentile slaves by Jews. Celsus, De Medic. 7.25.2.

11. Hippol., Tradit. 15; the late-5th-cent. Apost. Can. 10.63 ff. is stricter.

12. Col. 3.18 ff.; Ephes. 5.21; 1 Pet. 2.13; G. de Sainte Croix, S.C.H. (1975) 1–38, a fine study; Did. 4.10; Barn. 19.7; for the problems, P. Carrington, The Primitive Christian Catechism (1941), suggesting these advices were a common Christian feature, not Paul's invention. On the imperative participles, D. Daube, in First Epistle of Peter, ed. E. G. Selwyn, 467 ff.; for Jewish parallels, J. E. Crouch, Origin and Intention of Colossian Haustafel (1973).

13. 1. Tim. 6.1.

14. Act. Thom. 82–3

15. Clem., Paedag. 3.11, 74.1; cf. Seneca, Ep. 47.5.

16. C.J. 1.13.1; Cod. Theod. 4.7.1; Soz. H.E. 1.9.6: H. Langenfeld, Christianisierungspolitik u. Sklavengesetzgebung (1977) 26–31.

17. G. Sotgiu, Arch. Class. 25/6 (1973–4) 688.

18. Hippol., Trad. 11.4–5; Apost. Const. 8.32.73; Justin, Apol. 2.2.

19. 1 Clem. 55; Can. Gangra 3; A. J. Festugière, Moines d'Orient, vol. 2.ii. chap. 21 on Hypatius.

20. H. Bellen, Studien zur Sklavenflucht (1971) 74–5: "eine entscheidende Verschlechterung des Schutzes gegen die Willkür ihrer Herren." Cod. Theod. 9.45.3–5.

21. 1 Cor. 1.26; Orig., C. Cels. 3.55; Min. Felix (ed. J. Beaujeu, 1964); M. M. Sage, Cyprian (1975) 47 ff. for discussion.

22. M. M. Sage, Cyprian (1975) 64, for texts; Min. Fel. 5.4, 8.4; Octavius only partly answers at 31.6; cf. 15.5 and 36.3.

23. Acts of Peter, in Nag Hammadi Library, ed. J. M. Robinson (1977) 265–7.

24. Orig., C. Cels. 6.16.

25. M. Hengel, Property and Riches in the Early Church (1974) 11–22, suggesting a change in Jewish attitudes after 135.

26. Clem., Quis Dives, esp. 4–5, 34–5 (the praying army of poor without weapons), 41.

27. D. E. Groh, Studia Patristica 14 = Texte u. Unters. 117 (1976) 41; Tert., De Idol. 17–18.

28. Orig., C. Cels. 8.75, surely local offices: cf. Min. Fel. 8.4; A. R. Sheppard, Anat. Stud. (1979) 169, with bibliogr.

29. Cypr., Ep. 80.1–2; Eus., H.E. 7.16 with W. Eck, Chiron (1971) 381, a basic survey.

30. Paul, Phil. 4.22; 1 Clem. 65.1, with H. Gülzow, Christentum u. Sklaverei (1969) 77.

31. Iren., Adv. Haer. 4.30, with G. W. Clarke, H.T.R. (1966) 95; H. U. Instinsky, M. Aurelius Prosenes (1964); G. W. Clarke, H.T.R. (1971) 121, for inscriptions; on the graffito, J. Préaux, Latomus (1960) 639; Tert., Apol. 16; Min. Fel. 9.3; Cypr., Epist. 80.1–2; Eus., H.E. 7.10.3 (Dionysius).

32. J. G. C. Anderson, Studies in Hist. and Art of Eastern Roman Provinces (1906) 183.

33. Survey by J. Helgeland, L. J. Swift, A. N. R. W. 23.1 (1979) 724–868; note also L. Robert, Noms Indigènes (1963) 361 ff.; T. Drew-Bear, with discussion accessibly in L. Robert, B. Epig. 1982, 400. R. Freudenberger, Hist. (1970) 597, excellent on Tertullian's De Cor. Mil.

34. C. H. Roberts, The Birth of the Codex (1983), canvassing other explanations besides the obvious one, convenience; J. Stevenson, The Catacombs (1978) 104–5; Acta Scill. M. (ed. Musurillo) 12.
35. A. D. Nock, Essays I.125 ff.; II.828 ff.; Acts 24.3–5, very significant.
36. 1 Clem. 25 and W. Jaeger, Early Christianity and Greek Paideia (1962) 16 ff.
37. F. Millar, Emperor in Roman World (1977) 561–6 for apologists; E. Champlin, Fronto and Antonine Rome (1980), for culture and communication.
38. Against Barnes, J.T.S. (1975) p. 111, I agree with Brunt, Studies in Lat. Hist. . . . ed. C. Deroux I (1979) 506–7.
39. H. I. Marrou's ed. and introduction for Sources Chrét. (esp. pp. 78–93) and his valuable essay in Entretiens Fond. Hardt III (1955) 183 with Paed. 2.103.3, Luke 12.29 and his p. 186; also S. Lilla, Clement of Alexandria (1971) 96–7, 111–3 on the helping Word; Paedag. 2.10 (hyenas); 3.15.1 and 71.2 (mastic).
40. P. Oxy. 412: I cannot believe that any Jew would call "the colony Aelia Capitolina" his "archaia patris." J.-R. Viellefond, Les Cestes . . . (1970) 14 ff. is mistaken here. Eus., Chron. (ed. R. Helm, G.C.S., 1956) p. 214 for the embassy. Viellefond, 18 ff. for his life; most recently, F. C. R. Thee, Julius Africanus and the Early Christian View of Magic (1984), a survey only.
41. P. Amh. I.3A; P. Oxy. 907 with E. A. Judge, Jhb. Ant. u. Christ. (1977) 64–5: the case is not certain.
42. Hippol., Ref. 7.35; Eus., H.E. 5.28.1; Epiphan., Panar. 53.1.3; R. Walzer, Galen on Jews and Christians (1949) 75 ff.
43. Harnack, Mission and Expansion. II (1908) 64–84 is not surpassed. J. Gaudemet, Studi in Onore di U. E. Paoli (1956) 333, a classic study.
44. Tert., Ad Ux. 2.8; Can. Elv. 15; also W. Eck, Chiron (1971) 388–91 and 399 ff., with full lists; J. M. Demarolle, Jhb. A. u. C. (1970) 42; M. Fruct. 5.1 ff.; Tert., Ad Scap. 3; Orig., C. Cels. 3.9; Hippolyt., Comm. in Dan. 4.18; Eus. 8.14.16; Aug., C.D. 19.2.3. P. R. Weaver, Familia Caesaris (1972) 112–36.
45. Can. Co. Neocaes. 2; in general, my chap. 8.
46. Cod. Theod. 16.2.20 and 2.28.
47. G. Dagron, Byzance: Naissance d'une Capitale (1974) 496–509.
48. 1 Cor. 7.10; A. Harnack, Mission and Expansion II (1908) 68 ff., esp. 79, a basic account; Tert., Ad Uxor. 5; Optatus (C.S.E.L., ed Ziwsa, 1882), p. 187 lines 10 f.
49. Plut., Mor. 140D; Strabo, 1.2.8; Orig., C. Cels. 2.55.
50. 2 Tim. 3.6; e.g. Iren., Adv. Haer. 1.6.3, 1.13.3.
51. J. Vogt, in Ancient Slavery and Ideal of Man (1977) 146 ff., a brilliant study.
52. Optatus (ed. Ziwsa, C.S.E.L., 1893) 185 ff., for these people; E. Condi Guerri, Los Fossores di Roma Palaeocristiana (1979).
53. M. Perp. 8.3; Pontius, V. Cypr. 4; Justin, Dial. 3; Bardaisan, Book of Laws (1965, ed. Drijvers) p. 5.

## III

1. For what follows, M. E. Isaacs, The Concept of Spirit (1976), an admirable work; Y. Congar, Je Crois en l'Esprit Saint (1979–80) is more of a devotional study—I.31–105, II.76–81, 142–51 are relevant here.
2. Gen. 2.7 with Isaacs, 35–6 on Philo; cf. 41–2, on conscience; 45 ff., on revelation. Philo, Quis Rerum . . . 265, on "driving out"; Abrah. 35, Migr. 34,

Cherub. 27; Somn. II.252, on his own experience; in general, M. Harl, intro. to Quis Rerum . . . (ed. 1966) pp. 103 ff.

3. Isaacs, pp. 82–6, for Jewish views; J. D. G. Dunn, Jesus and the Spirit (1975) 84 ff. and 358, for continuity between Jesus and the first Christians.

4. 1 Cor. 14.23 ff. Y. Congar, Je Crois . . . , II (1979) 221 ff., for studies of glossolalia, with J. Sweet, N.T.S. 13 (1966–7) 240, on Paul's view; 1 Cor. 2.12 and Isaacs, 97 ff.; Rmn. 8.4–6; Rmn. 14.17, 15.13, 1 Thess. 1.6, Rmn. 8.14, 1 Cor. 3.1, 2 Cor. 2.2; 5.5.

5. Acts 8.19, cf. 8.29, 13.2–4, 16.6, 19.21, 20.22, 21.4.

6. Didasc. 12, p. 120 (ed. Connolly); Hippol., Trad. 15; Tert., De Cor. Mil. 13 and Ad Ux. II. 3 (equating marriage to a pagan with stuprum!), Ps. Cypr., Test. 3.62; 1 Cor. 7.39.

7. Tert., Apol. 50.15, rather rhetorically; M. Perp. 17.3 and M. Pion. 4–5.1.

8. E. Gibson, The Christians for Christians Inscriptions . . . (1978) 125; note, however, Orig., C. Cels. 6.27 on pagans' wariness of known Christians.

9. 1 Cor. 7.16; P. R. L. Brown, J.R.S. (1961) 6–8.

10. R. MacMullen, V.C. (1983) 185 ff. quotes no historical early texts, nor do I know any: p. 172 n. 63 are post-Constantinian stories. Note J. W. Barns, H. Chadwick, J.T.S. (1973) 449, for a conversion by persuasion, not miracle.

11. Hippol., Trad. 17; Orig., C. Cels. 3.51 ff. (important); Can. Elv. 42; M. Dujarier, Le Parrainage des Adultes aux Trois Premiers Siècles . . . (1962). Hippol., Trad. 15, 17, 18; Can. Elv. 4, 10, 11, 68; Nicaea 14; Neocaes. 5; Can. Co. Brag. 35, on their meagre rites if they died before baptism. Later saints, as in Sulp. Sev. Vita Mart. 2.5, were imagined acting differently.

12. Recent survey by E. A. Judge, J.R.S. (1980) 201; H. Gülzow, in Kirchengesch. als Missionsgesch., ed. H. Frohner, U. W. Knorr, 1 (1974) 189. Works by A. J. Malherbe, G. Theissen, W. A. Meeks are among the most recent.

13. A. T. Kraabel, Numen (1981) 113 and L. Robert, Nouv. Inscr. de Sardes (1964) 41–4 take the opposite view: obviously, "theosebēs" can apply to Jewish converts, but despite Acts 13.43, the participle phrases can also, I think, apply to "sympathizers." The question has been reopened by a recent (unpublished) text from Aphrodisias.

14. A. T. Kraabel, A.N.R.W. 19.1 (1979) 477, with bibliogr.; also Kraabel, J.J.S. (1982) 445. Note esp. G. Kittel, T.L.Z. (1944) 9; M.A.M.A. 6.264–5 for Julia Severa and Acmoneia; L.R., Hellenica 11–12 (1960) 393, 438 ff., with bibliogr; P. Bruneau, B.C.H. (1982) 465, for Delos.

15. N. R. M. de Lange, Origen and the Jews (1976); R. Wilken, Jo. Chrysostom and the Jews (1983); W. Horbury, J.T.S. (1972) 455.

16. J. Neusner, Early Rabbinic Judaism (1975) 188 ff., for ideas on this.

17. Most recently, W. A. Meeks, The First Urban Christians (1983) and earlier, E. A. Judge, Social Pattern of Christian Groups . . . (1960), a notable study, continued in J.R.H. (1980) 201.

18. A. H. M. Jones, in Conflict Between Paganism and Christianity . . . , ed. A. Momigliano (1963) 17, a classic study.

19. Act. Justini (Recension "B," ed. Musurillo) 4.7.

20. W. A. Meeks, First Urban Christians (1983) 191; B. Lifschitz, Donateurs et Fondateurs dans les Synag. Juives (1967); M. L. Gordon, J.R.S. (1931) 65; de Sainte Croix, C.S.A.G.W. (1981) 98 for women as a class, not a "status"; Averil Cameron, Greece–Rome (1980) 60, against "liberation" theories. Terms like

"patron" and "client" are used too freely in N.T. studies, where no converts in Paul's letters (except, on one view, Erastus) were of the high social standing where such concepts were applicable; G. Theissen, Social Setting of Pauline Christianity (1982) 158 ff. (cf. 95) is vulnerable here; Cameron makes a similar point, rightly, about the early Christian women.

21. L. W. Countryman, The Rich Christian (1980) 162 ff., very acutely.

22. Cypr., Ad Don. is stylized, but tellingly so, in my view; Tert., De Idol. 18 dissociates Christians from the exercise of power, not only because of idolatry but because of its very effect.

23. Acta Phileae Col. XI (Musurillo) 181 ff. with Latin Acta 6.4: the Bodmer version is only one of several, but a significant view, nonetheless, and exactly repeated in P. Chester Beatty, 15 (ed. A. Pietersma, 1984, p. 66).

24. M. Pion. 17; Tatian, Orat. 28, for "one law"; M. Hengel, Property and Riches . . . (1974) 65 ff.

25. A. Dihle, Die Goldene Regel . . . (1962).

26. Can. Elvir. 5, when "kindled with *furore zeli.*"

27. R. MacMullen, Paganism . . . (1981) 135 n. 14 raises this, but e.g. Lucian, Peregr. 13 and Tert., Apol. 39.

28. Best study is A. Dihle, R.A.C. 3 (1957) 736 ff. An exception in Plato, Laws 716A (but cf. 762E8; 791D8); others in Xen., Agesil. 11.11 and Lac., Pol. 8.2; more typical are Epict. 1.4.25, 2.16.18; I quote 1.3.1. On ptochoi, B. Grimm, Soziale Stellung . . . (1975) 255 ff.

29. T. R. Glover, Paul of Tarsus (1925) 177–80; Preisigke-Kiessling, Wörterbuch . . . s.v. Adelphos; P. Oxy. 3057 does not look Christian to me.

30. Paul, 1 Cor. 5.5, with Gal. 1.8–9; G. Forkman, Limits of the Religious Group . . . (1972), for the scrolls; R.A.C. 1.427, s.v. Anathema and 7, s.v. Exkommunikation; D. Feissel, B.C.H. (1977) 224, for the "anathema of Judas" on Christian tombstones.

31. S. C. Barton, G. H. R. Horsley, Jahrb. Ant. u. Christ. (1981) 7 on the Philadelphian oikos (Syll.[3] 985), which is, in my view, exceptional in its rules and membership.

32. On "catholic," P. Lemerle, Philippes et la Macédoine Orientale (1945) 94 is excellent.

33. Harnack, Mission and Expansion I (1908) 269 ff., excellently; Tert., Ad. Nat. 1.20 ff., for crowds.

34. L. W. Countryman, The Rich Christian (1980) 162–200, a very acute study; on alms, R. M. Grant, Early Christianity and Society (1977) 124.

35. Tatian, Orat. 16–19 is classic; cf. Athenag., Leg. 23 and 26; Tert., Apol. 22.8.

36. On Satan, G. B. Caird, Principalities and Powers (1958) and the essays in Satan (1951, E.T., publ. Sheed and Ward), incl. modern rituals and defences of exorcism.

37. On catacombs, F. Tolotti, Rev. Hist. Eccl. (1978) 281; J. Stevenson, The Catacombs (1978). J. Toynbee, Death and Burial in the Roman World (1971) 234 ff. Also, H. Brandenburg, Jhrb. A. u. C. Erganzbd. II (1984) 11.

38. Plut., Mor. 1104B; Orig., De Princip. 2.10.5; Acts 24.25.

39. K. Thraede, R.A.C. 7.43 ff. had all the sources: col. 49 (Homer); Iren., Adv. Haer. 2.6.2 and Justin, 2 Apol. 6 on successes; G. B. Caird, Principalities . . . (1958) 11 ff., 22, 80 ff.

40. Mk 9.23 (faith); Mk 6.5–6 (Mk's own narrative); Mk. 9.23–9, where the faith of

a father allows exorcism of his son. Iren., Adv. Haer. 2.32.4, no fee; Justin, 2 Apol. 6, no drugs; Ps.-Clem., De Virg. 1.12, with Orig., C. Cels. 7.4 (the "simpler" Christians do it too). C. Cels. 1.6: "histories" of Jesus used as a formula; Cypr., Ad Don. 5 and P. R. L. Brown, Cult of Saints (1981) 106–13.

41. Marcus, Med., pref. 6; Plotinus, 2.9.14.
42. Orig., Mthw. Comm. 13.6 with F. J. Dölger, A.u.C. 4 (1934) 95.
43. Tert., Ad Scap. 4; Hippol., Trad. 20 ff. with Tert., Spectac. 4, Anim. 35.2.
44. Thraede, col. 71–5; Iren., Adv. Haer. 2.32.4 ("very often" the cured person converts, not always). Acts 19.14; M. Lyons 49 (ed. Musurillo); Iren., Adv. Haer. 2.31.2; Orig., C. Cels. 1.2, 1.46, 2.8 and Hom. in Jer. 4.3; M. Pion. 13.6; Justin, Dial. 60.6; Thraede, cols. 100–2 (legends).
45. Eus., H.E. 6.43.14.
46. Acts 13.42–4, 17.2, 17.10–12, 17.17, 18.4, 18.19, 19.8–10, 20.20; Paul, 2 Cor. 10.4 and (e.g.) 1 Thess. 1.4–2.12. In Iconium, first the teaching (14.1), then the miracles (14.3): for others, 14.10, 16.14, 19.11–12. Notoriously, Paul himself does not emphasize these "wonders."
47. Acts 4.13; Cypr., Ep. 42; Eus., H.E. 7.24.6; H.E. 5.28.6.
48. H. Chadwick, Early Christian Thought . . . (1967) 51–4 on Clement's discussion of faith, considering pagans, Gnostics and simple believers.
49. J. Daniélou, Hist. of Early Christ. Doctrine II (1973) 166–83, on "recapitulation" and progress in Irenaeus; 398 ff., on education. H. Chadwick, B.J.R.L. (1964–5) 178, on Justin.
50. E.g., Justin, 1 Apol. 59; Eus., H.E. 1.2.
51. A. J. Festugière, Rév. Herm. Trismég. IV (1954); P. R. L. Brown, World of Late Antiquity (1971) 51–4: conversion, though, was a Christian phenomenon.
52. H. Puech, En Quête de la Gnose (1978) 1.215 ff., a classic study.
53. E. Conze, in Le Origini dello Gnosticismo, ed. U. Bianchi (1967) 651, esp. 666 n. 3.
54. A. Harnack, Marcion (1923), still unsurpassed; for followers in the East later, J. D. Fiey, Muséon (1970) 183.
55. P. Oxy. 3.405 with C. H. Roberts, Manuscript, Society, Belief . . . (1979) 53.
56. Justin, 1 Apol. 31–53; Theoph., Ad Aut. 1.14 ff.
57. A. D. Nock, Conversion (1933) 210.
58. Justin, Dial. 2–8; Tatian, Orat. 29–30; cf. (less clearly) Theophil., Ad Aut. 1.14; both are exceptions to Tert., Test. An. 1, on Christian texts for existing Christians only.

CHAPTER 7

The best survey of sexual perfectionism is H. Chadwick's article Enkrateia in Real-lexikon . . . Antike u. Christentum 5 (1962) 343, which covers much of my ground; on virginity as an ideal, the fullest survey is by D. B. Vismanos, Virgenes Cristianas de la Iglesia Primitiva (1949). M. Humbert, C. Préaux, Le Recensement dans l'Egypte Romaine (1952) is the starting point for views of age and marriage patterns. A. Rousselle's vigorous Porneia (1983) appeared after I had finished, but I retain doubts about her assumption that the doctors' texts reflect actual questions and concerns of their clients. Nor could I use M. Foucault, Histoire de Sexualité, vol. 2 (1983), which concerns many of the same authors.

I

1. Ep. James 1.9–10; 2.2–3; 5.1–6: note esp. Orig., Hom. in Jer. 12.8, a fine text.
2. H. Leclercq, D.A.C.L. 2 (1907) 2530 and 2579, for texts.
3. Tert., Paen. 6; e.g. Laodicea, Can. 19, 45, 46; Co. Constantinople, 7 (381 A.D.).
4. In general, B. Poschmann, Paenitentia Secunda (1940).
5. Tert., De Pud. 13.
6. Greg. Thaum, Can. Epist. 10 (P.G. 10.1047).
7. Eus. 6.43.6 (laikoi).
8. Orig., Hom. in Ps. 37.6 (P.G. 12.1386); Cypr., Ep. 15.1, 4.4; Leo, Ep. 168.2 (P.L. 54.1210–11).
9. Tert., De Pud. 13; Clem., Quis Div. 31–4; cf. Ecl. Proph. 19, Strom. 7.12.
10. E.g. Can. Elvira 47; 37; I quote Tert., De Bapt. 18.5–6; E. Nagel, Kindertaufe u. Taufaufschub (1980).
11. K. Aland, Die Sauglingstaufe im N.T. und der alten Kirche (1963) 36–44, 67–82.
12. Orig., Comm. in Matt. 15.26.
13. Above all, E. Bickerman, Riv. Fil. It. Class. (1973) 22; W. Speyer, Entretiens Fond. Hardt 18 (1972) 333 ff., with bibliogr., esp. 338–9.
14. Tert., Cult. Fem. 3.

II

1. For this, P. Veyne, Annales (1968) 35, a stimulating essay with which I disagree.
2. Ps.-Clem., Recog. 8.48.
3. Despite I. Kajanto, R.E.L. (1970) 99.
4. Most recently, K. Hopkins, Comp. Stud. Soc. and Hist. 20 (1980) 303; P. Brux. 5; P. Oxy. 528, 2858; P. Tebt. 317, 320; B.G.U. 183; P. Mil. Vogl. 85: note Theodoret, Epist. 8.79–81; H. Chadwick, in Early Christ. Lit. . . . R. M. Grant (ed. W. Schoedel, R. Wilken, 1979) esp. 145–53.
5. S. Lilja, Homosexuality in Rep. and Aug. Rome (1983), with bibliogr.; R. MacMullen, Historia (1982) 484.
6. Apul., Apol. 10; Artemid., e.g. 1.78; M. Aur., Medit. 1.17.6; cf. Firm. Mat., Math. 8.11.1.
7. K. J. Dover, Greek Homosexuality (1978) 19–34; mention of Lex Scantinia revived in texts of Tert., Monog. 12.3; Clem., Paed. 3.3.23 (vaguer); Prud., Peristeph. 10.203; J. Griffin, J.R.S. (1976) 99–101; S. Lilja, Homosexuality . . . (1983) 132–3; J. Boswell, Christianity, Social Tolerance . . . (1980) 61–87 and pp. 122–3 on the legal ruling in Paul, Sent. 2.27.12.
8. Artemid, 1.79–80; Ps.-Lucian, Erotes; Achill. Tat. 2.37–8; Plut., Mor. 750C. A. J. Festugière, Antioche Païenne et Chrétienne (1959) 197–203.
9. Tatian, Or. 18. Bardaisan, Book of Laws of Countries, ed. Drijvers (1965) 90–2.
10. A. D. Nock, Essays I.479.
11. P. A. Brunt, Italian Manpower (1971) 140; Musonius F13, 14, on exposure; Pliny, Ep. 8.10, with Sherwin-White, ad loc.; P. Veyne, J. Ramin, Historia (1981) 472.
12. E. Eyben, Family Planning in Antiquity, Anc. Soc. (1980–81) 1–81 is a major survey and bibliography. Also M. Th. Fontanille, Avortement et Contraception . . . (1977); J. T. Noonan, Contraception (1966).

13. J. Crook, Law and Life of Rome (1967) 47, 107 and R. Syme, Roman Papers, II (1979) 510, on bastards.

13A. For Rome, J. Gaudemet, R.I.D.A. (1949) 320; in Greek world, C. Vatin, Recherches sur le Mariage (1970), one out of many: against a "double standard," Ulpian, Dig. 48.5, 14.5 ("periniquum") and Plut., Mor. 144F, showing it was not unquestioned.

14. Ps.-Luc., Erotes 26.

15. Galen, IV (Kühn) 188; Ps.-Ar., Hist. An. 10.5; A. Rousselle, Annales (1980) 1085 ff.; Galen, IV.190, on eunuchs.

16. For Rome, M. Durry, R.E.L. (1970) 17–42, with bibliogr.; in the papyri, M. Humbert, C. Préaux, Le Recensement (1952) 160 ff.; M. K. Hopkins, Comp. Stud. Soc. Hist. (1980) 333.

17. Basic study now is M. Humbert, Remariage à Rome (1972) 31–50; 76–102; 138–59; epitaphs, pp. 63–6 and 102–13; univira, pp. 63–75; laws, pp. 138–59; astrologers' texts in Firm. Mat., Math. Bk. 5.3 under Saturn: e.g., 5.3.8; 5.3.41. Property, Humbert, pp. 188–283.

18. H. C. Youtie, in Le Monde Grec . . . Hommages à C. Préaux (1979) 723, a brilliant study of these effects. Full survey of concubinage and mod. study, in C. Tomulescu, Studi . . . Gaetano Scherillo, I (1972) 299.

19. Two-timers in (e.g.) C.I.L. 6.14027; 9.944; 14.4454; on divorce, M. Andreev, R.H.D. (1957) 7, with bibliogr.

20. Artemid., 1.78 (schooling); 79–80; 4.65; 5.62, 65, 68, 87, 95; 1.78, fin., on daughters.

21. Dio, Or. 33 with C. B. Welles, Mel. Univ. St. Jos. (1962) 43–75.

22. Artemid., 1.78; earlier, K. J. Dover, Arethusa (1973) 59.

23. Rufin., in Anth. Pal. (ed. Waltz) 2.37.

24. Rufus, in Oribas. 6.38.

25. Cael. Aurel., Tard. Pass. 4.9; Ps.-Luc., Erotes 26.

26. Beroean law, J. M. R. Cormack, Anc. Macedonia, II (1977) 139; B. Epig. (1978) 274.

27. Spirited study by L. Raditsa, A.N.R.W. 11.13 (1980) 278; on evasions, esp. R. Astolfi, Lex Julia et Papia (1970) and S.D.H.J. (1973) 187. "Chastity" in C.J. 9.9.9. (224 A.D.).

28. M. Molé, Novissimo Dig. Ital. 18 (1971) 582 on stuprum; the need to bring trial, Dig. 48.5.2 ff.

29. K. Schneider, R.A.C. 1 (1950) 55; Dig. 35.2.9.1.

30. Summary, now, in R. C. T. Parker, Miasma (1983) p. 74 n. 4, with the examples I cite; Lydian cult, again in S. C. Barton, G. H. Horsley, Jhb. Ant. u. Chr. (1981) 7.

31. In general, W. Speyer, Jhb. Ant. u. Chr. (1979) 30; vestals, in A. D. Nock, Essays I.252.

32. J. T. Milik, Dédicaces Faites par les Dieux . . . (1972) 371–5.

33. Alexandra, in L.R., B. Epig. (1950) no. 135 and esp. (1958) 303, promising a full commentary.

34. M. Beard, J.R.S. (1980) p. 14 n. 21.

35. M. J. Vermaseren, Cybele and Attis (1977) 132 with C.I.L. 13.525.

36. Esp. E. Bickel, Diatribe in Senecae Fragmenta, I: De Matrimonio (1915) esp. 204 ff.

37. E.g. Mus. Ruf., F12–14 (Lutz); Epictet., 1.11 and 3.22.60 ff.; also, I quote his Encheiridion 33.8.

38. Plut., Mor. 138A, esp. 144D.
39. Porph., Vita Plot. 15; S. Lilja, Homosexuality . . . (1983) 127–38.
40. Herstal vase, in F. Cumont, Ann. Soc. Arch. Brux. (1900) 401 ff.
41. Artemid., 5.95, with L. Robert, Entretiens Fond. Hardt (1967) 179 on "kataluein"; cf. Paul, in 1 Cor. 9.25.
42. T. Hägg, The Novel in Antiquity (E.T., 1983), s.v. chastity, ideal; Xen. Ephes., 5.14; Heliod., Ethiop. 3.15–20.
43. Galen, 8 (Kühn) 417–21, the classic passage; also 5.912 ff., with Oribasius 6.37–8, for Rufus's views too. For someone who "went off" sex, note Alypius, in Aug., Conf. 6.12.20.
44. Plato, Laws 838A ff., esp. 841B–C.

### III

1. In general, G. Delling, Geschlechtsverkehr, R.A.C. 10 (1978) 812.
2. Schneider, R.A.C., Abtreibung, for texts; Exod. 21.22–3; F. J. Dölger, Ant. u. Christ. (1934) 1–61, esp. 7; two stages, in Tert., Anim. 37 (with Waszink's note); Cypr., Ep. 52.2–3; Elvira, Can. 63, etc.
3. Act. Andr. 5 and esp. F. Nau, Rev. de l'Orient Chrétien (1909) pp. 25–6, canons 10, 11, 18, 20 (Antioch, 325 A.D.); Can. Neocaesarea 2 (on brothers).
4. P. Coleman, Christian Attitudes to Homosexuality (1980) restates the truth; J. Boswell, Christianity, Social Tolerance and Homosexuality (1980) is quite unconvincing: note esp. Rmn. 2.22; Tit. 1.10; 1 Tim. 1.10; 1 Cor. 6.9.
5. J. Boswell, Christianity, Social Tolerance (1980) 137–40, excellent on this; Lev. 11.5 with Ep. Barn. 10.
6. Most recently, M. Crouzel, Mariage et Divorce, Célibat et Caractère Sacerdotaux (1982).
7. In general, H. Crouzel, L'Egl. Primitive Face au Divorce (1971); Mk. 10.1–12; on Qumran, G. Vermes, J.J.S. (1974) 197; woman, D. Daube, N.T. and rabbinic Judaism (1956) 365; Jos., A.J. 4.253 and Vita 426; Mthw. 19.9–10 with the valuable study of J. A. Fitzmeyer, Theol. Stud. (1976) 197, though I still consider Mark to be the original text.
8. Epiph., Haer. 30.18 with H. J. Schoeps, Studia Theol. (1949) 99; A. H. M. Jones, Later Roman Emp. (1964) II.973–6.
9. Luke 2.36.
10. 1 Cor. 7.39 and 7.10–11; Rmn. 7.2–3; cf. 1 Tim. 5.2.
11. E.g. Hermas, Mand. 4.1; Clem., Strom. 3.12.82.3; Tert., Ad Ux. 5–8; Exh. Cast. 3; Monog. 1.4 with full survey by C. Munier, in the S. Chrét. edition of Ad Uxorem (1980), intro., passim.
12. B. Kötting, R.A.C. 3.1022, s.v. Digamoi.
13. M. Humbert, Remariage à Rome (1972) esp. 309–51.
14. Ps.-Clem., Recog. Bks. 9–10; I quote Ps.-Clem., Hom. 13.1.
15. Can. Elvira 70; Can. Elvira 72; M. Humbert, Le Remariage . . . (1972) 346–7.
16. E.g. Clem., Strom. 3.6.3.12: cf. Athenag., Leg. 33; on Origen, H. Crouzel, Virginité et Mariage Selon Origène (1963); J. T. Noonan, Contraception . . . (1966) 76–8, with Lactant., D.I. 6.23.13; on Gnostics, Noonan, pp. 95–6 and 121 (Manichees).
17. Dioscor., Mat. Med. 1.135: cf. Homer, Od. 10.510; Aristot., De Gen. An. 726A; Christian virgins, in Method., Symp. 4.3: cf. Orig., In Exod. 9.4 and in general, H. Rahner, Z.K.T. (1932) 231.

18. I owe this estimate to data from Father T. Radcliffe, of Blackfriars; Revel. 14.1 with John Sweet's note, p. 222.

19. Luke 20.35; Clem., Strom. 3.48.1; Nicaea, Can. 1; Justin, 1 Apol. 29 with Dig. 48.8.4.2.

20. 1 Cor. 7.25; Iren. 1.6.3; Hermas, Vis. 2.2.3 for "sisters"; cf. Tert., Ad Ux. 1.6 and Clem., Strom. 3.53.3 and 6.100; Method., Symp. 9.4; baptism, R. Murray, N.T.S. (1975) 58; S. P. Brock, Numen (1973) 1.

21. Clem., Strom. 3.12.81–2, with R. M. Grant, J.T.S. (1954) 62; Eus., H.E. 4.23 with P. Nautin, Lettres et Ecrivains Chrétiens (1961) 16.

22. R. M. Grant, V.C. (1961) 129, on Gosp. of Philip; Y. Tissot, in Les Actes Apocryphes des Apôtres, ed. F. Bovon (1981) 109; on Thecla, Tert., De Bapt. 17; Act. Paul et Thecl. 9; R. Söder, Die Apokr. Apostelakten u. die Romanhafte Literatur . . . (1932), still valid. Summing-up by P. J. Parsons, in a London book review.

23. A. Paul et Thecl. 7; Act. Andr. (trans. M. R. James, Apocryphal N.T., 1975), p. 352; in general, Y. Tissot, op. cit.

24. A. Thom. 12 and 98.

25. P. Nagel, in Gnosis u. Neues Testament, ed. K. W. Tröger (1973) 49–182.

26. M. R. James, Apocryphal N.T. (1975, ed.) 303; Aug., C. Adeim. 17.5.

27. S. L. Davies, The Revolt of the Widows . . . (1980) actually argues that "widows," or virginal women, were authors of our Apocryphal Acts.

28. Tert., Adv. Marc. 1.29; Iren. 1.27.3; R. Murray, Symbols of Church and Kingdom (1975) 74–5; 2 Clem. 12.1; Clem., Strom. 3.92.2; Gosp. Thom. 22 with A. F. J. Klijn, J.B.L. (1962) 271; Act. Thom. 147 (ed. Klijn).

29. H. Chadwick, in Alexandrian Christianity (1954) 25.

30. Clem., Strom. 7.70 and 6.100.3; in general, B. Prete, Matrimonio e Continenza (1981).

31. Hebr. 13.4, plainly hortatory, in view of following verses: B. F. Westcott (1889), ad loc.

32. C. Rambaux, Rev. Et. Aug. (1976) esp. 24; R. Braun, in Epektasis . . . J. Danielou (1972) 20.

33. Cypr., De Mort. 15; Ps.-Clem., Recogn. 9.10–11.

34. Tert., Virg. Vel. 14.

35. A. Voöbus, Hist. of Asceticism in Syr. Orient, I (1958) 64, for dating.

36. Ps.-Clem., De Virg. 1.3 (boasting); 1.10 (advice).

37. Ps.-Clem., 1.12 (exorcism); 2.1–5 (advice to travellers); 2.5 with Hippol., Ref. 9.11 and the brilliant study of E. Peterson, Frühkirche, Judentum . . . Gnosis (1959) 221.

38. E. R. Dodds, Pagan and Christian . . . (1965) 34; well diverted by J. Gager, Religion (1982) 358: "we need to ask not 'where does it come from?' but 'what does it say?'"

39. Ps.-Clem., De Virg. 2.6.

40. Athenag., Leg. 31.3 with M. Aur., Med. 6.13; R. Walzer, Galen on Jews and Christians (1949) 15; cf. Tatian, Or. 32.2; Tert., Apol. 9.19; Justin, Apol. 1.15.6.

41. Soranus, Gynaec. 1.28–33, esp. 30 ff.; Galen is still attacking Epicurus's view, in Oribas. 6.37.

42. P. Courcelle, Les Lettres Grecques en Occident (1948) 325.

43. 1 Cor. 7.5; Orig., On Prayer 21.4; 1 Pet. 2.9 with Exod. 19.5–6.

44. R. Schilling, R.S.R. (1961) 113, on their differences; contra, M. Beard, J.R.S. (1980) 26.
45. Tert., Praescr. Her. 40; cf. Exh. Cast. 13; Clem., Strom. 3.57 has difficulty in distinguishing Christian continence from pagan types.
46. T. Thornton, J.T.S. (1972) 444–5, most recently: Philo is not exactly a representative source, and Josephus had "dropped out" in his youth in the desert.
47. Protev. Jac. 20.1; Jer., Epist. 49; J. N. D. Kelly, Jerome (1975) 93–4, for the Roman girls.
48. W. Bauer, on Mth. 19.12, in Neutest. Studien für Georg Heinrici (1914) 235; on Luke, P. Nagel, Die Motivierung der Askese . . . (1966) 34–9.
49. On 1 Cor. 7, R. Braun, in Epektasis . . . J. Daniélou (1972) 20 and C. Jenkins, J.T.S. (1908) 500; I discuss 1 Cor. 7.9, 5, 29, 32–3, respectively. On Peter, Mth. 8.14 and prob. 1 Cor. 9.5.
50. J. Massingberd-Ford, N.T.S. (1964) 361–5.
51. Orig., Hom. in Jer. 20.4; Syriac texts in A. Voöbus, Hist. of Asceticism . . . I (1958) 40 ff., 45 ff. and p. 43.
52. Clem., Strom. 3.12.89; on T.'s deceit, good survey in detail by C. Rambaux, Rev. Et. Aug. (1976) 1 and (1977) 18–42.
53. Luke 23.29; Mark 13.17; 1 Cor. 7.28–9; full refs. to Dead Sea sect now in E. Schürer (rev. Vermes-Millar), Hist. of Jewish People vol. 2 (1979) esp. 570 and 578; R. Murray, Symbols of Church and Kingdom . . . (1975) 17; G. Vermes, J.J.S. (1974) 197; B. Janowski, H. Lichtenberger, J.J.S. (1983) 31, on purity and eschatology.
54. Method., Sympos. 2.
55. E. R. Dodds, Pagan and Christian . . . (1965) 27.
56. K. S. Frank, Angelikos Bios (1964) esp. 12–47; Ton H. C. van Eijk, in Epektasis . . . J. Daniélou (1972) 213, a good survey; P. Nagel, Die Motivierung der Askese . . . (1966) esp. 51 ff.; on androgyny and creation, M. Delcourt, Mélanges H. C. Puech (1976) 117; P. Pisi, Genesis e Phthora (1982).
57. J. Amstutz, Haplotes (1968) and F. J. Klijn, J.B.L. (1962) 271; Cypr., Hab. Virg. 20; Frank, Angelikos Bios (1964) 1–13.
58. Novatian, On Purity 7.
59. P. Schaefer, Rivalität zwischen Engeln u. Menschen . . . (1975), a fine study.
60. Ep. ad Diogn. 5.6–13, on not exposing children; age, C. Vogel, Rev. Droit Canonique 16 (1966) 355; M. K. Hopkins, Population Studies (1964–5) 319/20; Didasc. Apost. (ed. Connolly) chap. 17 p. 152; A. Rousselle, Annales (1980) 1108.
61. Aug. Epist. 3(e). J. Divjak, C.S.E.L. 1981; Tert., Virg. Vel. 13.2.
62. Ancyra, Can. 19; Elvira, Can. 13; B. Kötting, R.A.C. 9 (1976) 1055–99 with J. Schniewind, G. Friedrich, Epangelia, in G. Kittel, Th. Wb. 2.573–83.
63. A. Voöbus, History of Asceticism . . . I (1958) 64, 72, 104–5; S. P. Brock, J.J.S. (1979) 217–8 with bibliogr. and a possible Jewish model.
64. Tert., Exh. Cast. 1.
65. Tert., Exh. Cast. 12; De Monog. 16; tithes, in Apost. Const. 8.30.
66. E.g. Tert., Virg. Vel. 10; Cypr., De Hab. Virg. 9–11.
67. Eus., H.E. 7.30.12, for the 260s in Antioch; Tert., Virg. Vel. 13.2.
68. Cypr., Ep. 4 with Elvira, Can. 27; Nicaea, Can. 3; H. Koch, Virgines Christi (1907) 76.

69. 1 Cor. 7.36–8, with C. K. Barrett, ad loc. for the other views; I still follow H. Achelis, Virgines Subintroductae (1902) 7–9; 20–9; cf. Ign., Ad Smyrn. 13.17.
70. Ign., Ad Polyc. 5.2; Tert., Virg. Vel. 15.
71. Cypr., Hab. Virg. 24 (copycats).
72. Cypr., Hab. Virg. 17.
73. R. Murray, Symbols of Church and Kingdom (1975) p. 86 suggests this; "aphthartos," in G. W. Lampe, Patristic Lexicon.
74. Tert., De An. 41, with Waszink's note; 2 Cor. 11.2, with Eph. 5.27; Hermas, Vis. 4.2.1; H. Koch, Virgines Christi (1907) 97–112; F. C. Coneybeare, A.R.W. (1905) 376; (1906) 73. J. C. Plumpe, Mater Ecclesia (1943); J. Gager, Religion (1982) esp. 356 ff. for ideas of body symbolism. I would agree the "body stood for something else," but not that this "something" was a "condensed statement about the relation of society to the individual" (p. 347). "Society" seems wrong here.
75. Tert., Exh. Cast. 13; Res. Carn. 61; I quote Virg. Vel. 16; Cypr., Hab. Virg. 20; in general, D. B. Vismanos, Virgenes Cristianas de la Iglesia Primitiva (1949) 151 ff. and 161 ff. (adultery); Jer., Epist. 22.
76. M. Beard, J.R.S. (1980) 14–15; E. Giannelli, La Tipologia Femminile nella Biografia . . . Christiana . . . (1980) 28.
77. Most recently, A. Martimort, Les Diaconnesses (1983).
78. Tert., De Cult. Fem. 1.1 and 4; Irenae. 3.22.4 and 5.19.1; sects, in Epiph., Haer. 42.4 and my chap. 8, below.
79. Housework, Tert., Exh. Cast. 12; dowdy, Tert., C. Fem. 2.11; hair, A. Paul et Thecl. 25; Gangra, Can. 17.
80. Cypr., Hab. Virg. esp. 8–11 and 21.
81. Tert., Virg. Vel. 10; Exh. Cast. 3.4; Praescr. Her. 3.5.
82. A. Rousselle, Annales (1980) 1111–2, with texts; Galen, Util. Part. 14.10–11; on dreams, cf. my chap. 8 below, with a long text of John Cassian, Coll. 22. On fasting, H. Musurillo, Traditio (1956) 1 ff.
83. P. R. L. Brown, Augustine of Hippo (1967) p. 249, brilliantly expressed.
84. Didasc. 3, p. 26 (Connolly); Cypr., Hab. Virg. 19.
85. Greg. Naz., Epist. 246 and 248 (Budé).
86. E.g. Can. Elvira 7, 12–4, 47, 61, 64, 68–71, all fascinating. On bestiality, Ancyra, Can. 16 and the puzzling Can. 17, with the full note on textual and historical problems in J. Boswell, Christianity, Social Tolerance . . . (1980) 178 n. 33. My trans. is, I think, correct: the Latin West, esp. the Franks, cited it, wrongly, against homosexuals: cf. Boswell, p. 178.
87. Jo. Chrys., P.G. 58.677; in general, H. Selhorst, Die Platzanordnung im Gläubigenraum der altchristlichen Kirche (1931).

CHAPTER 8

No single book centres on this subject, but much is implied in Peter Brown's Making of Late Antiquity (1978) and E. R. Dodds's Pagan and Christian in an Age of Anxiety (1965) chaps. 2 and 3; I have been helped most of all by Martine Dulaey's Le Rêve dans la Vie et Pensée de S. Augustin (1973). There is an admirable survey of early medieval texts of visions and the subtle discussions by Gregory the Great: M. Aubrun, Cahiers de Civilisation Médiévale 23 (1980) 109; see now J. Amat, Songes et Visions: L'Au-Delà dans la Littérature Latine Tardive (1985).

I

1. Gosp. of Thomas 88; H. C. Puech, En Quête de la Gnose I (1978) 124–7 for interpretation; cf. Mth. 16.27; Didache 13.
2. B. Billet, ed. Vraies et Fausses Apparitions dans l'Eglise (1973); P. Marnham, Lourdes (1980) 184–5, which I owe to Kay Boswell. W. Christian, Apparitions in Late Medieval and Renaissance Spain (1981) is excellent here; p. 2, for what follows.
3. W. Christian (1981) p. 2.
4. Mth. 17.1; Mark 9.2; Origen, C. Cels. 2.64; C. Rowland, The Open Heaven (1982) p. 367, with bibliogr.; cf. Orig., Comm. in Mth. 12.36–40; Frag. in Luc. 5.243 (Lommatzsch).
5. H. C. Puech, En Quête de la Gnose I (1978) 133 (darkness); J. Jeremias, Theophanie (1965) esp. 87 ff. (effects on natural world); in general, E. Pax, R.A.C. 5.861–7; John 14.28–9 (thunder).
6. E. Pax, Epiphaneia (1955) 101–44 and esp. 159–71; C. Rowland, The Open Heaven (1982), esp. on visionaries' experiences.
7. P. Herrmann, Das Testament des Epikrates (1969); I.L.S. (Orelli) 4775; Lucian, Philops. 27 and Pliny, Ep. 7.27; note Plut., Cim. 1; Prop. 4.7.
8. Gal. 1.18; 1 Cor. 15.5; Luke 24.34 (Peter, 24.36 and John 21.4 and Mth. 28.16, possibly), to the Twelve; in general, J. D. G. Dunn, Jesus and the Spirit (1975) 95–132.
9. Mth. 28.9; John 20.27; Acts 1.4; John 21.9.
10. Mth. 28.17; I. P. Ellis, N.T.S. (1967/8) 574.
11. John 20.15–16 and 21.7; Luke 24.13–32.
12. Luke 24.49, with Acts 1.1–5 and E. Haenchen, commentary.
13. John 20.20, 20.26; E. Pax, Epiphaneia (1955) 136 and 164 on awe; Mark 16.8 with R. H. Lightfoot, Gospel Message of St. Mark (1950) 92.
14. Luke 27.47 ff.
15. Acts 12.7, 27.23; cf. Acts 7.59; E. Pax, Epiphaneia (1955) 217–21. A. Wikenhauser, in Pisciculi . . . F. J. Dölger (1939) 320; P.G. 85.565, 87.3469A and much else.
16. G. Vermes, Dead Sea Scrolls in English (1962) p. 76.
17. Acts 12.15; Hebr. 13.2; 2 Peter 1.16.
18. Coloss. 2.18 with a good study by A. L. Williams, J.T.S. 10 (1909) 413: esp. 435–7, as all travellers know. Despite the "sabbaths" in 2.16, I do not think this angel worship is necessarily Jewish (contra, Williams, Ramsay et al.); "embateuein" is a pagan word, and at Claros, see my chap. 5, part 1, note 20; F. O. Williams, W. Meeks, Conflict at Colossae (1975) 197 equate it too closely with "mysteries." I suspect a pagan angel (in general, L.R., Hellenica 11–12, 1960, 433 n. 1–3). For Michael nearby, Williams, op. cit., p. 436 and Robert, Villes d'Asie Mineure, p. 105.
19. Coloss. 2.15 with G. B. Caird, Principalities and Powers (1956) 80 and E. Peterson, Frühkirche, Judentum . . . (1959) 51.
20. 2 Cor. 3.18; on "glory," the Jewish Philo, De Spec. Leg. 1.45; 2 Cor. 12.1–7, with P. Schaefer, now in Jo. Jew. Studies (1984) 19.
21. Rev. 5.4.
22. Text, ed. M. Whittaker (G.C.S. 48, Berlin, 1967); review survey by H. Chadwick, J.T.S. (1957) 274; Orig., Comm in Rom. 10.31, on his identity in

Rmn. 16.14 (doubted by Chadwick, 276). I stand by Hermas, Vis. 2.4.3
against the "Muratorian Fragment" which alleges that H. was brother of Pius,
the bishop of Rome, c. 140 A.D. (on its character, Chadwick, 277–8): an old
and able defence of my view by G. Salmon, Dict. Christ. Biogr. 11 (1884) 912.
I reject the theory of a composite book, although the part from Vision 5
onwards did circulate independently (Michigan papyr., and K. Lake, H.T.R.
1925, 279–80): for the most recent Mss. study, I. Mazzini, Prometheus (1980)
181. I cannot pursue here the fascinating matter of Hermas's Greek style, its
Latinisms and "Semitisms": I think the "Semitisms" do not amount to much,
outside the LXX, but cf. A. Hilhorst, Semitismes et Latinismes dans le Pasteur
. . . (1979). Also the (indirect) analogies with themes in the Qumran texts.

23. Seventeen are now known: refs. in J. Lenaerts, Chron. d'Eg. (1979) 356.
24. Most recently, D. Hellholm, Das Visionenbuch des Hermas als Apokalypse
    (1982), whose bibliogr. I assume; M. Dibelius, Der Hirt des Hermas (1923),
    esp. 419–31, is ingenious, but I cannot follow him in his conclusions, and he
    disliked the book. J. Reiling, Hermas and Christian Prophecy (1973) is the best
    recent survey.
25. E. R. Dodds, Pagan and Christian . . . (1965) 59.
26. As, essentially, by W. J. Wilson, H.T.R. (1927) 21.
27. Despite E. Peterson, Frühkirche, Judentum . . . (1959) 275 n. 14, who
    overdoes the "traditional," non-biographical approach. His essays, however,
    are the outstanding studies of Hermas.
28. Peterson, Frühkirche . . . (1959) p. 266, on "aphypnosa."
29. Against Jungian "analysis" of Hermas, R. Joly, L'Antiquité Classique (1953)
    426–8, not, however, always cogently: Jung's wild, but entertaining,
    "analysis" is in Psychological Types (E.T., 1923) 276 ff.
30. E. Peterson, Frühkirche . . . (1959) 261–5; Artemid. 2.35.1.
31. E. Peterson (1959) 287, on text of Vis. 4.1.2, restoring "kampenos," acutely,
    from Cod. Athos and abolishing the "Via Campana"! M. Whittaker, in the
    G.C.S. ed., still retains it, without notice.
32. A. J. Festugière, Révélation d'Hermes . . . (1944) 1.317–24.
33. Vision 2.2.3–4.
34. Vis. 2.3.4.
35. L. Pernveden, The Concept of the Church in the Shepherd of Hermas (1966);
    cf. the Jewish Jos. and Asenath 8.11 (ed. Philonenko), for idea of the
    "pre-existent elect."
36. Vis. 3.5–7.
37. O. Seitz, J.B.L. (1947) 211 and N.T.S. (1958) 327.
38. Vis. 4.8–14 with R. J. Bauckham, J.T.S. (1974) 27; E. Peterson, Frühkirche
    . . . (1959) 299 is not convincing.
39. H. Musurillo, Traditio 12 (1956) p. 2, for evidence and texts on what follows;
    Basil P.G. 30. 684B connects eating and sexual desire; Apoc. Bar., Vis. 28.3.1;
    Apoc. Esdr., Vis. 3.29.2–4.
40. K. E. Kirk, Vision of God (1931) 167.
41. Mand. 4.4.
42. Simil. 5, esp. 5.3 with H. A. Musurillo, Traditio (1956) 35 ff.
43. Simil. 6.8–20; for correction, 7.4 and 7.7.
44. Simil. 2.7–11 (rich and poor); for progress, Simil. 9.1.
45. Simil. 9.5, never considered in Virgilian scholarship, for which see B. Snell,

Discovery of the Mind (1953) 281, not convincing; on the episode, W. Schmid, Convivium: Festgabe K. Ziegler (1954) 121.

46. Artemid. 1.50.

47. Simil. 10.4.5.

48. E.g. R. Joly, L'Antiquité Classique (1953) 427–8.

49. Hippol., Ref. 9.13.1–4: I accept the Trajanic date, and assume the book reached the West later. A. Henrichs, H.S.C.P. (1979) 362, for doubts about E.'s historicity (excessive); for the dating, A. F. J. Klijn, Patristic Evid. for Jewish-Christian Sects (1973) 56 n. 1, with Hippol., 9.16.4: the Parthian War may be relevant to E.'s vision.

50. Brilliantly seen by E. Peterson, Frühkirche, Judentum . . . (1959) pp. 259–61; 265–8; Mand. 11, with J. Reiling, Hermas and Christian Prophecy (1973); Act. Thom. 151, for a curious, magical "transfiguration" of Thomas.

51. For Hermas and Ep. to James, a speculative view by O. F. J. Seitz, J.B.L. (1944) 131.

52. Celsus, in Orig., C. Cels. 7.8–11.

53. In general, C. J. Lindblom, Gesichte und Offenbarungen (1968); Athanas., P.G. 25.169, on "merely" appearing.

54. Justin, Dial. 56–62; Iren., Adv. Haer. 4.10; Lindblom (1968) p. 104–12.

55. Revel. 2–3; Mth. 18.10; on Thera, most recently, D. Feissel, B.C.H. (1977) 209–14, with L.R., B. Epig. (1941) 106; P. R. L. Brown, Making of Late Antiquity (1978) 68–76; H. Grégoire, Byz. Ztsc. (1929–30) 641–4, a fine insight.

56. Tert., De Bapt. 6, with P. R. L. Brown, Making of Late Antiquity (1978) 52–3; Orig., De Princip. 3.3–4 and Hom. in Luc. 12.35, Comm. in Matt. 14.21: Comm. in John 20.36, all drawing on Hermas.

57. Hebr. 12.22–4; Orig., On Prayer 31.5; Hom. in Jos. 20.1; Hom. in Luc. 23; 32. J. Daniélou, Les Anges et Leur Mission (1952) 84–7; I owe this to K. T. Ware.

58. On the festival, E. Pax, R.A.C. 5.902.

59. Throughout, M. Dulaey, Le Rêve dans la Vie et Pensée de S. Augustin (1973), a fundamental book to which I am indebted; for later healing dreams and the problem of possible literary fiction, D. P. Antin, R.E.L. (1963) 358 ff.

60. Tatian, Oratio, passim, esp. 16–20; on wet dreams, Tert., De An. 45.4 and 47.1; Aug., De Gen. Ad Litt. 12.14 (cf. Confess. 10.30, 41, however); Dulaey, pp. 135 ff.

61. Aug., De Gen. Ad Litt. 12.18.

62. Hippol., Trad. 16; cf. Deut. 13.2–6.

63. Cypr., Epist. 11.4; Act. John 19.21 and 48; Acta Thom. 154; cf. Tert., De Anim. 47.2; cf. Miracl. St. Theclae 2, pref., for dreams of saint being "true, simple, coherent."

64. E.g. Pass. Mar. et Jac. (ed. Musurillo) 7.3–4; Perp. et Fel. 4.9; 10.2, and other dreams of combat.

65. Dulaey, pp. 110 ff. on "ostensio"; Aug., Gen. Ad Litt. 12.8.

66. Interesting inconsistency in Philo, heir to this school theme: does the soul reach "ecstasy" of its own accord, or with God's grace? Mig. Abr. 184–95, for former.

67. Tert., De An. 45.

68. Clem., Paedag. 3.1 with Isai. 53.2; contrast Origen, and C. Bigg, Christian Platonists (1913) 209 ff.; Tert., De Pud. 7.10.12 with A. Grabar, Christian

Iconography: A Study of Its Origins (1969) pp. 7 and 11.

69. W. Wishmeyer, V.C. (1981) 253 on the Cleveland Museum's statuettes: the dating is still an open question, though he argues well for c. 250–280.

70. Can. Elv. 36; Clem., Paed. 3.59.2, distorted by C. Murray, J.T.S. (1977) 322–4: (i) 3.12.1 is a false reference, (ii) C. is not answering "inquiring Christian converts, used to the iconographic oddities of Gnostic gems." He is attacking "licentious" (3.60.1) and "idolatrous" subjects, the living heart of great art. Murray, J.T.S. (1977) 303 ff. cites evidence from post- and pre-Constantinian dates without due distinction; she does not emphasize the absence of Christian figure sculpture and portraiture and is unconvincing in her contention that the "early" Church was not hostile to art.

71. Iren., Adv. Haer. 1.25.2–6 on Carpocratians; Acts of John 27 with A. Grabar, Christian Iconography . . . (1969) 66–9; on Roman objects, Grabar p. 69.

72. E. Kitzinger, in Age of Spirituality: A Symposium, ed. K. Weitzmann (1981) 142.

73. Epitaphs, e.g. W. Wishmeyer, Jhb. A. u. C. (1980) 22; E. Werner's marvellous musical study, The Sacred Bridge (1959).

74. E.g. Dan. 9.1; 4 Ezra 6.38; Aug., Conf. 8.12.29; Greg. Naz., P.G. 35.999.

75. Exod. 33.20; Orig., Homil. on Song of Songs 1.7; A. Louth, The Origins of the Christian Mystical Tradition (1981) 42–74; Orig., Comm. in John 32.27; Plato, Rep. 518C; Orig., Comm. in John 1.9 and the good studies by P. Rousselot, Les Yeux de la Foi, Rech. Sci. Relig. 1 (1919) 241 and 444.

76. Rev. 4.3; Iren., Adv. Haer. 4.9; Rev. 14.14; J. Sweet, Revelation (S.C.M. Pelican Bible Comm., 1979) p. 125 and passim, for an admirable discussion; Rev. 5.9, 7.14, 9.18, 5.6 and Sweet, p. 70, quoting Jung, Answer to Job (1979) p. 124.

77. Best in T. Boman, Das Hebräische Denken im Vergleich mit dem Griechischen (1952) 140 ff.

78. C. Rowland, The Open Heaven (1982) is excellent here: esp. pp. 85–6.

79. Cypr., Ep. 11.4; M. Perp. et Fel. 10.8; Pass. Mar. et Jac. 7.3; Mont. et Luc. 8.4.

80. In general, H. Musurillo, Traditio (1956) 1; esp. R. Arbesmann, Traditio 7 (1949) 32 ff. Did. 8; Socr., H.E. 5.22, 38 and Ps.-Ign., Philipp. 13; Eus., H.E. 5.3.2 is very nice; Iren., in Eus., H.E. 5.24.12; "superimposing," in Pass. Mar. et Jac. 8.1 with Greek "hypertithenai" in Dionysius. Ep. to Basileides (ed. Feltoe) p. 102 and Arbesmann p. 34 n. 29.

81. Apost. Const. 5.18; Jer., Ep. 41.3.

82. R. Arbesmann, Traditio 7 (1949–51) esp. 25 and 60 ff.; Galen 6.833 (Kühn); Tertull., De Jej. 12 ("extorting" a vision by xerophagy); Tert., De Anim. 48, passim, where 48.4 does not mean T. himself never dreamed when fasting, but that his dreams were so profuse that he no longer knew when they stopped. On "familarem dei," Arbesmann, p. 65 n. 76, acutely.

83. Literary visions, in my view, are Act. John 18; Act. Peter (Vercelli) 1, 5, 16, 17; Act. Thom. 29. At baptism, Act. Thom. 121 (voice); Act. Peter 5; Syriac setting, R. Murray, N.T.S. (1974) 59.

84. W. Christian, Apparitions in Late Medieval Spain (1981) 64–5; Act. John 88–9, 93; probably developing 1 John 1.1; for a similar tradition known to Clement (not, however, the Act. John), cf. T. Rüther, Theol. Quart. (1926) 251.

85. Act. Peter, 20–21, H. C. Puech, En Quête de la Gnose, II (1978) 84 ff.
86. A. D. Nock, Essays I.377; E. Peterson, Frühkirche, Judentum . . . (1959) 203; on Satan, Ps.-Ignat., Phil. IV.
87. G. G. Stroumsa, V.C. (1981) 412.
88. Gosp. Phil. 57.30–58.10; 61.30; on baptismal visions, E. Peterson, Frühkirche, Judentum . . . (1959) 194 ff.; Apocr. John 2.1–10; Orig., Excerp. ex Theod. 23.4; Comm. in Mth. 12.31.
89. Contra E. Pagels, Gnostic Gospels (1979) chap. 1 and also in Gnosis: Festschrift für H. Jonas, ed. B. Aland (1978) 415.
90. Orig., C. Cels. 1.46.
91. W. Christian, Apparitions . . . (1981), for later "lost" statues. For martyrs' altars, Codex Can. Eccles. Africa. 83 = Can. Co. of Carthage, 401, no. 17. Ps.-Clem, Homil. 17.14 and 19; Iren. 1.23.4; E. Pagels, in Gnosis . . . H. Jonas, ed. B. Aland (1978) 415. For Mani, see chap. 11, part II.
92. Ps.-Clem., Recog. 2.62; Homil. 17.14 and 19.
93. Acts 27.23.
94. Cypr., Ep. 16.4.
95. Tert., De Anim. 53.5 with Waszink's note; F. E. Brenk, In Mist Apparelled (1977) 214 ff.; for martyrdom and prisons, see my chap. 9, Part II, and for Jewish traditions of Isaac and his vision, R. Hayward, J.J.S. 32 (1981) 127. M. Dulaey, Le Rêve dans la Vie et Pensée du S. Aug. (1973) p. 44 quotes the First Circle.
96. W. H. C. Frend, J.E.H. (1954) 25–37; T. D. Barnes, Tertullian (1971) 167–8.
97. Proof of Greek, now, by L. Robert, C.R.A.I. (1982), esp. 253–6, the basic study; I quote M. Perp. et Fel. 4; there is no hint that P. was a Montanist herself, despite T. D. Barnes, Tertullian (1971) 77; E. Dodds, Pagan and Christian (1965) 51 n. 2, 53; F. J. Dölger, Ant. u. Christ. II (1930) 1–40; L. Robert, C.R.A.I. (1982) 254–66, fundamental on the "umpire."
98. Tert., De Cor. 3.3, on milk and baptism; Saturus, in M. Perp. 11 and 13; for the contrast, L. Robert, C.R.A.I. (1982) 276 n. 235; C. Rowland, Open Heaven (1982) mistakenly overinterprets P.'s own visions, at pp. 396–402; A. Fridh, Le Problème de la Passion des S. Perpétue et Félicité (1968) 58, arguing that Saturus, too, used Greek.
99. V. Lomanto, Forma Futuri . . . Studi M. Pellegrino (1975) 566 is best. P.'s influence; Pass. Mar. et Jac. (ed. Musurillo) 8.
100. Mar. et Jac. 7.
101. E.g. M. Polyc. 5.2; M. Perp. 10, 12; M. Pot. et Bas. 6; Mar. et Jas 6.5 and 11; Pontius, Vita Cypr. 12; Mont. et Luc. 5.2, 7, 21. Also the Donatist martyrs, P.L. 8.763B and 770; in fiction, A. Paul. et Theclae 21.
102. P. Mont. et Luc. 11; M. Perp. 12; on recapturing childhood, H. C. Puech, En Quête de la Gnose II.277–82, for apocryphal ideals.

## II

1. Hermas, Mand. 11.2–12 with the fine study of J. Reiling, Hermas and Christian Prophecy (1975), which I presuppose here.
2. C. H. E. Haspels, Highlands of Phrygia I (1971) no. 40, p. 313; she offers no commentary.
3. T. D. Barnes, J.T.S. (1970) 403, undermining Epiphanius, Panar, 48.1.2: we do not know the crucial date, Gratus's gov. of Asia (Eus., H.E. 5.16.7), but R.

Syme, Z.P.E. 53 (1983) 280–3 has ruled out Epiphanius's "156/7" and the 160s are filling up; a good argument, on other grounds, for the mid-150s by G. Salmon, Dict. Christ. Biogr. (1882) III.939.

4. Epiphan. 48.4.

5. There are two outstanding studies: P. Labriolle, La Crise Montaniste (1913), with the separate Les Sources de l'Histoire du Montanisme (1913), and the admirable article Montanus, by G. Salmon, Dict. of Christ. Biography (ed. Smith and Wace, 1882) III.935 ff.

6. Millennial, by T. D. Barnes, Tertullian (1971) p. 131; Phrygian, by W. Schepelern, Montanismus (1929): woman, Epiph., Panar. 49.1; on Pepuza, A. Strobel, Das Heilige Land der Montanisten . . . (1980) fails to establish a site, but evokes one part of Phrygia very well and prints many inscriptions, some new (pp. 117–8).

7. Jer., Epist. 49.4; A. Strobel, Das Heilige Land (1980) 234 ff., on these "parallels"; L. Robert, C.R.A.I. (1978) 267–9; Eus., H.E. 5.18.2 is by a critic, and perhaps excessive: "hōde" in Epiph. 49.1 is not clear.

8. Epiph. 48.4; 48.11; Eus., H.E. 5.16.17, "according to Urbanus," with Labriolle, Crise, p. 35; Tert., De Fuga 9; Epiph., 48.9; Hippol, Ref. 8.13 (fasts); Tert., De Res. Carn. 63; Tert., De Pud. 27.

9. "Uberior disciplina": Tert., De Virg. Vel. 1.

10. Lucian, Alex. 23.36; Eus., H.E. 5.18.2.

11. E. Gibson, G.R.B.S. (1975) 433–42; I am less sure than C. H. E. Haspels, Highlands of Phrygia, I (1971), pp. 215–6 and no. 107 is really Montanist. The text does not mention "ecstasy" (pace Haspels): lines 10–11 are of uncertain scope (whose is the voice? hers, or God's?) and not every biblical "prophetess" in Phrygia was Montanist. The question stays open.

12. Epiph., 49.2 (Eve, etc.) with Labriolle, Crise Montaniste, 509; Tert., De Fuga, 9; Montanist "militants" are further dispelled by E. Gibson, Christians for Christians . . . (1978), with S. Mitchell, J.T.S. (1980) 202–3.

13. Orig., C. Cels. 7.4–5.

14. K. Aland, Kirchengeschichtliche Entwürfe (1960) 105: on ecstasy, P. Labriolle, Crise Montaniste (1913), pp. 155–75, with all sources, and p. 338 n. 2 on Tert.'s lost work, De Ecstasi.

15. Labriolle, Crise Montaniste (1913) 324 ff., on Tert.'s use of "Paraclete" and its sense.

16. Apollonius, in Eus., H.E. 5.18.14; cf. Jerome, Ep. 41.1, to Marcella, rebutting the Montanists by citing Acts and Pentecost: it is this, in my view, the Montanists tried to outflank. For the arguments of "Alogoi" against the Apocalypse, Epiph. 51.33, with Labriolle, Crise Montaniste 196 ff.; L. assumes the Montanists, by contrast, accepted Revelation, but nothing in the early texts proves it; for Jezebel, Epiph., Panar. 51.33; Rev. 2.20.

17. Epiph. 48.4; for Philo and others, H. C. Puech, R.E.G. (1933) 311, a fine study, suggesting a Jewish origin (not convincing); cf. Quis Rerum Div. Heres 249 ff.; Labriolle, Crise Montaniste (1913) 165 ff., with Plut., Mor. 437D–E; Philostr., Imag. 1.7.20, for plectrum/lyre imagery in pagan contexts.

18. G. Salmon, Dict. Christ. Biography (1882) 3.937 for this acute suggestion.

19. Eus., H.E. 5.3–4; 5.6; 5.18.

20. G. Salmon, D. Christ. Biog. (1882) 3.938, 940–2, whom I accept on this; note the hint of glory for the "humble Christian" in Montanus's "oracles": Epiph.,

Panar. 48.10, very touchingly; J. Rezette, Antonianum (1974) 14, takes Tert., De Bapt. to show that the Spirit was manifest at baptism only.

21. G. Salmon, D.C.B. (1882) 3.941.
22. 2 Cor. 11.14.
23. Acts 15.28.
24. Apost. Const. 3.8; Cypr., Ep. 16.3. Cypr., Ep. 66.8 with A. Harnack, Z.N.T. (1902) 177 and P. R. L. Brown, Making of L.A. (1978) 79–80.
25. P. R. L. Brown, Making of L.A. (1978) 71 is, I think, misleading here: P.G. 11.44A is Africanus, not Origen, discussing Daniel's prophetic gifts, not contemporary Christians. Orig.'s answer, in P.G. 11.72B–C still leaves open the possibility of "inspiration" as well as dreams, guidance and so forth. The text does not reveal a watershed.
26. Cypr., Ep. 39.1; cf. Eus., H.E. 6.11.1–2 for the dream and the heavenly voice to the Christian community in Jerusalem, telling them whom to choose as bishop!
27. Tert., De An. 9.4: with Waszink, but I do not think "nos" means "we Montanists," nor does 48.4 prove T. was alluding in this work to specifically Montanist experiences.
28. Cypr., Ep. 11.3 and 66.10.
29. Dionys., ap Eus., H.E. 7.7; creed, for Gregory, in Greg. Nyss. P.G. 46.911C.
30. Cypr., De Mort. 19.
31. M. Himmelfarb, Tours of Hell (1983) for these differences and full bibliogr.: Holy Week reading, Soz. H.E.7.19.
32. Full summary of views and the few texts in J. Le Goff, The Birth of Purgatory (E.T., 1984) 29–57, rightly following the received view; Tert., Adv. Marc. 4.34 and L. De Bruyne, Riv. de Arch. Crist. (1958) 87 and (1959) 183 on the refrigerium debate.
33. J. Le Goff, Birth of Purgatory (1984) 82.
34. C. H. Roberts, Manuscript, Society, Belief (1979) 68–71, on Coptic; for the texts, J. Robinson, The Nag Hammadi Library in English (1979) with introduction p. 15: not a single "Library." Cod. 6.5 (Plato); 3.3 and 5.1 (Eugnostos); 6.6, 7, 8 (Hermes).
35. Codex 6.7 with Robinson's trans. p. 299; cf. p. 53, p. 194.
36. J. Barns, in Essays on N.H. Texts . . . In Honour of P. Labib, ed. M. Kruse (1975) 9.
37. F. Wisse, in Gnosis . . . Festschrift H. Jonas (1978) pp. 431–40, a brilliant study; in essentials, supported now by T. Orlandi, H.T.R. (1982) 85, another central discovery.
38. G. M. Browne, J. C. Shelton, the late J. Barns, ed. N.H. Codices: Greek and Coptic Papyri from the Cartonnage . . . (1981) 5–11 is much more sceptical, though Letter C6 is still suggestive, more than p. 11's conclusion allows.
39. R. M. Ogilvie, Library of Lactantius (1978) 33–6; earlier, Hermes in Athenag. Leg. 28.6.
40. Plato, Rep. 589A–B with J. Robinson, N.H. Library (1979) p. 291, for translation.
41. Mark Edwards reminds me that this slight Zostrianos can hardly be the same text as provoked forty books from the philosophic Amelius (Porph., V. Plot. 16).
42. V. Pachom. Prima 22; H. Chadwick, in the Byzantine Saint . . . , ed. S. Hackel

(1981) 23, Vita Prima 42–3, 122; Vita 1.135 (visions); H. Quecke, Die Briefe Pachoms (1975) for the "code" in letters.

43. M. Dulaey, Le Rêve dans la Vie et Pensée de S. Augustin (1973) on monks; cf. Pachom., Vita 1.60; F. Refoulé, Rêve et Vie Spirituelle Chez Evagre, Vie Spirituelle, Supplem. (1961) 470, is very pertinent.
44. J. Robinson, ed., N.H. Library in English (1977) 295.
45. In general, A. Meredith, J.T.S. (1976) 313; D. E. Groh, R. C. Gregg, Early Arianism: A View of Salvation (1981) 131–63 (unconvincing); Athan., V. Anton. 35, 36, 43.
46. H. Grégoire, Byz. Zeitschr. (1929) 641–4; "angelic state," e.g. Vie de Théodore de Sykeon, ed. and trans. Festugière (1970) chaps. 1–10.
47. Apophtheg. Patr., Antony, 1; cf. 12, a very subtle story.
48. Apophtheg. Patr., Olympius 1, with P. R. L. Brown, Making of Late Antiquity (1978) 92–5: the monks' own reaction is significant and not entirely suited to the case he presents.

CHAPTER 9

The outstanding study of the grounds of persecution is G. E. M. de Sainte Croix's "Why Were the Early Christians Persecuted?" in Past and Present 26 (1963) 6, reprinted in M. I. Finley, ed., Studies in Ancient Society (1974) 210. Recent work has mainly amplified its observations: T. D. Barnes, Tertullian (1971) 143–86 is a clear survey. D. Stockton, in The Ancient Historian and His Materials, ed. B. M. Levick (1975) 199 focusses on the 1st cent. A.D.; W. H. C. Frend, Martyrdom and Persecution (1965) is a spirited study, better on the former topic than the latter. I regret that G. W. Clarke's admirable commentary on the letters of Cyprian, S.C.M. (1984) reached me too late for use, here and elsewhere: we differ on the role of certificates in the Decian persecution. W. C. Weinrich, Spirit and Martyrdom (1981) is a recent survey of Christian and Jewish ideals. G. Lanata, Gli Atti dei Martiri Come Documenti Processuali (1973) is the most recent study of the texts' claims to authenticity. For Augustine's criteria, see the intriguing new letter 29, ed. J. Divjak, C.S.E.L. (1981).

I

1. K. T. Ware, Orthodox Church (1980) 20.
2. Migne, P.L. 115.703–870 (Eulogio, the eventual archbishop of Toledo); P.L. 221.500–56 (Alvaro). These fascinating texts were discussed most recently by N. Daniel, The Arabs and Medieval Europe (1975) chap. 2.
3. Passio Perp. et Fel. 21 with H. Musurillo, Acts of Christian Martyrs (1972) 131 n. 21.
4. L. Robert, Les Gladiateurs . . . (1940) 188; 301 ff.; pl. 12 and J.R.S. (1981) 137 with n. 222. Pass. Perp. et Fel. 20.
5. Marcus, Med. 11.3; P. A. Brunt, Studies in Lat. Lit. . . . , ed. C. Deroux I (1979) 484–94 is, I think, too logical in deleting this as a gloss.
6. M. Pion. 8.4; M. Polyc. 9–10, where I assume the "oath" is among the "other usual things they say."
7. Acta Phil., Col 8. 125 f.; M. Pion. 19.10.
8. E. A. Reymond and J. W. B. Barns, Four Martyrdoms from the Pierpont Morgan Coptic Codices (1973) pp. 146 and 148, with preface, 9 ff.

9. Acts 7.55; Aristot., Hist. An. 491B; Polemo, in Scriptores Physiog. Graeci (ed. Foerster-Hoffmann) 1.274; also "criminal," in Adeimant. (ed. Foerster-Hoffmann) 1.335 and 338. Didascalia (ed. Connolly) chap. 19, on martyr as God's "angel" and reflector. Mth. 10.32, on denying: a very favourite text in Cyprian's writings.

10. Eus., H.E. 5.1.20; M. Pal. 11.8–13.

11. G. E. M. de Sainte Croix, Past and Present (1963) 6–38 is fundamental; T. D. Barnes, J.R.S. (1968) 32, for the individual evidence, and Tertullian (1971) chap. 11, for general view.

12. Eus. 4.26.5–6, with de Sainte Croix, J.T.S. (1967) 219 and Brunt (1979, op. cit.) 501; M. Apollonii 24 (Greek text; ed. Musurillo); Eus. 6.28, with G. W. Clarke, Historia (1966) 445.

13. Pliny 10.96 f.; on Hadrian, E. Bickermann, Riv. di Fil. (1968) 296–315, a fine study.

14. N. Lewis, Life in Egypt under Roman Rule (1983) p. 140.

15. Justin, Apol. 2.2; Hippol., Trad. 9; M. Pion. 9; M. Agape, Chione et al., 1 and 5 (perhaps fearing denunciation by family to officials); M. Perp. et Fel. 3.

16. G. Lopuszanki, L'Antiqu. Classique (1951) 1 ff. is excellent on the texts and their meaning.

17. Melito, ap. Eus., H.E. 4.26.5; Marinus, ap. H.E. 7.15.2.

18. Dionys., Eus., H.E. 7.11.9; Tert., Ad Scap. 4.1–4; Cypr. Ep. 55.2, on incense.

19. Brunt, Studies in Lat. Lit. . . . , ed. C. Deroux 1 (1979) 514, for this point.

20. In detail, F. Millar, Entretiens du Fondat. Hardt 19 (1972) 145 ff.

21. Tert., Apol. 28.2–36.4; cf. Dionys., Eus., H.E. 7.11.8; Acta Scill. 3.

22. Acta Scill. 20; de Sainte Croix (1963) n. 209, showing that "flagitia" were known to Greek and Latin authors alike; on Fronto, Min. Fel. 9.6, ingeniously placed by E. Champlin, Fronto and Antonine Rome (1980) 64–6.

23. Insults, in Jos. C. Ap. II.79–96; 109–14: on converts, Mth. 23.15.

24. Gibbon, vol. II, chap. 16 (ed. Bury, 1909) 80.

25. On sacrifices, Philo, Leg. 157, 317; Jos., C. Ap. II.77, with E. M. Smallwood, Jews under Roman Rule (1976) 147 and n. 20; on views of Rome, esp. N. R. M. de Lange, in Imperialism in the Ancient World, ed. Garnsey-Whittaker (1978) 255–81; on prayer, E. Schürer, Hist. of Jewish People II (1979, rev.) 461 section 12. On loyalty formula, P. M. Fraser, Ptol. Alex. I (1972) 282 ff.; on Sardis, B.A.S.O.R. 187 (1967) p. 25, though the reading may be Severus, not Verus, and the exact context is unclear; M. F. Squarciapino, Archaeology (1963) 203.

26. E. M. Smallwood, Jews under Roman Rule (1976) 120 ff., for Jos. C. Ap. 2.44 and A.J. 12.147–53, both of which I accept, noting the later prominence of Jews in these areas. For Caesar's rulings, A.J. 14.215–6; 221: A.J. 13.27 ff. presumes military exemption.

27. A. Plassart, R.E.G. (1967) 372–8 for G.'s date: the older, "long" chronology, bringing Paul to Rome in 60 is now most implausible. E. Haenchen, The Acts (1970) p. 71, where I disagree with his interpretation of 24.27 (p. 68); M. T. Griffin, Seneca (1975) 449–51, for a short scheme, perhaps rightly, but 20.31 is then difficult, as she sees. I cannot pursue this open question here, but I reject Eus.-Jer.'s date for Festus's arrival.

28. Acts 27.24, refuting Cadbury's idea that Paul was never tried.

29. Acts 23.25; in papyri, H. Zilliacus, Unters. zu den abstrakten Andredeformen und Höflichkeitstiteln im Griech (1949) esp. 54 ff. is the best survey; in early Imperial epigraphy, note O.G.I.S. 614.4–5 (governor of Arabia); 629.168

(Corbulo); 667.4 (prefect of Egypt); in texts, Jos. A.J. 20.12 (governor of Syria). Josephus, C. Apion 1.1 is an exact parallel for use in a preface: on either view, Epaphroditus was a very prominent person.

30. Luke 23.47, with G. D. Kilpatrick, J.T.S. (1942) 34–6.

31. P. Garnsey, J.R.S. (1968) 51 stressed the delay, but denied the "appeal," suggesting the arcane "reiectio Romam" instead: its very existence is uncertain (H. M. Cotton, J.R.S. 1979, 39). A. W. Lintott, A.N.R.W. 1.2 (1972) esp. 263–7 restates the case for appeal, rightly, and notes the argument from language (Acts' epikaloumai = provoco): Acts 25.11.

32. H. J. Cadbury's excellent Making of Luke—Acts (1958) 310 ff. stressed the Gospel trial and Acts' apologetic hearings.

33. A. N. Sherwin-White, Rmn. Society and Rmn. Law in the N.T. (1963) 108 and n. 1 for discussion: I do not agree that Paul was tried long after the "two years" of open arrest, as that makes Acts' ending most odd. For Nero's laziness, cf. p. 111.

34. Juv., Sat. 1.155–7, no stray association of ideas, to my mind. Tac., Ann. 14.57 and M. Griffin, Seneca (1975) 363 for T. and an earlier scapegoat.

35. 1 Clem. 1.1, reasserted by L. W. Barnard, Studies in Church History and Patristics (1978) 139–42, convincingly.

36. Suet., Dom. 13.2.

37. Eus., Chronicon II.218 (P.G. 19.531), quoting Bruttius, on whom see R. Syme, Historia (1960) 374–6 and H.S.C.P. (1982) 189 with n. 50: a Bruttius also tried the Scillitan martyrs in 180: was he our source? Syncellus (ed. Dindorf, 1829) p. 650 uses Eus. E. M. Smallwood, C.P. (1956) 8–9 does not convince me (p. 13 n. 39 mistook Bruttius).

38. Eus., H.E. 3.19 ff., dismissed, admittedly, by T. D. Barnes, J.R.S. (1968) 35 and his Tertullian (1971) 105, not, I think, conclusively.

## II

1. Tert., De Fuga 5 and 12–14; L. W. Countryman, The Rich Christian . . . (1980) 135, 188. De Fuga 5.3, on Rutilius.

2. Cypr. 77.3 and J. G. Davies, Univ. Birmingham Hist. Jo. 6 (1957–8) 20.

3. Orig., C. Cels. 3.8.

4. A. M. Emmett, S. R. Pickering, Prudentia (1975) 95.

5. See now A. Pietersma, The Acts of Phileas (1984) 14–23.

6. M. Polyc. 18.3 with 22.3 ff. and W. Rordorf, Irenikon (1972) 315.

7. Cypr., Ep. 39; P. R. L. Brown, The Cult of the Saints (1981) for a brilliant study of the aftermath.

8. Melito F 10; cf. already Hermas 9.28.6; Hippol., Apost. Trad. 19.2; even a catechumen's sins are wiped out. Tert., De Anim. 55.4–5.

9. Justin, Apol. 1.57; on combat, F. J. Dölger, Ant. u. Christ. (1933) 177.

10. Mth. 10.19; Cypr., Ep. 10.4, in early April 250 (the Pythian games?).

11. M. Lyons (ed. Musurillo) section 41.

12. 4 Macc. 17.8; cf. 2 Macc. 7.9 ff.; on dating, A. Dupont-Sommer, Le Quatrième Livre des Macchabées (1939). I am indebted to lectures and discussion by G. E. M. de Sainte Croix, the connoisseur of this subject, for several points which follow.

13. 4 Macc. 16.25; 4 Macc. persistently uses athletic imagery for martyrs: e.g. 17.15 ff. St. Paul was not innovating.

14. Jos., B.J. 1.33.2–4; Schürer, Hist. of Jewish People (revised, 1973) 1, pp. 552–3 for Bar Kokhba martyrs; H. Fischel, J.Q.R. (1946–7) 265 and 363, and T. W. Manson, B.J.R.L. (1956–7) 463 for martyr prophets, some of whose texts are late and may be a response to Christian martyr writings; Hebr. 11.37, surely alludes to Isaiah's hideous death.

15. Acts 7.55–6; cf. Isaac, in G. Vermes, Scripture and Tradition (1961) 195 n. 6; Fischel, J.Q.R. (1946–7) 364–71; Rev. 7.14–15.

16. O. Perler, Riv. di Archeol. Crist. (1949) 47 emphasized this, at times too strongly.

17. Ign., Eph. 11.

18. 4 Macc. 17.22 with Ign., Eph. 8.1 and K. Bommes, Weizen Gottes (1976) esp. 221 ff.; Orig., Exh. Mart. 30 and 50 and esp. Comm. in John 6.54, on martyrs as "scapegoats."

19. H. von Campenhausen, Sitzb. Heidelb. (1957) Abh. 3, 1–48 wrongly presumed a later "Gospel redactor." Cf. Cypr., Ep. 27.3, 36.2 and 37.4 and H. Paulsen, Studien zur Theologie des Ignatius (1978) 180 ff.

20. E.g. M. Lyons 19 and 56 (ed. Musurillo).

21. M. Mar. and Jas. 6.12, 11.9.

22. Cypr., Ep. 10.2–3.

23. W. H. C. Frend, Religion Popular and Unpopular (1976) 27–37.

24. Acta Scill. 15 and the rose-bunch vision in M. Mar. and Jas. 11.5–6.

25. M. Perp. 10 with L. Robert, C.R.A.I. (1982) 228 ff.; feminists have overemphasized 10.7.

26. Against excessive theories of the text's influence, V. Lomanto, in Forma Futuri . . . Studi. M. Pellegrino (1975) 566–86; despite P. Godman, Poetry of the Carolingian Renaissance (1985) 66, I can see no evidence of Perpetua's influence on Notker's poetry.

27. Cypr., Ep. 31.3 ff.

28. Cypr., Ep. 21.1–2; Lucian, in Cypr., Ep. 22, an amazing letter: I assume the "claritas" in 22.2 is Christian, and symbolic.

29. Eus., H.E. 5.3.4; T. D. Barnes, Constantine and Eusebius (1981) 199.

30. Tert., Apol. 50.15 (rhetorical question) and Justin, Apol. 2.12, claiming only that martyrs made him doubt the tales of flagitia. M. Perp. 17.2–3, omitted, recently, by R. MacMullen, Christianizing the Roman Empire (1984) 29–30; cf. M. Pion. 7.1.

31. E.g. Cyprian Ep. 31.3 and M. Lods, Confesseurs et Martyrs (1958) 54.

32. Tert., Ad Scap. 5; G. de Sainte Croix, H.T.R. (1954) 83, 93, 101–4, a constant reminder of volunteers; Eus., H.E. 7.12.

33. Clem., Strom. 4.10.76–7; 7.11.66–7; Orig. in John 28.23; also M. Polyc. 4, Tertull. Cor. Mil. 1, on protesters at "cupido mori"; Acta Cypr. 1.6 and Cypr., Ep. 81.1; Ignat., Ad Rom. 4.

34. E.g. M. Ptol. and Luc. (Musurillo) 15; M. Lyons 9; Passio Perp. 4.5; M. Basileides 9.3–7; Eus., H.E. 6.41.16 and 22–3; Acta Cypr. 5.1; Mar. and Jas. 9.2–4; Acta Phileae (Latin) 7, Eus. M. Pal., is abundant in cases, listed by de Sainte Croix, H.T.R. (1954) 101–3; M. Pal. 5.2–3 and 11.15–19 for those I quote.

35. M.P. 3.2–4 and Acta Eupli (Musurillo), with T. D. Barnes, New Empire (1982) 177, doubting the concluding sections.

36. Petr. Alex., Canon. Epist. sections 8 and 11; G. W. Clarke, Historia (1973) 655–8 for texts.

37. Cyprian, De Lapsis 16; Ep. 21.2, on Lord's anger; importantly, compare Didascalia (ed. Connolly) chap. 19.
38. Mth. 10.23; Ign., Ad Rom. 1 and 4.
39. E. Dassmann, Sündenvergebung durch Taufe, Busse u. Martyrer Fürbitte (1973) 153 ff., for texts. E.g. Orig., Comm. in Cant. 3: In Lev. Hom. 4.4; Exh. Mart. 30.
40. M. Polyc. 7.2–3; M. Fruct. 3.6; Eus., M.P. 8.10; M. Mont. et Luc. 3.4; Ign., Ad Eph. 11.
41. M. Perp. 10.4–6 with F. Dölger, Vorträge der Bibliot. Warburg (1926) 196.
42. Ign., Rom. 4; M. Polyc. 17.1; M. Fruct. 6.3, where I cite only the short recension; Act. Thom. 170.
43. M. Perp. 8 with F. Dölger, Ant. u. Christ. 2 (1930) 1; M. Pot. and Bas. 6 ff.; Act. Paul. et Theclae 28–29; M. Perp. 17.
44. Survey in T. Klauser, Christlicher Märtyrerkult . . . , originally in Arbeitsgemeinsch. für Forsch. des Landes Nordrhein-Westfalen, Heft 91 (1960). He cites Num. 19.16, but pp. 37–8 look to problems of authority and tradition in the early Church for a further answer, to my mind unconvincingly. Mth. 23.29–31, with J. Jeremias, Heiligengräber in Jesu's Umwelt (1958), whom I follow here: these graves were not "official."
45. Didasc. 19 (Connolly), cited by Klauser, p. 34 n. 29.
46. V. Cronin, The Wise Man from the West (1984, ed.) p. 181.
47. Forgiveness, in mid-2nd-cent. texts, already: Eus., H.E. 5.1.45; 5.2.5; 5.18.6 (against Montanus's "martyrs"); cf. Cypr., Ep. 15–16; 17.2; 20–3; 27; 35–6; Dionys., H.E. 6.42.5–6.
48. Tert., De Pud. 22; Ad Ux. 2.4.1; with Ad Mart. 1.6; De Paen. 9.4; Scorp. 10.8.
49. I. Goldziher, Muslim Studies, II (1971 ed.) pp. 350–4. Shi'ite martyrs were, however, different.
50. Cypr. Ep. 37.1, for confession; note M. Perp. 7, when P. knows she must now die.
51. 1 John 5.16; continuing confessor letters, in Can. Elvira 25 and Arles 9.
52. A necessary preliminary to the great study by P. R. L. Brown, J.R.S. (1971) 80.

### III

1. G. W. Clarke, Historia (1966) 445 for this case.
2. Cypr. Ep. 16.4.
3. Orig., C. Cels. 3.15, with H. Chadwick's preface pp. xiv.
4. Eus., H. E. 6.41, "mantis kai poiētēs": the translation "prophet and cause" would also be possible.
5. P. J. Parsons, J.R.S. (1967) 134 and P. Oxyr. 3046–50; on the 290s, Optatus's edict and Domitian's revolt, T. D. Barnes, New Empire (1982) 11–12, 230–1, with bibliogr.
6. R. Syme, Emperors and Biography (1971) 195–8; on coins, K. J. J. Elks, The Coinage of Trajan Decius (1971), with bibliogr. to earlier studies.
7. J. H. Oliver, G.R.B.S. (1978) 375: the "Eis Basilea" is a mid-3rd-cent. work.
8. Syme, Emperors and Biography (1971) 198–9, for wars; on famine, Mart. Pionii 10.7–8, not isolated, I assume.
9. E.g. Greg. Nyss., P. G. 46.944B.
10. Ann. Epig. (1973) no. 235, with C. L. Babcock's suggestions, A.J.P. (1962) 157; Syme, op. cit. 197 and n. 7, on D.'s connections.

11. Eus. 6.39.1; Or. Sib. 13.86–8 is no support; (i) the reading "pistōn" is only Wilamowitz's in line 87; (ii) nothing else in the text requires a Christian author; (iii) the Ms. reading "autika d'au piptōn" inclines me to read "autika kappesetai" (cf. line 80) and thus carry on from the preceding gen. absolute. The next words then start a separate clause. This would ease the problems.

12. H. A. Pohlsander, Historia (1980) 463, for texts; G. W. Bowersock, Roman Arabia (1983) pp. 125–6 does not distinguish the "rumour" from E.'s other material.

13. Dionys., ap. Eus., H.E. 6.41.9 and H.E. 7.10.3, a very telling aside.

14. Cypr., Ep. 39.2 and 22.2 with the excellent study of G. W. Clarke, Antichthon (1969) 63 ff.; p. 64 n. 5: his ancestry.

15. Eus. 6.41.11; in Antioch, one of the festivals for Babylas's death falls in January, but he died in prison (H.E. 6.39.5 ff.) and it may be 251, not 250.

16. G. W. Clarke, B.I.C.S. (1973) 118; Historia (1973) 650; Latomus (1972) 1053 for details; the M. Pionii suffices to prove Jews were exempted.

17. Cypr., Ep. 20 is classic here; 20.2 mentions impious libelli and goes on to allude to what seems to be Letter 15. Its review of past letters is in sequence, and Ep. 15 is placed in May. "Libelli" were known (and first offered?) from mid-April, at least.

18. Most recently, P. Keresztes, Latomus (1975) 761; texts in J. R. Knipfing, H.T.R. (1923) 345; J. Schwarz, Rev. Biblique (1947) 365, with important discussion; P.S.I.778; P. Oxy. 2990.

19. Knipfing 11, 26: cf. Schwarz, op. cit. for other details; the Arsinoite one is numbered, whereas Theadelphian ones are not: perhaps they were discarded first.

20. P. Keresztes (1975), for this idea: I incline to it, as the Mart. Pionii does not mention "libelli," despite its exact observations in Feb./Mar. 250. Cypr., Ep. 20.2 is the first ref: ? early May 250.

21. Knipfing, H.T.R. (1923) no. 3; on scribes and papyri, Schwarz, p. 367.

22. Working from Knipfing (1923): some women do cite children too. P.S.I. 778: also females. Cf. Cypr., Ep. 6.3; 55.13; De Lapsis 2.

23. E.g. Knipfing (1923) nos. 5; 20; 21; Mart. Pion. 11.2, with part IV of this chapter; on households, Cypr. 55.13.

24. Cypr., Ad Don. 10.

25. Cypr., De Lapsis 11 with the notable comments of L. W. Countryman, The Rich Christian (1980) pp. 190 ff.

26. Slaves: e.g. Knipfing, no. 20; perhaps Cypr., De Lapsis 25 and Ep. 15.4; cf. Peter of Alexandria, Can. Epist. 5–8.

27. Cypr. Ep. 11.1; 13.4; 14.3; 15.3; De Laps. 16; De Unitate 20: "fraudes, stupra et adulteria."

28. I quote Cypr. Ep. 27.1; 15.4; 20.1; 15.4, again.

29. Cypr., Ep. 6.1.1–2.

30. Cypr., Ep. 21.4, on confessors; Ep. 66.8, end.

31. Acta Acaci (Knopf-Krüger) 57–60; Trypho, in Studi e Testi (1908) 27; Polyeuctus, Mon. of Early Christianity, ed. F. C. Conybeare (1894) 126; S. Binon, Essai sur le Cycle de S. Mercure (1937); on Cassian, J. B. Keates, Companion Guide to Shakespeare Country (1979) p. 111.

32. Eus. 4.15.46–7; H. A. Musurillo, Acts of the Christian Martyrs (1972) xxviii–xxix. On the texts, S. Gero, J.J.S. (1978) p. 164 n. 1, with bibliogr. The

Armenian, in M. Srapian, Wiener Ztschr. für d. Kunde d. Morgenlandes 28
(1914) 376, which was checked for me by Prof. C. Dowsett; the Slavonic, in
Codex Suprasliensis, ed. S. Severjanov, vol. I (1904) 124: Prof. J. Fennell kindly
translated it for me.

33. R. Naumann, S. Kantar, in Kleinasien u. Byzanz (Istanbuler Forsch. 17, 1950)
70–114 with L. Robert, O.M.S. IV.325; for a glimpse of the goddesses, L.
Robert, B.C.H. (1982) 376.

34. M. Pion. 3.7, with Musurillo's remarkable mistranslation. A. Chastagnol,
M.E.F.R.E. (1981) p. 386 line 28 (Orcistus); I.G.R.R. IV.1414; L.R., Op. Min.
Sel. II 1349–50 with n. 3; Chastagnol, p. 406. Prof. C. Dowsett has helped me
with the "kibotia"; Armenian "arkel" = cases, or boxes, but Srapian's "hütten"
is also possible: "kibotia" may derive from Iranian or Pahlavi "kywt," Turkic
(Tobol) "kibit" (booth); Russian "kibitka" (nomad felt tent); whence our
"caboodle" (German-Yiddish dim. in -l). "Whole caboodle" = German "der
ganze Kram" (tent, or booth cover, and thus booth, or stall).

## IV

L. Robert has long promised a full commentary on this martyrdom, which will
doubtless correct and enlarge what follows; Hellenica 11–12 (1960) 269 n. 9; R.E.A.
(1960) 319 n. 1; Ann. Collège de France (1960) 331; for an unpublished lecture in
Warsaw, 1968, see his Op. Min. Sel. IV, 325. Meanwhile, the most helpful discussion
and translation is by C. J. Cadoux, Ancient Smyrna (1938) pp. 374 ff.

1. Despite C. J. Cadoux, Anc. Smyrna (1938) 306 n. 1, the "Life of Polycarp" is a
patent fake, though a fascinating one: cf. H. Delehaye, Les Passions des Martyrs
(1966) 33 ff., decisively.

2. B.M.C. Ionia, p. 263.

3. M. Agape 5.8; Tert., De Monog. 15; Apolog. 50; Eus., H.E. 6.5; Jhb. Ant. u.
Christ. (1960) 70–111.

4. P. Herrmann, Denkschr. Akad. Wien 77 (1959) no. 7, pp. 10–11; L. Robert,
Villes d'Asie Mineure, 2nd ed., p. 410 n. 2 for the area; G. Barbieri, L'Albo
Senatorio (1952) no. 347 for husband.

5. J. B. Pighi, De Ludis Saecularibus (1965, rpr.) 140 ff.

6. J. B. Pighi (1965) 157.

7. G. Hanfmann, From Croesus to Constantine (1973) chaps. 3–4; B.A.S.O.R.
177 (1965) 24–5 and C. R. Morey, Sardis, 5.1.

8. W. M. Calder, B.J.R.L. (1923) esp. 29–41.

9. Cf. Orig., C. Cels. 5.20–1 (Socrates); Tatian, Or. 19.12 (Anaxarchus's
"doxomania"); Tert., Apol. 50.

10. (a) Mionnet, III.237; (b) "sophist": B.M.C. Ionia, 283–4; 287; 291; (c) Under
Gordian, Mionnet III.249. For a Rufinus, distinct from these, in Marcus's reign,
cf. C.I.G. II.3176. It is, of course, possible that "Rufinus the sophist" under
Gordian is a kinsman of the Claudius Rufinus under Severus.

11. R. Münsterberg, Num. Zeitschr. 8 (1915) 119, a very acute study, omitted,
however, by Bowersock's longer Greek Sophists (1969) and even by the
penetrating study of sophists by E. L. Bowie, Y.C.S. (1982) 29.

12. Str. 14.446, on books; Robert, Et. Anat. 137 ff.; Magie, Roman Rule II.1445 n.
47; I.G.R.R. IV.1446–7; 1449.

13. E.g. Claudius Proclus the sophist under Hadrian, Marcus and Verus. R. Münsterberg, Die Beamtennamen (1911) p. 105.

14. Philostr., V.S. 272; C. Habicht, Die Inschr. des Asklepeions (1969) 76–7.

15. B.M.C. Ionia, p. 283 and pl. 29.10; S.I.G.[3] 876; I differ on the detailed context from Bowersock, Greek Sophists (1969) 41 and V. Nutton, J.R.S. (1971) 54.

16. G. W. Lampe, Lexikon, s.v. kenodoxein, for a rich list of parallels, esp. in Jo. Chrys.

17. I.G. II/III[2] 4218–9 with Barnes, J.T.S. (1968) 531. The Chronicon Paschale (ed. Bonn) 1.504 tacks Pionius's death onto its year 251, but the connection is loose and clearly a derivative error for 250, stemming from its ultimate source, our text.

18. B.M.C. 265 and 294 with M. Pion. 18.3 and 8.

19. M. Pion. 11.2; P. Herrmann, Sitzb. Akad. Wien 265 (1969) 43–4 with L.R., Villes d'Asie Min., p. 32; B.C.H. (1887) p. 86 n. 5 and p. 311; on assizes, Pliny, N.H. 5.111; J.R.S. (1975) 71–2; cf. J. and L. Robert, Hellenica 6 (1948) 16–26.

20. Cypr., Ep. 10.1–2 and Eus., H.E. 6.41.16–21.

21. Monuments of Early Christianity, ed. F. C. Conybeare (1894) 146.

22. L. Robert, C.R.A.I. (1982) 228.

23. I forbear to give chapter and verse to the texts, printed in H. A. Musurillo, Acts of Christian Martyrs (1972); most recently, F. Dolbeau, Rev. Et. Aug. (1983) 39–82.

24. M. Pion. 10.5 and 18.13, for the "we" passages; H. Delehaye, Les Passions des Martyres et les Genres Littéraires (1921) 34.

25. M. Pion. 11.7; e.g. I.G.R.R. IV.1446–7.

26. Cypr., Ep. 31.4–5; Codex Sinaiticus, Fol. 19 with W. Bousset, Texte u. Unters. (1894) 45.

27. M. Pion. 9.1; Dionys., ap. Eus., H.E. 7.11.6.

28. M. Pion. 19.1; R. A. Coles, Atti dell' XI Congr. Internaz. di Papirol. (1968) 118–25; L.R., Et. Anat. 137 ff. with Ruinart, Acta Mart. (1859) 451 ff.

29. H. Delehaye, Les Passions des Martyrs . . . , pp. 33–6, most ingeniously; with him I accept the short ending (M. Polyc. 22.2–3), and also the longer one, in the Moscow Ms., which amplifies Irenaeus's part: I see no reason why P. could not have written this longer ending too. Contra, L. W. Barnard, Kyriakon (1970) 192–3. M. Polyc. 22.3 does not presuppose the (4th-cent.) bogus Vita Polycarpi. Discussion now in B. Dehandschutter, Martyrium Polycarpi (1979) 63.

30. Pliny, Ep. 3.5.4, with C. A. Behr, Aelius Ar. (1968) p. 46 n. 2.

31. Cypr., Ep. 21.3: "vel in terra dormiens" is, I think, a general reference to his dreams (like Joseph's), not to his dreams in prison only.

32. S. Byman, Amer. Hist. Rev. 83 (1978) 625, for ideas on this.

33. Ael. 16.15; 21.14; 22.8; C.I.G. II. 3165; L.R., Jo. des Sav. (1961) 155, praises of towns' sites.

34. C.I.G. II.3202.

35. M. Mar. and Jas. 12.7.

36. L. Robert, Villes d'Asie Min., pp. 280–317; also in Anatolia (1958) 33–4: I will discuss Typhon and his lairs elsewhere.

37. Ael. Ar. 16.11; Sacred Tales 2.7, 2.50, 3.43; L.R., Villes d'Asie Min., p. 291 n. 2.

38. H. Windisch, Ztschr. Deutsch. Palästin-Vereins 48 (1923) 145; A. E. Harvey, J.T.S. (1966) 401 and now, the superb study by E. D. Hunt, Holy Land Pilgrimage . . . (1982). Eus., H. E. 4.26.14 (Melito); Jer., De Vir. Illustr. 54 (Firm.); Orig., C. Cels. 1.51; 4.44; Comm. in John 6.41; for the Cave, Protev. Jac. 18. Note Eus., Dem. Ev. 6.13.7.

39. Orig., P.G. 11.604C; H. Kruse, Studien zur Offiz. Geltung des Kaiserbilds . . . (1934) 79–85; L.R., R.E.A. (1960) 319 n. 1; Reymond-Barns, Four Martyrdoms . . . , p. 21.

40. M. Pion. 8.4: for "kai" in this sense, cf. 7.2.

41. M. Pion. 7.1.

42. W. Jaeger, Early Christianity and Greek Paideia (1965) 24–5, but he underplays this continuing contrast.

43. Jos., B.J. 4.476; Tac., Hist. 5.6; Paus. 5.7.4–5; Galen 11.690 (Kuhn).

44. Cypr., Ep.11.1; De Laps. 5.

45. J. Parkes, Conflict of Church and Synagogue (1934) 144–5 nobly took the scene as an open offer of protection, but his reasons were unconvincing, and I cannot follow him.

46. M. Pion. 13.8, where the Christians "conjure up" Jesus (cf. 14.14; mistaken by Musurillo); "with the sign of the cross," surely, not "appearing with his cross" (despite S. Gero, J.J.S. 1978, 168, n. 3–4). E.g. Tert., Cor. Mil. 3, on use of sign of cross.

47. P. W. Van Der Horst, V.C. (1971) 282, for later discussion; cf. R. Hirzel, A.R.W. (1908).

48. Tert., De Anim. 56, with Waszink's full notes; E. Klostermann, Origenes, Eustathius u. Gregor v. Nyssa über die Hexe von Endor (1912), for details; Jos., A.J. 6.14.2 thinks a demon appeared; Justin, Dial. 105.4 and Orig., Hom. on I Kings 28 disagree. For more, K. A. Smelik, V.C. (1979) 60 and on Jewish texts, S. Gero, J.J.S. (1978) 164–8, with the Caesarea dialogue in B. Shab. 152B, at his p. 167 n. 20.

49. L.R., Hellenica 11–12 (1960) 260–2, esp. 262 n. 9; C.I.J. 739.

50. C.I.J. 742, well explained by A. T. Kraabel, J.J.S. (1982) 455.

51. C.I.J. 740–1 and 743; E. R. Goodenough, Jewish Symbols II, pp. 79–81, on buildings of Jews in Smyrna; L.R., Hellenica 11–12 (1960) 391 n. 2; S. Reinach, R.E.J. 7 (1883) 166 on Rufina's origins.

52. Rev. 2.9; M. Polyc. 17.2.

53. E.g. L.R., Hellenica 10, pp. 249–51 (Jew, strategos at Acmoneia); cf. L. R., Jo. des Sav. (1975) 158–9; Hellenica 11–12, p. 384 (Ephesus); 436 ff. (Eumeneia); H. Leclercq, D.A.C.L. 1.2 (1907) 2515 ff., on Apamea and the Ark; L.R., Nouvelles Inscr. de Sardes (1964) 56–7 and A. T. Kraabel, in Mélanges M. Simon, ed. A. Benoît (1978) 13–33, arguing on p. 19 for a possible late date for Jewish ownership of the Sardis building. Jos. 14.235 and 260 ff. for their "place" earlier in the city: the history of the complex is necessarily uncertain in its details.

54. A. T. Kraabel, Studies G.M.A. Hanfmann, ed. D. G. Milten (1971) 77, on Melito.

55. Jo. Chrys. P. G. 48.847, 861, 907 and M. Simon, Mélanges Cumont (1936) 403; J. Parkes, Conflict of Church and Synagogue (1934) 175–6; M. Simon, Verus Israel (1948) 144 ff.

56. E.g. Tert., Adv. Marc. 3.23, "seminarium infamiae nostrae"; Adv. Jud. 1.13;

Justin, Dial. 17.1 alleges a worldwide smear campaign in the Apostolic age.

57. N. R. M. de Lange, Origen and the Jews (1976), for texts, though his use of later rabbinic sources is questionable.

58. Orig., C. Cels. 1.28 ff.; on Panthera, Chadwick, C. Celsum, p. 31; Eus., Eccl. Proph. 3.10; on a possible early date for the "anti-Gospels," S. Gero, J.J.S. (1978) 164 ff.

59. P. Franchi de Cavalieri, Scritti Agiografici II, in Studi e Testi 222 (1962) 79 ff. is fundamental, linking the text to M. Nestor, and (p. 84) suggesting a local "laboratorio agiografico": p. 84 n. 1 does not prove dependence on our M. Pion., however. At M. Cononis (ed. Musurillo) 2.1, the "father," at this date, would have to be an honorary title, not a civic office. The "singularii" and the city's own "regiment of the Eirenarch" are convincing details. For the site, R.E. xiv (1928) 521; J. C. Mossop, N.C. (1970) 319–20.

60. L.R., Rev. Philol. (1958) 40–7, synagogue at Side, one of several: the Beth Shearim inscription cited on p. 40 n. 1 is differently punctuated, perhaps rightly, by M. Schwabe, Beth Shearim II (1974) 190–1.

61. M. Polyc. 3.1; for dating, T. D. Barnes, J.T.S. (1968) 512 and now R. Syme, Z.P.E. 51 (1983) 280–2, decisive on Quadratus's governorship: Eus.'s date is wrong again. On the Philippus crux, C. A. Behr, Aelius Ar. (1968) p. 98 n. 15, for solutions. 155/6 or 156/7 seem secure, now, for M. Polyc.

62. G. Talamanca, L'Organizzazione del "Conventus" del Praef. Egypti (1974), discussing changes over time and citing the basic works by Wilcken; G. P. Burton, J.R.S. (1975) 92 ff.; against C. P. Jones, Roman World of Dio (1978) p. 67, I doubt that Dio 35.15 means "in alternate years," for Phrygia's assizes: "par' etos" also means "yearly." On Asia, Pliny N.H. 5.110–20 with L.R., Hellenica 7 (1949) 206, a brilliant study confirmed by C. Habicht, J.R.S. (1975) 64; cf. N. Lewis, B.A.S.P. (1982) 119.

63. Dig. 1.16.6 (legates can only give prelim. hearing): cf. 1.16.11.

64. Plut., Mor. 501 E–F, with C. P. Jones, Plutarch and Rome (1971) 14.

65. Aelius Ar. 17 and 21 (Keil): 21.16, for governors.

66. M. Polyc. 12.2; L. Robert, Les Gladiateurs dans l'Orient Grec (1940) 202–14; 233; 284; 309 ff.

67. Moral. 501 E with Pliny N.H. 5.120 (Maced. Hyrcani in Smyrna's district) and A. B. Cook, Zeus II.2, p. 873 for Smyrna's Zeus; we should read "Akraios" not (with Wilamowitz) "Askraios" in Plut.'s text.

68. Ael. Ar. 17.6; Philostr., V.S. p. 106 (Loeb); L.R., B. Epig. 1968.402, for festivals and assizes.

69. Most recently, but unsuccessfully, W. Rordorf, Pietas . . . für B. Kötting, Jhrb. A. u. C. Erganzbd. 8 (1980) 243.

70. John 19.31.

71. I. Elbogen, Der Jüd. Gottesdienst . . . (1962) 155–9.

72. J. B. Lightfoot, Apostolic Fathers. Part II (1889) 710–12, for this theory: M. Goodman has helped me to accept it, citing C. Theod. 16.8.18, but pointing out that there are problems for 250, if we assume Purim fell on 14th or 15th Adar (depending on Smyrna's status: Danby, Mishnah p. 201). By E. J. Bickermann, Chronology (1968) pp. 139–40 and the table of new moons, Purim fell on February 22/23 in 251, not 250. I cannot reject our Martyrdom's firm consular dating, and the whole scene belongs in 250, when the edict was in its early days.

I assume some local complication in calendar equations; alternatively, as M. Goodman remarks, the Sabbath before Purim was Shabbat Zachor, when Deut. 25.17–19 was read to recall the past enemies of the Jews (Danby, Mishnah, p. 205). But I doubt if this was a "great Sabbath" and I stand by Purim 250.

73. Contrast W. H. C. Frend, Martyrdom and Persecution (1965) 130: a "people apart"; Abodah Zarah 1.1, on avoiding festivals; H. Chadwick, Early Christianity and Classical Culture (1967) 125.7 on "Iao Dionysus"; Plut., Qu. Conv. 4.6.1 with M. Stern, Gk. and Lat. Authors on Jews and Judaism 1 (1974) 259; Tac., Hist. 5.5.

74. Admirably seen by G. P. Burton, J.R.S. (1975) p. 96 n. 42–4; Tert., Ad Scap. 3.3; Cypr., Ep. 81.1; Acta Cypr. 2.3. I agree with G. W. Clarke, Latomus (1972) 1053 that T. D. Barnes, Tertullian (1971) 260–1 has not established a July arrival for governors in Africa in the 2nd–3rd cent.

75. Cypr., Ep. 82.1.

76. Pontius, Vita 12–13.

77. L.R., Rev. Phil. (1934) 276; Hellenica 7 (1949) 223; Dio Chrys. 35.15; Acts 19.38; Ael. Ar., Sacr. Tal. 4.77.

78. L. Robert, Et. Anatol. (1938) 147.

79. M. Fruct. 3.1; cf. A. Phileae col. 12.120; 13.205. Pontius, Vita 14.

80. M. Mar. and Jas. 6.5–10.

81. M. Pion. 10.4 (fasces); G. W. Clarke, Antichthon (1969) 73 n. 78 on Christian bribery in prisons, and esp. Libanius, Or. 45, esp. 9–10.

82. M. Pion. 15.4–5 for the princeps, with G. Lopuszanki, L'Ant. Class. (1951) 34–7 for his high rank; cf. A. Cypr. 2.4.

83. With H. Delehaye, Anal. Boll. (1940) 146, I prefer the Latin to the Greek text, poorly defended by H. Lietzmann, Kl. Schriften I.239 ff. The Greek makes Agathonice a "volunteer," against the Latin's sober account: Greek sec. 45 (ed. Mus.) is a stock theme in bogus Acts, e.g. A. Paul and Thecla 32. The Greek's October date conflicts with April in the early martyrologies. On "Optimus," Delehaye p. 147.

84. M. Carp., Pap., Agath. (Latin) 4.5. Note Carpus is not sentenced in his home assize district (Julia Gordos marches with Sardis, J.R.S. 1975, 65). J. den Boeft, J. Bremmer, V.C. (1982) 384–5 wrongly suggest a date before 215 because Papylus, from Thyatira, would have been tried there, not at Pergamum, once Thyatira became an assize centre. Martyrs in 250 were tried where they were arrested, cf. M. Pion., 11.2 for a Karenite at Smyrna, not Sardis. For Eleusis, I.G. II/III$^2$ 4218–9.

85. T. D. Barnes, Tertullian (1971) 163 n. 3.

86. M. Pion. 21.5, with E. Peterson, Frühkirche, Judentum . . . (1959) 15, for the East, and the Moscow Ms. ending to M. Polyc. 22.3, Pionius's own, I believe (with Delehaye). The 'Sabbath' in M. Pion. 23.1 is a mistake; P. was arrested on a Sabbath, Feb. 23 (2.1) and killed on Tuesday, Mar. 12. The Armenian rightly preserves the Tuesday: M. Srapian, Wien. Zts. Kunde des Morgenlandes 28 (1914) p. 405 n. 24.

CHAPTER 10

On bishops, I wrote without knowledge of The Role of the Christian Bishop in Ancient Society, ed. E. C. Hobbs and W. Wuellner (Center for Hermeneutical

Studies, Berkeley, Protocol of 35th Colloquy, 1980), with papers by Professors Brown, Grant, MacMullen and especially Chadwick, taking the subject into the 4th and 5th cents.; on Gregory, I was helped by the audience at an Oxford seminar in 1981: the panegyric and its stories then received an article by R. van Dam, in Calif. Stud. in Class. Antiquity 13 (1982) 272: he considers "Gregory may have been perceived as an 'icon' during his own lifetime." I doubt that. R. MacMullen, Christianizing the Roman Empire (1984) 59–61 has revived the argument that the most "trustworthy derivative" of lost early work on Gregory is a Syriac version of his career. This view, advanced by V. Ryssel in 1894, was refuted decisively by P. Koetschau, in Zts. für Wiss. Theol. (1898) 211: the Syriac is a variant of our legendary panegyric, with its own touches of imaginary colour.

# I

1. Apoc. Petr. in Nag Hammadi Library (ed. J. Robinson, 1977) p. 343; cf. Tripartite Tract. on pp. 64–9.
2. Hermas, Vis. 3.9.7–10.
3. M. Perp. et Fel. 13.
4. Cypr. 31.5: "gloriosus episcopus"; Cypr., Ep. 23.
5. B. Kötting, Jhrb. A. u. C. (1976) 7: Hippol., Trad. 9; Cypr., Ep. 61.3.
6. G. Vermes, Dead Sea Scrolls (1977) 90–9, on the mebaqqer; pp. 215–9, more generally.
7. E. Schürer, Hist. of Jewish People 2 (1979) 433–6, with texts; P. Bruneau, Recherches sur les Cultes de Delos . . . (1970) 489, for chairs; I.G.R. 4.655, for Acmoneia; Smyrna, I.G.R. IV.1452 and cf. R.E.J. (1901) 2; on buildings, e.g. C.I.J. 722.
8. See esp. L. Robert, Rev. Phil. (1958) 40 ff.; Cod. Theod. 16.8.1, 2, 4, 13–14; on Elders, an open question, A. E. Harvey, J. T. S. (1974) 318 and C. H. Roberts, J.T.S. (1975) 403.
9. On rulers, J. B. Frey, C.I.J. I (1956) LXXXII; J. Juster, Les Juifs dans l'Emp. Romain II (1914) 161–2, on floggings; both, in C.I.J. 265 and 553; entry fee, at Tlos, T.A.M. II (1930) 612, "fathers" etc., M. Hengel, Z.N.W. (1966) 176–8 and for civic (not cultic) use, most recently, R. van Bremen, Images of Women . . . , ed. A. Cameron, A. Kuhrt (1983) 241.
10. S. L. Greenslade, J.T.S. (1943) 162.
11. M. Goodman, State and Soc. in Rmn. Galilee (1983), pp. 97–8 and p. 120, with refs.; Cod. Theod. 16.8.2,4; in inscrips., E. R. Goodenough, J.Q.R. (1956–7) 221–4, inc. Dura, and L.R., Hellenica 10–11 (1960) 382–4, a brilliant note. "Priestess" in Rome: C.I.J. 615; in Sardis, Samoe the priest (late date); in Dura, C. Kraeling, The Synagogue . . . (1956) VIII.1 p. 263.
12. L. I. Levine, A.N.R.W. 19.2, pp. 649, esp. pp. 663–72, with refs.; against, M. Goodman, State . . . in Rmn. Galilee (1983), pp. 111–18 (excellent), although I trust Orig., P.G. 11.84; "apostles," in Justin, Dial. 17 (but cf. Cod. Theod. 16.8.14, 399 A.D.).
13. Best text in M. Hengel, Z.N.W. (1966) 145 ff.; I follow M. Goodman, p. 242 n. 296; cf. Cod. Theod. 16.8.1–2.
14. Cypr., Ep. 49.2, Eus. 6.43.11, both remarkably similar.
15. 1 Clem. 42.4–5 with Isai. 60.17 and C. A. Evans, V.C. (1982) 105; L. Abramowski, J.T.S. (1977) 103–4, on Iren.; Tert., De Praescr. Her. 32; Cypr., Ep. 33.1 and 3.3.

16. E.g. Ign., Eph. 5.3–6.1; Magn. 3; Trall. 2.1–2; Phil. 7; Smyrn. 8–9.1.
17. Jer., Ep. 146 with W. Telfer, J.E.H. (1952) 4–6, on Egypt's Elders; F. D. Gilliard, H.T.R. (1975) 17, on Gaul; in general, E. G. Jay, in The Second Century 1 (1981) 125.
18. I cite the Didascalia in Connolly's ed. and trans.: I presuppose chaps. 4–12, 17–18 on bishops.
19. Didasc. chap. 11, esp. p. 115 (murder court); 7.54 on threats.
20. Didasc. 7.56 (Last Day).
21. I quote 5.40; cf. pp. 52–3.
22. J. Gaudemet, Rev. Sc. Rel. (1949) 64; Gal. 1.8–9; 1 Cor. 5.9–13; 1 Cor. 16.22: 1 Tim. 1.19–20: in 3 John 10, "ekballein" is the action of wicked Diotrephes: for the orthodox, following suit, e.g. Can. Elvira 20, 41, 49, esp. 52, 62.
23. Didasc. 12.4–5; Orig., In Mth. 16.8 (P.G. 13.1393B).
24. Didasc. 9.
25. 1 Tim. 3.1–7; Tit. 1.7–9; Ign., Trall. 3.1; Magn. 3.2; Smyrn. 9.1.
26. H. Chadwick, H.T.R. (1950) 169, on silence; I quote Eph. 6.1 and 15; Trall. 3 and Magn. 6.
27. I differ from P. R. L. Brown, Making of Late Antiquity (1978) 58–9.
28. Ign., Ad Polyc. 2–4: Eus., H.E. 7.30.12, against Paul of Samosata; on virgins, L. Mitteis-U. Wilcken, Grundzüge u. Chrestomathie der Papyruskunde (1912) 1 no. 131, a marvellous text.
29. Ign., Ad Polyc. 5.2; Tert., De Pudic. 1.
30. Orig., Hom. in Num. 22.4.
31. M. Bevenot, J.T.S. (1979) 413–29; bishop as "God's elect," Cypr., Ep. 48.4, 49.2, 55.8, 59.4, 66.1; no opposition: Cypr., Ep. 3; cf. 59.4, 66.3.
32. H. Chadwick, The Early Church (1967) 49–50; C. H. Roberts, J.T.S. (1975) 404–5; W. Telfer, The Office of a Bishop (1952) 64–88.
33. Aug., Sermo 17.2 and Brown, Augustine (1967) 196–7.
34. Pontius, V. Cypr. 16; Cypr., Ep. 3.1, on the "chair"; Brown, Augustine (1967) 251.
35. Didasc. 11 (seating); Cypr., Ep. 4.4 and 52.3 (expulsion).
36. Didasc. 9 (choice); Cypr., Ep. 38–40; in general, R. Gryson, Rev. Hist. Ecc. (1973) 353.
37. Cypr., Ep. 29 and 32, on his clerics.
38. Cypr., Ep. 41.2 and 5.1.
39. A. H. M. Jones, Roman Economy (ed. Brunt 1974) 348 ff.; double share, 1 Tim. 5.17; first fruits, Hippol., Trad. 31; Didasc. 13.3–7; Orig., Hom. in Num. 11.2; tithes, R. M. Grant, Early Christianity and Society (1978) 139; Apost. Const. 8.30. Salaries: Eus., H.E. 5.18.2; 5.28.2; Hippol., Ref. 9.12.13.
40. Didasc. 9.86–7.
41. Cypr., Ep. 67.5.
42. Eus., H.E. 6.43.8; Cypr., Ep. 24.2; Nicaea, Can. 4; Arles, Can. 20.
43. Iren., Adv. Haer. 3.2.2; Hippolyt., Ref. Haer. 1. Praef. 6; Cypr., Ep. 3.3.
44. Cypr., Ep. 43.1, with more in J. Spiegl., Röm. Quart. (1974) 30 and R. Gryson, Rev. Hist. Eccles. (1973) 377 ff.
45. Hippol. Trad. 2–3, with K. Richter, Archiv. für Liturgiewiss. (1975–6) 7; E. Segelberg, Stud. Patr. (1975) 397.
46. Cypr., Ep. 72.3 and 73.22, for bishops' autonomy; K. M. Girardet, Historia (1977) 95, excellent on "bishop of bishops" with Tert., De Pud. 1.6, Cypr., Ep. 66.3 and the passage in his p. 97 n. 3.

47. On deposition, Cypr., Ep. 67; contrast Ep. 3.2!
48. C. Lepelley, Les Cités de l'Afrique . . . (1979), vol. I, 140 ff., esp. n. 94 for African evidence; Dig. 49.1.12 and 48.14.3–4, with Paul, Sent. 5.30, probably refer to these cities; Cod. Theod. 12.5.1 (325). Church historians have not made enough of this setting and usage.
49. Esp. the brilliant study by G. de Sainte Croix, Brit. Jo. Sociology (1954) 33, at p. 35, using Cyprian; cf. P. Granfield, Theol. Studies (1976) 41, for more on C.'s usage: Ep. 43.1–2; 55.8; 59.5; 67.3; 68.2.
50. Eus., H.E. 6.29; and H.E. 6.9–11; 6.11.1–2 on God's "oikonomia" and bishops' agreement.
51. Eus., H.E. 7.32.5 and 7.32.21.
52. Pontius, Vita 6.
53. Greg. Nyss., Ep. 17 on rich candidates.
54. E. Peterson, Heis Theos (1926) 144 ff., with Apul., Apol. 73 (see now C. Roueché, J.R.S. [1984] 187); Eus. 6.29.4; Cypr., Ep. 43.1; G. de Sainte Croix, Orig. of Pel. War (1972) 130–1 and Appendix 24 on "shouting, not vote."
55. J. Spiegl, Röm. Quart. (1974) 39, emphasizing that "iudicium Dei" does not overlap with popular "suffrage" in C.'s usage; "testimony," Cypr., Ep. 44.3.2; and note esp. Orig., Hom. in Lev. 6,3, quoting 1 Tim. 3.7. It is also used for "clergy and bishops" role: Ep. 8.4. For "agreement" after election, R. Gryson, Rev. Hist. Eccles. (1973) 384–5, cautiously.
56. Can. Co. Serdica (343) 2; Gesta Apud Zenoph., in C.S.E.L. edit. of Optatus (ed. Ziwsa, 1893) p. 189; cf. Orig., Hom. in Num. 9.1.
57. Cypr., Ep. 61.3; 63.1: "divina dignatio"; 3.1–3, for sanctions; cf. M. Bevenot, Rech. Sci. Rel. (1951) 397.
58. In general, E. Göller, in Ehrengabe für J.G.H. zu Sachsen (Freiburg, 1920) 603, a valuable collection of texts: esp., on bad bishops, Orig. Hom. in Judice. 4.3; Orig., Comm. in Mth. 16.21–2; C. Cels. 3.9; Hom. in Josh. 7.6.
59. Orig., Hom. in Num. 22.4 (Moses); Eus. 5.24.6, 7.32.2; Pass. Mont. et Luc. 23.4.
60. H. Chadwick, H.T.R. (1960) 171–95.
61. 1 Clem. 44–8.
62. Cypr., Ep. 68, 67; 44 ff.
63. Cypr., Ep. 29.1 and 80.1: clergy carry letters of bishop.
64. F. G. B. Millar, J.R.S. (1971) 1–17 and Eus. 7.27–30, for the affair; F. G. B. Millar, Emperor in Roman World (1977) 572–3.
65. Tert., De Praescr. Her. 4.1; Iren., Adv. Haer. 1.13.4.
66. Orig., Hom. in Josh. 23.2.
67. Jo. Chrys., Hom. in Act. III (P.G. 60.38–40); esp. 39, on inefficacy of "fear of God."
68. V. Tcherikover, Eos (1956) 169: the main audience, I think, not the sole one, though I cannot pursue this here.
69. Cf. H. Chadwick, Early Christian Thought and the Classical Tradition (1967) 26.
70. Greg. Nyss., P.G. 10.893–957; Latin legend, W. Telfer, J.T.S. (1930) 142 and 354; a Syriac legend, deriving from the panegyric's stories and of no independent historical value: P. Koetschau, Z. Wiss. Theol. (1898) 211 refuted V. Ryssel, Theol. Schweiz. (1894) 228 on this. On the letters, H. Crouzel's case, Gregorianum (1980) 745, is mine.

71. Eus., H.E. 6.30, where E.'s words on their concern for "Greek and Roman" studies can only derive from Greg.'s own surviving letter: in Pamphilus's library?; cf. 7.14, 7.28. Pace T. D. Barnes, Constantine and Eusebius (1981) 86, E. does not claim personal knowledge.

## II

1. Greg., Ep. ad Orig. (E.O.) 5.49–50.
2. Dig. 27.1.41.
3. P. Moraux, Imprécation Funéraire à Néocaesarée (1959), esp. 43–50.
4. L. Robert, C.R.A.I. (1978) 241, esp. 250–1.
5. Greg., E.O. 5.59–60; F. Millar, Emperor in Roman World (1977) 94–7; 251. Studia Pontica III. 129 no. 103, with Dig. 1.22.3.
6. F. Millar, in Colloque sur les Martyres de Lyons (1978) 187 ff., for one aspect; Greg., E.O. 5.65–8.
7. Men. Rhet. 2.432–3.
8. H. Crouzel, intro. to Gregory's Lettre de Remerciement, Sources Chrétiennes ed. (1969), esp. p. 22 (date): Eus., H.E. 6.27, on O. and Firmilian.
9. E.g. Orig., P.G. 11.61A; 12.1541C; 13.743; 11.381; 12.1269B.
10. Piety, E.O. 6.78; protreptics, 6.79–80; 6.85–92 (Jonathan).
11. E.O. 4.40–7; 5.71–2; P. R. L. Brown, Making of L.A. (1978) 71; Orig., De Princ. 3.6.9.
12. Eus., H.E. 6.14.8–9.
13. O.'s school: H. Crouzel, Bull. Lit. Eccles. (1970) 15; Greg., E.O. 11.143, with P. Courcelle, Connais-Toi Toi Même . . . (1974) 97–101; classes, E.O. 7.93–12.149; Bible, 15.173–88; philosophy, 13.150–73; barbarians, 13.153, with Epicurus, 13.152.
14. W. A. Bienert, Dionysius v. Alexandrien: Zur Frage des Origenismus (1978); creed, P.G. 10.912D–913A; H. Crouzel, Gregorianum (1980) 745 compares Greg., E.O. 4.35; L. Abramowski, Zts. für Kirchengesch. (1976) 145, argues against authenticity, too forcefully.
15. Text in V. Ryssel, Gregorius Thaumaturgus (1880) 73–99, with trans. Accepted by U. W. Knorr, Evangelisches Missionsmagazin, 110 (1966) 70, suggesting it shows G. with his catechumens (p. 75): nothing requires this. Dismissed, on theological grounds, by L. Abramowski, Zts. für Kirchengesch. 89 (1978) 279; reply by H. Crouzel, Gregorianum (1980) 754–5, not convincing.
16. P.G. 10.987 ff.
17. M. Hengel, Hellenism and Judaism (1974) 1.115–30, with II.143 n. 694 for D.S.S. fragments.
18. Greg., P.G. 10. 987 ff.; I refer to Eccles. 4.11, 12.1–4 and esp. P.G. 10.1016C.
19. E.g. Jer., P.L. 23.1048; E. Lucchesi, V.C. (1982) 292; Didymus, Kommentar zum Ecclesiastes, vols. I–IV (ed. G. Binder, 1969–79).
20. In general, S. Leanza, L'Esegesi di Origene al Libro dell'Ecclesiaste (Reggio, 1975); Orig., Exh. ad Mart. 22 misuses Eccles. 4.2; Orig., Comm. in Cant. (Rufinus) Prol. 3; P. Nautin, Origène (1977) 373–5.
21. Eus., H.E. 7.26.3, with W. Bienert, Dionysius . . . (1978) 56–8 and esp. in Kleronomia (1973) 305–14, for new evidence; I quote E. L. Feltoe, Dionysius of Alexandria (1904) 208.
22. Dionys., Comm. in Eccles. 2.24; Orig., On Prayer 23.4.

23. Orig., Sel. in Ps., P.G. 12.1080.
24. Greg., E.O. 15.179–80: W. Bienert, Dionysius . . . (1978) 119–23, on the question; Eus., H.E. 7.25.6.
25. Orig., Ep. ad Greg. (E.G.) 3, also in Crouzel's S.C. edition; on Ad Theop., see note 15.
26. Basil, Ep. 210.5, with H. Crouzel, R.S. Rel. (1963) 422.
27. Feltoe, Dionysius . . . (1904) 127–64, against Epicureans.
28. Greg., E.O. 1.7; cf. L. Robert, Rev. Phil. (1967) 60–61 and n. 1; on style, Crouzel, pp. 42–3.
29. Cf. Lucian, Alex. 48, How to Write Hist. 29, calling Roman troops "ours," with J. Palm, Rom, Römertum u. Imperium (1959) 54–5; Greg., E.O. 1.7, best analysed by J. Modrzjewski, Rév. Hist. du Droit Fr. et Etr. (1971) 313: on "synkeimenoi," I agree with M. p. 318 against A. M. Honoré, Tribonian (1978) 3; against M. p. 319, I see no obvious ref. to Imperial rescripts.
30. In general, M. Villey, Rech. sur la Litt. Didact. du Droit Rom. (1945), with R. Taubenschlag, Op. Min. II (1959) 159; on Gaius, A. M. Honoré, Gaius (1962), with P. Oxy. 2103 (his p. 126), and pp. 110–2 and 97–116 on the book's manner.
31. Ulp., Dig. 1.1.1, an analogy pressed (though too far) by P. Frezza, Studia et Doc. Hist. et Jur. (1968) at 367 ff.
32. Cf. J. Modrzjewski, R.H.D.F.E. (1971) 318; on Beirut (already "a trusted school," E.O. 5.62), esp. P. Collinet, Syria (1924) 359 and his fine Hist. de l'Ecole de Droit de Beyrouth (1925); cf. K. M. T. Atkinson, S. Afr. Law Jo. (1970) esp. 53–9; Lib., Ep. 652, on "mother"; Ep. 1652 on groups; Collinet, pp. 91–111 on ambience with Kugener's ed. of Zach. Schol., Vie de Sévère (P. Or., 1903) pp. 64–7. Eus., M.P. 4.3–5 specifically praises Appianus's self-control in Beirut.
33. L. R., Hellenica 11–12 (1960) 414–29; H. Leclerq, "Avocats" in D.A.C.L. I.3243.
34. Orig., Ep. Greg. 2–3 (Exodus); 1, where "eboulomén" and "an euxamén" are significant tenses.
35. Greg., E.O. 18.184–19.206.
36. Cf. Dionys., Eus., H.E. 7.22.1–10.
37. C.J. 10.50.1 (to "Arabi scolastici").
38. J. F. Gilliam, Z.P.E. 13 (1974) 147; name, Eus., H.E. 7.28.1, with Crouzel, p. 14; did the later Gregory, missionary to Armenia, copy ours deliberately?

III

1. Date, G. May, in Ecriture et Culture Philosophique dans la Pensée de Grégoire de Nysse, ed. M. Harl (1971) 56–9.
2. Creed: Greg. Nyss., P.G. 46.913A; Basil, Ep. 204.6; Basil, De Spir. Sanct. 74, on Greg. stories and "Moses."
3. On legend, W. Telfer, J.T.S. (1930) 142 and 354.
4. P.G. 46.909C and 953D; A. Harnack, Mission and Expansion II (1908) 206.
5. P.G. 46.899–909, with errors.
6. E.g. Greg. Nyss., Ep. 13; P.G. 46.920A–D, entry; 915C, the Emperor.
7. Comana, 933B–940B.
8. P.G. 940C, with P. Devos. An. Boll. (1975) 157.
9. W. J. Hamilton, Researches in Asia Minor . . . I (1842) 343, with P.G. 925D:

note the "army" they were preparing from their dependents, with Basil, Ep. 74–6, for similar action by rival bishops.

10. Musonius, in 920D–C, with Basil, Ep. 28.1 and 210.3; church, in 924 B–C.

11. Heretics, Eus., H.E. 7.2–9; Rome, Basil, Ep. 70 (citing documentary evidence); Paul, H.E. 7.28.1–2.

12. P. R. L. Brown, Cult of Saints (1981) 29.

13. Basil, De Spir. Sanct. 29; R. van Dam, C.S.C.A. (1982) 275 cites Lucian, Salt. 64, but this charming story is anecdotal and the "barbarian neighbours" would be Goths, Scyths, etc., not "Pontikoi."

14. X. Loriot, Bull. Soc. Nat. Ant. France (1976) 44, excellent study.

15. Greg. Nyss, Vita Macr. 8 (with P. Maraval's note, in the S.C. ed. p. 169), G. Mathew, Studies . . . D. Talbot Rice, ed. G. Robertson, G. Henderson (1975) 217; for bears in the forests (and arenas), S. Pontica II.168.

16. P.G. 913D; Studia Pontica (S.P.) II (1906) 259–95; 170–1; Basil 258.4, with L.R., Rev. Num. (1976) 37–8 n. 60, on Mithres the bishop at Nicaea.

17. X. Loriot, B.S.N.A.F. (1976) 44 ff.

18. M. Price, B. Trell, Coins and Their Cities (1977) 91 ff., 159–161; S.P. III.109.

19. Cabeira, Strabo 12.566; Price–Trell, figs. 178–9 (see below); W. J. Hamilton, Researches . . . I (1842) 365 and S.P. II. 145–8.

20. M. Price, B. Trell, Coins and Cities, pp. 92–3 with fig. 163 (sacrifice); 159 (hill); 159 and 164 (temples) and Strabo 12.561.

21. Strabo 11.512; with Price-Trell, Coins and Cities, figs. 263, 304, 362–3, 384; S.P. III.233–5; W.M. Ramsay, Hist. Geog. of Asia Minor (1890) 321.

22. J. Ebersolt, Sanctuaires de Byzance (1921) 54; in Cappadocia, the Comana shrine became a church (Procop., Wars 1.17.15).

23. Strabo 12.556; D. Magie, Roman Rule in Asia Minor I (1950) 180 and II p. 1071 n. 11. Against W. Ruge, Pauly R–E 16 (1939) 2409–13, I cite the double shrine in Price-Trell, figs. 178–9, explaining their problem by Cabeira's past.

24. Strab. 12.557–60; W. Ruge, Pauly R–E 11 (1922) 1126; Price-Trell, fig. 351 (198 A.D.) Greg. Nyss., P.G. 46.778A (wine).

25. B.M.C. Pontus, 32 no. 2, for league cities and constant "metropolis" slogan. C. Picard, B.C.H. (1922) 191; Claros, from "metropolis" already. Coins, Price-Trell, p. 123 with figs. 71, 165–75; 178–9; 414.

26. On Amaseia as metropolis, Samml. v. Aulock, Pontus, 20–44; G. C. Anderson, J.H.S. (1900) 153 and S.P. III.132–6. Asterius, Hom. IV, P.G. 40.218–9: I am not persuaded by M. Meslin, La Fête des Kalendes de Janvier (1970) that this is a late innovation. S.P. III. 152–3 (actor); 134–6 (gladiator).

27. P.G. 944C–D.

28. B.M.C. Pontus, 34.12–15 and Samml. v. Aulock, s.v. Pontus no. 107 (Aktia, first known under Gordian: earlier games, no. 104, Severus). For a parallel, C. Roueché, J.R.S. (1981) 119; afterlife, Samml. v. Aulock, Pontus 114, 116; B.M.C. Pontus, 35.17 (Gallienus). P.G. 953B–D, for motives: doubted, perhaps too fully, by P. R. L. Brown, Cult of Saints (1981) 31–3.

29. T. D. Barnes, Constantine and Eusebius (1981) 258, citing date and bibliogr.

30. P.G. 10.1020A ff., with J. Dräseke, Jhrb. für Prot. Theol. (1881) 724–56, on text.

31. A. Alföldi, Berytus (1937) 55–6, preferable to M. Salamon, Eos (1971) 116; Zos. 1.27.1 (253?): for boats, cf. Tac., Hist. 3.47.3.

32. A. M. Ramsay, in Studies in Hist. and Art of East Rmn. Prov., ed. W. Ramsay (1906) 22, on this title; also, E. W. Benson, Cyprian (1897) 29.

33. Greg., Can. Ep. 7 with Strabo 12.559 (emended to Pontikoi, rightly).
34. Not class war, despite de Sainte Croix, C.S.A.G.W. (1981) 477–8.
35. Greg., Can. 1 with Mth. 15.11 and Deut. 22.26–7.
36. Greg., Can. 4 with Deut. 22.1–3; Exod. 23.4; Josh. 7 and Can. 3.
37. Can. 2 and Can. 6 (thunderbolts).
38. Can. 8 (confession); Can. 7–9 and 11, which I accept as original.
39. Cypr., Ep. 30.3; 33–6; 43, Didasc. 6.52 (Connolly); Dionys., in Eus., H.E.
    6.46.1. Cf. Cypr., Ep. 32, sending copies of his views to other bishops: I am not
    sure that the "pappas" in the Can. Ep. would strictly rank in Greg.'s own
    episcopal "provincia."
40. J. Crook, Law and Life of Rome (1967) 169, on Roman law being less savage to
    thieves than English law before 1800. On "only the guilty," D. Halic. 8.80 and
    F. Schulz, Principles of Roman Law (1936) 203.
41. J. Danielou, Romanitas et Christianitas . . . J. H. Waszink (1973) 71; the fine
    C.S.L. ed., by G. F. Diercks (1972) is basic, now; Cypr., Ep. 60.3; Novat., De
    Spect. 2.1–3 and 2.10.
42. E. Gallicet, Forma Futuri . . . M. Pellegrino (1975) 43 and S. Deléani, Rev. Et.
    Aug. (1977) 221.
43. S. L. Greenslade, J.T.S. (1943) 172 ff.; I quote Cypr. 59.5 with Deut. 17.12–13
    and 1 Sam. 8.7; Cypr., Ep. 74.10 is another case.
44. Eus., H.E., 7.10.8.
45. C. Feltoe, Dionysius of Alexandria (1904) 102 ff.; de Sainte Croix, C.S.A.G.W.
    (1981) 557 n. 26.
46. Didascalia, ed. Connolly, pp. 68–74.
47. Cyprian, II (Ante-Nicene Library, xiii, 1869) 211.
48. Aug., Ep. 22.5.
49. So, acutely, P. Brown, Making of L.A. (1978) 71.
50. P. R. L. Brown, Religion and Society in the Age of Augustine (1972) 89.

CHAPTER 11

A stirring account of Christian triumph is given by W. H. C. Frend in his Martyrdom
and Persecution (1965) chaps. 14–15, citing a range of evidence which I would
interpret rather differently: Peter Brown's review in Religion and Society in the Age
of Augustine (1972) 74–93 and his fine chapters in The World of Late Antiquity (1971)
suggest other perspectives. R. MacMullen's Roman Government's Response to
Crisis (1976) is an essay on the other problems of the age; W. H. C. Frend, in M. I.
Finley, ed., Studies in Ancient Society (1974) 263 gives a fine study of the failure of
persecution.

I

1. Cypr., Ep. 11.1; Eus., H.E. 8.1.7 ff.
2. Dionys., ap. Eus. 6.42.5 (Antioch); 6.46.1 (generally): 6.46.2–5 (Rome, and
   Armenia, surely Armenia Minor, centred on Sebaste, just near his former
   schoolmate Gregory).
3. In general, M. M. Sage, Cyprian (1975) 212–65; pp. 295 ff.
4. Cypr., Ep. 54.3: Novatianists on "tares" in pure wheat of Church (cf. Orig.,
   Hom. in Josh. 22.1); Eus. 6.43.2, their ejection; T. Gregory, Byz. Studies 2

(1975) 1, their future; H. J. Vogt, Coetus Sanctorum (1968) 53, their ideals.

5. M. M. Sage, Cyprian (1975) 231–65; 280–5.
6. Cypr., Ep. 60; Sage, 284–7.
7. Eus., H.E. 7.11; Cypr., Ep. 80.1.
8. F. Millar, Emperor in Roman World (1977) p. 277 and p. 570 for this: Acta Cypriani 1.
9. Death as "koimesis" was not unknown in pagan epitaphs; on the word "cemetery," F. Blanchetière, Le Christianisme Asiate . . . (1981) 459.
10. Act. Cypr. 1 and 3; Eus., H.E. 7.11.
11. Firmil., ap. Cypr. Ep. 75.10; Orig., Comm. in Mth. 39; Cypr., Ad Dem. 2–3; Arnob., Adv. Gentes, 1.3.
12. M. Pion. 15.5; Act. Cypr. 2.2; M. Fructuos. 1; Mar. and Jas. 2.4, 3.1 and esp. 4.3.
13. Eus., H.E. 7.13, the edict: P. Keresztes, A.N.R.W. 23.1.375 ff., on aftermath; T. D. Barnes, however, thinks "Christianity remained technically a capital crime," Constantine and Eusebius (1981) 13. Martyr in Caesarea: Eus., H.E. 7.15; military martyrs listed in P. Keresztes, op. cit.
14. Dionys., ap. Eus. 7.10–11 and 7.23, esp. 7.23.4 where the "festival" is not necessarily Easter; C. Andresen, A.N.R.W. 23.1, esp. 416–28 and 420 for the dating: his entire study is important for what follows.
15. Eus., H.E. 7.11.8 and 7.10.8, with Ex. 20.5.
16. Eus., H.E., 7.21.2, with Andresen, A.N.R.W. 23.1.427/8 and pp. 428 ff.: the letter belongs with Aemilianus's revolt, during spring 262.
17. Eus., H.E., 7.32.5: this Eus. left Alexandria for Syria and the affair of Paul in Antioch, after the events of the siege (7.32.8). The siege is not, then, in Aurelian's reign, but belongs in the 260s: cf. W. H. C. Frend, Martyrdom and Persecution (1965) 446–7. In general, Andresen, op. cit., pp. 428 ff. and Eus., H.E. 7.32.10, for the vote and the council (synedrion): Eus. is perhaps exact in his formal language here.
18. Eus. 7.13, to others elsewhere.
19. W. H. C. Frend, Martyrdom and Persecution (1965) 440–77, most vigorous, but not convincing.
20. Orig., Hom. in Jer. 4.2–3: cf. Hom. in Jos. 21.1: Comm. in Mth. Series 61.
21. Tert., De Pud. 1.6; Hippol., Ref. 9.12.21, on adultery: Cypr., Ep. 55.6 and 55.13, Eus., H.E., on lapsing.
22. Cypr., De Laps. 35, on penance; J. Burnaby, Amor Dei (1938) 237.
23. L. W. Countryman, The Rich Christian (1980) 183 ff.
24. Cypr., De Laps. 28.1.
25. Didascalia Apostolorum, ed. R. H. Connolly (1929), the fundamental study to whose introduction, text and index I refer for what follows. On dating, P. Galtier, R.H.E. 42 (1947) 319: a pre-Decian date does not entirely affect my use of it.
26. Can. Elvira 67, on hairstyles (viri cinerarii!).
27. Bathing in R. Ginouvès, Balaneutike (1962) 220–2; Clem. Alex., Paedag. 3.5.
28. Didascalia, ed. Connolly, p. 120.

## II

Mani and his Gospel have attracted some of the outstanding scholarship of this century: the best brief book is still H. C. Puech, Le Manichéisme (1949), while F. C.

Burkitt, The Religion of the Manichees (1978, repr.) is also valuable. W. Sundermann, Mitteliranische Manichäische Texte Kirchengeschichtlichen Inhalts (Berlin, 1981), with bibliography of his earlier articles, and Mary Boyce, A Reader in Manichaean Middle Persian and Parthian (1975) are brilliant studies of the Central Asian material; the various papers by W. B. Henning, edited now by M. Boyce (1978, Acta Iranica 15–16) in two volumes, are masterpieces of wide learning and insight. The Greek Codex is published by A. Henrichs, L. Koenen in Z.P.E. 5 (1970) 97, 9 (1975) 1, 32 (1978) 87 and 48 (1982) 1; the first parts are translated into English by R. Cameron, A. J. Dewey, The Cologne Mani Codex . . . (1979) in Texts and Translations 15, of the Society of Biblical Literature, with bibliography. For the discovery, A. Henrichs, H.S.C.P. (1979) 339. In North Africa, F. Decret, L'Afrique Manichéenne (1978); in the Roman Empire, P. R. L. Brown, J.R.S. (1969) 92, a brilliant study of wide interest, and the memorable chap. 5 of his Augustine of Hippo (1967). I. Gruenewald, Manichaeism and Judaism, Z.P.E. 50 (1983) 29 has most of the recent bibliography; the studies of S. N. C. Lieu in J.T.S. (1981) 153, Jhb. Ant. u.Christ (1983) 152 esp. 190 ff. and B.J.R.L. (1979–80) 132 break new ground, especially on Manichaeism in China and the East. I owe a general debt to his advice and also to his introductory The Religion of Light (1979), published by the Centre of Asian Studies, Hong Kong University: his forthcoming book will greatly enlarge our knowledge of this subject.

1. H. I. Marrou, C.R.A.I. (1973) 533; in general, M. Simon, Early Christian Lit. . . . In Honor, R. M. Grant (ed. Schoedel, Wilken, 1979) 101.
2. Journeys, in A. Henrichs, L. Koenen, Z.P.E. 48 (1982) 1–3 and W. Sundermann, Acta Orientalia (Copenhagen) 1974, 135 ff. and Act. Orient. (Hungar., Budapest) (1971) 82 ff.
3. Advice, in W. Sundermann, Mitteliranische Manichäische Texte . . . (1981) 35.
4. F. F. Church, G. G. Stroumsa, V.C. (1981) esp. p. 49.
5. W. B. Henning, B.S.O.A.S. 10 (1942) 949 ff.; W. Sundermann, Mitteliranische Manich. Texte (1981) 130 ff. on Kustaios, the possible source for these traditions, and also M.'s interpreter, Bar Nuh.
6. S. N. C. Lieu, J.T.S. (1981) 161–2, on hierarchy; Kephalaia 154 and H. C. Puech, Le Manichéisme (1949) 62–4, on universality.
7. M.'s writings, esp. W. B. Henning, B.S.O.A.S. 11 (1943–6) 52–4; Parthian, in M. Boyce, A Reader in Manichaean Middle Persian . . . (1976) 40, "Greek, Indian, Syriac," in Sundermann, Mitteliranische Manich. Texte (1981) 87.
8. China, in S. Lieu, Religion of Light (1979) 26; Roman persecution, E. H. Kaden, in Festschr. H. Lewald (1953, Basel) 55; Byzant., now in Lieu, Jhb. A. u. C. (1983) 152; Aug., in Conf. 3.11.9.
9. Coptic Studies, surveyed by A. Böhlig, in Mysterion u.Wahrheit, Gesammelte Beiträge . . . (1968) 177–87; A. Henrichs, H.S.C.P. (1979) 352–4, on the new Codex as a "highly problematic source," a timely warning to historians.
10. A. Henrichs, H.S.C.P. (1973) 23, on Baptists; H.S.C.P. (1979) 354–67, on Elchesai with Eus., H.E. 6.38.
11. C.M.C. 3.2–5.3; 13.2, with L. Koenen, Illin. Class. Stud. (1978) 167–76; C.M.C. 18–23 and 63 (the great Vision); C.M.C. 63–8 (grace).
12. C.M.C. 89–91 (Baptists' attack); 77–9 (dark Vision).
13. C.M.C. 33.1, 40.1 (Helper); 45–62 (tradition).

14. Sundermann (1981) 117–9 and p. 41 (vision for the Syrian, probably sister of Zenobia); the Twin, e.g. C.M.C. 164.
15. Sundermann (1981) 102–4.
16. On hunting, Z.P.E. 48 (1982) 23–7 and Sundermann (1981) 116 for another hunter and tree pruner; Z.P.E. 48 (1982) 6 and n. 17 for important doubts (which I share) about these stories' historicity: they reinforce points in Manichaean teaching, which perhaps caused their invention.
17. Most recently, I. Gruenwald, Z.P.E. 50 (1983) 29; C.M.C. 48.1–63 (Baraies's defence of Mani).
18. C.M.C. 80–93, the quarrel; on M.'s debts to earlier thinkers, B. Aland and also A. Böhlig, in Syncretismus im Syrisch.-persisch. Kulturgebiet, ed. A. Dietrich (1975) pp. 123 and 144.
19. A. Henrichs, B.A.S.P. (1979) 85; Aug., De Morib. Manich. 29; S. N. C. Lieu, J.T.S. (1981) 168–72.
20. Best accounts in H. C. Puech (1949), P. R. L. Brown, Augustine (1967) chap. 5 and Brown, J.R.S. (1969) 92.
21. Charity, in S. Lieu, Jhb. A. u. C. (1983) 211 with Aug., Conf. 3.10.8. F. C. Burkitt, Religion of the Manichees (1925) 64–5 on the 1,468 years, known also to Al-Nadim, the bookseller-polymath in 10th-cent. Baghdad.
22. C.M.C. 66.4–7 and S. Lieu, Jhb. A. u. C. (1983) 197, on Christ; E. Rose, Die Manichäische Christologie (1979).
23. Well stressed by P. Brown, Augustine, p. 56.
24. V. Arnold-Doeben, Die Bildersprache des Manichäismus (1978), on imagery.
25. W. B. Henning, B.S.O.A.S. 12 (1947–8) 306, the folio; pp. 310–1, the drawings.
26. P. W. Van Der Horst, J. Mansfield, An Alexandrian Platonist Against Dualism (1974) chap. 12; on Mani's Book of Giants, a brilliant study by W. B. Henning, B.S.O.A.S. 11 (1943) 52–74, arguing for the importance of the Book of Enoch. Mani never used Iranian mythology.
27. F. Decret, L'Afrique Manichéenne 1 (1978) 176–7 (traders) and esp. 205–10, on ages, occupations and the "apologetique du souk." His pp. 354–77 give a prosopography, to which add S. and J. Lieu, J.T.S. (1981) 173; soldier, in Epiphan. Panar. 66.1.
28. F. Decret, L'Afr. Manichéenne 1 (1978) 205; Z.P.E. 48 (1982) 15.
29. W. Sundermann (1981) 92, with 105–6 (Shapur's letter of protection); cf. 58 ff.; on the Shahburagan, two fine recovery jobs by D. Mackenzie, B.S.O.A.S. (1979) 500 and (1980) 288.
30. Sundermann (1981) 39, on Mar Ammo.
31. On Zenobia, H. Schaeder, Gnomon (1933) 344; Sundermann, pp. 41 ff. and 123; on Z.'s Jewish/Christian "sympathies," F. Millar, J.R.S. (1971) 12–13, omitting, however, the Manichaean evidence.
32. Esp. Z.P.E. 48 (1982) 13–15; at Hira, J. S. Trimingham, Christianity Among the Arabs (1979) 157–8, with bibliogr.
33. C. H. Roberts, Rylands Papyr. 469.

### III

1. Generally, R. MacMullen, Roman Government's Response to Crisis (1976), for the issues. F. Millar, The Roman Empire and Its Neighbours (1981) 239–49, on

building; R. M. Harrison, Actes du Colloque sur la Lycie Antique (1980) 109; F. Millar, J.R.S. (1969) 12.

2. C. Foss, Ephesus after Antiquity (1979) 3 n. 3; L. Robert, Hellenica (1948) 119; P. M. Fraser, Ptolemaic Alexandria (1972) 16; W. H. C. Frend, Martyrdom and Persecution . . . (1965) 442–5 and 458–9; S. Johnson, Late Roman Fortifications (1983); Cod. J. 11.42.1, for funding.

3. A. H. M. Jones, Later Roman Empire 26–32; 37–70, with R. MacMullen, Klio (1981) 451; R. Duncan-Jones, Chiron (1978) 541 and P. A. Brunt, J.R.S. (1981) 170–1.

4. R. MacMullen, Response . . . (1976) 16–22 doubts the broader theories which have been built on art. However, in most cases, the patrons' tastes were relevant, and historically significant. The boldest account is still G. Mathew's brilliant Byzantine Aesthetics (1963) chaps. 1–3.

5. E. R. Dodds, Pagans and Christians . . . (1965) 137; W. H. C. Frend, Martyrdom and Persecution (1965) 461; cf. the legends of martyrs in Ancyra, of no historical worth for the 270s, in C. Foss, D.O.P. (1977) 32.3.

6. J. Geffcken, The Last Days of Greco-Roman Paganism (1978, Eng. ed.) 25.

7. On theology, J. H. Liebeschuetz, Continuity and Change . . . (1979) 243.

8. Inscr. Did. 159; Or. Sib. 13 (composed in the 260s), passim.

9. B.M.C. (Ionia) p. 45; Himerius, Or. 11.3, for 4th-cent. Claros: J. Geffcken, Last Days . . . (1978) 27, on Delphi.

10. I. Did. 159, with L. Robert, Hellenica 4 (1948) 25 and 75; 6 (1948) 119–21 and 10–11 (1960) 440, improving on Rehm's commentary; Makarios's paganism, in Milet 1.9 no. 339.

11. L. Vidmann, Syll. Inscr. Relig. Isiac. et Serapiac. (1969) no. 282, with bibliogr.

12. C. Roueché, J.R.S. (1981) 119; Wessely, Stud. Pal. 5.121, with L. Robert, Hellenica 5.61–2 and 11–12 (1960) 355; lines 14–15 show these Olympics were (revived by) the gift of Gallienus; P. Oxy. 2476 with Chron. d'Eg. (1971) 136 and L.R., B. Epig. (1972) 612; P. Oxy. 3367 and 3116 with J. D. Thomas, Collectanea Papyrologica (ed. A. E. Hanson, 1976) 471; P. Oslo 3.85.

13. J. D. Thomas, op. cit. (1976) 473, with G. Méautis, Hermopolis la Grande (1918) 152–5.

14. On a "grant," L. Robert, H.S.C.P. (1977) 33, Hellenica 11–12 (1960) 359–68 and B. Epig. (1972) 500 insists it is not financial, a more natural interpretation; Imperial victories and games in P. Oxy. 3116 and 3367.

15. Wilck., Chrest. 425 and P. Oxy. 2903, with P. J. Parsons, Collectanea Papyrologica (ed. A. E. Hanson, 1976) 438–40, importantly; cf. P. Oxy. 2892 with E. G. Turner, H.S.C.P. (1975) 16.

16. N. Cardus, Autobiography (1955) p. 137.

17. L. Robert, Hellenica 11–12 (1960) 365–7.

18. L. Robert, B. Epig. (1982) 420, for quotation.

19. P. Oxy. 1025; P. Mert. 1.26, with C. H. Roberts, J.E.A. (1934) 21–6; P. Oxy. 1256.12; for a Serapis festival at this date, F. Wormald, J.E.A. (1929) 239–42; G. Ronchi, Lexicon Theonymon . . . Fasc. 2 (Milan, 1974) 479–80, for letters, though the whole lexicon has many others too, a useful key; at Hermopolis, C.P. Hermopolis 125, with G. Méautis, Hermopolis (1918) 175–6.

20. C.I.L. 8.8457; H. Graillot, R.A. 3 (1904) 322.

21. W. H. C. Frend, Martyrdom and Persecution (1965) 452; but see A. Beschaouch, C.R.A.I. (1975) 117 for counter-evidence, with Ann. Ep. (1969–70) 657.

22. I.G.L.S. 1799–1800, with H. R. Baldus, Uranius Antoninus (1971) 250, for Cronos; H. Seyrig. Mél. Univ. St. Jos. 37 (1960–1) 261, for Nemesis.
23. P. Oxy. 2144.
24. P. A. Février, A.N.R.W. 10.2 (1982) 351–2, with texts; Thala, Ann. Epig. (1905) 35.
25. Above all, C. Lepelley, Les Cités de l'Afrique Romaine au Bas-Empire (1979), a fundamental study; vol. 1.304–6, for list, with pp. 345–6 for pagan cults; the sequel, Lepelley, 343–69 and 376 ff. (on Augustine).
26. Survey and bibliogr. in C. Lepelley, Les Cités de l'Afrique . . . (1979) 243–303; I am not denying the renewed "euergetism" in Africa from 275 to 439, summarized on his p. 303 and p. 315. In general, I am following A. H. M. Jones, e.g. Later Roman Empire, II. 726 ff. and, by implication, P. R. L. Brown, Making of L.A. (1978) 45–51; J.H. Liebeschuetz, Continuity and Change . . . (1979) 231–4, a clear statement.
27. Evidence all in C. Foss, Z.P.E. 26 (1977) 161; dating, in J.-M. Carrié, Z.P.E. 35 (1979) 213.
28. A. Laumonier, Les Cultes Indigènes en Carie (1958) 234 ff., esp. 286 ff., 322 ff. (the mysteries): I disagree with P. R. L. Brown, Making of L.A. (1978) 51: "the third century, as we know it, does not appear to have happened in Stratonikeia."

## IV

1. T. D. Barnes, J.T.S. (1973) 431 rightly reduces the fragments, but I do not accept his new dating; see now B. Croke, Journ. Rel. Hist. (1984) 1 for reasons, most of which I endorse.
2. J.-M. Demarolle, G.R.B.S. (1971) 49 for this, now invalid, evidence.
3. Lact., M.P. 12.2–4 on the "fanum editissimum"; Acta Purg. Felicis (in Optatus, ed. Ziwsa, C.S.E.L. 26, 1893) p. 199.10–11, basilicas at Zama and Furni; A. Ferrua, Riv. di Arch. Crist. (1977) 225–8, the text from Altava.
4. Eus., H.E. 8.11.1 with Lact., Div. Inst. 5.11.10, not, I think, big Eumeneia (though no bishop from E. is attested at Nicaea); A. Chastagnol, M.E.F.R.E. (1981) 381 toys with Orcistus as the place.
5. F. Blanchetière, Le Christianisme Asiate . . . (1977) 338–45 and esp. 473, best list of Phrygian texts, with bibliogr.
6. J. B. Segal, Edessa and Harran (1963); Eus., Onomast. s.v. Anaia, Jetheira, Kariatha; I will argue (against T. D. Barnes, Const. and Eus. 1981, pp. 110–1) for the traditional date elsewhere.
7. Gesta ap. Zenoph. (Optatus, ed. Ziwsa, in C.S.E.L. 26, 1893) p. 194, esp. 25; cf. W. H. C. Frend, The Donatist Church (1952) 11–12, considering the crowd to be "fanatically Christian." This cannot be right: the witnesses wish to contrast this rabble with the laity, the "populus dei."
8. J. J. Wilkes, Dalmatia (1969) 429–30 with P. R. L. Brown, J.R.S. (1969) 97; on army, A. H. M. Jones, in Conflict Between Paganism . . . ed. Momigliano (1963) 33. Cf. my chap. 12.
9. Porphyr., ap. Eus., Prep. Ev. 5.179D.
10. C. Pietri, Rev. Et. Aug. (1978) 3, an essential counter to the older views of R. Vielliard on the "identifiable" early tituli in Rome; on catacombs, a very open question, H. Brandenburg, Jhb. A. u. C., Ergänzbd. 11 (1984) 11; the Hypogaeum of the Aurelii does not, I think, show Christian influence, or

"syncretism," at this date: N. Himmelmann, Das Hypogäum der Aurelier (Mainz, 1975), but F. Bisconti, Augustinianum (1985) 889 still holds to this view, with good bibliogr.

11. Epiph., Panar. 69.2, with A. Martin, Rev. Et. Aug. (1984) 211, esp. 220–1: great uncertainty still remains; in Rome, note D. M. Novak, Anc. Society (1979) 281.

12. C. H. Roberts, Manuscript, Society and Belief . . . (1979) 1–25 and 64 ff.; list of papyri, some uncertainly Christian, in E. A. Judge, Jhrb A. u. C. (1977) 48–50; I reject his nos. 5 and 7, doubt 3 and cannot date 4. I cite P.S.I. 1492, dated 270–300 by J. Van Haelst, Proc. 12 Intern. Congr. Pap. (1970) 497; on Oxyrhynchus, P. Oxy. 1.43, with Judge 60–1 and A. Kasher, Jo. Jew. Stud. (1981) 151 (on Jews).

13. P. Bas. 17; P. Oxy. 2276 and wills in P. Oxy. 2404 and 907.

14. R. S. Bagnall, B.A.S.P. (1983) 105, for names; note, however, F. Blanchetière, Le Christianisme Asiate . . . (1981) 460–1 for pagan names in Christian families, attested on Phrygian epitaphs: B.'s "statistics" may on several counts be misleading.

15. A. Martin, Rev. Et. Aug. (1979) 6–7.

16. Cypr., Ep. 62.4; Eus. 7.22.7 ff. (not expressly to heathen too); Eus. 9.8.3–14, esp. 9.

17. On pagan grain distribution, note esp. the summary by E. G. Turner, H.S.C.P. (1975) 16–24.

18. Eus., H.E. 9.7 with R. M. Grant, in Christianity, Judaism . . . Studies for Morton Smith, ed. J. Neusner (1975) vol. 4, p. 161, n. 86 (very acute on multi/pleistoi in translation).

19. I quote T. D. Barnes, Cons. and Eus. (1981) 161.

20. Recent survey in Barnes, Cons. and Eus. (1981) 18 ff., 148 ff.

21. J. R. Fears, Princeps A Diis Electus (1977) 279; P. A. Brunt, J.R.S. (1979) 173–4.

22. J. H. Liebeschuetz, Continuity and Change . . . (1979) 237–44.

23. On Golden Age, Pan. Lat. 5.18.4–5 and A. D. Nock, J.R.S. (1947) 107 n. 57.

24. C.I.L. 3.4413, exaggerated by W. Seston, Bibl. Ec. Fr. d'Ath. et de Rome (1946) 225; in general, M. Simon, Acta Iranica (1978) 457, rightly minimizing Mithras as the main "opponent" of Christianity.

25. J. H. Liebeschuetz, Continuity and Change . . . (1979) 282–3; H. Seyrig, Syria (1971) 337 (important); Plato, Laws 945E–946; for Hadrian, M. Le Glay, B.C.H. (1976) 355.

26. Lib., Or. 61.7 with the portrait in J. Inan, E. Rosenbaum, Roman and Early Byz. Portrait Sculpture . . . (1966) pl. 39; T. D. Barnes, H.S.C.P. (1976) 240, G.R.B.S. (1978) 105 and J.T.S. (1973) 439 on the three persons; on Hierocles, Lact., Div. Inst. 5.2.12 does imply his book appeared after the persecution began, against Barnes, H.S.C.P. (1976) 240–3, unconvincing in his earlier dating.

27. E. J. Bickermann, Riv. di Filol. (1968) 298.

28. Mos. et Rom. Leg. Collatio 6.4, with H. Chadwick, in Studies in Hon. R. M. Grant (ed. W. Schoedel, R. L. Wilken) 1979. 135.

29. Collat. 15.3.2; T. D. Barnes, H.S.C.P. (1976) 246, for the dating, with bibliogr.; independently, I had concluded likewise, though I suppose it is not proven. R. M. Grant, in Ex Orbe Religionum . . . Studia G. Widengren (1972) 437, for opposite notions.

30. Eus., V.C. 2.50, on the philosopher-prophet. Eus., Prep. Ev. 4.135D–136A, an important text.

## V

1. T. D. Barnes, Const. and Eus. (1981) 150, for survey; G. E. M. de Sainte Croix, H.T.R (1954) 75 is still basic: I quote p. 104; on his pp. 91–2, I take the "natural view" of the mention of sacrifice in the African Passio Crispinae 4.1.
2. Eus., H.E. 9.5, with R. M. Grant, in Christianity, Judaism . . . Festschrift for Morton Smith, ed. J. Neusner (1975) vol. 4 p. 144, though white-robed priests are not a sign of Egyptianizing paganism; they were standard practice (contra his p. 159).
3. Gesta ap. Zenoph. (Optatus, C.S.E.L. 26, ed. Ziwsa), pp. 197–204 and C. Lepelley, Les Cités de l'Afr. Romaine . . . I (1979) 335 ff., an excellent treatment; compare Aug., Contr. Cresc. 3.30.
4. J. W. Barns, H. Chadwick, J.T.S. (1973) 445; Act. Phileae, Col. 2.
5. Canons, in M. Routh, Reliquiae Sacrae (1846) 23–45, 52 ff.; I cite Canon 3; 9 (volunteers); 11 (money); 10 (clergy); 14 (suffering); 6–7 (slaves); 5 (documents).
6. P. Oxy. 2601.
7. Eus., H.E. 9.7.2 and C.I.L. 3.12132.
8. Eus., H.E. 9, 9A.4 (images).
9. Eus., H.E. 9, 8.13–14.
10. Text in P. Franchi de Cavalieri, Studi e Testi 6 (1901): latest study by S. Mitchell, Anat. Studies (1982) 93, a very important addition: I differ only in doubting the full historicity.
11. Best in F. C. Burkitt, Euphemia and the Goth (1913); I quote pp. 105, 107 and 126 of his translation.
12. Habbib, p. 115 (Burkitt).
13. Burkitt, pp. 109 and 127–8 (I quote); records, on p. 101, p. 127.
14. Topography, brilliantly seen by S. Mitchell, Anat. Stud. (1982) 93 ff. and J. B. Segal, Edessa (1970) 83 ff. and Burkitt (1913) 43 ff.
15. I agree with Burkitt, p. 31, on the general reference of the synchronism in Shmona and Gurya 68; the prefatory dates may be corrupted by later tradition. The governors' names, Mysianus/Ausonius, are not yet verifiable: Burkitt, pp. 165 and 175, for their possible corruptions. The refs. to Constantine in the Habbib story are not credible if we accept a 312 dating: I am more uneasy about Habbib's authenticity than about the other text's but as yet Burkitt, pp. 5–34, is the basic summary of the case "for" and "against." Segal, p. 82, rightly contrasts other Edessene martyrdoms, patently glorifying families known in the 5th-cent. city, to give them a "Christian" ancestry. These two texts are not obviously of that type.
16. W. H. C. Frend, Past and Pres. (1959) 10.
17. Discussions in D. Chitty, The Desert a City (1966); A. Guillaumont, Aux Origines du Monachisme Chrétien (1979) 218–27; H. Chadwick, in The Byz. Saint, ed. S. Hackel (1981) 11.
18. Pachom., V. Prima (Greek) chap. 5 and Chitty p. 12.
19. E. A. Judge, Jhrb. A. u. C. (1977) 72–89, though I do not accept his tentative suggestions that Isaac was more an "apotaktikos" than a solitary like Antony and thus corrects Athanasius's emphasis. Athanas., V. Anton. 46, if historical,

already shows monks known to pagan officials before 312: D. Chitty, The
Desert . . . (1966) p. 6 n. 25.

20. Method., Sympos. 1.1.

21. On this aspect of Arius, R. C. Gregg and D. E. Groh, Early Arianism (1981) 88,
quoting Bishop Alexander. Their overall case is not convincing: see now E. F.
Osborn, Prudentia (1984) 51, for some counter-arguments.

22. Esp. S. N. C. Lieu, J.T.S. (1981) 153, with C.M.C. 89.9 and Z.P.E. 5 (1970)
169: food tests, P. Brown, J.R.S. (1969) 100 n. 100. Athan., V. Ant. 68 is
interesting, as R. M. Grant, Studia . . . G. Widengren (1972) 438 saw.

23. Esp. P. R. L. Brown, Making of L.A. (1978) 81–101; on changes in village
landholding, see A. K. Bowman, J.R.S. (1985) to appear, discussed previously
in Oxford seminars. Brown's thesis finds support, particularly, in the
Abinnaeus archive, ed. H. I. Bell (1962).

24. Eus., H.E. 6.42.2; Athan., V. Ant. 3; Mart. Agape, Chione . . . 5.5; Habbib
(ed. Burkitt) 6 ff.; Gesta ap. Zenophilum (C.S.E.L., vol. 26, 1893, ed. Ziwsa),
p. 186 line 6. On wanderers in Egypt, compare H. Braunert, Die
Binnenwanderung . . . (1964).

25. H. J. Drijvers, in The Byz. Saint (1981), ed. S. Hackel, p. 25 ff., for the religious
motivation; P. Brown's classic paper, J.R.S. (1971) 80, overstresses the social
function in accounting for the rise, to my mind: many holy men positively
shunned a role as "patron."

26. W. Till, ed., Koptische Heiligen und Martyrerlegende (1935–6) 69.

27. J. Monat, in his De Opificio (S. Chrét. ed. 1974) 12–15 for theories of his early
life. I owe a general debt to O. P. Nicholson and his Lactantius: Prophecy and
Politics in the Age of Constantine (Oxford, D.Phil. 1981) chaps. 1–3. On
retreat, Lact., Div. Inst. 4.18.2; the new Cicero, Div. Inst. 1.1.11; 6.1.2.

28. Lact., Div. Inst. 7.15–21, for the Sibyls; on the End, Div. Inst. 7.15.11.

29. T. D. Barnes, Constantine and Eusebius (1981) 106–58, for survey; he argues
for his datings in G.R.B.S. (1980) 191, but most of them are not convincing: I
cannot argue the traditional case here, but will publish it elsewhere.

30. Barnes, Constantine and Eusebius (1981) 111–20, for content: the synchronism
for 276/7 (Barnes p. 111) does not prove a first edition ended there. No Ms.
supports this notion: E. emphasized the dating, perhaps simply because he
borrowed it from Anatolius.

31. T. D. Barnes, Const. and Eus. (1981) 167–74, on form and content.

32. I will argue the datings of M. Pal. elsewhere, diverging from Barnes, 149–50.

33. Contra Barnes, G.R.B.S. (1980) 191; I cannot argue every point, but would
emphasize H.E. 6.32.3. E. refers to Pamphilus there as a martyr and, above all,
implies that the whole shape of his treatment of Origen in Bk. 6 has been
shortened because of *existing* work, done in the Life of Pamphilus. This destroys
the case for a Bk. 6 composed in the 290s. Note, too, the other post-Pamphilan
passages, in a footnote to Barnes, G.R.B.S. (1980) 201: they are "later
insertions," in his view. On pp. 110–11 of Const. and Eus. the argument for
Petra's early inclusion in Palestine attaches to the text now in P. Oxy. 3574: this
concerns Petra in Egypt, not Nabataea. Argument persists on its list, but not so
as to support B.'s argument. The Onomasticon belongs in the 320s, making
sense of Jerome's sequence (contra, Barnes, p. 111).

34. Eus., H.E. 8.1.7.

I

I have not multiplied primary references, as the fundamental book of T. D. Barnes, Constantine and Eusebius (1981) has recently brought them and the bibliography together so accessibly: the older account by A. H. M. Jones, Constantine the Great and the Conversion of Europe (1949) is the best short work. J. H. W. G. Liebeschuetz, Continuity and Change in Roman Religion (1979) 277–301 is also excellent; H. Dörries, Das Selbstzeugnis Kaiser Konstantins, Abhandl. der Akad. Wiss. Göttingen, Phil. Hist. Klasse, 3. Folge XXXIV (1954) is an indispensable work of cross-reference to the concepts and language in Constantine's writings. His Constantine and Religious Liberty (1960, trans. R. H. Bainton) discusses a central issue. H. Chadwick, Conversion in Constantine the Great, Studies in Church History, 15 (1878, Oxford), ed. Derek Baker, pp. 1–15 is the most recent English discussion I have used. The outstanding study remains N. H. Baynes, Constantine the Great and the Christian Church (1929, repr. 1972), a magisterial lecture with essential notes and bibliography.

1. Lact., M.P. 15.1: generally, these women are seen as crypto-Christians: e.g. J. Vogt (1963).
2. N. H. Baynes (1972) 3.
3. Barnes (1981) 38: Rome; prison disputes, Epiphan. Panar. 68.3.3. and Acta Saturnini 17.
4. H. I. Marrou (1973) 533, esp. 535–6 with Epiphan. Panar. 69.2.1–7. Marrou, p. 538 on Dionysius.
5. Eus., Vita Constantini (V.C. henceforward) 3.47.2. J. Vogt (1977) 135 produces no real evidence for his conjecture that Helena was a Jewess.
6. Contra, Barnes (1981) 4.n.11.
7. Barnes (1981) 194 thinks Helena and Const. "may have heard Lucian teach" in Nicomedia: no evidence of this. Lact., M.P. 24.9, with Barnes, J.R.S. (1973) 43.
8. Pan. Lat. 6 (ed. Mynors, henceforward) 21.4, with R. Syme, History in Ovid (1978) 17 n. 3: R. MacMullen, Constantine (1968) 67 is slightly too trusting.
9. Pan. Lat. 5.8.4.
10. V. C. de Clercq (1954), at length; A. Lippold (1981) and note F. Paschoud (1971) 342–3, citing a possible core of fact in Zos. 2.29. The list in O.'s keeping: Eus., H.E. 10.6.2.
11. Eus., H.E. 9.9A.4; Pan. Lat. 8.8.4.
12. Eus., H.E. 9.9.3; Pan. Lat. 9.14.3.
13. Pan. Lat. 12.2.4; cf. Arr. Anab. 4.4., or Suet., Otho 8.3 ff. for examples.
14. Eus., H.E. 9.9.
15. Lact., M.P. 44.5, with Barnes (1981) 306 n. 146: I reject Grégoire's insertion, translating the text as transmitted to refer to a "staurogram": its word "Christum" is inexact.
16. K. Aland (1967), developing the observation of J. de Savignac (1963); E. Dinkler (1951) on a more remote Jewish background to these sorts of sign.
17. Eus., V. C. 1.27, with Barnes (1981) 266 n. 69–70.
18. Eus., V.C. 2.49; Liebeschuetz (1979) 279 n. 7 and 280.
19. D. Hoffman (1969) 173, a shrewd insight.
20. Contra Baynes (1972) 63, I accept that "caeleste signum" does mean "sign seen

in the heavens": the alternative, "most high," is very strained. I accept, with M. Black (1970) 319 ff., that L. has muddled the "staurogram" with the "Christogram." For an early Eastern origin of L.'s De Mort. Pers, see the important study of T. D. Barnes (1973).

21. Baynes (1972) 58 n. 31 for "Times" reports; also Barnes (1981) 306 n. 148, citing "Sky and Telescope" (1977–8) 185.

22. M. Guarducci, The Tomb of St. Peter (1960), esp. 111, has not established that any of the "chi-rho" signs belong before 312, contrary to her own conclusions. For Phrygian inscriptions before 312, the same point emerges, summarized by F. Blanchetière, Le Christianisme Asiate . . . (1981) 470–3.

23. Grenfell-Hunt, note on P. Oxy. 1611.56; compare E. G. Turner, Greek Manuscripts of the Ancient World (1971) no. 58.

24. P. Bruun, R.I.C. VII (1966) 62.

25. Barnes (1981) 43 n. 150 is wrong to trust the etymology discussed by J.-J. Hatt, Latomus (1950) 427: philologically, "labarum" from Celtic "labar" is possible, but Hatt cannot evade the problem of meaning: "speaking" or "babbling," hardly therefore a "terrifying" sign (p. 429). H. Grégoire, Byzantion 4 (1927–8) 477 proposed "laureum," distorted into Greek. Baynes accepted this on p. 64, but the distortion is very irregular and the word "laureum" is indeed "un terme incorrect du latin des camps" for the object. Did a Greek misunderstand a poorly Romanized German or Gaul's pronunciation? It is a long shot, alas. I am grateful to Drs. J. H. Penney and J. B. Hainsworth for confirming these points.

26. Eus., H.E. 9.9.10 and V.C. 1.40.2 are decisive against the reinterpretations by A. Alföldi (1939): Baynes 62–3 also accepts the cross.

27. R. MacMullen (1969) 77–8 is a recent sceptical account of the "reality"; I draw less of a line between the psychological pattern and what, therefore, was noticed. At more length, his article in G.R.B.S. (1968).

28. B. Berenson (1954) 56–7.

29. S. MacCormack, C.Q. (1975) 131, esp. 137–8; 146–7. In 69 A.D., note Suet., Galba passim; Vitell. 14.4; F. A. Cramer, Astrology in Roman Law . . . (1954), esp. 81 ff.

30. Lact., M.P. 27.

31. Pan. Lat. 10.14.3–6 and Liebeschuetz, esp. 270–1; Christian's Livy in P. Oxy. 4.657 and 668 (an early- and late-3rd-cent. pair of texts).

32. I well remember this analogy in an Oxford lecture by Peter Brown, in 1970; it did not, of course, express his own view of C.'s religious position.

33. H. A. Drake (1976) 61–79 is the most recent exploration of this.

34. This cardinal point in H. P. L'Orange and A. von Gerkan (1939) 110–11.

35. H. P. L'Orange and A. von Gerkan (1939), with S. MacCormack (1981) 33 ff.; McC. implies the ceremonial changed (p. 35), but we only know that its depiction on one monument was different (p. 36). The change is less if seen not against Republican precedent, but against the scenes on Galerius's arch, admittedly with more pagan divinities: M. S. Pond Rothman (1977) 442.

36. Pan. Lat. 11.8.3–4.

37. Lact., M.P. 46.6 with V.C. 4.20 and A. Piganiol (1932) 76.

38. Lact., M.P. 48.1 with Eus., H.E. 10.5.4. ff.; L. has "quicquid (est) divinitatis" whereas E. has "ho ti pote theiotētos kai ouraniou pragmatos."

39. H. von Soden, Urkunde, no. 11. H. Grégoire, Byzantion (1932) 650 and F. Millar, Emperor . . . (1977) 585–7 air the early date of 311/2. This is untenable:

C. would not then have given the Christian reply, cited in Optatus 1.25. For a later date, Barnes (1975) 21. The double reference to Gaul suggests C. was there when the Donatists wrote: Barnes (1981) 65 and n. 26–7 reveal C. was in Gaul in spring/early summer 313. This solves the problem. The Donatists wrote in early 313; our text, I suspect, is their "libellus without a seal," handed in at Carthage on April 15: August., Ep. 88.2. Against Barnes, with Millar, I take "hoc facinore" as persecution, not schism, and I punctuate before, not after, "nam." Schism arose through persecution, so the distinction between the translations is slender.

40. Baynes (1972) 96 n. 3.
41. C. Theod. 7.20.2 with Barnes (1981) 309 n. 42 and (1982) chap. 5 n. 102, changing the date to 307. E. Gabba (1978) 45 proposes 326. B.'s early date is quite arbitrary: we cannot exclude a group of "Velovoci" in Thrace. If anything is wrong, may it not be "civitate"? Might not C. be addressing a Gallic group, one of many in his own army? Or perhaps Gauls had been settled as colonists in Thrace: Pan. Lat. 4.21 knows of settlements in the reverse direction, to (depopulated?) Velovoci. R. von Haehling (1978) helps to make the greeting unsurprising, even in 320.
42. Lib. Pontific. (ed. Duchesne) 172–5; 179–81; cf. C. Pietri, Roma Christiana I (1976) 6 ff., esp. 8 n. 1. and 11–7.
43. Eus., V.C. 2.46 ("apply to governors and Praet. Pref."): V.C. 3.31.
44. Eus., H.E. 10.7, to Anullinus (a pagan), with Baynes 10–11.
45. C. Theod. 16.2.1–6 and 14; Eus., H.E. 10.7.1–2; T. G. Elliott (1978) 326.
46. Orig., C. Cels. 8.75.
47. C. Theod. 16.2.3, 6.
48. C. Theod. 16.2.4: "decedens"; "supremae voluntatis."
49. Barnes (1981) 50–3; J. Gaudemet (1947); A. Watson (1983) 61, on C. Theod. 9.12.1–2; A. Ehrhardt (1955) 127, on role of drafters.
50. H. von Soden, Urkunde no. 31; for August.'s disgust, Ad Don. Post Gesta 31.54; 33.56.
51. Barnes (1981) 54–61; Millar (1977) 584–90.
52. H. Dörries, Das Selbstzeugnis (1954) 256–7 for "servant"; 76–7, for anger.
53. V.C. 2.28 and Optatus (C.S.E.L. XX, ed. C. Ziwsa, 1896) Appendix V.30.
54. Optatus (1893 ed.) 206.
55. Jerome, Chron. (ed. R. Helm, G.C.S. 1956) p.231 (Arnobius); Min. Fel., Octav. 16–40.
56. On Moses, Orig., C. Cels. 8.69 and Eus., H.E. 9.9.5.
57. Eus., V.C. 4.15.1, for C.'s involvement in one coin type: Eus. is perhaps exaggerating C.'s own role. P. Bruun, R.I.C. VII (1966) 61–4, on continuing Sun. S. Price, C.R. (1979) 278 for texts connecting Emps. to coins: it was surely exceptional.
58. Liban., Or. 30.6; Zos. 2.29; Julian, 336 A–B; F. Paschoud (1971); S. M. Stern (1968) esp. 171 ff.

## II

The Oration was first published by R. Stephanus in 1544 and discussed as genuine by J.-P. Rossignol, Virgile et Constantine le Grand (1845). My own view of it was given in an Oxford seminar in June, 1981; at that time, I was unaware that D. De Decker, in Lactance et Son Temps (1978) 85, ed. J. Fontaine, M. Perrin, had raised the possibility of a dating at the Antioch Council in April 325 ("peut fort bien constituer l'occasion"). He had, however, adduced no arguments for this suggestion. S. Mazzarino, Antico, Tardoantico ed Era Constantiniana I (Storia e Civilta 13, 1974) had also suggested 325, again not to my knowledge, but had thought of Constantinople as a venue, impossibly. Other discussions varied from 313 to "after 325," never, however, at Antioch. I owe my detailed interest in the text to the very important study by T. D. Barnes in J.T.S. (1976) 414, which opted, however, for Serdica in 317 (cf. Barnes [1981] 71 ff, suggesting 321–324 instead). As this book goes to final proof, H. A. Drake, A.J.P. 106 (1985) 335 has argued that "concern to find an exact date may be profoundly misleading." He also believes that the rejoicing people in Oratio 22.1 are the Christians of Rome: "a stunning admission with implications for interpreting the Oration, indeed for interpreting Constantine's whole career, that have yet to be assessed." This assessment is not needed: nothing in Drake's study makes me wish to modify the exact date and setting given in what follows.

1. A. H. M. Jones, T. C. Skeat (1954), following a suggestion by C. E. Stevens.
2. Eus., V.C. 4.32.
3. Baynes, Constantine the Great (1972) 56 n. 19.
4. Photius, Cod. 127.
5. John Lyd., De Magistr. 3.33.
6. V.C. 4.29 + 4.33.
7. E.g. E. Schwartz, P.-W. R.E. vi.1427 and the oratio obliqua with accusative reflexive pronouns as (e.g.) 179 line 8 (ed. Heikel); A. Kurfess, Theol. Quart. (1950) esp. 165 n. 38; further list of "Latinisms," in Kurfess (1920) 94. E. A. Fisher (1982) 173, esp. 178–82, on this and other Greek translations of Latin.
8. V.C. 3.13, e.g.
9. A. Kurfess, Mnemosyne (1912) 277, listing eight traces of Virgil's Latin, six of which are irrelevant and two not conclusive. Kurfess (1920) extends the argument to chap. 21, but it is clear that Oratio, p. 186, 21–2 in Heikel's text (G.C.S., Eusebius I, 1902) comment on the Greek Eclogue, lines 3 ff. of the page. K.'s case is unfounded: this issue is soluble, and I will survey it elsewhere.
10. E. Fisher (1982) 299–307; Eus., H.E. 8.17.2 or 2.2.4 and 2.25.3.
11. Barnes, Phoenix (1976) 184 on Oration, 16 and V.C. 1.19: a vital discovery.
12. Heikel, on p. 155.21, inserted a needless "ekklesia." The double "te" joins two figures: the "naukleros" (surely a person?) and then the "tithēnē" (Church), p. 154.5–6, for "leaders and the rest"; 155.30 ff., for experts.
13. Orig., C. Cels 3.51; Basil, Letter 243.2: syllogos as "Christian congregation." On saints, E. Williger, Hagios (1922) 83 ff.
14. Orat. 25; Heikel 191.27. On p. 156.16 the perfect passive has force; at p. 163 line 11, it does not. As I doubt the "independent Latin original," I do not believe it renders Latin "captus est."
15. Barnes (1981) 76–7; Licin. as Diocl.'s successor: the contemporary Praxagoras FGH 219 T1 line 16. Barnes (1981) 214: the strangling. Barnes (1976) 422–3 opts for Lic. on general grounds.
16. 188.1–2, whereas 188.10 names Rome in a detached manner; 190.1.24 names Nicomedia likewise. Both, then, are distinct from the "dearest city."
17. Barnes (1976) 418–20, but he then emends "Maximin" arbitrarily to "Maximian" (Galerius).
18. Barnes (1981) 39–41; 62–4.

19. Lact., M.P. 43–2, 44.10.
20. Eus., H.E. 9.2.2: 9.11.5: Prep. Ev. 4.2.10. Gelasius (in Theodoros Anagnostes, G.C.S. 1971, ed. F. C. Hansen) 158 connects Theotecnus with "Maximian," a cave and oracles; cf. Theophanes 9.30 (de Boor), who goes on to reveal confusion with Maximin (33 ff.). Neither mentions statues or images, and their story is a patent confusion of Maximin with Galerius and (probably) the Didyma affair. Barnes, H.S.C.P. (1976) 252 is more indulgent to it.
21. Liban., Or. 11.121, with P. Petit, Libanius (1959) 173; G. Dagron, Byzance: Naissance . . . (1974) 57. Both these are admittedly later.
22. Liban., Or. 11.94; Philostr., V.A. 1.16; Eustathius in Dionys. Perieg. 916, for the very laurel. D. Levi, Antioch Mosaic Pavements (1947) I.211 ff., for a local picture. This is one objection to the argument of R. P. C. Hanson, J.T.S. (1973) 505. There are others.

### III

1. V.C. 2.23; 2.24–42 (First Letter to Heathen); 2.46 (buildings); 2.48–60 (Second Letter to Heathen), with H. Kraft (1955) 74–86; also, in Eusebius's view, V.C. 2.44–45 (the bans on sacrifice).
2. V.C. 4.8–13, with Barnes (1981) 397 n. 144 and 212 with notes.
3. V.C. 2.28; 4.9–10 (Persia).
4. V.C. 2.55; 57–8; 60.
5. C.I.L. III.352 with A. Chastagnol (1981).
6. Barnes, A.J.A.H. 3 (1978) 53 has also discussed these details; he does not, however, bring C. to Antioch for Good Friday and thus my reconstruction differs.
7. P. Oxy. 1261; 1626; V.C. 2.72.
8. P. Bruun, R.I.C. VII (1966) 77 and 664; Malalas 318–9 (Bonn) does actually bring C. to Antioch, a local "fact" he may recall correctly.
9. Barnes (1975) 173; Porfyrius (ed. Polara) 1.1–9; Poem 24 (adultery).
10. Porfyr. 5.1 and 14.9–12 and 25.
11. Most recently, A. Wlosok (1984) 257–62, with the full doxography; Lact., Phoen. 151–2 (Loeb, Minor Latin Poets, ed. J. W. Duff). Wlosok airs a date of 303/4; note the phoenix coin in 326, at Rome: Bruun, R.I.C. VII.328.
12. John Salisb., Policratic. 411B (Webb, Oxford, 1909): three correct classical events precede this, all derived from Justin. I am indebted to O. P. Nicholson for the germ of what follows.
13. O.G.I.S. 720, and J. Baillet (1922) 282; Lact., Phoen. 169–70.
14. Barnes (1981) 202–6.
15. Baynes, 20–1 and C. Foss (1977) 29: note, too, p. 36 (possible visit by C. before 327), Barnes (1981) 2.
16. Barnes (1978) 53 for the evidence in detail: Opitz, Urkunde 18.3, for the new Antioch bishop. Athan., Apol. Sec. 74.; 76.3 for Ossius in Alexandria, an event which I date early in 325, before the Antioch Council.
17. E. Schwartz (1905) 271, with E. Seeberg (1913) and J. R. Nyman (1961); D. Holland, Z.K.G. (1970) 163 adds nothing of substance.
18. H. Chadwick (1958) 292; Athanas., Apol. De Fug. S. 2: Ossius presided at each council he attended.
19. Barnes, J.T.S. (1976) 417 lays weight on C.'s titles in the Oratio Mss. Const. became "Niketes/Victor" after Nov. 324: the longer Ms. ignores this honour.

However, so does the Eusebian heading to the Sapor letter (V.C. 4.9); the varying Mss. readings for the Oratio's heading suggest no one official, full titulature had been transmitted. The omission, then, is not evidence for a date before 324; the Sapor letter is probably after Nov. 324/5, perhaps long after, C. T. Ehrhardt, Z.P.E. 38 (1980) 180 n. 22 also observes that "victor" is used in several inscriptions dated before Nov. 324: the title then, is not a firm criterion. I forbear to quote each chapter and verse of the Oratio for the running analysis which follows.

20. Orat. 6, with Maximin, Eus., H.E. 9.7.8.
21. Orat. 7, with Pan. Lat. 6.22.1–2: an addition to the intriguing study of W. Speyer (1977) 39.
22. Orat. 16, with Barnes H.S.C.P. (1976) 251, a vital observation.
23. V.C. 3.49.
24. Orat. 18, with A. Kurfess (1936) and (1952); M. L. Guillaumin (1978), with bibliogr.
25. Orig., C. Cels. 7.53 and 56; Lact., Div. Inst. 4.15.28.
26. Cic., De Div. 2.56; Aug. Civ. Dei 18.23 quotes the acrostic, without the last seven lines, spelling "Stauros": this does not prove they have been interpolated into the Oratio: Baynes, Constantine the Great (1972) 51–2 for the controversy.
27. Orat. 19 line 25 (Heikel).
28. K. Prüm (1929); most recently, C. Monteleone (1975).
29. A. Kurfess, Mnemosyne (1912) 277 listed eight signs of the Latin, of which six are not evident, one is ambiguous and one is a single word ("epainoi" for "laudes": p. 184.10), which may be fortuitous.
30. At 183.18–19, I read "ollut' enīpē Loigios Assuriōn," against Wilamowitz's conjectures, and I punctuate before "thallei": Greek text and commentary then coincide neatly.
31. Orat. 21, with our Sib. Or. 8.195; at Ecl. 4.62, C. and his translators read "cui," not "qui," a useful addition to the text's history, omitted in the O.C.T. Virgil (ed. Mynors).
32. R. G. M. Nisbet (1978) 59 is most convincing: I presume Lact., Div. Inst. 7.24.12 quotes lines from a pre-Virgilian Sibyl, supporting Nisbet's argument. For Pollio, Jos. A.J. 14.388; 15.343.
33. Lact., M.P. 14.1.
34. Kraft (1955) 146: "kein Theologe oder Philosoph." J. M. Rist (1981) 155–9 suggests three near-Arian errors in Orat. 9: (i) the absence of the word "homoousios." This, he admits, only emerged after Nicaea. (ii) The speaker implies the second "ousia" owes its "hyparxis" to the first. This (he suggests) was already suspect at Antioch and its council's letter avoids "hyparxis" altogether. However, the Letter survives only in Syriac, in which these fine distinctions are not obviously expressible: Rist argues from the Greek version, composed in this century by E. Schwartz (Opitz, Urkunde 18). (iii) Father as "Father of the Logos" was denied already in the Antioch Letter. True, the Letter does have an anti-Arian tone, but the Son is expressly called the "begotten son of the Father." After Nicaea, Orat. 9 would seem dangerously Arian, but not (in my view) at Antioch, in a sermon in April, 325. For the ambiguities of Antioch, see esp. L. Abramowski, Zts. für Kirchengesch. 86 (1975) 356, an excellent study.

35. V.C. 2.69 and 71: a crafty letter, not to be taken literally. I must emphasize again that I date Ossius's synod in Alexandria to *before* the Antioch Council: above, n. 16.
36. Opitz, Urkunde 20: cf. V.C. 3.6, for haste. We do not know where C. was when he wrote this. Perhaps he left Antioch by ship (as Ossius would); Antioch to Nicaea is 706 miles by land (Itin. Bordeaux Pilgrim), quite manageable between April 18 and May 31.
37. Optatus 1.22.
38. I differ here from Millar (1977) 594–7 and 605–7, whose account tends to emphasize the role of petitions and independent Church activity, rather than C.'s own initiative.
39. V.C. 3.15–6.
40. V.C. 3.10 and 13.
41. H. Chadwick (1960) 371; Philostorgius 1.9A (G.C.S., ed. Bidez: 1981 ed.) p. 10 lines 25 ff.; Optatus 1.26, for his role in 315.
42. Socr., H.E. 1.10, diverging from the preface of Eus., V.C. 3.64, perhaps correctly.

## IV

1. Men. Rhet. 422.16 and 423.25 (ed. Russell-Wilson). Orat. 11.
2. M. R. Alföldi (1964) 10, a fine study, but I reject her choice on pp. 13 ff.
3. C. Theod. 16.10.1 and V.C. 4.62.
4. Baynes, Constantine the Great (1972) 29 n. 76, on C. and unity.
5. E. Heck (1972) on Div. Inst. 1.1.13 and 7.26.11; J. Gaudemet (1980) 401, reviewing the C.-Lact. question.
6. M. L. Guillaumin (1978) 185; Div. Inst. 4.15; 1.19.5; 7.24.
7. Lact., third book, "To Probus," in Jerome, Comm. in Ep. ad Gal. 50.2: cites Sib. and Virg. on whiteness of Gauls' bodies.
8. Justice, e.g. Bk. 5 and Div. Inst. 1.1.13.
9. M. Perrin (1978) 203 and R. M. Ogilvie (1978) 79–80, on Plato; J. M. Pfättisch (1910), esp. 411 ff., contrasting the Oratio's Plato with Eusebius's uses.
10. Barnes, J.R.S. (1973) 69, on these differences and dates.
11. Div. Inst. 2.3–5; 4.25; 7.5; 4.29; 4.21; Ogilvie (1978) 33 ff. on Hermes, with 6.25, 7.4, 7.9, 7.13 and 7.18. Cross: 4.26–7.
12. Pan. Lat. 6.21.4; Porfyr. 14.3 ff.: also P. Courcelle (1957) for other examples, including Carausius's earlier, Virgilian coin slogan.
13. M. Perrin (1978) 203, on L.'s Plato.
14. J. M. Dillon (1977) 401 ff. is decisive here, against J. Waszink.
15. Barnes (1981) 74 claims a "marked similarity"; nor is there any evidence of Numenius's On the Good (a dialogue: Numenius, F3–4, Des Places). N.'s Supreme god, notoriously, was not a Creator, or involved in Creation.
16. Ogilvie (1978) 79–80 acutely observed that Lact. (Epitome 63.1) did not use Calcid. 29E: did the trans. not yet exist?
17. I know of no study of the Const.-Lact.-Ossius axis which does justice to these personal elements, C.'s own, in his Oration; Heim (1978) 56, for C.'s other possible initiatives.
18. E. R. Dodds, Pagans and Christians . . . (1965) 80 n. 2, quoting Wilamowitz.
19. Orat. 2.2; 3.3.; 5.1; 15.2; 26.1–2 on God's benefits to C.

## BIBLIOGRAPHY: I

K. Aland, Bemerkungen zur Alter und Entstehung des Christogrammes, Studien zur Überlieferung des N.T. v Seines Textes (1967) 173.

A. Alföldi, Hoc Signo Victor Eris, Pisciculi . . . , F. J. Dölger, A. u. C. Ergänzbd. 1 (1939) 1.

T. D. Barnes, Lactantius and Constantine, J.R.S. (1973) 29.

T. D. Barnes, The Beginnings of Donatism, J.T.S. (1975) 13.

T. D. Barnes, Constantine and Eusebius (1981).

N. H. Baynes, Constantine the Great and the Christian Church (1972, 2nd ed.).

B. Berenson, The Arch of Constantine (1954).

M. Black, The Chi-Rho Sign: Christogram or Staurogram?, Biblical and Historical Essays . . . , F. F. Bruce, ed. Gasque and Martin (1970) 319.

V. C. de Clercq, Ossius of Cordova (1954).

E. Dinkler, Zur Geschichte des Kreuzsymbols, Z.T.K. (1951) 148.

H. A. Drake, In Praise of Constantine . . . , Univ. of California Publ. Class. Stud. 15 (1976).

A. Ehrhardt, Constantins des Grossen Religionspolitik u. Gesetzgebung, Z.S.S., Röm. Abt. 72 (1955) 127.

T. G. Elliott, Tax Exemptions Granted to Clerics by Constantine and Constantius, Phoenix (1978) 326.

E. Gabba, I Cristiani dell'Esercito Romano del Quarto Secolo, in Transformations et Conflits au IVème Siècle. Colloque 1970 (1978, Bonn) 35.

J. Gaudemet, La Législation Religieuse de Constantin, Rev. de l'Hist. de l'Eglise de France 33 (1947) 25.

R. von Haehling, Die Religionszugehörigkeit der Hohen Amtsträger . . . seit Constantin I bis 455 n. Chr. (1978).

J.-J. Hatt, La Vision de Constantin au Sanctuaire de Grand et l'Origine Celtique du Labarum, Latomus (1950) 427.

D. Hoffmann, Das Spätromische Bewegungsheer u. die Notitia, Epigraphische Studien, 7.1 (1969).

A. Lippold, Bischof Ossius von Cordova und Konstantin der Grosse, Ztschr. f. Kirchengesch. 92 (1881) 1.

S. MacCormack, Roma, Constantinopolis, the Emperor and His Genius, C.Q. (1975) 131.

S. MacCormack, Art and Ceremonial in Late Antiquity (1981).

R. MacMullen, Constantine and the Miraculous, G.R.B.S. (1968) 81.

H. I. Marrou, L'Arianisme Comme Phénomène Alexandrin, C.R.A.I. (1973) 533.

F. G. B. Millar, The Emperor in the Roman World (1977).

H. P. L'Orange and A. von Gerkan, Der Spätantike Bildschmuck des Konstantinbogens (1939).

F. Paschoud, Zosime 2.29 et la Version Païenne de la Conversion de Constantin, Historia (1971) 334.

A. Piganiol. L'Empereur Constantin (1932).

M. S. Pond Rothman, The Thematic Organization of the Panel-Reliefs on the Arch of Galerius, A.J.A. (1977) 442.

J. de Savignac, Bodmer Papyrus XIV and XV, Scriptorium 17 (1963) 50.

S. M. Stern, 'Abd al-Jabbar's Account of How Christ's Religion was Falsified, J.T.S. (1968) 128.

J. Vogt, Pagans and Christians in the Family of Constantine the Great, in Paganism and Christianity . . . , ed. A. Momigliano (1963) 38.

J. Vogt, Helena Augusta: The Cross and the Jews, Classical Folia 31 (1977) 135.

A. Watson, Roman Slave Law and Romanist Ideology, Phoenix (1983) 61.


BIBLIOGRAPHY: II

T. D. Barnes, The Emperor Constantine's Good Friday Sermon, J.T.S. (1976) 414.

T. D. Barnes, Sossianus Hierocles and the Antecedents of the Great Persecution, H.S.C.P. (1976) 239.

T. D. Barnes, Constantine and Eusebius (1981).

E. A. Fisher, Greek Translations of Latin Literature in the Fourth Century, Y.C.S. (1982) 173.

A. H. M. Jones, T. C. Skeat, Notes on the Genuineness of the Constantinian Documents in Eusebius's Life of Constantine, J.E.H. (1954) 196.

A. Kurfess, Observatiunculae ad Eclogae Quartae Interpretationem et Versionem Graecam, Mnemosyne (1912) 277.

A. Kurfess, Vergili Vierte Ekloge in Kaiser Konstantins Rede an die Heilige Versammlung, Jhrsber. des Philolog. Vereins zu Berlin 64 (1920) 90.

A. Kurfess, Zu Kaiser Konstantins Rede an die Versammlung der Heiligen, Theologische Quartalschrift (1950) 145.


BIBLIOGRAPHY: III

L. Abramowski, Die Synode von Antiochien 324/5 und ihr Symbol, Zts. für Kirchengesch. 86 (1975) 356.

J. Baillet, Constantin et le Dadouque d'Eleusis, C.R.A.I. (1922) 282.

T. D. Barnes, Publius Optatianus Porfyrius, A.J.P. (1975) 173.

T. D. Barnes, Emperors and Bishops, A.D. 324–44: Some Problems, A.J.A.H. 3 (1978) 53.

T. D. Barnes, Constantine and Eusebius (1981).

H. Chadwick, Ossius of Cordova and the Presidency of the Council of Antioch, J.T.S. (1958) 292.

H. Chadwick, Faith, Order and the Council of Nicaea, H.T.R. (1960) 171.

A. Chastagnol, L'Inscription Constantinienne d'Orcistus, M.E.F.R. (1981) 381.

C. Foss, Late Antique and Byzantine Ankara, D.O.P. (1977).

M. L. Guillaumin, L'Exploitation des Oracles Sibyllins par Lactance et par le Discours à l'Assemblée des Saints, in Lactance et Son Temps, ed. J. Fontaine, M. Perrin (1978) 185.

H. Kraft, Kaiser Konstantins Religiöse Entwicklung (1955).

A. Kurfess, Ad Vergilii Eclogae IV Versionem Graecam, Philolog. Wochenschr. (1936) 364.

A. Kurfess, Kaiser Konstantin und die Erythräische Sibylle, Zts. für Relig. u. Geistesgesch. (1952) 42.

C. Monteleone, L'Egloga Quarta da Virgilio a Constantino (1975).

R. G. M. Nisbet, Virgil's Fourth Eclogue: Easterners and Westerners, B.I.C.S. (1978) 59.

J. R. Nyman, The Synod at Antioch: 324/5. Studia Patristica IV (1961) 483.

K. Prüm, Das Prophetenamt der Sibyllen in kirchl. Lit. . . . , 4 Ekloge Virgili Scholastik 4 (1929) 54.

J. M. Rist. Basil's "Neoplatonism," in Basil of Caesarea: Christian, Humanist, Ascetic, ed. P. J. Fedwick, vol. 1 (1981) 155.

E. Schwartz, Gesammelte Schriften, vol. 3 (1959) 117–87.

E. Seeberg, Die Synode von Antioch in 324/5 (1913).

W. Speyer, Die Ursprung Warmer Quellen nach Heidn. und Christ. Deutung, Jhrb. A. u. C. (1977) 39.

A. Wlosok, Originalität, Kontinuität und Epigonentum in der Spätrömischen Literatur, in Proc. of VII Congress of Internat. Fed. of Soc. of Classical Studies, ed. J. Harmatta, vol. II (1984, Budapest) 297.

## BIBLIOGRAPHY: IV

M. R. Alföldi, Die Sol-Comes Münze vom Jahre 325 . . . , Mullus: Festschrift T. Klauser, Jhb. für A. u. C., Erganzbd. 1 (1964) 10.

A. Bolhuis, Die Rede Konstantins der Grossen an die Versammlung der Heiligen u. Lactantius, V.C. (1956) 25.

P. Courcelle, Les Exégèses Chrétiennes de la Quatrième Eglogue, R.E.A. (1957) 294.

D. de Decker, Le Discours à l'Assemblée des Saints . . . et l'Oeuvre de Lactance, in Lactance et Son Temps, ed. J. Fontaine, M. Perrin (1978) 75.

J. M. Dillon, The Middle Platonists (1977).

J. Gaudemet, Constantino e Lattanzio, Labeo XXVI (1980) 401.

M. L. Guillaumin, L'Exploitation des Oracles Sibyllins par Lactance . . . , in Lactance et Son Temps, ed. J. Fontaine, M. Perrin (1978) 185.

E. Heck, Die Dualistischen Zusätze u. die Kaiseranreden bei Lactantius (1972).

F. Heim, L'Influence Exercée par Constantin sur Lactance, in Lactance et Son Temps, ed. J. Fontaine, M. Perrin (1978) 56.

A. Kurfess, Zu Kaiser Konstantins Rede . . . , Theol. Quartalschr. (1950) 145.

R. M. Ogilvie, The Library of Lactantius (1978).

M. Perrin, Le Platon de Lactance, in Lactance et Son Temps, ed. J. Fontaine, M. Perrin (1978) 203.

J. M. Pfattisch, Plato's Einfluss auf die Rede Konstantins an die Versammlung der Heiligen, T.Q. (1910) 399.

J. Schwartz, A Propos des Ch. 4 et 6 du De Mortibus Persecutorum, in Lactance et Son Temps, ed. J. Fontaine, M. Perrin (1978) 91.

CHAPTER 13

1. Socr., H.E. 1.1.

2. Ruf., H.E. 10.2; Socr., H.E. 1.8.

3. G. Downey, History of Antioch . . . (1961) 342–6.

4. L. Duchesne, Mél. Renier (1887) 159–74 lies behind datings before 303, while H. Koch, Z.N.W. (1916) 61–7 is the basic study for a date c. 309; I have been encouraged in the preference for a later date by an important, long paper by G. de Sainte Croix, as yet unpublished; Elvira, Can. 25 (confessors); 60 (idols).

5. G. de Sainte Croix, H.T.R. (1954) 76, for the edicts in the West; Arles, Can. 13; Ancyra 1–9.

6. Elvira 70 (husbands); 64–5 (wives); 48 (deathbed); Neocaes., Can. 4 and bestiality in Ancyr. 16, with J. Boswell, Christian., Social Tolerance . . . (1980)

197. S. Laeuchli, Power and Sexuality . . . (1972) is an excessively hostile, but worthwhile, study of the council and its patterns.

7. I cite Elvira 79, 6, 49, 81, 62, 36.

8. Arles 7; Elvira 56.

9. Eus., V.C. 2.45, believed, however, by T. D. Barnes, Constantine and Eusebius (1981) 210.

10. E.g. the evidence in R. Bagnall, B.A.S.P. (1982) 10.5; J. A. Martin, Rev. Et. Aug. (1979) 1; J. H. Liebeschuetz, in Studies in Ch. History, ed. D. Baker, 16 (1979) 17; the rise of holy men is part of the same new presence in the countryside.

11. Cod. Theod. 16.2.2; Barnes, Constantine and Eusebius 51, with 318 n. 82; legacies, Cod. Theod. 16.2.4; dodgers, 16.2.3 and 6.

12. Eus., V.C. 3.31.1–3, 32.1–2; on melting down, Eus., Tric. Or. 8.

13. On doles to Christian poor, Eus., V.C. 4.28 and 3.58; E. Patlagean, Pauvreté Economique et Pauvreté Sociale . . . (1977) esp. 186 ff.

14. Father Gregory, the former "hypsistarius": note J. Bernardi, in the S.C. ed. of Greg. Naz., Orations (1978) I. p.8 and n. 3; Elvira, Can. 1–4.

15. P. R. L. Brown, J.R.S. (1961) esp. 8–9 on this.

16. Amm. Marc. 22.5.4; "gentleness" in 22.11.5, a very telling passage.

17. Cod. Theod. 15.12.1 and G. Ville, M.E.F.R. (1960) 312.

18. On churches, Cod. Theod. 4.22.1; 9.45.4 (asylum: 431 A.D.); Aug., Conf. 3.3.5, girlfriend.

19. Eus., V.C. 3.50; on Constantinople, caution advised by G. Dagron, Byzance . . . (1974) 388–400.

20. E.g. A. H. M. Jones, Later Roman Empire (1964) 732–57; J. H. Liebeschuetz, Antioch (1972) 167 ff.: Liebeschuetz, p. 60, on ephebes; on gymnasia, A. H. M. Jones, Roman Economy (1974) 106 and E. G. Turner, Greek Papyri (1968) 84, whom I quote; contrary views in Alan Cameron, Circus Factions (1976) 216–17.

21. J. F. Matthews, Western Aristocracies and the Imperial Court (1975) 99–100; K. Holum, Theodosian Empresses (1982), an outstanding study; on pagan–Christian contrasts in giving, note L. Robert, Hellenica 11–12 (1960) 571.

22. Cod. Theod. 16.2.20 and 2.28, on legacies.

23. Cod. Theod. 8.8.1; 3.7.2.

24. Eus., V.C. 3.25 f. (Jerusalem); 3.55–6 (Aphaca and Aigai); Eus., P.E. 4.135C–136A (Antioch and Didyma); Aigai, Philostr., V. Ap. 1.13 with, most plausibly, N. J. Richardson, P. Burian, G.R.B.S. (1981) 283–5.

25. Firmicus, De Errore 16.4, with R. Turcan, Budé ed. (1982) 7–28.

26. G. Fowden, J.T.S. (1978) 53, an excellent survey; on Shenoute, J. Barns, Actes du 10 Congr. Internat. des Papyrologues (1964) 151–9, very chilling.

27. J. J. O'Donnell, Traditio (1979) 45 ff., for this aspect and much else; Aug., Ep. 16, fin. for "discord," a very telling passage. Soc., H.E. 5.10, for a different response.

28. Eus., V.C. 3.57.4.

29. On Menas, M. Guarducci, Inscr. Creticae, II.303–4; A. Wilhelm, Jahreshefte 25 (1929) 54, a superb study of Attic examples; cf. B.C.H. (1958) 681, in Christian era; L. Robert, Hellenica 4.55–7, Philostr., V. Ap. 4.34.2; Damascius, ap. Phot. 131; L. Robert, B.C.H. (1977) 87, excellent.

30. Eus., V.C. 3.54.6.

31. Hiatus, in S. MacCormack, Art and Ceremony (1981) 35; tomb, in E. D. Hunt,

Holy Land Pilgrimage . . . (1982) 7–23, with V.C. 3.26; others, in V.C. 3.41–3.

32. V.C. 3.52.1, with E. D. Hunt, Holy Land . . . (1982).

33. E. D. Hunt, Holy Land . . . (1982) 131–5 is excellent, here.

34. Elvira, Can. 36 and R. Grigg, Viator (1977) 1–32, rejecting details in Lib. Pont., probably rightly; note V.C. 3.49 (Daniel); at Mambre, however, note Eus., Dem. Ev. 5.9.7–8.

35. Eus., Tricenn. Orat. 18; cf. Artemid. 2.35.1.

36. Suggestively sketched by P. R. L. Brown, Studies in Ch. History, ed. D. Baker, vol. 13 (1976) 14–15, with bibliogr.

37. On icons, Theod., Hist. Relig. 26 and the fine survey by E. Kitzinger, D.O.P. (1954) 85; his pp. 102–3 discuss the intensified interest in "presence." Saints' icons, best known in Thessalonica: R. S. Cormack, A.B.S.A. (1969) 17, esp. 22–3, 50–2; I suspect these were widespread elsewhere before 480–500, but cannot prove it. In Alexandria, before c. 600 A.D., Mir. Cyr. et Joh., P.G. 87.3560, with Kitzinger, 106 n. 66: icon of Christ.

38. N. Fernandez Marcos, Los Thaumata de Sofronio (1975); Basil, P.G. 85.608–12, with Philostr., V.S. p. 186 (Loeb); Therapon, in L. Deubner, De Incubatione (1900); on angelic presence and holy men, H. Chadwick, J.T.S. (1974) 63–5.

39. P. R. L. Brown, Making of Late Antiquity (1978) 92–3, 101.

40. Hermas, Mand. 11; Co. of Antioch, ed. F. Nau, Rév. de l'Orient Chrét. (1909) pp. 25–7, Can. 15, 23.

41. G. M. Brown, B.I.C.S. (1970) 96; cf. Ill. Class. Stud. (1976) 53–8; I quote questions 44.9 and 98.

42. H. C. Youtie, Z.P.E. (1975) 253, with P. Oxy. 925, 1150, 1926, etc.

43. P. R. L. Brown, The Cult of Saints (1981), with discussion by J. Fontaine, An. Boll. (1982) 16.

44. E. D. Hunt, Holy Land . . . (1982) 131 ff.

45. Oil, in (e.g.) P.G. 87.3669A; cf. T. Nissen, Byz. Zeitschr. (1939) 349–81; in general, L. Deubner, De Incubatione (1900); A. J. Festugière, Vie de Sainte Thecle; Côme et Damien; Cyr. et Jean (1971).

46. P. R. L. Brown, J.R.S. (1971) 80, esp. 87–8, slightly overstressing the social arbitration, as opposed to the intercession for sins before the Last Judgement; on Mary, Averil Cameron, J.T.S. (1978) 104–5.

47. G. Wolff, De Novissima Oraculorum Aetate (1854) 46–9, for texts; I accept his p. 36 on Claudian's evidence (cf. p. 48).

48. Eus., P. Ev. 4.135C–136A.

49. Theos. Tub. (ed. Erbse) 6; Lampe, Patristic Greek Lexikon, s.v. theosophia.

50. A. Grabar, C.R.A.I. (1969) 264.

51. In general, A. de Waal, Ara Coeli oder die Sibylle des Augustus (1902) and H. Leclercq, Marie in Ara Coeli, D.A.C.L. 10 (1931–2) 2075, with bibliogr. The earliest version may have cited a prophetic "pythoness," not a Sibyl.

# Index

The material within each entry is arranged alphabetically, with the following exceptions: (a) certain entries are arranged chronologically; (b) where entries are subdivided into PAGAN and CHRISTIAN, PAGAN precedes CHRISTIAN.

Abbahu, Rabbi, 481
Abercius (Phrygian bishop), 276–7
Abgar V, King of Edessa, 279
Abgar VIII, King of Edessa, 279–80, 307, 609
Abonouteichos (Ionopolis, Paphlagonia), 241–50
abortion, 343, 351, 355
abstract divinities: Aion, 116; Ammonius on, 186; in Anatolia, 33, 35, 404; Constantine and, 614–15; Iao (Yahweh), 190, 257; incense offerings, 70–71; Jewish, 35; magical invocation, 37; "merged," 35, 73; Oenoanda inscription, 169–77, 177; oracles on, 182, 190–200, 256–7; philosophers on, 170–71, 193; in Phrygia, 404; in Pontus, 534; Sun God, 575; "universal" gods, 34–5, 196
Acacius (legendary martyr), 459
Achan, sin of, 540–41
"Acts" of Apostles: spurious, 301, 339–40, 569–70; on relics, 446; on sex, 356–8; visions in, 396–9; see also Thomas
Acts of the Apostles: as Christian apology, 430–32; origin and aims, 305; quoted, 99–101, 140; see also Paul
administration, Roman, late C3 changes, 573, 582–3
adultery, 351, 386, 448, 556, 558
Aelian, on gods and nature, 42
Aelius Aristeides: Sacred Tales, 129–30, 159, 160–63, 170; at Smyrna, 485, 486
Africa, North: PAGAN: and Clarian oracle, 194, 195, 253; cults, 38; CHRISTIAN: arrival, 273–6; composition of church (180 A.D.) 291, (256 A.D.) 271–2, 280, 288, 289, (at Cirta, 303 A.D.) 310, 312, 588; penance in, 337–8; rural bishops, 288, 289; schisms in church, 250, 280; see also towns by name

Africanus, Julius (Christian writer), 307
afterlife, beliefs in, see death
agoraioi, local advisers to governor, 488–9
Aigai (Cilicia), 246, 247, 248, 253, 671, 676
Aizani, Phrygia, 41, 69, 222
Alexander of Cappadocia: in Judaea, 476, 508; meets Origen, 520–21
Alexander of Lycopolis, writes against Mani, 569
Alexandria: cult of Serapis, 75, 201; in C2nd (administration) 49–50, (population) 47; class of Christians (c. 200 A.D.), 301–2, 306–7; siege and plague (262 A.D.), 555–6, 573; games restored, 578; barbarians, 268–9, 572; and Diocletian (c. 300 A.D.), 594–5; 10 churches (310 A.D.), 589; heresy in, 609–10; Synod (325), 642; see also Arius; Dionysius
allegory, Origen and, 524
almsgiving, Christian: competition, 560, cf. pagan benefaction, 324–5; as penance, 254–5; see also charity
Altava (N. Africa), 587
Amaseia (Pontus), 534, 536
Ambrose (Augustine's teacher), 544
Ammianus, Marcellinus (historian), 669
Ammon: oracle at Siwah, Libya, 202, 230, 234, 238, 250, 252, 256
Ammonius (Origen's teacher), 271
Ammonius (Platonist philosopher), in Plutarch, 185–6
Amphicles (pupil of Herodes), 518
amulets, 36–7, 151, 160
Anahita (goddess), 535, 538
anathema, 501, 540
Anatolia: pagan cults, 33, 39; country bishops, 288
Anatolius (Alexandrian Christian), 555
Ancyra: games, 579–80; martyrs, 599–600; Synod, 641–2, 664–5

angels: PAGAN: 33, 169, 170, 191; CHRISTIAN: in *Acts* and *Epistles*, 101, 380; and chastity, 363, 366; in church art and liturgy, 676; guardian, 520; in Hermas' vision, 385–90; and monks, 417–18; protection by dead man's, 294–5

anger, divine: PAGAN: cause of misfortune, 34, 38, 95, 230–37, 326, 575; fear of, 98–101, 109–17, 122–3; Christians and, 425, 426, 474–6, 491–2, 552, 672; dreams, warning, 163; "limiting" invocation of god, 117; representations of gods, 159; CHRISTIAN: caused by sin, 475–6, 477–8, 678–9; and intercession, 679; and punishment, 554, 652–3

anger, personal, 65

Anthesteria (Athenian festival), 92–3

Antinoopolis, games, 578

Antioch (Syria): C2nd population, 47; Emperor Philip, 453; barbarians (c. 253), 572; Constantine (325), 634–5, 638; Council (325), 642–56; Church of Concord, 664

Antonine age: architecture, 56, 75; ethos, 64–6, 101; *see also* benefaction

Antony (Coptic hermit), 18, 20, 416–17, 601

Apamea (Syria), 47; oracle of Zeus, 197, 201, 228, 229–30

Aphaca (N. Africa), 671

apocalyptic texts, 340, 381, 412; *see also* Revelation

Apollo: Anexiomarus, 38–9; at Cyrene, 114–15; and Hierapolis, 233–6; Lairbenos, 41–2, 389; at Miletus, 102–3, 131–2; Mystes, 156; sacrifice to, 70–71; as Sun god, 216–17, 256; *see also* Claros; Delphi; Didyma; oracles

Apollonia (Epirus), oracle, 207

Apollonis (Lydia), 463

Apollonius of Tyana (wise man), 189, 191, 196, 245, 253–4; Christian attitude to, 671

apologists: Christian, 430–32, 305–6, 515–16; Jewish, 515

*apotaktikoi* (Christian perfectionists), 602

appearance of gods, *see* epiphany

Apphion (Milesian bull tamer), 227–8

Apuleius: afterlife, 96; gods' presence, 124, 138, 160; homosexuality, 341–2; on the nobility, 55; private cults, 55; trial for sorcery, 74

architecture, *see* building

arena, *see* games

Ares, 133–4, 575

Aristeides (C2nd Christian), 305

Arius: beliefs, 602, 610; Constantine writes to, 638; and Councils (Antioch) 641–3, 653–4, (Nicaea) 654–6

Arles, Council of, 664–6

Armenia, 281, 538

army: Christianity spread by, 277; Christians in, 304, 553, 588, 594; paganism in Constantine's, 622

Arsinoe (Egypt), 67

art, religious: PAGAN: and dreams, 153–5; C3rd change, 573–4; CHRISTIAN: 392–5, 676; *see also* statues

Artemidorus of Daldis, on dreams, 55, 95, 155–8, 342, 388

Artemis, 72, 90–91; "universal," 34

Arval Brothers, 29

Asclepius: cures, 118, 119; and dreams, 151–3, 161–2, 206; and Glycon's cult, 244–7; oracles, 206; at Pergamum, 34, 71, 75, 201; sacrifice to, 70–71; shrines "neutralized" by Christian churches, 676; Thessalos and, 39, 143

assemblies, civic, 51

assizes, 423, 484–9

Astrampsychus, *Fates*, 210–11, 677

astrology, 30, 212, 678

asylum at shrines: PAGAN, 127–8; CHRISTIAN, 669; for slaves, 299

"atheism," 30; Christian, 425–8, 551–2, 259; Epicurean, 168–9, 259; Jewish, 428

Athenagoras (Christian apologist), 136, 305–6

Athenodorus (bishop, brother of Gregory of Pontus), 532–3

Athens, 29; barbarians, 572; festivals, 81–2, 91–3; and oracles, 228, 231; T. Flavius Glaucus' career, 13–14; *see also* Eleusis

atonement in martyrdom, 437

Attis, cult of, 348

Augustine of Hippo, 57, 504; education, 544; "hearer" of Manichaeism, 563; on Latin/Punic bilingualism, 283, 286; scriptural authority, 544–5

Aurelian, Emperor, 513–14, 593

Autun (Gaul), panegyric to Constantine, 611–12

Babylon, Constantine visits, 630, 646, 652

Bacchus, 85–8, 96–7

baptism, 316–17, 337, 338–9; of Christ, 376–7

Baptists in Mesopotamia, 277–8, 564

barbarians, 539–40, 572–3, 575–7

Bardaisan (Christian teacher at Edessa), 278–9, 307, 312, 567

Barnabas (Paul's companion), 99–100, 140

Basil (Cappadocian bishop), 533

basilicas, Christian, 587

bathing, mixed, 373, 559

baths, heated, 54, 57

battles, gods' presence, 120–21

Baynes, N. H., 627

Beirut, law school, 519, 526–7

benefaction, public, 12–14, 52–7, 60–61,

79–80; C2nd and C3rd, 12–14, 15–16, 52–7, 60–61; religious and secular, 79–80; and oracular revival, 254–5; Christian, nature of, 325; late C3rd, 420, 582–5; Constantinian and later, 669–71; *see also* Bryonianus; Damianus; games; Glaucus; Herodes; "honour, love of"; Longinus; Opramoas; Politta; Rufinus

bequests, Christian, 309–10, 351–2, 589; Constantine's laws, 623–4, 667

Bes (Egyptian god), 205

*Birth of his Body, On the*, 563

bisexuality, 341–2

bishops: Apostolic succession, 498, 506; appointments by, 504–5; arbitration among, 507, 511–14; authority of, 455, 500–503, 507, 513–15, 543–5; "bishop of," 507; and confessors, 458–9, 494–5, 551; country, 288–9; emergence of, 498–9, 503–4; and Gnostics, 493–4, 561; ideal, 493–545; judicial role, 17, 494, 500–503, 540–41; and martyrs, 494–5; and pagan culture, 516–17, 542–3; cf. pagan prophets, 507; persecution of, 455, 495, 551; scriptural basis of doctrine, 542, 543–5; selection of, 503–4, 506–12, 514, 588; and sinners, 500–501; *see also* Augustine; Cyprian; Dionysius; Gregory of Pontus

Blandina (martyr), 436

books: Christian, 304–5; Manichaean, 569

bribery: of bishops by sinners, 501; in persecution, 457, 597

"brides of Christ," 371

Bruttius Praesens (historian), 433

Bryonianus Lollianus (benefactor, of Side), 583–4

building, 56, 72–4, 75–6; pagan religious, phases of, 75; late C3rd, 582; Christian basilicas, 587; Constantine, 620–21, 662–3, 667–9

Cabeira (Pontus), 534, 536

Caesarea (Mazaca, Cappadocia), 572

Caesarea Trochetta (Lydia), and Clarian oracle, 232, 240, 242–3

Calcidius (translator), 661

Callimachus, hymns, 114–15

Callipolis (Gallipoli), 232

Callistus (bishop of Rome), 308–9

Candida (martyr), 281

Candidus (Roman general), 180

Carthage: class of Christians (c. 200 A.D.), 302, 307; Council of, 544; Cyprian and, 14–16; extent of, 46; Greek culture, 32; plague (250s), 359, 573

Cassian (legendary martyr), 460

castration, 348, 355–6

catacombs in Rome, 312, 589

catechumen, 316–17, 387

caves, pagan cults, 41, 69, 673

Celerinus (martyr), 440, 454

celibacy, *see* chastity

Celsus (Platonist), on afterlife, 96; on Christians, 427, 482–3, 516; on Jews, 482–3

ceremonies, Roman, *see* cults

certificates, Decian, 455–7, 550

Chaldaean oracles, 185–6, 197–9

Chariton (novelist), 139–40

charity, Christian, 323–5, 591; Constantine and, 16, 17, 668–70; distribution, 325, 505; *see also* almsgiving

chastity, Christian virtue of, 340–74; bequests, 310; lapses in, 370–71, 373–4; in marriage, 356–7, 358–9, 363, 367–8; medical opinion on, 361; pagan attitude to, 157, 342–3; practical aspects, 366–72, 602; reasons for emphasis, 365–73; scriptures on, 362–4; vows of, 355–6, 367; *see also* virgins

chi-rho sign, 616

Christ: chastity of, 362–3; on divorce, 352–3; model of martyrdom, 441; visions of, 376–80, 390, 396–8, 402–3, 439

Church: buildings, 88–9, 269–70, 587, 622–3, 667–9; in cities, 272; organization, 63, 503–4; social structure, 291–3, 312; spread, 268–81, 272–3, 293–312, 586–92, 667–71; *see also* entries on individual aspects

churches, house, 88–9, 269–70

Cibyra Minor, 12

Cicero, Constantine misquotes, 648

circumcision, 271, 296–7

Cirta (N. Africa), church in 303 A.D., 310, 312, 588

cities and civic life: C2nd, 46–52; C3rd, 577–85; ceremonial and civic identity, 67, 80–82, 91–2; *see also* benefaction; councils; office; rivalry; society; town/country

claques, Christian electoral, 510–11

Claros, oracle of Apollo at, 171–80; area of influence, 177–8, 194–5; C2nd revival, 200–202, 250–53; C3rd influence, 576, 615; choirs, 178–9; enquiries, type of, 133–4, 177–80; method of consultation, 171–6; priests, 77, 171–6, 188; thespode, 172–6, 201, 240–41, 248–9

Clea (Delphic priestess), 184–5

Clement of Alexandria: on marriage and sex, 358–9; on mixed bathing, 559; *Paedogogus*, 306–7; repentance, 338; slavery, 298; structure of church, 301; *Whether the Rich Man can be Saved*, 302

codex, importance to Christianity, 304–5

cohabitation, 308–9, 344–5, 354

Collosseum, and Constantine, 658
Colossae (Phrygia), worship of angels by
    Christians, 380
Comana (Pontus), 536–7
Commagene, oracular inscription, 180
community, Christian sense of, 323–4; cf.
    cult societies, 88–9
concubinage, 344–5, 354
Condianus (senator), and oracle, 229–30
confession of sins, public, 337–8
confessors, 445, 448–50; authority, 408,
    440–41; and bishops, 458–9, 494–5, 551
Conon (martyr), and Jews, 483
Conon (law student), 528
Constantine I, Emperor: early life, 610–11;
    Tetrarch, 611–12; conversion, 611–18,
    625–7; vision of Cross, 613–18; defeats
    Maxentius, 618–19; sole Emperor, 607,
    608, 620
    accommodates pagan majority, 17,
    620–21, 626, 657–8, 666; authority over
    church, 512–14, 625, 656; building,
    622–3, 667–9, 620–21, at Council of
    Antioch, 642–53; and Donatists, 621–2,
    624–5; laws, 17–18, 623–4; letters, 635–7,
    653; and Persia, 636–7; reception of
    conversion, 620–22, 626–7; religious
    policy, 609, 610, 615–18; significance to
    church, 663–81; and suffrage, 508; travels
    in East, 630–31; *see also Oration to the
    Saints*
Constantius, 610–11, 614–15
contraception, 343, 355
conversion to Christianity, 314–16, 323–5; of
    Constantine, 613–18; and Jews, 318–19,
    271; means of, 314–16; by miracles, 270;
    opportunist, under Constantine, 668;
    social class of converts, 293–312, 317–18;
    social theories on, 317–23, 335
Coptic, Gospels in, 282–3
Cosa (Etruria), and Decius, 453
Councils, Church, *see* Antioch; Arles;
    Carthage; Elvira; Gangra; Nicaea
councils, civic, 50–51, 302
countryside, *see* town/country
crisis: divine epiphanies in, 142–3, 380,
    399–403; late C3rd civic, 572–4
Cronos, cult of, 581
Cross and Constantine, 613–18, 622–3
cult societies, 61, 84–9, 93, 206, 325
cults, pagan, 64–101; C1st decline, 74–5;
    C3rd vigour, 580–85; ceremonies, 31–2,
    66, 80–81, 89–90; Christians and, 130–32,
    259, 425–8, 551–2; Constantine and,
    669–70; cult acts and *religio*, 31–2;
    festivals, 66–8; household, 83, 88;
    "native" and imported, 38–9, 82–3; range
    of, 32–46, 82–3; Roman, in Greek East,
    39; rural, 41–3; sexual purity in, 347, 362;

tradition and change in, 29; urban, 66–89;
    *see also* Emperors; gods; mysteries; oracles
culture: Antonine, 305–6; Greek and Roman
    areas of, 32–3, 39; pagan, and Christians,
    304–8, 516–17, 542–3; at Smyrna, 477–8
Cybele, 71–2, 580–81
Cyprian (Thascius Cyprianus, bishop of
    Carthage), 14–16; chair of office, 504; and
    confessors, 495; and Decian persecution,
    451, 458–9; visions, 411, 451, 487–8; trial,
    487–8, 551; death, 552
    on bishops, 503; and Classical culture,
    543; on the End, 267; *On Mortality*, 574;
    on Novatian, 542; *On the Lapsed*, 443–4;
    on virginity, 359, 369
Cyrus and John, shrine of, 676, 679
Cyzicus (Phrygia), and oracles, 181, 202, 230,
    234, 250, 252, 256

*daimones, see* demons
Dalmatia, Clarian text, 194
Damianus (prophet at Didyma), 216–17
Daniel, Book of, 476, 647
Daphne, at Antioch, 634–5, 647
Dead Sea, Pionius on, 474–5, 478
Dead Sea Scrolls: on angels, 380; on authority
    of leader, 495; on celibacy, 365; on Holy
    Spirit, 313
death, the dead, 48; PAGAN: afterlife, 95–8,
    192–3; commemoration of dead, 61,
    83–4, 98, 132, 142–3; funerals, 61;
    funerary foundations, 61, 84–8, 93, 325;
    visions of dead, 377; CHRISTIAN: afterlife,
    326–7; burial beside holy man, 294–5;
    intercession for, 97–8; Jewish influence on
    beliefs, 447–8; veneration of martyrs,
    47–8; visions of dead, 412–13
Decius, Emperor: persecution of Christians,
    450–92, 532, 549–50; death, 457, 652
Delphi, oracle of Apollo at, 178; on god, 171;
    philosophers on, 184–8, 197; C2nd text,
    233–6; in C3rd, 576; demise, 681
demons: *daimones*, 129, 132, 137; exorcism,
    327–30; Satanic, 137, 326, 327–30, 444
*Didascalia* (C3rd text), 499, 557
Didyma, oracle of Apollo at, 34, 180–83;
    C1st revival, 250–51; barbarians, 576–7;
    and Christians, 595, 618, 671–2; demise,
    679
    consultation, method of, 182–3; choirs,
    183, 219–22; enquiries, 180–82, 192–3,
    194; procession, 72; prophets, 181–3, 188,
    220–25
Dio of Prusa (orator), 45–6, 50, 110, 122,
    123, 345
Dio, Cassius (historian), 123
dioceses, Imperial and Christian, 573
Diocletian, Emperor: consults oracle at
    Didyma, 595; family, 609; Great

Persecution, 592, 594; and Manichaeans, 594–5; provincial administration, 573

Dionysia, at Smyrna, 485–6

Dionysius (bishop of Alexandria): and Classical culture, 543; and debate on resurrection, 265–6; on Decian persecution, 454–5; on Ecclesiastes, 523–4; and Gallienus, 554–6, 609; on Emperor Philip, 454; on philosophy, 525; scriptural authority, 543; source for Eusebius, 607; trial, 471, 551, 552–3

Dionysus, 96–7, 206; and Iobacchi, 85–8

disasters, civic (C2nd) 231–5, (C3rd) 572–4, 577, 599

disguise, gods in: PAGAN: 123, 129, 137–41, 148, 161, 164; Homer on, 104–7, 108; CHRISTIAN: 378–9, 390

divination: PAGAN: 208–13, 236; CHRISTIAN: 389, 404–12, 677

divinity, Supreme, *see* abstract divinities

divorce, 345, 352–4, 386

doctrine, popular interest, 265–6, 330

Domitian, Emperor, 433

Donatists, 609, 621–2, 624, 655

dreams, divine: PAGAN: 102–3, 108–9, 149–66; influence of art, 161–2; philosophers on, 150; promotion of, 151–5; CHRISTIAN: 391–403; influence of art, 676; literary inspiration, 472–3; prophetic, of martyrdom, 451, 488–9

dreams, erotic, 155, 157, 345, 373, 392, 543

dualism, Manichaean, 567–9

Dugga, revival in 260s, 582

Dura-Europus, 269–70, 277


east, prayer towards, 168–70, 190

Ecclesiastes, 522–4

Edessa (Syria), 276, 279–80, 284, 307; martyrs, 587, 600–601

education, in Church, 265–6, 304–8

Egypt: Christians, 265–6, 589–90; civic administration, 50; civic entertainment, 578–80, 581; cults, 33, 37, 70–71, 166–7, 187; magic, 37, 135; mechanical effects in temples, 136; oracles, 214–15; priests, 77, 138, 187; *see also* Dionysius; monasticism; towns by name

Elchesai (heretic), 277, 360, 388; and Mani, 564–5, 567

Elders, Christian, 495, 503–4

Eleusis, cult of Demeter, 14, 72; afterlife, 96, 97; initiates, 491, 640–41

Elvira (Spain), Council of, 664–7, 675

Emperors: authority over Church, 512–14, 625, 656; Christians and cult, 426, 431–2, 476–7; cult of, 39–41, 72, 90, 141; popular image, 48–9; *see also* individual names

end of world: Christian expectations, 226–7,

331, 333–4, 363, 474–5, 605; Last Judgement, 327, 412, 500, 647–8

Endor, witch of, 480–83

Ephebes, 670

*Ephesian Tales* (novel), 139

Ephesus (Lydia): barbarians, 572; benefactors (Damianus), 56; C2nd population, 46–7; Decian martyrs, 459, 490; Gordian at, 12; oracular texts, 176–82, 190

epic poems, Greek, 103–110

Epicrates (C1st Lydian), inscription to son, 142–3

Epicureanism, 30, 123, 168–9

epigraphy, 14, 251; C2nd oracles, 177–9, 231–6; C3rd decline, 572, 574, 575; C3rd–4th, 580–81, 583

epilepsy, exorcism of, 328

*epiphaneia, epiphanes*, 127

epiphany, Christian, *see* visions

Epiphany, feast of, 116

epiphany of pagan gods, 98–167 (summarized, 164–5): before Christian era, 102–23; Imperial era, 123–67 accommodation to recipient, 109; in battle, 120–22, 618–19; C3rd, 575; in crises, 117–18; cults to mark, 111, 379; educated attitude, 144–8; emotional response, 112–13; face to face, 142–9; "limiting" invocations, 117; and moral worth, 129; Paul and Peter mistaken as, 100–101; as personal companions, 104–5, 128–9, 678; philosophers on, 123; places, special, 144–7; simulated in temples, 133, 166, 248; spiritual experience, 126; through statues, 115, 133–5; "traces," 140–41, 138; unseen presence, 127–37, 390–91; voices, 111–12, 166–7, 168; *see also* disguise; dreams

episcopacy, *see* bishops

Erythrae (Lydia), Sibyl, 203

eschatology, *see* end of world

Euergetis (Egypt), festival, 580

Eumeneia (Phrygia), 295, 302

Eumolpids, 491, 640–41

Euplus (voluntary martyr), 443

Eusebius (Christian bishop and historian): and Arianism, 653–4, 656; and Bruttius' *History*, 433; on Christian expansion, 271–2, 278; *Church History*, 273–4, 607–8; on Constantine, 17, 613, 615–16; *On the Life of Constantine*, 17, 627; and *Oration to the Saints*, 627–30; writings and education, 605–8

Eusebius (deacon), 555

Eutropia (Constantine's mother-in-law), 674

evil, idea of, 326–7

excommunication, 501, 540, 550; of Paul of Samosata, 512–13

exorcism, 327–8, 329–30, 337
exposure of babies, 48, 343, 351, 382

fabrications, Christian literary, *see* "Acts,"
    spurious
fairies, 120
faith, "the faithful," 31
family: conversion in, 312, 316; persecution
    in, 423–4; *see also* marriage
fasting and epiphany/visions, 151, 173, 175,
    182, 205, 386, 395–6, 400
*Fates* (oracular books), 210–11
fear, *see* anger, divine
Felix, Antonius (governor of Judaea), 431
festivals, pagan, 66–8, 90–92; *see also* games;
    festivals by name
Festus, Porcius (governor of Judaea), 431
Firmicus Maternus, on persecution of
    pagans, 672
Firmilian of Cappadocia, 530
Flavian (martyr), 469–70, 511
footprints: dedicated to gods, 83; *see also*
    "traces"
freedom, civil, 49
Fronto (Emperor Marcus' tutor), 427
Fructuosus (martyr), 445, 446, 488
funeral associations, 61, 84–9, 93, 325

Gaius (Christian lawyer), 518, 526, 527
Galen (medical writer), 65, 123, 344
Galerius, Emperor, 592, 630, 660
Gallienus, Emperor, 578, 592; and
    Christians, 550–51, 553–6
Gallio (governor of Achaea), 430
games, 11–13, 537–8, 578–80; in Christian
    imagery, 436; gladiatorial, 54–5, 485, 669;
    *see also* martyrs
Gangra, Council of, 325, 372
Gaza (Syria), 18–19, 270
Gerasa (Jerash, Syria), 72–3
Gibbon, Edward, 314
Glaucus, T. Flavius (Athenian noble), 13–14
Gnosticism, 332, 493–4, 561
"goddesses" (beautiful women), 106, 139
gods: household, 83, 88; imported, 38–9,
    82–3; rural, 41–5; "universal," 34–5, 196;
    *see also* abstract divinities; individual
    names
Golden Age, 111, 165
Gordian III, Emperor, 11–13, 60
"Gospel of Light," *see* Mani
Gospel, third, as apology, 430–31
Goths, 539–40, 575–6
governors, Roman, 49; and Christians, 424,
    425–8, 434, 552–3
Greek and Latin cultural areas, 32–3, 39
Gregory of Nyssa, panegyric on Gregory of
    Pontus, 516, 528–39, 574
Gregory of Pontus (bishop of Neocaesarea),
    516–42, *529*: early life, 517–28, 542; and
    Origen, 516–17, 519–28; in Neocaesarea,
    533–8; at Council of Antioch, 532; in
    persecution, 532; Gregory of Nyssa's
    panegyric, 516, 528–39, 574
    *Canonical Letter*, 539–42; on Ecclesiastes,
    522–4; on Roman law, 525–6; scriptural
    authority, 542; theological creed, 521,
    532; *To Theopompus* (prob. spurious),
    521–2, 525, 539, 542
groves, pagan, 43–4
Gryneum (Asia Minor), 231
Gurya (martyr), 600
gymnasia, C4th demise, 670

Habbib (martyr), 600
Hadrian, Emperor, 189, 201
hagiography, 18–19
hairesis, *see* heresy
Hamilton, William, in Pontus, 531
Harran (Carrhae), 280, 587, 627
Hegesippus (writer), 506
Helena (Constantine's mother), 609, 610–11,
    670–71, 674
Heliodorus, *Ethiopic Tales*, 137–8, 186–7
Heraclea (Caria), 179, 252
heretics and heresy: appointments by lot, 514;
    baptism of, 532; Constantine's attitude,
    626, 656; Council of Carthage on, 544;
    Council of Nicaea on, 654–6; in Egypt,
    265–6; Gnosticism, 332, 493–4, 561;
    Heavenly Twin, 565–6; Montanism,
    404–10; orthodox doctrine hardens in
    C3rd, 561; pagan concept of, 31; on sex,
    357–8; spread of, 276; and tradition,
    332–3; value to Church, 571; *see also*
    Arius; Manichaeism; Marcion
Hermas, *Shepherd*, 381–90, 493–4
Hermes, Thrice-great, 94, 126, 414–16
Hermias (of Didyma), 216, 258
hermits, 18–20, 601–4
Hermopolis (Egypt), 578–9, 580
Hero of Alexandria (writer), 136
Herodes Atticus (benefactor), 79, 85, 86, 88,
    518
Herodian (historian), 121
Hesiod, 108
Hierapolis (Phrygia), oracular text, 233–6,
    238, 255–6
Hierocles (voluntary martyr), 442
Hierocles (pagan writer), 593, 606, 671
Hilarion (holy man), 18–20
Hinton St. Mary, mosaic, 676
Hippolytus (bishop of Rome), 267
Hira (Arab kingdom), Manichees at, 570
Holy and Just divinity, *see* abstract divinities
holy men, 449–50; *see also* Antony; Hilarion;
    monasticism
Holy Sepulchre, discovery of, 674

Homer, 103–110, 150, 151, 164–5
homosexuality, 341–2, 346, 352
honour: and gods, 38, 425; in sexuality, 346
"honour, love of" (*philotimia*), 15–16, 53,
    75–6, 89, 92, 173
house churches, 88–9, 269–70
Housesteads, 179, 194, 253
humility, Christian, 324
hymns, pagan, 114–16, 198

Iamblichus (philosopher), on oracles, 171–5
    *passim*, 182–3
iconoclasm, 671–4
icons, rise of, 676
ideals: Christian, 18–20; Christian and pagan,
    motivation, 544–5
identity, civic, 67, 80–82, 91–2
Ignatius (martyr), 437, 446, 498–9, 502
illness, cured by exorcism, 328
Imperial cult, *see* Emperors
incense, in sacrifice, 70–71, 426, 581
India, missions to, 278
inflation (late C3rd), 573, 577–85
inheritance, 62; Christianity and, 309–10,
    351–2, 589, 623–4, 667
inscriptions, *see* epigraphy
intolerance, religious, 23, 656, 671, 672–4
invasions, barbarian, 539–40, 572–3, 575–7
Iobacchi (cult society), 85–8
Ionopolis (Abonouteichos), 241–50
Irenaeus, 266, 285; on Apostolic succession,
    506; on heresy, 332–3, 408, 492
Isaac (monk), 601
Isis, 93; "universal," 34
Islam: martyrs, 449; and oracles, 205

James (martyr), 470
Jerash, *see* Gerasa
Jerome (theologian): on Ecclesiastes, 522,
    523; on Hilarion, 18–20; on virgins, 371
Jerusalem, the New, 422
Jesus, *see* Christ
Jews and Judaism, 35; antiquity of, 94, 428–9;
    apocalyptic texts, 381, 412; Celsus on,
    482–3; Christianity spread through,
    272–7; and Christians, 428–34, 474,
    479–83, 486–7, 671; civic status, 51, 433,
    453, 456, 671; conversion to and from, 88,
    271, 296–7, 318–19, 479–80, 482; on
    death, 98, 412, 447–8; on demons, 327; of
    Diaspora, 51, 317–19; on end of world,
    267; on epiphany, 112, 377; leaders,
    496–8; martyrdom, 436–7, 447–9;
    monotheism and pagans, 34–5; oracles
    and, 257–8; persecution, exempt from
    Decian, 456; privileges, legal, 51, 428–30,
    453; Purim, 486–7; Roman attitude to,
    428–34; Scriptures quoted by Christians,
    476, 480–83, 540–41, 544, 647; on sex,

351–2; on slavery, 296–7; wars with
    Rome, 428, 429; Yahweh (Greek Iao),
    190, 257; *see also* Miletus; Pionius;
    synagogues
John (bishop of Ephesus), 289–90
John Chrysostom, 101, 286, 374, 514–15
John Malalas, 171
Judgement, Last, *see* end of world
Julian, Emperor: apostasy, 20, 199, 271; on
    epiphany, 137, 148–9
justice: local gods' role, 128; *see also* assizes;
    bishops; governors
Justin (Christian writer), 266, 267, 333, 356
Justinian, Emperor, 681

Kalends of January (Roman festival), 39, 537
Karanis (Egyptian village), 602
Karine (village near Smyrna), 468
knights/equites, Christian, 302, 303

*labarum*, Constantine's standard, 616
Labeo, Cornelius, *On the Oracle of Clarian
    Apollo*, 180
Lactantius: on Constantine's vision, 613–14,
    616–17; life and writings, 604–5, 607; and
    oracles, 171, 680, 681; and *Oration to the
    Saints*, 659–61, 681; "phoenix" poem,
    639–40
languages: areas, Greek and Latin, 32–3;
    Christians and, 282–7, 533, 589;
    Manichaeans and, 282, 563
Lagina (Caria), cult of Hecate, 584
Laodicea (Phrygia), oracle, 235
Laphria (festival at Patras), 90–91
lapses from Christianity: causes, 270–71;
    Decian persecution, 456–7, 479, 489,
    549–50, 556–7; Great persecution, 597,
    609; reception by Church, 427, 549–50,
    556–7, 609; voluntary martyrdom to
    purge, 443
Last Judgement, *see* end of world
Latin and Greek cultural areas, 32–3
Laura (village), and priests, 580
law, Roman, education in, 518–19, 525–6
laws, Constantine's, 17–18, 623–4
legal system, *see* assizes; governors; trials
Lepcis Magna (N. Africa), 82
*Leucippe and Cleitophon* (novel), 131
Libanius (orator), 29, 149, 159–60
Licinius (Emperor), 621, 632, 651
liturgies (voluntary services), 52
liturgy, Christian, 676
Longinus, Aurelius (of Side), 12–13
Longus, *Daphnis and Chloë*, 131
lot, choice by, 208–9, 514
Lucian (martyr), 440, 473
Lucian (bishop of Rucuma), 544
Lucian (pagan writer), on cult of Glycon,
    243–50

Lucius (African martyr), 445–6, 469
Lucretius, 95
Lydia, Burnt, 475, 478
Lyons: Blandina's martyrdom, 436; confessors at, 408, 440–41; early church, 273, 276; Greek culture, 32, 285; and Montanism, 408
Lystra, Paul and Barnabas in, 99–100, 140

Ma (goddess), 535–6
Maccabean martyrs, 436–7
Macer, Ambeibios (prophet at Didyma), 220–22, 255, 256, 258–9, 575
magic, 36–8, 117, 125, 143, 151
magistracies, 52–7
Magnesia (Caria), 226
Mallos (Cilicia), dream oracle, 230, 253
Mambre (Judaea), 671, 674
Manasseh, prayer of, 544
Mandulis (Egyptian god), 166–7, 195
Mani, life of: and Edessa, 279; education, 564; miracles, 570–71; and the nobility, 570–71; teaching, 567–9; travels, 548, 562, 567; visions, 399, 565–7
Manichaeism, 561–71, 548; and apocryphal "Acts," 357; books, 569; church structure, 563, 568, 571; conduct, 357, 566–7, 571; and Diocletian, 594–5; dualism, 567–8; Elect and "hearers," 568, 571; followers, range of, 569–71; and Greek culture, 569; languages, 282, 563; mission, 281–2, 561–2, 570–71; and monks, 563–4; persecution of, 563, 594–5; sources on, 563–4; summary, 571
Mappalicus (martyr), 468
Mar Ammo (Manichaean), 563, 570
Marcion, heresy of, 332, 358, 364, 492, 516
Marcus Aurelius, Emperor: on afterlife, 97; on anger, 65; on epiphany, 123, 150; cf. *Oration to the Saints*, 662
Maria in Ara Coeli (church), 681
Marian (martyr), 438–9, 470, 474, 488–9
marriage: age at, 47–8, 343–4, 367; chastity in, 356–7, 358–9, 363, 367–8; cohabitation, 308–9, 344–5, 354; incestuous, 341, 351–2; laws of, 308–9, 346–7, 386; mixed, 308–9, 310, 315, 344–5; remarriage, 344, 353–4, 386; *see also* divorce
martyrs and martyrdom, 419–92; in arena, 55, 420–21, 436, 485; in army, 304, 553; authority of, 440–41, 511; and bishops, 16, 455, 494–5, 511, 551; Christ as model, 437–8; conversions by, 315; cult of, 435, 445–6, 601; female, 419, 420; ideal, 435–41; intercession through, 445–6, 448–50; Jewish, 436–7; motivation, 422, 437–8; in prison, 458, 468–71; remission

of sins by confessors and, 338, 448–9, 458–9; rewards, 419, 435; "steadfast face," 422, 427; subsequent history, 419–20; texts of, 434–5, 468–71; theology of, 435–41; tranquillity, 438–9; trials, 421–2, 425–6, 471–2; uniting factor in Church, 445–6; visions, 400–403; voluntary, 442–5, 461, 600; *see also* martyrs by name; persecution; prison; relics
Mary, Virgin: idealized view, 311, 363, 535, 651; modern epiphany, 102, 104, 375–6, 409–10
matrons, Christian, 308–9
Maxentius, Emperor, 612–14, 618
Maximin Thrax, Emperor: and Licinius, 585, 621, 644; in *Oration to the Saints*, 632–4, 652; and persecution, 450, 591–2, 596–8, 612
Maximus (legendary martyr), 459, 490
Maximus of Tyre (orator), 129, 137
meat, eating of, 70
medical writers, pagan, 350–51, 361
Meletius (schismatic), 609–10
Melito (bishop of Sardis), 476
Memnon, statue of, 166–7
Memphis, Constantine at, 630, 646
Men (goddess), 82, 535–6
menstruation, and Eucharist, 543, 558
Mercurius (legendary martyr), 460
Mesopotamia: Christians flee to, 280–81; sects in, 277–8, 564, 566
Methodius (Lycian bishop), 602
Miletus (Caria): barbarians, 572, 576; cults at, 102–3, 254, 256–7; epiphanies of gods, 102–4, 141–4, 149, 164; Jews in, 257–8; oracles and, 226–8, 240; sale of priesthoods, 77; *see also* Didyma
millennium, 265–6, 405–6, 605
mines, Christians in, 434, 441
Minucius, *Octavius*, 300–301
miracles, 118–19, 329, 570–71
mission: Christian, 282, 289–91; Manichaean, 281–2, 561–2, 570–71
Mithras, 29, 83, 575, 593; afterlife, 96; and army, 304; mechanical effects in temples, 136; and myths, 93
monasticism, 18–20, 601–4; beginnings, 370; and charity, 668; communities, 603–4; Hilarion, 18–20; *monachos*, 601–2; Nag Hammadi library, 414–16; perfectionism, 603–4; visions, 415–18; *see also* Antony; virgins
monotheism, 34–5; *see also* abstract divinities
Montanus (martyr), 469
Montanus (heretic), 404–10
Most High God, *see* abstract divinities
mystery cults, 93–4, 96–7, 124–5, 260; *see also* Attis; Eleusis; Mithras; Oriental

Nag Hammadi library, 414–15
names, Christian, 590, 611
Narcissus (bishop of Jerusalem), 508–9
Nemesis, cult at Smyrna, 461
Neocaesarea (Pontus), 531, 536; culture, 517–18; games, 537–8, 578; Synod of, 664, 665; *see also* Gregory of Pontus
Nero, Emperor, and Christians, 432
Nestor, Septimius (antiquarian), 189
Nicaea, Council of, 629, 654–6, 663–4
Nicagoras (Athenian noble), 640–1
Nicomedia (Bithynia): and Clarian oracle, 231; church destroyed, 587, 595; and Constantine, 638; and Diocletian, 593, 595–6, 652; and Lactantius, 605; and Maximin, 598
Nilus (Christian author), 599
Nisibis (Mesopotamia), 276–7
Nora (Sardinia), 194, 201, 253
Novatian (heretic), 542–3, 549–50, 656
novels, *see* Apuleius; Chariton; *Ephesian Tales*; Heliodorus; *Leucippe and Cleitophon*; Longus; Minucius; *Recognitions*

Odessos (Thrace), 231
Oenoanda (Lycia): alphabetic oracle, 209–10; oracular inscription, 168–77, 190–91
offerings to gods, *see* sacrifice
office, public, 52–7; Christian clergy exempt, 623, 667
Old Testament, quoted by Christians, 476, 480–83, 540–41, 544, 647
omens, Constantine and pagan, 613
Opramoas (benefactor), 60–61, 79, 255
oracles, 168–261; ambiguous, 228–9, 238–9; atmosphere, 204–5, 206–7; "bidding" (referral to other shrines), 202, 234, 247, 252; in C3rd troubles, 576–7; choirs, 178–9, 183, 219–22; in Christian texts, 171, 190–93; and Christians, 258–9, 452, 595, 671–2, 677–8, 680–81; conservatism, 239, 258–9; demise, 679–81; and divination, range of, 205–15; and Emperors, 228–9; enquiries, range of, 133–4, 215–41; forgery of, 202–4; place, importance of, 204–5, 206–7; prophets, 171–6, 181–3, 188, 204–5, 219–25, 584–5; replies, style of, 237–41; revival, C2nd, 75, 200–241, 250–56; on theology and philosophy, 190–97, 200, 256–7; water at, 172, 175, 183–4; *see also* Chaldaean; Claros; Delphi; Didyma; divination; Oenoanda
*Oration to the Saints*, 21, 642–53; ascription, 627–9; content, 643–53; influences on, 659–62; Marcus' *Meditations* compared, 662; misuse of Latin literature, 648–52
Orcistus (Phrygia), 587, 638

"Oriental" gods, 35, 36, 38–9, 88; epiphany, 124; establishment, 82–3; late C3rd, 574–5; myths, 93; *see also* Attis; Dionysus; Mithras; Serapis
Origen, 520–25; uses allegory, 524; on bishops, 501, 503, 511; on Ecclesiastes, 523–4; Eusebius' *Defence of*, 606–7; *Exhortation to Martyrs*, 476; and Gregory of Pontus, 516–17, 519–28; on Jews, 482, 497, 520; on persecution, 451, 556; on the poor, 300–301; on rural missionaries, 287–9; teaching, 520–25
Ossius, bishop of Cordova: and Constantine, 612, 617, 624, 638, 642, 654; at Councils (Antioch) 642–3, 644; (Nicæa) 655–6, (Elvira) 664; and Plato, 661
"overachievement," *see* perfectionism
Oxyrhynchus (Egypt): Christians in, 587, 590; games, 578, 579, 580

Pachomius (Coptic monk), 414–16, 601
pagans, *pagani*, 30–31
"pageantry, consensual," 80–81, 92, 582
Palmyra (Syria), 47, 205, 233, 570, 572
Pamphilus (martyr), 443, 471, 606
Pan, 120, 130–32, 673
Panamara (Asia), 67, 72, 577, 584–5
panegyrics: on Constantine, 611–13, 618–19, 645; on Gregory, 516, 528–39, 574
Panopolis (Egypt), 578
Pantaenus (missionary), 278
*pappas* (Christian title), 539
Papylus (martyr), 491
Patara (Lycia), oracle, 201, 253, 256
patronage, *see* benefaction
Paul (apostle): arrest and trial, 430–32; on authority, 422; on bishops, 502; on Christian community, 324; letters from prison, 468–9; in Lystra, 99–100, 140; Mani and, 567; on Melite, 100, 140; and the nobility, 293–4; and pagan philosophy, 305; on remarriage, 353–4; on sex, 363–4; visions, 381, 401
Paul of Samosata (bishop of Antioch), 513–14, 561
Paul (Palestinian confessor), 445
Paulus, Sergius (Roman governor), 293–4
Pausanias, 90–91, 95, 110–11, 123
Pelagianus (bishop of Luperciana), 544
penance: Christian, 337–8, 500–501, 541, 549–50, 556–7; Novatianism, 594–50
perfectionism: Christian, 336–40; holy men, 449–50; Manichaeism, 562, 568, 571; monasticism, 602–4; tempered for majority, 557–60; *see also* chastity; martyrdom; visions
Pergamum (Mysia): Asclepius' shrine, 71, 75, 201, 247, 248; C2nd population, 47; and

Pergamum (Mysia) – *cont.*
  Clarian oracle, 232–3, 240; martyrs,
  490–91
Perinthus (Thrace), 177, 202, 226
Permissos (father and son, poets), at Claros,
  178
Perpetua (martyr), 312, 401, 420, 487; diary,
  438–40, 469
persecution, of Christians, 419–92; before
  250 A.D., 423–49; Decian, 450–92, 532,
  549–50; Valerian's, 550–53; "Great,"
  592–608
  causes, 422, 424–8, 430–32, 433–4
  consequences, long-term, 601; dispersal
  of Christians, 280–81, 287, 288, 601, 603;
  the end of the world, Christian
  expectations of, 266–7; governors and,
  424, 425–8; intellectuals, Greek, and,
  593–5; legal framework, 422–3, 450–51,
  594–5; oracles and, 259, 452, 595; popular
  attitude, 423–5, 552–3, 598–601;
  punishment for sin, 549; *see also* lapsing;
  martyrs
Persia, 281, 562, 570, 593–4, 646–7
Peter (apostle), 100–101, 140
Peter (bishop of Alexandria), canons
  on lapsed Christians, 443, 597–8
Petronius, *Satyricon*, 141–2
Pharai (Achaea), 208–9
Phileas (martyr), 434–5
Philip, Emperor, 451–2, 579, 609
Philo (Alexandrian Jew), 49, 313
philosophy, Greek: afterlife, 95–6; Christian
  apologists and, 305–8, 334, 516; Christian
  apostasy to, 271; Christianity more
  confident, 330–31, 335; Constantine on,
  645–6; and cult, 29–30, 94; and epiphanies
  of gods, 123, 126, 164–5; and
  Manichaeism, 569; and oracles, 170–71,
  184–8, 248–9; on sex, 348–50; and
  theology, 170–71, 193
Philostratus, *On Heroes*, 144–8, 189–90
*philotimia, see* "honour"
Philumenus ("master of the offices" at
  Nicaea), 656
phoenix (mythical bird), 639–41
Phrygia, Christians in, 587
pilgrimage, early practice, 476
Pindar, 112
Pionius (martyr), 460–92; authenticity of
  text, 460–68, 471–2; and Jews, 474,
  479–83; speeches, 473–81; trial and death,
  472, 483–93
plague (C3rd), 550, 573, 574; oracles on,
  194–5, 219, 222, 231–5
Plato: on afterlife, 95–6; on epiphanies, 119,
  150; God, sense of, 94, 164; against
  private cults, 88; on sex, 351
Platonists: on afterlife, 96, 97; and oracles,

199–200, (Chaldaean) 198, (Delphic)
  184–6, 187–8, 197; epiphany of gods,
  123, 164–5; theurgy, 126; *see also*
  Plutarch
Pliny (the Younger), 43, 287, 294, 427
Plotinus (Platonist), 187–8
Plutarch: on afterlife, 96, 97; on Delphi,
  184–6; on epiphany, 123; on passions,
  484; on sex, 349
Polites (of Miletus), and oracle at Didyma,
  192–3, 256
Politta, Flavia (benefactor), 463–5
Pollio, Pomponius, at Didyma, 181
pollution, 83, 543
Polycarp (martyr): intercession by, 445; and
  Marcionism, 492; martyrdom, 435, 446,
  472–3, 481, 485
Polyeuctus (legendary martyr), 459–60, 468
Pontus, 178, 287, 288, 533–8, 539
Poplas, Aelianus (prophet at Didyma), 192,
  228; family, 219–21
population of cities, C2nd, 46–8
Porfyrius, P. Optatianus (poet), 639
Porphyry: *Philosophy from Oracles*, 171, 191,
  196–7, 198, 256–7, 362; *Against the
  Christians*, 586, 589, 593, 606, 671
Potamiaena (martyr), 447
poverty (*ptocheia*), Christian virtue, 324
power, Christian attitude to, 321–2
prayers, pagan, 116–17
preaching, Christian, 284
priesthood, pagan: and civic status, 12–14,
  39; of Oriental cults, 33, 36; sale of, 76–8;
  virgin, 347–8, 362, *see also* oracles
prison, martyrs in; remit sins, 338, 448–9,
  458–9; tips to warders, 489; visions,
  400–403; writings, 468–71; *see also*
  confessors
privacy, lack of, 61–2, 315–16
privileges, legal: for Christians under
  Constantine, 17, 610, 623–4, 667; for
  Jews, 51, 428–9, 453
processions, 72, 679; pagan and modern
  Spanish compared, 67–8, 114
"promising" to pagan gods, 76, 582
prophecy: by martyrs, 483–4, 487–8; pagan,
  208, 213; *see also* oracles
prostitutes, 67, 68, 342–3, 346, 671
Protesilaus (hero), 144–7
Punic language, 283–4
purgatory, 412, 418
purification, 83, 543
Purim, at Smyrna, 486–7
Pythagoreanism, 70, 95, 189–90, 245–9

Quintilianus (governor of Asia), 490–92
Qumran sect, *see* Dead Sea scrolls

rabbis, 481, 497

*Recognitions, The* (Christian fiction), 30, 193–4, 333, 354, 359, 399
relics, 16, 446–8, 535, 599, 600
*religio*, 31–2, 95, 551
remarriage, *see* marriage
resurrection of the body, 265–6, 326
Revelation, Book of, 355, 381, 394
Rhodes, 218
Riace, statues from, 153–4, 159
rivalry, inter-city, 54, 68–9, 201–2, 252, 280, 582
Rome: c. 200 A.D. (administration) 50, (population) 47; Church in 251 A.D., 268–9, 272, 589; plague in 250s A.D., 573; primacy of bishop, 511–12
Rufinus, Claudius, and Smyrna, 465–7
Rufinus (Roman consul), 218–19
ruler, cult of living, 39–41, 72, 90, 127, 139, 141
Rutilius (martyr), 434

Sabbath, 482; "Great," at Smyrna, 486
Sabina (Christian slave), 463, 465
Sabratha (Tripoli), 73–4
sacrifice: of animals, 69–72, 90, 219–22; in Christian imagery, 89; by Christians during persecution, 425–6, 455–8, 597; of incense, 70–71, 425–6
salaries, clerical, 505
Salona (Split, Dalmatia), 588
Samuel, at Endor, 482–3
sanctuary, *see* asylum
Sappho, 112
Sardis, 464–5, 468, 482
Sartre, Jean-Paul, 112–13, 162
Satan, 30–31, 326, 436; *see also* demons
Saturn, worship, C3rd–4th, 581
Saturus (martyr), 402, 446, 447, 469, 494
scent, and god's presence, 105, 112
Sceptics, 29–30
schisms, 280, 550, 590, 601; Constantine and, 626, 641; Meletius, 609–10; *see also* Donatists; Novatian
Scriptures: and bishops, 15, 544–5; distortion of, 364; *see also* Old Testament
sea journeys, and epiphany, 118, 144
Seleucia-on-the-Tigris, 47
Serapis, 73, 75, 82, 201, 205, 227–8; "universal," 34–5, 36
Setif (N. Africa), 578–9
Seven Sleepers (legendary martyrs), 490
Severus, Emperor, 213, 228, 229
sexual mores: Christian, 339, 351–74, 382; pagan, 340–51; *see also* chastity; homosexuality; marriage; prostitution
Shapur (king of Persia), 637, 653
Shenoute (Egypt), idol smashing, 672
Shmona (martyr), 600
shorthand, 176, 472

shrines: asylum, 127–8; and epiphany, 376, 676; pagan, "neutralized" by Christian, 206, 673–4, 676; in special places, 41–2
Sibyl, 202–3, 240, 464, 605, 681; and Constantine, 647–9, 651; "oracles," Jewish, 176
Side: Aurelius Longinus and, 12–13; benefactors, 583–4; Jews, 483; and oracles, 225, 238, 255, 256, 576, 580; temples, 73
Simon Magus, in *The Recognitions*, 399
sin: Christian concept of, 22–3, 326–7, 556; church, sinners at, 337–8, 500–501, 541; intercessors (C4th onwards), 679; persecution caused by, 549; remission of, 338, 448–9, 458; of thought, 327; vainglory, 336; *see also* adultery; lapsing; penance
slavery, 44, 51, 59, 82; Christianity and, 295–9, 303, 317–18, 465; and Decian persecution, 456, 458
Smyrna (Izmir), 460–92 *passim*; assizes, 484–6; buildings, 461–2, 471, 477; culture, 466, 471–4; famine, 477–8; synagogue, 481–2; *see also* Pionius; Polycarp
society, structure of, 46–63, 80–82, 299–300; Christianity and, 293–312, 319–20, 322–3, 334–5, 590–91
Soknopaiou Nesos (Egypt), 33
Solon, T. Statilius (Clarian choir boy), 179
sophists, 212, 466–7
Soranus (medical writer), 361
sorcery, 37, 143, 205
Sozomen (Christian writer), 19
Spirit, Holy, 312–14, 409–10, 494; and bishops, 502, 506; and martyrs, 436, 437, 439–41, 448–9
springs, and oracles, 206–7
statues of gods, 153–5, 159–60; and dreams, 153–5, 161–2; gods' presence in, 133–5, 136–7, 230, 673–5; at oracles, 172, 173, 181
Stobi (Macedonia): Jewish patriarch, 497–8; oracles, 178, 222
Stoicism: and afterlife 97, 123, 150, 306–7; *see also* Marcus
Strabo (geographer), on Pontus, 533–7
Stratonicea (Caria), 135, 577
Stratonicus (of Didyma), 192
suffrage, 507–11
Sun god, 575; Apollo, 216–17; Emperors and, 593, 615, 657–8; Mandulis, 166–7
Syedra (Cilicia), 240
Symeon the Mountaineer, 289–90
synagogues: as "cult society," 88; Dura-Europus, 277; officials, 496–8; Ostia, 429; Oxyrynchus, 590; Pamphylia, 483; Sardis, 429; Smyrna, 481–2; Stobi, 497
syncretism, 35

Synesius of Cyrene, 48–9, 149–50
synods of bishops, 512, 513; *see also*
    Alexandria; Ancyra; Antioch; Elvira;
    Neocaesarea
Syria, 28–9; cults, 33–4, 35, 557, 581; rural
    mission, 288–9; *see also* towns and cities
    by name

Tabai (Caria), 252
Tacitus, on Claros oracle, 172–5 *passim*
Tarsus, 345
Tatian (Christian writer), 333, 342, 356, 364
taxation, 53
temple- and statue-breakers, 671–4
Tertullian: on "bishop of bishops," 507; on
    class of Christians, 294; on education, 83;
    on election by lot, 514; on the end of the
    world, 269; on marriage, 310, 359, 364;
    on martyrs in prison, 448; and
    Montanism, 409–11; on repentance,
    337–9; on widows, 368, 369
Tetrarchy, 573, 574, 612; tolerance of
    Christians, 611, 612
Thala (N. Africa), benefactor at, 582
Theadelphia (Egypt), 455–6
Theodotus (martyr), 599–600
Theodotus, Sempronius Arruncius (priest at
    Panamara), 584–5
theophany, 675, 680
Theophilus (of Acts), 303–4, 430
Theophilus (Edessan Christian), 600–601
Theophilus, Julius, and oracle at Didyma,
    171, 193, 194, 197
"theosophy," Christian coinage?, 680
thespode, oracular, *see* Claros
Thessalus (student), and magic, 37, 143
theurgy, 124, 126, 207–8
*Thomas, Acts of*, 278, 297–8, 340, 446
Thrace, and oracles, 231, 232, 247
Tigellinus, 432
tithes, Christian, 505
tolerance, *see* intolerance
town/country, 41–6, 132, 139, 287–93
"traces" of the gods (footprints), 138,
    140–41, 207
trade and commerce, 58–9, 272–3
tradition: in pagan religion, 29, 80, 148,
    258–60, 551; in Christianity, 331–3
Trajan, Emperor, 201, 228, 229, 251
Tralles (Lydia), 235, 238
Transfiguration of Christ, 376–7, 397, 380
translation, of Christian texts, 282–4
Trapezus (Pontus), and Goths, 539
travel, Christians, 268, 277–8, 476
trees, around shrines, 43–4, 127–8
trials, *see* assizes; Dionysius; governors;
    martyrs; Paul; Pionius
Trier (Gaul); panegyric to Constantine, 611,
    613, 645

*Trinity, On the* (sermon), 191
Trophonius (Greece), oracle of, 189, 206
Troy, 144–7
*True Belief, On*, 171, 190–93, 253, 258, 680
Twin, Heavenly, in heresies, 565–6
Typhon (monster), 475, 478
Tyre, and oracle at Didyma, 251

Ulpianus, Flavius (prophet at Didyma), 220,
    224–5, 256, 258–9
Utica (N. Africa), assizes, 487

Vahram, King of Persians, 562
vainglory, sin of, 336
Valerian, Emperor: persecution, 302–3,
    550–51, 594; death, 553, 652
values, attraction of Christian, 323–5
Vestal Virgins, 29, 347–8, 362
*vicarius*/vicar, 573
virginity, *see* chastity
*Virginity, On* (Syriac texts), 359–61
virgins in Church: and bequests, 310;
    communities of, 368–70; honoured, 359;
    lapsed, 370–71, 373–4; provided for, 359,
    368–9; role, 372–3
visions, Christian, 339, 340, 375–418;
    accounts amplified to counter doubt,
    377–8; art, legend and, 676–7, 392–5;
    compared with pagan, 376, 398, 618–19,
    678; of Constantine, 611–19, 674–81; in
    crises, 399–403; criticism of Church
    suppressed, 409–11; fasting, 395–6;
    heretics and, 399, 565; Jewish antecedents,
    376–7; monks and, 415–18; Montanism
    and, 404–10; monuments to, 379, 398;
    Nag Hammadi library, 414–16; response
    to, 379–80; true and false, 409–11,
    416–17; variations between, 396–8,
    401–2, 565; worthiness for, 416, 417–18;
    *see also* Christ; epiphany; Mary
votive sculpture, 118–19, 140–41, 162–3

war, spread of Christianity by, 281
Wars, Jewish, 428, 429
widows, in Church, 309–10, 354; in
    *Didascalia*, 559–60; Jewish models, 353;
    provision for, 368–9, 505
women, in Church, 308–11; in *Didascalia*,
    559–60; martyrs, 419–20; and spread of
    Christianity, 281; virginity and role in
    church, 372–3; *see also* marriage; virgins;
    widows

Yahweh (Greek Iao), 190, 257
Yaliniz-Serai (Phrygia), 180
Yohanan (rabbi), 51

Zela (Pontus), 535

Zenobia (Queen of Palmyra), 570
Zeus, cults of: at Amaseia, 534–5; at Apamea, 197, 228, 229; at Baalbek, 229, 236; in caves, 41, 69, 673; at Gerasa, 73; at Panamara, 67, 72, 577, 584–5; at Pergamum, 232; at Side, 73; at Smyrna, 485
Zosimus (diviner), 404